LIFE-SPAN DEVELOPMENT

TWELFTH EDITION

John W. Santrock

Uiversity of Texas at Dallas

Boston   Burr Ridge, IL   Dubuque, IA   Madison, WI   New York   San Francisco   St. Louis
Bangkok   Bogotá   Caracas   Kuala Lumpur   Lisbon   London   Madrid   Mexico City
Milan   Montreal   New Delhi   Santiago   Seoul   Singapore   Sydney   Taipei

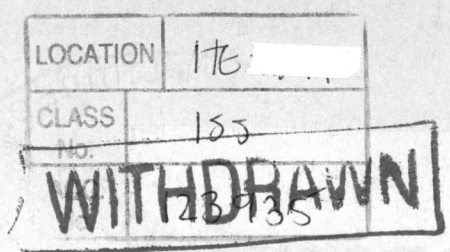

McGraw-Hill
Higher Education

Published by McGraw-Hill, an imprint of The McGraw-Hill Companies, Inc., 1221 Avenue of the Americas, New York, NY 10020. Copyright © 2009 by The McGraw-Hill Companies, Inc. All rights reserved. No part of this publication may be reproduced or distributed in any form or by any means, or stored in a database or retrieval system, without the prior written consent of The McGraw-Hill Companies, Inc., including, but not limited to, in any network or other electronic storage or transmission, or broadcast for distance learning.

Some ancillaries, including electronic and print components, may not be available to customers outside the United States.

This book is printed on acid-free paper.

1 2 3 4 5 6 7 8 9 0 VNH/VNH 0 9 8

ISBN 978-0-07-128083-9
MHID 0-07-128083-9

www.mhhe.com

*With special appreciation to
my mother, Ruth Santrock and
the memory of my father, John Santrock*

About the Author

John W. Santrock

John Santrock received his Ph.D. from the University of Minnesota in 1973. He taught at the University of Charleston and the University of Georgia before joining the Program in Psychology and Human Development at the University of Texas at Dallas, where he currently teaches a number of undergraduate courses and was given the University's Effective Teaching Award in 2006.

John has been a member of the editorial boards of *Child Development* and *Developmental Psychology*. His research on father custody is widely cited and used in expert witness testimony to promote flexibility and alternative considerations in custody disputes. John also has authored these exceptional McGraw-Hill texts: *Psychology* (7th edition), *Children* (10th edition), *Adolescence* (12th edition), *Topical Life-Span Development* (4th edition), and *Educational Psychology* (4th edition).

For many years, John was involved in tennis as a player, teaching professional, and coach of professional tennis players. He has been married for more than 35 years to his wife, Mary Jo, who is a realtor. He has two daughters—Tracy, who is studying to become a financial planner at Duke University, and Jennifer, who is a medical sales specialist at Medtronic. He has one granddaughter, Jordan, age 17, and two grandsons, Alex, age 4, and Luke, age 3. Tracy recently completed the New York Marathon, and Jennifer was in the top 100 ranked players on the Women's Professional Tennis Tour. In the last decade, John also has spent time painting expressionist art.

John Santrock, teaching in his undergraduate course in life-span development.

Brief Contents

Contents

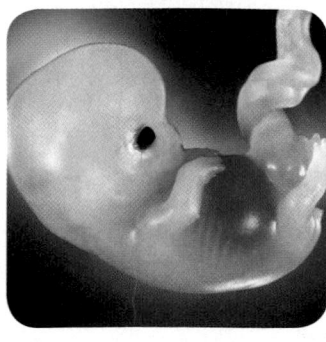

SECTION 3

INFANCY 111

SECTION 4   EARLY CHILDHOOD 207

SECTION 6

ADOLESCENCE 351

SECTION 7 EARLY ADULTHOOD 413

SECTION 8   # MIDDLE ADULTHOOD 471

SECTION 9   **LATE ADULTHOOD 525**

SECTION 10   ENDINGS 613

CHAPTER 20
Death, Dying, and Grieving 615

Expert Consultants

Life-span development has become an enormous, complex field, and no single author, or even several authors, can possibly keep up with the rapidly changing content in the many different areas of life-span development. To solve this problem, author John Santrock sought the input of leading experts about content in numerous aspects of human development. The experts provided detailed evaluations and recommendations for a chapter(s) in their areas of expertise. The biographies and photographs of the experts, who literally represent a who's who in the field of life-span development, follow.

K. Warner Schaie

Dr. Schaie is widely recognized as one of the pioneers who created the field of life-span development and continues to be one of its leading experts. He currently is the Evan Pugh Professor Emeritus of Human Development and Psychology at Pennsylvania State University. Dr. Schaie also holds an appointment as Affiliate Professor of Psychiatry and Behavioral Sciences at the University of Washington. He received his Ph.D. in psychology from the University of Washington, an honorary D.phil. from the Friedrich-Schiller University of Jena, Germany, and an honorary Sc.D. degree from West Virginia University. He received the Kleemeier Award for Distinguished Research Contributions from the Gerontological Society of America, the MENSA Lifetime Career Award, and the Distinguished Scientific Contributions Award from the American Psychological Association. Dr. Schaie is author or editor of 54 books including the textbook *Adult Development and Aging* (with Sherry Willis) and the *Handbook of the Psychology of Aging* (with James Birren). He has directed the Seattle Longitudinal Study of cognitive aging since 1956 and is the author of more than 275 journal articles and chapters on the psychology of aging. His current research focuses on the life course of adult intelligence, its antecedents and modifiability, the early detection of risk for dementia, as well as methodological issues in the developmental sciences.

This excellent chapter (Chapter 18: Cognitive Development in Late Adulthood) *has been carefully brought up to date.*

—K. WARNER SCHAIE

Maria Hernandez-Reif

Dr. Hernandez-Reif is a leading expert on prenatal development, birth, and infant development. She currently is a Professor in the Department of Human Development and Families at the University of Alabama and is Director of the Pediatric Development Research Laboratory. She previously was a research scientist at the Touch Research Institute at the University of Miami School of Medicine, where she conducted a number of research studies with Dr. Tiffany Field on the importance of touch and massage therapy in improving the development of newborns and infants with varied developmental and medical problems.

Overall, I found the chapters (Chapter 3: Prenatal Development and Birth; Chapter 4: Physical Development in Infancy) *to be clearly written and to cover basic information for an undergraduate course that generally reviews prenatal and physical development in infancy.*

—MARIA HERNANDEZ-REIF

Andrew Meltzoff

Dr. Meltzoff is widely recognized as one of the world's leading experts on infant learning and cognition. He currently holds the Job and Gertrud Tamaki Endowed Chair in Developmental Science at the University of Washington and is the Codirector of the Institute for Learning and Brain Sciences. Dr. Meltzoff's research focuses on children's cognitive development, and he recently has proposed a theory of social cognitive development called the "Like Me" developmental framework. He has coauthored *Words Thoughts, and Theories* and *Scientist in the Crib: Minds, Brains, and How Children Learn*, and is Coeditor of *The Imitative Mind: Development, Evolution, and Brain Bases*. Dr. Meltzoff has received the National Institutes of Health Merit Award for outstanding research and the Kenneth Craik Research Award. He is a Fellow in American Association for the Advancement of Science, the American Psychological Association, Association for Psychological Science, and the Norwegian Academy of Science and Letters.

The improvements that are described are excellent additions. They will help bring the book up-to-date with key new advances in the field. I teach a large undergraduate course and am very appreciative of the pedagogical style adopted in the book.

—ANDREW MELTZOFF

Ross Thompson

Dr. Thompson is one of the world's leading experts on children's socioemotional development. He currently is Professor of Psychology at the University of California–Davis. His research interests are in two fields. First, as a developmental psychologist, he studies early parent-child relationships, the development of emotional understanding and emotion regulation, conscience development, and the growth of self-understanding. Second, as a psycholegal scholar, he works on the applications of developmental research to public policy concerns, including the effects of divorce and custody arrangements on children, child maltreatment prevention, school readiness, research ethics, and early brain development and early intervention. Dr. Thompson is a founding member of the National Scientific Council on the Developing Child, and was a member of the Committee on Integrating the Science of Early Childhood Development of the National Academy of Sciences that produced the report, *From Neurons to Neighborhoods: The Science of Early Childhood Development*. He is a member of the Board of Directors of Zero to Three: National Center for Infants, Toddlers, and Families, and is on the Editorial Advisory Board of *Wondertime* magazine. Dr. Thompson has twice been Associate Editor of *Child Development*, and is Consulting Editor for a series of topical texts in developmental psychology published by McGraw-Hill. His books include *Preventing Child Maltreatment Through Social Support: A Critical Analysis*; *The Postdivorce Family: Children, Families, and Society* (coedited with Paul Amato); and *Toward a Child-Centered, Neighborhood-Based Child Protection System* (coedited with Gary Melton and Mark Small). He is currently working on two books: *Early Brain Development, the Media, and Public Policy* and *Emotional Development*. Dr. Thompson has been a Visiting Scientist at the Max Planck Institute for Human Development and Education in Berlin, a Senior NIMH Fellow in Law and Psychology at Stanford University, and a Harris Visiting Professor at the University of Chicago. He received the Boyd McCandless Young Scientist Award for Early Distinguished Achievement from the American Psychological Association, the Scholarship in Teaching Award, and the Outstanding Research and Creative Activity Award from the University of Nebraska, where he was also a lifetime member of the Academy of Distinguished Teachers.

Reading the dual chapters on socioemotional development (infancy and early childhood) was a joy. The writing is engaging and inviting, the coverage is accurate and timely . . . . Time and again I would read a section and anticipate making a suggestion for updating the discussion, only to find John Santrock had already done so. This text comes closer than any I have previously read to combining state-of-the art representation of the field with writing quality that undergraduate readers will find captivating.

—ROSS THOMPSON

Candice Mills

Dr. Mills is a leading expert on social cognition in children's development. She obtained her Ph.D. in developmental psychology from Yale University and currently is an Assistant Professor in the School of Behavioral and Brain Sciences at the University of Texas at Dallas. Dr. Mills' research explores how children evaluate the knowledge and beliefs of others as well as themselves, and what changes over the course of development. Her recent publications (with coauthor Frank Keil) include articles in these research journals: *Cognition, Psychological Science*, and *Journal of Experimental Child Psychology*. For the current edition of *Life-Span Development*, Dr. Mills updated and expanded the section on children's theory of mind.

The additions to this textbook show the remarkable advances made in the field the last several years. Students will also benefit from the learning system, which encourages them to preview each chapter's main themes and then review and reflect on the learning goals for each chapter.

—CANDICE MILLS

L. Monique Ward

Dr. Ward is a leading expert on adolescent development, gender, and sexuality. She currently is a Professor of Psychology at the University of Michigan. Her research examines children's and adolescents' developing conceptions of both gender and sexuality, and explores the contributions of these notions to their social and sexual decision making. Dr. Ward is especially interested in the media's role in sexual socialization and has published extensively on this topic in various academic journals, including *Developmental Review, Psychology of Women Quarterly,* and the *Journal of Research on Adolescence.* She served as a member of APA's Task Force on the Sexualization of Girls and is on the editorial board of both the *Journal of Adolescent Research* and *Media Psychology.* Dr. Ward was also an Associate Editor for the *Encyclopedia of Children, Adolescents, and the Media.*

> *. . . I appreciate the author's attempt to update findings and references.*
>
> —L. MONIQUE WARD

John Schulenberg

Dr. Schulenberg is a leading expert on adolescent development and emerging adulthood. He currently is Professor in the Department of Psychology, and Research Professor in the Institute for Social Research and Center for Human Growth and Development, all at the University of Michigan. He has published widely on adolescent development and the transition to adulthood, focusing on how developmental transitions and tasks relate to health risks and adjustment difficulties. His current research examines factors involved substance use and psychopathology with a particular emphasis on continuities and discontinuities in adolescence and emerging adulthood. Dr. Schulenberg is a co-Principal Investigator of the National Institute of Drug Abuse–funded national Monitoring the Future Study involving substance use by U.S. adolescents and young adults. Dr. Schulenberg has served on a number of advisory and review committees for the National Institutes of Health, the National Science Foundation, and the Society for Research on Adolescence. He is a Fellow of the American Psychological Association.

> *Overall, these are excellent chapters* (Chapter 13: Physical and Cognitive Development in Early Adulthood; Chapter 14: Socioemotional Development in Early Adulthood) *that I suspect do very well in terms of engaging college students and conveying current themes and research on early adulthood. I enjoyed reading these, and learned quite a bit.*
>
> —JOHN SCHULENBERG

Phyllis Moen

Dr. Moen is one of the world's leading experts on the adult life course of work, family, health, and gender. She currently the McKnight Presidential Chair in Sociology at the University of Minnesota. Her extensive research studies and numerous books emphasize public and organizational policies and practices as they shape the life course of work, family, health, and gender. Her two most recent books are *It's About Time: Couples and Careers* (2003) and the award-winning *Career Mystique: Cracks in the American Dream* (2005, with Pat Roehling). Dr. Moen is currently engaged (with Erin Kelly) in the Flexible Work and Well-Being Study, a study of a results-only work environment (ROWE) at Best Buy. As part of a larger National Institutes of Health–funded network initiative, she and Erin Kelly are investigating the family, health, and productivity impacts of shifts in the way work is organized so as to offer employees greater control over their working time. Dr. Moen is the 2008 recipient of the Work-Life Legacy Award from the Families and Work Institute.

> *Good chapter!* (Chapter 15: Physical and Cognitive Development in Middle Adulthood); *Good chapter!* (Chapter 18: Cognitive Development in Late Adulthood)
>
> —PHYLLIS MOEN

Arthur Kramer

Dr. Kramer is one of the world's leading experts on cognitive neuroscience, exercise, and aging. He currently is the Swanlund Chair and Professor of Psychology at the University of Illinois, where he obtained his Ph.D. in cognitive/experimental psychology. He also is the Director of the Biomedical Imaging Center and Codirector of the National Institutes of Health Center for Healthy Minds. Dr. Kramer holds appointments in the Department of Psychology, Neuroscience Program, Institute of Aviation, and the Beckman Institute. Dr. Kramer's research focuses on cognitive psychology, cognitive neuroscience, and human factors. A major emphasis in his recent research is the understanding and enhancement of cognitive and neural plasticity across the life span. Dr. Kramer served as Associate Editor of *Perception and Psychophysics* and currently is on the Editorial Boards of seven research journals. He is a Fellow of the American Psychological Association, a member of the International Society of Attention and Performance, and a recipient of a NIH Ten Year MERIT Award. Dr. Kramer's research has been featured in numerous print and electronic media including the *New York Times, Wall Street Journal, Washington Post, Chicago Tribune, CBS Evening News, NBC Today Show,* and *Saturday Night Live.*

> *Middle age is the least studied period of the life span. Despite the sparsity of research for this age group, the present chapter* (Chapter 15: Physical and Cognitive Development in Middle Adulthood) *provides a thorough and informative review of this important portion of our life span. . . . Similar to Chapter 15, I found this chapter* (Chapter 18: Cognitive Development in Late Adulthood) *to be well written with information that should appeal to those readers interested in theories of cognitive aging as well as practical information geared toward understanding what we can do now (without waiting for the next wonder drug . . .) to ensure that both our bodies and minds age well.*
>
> —ARTHUR KRAMER

Margie Lachman

Dr. Lachman is one of the world's leading experts on midlife development. She currently is Professor and Chair of Psychology and Director of the Lifespan Developmental Psychology Laboratory at Brandeis University. Dr. Lachman is Codirector of the NIH-funded predoctoral and postdoctoral training program, Cognitive Aging in a Social Context. She recently was Editor of the *Journal of Gerontology: Psychological Sciences* and has edited two volumes on midlife development. She also is a Fellow of the American Psychological Association, Division 20 (Adult Development and Aging), and of the Gerontological Society of America. Dr. Lachman's research especially focuses on how personal control is linked to memory, physical activity, work and family life, and health as adults age. Dr. Lachman was a member of the MacArthur Foundation Research Network on Successful Midlife Development and is currently collaborating on a 10-year longitudinal follow-up of the original MacArthur midlife

sample. She has conducted intervention studies to enhance the sense of control over memory and physical exercise, and one of the programs designed to increase control over falling won the Archstone Award for Excellence in Program Innovation from the American Public Health Association. Dr. Lachman has served as an advisor to organizations such as the AARP and the Boston Museum of Science for the traveling exhibit on the Secrets of Aging. She has presented her research on the *CBS Evening News* and the *NBC Today Show.* Dr. Lachman also recently received the Distinguished Research Achievement Award from the American Psychological Association, Division on Adult Development and Aging.

> *I found the chapter* (Chapter 16: Socioemotional Development in Middle Adulthood) *to be excellent. It has a good balance of coverage. . . . The literature John Santrock covers is up-to-date and central to the field. . . . I enjoyed reading the chapter. Thank you for the opportunity.*
>
> —MARGIE LACHMAN

Karen Fingerman

Dr. Fingerman is a leading expert on socioemotional processes in adult development and aging. She is currently the Berner Hanley Scholar and a Professor in the Child Development and Family Studies Program at Purdue University, where she also is Head of the Graduate Program. She obtained her Ph.D. at the University of Michigan, was a postdoctoral Fellow at Stanford University, and was a Professor at Pennsylvania State University before coming to Purdue. Her research focuses on social relationships, emotions, and aging with a special interest in relationships between adults and their parents. Dr. Fingerman's research has been funded by the Brookdale Foundation and the National Institutes of Health. The National Institute of Aging and the MacArthur Network on Transitions to Adulthood are currently funding Dr. Fingerman's

intergenerational research on middle-aged adults, their young adult children, and their aging parents. She received the Margaret Baltes Award for Early Career Achievement in Social and Behavioral Gerontology and the Springer Award for Early Career Achievement from the American Psychological Association. Dr. Fingerman currently serves on the Editorial Boards of the *Journal of the Marriage and the Family, International Journal for Aging and Human Development,* and *Journals of Gerontology: Psychological Sciences.*

> *The great strength of this book is that it fully covers theory and cutting-edge research throughout the life span in a manner that is completely accessible to beginning college students.*
>
> —KAREN FINGERMAN

Wolfgang Stroebe

Dr. Stroebe is one of the world's leading experts on dying and grieving. He has held academic positions in the United States, Great Britain, and Germany and is now Professor of Social Psychology at Utrecht University in the Netherlands. A past president of the European Association of Social Psychology and Fellow of numerous international scientific societies, he has published widely on topics of social and health psychology. His many awards include an honorary doctorate from the University of Louvain (Belgium) and the Tajfel Award for Distinguished Contributions to Social Psychology from the European Association of Experimental Social Psychology.

An informative chapter (Chapter 20: Death, Dying, and Grieving) *that covers a great deal of important literature.*

—**Wolfgang Stroebe**

Preface

Preparing a new edition of *Life-Span Development* is both a joy and a challenge. I enjoy revising this text because I continue to learn more about the human life span and the journey of life each of us takes. It also is gratifying to revise the text because the feedback from students and instructors has been consistently enthusiastic. The challenge of revising a successful text is always to continue meeting readers' needs and expectations, while keeping the material fresh and up to date. For the twelfth edition of *Life-Span Development*, I have reduced the book's length, expanded coverage in a number of key areas (such as the development of brain), incorporated the latest research and applications, and fine-tuned the aspects of the book that make learning easier and more engaging.

REDUCED LENGTH

At the request of numerous adopters and reviewers, I reduced the length of the book for the new twelfth edition. To accomplish this reduction in length, I combined Chapter 1 (Introduction) and Chapter 2 (The Science of Life-Span Development) from the eleventh edition into a single chapter (Introduction) in the twelfth edition. I also carefully examined each chapter and reduced content that was dated or less central to current thinking in the field of life-span development.

INCREASED COVERAGE OF BRAIN DEVELOPMENT

The creation of brain-imaging techniques such as fMRI have led to remarkable increases in our knowledge about brain development in recent years. I have substantially expanded the coverage of brain development in this new edition and where appropriate incorporated images of brains scans. Here are some of the main changes related to brain development:

Chapter 2   Biological Beginnings

- New coverage of the increasing use of fetal MRI to detect fetal malformations (Garel, 2008; Obenauer & Maestre, 2008)
- New Figure 2.12 with a photograph of a fetal MRI

Chapter 3   Prenatal Development and Birth

- Important new section on the development of the brain in the prenatal period, including a photo of the tubular appearance of the human nervous system six weeks after conception in Figure 3.4 (Moulson & Nelson, 2008; Nelson 2009)

- New discussion of neural tube defects and what characterizes anencephaly and spina bifida
- Description of recent MRI study of brain deficiencies in children born very preterm (Narberhus & others, 2008)

Chapter 4   Physical Development in Infancy

- Updated coverage of the development of the brain (Fischer, & Immordino Yang, 2008; Nelson, 2009)
- Expanded description of the function of myelination (Haynes & others, 2006)
- Expanded and updated discussion of links between spurts in brain growth and cognitive functioning (Immordino-Yang & Fischer, 2007)

Chapter 5   Cognitive Development in Infancy

- New description of the main region of the brain involved in infant attention
- New discussion of connections between development of the brain and development of memory in infancy, including new figure
- New description of the numerous areas of the brain likely involved in infant imitation, including the role that mirror neurons might play in infant imitation (Jackson, Meltzoff, & Decety, 2006; Nash, 2006)

Chapter 7   Physical and Cognitive Development in Early Childhood

- New Figure 7.1 that shows an electron microscope image of myelination

Chapter 9   Physical and Cognitive Development in Middle and Late Childhood

- Important new section, The Brain, including recent research on changes in the prefrontal cortex and diffuse/focused activation in the brain, as well as the connection of these changes to cognitive functioning in areas such as cognitive control (Durston & others, 2006)
- Discussion of cortical thickening in children 5 to 11 years of age (Toga, Thompson, & Sowell, 2006)
- New discussion of brain pathways involved in reading disabilities based on recent MRI brain scans (Shaywitz, Lyon, & Lyon, 2006)

- New Figure 9.5 of a 9-year-old boy with dyslexia going through an MRI scanner in a research study focused on learning disabilities
- New material documenting a three-year delay in the thickening of the cerebral cortex in children with ADHD, including a new figure

Chapter 10   Socioemotional Development in Middle and Late Childhood

- Connection of increased self-regulation to the discussion of developmental advances in the brain's prefrontal cortex in Chapter 9

Chapter 11   Physical and Cognitive Development in Adolescence

- Updating and expansion of changes in the brain's development in adolescence, including new Figure 11.4 (Giedd, 2008)
- New discussion of the implications of recent research on brain development in adolescence for the legal system, including whether this research can be used to decide whether an adolescent should be given the death penalty (Ash, 2006)
- Coverage of recent research on changes in the brain in adolescence and resistance to peer pressure (Paus & others, 2008)

Chapter 17   Physical Development in Late Adulthood

- Coverage of recent neuroimaging study on the slowing of activity in the prefrontal cortex of older adults during retrieval of information on a cognitive task (Rypma, Eldreth, & Rebbechi, 2007)
- Considerable expansion and updating of research and current knowledge about various aspects of the aging brain (Hillman, Erikson, & Kramer, 2008; Libert, Cohen, & Guarente, 2008; Yuan, 2008)
- Updated description of the current status of knowledge about the limitations of neurogenesis in humans to the hippocampus and olfactory bulb, as well as what is known about neurogenesis and the functioning of neurons (Nelson, 2006)
- Coverage of recent study linking exercise with an increase in brain volume in older adults (Colcombe & others, 2006)
- New material on individual differences in brain lateralization and aging, including a new Figure 17.7 showing an fMRI scan of 80-year-old T. Boone Pickens' brain (Helman, 2008)

Chapter 18   Cognitive Development in Late Adulthood

- Expanded and updated material on cognitive neuroscience and aging, including discussion of recent research on the role of exercise in cognitive advances related to changes in brain functioning assessed by neuroimaging techniques (Kramer & Erickson, 2007)
- New material on older adults' frontal and parietal regions while they are engaging in tasks that require cognitive control processes, such as attention (Grady, 2008)

RESEARCH AND APPLICATIONS

While reducing the book's overall length, I replaced dated material and significantly updated research in virtually every age period and topic in the text. The twelfth edition continues my view, that above all, a text on life-span development must include a solid research foundation.

Recent Research

This edition of *Life-Span Development* presents the latest, most contemporary research on each period of the human life span. The new twelfth edition includes more than 1,200 citations from 2007, 2008, and 2009. Shortly, I will list the main chapter-by-chapter content changes.

Research in Life-Span Development Interludes

Research in Life-Span Development interludes appear once in each chapter and provide a more in-depth look at research related to a topic in the chapter. I call them interludes rather than boxes because they follow directly in the text after they have been introduced. In most instances, they consist of a description of a research study, including the identity of the participants, the methods used to obtain data, and the main results. In most cases, they are research studies that have been conducted in the twenty-first century. Because students often have more difficulty reading about research studies than other text material, I wrote these with an eye toward student understanding. Several new and updated research interludes appear in this new edition, including Tiffany Field and her colleagues recent research on massage therapy with preterm infants (Diego, Field, & Hernandez-Reif, 2008; Field, Diego, & Hernandez-Reif, 2008) (Chapter 3), and recent research on the Fast Track intervention with high risk children and adolescents (The Conduct Problems Prevention Research Group, 2007) (Chapter 12).

Expert Research Consultants

Life-span development has become an enormous, complex field, and no single author, or even several authors, can possibly be an expert in many different areas of life-span development. To solve this problem, I sought the input of leading experts in many different research areas of life-span development. The experts provided me with detailed evaluations and recommendations for a chapter(s) or topics in their area(s) of expertise. The expert research consultants for *Life-Span Development,* twelfth edition, were:

Expert	*Chapters and Topics*
Maria Hernandez-Reif *University of Alabama*	Chapters 3 (Prenatal Development and Birth) and Chapter 4 (Physical Development in Infancy)
Andrew Meltzoff *University of Washington*	Chapter 5 (Cognitive Development in Infancy)

Ross Thompson *University of California— Davis*	Chapter 6 (Socioemotional Development in Infancy) and Chapter 8 (Socioemotional Development in Early Childhood)
Candice Mills *University of Texas at Dallas*	Chapter 17 (Physical and Cognitive Development in Early Childhood)
L. Monique Ward *University of Michigan*	Chapter 11 (Physical and Cognitive Development in Adolescence) and Chapter 12 (Socioemotional Development in Adolescence)
John Schulenberg *University of Michigan*	Chapter 13 (Physical and Cognitive Development in Early Adulthood) and Chapter 14 (Socioemotional Development in Early Adulthood)
Phyllis Moen *University of Minnesota*	Careers, Work, and Gender in Adulthood and Aging (Chapters 14, 15, and 18)
Karen Fingerman *Purdue University*	Social Relationships (Chapters 14, 16, and 19)
K. Warner Schaie *Pennsylvania State University*	Chapter 18 (Cognitive Development in Late Adulthood)
Margie Lachman *Brandeis University*	Chapter 16 (Socioemotional Development in Middle Adulthood)
Arthur Kramer *University of Illinois*	Chapter 17 (Physical Development in Late Adulthood) and Chapter 18 (Cognitive Development in Late Adulthood)
Wolfgang Stroebe *University of Utrecht, The Netherlands*	Chapter 20 (Death, Dying, and Grieving)

Applications

It is important to not only present the scientific foundations of life-span development to students, but also to provide applied examples of concepts and to give students a sense that the field of life-span development has personal meaning for them. To underscore the importance of applications, I have included an *Applications in Life-Span Development* interlude in every chapter that focuses on health and well-being, parenting, and education. A new *Applications* interlude appears in Chapter 3: From Waterbirth to Music Therapy (Field, 2007).

In addition to giving special attention throughout the text to health and well-being, parenting, and educational applications, the twelfth edition of *Life-Span Development* also includes a *Careers in Life-Span Development* profile in every chapter. They describe an individual whose career relates to the chapter's content. Most of these profiles have a photograph of the person at work. In addition, a *Careers in Life-Span Development* appendix follows Chapter 1 and describes a number of careers in education/ research, clinical/counseling, medical/nursing/physical development, and family/relationships categories. Several new *Career* profiles appear in this new edition, including Helen Schwe, Developmental Psychologist and Toy Designer (Chapter 7).

ADULT DEVELOPMENT, AGING, AND DIVERSITY

Two very important aspects of a text on life-span development are strong coverage of adult development and aging, as well as diversity.

Adult Development and Aging

Instructors have repeatedly told me that most life-span texts don't give adequate attention to adult development and aging. In the twelfth edition, I have substantially modified, expanded, and updated the adult development and aging content, continuing a process I began a number of editions ago. Examples of new coverage include:

- Coverage of a longitudinal study on the charateristics of emerging adults who became competent after experiencing difficulties while growing up (Masten, Obradovic, & Burt, 2006)
- New description of research on college students' mental health problems, including new Figure 13.1 (American College Health Association, 2008)
- Updated material on obesity in emerging and early adulthood, including longitudinal data and new Figure 13.3 (Centers for Disease Control and Prevention, 2006), and also coverage of recent large-scale study of more than 168,000 adults in 63 countries (Balkau & others, 2007)
- Description of recent research on stress in the U.S. workplace (American Psychological Association, 2007)
- Extensively updated and expansion of material on adult attachment based on a recent research review by leading experts (Mikulincer & Shaver, 2007, 2009)
- Coverage of two recent studies on gender differences and similarities in the use of words for various purposes (Mehl & others, 2007; Nelson & others, 2008)
- Description of longitudinal study that compared the risk of dying for married and never-married individuals (Ikeda & others, 2007)
- Updated description of gender differences in attraction (Eastwick & Finkel, 2008)
- Coverage of recent research comparing same-sex couples with opposite-sex dating, engaged, and married dyads (Roisman & others, 2008)
- New Figure 15.3 showing NK cells destroying a tumor and coverage of a recent study revealing high NK cell levels in persistently unemployed young and middle-aged adults (Cohen & others, 2007)
- Coverage of the increasing trend for midlife couples to have to plan for two retirements, his and hers (Moen, Kelly, & Magennis, 2008)

- Expanded and updated coverage of menopause (Gosden, 2007; Zaborowska & others, 2007)

- Inclusion of new data from K. Warner Schaie's (2007) Seattle Longitudional Study on generational differences in parents and their offspring at 60 to 67 years of age

- Coverage of a recent study on developmental comparisons of older, middle-aged, and younger adults on the Big Five factors of personality (Allemand, Zimprich, & Hendriks, 2008)

- Substantial updating and expansion of conclusions about stability and change in personality development based on a recent review by Brent Roberts and Daniel Mroczek (2008)

- Description of a recent study on support between adult siblings (Voorpostel & Blieszner, 2008)

- Coverage of a recent study documenting the stronger role of mothers in intergenerational connections than fathers (Monserud, 2008)

- Inclusion of information about two recent studies that document how various characteristics influence the degree individuals have intergenerational contact (Bucx & others, 2008; Sarkisian & Gerstel, 2008)

- Description of recent study linking parental generativity with young adult offsprings' conscientiousness and agreeableness (Peterson, 2006)

- Discussion of recent study on the intergenerational transmission of conduct disorder (D'Onofrio & others, 2007)

- New coverage of a gender difference in health that suprisingly favors men (Perls, 2007)

- Updated and expanded discussion of the role that telomerase inhibition might play in reducing cancerous cells (Chen, Yang, & Zhang, 2008; Fakhoury, Nimmo, & Autexier, 2007)

- Coverage of a recent study linking smoking with a higher concentrations of free radicals (Reddy Thavanti & others, 2008)

- New illustration of mitochondria to accompany the mitochondrial theory of aging (Figure 17.4)

- Coverage of recent neuroimaging study on slowing prefrontal cortex activity during retrieval of information (Rypma, Eldreth, & Rebbechi, 2007)

- Considerable expansion and updating of research and current knowledge about various aspects of the aging brain (Chen & others, 2007; Gould, 2007; Mora & others, 2007)

- Updated description of the limitations of neurogenesis in the aging brain (Nelson, 2006)

- Coverage of recent study on exercise and brain volume in older adults (Colcombe & others, 2006)

- New description of falls as the leading cause of injury death in 65-year and older adults (National Center for Health Statistics, 2008)

- Considerable expansion and updating of research and current knowledge about various aspects of the aging brain

(Hillman, Erikson, & Kramer, 2008; Libert, Cohen, & Guarente, 2008; Yuan, 2008)

- New material on individual differences in brain lateralization and aging, including new Figure 17.7 showing an fMRI scan of 80-year-old T. Boone Pickens' brain (Helman, 2008)

- Coverage of recent national study revealing that older adults have only slightly increased their level of exercise in recent years, including new Figure 17.9 (Centers for Disease Control and Prevention, 2008)

- New discussion of the role that resveratrol plays in increasing longevity through moderate drinking and description of its link to a key enzyme, SIRT1 (Pallas & others, 2008; Putics & others, 2008)

- Discussion of recent longitudinal study on physical fitness, weight, and longevity across a 12-year period (Sui & others, 2007)

- New material from recent large-scale study on the sexual activity of older adults, including new Figure 17.13 (Lindau & others, 2007)

- Description of three factors most likely to contribute to cognitive decline in fluid mechanics in late adulthood (Lovden & Lindenberger, 2007)

- Discussion of recent research indicating that trial-to-trial variablity on perceptual speed tasks signals impending decline in the cognitive performance of older adults (Lovden & others, 2007)

- Revised conclusion about age differences in sustained attention and vigilence (Isella & others, 2008)

- Coverage of Sherry Willis and her colleagues' (2006) extensive cognitive aging intervention study with older adults

- Inclusion of recent ideas about the engagement model of cognitive optimization in older adults and recent research on the Senior Odyssey program that implements this model (Stine-Morrow & others, 2007)

- Coverage of recent research on how important cohort effects are in cognitive aging (Zelinski & Kennison, 2007)

- Expanded and updated coverage of cognitive neuroscience and aging, including activity increases in older adults' frontal and parietal regions while they are engaging in tasks that require cognitive control processes, such as attention (Grady, 2008)

- Description of recent study on the role of sustained attention in older adults' decision making (Isella & others, 2008)

- Inclusion of research in men in their seventies, indicating that reading daily reduced their mortality (Jacobs & others, 2008)

- New photo and description of the Young@Heart Chorus to illustrate the "use it" side of "use it or lose it"

- Inclusion of recent research on the *apoE* gene and onset of Alzheimer disease (Sando & others, 2008)

- Coverage of recent research on the use of deep brain stimulation in treating Parkinson disease (Ellrichmann, Harati, & Müller, 2008)

- Coverage of a recent study linking years of education and cognitive ability in 79-year-olds (Gow & others, 2008)

- Inclusion of recent research on a link between on regular religious attendance and a lower risk of mortality (Gillum & others, 2008)

- New *Diversity in Life-Span Development* interlude, Work and Retirement Around the World, describing a recent large-scale study of 21,000 40- to 79-year-old adults in 21 countries (HSBC Insurance, 2007)

- Description of information about ibuprofen and coffee being linked to a lower risk of developing Parkinson disease (Chand & Litvan, 2007)

- Discussion of five characteristics in late adulthood that are linked to low self-esteem (Giarrusso & Bengtson, 2007)

- Coverage of 12-year longitudinal study of older men linking aspects of neuroticism to a lower level of survival (Mroczek & Spiro, 2007)

- Inclusion of research on consientiousness as a predictor of mortality risk from childhood through late adulthood (Martin, Friedman, & Schwartz, 2007)

- Description of recent studies indicating that older adults are more inclined to use passive emotion regulation strategies (such as distracting themselves from the problem and suppressing feelings) and less inclined to express anger in solving interpersonal problems than younger adults are (Blanchard-Fields & Coats, 2007; Coats & Blanchard-Fields, 2008)

- Inclusion of recent study on positive and negative emotions in older and younger adults (Lochenhoff, Costa, & Lane, 2008)

- Inclusion of recent study on relationships between aging parents and their children (Fingerman & others, 2008)

- Description of recent study on older adults' social networks (Cornwell, Laumann, & Schumm, 2008)

- Discussion of recent study on the types of emotions experienced with new and established friends in younger and older adults, including new Figure 19.7 (Charles & Piazza, 2007)

- Coverage of recent research on the importance of unmarried older adults being embedded in a friendship network (Fiori, Smith, & Antonucci, 2007)

- New description of three factors most often related with living the "good life" as an older adult in most cultures (Fry, 2007)

- New section on Kastenbaum's (2007) view of the death system

- New Figure 20.1 that focuses on how the death system was involved in Hurricane Katrina (Kastenbaum, 2007)

- Recently proposed ideas about what might constitute a "good death" (Brink & Smith, 2008)

- New section, Coping and Type of Death (Wortman & Boerner, 2007)

- Description of a recent study indicating that when older adults engaged in helping behavior following a spouse's death, they experienced an accelerated decline in depressive symptoms (Brown & others, 2008)

- New coverage of the increasingly used terms of complicated grief and disenfrancised grief (Zuckoff & others, 2006; Read & Elliott, 2007)

- Description of the outpouring of support and forgiveness to the widow of Charles Roberts by the Amish following his murder of five Amish school girls in October 2006

Diversity

Diversity is another key aspect of life-span development. I made every effort to explore diversity issues in a sensitive manner in each chapter. In addition to weaving diversity into discussions of life-span topics, I've included *Diversity in Life-Span Development* interludes in each chapter. Several new and updated *Diversity* interludes appear in this new edition, including recent research by Aletha Huston and her colleagues (2006) on interviewing in improverished families (Chapter 10) the "I Have a Dream" Program ("I Have a Dream" Foundation, 2008) (Chapter 11) and Work and Retirement Around the World (HSBC Insurance, 2007) (Chapter 18). The discussion of diversity also includes new material on these topics:

- Expanded discussion of poverty and children, including updated statistics (Federal Interagency Forum on Child and Family Statistics, 2007)

- Updated coverage of cultural variation in infant motor development (Adolph, 2008)

- Updated and expanded description of cultural variations in infant emotion (Cole & Tan, 2007)

- Discussion of recent research on acculturation of Latino families and links to infant cognitive development (Cabrera & others, 2007)

- Expanded and updated coverage of young children's nutrition in low-income families (Darton-Hill & others, 2007; Sausenthaler & others, 2007)

- New description of low-income families having fewer resources than higher-income families (Conger & Dogan, 2007; Patterson & Hastings, 2007)

- Coverage of recent study in four developing countries linking caregiver depression with childhood injuries (Howe, Hutley, & Abramsky, 2007)

- Description of recent study of parental monitoring of Latino children's eating habits (Arrendondo & others, 2006)

- Updated and expanded coverage of family leave policies around the world related to childbirth in the *Diversity in Life-Span Development* interlude (Tolani & Brooks-Gunn, 2008)

- New coverage of Marva Collin's work with children from impoverished areas

- Inclusion of recent research on factors involved in inconsistent contraceptive use by female adolescents living in low-income circumstances (Davies & others, 2006)

- Updating of the continuing improvement in school dropout rates for different ethnic groups (National Center for Education Statistics, 2007)

- Description of the recent initiative by the Bill and Melinda Gates Foundation (2008) to reduce the dropout rate in schools with high dropout rates

- Coverage of recent study on the bicultural identity of Mexican American and Asian American college students (Devos, 2006)

- Inclusion of recent studies linking discrimination of African American and Latino adoelscents to more problems and lower academic achievement, including new Figure 12.5, showing the types of racial hassles African American adolescents experience (DeGarmo & Martinez, 2006; Sellers & others, 2006)

- Inclusion of recent research comparing the religion and spirituality of African American, Caribbean Black, and non-Latino White older adults (Taylor, Chatters, & Jackson, 2007)

- New description of cultural variations in social support for older adults (Antonucci, Akiyama, & Sherman, 2007)

WRITING, ORGANIZATION, AND THE LEARNING SYSTEM

The new edition of this text should be accessible to students because of the extensive rewriting, organization, and learning system. Every sentence, paragraph, section, and chapter of this book was carefully examined and, when appropriate, revised and rewritten. The result is a much clearer, better-organized presentation of material in this new edition.

Students should not only be challenged to study hard and think more deeply and productively about life-span development, but also be provided with an effective learning system. Instructors and students have commented about how student-friendly this book has become in recent editions.

Now more than ever, students struggle to find the main ideas in their courses, especially in courses like life-span development, which include so much material. The learning system centers on learning goals that, together with the main text headings, keep the key ideas in front of the reader from the beginning to the end of the chapter. Each chapter has no more than six main headings and corresponding learning goals, which are presented in the chapter-opening spread. At the end of each main section of a chapter, the learning goal is repeated in a featured called Review and Reflect, which prompts students to review the key topics in the section and poses a question to encourage them to think critically about what they have read. At the end of the chapter, under the heading Reach Your Learning Goals, the learning goals guide students through the chapter review.

In addition to the verbal tools just described, mini–chapter maps that link up with the learning goals are presented at the beginning of each major section in the chapter. The complete learning system, including many additional features not mentioned here, is presented later in a section titled Visual tour for Students.

CHAPTER 1
INTRODUCTION

- Extensively revised Chapter 1, which in this new edition combines Chapters 1 and 2 from the previous edition; change requested by a number of adopters and reviewers to help shorten the early part of the text

- Significant updating of research and citations

- Revised definition of gender

- Expanded discussion of poverty and children, including updated statistics on the percentage of U.S. children living in poverty (Federal Interagency Forum on Child and Family Statistics, 2007)

- Updated coverage of family policy (Coltrane & others, 2008; Conger & Conger, 2008)

- Description of recent research revealing the cumulative effects of poverty on physiological indices of stress in children (Evans & Kim, 2007)

- Deleted section on history of interest in children and aging

- Reduced amount of material on Freud's theory at reviewers' and adopters' requests

CHAPTER 2
BIOLOGICAL BEGINNINGS

- Considerable rewriting and editing to make chapter shorter in length without sacrificing any content

- Description of recent search documenting how stress hormones can damage DNA (Flint & others, 2007)

- Updated material on the approximate number of genes that humans possess (20,500) (Science Daily, 2008)

- Description of recent research on the characteristics of boys with Klinefelter syndorme (Ross & others, 2008)

- Updated and expanded coverage of fragile X syndrome, including a new photograph of a boy with fragile X syndrome (One, Farzin, & Hagerman, 2008)

- Inclusion of recent research on cognitive deficits in boys with fragile X syndrome (Hooper & others, 2008)

- New coverage of the underutilization of the only drug (hydroxyurea) approved to treat sickle-cell anemia in adolescents and adults, and current research that is under way to determine if the drug is effective in treating babies

- New section on the extensive recent research on the potential for using noninvasive prental diagnosis (NIPD) as an alternative to chorionic villus sampling and aminocentesis (Avent & others, 2008; Finning & Chitty, 2008)

- New coverage of the increasing use of fetal MRI for detecting fetal malformations (Laifer-Narin & others, 2007; Muhler & others, 2007)

- New Figure 2.12 showing a fetal fMRI

- Description of recent large-scale study that found no difference in pregnancy loss between chronic villus sampling and amniocentesis (Caughey, Hopkins, & Norton, 2006).

- New information about the success rates of in vitro fertilization at different ages, including new Figure 2.9 (Centers for Disease Control and Prevention, 2006)

- New coverage of recent large-scale study on adoption and learning disabilities (Altarac & Saroha, 2007)

- Coverage of recent study of the antisocial behavior of adopted and nonadopted young adults (Grotevant & others, 2006)

- Description of recent research review on the self-esteem of adopted and nonadopted children, and transracial and same-race adoptees (Juffer & IJzendoorn, 2007)

- Updated and expanded discussion of the epigenetic view (Gottlieb, 2007)

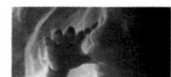

CHAPTER 3
PRENATAL DEVELOPMENT AND BIRTH

- Extensive editing and updating of chapter based on recommendations by expert consultant Maria Hernandez-Reif

- Important new section on the development of the brain in the prenatal period, including a photo of the tubular appearance of the human nervous system six weeks after conception (Moulson & Nelson, 2008; Nelson, 2009)

- New discussion of neural tube defects and what characterizes anencephaly and spina bifida

- Inclusion of information from a recent research review of aspirin and reproductive outcomes (James, Brancazio, & Price, 2008)

- Coverage of recent study on caffeine intake during pregnancy and risk for miscarriage (Weng, Odouli, & Li, 2008)

- Change of label from FAS to FASD (fetal alcohol spectrum disorders) in keeping with recently developed terminology and expanded coverage of FASD (Olson, King, & Jirikowic, 2008)

- Description of recent research on environmental tobacco smoke and risk of low birth weight (Leonardi-Bee & others, 2008)

- Coverage of recent research on the harmful effects of cocaine use during pregnancy on growth, language development, and attention (Acconero & others, 2007; Lewis & others, 2008; Richardson, Goldschmidt, & Willford, 2008)

- Inclusion of information about a recent study that revealed negative neonatal outcomes following exposure to methamphetamine in the prenatal period (Smith & others, 2008)

- Updated and revised conclusions about the effects of marijuana use by pregnant women on offspring (Williams & Ross, 2007)

- Description of recent study on prenatal marijuana exposure and lower intelligence in childhood (Goldschmidt & others, 2008)

- Coverage of recent analysis proposing that fetal programming from an overweight pregnant woman is likely linked to the offspring being overweight in childhood and adolescence (McMillen & others, 2008)

- Inclusion of recent research on a link between folic acid and a reduction in preterm birth (Bukowski & others, 2008).

- Updated research on fetal mercury exposure and developmental outcomes (Triche & Hossain, 2007; Xue & others, 2007)

- Description of a recent research review on maternal stress during pregnancy and negative developmental outcomes in offspring (Talge & others, 2007)

- Coverage of recent study showing that a decline in stress during pregnancy was linked to a lower incidence of preterm birth (Glynn & others, 2008)

- New *Applications in Life-Span Development* interlude, From Waterbirth to Music Therapy (Field, 2007)

- Description of recent studies on the benefits of massage and acupuncture during labor (Beckmann & Garrett, 2006; Gaudernack, Forbord, & Hole, 2006)

- Expanded and updated coverage of why cesarean delivery has increased in the United States and recent data on trends in cesarean delivery (National Center for Health Statistics, 2007)

- Updated coverage of trends in cesarean delivery (National Center for Health Statistics, 2007)

- Description of recent study linking preterm birth with dropping out of school, including new research figure (Geeta & others, 2008)

- Description of recent MRI study of brain deficiencies in children born very preterm (Narberhus & others, 2008)

- Coverage of the factors involved in why poverty continues to contribute to preterm birth in the United States (Goldenberg & Nagahawatte, 2008)

- Considerably expanded and updated material on the consequences of preterm birth (Minde & Zelkowitz, 2008)

- New coverage of a recent survey on techniques used in the NICU (Field & others, 2006)

- Description of recent national study on the incidence of depressive symptoms in mothers and fathers in the postpartum period (Paulson, Dauber, & Leiferman, 2006)

- Updated research about the use of progestin in reducing the risk of preterm birth (Fonseca & others, 2007; Lamant & Jaggat, 2007)

- Coverage of a recent study that revealed a substantial reduction in preterm birth when women took folic acid for one year prior to delivering (Bukowski & others, 2008)

- Description of two recent experimental studies revealing the benefits of kangaroo care (Gathwala, Singh, & Balhara, 2008; Suman, Udani, & Nanavati, 2008)

- Updated coverage of the *Research in Life-Span Development* interlude on Tiffany Field's massage therapy research, including recent research on the effects of massage therapy on preterm infants' stress behaviors with new Figure 3.10 illustrating the results (Field, Diego, & Hernandez-Reif, 2008; Hernandez-Reif, Diego, & Field, 2007)

- New coverage of the sleep deprivation experienced by post-partum women, including new research Figure 3. (Gunderson & others, 2008; National Sleep Foundation, 2007)

- Expanded and updated description of postpartum mothers' patterns of interaction with their infants (Teti & Towe-Goodman, 2008)

- Coverage of recent study on mothers' postpartum depression, preterm/full-term infants, and maternal synchrony (Feldman & Eidelman, 2007)

- Description of the unsettled issue of the optimal course of therapy for the depressed, breast feeding mother, and breast fed infant (Field, 2008)

CHAPTER 4
PHYSICAL DEVELOPMENT IN INFANCY

- Extensive rewriting and editing of chapter for improved student understanding, including a number of changes based on input from expert consultant Maria Hernandez-Reif

- Updated coverage of the development of the brain (Fischer & Immordino-Yang, 2008; Nelson, 2009)

- Expanded description of the function of myelination (Haynes & others, 2006)

- Expanded and updated discussion of links between spurts in brain growth and cognitive functioning (Immordino-Yang & Fischer, 2007)

- Description of recent research on factors related to infant night waking (DeLeon & Karraker, 2007)

- Expanded discussion of REM sleep in infancy and question raised about whether we can know for sure whether infants dream

- Updated and expanded discussion of the shared sleeping and SIDS controversy (Bajanowoski & others, 2007; Mitchell, 2007)

- Expanded and updated research on SIDS, including recent information about the role of the neurotransmitter serotonin in the brain stem (Shani, Fifer, & Myers, 2007)

- New discussion of a recent research on the percentage of overweight babies in the United States, including new Figure 4.11 (Kim & others, 2006)

- Expanded and updated material on developmental changes in infants' eating patterns (Black & Hurley, 2007; Black & Lozoff, 2008; Chatoor & Macoay, 2008)

- Coverage of recent information about breast feeding and type 2 diabetes (Villegas & others, 2008)

- Inclusion of material from a recent research review by the American Academy of Pediatrics indicating no link between breast feeding and children's allergies (Greer & others, 2008)

- Extensive updating, revision, and expansion of material on breast feeding based on a recent large-scale research review (Agency for Healthcare Quality and Research, 2007)

- Description of recent research linking longer breast feeding with a lower incidence of metabolic syndrome in midlife women (Ram & others, 2008)

- Discussion of an important issue related to the correlational nature of breast versus bottle feeding studies (Agency for Healthcare Research and Quality, 2007)

- Description of recent research on infants' walking patterns and their occasional large steps (Badaly & Adolph, 2008)

- Updated coverage of cultural variation in infant motor development (Adolph, 2008)

- Updated information about the development of visual acuity in young infants (Aslin & Lathrop, 2008)

- New discussion of recent research on face perception in young infants (Kelly & others, 2007a, b; Slater, Field, & Hernandez-Reif, 2007)

CHAPTER 5
COGNITIVE DEVELOPMENT INFANCY

- Extensive editing and rewriting of Piagetian material for improved student understanding

- Recent revised interpretation of A-not-B error (Clearfield & others, 2006)

- Updated and expanded evaluation of Piaget's view of infant cognitive development (Slater, Field, & Hernandez-Reif, 2007)

- Expanded analysis of object permanence, including Andrew Meltzoff's (2008; Meltzoff & Moore, 1998) criticisms of the violation of expectations method as an accurate measure of object permanence

- Expanded and updated coverage of attention, including developmental changes in orienting/investigative and sustained attention (Courage & Richards, 2008)

- New description of the main region of the brain involved in infant attention

- Expanded and updated discussion of habituation and its importance in infant development (Slater, Field, & Hernandez-Reif, 2007)

- New coverage of joint attention and its role in infants' language development (Tomasello & Carpenter, 2007)

- Coverage of recent research on the emergence of gaze following in infants, including new Figure 5.5 showing the research setting and sequence involved in the study (Brooks & Meltzoff, 2005)

- Updated and expanded information on Meltzoff's (2007) view of infant imitation

- Description of recent research on deferred imitation as a predictor of communicative gestures (Heimann & others, 2006)

- New discussion of connections between development of the brain and development of memory in infancy, including new figure

- Expanded and updated coverage of concept formation and categorization in infancy (Booth, 2006; Quinn, Bhatt, & Hayden, 2008)

- New description of the Bayley-III, including its two new scales—socioemotional and adaptive, that are assessed by questionnaires given to the infant's primary caregiver (Lennon & others, 2008)

- Inclusion of two recent studies on the prediction of language skills at 24 months of age by joint attention as early as 10 to 12 months (Brooks & Meltzoff, 2007; Mundy & others, 2007)

- Description of recent research on the early development of intense interests in particular categories, including strong gender differences, including new Figure 5.9 (DeLoache, Simcock, & Macari, 2007)

- Revised, updated, and expanded coverage of early language development based on leading expert Beverly Goldfield's (Goldfield & Snow, 2009) recommendations

- Movement of recognizing speech sounds before babbling in the section on early development of language in infancy

- New section on gestures to indicate their importance in early language development and expansion of this topic

- Expanded discussion of infant understanding of words before speaking first word

 **CHAPTER 6**
SOCIOEMOTIONAL DEVELOPMENT IN INFANCY

- Extensive rewriting of chapter for improved student understanding, including addition of numerous concrete examples of concepts and more descriptions of infants' behaviors and emotions

- Expanded and updated coverage of the controversy regarding the onset of early emotions (Lewis, 2007)

- Description of cultural variations in infant emotion (Cole & Tan, 2007)

- Inclusion of new material on links between infant fear and guilt, empathy, and low aggression in childhood (Rothbart, 2007)

- New discussion of why studying the self in infancy is difficult based on the view of leading expert Ross Thompson (2007)

- Updated and expanded description of separation protest in infants (Kagan, 2008)

- Expanded and updated coverage of infant smiling, including new Figure 6.3 on showing the characteristics of an intense smile by a 6-month-old (Messinger, 2008)

- New description of cultural variations in how parents handle infant emotions (Cole & Tan, 2007)

- Description of recent research review on swaddling (van Sleuwen & others, 2007)

- New discussion of developmental changes in temperament characteristics (Rothbart & Gartstein, 2008)

- Description of recent research on factors that benefited children with a difficult temperament (Bradley & Corwyn, 2008)

- Important new major section, Social Orientation/ Understanding, that includes coverage of infants' developing social interest, locomotion, joint attention, and social referencing (Laible & Thompson, 2007; Thompson, 2006, 2008)

- New discussion of recent research on becoming a social partner with a peer in 1-and 2-year-olds, including a photograph of the research setting and task (Figure 6.6) (Brownell, Ramani, & Zerwas, 2006)

- Description of recent study on links between joint attention in infancy and social competence at 30 months of age (Vaughn Van Hecke & others, 2007)

- New description of Bowlby's internal working model of attachment based on expert consultant Ross Thompson's recommendation

- Expanded discussion of cultural variations in attachment (Saami & others, 2006)

- Connection of turn-taking and games like peek-a-boo to the development of joint attention (Chapter 6) (Tomasello & Carpenter, 2007)

- Expanded coverage of the role of locomotion in social orientation and motivation (Thompson, 2008).

- New summary section, Infants' Social Sophistication and Insight (Thompson, 2008)

- New commentary about how recent findings regarding infants' earlier social understanding may be linked to understanding goals and intentions in Bowlby's phase 3 of attachment rather than phase 4 (Thompson, 2008)

- New coverage of John Gottman and his colleagues (2004) Bringing Home Baby project

- Description of recent research on parent-infant synchrony and children's self-regulation (Feldman, 2007)

- Coverage of recent longitudinal study on infant attachment and cognitive development in the elementary school years (O'Connor & McCartney, 2007)

- New Figure 6.10 on the dramatic increase in the percentage of U.S. fathers staying at home full-time with their children and the results of a recent study of stay-at-home fathers (Rochlen & others, 2008)

- New Figure 6.11 on the primary care arrangements for children under 5 years of age with employed mothers (Clarke-Stewart & Miner, 2008)

- Updated and expanded coverage of family leave policies around the world related to childbirth in the *Diversity in Life-Span Development* interlude (Tolani & Brooks-Gunn, 2008)

- Inclusion of recent research on the positive outcomes that develop when low-income parents select higher-quality child care (McCartney & others, 2007)

- Description of recent research on quality of child care and children's vocabulary development (Belsky & others, 2007)

CHAPTER 7
PHYSICAL AND COGNITIVE DEVELOPMENT IN EARLY CHILDHOOD

- New Figure 7.1 that shows an electron microscope image of myelination

- Inclusion of information about three recent studies focused on increasing young children's physical activity (Beets & Foley, 2008; Bower & others, 2008; Trost, Fees, & Dzewaltowski, 2008)

- New *Research in Life-Span Development* interlude, Physical Activity in Young Children Attending Preschools

- New description of the recent trend in reducing physical activity opportunities in preschool and kindergarten programs (American Academy of Pediatrics, 2006)

- Added description of what body mass index is and how it is used to categorize a child as being obese, overweight, or at risk for being overweight (Centers for Disease Control and Prevention, 2008)

- Coverage of recent large-scale U.S. study on the percentage of children 2 to 19 years of age who have weight problems and the recent leveling off in overweight categories (Odgen, Carroll, & Flegal, 2008)

- Discussion of recent research linking being overweight at age 3 with being overweight at age 12 (Nader & others, 2006)

- Coverage of recent study of ethnic variations in being overweight in 3-year-old children (Kimbro, Brooks-Gunn, & McLanahan, 2006)

- New discussion of the role of caregiver feeding behavior and styles in young children's eating behavior (Black & Hurley, 2007; Black & Lozoff, 2008)

- Recent research on iron deficiency anemia in children and their affective behavior (Lozoff & others, 2007)

- Expanded and updated coverage of young children's nutrition in low-income families (Sausenthaler & others, 2007)

- Revised, improved Figure 7.4 on Piaget's three mountains task that provides students with a better understanding of the concept of egocentrism

- Expanded description of criticisms of Vygotsky (Gauvain, 2008)

- New coverage of advances in executive attention and sustained attention in early childhood (Rothbart & Gartstein, 2008)

- New description of exercises used in some European kindergartens to improve young children's attention (Mills & Mills, 2000; Posner & Rothbart, 2007)

- Much expanded and updated coverage of the young child's theory of mind with considerable input from leading expert Candice Mills

- Description of recent study linking infant attention to 4-year-olds' theory of mind (Wellman & others, 2008)

- Coverage of recent study linking young children's theory of mind competence with later metamemory skills (Lockl & Schneider, 2007)

- New discussion of reasons to question false-belief understanding as a pivotal point in the development of a theory of mind

- Two new figures that show stimuli used in theory of mind research

- New section, Theory of Mind and Autism

- New *Careers in Life-Span Development* profile, Helen Schwe, Developmental Psychologist and Toy Designer

- Updated description of 3-year-olds' phonological advances (Menn & Stoel-Gammon, 2009)

- Expanded and updated coverage of young children's improvements in pragmatics (Aktar & Herold, 2008)

- Description of how not all developmentally appropriate programs show significant benefits for children and recent changes in the concept of developmentally appropriate education (Hyson, 2007)

- Updated material on Project Head Start, including information about it being the largest federally funded program for U.S. children (Hagen & Lamb-Parker, 2008)

CHAPTER 8
SOCIOEMOTIONAL DEVELOPMENT IN EARLY CHILDHOOD

- Expanded explanation of why young children have unrealistically positive self-descriptions (Thompson, 2008)

- New description of young children's use of psychological traits in their self-descriptions at about 4 to 5 years of age (Thompson, 2006)

- Expansion of section on Self-Understanding to Self-Understanding and Understanding Others, including new introduction on how young children are more psychologically sophisticated than used to be thought (Labile & Thompson, 2007)

- Coverage of research on how even 4-year-olds understand that people will sometimes make statements that aren't true to get what they want or to avoid trouble (Gee & Heyman, 2007; Lee & others, 2002)

- Description of recent research on the age at which young children take into account the relative frequency of errors informants make in deciding whether to trust the person (Pasquini & others, 2007)

- Reorganization of emotion regulation coverage with a new introductory paragraph on its importance in children's development.

- Coverage of recent research on emotion-dismissing parents and children's poor emotion regulation (Lunkenheimer, Shields, & Cortina, 2007)

- New section on young children's development of a conscience (Kochanska & Aksan, 2007)

- Important new section, Parenting and Young Children's Moral Development, that focuses on the quality of parent-child relationships, parents' use of proactive strategies, and conversational dialogue about moral issues (Laible & Thompson, 2007; Thompson, 2006)

- Coverage of recent study linking an early mutually responsive orientation between parents and their infant, a decrease in power assertive discipline in early childhood, and an increase in the young child's internalization and self-regulation (Kochanska & others, 2008)

- New description of recent research review of mothers' and fathers' socialization strategies (Bronstein, 2006)

- Discussion of the increasing number of recent research studies that have found negative developmental outcomes for children who have been physically punished by their parents (Bender & others, 2007; Mulvaney & Mebert, 2007)

- New coverage of data indicating that child neglect occurs up to three times as often as child abuse (Benoit, Coolbear, & Crawford, 2008)

- New information about abnormal stress hormone levels in children who have been maltreated (Gunnar & Fisher, 2006), including new Figure 8.4

- New description of three main characteristics of sibling relationships (Dunn, 2007)

- Inclusion of recent research on mediating training for parents and positive sibling outcomes (Smith & Ross, 2007)

- Updated coverage of birth order based on a recent review (Paulhus, 2008)

- Coverage of Ann Crouter's (2006) recent research on how parents' poor conditions at work can be brought home to negatively influence parenting behavior and child outcomes

- New description of a link between working mothers and a reduction in children's (especially girls') gender stereotyping (Goldberg & Lucas-Thompson, 2008)

- Added commentary that the problems children from divorced families experience often stem from active marital conflict in the predivorce period (Thompson, 2008)

- Description of Paul Amato's (2006) longitudinal research on adult outcomes of individuals who experienced their parents' divorce in childhood and adolescence

- New description of low-income families having less resources than higher-income families (Conger & Dogan, 2007; Patterson & Hastings, 2007)

- Expanded coverage of pretend play, including Catherine Garvey's and Angeline Lillard's views

CHAPTER 9

PHYSICAL AND COGNITIVE DEVELOPMENT IN MIDDLE AND LATE CHILDHOOD

- Important new section, The Brain, including recent research on changes in the prefrontal cortex and diffuse/focused activation in the brain, as well as the connection of these changes to cognitive functioning in areas such as cognitive control (Durston & Casey, 2006; Durston & others, 2006)

- Discussion of cortical thickening in children 5 to 11 years of age (Toga, Thompson, & Sowell, 2006)

- Inclusion of recent data regarding the incidence and treatment of childhood cancer in the United States (National Cancer Institute, 2008a, b)

- Description of recent study of significant underdiagnosis of high blood pressure in a large percentage of children with the disease (Hansen, Gunn, & Kaelber, 2007)

- Coverage of recent study in four developing countries linking caregiver depression with child injuries (Howe, Hutley, & Abramsky, 2006)

- Description of recent research on factors linked with whether children will be physically active when they have free time (Heitzler & others, 2006)

- Discussion of recent research linking TV viewing in childhood with exercising less and eating fewer servings of fruit per day (Salmon, Campbell, & Crawford, 2006)

- Description of large-scale U.S. study showing recent leveling off in child obesity (Ogden, Carroll, & Flegal, 2008)

- Coverage of recent research on the benefits of an intensive resistance training program on reducing children's body fat and increasing their muscle strength (Benson, Torodes, & Fiatarone Singh, 2008)

- Inclusion of recent research indicating the amount of daily physical activity that is associated with lower odds of childhood obesity (Wittmeier, Mollard, & Kriellaars, 2008)

- Description of recent study linking aerobic exercise to an increase in planning skills in overweight children (Davis & others, 2007)

- Updated material on the increase in overweight children in many countries around the world (Fogelholm, 2008; Liu & others, 2008)

- Expanded and updated coverage of the developmental outcomes of children who are overweight

- Coverage of recent study indicating a link between body mass index and waist circumference in childhood and metabolic syndrome in adulthood (Sun & others, 2008)

- Description of recent study on how peers perceived obese children (Zeller, Reiter-Purtill, & Ramey, 2008)

- Description of recent study of parental monitoring of Latino children's eating habits (Arrendondo & others, 2006)

- Considerable editing of material on children with disabilities based on expert consultant Karen Harris' recommendations

- Updated description of the percentage of students with disabilities receiving special Services (National Center for Education Statistics, 2007)

- Revised definition of learning disabilities to more closely approximate the U.S. government's definition

- Coverage of trends in the percentage of students with learning disabilities who receive special services (National Center for Education Statistics, 2007)

- New discussion of the brain pathways that are involved in reading disabilities based on recent MRI brain scans (Shaywitz, Lyon, & Lyon, 2006)

- New Figure 9.5 of a 9-year-old boy with dyslexia going through an MRI scanner in a research study focused on learning disabilities

- New description of variation that occur across states and school systems in how learning disabilities are defined and diagnosed (Bender, 2008)

- Description of recent intensive 16-week instruction program that increased the reading skills of first-grade students with severe reading problems who had not responded to adequately to reading instruction (Simos & others, 2007)

- New material documenting a three-year delay in the thickening of the cerebral cortex in children with ADHD, including new Figure 9.6

- Updated coverage of new stimulant and nonstimulant drugs that are being evaluated in the treatment of ADHD (Bhatara & Aparasu, 2007; Faraone, 2007)

- New section, Autism Spectrum Disorders, including research linking autism spectrum disorders to genetic mutations on chromosome 16 in approximately 1 out of 100 cases of these disorders (Weiss & others, 2008)

- New Figure 9.7 showing the percentage of U.S. students with disabilities who spend time in the regular classroom in a recent school year (National Center for Education Statistics, 2007)

- Inclusion of new strategies parents and teachers can use to encourage students' creativity: (1) build students' self-confidence, (2) encourage students to take intellectual risks, and (3) guide students to be persistent and delay gratification

- Expanded and updated coverage of children's scientific thinking, including educational issues in teaching science to children (Gallagher, 2007; Moyer, Hackett, & Everett, 2007)

- Description of recent research on more than 107,000 students in 41 countries linking family, economic, and cultural influences to science achievement (Chiu, 2007)

- Expansion of discussion on what intelligence is, including variations of what Sternberg and Vygotsky might include in their views of what intelligence involves

- Updated discussion of the Wechsler scales to include recently introduced composite indexes such as the Verbal Comprehension Index, the Working Memory Index, and the Processing Speed Index

- Considerable editing and updating of the discussion of intelligence based on feedback from expert consultant Robert J. Sternberg

- Expanded and updated coverage of evaluating general tests of intelligence and the concept of general intelligence in comparison to the concept of multiple intelligencs, including Sternberg's (2008) most recent position on these topics

- New description of Sternberg and his colleagues (Sternberg & Grigorenko, 2008; Zhang & Sternberg, 2008) that there are no culture-fair tests, only culture-reduced tests

- Expanded and updated coverage of gifted education, including recent concerns that the No Child Left Behind Policy may be harming students who are gifted (Clark, 2008; Cloud, 2007)

- Extensively revised and updated discussion of sensitive periods in learning a second language (Thomas & Johnson, 2008)

CHAPTER 10

SOCIOEMOTIONAL DEVELOPMENT IN MIDDLE AND LATE CHILDHOOD

- Updated coverage of developmental changes in self-descriptions during middle and late childhood (Harter, 2006)

- New section, Understanding Others, including information about perspective taking and recent research on children's increasing psychological sophistication in understanding others, especially showing more skepticism of others' self-reports of value-laden terms (Heyman, Fu, & Lee, 2007)

- New section, Self-Regulation, describing the increased capacity for self-regulation in middle and late childhood, including its link to advances in managing one's own behavior, emotions, and thoughts that lead to increased social competence and achievement (Laible & Thompson, 2007)

- Connection of increased self-regulation to the discussion of developmental advances in the brain's prefrontal cortex in Chapter 9, "Physical and Cognitive Development in Middle and Late Childhood" (Durston & others, 2006)

- Description of recent research on the downside of high self-esteem in aggressive children (Menon & others, 2007)

- Coverage of recent research review of cross-cultural studies of Kohlberg's moral judgment stages, including the role of perspective taking (Gibbs & others, 2007)

- Updated summary of experts' conclusions about gender and Gilligan's approach to moral thinking (Hyde, 2005, 2007a, b; Walker, 2006)

- Description of recent research on an increase in gender stereotyping from preschool through the fifth grade (Miller & others, 2007)

- Description of recent research review on gender and visuo-spatial skills (Halpern & others, 2007)

- Coverage of the subtantial gender difference in literacy skills of boys and girls in the most recent National Assessment of Educational Progress (2007)

- Updating of discussion of relational aggression, including research that indicates relational aggression comprises a greater percentage of girls' total aggression than is the case for boys (Putallaz & others, 2007; Young, Boye, & Nelson, 2006)

- New coverage of the importance of parenting in middle and late childhood as gatekeepers for children's behavior as children spend less time with parents (Huston & Ripke, 2006)

- New section, Parents as Managers, describing the important roles that parents play as managers of children's opportunities, monitors of their behavior, and social initiators and arrangers (Eccles, 2007; Parke & Buriel, 2006)

- Discusssion of Hetherington's (2006) recent conclusions about which type of stepfamily arrangement is linked to better adjustment in children and adolescents

- New discussion of two longitudinal studies linking peer competence in middle and late childhood with competence at work and in close relationships in adulthood (Collins & van Dulmen, 2006; Huesmann & others, 2006)

- New description of two promising bullying intervention programs (Frey & others, 2005; Olweus, 2003)

- New coverage of recent conclusions by experts in educational psychology that the most effective teachers often use both constructivist and direct instruction approaches (Bransford & others, 2006)

- New *Diversity in Life-Span Development* interlude, Improving Resources for Schools and Families in Impoverished Areas, including recent research by Aletha Huston and her colleagues (Huston & others, 2006) on intervening in impoverished families

- Updated discussion of accountability and the No Child Left Behind legislation, including recent research on how many states actually have lowered rather than raised standards because of NCLB and NCLB's failure to meet its goal of reducing the ethnic achievement gap (Birman & others, 2007; Darling-Hammond, 2007)

- New description of Carol Dweck's (2006) recent concept of mindset

- New coverage of Marva Collin's work with children from impoverished areas

 **CHAPTER 11**
PHYSICAL AND COGNITIVE DEVELOPMENT IN ADOLESCENCE

- New *Images of Life-Span Development*, Latisha, Arnie, and Katie
- Coverage of recent research studies on body image and body dissatisfaction during adolescence that focus on appearance, physical and mental health problems, and the best and worst aspects of being a boy or a girl (Dyl & others, 2006; Gillen, Lefkowitz, & Shearer, 2006; Neumark-Sztainer & others, 2006; Zittleman, 2006)

- New section, Body Art, describing the increased use of tattooing and body piercing by adolescents and college students (Armstrong, Caliendo, & Roberts, 2006; Deschesnes, Fines, & Demers, 2006; Suris & others, 2007)

- Inclusion of information about recent study on early-maturing girls and their trying cigarettes and alcohol without their parents' knowledge (Westling & others, 2008)

- Updating and expansion of changes in the brain's development in adolescence, including new Figure 11.4

- New discussion of the implications of recent research on brain development in adolescence for the legal system, including whether this research can be used to decide whether an adolescent should be given the death penalty (Ash, 2006)

- Coverage of recent research on changes in the brain in adolescence and resistance to peer pressure (Paus & others, 2008)

- Description of recent research on patterns of TV viewing by high school students and links to their sexual experience (Ward & Friedman, 2006)

- Updated data on developmental changes in adolescents' sexual activities, including new Figure 11.5, illustrating these changes (MMWR, 2006)

- New discussion of the dramatic increase in oral sex by U.S. adolescents (Bersamin & others, 2006)

- Description of longitudinal study from 10 to 12 years of age to 25 years of age indicating a link between early sexual intercourse and problems in emerging adulthood (Cornelius & others, 2007)

- Coverage of recent research on a link between various risk factors and early sexual intercourse (Hyde & Price, 2007)

- Description of recent research review on factors linked to having early sexual intercourse (Zimmer-Gembeck & Helfand, 2008)

- Discussion of large-scale U.S. study on the increase in the use of a contraceptive during the last time high school students had sexual intercourse (Centers for Disease Control and Prevention, 2008).

- Inclusion of recent research on factors involved in inconsistent contraceptive use by female adolescents living in low-income circumstances (Davies & others, 2006)

- Coverage of recent research reviews indicating that abstinence-only education is not effective in delaying sexual intercourse in adolescence and is not effective in reducing HIV risk behaviors (Kirby, Laris, & Rolleir, 2007; Underhill, Montgomery, & Operario, 2007)

- Description of recent study that revealed that adolescents who experienced comprehensive sex education reported fewer pregnancies than adolescents who were given abstinence-only or no sex education (Kohler, Manhart, & Lafferty, 2008)

- Coverage of recent study indicating a gender difference in adolescents in meeting U.S. guidelines for physical activity (Butcher & others, 2008)

- Description of recent study indicating the percent of over-weight male and female adolescents who become obese adults (Wang & others, 2008)

- Description of recent research on adolescents eating dinner with their families and lower incidences of drug abuse (CASA, 2007)

- Coverage of the National Youth Risk Survey, indicating that U.S. high school students are decreasing their intake of fruits and vegetables (MMWR, 2006)

- Description of recent data on the increase in the percentage of adolescents who are overweight (Eaton & others, 2006)

- Discussion of recent data from the National Youth Risk Survey (2005) on adolescents' exercise patterns with a special focus on gender and ethnic variations, including new Figure 11.7 (MMWR, 2006)

- Coverage of recent study indicating that higher physical activity at 9 and 11 years of age predicted higher self-esteem at 11 and 13 years of age (Schmalz & others, 2007)

- Description of results from the recent National Sleep Foundation (2006) survey on adolescent sleep patterns and new research photo of an adolescent being assessed in Mary Carskadon's sleep laboratory

- Coverage of recent research study that linked sleep deprivation in adolescence to health-compromising behaviors (Fuligni & Hardway, 2006)

- Description of recent study on factors linked to adolescents' negative body images (Ata, Ludden, & Lally, 2007)

- Updated results from the Monitoring the Future Study regarding adolescent substance use and abuse (Johnston & others, 2008)

- Coverage of recent research on the protective role of educational success in reducing adolescents' drug use (Bachman & others, 2008)

- Recent research on the increasing recognition of the importance of family functioning in anorexia nervosa and its treatment (Benninghoven & others, 2007; Bulik & others, 2007)

- Much expanded and updated discussion of adolescent decision making, including recent research and views (Gerrard & others, 2008; Reyna & Rivers, 2008)

- Inclusion of new material about the importance of social contexts, especially peers and how their presence activates the brain's reward pathways, in adolescent decision-making (Steinberg, 2008)

- Description of how graduated driver licensing (GDL) reduces adolescent crashes and fatalities (Keating, 2007)

- Updated coverage of the continuing decline in school drop-out rates for different ethnic groups (National Center for Education Statistics, 2007)

- Description of recent initiative by the Bill and Melina Gates Foundation (2008) to reduce the dropout rate in schools with high dropout rates by keeping high-risk students with the same teachers across the high school years

- New *Diversity in Life-Span Development* interlude, the "I Have a Dream" Program to reduce dropping out of school ("I Have a Dream" Foundation, 2008)

- New material on two conditions that improve the likelihood that service learning will generate positive outcomes (Nucci, 2006)

- Updated and expanded coverage of service learning outcomes, including recent research on different outcomes for adolescents, depending on the type of service learning (Schmidt, Shumow, & Kackar, 2007)

- Inclusion of recent study of gender differences in service learning (Webster & Worrell, 2008)

CHAPTER 12
SOCIOEMOTIONAL DEVELOPMENT IN ADOLESCENCE

- Description of longitudinal study linking low self-esteem with a number of problems in adulthood (Trzesniewski & others, 2006)

- New coverage of James Cote's (2006) view on identity development in emerging adulthood

- Description of recent study on the bicultural identity of Mexican American and Asian American college students (Devos, 2006)

- Inclusion of recent research on ethnic identity in Navajo adolescents (Jones & Galliher, 2007)

- New major section, Religious and Spiritual Development

- New section on religion and identity development in adolescence and emerging adulthood (Kroger, 2007; Templeton & Eccles, 2006)

- Discussion of recent study of changes in religiousness and attending religious services from 14 to 24 years of age, including new Figure 12.2 (Koenig, McGue, & Iacono, 2008)

- Coverage of recent study of Indonesian Muslim 13-year-olds' religious involvement and social competence (French & others, 2008)

- Coverage of recent research on the positive role of religion in adolescent development (Cotton & others, 2006)

- Description of recent large-scale random sample connecting religiosity in adolescents to lower levels of problem behaviors (Sinha, Cnaan, & Gelles, 2007)

- Coverage of recent World Values Survey (Lippman & Keith, 2006)

- Description of recent research on secure attachment in adolescence and capacity for romantic intimacy in emerging adulthood (Mayseless & Scharf, 2007)

- Discussion of recent research on age differences in resistance to peer influence (Steinberg & Monahan, 2007)

- Description of recent research on girls and friendships with older boys (Poulin & Pedersen, 2007)

- Coverage of recent research indicating the importance of friends' grade-point average in adolescent development (Cook, Deng, & Morgano, 2007)

- Discussion of two recent studies of adolescent girls' romantic involvement and its link to co-rumination, depressive symptoms, and emotionally unavailable parents (Starr & Davila, 2008; Steinberg & Davila, 2008)

- Inclusion of recent studies linking discrimination of African American and Latino adolescents to more problems and lower-level academic achievement, including new Figure 12.5, showing the types of racial hassles African American adolescents experience (DeGarmo & Martinez, 2006; Sellers & others, 2006)

- New discussion of early-onset and late-onset antisocial behavior and their links with outcomes in emerging adulthood (Loeber & others, 2007; Schulenberg & Zarrett, 2006)

- Description of recent research on maternal monitoring and a lower incidence of delinquency in Latino girls (Loukas, Suizzo, & Prelow, 2007)

- Inclusion of recent research on the role of deviant peers in predicting delinquency in African American males (Bowman, Prelow, & Weaver, 2007)

- Updated and expanded coverage of early onset of depression in adolescence and developmental changes in depression during emerging adulthood (Schulenberg & Zarrett, 2006)

- Coverage of recent study linking adolescent depression to parent-adolescent conflict and low parental support (Sheeber & others, 2007)

- Description of recent studies on protective factors linked with a lower incidence of depressed mood in adolescence (Costello & others, 2008)

- Coverage of recent research that examined variations in therapies to reduce adolescent depression (The TADS Team, 2007)

- Updated description of suicide rates in adolescence and new information about the increase in suicide in emerging adulthood (Minino, Heron, & Smith, 2006; Park & others, 2006)

- New Figure 12.6 on the percentage of adolescents who say they have seriously considered suicide or attempted it unsuccessfully (Eaton & others, 2006)

- New discussion of the cultural contexts of suicide attempts, including new Figure 12.7 on ethnic variations in suicide attempts by U.S. adolescents (Goldston & others, 2007)

- Coverage of recent study on the influence of suicide attempts by members of an adolescent's social groups on the adolescent's probability of attempting suicide (de Leo & Heller, 2008)

- Inclusion of recent research linking thwarted belongingness and perception of being a burden to others with suicidal thoughts (Van Orden & others, 2008)

- Description of recent study on preteen alcohol use and suicide attempts in adolescence (Swahn, Bossarte, & Sullivent, 2008)

- Coverage of recent research linking suicidal thoughts to eating disorders in adolescence (Whetstone, Morrissey, & Cummings, 2007)

- Extensively updated discussion of juvenile delinquency, including research on cognitive factors such as IQ, self-control, and sustained attention (Koolhof & others, 2007; Loeber & others, 2007), physical abuse (Lansford & others, 2007), peer rejection and deviant friends (Vitaro, Pedersen, & Brengden, 2007)

- New *Research in Life-Span Development* interlude, Fast Track, providing very recent information about an extensive intervention with high-risk kindergarten children and outcomes of the intervention in adolescence (The Conduct Problems Prevention Research Group, 2007; Dodge & the Conduct Problems Prevention Research Group, 2007)

 **CHAPTER 13**
PHYSICAL AND COGNITIVE DEVELOPMENT IN EARLY ADULTHOOD

- New material on the fascinating life of Dr. Michael Maddaus, who turned his life around as an emerging adult

- Description of recent research on the criteria that parents and college students perceive to be important in determining when an individual should be considered an adult (Nelson & others, 2007)

- Coverage of longitudinal study on the characteristics of emerging adults who became competent after experiencing difficulties while growing up (Masten, Obradovic, & Burt, 2006)

- New description of research on college students' mental health problems, including new Figure 13.1 (American College Health Association, 2008)

- Updated description of the percentage of college freshmen who experience stress and depression (Pryor & others, 2007)

- New discussion of emerging adults' mortality rate, including new Figure 13.2 (Park & others, 2006)

- Coverage of longitudinal study indicating that bad health habits engaged in during adolescence tend to increase in emerging adulthood (Harris & others, 2006)

- Updated material on obesity in emerging and early adulthood, including longitudinal data and new Figure 13.3 (Centers for Disease Control and Prevention, 2006)

- Description of recent large-scale study of overweight and obesity in more than 168,000 adults in 63 countries (Balkau & others, 2007)

- Updated description of the prevalence of smoking in the United States (Centers for Disease Control and Prevention, 2006)

- Discussion of recent data on the percentage of college students who binge drink and are current smokers (Johnston & others, 2007)

- Description of recent research on the percentage of young adults 19 to 28 years of age who are current smokers (Johnston & others, 2007)

- Coverage or recent research on a decrease in lung cancer deaths following smoking cessation (Wakai & others, 2007)

- New section, Sexual Activity in Emerging Adulthood

- Comparison of sexual activity in emerging adulthood with early adulthood (Leftkowitz & Gillen, 2006)

- Coverage of recent research comparing same-sex couples with opposite-sex dating, engaged, and married dyads (Roisman & others, 2008)

- Inclusion of recent research on the percentage of lesbian and gay males who have encountered various forms of harassment and discrimination (Herek, 2008)

- Updated coverage of the number of U.S. AIDS cases (Centers for Disease Control and Prevention, 2008)

- Updated description of the number of individuals with HIV in the world (UNAIDS, 2006)

- Discussion of recent American Association of University Women (2006) survey of sexual harassment in the lives of college women

- Description of how many adults today have changing expectations for work, yet too often employers aren't meeting those expectations (Moen, 2007; Orrange, 2007)

- Updated description of occupational trends (*Occupational Outlook Handbook, 2008–2009* [2008])

- Coverage of recent national survey on stress in the workplace (American Psychological Association, 2007)

- Updated research on the physical problems of individuals who are unemployed (Gallo & others, 2006)

- Description of recent study of immune system functioning and unemployment (Cohen & others, 2007)

CHAPTER 14
SOCIOEMOTIONAL DEVELOPMENT
IN EARLY ADULTHOOD

- Extensively updated and expanded of material on adult attachment (Feeney, 2009; Mikulincer & Shaver, 2007, 2009)

- New high-interest self-assessment (Hazan & Shaver, 1987, p. 515) embedded in the text that gives students an opportunity to assess their attachment style

- Description of recent study on adult attachment patterns in women and female orgasm (Cohen & Belsky, 2008)

- Updated description of gender differences in attraction (Eastwick & Finkel, 2008)

- Coverage of recent study that revealed the matching hypothesis does not hold up in established marital relation-

ships but that differences in spouses' attractiveness have important influences on marital behavior and outcomes (McNulty, Karney, & Neff, 2008)

- New description of recent research on lower remarital happiness for individuals who cohabited postdivorce (Xu, Hudspeth, & Bartkowski, 2006)

- Coverage of recent census data on the significant increase in single adults in their twenties (U.S. Census Bureau, 2006)

- Inclusion of recent research comparing stressful recent experiences in single, married, and divorced adults (American Psychological Association, 2007)

- Coverage of recent research on the role of equal decision making in a successful marriage (Amato & others, 2007)

- Discussion of the importance of forgiveness and commitment in a successful marriage (Amato, 2007; Fincham, Stanley, & Beach, 2007)

- Inclusion of recent research on length of marriage and its relation to the onset of chronic health problems and disease (Dupre & Meadows, 2007)

- Description of 10-year longitudinal study that compared the risk of dying for married and never-married individuals (Ikeda & others, 2007)

- Information about the increasing age at which U.S. women have their first child (Joint Economics Committee, 2007)

- Added commentary about the best age to get married (Cherlin, 2006)

- New discussion of whether there is a best age to get married (Glenn, 2005; Furstenberg, 2007)

- Description of recent study on the risk of becoming depressed following the dissolution of a marriage (Rotermann, 2007)

- Discussion of two recent studies on gender differences and similarities in the use of words for various purposes, such as describing people, internal states, and so on (Mehl & others, 2007; Newman & others, 2008)

- Coverage of recent research on trends in housework and caring for children in U.S. families (Bianchi, Robinson, & Milkie, 2006)

CHAPTER 15
PHYSICAL AND COGNITIVE DEVELOPMENT
IN MIDDLE ADULTHOOD

- Added explanation of why there has been an increased rectangularization of the population (Moen, 2007)

- New coverage of how midlife changes today also involve the lack of senority protection in jobs and strong encouragement to take early retirement (Sweet, Moen, & Meiksins, 2007)

- Updated description of the incidence of hearing loss in individuals 50 years of age and older (Fowler & Leigh-Paffenroth, 2007)

- Expanded and updated information about factors that affect cholesterol and aging (Masley & others, 2008)

- Coverage of recent national survey on the percentage of U.S. middle-aged individuals classifed as obese (Centers for Disease Control and Prevention, 2006)

- Desription of recent large-scale longitudional study linking obesity in middle age with an increased risk of dying (Adams & others, 2006)

- Coverage of recent study that revealed a link between emotional stress and anger at work and the occurrence of acute coronary syndrome (Lipovetsky & others, 2007)

- Discussion of recent research and the increasing study of metabolic syndrome (Hong & others, 2007; You & others, 2008)

- Description of recent research review indicating that reducing risk factors such smoking and high blood pressure saves as many lives as high-tech surgical treatments (Ford & others, 2007)

- New Figure 15.3 showing NK cells destroying a tumor and coverage of recent study revealing higher NK cells levels in persistently unemployed young and middle-aged adults compared with their previously unemployed counterparts who became reemployed (Cohen & others, 2007)

- Expanded and updated coverage of menopause, including factors that contribute to its onset and whether, like menarche, menopause has been coming earlier, as well as alternatives to hormone replacement therapy (Gosden, 2007; Zaborowska & others, 2007)

- Description of recent research on exercise, smoking, and menopausal onset and menopausal symptoms (Gosden, 2007; Nelson & others, 2008; Santoro & others, 2007)

- Description of recent study of menopausal transition on the quality on women's quality of life in Taiwan (Cheng & others, 2008)

- Coverage of recent study on factors that increase menopausal symptoms (Sabia & others, 2008)

- New discussion of the likely protective effect of estrogen on cognitive aging in women when initiated soon after menopause begins (Sherwin, 2007)

- Updated description of recent studies documenting the effectiveness and sexual satisfaction of men with erectile dysfunction after taking Viagra (Abdo & others, 2008)

- Description of recent national study of the percentage of U.S. men 40 years of age and older who say they have erectile dysfunction (Laumann & others, 2007)

- Expanded and updated coverage of sexual attitudes and behaviors in middle-aged adults, including gender similarities and differences (Stones & Stones, 2007)

- Inclusion of new data from K. Warner Schaie's (2007) Seattle Longitudinal Study on generational differences in parents and their offspring at 60 to 67 years of age

- Coverage of the increasing trend for midlife couples to have to plan for two retirements, his and hers (Moen & Altobelli, 2007; Moen, Kelly, & Magennis, 2008)

- Description of recent research documenting links between religious attendance and a reduction in hypertension, as well as an increase in longevity (Gillum & Ingram, 2007; Oman & Thoresen, 2006)

CHAPTER 16
SOCIOEMOTIONAL DEVELOPMENT
IN MIDDLE ADULTHOOD

- Description of recent study linking parental generativity with young adult offsprings' conscientiousness and agreeableness (Peterson, 2006)

- New Figure 16.5 added to illustrate the increase in environmental mastery, positive relations, and autonomy in middle age

- Coverage of recent study on psychological and physical reactions to daily stressors in young, middle-aged, and older adults (Neupert, Almeida, & Charles, 2007)

- Expanded discussion of information about why midlife is not characterized by a crisis for most people

- Coverage of recent study on development comparisons of older, middle-aged, and younger adults on the Big Five factors of personality (Allemand, Zimprich, & Hendriks, 2008)

- Substantial updating and expansion of a conclusions about stability and change in personality development based on recent review by Brent Roberts and Daniel Mroczek (2008)

- Description of recent study on support between adult siblings (Voorpostel & Blieszner, 2008)

- New discussion of the potential negative influence on the economic circumstances of middle-aged women who become divorced (Mitchell, 2007)

- Coverage of recent research on children's relationship with their father following a divorce and how this affects the children's relationship with their paternal grandparents (Ahrons, 2007)

- Inclusion of recent research on why the grandparent role is important in midlife (Thiele & Whelan, 2008)

- Description of recent research on the influence of caring for grandchildren on grandparents' health (Hughes & others, 2007)

- Updated coverage of the number of grandchildren living with their grandparents (U.S. Census Bureau, 2006)

- Inclusion of information about two recent studies that document how various characteristics influence the degree to which individuals have intergenerational contact (Bucx & others, 2008; Sarkisian & Gerstel, 2008)

- Description of recent large-scale study in 21 countries on intergenerational ties and family responsibility (HSBC Insurance, 2007)

- Discussion of recent study on the intergenerational transmission of conduct disorder (D'Onofrio & others, 2007)
- Coverage of recent study documenting the stronger role of mothers in intergenerational connections than fathers (Monserud, 2008)

 **CHAPTER 17**

PHYSICAL DEVELOPMENT IN LATE ADULTHOOD

- New coverage of a surprising gender difference in centenarians' physical and cognitive functioning that favors men (Perls, 2007; Terry & others, 2008)
- New description of the percentage of individuals in the New England Centenarian Study who are living independently, with family or in assisted living, and in nursing homes (Perls, 2007)
- Updated and expanded discussion of the role that telomerase inhibition might play in reducing cancerous cells (Chen, Yang, & Zhang, 2008; Fakhoury, Nimmo, & Autexier, 2007)
- Coverage of recent study linking smoking with higher concentrations of free radicals (Reddy Thavanati & others, 2008)
- New illustration of mitochondria to accompany the mitochondrial theory of aging (Figure 17.4)
- New description of falls as the leading cause of injury death among adults 65 years and older (National Center for Health Statistics, 2008)
- Coverage of recent neuroimaging study on the slowing of activity in the prefrontal cortex of older adults during retrieval of information on a cognitive task (Rypma, Eldreth, & Rebbechi, 2007)
- Considerable expansion and updating of research and current knowledge about various aspects of the aging brain (Chen & others, 2007; Gould, 2007; Mora & others, 2007; Sun & Bartke, 2007)
- Updated description of the current status of knowledge about the limitations of neurogenesis in humans to the hippocampus and olfactory bulb, as well as what is known about neurogenesis and the functioning of neurons (Nelson, 2006)
- New material on individual differences in brain lateralization and aging, including new Figure 17.7 showing an fMRI scan of 80-year-old T. Boone Pickens' brain (Helman, 2008)
- Coverage of eight-year longitudinal study of 70-plus-year-olds that revealed the greatest functional decline occurred in mobility (Holstein & others, 2007)
- Coverage of recent experimental study of physical activity in older adults at risk for mobility disability (Rejeski & others, 2008)

- Inclusion of recent study on mobility restrictions in older adults predicted by a lower level of physical activity and a higher level of adiposity (Koster & others, 2008)
- New information about the decline in the amount of light the retina receives at 60 years of age compared with 20 years of age (Scialfa & Kline, 2007)
- Expanded coverage of hearing problems in older adults (Fowler & Leigh-Paffenroth, 2007)
- New material on the use of stem cells as an alterative to cochlear implants in neurosensory hearing loss (Pauley & others, 2008)
- New coverage of information about older adults showing a greater decline in their sense of smell than taste (Schiffman, 2007)
- Description of recent study indicating a decline in the detection of smells in older adults but an increase in perceived pleasantness of a smell (Markovic & others, 2007)
- New coverage of the benefits of exercise in older adults with arthritis (Bulthuis & others, 2007; Metsios & others, 2008)
- Description of the percentage of women and men in their eighties who have hypertension and who have experienced a stroke (Aronow, 2007)
- Inclusion of recent research linking regular exercise at 72 years of age with a nearly 30 percent increase in the probability of still being alive at 90 years of age (Yates & others, 2008)
- Coverage of recent study on exercise and brain volume in older adults (Colcombe & others, 2006)
- Discussion of how exercise benefits in older adults may not always be independent of other lifestyle factors such as diet and engagement in social activities (Kramer & Erickson, 2007)
- Description of recent longitudinal study on physical fitness, weight, and longevity across a 12-year period (Sui & others, 2007)
- New material on the positive role of exercise in older adults' cellular functioning, including recent study on exercise and telomere length (Cherkas & others, 2008)
- Coverage of recent national study revealing that older adults have only slightly increased their level of exercise in recent years, including new Figure 17.19 (Centers for Disease Control and Prevention, 2008)
- New Figure 17.14 showing the percentage of U.S. individuals 65 and older who have chronic conditions
- Description of recent large-scale research study on the sexual activity of older adults, including new Figure 17.13 (Lindau & others, 2007)
- Coverage of two recent research studies that found a protective effect of moderate drinking on the health and longevity of older adults (Rozinni, Ranhoff, & Trabucchi, 2007; Stranberg & others, 2007)

- New discussion of the role that resveratrol plays in increasing longevity through moderate drinking and description of its link to a key enzyme, SIRT1 (Pallas & others, 2008; Putics & others, 2008)

- New commentary about the increasing demand for home health-care workers because of the increase in the population of older adults and their preference to stay out of nursing homes (Moos, 2007)

- Expanded coverage of the importance of different types of exercise, including flexibility and balance exercise (Der Ananian & Prohaska, 2007)

- Expanded description of the evolutionary perspective on why calorie restriction might increase longevity over the long haul (Chen & Guarente, 2007)

- Inclusion of information about recent study linking higher level intake of antioxidants and less cognitive decline in older adults (Wengreen & others, 2007)

CHAPTER 18
COGNITIVE DEVELOPMENT IN LATE ADULTHOOD

- Introduction of new combined terms to illustrate the similarity of fluid and crystallized intelligence and cognitive mechanics and cognitive pragmatics: fluid mechanics and crystallized pragmatics (Lovden & Lindenberger, 2007)

- Description of three factors most likely to contribute to the decline in fluid mechanics in late adulthood (Lovden & Lindenberger, 2007)

- New discussion of the concept of terminal decline in understanding changes in cognitive functioning in older adults (Lovden & Lindenberger, 2007)

- Description of recent research indicating that trial-to-trial variability on perceptual speed tasks signals impending decline in the cognitive performance of older adults (Lovden & others, 2007)

- Coverage of recent research on decline in processing speed as a leading indicator of subsequent decline in memory and spatial ability (Finkel & others, 2007)

- Inclusion of results from a study of episodic memory in 18- to 94-year-olds (Siedlecki, 2007)

- Description of recent study on the role of sustained attention in older adults' decision making (Isella & others, 2008)

- New coverage of the reminiscence bump in autobiographical memory, including recent research on the role of perceived control and influence on later development in such memories (Gluck & Bluck, 2007)

- Expanded coverage of semantic memory, including examples of the measures used to assess semantic memory and the tip-of-the-tongue (TOT) phenomenon (Bucur & Madden, 2007)

- Revised conclusion about age differences in sustained attention and vigilance (Bucur & Madden, 2007)

- Discussion of cross-sectional study that supported the distinction between fluid mechanics and crystallized pragmatics, including new Figure 18.2, which illustrates the findings (Li & others, 2004; Lovden & Lindenberger, 2007)

- Description of Sherry Willis and her colleagues' (2006) extensive cognitive aging intervention study with older adults

- Inclusion of recent ideas about the engagement model of cognitive optimization in older adults and recent research on the Senior Odyssey program, which implements the model (Stine-Morrow & others, 2007)

- Coverage of recent processing speed training study that resulted in improvement in daily living activities, including safer driving performance (Ball, Edwards, & Ross, 2007)

- Expanded and updated coverage of cognitive neuroscience and aging, including activity increases in older adults' frontal and parietal regions while they are engaging in tasks that require cognitive control processes, such as attention (Grady, 2008)

- Coverage of recent research involving data from the Victoria Longitudinal Study that supports the "use it or lose it" concept (Bielak & others, 2007)

- Inclusion of research in men in their seventies, indicating that reading daily reduced their mortality (Jacobs & others, 2008)

- New photo and description of the Young@Heart Chorus to illustrate the "use it" side of "use it or lose it"

- New coverage of Sternberg's (2003, 2008) balance theory of wisdom

- Coverage of recent study linking years of education and cognitive ability in 79-year-olds (Gow & others, 2008)

- Description of age-related cognitive decline in adults with mood disorders, such as depression (Chodosh & others, 2007; Gualtieri & Johnson, 2008)

- Description of recent large-scale study that assessed the incidence of depression in older adult women (McGuire & others, 2008)

- Coverage of recent research documenting how important cohort effects are in cognitive aging (Zelinksi & Kennison, 2007)

- Expanded and updated coverage of language development in older adults, including new material on understanding speech, phonological skills, and discourse (Clark-Cotton, Williams, & Goral, 2007)

- New material on the projection of an increase in the number of workers when the largest of the baby-boom cohorts reaches 70 in 2034 (Manton & others, 2007)

- Updated and expanded coverage of the complexity of life paths older adults follow when they reach retirement age, as well as the varied reasons some older adults continue to work when they reach retirement age, based on expert consultant Phyllis Moen's (2007) ideas

- Description of baby boomers' delayed retirement plans (Frey, 2007)

- New *Diversity in Life-Span Development* interlude, Work and Retirement Around the World, describing a recent large-scale study of 21,000 40- to 79-year-old adults in 21 countries (HSBC Insurance, 2007)

- Coverage of 2007 U.S. retirement survey indicating how workers have some misconceptions about retirement and the income and long-term care they will receive (Helman, VanDerhei, & Copeland, 2007)

- Description of how important planning is for adjustment in retirement, especially for women, who are more likely to live longer than men and more likely to be alone (Moen, 2007)

- Inclusion of new information that the number of older adults with depression will likely increase as the current large cohort of baby boomers moves through late adulthood (Parmelee, 2007)

- Description of recent research on the positive role of exercise in alleviating or reducing depression in older adults (Kostka & Praczko, 2007; Mavandadi & others, 2007)

- Added commentary about the global nature of the term *dementia* and the importance of narrowing the diagnosis to a more specific disorder (Whitehouse, 2007a)

- Inclusion of recent research on the *apoE* gene and onset of Alzheimer disease (Sando & others, 2008)

- Coverage of recent research on the use of deep brain stimulation in treating Parkinson disease (Ellrichmann, Harati, & Müller, 2008)

- Description of information about ibuprofen and coffee being linked to a lower risk of developing Parkinson disease (Chand & Litvan, 2007)

- New information about the incidence of elder abuse (Cooper, Selwood, & Livingston, 2008)

- New coverage of institutional abuse in elder maltreatment (MacDonald, 2007)

- Inclusion of recent research on a link between on regular religious attendance and a lower risk of mortality (Gillum & others, 2008)

- Description of recent research comparing aspects of religion in African American, Caribbean Black, and non-Latino White older adults (Taylor, Chatters, & Jackson, 2007)

- Inclusion of information about recent study linking higher spirituality/religiousness with a lower incidence of depression (Yoon & Lee, 2007)

CHAPTER 19
SOCIOEMOTIONAL DEVELOPMENT
IN LATE ADULTHOOD

- Inclusion of recent commentary by leading expert Robert Butler (2007) on the nature of the life review

- Coverage of recent ideas about the importance of including regrets as part of a life review that may lead to developing

a more complex, mature self-understanding (King & Hicks, 2007)

- Description of five characteristics in late adulthood that are linked to low self-esteem, (Giarrusso & Bengtson, 2007)

- Coverage of recent large-scale study comparing older and middle-aged adults' peeceived control over their lives (HSBC Insurance, 2007)

- Inclusion of study on conscientiousness as a predictor of mortality risk from childhood through late adulthood (Martin, Friedman, & Schwartz, 2007)

- Coverage of 12-year longitudinal study of older men linking aspects of neuroticism to a lower level of survival (Mroczek & Spiro, 2007)

- New section, Possible Selves, including recent research on the possible selves of older adults (Hoppmann & others, 2007)

- Discussion of recent study on the type of emotions experienced with new and established friends in younger adults and older adults, including new Figure 19.7 (Charles & Piazza, 2007)

- Coverage of recent study on aging stereotypes by older adults and hearing decline (Levy, Slade, & Gill, 2006)

- Description of recent research revealing that older adults are clearly capable of being trained to learn new technologies (Hickman, Rogers, & Fisk, 2007)

- Coverage of recent study focused on marital satisfaction in older adults and middle-aged adults (Henry & others, 2007)

- Description of recent study of the sexual activities of older adults in Greece (Papaharitou & others, 2008)

- Inclusion of recent study on relationships between aging parents and their children (Fingerman & others, 2007)

- Coverage of recent study on the importance for unmarried older adults of being embedded in a friendship network (Fiori, Smith, & Antonucci, 2007)

- New description of three factors most often associated with living the "good life" as an older adult in most cultures (Fry, 2007)

- Updated coverage of the importance of social support and social integration in late adulthood, including cultural variations in social support (Antonucci, Akiyama, & Sherman, 2007; Loucks & others, 2006; Rook & others, 2007)

- Description of recent research on older adults' volunteerism in 21 countries (HSBC Insurance, 2007)

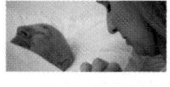

CHAPTER 20
DEATH, DYING, AND GRIEVING

- New chapter title: Death, Dying and Grieving

- New section on Kastenbaum's (2004, 2007) view of the death system, including its components, functions, and cultural variations; this new section is now the opening section in the chapter and provides a framing for the chapter

- New Figure 20.1, focusing on how the death system was involved in Hurricane Katrina (Kastenbaum, 2007)

- Recently proposed ideas about what might characterize a "good death" (Brink & Smith, 2008)

- New description of the contexts of hospice care (Hayslip & Hansson, 2007)

- Coverage of recent research on hospices (Harrison & Ford, 2007)

- 2006 update of the Oregon euthanasia law

- Discussion of recent study of the factors that predicted whether older adults had engaged in end-of-life planning activities (Carr & Khodyakov, 2007)

- Coverage of recent study of terminally ill cancer patients' views on physician-assisted suicide (Wilson & others, 2007)

- Description of recent research on the concerns of dying patients (Terry & others, 2006)

- New section, Coping and Type of Death (Murphy & others, 2003; Wortman & Boerner, 2007)

- Description of recent research indicating that yearning and acceptance are more common responses than depression following the death of a loved one (Maciejewski & others, 2007)

- New coverage of the increasingly used term of prolonged grief by Holly Prigerson and others (Maciejewski & others, 2007)

- New inclusion of the concept of disenfranchised grief (Read & Elliott, 2007)

- Description of recent therapy that was effective in reducing complicated grief (Zuckoff & others, 2006)

- Discussion of research on sense making and grief (Currier, Holland, & Neimeyer, 2006)

- Description of recent research on risk of death in Mexican American widows following a spouse's death (Stimpson & others, 2007)

- Inclusion of information about recent study on chronic grief in bereaved spouses (Ott & others, 2007)

- Discussion of recent study on the benefits of volunteering for widows following the death of a spouse (Li, 2007)

- Description of recent study indicating that when older adults engaged in helping behavior following a spouse's death, they experienced an accelerated decline in depressive symptoms (Brown & others, 2008)

- Coverage of the outpouring of support and forgiveness to the widow of Charles Roberts by the Amish following his murder of five Amish schoolgirls in October 2006

ACKNOWLEDGMENTS

I very much appreciate the support and guidance provided to me by many people at McGraw-Hill. Mike Ryan, Editor in Chief, and Beth Mejia, Publisher, have made some important strategic changes that have helped to make this a much better text. Mike Sugarman, Executive Editor, has brought a wealth of publishing knowledge and vision to bear on improving my texts. Dawn Groundwater, Director of Development, has done a superb job of organizing and monitoring the many tasks necessary to move this book through the editorial process. Jillian Allison, Editorial Coordinator, has handled a number of editorial contributions in a highly competent manner; Maureen Spada, the development editor for this text, provided very helpful feedback about many aspects of the text. James Headley, Marketing Manager, has contributed in numerous positive ways to promoting this book. Kim Menning created a beautiful design for the text. Beatrice Sussman did an outstanding job as the book's copy editor. Marilyn Rothenberger did a terrific job in coordinating the book's production.

I also want to thank my parents, John and Ruth Santrock, my wife, Mary Jo, our children, Tracy and Jennifer, and our grandchildren, Jordan, Alex, and Luke, for their wonderful contributions to my life and for helping me to better understand the marvels and mysteries of life-span development.

REVIEWERS

I owe a special gratitude to the reviewers who provided detailed feedback about the book.

Expert Consultants

I already listed the expert consultants earlier in the preface. Their photographs and biographies appear on pages xv through xix. Life-span development has become an enormous, complex field, and no single author can possibly be an expert in all areas of the field. To solve this problem, beginning with the sixth edition, I have sought the input of leading experts in many different areas of life-span development. This tradition continues in the twelfth edition. The experts have provided me with detailed recommendations of new research to include in every period of the life span. The panel of experts is literally a who's who in the field of life-span development.

General Text Reviewers

Paul Anderer Castillo—*SUNY Canton*
John Bauer—*University of Dayton*
William Blackston—*Baltimore City Community College*
Yiwei Chen—*Bowling Green State University*
Kevin Clark—*Indiana University, Kokomo*
Karen Davis—*Chippewa Valley Technical College*
Charles H. Huber—*New Mexico State University*
Ulas Kaplan—*Harvard University*
Deborah H. McMurtrie—*University of South Carolina, Aiken*
Rachel Schremp—*Santa Fe Community College*

Reviewers of Previous Editions

Patrick K. Ackles, *Michigan State University;* **Berkeley Adams,** *Jamestown Community College;* **Jackie Adamson,** *South Dakota School of Mines & Technology;* **Pamela Adelmann,** *Saint Paul Technical College;* **Joanne M. Alegre,** *Yavapai College;* **Gary L. Allen,** *University of South Carolina;* **Kristy Allen,** *Ozark Technical*

College; **Lilia Allen,** *Charles County Community College;* **Ryan Allen,** *The Citadel;* **Susan E. Allen,** *Baylor University;* **Toni C. Antonucci,** *University of Michigan–Ann Arbor;* **Doreen Arcus,** *University of Massachusetts–Lowell;* **Frank. R. Ashbur,** *Valdosta State College;* **Leslie Ault,** *Hostos Community College–CUNY;* **Renee L. Babcock,** *Central Michigan University;* **Paul Baltes—***Max Plank Institute, Berlin Germany;* **Diana Baumrind,** *University of California–Berkeley;* **Carol Beal,** *University of Massachusetts at Amherst;* **Daniel R. Bellack,** *Trident Technical College;* **Helen E. Benedict,** *Baylor University;* **Alice D. Beyrent,** *Hesser College;* **James Birren,** *University of California–Los Angeles;* **John Biondo,** *Community College of Allegheny County–Boyce Campus;* **James A. Blackburn,** *University of Wisconsin–Madison;* **Stephanie Blecharczyk,** *Keene State College;* **Belinda-Blevin Knabe,** *University of Arkansas–Little Rock;* **Marc H. Bornstein,** *National Institute of Child Health & Development;* **Karyn Mitchell Boutlin,** *Massasoit Community College;* **Donald Bowers,** *Community College of Philadelphia;* **Saundra Y. Boyd,** *Houston Community College;* **Michelle Boyer-Pennington,** *Middle Tennessee State University;* **Ann Brandt-Williams,** *Glendale Community College;* **Julia Braungart-Rieke,** *University of Notre Dame;* **Gregory Braswell,** *Illinois State University* **Sue Bredekamp,** *National Association for the Education of Young Children;* **Urie Bronfenbrenner,** *Cornell University;* **Kathy Brown,** *California State University at Fullerton;* **Jack Busky,** *Harrisburg Area Community College;* **Joesph Campos—***University of California—Berkeley,* **Joan B. Cannon,** *University of Lowell;* **Jeri Carter,** *Glendale Community College;* **Vincent Castranovo,** *Community College of Philadelphia;* **Ginny Chappeleau,** *Muskingum Area Technical College;* **Dominique Charlotteaux,** *Broward Community College;* **Rosalind Charlesworth,** *Weber State University;* **Yiwei Chen,** *Bowling Green State University;* **Bill Cheney,** *Crichton College;* **M. A. Christenberry,** *Augusta College;* **Saundra Ciccarelli,** *Florida Gulf University;* **Andrea Clements,** *East Tennessee State University;* **Meredith Cohen,** *University of Pittsburgh;* **Diane Cook,** *Gainesville College;* **Ava Craig,** *Sacramento City College;* **Kathleen Crowley-Long,** *College of Saint Rose;* **Cynthia Crown,** *Xavier University;* **Dana Davidson,** *University of Hawaii at Manoa;* **Diane Davis,** *Bowie State University;* **Tom L. Day,** *Weber State University;* **Florence Denmark,** *Pace University;* **Doreen DeSantio,** *West Chester University;* **Jill De Villiers,** *Smith College;* **Darryl M. Dietrich,** *College of St. Scholastica;* **Bailey Drechsler,** *Cuesta College;* **Joseph Durlack,** *Loyola University;* **Mary B. Eberly,** *Oakland University;* **Margaret Sutton Edmonds,** *University of Massachusetts–Boston;* **Glen Elder,** *University of North Carolina–Chapel Hill;* **Martha M. Ellis,** *Collin County Community College;* **Lena Eriksen,** *Western Washington University;* **Richard Ewy,** *Pennsylvania State University;* **Dan Fawaz,** *Georgia Perimeter College;* **Shirley Feldman,** *Stanford University;* **Roberta Ferra,** *University of Kentucky;* **Tiffany Field—***University of Miami* **Alan Fogel,** *University of Utah;* **Linda E. Flickinger,** *St. Claire Community College;* **Lynne Andreozzi Fontaine,** *Community College of Rhode Island;* **Tom Frangicetto,** *Northampton Community College;* **Kathleen Corrigan Fuhs,** *J. Sargeant Reynolds Community College;* **J. Steven Fulks,** *Utah State University;* **Cathy Furlong,** *Tulsa Junior College;* **Duwayne Furman,** *Western Illinois University;* **John Gat,** *Humboldt State University;* **Marvin Gelman,** *Montgomery County College;* **Rebecca J. Glare,** *Weber State College;* **Jean Berko Gleason,** *Boston University;* **David Goldstein,** *Temple University;* **Arthur Gonchar,** *University of LaVerne* **Judy Goodell,** *National University;* **Mary Ann Goodwyn,** *Northeast Louisiana University;* **Gilbert Gottlieb,** *University of North Carolina;* **Caroline Gould,** *Eastern Michigan University;* **Julia Graber,** *Columbia University;* **Sandra Graham,** *University of California–Los Angeles;* **Peter C. Gram,** *Pensacola Junior College;* **Dan Grangaard,** *Austin Community College;* **Tom Gray,** *Laredo Community College;* **Michele Gregoire,** *University of Florida at Gainesville;* **Michael Green,** *University of North Carolina;* **Rea Gubler,** *Southern Utah University;* **Gary Gute,** *University of Northern Iowa;* **Jane Halonen,** *Alverno College;* **Laura Hanish,** *Arizona State University;* **Ester Hanson,** *Prince George's Community College;* **Marian S. Harris,** *University of Illinois at Chicago;* **Yvette R. Harris,** *Miami University–Ohio;* **Algea O. Harrison-Hale,** *Oakland University;* **Amanda W. Harrist,** *Oklahoma State University;* **Craig Hart,** *Brigham Young University;* **Bert Hayslip,** *University of North Texas;* **Robert Heavilin,** *Greater Hartford Community College;* **Ravenna Helson,** *University of California–Berkeley;* **Donna Henderson,** *Wake Forest University;* **Debra Hollister,** *Valencia Community College;* **Heather Holmes-Lonergan,** *Metropolitan State College of Denver;* **Ramona O. Hopkins,** *Brigham Young University;* **Donna Horbury,** *Appalachian State University;* **Susan Horton,** *Mesa Community College;* **Sharon C. Hott,** *Allegany College of Maryland;* **John Hotz,** *Saint Cloud State University;* **Tasha Howe,** *Humboldt State University;* **Kimberley Howe-Norris,** *Cape Fear Community College;* **Stephen Hoyer,** *Pittsburgh State University;* **William Hoyer—***Syracuse University* **Kathleen Day Hulbert,** *University of Massachusetts–Lowell;* **Derek Isaacowitz,** *Brandeis University;* **Kathryn French Iroz,** *Utah Valley State College;* **Terry Isbell,** *Northwestern State University of Louisiana;* **Erwin Janek,** *Henderson State University;* **James Jasper-Jacobsen,** *Indiana University–Purdue;* **Christina Jose-Kampfner,** *Eastern Michigan University;* **Ursula Joyce,** *St. Thomas Aquinas College;* **Cigdem Kagitcibasi,** *Koc University (Turkey);* **Seth Kalichman,** *Loyola University;* **Barbara Kane,** *Indiana State University;* **Robert Kastenbaum,** *Arizona State University;* **Kevin Keating,** *Broward Community College;* **James L. Keeney,** *Middle Georgia College;* **Elinor Kinarthy,** *Rio Hondo College;* **Karen Kirkendall,** *Sangamon State University;* **A. Klingner,** *Northwest Community College;* **Steven J. Kohn,** *Nazareth College;* **Amanda Kowal,** *University of Missouri;* **Jane Krump,** *North Dakota State College of Science;* **Nadene L'Amoreaux,** *Indiana University of Pennsylvania;* **Gisela Labouvie-Vief,** *Wayne State University;* **Joseph C. LaVoie,** *University of Nebraska at Omaha;* **Kathy Lein,** *Community College of Denver;* **Barry M. Lester,** *Women and Infants' Hospital;* **Jean Hill Macht,** *Montgomery County Community College;* **James Marcia,** *Simon Fraser University;* **Salvador Macias,** *University of South Carolina–Sumter;* **Karen Macrae,** *University of South Carolina;* **Christine Malecki,** *Northern Illinois University;* **Jean Mandler—***University of California—San Diego* **Kathy Manuel,** *Bossier Parish Community College;* **Myra Marcus,** *Florida Gulf Coast University;* **Allan Mayotte,** *Riverland*

Community College; **Susan McClure,** *Westmoreland Community College;* **Dorothy H. McDonald,** *Sandhills Community College;* **Robert C. McGinnis,** *Ancilla College;* **Clara McKinney,** *Barstow College;* **Robert McLaren,** *California State University at Fullerton;* **Sharon McNeeley,** *Northeastern Illinois University;* **Daysi Mejia,** *Florida Gulf Coast University* **James Messina,** *University of Phoenix;* **Heather E. Metcalfe,** *University of Windsor;* **Karla Miley,** *Black Hawk College;* **Jessica Miller,** *Mesa State College;* **Scott Miller,** *University of Florida;* **Teri M. Miller-Schwartz,** *Milwaukee Area Technical College;* **David B. Mitchell,** *Loyola University;* **Joann Montepare,** *Emerson College;* **Phyllis Moen,** *Cornell University;* **David Moore—***Pitzer College and Claremont Graduate University* **Martin D. Murphy,** *University of Akron;* **Malinda Muzi,** *Community College of Philadelphia;* **Gordon K. Nelson,** *Pennsylvania State University;* **Michael Newton,** *Sam Houston State University;* **Charisse Nixon,** *Pennsylvania State University at Erie* **Beatrice Norrie,** *Mount Royal College;* **Jean O'Neil,** *Boston College;* **Laura Overstreet,** *Tarrant County College–Northeast;* **Ross Parke—***University of California—***Riverside Jennifer Parker,** *University of South Carolina;* **Barba Patton,** *University of Houston–Victoria;* **Susan Perez,** *University of North Florida* **Pete Peterson,** *Johnson County Community College;* **Richard Pierce,** *Pennsylvania State University–Altoona;* **David Pipes,** *Caldwell Community College;* **Leslee Pollina,** *Southeast Missouri State University;* **Robert Poresky,** *Kansas State University;* **Christopher Quarto,** *Middle Tennessee State University;* **Bob Rainey,** *Florida Community College;* **Nancy Rankin,** *University of New England;* **H. Ratner,** *Wayne State University;* **Cynthia Reed,** *Tarrant County College–Northeast;* **James Reid,** *Washington University;* **Russell Riley,** *Lord Fairfax Community College;* **Mark P. Rittman,** *Cuyahoga Community College;* **Cathie Robertson,** *Grossmont College* **Clarence Romeno,** *Riverside Community College;* **Paul Roodin,** *SUNY–Oswego;* **Ron Rossac,** *University of North Florida;* **Julia Rux,** *Georgia Perimeter College;* **Carolyn Saarni,** *Sonoma State University;* **Karen Salekin,** *University of Alabama* **Gayla Sanders,** *Community College of Baltimore County–Essex;* **Toru Sato,** *Shippensburg University;* **Nancy Sauerman,** *Kirkwood Community College;* **K. Warner Schaie,** *Pennsylvania State University;* **Cynthia Scheibe,** *Ithaca College;* **Robert Schell,** *SUNY–Oswego;* **Pamela Schuetze,** *Buffalo State College* **John Schulenberg—***University of Michigan* **Edythe Schwartz,** *California State University at Sacramento;* **Lisa Scott,** *University of Minnesota–Twin Cities;* **Owen Sharkey,** *University of Prince Edward Island;* **Elisabeth Shaw,** *Texarkana College;* **Susan Nakayama Siaw,** *California State Polytechnical University;* **Vicki Simmons,** *University of Victoria;* **Jan Sinnott,** *Towson State University;* **Gregory Smith,** *University of Maryland;* **Jon Snodgrass,** *California State University–Los Angeles;* **Donald Stanley,** *North Dallas Community College;* **Jean A. Steitz,** *University of Memphis;* **Margaret Beale Spencer,** *University of Pennsylvania;* **Collier Summers,** *Florida Community College at Jacksonville;* **Barbara Thomas,** *National University;* **Ross A. Thompson,** *University of Nebraska–Lincoln;* **Stacy D. Thompson,** *Oklahoma State University;* **Debbie Tindell,** *Wilkes University;* **Stephen Truhon,** *Winston-Salem State University;* **James Turcott,** *Kalamazoo Valley Community College;* **Marian Underwood,** *University of Texas at Dallas;* **Dennis Valone,** *Pennsylvania State University at Erie* **Gaby Vandergiessen,** *Fairmount State College;* **Elisa Velasquez—***Sonoma State University,* **L. Monique Ward—***University of Michiga* **Stephen Werba,** *Community College of Baltimore County–Catonsville;* **B. D. Whetstone,** *Birmingham Southern College;* **Susan Whitbourne,** *University of Massachusetts–Amherst.* **Nancy C. White,** *Reynolds Community College;* **Lyn W. Wickelgren,** *Metropolitan State College;* **Ann M. Williams,** *Luzerne County Community College;* **Myron D. Williams,** *Great Lakes Bible College;* **Linda B. Wilson,** *Quincy College;* **Mark Winkel,** *University of Texas—Pan American;* **Mary Ann Wisniewski,** *Carroll College* **Camille Wortman—***State University of New York—Stony Brook.*

SUPPLEMENTS

The supplements listed here may accompany *Lifespan Development,* twelfth edition. Please contact your McGraw-Hill representative for details concerning policies, prices, and availability.

For the Instructor

The instructor side of the Online Learning Center at http://www.mhhe.com/santrockld12e contains the Instructor's Manual, Test Bank files, PowerPoint slides, Image Gallery, and other valuable material to help you design and enhance your course. Ask your local McGraw-Hill representative for your password.

Instructor's Manual *by Rebecca Fraser-Thill, Bates College* Each chapter of the *Instructor's Manual* is introduced by a Resources Overview. This fully integrated tool helps instructors more easily locate and choose among the many resources available for the course by linking each element of the Instructor's Manual to a particular teaching topic within the chapter. These elements include lecture suggestions, classroom activities, personal applications, research project ideas, video suggestions, and handouts.

Test Bank and Computerized Test Bank *by Virginia Powers-Lagac, Westfield State College* This comprehensive Test Bank includes more than 2,000 multiple-choice and short answers questions and 5-10 essay questions per chapter. Organized by chapter, the questions are designed to test factual, applied, and conceptual understanding and are keyed to Bloom's taxonomy. All test questions are compatible with EZ Test, McGraw-Hill's Computerized Test Bank program.

PowerPoint Slides *by Jenel Cavazos, University of Oklahoma* These presentations cover the key points of each chapter and include charts and graphs from the text. They can be used as is, or you may modify them to meet your specific needs.

CPS Questions These questions, formatted for use with the interactive Classroom Performance System, are organized by chapter and designed to test factual, applied, and conceptual understanding. These test questions are also compatible with EZTest, McGraw-Hill's Computerized Test Bank program.

McGraw-Hill's Visual Asset Database for Lifespan Develpoment ("VAD") McGraw-Hill's Visual Assets Database for Lifespan Development (VAD 2.0) (www.mhhe.com/vad) is an on-line database of videos for use in the developmental psychology classroom, created specifically for instructors. You can customize classroom presentations by downloading the videos to your computer and showing the videos on their own or insert them into your course cartridge or PowerPoint presentations. All of the videos are available with or without captions. Ask your McGraw-Hill representative for access information.

McGraw-Hill Contemporary Learning Series *Annual Editions: Human Development* This reader is a collection of articles on topics related to the latest research and thinking in human development. Annual Editions are updated regularly and include useful features such as a topic guide, an annotated table of contents, unit overviews, and a topical index.

Taking Sides: Clashing Views on Controversial Issues in Life-Span Development Current controversial issues are presented in a debate-style format designed to stimulate student interest and develop critical thinking skills. Each issue is thoughtfully framed with an issue summary, an issue introduction, and a postscript.

For the Student

Online Learning Center (OLC) This companion website, at www.mhhe.com/santrockld12e offers a wide variety of student resources. **Multiple Choice, True/False, and Matching Tests** for each chapter reinforce key principles, terms, and ideas, and cover all the major concepts discussed throughout the text. Entirely different from the test items in the Test Bank, the questions have been written to quiz students but also to help them learn. Key terms from the text are reproduced in a **Glossary of Key Terms** where they can be accessed in alphabetical order for easy reference and review. **Decision Making Scenarios** present students with the opportunity to apply the information in the chapter to realistic situations, and see what effects their decisions have. Streamable online **Videos** reinforce chapter content.

A Visual Tour for Students

This book provides you with important study tools to help you more effectively learn about life-span development. Especially important is the learning goals system that is integrated throughout each chapter. In the visual walk-through of features, pay special attention to how the learning goals system works.

THE LEARNING GOALS SYSTEM

Using the learning goals system will help you to learn the material more easily. Key aspects of the learning goals system are the learning goals, chapter maps, Review and Reflect, and Reach Your Learning Goals sections, which are all linked together.

At the beginning of each chapter, you will see a page that includes both a chapter outline and three to six learning goals that preview the chapter's main themes and underscore the most important ideas in the chapter. Then, at the beginning of each major section of a chapter, you will see a mini–chapter map that provides you with a visual organization of the key topics you are about to read in the section. At the end of each section is Review and Reflect, in which the learning goal for the section is restated, a series of review questions related to the mini–chapter map are asked, and a question that encourages you to think critically about a topic related to the section appears. At the end of the chapter, you will come to a section titled Reach Your Learning Goals. This includes an overall chapter map that visually organizes all of the main headings, a restatement of the chapter's learning goals, and a summary of the chapter's content that is directly linked to the chapter outline at the beginning of the chapter and the questions asked in the Review part of Review and Reflect within the chapter. The summary essentially answers the questions asked in the within-chapter Review sections.

**CHAPTER-OPENING
OUTLINE AND LEARNING
GOALS**

MINI–CHAPTER MAP

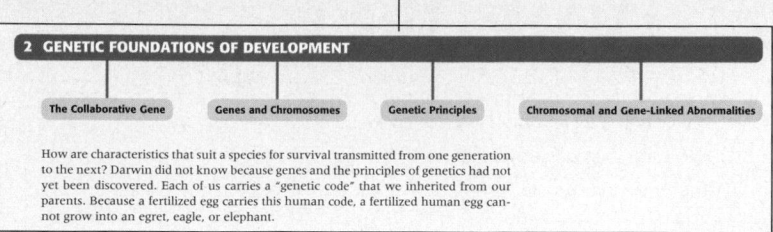

2 GENETIC FOUNDATIONS OF DEVELOPMENT

| The Collaborative Gene | Genes and Chromosomes | Genetic Principles | Chromosomal and Gene-Linked Abnormalities |

How are characteristics that suit a species for survival transmitted from one generation to the next? Darwin did not know because genes and the principles of genetics had not yet been discovered. Each of us carries a "genetic code" that we inherited from our parents. Because a fertilized egg carries this human code, a fertilized human egg cannot grow into an egret, eagle, or elephant.

REVIEW AND REFLECT

Review and Reflect: Learning Goal 1

1 Discuss the Evolutionary Perspective on Life-Span Development

REVIEW

- How can natural selection and adaptive behavior be defined?
- What is evolutionary psychology? What are some basic ideas about human development proposed by evolutionary psychologists? How might evolutionary influences have different effects at different points in the life span? How can evolutionary psychology be evaluated?

REFLECT

- Which is more persuasive to you: the views of evolutionary psychologists or their critics? Why?

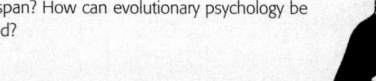

REACH YOUR LEARNING GOALS

Reach Your Learning Goals

Introduction

1 THE LIFE-SPAN PERSPECTIVE: DISCUSS THE DISTINCTIVE FEATURES OF A LIFE-SPAN PERSPECTIVE ON DEVELOPMENT

The Importance of Studying Life-Span Development

Characteristics of the Life-Span Perspective

Some Contemporary Concerns

- Development is the pattern of change that begins at conception and continues through the human life span. It includes both growth and decline. Studying life-span development helps prepare us to take responsibility for children, gives us insight about our own lives, and gives us knowledge about what our lives will be like as we age.

- The life-span perspective includes these basic conceptions: Development is lifelong, multidimensional, multidirectional, and plastic; its study is multidisciplinary; it is contextual; it involves growth, maintenance, and regulation of loss; and it is a co-construction of biological, sociocultural, and individual factors. Three important sources of contextual influences are (1) normative age-graded influences, (2) normative history-graded influences, and (3) nonnormative life events.

- Health and well-being, parenting, education, sociocultural contexts and diversity, and social policy are all areas of contemporary concern that are closely tied to life-span development. Important dimensions of the sociocultural context include culture, ethnicity, socioeconomic status, and gender. There is increasing interest in social policy issues related to children and to older adults.

OTHER LEARNING SYSTEM FEATURES

RESEARCH IN LIFE-SPAN DEVELOPMENT INTERLUDE

One *Research in Life-Span Development* interlude appears in every chapter. The research interludes describe a research study or program and are designed to acquaint you with how research in life-span development is conducted.

Research In Life-Span Development
In Vitro Fertilization and Developmental Outcomes in Adolescence

A longitudinal study examined 34 in vitro fertilization families, 49 adoptive families, and 38 families with a naturally conceived child (Golombok, MacCallum, & Goodman, 2001). Each type of family included a similar portion of boys and girls. Also, the age of the young adolescents did not differ according to family type (mean age of 11 years, 11 months).

Children's socioemotional development was assessed by (1) interviewing the mother and obtaining detailed descriptions of any problems the child might have; (2) administering a Strengths and Difficulties questionnaire to the child's mother and teacher; and (3) administering the Social Adjustment Inventory for Children and Adolescents, which examines functioning in school, peer relationships, and self-esteem.

No sigificant differences between the children from the in vitro fertilization, adoptive, and naturally conceiving families were found. The results from the Social Adjustment Inventory for Children

APPLICATIONS IN LIFE-SPAN DEVELOPMENT INTERLUDE

Every chapter has one *Applications in Life-Span Development* interlude, which provides applied information about parenting, education, or health and well-being related to a topic in the chapter.

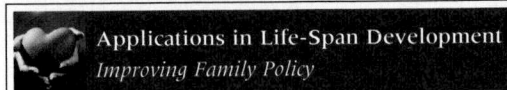

Applications in Life-Span Development
Improving Family Policy

In the United States, the national government, state governments, and city governments all play a role in influencing the well-being of children (Children's Defense Fund, 2007). When families fail or seriously endanger a child's well-being, governments often step in to help (Corbett, 2007). At the national and state levels, policy makers have debated for decades whether helping poor parents ends up helping their children as well. Researchers are providing some answers by examining the effects of specific policies (Coltrane & others, 2008; Gupta, Thornton, & Huston, 2008).

For example, the Minnesota Family Investment Program (MFIP) was designed in the 1990s primarily to influence the behavior of adults—specifically, to move adults off the welfare rolls and into paid employment. A key element of the program was that it guaranteed that adults participating in the program would receive more income if they worked than if they did not. When the adults' income rose, how did that affect their children? A study of the effects of MFIP found that increases in the incomes of working poor parents were linked with benefits for their children (Gennetian & Miller, 2002). The children's achievement in school improved, and their behavior problems decreased.

Developmental psychologists and other researchers have examined the effects of many other government policies. They are seeking ways to help families living in poverty improve their well-being, and they have offered many suggestions for improving government policies (Conger & Conger, 2008; Johnson, Tarrant, & Brooks-Gunn, 2008).

DIVERSITY IN LIFE-SPAN DEVELOPMENT INTERLUDE

Once each chapter, a *Diversity in Life-Span Development* interlude appears to provide information about diversity related to a chapter topic.

Diversity in Life-Span Development
Language Environment, Poverty, and Language Development

What characteristics of a family make a difference to a child's language development? Socioeconomic status has been linked with how much parents talk to their children and with young children's vocabulary. Betty Hart and Todd Risley (1995) observed the language environments of children whose parents were professionals and children whose parents were on welfare. Compared with the professional parents, the parents on welfare talked much less to their young children, talked less about past events, and provided less elaboration. As indicated in Figure 5.16, the children of the professional parents had a much larger vocabulary at 36 months of age than the children of the welfare parents.

Other research has linked how much mothers speak to their infants and the infants' vocabularies. For example, in one study by Janellen Huttenlocher and her colleagues (1991), infants whose mothers spoke more often to them had markedly higher vocabularies. By the second birthday, vocabulary differences were substantial.

However, a recent study of 1- to 3-year-old children living in low-income families found that the sheer amount of maternal talk was not the best predictor of a child's vocabulary growth (Pan & others, 2005). Rather, it was maternal language and literacy skills that were positively related to the children's vocabulary development. For example, when mothers used a more diverse vocabulary when talking with their children, their children's vocabulary benefited, but their children's vocabulary was not related to the total amount of their talkativeness with their children. Also, mothers who frequently

KEY TERMS AND GLOSSARY

Key terms appear in boldface. Their definitions appear in the margin near where they are introduced.

Individual Differences in Attachment

Although attachment to a caregiver intensifies midway through the first year, isn't it likely that that quality of babies' attachment experiences varies? Mary Ainsworth (1979) thought so. Ainsworth created the **Strange Situation**, an observational measure of infant attachment in which the infant experiences a series of introductions, separations, and reunions with the caregiver and an adult stranger in a prescribed order. In using the Strange Situation, researchers hope that their observations will provide information about the infant's motivation to be near the caregiver and the degree to which the caregiver's presence provides the infant with security and confidence.

Strange Situation An observational measure of infant attachment that requires the infant to move through a series of introductions, separations, and reunions with the caregiver and an adult stranger in a prescribed order.

Key terms also are listed and page-referenced at the end of each chapter.

KEY TERMS

evolutionary psychology 53	phenotype 58	twin study 69	active (niche-picking)
chromosomes 56	Down syndrome 60	adoption study 69	genotype-environment
DNA 56	Klinefelter syndrome 60	passive genotype-	correlations 70
genes 56	fragile X syndrome 60	environment	shared environmental
mitosis 57	Turner syndrome 60	correlations 69	experiences 70
meiosis 57	XYY syndrome 60	evocative genotype-	nonshared environmental
fertilization 57	phenylketonuria (PKU) 60	environment	experiences 70
zygote 57	sickle-cell anemia 61	correlations 69	epigenetic view 71
genotype 58	behavior genetics 69		

A

acceptance Kübler-Ross' fifth stage of dying, in which the dying person develops a sense of peace, an acceptance of her or his fate, and, in many cases, a desire to be left alone.

accommodation Piagetian concept of adjusting schemes to fit new information and experiences.

active (niche-picking) genotype-environment correlations Correlations that exist when children seek out environments they find

Alzheimer disease A progressive, irreversible brain disorder characterized by a gradual deterioration of memory, reasoning, language, and eventually physical function.

amnion The life-support system that is a bag or envelope that contains a clear fluid in which the developing embryo floats.

amygdala The region of the brain that is the seat of emotions.

androgyny The presence of positive masculine and feminine characteristics in the same individual.

assimilation Piagetian concept of using existing schemes to deal with new information or experiences.

assimilation The absorption of ethnic minority groups into the dominant group, which often involves the loss of some or virtually all of the behavior and values of the ethnic minority group.

attachment A close emotional bond between two people.

attention The focusing of mental resources on select information.

Key terms are alphabetically listed, defined, and page-referenced in a Glossary at the end of the book.

QUOTATIONS

These appear occasionally in the margins to stimulate further thought about a topic.

How old would you be if you didn't know how old you were?

—Satchel Paige
American Baseball Pitcher, 20th Century

occur. However, chronological age has become a less accurate predictor of these life events in our society. Moreover, issues such as how to deal with intimacy and how to cope with success and failure appear and reappear throughout the life span.

From a life-span perspective, an overall age profile of an individual involves not just chronological age but also biological age, psychological age, and social age. For example, a 70-year-old man (chronological age) might be in good physical health (biological age), be experiencing memory problems and not be coping well with the demands placed on him by his wife's recent hospitalization (psychological age), and have a number of friends with whom he regularly golfs (social age).

What is the nature of the early- and later-experience issue in development?

smoother ebbs and flows? These questions point to three issues about the nature of development: the roles played by nature and nurture, stability and change, and continuity and discontinuity.

Nature and Nurture The **nature-nurture issue** involves the extent to which development is influenced by nature and by nurture. *Nature* refers to an organism's biological inheritance, *nurture* to its environmental experiences.

According to those who emphasize the role of nature, just as a sunflower grows in an orderly way—unless flattened by an unfriendly environment—so too the human grows in an orderly way. An evolutionary and genetic foundation produces commonalities in growth and development (D'Onofrio, 2008; Hartwell, 2008). We walk before we talk, speak one word before two words, grow rapidly in infancy and less so in early childhood, experience a rush of sex hormones in puberty, reach the peak of our physical strength in late adolescence and early adulthood, and then physically decline. Proponents of the importance of nature acknowledge that extreme environments—those that are psychologically barren or hostile—can depress development. However, they believe that basic growth tendencies are genetically programmed into humans (Balasubramanian, Koontz, & Reynolds, 2008; Plomin & Schalkwyk, 2007).

By contrast, other psychologists emphasize the importance of nurture, or environmental experiences, in development (Cannides, 2009; Crane & Heaton, 2008). Experiences run the gamut from the individual's biological environment (nutrition, medical care, drugs, and physical accidents) to the social environment (family, peers, schools, community, media, and culture).

CRITICAL-THINKING AND CONTENT QUESTIONS IN PHOTOGRAPH CAPTIONS

Most photographs have a caption that ends with a critical-thinking or knowledge question in italic to stimulate further thought about a topic.

CAREERS IN LIFE-SPAN DEVELOPMENT APPENDIX

A *Careers in Life-Span Development* appendix that describes a number of careers appears following Chapter 1.

Appendix

Careers in Life-Span Development

The field of life-span development offers an amazing breadth of careers that can provide extremely satisfying work. College and university professors teach courses in many areas of life-span development. Teachers impart knowledge, understanding, and skills to children and adolescents. Counselors, clinical psychologists, nurses, and physicians help people of different ages to cope more effectively with their lives and improve their well-being.

These and many other careers related to life-span development offer many rewards. By working in the field of life-span development, you can help people to improve their lives, understand yourself and others better, possibly advance the state of knowledge in the field, and have an enjoyable time while you are doing these things. Many careers in life-span development pay reasonably well. For example, psychologists earn well above the median salary in the United States.

In the upcoming sections, we will profile a number of careers in four areas: education/research; clinical/counseling; medical/nursing/physical development; and families/relationships. These are not the only career options in life-span development, but the profiles should give you an idea of the range of opportunities available. For each career, we will describe the work and address the amount of education required and the nature of the training. The Web site for this book gives more detailed information about these careers in life-span development.

EDUCATION/RESEARCH

Numerous careers in life-span development involve education or research. The opportunities range from college professor to preschool teacher to school psychologist.

CAREERS IN LIFE-SPAN DEVELOPMENT PROFILES

Throughout the book, *Careers in Life-Span Development* profiles feature a person working in a life-span field related to the chapter's content.

Careers in Life-Span Development

Pam Reid, Educational and Developmental Psychologist

When she was a child, Pam Reid liked to play with chemistry sets. Reid majored in chemistry during college and wanted to become a doctor. However, when some of her friends signed up for a psychology class as an elective, she decided to take the course. She was intrigued by learning about how people think, behave, and develop—so much so that she changed her major to psychology. Reid went on to obtain her Ph.D. in psychology (American Psychological Association, 2003, p. 16).

For a number of years, Reid was a professor of education and psychology at the University of Michigan, where she also was a research scientist at the Institute for Research on Women and Gender. Her main focus has been on how children and adolescents develop social skills, with a special interest in the development of African American girls (Reid & Zalk, 2001). In 2004, Reid became provost and executive vice-president at Roosevelt University in Chicago.

Pam Reid (*back row, center*), with graduate students she mentored at the University of Michigan.

KEY PEOPLE

Paul Baltes 8	Erik Erikson 23	B. F. Skinner 26	Urie Bronfenbrenner 28
Marian Wright Edelman 13	Jean Piaget 24	Albert Bandura 27	Ross Parke and Raymond
Bernice Neugarten 19	Lev Vygotsky 25	Konrad Lorenz 27	Buriel 37
Sigmund Freud 22	Robert Siegler 26	John Bowlby 27	

KEY PEOPLE

The most important theorists and researchers in the chapter are listed and page-referenced at the end of each chapter.

E-LEARNING TOOLS

This feature appears at the end of each chapter and consists of four parts: *Self-Assessment*, which consists of one or more self-evaluations: *Taking It to the Net* Internet problem-solving exercises; and Video Clips of relevant material also are described and *Health and Well-Being, Parenting, and Education*, which provides an opportunity to practice, decision-making skills related to real-world applications. By going to the OnLine Learning Center (**www.mhhe. com/santrockld12**), where you will find many learning activities to improve your knowledge and understanding of the chapter, you can complete the valuable and enjoyable exercises of this book.

E-LEARNING TOOLS

To help you master the material in this chapter, you'll find a number of valuable study tools on the student Online Learning Center for *Life-Span Development*, twelfth edition, at **www.mhhe. com/santrockld12**.

Self-Assessment

Connect to **www.mhhe.com/santrockld12** to learn more about your career options by completing the self-assessment, *Evaluating My Interest in a Career in Life-Span Development*.

Taking It to the Net

Connect to **www.mhhe.com/santrockld12** to research the answers to these questions:

1. Janice plans to join a small family practice group on completion of her pediatrics residency. Why should Janice, as a pediatrician, be involved in detecting and helping to prevent violence in the lives of her young patients?

2. Derrick was assigned to write about the challenges of caring for aging adults in the United States in the twenty-first century. What are some important issues he should address?

3. Carmen is completing her Ph.D. in clinical psychology. She is interested in geropsychology. What are some of the areas in which geropsychologists might conduct research and practice?

Video Clips

At the Online Learning Center, you'll find a video called "Intelligence: The Nature and Nurture of Twins." This segment examines the nature-nurture connection by tracing the development of identical twins Cory and Eric.

Health and Well-Being, Parenting, and Education Exercises

Build your decision-making skills by trying your hand at the health and well-being, parenting, and education exercises. Connect to **www.mhhe.com/santrockld12** to research the answers and complete the exercises.

LIFE-SPAN DEVELOPMENT

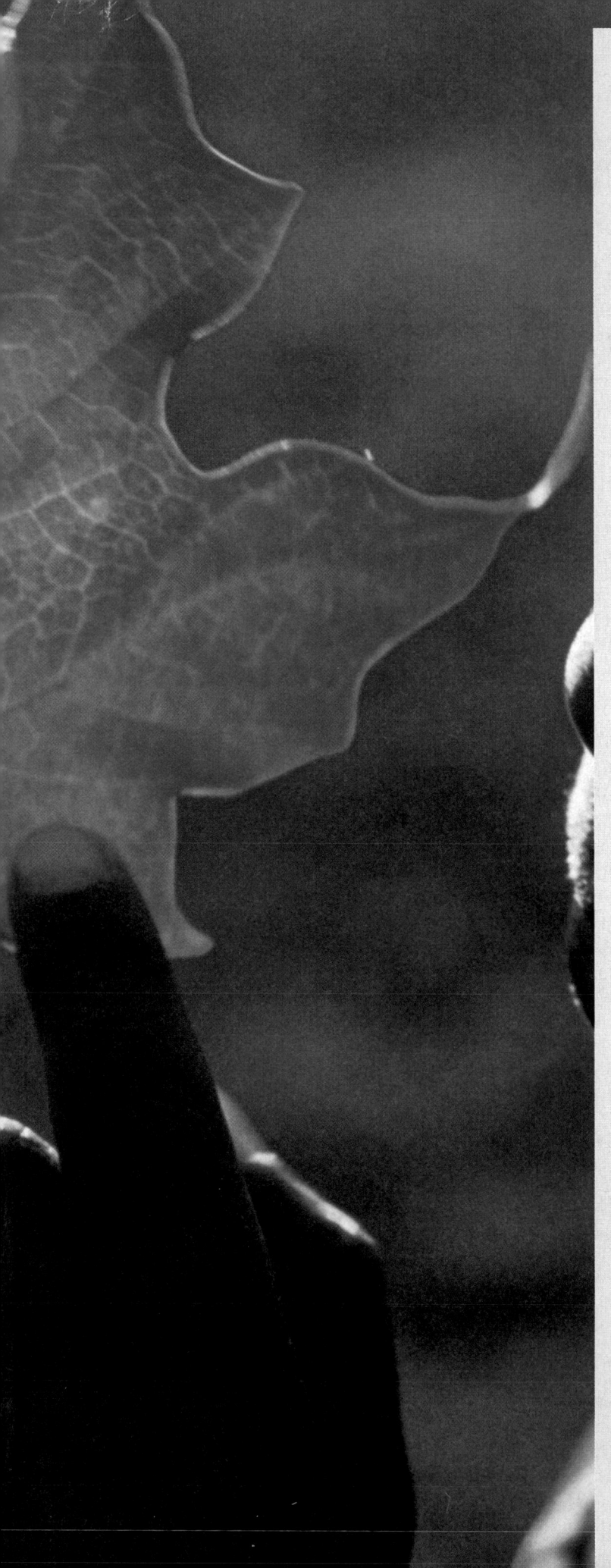

THE LIFE-SPAN PERSPECTIVE

*All the world's a stage.
And all the men and
women merely players.
They have their exits and
their entrances, and one
man in his time plays
many parts.*

—WILLIAM SHAKESPEARE
English Playwright, 17th Century

This book is about human development—its universal features,

its individual variations, its nature. Every life is distinct, a new

biography in the world. Examining the shape of life-span

development allows us to understand it better. *Life-Span*

Development is about the rhythm and meaning of people's

lives, about turning mystery into understanding, and about

weaving a portrait of who each of us was, is, and will be. In

Section 1, you will read "Introduction" (Chapter 1).

1

We reach backward to our parents and forward to our children, and through their children to a future we will never see, but about which we need to care.

—CARL JUNG
Swiss Psychiatrist, 20th Century

LEARNING GOALS

◆ Discus the distinctive features of a life-span perspective on development.

◆ Identify the most important processes, periods, and issues in development.

◆ Describe the main theories of human development.

◆ Explain how research in life-span development is conducted.

INTRODUCTION

CHAPTER OUTLINE

Images of Life-Span Development
How Did Ted Kaczynski Become Ted Kaczynski and Alice Walker Become Alice Walker?

Ted Kaczynski, the convicted unabomber, traced his difficulties to growing up as a genius in a kid's body and not fitting in when he was a child.

Ted Kaczynski sprinted through high school, not bothering with his junior year and making only passing efforts at social contact. Off to Harvard at age 16, Kaczynski was a loner during his college years. One of his roommates at Harvard said that he avoided people by quickly shuffling by them and slamming the door behind him. After obtaining his Ph.D. in mathematics at the University of Michigan, Kaczynski became a professor at the University of California at Berkeley. His colleagues there remember him as hiding from social circumstances—no friends, no allies, no networking.

After several years at Berkeley, Kaczynski resigned and moved to a rural area of Montana where he lived as a hermit in a crude shack for 25 years. Town residents described him as a bearded eccentric. Kaczynski traced his own difficulties to growing up as a genius in a kid's body and sticking out like a sore thumb in his surroundings as a child. In 1996, he was arrested and charged as the notorious Unabomber, America's most wanted killer. Over the course of 17 years, Kaczynski had sent 16 mail bombs that left 23 people wounded or maimed, and 3 people dead. In 1998, he pleaded guilty to the offenses and was sentenced to life in prison.

A decade before Kaczynski mailed his first bomb, Alice Walker spent her days battling racism in Mississippi. She had recently won her first writing fellowship, but rather than use the money to follow her dream of moving to Senegal, Africa, she put herself into the heart and heat of the civil rights movement. Walker had grown up knowing the brutal effects of poverty and racism. Born in 1944, she was the eighth child of Georgia sharecroppers who earned $300 a year. When Walker was 8, her brother accidentally shot her in the left eye with a BB gun. By the time her parents got her to the hospital a week later (they had no car), she was blind in that eye, and it had developed a disfiguring layer of scar tissue. Despite the counts against her, Walker overcame pain and anger and went on to win a Pulitzer Prize for her book *The Color Purple*. She became not only a novelist but also an essayist, a poet, a short-story writer, and a social activist.

Alice Walker won the Pulitzer Prize for her book *The Color Purple*. Like the characters in her book, Walker overcome pain and anger to triumph and celebrate the human spirit.

PREVIEW

What leads one individual, so full of promise, to commit brutal acts of violence and another to turn poverty and trauma into a rich literary harvest? If you have ever wondered why people turn out the way they do, you have asked yourself the central question we will explore in this book. This book is a window into the journey of human development—your own and that of every other member of the human species. In this first chapter, we will explore what it means to take a life-span perspective on development, examine the nature of development, and outline how science helps us to understand it.

1 THE LIFE-SPAN PERSPECTIVE

| The Importance of Studying Life-Span Development | Characteristics of the Life-Span Perspective | Some Contemporary Concerns |

Each of us develops partly like all other individuals, partly like some other individuals, and partly like no other individuals. Most of the time our attention is directed to an individual's uniqueness. But as humans, we have all traveled some common paths. Each of us—Leonardo da Vinci, Joan of Arc, George Washington, Martin Luther King, Jr., and you—walked at about 1 year, engaged in fantasy play as a young child, and became more independent as youth. Each of us, if we live long enough, will experience hearing problems and the death of family members and friends. This is the general course of our **development**, the pattern of movement or change that begins at conception and continues through the human life span.

In this section, we will explore what is meant by the concept of development and why the study of life-span development is important. We will outline the main characteristics of the life-span perspective and discuss various sources of contextual influences. In addition, we will examine some contemporary concerns in life-span development.

The Importance of Studying Life-Span Development

How might people benefit from examining life-span development? Perhaps you are, or will be, a parent or teacher. If so, responsibility for children is, or will be, a part of your everyday life. The more you learn about them, the better you can deal with them. Perhaps you hope to gain some insight about your own history—as an infant, a child, an adolescent, or a young adult. Perhaps you want to know more about what your life will be like as you grow through the adult years—as a middle-aged adult, or as an adult in old age, for example. Or perhaps you just stumbled onto this course, thinking that it sounded intriguing and that the study of the human life span might raise some provocative issues. Whatever your reasons, you will discover that the study of life-span development is intriguing and filled with information about who we are, how we came to be this way, and where our future will take us.

Most development involves growth, but it also includes decline (as in dying). In exploring development, we will examine the life span from the point of conception until the time when life (at least, life as we know it) ends. You will see yourself as an infant, as a child, and as an adolescent, and be stimulated to think about how those years influenced the kind of individual you are today. And you will see yourself as a young adult, as a middle-aged adult, and as an adult in old age, and be motivated to think about how your experiences today will influence your development through the remainder of your adult years.

PEANUTS © United Features Syndicate, Inc.

development The pattern of movement or change that begins at conception and continues through the human life span.

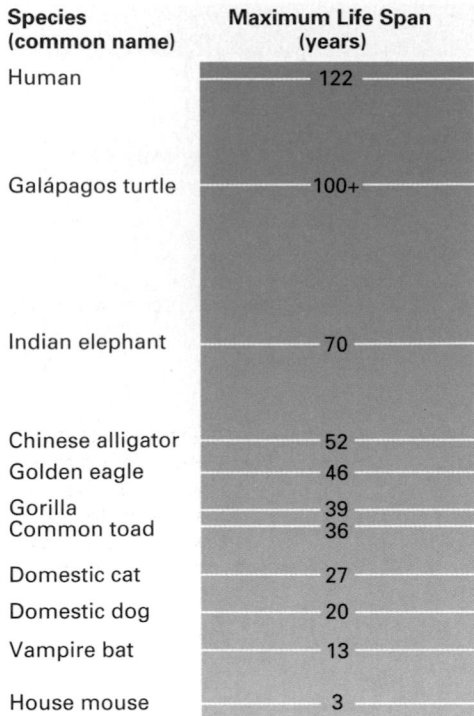

Species (common name)	Maximum Life Span (years)
Human	122
Galápagos turtle	100+
Indian elephant	70
Chinese alligator	52
Golden eagle	46
Gorilla	39
Common toad	36
Domestic cat	27
Domestic dog	20
Vampire bat	13
House mouse	3

FIGURE 1.1 Maximum Recorded Life Span for Different Species. Our only competitor for the maximum recorded life span is the Galápagos turtle.

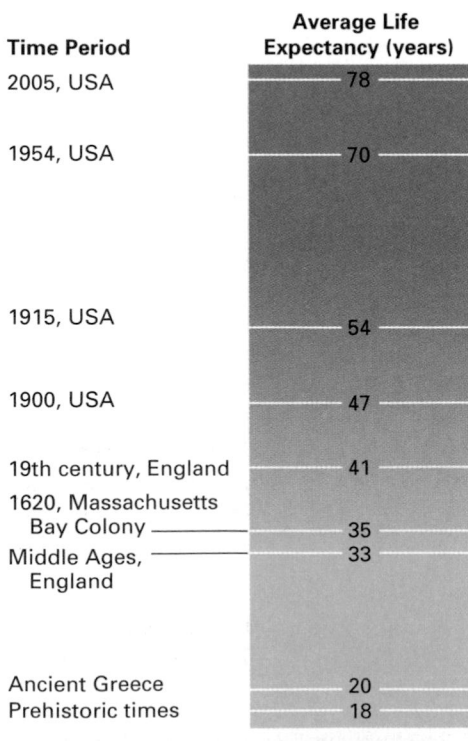

Time Period	Average Life Expectancy (years)
2005, USA	78
1954, USA	70
1915, USA	54
1900, USA	47
19th century, England	41
1620, Massachusetts Bay Colony	35
Middle Ages, England	33
Ancient Greece	20
Prehistoric times	18

FIGURE 1.2 Human Life Expectancy at Birth from Prehistoric to Contemporary Times. It took 5,000 years to extend human life expectancy from 18 to 41 years of age.

Characteristics of the Life-Span Perspective

Although growth and development are dramatic during the first two decades of life, development is not something that happens only to children and adolescents. The *traditional approach* to the study of development emphasizes extensive change from birth to adolescence (especially during infancy), little or no change in adulthood, and decline in old age. But a great deal of change does occur in the five or six decades after adolescence. The *life-span approach* emphasizes developmental change throughout adulthood as well as childhood (Park & Schwarz, 2009; Birren, 2007; Baltes, 2009; Schaie, 2007).

Recent increases in human life expectancy contributed to the popularity of the life-span approach to development. The upper boundary of the *human life span* (based on the oldest age documented) is 122 years, as indicated in Figure 1.1; this maximum life span of humans has not changed since the beginning of recorded history. What has changed is *life expectancy*: the average number of years that a person born in a particular year can expect to live (Manton, 2007). In the twentieth century alone, life expectancy in the United States increased by 30 years, thanks to improvements in sanitation, nutrition, and medicine (see Figure 1.2). As we move toward the end of the first decade of the twenty-first century, the life expectancy in the United States is 78 years of age (Centers for Disease Control and Prevention, 2008). Today, for most individuals in developed countries, childhood and adolescence represent only about one-fourth of their lives.

The belief that development occurs throughout life is central to the life-span perspective on human development, but this perspective has other characteristics as well. According to life-span development expert Paul Baltes (1939–2006), the **life-span perspective** views development as lifelong, multidimensional, multidirectional, plastic, multidisciplinary, and contextual, and as a process that involves growth, maintenance, and regulation of loss (Baltes, 1987, 2003, 2009; Baltes, Lindenberger, & Staudinger, 2006). In Baltes' view, is important to understand that development is constructed through biological, sociocultural, and individual factors working together (Baltes, Reuter-Lorenz, & Rosler, 2006). Let's look at each of these characteristics.

Development Is Lifelong In the life-span perspective, early adulthood is not the endpoint of development; rather, no age period dominates development. Researchers increasingly study the experiences and psychological orientations of adults at different points in their lives. Later in this chapter, we will describe the age periods of development and their characteristics.

Development Is Multidimensional Whatever your age, your body, your mind, your emotions, and your relationships are changing and affecting each other. Consider the development of Ted Kaczynski, the bomber discussed at the opening of the chapter. When he was 6 months old, he was hospitalized with a severe allergic reaction, and his parents were rarely allowed to visit the baby. According to his mother, the previously happy baby was never the same. The infant became withdrawn and unresponsive. As Ted grew up, he had periodic "shutdowns" accompanied by rage. In his mother's view, a biological event in infancy warped the development of her son's mind and emotions.

Development consists of biological, cognitive, and socioemotional dimensions. Even within a dimension, there are many components—for example, attention, memory, abstract thinking, speed of processing information, and social intelligence are just a few of the components of the cognitive dimension.

Development Is Multidirectional Throughout life, some dimensions or components of a dimension expand and others shrink. For example, when one language (such as English) is acquired early in development, the capacity for acquiring second and third languages (such as Spanish and Chinese) decreases later in development, especially after early childhood (Levelt, 1989). During adolescence, as individuals establish romantic relationships, their time spent with friends may decrease. During late adulthood, older adults might become wiser by being able to call on experience to guide their intellectual decision making, but they perform more poorly on tasks that require speed in processing information (Baltes, 2009; Baltes & Kuntzman, 2007; Salthouse, 2009).

Paul Baltes, a leading architect of the life-span perspective of development, conversing with one of the long-time research participants in the Berlin Aging Study that he directs. She joined the study in the early 1990s and has participated six times in extensive physical, medical, psychological, and social assessments. In her professional life, she was a practicing medical doctor.

Development Is Plastic Even at 10 years old, Ted Kaczynski was extraordinarily shy. Was he destined to remain forever uncomfortable with people? Developmentalists debate how much plasticity people have in various dimensions at different points in their development. *Plasticity* means the capacity for change. For example, can you still improve your intellectual skills when you are in your seventies or eighties? Or might these intellectual skills be fixed by the time you are in your thirties so that further improvement is impossible? Researchers have found that the cognitive skills of older adults can be improved through training and developing better strategies (Boron, Willis, & Schaie, 2007; Kramer, 2009). However, possibly we possess less capacity for change when we become old (Baltes, Reuter-Lorenz, & Rosler, 2006). The search for plasticity and its constraints is a key element on the contemporary agenda for developmental research (Kramer & Morrow, 2009).

Developmental Science Is Multidisciplinary Psychologists, sociologists, anthropologists, neuroscientists, and medical researchers all share an interest in unlocking the mysteries of development through the life span. How do your heredity and health limit your intelligence? Do intelligence and social relationships change with age in the same way around the world? How do families and schools influence intellectual development? These are examples of research questions that cut across disciplines.

Development Is Contextual All development occurs within a *context,* or setting. Contexts include families, schools, peer groups, churches, cities, neighborhoods, university laboratories, countries, and so on. Each of these settings is influenced by historical, economic, social, and cultural factors (Matsumoto & Juang, 2008; Mehrotra & Wagner, 2009).

Contexts, like individuals, change. Thus, individuals are changing beings in a changing world. As a result of these changes, contexts exert three types of influences (Baltes, 2003): (1) normative age-graded influences, (2) normative history-graded influences, and (3) nonnormative or highly individualized life events. Each of these types can have a biological or environmental impact on development. **Normative age-graded influences** are similar for individuals in a particular age group. These influences include biological processes such as puberty and menopause. They also include sociocultural, environmental processes such as beginning formal education (usually at about age 6 in most cultures) and retirement (which takes place in the fifties and sixties in most cultures).

Normative history-graded influences are common to people of a particular generation because of historical circumstances. For example, in their youth American baby boomers shared the experience of the Cuban missile crisis, the assassination

life-span perspective Views development as lifelong, multidimensional, multidirectional, plastic, multidisciplinary, and contextual, and as a process that involves growth, maintenance, and regulation of loss.

normative age-graded influences Describes influences that are similar for individuals in a particular age group.

normative history-graded influences Describes influences common to individuals of a particular generation because of historical circumstances.

Nonnormative life events, such as Hurricane Katrina in August 2005, are unusual circumstances that have a major impact on a person's life. Here a woman and her children are shown in a Houston shelter for those left homeless by the devastating hurricane.

of John F. Kennedy, and the Beatles invasion. Other examples of normative history-graded influences include economic, political, and social upheavals such as the Great Depression in the 1930s, World War II in the 1940s, the civil rights and women's rights movements of the 1960s and 1970s, the terrorist attacks of 9/11/2001, as well as the integration of computers and cell phones into everyday life during the 1990s (Elder & Shanahan, 2006; Schaie, 2007). Long-term changes in the genetic and cultural makeup of a population (due to immigration or changes in fertility rates) are also part of normative historical change.

Nonnormative life events are unusual occurrences that have a major impact on the individual's life. These events do not happen to all people, and when they do occur they can influence people in different ways. Examples include the death of a parent when a child is young, pregnancy in early adolescence, a fire that destroys a home, winning the lottery, or getting an unexpected career opportunity.

Development Involves Growth, Maintenance, and Regulation of Loss   Baltes and his colleagues (2006) assert that the mastery of life often involves conflicts and competition among three goals of human development: growth, maintenance, and regulation of loss. As individuals age into middle and late adulthood, the maintenance and regulation of loss in their capacities takes center stage away from growth. Thus, a 75-year-old man might aim not to improve his memory or his golf swing but to maintain his independence and his ability to play golf at all. In Chapters 15 and 16, we will discuss these ideas about maintenance and regulation of loss in greater depth.

Development Is a Co-Construction of Biology, Culture, and the Individual
Development is a co-construction of biological, cultural, and individual factors working together (Baltes, 2009; Baltes, Reuter-Lorenz, & Rosler, 2006). For example, the brain shapes culture, but it is also shaped by culture and the experiences that individuals have or pursue. In terms of individual factors, we can go beyond what our genetic inheritance and environment give us. We can author a unique developmental path by actively choosing from the environment the things that optimize our lives (Rathunde & Csikstentmihalyi, 2006).

How might growth versus maintenance and regulation be reflected in the development of this grandfather and his two grandchildren?

Some Contemporary Concerns

Pick up a newspaper or magazine and you might see headlines like these: "Political Leanings May Be Written in the Genes," "Mother Accused of Tossing Children into Bay," "Gender Gap Widens," "FDA Warns About ADHD Drug," "Heart Attack Deaths Higher in Black Patients," "Test May Predict Alzheimer disease." Researchers using the life-span perspective are examining these and many other topics of contemporary concern. The roles that health and well-being, parenting, education, and sociocultural contexts play in life-span development, as well as how social policy is related to these issues, are a particular focus of this textbook.

Health and Well-Being   Health professionals today recognize the power of lifestyles and psychological states in health and well-being (Fahey, Insel, & Roth, 2009; Hahn, Payne, & Lucas, 2009). In every chapter of this book, issues of health and well-being are integrated into our discussion.

Clinical psychologists are among the health professionals who help people improve their well-being. Read about one clinical psychologist who helps adolescents who have become juvenile delinquents or substance abusers in the *Careers in Life-Span Development* profile.

nonnormative life events Unusual events that have a major impact on an individual's life.

Careers in Life-Span Development

Luis Vargas, Child Clinical Psychologist

Luis Vargas is Director of the Clinical Child Psychology Internship Program and a professor in the Department of Psychiatry at the University of New Mexico Health Sciences Center. He also is Director of Psychology at the University of New Mexico children's Psychiatric Hospital.

Vargas obtained an undergraduate degree in psychology from St. Edwards University in Texas, a master's degree in psychology from Trinity University in Texas, and a Ph.D. in clinical psychology from the University of Nebraska–Lincoln.

Vargas' main interests are cultural issues and the assessment and treatment of children, adolescents, and families. He is motivated to find better ways to provide culturally responsive mental health services. One of his special interests is the treatment of Latino youth for delinquency and substance abuse.

Luis Vargas (*left*) conducting a child therapy session.

Parenting and Education   Can two gay men raise a healthy family? Are children harmed if both parents work outside the home? Are U.S. schools failing to teach children how to read and write and calculate adequately? We hear many questions like these related to pressures on the contemporary family and the problems of U.S. schools (Ballantine & Hammock, 2009; Parke & others, 2008). In later chapters, we will analyze child care, the effects of divorce, parenting styles, intergenerational relationships, early childhood education, relationships between childhood poverty and education, bilingual education, new educational efforts to improve lifelong learning, and many other issues related to parenting and education (Tolani & Brooks-Gunn, 2008; Wallerstein, 2008).

Sociocultural Contexts and Diversity   Health, parenting, and education—like development itself—are all shaped by their sociocultural context. To analyze this context, four concepts are especially useful: culture, ethnicity, socioeconomic status, and gender.

Culture encompasses the behavior patterns, beliefs, and all other products of a particular group of people that are passed on from generation to generation. Culture results from the interaction of people over many years. A cultural group can be as large as the United States or as small as an isolated Appalachian town. Whatever its size, the group's culture influences the behavior of its members (Taylor & Whitaker, 2009). **Cross-cultural studies** compare aspects of two or more cultures. The comparison provides information about the degree to which development is similar, or universal, across cultures, or is instead culture-specific (Rothbaum & Trommsdorff, 2007).

Ethnicity (the word *ethnic* comes from the Greek word for "nation") is rooted in cultural heritage, nationality, race, religion, and language. African Americans, Latinos, Asian Americans, Native Americans, European Americans, and Arab Americans are a few examples of broad ethnic groups in the United States. Diversity exists within each ethnic group (Banks, 2008; Kim & others, 2009; Gollnick & Chinn, 2009).

Socioeconomic status (SES) refers to a person's position within society based on occupational, educational, and economic characteristics. Socioeconomic status implies certain inequalities. Differences in the ability to control resources and to participate in society's rewards produce unequal opportunities (Coltrane & others, 2008; Crane & Heaton, 2008; Philipsen, Johnson, & Brooks-Gunn, 2009).

culture The behavior patterns, beliefs, and all other products of a group that are passed on from generation to generation.

cross-cultural studies Comparisons of one culture with one or more other cultures. These provide information about the degree to which children's development is similar, or universal, across cultures, and to the degree to which it is culture-specific.

ethnicity A characteristic based on cultural heritage, nationality, race, religion, and language.

socioeconomic status (SES) Refers to a person's position within society based on occupational, educational, and economic characteristics.

Two Korean-born children on the day they became United States citizens. Asian American and Latino children are the fastest-growing immigrant groups in the United States. *How diverse are the students in your class on lifespan development that you now are taking? How are their experiences in growing up likely similar to or different from yours?*

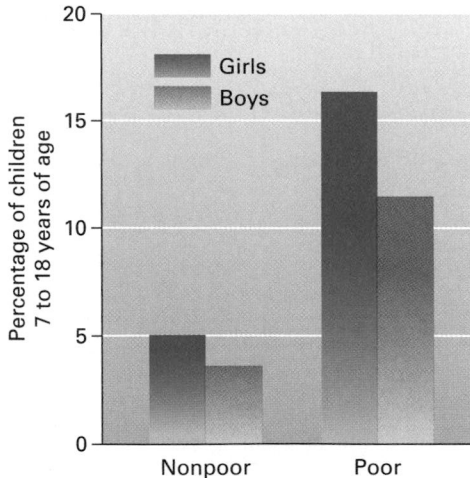

FIGURE 1.3 Percentage of Children 7 to 18 Years of Age Around the World Who Have Never Been to School of Any Kind. When UNICEF (2004) surveyed the education that children around the world are receiving, it found that far more girls than boys receive no formal schooling at all.

gender Refers to the characterists of people as males or females.

Gender refers to the characteristics of people as males and females. Few aspects of our development are more central to our identity and social relationships than gender (Blakemore, Barenbaum, & Liben, 2009; Matlin, 2008; Zosuls, Lurye, & Ruble, 2008).

In the United States, the sociocultural context has become increasingly diverse in recent years. Its population includes a greater variety of cultures and ethnic groups than ever before. This changing demographic tapestry promises not only the richness that diversity produces but also difficult challenges in extending the American dream to all individuals (Banks, 2008; Spring, 2008). We will discuss sociocultural contexts and diversity in each chapter. In addition, a *Diversity in Life-Span Development* interlude appears in every chapter. The first one, about women's international struggle for equality, appears next.

Diversity in Life-Span Development
Women's Struggle for Equality: An International Journey

The educational and psychological conditions of women around the world are a serious concern (UNICEF, 2008). Inadequate educational opportunities, violence, and mental health issues are just some of the problems faced by many women.

One analysis found that a higher percentage of girls than boys around the world have never had any education (UNICEF, 2004) (see Figure 1.3). The countries with the fewest females being educated are in Africa, where in some areas, girls and women are receiving no education at all. Canada, the United States, and Russia have the highest percentages of educated women. In developing countries, 67 percent of women over the age of 25 (compared with 50 percent of men) have never been to school. At the beginning of the twenty-first century, 80 million more boys than girls were in primary and secondary educational settings around the world (United Nations, 2002).

Women in every country experience violence, often from someone close to them (Humphreys, 2007). Abuse by partners occurs in one of every six households in the United States, with the vast majority of the abuse being directed at women by men (White & Frabutt, 2006). Although most countries around the world now have battered women's shelters, beating women continues to be accepted and expected behavior in some countries (UNICEF, 2008).

Gender also influences mental health. A study of depression in high-income countries found women were twice as likely as men to be diagnosed as depressed (Nolen-Hoeksema, 2007). In the United States, from adolescence through adulthood, females are more likely than males to be depressed (Davison & Neale, 2007). Why? Some experts suggest that more women are diagnosed with depression than actually have depression (Nolen-Hoeksema, 2007). Some argue that inequities such as low pay and unequal employment opportunities have contributed to the greater incidence of depression in females than males (Whiffen, 2001). In the view of some researchers and policy makers problems like these are likely to be addressed only when women share equal power with men (UNICEF, 2008).

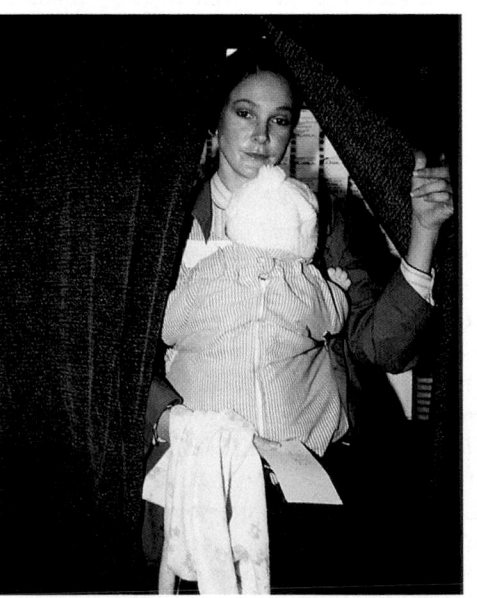

Around the world women too often are treated as burdens rather than assets in the political process. *What can be done to strengthen women's roles in the political process?*

Marian Wright Edelman, president of the Children's Defense Fund (shown here interacting with young children), has been a tireless advocate of children's rights and has been instrumental in calling attention to the needs of children. *What are some of these needs?*

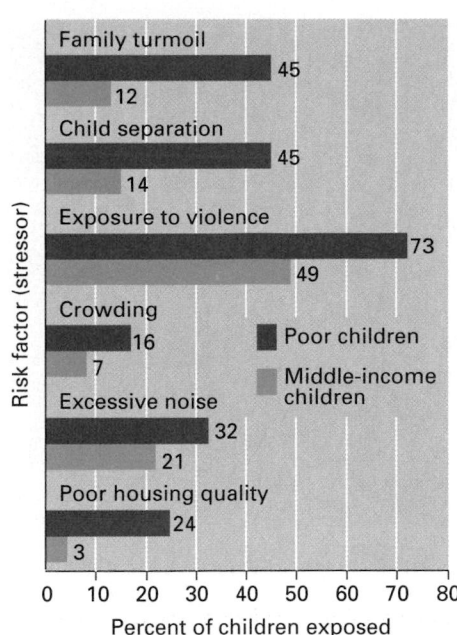

FIGURE 1.4 Exposure to Six Stressors Among Poor and Middle-Income Children. One recent study analyzed the exposure to six stressors among poor children and middle-income children (Evans & English, 2002). Poor children were much more likely to face each of these stressors

Social Policy   **Social policy** is a government's course of action designed to promote the welfare of its citizens. Values, economics, and politics all shape a nation's social policy (Kelly & Marshall, 2007). Out of concern that policy makers are doing too little to protect the well-being of children and older adults, life-span researchers are increasingly undertaking studies that they hope will lead to effective social policy (Coltrane & others, 2008; Gupta, Thorton, & Huston, 2008).

Statistics such as infant mortality rates, mortality among children under 5, and the percentage of children who are malnourished or living in poverty provide benchmarks for evaluating how well children are doing in a particular society. Marian Wright Edelman (1997), a tireless advocate of children's rights, has pointed out that indicators like these place the United States at or near the lowest rank for industrialized nations in the treatment of children.

Children who grow up in poverty represent a special concern (Conger & Conger, 2008; Crane & Heaton, 2008). In 2006, approximately 17.4 percent of U.S. children were living in families below the poverty line (Federal Interagency Forum on Child and Family Statistics, 2007). This is an increase from 2001 (16.2 percent) but down from a peak of 22.7 percent in 1993. As indicated in Figure 1.4, one study found that a higher percentage of U.S. children in poor families than in middle-income families were exposed to family turmoil, separation from a parent, violence, crowding, excessive noise, and poor housing (Evans & English, 2002). A recent study also revealed that the more years children spent living in poverty, the more their physiological indices of stress were elevated (Evans & Kim, 2007).

The U.S. figure of 17.4 percent of children living in poverty is much higher than those from other industrialized nations. For example, Canada has a child poverty rate of 9 percent and Sweden has a rate of 2 percent.

Edelman says that parenting and nurturing the next generation of children is our society's most important function and that we need to take it more seriously than we have in the past. To read about efforts to improve the lives of children through social policies, see the *Applications in Life-Span Development* interlude that follows.

social policy The laws, regulations, and government programs designed to promote the welfare of its citizens.

These children live in a slum area of a small Vermont town where the unemployment rate is very high because of a decline in industrial jobs. *What should be the government's role in improving the lives of these children?*

Applications in Life-Span Development
Improving Family Policy

In the United States, the national government, state governments, and city governments all play a role in influencing the well-being of children (Children's Defense Fund, 2007). When families fail or seriously endanger a child's well-being, governments often step in to help (Corbett, 2007). At the national and state levels, policy makers have debated for decades whether helping poor parents ends up helping their children as well. Researchers are providing some answers by examining the effects of specific policies (Coltrane & others, 2008; Gupta, Thornton, & Huston, 2008).

For example, the Minnesota Family Investment Program (MFIP) was designed in the 1990s primarily to influence the behavior of adults—specifically, to move adults off the welfare rolls and into paid employment. A key element of the program was that it guaranteed that adults participating in the program would receive more income if they worked than if they did not. When the adults' income rose, how did that affect their children? A study of the effects of MFIP found that increases in the incomes of working poor parents were linked with benefits for their children (Gennetian & Miller, 2002). The children's achievement in school improved, and their behavior problems decreased.

Developmental psychologists and other researchers have examined the effects of many other government policies. They are seeking ways to help families living in poverty improve their well-being, and they have offered many suggestions for improving government policies (Conger & Conger, 2008; Johnson, Tarrant, & Brooks-Gunn, 2008).

Maggie Kuhn is founder of the Gray Panthers, an international advocacy group that began in 1970 with five older women committed to improving the social conditions of older adults.

At the other end of the life span, the well-being of older adults also creates policy issues (Branch, 2007; Nemund & Kolland, 2007). Key concerns are escalating health-care costs and the access of older adults to adequate health care (Ferrini & Ferrini, 2008). One study found that the health-care system fails older adults in many areas (Wenger & others, 2003). For example, older adults received the recommended care for general medical conditions such as heart disease only 52 percent of the time; they received appropriate care for undernutrition and Alzheimer disease only 31 percent of the time.

These concerns about the well-being of older adults are heightened by two facts. First, the number of older adults in the United States is growing dramatically, as Figure 1.5 shows. Second, many of these older Americans are likely to need society's help. Compared with earlier decades, U.S. adults today are less likely to be married, more likely to be childless, and more likely to be living alone. As the older population continues to expand in the twenty-first century, an increasing number of older adults will

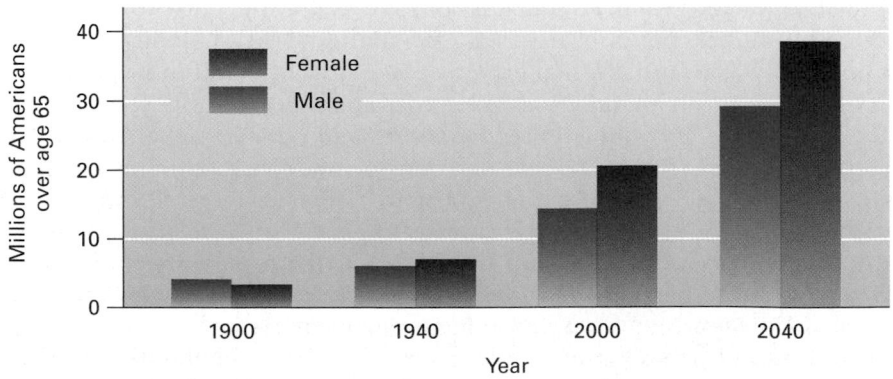

FIGURE 1.5 The Aging of America. The number of Americans over 65 has grown dramatically since 1900 and is projected to increase further from the present to the year 2040. A significant increase will also occur in the number of individuals in the 85-and-over group. Centenarians—persons 100 years of age or older—are the fastest-growing age group in the United States, and their numbers are expected to swell in the coming decades (Perls, 2007).

be without either a spouse or children—traditionally the main sources of support for older adults (Martin-Matthews & Davidson, 2007). These individuals will need social relationships, networks, and supports (Askham, Ferring, & Lamura, 2007).

Review and Reflect: Learning Goal 1

1 **Discuss the Distinctive Features of a Life-Span Perspective on Development**

REVIEW

- What is meant by the concept of development? Why is the study of life-span development important?
- What are the main characteristics of the life-span perspective? What are three sources of contextual influences?
- What are some contemporary concerns in life-span development?

REFLECT

- Imagine what your development would have been like in a culture that offered fewer or distinctly different choices. How might your development have been different if your family had been significantly richer or poorer?

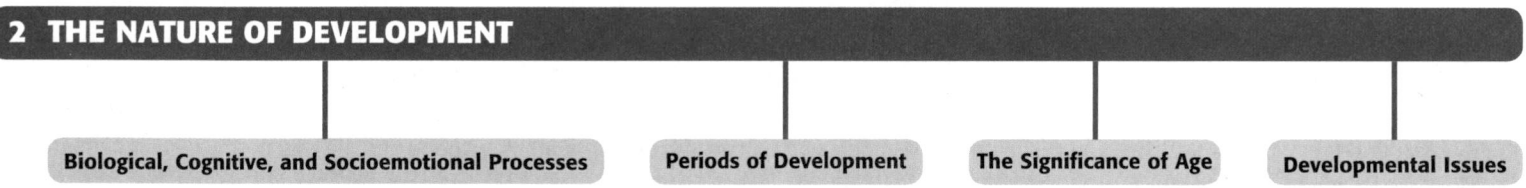

2 THE NATURE OF DEVELOPMENT

| Biological, Cognitive, and Socioemotional Processes | Periods of Development | The Significance of Age | Developmental Issues |

In this section, we will explore what is meant by developmental processes and periods, as well as variations in the way age is conceptualized. We will examine key developmental issues, how they describe development, and strategies we can use to evaluate them.

If you wanted to describe how and why Alice Walker or Ted Kaczynski developed during their lifetimes, how would you go about it? A chronicle of the events in any person's life can quickly become a confusing and tedious array of details. Two concepts help provide a framework for describing and understanding an individual's development: developmental processes and periods.

Biological, Cognitive, and Socioemotional Processes

At the beginning of this chapter, we defined *development* as the pattern of change that begins at conception and continues through the life span. The pattern is complex because it is the product of biological, cognitive, and socioemotional processes (see Figure 1.6).

Biological processes produce changes in an individual's physical nature. Genes inherited from parents, the development of the brain, height and weight gains, changes in motor skills, the hormonal changes of puberty, and cardiovascular decline are all examples of biological processes that affect development.

Cognitive processes refer to changes in the individual's thought, intelligence, and language. Watching a colorful mobile swinging above the crib, putting together a two-word sentence, memorizing a poem, imagining what it would be like to be a movie star, and solving a crossword puzzle all involve cognitive processes.

Socioemotional processes involve changes in the individual's relationships with other people, changes in emotions, and changes in personality. An infant's smile in

biological processes Changes in an individual's physical nature

cognitive processes Changes in an individual's thought, intelligence, and language.

socioemotional processes Changes in an individual's relationships with other people, emotions, and personality.

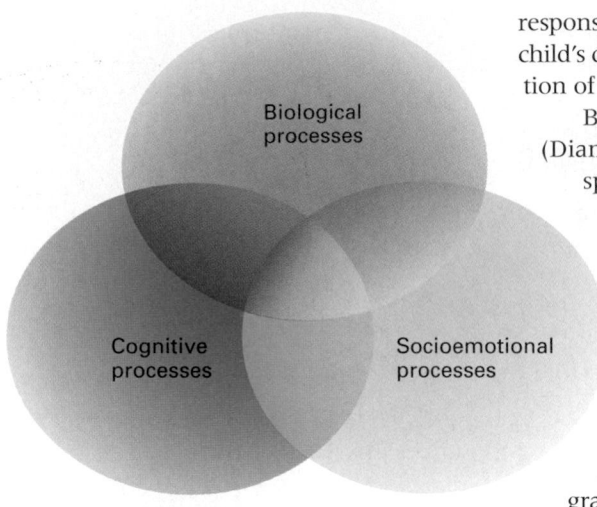

FIGURE 1.6 Processes Involved in Developmental Changes. Biological, cognitive, and socioemotional processes interact as individuals develop.

response to a parent's touch, a toddler's aggressive attack on a playmate, a school-age child's development of assertiveness, an adolescent's joy at the senior prom, and the affection of an elderly couple all reflect the role of socioemotional processes in development.

Biological, cognitive, and socioemotional processes are inextricably intertwined (Diamond, 2007). Consider a baby smiling in response to a parent's touch. This response depends on biological processes (the physical nature of touch and responsiveness to it), cognitive processes (the ability to understand intentional acts), and socioemotional processes (the act of smiling often reflects a positive emotional feeling, and smiling helps to connect us in positive ways with other human beings).

In many instances, biological, cognitive, and socioemotional processes are bidirectional. For example, biological processes can influence cognitive processes and vice versa. Thus, although usually we will study the different processes of development (biological, cognitive, and socioemotional) in separate locations, keep in mind that we are talking about the development of an integrated individual with a mind and body that are interdependent.

Periods of Development

The interplay of biological, cognitive, and socioemotional processes produces the periods of the human life span (see Figure 1.7). A *developmental period* refers to a time frame in a person's life that is characterized by certain features. For the purposes of organization and understanding, we commonly describe development in terms of these periods. The most widely used classification of developmental periods involves the eight-period sequence shown in Figure 1.7. Approximate age ranges are listed for the periods to provide a general idea of when a period begins and ends.

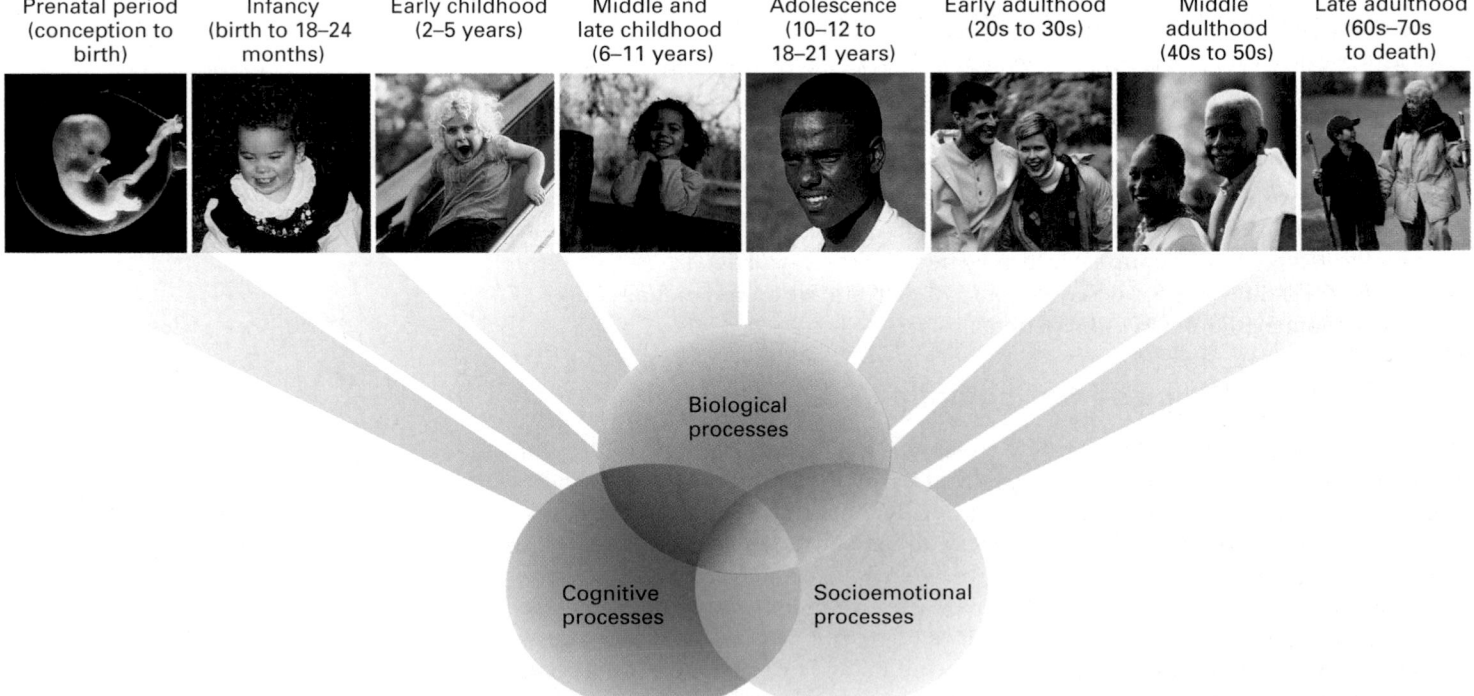

FIGURE 1.7 Processes and Periods of Development. The unfolding of life's periods of development is influenced by the interaction of biological, cognitive, and socioemotional processes.

The *prenatal period* is the time from conception to birth. It involves tremendous growth—from a single cell to an organism complete with brain and behavioral capabilities—and takes place in approximately a nine-month period.

Infancy is the developmental period from birth to 18 or 24 months. Infancy is a time of extreme dependence upon adults. During this period, many psychological activities—language, symbolic thought, sensorimotor coordination, and social learning, for example—are just beginning.

Early childhood is the developmental period from the end of infancy to age 5 or 6. This period is sometimes called the "preschool years." During this time, young children learn to become more self-sufficient and to care for themselves, develop school readiness skills (following instructions, identifying letters), and spend many hours in play with peers. First grade typically marks the end of early childhood.

Middle and late childhood is the developmental period from about 6 to 11 years of age, approximately corresponding to the elementary school years. During this period, the fundamental skills of reading, writing, and arithmetic are mastered. The child is formally exposed to the larger world and its culture. Achievement becomes a more central theme of the child's world, and self-control increases.

Adolescence is the developmental period of transition from childhood to early adulthood, entered at approximately 10 to 12 years of age and ending at 18 to 21 years of age. Adolescence begins with rapid physical changes—dramatic gains in height and weight, changes in body contour, and the development of sexual characteristics such as enlargement of the breasts, growth of pubic and facial hair, and deepening of the voice. At this point in development, the pursuit of independence and an identity are prominent. Thought is more logical, abstract, and idealistic. More time is spent outside the family.

Early adulthood is the developmental period that begins in the early twenties and lasts through the thirties. It is a time of establishing personal and economic independence, career development, and, for many, selecting a mate, learning to live with someone in an intimate way, starting a family, and rearing children.

Middle adulthood is the developmental period from approximately 40 years of age to about 60. It is a time of expanding personal and social involvement and responsibility; of assisting the next generation in becoming competent, mature individuals; and of reaching and maintaining satisfaction in a career.

Late adulthood is the developmental period that begins in the sixties or seventies and lasts until death. It is a time life review, retirement, and adjustment to new social roles involving decreasing strength and health.

Late adulthood has the longest span of any period of development, and as noted earlier, the number of people in this age group has been increasing dramatically. As a result, life-span developmentalists have been paying more attention to differences within late adulthood (Scheibe, Freund, & Baltes, 2007). Paul Baltes and Jacqui Smith (2003) argue that a major change takes place in older adults' lives as they become the "oldest-old," on average at about 85 years of age. For example, the "young-old" (classified as 65 through 84 in this analysis) have substantial potential for physical and cognitive fitness, retain much of their cognitive capacity, and can develop strategies to cope with the gains and losses of aging. In contrast, the oldest-old (85 and older) show considerable loss in cognitive skills, experience an increase in chronic stress, and are more frail (Baltes & Smith, 2003). Nonetheless, as we will see in later chapters, considerable variation exists in how much the oldest-old retain their capabilities.

Thus, Baltes and Smith concluded that considerable plasticity and adaptability characterize adults from their sixties until their mid-eighties but that the oldest-old have reached the limits of their functional capacity, which makes interventions to improve their lives difficult. Nonetheless, as will be described in later chapters, considerable variation exists in how much the oldest-old retain their capabilities (Perls, 2007). As you will see next in the *Research in Life-Span Development* interlude, contexts play an important role in how well older adults perform.

*O*ne's children's children's children. Look back to us as we look to you; we are related by our imaginations. If we are able to touch, it is because we have imagined each other's existence, our dreams running back and forth along a cable from age to age.

—ROGER ROSENBLATT
American Writer, 20th Century

Research in Life-Span Development
Memory in the A.M. *and* P.M. *and Memory for Something Meaningful*

Laura Helmuth (2003) described how researchers are finding that certain testing conditions have exaggerated age-related declines in performance in older adults. Optimum testing conditions are not the same for young adults as they are for older adults. Most researchers conduct their studies in the afternoon, a convenient time for researchers and undergraduate participants. Traditional-aged college students in their late teens and early twenties are often more alert and function more optimally in the afternoon, but about 75 percent of older adults are "morning people," performing at their best early in the day (Helmuth, 2003).

Lynn Hasher and her colleagues (2001) tested the memory of college students 18 to 32 years of age and community volunteers 58 to 78 years of age in the late afternoon (about 4 to 5 P.M.) and in the morning (about 8 to 9 A.M.). Regardless of the time of day, the younger college students performed better than the older adults on the memory tests, which involved recognizing sentences from a story and memorizing a list of words. However, when the participants took the memory tests in the morning rather than in the late afternoon, the age difference in performance decreased considerably (see Figure 1.8).

The relevance of information also affects memory. Thomas Hess and his colleagues (2003) asked younger adults (18 to 30 years of age) and older adults (62 to 84 years of age) to listen to a drawn-out description that was identified as either someone's experiences on a first job or their experiences while searching for a retirement home. The younger adults remembered the details of both circumstances. However, the older adults showed a keen memory for the retirement-home search but not for the first-job experience.

In short, researchers have found that age differences in memory are robust when researchers ask for information that doesn't matter much, but when older adults are asked about information that is relevant to their lives, differences in the memory of younger and older adults often decline considerably (Hasher, 2003). Thus, the type of information selected by researchers may produce an exaggerated view of declines in memory with age.

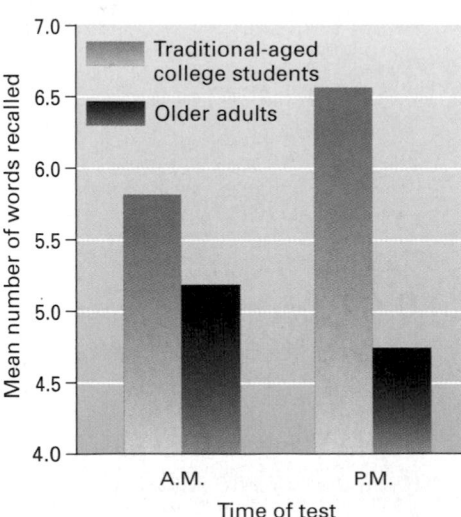

FIGURE 1.8 Memory, Age, and Time of Day Tested (A.M. or P.M.). In one study, traditional-aged college students performed better than older adults in both the A.M. and the P.M. Note, however, that the memory of the older adults was better when they were tested in the morning than in the afternoon, whereas the memory of the traditional-aged college students was not as good in the morning as it was in the afternoon (Hasher & others, 2001).

Life-span developmentalists who focus on adult development and aging increasingly describe life-span development in terms of four "ages" (Baltes, 2006; Willis & Schaie, 2006):

First age: Childhood and adolescence

Second age: Prime adulthood, twenties through fifties

Third age: Approximately 60 to 79 years of age

Fourth age: Approximately 80 years and older

The major emphasis in this conceptualization is on the third and fourth ages, especially the increasing evidence that individuals in the third age are healthier and can lead more active, productive lives than their precedessors in earlier generations. However, when older adults reach their eighties, especially 85 and over (fourth age), health and well-being decline for many individuals.

The Significance of Age

In our description of developmental periods, we linked an approximate age range with each period. But we also have noted that there are variations in the capabilities of individuals of the same age, and we have seen how changes with age can be exaggerated. How important is age when we try to understand an individual?

Age and Happiness   Is one age in life better than another? When researchers have studied this question, consistent answers have not been forthcoming. Some studies of adults have indicated that happiness increases with age (Rodgers, 1982), others reveal no differences in happiness for adults of different ages (Inglehart, 1990), and yet others have found a U-shaped result with the lowest happiness occurring at 30 to 40 years of age (Mroczek & Kolarz, 1998). However, an increasing number of studies indicate that at least in the United States adults are happier as they age (Charles, Reynolds, & Gatz, 2001; Erlich & Isaacowitz, 2002). Consider a recent large-scale U.S. study of approximately 28,000 individuals from 18 to 88 that revealed happiness increased with age (Yang, 2008). For example, about 33 percent were very happy at 88 years of age compared with only about 24 percent in their late teens and early twenties. Why might older people report as much or more happiness and life satisfaction as younger people? Despite the increase in physical problems and losses older adults experience, they are more content with what they have in their lives, have better relationships with the people who matter to them, are less pressured to achieve, have more time for leisurely pursuits, and have many years of experience that may help them adapt to their circumstances with wisdom than younger adults do (Cornwell, Schumm, & Laumann, 2008; Ram & others, 2008). Also in the study, baby boomers (those born from 1946 to 1964) reported being less happy than individuals born earlier, possibly because they are not lowering their aspirations and idealistic hopes as they age as earlier generations did. Because growing older is a certain outcome of living, it is good to know that we are likely to be just as happy or happier as older adults as when we were younger.

Conceptions of Age   According to some life-span experts, chronological age is not very relevant to understanding a person's psychological development (Botwinick, 1978). *Chronological age* is the number of years that have elapsed since birth. But time is a crude index of experience, and it does not cause anything. Chronological age, moreover, is not the only way of measuring age. Just as there are different domains of development, there are different ways of thinking about age.

Age has been conceptualized not just as chronological age but also as biological age, psychological age, and social age (Hoyer & Roodin, 2003). *Biological age* is a person's age in terms of biological health. Determining biological age involves knowing the functional capacities of a person's vital organs (Westendorp & Kirkwood, 2007). One person's vital capacities may be better or worse than those of others of comparable age. The younger the person's biological age, the longer the person is expected to live, regardless of chronological age.

Psychological age is an individual's adaptive capacities compared with those of other individuals of the same chronological age. Thus, older adults who continue to learn, are flexible, are motivated, control their emotions, and think clearly are engaging in more adaptive behaviors than their chronological age-mates who do not continue to learn, are rigid, are unmotivated, do not control their emotions, and do not think clearly (Marcoen, Coleman, & O'Hanlon, 2007).

Social age refers to social roles and expectations related to a person's age (Phillipson & Baars, 2007). Consider the role of "mother" and the behaviors that accompany the role (Huyck & Hoyer, 1982). In predicting an adult woman's behavior, it may be more important to know that she is the mother of a 3-year-old child than to know whether she is 20 or 30 years old.

Life-span expert Bernice Neugarten (1988) argues that in U.S. society chronological age is becoming irrelevant. The 28-year-old mayor, the 35-year-old grandmother, the 65-year-old father of a preschooler, the 55-year-old widow who starts a business, and the 70-year-old student illustrate that old assumptions about the proper timing of life events no longer govern our lives. We still have some expectations for when certain life events—such as getting married, having children, and retiring—should

(*Top*) Dawn Russel, competing in the broad jump in a recent Senior Olympics competition in Oregon; (*bottom*) a sedentary, overweight middle-aged man. *Even if Dawn Russel's chronological age is older, might her biological age be younger than the middle-aged man's?*

How old would you be if you didn't know how old you were?

—SATCHEL PAIGE
American Baseball Pitcher, 20th Century

occur. However, chronological age has become a less accurate predictor of these life events in our society. Moreover, issues such as how to deal with intimacy and how to cope with success and failure appear and reappear throughout the life span.

From a life-span perspective, an overall age profile of an individual involves not just chronological age but also biological age, psychological age, and social age. For example, a 70-year-old man (chronological age) might be in good physical health (biological age), be experiencing memory problems and not be coping well with the demands placed on him by his wife's recent hospitalization (psychological age), and have a number of friends with whom he regularly golfs (social age).

Developmental Issues

Was Ted Kaczynski born a killer, or did his life turn him into one? Kaczynski himself thought that his childhood was the root of his troubles. He grew up as a genius in a boy's body and never fit in with other children. Did his early experiences determine his later life? Is your own journey through life marked out ahead of time, or can your experiences change your path? Are the experiences you have early in your journey more important than later ones? Is your journey more like taking an elevator up a skyscraper with distinct stops along the way or more like a cruise down a river with smoother ebbs and flows? These questions point to three issues about the nature of development: the roles played by nature and nurture, stability and change, and continuity and discontinuity.

Nature and Nurture   The **nature-nurture issue** involves the extent to which development is influenced by nature and by nurture. *Nature* refers to an organism's biological inheritance, *nurture* to its environmental experiences.

According to those who emphasize the role of nature, just as a sunflower grows in an orderly way—unless flattened by an unfriendly environment—so too the human grows in an orderly way. An evolutionary and genetic foundation produces commonalities in growth and development (D'Onofrio, 2008; Hartwell, 2008). We walk before we talk, speak one word before two words, grow rapidly in infancy and less so in early childhood, experience a rush of sex hormones in puberty, reach the peak of our physical strength in late adolescence and early adulthood, and then physically decline. Proponents of the importance of nature acknowledge that extreme environments—those that are psychologically barren or hostile—can depress development. However, they believe that basic growth tendencies are genetically programmed into humans (Balasubramanian, Koontz, & Reynolds, 2008; Plomin & Schalkwyk, 2007).

By contrast, other psychologists emphasize the importance of nurture, or environmental experiences, in development (Cannides, 2009; Crane & Heaton, 2008). Experiences run the gamut from the individual's biological environment (nutrition, medical care, drugs, and physical accidents) to the social environment (family, peers, schools, community, media, and culture).

What is the nature of the early- and later-experience issue in development?

Stability and Change   Is the shy child who hides behind the sofa when visitors arrive destined to become a wallflower at college dances, or might the child become a sociable, talkative individual? Is the fun-loving, carefree adolescent bound to have difficulty holding down a 9-to-5 job as an adult? These questions reflect the **stability-change issue**, which involves the degree to which early traits and characteristics persist through life or change.

Many developmentalists who emphasize stability in development argue that stability is the result of heredity and possibly early experiences in life. For example, many argue that if an individual is shy throughout life (as Ted Kaczynski was), this stability is due to heredity and possibly early experiences in which the infant or young child encountered considerable stress when interacting with people.

Developmentalists who emphasize change take the more optimistic view that later experiences can produce change. Recall that in the life-span perspective, plasticity, the

nature-nurture issue The issue that involves the extent to which development is influenced by nature and by nurture. The "nature" proponents claim biological inheritance is the most important influence on development; the "nurture" proponents claim that environmental experiences are the most important.

stability-change issue Involves the degree to which early traits and characteristics persist through life or change.

potential for change, exists throughout the life span. Experts such as Paul Baltes (2003) argue that with increasing age and on average older adults often show less capacity for change in the sense of learning new things than younger adults. However, many older adults continue to be good at practicing what they have learned in earlier times.

The roles of early and later experience are an aspect of the stability-change issue that has long been hotly debated (Caspi & Shiner, 2006). Some argue that unless infants experience warm, nurturant caregiving in the first year or so of life, their development will never be optimal (Sroufe, 2007). The later-experience advocates see children as malleable throughout development and later sensitive caregiving as equally important to earlier sensitive caregiving.

Continuity and Discontinuity When developmental change occurs, is it gradual or abrupt? Think about your own development for a moment. Did you become the person you are gradually? Or did you experience sudden, distinct changes in your growth? For the most part, developmentalists who emphasize nurture describe development as a gradual, continuous process. Those who emphasize nature often describe development as a series of distinct stages.

The **continuity-discontinuity issue** focuses on the degree to which development involves either gradual, cumulative change (continuity) or distinct stages (discontinuity). In terms of continuity, as the oak grows from seedling to giant oak, it becomes more oak—its development is continuous (see Figure 1.9). Similarly, a child's first word, though seemingly an abrupt, discontinuous event, is actually the result of weeks and months of growth and practice. Puberty might seem abrupt, but it is a gradual process that occurs over several years.

In terms of discontinuity, as an insect grows from a caterpillar to a chrysalis to a butterfly, it passes through a sequence of stages in which change is qualitatively rather than quantitatively different. Similarly, at some point a child moves from not being able to think abstractly about the world to being able to. This is a qualitative, discontinuous change in development rather than a quantitative, continuous change.

Evaluating the Developmental Issues Most life-span developmentalists acknowledge that development is not all nature or all nurture, not all stability or all change, and not all continuity or all discontinuity (Gottlieb, 2007; Rutter, 2007). Nature *and* nurture, stability *and* change, continuity *and* discontinuity characterize development throughout the human life span.

Although most developmentalists do not take extreme positions on these three important issues, there is spirited debate regarding how strongly development is influenced by each of these factors (Blakemore, Berenbam, & Liben, 2009; Plomin, DeFries, & Fulker, 2007).

FIGURE 1.9 Continuity and Discontinuity in Development. *Is our development like that of a seedling gradually growing into a giant oak? Or is it more like that of a caterpillar suddenly becoming a butterfly?*

Review and Reflect: Learning Goal 2

2 **Identify the Most Important Processes, Periods, and Issues in Development**

REVIEW

- What are three key developmental processes?
- What are eight main developmental periods?
- How is age related to development?
- What are three main developmental issues?

REFLECT

- Do you think there is a best age to be? If so, what is it? Why?

continuity-discontinuity issue The issue regarding whether development involves gradual, cumulative change (continuity) or distinct stages (discontinuity).

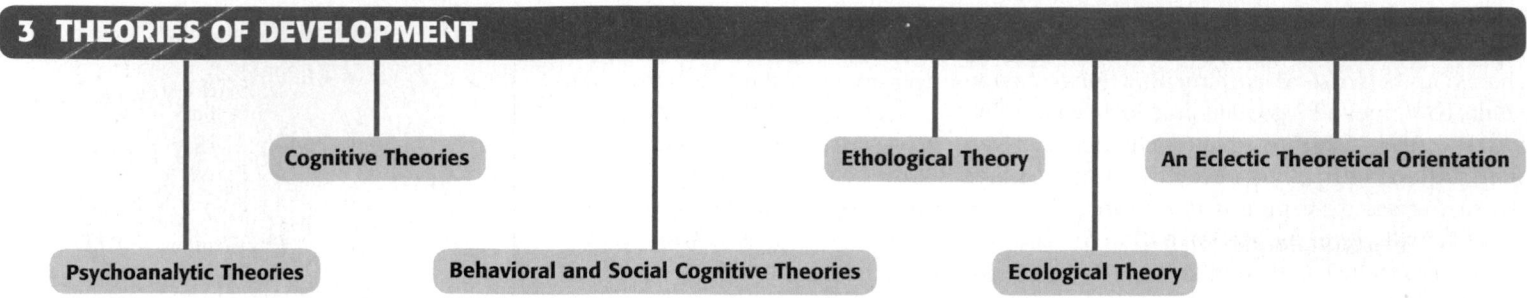

3   THEORIES OF DEVELOPMENT

Cognitive Theories

Ethological Theory

An Eclectic Theoretical Orientation

Psychoanalytic Theories

Behavioral and Social Cognitive Theories

Ecological Theory

*T*here is nothing quite so practical as a good theory.

—KURT LEWIN
American Social Psychologist, 20th Century

Sigmund Freud, the pioneering architect of psychoanalytic theory. *How did Freud portray the organization of an individual's personality?*

scientific method An approach that can be used to obtain accurate information. It includes these steps: (1) conceptualize the problem, (2) collect data, (3) draw conclusions, and (4) revise research conclusions and theory.

theory An interrelated, coherent set of ideas that helps to explain phenomena and make predictions.

hypotheses Specific assertions and predictions that can be tested to determine their accuracy.

How can we answer questions about the roles of nature and nurture, stability and change, and continuity and discontinuity in development? How can we determine, for example, whether memory declines in older adults can be prevented or whether special care can repair the harm inflicted by child neglect? The scientific method is the best tool we have to answer such questions.

The **scientific method** is essentially a four-step process: (1) Conceptualize a process or problem to be studied, (2) collect research information (data), (3) analyze data, and (4) draw conclusions.

In step 1, when researchers are formulating a problem to study, they often draw on theories and develop hypotheses. A **theory** is an interrelated, coherent set of ideas that helps to explain phenomena and make predictions. It may suggest **hypotheses**, which are specific assertions and predictions that can be tested. For example, a theory on mentoring might state that sustained support and guidance from an adult makes a difference in the lives of children from impoverished backgrounds because the mentor gives the children opportunities to observe and imitate the behavior and strategies of the mentor.

This section outlines key aspects of five theoretical orientations to development: psychoanalytic, cognitive, behavioral and social cognitive, ethological, and ecological. Each contributes an important piece to the life-span development puzzle. Although the theories disagree about certain aspects of development, many of their ideas are complementary rather than contradictory. Together they let us see the total landscape of life-span development in all its richness (Newman & Newman, 2007).

Psychoanalytic Theories

Psychoanalytic theories describe development as primarily unconscious (beyond awareness) and heavily colored by em otion. Psychoanalytic theorists emphasize that behavior is merely a surface characteristic and that a true understanding of development requires analyzing the symbolic meanings of behavior and the deep inner workings of the mind. Psychoanalytic theorists also stress that early experiences with parents extensively shape development. These characteristics are highlighted in the main psychoanalytic theory, that of Sigmund Freud (1856–1939).

Freud's Theory   As Freud listened to, probed, and analyzed his patients, he became convinced that their problems were the result of experiences early in life. He thought that as children grow up, their focus of pleasure and sexual impulses shifts from the mouth to the anus and eventually to the genitals. As a result, we go through five stages of psychosexual development: oral, anal, phallic, latency, and genital (see Figure 1.10). Our adult personality, Freud (1917) claimed, is determined by the way we resolve conflicts between sources of pleasure at each stage and the demands of reality.

Freud's theory has been significantly revised by a number of psychoanalytic theorists. Many of today's psychoanalytic theorists maintain that Freud overemphasized sexual instincts; they place more emphasis on cultural experiences as determinants of an individual's development. Unconscious thought remains a central theme, but

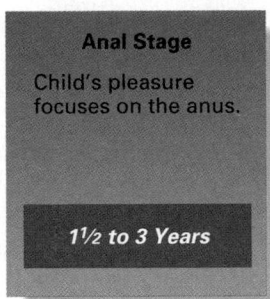
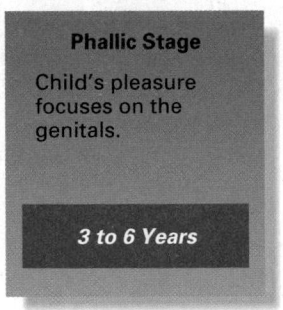
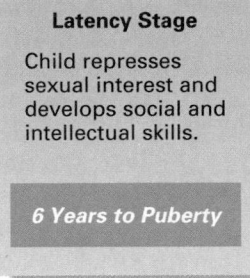
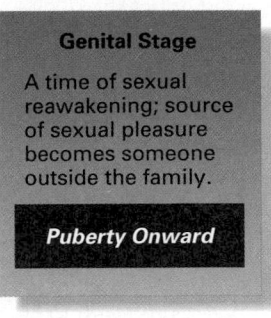

Oral Stage	**Anal Stage**	**Phallic Stage**	**Latency Stage**	**Genital Stage**
Infant's pleasure centers on the mouth.	Child's pleasure focuses on the anus.	Child's pleasure focuses on the genitals.	Child represses sexual interest and develops social and intellectual skills.	A time of sexual reawakening; source of sexual pleasure becomes someone outside the family.
Birth to 1½ Years	*1½ to 3 Years*	*3 to 6 Years*	*6 Years to Puberty*	*Puberty Onward*

FIGURE 1.10 Freudian Stages. Because Freud emphasized sexual motivation, his stages of development are known as *psychosexual stages.* In his view, if the need for pleasure at any stage is either undergratified or overgratified, an individual may become *fixated,* or locked in, at that stage of development.

thought plays a greater role than Freud envisioned. Next, we will outline the ideas of an important revisionist of Freud's ideas—Erik Erikson.

Erikson's Psychosocial Theory   Erik Erikson recognized Freud's contributions but believed that Freud misjudged some important dimensions of human development. For one thing, Erikson (1950, 1968) said we develop in *psychosocial* stages, rather than in *psychosexual* stages, as Freud maintained. According to Freud, the primary motivation for human behavior is sexual in nature; according to Erikson, it is social and reflects a desire to affiliate with other people. According to Freud, our basic personality is shaped in the first five years of life; according to Erikson, developmental change occurs throughout the life span. Thus, in terms of the early-versus-later-experience issue described in earlier in the chapter, Freud viewed early experience as far more important than later experiences, whereas Erikson emphasized the importance of both early and later experiences.

In **Erikson's theory**, eight stages of development unfold as we go through life (see Figure 1.11). At each stage, a unique developmental task confronts individuals with a crisis that must be resolved. According to Erikson, this crisis is not a catastrophe but a turning point marked by both increased vulnerability and enhanced potential. The more successfully an individual resolves the crises, the healthier development will be.

Trust versus mistrust is Erikson's first psychosocial stage, which is experienced in the first year of life. Trust in infancy sets the stage for a lifelong expectation that the world will be a good and pleasant place to live.

Autonomy versus shame and doubt is Erikson's second stage. This stage occurs in late infancy and toddlerhood (1 to 3 years). After gaining trust in their caregivers, infants begin to discover that their behavior is their own. They start to assert their sense of independence or autonomy. They realize their *will.* If infants and toddlers are restrained too much or punished too harshly, they are likely to develop a sense of shame and doubt.

Initiative versus guilt, Erikson's third stage of development, occurs during the preschool years. As preschool children encounter a widening social world, they face new challenges that require active, purposeful, responsible behavior. Feelings of guilt may arise, though, if the child is irresponsible and is made to feel too anxious.

Industry versus inferiority is Erikson's fourth developmental stage, occurring approximately in the elementary school years. Children now need to direct their energy toward mastering knowledge and intellectual skills. The negative outcome is that the child may develop a sense of inferiority—feeling incompetent and unproductive.

During the adolescent years, individuals face finding out who they are, what they are all about, and where they are going in life. This is Erikson's fifth developmental stage, *identity versus identity confusion.* If adolescents explore roles in a healthy manner

Erik Erikson with his wife, Joan, an artist. Erikson generated one of the most important developmental theories of the twentieth century. *Which stage of Erikson's theory are you in? Does Erikson's description of this stage characterize you?*

psychoanalytic theories Describe development as primarily unconscious and heavily colored by emotion. Behavior is merely a surface characteristic, and the symbolic workings of the mind have to be analyzed to understand behavior. Early experiences with parents are emphasized.

Erikson's theory Includes eight stages of human development. Each stage consists of a unique developmental task that confronts individuals with a crisis that must be resolved.

Erikson's Stages	Developmental Period
Integrity versus despair	Late adulthood (60s onward)
Generativity versus stagnation	Middle adulthood (40s, 50s)
Intimacy versus isolation	Early adulthood (20s, 30s)
Identity versus identity confusion	Adolescence (10 to 20 years)
Industry versus inferiority	Middle and late childhood (elementary school years, 6 years to puberty)
Initiative versus guilt	Early childhood (preschool years, 3 to 5 years)
Autonomy versus shame and doubt	Infancy (1 to 3 years)
Trust versus mistrust	Infancy (first year)

FIGURE 1.11 Erikson's Eight Life-Span Stages. Like Freud, Erikson proposed that individuals go through distinct, universal stages of development. Thus, in terms of the continuity–discontinuity issue discussed in Chapter 1, both favor the discontinuity side of the debate. Notice that the timing of Erikson's first four stages is similar to that of Freud's stages. *What are implications of saying that people go through stages of development?*

Piaget's theory States that children actively construct their understanding of the world and go through four stages of cognitive development.

and arrive at a positive path to follow in life, then they achieve a positive identity; if not, then identity confusion reigns.

Intimacy versus isolation is Erikson's sixth developmental stage, which individuals experience during the early adulthood years. At this time, individuals face the developmental task of forming intimate relationships. If young adults form healthy friendships and an intimate relationship with another, intimacy will be achieved; if not, isolation will result.

Generativity versus stagnation, Erikson's seventh developmental stage, occurs during middle adulthood. By *generativity* Erikson means primarily a concern for helping the younger generation to develop and lead useful lives. The feeling of having done nothing to help the next generation is stagnation.

Integrity versus despair is Erikson's eighth and final stage of development, which individuals experience in late adulthood. During this stage, a person reflects on the past. If the person's life review reveal a life well spent, integrity will be achieved; if not, the retrospective glances likely will yield doubt or gloom—the despair Erikson described.

Evaluating Psychoanalytic Theories Contributions of psychoanalytic theories include an emphasis on a developmental framework, family relationships, and unconscious aspects of the mind. Criticisms include a lack of scientific support, too much emphasis on sexual underpinnings, and an image of people that is too negative.

Cognitive Theories

Whereas psychoanalytic theories stress the importance of the unconscious, cognitive theories emphasize conscious thoughts. Three important cognitive theories are Piaget's cognitive adevelopmental theory, Vygotsky's sociocultural cognitive theory, and information-processing theory.

Jean Piaget, the famous Swiss developmental psychologist, changed the way we think about the development of children's minds. *What are some key ideas in Piaget's theory?*

Piaget's Cognitive Developmental Theory Piaget's **theory** states that children go through four stages of cognitive development as they actively construct their understanding of the world. Two processes underlie this cognitive construction of the world: organization and adaptation. To make sense of our world, we organize our experiences (Carpendale, Muller, & Bibok, 2008). For example, we separate important ideas from less important ideas, and we connect one idea to another. In addition to organizing our observations and experiences, we *adapt,* adjusting to new environmental demands (Byrnes, 2008).

Piaget (1954) also held that we go through four stages in understanding the world (see Figure 1.12). Each stage is age-related and consists of a distinct way of thinking, a *different* way of understanding the world. Thus, according to Piaget, the child's cognition is *qualitatively* different in one stage compared with another. What are Piaget's four stages of cognitive development?

- The *sensorimotor stage,* which lasts from birth to about 2 years of age, is the first Piagetian stage. In this stage, infants construct an understanding of the world by coordinating sensory experiences (such as seeing and hearing) with physical, motoric actions—hence the term *sensorimotor.*

- The *preoperational stage,* which lasts from approximately 2 to 7 years of age, is Piaget's second stage.

Sensorimotor Stage	Preoperational Stage	Concrete Operational Stage	Formal Operational Stage
The infant constructs an understanding of the world by coordinating sensory experiences with physical actions. An infant progresses from reflexive, instinctual action at birth to the beginning of symbolic thought toward the end of the stage.	The child begins to represent the world with words and images. These words and images reflect increased symbolic thinking and go beyond the connection of sensory information and physical action.	The child can now reason logically about concrete events and classify objects into different sets.	The adolescent reasons in more abstract, idealistic, and logical ways.
Birth to 2 Years of Age	*2 to 7 Years of Age*	*7 to 11 Years of Age*	*11 Years of Age Through Adulthood*

FIGURE 1.12 Piaget's Four Stages of Cognitive Development. According to Piaget, how a child thinks—not how much the child knows—determines the child's stage of cognitive development.

In this stage, children begin to go beyond simply connecting sensory information with physical action and represent the world with words, images, and drawings. However, according to Piaget, preschool children still lack the ability to perform what he calls *operations,* which are internalized mental actions that allow children to do mentally what they previously could only do physically. For example, if you imagine putting two sticks together to see whether they would be as long as another stick, without actually moving the sticks, you are performing a concrete operation.

- The *concrete operational stage,* which lasts from approximately 7 to 11 years of age, is the third Piagetian stage. In this stage, children can perform operations that involve objects, and they can reason logically when the reasoning can be applied to specific or concrete examples. For instance, concrete operational thinkers cannot imagine the steps necessary to complete an algebraic equation, which is too abstract for thinking at this stage of development.

- The *formal operational stage,* which appears between the ages of 11 and 15 and continues through adulthood, is Piaget's fourth and final stage. In this stage, individuals move beyond concrete experiences and think in abstract and more logical terms. As part of thinking more abstractly, adolescents develop images of ideal circumstances. They might think about what an ideal parent is like and compare their parents to this ideal standard. They begin to entertain possibilities for the future and are fascinated with what they can be. In solving problems, they become more systematic, developing hypotheses about why something is happening the way it is and then testing these hypotheses. We will examine Piaget's cognitive developmental theory further in Chapters 5, 7, 9, and 11.

Vygotsky's Sociocultural Cognitive Theory Like Piaget, the Russian developmentalist Lev Vygotsky (1896–1934) argued that children actively construct their knowledge. However, Vygotsky (1962) gave social interaction and culture far more important roles in cognitive development than Piaget did. **Vygotsky's theory** is a sociocultural cognitive theory that emphasizes how culture and social interaction guide cognitive development.

Vygotsky portrayed the child's development as inseparable from social and cultural activities (Cole & Gajdamaschko, 2007; Gredler, 2008). He maintained that cognitive development involves learning to use the inventions of society, such as language, mathematical systems, and memory strategies. Thus in one culture, children might learn to count with the help of a computer; in another, they might learn by using

Lev Vygotsky was born the same year as Piaget, but he died much earlier, at the age of 37. There is considerable interest today in Vygotsky's sociocultural cognitive theory of child development. *What are some key characteristics of Vygotsky's theory?*

Vygotsky's theory A sociocultural cognitive theory that emphasizes how culture and social interaction guide cognitive development.

beads. According to Vygotsky, children's social interaction with more-skilled adults and peers is indispensable to their cognitive development (Holzman, 2009). Through this interaction, they learn to use the tools that will help them adapt and be successful in their culture. In Chapter 7, we examine ideas about learning and teaching that are based on Vygotsky's theory.

The Information-Processing Theory **Information-processing theory** emphasizes that individuals manipulate information, monitor it, and strategize about it. Unlike Piaget's theory, but like Vygotsky's theory, information-processing theory does not describe development as stage-like. Instead, according to this theory, individuals develop a gradually increasing capacity for processing information, which allows them to acquire increasingly complex knowledge and skills (Halford, 2008; Vallotton & Fischer, 2008).

Robert Siegler (2006, 2007), a leading expert on children's information processing, states that thinking is information processing. In other words, when individuals perceive, encode, represent, store, and retrieve information, they are thinking. Siegler emphasizes that an important aspect of development is learning good strategies for processing information. For example, becoming a better reader might involve learning to monitor the key themes of the material being read.

Evaluating Cognitive Theories Contributions of cognitive theories include a positive view of development and an emphasis on the active construction of understanding. Criticisms include skepticism about the pureness of Piaget's stages and too little attention to individual variations.

Behavioral and Social Cognitive Theories

Behaviorism essentially holds that we can study scientifically only what can be directly observed and measured. Out of the behavioral tradition grew the belief that development is observable behavior that can be learned through experience with the environment (Watson & Tharp, 2007). In terms of the continuity-discontinuity issue discussed earlier in this chapter, the behavioral and social cognitive theories emphasize continuity in development and argue that development does not occur in stage-like fashion. Let's explore two versions of behaviorism: Skinner's operant conditioning and Bandura's social cognitive theory.

Skinner's Operant Conditioning According to B. F. Skinner (1904–1990), through *operant conditioning* the consequences of a behavior produce changes in the probability of the behavior's occurrence. A behavior followed by a rewarding stimulus is more likely to recur, whereas a behavior followed by a punishing stimulus is less likely to recur. For example, when an adult smiles at a child after the child has done something, the child is more likely to engage in that behavior again than if the adult gives the child a disapproving look.

In Skinner's (1938) view, such rewards and punishments shape development. For Skinner the key aspect of development is behavior, not thoughts and feelings. He emphasized that development consists of the pattern of behavioral changes that are brought about by rewards and punishments. For example, Skinner would say that shy people learned to be shy as a result of experiences they had while growing up. It follows that modifications in an environment can help a shy person become more socially oriented.

Bandura's Social Cognitive Theory Some psychologists agree with the behaviorists' notion that development is learned and is influenced strongly by environmental interactions. However, unlike Skinner, they also see cognition as important in understanding development (Mischel, 2004). **Social cognitive theory** holds that behavior, environment, and cognition are the key factors in development.

B. F. Skinner was a tinkerer who liked to make new gadgets. The younger of his two daughters, Deborah, was raised in Skinner's enclosed Air-Crib, which he invented because he wanted to control her environment completely. The Air-Crib was sound-proofed and temperature controlled. Debbie, shown here as a child with her parents, is currently a successful artist, is married, and lives in London. *What do you think about Skinner's Air-Crib?*

information-processing theory Emphasizes that individuals manipulate information, monitor it, and strategize about it. Central to this theory are the processes of memory and thinking.

social cognitive theory The view of psychologists who emphasize behavior, environment, and cognition as the key factors in development.

American psychologist Albert Bandura (1925–) is the leading architect of social cognitive theory. Bandura (1986, 2004, 2007, 2008, 2009) emphasizes that cognitive processes have important links with the environment and behavior. His early research program focused heavily on *observational learning* (also called *imitation* or *modeling*), which is learning that occurs through observing what others do. For example, a young boy might observe his father yelling in anger and treating other people with hostility; with his peers, the young boy later acts very aggressively, showing the same characteristics as his father's behavior. Social cognitive theorists stress that people acquire a wide range of behaviors, thoughts, and feelings through observing others' behavior and that these observations form an important part of life-span development.

What is *cognitive* about observational learning in Bandura's view? He proposes that people cognitively represent the behavior of others and then sometimes adopt this behavior themselves.

Bandura's (2004, 2007, 2008, 2009) most recent model of learning and development includes three elements: behavior, the person/cognition, and the environment. An individual's confidence that he or she can control his or her success is an example of a person factor; strategies are an example of a cognitive factor. As shown in Figure 1.13, behavior, person/cognitive, and environmental factors operate interactively.

Evaluating Behavioral and Social Cognitive Theories   Contributions of the behavioral and social cognitive theories include an emphasis on scientific research and environmental determinants of behavior. Criticisms include too little emphasis on cognition in Skinner's view and giving inadequate attention to developmental changes.

Ethological Theory

Ethology stresses that behavior is strongly influenced by biology, is tied to evolution, and is characterized by critical or sensitive periods. These are specific time frames during which, according to ethologists, the presence or absence of certain experiences has a long-lasting influence on individuals.

European zoologist Konrad Lorenz (1903–1989) helped bring ethology to prominence. In his best-known research, Lorenz (1965) studied the behavior of greylag geese, which will follow their mothers as soon as they hatch. Lorenz separated the eggs laid by one goose into two groups. One group he returned to the goose to be hatched by her. The other group was hatched in an incubator. The goslings in the first group performed as predicted. They followed their mother as soon as they hatched. However, those in the second group, which saw Lorenz when they first hatched, followed him everywhere, as though he were their mother. Lorenz marked the goslings and then placed both groups under a box. Mother goose and "mother" Lorenz stood aside as the box lifted. Each group of goslings went directly to its "mother." Lorenz called this process *imprinting*, the rapid, innate learning that involves attachment to the first moving object seen.

John Bowlby (1969, 1989) illustrated an important application of ethological theory to human development. Bowlby stressed that attachment to a caregiver over the first year of life has important consequences throughout the life span. In his view, if this attachment is positive and secure, the individual will likely develop positively in childhood and adulthood. If the attachment is negative and insecure, life-span development will likely not be optimal. In Chapter 6, we will explore the concept of infant attachment in much greater detail.

In Lorenz's view, imprinting needs to take place at a certain, very early time in the life of the animal, or else it will not take place. This point in time is called a *critical period*. A related concept is that of a *sensitive period*, and an example of this is the time during infancy when, according to Bowlby, attachment should occur in order to promote optimal development of social relationships.

Another theory that emphasizes biological foundations of development—evolutionary psychology—will be presented in Chapter 2, along with views on the role of heredity in development. In addition, we will examine a number of biological theories of aging in Chapter 17.

Albert Bandura has been one of the leading architects of social cognitive theory. *How does Bandura's theory differ from Skinner's?*

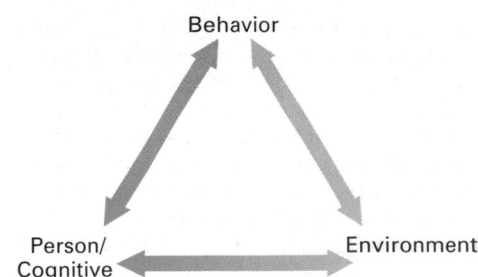

FIGURE 1.13 Bandura's Social Cognitive Model. The arrows illustrate how relations between behavior, person/cognitive, and environment are reciprocal rather than one way. *Person/cognitive* refers to cognitive processes (for example, thinking and planning) and personal characteristics (for example, believing that you can control your experiences).

ethology Stresses that behavior is strongly influenced by biology, is tied to evolution, and is characterized by critical or sensitive periods.

Konrad Lorenz, a pioneering student of animal behavior, is followed through the water by three imprinted greylag geese. Describe Lorenz's experiment with the geese. *Do you think his experiment would have the same results with human babies? Explain.*

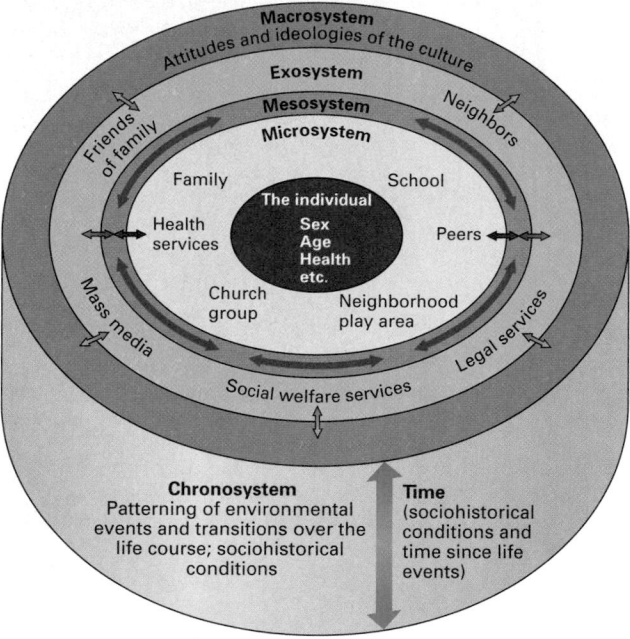

FIGURE 1.14 Bronfenbrenner's Ecological Theory of Development. Bronfenbrenner's ecological theory consists of five environmental systems: microsystem, mesosystem, exosystem, macrosystem, and chronosystem.

Bronfenbrenner's ecological theory Maintains that development reflects the influence of five environmental systems: microsystem, mesosystem, exosystem, macrosystem, and chronosystem.

Evaluating Ethological Theory Contributions of ethological theory include a focus on the biological and evolutionary basis of development, and the use of careful observations in naturalistic settings. Criticisms include too much emphasis on biological foundations and a belief that the critical and sensitive period concepts might be too rigid.

Ecological Theory

While ethological theory stresses biological factors, ecological theory emphasizes environmental factors. One ecological theory that has important implications for understanding life-span development was created by Urie Bronfenbrenner (1917–2005).

Bronfenbrenner's ecological theory (1986, 2004; Bronfenbrenner & Morris, 1998, 2006) holds that development reflects the influence of several environmental systems. The theory identifies five environmental systems: microsystem, mesosystem, exosystem, macrosystem, and chronosystem (see Figure 1.14).

The *microsystem* is the setting in which the individual lives. These contexts include the person's family, peers, school, and neighborhood. It is in the microsystem that the most direct interactions with social agents take place—with parents, peers, and teachers, for example. The individual is not a passive recipient of experiences in these settings, but someone who helps to construct the settings.

The *mesosystem* involves relations between microsystems or connections between contexts. Examples are the relation of family experiences to school experiences, school experiences to church experiences, and family experiences to peer experiences. For example, children whose parents have rejected them may have difficulty developing positive relations with teachers.

The *exosystem* consists of links between a social setting in which the individual does not have an active role and the individual's immediate context. For example, a husband's or child's experience at home may be influenced by a mother's experiences at work. The mother might receive a promotion that requires more travel, which might increase conflict with the husband and change patterns of interaction with the child.

The *macrosystem* involves the culture in which individuals live. Remember from earlier in the chapter that culture refers to the behavior patterns, beliefs, and all other products of a group of people that are passed on from generation to generation. Remember also that cross-cultural studies—the comparison of one culture with one or more other cultures—provide information about the generality of development.

The *chronosystem* consists of the patterning of environmental events and transitions over the life course, as well as sociohistorical circumstances. For example, divorce is one transition. Researchers have found that the negative effects of divorce on children often peak in the first year after the divorce (Hetherington, 1993, 2006). By two years after the divorce, family interaction is more stable. As an example of sociohistorical circumstances, consider how the opportunities for women to pursue a career have increased since the 1960s.

Bronfenbrenner (2004; Bronfenbrenner & Morris, 2006) subsequently added biological influences to his theory, describing it as a *bioecological* theory. Nonetheless, it is still dominated by ecological, environmental contexts (Ceci, 2000).

Evaluating Ecological Theory Contributions of the theory include a systematic examination of macro and micro dimensions of environmental systems, and attention to connections between environmental systems. Criticisms include giving inadequate attention to biological factors, as well as too little emphasis on cognitive factors.

An Eclectic Theoretical Orientation

No single theory described in this chapter can explain entirely the rich complexity of life-span development, but each has contributed to our understanding of development. Psychoanalytic theory best explains the unconscious mind. Erikson's theory best describes the changes that occur in adult development. Piaget's, Vygotsky's, and the information-processing views provide the most complete description of cognitive development. The behavioral and social cognitive and ecological theories have been the most adept at examining the environmental determinants of development. The ethological theories have highlighted biology's role and the importance of sensitive periods in development.

In short, although theories are helpful guides, relying on a single theory to explain development is probably a mistake. This book instead takes an **eclectic theoretical orientation**, which does not follow any one theoretical approach but rather selects from each theory whatever is considered its best features. In this way, you can view the study of development as it actually exists—with different theorists making different assumptions, stressing different empirical problems, and using different strategies to discover information. Figure 1.15 compares the main theoretical perspectives in terms of how they view important developmental issues in children's development.

Urie Bronfenbrenner developed ecological theory, a perspective that is receiving increased attention today. His theory emphasizes the importance of both micro and macro dimensions of the environment in which the child lives.

eclectic theoretical orientation An orientation that does not follow any one theoretical approach, but rather selects from each theory whatever is considered the best in it.

THEORY	ISSUES	
	Continuity/discontinuity, early versus later experiences	**Biological and environmental factors**
Psychoanalytic	Discontinuity between stages—continuity between early experiences and later development; early experiences very important; later changes in development emphasized in Erikson's theory	Freud's biological determination interacting with early family experiences; Erikson's more balanced biological-cultural interaction perspective
Cognitive	Discontinuity between stages in Piaget's theory; continuity between early experiences and later development in Piaget's and Vygotsky's theories; no stages in Vygotsky's theory or information-processing theory	Piaget's emphasis on interaction and adaptation; environment provides the setting for cognitive structures to develop; information-processing view has not addressed this issue extensively but mainly emphasizes biological-environmental interaction
Behavioral and social cognitive	Continuity (no stages); experience at all points of development important	Environment viewed as the cause of behavior in both views
Ethological	Discontinuity but no stages; critical or sensitive periods emphasized; early experiences very important	Strong biological view
Ecological	Little attention to continuity/discontinuity; change emphasized more than stability	Strong environmental view

FIGURE 1.15 A Comparison of Theories and Issues in Life-Span Development.

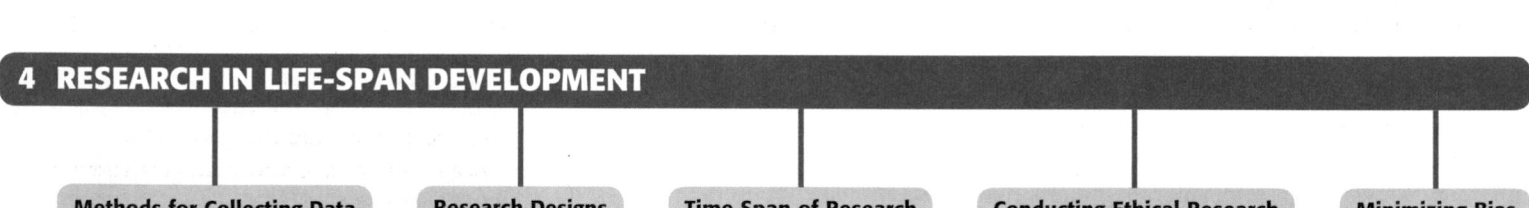

Review and Reflect: Learning Goal 3

3 **Describe the Main Theories of Human Development**

REVIEW

- What are the four steps of the scientific method? How can theory and hypotheses be defined? What are two main psychoanalytic theories? What are some contributions and criticisms of the psychoanalytic theories?
- What are three main cognitive theories? What are some contributions and criticisms of the cognitive theories?
- What are two main behavioral and social cognitive theories? What are some contributions and criticisms of the behavioral and social cognitive theories?
- What is the nature of ethological theory? What are some contributions and criticisms of the theory?
- What characterizes ecological theory? What are some contributions and criticisms of the theory?
- What is an eclectic theoretical orientation?

REFLECT

- Which of the life-span theories do you think best explains your own development? Why?

4 RESEARCH IN LIFE-SPAN DEVELOPMENT

| Methods for Collecting Data | Research Designs | Time Span of Research | Conducting Ethical Research | Minimizing Bias |

What are some important strategies in conducting observational research with children?

If they follow an eclectic orientation, how do scholars and researchers determine that one feature of a theory is somehow better than another? The scientific method discussed at the beginning of this chapter provides the guide. Through scientific research, the features of theories can be tested and refined.

Generally, research in life-span development is designed to test hypotheses, which in some cases are derived from the theories just described. Through research, theories are modified to reflect new data, and occasionally new theories arise. How are data about life-span development collected? What types of research designs are used to study life-span development? And what are some ethical considerations in conducting research on life-span development?

Methods for Collecting Data

Whether we are interested in studying attachment in infants, the cognitive skills of children, or social relationships in older adults, we can choose from several ways of collecting data. Here we outline the measures most often used, beginning with observation.

Observation Scientific observation requires an important set of skills (Rosnow & Rosenthal, 2008; Wiersma & Jurs, 2009). For observations to be effective, they have to be systematic. We have to have some idea of what we are looking for. We have to know whom we are observing, when and where we will observe, how the observations will be made, and how they will be recorded.

Where should we make our observations? We have two choices: the laboratory and the everyday world.

When we observe scientifically, we often need to control certain factors that determine behavior but are not the focus of our inquiry (McMillan, 2008). For this reason, some research in life-span development is conducted in a **laboratory**, a controlled setting where many of the complex factors of the "real world" are absent. For example, suppose you want to observe how children react when they see other people act aggressively. If you observe children in their homes or schools, you have no control over how much aggression the children observe, what kind of aggression they see, which people they see acting aggressively, or how other people treat the children. In contrast, if you observe the children in a laboratory, you can control these and other factors and therefore have more confidence about how to interpret your observations.

Laboratory research does have some drawbacks, however, including the following:

1. It is almost impossible to conduct research without the participants' knowing they are being studied.

2. The laboratory setting is unnatural and therefore can cause the participants to behave unnaturally.

3. People who are willing to come to a university laboratory may not fairly represent groups from diverse cultural backgrounds.

4. People who are unfamiliar with university settings, and with the idea of "helping science," may be intimidated by the laboratory setting.

Naturalistic observation provides insights that we sometimes cannot achieve in the laboratory (Jackson, 2008). **Naturalistic observation** means observing behavior in real-world settings, making no effort to manipulate or control the situation. Life-span researchers conduct naturalistic observations at sporting events, child-care centers, work settings, malls, and other places people live in and frequent.

Naturalistic observation was used in one study that focused on conversations in a children's science museum (Crowley & others, 2001). When visiting exhibits at the science museum, parents were far more likely to engage boys than girls in explanatory talk. This finding suggests a gender bias that encourages boys more than girls to be interested in science (see Figure 1.16).

Survey and Interview   Sometimes the best and quickest way to get information about people is to ask them for it. One technique is to *interview* them directly. A related method is the *survey* (sometimes referred to as a questionnaire), which is especially useful when information from many people is needed. A standard set of questions is used to obtain peoples' self-reported attitudes or beliefs about a particular topic. In a good survey, the questions are clear and unbiased, allowing respondents to answer unambiguously.

Surveys and interviews can be used to study a wide range of topics from religious beliefs to sexual habits to attitudes about gun control to beliefs about how to improve schools. Surveys and interviews may be conducted in person, over the telephone, and over the Internet.

One problem with surveys and interviews is the tendency of participants to answer questions in a way that they think is socially acceptable or desirable rather than to say what they truly think or feel (Creswell, 2008). For example, on a survey or in an interview some individuals might say that they do not take drugs even though they do.

Standardized Test   A **standardized test** has uniform procedures for administration and scoring. Many standardized tests allow a person's performance to be compared with that of other individuals; thus they provide information about individual differences among people (Kingston, 2008). One example is the Stanford-Binet intelligence test, which is described in Chapter 9. Your score on the Stanford-Binet test tells you how your performance compares with that of thousands of other people who have taken the test (Bart & Peterson, 2008).

> *S*cience refines everyday thinking.
>
> —ALBERT EINSTEIN
> *German-born American Physicist, 20th Century*

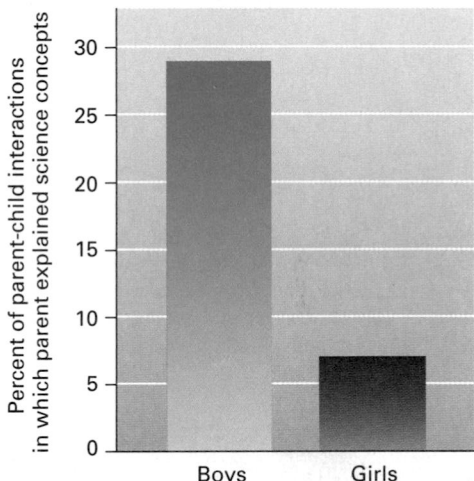

FIGURE 1.16 Parents' Explanations of Science to Sons and Daughters at a Science Museum. In a naturalistic observation study at a children's science museum, parents were three times more likely to explain science to boys than to girls (Crowley & others, 2001). The gender difference occurred regardless of whether the father, the mother, or both parents were with the child, although the gender difference was greatest for fathers' science explanations to sons and daughters.

laboratory A controlled setting in which many of the complex factors of the "real world" are removed.

naturalistic observation Observing behavior in real-world settings.

standardized test A test with uniform procedures for administration and scoring. Many standardized tests allow a person's performance to be compared with the performance of other individuals.

One criticism of standardized tests is that they assume a person's behavior is consistent and stable, yet personality and intelligence—two primary targets of standardized testing—can vary with the situation. For example, a person may perform poorly on a standardized intelligence test in an office setting but score much higher at home, where he or she is less anxious.

Mahatma Gandhi was the spiritual leader of India in the middle of the twentieth century. Erik Erikson conducted an extensive case study of Gandhi's life to determine what contributed to his identity devlopment. *What are some limitations of the case study approach?*

Case Study   A **case study** is an in-depth look at a single individual. Case studies are performed mainly by mental health professionals when, for either practical or ethical reasons, the unique aspects of an individual's life cannot be duplicated and tested in other individuals. A case study provides information about one person's experiences; it may focus on nearly any aspect of the subject's life that helps the researcher understand the person's mind, behavior, or other attributes. A researcher may gather information for a case study from interviews and medical records. In later chapters, we discuss vivid case studies, such as that of Michael Rehbein, who had much of the left side of his brain removed at 7 years of age to end severe epileptic seizures.

A case study can provide a dramatic, in-depth portrayal of an individual's life, but we must be cautious when generalizing from this information. The subject of a case study is unique, with a genetic makeup and personal history that no one else shares. In addition, case studies involve judgments of unknown reliability. Researchers who conduct case studies rarely check to see if other professionals agree with their observations or findings.

Physiological Measures   Researchers are increasingly using physiological measures when they study development at different points in the life span. For example, as puberty unfolds, the blood levels of certain hormones increase. To determine the nature of these hormonal changes, researchers analyze blood samples from adolescent volunteers (Dorn & others, 2006).

Another physiological measure that is increasingly being used is neuroimaging, especially *functional magnetic resonance imaging (fMRI)*, in which electromagnetic waves are used to construct images of a person's brain tissue and biochemical activity (Hofheimer & Lester, 2008; Moulson & Nelson, 2008). We will have much more to say about neuroimaging and other physiological measures in later chapters.

Research Designs

In conducting research on life-span development, in addition to a method for collecting data, you also need a research design. There are three main types of research design: descriptive, correlational, and experimental.

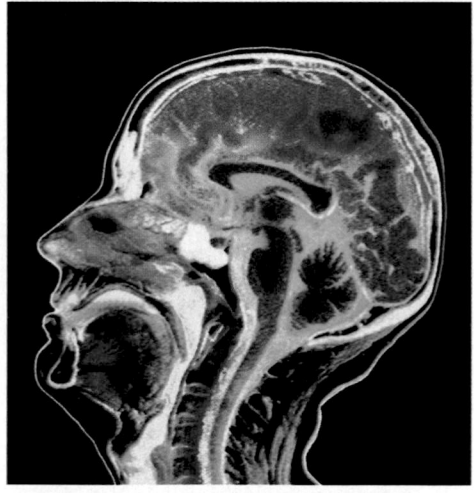

This fMRI scan of a 51-year-old male shows atrophy in the cerebral cortex of the brain, which occurs in various disorders including stroke and Alzheimer disease. The area of the upper cerebral cortex (where higher-level brain functioning such as thinking and planning occur) is colored dark red. Neuro-imaging techniques such as the fMRI are helping researchers to learn more about how the brain functions as people develop and age, as well as what happens to the brain when aging diseases such as stroke and Alzheimer disease are present.

case study An in-depth look at a single individual.

Descriptive Research   All of the data-collection methods that we have discussed can be used in **descriptive research**, which aims to observe and record behavior. For example, a researcher might observe the extent to which people are altruistic or aggressive toward each other. By itself, descriptive research cannot prove what causes some phenomenon, but it can reveal important information about people's behavior (Given, 2008).

Correlational Research   In contrast to descriptive research, correlational research goes beyond describing phenomena; it provides information that will help us to predict how people will behave. In **correlational research**, the goal is to describe the strength of the relationship between two or more events or characteristics. The more strongly the two events are correlated (or related or associated), the more effectively we can predict one event from the other (Jackson, 2008; & Kraska, 2008).

For example, to study if children of permissive parents have less self-control than other children, you would need to carefully record observations of parents'

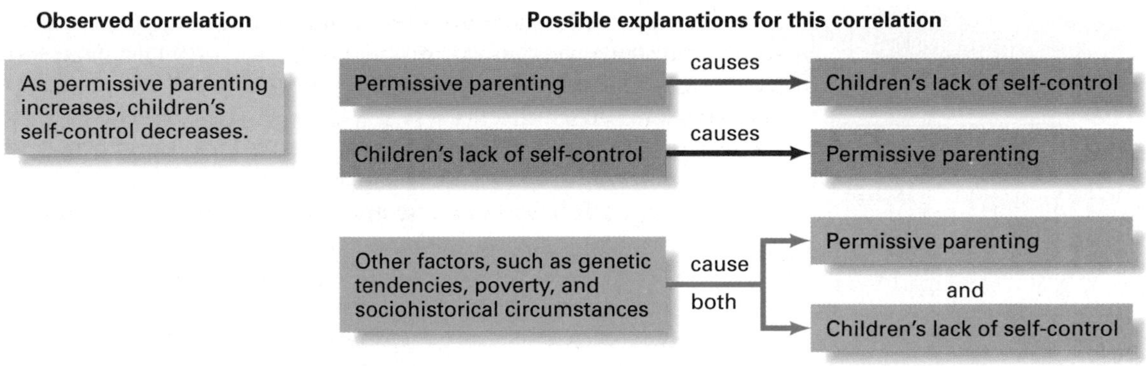

Observed correlation   **Possible explanations for this correlation**

FIGURE 1.17 **Possible Explanations for Correlational Data.** An observed correlation between two events cannot be used to conclude that one event caused the other. Some possibilities are that the second event caused the first event or that a third, unknown event caused the correlation between the first two events.

permissiveness and their children's self-control. You might observe that the higher a parent was in permissiveness, the lower the child was in self-control. You would then analyze these data statistically to yield a numerical measure, called a **correlation coefficient**, a number based on a statistical analysis that is used to describe the degree of association between two variables. The correlation coefficient ranges from $+1.00$ to -1.00. A negative number means an inverse relation. In this example, you might find an inverse correlation between permissive parenting and children's self-control with a coefficient of, say, $-.30$. By contrast, you might find a positive correlation of $+.30$ between parental monitoring of children and children's self-control.

The higher the correlation coefficient (whether positive or negative), the stronger the association between the two variables. A correlation of 0 means that there is no association between the variables. A correlation of $-.40$ is stronger than a correlation of $+.20$ because we disregard whether the correlation is positive or negative in determining the strength of the correlation.

A caution is in order, however. Correlation does not equal causation (Aron, Aron, & Coupos, 2008). The correlational finding just mentioned does not mean that permissive parenting necessarily causes low self-control in children. It could mean that, but it also could mean that a child's lack of self-control caused the parents to throw up their arms in despair and give up trying to control the child. It also could mean that other factors, such as heredity or poverty, caused the correlation between permissive parenting and low self-control in children. Figure 1.17 illustrates these possible interpretations of correlational data.

Experimental Research   To study causality, researchers turn to *experimental research*. An **experiment** is a carefully regulated procedure in which one or more factors believed to influence the behavior being studied are manipulated while all other factors are held constant. If the behavior under study changes when a factor is manipulated, we say that the manipulated factor has caused the behavior to change. In other words, the experiment has demonstrated cause and effect. The cause is the factor that was manipulated. The effect is the behavior that changed because of the manipulation. Nonexperimental research methods (descriptive and correlational research) cannot establish cause and effect because they do not involve manipulating factors in a controlled way (Martin, 2008).

Independent and Dependent Variables   Experiments include two types of changeable factors, or variables: independent and dependent. An independent variable is a manipulated, influential, experimental factor. It is a potential cause. The label "independent" is used because this variable can be manipulated independently of other factors to determine its effect. An experiment may include one independent variable or several of them.

descriptive research Has the purpose of observing and recording behavior.

correlational research The goal is to describe the strength of the relationship between two or more events or characteristics.

correlation coefficient A number based on statistical analysis that is used to describe the degree of association between two variables.

experiment A carefully regulated procedure in which one or more of the factors believed to influence the behavior being studied are manipulated while all other factors are held constant.

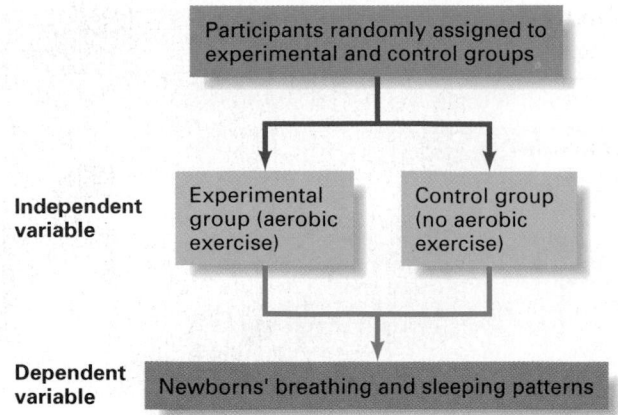

Independent variable

Dependent variable

FIGURE 1.18 Principles of Experimental Research. Imagine that you decide to conduct an experimental study of the effects of aerobic exercise by pregnant women on their newborns' breathing and sleeping patterns. You would randomly assign pregnant women to experimental and control groups. The experimental-group women would engage in aerobic exercise over a specified number of sessions and weeks. The control group would not. Then, when the infants are born, you would assess their breathing and sleeping patterns. If the breathing and sleeping patterns of newborns whose mothers were in the experimental group are more positive than those of the control group, you would conclude that aerobic exercise caused the positive effects.

A dependent variable is a factor that can change in an experiment, in response to changes in the independent variable. As researchers manipulate the independent variable, they measure the dependent variable for any resulting effect.

For example, suppose that you conducted a study to determine whether pregnant women could change the breathing and sleeping patterns of their newborn babies by meditating during pregnancy. You might require one group of pregnant women to engage in a certain amount and type of meditation each day while another group would not meditate; the meditation is thus the independent variable. When the infants are born, you would observe and measure their breathing and sleeping patterns. These patterns are the dependent variable, the factor that changes as the result of your manipulation.

Experimental and Control Groups   Experiments can involve one or more experimental groups and one or more control groups. An experimental group is a group whose experience is manipulated. A control group is a comparison group that is as much like the experimental group as possible and that is treated in every way like the experimental group except for the manipulated factor (independent variable). The control group serves as a baseline against which the effects of the manipulated condition can be compared.

Random assignment is an important principle for deciding whether each participant will be placed in the experimental group or in the control group. Random assignment means that researchers assign participants to experimental and control groups by chance. It reduces the likelihood that the experiment's results will be due to any pre-existing differences between groups (Martin, 2008). In the example of the effects of meditation by pregnant women on the breathing and sleeping patterns of their newborns, you would randomly assign half of the pregnant women to engage in meditation over a period of weeks (the experimental group) and the other half to not meditate over the same number of weeks (the control group). Figure 1.18 illustrates the nature of experimental research.

Time Span of Research

Researchers in life-span development have a special concern with studies that focus on the relation of age to some other variable. We have several options: Researchers can study different individuals of different ages and compare them or they can study the same individuals as they age over time.

Cross-Sectional Approach   The **cross-sectional approach** is a research strategy that simultaneously compares individuals of different ages. A typical cross-sectional study might include three groups of children: 5-year-olds, 8-year-olds, and 11-year-olds. Another study might include a group of 15-year-olds, 25-year-olds, and 45-year-olds. The groups can be compared with respect to a variety of dependent variables: IQ, memory, peer relations, attachment to parents, hormonal changes, and so on. All of this can be accomplished in a short time. In some studies, data are collected in a single day. Even in large-scale cross-sectional studies with hundreds of subjects, data collection does not usually take longer than several months to complete.

The main advantage of the cross-sectional study is that the researcher does not have to wait for the individuals to grow up or become older. Despite its efficiency, though, the cross-sectional approach has its drawbacks. It gives no information about how individuals change or about the stability of their characteristics. It can obscure the increases and decreases of development—the hills and valleys of growth and development. For example, a cross-sectional study of life satisfaction might reveal average increases and decreases, but it would not show how the life satisfaction of individual adults waxed and waned over the years. It also would not tell us whether the same

cross-sectional approach A research strategy in which individuals of different ages are compared at one time.

adults who had positive or negative perceptions of life satisfaction in early adulthood maintained their relative degree of life satisfaction as they became middle-aged or older adults.

Longitudinal Approach   The **longitudinal approach** is a research strategy in which the same individuals are studied over a period of time, usually several years or more. For example, in a longitudinal study of life satisfaction, the same adults might be assessed periodically over a 70-year time span—at the ages of 20, 35, 45, 65, and 90, for example.

Longitudinal studies provide a wealth of information about vital issues such as stability and change in development and the importance of early experience for later development, but they do have drawbacks (Hofer & Piccinin, 2007; Hofer & Sliwinski, 2006). They are expensive and time consuming. The longer the study lasts, the more participants drop out—they move, get sick, lose interest, and so forth. The participants who remain may be dissimilar to those who drop out, biasing the outcome of the study. Those individuals who remain in a longitudinal study over a number of years may be more responsible and conformity-oriented, for example, or they might have more stable lives.

Cohort Effects   A *cohort* is a group of people who are born at a similar point in history and share similar experiences as a result, such as living through the Vietnam War or growing up in the same city around the same time. These shared experiences may produce a range of differences among cohorts. For example, people who were teenagers during the Great Depression are likely to differ from people who were teenagers during the booming 1990s in their educational opportunities and economic status, in how they were raised, and in their attitudes toward sex and religion. In life-span development research, **cohort effects** are due to a person's time of birth, era, or generation but not to actual age.

Cohort effects are important because they can powerfully affect the dependent measures in a study ostensibly concerned with age (Schaie, 2007). Researchers have shown it is especially important to be aware of cohort effects when assessing adult intelligence (Schaie, 1996). Individuals born at different points in time—such as 1920, 1940, and 1960—have had varying opportunities for education. Individuals born in earlier years had less access to education, and this fact may have a significant effect on how this cohort performs on intelligence tests.

Cross-sectional studies can show how different cohorts respond, but they can confuse age changes and cohort effects. Longitudinal studies are effective in studying age changes but only within one cohort.

Conducting Ethical Research

Ethics in research may affect you personally if you ever serve as a participant in a study. In that event, you need to know your rights as a participant and the responsibilities of researchers to assure that these rights are safeguarded.

If you ever become a researcher in life-span development yourself, you will need an even deeper understanding of ethics. Even if you only carry out experimental projects in psychology courses, you must consider the rights of the participants in those projects. A student might think, "I volunteer in a home for the mentally retarded several hours per week. I can use the residents of the home in my study to see if a particular treatment helps improve their memory for everyday tasks." But without proper permissions, the most well-meaning, kind, and considerate studies still violate the rights of the participants.

Today, proposed research at colleges and universities must pass the scrutiny of a research ethics committee before the research can be initiated. In addition, the American Psychological Association (APA) has developed ethics guidelines for its members. The code of ethics instructs psychologists to protect their participants from mental and

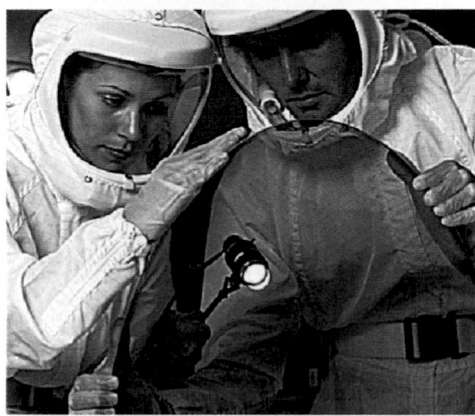

Cohort effects are due to a person's time of birth or generation but not actually to age. Think for a moment about growing up in (a) the Great Depression and (b) today. *How might your development be different depending on which of these time frames has dominated your life? your parents' lives? your grandparents' lives?*

longitudinal approach A research strategy in which the same individuals are studied over a period of time, usually several years or more.

cohort effects Describe effects due to a person's time of birth, era, or generation but not to actual age.

physical harm. The participants' best interests need to be kept foremost in the researcher's mind (Fisher, 2009; Gay, Mills, & Airasian, 2009; Rosnow & Rosenthal, 2008). APA's guidelines address four important issues:

1. *Informed consent.* All participants must know what their research participation will involve and what risks might develop. Even after informed consent is given, participants must retain the right to withdraw from the study at any time and for any reason.

2. *Confidentiality.* Researchers are responsible for keeping all of the data they gather on individuals completely confidential and, when possible, completely anonymous.

3. *Debriefing.* After the study has been completed, participants should be informed of its purpose and the methods that were used. In most cases, the experimenter also can inform participants in a general manner beforehand about the purpose of the research without leading participants to behave in a way they think that the experimenter is expecting.

4. *Deception.* In some circumstances, telling the participants beforehand what the research study is about substantially alters the participants' behavior and invalidates the researcher's data. In all cases of deception, however, the psychologist must ensure that the deception will not harm the participants and that the participants will be *debriefed* (told the complete nature of the study) as soon as possible after the study is completed.

Minimizing Bias

Studies of life-span development are most useful when they are conducted without bias or prejudice toward any particular group of people. Of special concern is bias based on gender and bias based on culture or ethnicity.

Gender Bias For most of its existence, our society has had a strong gender bias, a preconceived notion about the abilities of women and men that prevented individuals from pursuing their own interests and achieving their potential (Matlin, 2008; UNICEF, 2008). Gender bias also has had a less obvious effect within the field of life-span development (Etaugh & Bridges, 2006). For example, it is not unusual for conclusions to be drawn about females' attitudes and behaviors from research conducted with males as the only participants (Hyde, 2007).

Furthermore, when researchers find gender differences, their reports sometimes magnify those differences (Denmark & others, 1988). For example, a researcher might report that 74 percent of the men in a study had high achievement expectations versus only 67 percent of the women and go on to talk about the differences in some detail. In reality, this might be a rather small difference. It also might disappear if the study were repeated or the study might have methodological problems that don't allow such strong interpretations.

Pam Reid is a leading researcher who studies gender and ethnic bias in development. To read about Pam's interests, see the *Careers in Life-Span Development* profile.

Cultural and Ethnic Bias The realization that research on life-span development needs to include more people from diverse ethnic groups has also been building (Graham, 2006; Mehrotra & Wagner, 2009). Historically, people from ethnic minority groups (African American, Latino, Asian American, and Native American) were excluded from most research in the United States and simply thought of as variations from the norm or average. If minority individuals were included in samples and their scores didn't fit the norm, they were viewed as confounds or "noise" in data and discounted. Given the fact that individuals from diverse ethnic

Careers in Life-Span Development

Pam Reid, Educational and Developmental Psychologist

When she was a child, Pam Reid liked to play with chemistry sets. Reid majored in chemistry during college and wanted to become a doctor. However, when some of her friends signed up for a psychology class as an elective, she decided to take the course. She was intrigued by learning about how people think, behave, and develop—so much so that she changed her major to psychology. Reid went on to obtain her Ph.D. in psychology (American Psychological Association, 2003, p. 16).

For a number of years, Reid was a professor of education and psychology at the University of Michigan, where she also was a research scientist at the Institute for Research on Women and Gender. Her main focus has been on how children and adolescents develop social skills, with a special interest in the development of African American girls (Reid & Zalk, 2001). In 2004, Reid became provost and executive vice-president at Roosevelt University in Chicago.

Pam Reid (*back row, center*), with graduate students she mentored at the University of Michigan.

groups were excluded from research on life-span development for so long, we might reasonably conclude that people's real lives are perhaps more varied than research data have indicated in the past.

Researchers also have tended to overgeneralize about ethnic groups (Banks, 2008; Markides, Rudkin, & Wallace, 2007). **Ethnic gloss** is using an ethnic label such as African American or Latino in a superficial way that portrays an ethnic group as being more homogeneous than it really is (Trimble, 1988). For example, a researcher might describe a research sample like this: "The participants were 60 Latinos." A more complete description of the Latino group might be something like this: "The 60 Latino participants were Mexican Americans from low-income neighborhoods in the southwestern area of Los Angeles. Thirty-six were from homes in which Spanish is the dominant language spoken, 24 from homes in which English is the main language spoken. Thirty were born in the United States, 30 in Mexico. Twenty-eight described themselves as Mexican American, 14 as Mexican, 9 as American, 6 as Chicano, and 3 as Latino." Ethnic gloss can cause researchers to obtain samples of ethnic groups that are not representative of the group's diversity, which can lead to overgeneralization and stereotyping.

Ross Parke and Raymond Buriel (2006) recently described how research on ethnic minority children and their families has not been given adequate attention, especially in light of their significant rate of growth. Until recently, ethnic minority families were combined in the category "minority," which masks important differences among ethnic groups as well as diversity within an ethnic group. When research has been conducted on ethnic groups, most often they are compared to non-White Latinos to identify group differences. An assumption in two-group studies is that ethnic minority children have not advanced far enough to be the same as non-White Latino children and that this developmental lag contributes to ethnic minority children's problems. Recently, some researchers have replaced two-group studies with more in-depth examination of variations within a single ethnic group. For example, a researcher might study how parents in an ethnic group adapt to the challenges they face as a minority

ethnic gloss Using an ethnic label such as African American or Latino in a superficial way that portrays an ethnic group as being more homogeneous than it really is.

Look at these two photographs, one of all White males, the other of a diverse group of females and males from different ethnic groups, including some White individuals. Consider a topic in life-span development, such as parenting love, or cultural values. *If you were conducting research on this topic, might the results of the study be different depending on whether the participants in your study were the individuals in the photograph on the left or the right?*

in U.S. society and how these experiences contribute to the goals they have for their children.

The continued growth of minority families in the United States in approaching decades will mainly be due to the immigration of Latino and Asian families. Researchers need "to take into account their acculturation level and generational status of parents and children," and how they influence family processes and child outcomes (Parke & Buriel, 2006, p. 487). More attention also needs to be given to biculturalism because the complexity of diversity means that some children of color identify with two or more ethnic groups. And language development research needs to focus more on second-language acquisition (usually English) and bilingualism and how they are linked to school achievement (Levine & McCloskey, 2009).

Review and Reflect: Learning Goal 4

 Explain How Research in Life-Span Development Is Conducted

REVIEW

- What methods do researchers use to collect data on life-span development?
- What research designs are used to study human development?
- How is research conducted on the time span of people's lives?
- What are researchers' ethical responsibilities to the people they study?
- How can gender, cultural, and ethnic bias affect the outcome of a research study?

REFLECT

- Imagine that you are conducting a research study on the sexual attitudes and behaviors of adolescents. What ethical safeguards should you use in conducting the study?

Introduction

1 THE LIFE-SPAN PERSPECTIVE: DISCUSS THE DISTINCTIVE FEATURES OF A LIFE-SPAN PERSPECTIVE ON DEVELOPMENT

The Importance of Studying Life-Span Development

Characteristics of the Life-Span Perspective

Some Contemporary Concerns

- Development is the pattern of change that begins at conception and continues through the human life span. It includes both growth and decline. Studying life-span development helps prepare us to take responsibility for children, gives us insight about our own lives, and gives us knowledge about what our lives will be like as we age.

- The life-span perspective includes these basic conceptions: Development is lifelong, multidimensional, multidirectional, and plastic; its study is multidisciplinary; it is contextual; it involves growth, maintenance, and regulation of loss; and it is a co-construction of biological, sociocultural, and individual factors. Three important sources of contextual influences are (1) normative age-graded influences, (2) normative history-graded influences, and (3) nonnormative life events.

- Health and well-being, parenting, education, sociocultural contexts and diversity, and social policy are all areas of contemporary concern that are closely tied to life-span development. Important dimensions of the sociocultural context include culture, ethnicity, socioeconomic status, and gender. There is increasing interest in social policy issues related to children and to older adults.

2 THE NATURE OF DEVELOPMENT: IDENTIFY THE MOST IMPORTANT PROCESSES, PERIODS, AND ISSUES IN DEVELOPMENT

Biological, Cognitive, and Socioemotional Processes

Periods of Development

The Significance of Age

Developmental Issues

- Three key developmental processes are biological, cognitive, and socioemotional. Development is influenced by an interplay of these processes.

- The life-span is commonly divided into these periods of development: prenatal, infancy, early childhood, middle and late childhood, adolescence, early adulthood, middle adulthood, and late adulthood. Recently, life-span developmentalists have described the human life span in terms of four ages with a special focus on the third and fourth ages (young-old and oldest-old).

- According to some experts on life-span development, too much emphasis is placed on chronological age. In studies covering adolescence through old age, people report that they are not happier at one point in development than at others. We often think of age only in terms of chronological age, but a full evaluation of age requires consideration of chronological, biological, psychological, and social age. Neugarten emphasizes that we are moving toward a society in which chronological age is only a weak predictor of development in adulthood.

- The nature-nurture issue focuses on the extent to which development is mainly influenced by nature (biological inheritance) or nurture (experience). The stability-change issue focuses on the degree to which we become older renditions of our early experience or develop into someone different from who we were earlier in development. A special aspect of the stability-change issue is the extent to which development is determined by early versus later experiences. Developmentalists describe development as continuous (gradual, a cumulative change) or as discontinuous (abrupt, a sequence of stages). Most developmentalists recognize that extreme positions on the nature-nurture, stability-change, and continuity-discontinuity issues are unwise. Despite this consensus, there is still spirited debate on these issues.

3   THEORIES OF DEVELOPMENT: DESCRIBE THE MAIN THEORIES OF HUMAN DEVELOPMENT

Psychoanalytic Theories

- The scientific method involves four main steps: (1) conceptualize a problem, (2) collect data, (3) analyze data, and (4) draw conclusions. Theory is often involved in conceptualizing a problem. A theory is an interrelated, coherent set of ideas that helps to explain phenomena and to make predictions. Hypotheses are specific assertions and predictions, often derived from theory, that can be tested. According to psychoanalytic theories, development primarily depends on the unconscious mind and is heavily couched in emotion. Freud also argued that individuals go through five psychosexual stages. Erikson's theory emphasizes eight psychosocial stages of development: trust versus mistrust, autonomy versus shame and doubt, initiative versus guilt, industry versus inferiority, identity versus identity confusion, intimacy versus isolation, generativity versus stagnation, and integrity versus despair. Contributions of psychoanalytic theories include an emphasis on a developmental framework, family relationships, and unconscious aspects of the mind. Criticisms include a lack of scientific support, too much emphasis on sexual underpinnings, and an image of people that is too negative.

Cognitive Theories

- Three main cognitive theories are Piaget's, Vygotsky's, and information processing. Cognitive theories emphasize thinking, reasoning, language, and other cognitive processes. Piaget proposed a cognitive developmental theory in which children use their cognition to adapt to their world. In Piaget's theory, children go through four cognitive stages: sensorimotor, preoperational, concrete operational, and formal operational. Vygotsky's sociocultural cognitive theory emphasizes how culture and social interaction guide cognitive development. The information-processing approach emphasizes that individuals manipulate information, monitor it, and strategize about it. Contributions of cognitive theories include an emphasis on the active construction of understanding and a positive view of development. Criticisms include giving too little attention to individual variations and skepticism about the pureness of Piaget's stages.

Behavioral and Social Cognitive Theories

- Two main behavioral and social cognitive theories Skinner's operant conditioning and Bandura's social cognitive theory. In Skinner's operant conditioning, the consequences of a behavior produce changes in the probability of the behavior's occurrence. In Bandura's social cognitive theory, observational learning is a key aspect of life-span development. Bandura emphasizes reciprocal interactions among person/cognition, behavior, and environment. Contributions of the behavioral and social cognitive theories include an emphasis on scientific research and a focus on environmental factors. Criticisms include inadequate attention to developmental changes and, in Skinner's view, too little attention to cognition.

Ethological Theory

- Ethology stresses that behavior is strongly influenced by biology, is tied to evolution, and is characterized by critical or sensitive periods. Contributions of ethological theory include a focus on the biological and evolutionary basis of development. Criticisms include a belief that the concepts of critical and sensitive periods may be too rigid.

Ecological Theory

- Ecological theory emphasizes environmental contexts. Bronfenbrenner's environmental systems view of development proposes five environmental systems: microsystem, mesosystem, exosystem, macrosystem, and chronosystem. Contributions of the theory include a systematic examination of macro and micro dimensions of environmental systems and attention to connections between them. Criticisms include giving inadequate attention to biological factors, as well as a lack of emphasis on cognitive factors.

An Eclectic Theoretical Orientation

- An eclectic theoretical orientation does not follow any one theoretical approach but rather selects from each theory whatever is considered the best in it.

4   RESEARCH IN LIFE-SPAN DEVELOPMENT: EXPLAIN HOW RESEARCH IN LIFE-SPAN DEVELOPMENT IS CONDUCTED.

Methods for Collecting Data

- Methods for collecting data about life-span development include observation (in a laboratory or a naturalistic setting), survey (questionnaire) or interview, standardized test, case study, and physiological measures.

Research Designs

- Three main research designs are descriptive, correlational, and experimental. Descriptive research aims to observe and record behavior. In correlational research, the goal is to describe the strength of the relationship between two or more events or characteristics. Experimental research involves conducting an experiment, which can determine cause and effect. An independent variable is the manipulated, influential, experimental factor. A dependent variable is a factor that can change in an experiment, in response to changes in the independent variable. Experiments can involve one or more experimental groups and control groups. In random assignment, researchers assign participants to experimental and control groups by chance.

Time Span of Research

- When researchers decide about the time span of their research, they can conduct cross-sectional or longitudinal studies. Life-span researchers are especially concerned about cohort effects.

Conducting Ethical Research

- Researchers' ethical responsibilities include seeking participants' informed consent, ensuring their confidentiality, debriefing them about the purpose and potential personal consequences of participating, and avoiding unnecessary deception of participants.

Minimizing Bias

- Researchers need to guard against gender, cultural, and ethnic bias in research. Every effort should be made to make research equitable for both females and males. Individuals from varied ethnic backgrounds need to be included as participants in life-span research, and overgeneralization about diverse members within a group must be avoided.

KEY TERMS

development 7
life-span perspective 9
normative age-graded influences 9
normative history-graded influences 9
nonnormative life events 10
culture 11
cross-cultural studies 11
ethnicity 11
socioeconomic status (SES) 11

gender 13
social policy 13
biological processes 15
cognitive processes 15
socioemotional processes 15
nature-nurture issue 20
stability-change issue 20
continuity-discontinuity issue 21
scientific method 22
theory 22
hypotheses 22

psychoanalytic theories 23
Erikson's theory 23
Piaget's theory 24
Vygotsky's theory 25
information-processing theory 26
social cognitive theory 26
ethology 27
Bronfenbrenner's ecological theory 28
eclectic theoretical orientation 29
laboratory 31

naturalistic observation 31
standardized test 31
case study 32
descriptive research 33
correlational research 33
correlation coefficient 33
experiment 33
cross-sectional approach 34
longitudinal approach 35
cohort effects 35
ethnic gloss 37

KEY PEOPLE

Paul Baltes 8
Marian Wright Edelman 13
Bernice Neugarten 19
Sigmund Freud 22

Erik Erikson 23
Jean Piaget 24
Lev Vygotsky 25
Robert Siegler 26

B. F. Skinner 26
Albert Bandura 27
Konrad Lorenz 27
John Bowlby 27

Urie Bronfenbrenner 28
Ross Parke and Raymond Buriel 37

E-LEARNING TOOLS

To help you master the material in this chapter, you'll find a number of valuable study tools on the student Online Learning Center for *Life-Span Development*, twelfth edition, at **www.mhhe.com/santrockld12**.

Self-Assessment

Connect to **www.mhhe.com/santrockld12** to learn more about your career options by completing the self-assessment, *Evaluating My Interest in a Career in Life-Span Development*.

Taking It to the Net

Connect to **www.mhhe.com/santrockld12** to research the answers to these questions:

1. Janice plans to join a small family practice group on completion of her pediatrics residency. Why should Janice, as a pediatrician, be involved in detecting and helping to prevent violence in the lives of her young patients?

2. Derrick was assigned to write about the challenges of caring for aging adults in the United States in the twenty-first century. What are some important issues he should address?

3. Carmen is completing her Ph.D. in clinical psychology. She is interested in geropsychology. What are some of the areas in which geropsychologists might conduct research and practice?

Video Clips

At the Online Learning Center, you'll find a video called "Intelligence: The Nature and Nurture of Twins." This segment examines the nature-nuture connection by tracing the development of identical twins Cory and Eric.

Health and Well-Being, Parenting, and Education Exercises

Build your decision-making skills by trying your hand at the health and well-being, parenting, and education exercises. Connect to **www.mhhe.com/santrockld12** to research the answers and complete the exercises.

Appendix

Careers in Life-Span Development

The field of life-span development offers an amazing breadth of careers that can provide extremely satisfying work. College and university professors teach courses in many areas of life-span development. Teachers impart knowledge, understanding, and skills to children and adolescents. Counselors, clinical psychologists, nurses, and physicians help people of different ages to cope more effectively with their lives and improve their well-being.

These and many other careers related to life-span development offer many rewards. By working in the field of life-span development, you can help people to improve their lives, understand yourself and others better, possibly advance the state of knowledge in the field, and have an enjoyable time while you are doing these things. Many careers in life-span development pay reasonably well. For example, psychologists earn well above the median salary in the United States.

If you are considering a career in life-span development, would you prefer to work with infants? children? adolescents? older adults? As you go through this term, try to spend some time with people of different ages. Observe their behavior. Talk with them about their lives. Think about whether you would like to work with people of this age in your life's work.

In addition, to find out about careers in life-span development you might talk with people who work in various jobs. For example, if you have some interest in becoming a school counselor, call a school, ask to speak with a counselor, and set up an appointment to discuss the counselor's career and work. If you have an interest in becoming a nurse, call the nursing department at a hospital and set up an appointment to speak with the nursing coordinator about a nursing career.

Another way of exploring careers in life-span development is to work in a related job while you are in college. Many colleges and universities offer internships or other work experiences for students who major in specific fields. Course credit or pay is given for some of these jobs. Take advantage of these opportunities. They can help you decide if this is the right career for you, and they can help you get into graduate school, if you decide you want to go.

An advanced degree is not absolutely necessary for some careers in life-span development, but usually you can considerably expand your opportunities (and income) by obtaining a graduate degree. If you think you might want to go to graduate school, talk with one or more professors about your interests, keep a high grade point average, take appropriate courses, and realize that you likely will need to take the Graduate Record Examination at some point.

In the upcoming sections, we will profile a number of careers in four areas: education/research; clinical/counseling; medical/nursing/physical development; and families/relationships. These are not the only career options in life-span development, but the profiles should give you an idea of the range of opportunities available. For each career, we will describe the work and address the amount of education required and the nature of the training. The Web site for this book gives more detailed information about these careers in life-span development.

EDUCATION/RESEARCH

Numerous careers in life-span development involve education or research. The opportunities range from college professor to preschool teacher to school psychologist.

College/University Professor

Professors teach courses in life-span development at many types of institutions, including research universities with master's or Ph.D. programs in life-span development, four-year colleges with no graduate programs, and community colleges. The courses in life-span development are offered in many different programs and schools, including psychology, education, nursing, child and family studies, social work, and medicine. In addition to teaching at the undergraduate or graduate level (or both), professors may conduct research, advise students or direct their research, and serve on college or university committees. Research is part of a professor's job description at most universities with master's and Ph.D. programs, but some college professors do not conduct research and focus instead on teaching.

Teaching life-span development at a college or university almost always requires a Ph.D. or master's degree. Obtaining a Ph.D. usually takes four to six years of graduate work; a master's degree requires approximately two years. The training involves taking graduate courses, learning to conduct research, and attending and presenting papers at professional meetings. Many graduate students work as teaching or research assistants for professors in an apprenticeship relationship that helps them to become competent teachers and researchers.

Researcher

Some individuals in the field of life-span development work in research positions. They might work for a university, a government agency such as the National Institute of Mental Health, or private industry. They generate research ideas, plan studies, carry out the research, and usually attempt to publish the research in a scientific journal. A researcher often works in collaboration with other researchers. One researcher might spend much of his or her time in a laboratory; another researcher might work out in the field, such as in schools, hospitals, and so on. Most researchers in life-span development have either a master's or a Ph.D.

Elementary or Secondary School Teacher

Elementary and secondary school teachers teach one or more subject areas, preparing the curriculum, giving tests, assigning grades, monitoring students' progress, conducting parent-teacher conferences, and attending workshops. Becoming an elementary or secondary school teacher requires a minimum of an undergraduate degree. The training involves taking a wide range of courses with a major or concentration in education as well as completing supervised practice teaching.

Exceptional Children (Special Education) Teacher

Teachers of exceptional children spend concentrated time with children who have a disability such as ADHD, mental retardation, or cerebral palsy or with children who are gifted. Usually some of their work occurs outside of the students' regular classroom and some of it inside the students' regular classroom. The exceptional children teacher works closely with the student's regular classroom teacher and parents to create the best educational program for the student. Teachers of exceptional children often continue their education after obtaining their undergraduate degree and attain a master's degree.

Early Education Educator

Early childhood educators work on college faculties and usually teach in community colleges that award an associate degree in early childhood education. They have a minimum of a master's degree in their field. In graduate school, they take courses in early child education and receive supervisory training in child-care or early childhood programs.

Preschool/Kindergarten Teacher

Preschool teachers teach mainly 4-year-old children, and kindergarten teachers primarily teach 5-year-old children. They usually have an undergraduate degree in education, specializing in early childhood education. State certification to become a preschool or kindergarten teacher usually is required.

Family and Consumer Science Educator

Family and consumer science educators may specialize in early childhood education or instruct middle and high school students about such matters as nutrition, interpersonal relationships, human sexuality, parenting, and human development. Hun-

dreds of colleges and universities throughout the United States offer two- and four-year degree programs in family and consumer science. These programs usually require an internship. Additional education courses may be needed to obtain a teaching certificate. Some family and consumer educators go on to graduate school for further training, which provides a background for possible jobs in college teaching or research.

Educational Psychologist

Educational psychologists most often teach in a college or university and conduct research in such areas of educational psychology as learning, motivation, classroom management, and assessment. They help train students for positions in educational psychology, school psychology, and teaching. Most educational psychologists have a doctorate in education, which takes four to six years of graduate work.

School Psychologist

School psychologists focus on improving the psychological and intellectual well-being of elementary, middle/junior, and high school students. They give psychological tests, interview students and their parents, consult with teachers, and may provide counseling to students and their families. They may work in a centralized office in a school district or in one or more schools.

School psychologists usually have a master's or doctoral degree in school psychology. In graduate school, they take courses in counseling, assessment, learning, and other areas of education and psychology.

Gerontologist

Gerontologists usually work in research in some branch of the federal or state government. They specialize in the study of aging with a particular focus on government programs for older adults, social policy, and delivery of services to older adults. In their research, gerontologists define problems to be studied, collect data, interpret the results, and make recommendations for social policy. Most gerontologists have a master's or doctoral degree and have taken a concentration of coursework in adult development and aging.

CLINICAL/COUNSELING

There are a wide variety of clinical and counseling jobs that are linked with life-span development. These range from child clinical psychologist to adolescent drug counselor to geriatric psychiatrist.

Clinical Psychologist

Clinical psychologists seek to help people with psychological problems. They work in a variety of settings, including colleges and universities, clinics, medical schools, and private practice. Some clinical psychologists only conduct psychotherapy; others do psychological assessment and psychotherapy; some also do research. Clinical psychologists may specialize in a particular age group, such as children (child clinical psychologist) or older adults (often referred to as a geropsychologist).

Clinical psychologists have either a Ph.D. (which involves clinical and research training) or a Psy.D. degree (which only involves clinical training). This graduate training usually takes five to seven years and includes courses in clinical psychology and a one-year supervised internship in an accredited setting toward the end of the training. Many geropsychologists pursue a year or two of postdoctoral training. Most states require clinical psychologists to pass a test in order to become licensed in the state and to call themselves clinical psychologists.

Psychiatrist

Psychiatrists obtain a medical degree and then do a residency in psychiatry. Medical school takes approximately four years and the psychiatry residency another three to four years. Unlike most psychologists (who do not go to medical school), psychiatrists can administer drugs to clients. (Recently, several states gave clinical psychologists the right to prescribe drugs.)

Like clinical psychologists, psychiatrists might specialize in working with children (child psychiatry) or with older adults (geriatric psychiatry). Psychiatrists might work in medical schools in teaching and research roles, in a medical clinic or hospital, or in private practice. In addition to administering drugs to help improve the lives of people with psychological problems, psychiatrists also may conduct psychotherapy.

Counseling Psychologist

Counseling psychologists work in the same settings as clinical psychologists and may do psychotherapy, teach, or conduct research. Many counseling psychologists do not do therapy with individuals who have severe mental disorders, such as schizophrenia.

Counseling psychologists go through much the same training as clinical psychologists, although in a graduate program in counseling rather than clinical psychology. Counseling psychologists have either a master's degree or a doctoral degree. They also must go through a licensing procedure. One type of master's degree in counseling leads to the designation of licensed professional counselor.

School Counselor

School counselors help students to cope with adjustment problems, identify their abilities and interests, develop academic plans, and explore career options. The focus of the job depends on the age of the children. High school counselors advise students about vocational and technical training and admissions requirements for college, as well as about taking entrance exams, applying for financial aid, and choosing a major. Elementary school counselors mainly counsel students about social and personal problems. They may observe children in the classroom and at play as part of their work.

School counselors may work with students individually, in small groups, or even in a classroom. They often consult with parents, teachers, and school administrators when trying to help students. School counselors usually have a master's degree in counseling.

Career Counselor

Career counselors help individuals to identify their best career options and guide them in applying for jobs. They may work in private industry or at a college or university. They usually interview individuals and give them vocational and/or psychological tests to identify appropriate careers that fit their interests and abilities. Sometimes they help individuals to create résumés or conduct mock interviews to help them feel comfortable in a job interview. They might arrange and promote job fairs or other recruiting events to help individuals obtain jobs.

Rehabilitation Cou nselor

Rehabilitation counselors work with individuals to identify career options, develop adjustment and coping skills to maximize independence, and resolve problems created by a disability. A master's degree in rehabilitation counseling or guidance or counseling psychology is generally considered the minimum education requirement.

Social Worker

Many social workers are involved in helping people with social or economic problems. They may investigate, evaluate, and attempt to rectify reported cases of abuse, neglect, endangerment, or domestic disputes. They may intervene in families and provide counseling and referral services to individuals and families. Some social workers specialize in a certain area. For example, a medical social worker might coordinate support services to people with a long-term disability; family-care social workers often work with families with children or an older adult who needs support services. Social workers often work for publicly funded agencies at the city, state, or national level, although increasingly they work in the private sector in areas such as drug rehabilitation and family counseling.

Social workers have a minimum of an undergraduate degree from a school of social work that includes coursework in sociology and psychology. Some social workers also have a master's or doctoral degree. For example, medical social workers have a master's degree in social work (M.S.W.) and complete graduate coursework and supervised clinical experiences in medical settings.

Drug Counselor

Drug counselors provide counseling to individuals with drug-abuse problems. Some drug counselors specialize in working with adolescents or older adults. They may work on an individual basis with a substance abuser or conduct group therapy.

They may work in private practice, with a state or federal government agency, with a company, or in a hospital.

At a minimum, drug counselors complete an associate's or certificate program. Many have an undergraduate degree in substance-abuse counseling, and some have master's and doctoral degrees. Most states provide a certification procedure for obtaining a license to practice drug counseling.

MEDICAL/NURSING/PHYSICAL DEVELOPMENT

This third main area of careers in life-span development includes a wide range of choices in the medical and nursing areas, as well as jobs pertaining to improving some aspect of a person's physical development.

Obstetrician/Gynecologist

An obstetrician/gynecologist prescribes prenatal and postnatal care, performs deliveries in maternity cases, and treats diseases and injuries of the female reproductive system. Becoming an obstetrician/gynecologist requires a medical degree plus three to five years of residency in obstetrics/gynecology. Obstetricians may work in private practice, a medical clinic, a hospital, or a medical school.

Pediatrician

A pediatrician monitors infants' and children's health, works to prevent disease or injury, helps children attain optimal health, and treats children with health problems. Pediatricians have earned a medical degree and completed a three- to five-year residency in pediatrics.

Pediatricians may work in private practice, a medical clinic, a hospital, or a medical school. Many pediatricians on the faculty of medical schools also teach and conduct research on children's health and diseases.

Geriatric Physician

Geriatric physicians diagnose medical problems of older adults, evaluate treatment options, and make recommendations for nursing care or other arrangements. They have a medical degree and specialized in geriatric medicine by doing a three- to five-year residency. Like other doctors, geriatric physicians may work in private practice, a medical clinic, a hospital, or a medical school. Those in medical school settings may not only treat older adults but also teach future physicians and conduct research.

Neonatal Nurse

Neonatal nurses deliver care to newborn infants. They may work with infants born under normal circumstances or premature and critically ill neonates. A minimum of an undergraduate degree in nursing with a specialization in the newborn is required. This training involves coursework in nursing and the biological sciences, as well as supervised clinical experiences.

Nurse-Midwife

A nurse-midwife formulates and provides comprehensive care to expectant mothers as they prepare to give birth, guides them through the birth process, and cares for them after the birth. The nurse-midwife also may provide care to the newborn, counsel parents on the infant's development and parenting, and provide guidance about health practices. Becoming a nurse-midwife generally requires an undergraduate degree from a school of nursing. A nurse-midwife most often works in a hospital setting.

Pediatric Nurse

Pediatric nurses monitor infants' and children's health, work to prevent disease or injury, and help children attain optimal health. They may work in hospitals, schools of nursing, or with pediatricians in private practice or at a medical clinic.

Pediatric nurses have a degree in nursing that takes two to five years to complete. They take courses in biological sciences, nursing care, and pediatrics, usually in a school of nursing. They also undergo supervised clinical experiences in medical settings. Some pediatric nurses go on to earn a master's or doctoral degree in pediatric nursing.

Geriatric Nurse

Geriatric nurses seek to prevent or intervene in the chronic or acute health problems of older adults. They may work in hospitals, nursing homes, schools of nursing, or with geriatric medical specialists or psychiatrists in a medical clinic or in private practice.

Like pediatric nurses, geriatric nurses take courses in a school of nursing and obtain a degree in nursing, which takes from two to five years. They complete courses in biological sciences, nursing care, and mental health as well as supervised clinical training in geriatric settings. They also may obtain a master's or doctoral degree in their specialty.

Physical Therapist

Physical therapists work with individuals who have a physical problem due to disease or injury to help them function as competently as possible. They may consult with other professionals and coordinate services for the individual. Many physical therapists work with people of all ages, although some specialize in working with a specific age group, such as children or older adults.

Physical therapists usually have an undergraduate degree in physical therapy and are licensed by a state. They take courses and experience supervised training in physical therapy.

Occupational Therapist

Occupational therapists initiate the evaluation of clients with various impairments and manage their treatment. They help people regain, develop, and build skills that are important for independent functioning, health, well-being, security, and happiness.

An "Occupational Therapist Registered" (OTR) must have a master's and/or doctoral degree with education ranging from two to six years. Training includes occupational therapy courses in a specialized program. National certification is required and licensing/registration is required in some states.

Therapeutic/Recreation Therapist

Therapeutic/recreation therapists maintain or improve the quality of life for people with special needs through intervention, leisure education, and recreation. They work in hospitals, rehabilitation centers, local government agencies, at-risk youth programs, as well as other settings. Becoming a therapeutic/recreation therapist requires an undergraduate degree with coursework in leisure studies and a concentration in therapeutic recreation. National certification is usually required. Coursework in anatomy, special education, and psychology is beneficial.

Audiologist

Audiologists assess and identify the presence and severity of hearing loss, as well as problems in balance. They may work in a medical clinic, with a physician in private practice, in a hospital, or in a medical school.

An audiologist completes coursework and supervised training to earn a minimum of an undergraduate degree in hearing science. Some audiologists also go on to obtain a master's or doctoral degree.

Speech Therapist

Speech therapists identify, assess, and treat speech and language problems. They may work with physicians, psychologists, social workers, and other health-care professionals in a team approach to help individuals with physical or psychological problems that involve speech and language. Some speech therapists specialize in working with individuals of a particular age or people with a particular type of speech disorder.

Speech therapists have a minimum of an undergraduate degree in speech and hearing science or in a type of communications disorder. They may work in private practice, hospitals and medical schools, and government agencies.

Genetic Counselor

Genetic counselors identify and counsel families at risk for genetic disorders. They work as members of a health-care team, providing information and support to families who have members who have genetic defects or disorders or are at risk for a variety of inherited conditions. They also serve as educators and resource people for other health-care professionals and the public. Almost one-half work in university medical centers; one-fourth work in private hospital settings.

Genetic counselors have specialized graduate degrees and experience in medical genetics and counseling. Most enter the field after majoring in undergraduate school in such disciplines as biology, genetics, psychology, nursing, public health, or social work.

FAMILIES/RELATIONSHIPS

A number of careers and jobs related to life-span development focus on working with families and relationship problems. These range from home health aide to marriage and family therapist.

Home Health Aide

A home health aide provides services to older adults in the older adults' homes, helping them with basic self-care tasks. No higher education is required for this position. There is brief training by an agency.

Child Welfare Worker

Child protective services in each state employ child welfare workers. They protect children's rights, evaluate any maltreatment, and may have children removed from their homes if necessary. A child social worker has a minimum of an undergraduate degree in social work.

Child Life Specialist

Child life specialists work with children and their families when the child needs to be hospitalized. They monitor the child's activities, seek to reduce the child's stress, and help the child to cope and to enjoy the hospital experience as much as possible. Child life specialists may provide parent education and develop individualized treatment plans based on an assessment of the child's development, temperament, medical plan, and available social supports. Child life specialists have an undergraduate degree. They have taken courses in child development and education and usually completed additional courses in a child life program.

Marriage and Family Therapist

Marriage and family therapists work on the principle that many individuals who have psychological problems benefit when psychotherapy is provided in the context of a marital or family relationship. Marriage and family therapists may provide marital therapy, couple therapy to individuals in a relationship who are not married, and family therapy to two or more members of a family.

Marriage and family therapists have a master's or a doctoral degree. They complete a training program in graduate school similar to a clinical psychologist's but with the focus on marital and family relationships. In most states, it is necessary to go through a licensing procedure to practice marital and family therapy.

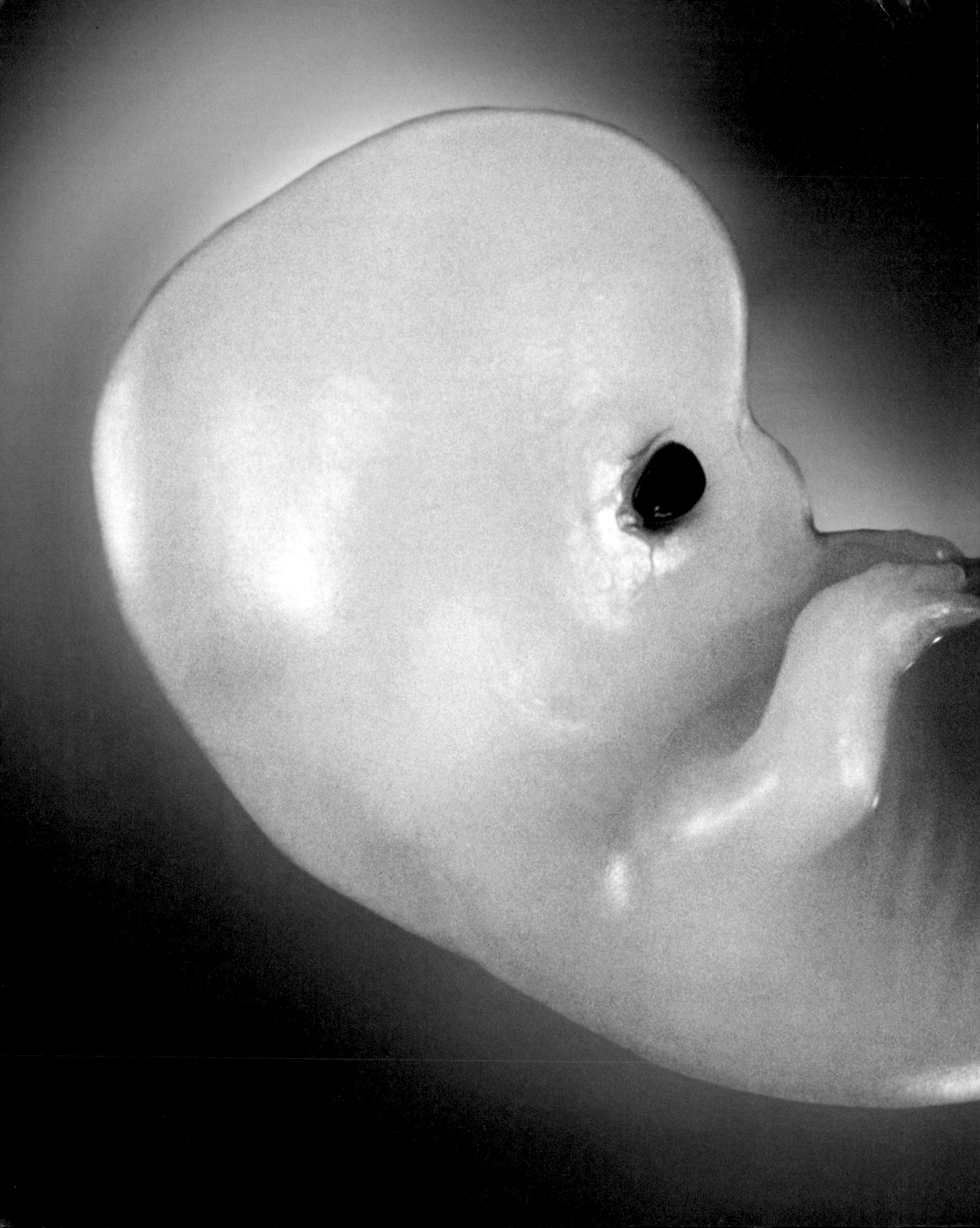

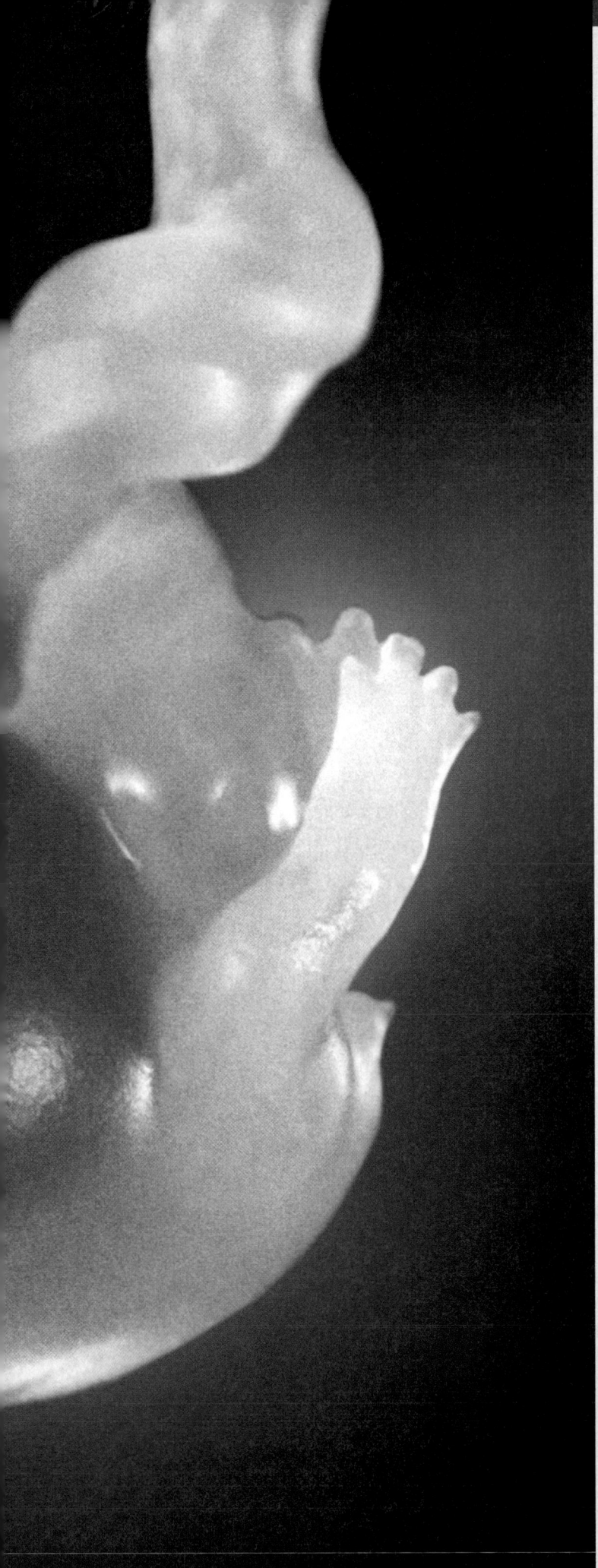

BEGINNINGS

There are one hundred and ninety-three living species of monkeys and apes. One hundred and ninety-two of them are covered with hair. The exception is the naked ape, self-named Homo sapiens.

—DESMOND MORRIS
British Zoologist, 20th Century

The rhythm and meaning of life involve beginnings. Questions

are raised about how, from so simple a beginning, endless

forms develop, grow, and mature. What was this organism,

what is the organism, and what will this organism be? In

Section 2, you will read two chapters: "Biological Beginnings"

(Chapter 2) and "Prenatal Development Birth" (Chapter 3).

2

What endless questions vex the thought, of whence and whither, when and how.

—SIR RICHARD BURTON
British Explorer, 19th Century

LEARNING GOALS

◆ Discuss the evolutionary perspective on life-span development.

◆ Describe what genes are and how they influence human development.

◆ Identify some important reproductive challenges and choices.

◆ Explain some of the ways that heredity and environment interact to produce individual differences in development.

BIOLOGICAL BEGINNINGS

CHAPTER OUTLINE

1

THE EVOLUTIONARY PERSPECTIVE
Natural Selection and Adaptive Behavior

Evolutionary Psychology

2

GENETIC FOUNDATIONS OF DEVELOPMENT
The Collaborative Gene

Genes and Chromosomes

Genetic Principles

Chromosomal and Gene-Linked Abnormalities

3

REPRODUCTIVE CHALLENGES AND CHOICES
Prenatal Diagnostic Tests

Infertility and Reproductive Technology

Adoption

4

HEREDITY AND ENVIRONMENT INTERACTION: THE NATURE-NURTURE DEBATE
Behavior Genetics

Heredity-Environment Correlations

Shared and Nonshared Environmental Experiences

The Epigenetic View

Conclusions About Heredity-Environment Interaction

Images of Life-Span Development
The Jim and Jim Twins

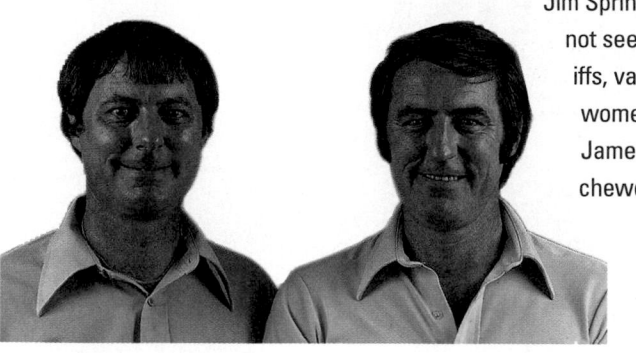

Jim Lewis (*left*) and Jim Springer (*right*).

Jim Springer and Jim Lewis are identical twins. They were separated at 4 weeks of age and did not see each other again until they were 39 years old. Both worked as part-time deputy sheriffs, vacationed in Florida, drove Chevrolets, had dogs named Toy, and married and divorced women named Betty. One twin named his son James Allan, and the other named his son James Alan. Both liked math but not spelling, enjoyed carpentry and mechanical drawing, chewed their fingernails down to the nubs, had almost identical drinking and smoking habits, had hemorrhoids, put on 10 pounds at about the same point in development, first suffered headaches at the age of 18, and had similar sleep patterns.

Jim and Jim do have some differences. One wears his hair over his forehead, the other slicks it back and has sideburns. One expresses himself best orally; the other is more proficient in writing. But, for the most part, their profiles are remarkably similar.

Another pair of identical twins, Daphne and Barbara, are called the "giggle sisters" because, after being reunited, they were always making each other laugh. A thorough search of their adoptive families' histories revealed no gigglers. The giggle sisters ignored stress, avoided conflict and controversy whenever possible, and showed no interest in politics.

Jim and Jim and the giggle sisters were part of the Minnesota Study of Twins Reared Apart, directed by Thomas Bouchard and his colleagues. The study brings identical twins (identical genetically because they come from the same fertilized egg) and fraternal twins (who come from different fertilized eggs) from all over the world to Minneapolis to investigate their lives. There the twins complete personality and intelligence tests, and they provide detailed medical histories, including information about diet and smoking, exercise habits, chest X-rays, heart stress tests, and EEGs. The twins are asked more than 15,000 questions about their family and childhood, personal interests, vocational orientation, values, and aesthetic judgments. (Bouchard & others, 1990).

When genetically identical twins who were separated as infants show such striking similarities in their tastes and habits and choices, can we conclude that their genes must have caused the development of those tastes and habits and choices? Other possible causes need to be considered. The twins shared not only the same genes but also some experiences. Some of the separated twins lived together for several months prior to their adoption; some of the twins had been reunited prior to testing (in some cases, many years earlier); adoption agencies often place twins in similar homes; and even strangers who spend several hours together and start comparing their lives are likely to come up with some coincidental similarities (Joseph, 2006). The Minnesota study of identical twins points to both the importance of the genetic basis of human development and the need for further research on genetic and environmental factors (Lykken, 2001).

PREVIEW

The examples of Jim and Jim and the giggle sisters stimulate us to think about our genetic heritage and the biological foundations of our existence. However, organisms are not like billiard balls, moved by simple external forces to predictable positions on life's table. Environmental experiences and biological foundations work together to make us who we are. Our coverage of life's biological beginnings focuses on evolution, genetic foundations, challenges and choices regarding reproduction, and the interaction of heredity and environment.

1 THE EVOLUTIONARY PERSPECTIVE

Natural Selection and Adaptive Behavior　　　**Evolutionary Psychology**

In evolutionary time, humans are relative newcomers to Earth. As our earliest ancestors left the forest to feed on the savannahs, and then to form hunting societies on the open plains, their minds and behaviors changed, and they eventually established humans as the dominant species on Earth. How did this evolution come about?

Natural Selection and Adaptive Behavior

Natural selection is the evolutionary process by which those individuals of a species that are best adapted are the ones that survive and reproduce. To understand what this means, let's return to the middle of the nineteenth century, when the British naturalist Charles Darwin was traveling around the world, observing many different species of animals in their natural surroundings. Darwin, who published his observations and thoughts in *On the Origin of Species* (1859), noted that most organisms reproduce at rates that would cause enormous increases in the population of most species and yet populations remain nearly constant. He reasoned that an intense, constant struggle for food, water, and resources must occur among the many young born each generation, because many of the young do not survive. Those that do survive and reproduce pass on their characteristics to the next generation. Darwin argued that these survivors are better *adapted* to their world than are the nonsurvivors (Johnson, 2008). The best-adapted individuals survive to leave the most offspring. Over the course of many generations, organisms with the characteristics needed for survival make up an increased percentage of the population. Over many, many generations, this could produce a gradual modification of the whole population. If environmental conditions change, however, other characteristics might become favored by natural selection, moving the species in a different direction (Mader, 2009).

All organisms must adapt to particular places, climates, food sources, and ways of life. An eagle's claws are a physical adaptation that facilitates predation. *Adaptive behavior* is behavior that promotes an organism's survival in the natural habitat (Enger, Ross, & Bailey, 2009). For example, attachment between a caregiver and a baby ensures the infant's closeness to a caregiver for feeding and protection from danger, thus increasing the infant's chances of survival.

How does the attachment of this Vietnamese baby to its mother reflect the evolutionary process of adaptive behavior?

Evolutionary Psychology

Although Darwin introduced the theory of evolution by natural selection in 1859, his ideas only recently have become a popular framework for explaining behavior. Psychology's newest approach, **evolutionary psychology**, emphasizes the importance of adaptation, reproduction, and "survival of the fittest" in shaping behavior. "Fit" in this sense refers to the ability to bear offspring that survive long enough to bear offspring of their own (Rose & Rauser, 2007). In this view, natural selection favors behaviors that increase reproductive success, the ability to pass your genes to the next generation (Bjorklund, 2006, 2007).

David Buss (1995, 2000, 2004, 2008) has been especially influential in stimulating new interest in how evolution can explain human behavior. He reasons that just as evolution shapes our physical features, such as body shape and height, it also pervasively influences how we make decisions, how aggressive we are, our fears, and our mating patterns. For example, assume that our ancestors were hunterers and gatherers on the plains and that men did most of the hunting and women stayed close to home gathering seeds and plants for food. If you have to travel some distance from

evolutionary psychology Emphasizes the importance of adaptation, reproduction, and "survival of the fittest" in shaping behavior.

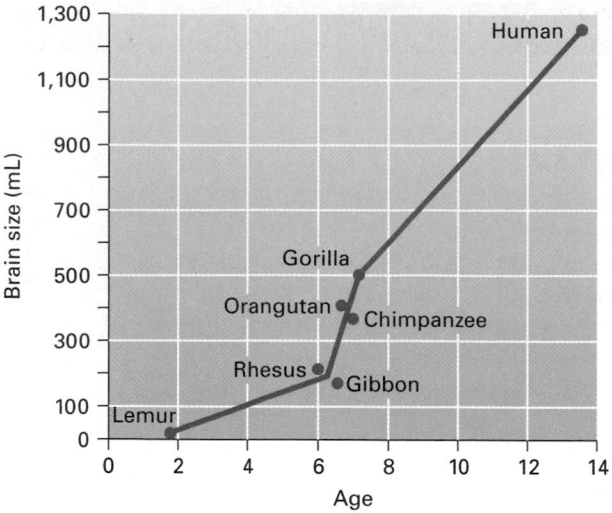

FIGURE 2.1 The Brain Sizes of Various Primates and Humans in Relation to the Length of the Childhood Period. Compared with other primates, humans have both a larger brain and a longer childhood period. *What conclusions can you draw from the relationship indicated by this graph?*

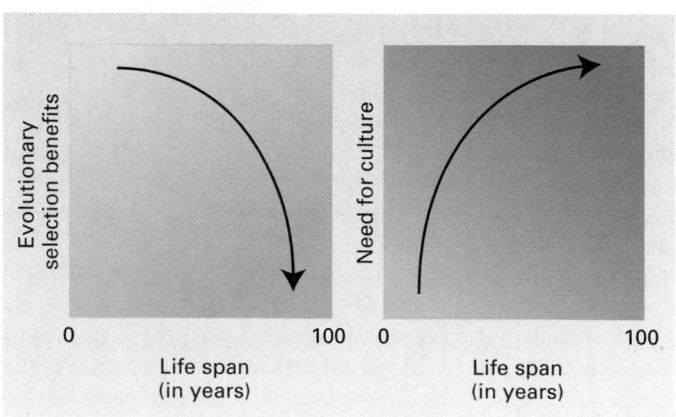

FIGURE 2.2 Baltes' View of Evolution and Culture Across the Life Span. Benefits derived from evolutionary selection decrease as we age, whereas the need for culture increases with age.

your home in an effort to find and slay a fleeing animal, you need not only certain physical traits but also the ability for certain types of spatial thinking. Men born with these traits would be more likely than men without them to survive, to bring home lots of food, and to be considered attractive mates—and thus to reproduce and pass on these characteristics to their children. In other words, these traits would provide a reproductive advantage for males—over many generations, men with good spatial thinking skills might become more numerous in the population. Critics point out that this scenario might or might not have actually happened.

Evolutionary Developmental Psychology Recently, interest has grown in using the concepts of evolutionary psychology to understand human development (Bjorklund, 2006, 2007). Here we discuss some ideas proposed by evolutionary developmental psychologists (Bjorklund & Pellegrini, 2002).

An extended childhood period evolved because humans require time to develop a large brain and learn the complexity of human societies. Humans take longer to become reproductively mature than any other mammal (see Figure 2.1). During this extended childhood period, they develop a large brain and the experiences needed to become competent adults in a complex society.

Many evolved psychological mechanisms are domain-specific. That is, the mechanisms apply only to a specific aspect of a person's makeup. According to evolutionary psychology, information processing is one example. In this view, the mind is not a general-purpose device that can be applied equally to a vast array of problems. Instead, as our ancestors dealt with certain recurring problems, such as hunting and finding [fo]r, specialized modules evolved that process information related to those prob[lems]. For example, a module for physical knowledge for tracking animals, a module for [math]ematical knowledge for trading, and a module for language.

Evolved mechanisms are not always adaptive in contemporary society. Some be[hav]iors that were adaptive for our prehistoric ancestors may not serve us well today. For [ex]ample, the food-scarce environment of our ancestors likely led to humans' propen[s]ity to gorge when food is available and to crave high-caloric foods, a trait that might lead to an epidemic of obesity when food is plentiful.

Evolution and Life-Span Development In evolutionary theory, what matters is that individuals live long enough to reproduce and pass on their characteristics (Enger, Ross, & Bailey, 2009). So why do humans live so long after reproduction? Perhaps evolution favored longevity because having older people around improves the survival rates of babies. Possibly having grandparents alive to care for the young while parents were out hunting and gathering food created an evolutionary advantage.

According to life-span developmentalist Paul Baltes (2003; Baltes, Lindenberger, & Staudinger, 2006), the benefits conferred by evolutionary selection decrease with age. Natural selection has not weeded out many harmful conditions and nonadaptive characteristics that appear among older adults. Why? Natural selection operates primarily on characteristics that are tied to reproductive fitness, which extends through the earlier part of adulthood. Thus, says Baltes, selection primarily operates during the first half of life.

As an example, consider Alzheimer disease, an irreversible brain disorder characterized by gradual deterioration. This disease typically does not appear until age 70 or later. If it were a disease that struck 20-year-olds, perhaps natural selection would have eliminated it eons ago.

Thus, unaided by evolutionary pressures against nonadaptive conditions, we suffer the aches, pains, and infirmities of aging. And as the benefits of evolutionary selection decrease with age, argues Baltes, the need for culture increases (see Figure 2.2). That is, as older adults weaken biologically, they need culture-based resources such as cognitive skills, literacy, medical technology, and social support. For example, older adults may need help and training from other people to maintain their cognitive skills (Boron, Willis, & Schaie, 2007; Kramer & Morrow, 2009).

Evaluating Evolutionary Psychology   Although the popular press gives a lot of attention to the ideas of evolutionary psychology, it remains just one theoretical approach. Like the theories described in Chapter 1, it has limitations, weaknesses, and critics. Albert Bandura (1998), whose social cognitive theory was described in Chapter 1, acknowledges the important influence of evolution on human adaptation. However, he rejects what he calls "one-sided evolutionism," which sees social behavior as the product of evolved biology. An alternative is a *bidirectional view*, in which environmental and biological conditions influence each other. In this view, evolutionary pressures created changes in biological structures that allowed the use of tools, which enabled our ancestors to manipulate the environment, constructing new environmental conditions. In turn, environmental innovations produced new selection pressures that led to the evolution of specialized biological systems for consciousness, thought, and language.

In other words, evolution gave us bodily structures and biological potentialities; it does not dictate behavior. People have used their biological capacities to produce diverse cultures—aggressive and pacific, egalitarian and autocratic. As American scientist Steven Jay Gould (1981) concluded, in most domains of human functioning, biology allows a broad range of cultural possibilities.

Children in all cultures are interested in the tools that adults in their cultures use. For example, this 11-month-old boy from the Efe culture in the Democratic Republic of the Congo in Africa is trying to cut a papaya with an *apopau* (a smaller version of a machete). *Might the infant's behavior be evolutionary-based or be due to both biological and environmental conditions?*

Review and Reflect: Learning Goal 1

1   **Discuss the Evolutionary Perspective on Life-Span Development**

REVIEW

- How can natural selection and adaptive behavior be defined?
- What is evolutionary psychology? What are some basic ideas about human development proposed by evolutionary psychologists? How might evolutionary influences have different effects at different points in the life span? How can evolutionary psychology be evaluated?

REFLECT

- Which is more persuasive to you: the views of evolutionary psychologists or their critics? Why?

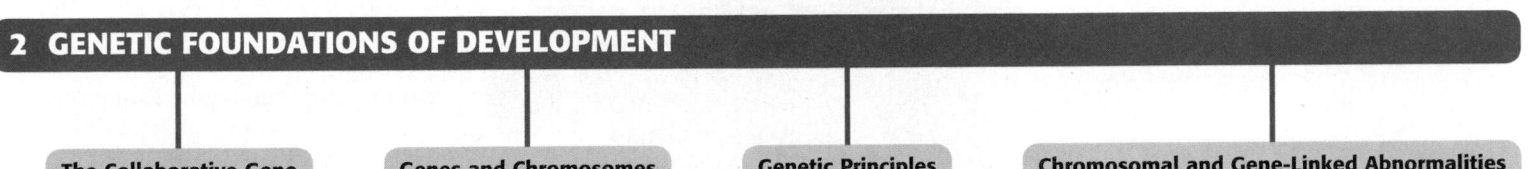

2   GENETIC FOUNDATIONS OF DEVELOPMENT

| The Collaborative Gene | Genes and Chromosomes | Genetic Principles | Chromosomal and Gene-Linked Abnormalities |

How are characteristics that suit a species for survival transmitted from one generation to the next? Darwin did not know because genes and the principles of genetics had not yet been discovered. Each of us carries a "genetic code" that we inherited from our parents. Because a fertilized egg carries this human code, a fertilized human egg cannot grow into an egret, eagle, or elephant.

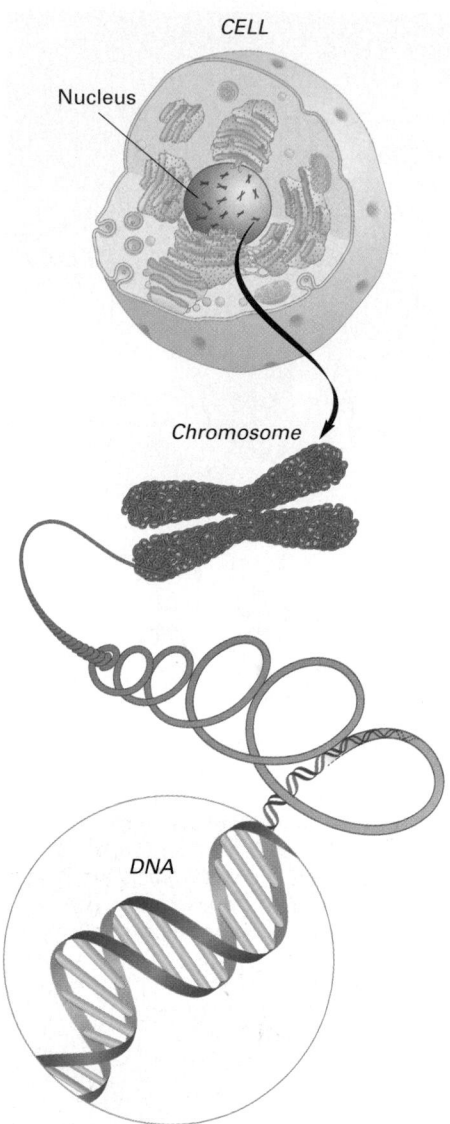

CELL

Nucleus

Chromosome

DNA

FIGURE 2.3 Cells, Chromosomes, DNA, and Genes. (*Top*) The body contains trillions of cells. Each cell contains a central structure, the nucleus. (*Middle*) Chromosomes are thread-like structures located in the nucleus of the cell. Chromosomes are composed of DNA. (*Bottom*) DNA has the structure of a spiral staircase. A gene is a segment of DNA.

chromosomes Threadlike structures that come in 23 pairs, one member of each pair coming from each parent. Chromosomes contain the genetic substance DNA.

DNA A complex molecule that contains genetic information.

genes Units of hereditary information composed of short segments of DNA. Genes direct cells to reproduce themselves and manufacture the proteins that maintain life.

The Collaborative Gene

Each of us began life as a single cell weighing about one twenty-millionth of an ounce! This tiny piece of matter housed our entire genetic code—instructions that orchestrated growth from that single cell to a person made of trillions of cells, each containing a replica of the original code. That code is carried by our genes. What are genes and what do they do? For the answer, we need to look into our cells.

The nucleus of each human cell contains **chromosomes**, which are threadlike structures made up of deoxyribonucleic acid, or DNA. **DNA** is a complex molecule with a double helix shape, like a spiral staircase, and contains genetic information. **Genes,** the units of hereditary information, are short segments of DNA, as you can see in Figure 2.3. They direct cells to reproduce themselves and to assemble proteins. Proteins, in turn, are the building blocks of cells as well as the regulators that direct the body's processes (Hartwell, 2008; Hoefnagels, 2009).

Each gene has its own location, its own designated place on a particular chromosome. Today, there is a great deal of enthusiasm about efforts to discover the specific locations of genes that are linked to certain functions (Brooker, 2009; Plomin & Schalkwyk, 2007; Weaver, 2008). An important step in this direction is the Human Genome Project's efforts to map the human *genome*—the complete set of developmental instructions for creating proteins that initiate the making of a human organism.

One of the big surprises of the Human Genome Project was an early report indicating that humans have only about 30,000 genes (U.S. Department of Energy, 2001). More recently, the number of human genes has been revised further downward to approximately 20,500 (*Science Daily*, 2008). Scientists had thought that humans had as many as 100,000 or more genes. They had also maintained that each gene programmed just one protein. In fact, humans have far more proteins than they have genes, so there cannot be a one-to-one correspondence between genes and proteins (Commoner, 2002). Each gene is not translated, in automaton-like fashion, into one and only one protein. A gene does not act independently, as developmental psychologist David Moore (2001) emphasized by titling his book *The Dependent Gene.*

Rather than being a group of independent genes, the human genome consists of many genes that collaborate both with each other and with nongenetic factors inside and outside the body. The collaboration operates at many points. For example, the cellular machinery mixes, matches, and links small pieces of DNA to reproduce the genes—and that machinery is influenced by what is going on around it.

Whether a gene is turned "on," working to assemble proteins, is also a matter of collaboration. The activity of genes (*genetic expression*) is affected by their environment (Gottlieb, 2007). For example, hormones that circulate in the blood make their way into the cell where they can turn genes "on" and "off." And the flow of hormones can be affected by environmental conditions, such as light, day length, nutrition, and behavior. Numerous studies have shown that external events outside of the original cell and the person, as well as events inside the cell, can excite or inhibit gene expression (Gottlieb, Wahlsten, & Lickliter, 2006). For example, one recent study revealed that an increase in the concentration of

A positive result from the Human Genome Project. Shortly after Andrew Gobea was born, his cells were genetically altered to prevent his immune system from failing.

Calvin and Hobbes   by Bill Watterson

stress hormones such as cortisol produced a fivefold increase in DNA damage (Flint & others, 2007).

In short, a single gene is rarely the source of a protein's genetic information, much less of an inherited trait (Gottlieb, 2007).

Genes and Chromosomes

Genes are not only collaborative, they are enduring. How do the genes manage to get passed from generation to generation and end up in all of the trillion cells in the body? Three processes explain the heart of the story: mitosis, meiosis, and fertilization.

Mitosis, Meiosis, and Fertilization All cells in your body, except the sperm and egg, have 46 chromosomes arranged in 23 pairs. These cells reproduce by a process called **mitosis**. During mitosis, the cell's nucleus—including the chromosomes—duplicates itself and the cell divides. Two new cells are formed, each containing the same DNA as the original cell, arranged in the same 23 pairs of chromosomes.

However, a different type of cell division—**meiosis**—forms eggs and sperm (or *gametes*). During meiosis, a cell of the testes (in men) or ovaries (in women) duplicates its chromosomes but then divides *twice*, thus forming four cells, each of which has only half of the genetic material of the parent cell (Balasubramanian, Koontz, & Reynolds, 2008). By the end of meiosis, each egg or sperm has 23 *unpaired* chromosomes.

During **fertilization**, an egg and a sperm fuse to create a single cell, called a **zygote** (see Figure 2.4). In the zygote, the 23 unpaired chromosomes from the egg and the 23 unpaired chromosomes from the sperm combine to form one set of 23 paired chromosomes—one chromosome of each pair from the mother's egg and the other from the father's sperm. In this manner, each parent contributes half of the offspring's genetic material.

Figure 2.5 shows 23 paired chromosomes of a male and a female. The members of each pair of chromosomes are both similar and different: Each chromosome in the pair contains varying forms of the same genes, at the same location on the chromosome. A gene for hair color, for example, is located on both members of one pair of chromosomes, in the same location on each. However, one of those chromosomes might carry the gene for blond hair; the other chromosome in the pair might carry the gene for brown hair.

Do you notice any obvious differences between the chromosomes of the male and the chromosomes of the female in Figure 2.5? The difference lies in the 23rd pair. Ordinarily, in females this pair consists of two chromosomes called *X chromosomes*; in males the 23rd pair consists of an X and a *Y chromosome*. The presence of a Y chromosome is what makes an individual male.

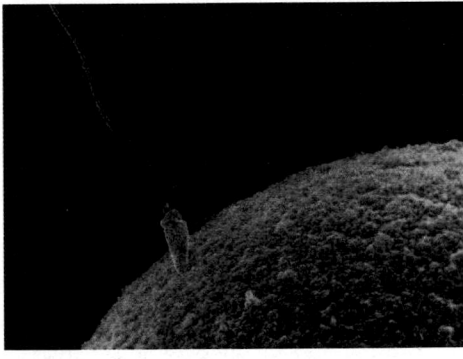

FIGURE 2.4 A Single Sperm Penetrating an Egg at the Point of Fertilization

mitosis Cellular reproduction in which the cell's nucleus duplicates itself with two new cells being formed, each containing the same DNA as the parent cell, arranged in the same 23 pairs of chromosomes.

meiosis A specialized form of cell division that occurs to form eggs and sperm (or gametes).

fertilization A stage in reproduction whereby an egg and a sperm fuse to create a single cell, called a zygote.

zygote A single cell formed through fertilization.

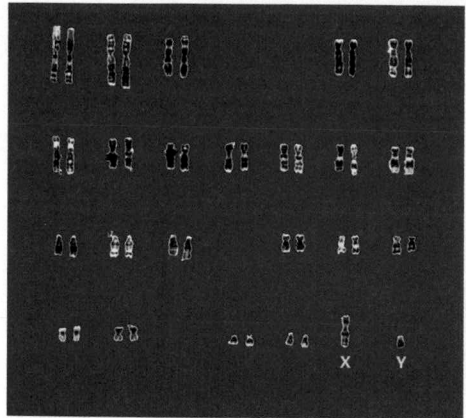

(a)

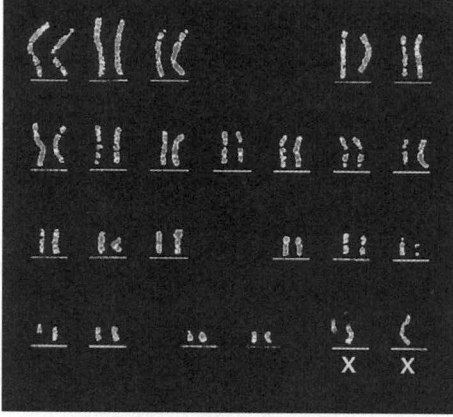

(b)

FIGURE 2.5 The Genetic Difference Between Males and Females. Set (*a*) shows the chromosome structure of a male, and set (*b*) shows the chromosome structure of a female. The last pair of 23 pairs of chromosomes is in the bottom right box of each set. Notice that the Y chromosome of the male is smaller than the X chromosome of the female. To obtain this kind of chromosomal picture, a cell is removed from a person's body, usually from the inside of the mouth. The chromosomes are stained by chemical treatment, magnified extensively, and then photographed.

genotype A person's genetic heritage; the actual genetic material.

phenotype The way an individual's genotype is expressed in observable and measurable characteristics.

Sources of Variability   Combining the genes of two parents in offspring increases genetic variability in the population, which is valuable for a species because it provides more characteristics for natural selection to operate on (Brooker, 2009; Mader, 2009). In fact, the human genetic process creates several important sources of variability.

First, the chromosomes in the zygote are not exact copies of those in mother's ovaries and the father's testes. During the formation of the sperm and egg in meiosis, the members of each pair of chromosomes are separated, but which chromosome in the pair goes to the gamete is a matter of chance. In addition, before the pairs separate, pieces of the two chromosomes in each pair are exchanged, creating a new combination of genes on each chromosome (Hyde, 2009). Thus, when chromosomes from the mother's egg and the father's sperm are brought together in the zygote, the result is a truly unique combination of genes (Raven & others, 2008).

If each zygote is unique, how do identical twins like those discussed in the opening of the chapter exist? *Identical twins* (also called monozygotic twins) develop from a single zygote that splits into two genetically identical replicas, each of which becomes a person. *Fraternal twins* (called dizygotic twins) develop from separate eggs and separate sperm, making them genetically no more similar than ordinary siblings.

Another source of variability comes from DNA (Weaver, 2008). Chances, a mistake by cellular machinery, or damage from an environmental agent such as radiation may produce a *mutated gene*, which is a permanently altered segment of DNA (Enger, Ross, & Bailey, 2009).

Even when their genes are identical, however, people vary. The difference between genotypes and phenotypes helps us to understand this source of variability. All of a person's genetic material makes up his or her **genotype**. However, not all of the genetic material is apparent in our observed and measurable characteristics. A **phenotype** consists of observable characteristics. Phenotypes include physical characteristics (such as height, weight, and hair color) and psychological characteristics (such as personality and intelligence).

For each genotype, a range of phenotypes can be expressed, providing another source of variability (Gottlieb, 2007). An individual can inherit the genetic potential to grow very large, for example, but good nutrition, among other things, will be essential to achieving that potential.

Genetic Principles

What determines how a genotype is expressed to create a particular phenotype? Much is unknown about the answer to this question (Hartwell, 2008; Talaro, 2008). However, a number of genetic principles have been discovered, among them those of dominant-recessive genes, sex-linked genes, genetic imprinting, and polygenically determined characteristics.

Dominant-Recessive Genes Principle   In some cases, one gene of a pair always exerts its effects; it is *dominant*, overriding the potential influence of the other gene, called the *recessive* gene. This is the *dominant-recessive genes principle*. A recessive gene exerts its influence only if the two genes of a pair are both recessive. If you inherit a recessive gene for a trait from each of your parents, you will show the trait. If you inherit a recessive gene from only one parent, you may never know you carry the gene. Brown hair, farsightedness, and dimples rule over blond hair, nearsightedness, and freckles in the world of dominant-recessive genes.

Can two brown-haired parents have a blond-haired child? Yes, they can. Suppose that each parent has a dominant gene for brown hair and a recessive gene for blond hair. Since dominant genes override recessive genes, the parents have brown hair, but both are carriers of blondness and pass on their recessive genes for blond hair. With no dominant gene to override them, the recessive genes can make the child's hair blond.

Sex-Linked Genes   Most mutated genes are recessive. When a mutated gene is carried on the X chromosome, the result is called *X-linked inheritance*. The implications for males may be very different from those for females. (Peterson, Wang, & Williams, 2008). Remember that males have only one X chromosome. Thus, if there is an altered, disease-creating gene on the X chromosome, males have no "backup" copy to counter the harmful gene and therefore may carry an X-linked disease. However, females have a second X chromosome, which is likely to be unchanged. As a result, they are not likely to have the X-linked disease. Thus, most individuals who have X-linked diseases are males. Females who have one changed copy of the X gene are known as "carriers," and they usually do not show any signs of the X-linked disease. Hemophilia and fragile-X syndrome, which we will discuss later in the chapter, are examples of X-linked inheritance diseases (Pierce & others, 2007).

Genetic Imprinting   *Genetic imprinting* occurs when the expression of a gene has different effects depending on whether the mother or the father passed on the gene (Horsthemke & Bunting, 2008). A chemical process "silences" one member of the gene pair. For example, as a result of imprinting, only the maternally derived copy of the Expressed gene might be active, while the paternally derived copy of the same Expressed gene is silenced— or vice versa. Only a small percentage of human genes appear to undergo imprinting, but it is a normal and important aspect of development (Hampton, 2008). When imprinting goes awry, development is disturbed, as in the case of Beckwith-Wiedemann syndrome, a growth disorder, and Wilms tumor, a type of cancer (Gropman & Adams, 2007).

Polygenic Inheritance   Genetic transmission is usually more complex than the simple examples we have examined thus far (Hartwell, 2008; Weaver, 2008). Few characteristics reflect the influence of only a single gene or pair of genes. Most are determined by the interaction of many different genes; they are said to be *polygenically determined*. Even a simple characteristic such as height, for example, reflects the interaction of many genes, as well as the influence of the environment.

Chromosomal and Gene-Linked Abnormalities

Sometimes, abnormalities characterize the genetic process. Some of these abnormalities involve whole chromosomes that do not separate properly during meiosis. Other abnormalities are produced by harmful genes.

Chromosomal Abnormalities   Sometimes, when a gamete is formed, the male's sperm and the female's ovum do not have their normal set of 23 chromosomes. The most notable examples involve Down syndrome and abnormalities of the sex chromosomes (see Figure 2.6).

FIGURE 2.6 Some Chromosomal Abnormalities. The treatments for these abnormalities do not necessarily erase the problem but may improve the individual's adaptive behavior and quality of life.

Name	Description	Treatment	Incidence
Down syndrome	An extra chromosome causes mild to severe retardation and physical abnormalities.	Surgery, early intervention, infant stimulation, and special learning programs	1 in 1,900 births at age 20 1 in 300 births at age 35 1 in 30 births at age 45
Klinefelter syndrome (XXY)	An extra X chromosome causes physical abnormalities.	Hormone therapy can be effective	1 in 600 male births
Fragile X syndrome	An abnormality in the X chromosome can cause mental retardation, learning disabilities, or short attention span.	Special education, speech and language therapy	More common in males than in females
Turner syndrome (XO)	A missing X chromosome in females can cause mental retardation and sexual underdevelopment.	Hormone therapy in childhood and puberty	1 in 2,500 female births
XYY syndrome	An extra Y chromosome can cause above-average height.	No special treatment required	1 in 1,000 male births

These athletes, many of whom have Down syndrome, are participating in a Special Olympics competition. Notice the distinctive facial features of the individuals with Down syndrome, such as a round face and a flattened skull. *What causes Down syndrome?*

Down Syndrome An individual with **Down syndrome** has a round face, a flattened skull, an extra fold of skin over the eyelids, a protruding tongue, short limbs, and retardation of motor and mental abilities (Fidler, 2008). The syndrome is caused by the presence of an extra copy of chromosome 21. It is not known why the extra chromosome is present, but the health of the male sperm or female ovum may be involved.

Down syndrome appears approximately once in every 700 live births. Women between the ages of 16 and 34 are less likely to give birth to a child with Down syndrome than are younger or older women. African American children are rarely born with Down syndrome.

Sex-Linked Chromosomal Abnormalities Recall that a newborn normally has either an X and a Y chromosome, or two X chromosomes. Human embryos must possess at least one X chromosome to be viable. The most common sex-linked chromosomal abnormalities involve the presence of an extra chromosome (either an X or Y) or the absence of one X chromosome in females.

Klinefelter syndrome is a genetic disorder in which males have an extra X chromosome, making them XXY instead of XY. Males with this disorder have undeveloped testes, and they usually have enlarged breasts and become tall (Ross & others, 2008). Klinefelter syndrome occurs approximately once in every 600 live male births.

Fragile X syndrome is a genetic disorder that results from an abnormality in the X chromosome, which becomes constricted and often breaks (Penagarikano, Mulle, & Warren, 2007). Mental deficiency often is an outcome, but it may take the form of mental retardation, a learning disability, or a short attention span. A recent study revealed that boys with fragile X syndrome were characterized by cognitive deficits in inhibition, memory, and planning (Hooper & others, 2008). This disorder occurs more frequently in males than in females, possibly because the second X chromosome in females negates the effects of the other abnormal X chromosome (Ono, Farzin, & Hagerman, 2008).

Turner syndrome is a chromosomal disorder in females in which either an X chromosome is missing, making the person XO instead of XX, or part of one X chromosome is deleted. Females with Turner syndrome are short in stature and have a webbed neck. They might be infertile and have difficulty in mathematics, but their verbal ability is often quite good (Murphy & Mazzocco, 2008). Turner syndrome occurs in approximately 1 of every 2,500 live females births.

The **XYY syndrome** is a chromosomal disorder in which the male has an extra Y chromosome (Isen & Baker, 2008). Early interest in this syndrome focused on the belief that the extra Y chromosome found in some males contributed to aggression and violence. However, researchers subsequently found that XYY males are no more likely to commit crimes than are XY males (Witkin & others, 1976).

Gene-Linked Abnormalities Abnormalities can be produced not only by an uneven number of chromosomes, but also by harmful genes (Presson & Jenner, 2008). More than 7,000 such genetic disorders have been identified, although most of them are rare.

Phenylketonuria (PKU) is a genetic disorder in which the individual cannot properly metabolize phenylalanine, an amino acid. It results from a recessive gene and occurs about once in every 10,000 to 20,000 live births. Today, phenylketonuria is easily detected, and it is treated by a diet that prevents an excess accumulation of phenylalanine. If phenylketonuria is left untreated, however, excess phenylalanine builds up in the child, producing mental retardation and hyperactivity. Phenylketonuria accounts for approximately 1 percent of institutionalized individuals who are mentally retarded, and it occurs primarily in Whites.

The story of phenylketonuria has important implications for the nature-nurture issue. Although phenylketonuria is a genetic disorder (nature), how or whether a gene's influence in phenylketonuria is played out depends on environmental influences since the disorder can be treated (nurture) (Ney & others, 2008). That is, the

Down syndrome A chromosomally transmitted form of mental retardation, caused by the presence of an extra copy of chromosome 21.

Klinefelter syndrome A chromosomal disorder in which males have an extra X chromosome, making them XXY instead of XY.

fragile X syndrome A genetic disorder involving an abnormality in the X chromosome, which becomes constricted and often breaks.

Turner syndrome A chromosomal disorder in females in which either an X chromosome is missing, making the person XO instead of XX, or part of one X chromosome is deleted.

XYY syndrome A chromosomal disorder in which males have an extra Y chromosome.

phenylketonuria (PKU) A genetic disorder in which an individual cannot properly metabolize phenylalanine, an amino acid. PKU is now easily detected but, if left untreated, results in mental retardation and hyperactivity.

presence of a genetic defect *does not* inevitably lead to the development of the disorder *if* the individual develops in the right environment (one free of phenylalanine) (Cipriano, Rupar, & Zaric, 2007). This is one example of the important principle of heredity-environment interaction. Under one environmental condition (phenylalanine in the diet), mental retardation results, but when other nutrients replace phenylalanine, intelligence develops in the normal range. The same genotype has different outcomes depending on the environment (in this case, the nutritional environment).

Sickle-cell anemia, which occurs most often in African Americans, is a genetic disorder that impairs the body's red blood cells. Red blood cells carry oxygen to the body's cells and are usually shaped like a disk. In sickle-cell anemia, a recessive gene causes the red blood cell to beome a hook-shaped "sickle" that cannot carry oxygen properly and dies quickly. As a result, the body's cells do not receive adequate oxygen, causing anemia and early death (King, DeBraun, & White, 2008). About 1 in 400 African American babies is affected by sickle-cell anemia. One in 10 African Americans is a carrier, as is 1 in 20 Latin Americans. A National Institutes of Health (2008) panel recently concluded that the only FDA-approved drug (hydroyurea) to treat sickle-cell anemia in adolescents and adults has been underutilized. Research is currently being conducted in a study named Baby HUG to determine if the drug works with babies.

Other diseases that result from genetic abnormalities include cystic fibrosis, diabetes, hemophilia, Huntington disease, spina bifida, and Tay-Sachs disease (Dunn & others, 2008). Figure 2.7 provides further information about these diseases. Someday, scientists may identify why these and other genetic abnormalities occur and discover how to cure them. The Human Genome Project has already linked specific DNA variations with increased risk of a number of diseases and conditions, including

During a physical examination for a college football tryout, Jerry Hubbard, 32, learned that he carried the gene for sickle-cell anemia. Daughter Sara is healthy but daughter Avery (in the print dress) has sickle-cell anemia. *If you were a genetic counselor would you recommend that this family have more children? Explain.*

sickle-cell anemia A genetic disorder that affects the red blood cells and occurs most often in African Americans.

Name	Description	Treatment	Incidence
Cystic fibrosis	Glandular dysfunction that interferes with mucus production; breathing and digestion are hampered, resulting in a shortened life span.	Physical and oxygen therapy, synthetic enzymes, and antibiotics; most individuals live to middle age.	1 in 2,000 births
Diabetes	Body does not produce enough insulin, which causes abnormal metabolism of sugar.	Early onset can be fatal unless treated with insulin.	1 in 2,500 births
Hemophilia	Delayed blood clotting causes internal and external bleeding.	Blood transfusions/injections can reduce or prevent damage due to internal bleeding.	1 in 10,000 males
Huntington disease	Central nervous system deteriorates, producing problems in muscle coordination and mental deterioration.	Does not usually appear until age 35 or older; death likely 10 to 20 years after symptoms appear.	1 in 20,000 births
Phenylketonuria (PKU)	Metabolic disorder that, left untreated, causes mental retardation.	Special diet can result in average intelligence and normal life span.	1 in 10,000 to 1 in 20,000 births
Sickle-cell anemia	Blood disorder that limits the body's oxygen supply; it can cause joint swelling, as well as heart and kidney failure.	Penicillin, medication for pain, antibiotics, and blood transfusions.	1 in 400 African American children (lower among other groups)
Spina bifida	Neural tube disorder that causes brain and spine abnormalities.	Corrective surgery at birth, orthopedic devices, and physical/medical therapy.	2 in 1,000 births
Tay-Sachs disease	Deceleration of mental and physical development caused by an accumulation of lipids in the nervous system.	Medication and special diet are used, but death is likely by 5 years of age.	One in 30 American Jews is a carrier.

FIGURE 2.7 Some Gene-Linked Abnormalities

Huntington disease (in which the central nervous system deteriorates), some forms of cancer, asthma, diabetes, hypertension, and Alzheimer disease (Knowles, 2004).

Dealing with Genetic Abnormalities Every individual carries DNA variations that might predispose the person to serious physical disease or mental disorder. But not all individuals who carry a genetic disorder display the disorder. Other genes or developmental events sometimes compensate for genetic abnormalities (Gottlieb, Wahlsten, & Lickliter, 2006). For example, recall the earlier example of phenylketonuria: Even though individuals might carry the genetic disorder of phenylketonuria, it is not expressed when phenylalanine is replaced by other nutrients in their diet.

Thus, genes are not destiny, but genes that are missing, nonfunctional, or mutated can be associated with disorders (Gaff, Williams, & McInerney, 2008). Identifying such genetic flaws could enable doctors to predict an individual's risks, recommend healthy practices, and prescribe the safest and most effective drugs (Blaine & others, 2008). A decade or two from now, parents of a newborn baby may be able to leave the hospital with a full genome analysis of their offspring that reveals disease risks.

However, this knowledge might bring important costs as well as benefits. Who would have access to a person's genetic profile? An individual's ability to land and hold jobs or obtain insurance might be threatened if it is known that a person is considered at risk for some disease. For example, should an airline pilot or a neurosurgeon who is predisposed to develop a disorder that makes one's hands shake be required to leave that job early?

Genetic counselors, usually physicians or biologists who are well-versed in the field of medical genetics, understand the kinds of problems just described, the odds of encountering them, and helpful strategies for offseting some of their effects (Sivell & others, 2008). To read about the career and work of a genetic counselor, see the *Careers in Life-Span Development* profile.

Careers in Life-Span Development

Holly Ishmael, Genetic Counselor

Holly Ishmael is a genetic counselor at Children's Mercy Hospital in Kansas City. She obtained an undergraduate degree in psychology and then a master's degree in genetic counseling from Sarah Lawrence College.

Genetic counselors, like Ishmael, work as members of a health-care team, providing information and support to families with birth defects or genetic disorders. They identify families at risk by analyzing inheritance patterns and explore options with the family. Some genetic counselors, like Ishmael, become specialists in prenatal and pediatric genetics; others might specialize in cancer genetics or psychiatric genetic disorders.

Ishmael says, "Genetic counseling is a perfect combination for people who want to do something science-oriented, but need human contact and don't want to spend all of their time in a lab or have their nose in a book" (Rizzo, 1999, p. 3).

Genetic counselors have specialized graduate degrees in the areas of medical genetics and counseling. They enter graduate school with undergraduate backgrounds from a variety of disciplines, including biology, genetics, psychology, public health, and social work. There are approximately thirty graduate genetic counseling programs in the United States. If you are interested in this profession, you can obtain further information from the National Society of Genetic Counselors at www.nsgc.org.

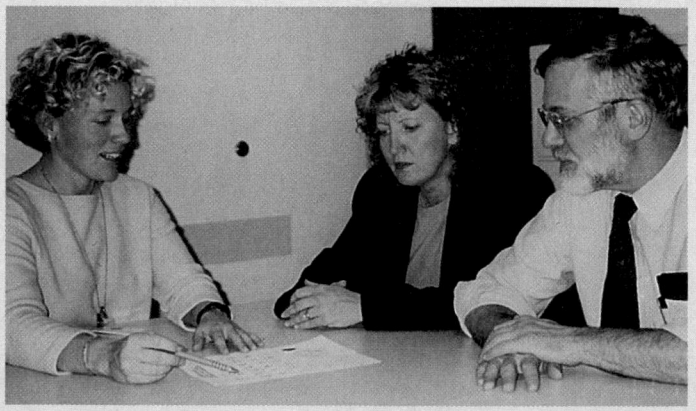

Holly Ishmael (*left*) in a genetic counseling session.

Review and Reflect: Learning Goal 2

2 **Describe What Genes Are and How They Influence Human Development**

REVIEW

- What are genes?
- How are genes passed on?
- What basic principles describe how genes interact?
- What are some chromosomal and gene-linked abnormalities?

REFLECT

- What are some possible ethical issues regarding genetics and development that might arise in the future?

3 REPRODUCTIVE CHALLENGES AND CHOICES

| Prenatal Diagnostic Tests | Infertility and Reproductive Technology | Adoption |

The facts and principles we have discussed regarding meiosis, genetics, and genetic abnormalities are a small part of the recent explosion of knowledge about human biology. This knowledge not only helps us understand human development but also opens up many new choices to prospective parents, choices that can also raise ethical questions.

Prenatal Diagnostic Tests

One choice open to prospective mothers is the extent to which they should undergo prenatal testing. A number of tests can indicate whether a fetus is developing normally, including ultrasound sonography, fetal MRI, chorionic villus sampling, amniocentesis, maternal blood screening, and noninvasive prenatal diagnosis (Lenzi & Johnson, 2008).

An ultrasound test is often conducted seven weeks into a pregnancy and at various times later in pregnancy. *Ultrasound sonography* is a prenatal medical procedure in which high-frequency sound waves are directed into the pregnant woman's abdomen. The echo from the sounds is transformed into a visual representation of the fetus's inner structures. This technique can detect many structural abnormalities in the fetus, including microencephaly, a form of mental retardation involving an abnormally small brain; it can also determine the number of fetuses and give clues to the baby's sex (Gerards & others, 2008). There is virtually no risk to the woman or fetus in this test.

The development of brain-imaging techniques has led to increasing use of *fetal MRI* to diagnose fetal malformations (Garel, 2008; Huisman & Kellenberger, 2008) (see Figure 2.8). MRI stands for magnetic resonance imaging and uses a powerful magnet and radio images to generate detailed images of the body's organs and structures. Currently, ultrasound is still the first choice in fetal screening, but fetal MRI can provide more detailed images than ultrasound. In many instances, ultrasound will indicate a possible abnormality and then fetal MRI will be used to obtain

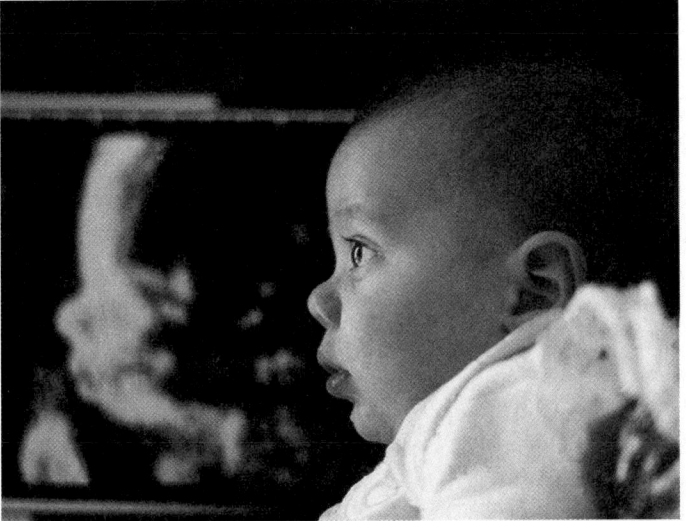

A 6-month-old infant poses with the ultrasound sonography record taken four months into the baby's prenatal development. *What is ultrasound sonography?*

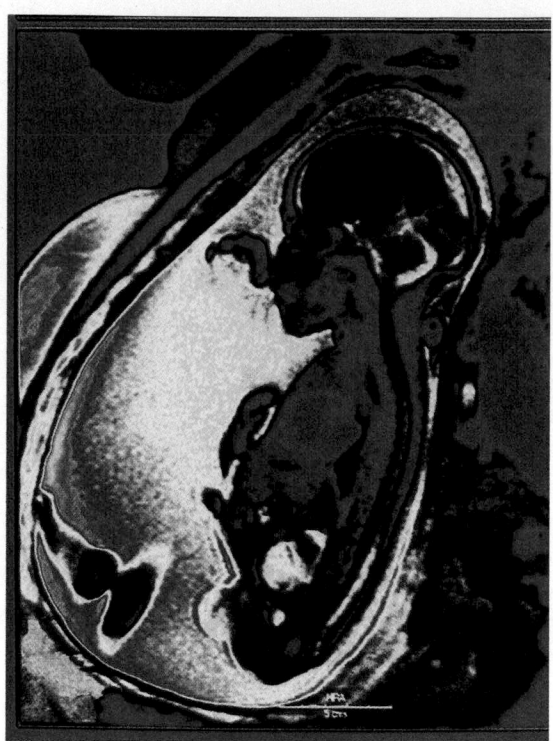

FIGURE 2.8 A Fetal MRI, Which Is Increasingly Being Used in Prenatal Diagnosis of Fetal Malformations

a clearer, more detailed image (Obenauer & Maestre, 2008). Among the fetal malformations that fetal MRI may be able to detect better than ultrasound sonography are certain central nervous system, chest, gastrointestinal, genital/urinary, and placental abnormalities (Fratelli & others, 2007; Laifer-Narin & others, 2007).

At some point between the 10th and 12th weeks of pregnancy, chorionic villus sampling may be used to detect genetic defects and chromosomal abnormalities, such as the ones discussed in the previous section. (Csaba, Bush, & Saphier, 2006). *Chorionic villus sampling (CVS)* is a prenatal medical procedure in which a small sample of the placenta (the vascular organ that links the fetus to the mother's uterus) is removed. Diagnosis takes about 10 days. There is a small risk of limb deformity when CVS is used.

Between the 15th and 18th weeks of pregnancy, amniocentesis may be performed. *Amniocentesis* is a prenatal medical procedure in which a sample of amniotic fluid is withdrawn by syringe and tested for chromosomal or metabolic disorders (Nagel & others, 2007). The amnionic fluid is found within the amnion, a thin sac in which the embryo is suspended. Ultrasound sonography is often used during amniocentesis so that the syringe can be placed precisely. The later amniocentesis is performed, the better its diagnostic potential. The earlier it is performed, the more useful it is in deciding how to handle a pregnancy. It may take two weeks for enough cells to grow and amniocentesis test results to be obtained. Amniocentesis brings a small risk of miscarriage: about 1 woman in every 200 to 300 miscarries after amniocentesis.

Both amniocentesis and chorionic villus sampling provide valuable information about the presence of birth defects, but they also raise difficult issues for parents about whether an abortion should be obtained if birth defects are present (Quadrelli & others, 2007). Chorionic villus sampling allows a decision to made sooner, near the end of the first 12 weeks of pregnancy, when abortion is safer and less traumatic than later. Although earlier reports indicated that chorionic villus sampling brings a slightly higher risk of pregnancy loss than amniocentesis, a recent U.S. study of more than 40,000 pregnancies found that loss rates for CVS decreased from 1998–2003 and that there is no longer a difference in pregnancy loss risk between CVS and amniocentesis (Caughey, Hopkins, & Norton, 2006).

During the 16th to 18th weeks of pregnancy, maternal blood screening may be performed. *Maternal blood screening* identifies pregnancies that have an elevated risk for birth defects such as spina bifida (a defect in the spinal cord) and Down syndrome (Palomaki & others, 2006). The current blood test is called the *triple screen* because it measures three substances in the mother's blood. After an abnormal triple screen result, the next step is usually an ultrasound examination. If an ultrasound does not explain the abnormal triple screen results, amniocentesis is typically used.

Noninvasive prenatal diagnosis (NIPD) is increasingly being explored as an alternative to such procedures as chorionic villus sampling and amniocentesis (Avent & others, 2008). At this point, NIPD has mainly focused on the isolation and examination of fetal cells circulating in the mother's blood and analysis of cell-free fetal DNA in maternal plasma (Finning & Chitty, 2008; Norbury & Norbury, 2008).

Researchers already have used NIPD to successfully test for genes inherited from a father that cause cystic fibrosis and Huntington disease. They also are exploring the potential for using NIPD to diagnose a baby's sex, as early as five weeks after conception, and Down syndrome (Avent & others, 2008; Hahn, Zhong, & Holzgreve, 2008). Being able to detect an offspring's sex and various diseases and defects so early raises ethical concerns about couples' motivation to terminate a pregnancy (Newson, 2008; van den Heuvel & Marteau, 2008).

Technical challenges still characterize the use of NIPD, but its benefit in reducing risk make it an attractive diagnostic candidate (van der Schoot, Hahn, & Chitty, 2008). The main technical challenge is to efficiently separate out the fetal cells, which comprise only about one of every million cells in a mother's blood.

Infertility and Reproductive Technology

Recent advances in biological knowledge have also opened up many choices for infertile people. Approximately 10 to 15 percent of couples in the United States experience infertility, which is defined as the inability to conceive a child after 12 months of regular intercourse without contraception. The cause of infertility can rest with the woman or the man. The woman may not be ovulating (releasing eggs to be fertilized), she may be producing abnormal ova, her fallopian tubes by which ova normally reach the womb may be blocked, or she may have a disease that prevents implantation of the embyro into the uterus. The man may produce too few sperm, the sperm may lack motility (the ability to move adequately), or he may have a blocked passageway (Hesmet & Lo, 2006).

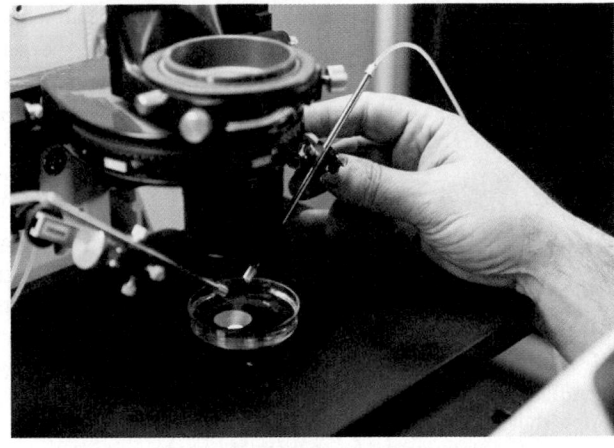

A technician using a micro-needle to inject human sperm into a human egg cell as part of an in vitro fertilization procedure. The injected sperm fertilizes the egg, and the resulting zygote is then grown in the laboratory until it reaches an early stage of embryonic development. Then it is implanted in the uterus.

In the United States, more than 2 million couples seek help for infertility every year. In some cases of infertility, surgery may correct the cause; in others, hormone-based drugs may improve the probability of having a child. Of the 2 million couples who seek help for infertility every year, about 40,000 try high-tech assisted reproduction. By far the most common technique used is *in vitro fertilization (IVF)*, in which eggs and sperm are combined in a laboratory dish. If any eggs are successfully fertilized, one or more of the resulting fertilized eggs is transferred into the woman's uterus. A national study in the United States by the Centers for Disease Control and Prevention (2006) found the success rate of IVF depends on the mother's age (see Figure 2.9).

The creation of families by means of the new reproductive technologies raises important questions about the physical and psychological consequences for children (Gurgan & Demirol, 2007). One result of fertility treatments is an increase in multiple births (Jones, 2007; Reddy & others, 2007). Twenty-five to 30 percent of pregnancies achieved by fertility treatments—including in vitro fertilization—now result in multiple births. Any multiple birth increases the likelihood that the babies will have life-threatening and costly problems, such as extremely low birth weight (Ito & others, 2006).

Not nearly as many studies have examined the psychological outcomes of IVF as the physical outcomes. To read about a study that addresses these consequences, see the *Research in Life-Span Development* interlude that follows.

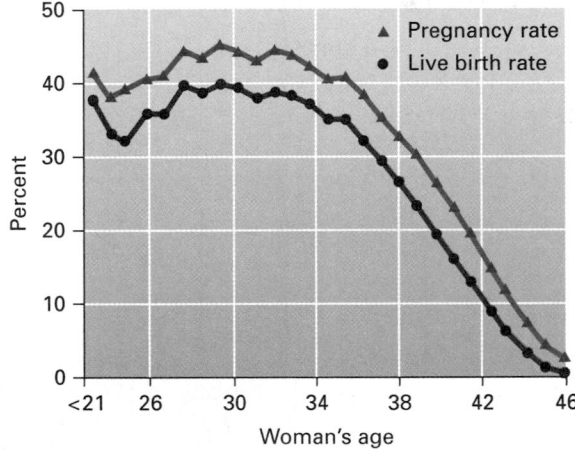

FIGURE 2.9 Success Rates of In Vitro Fertilization Vary According to the Woman's Age

Research In Life-Span Development
In Vitro Fertilization and Developmental Outcomes in Adolescence

A longitudinal study examined 34 in vitro fertilization families, 49 adoptive families, and 38 families with a naturally conceived child (Golombok, MacCallum, & Goodman, 2001). Each type of family included a similar portion of boys and girls. Also, the age of the young adolescents did not differ according to family type (mean age of 11 years, 11 months).

Children's socioemotional development was assessed by (1) interviewing the mother and obtaining detailed descriptions of any problems the child might have; (2) administering a Strengths and Difficulties questionnaire to the child's mother and teacher; and (3) administering the Social Adjustment Inventory for Children and Adolescents, which examines functioning in school, peer relationships, and self-esteem.

No sigificant differences between the children from the in vitro fertilization, adoptive, and naturally conceiving families were found. The results from the Social Adjustment Inventory for Children

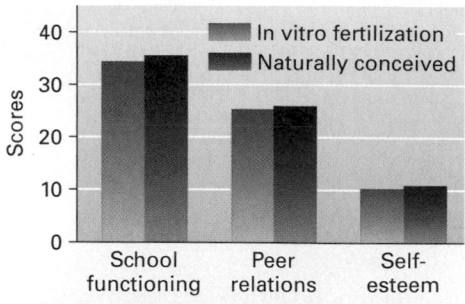

FIGURE 2.10 Socioemotional Functioning of Children Conceived Through In Vitro Fertilization or Naturally Conceived. This graph shows the results of a study that compared the socioemotional functioning of young adolescents who had either been conceived through in vitro fertilization (IVF) or naturally conceived (Golombok, MacCallum, & Goodman, 2001). For each type of family, the study included a similar portion of boys and girls and children of similar age (mean age of 11 years, 11 months). Although the means for the naturally conceived group were slightly higher, this is likely due to chance: there were no significant differences between the groups.

An increasing number of Hollywood celebrities are adopting children from developing countries. Actress Angelina Jolie recently adopted a baby girl, Zahara (above), in Ethiopia.

and Adolescents are shown in Figure 2.10. Another study also revealed no psychological differences between IVF babies and those not conceived by IVF, but more research is needed to reach firm conclusions in this area (Hahn & Dipietro, 2001).

Adoption

Although surgery and fertility drugs can sometimes solve the infertility problem, another choice is to adopt a child (Bernard & Dozier, 2008; Cohen & others, 2008). Adoption is the social and legal process by which a parent-child relationship is established between persons unrelated at birth. As we see next in the *Diversity in Life-Span Development* interlude, an increase in diversity has characterized the adoption of children in the United States in recent years.

Diversity in Life-Span Development
The Increased Diversity of Adopted Children and Adoptive Parents

Several changes occurred during the last several decades of the twentieth century in the characteristics both of adopted children and of adoptive parents (Brodzinsky & Pinderhughes, 2002, pp. 280–282). Until the 1960s, most U.S. adopted children were healthy, European American infants, who were adopted within a few days or weeks after birth. However, in recent decades, an increasing number of unmarried U.S. mothers decided to keep their babies, and the number of unwanted births decreased as contraception became readily available and abortion was legalized. As a result, the number of healthy European American infants available for adoption dropped dramatically. Increasingly, U.S. couples adopted children who were not European Americans, children from other countries, and children in foster care whose characteristics—such as age, minority status, exposure to neglect or abuse, or physical or mental health problems—"were once thought to be barriers to adoption" (p. 281).

Changes also have characterized adoptive parents. Until the last several decades of the twentieth century, most adoptive parents had a middle or upper socioeconomic status and were "married, infertile, European American couples, usually in their 30s and 40s, and free of any disability. Adoption agencies *screened out* couples who did not have these characteristics" (p. 281). Today, however, many adoption agencies *screen in* as many applicants as possible and have no income requirements for adoptive parents. Many agencies now permit single adults, older adults, and gay and lesbian adults to adopt children (Matthews & Cramer, 2006; Ryan, Pearlmutter, & Groza, 2004).

Do these changes matter? They open opportunities for many children and many couples, but possible effects of changes in the characteristics of parents on the outcomes for children are still unknown. For example, in one study, adopted adolescents were more likely to have problems if the adoptive parents had low levels of education (Miller & others, 2000). In another study, international adoptees showed fewer behavior problems and were less likely to be using mental health services than domestic adoptees (Juffer & van IJzendoorn, 2005). More research is needed before definitive conclusions can be reached about the changing demographic characteristics of adoption.

The changes in adoption practice over the last several decades make it difficult to generalize about the average adopted child or average adoptive parent. As we see next, though, some researchers have provided useful comparisons between adopted children and non adopted children and their families.

How do adopted children fare after they are adopted? Children who are adopted very early in their lives are more likely to have positive outcomes than children adopted later in life. In one study, the later adoption occurred, the more problems the adoptees had. Infant adoptees had the fewest adjustment difficulties; those adopted after they were 10 years of age had the most problems (Sharma, McGue, & Benson, 1996).

In general, adopted children and adolescents are more likely to show experience psychological and school-related problems than nonadopted children (Brodzinsky & Pinderhuges, 2002). For example, a recent meta-analysis (a statistical procedure that combines the results of a number of studies) revealed that adoptees were far more likely to be using mental health services than their nonadopted counterparts. (Juffer & van IJzendoorn, 2005). Adopted children also showed more behavior problems than nonadoptees, but this difference was small. A recent large-scale study found that adopted children are more likely to have a learning disability than nonadopted children (Altarac & Saroha, 2007).

Research that contrasts adopted and nonadopted adolescents has also found positive characteristics among the adopted adolescents. For example, in one study, although adopted adolescents were more likely than nonadopted adolescents to use illicit drugs and to engage in delinquent behavior, the adopted adolescents were also less likely to be withdrawn and engaged in more prosocial behavior, such as being altruistic, caring, and supportive of others (Sharma, McGue, & Benson, 1996).

In short, the vast majority of adopted children (including those adopted at older ages, transracially, and across national borders) adjust effectively, and their parents report considerable satisfaction with their decision to adopt (Brodzinsky & Pinderhughes, 2002). In one recent national study, there were no differences in the antisocial behavior of adopted and nonadopted young adults (Grotevant & others, 2006). A recent research review of 88 studies also revealed no difference in the self-esteem of adopted and nonadopted children, as well as no differences between transracial and same-race adoptees (Juffer & van IJzendoorn, 2007). Furthermore, adopted children fare much better than children in long-term foster care or in an institutional environment (Bernard & Dozier, 2008). To read more about adoption, see the *Applications in Life-Span Development* interlude in which we discuss effective parenting strategies with adopted children.

Applications in Life-Span Development
Parenting Adopted Children

Many of the keys to effectively parenting adopted children are no different from those for effectively parenting biological children: Be supportive and caring, be involved and monitor the child's behavior and whereabouts, be a good communicator, and help the child to learn to develop self-control. However, parents of adopted children face some unique circumstances (Fontenot, 2007). These parents need to recognize the differences involved in adoptive family life, communicate about these differences, show respect for the birth family, and support the child's search for self and identity.

David Brodzinsky and Ellen Pinderhughes (2002, pp. 288–292) discussed how to handle some of the challenges that parents face when their adopted children are at different points in development:

- *Infancy.* Researchers have found few differences in the attachment that adopted and non-adopted infants form with their parents, but attachmemt can be compromised "when parents have difficulty in claiming the child as their own either because of unresolved fertility issues, lack of support from family and friends, and/or when their expectations about the child have not been met" p. 288. Competent adoption agencies or counselors can help prospective adoptive parents develop realistic expectations.

- *Early childhood.* Because many children begin to ask where they came from when they are about 4 to 6 years old, this is a natural time to begin to talk in simple ways to children about their adoption status (Warshak, 2007). Some parents (although not as many as in the past) decide not to tell their children about the adoption. This secrecy may create psychological risks for the child if he or she later finds out about the adoption.

What are some strategies for parenting adopted children at different points in their development?

• ***Middle and late childhood.*** During the elementary school years, children begin to express "much more curiosity about their origins: *Where did I come from? What did my birthmother and birthfather look like? Why didn't they keep me? Where are they now? Can I meet them?"* (p. 290). As they grow older, children may become more ambivalent about being adopted and question their adoptive parents' explanations. It is important for adoptive parents to recognize that this ambivalence is normal. Also, problems may come from the desire of adoptive parents to make life too perfect for the adoptive child and to present a perfect image of themselves to the child. The result too often is that adopted children feel that they cannot release any angry feelings and openly discuss problems (Warshak, 2007).

• ***Adolescence.*** Adolescents are likely to develop more abstract and logical thinking, to focus their attention on their bodies, and to search for an identity. These characteristics provide the foundation for adopted adolescents to reflect on their adoption status in more complex ways, to become "preoccupied with the lack of physical resemblance between themselves and others in the family" (p. 291), and to explore how the fact that they were adopted fits into their identity. Adoptive parents "need to be aware of these many complexities and provide teenagers with the support they need to cope with these adoption-related tasks" (p. 292).

Review and Reflect: Learning Goal 3

3 **Identify Some Important Reproductive Challenges and Choices**

REVIEW

• What are some common prenatal diagnostic tests?
• What are some techniques that help infertile people to have children?
• How does adoption affect children's development?

REFLECT

• We discussed a number of studies indicating that adoption is linked with negative outcomes for children. Does that mean that all adopted children have more negative outcomes than all nonadopted children? Explain.

---

4 HEREDITY AND ENVIRONMENT INTERACTION: THE NATURE-NURTURE DEBATE

Behavior Genetics

Shared and Nonshared Environmental Experiences

Conclusions About Heredity-Environment Interaction

Heredity-Environment Correlations

The Epigenetic View

Is it possible to untangle the influence of heredity from that of environment and discover the role of each in producing individual differences in development? When heredity and environment interact, how does heredity influence the environment, and vice versa?

Behavior Genetics

Behavior genetics is the field that seeks to discover the influence of heredity and environment on individual differences in human traits and development (Derks & others, 2008). Note that behavior genetics does not determine the extent to which genetics or the environment affects an individual's traits. Instead, what behavior geneticists try to do is to figure out what is responsible for the differences among people—that is, to what extent do people differ because of differences in genes, environment, or a combination of these. To study the influence of heredity on behavior, behavior geneticists often use either twins or adoption situations (Goldsmith, 2008).

In the most common **twin study**, the behavioral similarity of identical twins (who are genetically identical) is compared with the behavioral similarity of fraternal twins. Recall that although fraternal twins share the same womb, they are no more genetically alike than brothers or sisters. Thus by comparing groups of identical and fraternal twins, behavior geneticists capitalize on the basic knowledge that identical twins are more similar genetically than are fraternal twins (Wood & others, 2008). For example, one study found that conduct problems were more prevalent in identical twins than fraternal twins; the researchers concluded that the study demonstrated an important role for heredity in conduct problems (Scourfield & others, 2004).

However, several issues complicate interpretation of twin studies (Vogler, 2006). For example, perhaps the environments of identical twins are more similar than the environments of fraternal twins. Adults might stress the similarities of identical twins more than those of fraternal twins, and identical twins might perceive themselves as a "set" and play together more than fraternal twins do. If so, the influence of the environment on the observed similarities between identical and fraternal twins might be very significant.

In an **adoption study**, investigators seek to discover whether the behavior and psychological characteristics of adopted children are more like those of their adoptive parents, who have provided a home environment, or more like those of their biological parents, who have contributed their heredity (Loehlin, Horn, & Ernst, 2007). Another form of the adoption study compares adoptive and biological siblings.

Twin studies compare identical twins with fraternal twins. Identical twins develop from a single fertilized egg that splits into two genetically identical organisms. Fraternal twins develop from separate eggs, making them genetically no more similar than nontwin siblings. *What is the nature of the twin study method?*

Heredity-Environment Correlations

The difficulties that researchers encounter when they interpret the results of twin studies and adoption studies reflect the complexities of heredity-environment interaction. Some of these interactions are *heredity-environment correlations*, which means that individuals' genes may influence the types of environments to which they are exposed. In a sense, individuals "inherit" environments that may be related or linked to genetic "propensities." Behavior geneticist Sandra Scarr (1993) described three ways that heredity and environment are correlated (see Figure 2.11):

- **Passive genotype-environment correlations** occur because biological parents, who are genetically related to the child, provide a rearing environment for the child. For example, the parents might have a genetic predisposition to be intelligent and read skillfully. Because they read well and enjoy reading, they provide their children with books to read. The likely outcome is that their children, given their own inherited predispositions from their parents and their book-filled environment, will become skilled readers.

- **Evocative genotype-environment correlations** occur because a child's characteristics elicit certain types of environments. For example, active, smiling children receive more social stimulation than passive, quiet children do. Cooperative, attentive children evoke more pleasant and instructional responses from the adults around them than uncooperative, distractible children do.

behavior genetics The field that seeks to discover the influence of heredity and environment on individual differences in human traits and development.

twin study A study in which the behavioral similarity of identical twins is compared with the behavioral similarity of fraternal twins.

adoption study A study in which investigators seek to discover whether, in behavior and psychological characteristics, adopted children are more like their adoptive parents, who provided a home environment, or more like their biological parents, who contributed their heredity. Another form of the adoption study is to compare adoptive and biological siblings.

passive genotype-environment correlations Correlations that exist when the natural parents, who are genetically related to the child, provide a rearing environment for the child.

evocative genotype-environment correlations Correlations that exist when the child's genotype elicits certain types of physical and social environments.

Heredity-Environment Correlation	Description	Examples
Passive	Children inherit genetic tendencies from their parents, and parents also provide an environment that matches their own genetic tendencies.	Musically inclined parents usually have musically inclined children and they are likely to provide an environment rich in music for their children.
Evocative	The child's genetic tendencies elicit stimulation from the environment that supports a particular trait. Thus genes evoke environmental support.	A happy, outgoing child elicits smiles and friendly responses from others.
Active (niche-picking)	Children actively seek out "niches" in their environment that reflect their own interests and talents and are thus in accord with their genotype.	Libraries, sports fields, and a store with musical instruments are examples of environmental niches children might seek out if they have intellectual interests in books, talent in sports, or musical talents, respectively.

FIGURE 2.11 Exploring Heredity-Environment Correlations

- **Active (niche-picking) genotype-environment correlations** occur when children seek out environments that they find compatible and stimulating. *Niche-picking* refers to finding a setting that is suited to one's abilities. Children select from their surrounding environment some aspect that they respond to, learn about, or ignore. Their active selections of environments are related to their particular genotype. For example, outgoing children tend to seek out social contexts in which to interact with people, whereas shy children don't. Children who are musically inclined are likely to select musical environments in which they can successfully perform their skills. How these "tendencies" come about will be discussed shortly under the topic of the epigenetic view.

Scarr observes that the relative importance of the three genotype-environment correlations changes as children develop from infancy through adolescence. In infancy, much of the environment that children experience is provided by adults. Thus, passive genotype-environment correlations are more common in the lives of infants and young children than they are for older children and adolescents who can extend their experiences beyond the family's influence and create their environments to a greater degree.

Notice that this analysis gives the preeminent role in development to heredity: The analysis describes how heredity may influence the types of environments that children experience. Critics argue that the concept of heredity-environment correlation gives heredity too much of a one-sided influence in determining development because it does not consider the role of prior environmental influences in shaping the correlation itself (Gottlieb, Wahlsten, & Lickliter, 2006). Before considering this criticism and a different view of the heredity-environment linkage, let's take a closer look at how behavior geneticists analyze the environments involved in heredity.

Shared and Nonshared Environmental Experiences

Behavior geneticists have argued that to understand the environment's role in differences between people, we should distinguish between shared and nonshared environments. That is, we should consider experiences that children share in common with other children living in the same home, and experiences that are not shared (Gelhorn & others, 2006).

Shared environmental experiences are siblings' common experiences, such as their parents' personalities or intellectual orientation, the family's socioeconomic status, and the neighborhood in which they live. By contrast, **nonshared environmental experiences** are a child's unique experiences, both within the family and outside the family, that are not shared with a sibling. Even experiences occurring within the family can be part of the "nonshared environment." For example, parents often interact differently with

active (niche-picking) genotype-environment correlations Correlations that exist when children seek out environments they find compatible and stimulating.

shared environmental experiences Siblings' common environmental experiences, such as their parents' personalities and intellectual orientation, the family's socioeconomic status, and the neighborhood in which they live.

nonshared environmental experiences The child's own unique experiences, both within the family and outside the family, that are not shared by another sibling. Thus, experiences occurring within the family can be part of the "nonshared environment."

each sibling, and siblings interact differently with parents. Siblings often have different peer groups, different friends, and different teachers at school.

Behavior geneticist Robert Plomin (2004) has found that shared environment accounts for little of the variation in children's personality or interests. In other words, even though two children live under the same roof with the same parents, their personalities are often very different. Further, Plomin argues that heredity influences the nonshared environments of siblings through the heredity-environment correlations we described earlier (Plomin, DeFries, & Fulker, 2007). For example, a child who has inherited a genetic tendency to be athletic is likely to spend more time in environments related to sports, and a child who has inherited a tendency to be musically inclined is more likely to spend time in environments related to music.

What are the implications of Plomin's interpretation of the role of shared and nonshared environments in development? In the *Nurture Assumption*, Judith Harris (1998) argued that what parents do does not make a difference in their children's and adolescents' behavior. Yell at them. Hug them. Read to them. Ignore them. Harris says it won't influence how they turn out. She argues that genes and peers are far more important than parents in children's and adolescents' development.

Genes and peers do matter, but Harris' descriptions of peer influences do not take into account the complexity of peer contexts and developmental trajectories (Hartup, 1999). In addition, Harris is wrong in saying that parents don't matter. For example, in the early child years parents play an important role in selecting children's peers and indirectly influencing children's development (Baumrind, 1999). A large volume of parenting literature with many research studies documents the importance of parents in children's development (Clarke-Stewart & Dunn, 2006; Grusec & Davidov, 2007; Maccoby, 2007; Parke & others, 2008). We will discuss parents' important roles throughout this book.

Tennis stars Venus and Serena Williams. *What might be some shared and nonshared environmental experiences they had while they were growing up that contributed to their tennis stardom?*

The Epigenetic View

Does the concept of heredity-environment correlation downplay the importance of environment in our development? The concept emphasizes how heredity directs the kind of environmental experiences individuals have. However, earlier in the chapter we discussed how genes are collaborative, not determining an individual's traits in an independent manner, but rather in an interactive manner with the environment. In line with the concept of a collaborative gene, Gilbert Gottlieb (2007) emphasizes the **epigenetic view**, which states that development is the result of an ongoing, bidirectional interchange between heredity and the environment. Figure 2.12 compares the heredity-environment correlation and epigenetic views of development.

Let's look at an example that reflects the epigenetic view. A baby inherits genes from both parents at conception. During prenatal development, toxins, nutrition, and stress can influence some genes to stop functioning while others become stronger or weaker. During infancy, the same environmental experiences such as toxins, nutrition, stress, learning, and encouragement continue to modify genetic activity and the activity of the nervous system that directly underlies behavior. Heredity and environment operate together—or collaborate—to produce a person's intelligence, temperament, height, weight, ability to pitch a baseball, ability to read, and so on (Gottlieb, 2007).

Heredity-Environment Correlation View
Heredity ————▶ Environment

Epigenetic View
Heredity ◀————▶ Environment

FIGURE 2.12 Comparison of the Heredity-Environment Correlation and Epigenetic Views

Conclusions About Heredity-Environment Interaction

If an attractive, popular, intelligent girl is elected president of her senior class in high school, is her success due to heredity or to environment? Of course, the answer is both.

The relative contributions of heredity and environment are not additive. That is, we can't say that such-and-such a percentage of nature and such-and-such a percentage

epigenetic view Emphasizes that development is the result of an ongoing, bidirectional interchange between heredity and environment.

of experience make us who we are. Nor is it accurate to say that full genetic expression happens once, around conception or birth, after which we carry our genetic legacy into the world to see how far it takes us. Genes produce proteins throughout the life span, in many different environments. Or they don't produce these proteins, depending in part on how harsh or nourishing those environments are.

The emerging view is that complex behaviors have some *genetic loading* that gives people a propensity for a particular developmental trajectory (Plomin, DeFries, & Fulker, 2007). However, the actual development requires more: an environment. And that environment is complex, just like the mixture of genes we inherit (Parke & others, 2008). Environmental influences range from the things we lump together under "nurture" (such as parenting, family dynamics, schooling, and neighborhood quality) to biological encounters (such as viruses, birth complications, and even biological events in cells).

Imagine for a moment that there is a cluster of genes somehow associated with youth violence (this example is hypothetical because we don't know of any such combination). The adolescent who carries this genetic mixture might experience a world of loving parents, regular nutritious meals, lots of books, and a series of masterful teachers. Or the adolescent's world might include parental neglect, a neighborhood in which gunshots and crime are everyday occurrences, and inadequate schooling. In which of these environments are the adolescent's genes likely to manufacture the biological underpinnings of criminality?

Review and Reflect: Learning Goal 4

 Explain Some of the Ways That Heredity and Environment Interact to Produce Individual Differences in Development

REVIEW

- What is behavior genetics?
- What are three types of heredity-environment correlations?
- What is meant by the concepts of shared and nonshared environmental experiences?
- What is the epigenetic view of development?
- What conclusions can be reached about heredity-environment interaction?

REFLECT

- Someone tells you that she has analyzed her genetic background and environmental experiences and reached the conclusion that environment definitely has had little influence on her intelligence. What would you say to this person about her ability to make this self-diagnosis?

Biological Beginnings

1 THE EVOLUTIONARY PERSPECTIVE: DISCUSS THE EVOLUTIONARY PERSPECTIVE ON LIFE-SPAN DEVELOPMENT

Natural Selection and Adaptive Behavior

- Natural selection is the process by which those individuals of a species that are best adapted survive and reproduce. Darwin proposed that natural selection fuels evolution. In evolutionary theory, adaptive behavior is behavior that promotes the organism's survival in a natural habitat.

Evolutionary Psychology

- Evolutionary psychology holds that adaptation, reproduction, and "survival of the fittest" are important in shaping behavior. Ideas proposed by evolutionary developmental psychology include the view that an extended childhood period is needed to develop a large brain and learn the complexity of human social communities. According to Baltes, the benefits resulting from evolutionary selection decrease with age mainly because of a decline in reproductive fitness. At the same time, cultural needs increase. Like other theoretical approaches to development, evolutionary psychology has limitations. Bandura rejects "one-sided evolutionism" and argues for a bidirectional link between biology and environment. Biology allows for a broad range of cultural possibilities.

2 GENETIC FOUNDATIONS OF DEVELOPMENT: DESCRIBE WHAT GENES ARE AND HOW THEY INFLUENCE HUMAN DEVELOPMENT

The Collaborative Gene

- Short segments of DNA constitute genes, the units of hereditary information that direct cells to reproduce and manufacture proteins. Genes act collaboratively, not independently.

Genes and Chromosomes

- Genes are passed on to new cells when chromosomes are duplicated during the process of mitosis and meiosis, which are two ways in which new cells are formed. When an egg and a sperm unite in the fertilization process, the resulting zygote contains the genes from the chromosomes in the father's sperm and the mother's egg. Despite this transmission of genes from generation to generation, variability is created in several ways, including the exchange of chromosomal segments during meiosis, mutations, and the distinction between a genotype and a phenotype.

Genetic Principles

- Genetic principles include those involving dominant-recessive genes, sex-linked genes, genetic imprinting, and polygenic inheritance.

Chromosomal and Gene-Linked Abnormalities

- Chromosomal abnormalities produce Down syndrome, which is caused by the presence of an extra copy of chromosome 21, as well as sex-linked chromosomal abnormalities such as Klinefelter syndrome, fragile X syndrome, Turner syndrome, and XYY syndrome. Gene-linked abnormalities involve harmful genes. Gene-linked disorders include phenylketonuria (PKU) and sickle-cell anemia. Genetic counseling offers couples information about their risk of having a child with inherited abnormalities.

3 REPRODUCTIVE CHALLENGES AND CHOICES: IDENTIFY SOME IMPORTANT REPRODUCTIVE CHALLENGES AND CHOICES

Prenatal Diagnostic Tests

- Ultrasound sonography, fetal MRI, chorionic villus sampling, amniocentesis, and maternal blood screening are used to determine whether a fetus is developing normally. Noninvasive prenatal diagnosis is increasingly being Explored.

Infertility and Reproductive Technology

- Approximately 10 to 15 percent of U.S. couples have infertility problems, some of which can be corrected through surgery or fertility drugs. An additional option is in vitro fertilization.

Adoption

- Although adopted children and adolescents have more problems than their nonadopted counterparts, the vast majority of adopted children adapt effectively. When adoption occurs very early in development, the outcomes for the child are improved. Because of the dramatic changes that occurred in adoption in recent decades, it is difficult to generalize about the average adopted child or average adoptive family.

4 HEREDITY AND ENVIRONMENT INTERACTION: THE NATURE-NURTURE DEBATE: EXPLAIN SOME OF THE WAYS THAT HEREDITY AND ENVIRONMENT INTERACT TO PRODUCE INDIVIDUAL DIFFERENCES IN DEVELOPMENT

Behavior Genetics

- Behavior genetics is the field concerned with the influence of heredity and environment on individual differences in human traits and development. Methods used by behavior geneticists include twin studies and adoption studies.

Heredity-Environment Correlations

- In Scarr's heredity-environment correlations view, heredity directs the types of environments that children experience. She describes three genotype-environment correlations: passive, evocative, and active (niche-picking). Scarr argues that the relative importance of these three genotype-environment correlations changes as children develop.

Shared and Nonshared Environmental Experiences

- Shared environmental experiences refer to siblings' common experiences, such as their parents' personalities and intellectual orientation, the family's socioeconomic status, and the neighborhood in which they live. Nonshared environmental experiences involve the child's unique experiences, both within a family and outside a family, that are not shared with a sibling. Many behavior geneticists argue that differences in the development of siblings are due to nonshared environmental experiences (and heredity) rather than shared environmental experiences.

The Epigenetic View

- The epigenetic view emphasizes that development is the result of an ongoing, bidirectional interchange between heredity and environment.

Conclusions About Heredity-Environment Interaction

- Complex behaviors have some genetic loading that gives people a propensity for a particular developmental trajectory. However, actual development also requires an environment, and that environment is complex. The interaction of heredity and environment is extensive. Much remains to be discovered about the specific ways that heredity and environment interact to influence development.

KEY TERMS

evolutionary psychology 53
chromosomes 56
DNA 56
genes 56
mitosis 57
meiosis 57
fertilization 57
zygote 57
genotype 58

phenotype 58
Down syndrome 60
Klinefelter syndrome 60
fragile X syndrome 60
Turner syndrome 60
XYY syndrome 60
phenylketonuria (PKU) 60
sickle-cell anemia 61
behavior genetics 69

twin study 69
adoption study 69
passive genotype-
  environment
  correlations 69
evocative genotype-
  environment
  correlations 69

active (niche-picking)
  genotype-environment
  correlations 70
shared environmental
  experiences 70
nonshared environmental
  experiences 70
epigenetic view 71

KEY PEOPLE

Thomas Bouchard 52
Charles Darwin 53
David Buss 53

Paul Baltes 54
Albert Bandura 55
Steven Jay Gould 55

David Moore 56
Sandra Scarr 69
Robert Plomin 71

Judith Harris 71
Gilbert Gottlieb 71

E-LEARNING TOOLS

To help you master the material in this chapter, visit the Online Learning Center for *Life-Span Development,* twelfth edition, at **www.mhhe.com/santrockld12**.

Self-Assessment

Connect to **www.mhhe.com/santrockld12** to learn more about how genetic screening is done by reviewing the sample assessment, *Prenatal Genetic Screening Questionnaire.* Then try your hand at developing a family health tree by completing the self-assessment, *My Family Health Tree.*

Taking It to the Net

Connect to **www.mhhe.com/santrockld12** to research the answers to these questions:

1. Ahmahl, a biochemistry major, is writing a psychology paper on the potential dilemmas that society and scientists may face as a result of the decoding of the human genome. What are some of the main issues or concerns that Ahmahl should address in his class paper?

2. Brandon and Katie are thrilled to learn that they are expecting their first child. They are curious about the genetic makeup of their unborn child and want to know (a) what disorders might be identified through prenatal genetic testing; and (b) which tests, if any, Katie should undergo to help determine this information?

3. Greg and Courtney have three boys. They would love to have a girl. Courtney read that there is a clinic in Virginia where you can pick the sex of your child. How successful are such efforts? Would you want to have this choice available to you?

Video Clips

The Online Learning Center includes video clips of key researchers, including David Buss as he discusses the importance of evolutionary psychology.

Health and Well-Being, Parenting, and Education Exercises

Build your decision-making skills by trying your hand at the health and well-being, parenting, and education exercises. Connect to **www.mhhe.com/santrockld12** to research the answers and complete the exercises.

3

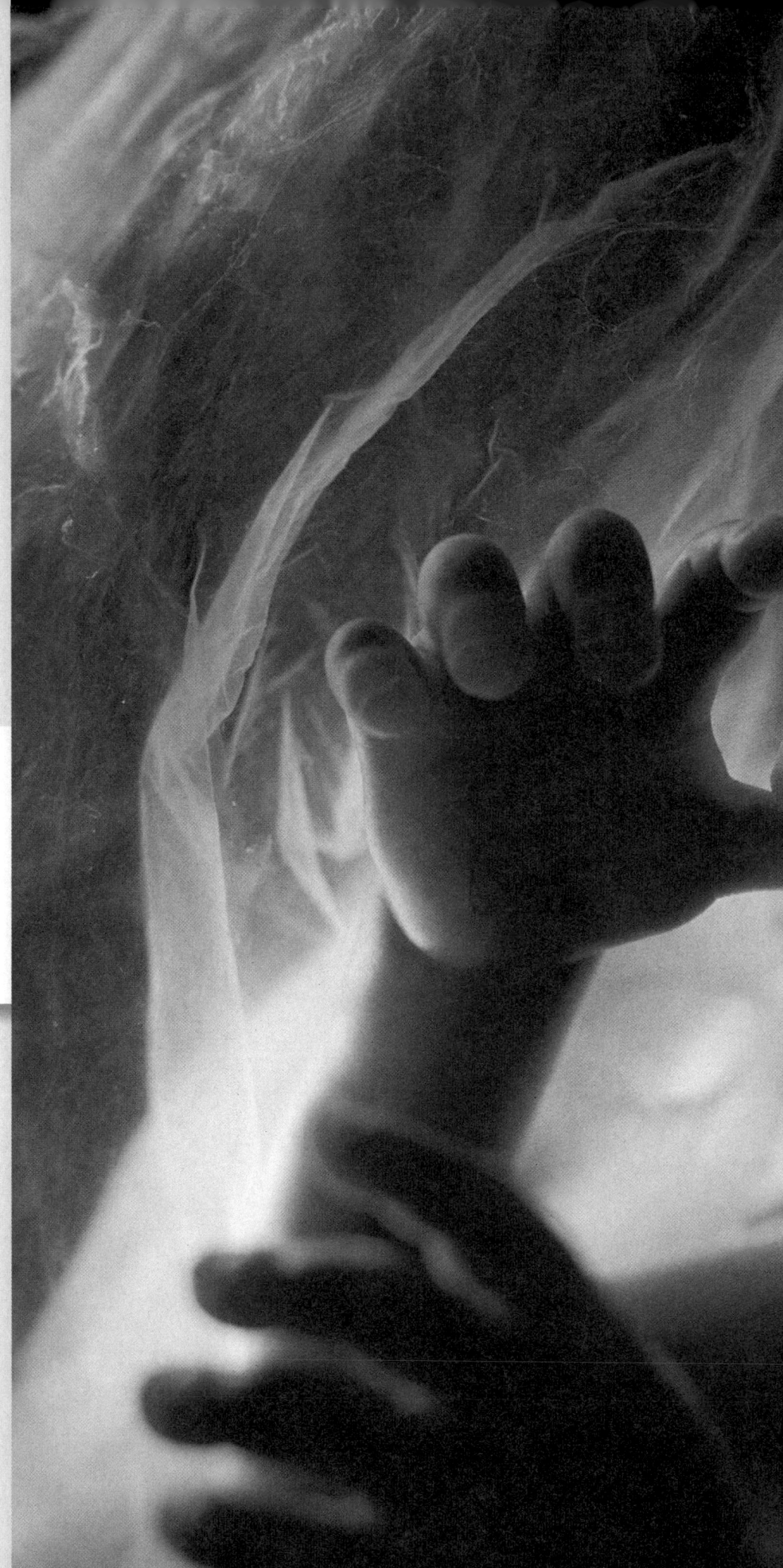

There was a star danced, and under that I was born.

—William Shakespeare
English Playwright, 17th Century

LEARNING GOALS

- ◆ Describe prenatal development.

- ◆ Discuss the birth process.

- ◆ Explain the changes that take place in the postpartum period.

PRENATAL DEVELOPMENT AND BIRTH

CHAPTER OUTLINE

1 PRENATAL DEVELOPMENT

The Course of Prenatal Development

Teratology and Hazards to Prenatal Development

Prenatal Care

Normal Prenatal Development

2 BIRTH

The Birth Process

Assessing the Newborn

Preterm and Low Birth Weight Infants

3 THE POSTPARTUM PERIOD

Physical Adjustments

Emotional and Psychological Adjustments

Bonding

Images of Life-Span Development
The Story of Mr. Littles

Diana and Roger married when he was 38 and she was 34. Both worked full-time and were excited when Diana became pregnant. Two months later, Diana began to have some unusual pains and bleeding. Just two months into her pregnancy she had lost the baby. Diana thought deeply about why she was unable to carry the baby to full term. It was about the time she became pregnant that the federal government began to warn that eating certain types of fish with a high mercury content during pregnancy on a regular basis can cause a miscarriage. Now she eliminated these fish from her diet.

Six months later, Diana became pregnant again. She and Roger read about pregnancy and signed up for birth preparation classes. Each Friday night for eight weeks they practiced simulated contractions. They talked about what kind of parents they wanted to be and discussed what changes in their lives the baby would make. When they found out that their offspring was going to be a boy, they gave him a name: Mr. Littles.

This time, Diana's pregnancy went well, and Alex, also known as Mr. Littles, was born. During the birth, however, Diana's heart rate dropped precipitously, and she was given a stimulant to raise it. Apparently the stimulant also increased Alex's heart rate and breathing to a dangerous point, and he had to be placed in a neonatal intensive care unit (NICU).

Several times a day, Diana and Roger visited Alex in the NICU. A number of babies in the NICU who had a very low birth weight had been in intensive care for weeks, and some of these babies were not doing well. Fortunately, Alex was in better health. After several days in the NICU, his parents were permitted to take home a very healthy Alex.

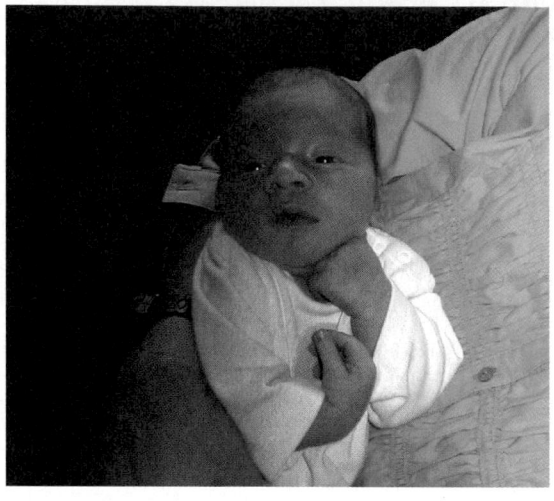

Alex, also known as "Mr. Littles."

PREVIEW

This chapter chronicles the truly remarkable developments from conception through birth. Imagine . . . at one time you were an organism floating in a sea of fluid in your mother's womb. Let's now explore what your development was like from the time you were conceived through the time you were born.

---

1 PRENATAL DEVELOPMENT

The Course of Prenatal Development **Teratology and Hazards to Prenatal Development** **Prenatal Care** **Normal Prenatal Development**

Imagine how Alex ("Mr. Littles") came to be. Out of thousands of eggs and millions of sperm, one egg and one sperm united to produce him. Had the union of sperm and egg come a day or even an hour earlier or later, he might have been very different—maybe even of the opposite sex. *Conception* occurs when a single sperm cell from the male unites with an ovum (egg) in the female's fallopian tube in a process called fertilization. Over the next few months, the genetic code discussed in Chapter 2 directs a series of changes in the fertilized egg, but many events and hazards will influence how that egg develops and becomes tiny Alex.

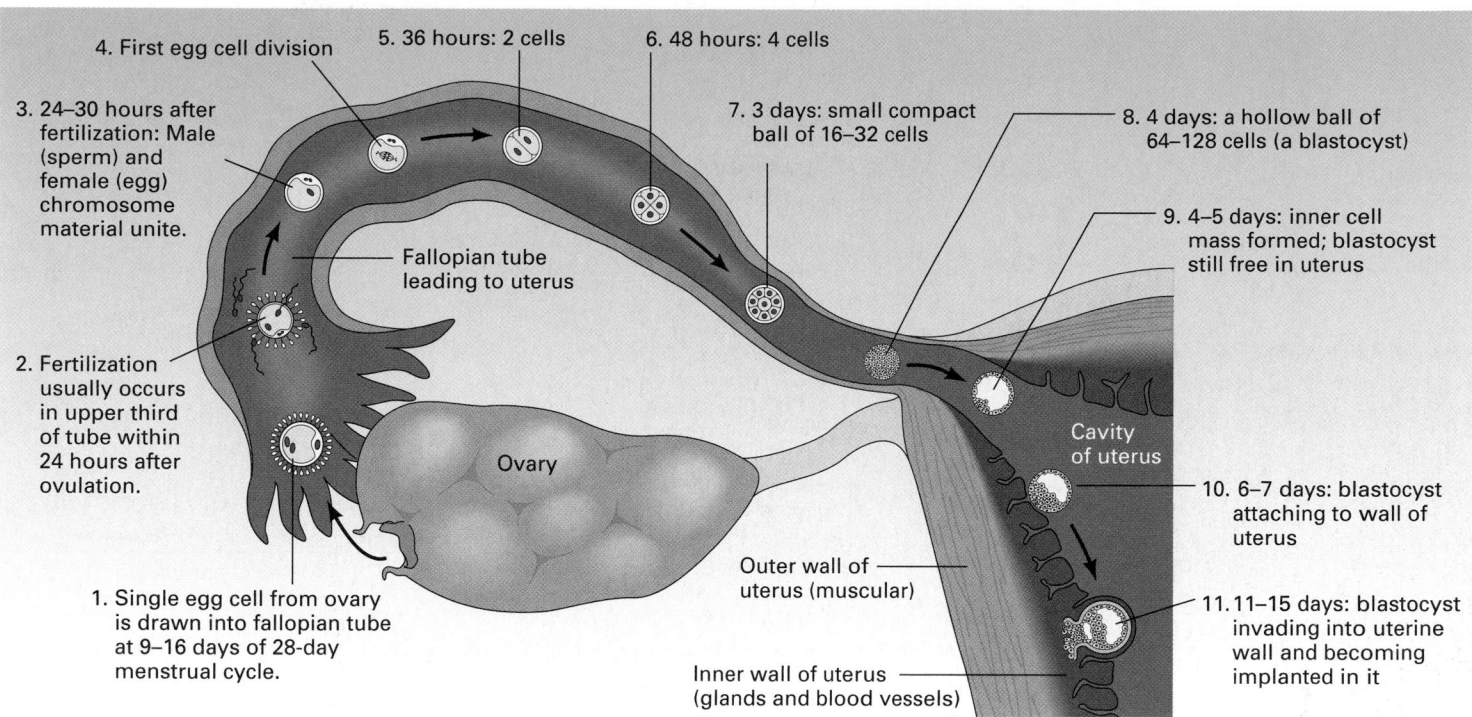

4. First egg cell division

5. 36 hours: 2 cells

6. 48 hours: 4 cells

3. 24–30 hours after fertilization: Male (sperm) and female (egg) chromosome material unite.

7. 3 days: small compact ball of 16–32 cells

8. 4 days: a hollow ball of 64–128 cells (a blastocyst)

Fallopian tube leading to uterus

9. 4–5 days: inner cell mass formed; blastocyst still free in uterus

2. Fertilization usually occurs in upper third of tube within 24 hours after ovulation.

Ovary

Cavity of uterus

10. 6–7 days: blastocyst attaching to wall of uterus

1. Single egg cell from ovary is drawn into fallopian tube at 9–16 days of 28-day menstrual cycle.

Outer wall of uterus (muscular)

11. 11–15 days: blastocyst invading into uterine wall and becoming implanted in it

Inner wall of uterus (glands and blood vessels)

FIGURE 3.1 Significant Developments in the Germinal Period. Just one week after conception, cells of the blastocyst have already begun specializing. The germination period ends when the blastocyst attaches to the uterine wall. *Which of the steps shown in the drawing occur in the laboratory when IVF (described in Chapter 2) is used?*

The Course of Prenatal Development

Typical prenatal development begins with fertilization and ends with birth, lasting between 266 and 280 days (from 38 to 40 weeks). It can be divided into three periods: germinal, embryonic, and fetal.

The Germinal Period

The **germinal period** is the period of prenatal development that takes place in the first two weeks after conception. It includes the creation of the fertilized egg, called a zygote, cell division, and the attachment of the zygote to the uterine wall.

Rapid cell division by the zygote continues throughout the germinal period (recall from Chapter 2 that this cell divison occurs through a process called *mitosis*). By approximately one week after conception, the differentiation of these cells—their specialization for different tasks—has already begun. At this stage, the group of cells, now called the **blastocyst**, consists of an inner mass of cells that will eventually develop into the embryo, and the **trophoblast**, an outer layer of cells that later provides nutrition and support for the embryo. *Implantation*, the attachment of the zygote to the uterine wall, takes place about 11 to 15 days after conception. Figure 3.1 illustrates some of the most significant developments during the germinal period.

The Embryonic Period

The **embryonic period** is the period of prenatal development that occurs from two to eight weeks after conception. During the embryonic period, the rate of cell differentiation intensifies, support systems for cells form, and organs appear.

This period begins as the blastocyst attaches to the uterine wall. The mass of cells is now called an *embryo*, and three layers of cells form. The embryo's *endoderm* is the inner layer of cells, which will develop into the digestive and respiratory systems. The *mesoderm* is the middle layer, which will become the circulatory system, bones, muscles,

germinal period The period of prenatal development that takes place in the first two weeks after conception. It includes the creation of the zygote, continued cell division, and the attachment of the zygote to the uterine wall.

blastocyst The inner layer of cells that develops during the germinal period. These cells later develop into the embryo.

trophoblast The outer layer of cells that develops in the germinal period. These cells provide nutrition and support for the embryo.

embryonic period The period of prenatal development that occurs two to eight weeks after conception. During the embryonic period, the rate of cell differentiation intensifies, support systems for the cells form, and organs appear.

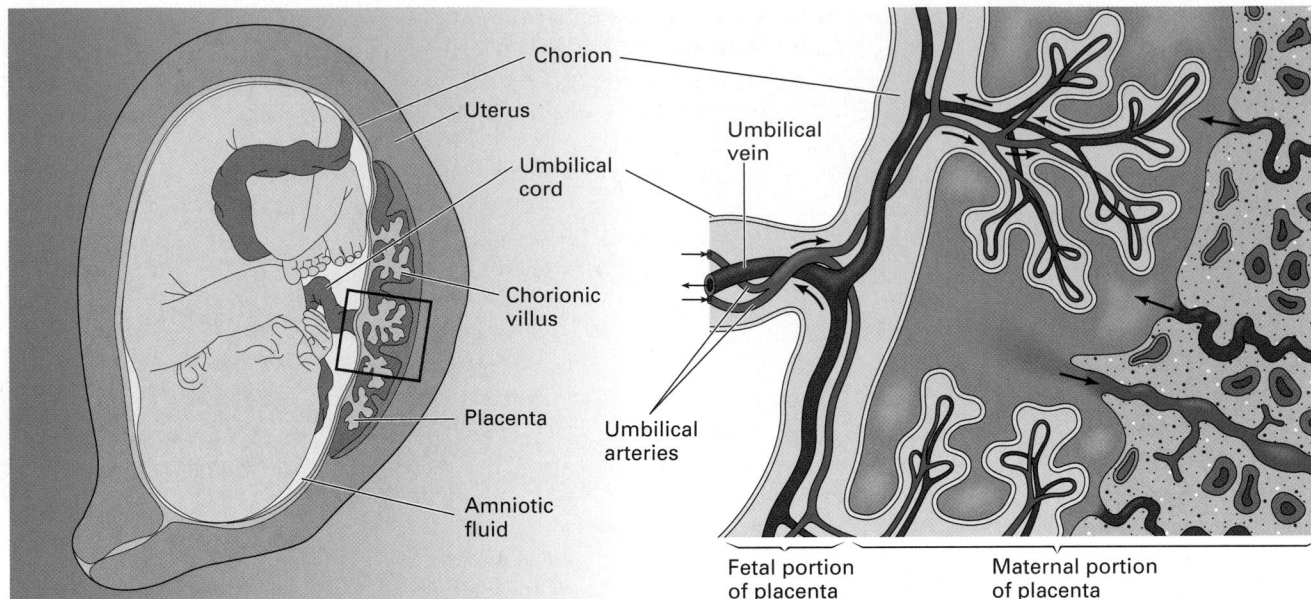

FIGURE 3.2 The Placenta and the Umbilical Cord. The area bound by the square is enlarged in the right half of the illustration. Arrows indicate the direction of blood flow. Maternal blood flows through the uterine arteries to the spaces housing the placenta, and it returns through the uterine veins to the maternal circulation. Fetal blood flows through the umbilical arteries into the capillaries of the placenta and returns through the umbilical vein to the fetal circulation. The exchange of materials takes place across the layer separating the maternal and fetal blood supplies, so the bloods never come into contact. *What is known about how the placental barrier works and its importance?*

excretory system, and reproductive system. The *ectoderm* is the outermost layer, which will become the nervous system and brain, sensory receptors (ears, nose, and eyes, for example), and skin parts (hair and nails, for example). Every body part eventually develops from these three layers. The endoderm primarily produces internal body parts, the mesoderm primarily produces parts that surround the internal areas, and the ectoderm primarily produces surface parts.

As the embryo's three layers form, life-support systems for the embryo develop rapidly. These life-support systems include the amnion, the umbilical cord (both of which develop from the fertilized egg, not the mother's body), and the placenta. The **amnion** is like a bag or an envelope and contains a clear fluid in which the developing embryo floats. The amniotic fluid provides an environment that is temperature and humidity controlled, as well as shockproof. The **umbilical cord** contains two arteries and one vein, and connects the baby to the placenta. The **placenta** consists of a disk-shaped group of tissues in which small blood vessels from the mother and the offspring intertwine but do not join.

Figure 3.2 illustrates the placenta, the umbilical cord, and the blood flow in the expectant mother and developing organism. Very small molecules—oxygen, water, salt, food from the mother's blood, as well as carbon dioxide and digestive wastes from the offspring's blood—pass back and forth between the mother and embryo or fetus. Large molecules cannot pass through the placental wall; these include red blood cells and harmful substances, such as most bacteria, maternal wastes, and hormones. The mechanisms that govern the transfer of substances across the placental barrier are complex and are still not entirely understood (Klieger, Pollex, & Koren, 2008; Nanovskaya & others, 2008).

By the time most women know they are pregnant, the major organs have begun to form. **Organogenesis** is the name given to the process of organ formation during the first two months of prenatal development. While they are being formed, the organs are especially vulnerable to environmental changes (Mullis & Tonella, 2008). In the third week after conception, the neural tube that eventually becomes the spinal cord forms. At about 21 days, eyes begin to appear, and at 24 days the cells for the

amnion The life-support system that is a bag or envelope that contains a clear fluid in which the developing embryo floats.

umbilical cord A life-support system containing two arteries and one vein that connects the baby to the placenta.

placenta A life-support system that consists of a disk-shaped group of tissues in which small blood vessels from the mother and offspring intertwine.

organogenesis Organ formation that takes place during the first two months of prenatal development.

heart begin to differentiate. During the fourth week, the urogenital system becomes apparent, and arm and leg buds emerge. Four chambers of the heart take shape, and blood vessels appear. From the fifth to the eighth week, arms and legs differentiate further; at this time, the face starts to form but still is not very recognizable. The intestinal tract develops and the facial structures fuse. At eight weeks, the developing organism weighs about 1/30 ounce and is just over 1 inch long.

The Fetal Period   The **fetal period**, lasting about seven months, is the prenatal period between two months after conception and birth in typical pregnancies. Growth and development continue their dramatic course during this time.

Three months after conception, the fetus is about 3 inches long and weighs about 3 ounces. It has become active, moving its arms and legs, opening and closing its mouth, and moving its head. The face, forehead, eyelids, nose, and chin are distinguishable, as are the upper arms, lower arms, hands, and lower limbs. In most cases, the genitals can be identified as male or female. By the end of the fourth month of pregnancy, the fetus has grown to 6 inches in length and weighs 4 to 7 ounces. At this time, a growth spurt occurs in the body's lower parts. For the first time, the mother can feel arm and leg movements.

By the end of the fifth month, the fetus is about 12 inches long and weighs close to a pound. Structures of the skin have formed—toenails and fingernails, for example. The fetus is more active, showing a preference for a particular position in the womb. By the end of the sixth month, the fetus is about 14 inches long and has gained another half pound to a pound. The eyes and eyelids are completely formed, and a fine layer of hair covers the head. A grasping reflex is present and irregular breathing movements occur.

As early as six months of pregnancy (about 24 to 25 weeks after conception), the fetus for the first time has a chance of surviving outside of the womb—that is, it is *viable* (Hernandez-Reif, 2007). Infants are born early, or between 24 and 37 weeks of pregnancy, usually need help breathing because their lungs are not yet fully mature. By the end of the seventh month, the fetus is about 16 inches long and now weighs about 3 pounds.

During the last two months of prenatal development, fatty tissues develop, and the functioning of various organ systems—heart and kidneys, for example—steps up. During the eighth and ninth months, the fetus grows longer and gains substantial weight—about another 4 pounds. At birth, the average American baby weighs $7\frac{1}{2}$ pounds and is about 20 inches long.

Figure 3.3 gives an overview of the main events during prenatal development. Notice that instead of describing development in terms of germinal, embryonic, and fetal periods, Figure 3.3 divides prenatal development into equal periods of three months, called *trimesters*. Remember that the three trimesters are not the same as the three prenatal periods we have discussed. The germinal and embryonic periods occur in the first trimester. The fetal period begins toward the end of the first trimester and continues through the second and third trimesters. Viability (the chances of surviving outside the womb) occurs at the very end of the second trimester.

The Brain   One of the most remarkable aspects of the prenatal period is the development of the brain (Fair & Schlaggar, 2008; Nelson, 2009). By the time babies are born, they have approximately 100 billion **neurons**, or nerve cells, which handle information processing at the cellular level in the brain. During prenatal development, neurons spend time moving to the right locations and are starting to become connected. The basic architecture of the human brain is assembled during the first two trimesters of prenatal development. In typical development, the third trimester of prenatal development and the first two years of postnatal life are characterized by connectivity and functioning of neurons (Moulson & Nelson, 2008).

As the human embryo develops inside its mother's womb, the nervous system begins forming as a long, hollow tube located on the embryo's back. This pear-shaped

> *The history of man for nine months preceding his birth would, probably, be far more interesting, and contain events of greater moment than all three score and ten years that follow it.*
>
> —SAMUEL TAYLOR COLERIDGE
> *English Poet, Essayist, 19th Century*

fetal period Lasting about seven months, the prenatal period between two months after conception and birth in typical pregnancies.

neurons Nerve cells, which handle information processing at the cellular level in the brain.

First trimester (first 3 months)

Prenatal growth

Conception to 4 weeks

- Is less than $1/10$ inch long
- Beginning development of spinal cord, nervous system, gastrointestinal system, heart, and lungs
- Amniotic sac envelopes the preliminary tissues of entire body
- Is called a "zygote"

8 weeks

- Is just over 1 inch long
- Face is forming with rudimentary eyes, ears, mouth, and tooth buds
- Arms and legs are moving
- Brain is forming
- Fetal heartbeat is detectable with ultrasound
- Is called an "embryo"

12 weeks

- Is about 3 inches long and weighs about 1 ounce
- Can move arms, legs, fingers, and toes
- Fingerprints are present
- Can smile, frown, suck, and swallow
- Sex is distinguishable
- Can urinate
- Is called a "fetus"

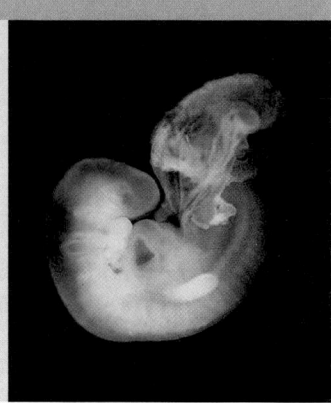

Second trimester (middle 3 months)

Prenatal growth

16 weeks

- Is about 6 inches long and weighs about 4 to 7 ounces
- Heartbeat is strong
- Skin is thin, transparent
- Downy hair (lanugo) covers body
- Fingernails and toenails are forming
- Has coordinated movements; is able to roll over in amniotic fluid

20 weeks

- Is about 12 inches long and weighs close to 1 pound
- Heartbeat is audible with ordinary stethoscope
- Sucks thumb
- Hiccups
- Hair, eyelashes, eyebrows are present

24 weeks

- Is about 14 inches long and weighs 1 to $1\frac{1}{2}$ pounds
- Skin is wrinkled and covered with protective coating (vernix caseosa)
- Eyes are open
- Waste matter is collected in bowel
- Has strong grip

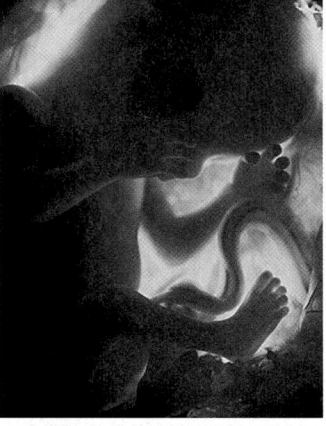

Third trimester (last 3 months)

Prenatal growth

28 weeks

- Is about 16 inches long and weighs about 3 pounds
- Is adding body fat
- Is very active
- Rudimentary breathing movements are present

32 weeks

- Is $16\frac{1}{2}$ to 18 inches long and weighs 4 to 5 pounds
- Has periods of sleep and wakefulness
- Responds to sounds
- May assume the birth position
- Bones of head are soft and flexible
- Iron is being stored in liver

36 to 38 weeks

- Is 19 to 20 inches long and weighs 6 to $7\frac{1}{2}$ pounds
- Skin is less wrinkled
- Vernix caseosa is thick
- Lanugo is mostly gone
- Is less active
- Is gaining immunities from mother

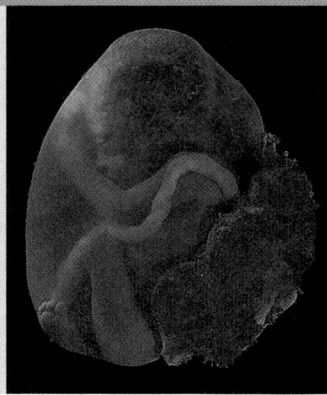

FIGURE 3.3 The Three Trimesters of Prenatal Development. Both the germinal and embryonic periods occur during the first trimester. The end of the first trimester as well as the second and third trimesters are part of the fetal period.

neural tube, which forms at about 18 to 24 days after conception, develops out of the ectoderm. The tube closes at the top and bottom ends at about 24 days after conception. Figure 3.4 shows that the nervous system still has a tubular appearance six weeks after conception.

Two birth defects related to a failure of the neural tube to close are anencephaly and spina bifida. The highest regions of the brain fail to develop when fetuses have anencephaly or when the head end of neural tube fails to close, and they die in the womb, during childbirth, or shortly after birth (Koukoura & others, 2006). Spina bifida results in varying degrees of paralysis of the lower limbs. Individuals with spina bifida usually need assistive devices such as crutches, braces, or wheelchairs. A strategy that can help to prevent neural tube defects is for women to take adequate amounts of the B vitamin folic acid, a topic we will further discuss later in the chapter (Johnston, 2008; Ryan-Harshman & Aldoori, 2008).

In a normal pregnancy, once the neural tube has closed, a massive proliferation of new immature neurons begins to takes place about the fifth prenatal week and continues throughout the remainder of the prenatal period. The generation of new neurons is called *neurogenesis*. At the peak of neurogenesis, it is estimated that as many as 200,000 neurons are being generated every minute.

At approximately 6 to 24 weeks after conception, *neuronal migration* occurs (Nelson, 2009). This involves cells moving outward from their point of origin to their appropriate locations and creating the different levels, structures, and regions of the brain (Hepper, 2007). Once a cell has migrated to its target destination, it must mature and develop a more complex structure.

At about the 23rd prenatal week, connections between neurons begin to occur, a process that continues postnatally (Moulson & Nelson, 2008). We will have much more to say about the structure of neurons, their connectivity, and the development of the infant brain in Chapter 4.

Teratology and Hazards to Prenatal Development

For Alex, the baby discussed at the opening of this chapter, the course of prenatal development went smoothly. His mother's womb protected him as he developed. Despite this protection, the environment can affect the embryo or fetus in many well-documented ways.

General Principles A **teratogen** is any agent that can potentially cause a birth defect or negatively alter cognitive and behavioral outcomes. (The word comes from the Greek word *tera,* meaning "monster.") The field of study that investigates the causes of birth defects is called *teratology.* Teratogens include drugs, incompatible blood types, environmental pollutants, infectious diseases, nutritional deficiencies, maternal stress, advanced maternal and paternal age, and environmental pollutants. In fact, thousands of babies are born deformed or mentally retarded every year as a result of events that occurred in the mother's life as early as one or two months *before* conception. As we further discuss teratogens, you will see that factors related to the father also can influence prenatal development.

So many teratogens exist that practically every fetus is exposed to at least some teratogens. For this reason, it is difficult to determine which teratogen causes which problem. In addition, it may take a long time for the effects of a teratogen to show up. Only about half of all potential effects appear at birth.

The dose, genetic susceptibility, and the time of exposure to a particular teratogen influence both the severity of the damage to an embryo or fetus and the type of defect:

- *Dose.* The dose effect is rather obvious—the greater the dose of an agent, such as a drug, the greater the effect.
- *Genetic susceptibility.* The type or severity of abnormalities caused by a teratogen is linked to the genotype of the pregnant woman and the genotype of the embryo or fetus (Lidral & Murray, 2005). For example, how a mother metabolizes a particular drug can influence the degree to which the drug effects are transmitted to the embryo or fetus. Differences in placental membranes and placental transport also affect exposure. The extent to which an embryo or fetus is vulnerable to a teratogen may also depend on its genotype (Graham & Shaw, 2006).

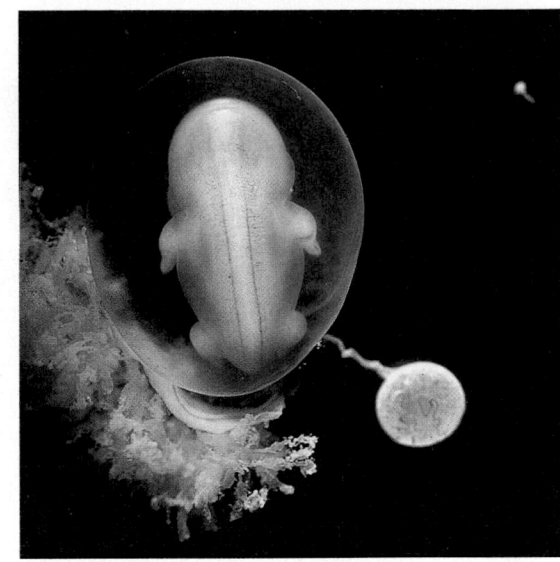

FIGURE 3.4 Early Formation of the Nervous System. The photograph shows the primitive, tubular appearance of the nervous system at six weeks in the human embryo.

These individuals are members of the Spina Bifida Association of Greater New Orleans. The association is made up of parents, family members, children, and adults with spina bifida, and health professionals who provide care for individuals born with spina bifida and their families.

teratogen From the Greek word *tera,* meaning "monster." Any agent that causes a birth defect. The field of study that investigates the causes of birth defects is called teratology.

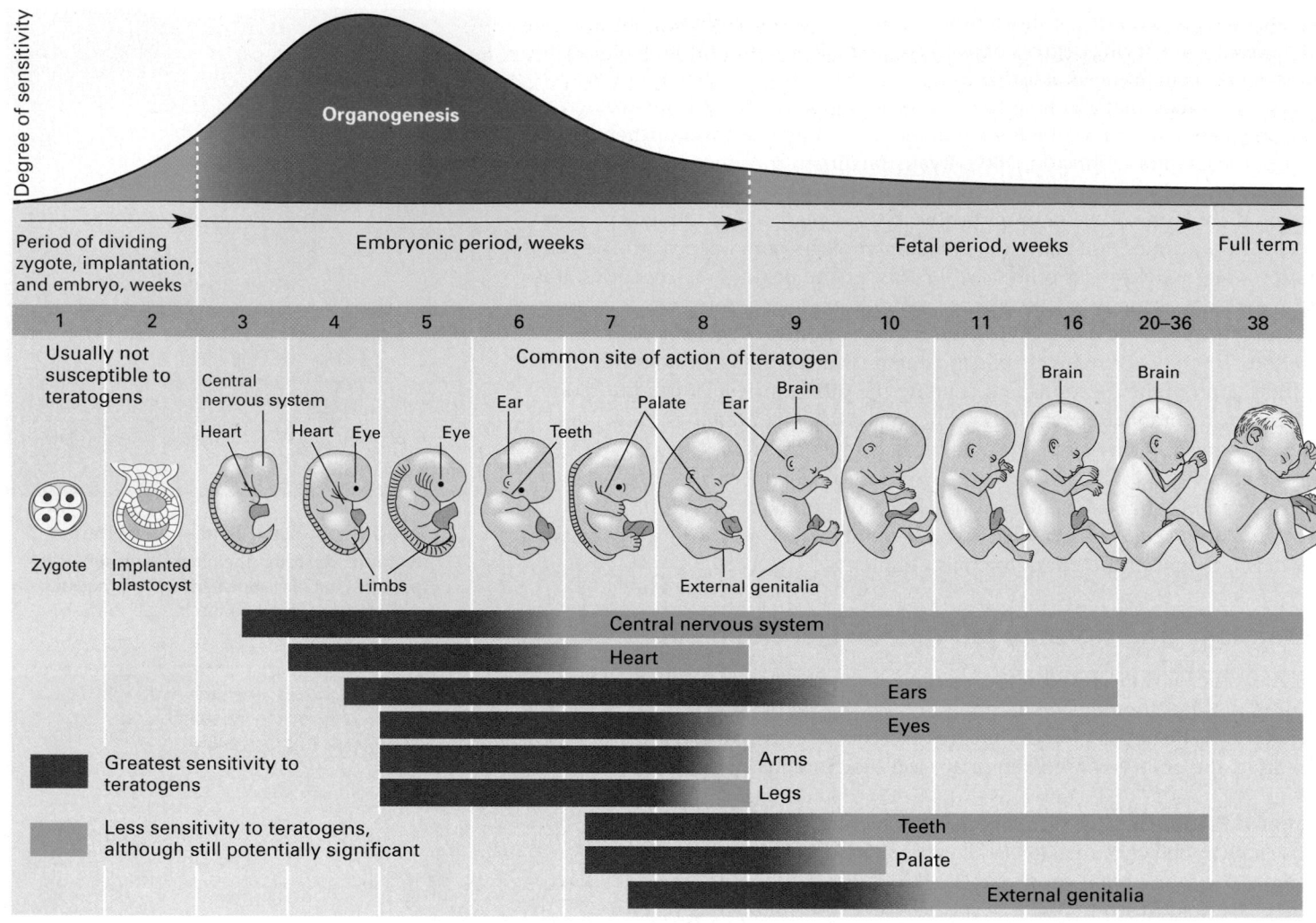

FIGURE 3.5 Teratogens and the Timing of Their Effects on Prenatal Development. The danger of structural defects caused by teratogens is greatest early in embryonic development. The period of organogenesis (red color) lasts for about six weeks. Later assaults by teratogens (blue-green color) mainly occur in the fetal period and instead of causing structural damage are more likely to stunt growth or cause problems of organ function.

- *Time of exposure.* Teratogens do more damage when they occur at some points in development than at others (Nava-Ocampo & Koren, 2007; Rifas-Shiman & others, 2006). Damage during the germinal period may even prevent implantation. In general, the embryonic period is more vulnerable than the fetal period.

Figure 3.5 summarizes additional information about the effects of time of exposure to a teratogen. The probability of a structural defect is greatest early in the embryonic period, when organs are being formed (Hill, 2007). Each body structure has its own critical period of formation. Recall from Chapter 1 that a *critical period* is a fixed time period very early in development during which certain experiences or events can have a long-lasting effect on development. The critical period for the nervous system (week 3) is earlier than for arms and legs (weeks 4 and 5).

After organogenesis is complete, teratogens are less likely to cause anatomical defects. Instead, exposure during the fetal period is more likely instead to stunt growth or to create problems in the way organs function. To examine some key teratogens and their effects, let's begin with drugs.

Prescription and Nonprescription Drugs Many U.S. women are given prescriptions for drugs while they are pregnant—especially antibiotics, analgesics, and asthma medications (Riley & others, 2005). Prescription as well as nonprescription drugs, however, may have effects on the embryo or fetus that the women never imagine.

Prescription drugs that can function as teratogens include antibiotics, such as streptomycin and tetracycline; some antidepressants; certain hormones, such as progestin and synthetic estrogen; and Accutane (which often is prescribed for acne) (Garcia-Bournissen & others, 2008). Nonprescription drugs that can be harmful include diet pills and aspirin (Norgard & others, 2006). A recent research review indicated that low doses of aspirin pose no harm for the fetus but that high doses can contribute to maternal and fetal bleeding (James, Brancazio, & Price, 2008).

Psychoactive Drugs *Psychoactive drugs* are drugs that act on the nervous system to alter states of consciousness, modify perceptions, and change moods. Examples include caffeine, alcohol, and nicotine, as well as illicit drugs such as cocaine, methamphetamine, marijuana, and heroin.

Caffeine People often consume caffeine by drinking coffee, tea, or colas, or by eating chocolate. A recent study revealed that pregnant women who consumed 200 or more milligrams of caffeine a day had an increased risk of miscarriage (Weng, Odouli, & Li, 2008). Taking into account such results, the Food and Drug Administration recommends that pregnant women either not consume caffeine or consume it only sparingly.

Alcohol Heavy drinking by pregnant women can be devastating to offspring. **Fetal alcohol spectrum disorders (FASD)** are a cluster of abnormalities and problems that appear in the offspring of mothers who drink alcohol heavily during pregnancy (Olson, King, & Jirikowic, 2008). The abnormalities include facial deformities and defective limbs, face, and heart. Most children with FASD have learning problems and many are below average in intelligence with some that are mentally retarded (Caley & others, 2008; Cuzon & others, 2008). Although many mothers of FASD infants are heavy drinkers, many mothers who are heavy drinkers do not have children with FASD or have one child with FASD and other children who do not have it.

Drinking alcohol during pregnancy, however, can have serious effects on offspring even when they are not afflicted with FASD (Pollard, 2007; Sayal & others, 2007). Serious malformations, such as those produced by FASD are not found in infants born to mothers who are moderate drinkers, but even moderate drinking can have a negative effect on the offspring.

What are some guidelines for alcohol use during pregnancy? Even drinking just one or two servings of beer or wine or one serving of hard liquor a few days a week can have negative effects on the fetus, although it is generally agreed that this level of alcohol use will not cause fetal alcohol syndrome. The U.S. Surgeon General recommends that *no* alcohol be consumed during pregnancy. And research suggests that it may not be wise to consume alcohol at the time of conception. One study revealed that intakes of alcohol by both men and women during the weeks of conception increased the risk of early pregnancy loss (Henriksen & others, 2004).

Nicotine Cigarette smoking by pregnant women can also adversely influence prenatal development, birth, and postnatal development (Cooper & Moley, 2008). Preterm births and low birth weights, fetal and neonatal deaths, respiratory problems and sudden infant death syndrome (SIDS, also known as crib death) are all more common among the offspring of mothers who smoked during pregnancy (Henderson, 2008; Landau, 2008). One study linked heavy smoking during pregnancy to nicotine withdrawal symptoms in newborns (Godding & others, 2004). Prenatal exposure to cigarette smoking during pregnancy is also related to increased incidence of attention deficit hyperactivity disorder at 5 to 16 years of age (Thapar & others, 2003). A recent

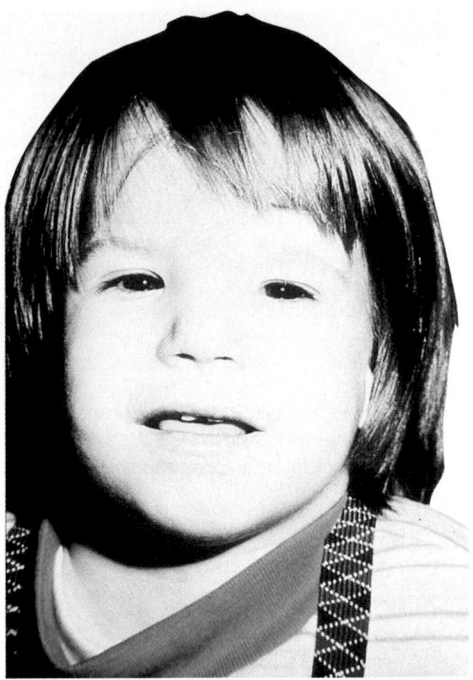

Fetal alcohol spectrum disorders (FASD) are characterized by a number of physical abnormalities and learning problems. Notice the wide-set eyes, flat cheekbones, and thin upper lip in this child with FASD.

What are some links between expectant mothers' cigarette smoking and outcomes for their offspring?

fetal alcohol spectrum disorders (FASD) A cluster of abnormalities that appears in the offspring of mothers who drink alcohol heavily during pregnancy.

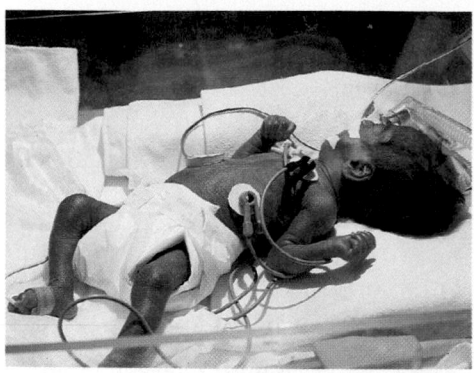

This baby was exposed to cocaine prenatally. *What are some of the possible effects on development of being exposed to cocaine prenatally?*

study also revealed that environmental tobacco smoke was linked to increased risk of low birth weight in offspring (Leonardi-Bee & others, 2008).

Intervention programs designed to help pregnant women stop smoking can reduce some of smoking's negative effects, especially by raising birth weights (Barron & others, 2007). A recent study revealed that women who quit smoking during pregnancy had offspring with higher birth weight than their counterparts who continued smoking (Jaddoe & others, 2008).

Cocaine   Does cocaine use during pregnancy harm the developing embryo and fetus? The most consistent finding is that cocaine exposure during prenatal development is associated with reduced birth weight, length, and head circumference (Smith & others, 2001). Also, in other studies, prenatal cocaine exposure has been linked to lower arousal, less effective self-regulation, higher excitability, and lower quality of reflexes at 1 month of age (Lester & others, 2002); to impaired motor development at 2 years of age and a slower rate of growth through 10 years of age (Richardson, Goldschmidt, & Willford, 2008); to impaired language development and information processing (Beeghly & others, 2006), including attention deficits in preschool and elementary school children (Accornero & others, 2007; Noland & others, 2005).

Some researchers argue that these findings should be interpreted cautiously (Accornero & others, 2006). Why? Because other factors in the lives of pregnant women who use cocaine (such as poverty, malnutrition, and other substance abuse) often cannot be ruled out as possible contributors to the problems found in their children (Hurt & others, 2005). For example, cocaine users are more likely than nonusers to smoke cigarettes, use marijuana, drink alcohol, and take amphetamines.

Despite these cautions, the weight of research evidence indicates that children born to mothers who use cocaine are likely to have neurological and cognitive deficits (Field, 2007; Richardson, Goldschmidt, & Larkby, 2008). Cocaine use by pregnant women is never recommended.

Methamphetamine   Methamphetamine, like cocaine, is a stimulant, speeding up an individual's nervous system. Babies born to mothers who use methamphetamine, or "meth," during pregnancy are at risk for a number of problems, including high infant mortality, low birth weight, and developmental and behavioral problems (Forester & Merz, 2007). Meth use during pregnancy is increasing, and some experts conclude that meth use during pregnancy has become a greater problem in the United States than cocaine use (Elliott, 2004). A recent study revealed that meth exposure during prenatal development was linked to decreased arousal, increased stress, and poor movement quality in newborns (Smith & others, 2008).

Marijuana   An increasing number of studies find that marijuana use by pregnant women also has negative outcomes for offspring (Huizink & Mulder, 2006; Williams & Ross, 2007). A recent study found that prenatal marijuana exposure was related to lower intelligence in children (Goldschmidt & others, 2008). Another study revealed that prenatal marijuana exposure was linked with depressive symptoms at 10 years of age (Gray & others, 2005). Further, a recent study indicated that prenatal exposure to marijuana was linked to marijuana use at 14 years of age (Day, Goldschmidt, & Thomas, 2006). In sum, marijuana use is not recommended for pregnant women.

Heroin   It is well documented that infants whose mothers are addicted to heroin show several behavioral difficulties at birth (Steinhausen, Blattmann, & Pfund, 2007). The difficulties include withdrawal symptoms, such as tremors, irritability, abnormal crying, disturbed sleep, and impaired motor control. Many still show behavioral problems at their first birthday, and attention deficits may appear later in development. The most common treatment for heroin addiction, methadone, is associated with very severe withdrawal symptoms in newborns (Binder & Vavrinkova, 2008). A recent study revealed that when compared to pregnant women who entered methadone treatment late (less than six months prior to birth), continuous methadone treatment during pregnancy was linked to improved neonatal outcomes (Burns & others, 2007).

Incompatible Blood Types Incompatibility between the mother's and father's blood type poses another risk to prenatal development. Blood types are created by differences in the surface structure of red blood cells. One type of difference in the surface of red blood cells creates the familiar blood groups—A, B, O, and AB. A second difference creates what is called Rh-positive and Rh-negative blood. If a surface marker, called the *Rh-factor,* is present in an individual's red blood cells, the person is said to be Rh-positive; if the Rh-marker is not present, the person is said to be Rh-negative. If a pregnant woman is Rh-negative and her partner is Rh-positive, the fetus may be Rh-positive. If the fetus' blood is Rh-positive and the mother's is Rh-negative, the mother's immune system may produce antibodies that will attack the fetus. This can result in any number of problems, including miscarriage or stillbirth, anemia, jaundice, heart defects, brain damage, or death soon after birth (Moise, 2005).

Generally, the first Rh-positive baby of an Rh-negative mother is not at risk, but with each subsequent pregnancy the risk increases. A vaccine (RhoGAM) may be given to the mother within three days of the first child's birth to prevent her body from making antibodies that will attack any future Rh-positive fetuses in subsequent pregnancies. Also, babies affected by Rh incompatibility can be given blood transfusions before or right after birth (Flegal, 2007).

Environmental Hazards Many aspects of our modern industrial world can endanger the embryo or fetus (O'Connor & Roy, 2008). Some specific hazards to the embryo or fetus that are worth a closer look include radiation, toxic wastes, and other chemical pollutants (Orecchia, Lucignani, & Tosi, 2008; Raabe & Muller, 2008).

Radiation can cause a gene mutation (an abrupt, permanent change in DNA). Chromosomal abnormalities are elevated among the offspring of fathers exposed to high levels of radiation in their occupations (Schrag & Dixon, 1985). X-ray radiation also can affect the developing embryo or fetus, especially in the first several weeks after conception, when women do not yet know they are pregnant (Urbano & Tait, 2004). Possible effects include microencephaly (an abnormally small brain), mental retardation, and leukemia. Women and their physicians should weigh the risk of an X-ray when an actual or potential pregnancy is involved (Menias & others, 2007). However, a routine diagnostic X-ray of a body area other than the abdomen, with the woman's abdomen protected by a lead apron, is generally considered safe (Loughlin, 2007).

Environmental pollutants and toxic wastes are also sources of danger to unborn children. Among the dangerous pollutants are carbon monoxide, mercury, and lead, as well as certain fertilizers and pesticides. Exposure to lead can come from lead-based paint that flakes off the walls of a home or from leaded gasoline emitted by cars on a nearby busy highway. Early exposure to lead can affect children's mental development. For example, a recent study revealed that a moderately high maternal lead level in the first trimester of pregnancy was linked to lower scores on an index of mental development in infancy (Hu & others, 2006).

Maternal Diseases Maternal diseases and infections can produce defects in offspring by crossing the placental barrier, or they can cause damage during birth. Rubella (German measles) is one disease that can cause prenatal defects. Women who plan to have children should have a blood test before they become pregnant to determine if they are immune to the disease (Dontigny & others, 2008).

Syphilis (a sexually transmitted infection) is more damaging later in prenatal development—four months or more after conception. Rather than affecting organogenesis, as rubella does, syphilis damages organs after they have formed. Damage includes eye lesions, which can cause blindness, and skin lesions. When syphilis is present at

An explosion at the Chernobyl nuclear power plant in the Ukraine produced radioactive contamination that spread to surrounding areas. Thousands of infants were born with health problems and deformities as a result of the nuclear contamination, including this boy whose arm did not form. *Other than radioactive contamination, what are some other types of environmental hazards to prenatal development?*

birth, problems can develop in the central nervous system and gastrointestinal tract (Johnson, Erbelding, & Ghanem, 2007). Most states require that pregnant women be given a blood test to detect the presence of syphilis.

Another infection that has received widespread attention recently is genital herpes. Newborns contract this virus when they are delivered through the birth canal of a mother with genital herpes (Hollier & Wendel, 2008). About one-third of babies delivered through an infected birth canal die; another one-fourth become brain damaged. If an active case of genital herpes is detected in a pregnant woman close to her delivery date, a cesarean section can be performed (in which the infant is delivered through an incision in the mother's abdomen) to keep the virus from infecting the newborn (Baker, 2007).

AIDS is a sexually transmitted infection that is caused by the human immunodeficiency virus (HIV), which destroys the body's immune system. A mother can infect her offspring with HIV/AIDS in three ways: (1) during gestation across the placenta, (2) during delivery through contact with maternal blood or fluids, and (3) postpartum (after birth) through breast feeding. The transmission of AIDS through breast feeding is especially a problem in many developing countries (Lunney & others, 2008; UNICEF, 2008). Babies born to HIV-infected mothers can be (1) infected and symptomatic (show HIV symptoms), (2) infected but asymptomatic (not show HIV symptoms), or (3) not infected at all. An infant who is infected and asymptomatic may still develop HIV symptoms up until 15 months of age.

The more widespread disease of diabetes, characterized by high levels of sugar in the blood, also affects offspring. A recent research review concluded that the offspring of diabetic mothers are at risk for metabolic disease (Dobaldo & Moley, 2007). And one study revealed that both chronic (long-standing) and gestational (onset or first recognition during pregnancy) diabetes were significant risks for cesarean delivery and preterm birth (Rosenberg & others, 2005). Women who have gestational diabetes also may deliver very large infants (weighing 10 pounds or more), and the infants may be at risk for diabetes themselves.

Other Parental Factors So far we have discussed a number of drugs, environmental hazards, maternal diseases, and incompatible blood types that can harm the embryo or fetus. Here we will explore other characteristics of the mother and father that can affect prenatal and child development, including nutrition, age, and emotional states and stress.

Maternal Diet and Nutrition A developing embryo or fetus depends completely on its mother for nutrition, which comes from the mother's blood (Derbyshire, 2007a, b). The nutritional status of the embryo or fetus is determined by the mother's total caloric intake, and her intake of proteins, vitamins, and minerals. Children born to malnourished mothers are more likely than other children to be malformed.

Being overweight before and during pregnancy can also put the embryo or fetus at risk, and an increasing number of pregnant women in the United States are overweight (Reece, 2008). Researchers have found that obese women have a significant risk of fetal death (Nohr & others, 2005). Recent studies indicate that prepregnancy maternal obesity doubles the risk of stillbirth and neonatal death and is linked with defects in the central nervous system of offspring (Frederick & others, 2008; Guelinckx, 2008). Further, a recent analysis proposed that overeating by pregnant women results in a series of neuroendocrine changes in the fetus that in turn program the development of fat cells and appetite regulation system (McMillen & others, 2008). In this analysis, it was predicted that such early fetal programming is likely linked to being overweight in childhood and adolescence.

One aspect of maternal nutrition that is important for normal prenatal development is folic acid, a B-complex vitamin (Goh & Koren, 2008). A recent study of more

Because the fetus depends entirely on its mother for nutrition, it is important for the pregnant woman to have good nutritional habits. In Kenya, this government clinic provides pregnant women with information about how their diet can influence the health of their fetus and offspring. *What might the information about diet be like?*

than 34,000 women taking folic acid either alone or as part of a multivitamin for at least one year prior to conceiving was linked with a 70 percent lower risk of delivering from 20 to 28 weeks and a 50 percent lower risk of delivering between 28 to 32 weeks (Bukowski & others, 2008). As we indicated earlier in the chapter, a lack of folic acid is linked with neural tube defects in offspring, such as spina bifida (a defect in the spinal cord) (Ryan-Harshman & Aldoori, 2008). The U.S. Department of Health and Human Services (2008) recommends that pregnant women consume a minimum of 400 micrograms of folic acid per day (about twice the amount the average woman gets in one day). Orange juice and spinach are examples of foods rich in folic acid.

Eating fish is often recommended as part of a healthy diet, but pollution has made many fish a risky choice for pregnant women. Some fish contain high levels of mercury, which is released into the air both naturally and by industrial pollution (Oken & Bellinger, 2008). When mercury falls into the water it can become toxic and accumulate in large fish, such as shark, swordfish, king mackerel, and some species of large tuna. Mercury is easily transferred across the placenta, and the embryo's developing brain and nervous system are highly sensitive to the metal (Gliori & others, 2006). Researchers have found that prenatal mercury exposure is linked to adverse outcomes, including miscarriage, preterm birth, and lower intelligence (Triche & Hossain, 2007; Xue & others, 2007). The U.S. Food and Drug Administration (2004) gave the following recommendations for women of childbearing age and young children: Don't eat shark, swordfish, king mackerel or tilefish; eat up to 12 ounces (two average meals) a week of fish and shellfish that are lower in mercury, such as shrimp, canned light tuna, salmon, pollock, and catfish.

PCBs (polychlorinated biphenyls) are chemicals that were used in manufacturing until they were banned in the 1970s in the United States, but they are still present in landfills, sediments, and wildlife. One concern focuses on pregnant women eating PCB-polluted fish (Hertz-Picciotto & others, 2008). A recent research review concluded that PCB-polluted fish pose a potential risk to prenatal neurodevelopment (Korrick & Sagiv, 2008).

Maternal Age   When possible harmful effects on the fetus and infant are considered, two maternal ages are of special interest: adolescence and 35 and older (Chen & others, 2007a; Maconochie & others, 2007). One recent study revealed that the rate of stillbirth was elevated for adolescent girls and women 35 years and older (Bateman & Simpson, 2006).

The mortality rate of infants born to adolescent mothers is double that of infants born to mothers in their twenties. Although this high rate probably reflects the immaturity of the mother's reproductive system, poor nutrition, lack of prenatal care, and low socioeconomic status may also play a role (Smithbattle, 2007). Adequate prenatal care decreases the probability that a child born to an adolescent girl will have physical problems. However, adolescents are the least likely of women in all age groups to obtain prenatal assistance from clinics and health services.

Maternal age is also linked to the risk that a child will have Down syndrome (Soergel & others, 2006). As discussed in Chapter 2, an individual with *Down syndrome* has distinctive facial characteristics, short limbs, and retardation of motor and mental abilities. A baby with Down syndrome rarely is born to a mother 16 to 34 years of age. However, when the mother reaches 40 years of age, the probability is slightly over 1 in 100 that a baby born to her will have Down syndrome, and by age 50 it is almost 1 in 10.

When mothers are 35 years and older, risks also increase for low birth weight, for preterm delivery, and for fetal death (Fretts, Zera, & Heffner, 2008). One study found that low birth weight delivery increased 11 percent and preterm delivery increased 14 percent in women 35 years and older (Tough & others, 2002). In another study, fetal death was low for women 30 to 34 years of age but increased progressively for women 35 to 44 years of age (Canterino & others, 2004).

What are some of the risks for infants born to adolescent mothers?

We still have much to learn about the role of the mother's age in pregnancy and childbirth (Montan, 2007). As women remain active, exercise regularly, and are careful about their nutrition, their reproductive systems may remain healthier at older ages than was thought possible in the past. For example, in one study, two-thirds of the pregnancies of women 45 years and older in Australia were free of complications (Callaway, Lust, & McIntrye, 2005).

Emotional States and Stress   When a pregnant woman experiences intense fears, anxieties, and other emotions or negative mood states, physiological changes occur that may affect her fetus (Taige & others, 2007). Maternal stress may increase the level of corticotropin-releasing hormone (CRH), a precursor of the the the stress hormone cortisol, early in pregnancy (Nakamura, Sheps, & Clara Auck, 2008). Elevated levels of CRH and cortisol in the fetus have been linked to premature delivery in infants (Field, 2007). A recent study also revealed that a decline in stress during pregnancy was linked to a lower incidence of preterm birth (Glynn & others, 2008). A mother's stress may also influence the fetus indirectly by increasing the likelihood that the mother will engage in unhealthy behaviors, such as taking drugs and engaging in poor prenatal care.

The mother's emotional state during pregnancy can influence the birth process, too. An emotionally distraught mother might have irregular contractions and a more difficult labor, which can cause irregularities in the supply of oxygen to the fetus or other problems after birth. Babies born after extended labor also may adjust more slowly to their world and be more irritable.

High maternal anxiety and stress during pregnancy can have long-term consequences for the offspring (Davis & others, 2007). A recent research review indicated that pregnant women with high levels of stress are at increased risk for having a child with emotional or cognitive problems, attention deficit hyperactivity disorder (ADHD), and language delay (Taige & others, 2007). In this review, it was concluded that still unknown is the type of stress that is most detrimental, but research suggests stress in the woman's relationship with a partner is one candidate.

Positive emotional states also appear to make a difference to the fetus. Pregnant women who are optimistic thinkers have less adverse outcomes than pregnant women who are pessimistic thinkers (Loebel & Yali, 1999). Optimists are more likely to believe that they have control over the outcomes of their pregnancies.

Paternal Factors   So far, we have discussed how characteristics of the mother—such as drug use, disease, diet and nutrition, age, and emotional states—can influence prenatal development and the development of the child. Might there also be some paternal risk factors? Indeed, there are several. Men's exposure to lead, radiation, certain pesticides, and petrochemicals may cause abnormalities in sperm that lead to miscarriage or diseases, such as childhood cancer (Cordier, 2008; Monge & others, 2007). When fathers have a diet low in vitamin C, their offspring have a higher risk of birth defects and cancer (Fraga & others, 1991). Also, it has been speculated that, when fathers take cocaine, it may attach itself to sperm and cause birth defects, but the evidence for this effect is not yet strong. In one study, long-term use of cocaine by men was related to low sperm count, low motility, and a higher number of abnormally formed sperm (Bracken & others, 1990). Cocaine-related infertility appears to be reversible if users stop taking the drug for at least one year.

The father's smoking during the mother's pregnancy also can cause problems for the offspring. In one study, in China, the longer the fathers smoked, the stronger the risk that their children would develop cancer (Ji & others, 1997). In another study, heavy paternal smoking was associated with the risk of early pregnancy loss (Venners & others, 2004). All of these negative effects may be related to secondhand smoke.

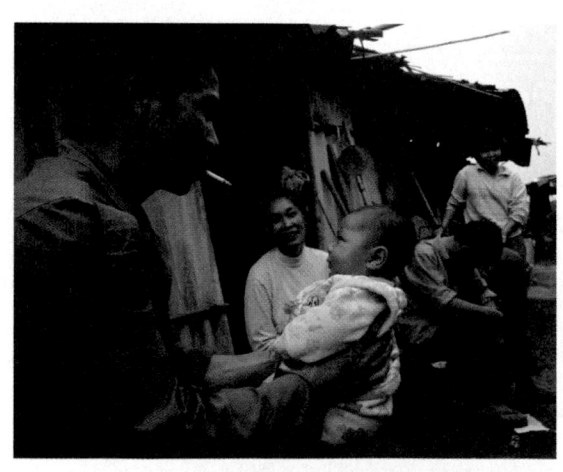

In one study, in China, the longer fathers smoked the greater the risk that their children would develop cancer (Ji & others, 1997). *What are some other paternal factors that can influence the development of the fetus and the child?*

The father's age also makes a difference (Maconochie & others, 2007; Yang & others, 2007). About 5 percent of children with Down syndrome have older fathers. The offspring of older fathers also face increased risk for other birth defects, including dwarfism and Marfan syndrome, which involves head and limb deformities.

Prenatal Care

Although prenatal care varies enormously, it usually involves a defined schedule of visits for medical care, which typically includes screening for manageable conditions and treatable diseases that can affect the baby or the mother (Lu & Lu, 2008; Mennuti, 2008). In addition to medical care, prenatal programs often include comprehensive educational, social, and nutritional services (Moos, 2006).

The education provided in prenatal care varies during the course of pregnancy. Those in the early stages of pregnancy, as well as couples who are anticipating a pregnancy, may participate in early prenatal classes (Davidson, London, & Ladewig, 2008). In addition to providing information on dangers to the fetus, early prenatal classes often discuss the development of the embryo and the fetus; sexuality during pregnancy; choices about the birth setting and care providers; nutrition, rest, and exercise; common discomforts of pregnancy and relief measures; psychological changes in the expectant mother and her partner; and factors that increase the risk of preterm labor and possible symptoms of preterm labor. Early classes also may include information about the advantages and disadvantages of breast feeding and bottle feeding (fifty to eighty percent of expectant mothers decide how they will feed their infant prior to the sixth month of pregnancy). During the second or third trimester of pregnancy, prenatal classes focus on preparing for the birth, infant care and feeding, choices about birth, and postpartum self-care.

An innovative program that is rapidly expanding in the United States is Centering Pregnancy (Massey, Rising, & Ickovics, 2006; Reid, 2007). This program is relationship-centered and provides complete prenatal care in a group setting. Centering Pregnancy replaces traditional 15-minute physician visits with 90-minute peer group support settings and self-examination led by a physician or certified nurse-midwife. Groups of up to 10 women (and often their partners) meet regularly beginning at 12 to 16 weeks of pregnancy. The sessions emphasize empowering women to play an active role in experiencing a positive pregnancy.

Does prenatal care matter? Information about pregnancy, labor, delivery, and caring for the newborn can be especially valuable for first-time mothers (Chang & others, 2003). Prenatal care is also very important for women in poverty because it links them with other social services (Hogan & others, 2007). The legacy of prenatal care continues after the birth because women who experience this type of care are more likely to get preventive care for their infants (Bates & others, 1994).

Research contrasting the experiences of mothers who had prenatal care, and those who did not supports the importance of prenatal care (Chen & others, 2007b; Daniels, Noe, & Mayberry, 2006). One study found that U.S. women who had no prenatal care were far more likely than their counterparts who received prenatal care to have infants who had low birth weight, increased mortality, and a number of other physical problems (Herbst & others, 2003). In other recent studies, low birth weight and preterm deliveries were common among U.S. mothers who received no prenatal care, and the absence of prenatal care, increased the risk for preterm birth by almost threefold in both non-Latino White and African American women (Stringer & others, 2005).

Inadequate prenatal care may help explain a disturbing fact: Rates of infant mortality and low birth weight indicate that many other nations have healthier babies than the United States (Flynn, Budd, & Modelski, 2008; Goldenberg & Nagahawatte, 2008). In many countries that have a lower percentage of low birth weight infants than the United States, mothers receive either free or very low cost prenatal and postnatal care, and can receive paid maternity leave from work that ranges from 9 to 40 weeks. In Norway and the Netherlands, prenatal care is coordinated with a general practitioner, an obstetrician, and a midwife.

Why do some U.S. women receive inadequate prenatal care? Sometimes the reasons are tied to the health-care system, to provider practices, and to their own individual and social characteristics (Conway & Kutinova, 2006). Women who do not

Many husbands, or coaches take childbirth classes with their wives or friends.

A Centering Pregnancy program. This rapidly increasing program alters routine prenatal care by bringing women out of exam rooms and into relationship-oriented groups.

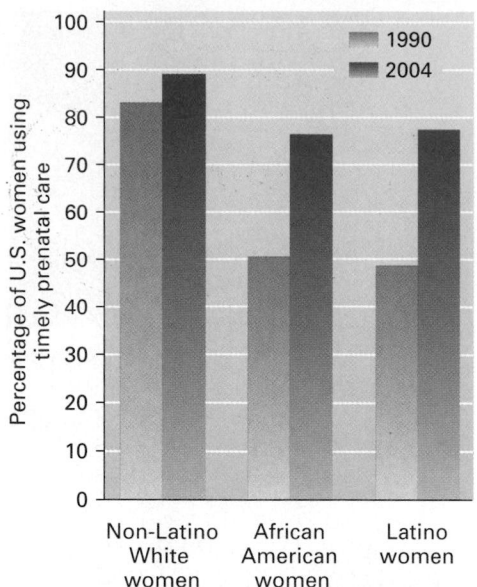

FIGURE 3.6 Percentage of U.S. Women Using Timely Prenatal Care: 1990 to 2004. From 1990 to 2004, the use of timely prenatal care increased by 7 percent (to 89.1) for non-Latino White women, by 25 percent (to 76.5) for African American women, and by 28 percent (to 77.4) for Latino women in the United States.

want to be pregnant, who have negative attitudes about being pregnant, or who unintentionally become pregnant are more likely to delay prenatal care or to miss appointments. As we noted earlier, adolescent girls are less likely than adult women to obtain prenatal care (Hueston, Geesey, & Diaz, 2008). Within the United States, there are differences among ethnic groups both in the health of babies and in prenatal care (Park, Vincent, & Hastings-Tolsma, 2007; Wasserman, Bender, & Lee, 2007). In the 1980s, more than one-fifth of all non-Latino White mothers and one-third of all African American mothers did not receive prenatal care in the first trimester of their pregnancy, and five percent of White mothers and 10 percent of African American mothers received no prenatal care at all (Wegman, 1987).

The situation has been improving. From 1990 to 2004, the use of timely prenatal care increased for women from a variety of ethnic backgrounds in the United States, although non-Latino White women were still more likely to obtain prenatal care than African American and Latino women (Martin & others, 2005) (see Figure 3.6). The United States needs more comprehensive medical and educational services to improve the quality of prenatal care and to reduce the number of low birth weight and preterm infants (Johnson & others, 2007).

Cultures around the world have views of pregnancy that differ from those of the United States. In the *Diversity in Life-Span Development* interlude that follows, we will explore these beliefs.

Diversity in Life-Span Development
Cultural Beliefs About Pregnancy

All cultures have beliefs and practices that surround life's major events, and one such event is pregnancy. When a woman who immigrated to the United States becomes pregnant, the beliefs and practices of her native culture may be as important as, or more so than, those of the mainstream U.S. culture that now surrounds her. The conflict between cultural tradition and Western medicine may pose a risk for the pregnancy and a challenge for the health-care professional who wishes to give proper care while respecting the woman's values.

The American Public Health Association (2006) has identified a variety of cultural beliefs and practices that are observed among various immigrant groups, such as:

In India, a midwife checks on the size, position, and heartbeat of a fetus. Midwives deliver babies in many cultures around the world. *What are some cultural variations in prenatal care?*

- *Food cravings.* Latin American, Asian, and some African cultures believe that it is important for a pregnant woman's food cravings to be satisfied because they are thought to be the cravings of the baby. If cravings are left unsatisfied, the baby might take on certain unpleasant personality and/or physical traits, perhaps characteristic of the food (Taylor, Ko, & Pan, 1999). As an example, in African cultures women often eat soil, chalk, or clay during pregnancy—this is believed to satisfy the baby's hunger as well as affirming soil as a symbol of female fertility (American Public Health Association, 2006).

- *"Hot-cold" theory of illness.* Many cultures in Latin America, Asia, and Africa characterize foods, medications, and illnesses as "hot" or "cold"; this has nothing to do with temperature or spiciness, but with traditional definitions and categories. Most of these cultures view pregnancy as a "hot" condition, although the Chinese view it as "cold" (Taylor, Ko, & Pan, 1999). As a result, a woman may resist taking a prescribed medication because of concern that it could create too much "heat" and cause a miscarriage; in Indian culture, iron-rich foods are also considered unacceptably "hot" for pregnant women (DeSantis, 1998).

- *Extended family.* In many immigrant cultures, the extended family is a vital support system, and health-care decisions are made based on the needs of the family over those of the individual.

Western health-care providers need to be sensitive to this dynamic, which runs counter to today's practices of protecting patient confidentiality and autonomy.

- *Stoicism.* In many Asian cultures, stoicism is valued, as suffering is seen as part of life (Uba, 1992). Physicians are also viewed with great respect. As a result, a pregnant Asian woman may behave submissively and avoid voicing complaints to her health-care provider, but may privately fail to follow the provider's advice (Assanand & others, 1990).

Some cultures treat pregnancy simply as a natural occurrence; others see it as a medical condition (Walsh, 2006). How expectant mothers behave during pregnancy may depend in part on the prevalence of traditional home-care remedies and folk beliefs, the importance of indigenous healers, and the influence of health-care professionals in their culture. In various cultures, women may consult herbalists and/or faith healers during pregnancy (Mbonye, Neema, & Magnussen, 2006).

Health-care workers should assess whether a woman's beliefs or practices pose a threat to her or the fetus. If they do, health-care professionals should consider a culturally sensitive way to handle the problem (Kenner, Sugrue, & Finkelman, 2007).

Normal Prenatal Development

Much of our discussion so far in this chapter has focused on what can go wrong with prenatal development. Prospective parents should take steps to avoid the vulnerabilities to fetal development that we have described. But it is important to keep in mind that most of the time, prenatal development does not go awry, and development occurs along the positive path that we described at the beginning of the chapter.

Review and Reflect: Learning Goal 1

 1 **Describe Prenatal Development**

REVIEW

- What is the course of prenatal development?
- What is teratology, and what are some of the main hazards to prenatal development?
- What are some good prenatal care strategies?
- Why is it important to take a positive approach to prenatal development?

REFLECT

- What can be done to convince women who are pregnant not to smoke or drink? Consider the role of health-care providers, the role of insurance companies, and specific programs targeted at women who are pregnant.

---

2 BIRTH

| The Birth Process | Assessing the Newborn | Preterm and Low Birth Weight Infants |

Nature writes the basic script for how birth occurs, but parents make important choices about conditions surrounding birth. We look first at the sequence of physical steps when a child is born.

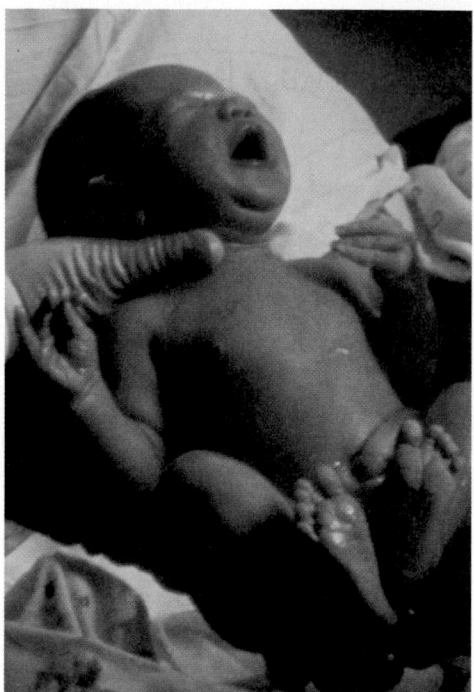

After the long journey of prenatal development, birth takes place. During birth the baby is on a threshold between two worlds. *What is the fetus/newborn transition like?*

A woman in the African !Kung culture giving birth in a sitting position. Notice the help and support being given by another woman. *What are some cultural variations in childbirth?*

afterbirth The third stage of birth, when the placenta, umbilical cord, and other membranes are detached and expelled.

The Birth Process

The birth process occurs in stages, occurs in different contexts, and in most cases involves one or more attendants.

Stages of Birth   The birth process occurs in three stages. The first stage is the longest of the three stages. Uterine contractions are 15 to 20 minutes apart at the beginning and last up to a minute. These contractions cause the woman's cervix to stretch and open. As the first stage progresses, the contractions come closer together, appearing every two to five minutes. Their intensity increases. By the end of the first birth stage, contractions dilate the cervix to an opening of about 10 centimeters (4 inches), so that the baby can move from the uterus to the birth canal. For a woman having her first child, the first stage lasts an average of 6 to 12 hours; for subsequent children, this stage typically is much shorter.

The second birth stage begins when the baby's head starts to move through the cervix and the birth canal. It terminates when the baby completely emerges from the mother's body. With each contraction, the mother bears down hard to push the baby out of her body. By the time the baby's head is out of the mother's body, the contractions come almost every minute and last for about a minute. This stage typically lasts approximately 45 minutes to an hour.

Afterbirth is the third stage, at which time the placenta, umbilical cord, and other membranes are detached and expelled. This final stage is the shortest of the three birth stages, lasting only minutes.

Childbirth Setting and Attendants   In the United States, 99 percent of births take place in hospitals, a figure that has remained constant for several decades (Martin & others, 2005). Some women with good medical histories and low risk for problems may choose a delivery at home or in a freestanding birth center, which is usually staffed by nurse-midwives. Births at home are far more common in many other countries—for example, in Holland, 35 percent of the babies are born at home. Some critics worry that the U.S. tendency to view birth through a medical lens may lead to unnecessary medical procedures (Hausman, 2005).

Who helps a mother during birth varies across cultures. In U.S. hospitals, it has become the norm for fathers or birth coaches to be with the mother throughout labor and delivery. In the East African Nigoni culture, men are completely excluded from the childbirth process. When a woman is ready to give birth, female relatives move into the woman's hut and the husband leaves, taking his belongings (clothes, tools, weapons, and so on) with him. He is not permitted to return until after the baby is born. In some cultures, childbirth is an open, community affair. For example, in the Pukapukan culture in the Pacific Islands, women give birth in a shelter that is open for villagers to observe.

Midwives   Midwifery is the norm throughout most of the world (Parfitt, Mughal, & Thomas, 2008). In Holland, more than 40 percent of babies are delivered by midwives rather than doctors. But in 2003, 91 percent of U.S. births were attended by physicians, and only 8 percent of women who delivered baby were attended by a *midwife* (Martin & others, 2005). However, the 8 percent figure in 2003 represents a substantial increase from less than 1 percent of U.S. women attended by a midwife in 1975 (Martin & others, 2005). Ninety-five percent of the midwives who delivered babies in the United States in 2003 were certified nurse-midwives. Compared to physicians, certified nurse-midwives generally spend more time with patients during prenatal visits, place more emphasis on patient counseling and education, provide more emotional support, and are more likely to be with the patient one-on-one during the entire labor and delivery process, which may explain the more positive outcomes for babies delivered by certified nurse-midwives (Davis, 2005).

Doulas   In many countries, a doula attends a childbearing woman. *Doula* is a Greek word that means "a woman who helps." A **doula** is a caregiver who provides continuous physical, emotional, and educational support for the mother before, during, and after childbirth. Doulas remain with the mother throughout labor, assessing and responding to her needs. Researchers have found positive effects when a doula is present at the birth of a child (Campbell & others, 2007; Stein, Kennell, & Fulcher, 2004). In a recent study, low-income pregnant women who were given doula support spent a shorter time in labor and their newborn had a higher health rating at 1 and 5 minutes after birth than their low-income counterparts who did not receive doula support (Campbell & others, 2006).

In the United States, most doulas work as independent providers hired by the expectant mother. Doulas typically function as part of a "birthing team," serving as an adjunct to the midwife or the hospital's obstetric staff (Dundek, 2006). Managed care organizations are increasingly offering doula support as a part of regular obstetric care.

Methods of Childbirth   U.S. hospitals often allow the mother and her obstetrician a range of options regarding their method of delivery. Key choices involve the use of medication, whether to use any of a number of nonmedicated techniques to reduce pain, and when to resort to a cesarean delivery.

Medication   Three basic kinds of drugs that are used for labor are analgesia, anesthesia, and oxytocics.

Analgesia is used to relieve pain. Analgesics include tranquilizers, barbiturates, and narcotics (such as Demerol).

Anesthesia is used in late first-stage labor and during expulsion of the baby to block sensation in an area of the body or to block consciousness. There is a trend toward not using general anesthesia, which blocks consciousness, in normal births because general anesthesia can be transmitted through the placenta to the fetus (Lieberman & others, 2005). An *epidural block* is regional anesthesia that numbs the woman's body from the waist down. Even this drug, thought to be relatively safe, has come under recent criticism because it is associated with fever, extended labor, and increased risk for cesarean delivery (Glantz, 2005).

Oxytocin is a synthetic hormone that is used to stimulate contractions; pitocin is the most widely used oxytocin. The benefits and risks of oxytocin as a part of childbirth continues to be debated (Vasdev, 2008).

Predicting how a drug will affect an individual woman and her fetus is difficult (Funai, Evans, & Lockwood, 2008). A particular drug might have only a minimal effect on one fetus yet have a much stronger effect on another. The drug's dosage also is a factor. Stronger doses of tranquilizers and narcotics given to decrease the mother's pain potentially have a more negative effect on the fetus than mild doses. It is important for the mother to assess her level of pain and have a voice in the decision of whether she should receive medication.

Natural and Prepared Childbirth   For a brief time not long ago, the idea of avoiding all medication during childbirth gained favor in the United States. Instead, many women chose to reduce the pain of childbirth through techniques known as natural childbirth and prepared childbirth. Today, at least some medication is used in the typical childbirth, but elements of natural childbirth and prepared childbirth remain popular (Davidson, London, & Ladewig, 2008; Hogan & others, 2007).

Natural childbirth is the method that aims to reduce the mother's pain by decreasing her fear through education about childbirth and by teaching her to use breathing methods and relaxation techniques during delivery (Sandiford, 2006). This approach was developed in 1914 by English obstetrician Grantley Dick-Read. Dick-Read argued that the doctor's relationship with the mother plays an important role in

A doula assisting a birth. *What types of support do doulas provide?*

doula A caregiver who provides continuous physical, emotional, and educational support for the mother before, during, and after childbirth.

natural childbirth Developed in 1914 by Dick-Read, this method attempts to reduce the mother's pain by decreasing her fear through education about childbirth and relaxation techniques during delivery.

reducing her perception of pain and that the doctor should be present, providing reassurance, during her active labor prior to delivery.

French obstetrician Ferdinand Lamaze developed a method similar to natural childbirth that is known as **prepared childbirth**, or the Lamaze method. It includes a special breathing technique to control pushing in the final stages of labor, as well as more detailed education about anatomy and physiology than Dick-Read's approach provides. The Lamaze method has become very popular in the United States. The pregnant woman's partner usually serves as a coach, who attends childbirth classes with her and helps her with her breathing and relaxation during delivery.

Many other prepared childbirth techniques have been developed (Davidson, London, & Ladewig, 2008). They usually include elements of Dick-Read's natural childbirth or Lamaze's method, plus one or more other components. For instance, the Bradley method emphasizes the father's role as a labor coach (Signore, 2004). Virtually all of the prepared childbirth methods emphasize education, relaxation and breathing exercises, and support.

In sum, proponents of current prepared childbirth methods believe that when information and support are provided, women *know* how to give birth. To read about one nurse whose research focuses on fatigue during childbearing and breathing exercises during labor, see the *Careers in Life-Span Development* profile. And to read about the increased variety of techniques now being used to reduce stress and control pain during labor, see the *Applications in Life-Span Development* interlude.

Careers in Life-Span Development

Linda Pugh, Perinatal Nurse

Perinatal nurses work with childbearing women to support health and growth, during the childbearing experience. Linda Pugh, Ph.D., R.N.C., is a perinatal nurse on the faculty at The John Hopkins University School of Nursing. She is certified as an inpatient obstetric nurse and specializes in the care of women during labor and delivery. She teaches undergraduate and graduate students, educated professional nurses, and conducts research. In addition, Pugh consults with hospitals and organizations about women's health issues and topics we discuss in this chapter.

Her research interests include nursing interventions with low-income breast feeding women, discovering ways to prevent and ameliorate fatigue during childbearing, and using breathing exercises during labor.

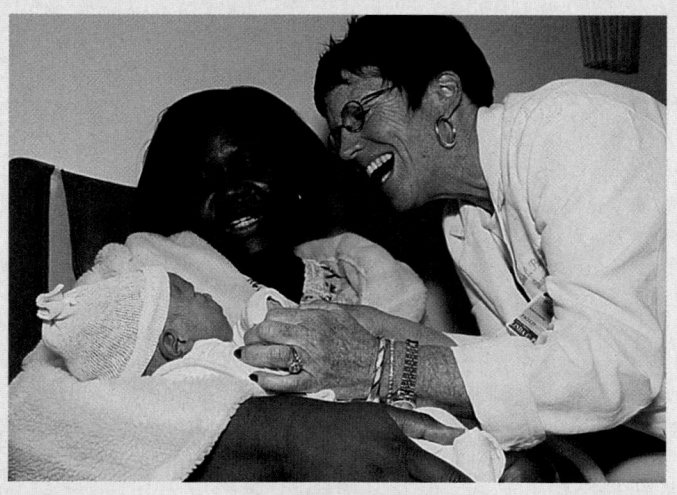

Linda Pugh (*right*) a perinatal nurse, with a mother and her newborn.

prepared childbirth Developed by French obstetrician Ferdinand Lamaze, this childbirth strategy is similar to natural childbirth but includes a special breathing technique to control pushing in the final stages of labor and a more detailed anatomy and physiology course.

Applications in Life-Span Development
From Waterbirth to Music Therapy

The effort to reduce stress and control pain during labor has recently led to an increase in the use of some older and some newer nonmedicated techniques (Field, 2007; Simkin & Bolding, 2004; Smith & others, 2006). These include waterbirth, massage, acupuncture, hypnosis, and music therapy.

Waterbirth

Waterbirth involves giving birth in a tub of warm water. Some women go through labor in the water and get out for delivery, others remain in the water for delivery. The rationale for waterbirth is that the baby has been in an amniotic sac for many months and that delivery in a similar environment is likely to be less stressful for the baby and the mother. Mothers get into the warm water when contractions become closer together and more intense. Getting into the water too soon can cause labor to slow or stop. Reviews of research have indicated mixed results for waterbirths (Field, 2007; Pinette, Wax, & Wilson, 2004; Thöni & Moroder, 2004). In a recent comparison of almost 6,000 landbirths and more than 3,500 waterbirths, waterbirths resulted in a lower incidence of episiotomies (an incision made to widen the vagina for delivery), fewer perineal lacerations (the perineum is a muscle between the vagina and the rectum), fewer vaginal tears, and a lower rate of newborn complications (Geissbuehler, Stein, & Eberhard, 2004). Critics of waterbirth indicate that in some cases drowning and infectious disease may result (Pinnette, Wax, & Wilson, 2004). Waterbirth has been practiced more often in European countries such as Switzerland and Sweden in recent decades than in the United States but is increasingly being included in U.S. birth plans.

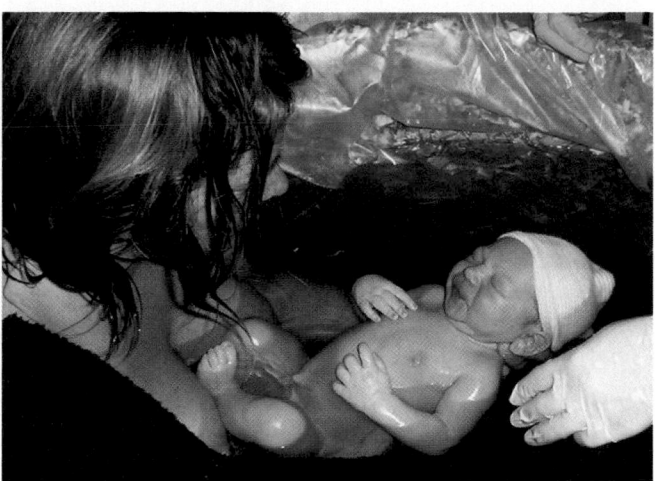

What characterizes the use of waterbirth in delivering a baby?

Massage

Massage is increasingly used as a procedure prior to and during delivery (Field, 2007; Kimber & others, 2008). Researchers have found that massage can reduce pain and anxiety during labor (Chang, Chen, & Huang, 2006). A recent research review concluded that massage reduces the incidence of perineal trauma (damage to genitalia) following birth (Beckmann & Garrett, 2006).

Acupuncture

Acupuncture, the insertion of very fine needles into specific locations in the body, is used as a standard procedure to reduce the pain of childbirth in China, although it only recently has begun to be used in the United States for this purpose (Pennick & Young, 2007). A research review indicated that only a limited number of studies had been conducted on the use of acupuncture in childbirth but that it appears to be safe and may have positive effects (Smith & Crowther, 2004). One recent study revealed that acupuncture resulted in less time spent in labor and a reduction in the need for oxytocin to augment labor (Gaudernack, Forbord, & Hole, 2006). Further research is needed to determine the effectiveness of acupuncture as childbirth procedure (Lee & Chan, 2006).

Hypnosis

Hypnosis, the induction of a psychological state of altered attention and awareness in which the individual is unusually responsively to suggestions, is also increasingly being used during childbirth (Mottershead, 2006). Some studies have indicated positive effects of hypnosis for reducing pain during childbirth (Barabasz & Perez, 2007; Cyna, Andrew, & McAuliffe, 2006). However, reviews indicate that further research is needed to determine the risks and benefits of this procedure (Cyna, McAuliffe, & Andrew, 2004; Simpkin & Bolding, 2004).

Music Therapy

Music therapy during childbirth, which involves the use of music to reduce stress and manage pain, is increasingly used (Cepeda & others, 2006). Few research studies have been conducted to determine its effectiveness (Simpkin & Bolding, 2004).

Cesarean Delivery Normally, the baby's head comes through the vagina first. But if the baby is in a **breech position**, the baby's buttocks are the first part to emerge from the vagina. In 1 of every 25 deliveries, the baby's head is still in the uterus when the rest of the body is out. Breech births can cause respiratory problems. As a result, if the baby is in a breech position, a surgical procedure known as a cesarean section, or

breech position The baby's position in the uterus that causes the buttocks to be the first part to emerge from the vagina.

a cesarean delivery, is usually preformed. In a **cesarean delivery**, the baby is removed from the mother's uterus through an incision made in her abdomen (Lee, El-Sayed, & Gould, 2008).

Cesarean deliveries are safer than breech deliveries. Cesarean deliveries also are performed if the baby is lying crosswise in the uterus, if the baby's head is too large to pass through the mother's pelvis, if the baby develops complications, or if the mother is bleeding vaginally. Cesarean deliveries can be life-saving, but they do bring risks. Compared with vaginal deliveries, they involve a higher infection rate, longer hospital stays, and the greater expense and stress that accompany any surgery.

The benefits and risks of cesarean sections continue to be debated (Declercq & others, 2008; Vendittelli & others, 2008). Some critics stress that too many babies are delivered by cesarean section in the United States (Chaillet & Dumont, 2007). More cesarean sections are performed in the United States than in any other country in the world. The cesarean delivery rate jumped 5 percent from 2002 to 2006 in the United States to 31 percent of all births, the highest level since these data began to be reported on birth certificates in 1989 (National Center for Health Statistics, 2007). Higher cesarean delivery rates may be due to a better ability to identify infants in distress during birth and the increase in overweight and obese pregnant women (Coleman & others, 2005). Also, some doctors may be overly cautious and recommend a cesarean delivery to defend against a potential lawsuit.

The Transition from Fetus to Newborn Much of our discussion of birth so far has focused on the mother. Being born also involves considerable stress for the baby. During each contraction, when the placenta and umbilical cord are compressed as the uterine muscles draw together, the supply of oxygen to the fetus is decreased. If the delivery takes too long, the baby can develop *anoxia*, a condition in which the fetus or newborn has an insufficient supply of oxygen. Anoxia can cause brain damage (Smith, 2008).

The baby has considerable capacity to withstand the stress of birth. Large quantities of adrenaline and noradrenaline, hormones that protect the fetus in the event of oxygen deficiency, are secreted in stressful circumstances. These hormones increase the heart's pumping activity, speed up heart rate, channel blood flow to the brain, and raise the blood-sugar level. Never again in life will such large amounts of these hormones be secreted. This circumstance underscores how stressful it is to be born and also how well prepared and adapted the fetus is for birth (Van Beveren, 2008).

At the time of birth, the baby is covered with a protective skin greased called *vernix caseosa*. This vernix consists of fatty secretions and dead cells, thought to help protect the baby's skin against heat loss before and during birth.

Immediately after birth, the umbilical cord is cut and the baby is on its own. Before birth, oxygen came from the mother via the umbilical cord, but now the baby is self-sufficient and can breathe on its own. Now 25 million little air sacs in the lungs must be filled with air. These first breaths may be the hardest ones an individual takes.

Assessing the Newborn

Almost immediately after birth, after the baby and mother have been introduced, a newborn is taken to be weighed, cleaned up, and tested for signs of developmental problems that might require urgent attention (Als & Butler, 2008). The **Apgar Scale** is widely used to assess the health of newborns at one and five minutes after birth. The Apgar Scale evaluates infants' heart rate, respiratory effort, muscle tone, body color, and reflex irritability. An obstetrician or a nurse does the evaluation and gives the newborn a score, or reading, of 0, 1, or 2 on each of these five health signs (see Figure 3.7). A total score of 7 to 10 indicates that the newborn's condition is good. A score of 5 indicates there may be developmental difficulties. A score of 3 or below signals an emergency and indicates that the baby might not survive. The percentage of U.S. newborns with five-minute Apgar scores of 9 or 10, indicating excellent health, increased slowly from 88.6 percent in 1978 to 91.1 percent in 2003 (Martin & others, 2005). In

cesarean delivery The baby is removed from the mother's uterus through an incision made in her abdomen.

Apgar Scale A widely used method to assess the health of newborns at one and five minutes after birth. The Apgar Scale evaluates infants' heart rate, respiratory effort, muscle tone, body color, and reflex irritability.

Score	0	1	2
Heart rate	Absent	Slow—less than 100 beats per minute	Fast—100–140 beats per minute
Respiratory effort	No breathing for more than one minute	Irregular and slow	Good breathing with normal crying
Muscle tone	Limp and flaccid	Weak, inactive, but some flexion of extremities	Strong, active motion
Body color	Blue and pale	Body pink, but extremities blue	Entire body pink
Reflex irritability	No response	Grimace	Coughing, sneezing and crying

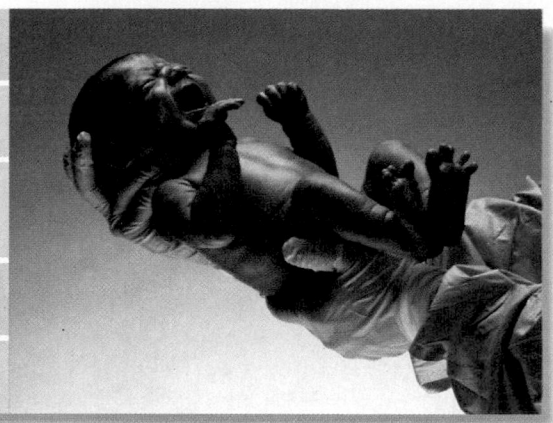

FIGURE 3.7 The Apgar Scale. A newborn's score on the Apgar Scale indicates whether the baby has urgent medical problems. *What are some trends in the Apgar scores of U.S. babies?*

this survey, five-minute Apgar scores of 7 or less decreased from 2.1 percent in 1978 to 1.4 percent in 1993 but have been unchanged since.

The Apgar Scale is especially good at assessing the newborn's ability to respond to the stress of delivery and the new environment (Oberlander & others, 2008). It also identifies high-risk infants who need resuscitation. For a more thorough assessment of the newborn, the Brazelton Neonatal Behavioral Assessment Scale or the Neonatal Intensive Care Unit Network Neurobehavioral Scale may be used.

The **Brazelton Neonatal Behavioral Assessment Scale (NBAS)** is typically performed within 24 to 36 hours after birth. It is also used as a sensitive index of neurological competence up to one month after birth for typical infants and as a measure in many studies of infant development (Mamtani, Patel, & Kulkarni, 2008). The NBAS assesses the newborn's neurological development, reflexes, and reactions to people and objects. Sixteen reflexes, such as sneezing, blinking, and rooting, are assessed, along with reactions to circumstances, such as the infant's reaction to a rattle. (We will have more to say about reflexes in Chapter 5, when we discuss motor development in infancy.)

A very low NBAS score can indicate brain damage, or stress to the brain that may heal in time. If an infant merely seems sluggish, parents are encouraged to give the infant attention and become more sensitive to the infant's needs. Parents are shown how the newborn can respond to people and how to stimulate such responses. These communications with parents can improve their interaction skills with both high-risk infants and healthy, responsive infants (Girling, 2006).

An "offspring" of the NBAS, the **Neonatal Intensive Care Unit Network Neurobehavioral Scale (NNNS)** provides a more comprehensive analysis of the newborn's behavior, neurological and stress responses, and regulatory capacities (Brazelton, 2004; Lester, Tronick, & Brazelton, 2004). Whereas the NBAS was developed to assess normal, healthy, term infants, T. Berry Brazelton, along with Barry Lester and Edward Tronick, developed the NNNS to assess the "at-risk" infant. It is especially useful for evaluating preterm infants (although it may not be appropriate for those less than 30 weeks' gestational age) and substance-exposed infants (Boukydis & Lester, 2008; Smith & others, 2008).

Preterm and Low Birth Weight Infants

Different conditions that pose threats for newborns have been given different labels. We will examine these conditions and discuss interventions for improving outcomes of preterm infants.

Preterm and Small for Date Infants Three related conditions pose threats to many newborns: low birth weight, being preterm, and being small for date. **Low birth weight infants** weigh less than 5½ pounds at birth. *Very low birth weight* newborns

Brazelton Neonatal Behavioral Assessment Scale (NBAS) A measure that is used in the first month of life to assess the newborn's neurological development, reflexes, and reactions to people and objects.

Neonatal Intensive Care Unit Neurobehavioral Scale (NNNS) An "offspring" of the NBAS, the NNNS provides a more comprehensive analysis of the newborn's behavior, neurological and stress responses, and regulatory capacities.

low birth weight infants An infant that weighs less than 5½ pounds at birth.

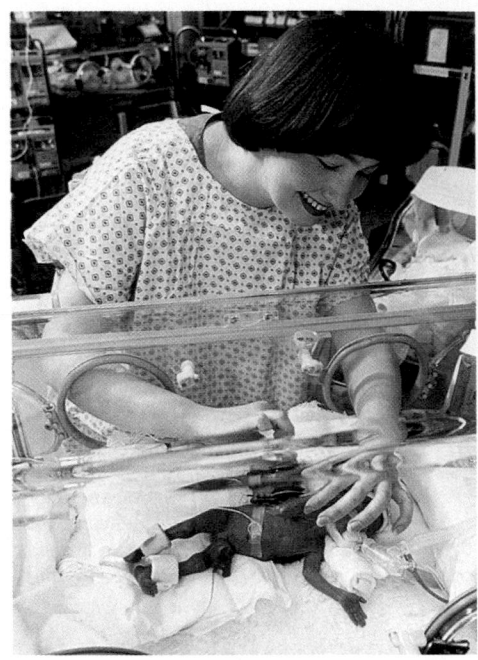

A "kilogram kid," weighing less than 2.3 pounds at birth. *What are some long-term outcomes for weighing so little at birth?*

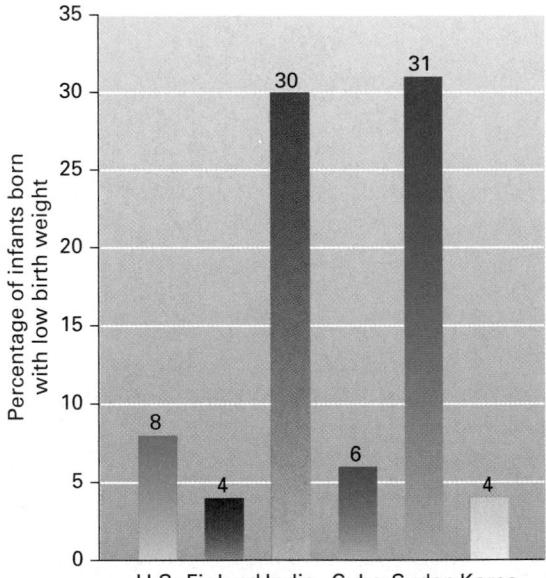

FIGURE 3.8 Percentage of Infants Born with Low Birth Weight in Selected Countries

preterm infants Those born before the completion of 37 weeks of gestation (the time between fertilization and birth).

small for date infants Also called small for gestational age infants, these infants' birth weights are below normal when the length of pregnancy is considered. Small for date infants may be preterm or full term.

weigh under 3½ pounds, and *extremely low birth weight* newborns weigh under 2 pounds. **Preterm infants** are those born three weeks or more before the pregnancy has reached its full term—in other words, before the completion of 37 weeks of gestation (the time between fertilization and birth). **Small for date infants** (also called *small for gestational age infants*) are those whose birth weight is below normal when the length of the pregnancy is considered. They weigh less than 90 percent of all babies of the same gestational age. Small for date infants may be preterm or full term. One study found that small for date infants had more than a fourfold risk of death (Regev & others, 2004).

The preterm birth rate in the United States increased 18 percent from 1990 to 2004 (Hoyert & others, 2006). One of every eight U.S. births is now preterm (Ashton, 2006). The increase in preterm birth is likely due to such factors as the increasing number of births to women 35 years and older, increasing rates of multiple births, increased management of maternal and fetal conditions (for example, inducing labor preterm if medical technology indicates it will increase the likelihood of survival), increased substance abuse (tobacco, alcohol), and increased stress (Goldenberg & Culcane, 2007). Ethnic variations characterize preterm birth (Balchin & Steer, 2007). For example, in 2003, the likelihood of being born preterm was one in eight for all U.S. infants, but the rate was one in six for African American infants (Ashton, 2006).

Recently, there has been considerable interest generated in the role that progestin might play in reducing preterm births (Basaran, 2007; Thornton, 2007). In one study, weekly injections of the hormone progesterone, which is naturally produced by the ovaries, lowered the rate of preterm births by one-third (Meis & Peaceman, 2003). Other recent studies provide further support for the use of progestin in the second trimester of pregnancy in reducing the risk of preterm delivery (Fonseca & others, 2007; Lamont & Jaggat, 2007). However, one recent study did not find a reduction in preterm labor when progestin was given to women who were pregnant with twins (Rouse & others, 2007). A recent survey indicated that the use of progestin to prevent preterm birth increased from 38 percent of maternal-fetal medicine specialists in 2003 to 67 percent in 2005 (Ness & others, 2006).

The incidence of low birth weight varies considerably from country to country. In some countries, such as India and Sudan, where poverty is rampant and the health and nutrition of mothers are poor, the percentage of low birth weight babies reaches as high as 31 percent (see Figure 3.8). In the United States, there has been an increase in low birth weight infants in the last two decades. The U.S. low birth weight rate of 8 percent in 2004 is considerably higher than that of many other developed countries (Hoyert & others, 2006). For example, only 4 percent of the infants born in Sweden, Finland, Norway, and Korea are low birth weight, and only 5 percent of those born in New Zealand, Australia, and France are low birth weight.

The causes of low birth weight also vary. In the developing world, low birth weight stems mainly from the mother's poor health and nutrition (Lasker & others, 2005). For example, diarrhea and malaria, which are common in developing countries, can impair fetal growth if the mother becomes affected while she is pregnant. In developed countries, cigarette smoking during pregnancy is the leading cause of low birth weight (Nabet & others, 2007). In both developed and developing countries, adolescents who give birth when their bodies have not fully matured are at risk for having low birth weight babies (Malamitsi-Puchner & Boutsikou, 2006). In the United States, the increase in the number of low birth weight infants is due to such factors as the use of drugs, poor nutrition, multiple births, reproductive technologies, and improved technology and prenatal care that result in more high-risk babies surviving (Chen & others, 2007b). Nonetheless, poverty still is a major factor is preterm birth in the United States. Women living in poverty conditions are more likely to be obese, have diabetes and hypertension, smoke cigarettes and use illicit drugs, and be less likely to have regular prenatal care (Goldenberg & Nagahawatte, 2008).

Consequences of Preterm Birth and Low Birth Weight   Although most preterm and low birth weight infants are healthy, as a group they have more health and developmental problems than normal birth weight infants (Minde & Zelkowitz, 2008; van de Weijer-Bergsma, Wijnroks, & Jongmans, 2008). For preterm birth, the terms *extremely preterm* and *very preterm* are increasingly used (Smith, 2008). *Extremely preterm infants* are those born less than 28 weeks preterm, and *very preterm infants* are those born less than 33 weeks of gestational age. Figure 3.9 shows the results of a recent Norwegian study indicating that the earlier preterm infants are born the more likely they will drop out of school (Swamy, Osbye, & Skjaerven, 2008). Another, a recent study found that extremely preterm infants were more likely to show pervasive delays in early language development (such as vocabulary size and quality of word use) than very preterm infants, who in turn showed more early language delays than full-term infants (Foster-Cohen & others, 2007). A recent research review also revealed that very preterm infants had lower IQ scores, less effective information-processing skills, and were more at risk for behavioral problems than full-term infants (Johnson, S., 2007).

The number and severity of these problems increase when infants are born very early and as their birth weight decreases (Marlow & others, 2007). Survival rates for infants who are born very early and very small have risen, but with this improved survival rate have come increases in rates of severe brain damage (Allen, 2008; Casey, 2008). A recent MRI study revealed that adolescents who had experienced very preterm birth were more likely to show reduced prefrontal lobe and corpus callosum functioning than full-term adolescents (Narberhaus & others, 2008).

At school age, children who were born low in birth weight are more likely than their normal birth weight counterparts to have a learning disability, attention deficit hyperactivity disorder, or breathing problems such as asthma (Greenough, 2007; Joshi & Kotecha, 2007). One study revealed that 17-year-olds who were born with low birth weight were 50 percent more likely than normal birth weight individuals to have reading and mathematics deficits (Breaslau, Paneth, & Lucia, 2004). Approximately 50 percent of all low birth weight children are enrolled in special education programs.

Nurturing Preterm Infants   Some effects of being born low in birth weight can be reversed. Intensive enrichment programs that provide medical and educational services for both the parents and children can improve short-term outcomes for low birth weight children. Federal laws mandate that services for school-age children be expanded to include family-based care for infants. At present, these services are aimed at children born with severe disabilities. The availability of services for moderately low birth weight children who do not have severe physical problems varies, but most states do not provide these services.

Currently, the two most popular neonatal intensive care unit (NICU) interventions that involve parents are breast feeding and **kangaroo care**, treatment for preterm infants that involves skin-to-skin contact. Both of these interventions were uncommon until recently.

A recent survey revealed that breast feeding is now virtually universally encouraged for mothers with newborns in U.S. NICUs (Field & others, 2006). Recent surveys indicated that kangaroo care is used from 82 to 97 percent by nurses in NICUs (Engler & others, 2002; Field & others, 2006). Also in one of these surveys, massage therapy was used in 37 percent of the NICUs (Field & others, 2006).

Let's further examine kangaroo care and massage therapy. In kangaroo care, the baby, wearing only a diaper, is held upright against the parent's bare chest, much as a baby kangaroo is carried by its mother. Kangaroo care is typically practiced for two to three hours per day, skin-to-skin over an extended time in early infancy (Johnson, A. N., 2007).

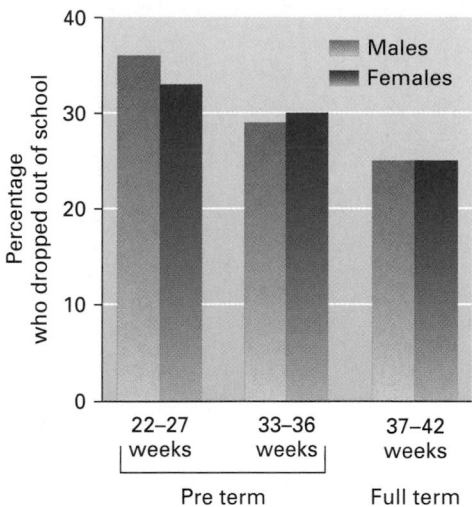

FIGURE 3.9 Percentage of Preterm and Full-Term Birth Infants Who Dropped Out of School

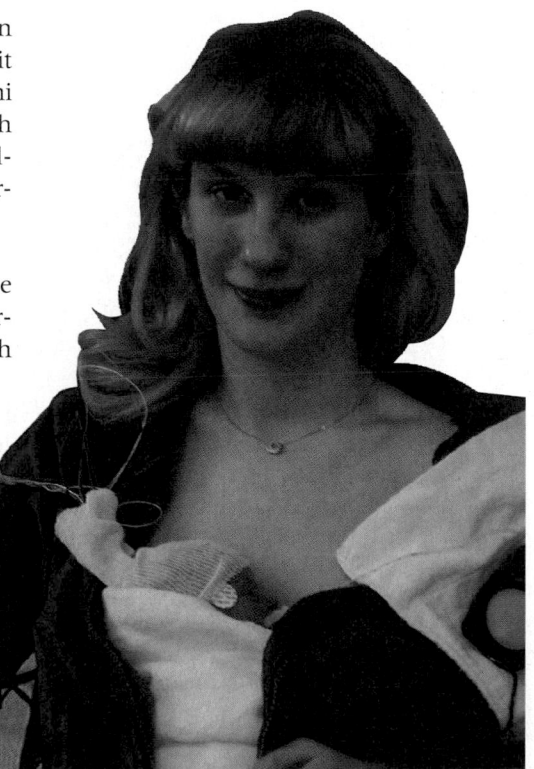

A new mother practicing kangaroo care. *What is kangaroo care?*

kangaroo care   Treatment for preterm infants that involves skin-to-skin contact.

Why use kangaroo care with preterm infants? Preterm infants often have difficulty coordinating their breathing and heart rate, and the close physical contact with the parent provided by kangaroo care can help to stabilize the preterm infant's heartbeat, temperature, and breathing (Walters & others, 2007). Further, preterm infants who experience kangaroo care have longer periods of sleep, gain more weight, decrease their crying, have longer periods of alertness, and earlier hospital discharge (Ludington-Hoe & others, 2006). Two recent experimental studies revealed that low birth weight infants randomly assigned to kangaroo mother care compared with traditional mother care gained more weight, were less likely to experience hypothermia and hypglycemia, and were more strongly attached to their mother (Gathwala, Singh, & Balhara, 2008; Suman, Udani, & Nanavati, 2008). Increasingly kangaroo care is being recommended for full-term infants as well (Ferber & Makhoul, 2008; Walters & others, 2007).

Many preterm infants experience less touch than full-term infants because they are isolated in temperature-controlled incubators (Chia, Selleck, & Gans, 2006). The research of Tiffany Field has led to a surge of interest in the role that massage might play in improving the developmental outcomes for preterm infants. To read about her research, see the following *Research in Life-Span Development* interlude.

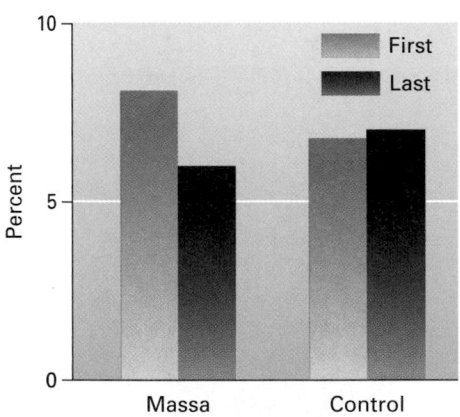

FIGURE 3.10 Preterm Infants Show Reduced Stress Behaviors and Activity After Five Days of Massage Therapy, (Hernandez-Reif, Diego, & Field, 2007). Infant Behavior and Development, 30.

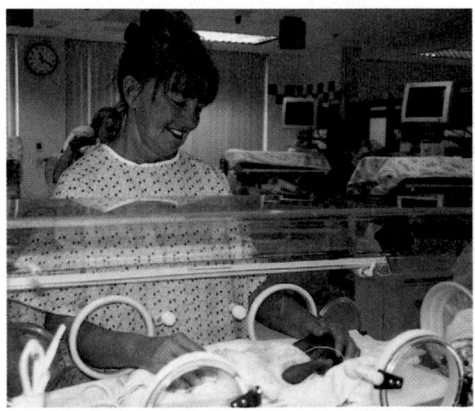

Shown here is Tiffany Field massaging a newborn infant. *What types of infants has massage therapy been shown to help?*

Research in Life-Span Development
Tiffany Field's Research on Massage Therapy

Throughout history and in many cultures, caregivers have massaged infants. In Africa and Asia, infants are routinely massaged by parents or other family members for several months after birth. In the United States, interest in using touch and massage to improve the growth, health, and well-being of infants has been stimulated by the research of Tiffany Field (2001, 2007; Diego, Field, & Hernandez-Reif, 2008; Field, Diego, & Hernandez-Reif, 2008; Field & others, 2006; Hernandez-Reif, Diego, & Field, 2007), director of the Touch Research Institute at the University of Miami School of Medicine.

In a recent study, preterm infants in a neonatal intensive care unit (NICU) were randomly assigned to a massage therapy group or a control group. For five consecutive days, the preterm infants in the massage group were given three 15-minute moderate pressure massages. Behavioral observations of the following stress behaviors were made on the first and last days of the study: crying, grimacing, yawning, sneezing, jerky arm and leg movements, startles, and finger flaring. The various stress behaviors were summarized in a composite stress behavior index. As indicated in Figure 3.10, massage had a stress-reducing effect on the preterm infants, which is especially important because they encounter numerous stressors while they are hospitalized.

In another study, Field and her colleagues (2004) tested a more cost-effective massage strategy. They taught mothers how to massage their full-term infants rather than having health-care professionals do the massage. Beginning from day one of the newborn's life to the end of the first month, once a day before bedtime the mothers massaged the babies using either light or moderate pressure. Infants who were massaged with moderate pressure gained more weight, performed better on the orientation scale of the Brazelton, were less excitable and less depressed, and were less agitated during sleep.

Field has demonstrated the benefits of massage therapy for infants who face a variety of problems. For example, preterm infants exposed to cocaine in utero who received massage therapy gained weight and improved their scores on developmental tests (Wheeden & others, 1993). Another study investigated 1- to 3-month-old infants born to depressed adolescent mothers (Field & others, 1996). The infants of depressed mothers who received massage therapy had lower stress—as well as improved emotionality, sociability, and soothability—compared with the nonmassaged infants of depressed mothers.

In a research review of massage therapy with preterm infants, Field and her colleagues (2004) concluded that the most consistent findings involve two positive results: (1) increased weight gain and (2) discharge from the hospital from three to six days earlier.

Infants are not the only ones who may benefit from massage therapy (Field, 2007). In other studies, Field and her colleagues have demonstrated the benefits of massage therapy with women in reducing labor pain (Field, Hernandez-Rief, Taylor, & others, 1997), with children who have asthma (Field, Henteleff, & others, 1998), with autistic children's attentiveness (Field, Lasko, & others, 1997), and with adolescents who have attention deficit hyperactivity disorder (Field, Quintino, & others, 1998).

Review and Reflect: Learning Goal 2

 2 Discuss the Birth Process

REVIEW

- What are the three main stages of birth? What are some different birth strategies? What is the transition from fetus to newborn like for the infant?
- What are three measures of neonatal health and responsiveness?
- What are the outcomes for children if they are born preterm or with a low birth weight?

REFLECT

- If you are a female, which birth strategy do you prefer? Why? If you are a male, how involved would you want to be in helping your partner through pregnancy and the birth of your baby?

3 THE POSTPARTUM PERIOD

| Physical Adjustments | Emotional and Psychological Adjustments | Bonding |

The weeks after childbirth present challenges for many new parents and their offspring. This is the **postpartum period**, the period after childbirth or delivery that lasts for about six weeks or until the mother's body has completed its adjustment and has returned to a nearly prepregnant state. It is a time when the woman adjusts, both physically and psychologically, to the process of childbearing.

The postpartum period involves a great deal of adjustment and adaptation. The baby has to be cared for. The mother has to recover from childbirth, to learn how to take care of the baby, and to learn to feel good about herself as a mother. The father needs to learn how to take care of his recovering wife, to learn how to take care of the baby, and to learn how to feel good about himself as a father. Many health professionals believe that the best way to meet these challenges is with a family-centered approach that uses the family's resources to support an early and smooth adjustment to the newborn by all family members. The adjustments needed are physical, emotional, and psychological.

Physical Adjustments

A woman's body makes numerous physical adjustments in the first days and weeks after childbirth (London & others, 2007). She may have a great deal of energy or feel exhausted and let down. Most new mothers feel tired and need rest. Though these changes

postpartum period The period after childbirth when the mother adjusts, both physically and psychologically, to the process of childbirth. This period lasts for about six weeks or until her body has completed its adjustment and returned to a near prepregnant state.

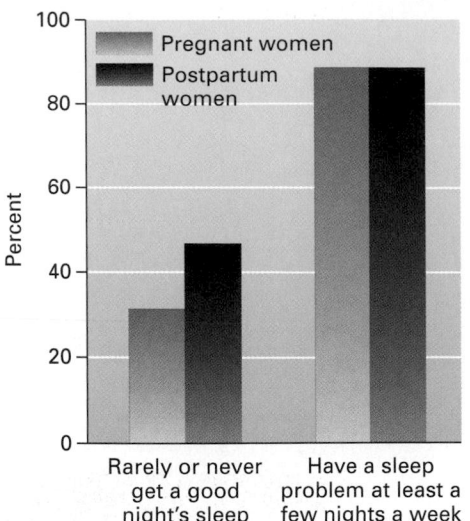

FIGURE 3.11 Sleep Deprivation in Pregnant and Postpartum Women

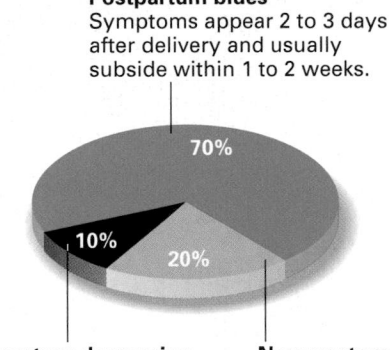

Postpartum blues
Symptoms appear 2 to 3 days after delivery and usually subside within 1 to 2 weeks.

Postpartum depression
Symptoms linger for weeks or months and interfere with daily functioning.

No symptoms

FIGURE 3.12 Postpartum Blues and Postpartum Depression Among U.S. Women. Some health professionals refer to the postpartum period as the "fourth trimester." Though the time span of the postpartum period does not necessarily cover three months, the term "fourth trimester" suggests continuity and the importance of the first several months after birth for the mother.

postpartum depression Characteristic of women who have such strong feelings or sadness, anxiety, or despair that they have trouble coping with daily tasks in the postpartum period.

are normal, the fatigue can undermine the new mother's sense of well-being and confidence in her ability to cope with a new baby and a new family life (Runquist, 2007).

A concern is the loss of sleep that the primary caregiver experiences in the postpartum period (Gunderson & others, 2008; Signal & others, 2007). A recent analysis indicated that the primary caregiver loses as much as 700 hours of sleep in the first year following the baby's birth (Maas, 2008). In the 2007 Sleep in America survey, a substantial percentage of women reported loss of sleep during pregnancy and in the postpartum period (National Sleep Foundation, 2007) (see Figure 3.11). The loss of sleep can contribute to stress, marital conflict, and impaired decision making (Meerlo, Sgoifo, & Suchecki, 2008). Even after their newborn begins to sleep better through the night by the middle of the baby's first year, many mothers report waking up several times a night even when their baby is asleep. Sleep experts say it takes several weeks to several months for parents' internal sleep clocks to adjust.

After delivery, a mother's body undergoes sudden and dramatic changes in hormone production. When the placenta is delivered, estrogen and progesterone levels drop steeply and remain low until the ovaries start producing hormones again. The woman will probably begin menstruating again in four to eight weeks if she is not breast feeding. If she is breast feeding, she might not menstruate for several months to a year or more, though ovulation usually occurs during this time. The first several menstrual periods following delivery might be heavier than usual, but periods soon return to normal.

Involution is the process by which the uterus returns to its prepregnant size five or six weeks after birth. Immediately following birth, the uterus weighs 2 to 3 pounds. By the end of five or six weeks, the uterus weighs 2 to $3\frac{1}{2}$ ounces. Nursing the baby helps contract the uterus at a rapid rate.

If the woman regularly engaged in conditioning exercises during pregnancy, exercise will help her recover her former body contour and strength. With a caregiver's approval, the new mother can begin some exercises as soon as one hour after delivery. One study found that women who maintained or increased their exercise from prepregnancy to postpartum had better maternal well-being than women who engaged in no exercise or decreased their exercise from prepregnancy to postpartum (Blum, Beaudoin, & Caton-Lemos, 2005).

Relaxation techniques are also helpful during the postpartum period. Five minutes of slow breathing on a stressful day in the postpartum period can relax and refresh the new mother, which will indirectly benefit the new baby.

Emotional and Psychological Adjustments

Emotional fluctuations are common for mothers in the postpartum period. For some women, emotional fluctuations decrease within several weeks after the delivery, but other women experience more long-lasting emotional swings.

As shown in Figure 3.12, about 70 percent of new mothers in the United States have what are called the postpartum blues. About two to three days after birth, they begin to feel depressed, anxious, and upset. These feelings may come and go for several months after the birth, often peaking about three to five days after birth. Even without treatment, these feelings usually go away after one or two weeks.

For other women, emotional fluctuations persist and can produce feelings of anxiety, depression, and difficulty in coping with stress (Morrissey, 2007; Tam & Chung, 2007). Mothers who have such feelings, even when they are getting adequate rest, may benefit from professional help in dealing with their problems. Indications of a need for professional counseling about postpartum adaptation include excessive worrying, depression, extreme changes in appetite, crying spells, and inability to sleep.

Postpartum depression involves a major depressive episode that typically occurs about four weeks after delivery. In other words, women with postpartum depression have such strong feelings of sadness, anxiety, or despair that for at least a two-week period they have trouble coping with their daily tasks. Without treatment, postpartum depression may become worse and last for many months (Gjeringem, Katon, & Rich, 2008). About 10 percent of new mothers experience postpartum depression. Between 25 to 50 percent of these depressed new mothers have episodes that last six months or longer (Beck, 2002). If untreated, approximately 25 of these women are still depressed a year later.

Hormonal changes that occur after childbirth are believed to play a role in postpartum depression (Groer & Morgan, 2007; Jolley & others, 2007). Estrogen helps some women with postpartum depression, but estrogen also has some possible problematic side effects (Grigoriadis & Kennedy, 2002). Several antidepressant drugs are effective in treating postpartum depression and appear to be safe for breast feeding women (Horowitz & Cousins, 2006). Psychotherapy, especially cognitive therapy, also is an effective treatment of postpartum depression for many women (Beck, 2006). Also, engaging in regular exercise may help in treating postpartum depression (Daley, Macarthur, & Winter, 2007).

One concern about postpartum depression is that breast feeding is less common among postpartum depressed women. They may not breast feed because of their concern about potentially negative effects of antidepressants that can be transmitted to their young infant through breast milk (Einarson & Ito, 2007). Currently, little research has been conducted on whether the positive effects of breast feeding might outweigh the positive effects of antidepressants for both the mother and the infant (Field, 2008).

Can a mother's postpartum depression affect the way mothers interact with their infants? Researchers have found that depressed mothers interact less with their infants and are less likely to respond to their infants' effort to get attention (Teti & Towe-Goodman, 2008). A recent national survey indicated that mothers who were depressed were 1.5 times more likely to provide less healthy feeding and sleeping practices for their newborns (Paulson, Dauber, & Leiferman, 2006). Another recent study revealed that postpartum depression was more common in mothers who had preterm than full-term infants (Feldman & Eidelman, 2007). In this study, with both preterm and full-term infants, mothers with postpartum depression showed a low level of maternal-infant synchrony.

Fathers also undergo considerable adjustment in the postpartum period, even when they work away from home all day (Cox, 2006). Many fathers feel that the baby comes first and gets all of the mother's attention; some feel that they have been replaced by the baby.

To help the father adjust, parents should set aside some special time to be together with each other. The father's postpartum reaction also likely will be improved if he has taken childbirth classes with the mother and is an active participant in caring for the baby.

Bonding

A special component of the parent-infant relationship is **bonding**, the formation of a connection, especially a physical bond between parents and the newborn in the period shortly after birth. Sometimes hospitals seem determined to deter bonding. Drugs given to the mother to make her delivery less painful can make the mother drowsy, interfering with her ability to respond to and stimulate the newborn. Mothers and newborns are often separated shortly after delivery, and preterm infants are isolated from their mothers even more than full-term mothers.

Do these practices do any harm? Some physicians believe that during the period shortly after birth, the parents and newborn need to form an emotional attachment as a foundation for optimal development in years to come (Kennell, 2006; Kennell & McGrath, 1999). Is there evidence that close contact between mothers in the first several days after birth is critical for optimal development later in life? Although some research supports this bonding hypothesis (Klaus & Kennell, 1976), a body of research challenges the significance of the first few days of life as a critical period (Bakeman & Brown, 1980; Rode & others, 1981). Indeed, the extreme form of the bonding hypothesis—that the newborn must have close contact with the mother in the first few days of life to develop optimally—simply is not true.

The postpartum period is a time of considerable adjustment and adaptation for both the mother and the father. Fathers can provide an important support system for mothers, especially in helping mothers care for young infants. *What kinds of tasks might the father of a newborn do to support the mother?*

bonding The formation of a close connection, especially a physical bond between parents and their newborn in the period shortly after birth.

A mother bonds with her infant moments after it is born. *How critical is bonding for the development of social competence later in childhood?*

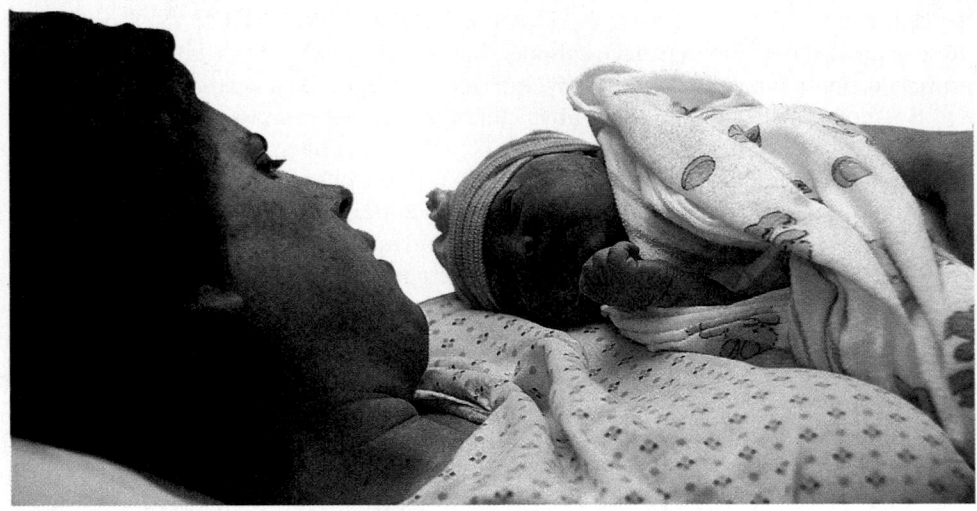

Nonetheless, the weakness of the bonding hypothesis should not be used as an excuse to keep motivated mothers from interacting with their newborns. Such contact brings pleasure to many mothers. In some mother-infant pairs—including preterm infants, adolescent mothers, and mothers from disadvantaged circumstances—early close contact may establish a climate for improved interaction after the mother and infant leave the hospital.

Many hospitals now offer a *rooming-in* arrangement, in which the baby remains in the mother's room most of the time during its hospital stay. However, if parents choose not to use this rooming-in arrangement, the weight of the research suggests that this decision will not harm the infant emotionally (Lamb, 1994).

Review and Reflect: Learning Goal 3

 Explain the Changes That Take Place in the Postpartum Period

REVIEW

- What does the postpartum period involve? What physical adjustments does the woman's body make in this period?
- What emotional and psychological adjustments characterize the postpartum period?
- Is bonding critical for optimal development?

REFLECT

- If you are a female, what can you do to adjust effectively in the postpartum period? If you are a male, what can you do to help in the postpartum period?

Prenatal Development and Birth

1   PRENATAL DEVELOPMENT: DESCRIBE PRENATAL DEVELOPMENT

The Course of Prenatal Development

- Prenatal development is divided into three periods: germinal (conception until 10 to 14 days later), which ends when the zygote (a fertilized egg) attaches to the uterine wall; embryonic (two to eight weeks after conception), during which the embryo differentiates into three layers, life-support systems develop, and organ systems form (organogenesis); and fetal (two months after conception until about nine months, or when the infant is born), a time when organ systems have matured to the point at which life can be sustained outside of the womb. The growth of the brain during prenatal development is nothing short of remarkable. By the time babies are born they have approximately 100 billion neurons, or nerve cells. Neurogenesis is the term that means the formation of new neurons. The nervous system begins with the formation of a neural tube at 18 to 24 days after conception. Proliferation and migration are two processes that characterize brain development in the prenatal period. The basic architecture of the brain is formed in the first two trimesters of prenatal development

Teratology and Hazards to Prenatal Development

- Teratology is the field that investigates the causes of congenital (birth) defects. Any agent that causes birth defects is called a teratogen. The dose, genetic susceptibility, and time of exposure influence the severity of the damage to an unborn child and the type of defect that occurs. Prescription drugs that can be harmful include antibiotics. Nonprescription drugs that can be harmful include diet pills, aspirin, and caffeine. Legal psychoactive drugs that are potentially harmful to prenatal development include alcohol and nicotine. Fetal alcohol spectrum disorders are a cluster of abnormalities that appear in offspring of mothers who drink heavily during pregnancy. Even when pregnant women drink moderately (one to two drinks a few days a week), negative effects on their offspring have been found. Cigarette smoking by pregnant women has serious adverse effects on prenatal and child development (such as low birth weight). Illegal psychoactive drugs that are potentially harmful to offspring include methamphetamine, marijuana, cocaine, and heroin. Incompatibility of the mother's and the father's blood types can also be harmful to the fetus. Environmental hazards include radiation, environmental pollutants, and toxic wastes. Syphilis, rubella (German measles), genital herpes, and AIDS are infectious diseases that can harm the fetus. Other parental factors include maternal diet and nutrition, age, emotional states and stress, and paternal factors. A developing fetus depends entirely on its mother for nutrition. Maternal age can negatively affect the offspring's development if the mother is an adolescent or over 35. High stress in the mother is linked with less than optimal prenatal and birth outcomes. Paternal factors that can adversely affect prenatal development include exposure to lead, radiation, certain pesticides, and petrochemicals.

Prenatal Care

- Prenatal care varies extensively but usually involves medical care services with a defined schedule of visits.

Normal Prenatal Development

- It is important to remember that, although things can and do go wrong during pregnancy, most of the time pregnancy and prenatal development go well.

2   BIRTH: DISCUSS THE BIRTH PROCESS

The Birth Process

- Childbirth occurs in three stages. The first stage, which lasts about 6 to 12 hours for a woman having her first child, is the longest stage. The cervix dilates to about 10 centimeters (4 inches) at the end of the first stage. The second stage begins when the baby's head starts to move through the cervix and ends with the baby's complete emergence. The third stage involves the delivery of the placenta after birth. Childbirth strategies involve the childbirth setting and attendants. In many countries, a doula attends a childbearing woman. Methods of delivery include medicated, natural and prepared, and cesarean. Being born involves considerable stress for the baby, but the baby is well prepared and adapted to handle the stress. Anoxia—insufficient oxygen supply to the fetus/newborn—is a potential hazard.

Assessing the Newborn

- For many years, the Apgar Scale has been used to assess the newborn's health. The Brazelton Neonatal Behavioral Assessment Scale examines the newborn's neurological development, reflexes, and reactions to people. Recently, the Neonatal Intensive Care Unit Network Neurobehavioral Scale (NNNS) was created to assess the at-risk infant.

Preterm and Low Birth Weight Infants

- Low birth weight infants weigh less than $5\frac{1}{2}$ pounds, and they may be preterm (born before the completion of 37 weeks of gestation) or small for date (also called small for gestational age, which refers to infants whose birth weight is below normal when the length of pregnancy is considered). Small for date infants may be preterm or full term. Although most low birth weight and preterm infants are normal and healthy, as a group they have more health and developmental problems than normal birth weight infants. Kangaroo care and massage therapy have been shown to have benefits for preterm infants.

3 THE POSTPARTUM PERIOD: EXPLAIN THE CHANGES THAT TAKE PLACE IN THE POSTPARTUM PERIOD

Physical Adjustments

- The postpartum period is the name given to the period after childbirth or delivery. The period lasts for about six weeks or until the woman's body has completed its adjustment. Physical adjustments in the postpartum period include fatigue, involution (the process by which the uterus returns to its prepregnant size five or six weeks after birth), hormonal changes, when to resume sexual intercourse, and exercises to recover body contour and strength.

Emotional and Psychological Adjustments

- Emotional fluctuations on the part of the mother are common in this period, and they can vary a great deal from one mother to the next. Postpartum depression characterizes women who have such strong feelings of sadness, anxiety, or despair that they have trouble coping with daily tasks in the postpartum period. Postpartum depression occurs in about 10 percent of new mothers. The father also goes through a postpartum adjustment.

Bonding

- Bonding is the formation of a close connection, especially a physical bond between parents and the newborn shortly after birth. Early bonding has not been found to be critical in the development of a competent infant.

KEY TERMS

germinal period 79
blastocyst 79
trophoblast 79
embryonic period 79
amnion 80
umbilical cord 80
placenta 80
organogenesis 80
fetal period 81

neurons 81
teratogen 83
fetal alcohol spectrum disorders (FASD) 85
afterbirth 94
doula 95
natural childbirth 95
prepared childbirth 96
breech position 97

cesarean delivery 98
Apgar Scale 98
Brazelton Neonatal Behavioral Assessment Scale (NBAS) 99
Neonatal Intensive Care Unit Network Neurobehavioral Scale (NNNS) 99

low birth weight infants 99
preterm infants 100
small for date infants 100
kangaroo care 101
postpartum period 103
postpartum depression 104
bonding 105

KEY PEOPLE

Grantley Dick-Read 95   Ferdinand Lamaze 96   T. Berry Brazelton 99   Tiffany Field 102

E-LEARNING TOOLS

To help you master the material in this chapter, visit the Online Learning Center for *Life-Span Development*, twelfth edition, at **www.mhhe.com/santrockld12**.

Self-Assessment

Connect to **www.mhhe.com/santrockld12** and complete the self-assessment *Pregnancy Screening for Alcohol Use* to learn more about how alcohol can affect an unborn baby.

Taking It to the Net

Connect to **www.mhhe.com/santrockld12** to research the answers to these questions:

1. Denise's sister, Doreen, is pregnant for the first time. Doreen is not particularly known for her healthy lifestyle. What particular things can Denise encourage Doreen to do in order to give birth to a healthy baby?

2. Sienne told her fiancé, Jackson, that he had better stop smoking before they begin trying to conceive a child. Why is Sienne concerned about Jackson's smoking and its effect on their children before they have even started planning their family?

3. Hannah, who gave birth to a healthy baby boy—her first child—two weeks ago, appears to her husband Sean to be sad and lethargic and is having trouble sleeping. How can Sean determine if Hannah is just going through a natural period of postpartum "blues" or if she might be suffering from postpartum depression?

Video Clips

The Online Learning Center includes a video for Chapter 3 called "Transitions to Parenting—Heterosexual Married Couples." In an interview conducted only weeks before the birth of their first child, a couple anticipates some of the transitional issues that all parents must deal with in the weeks immediately following the birth of the child.

Health and Well-Being, Parenting, and Education Exercises

Build your decision-making skills by trying your hand at the health and well-being, parenting, and education exercises. Connect to **www.mhhe.com/santrockld12** to research the answers and complete the exercises.

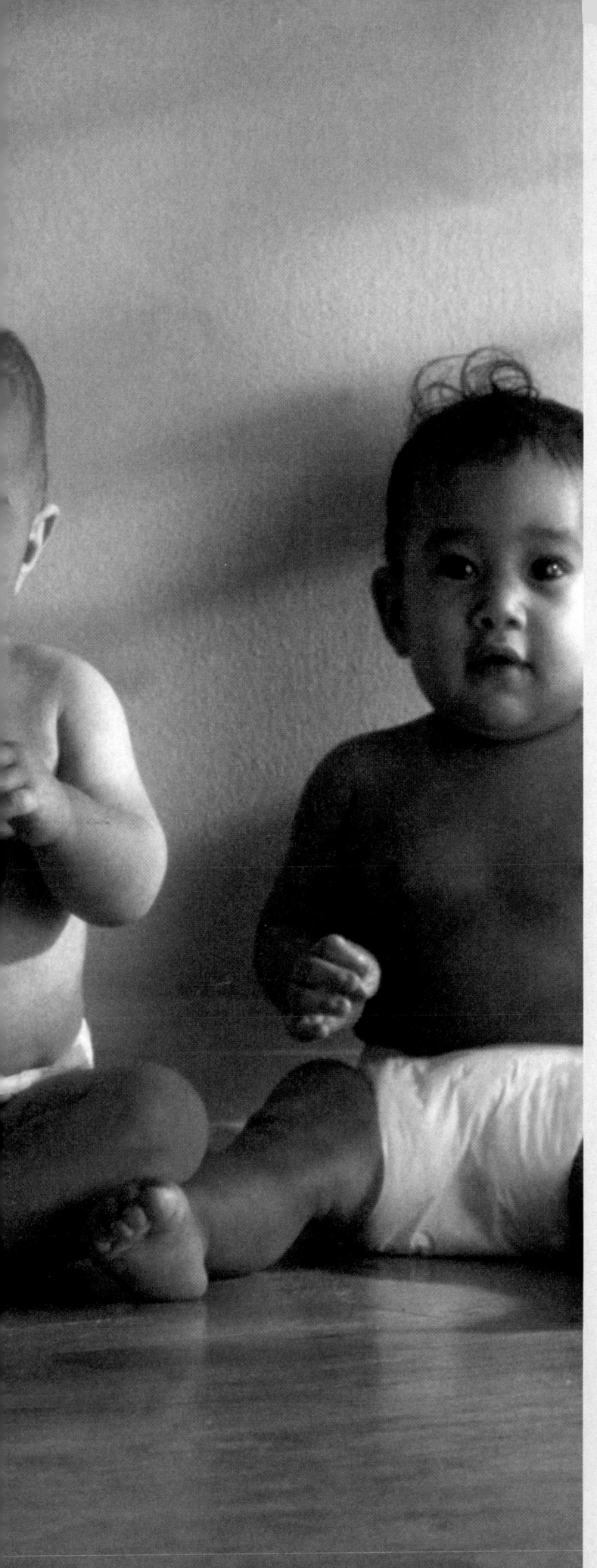

INFANCY

*Babies are such a nice
way to start people.*

—DON HEROLD
American Writer, 20th Century

As newborns, we were not empty-headed organisms. We had some basic reflexes, among them crying, kicking, and coughing. We slept a lot, and occasionally we smiled, although the meaning of our first smiles was not entirely clear. We ate and we grew. We crawled and then we walked, a journey of a thousand miles beginning with a single step. Sometimes we conformed; sometimes others conformed to us. Our development was a continuous creation of more complex forms. Our helpless kind demanded the meeting eyes of love. We juggled the necessity of curbing our will with becoming what we could will freely. Section 3 contains three chapters: "Physical Development in Infancy" (Chapter 4), "Cognitive Development in Infancy" (Chapter 5), and "Socioemotional Development in Infancy" (Chapter 6).

4

A baby is the most complicated object made by unskilled labor.

—Anonymous

LEARNING GOALS

◆ Discuss physical growth and development in infancy.

◆ Describe infants' motor development.

◆ Summarize the course of sensory and perceptual development in infancy.

PHYSICAL DEVELOPMENT IN INFANCY

CHAPTER OUTLINE

Images of Life-Span Development
The Stories of Latonya and Ramona: Breast and Bottle Feeding in Africa

Latonya is a newborn baby in Ghana. During her first days of life, she has been kept apart from her mother and bottle fed. Manufacturers of infant formula provide the hospital where she was born with free or subsidized milk powder. Her mother has been persuaded to bottle feed rather than breast feed her. When her mother bottle feeds Latonya, she overdilutes the milk formula with unclean water. Latonya's feeding bottles have not been sterilized. Latonya becomes very sick. She dies before her first birthday.

Ramona was born in Nigeria with a "baby-friendly" program. In this program, babies are not separated from their mothers when they are born, and the mothers are encouraged to breast feed them. The mothers are told of the perils that bottle feeding can bring because of unsafe water and unsterilized bottles. They also are informed about the advantages of breast milk, which include its nutritious and hygienic qualities, its ability to immunize babies against common illnesses, and its role in reducing the mother's risk of breast and ovarian cancer. Ramona's mother is breast feeding her. At 1 year of age, Ramona is very healthy.

For many years, maternity units in hospitals favored bottle feeding and did not give mothers adequate information about the benefits of breast feeding. In recent years, the World Health Organization and UNICEF have tried to reverse the trend toward bottle feeding of infants in many impoverished countries. They instituted the "baby-friendly" program in many countries (Grant, 1993). They also persuaded the International Association of Infant Formula Manufacturers to stop marketing their baby formulas to hospitals in countries where the governments support the baby-friendly initiatives (Grant, 1993). For the hospitals themselves, costs actually were reduced as infant formula, feeding bottles, and separate nurseries become unnecessary. For example, baby-friendly Jose Fabella Memorial Hospital in the Philippines reported saving 8 percent of its annual budget. Still, there are many places in the world where the baby-friendly initiatives have not been implemented (UNICEF, 2004).

The advantages of breast feeding in impoverished countries are substantial. However, these advantages must be balanced against the risk of passing HIV to the babies through breast milk if the mothers have the virus; the majority of mothers don't know that they are infected (Doherty & others, 2006; Dube & others, 2008). In some areas of Africa, more than 30 percent of mothers have the human immuno deficiency virus (HIV).

(*Top*) An HIV-infected mother breast feeding her baby in Nairobi, Africa. (*Bottom*) A Rhwandan mother bottle feeding her baby. *What are some concerns about breast versus bottle feeding in impoverished African countries?*

PREVIEW

It is very important for infants to get a healthy start. When they do, their first two years of life are likely to be a time of amazing development. In this chapter, we focus on the biological domain and the infant's physical development, exploring physical growth, motor development, and sensory and perceptual development.

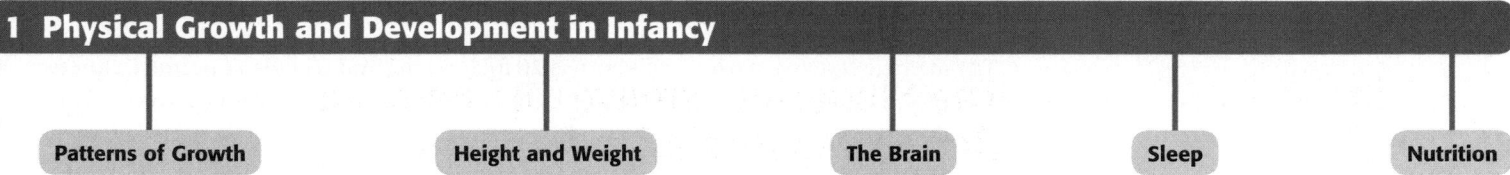

1 Physical Growth and Development in Infancy

| Patterns of Growth | Height and Weight | The Brain | Sleep | Nutrition |

Infants' physical development in the first two years of life is extensive. Newborns heads are quite large when compared with the rest of their bodies. They have little strength in their necks and cannot hold their heads up. They have some basic reflexes. In the span of 12 months, infants become capable of sitting anywhere, standing, stooping, climbing, and usually walking. During the second year, growth decelerates, but rapid increases in such activities as running and climbing take place. Let's now examine in greater detail the sequence of physical development in infancy.

Patterns of Growth

An extraordinary proportion of the total body is occupied by the head during prenatal development and early infancy (see Figure 4.1). The **cephalocaudal pattern** is the sequence in which the earliest growth always occurs at the top—the head—with physical growth and differentiation of features gradually working their way down from top to bottom (for example, shoulders, middle trunk, and so on) (Pedroso, 2008). This same pattern occurs in the head area, because the top parts of the head—the eyes and brain—grow faster than the lower parts, such as the jaw.

Motor development generally proceeds according to the cephalocaudal principle. For example, infants see objects before they can control their torso, and they can use their hands long before they can crawl or walk. However, development does not follow a rigid blueprint. One study found that infants reached for toys with their feet prior to reaching with their hands (Galloway & Thelen, 2004). On average, infants first touched the toy with their feet when they were 12 weeks old and with their hands when they were 16 weeks old.

Growth also follows the **proximodistal pattern**, the sequence in which growth starts at the center of the body and moves toward the extremities. For example, infants control the muscles of their trunk and arms before they control their hands and fingers, and they use their whole hands before they can control several fingers.

cephalocaudal pattern The sequence in which the earliest growth always occurs at the top—the head—with physical growth in size, weight, and feature differentiation gradually working from top to bottom.

proximodistal pattern The sequence in which growth starts at the center of the body and moves toward the extremities.

FIGURE 4.1 Changes in Proportions of the Human Body During Growth. As individuals develop from infancy through adulthood, one of the most noticeable physical changes is that the head becomes smaller in relation to the rest of the body. The fractions listed refer to head size as a proportion of total body length at different ages.

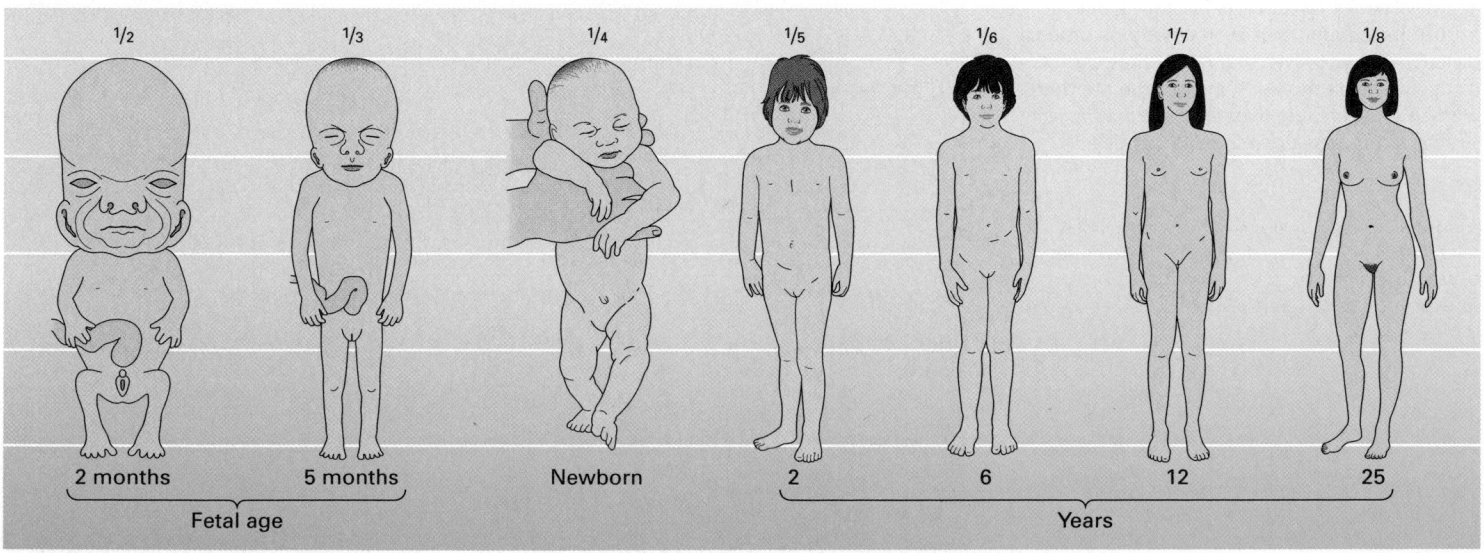

Height and Weight

The average North American newborn is 20 inches long and weighs $7\frac{1}{2}$ pounds. Ninety-five percent of full-term newborns are 18 to 22 inches long and weigh between $5\frac{1}{2}$ and 10 pounds.

In the first several days of life, most newborns lose 5 to 7 percent of their body weight before they adjust to feeding by sucking, swallowing, and digesting. Then they grow rapidly, gaining an average of 5 to 6 ounces per week during the first month. They have doubled their birth weight by the age of 4 months and have nearly tripled it by their first birthday. Infants grow about 1 inch per month during the first year, reaching approximately $1\frac{1}{2}$ times their birth length by their first birthday.

Growth slows considerably in the second year of life (Hockenberry & Wilson, 2009). By 2 years of age, infants weigh approximately 26 to 32 pounds, having gained a quarter to half a pound per month during the second year; now they have reached about one-fifth of their adult weight. At 2 years of age, the average infant is 32 to 35 inches in height, which is nearly half of their adult height.

The Brain

We described the amazing growth of the brain from conception to birth in Chapter 3. By the time it is born, the infant that began as a single cell is estimated to have a brain that contains approximately 100 billion nerve cells, or neurons. Extensive brain development continues after birth, through infancy and later (de Haan & Martinos, 2008; Nelson, 2009). Because the brain is still developing so rapidly in infancy, the infant's head should be protected from falls or other injuries and the baby should never be shaken. *Shaken baby syndrome,* which includes brain swelling and hemorrhaging, affects hundreds of babies in the United States each year (Altimer, 2008; Squire, 2008).

Studying the brain's development in infancy is not as easy as it might seem. Even the latest brain-imaging technologies (described in Chapter 1) cannot make out fine details in adult brains and cannot be used with babies (Nelson, 2009). Positron-emission tomography (PET) scans pose a radiation risk to babies, and infants wriggle too much to capture accurate images using magnetic resonance imaging (MRI) (Marcus, Mulrine, & Wong, 1999). However, among the researchers who are making strides in finding out more about the brain's development in infancy are Charles Nelson and his colleagues (2007, 2009; Moulson & Nelson, 2008; Nelson, Zeanah, & Fox, 2007) (see Figure 4.2).

FIGURE 4.2 Measuring the Activity of an Infant's Brain. By attaching up to 128 electrodes to a baby's scalp to measure the brain's activity, Charles Nelson and his colleagues (2006) have found that even newborns produce distinctive brain waves that reveal they can distinguish their mother's voices from another woman's, even while they are asleep. *Why is it so difficult to measure infants' brain activity?*

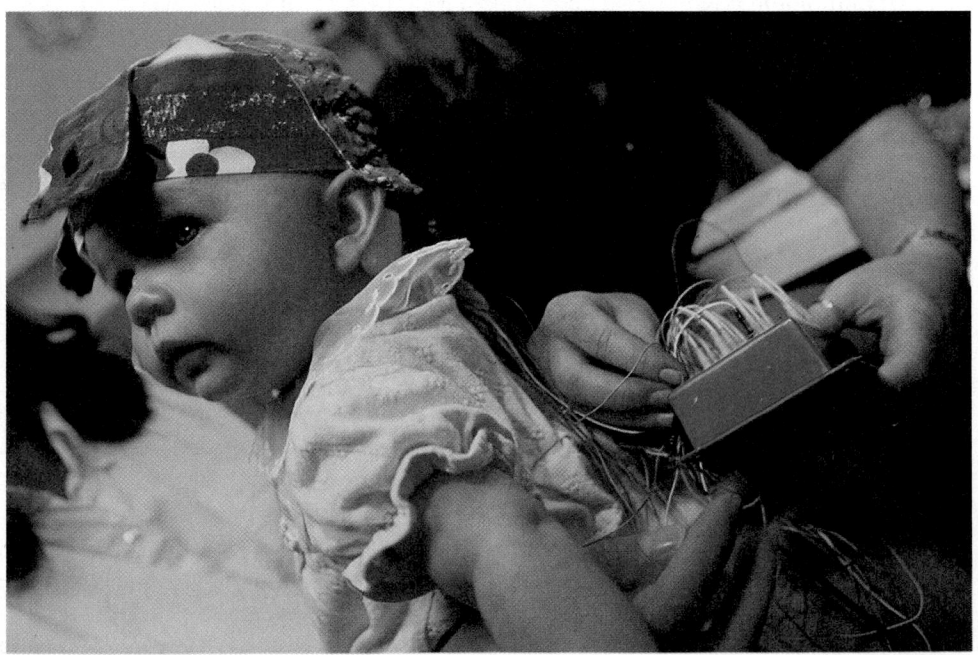

Using the electroencephalogram (EEG), which measures the brain's electrical activity, researchers have found that a spurt in EEG activity occurs at about $1\frac{1}{2}$ to 2 years of age (Fischer & Bidell, 2006; Fischer & Rose, 1995). Other spurts seem to take place at about 9, 12, 15, and 20 years of age. Researchers maintain that these spurts of brain activity may coincide with important changes in cognitive development. For example, the increase in EEG brain activity at $1\frac{1}{2}$ to 2 years of age is associated with an increase in the infant's capacity for conceptualization and language, and the spurts at 15 and 20 years of age are linked to increases in reflective thinking (Fischer & Immordino-Yang, 2008; Immordino-Yang & Fischer, 2007).

The Brain's Development   At birth, the newborn's brain is about 25 percent of its adult weight. By the second birthday, the brain is about 75 percent of its adult weight. However, the brain's areas do not mature uniformly.

Mapping the Brain   Scientists analyze and categorize areas of the brain in numerous ways (Fischer & Immordino-Yang, 2008; Nelson, 2009). We are most concerned with the portion farthest from the spinal cord known as the *forebrain,* which includes the cerebral cortex and several structures beneath it. The *cerebral cortex* covers the forebrain like a wrinkled cap. It has two halves, or hemispheres (see Figure 4.3). Based on ridges and valleys in the cortex, scientists distinguish four main areas, called lobes, in each hemisphere. Although the lobes usually work together, each has a somewhat different primary function (see Figure 4.4):

- *Frontal lobes* are involved in voluntary movement, thinking, personality, and intentionality or purpose.
- *Occipital lobes* function in vision.
- *Temporal lobes* have an active role in hearing, language processing, and memory.
- *Parietal lobes* play important roles in registering spatial location, attention, and motor control.

To some extent, the type of information handled by neurons depends on whether they are in the left or right hemisphere of the cortex (Bianco & others, 2008; Spironelli & Angrilli, 2008). Speech and grammar, for example, depend on activity in the left hemisphere in most people; humor and the use of metaphors depends on activity in the right hemisphere (Imada & others, 2007). This specialization of function in one hemisphere of the cerebral cortex or the other is called **lateralization**. However, most neuroscientists agree that complex functions such as reading or performing music involve both hemispheres. Labeling people as "left-brained" because they are logical thinkers and "right-brained" because they are creative thinkers does not correspond to the way the brain's hemispheres work. Complex thinking in normal people is the outcome of communication between both hemispheres of the brain (Liegeois & others, 2008).

At birth, the hemispheres of the cerebral cortex already have started to specialize: Newborns show greater electrical brain activity in the left hemisphere than the right hemisphere when they are listening to speech sounds (Hahn, 1987). How are the areas of the brain different in the newborn and the infant from those in an adult, and why do the differences matter? Important differences have been documented at both the cellular and the structural level.

Changes in Neurons   Within the brain, the type of nerve cells called neurons send electrical and chemical signals, communicating with each other. As we indicated in Chapter 3, a *neuron* is a nerve cell that handles information processing (see Figure 4.5). Extending from the neuron's cell body are two types of fibers known as axons and

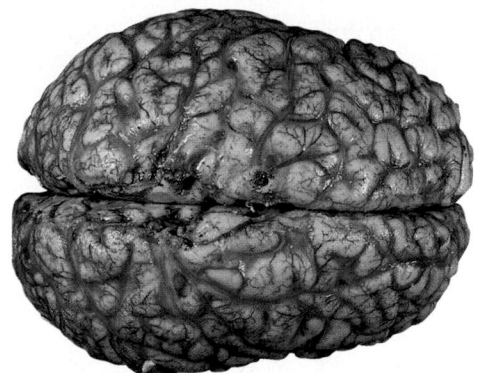

FIGURE 4.3 The Human Brain's Hemispheres. The two hemispheres of the human brain are clearly seen in this photograph. It is a myth that the left hemisphere is the exclusive location of language and logical thinking or that the right hemisphere is the exclusive location of emotion and creative thinking.

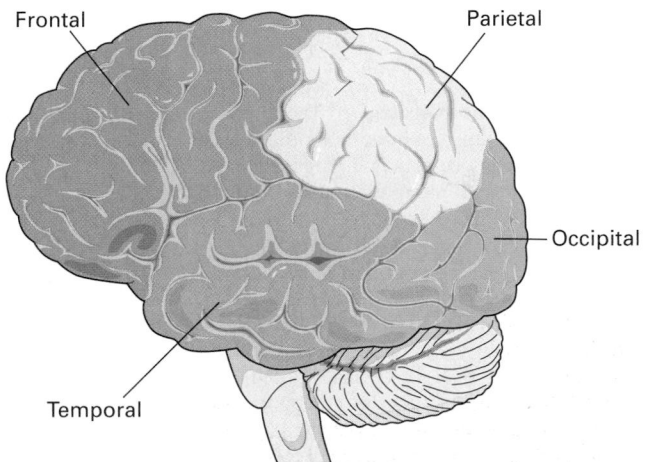

FIGURE 4.4 The Brain's Four Lobes. Shown here are the locations of the brain's four lobes: frontal, occipital, temporal, and parietal.

lateralization Specialization of function in one hemisphere of the cerebral cortex or the other.

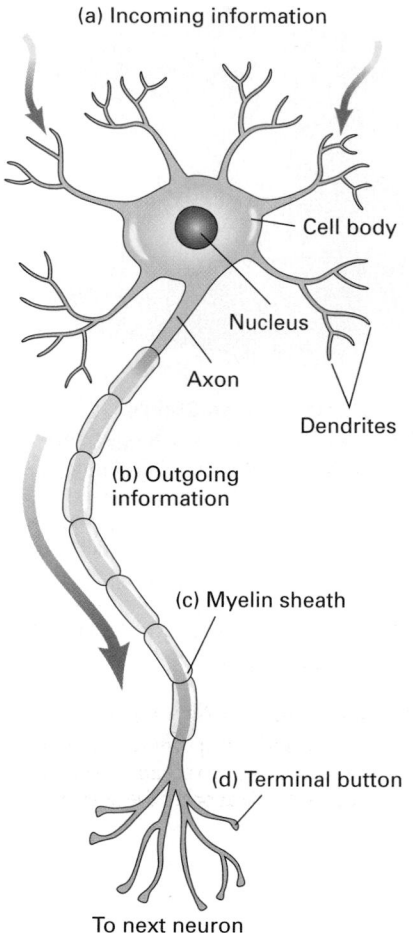

(a) Incoming information

Cell body

Nucleus

Axon

Dendrites

(b) Outgoing information

(c) Myelin sheath

(d) Terminal button

To next neuron

FIGURE 4.5 The Neuron. (*a*) The dendrites of the cell body receive information from other neurons, muscles, or glands through the axon. (*b*) Axons transmit information away from the cell body. (*c*) A myelin sheath covers most axons and speeds information transmission. (*d*) As the axon ends, it branches out into terminal buttons.

FIGURE 4.6 The Development of Dendritic Spreading. Note the increase in connectedness between neurons over the course of the first two years of life.
Reprinted by permission of the publisher from *The Postnatal Development of the Human Cerebral Cortex, Vols. I-VIII* by Jesse LeRoy Conel, Cambridge, Mass.: Harvard University Press. Copyright © 1939, 1975 by the President and Fellows of Harvard College.

dendrites. Generally, the axon carries signals away from the cell body and dendrites carry signals toward it. A *myelin sheath*, which is a layer of fat cells, encases many axons (see Figure 4.5). The myelin sheath insulates axons and helps electrical signals travel faster down the axon (Zalc, 2006). Myelination also may be involved in providing energy to neurons and in communication (Haynes & others, 2006). At the end of the axon are terminal buttons, which release chemicals called *neurotransmitters* into *synapses,* which are tiny gaps between neurons' fibers. Chemical interactions in synapses connect axons and dendrites, allowing information to pass from neuron to neuron. Think of the synapse as a river that blocks a road. A grocery truck arrives at one bank of the river, crosses by ferry, and continues its journey to market. Similarly, a message in the brain is "ferried" across the synapse by a neurotransmitter, which pours out information contained in chemicals when it reaches the other side of the river.

Neurons change in two very significant ways during the first years of life. First, *myelination,* the process of encasing axons with fat cells, begins prenatally and continues after birth, even into adolescence (Dubois & others, 2008; Fair & Schlaggar, 2008). Second, connectivity among neurons increases, creating new neural pathways, as Figure 4.6 illustrates. New dendrites grow, connections among dendrites increase, and synaptic connections between axons and dendrites proliferate. Whereas myelination speeds up neural transmissions, the expansion of dendritic connections facilitates the spreading of neural pathways in infant development.

Researchers have discovered an intriguing aspect of synaptic connections. Nearly twice as many of these connections are made as will ever be used (Huttenlocher & Dabholkar, 1997). The connections that are used become strengthened and survive, while the unused ones are replaced by other pathways or disappear. In the language of neuroscience, these connections will be "pruned" (Giedd, 2008). For example, the more babies engage in physical activity or use language, the more those pathways will be strengthened.

Changes in Regions of the Brain   Figure 4.7 vividly illustrates the dramatic growth and later pruning of synapses in the visual, auditory, and prefrontal cortex (Huttenlocher & Dabholkar, 1997). Notice that "blooming and pruning" vary considerably by brain region (Thompson & Nelson, 2001). For example, the peak of synaptic overproduction in the visual cortex occurs at about the fourth postnatal month, followed by a gradual retraction until the middle to end of the preschool years (Huttenlocher & Dabholkar, 1997). In areas of the brain involved in hearing and language, a similar, though somewhat later, course is detected. However, in the *prefrontal cortex,* the area of the brain where higher-level thinking and self-regulation occur, the peak of overproduction takes place at about 1 year of age; it is not until middle to late adolescence that the adult density of synapses is achieved. Both heredity and environment are thought to influence the timing and course of synaptic overproduction and subsequent retraction.

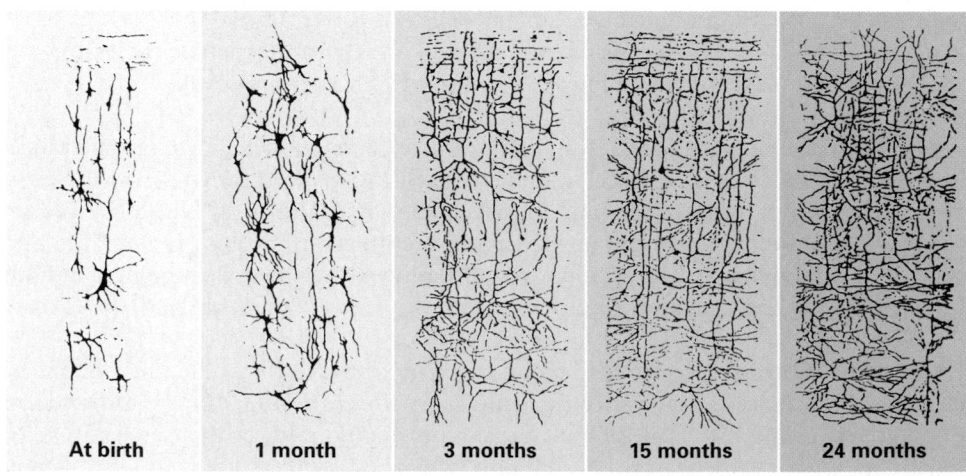

At birth   1 month   3 months   15 months   24 months

Meanwhile, the pace of myelination also varies in different areas of the brain (Dubois & others, 2007). Myelination for visual pathways occurs rapidly after birth and is completed in the first six months. Auditory myelination is not completed until 4 or 5 years of age.

In general, some areas of the brain, such as the primary motor areas, develop earlier than others, such as the primary sensory areas. The frontal lobes are immature in the newborn. However, as neurons in the frontal lobes become myelinated and interconnected during the first year of life, infants develop an ability to regulate their physiological states, such as sleep, and gain more control over their reflexes. Cognitive skills that require deliberate thinking do not emerge until later (Bell & Fox, 1992). Indeed, the prefrontal region of the frontal lobe has the most prolonged development of any brain region, with changes detectable at least into emerging adulthood (Steinberg, 2009).

Early Experience and the Brain

Children who grow up in a deprived environment may have depressed brain activity (Nelson, Zeanah, & Fox, 2007; Reeb & others, 2008). As shown in Figure 4.8, a child who grew up in the unresponsive and unstimulating environment of a Romanian orphanage showed considerably depressed brain activity compared with a normal child.

Are the effects of deprived environments irreversible? There is reason to think the answer is no. The brain demonstrates both flexibility and resilience. Consider 14-year-old Michael Rehbein. At age 7, he began to experience uncontrollable seizures—as many as 400 a day. Doctors said the only solution was to remove the left hemisphere of his brain where the seizures were occurring. Recovery was slow, but his right hemisphere began to reorganize and take over functions that normally occur in the brain's left hemisphere, including speech (see Figure 4.9).

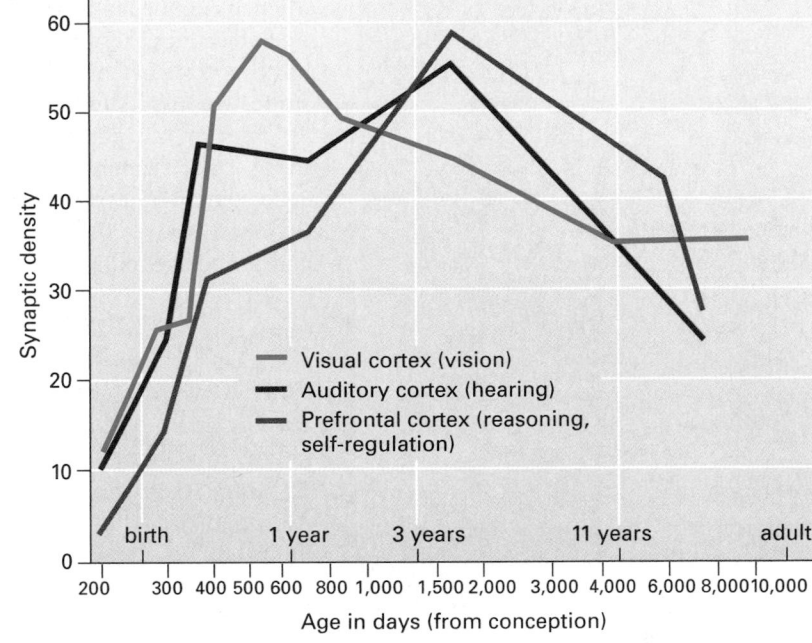

FIGURE 4.7 Synaptic Density in the Human Brain from Infancy to Adulthood. The graph shows the dramatic increase and then pruning in synaptic density for three regions of the brain: visual cortex, auditory cortex, and prefrontal cortex. Synaptic density is believed to be an important indication of the extent of connectivity between neurons.

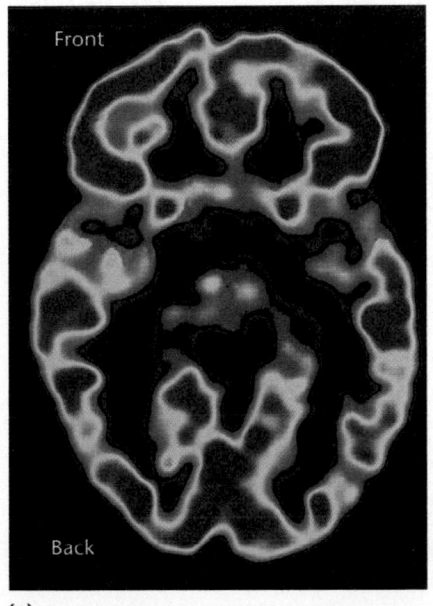

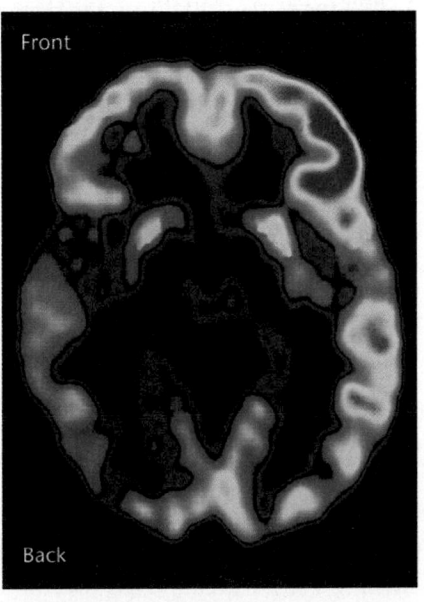

(a)   (b)

FIGURE 4.8 Early Deprivation and Brain Activity. These two photographs are PET (positron emission tomography) scans—which use radioactive tracers to image and analyze blood flow and metabolic activity in the body's organs. These scans show the brains of (a) a normal child and (b) an institutionalized Romanian orphan who experienced substantial deprivation since birth. In PET scans, the highest to lowest brain activity is reflected in the colors of red, yellow, green, blue, and black, respectively. As can be seen, red and yellow show up to a much greater degree in the PET scan of the normal child than the deprived Romanian orphan.

(a)

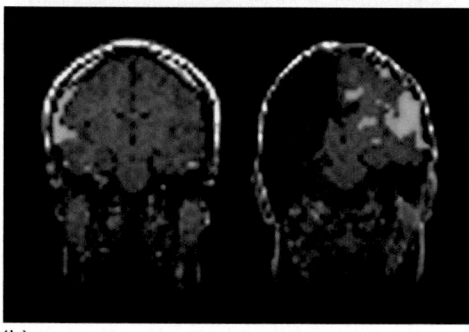

(b)

FIGURE 4.9 Plasticity in the Brain's Hemispheres. (*a*) Michael Rehbein at 14 years of age. (*b*) Michael's right hemisphere (*top*) has reorganized to take over the language functions normally carried out by corresponding areas in the left hemisphere of an intact brain (*bottom*). However, the right hemisphere is not as efficient as the left, and more areas of the brain are recruited to process speech.

*S*leep that knits up the
ravelled sleave of care . . .
Balm of hurt minds, nature's
second course. Chief nourisher
in life's feast.

—**William Shakespeare**
English Playwright, 17th Century

Neuroscientists believe that what wires the brain—or rewires it, in the case of Michael Rehbein—is repeated experience. Each time a baby tries to touch an attractive object or gazes intently at a face, tiny bursts of electricity shoot through the brain, knitting together neurons into circuits. The results are some of the behavioral milestones we discuss in this chapter.

In sum, the infant's brain depends on experiences to determine how connections are made (Dalton & Bergenn, 2007). Before birth, it appears that genes mainly direct basic wiring patterns. Neurons grow and travel to distant places awaiting further instructions (Sheridan & Nelson, 2008). After birth, the inflowing stream of sights, sounds, smells, touches, language, and eye contact help shape the brain's neural connections (Nelson, 2009).

Sleep

When we were infants, sleep consumed more of our time than it does now (Sadeh, 2008; Taveras, 2008). The typical newborn sleeps 16 to 17 hours a day, but newborns vary a lot in how much they sleep. The range is from about 10 hours to about 21 hours.

Infants also vary in their preferred times for sleeping and their patterns of sleep. Although the total amount of time spent sleeping remains somewhat consistent, an infant may change from sleeping seven or eight hours several times a day to sleeping for only a few hours three or four times a day. By about 1 month of age, many American infants have begun to sleep longer at night. By about 4 months of age, they usually have moved closer to adultlike sleep patterns, spending the most time sleeping at night and the most time awake during the day (Sadeh, 2008).

What factors are involved in infant night waking? A recent study of 9-month-old infants revealed that more time awake at night was linked to intrinsic factors such as daytime crying and fussing, and extrinsic factors such as being distressed when separated from the mother, breast feeding, and co-sleeping (DeLeon & Karraker, 2007).

Cultural variations influence infant sleeping patterns. For example, in the Kipsigis culture in Kenya, infants sleep with their mothers at night and are permitted to nurse on demand (Super & Harkness, 1997). During the day, they are strapped to their mothers' backs, accompanying them on daily rounds of chores and social activities. As a result, the Kipsigis infants do not sleep through the night until much later than American infants do. During the first eight months of postnatal life, Kipsigis infants rarely sleep longer than three hours at a stretch, even at night. This sleep pattern contrasts with that of American infants, many of whom begin to sleep up to eight hours a night by 8 months of age.

REM Sleep   In *REM sleep*, the eyes flutter beneath closed lids; in *non-REM sleep*, this type of eye movement does not occur and sleep is more quiet. Figure 4.10 shows developmental changes in the average number of total hours spent in REM and non-REM sleep. By the time they reach adulthood, individuals spend about one-fifth of their night in REM sleep, and REM sleep usually appears about one hour after non-REM sleep. However, about half of an infant's sleep is REM sleep, and infants often begin their sleep cycle with REM sleep rather than non-REM sleep. A much greater amount of time is taken up by REM sleep in infancy than at any other point in the life span. By the time infants reach 3 months of age, the percentage of time they spend in REM sleep falls to about 40 percent, and REM sleep no longer begins their sleep cycle.

Why do infants spend so much time in REM sleep? Researchers are not certain. The large amount of REM sleep may provide infants with added self-stimulation, since they spend less time awake than do older children. REM sleep also might promote the brain's development in infancy (Graven, 2006).

When adults are awakened during REM sleep, they frequently report that they have been dreaming, but when they are awakened during non-REM sleep they are much less likely to report they have been dreaming (Cartwright & others, 2006; Dement, 2005). Since infants spend more time than adults in REM sleep, can we conclude that they dream a lot? We don't know whether infants dream or not, because they don't have any way of reporting dreams.

Shared Sleeping Sleeping arrangements for newborns vary from culture to culture. For example, sharing a bed with a mother is a common practice in many cultures, such as Guatamala and China, whereas in others, such as the United States and Great Britain, newborns sleep in a crib, either in the same room as the parents or in a separate room. In some cultures, infants sleep with the mother until they are weaned, after which they sleep with siblings until middle and late childhood (Walker, 2006). Whatever the sleeping arrangements, it is recommended that the infant's bedding provide firm support and that cribs should have side rails.

Shared sleeping, or co-sleeping, is a controversial issue among experts (Sadeh, 2008). According to some child experts, shared sleeping brings several benefits: It promotes breast feeding and a quicker response to the baby's cries, and it allows the mother to detect potentially dangerous breathing pauses in the baby (Pelayo & others, 2006). However, shared sleeping remains a controversial issue, with some experts recommending it, others arguing against it (Mitchell, 2007; Newton & Vandeven, 2006). The American Academy of Pediatrics Task Force on Infant Positioning and SIDS (AAPTFIPS) (2000) discourages shared sleeping. The Task Force concluded that bed sharing increases the risk that the sleeping mother will roll over onto her baby or increase the risk of sudden infant death syndrome (SIDS). Recent studies have found that bed sharing is linked with a greater incidence of SIDS, especially when parents smoke (Alm, Lagercrantz, & Wennergren, 2006; Bajanowski & others, 2007). Also, shared sleeping is likely to place the infant at risk more if the caregivers are impaired by alcohol, smoking, or being overly tired (Baddock & others, 2007).

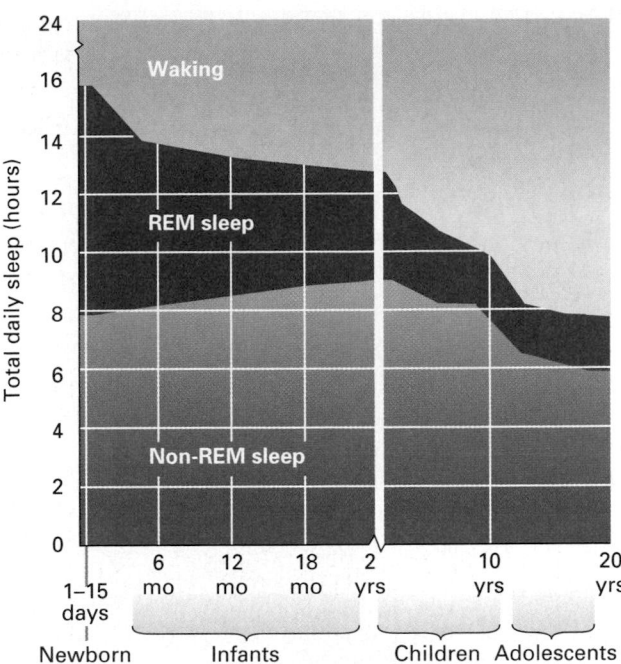

FIGURE 4.10 Developmental Changes in REM and Non-REM Sleep

SIDS **Sudden infant death syndrome (SIDS)** is a condition that occurs when infants stop breathing, usually during the night, and die suddenly without an apparent cause. SIDS remains the highest cause of infant death in the United States with nearly 3,000 infant deaths annually attributed to SIDS. Risk of SIDS is highest at 2 to 4 months of age (Centers for Disease Control and Prevention, 2008).

Since 1992, The American Academy of Pediatrics (AAP) has recommended that infants be placed to sleep on their backs to reduce the risk of SIDS, and the frequency of prone sleeping among U.S. infants has dropped dramatically (AAPTFIPS, 2000). Researchers have found that SIDS does indeed decrease when infants sleep on their backs rather than their stomachs or sides (Keens & Gimmill, 2008; Sharma, 2007). Among the reasons given for prone sleeping being a high risk factor for SIDS are that it impairs the infant's arousal from sleep and restricts the infant's ability to swallow effectively (Keens & Gimmill, 2008).

In addition to sleeping in a prone position, researchers have found that the following are risk factors for SIDS:

- SIDS is less likely to occur in infants who use a pacifier when they go to sleep (Li & others, 2006).

- Low birth weight infants are 5 to 10 times more likely to die of SIDS than are their normal-weight counterparts (Horne & others, 2002).

- Infants whose siblings have died of SIDS are two to four times as likely to die of it (Lenoir, Mallet, & Calenda, 2000).

- Six percent of infants with *sleep apnea,* a temporary cessation of breathing in which the airway is completely blocked, usually for 10 seconds or longer, die of SIDS (McNamara & Sullivan, 2000).

sudden infant death syndrome (SIDS) A condition that occurs when an infant stops breathing, usually during the night, and suddenly dies without an apparent cause.

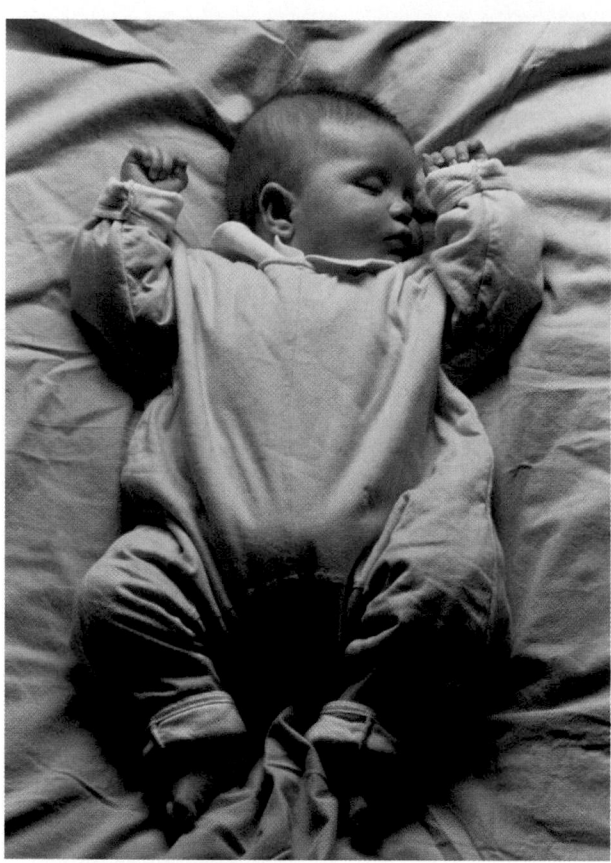

Is this a good sleep position for infants? Why or why not?

- African American and Eskimo infants are four to six times more likely than all others to die of SIDS (Ige & Shelton, 2004).

- SIDS is more common in lower socioeconomic groups (Mitchell & others, 2000).

- SIDS is more common in infants who are passively exposed to cigarette smoke (Shea & Steiner, 2008).

- SIDS is more common if infants sleep in soft bedding (McGarvey & others, 2006).

- SIDS occurs more often in infants with abnormal brain stem functioning involving the neurotransmitter serotonin (Shani, Fifer, & Myers, 2007; Shea & Steiner, 2008).

Nutrition

From birth to 1 year of age, human infants nearly triple their weight and increase their length by 50 percent. What do they need to sustain this growth?

Nutritional Needs Individual differences among infants in terms of their nutrient reserves, body composition, growth rates, and activity patterns make defining actual nutrient needs difficult (Burns & others, 2008; Wardlaw & Smith, 2009). However, because parents need guidelines, nutritionists recommend that infants consume approximately 50 calories per day for each pound they weigh—more than twice an adult's requirement per pound.

A number of developmental changes involving eating characterize the infant's first year (Black & Hurley, 2007). As infants' motor skills improve, they change from using suck-and-swallow movements with breast milk or formula to chew-and-swallow movements with semisolid and then more complex foods. As their fine motor control improves in the first year, they transition from being fed by others toward self-feeding. "By the end of the first year of life, children can sit independently, can chew and swallow a range of textures, are learning to feed themselves, and are making the transition to the family diet and meal patterns" (Black & Hurley, 2007, p. 1). At this point, infants need to have a diet that includes a variety of foods that especially includes fruits and vegetables.

Caregivers play very important roles in infants' early development of eating patterns (Bolling & Daniels, 2008; Chatoor & Macaoay, 2008; Farrow & Blissett, 2008). Caregivers who are not sensitive to developmental changes in infants' nutritional needs, neglectful caregivers, and conditions of poverty can contribute to the development of eating problems in infants (Black & Lozoff, 2008).

A national study of more than 3,000 randomly selected 4- to 24-month-olds documented that many U.S. parents aren't feeding their babies enough fruits and vegetables, but are feeding them too much junk food (Fox & others, 2004). Up to one-third of the babies ate no vegetables and fruit, frequently ate french fries, and almost half of the 7- to 8-month-old babies were fed desserts, sweets, or sweetened drinks. By 15 months, french fries were the most common vegetables the babies ate.

Are U.S. babies becoming increasingly overweight? A recent analysis revealed that in 1980 3.4 percent of U.S. babies less than 6 months old were overweight, a percentage that increased to 5.9 percent in 2001

(Kim & others, 2006). As shown in Figure 4.11, as younger infants become older infants, an even greater percentage are overweight. Also in this study, in addition to the 5.9 percent of infants less than 6 months old who were overweight in 2001, another 11 percent were categorized as at risk for being overweight. In this study, infants were categorized as overweight if they were above the 95th percentile for their age and gender on a weight-for-height index; they were labeled at risk for being overweight if they were between the 85th and 95th percentile.

In addition to eating too many french fries, sweetened drinks, and desserts, are there other factors that might explain this increase in overweight U.S. infants? A mother's weight gain during pregnancy, and a mother's own high weight before pregnancy, may be factors (Hockenberry & Wilson, 2009; Wardlaw & Smith, 2009). One likely important factor is whether an infant is breast fed or bottle fed. Breast fed infants have lower rates of weight gain than bottle fed infants by school age, and it is estimated that breast feeding reduces the risk of obesity by approximately 20 percent (Li & others, 2006).

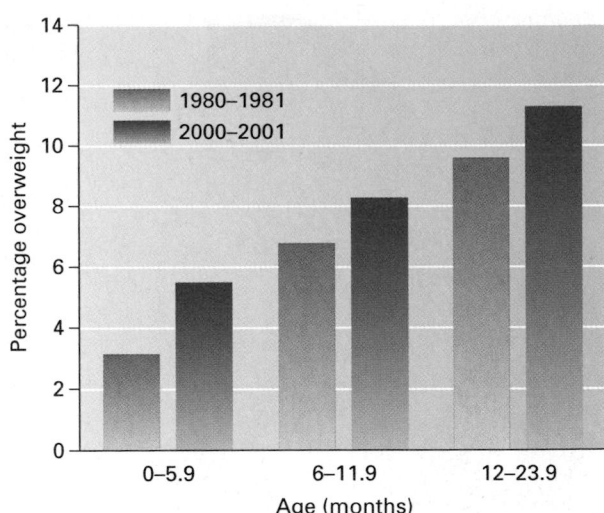

FIGURE 4.11 Percentage of Overweight U.S. Infants in 1980–1981 and 2000–2001. Note: Infants above the 95th percentile for their age and gender on a weight-for-height index were categorized as overweight.

Breast Versus Bottle Feeding   For the first four to six months of life, human milk or an alternative formula is the baby's source of nutrients and energy. For years, debate has focused on whether breast feeding is better for the infant than bottle feeding. The growing consensus is that breast feeding is better for the baby's health (Hosea Blewett & others, 2008; Lawrence, 2008). Since the 1970s, breast feeding by U.S. mothers has soared (see Figure 4.12). In 2004 more than two-thirds of U.S. mothers breast fed their newborns, and more than a third breast fed their 6-month-olds The American Academy of Pediatrics (AAP) and the American Dietetic Association strongly endorse breast feeding throughout the infant's first year (AAP Work Group on Breastfeeding, 1997; James & Dobson, 2005).

What are some of the benefits of breast feeding? The following conclusions have been reached based on the current state for research:

Benefits for Child

- *Gastrointestinal infections.* Breast fed infants have fewer gastrointestinal infections (Newburg & Walker, 2007).

- *Lower respiratory tract infections.* Breast fed infants have fewer lower respiratory tract infections (Ip & others, 2007).

- *Allergies.* A recent research review by the American Academy of Pediatrics indicated that there is no evidence that breast feeding reduces the risk of allergies in children (Greer & others, 2008). The research review also concluded that modest evidence exists for feeding hyperallergenic formulas to susceptible babies if they are not soley breast fed.

- *Asthma.* The recent research review by the American Academy of Pediatrics concluded that exclusive breast feeding for three months protects against wheezing in babies, but whether it prevents asthma in older children is unclear (Greer & others, 2008).

- *Otitis media.* Breast fed infants are less likely to develop this middle ear infection (Rovers, de Kok, & Schilder, 2006).

- *Atopic dermatitis.* Breast fed babies are less likely to have this chronic inflammation of the skin (Snijders & others, 2007). The recent research review by the American Academy of Pediatrics also concluded that for infants with a family history of allergies, breast

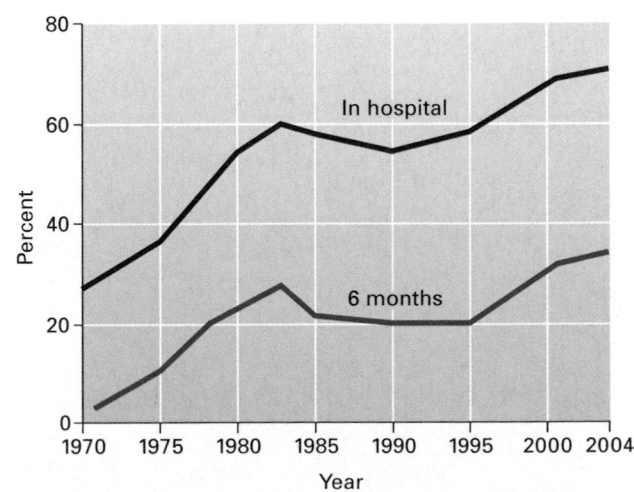

FIGURE 4.12 Trends in Breast Feeding in the United States: 1970–2004

Human milk or an alternative formula is a baby's source of nutrients for the first four to six months. The growing consensus is that breast feeding is better for the baby's health, although controversy still swirls about the issue of breast feeding versus bottle feeding. *Why is breast feeding strongly recommended by pediatricians?*

feeding exclusively for at least four months is linked to a lower risk of skin rashes (Greer & others, 2008).

- *Overweight and obesity.* Consistent evidence indicates that breast fed infants are less likely to become overweight or obese in childhood, adolescence, and adulthood (Moschonis, Grammatikaki, & Manios, 2008).

- *Diabetes.* Breast fed infants are less likely to develop type 1 diabetes in childhood (Ping & Hagopian, 2006) and type 2 diabetes in adulthood (Villegas & others, 2008).

- *SIDS.* Breast fed infants are less likely to experience SIDS (Alm, Lagercrantz, & Wennergen, 2006).

In a large-scale research review, no conclusive evidence for the benefits of breast feeding was found for children's cognitive development and cardiovascular system (Agency for Healthcare Research and Quality, 2007).

Benefits for Mother

- *Breast cancer.* Consistent evidence indicates a lower incidence of breast cancer in women who breast feed their infants (Shema & others, 2007).

    - *Ovarian cancer.* Evidence also reveals a reduction in ovarian cancer in women who breast feed their infants (Jordan & others, 2008).

    - *Type 2 diabetes.* Some evidence suggests a small reduction in type 2 diabetes in women who breast feed their infants (Ip & others, 2007).

In a large-scale research review, no conclusive evidence could be found for the maternal benefits of breast feeding on return to prepregnancy weight, osteorporosis, and postpartum depression (Agency for Healthcare Research and Quality, 2007). However, a recent study revealed that women who breast fed their infants had a lower incidence of metabolic syndrome (a disorder characterized by obesity, hypertension, and insulin resistance) in midlife (Ram & others, 2008).

Which women are least likely to breast feed? They include mothers who work full-time outside of the home, mothers under age 25, mothers without a high school education, African American mothers, and mothers in low-income circumstances (Merewood & others, 2007). In one study of low-income mothers in Georgia, interventions (such as counseling focused on the benefits of breast feeding and the free loan of a breast pump) increased the incidence of breast feeding (Ahluwalia & others, 2000). Increasingly, mothers who return to work in the infant's first year of life use a breast pump to extract breast milk that can be stored for later feeding of the infant when the mother is not present.

The AAP Work Group on Breastfeeding strongly endorses breast feeding throughout the first year of life (AAPWGB, 1997). Are there circumstances when mothers should not breast feed? Yes, a mother should not breast feed (1) when she is infected with HIV or some other infectious disease that can be transmitted through her milk, (2) if she has active tuberculosis, or (3) if she is taking any drug that may not be safe for the infant (Chatzimichael & others, 2007; Dube & others, 2008).

Some women cannot breast feed their infants because of physical difficulties; others feel guilty if they terminate breast feeding early. Mothers may also worry that they are depriving their infants of important emotional and psychological benefits if they bottle feed rather than breast feed. Some researchers have found, however, that there are no psychological differences between breast fed and bottle fed infants (Ferguson, Harwood, & Shannon, 1987; Young, 1990).

A further issue in interpreting the benefits of breast feeding was underscored in a recent large-scale research review (Agency for Healthcare Quality and Research, 2007). While highlighting a number of breast feeding benefits for children and mothers, the report issued a caution about breast feeding research: None of the findings imply causality. Breast versus bottle feeding studies are correlational not experimental, and women who breast feed are wealthier, older, more educated, and likely more health-conscious than their bottle feeding counterparts, which could explain why breast fed children are healthier.

Malnutrition in Infancy   Early weaning of infants from breast milk to inadequate sources of nutrients, such as unsuitable and unsanitary cow's milk formula, can cause protein deficiency and malnutrition in infants (Kramer, 2003). Something that looks like milk but is not, usually a form of tapioca or rice, is also often substituted for breast milk. In many of the world's developing countries, mothers used to breast feed their infants for at least two years. To become more modern, they stopped breast feeding much earlier and replaced it with bottle feeding. Comparisons of breast fed and bottle fed infants in such countries as Afghanistan, Haiti, Ghana, and Chile document that the mortality rate of bottle fed infants is as much as five times that of breast fed infants (Grant, 1997). However, as we saw in the *Images of Life-Span Development* opening story, a concern in developing countries is the increasing number of women who are HIV-positive and the fear that they will transmit this virus to their offspring (Doherty & others, 2006). Breast feeding is more optimal for mothers and infants in developing countries, except for mothers with HIV/AIDS or those suspected of having HIV/AIDS.

Two life-threatening conditions that can result from malnutrition are marasmus and kwashiorkor. **Marasmus** is caused by a severe protein-calorie deficiency and results in a wasting away of body tissues in the infant's first year. The infant becomes grossly underweight and his or her muscles atrophy. **Kwashiorkor**, caused by severe protein deficiency, usually appears between 1 and 3 years of age. Children with kwashiorkor sometimes appear to be well fed even though they are not because the disease can cause the child's abdomen and feet to swell with water. Kwashiorkor causes a child's vital organs to collect the nutrients that are present and deprive other parts of the body of them. The child's hair also becomes thin, brittle, and colorless, and the child's behavior often becomes listless.

Even if not fatal, severe and lengthy malnutrition is detrimental to physical, cognitive, and social development (de Onis & others, 2006). In a longitudinal study over two decades in rural Guatemala, Ernesto Pollitt and his colleagues (1993) found that early nutritional supplements in the form of protein and increased calories can have positive long-term effects on cognitive development. The researchers also found that the relation of nutrition to cognitive performance is moderated both by the time period during which the supplement is given and by socioeconomic status. Although there still was a positive nutritional influence when supplementation began after 2 years of age, the effect on cognitive development was less powerful. Also, the children in the lowest socioeconomic groups benefited more than did the children in higher socioeconomic groups

Another study linked the diets of rural Guatemalan infants with their social development at the time they entered elementary school (Barrett, Radke-Yarrow, & Klein, 1982). Children whose mothers had been given nutritious supplements during pregnancy, and who themselves had been given more nutritious, high-calorie foods in their first two years of life, were more active, more involved, more helpful with their peers, less anxious, and happier than their counterparts who had not been given nutritional supplements.

Adequate early nutrition is an important aspect of healthy development (Schiff, 2009). In addition to sound nutrition, children need a nurturant, supportive environment (Floyd, Mimms, & Yelding, 2008). One individual who has stood out as an advocate of caring for children is T. Berry Brazelton, who is featured in the *Careers in Life-Span Development* profile.

We have discussed many aspects of the infant's health in this chapter. In the following *Applications in Life-Span Development* interlude, we will further explore aspects of getting infants off to a healthy start in life.

This Honduran child has kwashiorkor. Notice the telltale sign of kwashiorkor—a greatly expanded abdomen. *What are some other characteristics of kwashiorkor?*

marasmus A wasting away of body tissues in the infant's first year, caused by severe protein-calorie deficiency.

kwashiorkor A condition caused by severe protein deficiency in which the child's abdomen and feet become swollen with water; usually appears between 1 to 3 years of age.

Careers in Life-Span Development

T. Berry Brazelton, Pediatrician

T. Berry Brazelton is America's best-known pediatrician as a result of his numerous books, television appearances, and newspaper and magazine articles about parenting and children's health. He takes a family-centered approach to child development issues and communicates with parents in easy to understand ways.

Dr. Brazelton founded the Child Development Unit at Boston Children's Hospital and created the Brazelton Neonatal Behavioral Assessment Scale, a widely used measure of the newborn's health and well-being (which you read about in Chapter 3). He also has conducted a number of research studies on infants and children and has been president of the Society for Research in Child Development, a leading research organization.

T. Berry Brazelton, pediatrician, with a young child.

Applications in Life-Span Development
A Healthy Start

The Hawaii Family Support/Healthy Start Program began in 1985 (Allen, Brown, & Finlay, 1992). It was designed by the Hawaii Family Stress Center in Honolulu, which already had been making home visits to improve family functioning and reduce child abuse for more than a decade. Participation is voluntary. Families of newborns are screened for family risk factors, including unstable housing, histories of substance abuse, depression, parents' abuse as a child, late or no prenatal care, fewer than 12 years of schooling, poverty, and unemployment. Healthy Start workers screen and interview new mothers in the hospital. They also screen families referred by physicians, nurses, and others. Because the demand for services outstrips available resources, only families with a substantial number of risk factors can participate.

Each new participating family receives a weekly visit from a family support worker. Each of the program's eight home visitors works with approximately 25 families at a time. The worker helps the family cope with any immediate crises, such as unemployment or substance abuse. The family also is linked directly with a pediatrician to ensure that the children receive regular health care. Infants are screened for developmental delays and are immunized on schedule. Pediatricians are notified when a child is enrolled in Healthy Start and when a family at risk stops participating.

The Family Support/Healthy Start Program recently hired a child development specialist to work with families of children with special needs. And, in some instances, the program's male family support worker visits a father to talk about his role in the family. The support workers encourage parents to participate in group activities held each week at the program center located in a neighborhood shopping center.

Over time, parents are encouraged to assume more responsibility for their family's health and well-being. Families can participate in Healthy Start until the child is 5 and enters public school. One recent study found that the Hawaiian Healthy Start program produced a lower incidence of maternal alcohol abuse and partner violence but did not reduce child abuse (Duggan & others, 2004).

The Hawaii Family Support/Healthy Start Program provides overburdened families of newborns and young children many home-visitor services. This program has been very successful in reducing abuse and neglect in families.

Review and Reflect: Learning Goal 1

1 **Discuss Physical Growth and Development in Infancy**

REVIEW

- What are cephalocaudal and proximodistal patterns?
- What changes in height and weight take place in infancy?
- What are some key features of the brain and its development in infancy?
- What changes occur in sleep during infancy?
- What are infants' nutritional needs?

REFLECT

- What three pieces of advice about the infant's physical development would you want to give a friend who has just had a baby? Why those three?

2 MOTOR DEVELOPMENT

| The Dynamic Systems View | Reflexes | Gross Motor Skills | Fine Motor Skills |

As a newborn, Ramona, whom we met in the chapter opening, could suck, fling her arms, and tightly grip a finger placed in her tiny hand. Within just two years, she would be toddling around on her own, opening doors and jars as she explored her little world. Are her accomplishments inevitable? How do infants develop their motor skills, and which skills do they develop when?

The Dynamic Systems View

Developmentalist Arnold Gesell (1934) thought his painstaking observations had revealed how people develop their motor skills. He had discovered that infants and children develop rolling, sitting, standing, and other motor skills in a fixed order and within specific time frames. These observations, said Gesell, show that motor development comes about through the unfolding of a genetic plan, or *maturation.*

Later studies, however, demonstrated that the sequence of developmental milestones is not as fixed as Gesell indicated and not due as much to heredity as Gesell argued (Adolph, 2008; Adolph & Joh, 2008). In the last two decades, the study of motor development experienced a renaissance as psychologists developed new insights about *how* motor skills develop (Thelen & Smith, 1998, 2006). One increasingly influential theory is dynamic systems theory, proposed by Esther Thelen.

According to **dynamic systems theory**, infants assemble motor skills for perceiving and acting. Notice that perception and action are coupled according to this theory (Smith & Breazeal, 2007; Thelen & Smith, 2006). To develop motor skills, infants must perceive something in the environment that motivates them to act and use their perceptions to fine-tune their movements. Motor skills represent solutions to the infant's goals.

How is a motor skill developed according to this theory? When infants are motivated to do something, they might create a new motor behavior. The new behavior is

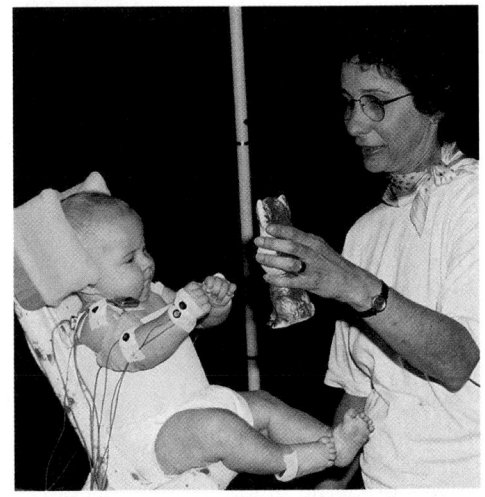

Esther Thelen is shown conducting an experiment to discover how infants learn to control their arms to reach and grasp for objects. A computer device is used to monitor the infant's arm movements and to track muscle patterns. Thelen's research is conducted from a dynamic systems perspective. *What is the nature of this perspective?*

dynamic systems theory The perspective on motor development that seeks to explain how motor behaviors are assembled for perceiving and acting.

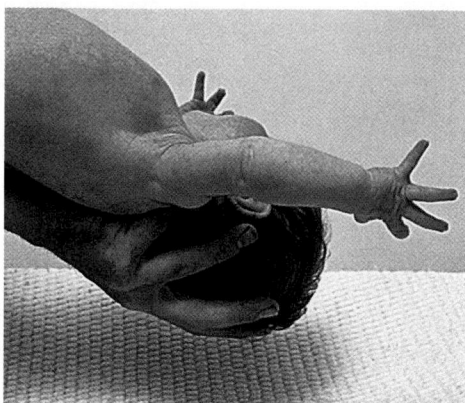

Moro reflex

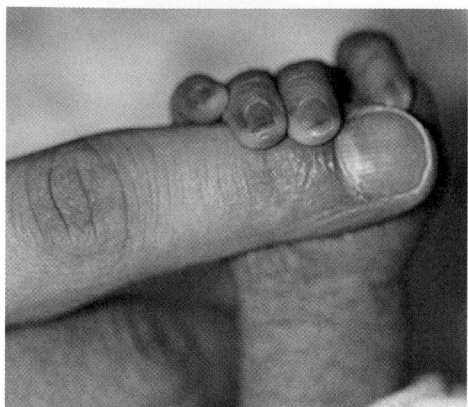

Grasping reflex

FIGURE 4.13 Moro Reflex and Grasping Reflex

reflexes Built-in reactions to stimuli that govern the newborn's movements, which are automatic and beyond the newborn's control.

rooting reflex A newborn's built-in reaction that occurs when the infant's cheek is stroked or the side of the mouth is touched. In response, the infant turns his or her head toward the side that was touched, in an apparent effort to find something to suck.

sucking reflex A newborn's built-in reaction to automatically suck an object placed in its mouth. The sucking reflex enables the infant to get nourishment before he or she has associated a nipple with food and also serves as a self-soothing or self-regulating mechanism.

Moro reflex A neonatal startle response that occurs in reaction to a sudden, intense noise or movement. When startled, the newborn arches its back, throws its head back, and flings out its arms and legs. Then the newborn rapidly closes its arms and legs to the center of the body.

the result of many converging factors: the development of the nervous system, the body's physical properties and its possibilities for movement, the goal the child is motivated to reach, and the environmental support for the skill (Bertenthal, 2008; Von Hofsten, 2008). For example, babies learn to walk only when maturation of the nervous system allows them to control certain leg muscles, when their legs have grown enough to support their weight, and when they want to move.

Mastering a motor skill requires the infant's active efforts to coordinate several components of the skill. Infants explore and select possible solutions to the demands of a new task; they assemble adaptive patterns by modifying their current movement patterns. The first step occurs when the infant is motivated by a new challenge—such as the desire to cross a room—and gets into the "ballpark" of the task demands by taking a couple of stumbling steps. Then, the infant "tunes" these movements to make them smoother and more effective. The tuning is achieved through repeated cycles of action and perception of the consequences of that action. According to the dynamic systems view, even universal milestones, such as crawling, reaching, and walking, are learned through this process of adaptation: Infants modulate their movement patterns to fit a new task by exploring and selecting possible configurations (Adolph & Joh, 2008; Thelen & Smith, 2006).

To see how dynamic systems theory explains motor behavior, imagine that you offer a new toy to a baby named Gabriel (Thelen & others, 1993). There is no exact program that can tell Gabriel ahead of time how to move his arm and hand and fingers to grasp the toy. Gabriel must adapt to his goal—grasping the toy—and the context. From his sitting position, he must make split-second adjustments to extend his arm, holding his body steady so that his arm and torso don't plow into the toy. Muscles in his arm and shoulder contract and stretch in a host of combinations, exerting a variety of forces. He improvises a way to reach out with one arm and wrap his fingers around the toy.

Thus, according to dynamic systems theory, motor development is not a passive process in which genes dictate the unfolding of a sequence of skills over time. Rather, the infant actively puts together a skill to achieve a goal within the constraints set by the infant's body and environment. Nature and nurture, the infant and the environment, are all working together as part of an ever-changing system.

As we examine the course of motor development, we will describe how dynamic systems theory applies to some specific skills. First, though, let's examine how the story of motor development begins with reflexes.

Reflexes

The newborn is not completely helpless. Among other things, it has some basic reflexes. For example, the newborn automatically holds its breath and contracts its throat to keep water out. **Reflexes** are built-in reactions to stimuli; they govern the newborn's movements, which are automatic and beyond the newborn's control. Reflexes are genetically carried survival mechanisms. They allow infants to respond adaptively to their environment before they have had the opportunity to learn.

The rooting and sucking reflexes are important examples. Both have survival value for newborn mammals, who must find a mother's breast to obtain nourishment. The **rooting reflex** occurs when the infant's cheek is stroked or the side of the mouth is touched. In response, the infant turns its head toward the side that was touched in an apparent effort to find something to suck. The **sucking reflex** occurs when newborns automatically suck an object placed in their mouth. This reflex enables newborns to get nourishment before they have associated a nipple with food and also serves as a self-soothing or self-regulating mechanism.

Another example is the **Moro reflex**, which occurs in response to a sudden, intense noise or movement (see Figure 4.13). When startled, the newborn arches its back, throws back its head, and flings out its arms and legs. Then the newborn rapidly

closes its arms and legs. The Moro reflex is believed to be a way of grabbing for support while falling; it would have had survival value for our primate ancestors.

Some reflexes—coughing, sneezing, blinking, shivering, and yawning, for example—persist throughout life. They are as important for the adult as they are for the infant. Other reflexes, though, disappear several months following birth, as the infant's brain matures, and voluntary control over many behaviors develops (Pedroso, 2008). The rooting and Moro reflexes, for example, tend to disappear when the infant is 3 to 4 months old.

The movements of some reflexes eventually become incorporated into more complex, voluntary actions. One important example is the **grasping reflex**, which occurs when something touches the infant's palms (see Figure 4.13). The infant responds by grasping tightly. By the end of the third month, the grasping reflex diminishes, and the infant shows a more voluntary grasp. As its motor development becomes smoother, the infant will grasp objects, carefully manipulate them, and explore their qualities.

Although reflexes are automatic and inborn, differences in reflexive behavior are soon apparent. For example, the sucking capabilities of newborns vary considerably. Some newborns are efficient at forceful sucking and obtaining milk; others are not as adept and get tired before they are full. Most infants take several weeks to establish a sucking style that is coordinated with the way the mother is holding the infant, the way milk is coming out of the bottle or breast, and the infant's temperament (Blass, 2008).

Pediatrician T. Berry Brazelton (1956) observed how infants' sucking changed as they grew older. Over 85 percent of the infants engaged in considerable sucking behavior unrelated to feeding. They sucked their finger, their fists, and pacifiers. By the age of 1 year, most had stopped the sucking behavior, but as many as 40 percent of children continue to suck their thumbs after they have started school (Kessen, Haith, & Salapatek, 1970). Most developmentalists do not attach a great deal of significance to this behavior.

Gross Motor Skills

Ask any parents about their baby, and sooner or later you are likely to hear about one or more motor milestone, such as "Cassandra just learned to crawl," "Jesse is finally sitting alone," or "Angela took her first step last week." Parents proudly announce such milestones as their children transform themselves from babies unable to lift their heads to toddlers who grab things off the grocery store shelf, chase a cat, and participate actively in the family's social life (Thelen, 2000). These milestones are examples of **gross motor skills**, which are skills that involve large-muscle activities, such as moving one's arms and walking.

The Development of Posture   How do gross motor skills develop? As a foundation, these skills require postural control (Thelen & Smith, 2006). For example, to track moving objects, you must be able to control your head in order to stabilize your gaze; before you can walk, you must be able to balance on one leg.

Posture is more than just holding still and straight. Posture is a dynamic process that is linked with sensory information in the skin, joints, and muscles, which tell us where we are in space; in vestibular organs in the inner ear that regulate balance and equilibrium; and in vision and hearing (Thelen & Smith, 2006).

Newborn infants cannot voluntarily control their posture. Within a few weeks, though, they can hold their heads erect, and soon they can lift their heads while prone. By 2 months of age, babies can sit while supported on a lap or an infant seat, but they cannot sit independently until they are 6 or 7 months of age. Standing also develops gradually during the first year of life. By about 8 to 9 months of age, infants usually learn to pull themselves up and hold on to a chair, and they often can stand alone by about 10 to 12 months of age.

What are some developmental changes in posture during infancy?

grasping reflex A neonatal reflex that occurs when something touches the infant's palms. The infant responds by grasping tightly.

gross motor skills Motor skills that involve large-muscle activities, such as walking.

Newly crawling infant

Experienced walker

FIGURE 4.14 The Role of Experience in Crawling and Walking Infants' Judgments of Whether to Go Down a Slope. Karen Adolph (1997) found that locomotor experience rather than age was the primary predictor of adaptive responding on slopes of varying steepness. Newly crawling and walking infants could not judge the safety of the various slopes. With experience, they learned to avoid slopes where they would fall. When expert crawlers began to walk, they again made mistakes and fell, even though they had judged the same slope accurately when crawling. Adolph referred to this as the *specificity of learning* because it does not transfer across crawling and walking.

Learning to Walk   Locomotion and postural control are closely linked, especially in walking upright (Adolph, 2008; Adolph & Joh, 2008). To walk upright, the baby must be able both to balance on one leg as the other is swung forward and to shift the weight from one leg to the other.

Even young infants can make the alternating leg movements that are needed for walking. The neural pathways that control leg alternation are in place from a very early age, possibly even at birth or before. Infants engage in frequent alternating kicking movements throughout the first six months of life when they are lying on their backs. Also when 1- to 2-month-olds are given support with their feet in contact with a motorized treadmill, they show well-coordinated, alternating steps. Despite these early abilities, most infants do not learn to walk until about the time of their first birthday.

If infants can produce forward stepping movements so early, why does it take them so long to learn to walk? The key skills in learning to walk appear to be stabilizing balance on one leg long enough to swing the other forward and shifting the weight without falling. This is a difficult biomechanical problem to solve, and it takes infants about a year to do it.

When infants learn to walk, they typically take small steps because of their limited balance control and strength. However, a recent study revealed that infants occasionally take a few large steps that even exceed their leg length, and these large steps indicate increased balance and strength (Badaly & Adolph, 2008).

In learning to locomote, infants learn what kinds of places and surfaces are safe for locomotion (Adolph, 2008; Adolph & Joh, 2008). Karen Adolph (1997) investigated how experienced and inexperienced crawling infants and walking infants go down steep slopes (see Figure 4.14). Newly crawling infants, who averaged about $8\frac{1}{2}$ months in age, rather indiscriminately went down the steep slopes, often falling in the process (with their mothers next to the slope to catch them). After weeks of practice, the crawling babies became more adept at judging which slopes were too steep to crawl down and which ones they could navigate safely. New walkers also could not judge the safety of the slopes, but experienced walkers accurately matched their skills with the steepness of the slopes. They rarely fell downhill, either refusing to go down the steep slopes or going down backward in a cautious manner. Experienced walkers perceptually assessed the situation—looking, swaying, touching, and thinking before they moved down the slope. With experience, both the crawlers and the walkers learned to avoid the risky slopes where they would fall, integrating perceptual information with the development of a new motor behavior. In this research, we again see the importance of perceptual-motor coupling in the development of motor skills.

Practice is especially important in learning to walk (Adolph & Joh, 2008). "Thousands of daily walking steps, each step slightly different from the last because of variations in the terrain and the continually varying bio- mechanical constraints on the body, may help infants to identify the relevant" combination of strength and balance required to improve their walking skills (Adolph, Vereijken, & Shrout, 2003, p. 495).

The First Year: Motor Development Milestones and Variations   Figure 4.15 summarizes important accomplishments in gross motor skills during the first year, culminating in the ability to walk easily. The timing of these milestones, especially the later ones, may vary by as much as two to four months, and experiences can modify the onset of these accomplishments (Eaton, 2008). For example, since 1992, when pediatricians began recommending that parents place their babies on their backs when they sleep, fewer babies crawled, and those who did crawled later (Davis & others, 1998). Also, some infants do not follow the standard sequence of motor accomplishments. For example, many American infants never crawl on their belly or on their hands and knees. They may discover an idiosyncratic form of locomotion

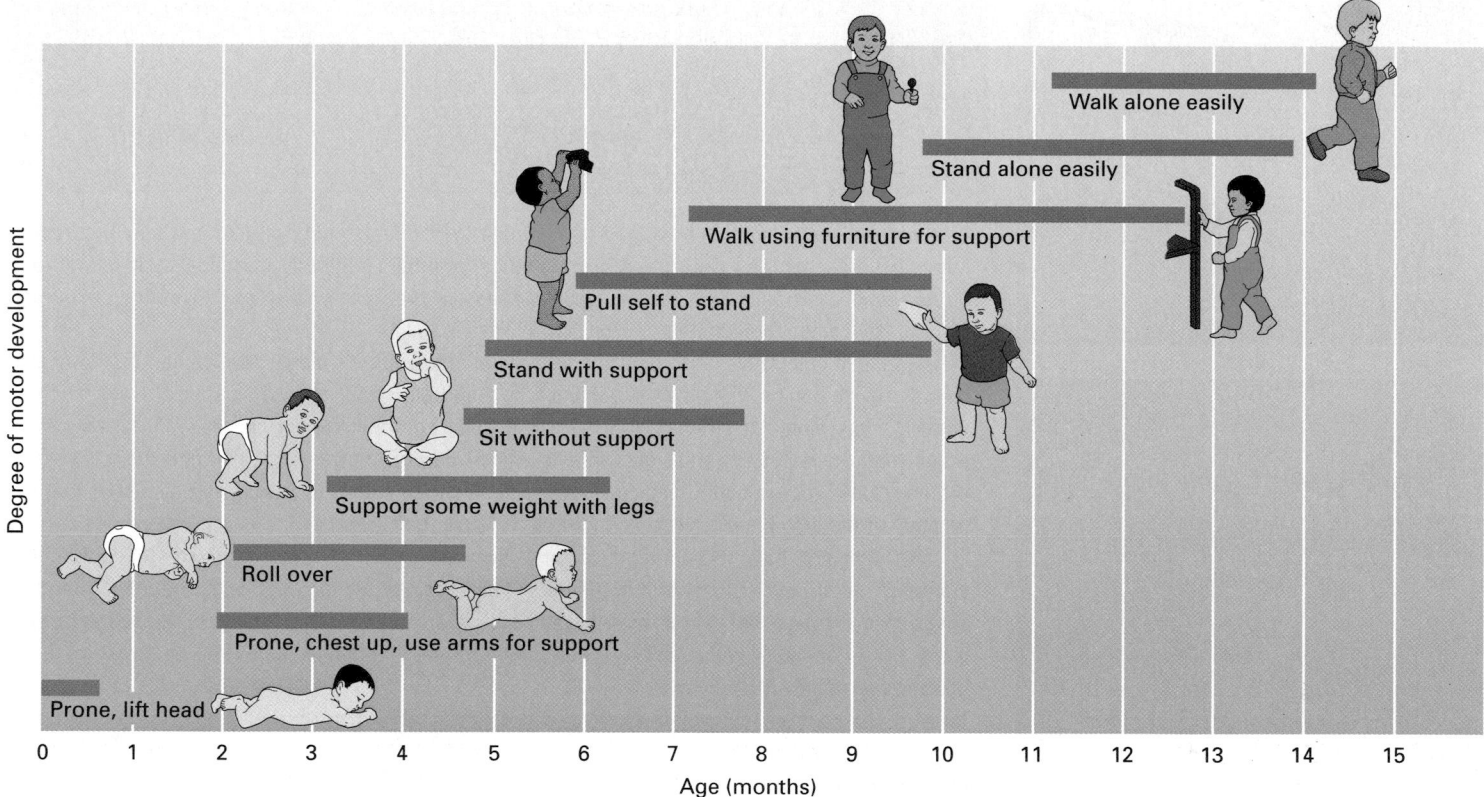

FIGURE 4.15 Milestones in Gross Motor Development. The horizontal blue bars indicate the range in which most infants reach various milestones in gross motor development.

before walking, such as rolling, or they might never locomote until they get upright (Adolph & Joh, 2007, 2008). In the African Mali tribe, most infants do not crawl (Bril, 1999).

According to Karen Adolph and Sarah Berger (2005), "the old-fashioned view that growth and motor development reflect merely the age-related output of maturation is, at best, incomplete. Rather, infants acquire new skills with the help of their caregivers in a real-world environment of objects, surfaces, and planes."

Development in the Second Year   The motor accomplishments of the first year bring increasing independence, allowing infants to explore their environment more extensively and to initiate interaction with others more readily. In the second year of life, toddlers become more motorically skilled and mobile. Motor activity during the second year is vital to the child's competent development, and few restrictions, except for safety, should be placed on their adventures.

By 13 to 18 months, toddlers can pull a toy attached to a string and use their hands and legs to climb up a number of steps. By 18 to 24 months, toddlers can walk quickly or run stiffly for a short distance, balance on their feet in a squat position while playing with objects on the floor, walk backward without losing their balance, stand and kick a ball without falling, stand and throw a ball, and jump in place.

Can parents give their babies a head start on becoming physically fit and physically talented through structured exercise classes? Most infancy experts recommend against structured exercise classes for babies. But there are other ways of guiding infants' motor development. Caregivers in some cultures do handle babies vigorously, and this might advance motor development, as we discuss in the *Diversity in Life-Span Development* interlude.

A baby is an angel whose wings decrease as his legs increase.

—FRENCH PROVERB

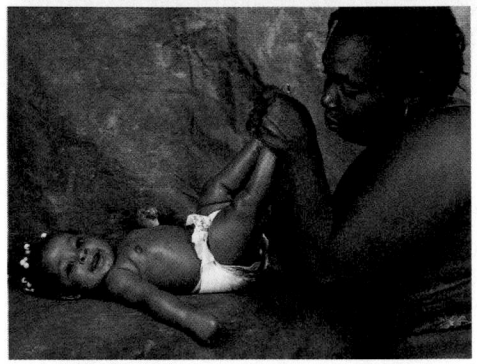

Diversity in Life-Span Development
Cultural Variations in Guiding Infants' Motor Development

Mothers in developing countries tend to stimulate their infants' motor skills more than mothers in more modern countries (Hopkins, 1991). Jamaican mothers regularly massage their infants and stretch their arms and legs (Adolph, 2008). Mothers in the Gusii culture of Kenya also encourage vigorous movement in their babies (Hopkins & Westra, 1988).

Do these cultural variations make a difference in the infant's motor development? When caregivers provide babies with physical guidance by physically handling them in special ways (such as stroking, massaging, or stretching) or by giving them opportunities for exercise, the infants often reach motor milestones earlier than infants whose caregivers have not provided these activities (Adolph, 2008). For example, Jamaican mothers expect their infants to sit and walk alone two to three months earlier than English mothers do (Hopkins & Westra, 1990).

Nonetheless, even when infants' motor activity is restricted, many infants still reach the milestones of motor development at a normal age. For example, Algonquin infants in Quebec, Canada, spend much of their first year strapped to a cradle board. Despite their inactivity, these infants still sit up, crawl, and walk within an age range similar to that of infants in cultures who have had much greater opportunity for activity.

(*Top*) In the Algonquin culture in Quebec, Canada, babies are strapped to a cradle board for much of their infancy. (*Bottom*) In Jamaica, mothers massage and stretch their infants' arms and legs. *To what extent do cultural variations in the activity infants engage in influence the time at which they reach motor milestones?*

Fine Motor Skills

Whereas gross motor skills involve large muscle activity, **fine motor skills** involve finely tuned movements. Grasping a toy, using a spoon, buttoning a shirt, or anything that requires finger dexterity demonstrates fine motor skills. Infants have hardly any control over fine motor skills at birth, but newborns do have many components of what will become finely coordinated arm, hand, and finger movements.

The onset of reaching and grasping marks a significant achievement in infants' ability to interact with their surroundings (Van Hof, Vander Kamp, & Savelsbergh, 2008). During the first two years of life, infants refine how they reach and grasp (Barrett & Needham, 2008). Initially, infants reach by moving their shoulders and elbows crudely, swinging toward an object. Later, when infants reach for an object they move their wrists, rotate their hands, and coordinate their thumb and forefinger. Infants do not have to see their own hands in order to reach for an object (Clifton & others, 1993). Cues from muscles, tendons, and joints, not sight of the limb, guide reaching by 4-month-old infants.

Infants refine their ability to grasp objects by developing two types of grasps. Initially, infants grip with the whole hand, which is called the *palmer grasp*. Later, toward the end of the first year, infants also grasp small objects with their thumb and forefinger, which is called the *pincer grip*. Their grasping system is very flexible. They vary their grip on an object depending on its size, shape, and texture, as well as the size of their own hands relative to the object's size. Infants grip small objects with their thumb and forefinger (and sometimes their middle finger too), whereas they grip large objects with all of the fingers of one hand or both hands.

Perceptual-motor coupling is necessary for the infant to coordinate grasping (Barrett, Traupman, & Needham, 2008). Which perceptual system the infant is most likely to use in coordinating grasping varies with age. Four-month-old infants rely greatly on touch to determine how they will grip an object; 8-month-olds are more likely to use vision as a guide (Newell & others, 1989). This developmental change is efficient because vision lets infants preshape their hands as they reach for an object.

Experience plays a role in reaching and grasping. In one study, three-month old infants participated in play sessions wearing "sticky mittens"—"mittens with palms

A young girl using a pincer grip to pick up puzzle pieces.

fine motor skills Motor skills that involve more finely tuned movements, such as finger dexterity.

that stuck to the edges of toys and allowed the infants to pick up the toys" (Needham, Barrett, & Peterman, 2002, p. 279) (see Figure 4.16). Infants who participated in sessions with the mittens grasped and manipulated objects earlier in their development than a control group of infants who did not receive the "mitten" experience. The experienced infants looked at the objects longer, swatted at them more during visual contact, and were more likely to mouth the objects.

Just as infants need to exercise their gross motor skills, they also need to exercise their fine motor skills (Barrett, Davis, & Needham, 2007; Needham, 2008). Especially when they can manage a pincer grip, infants delight in picking up small objects. Many develop the pincer grip and begin to crawl at about the same time, and infants at this time pick up virtually everything in sight, especially on the floor, and put the objects in their mouth. Thus, parents need to be vigilant in regularly monitoring what objects are within the infant's reach (Keen, 2005a).

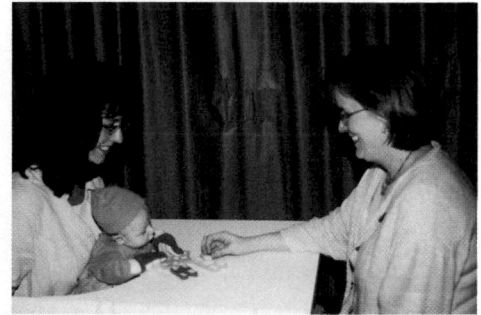

FIGURE 4.16 Infants' Use of "Sticky Mittens" to Explore Objects. Amy Needham and her colleagues (2002) found that "sticky mittens" enhanced young infants' object exploration skills.

Review and Reflect: Learning Goal 2

 Describe Infants' Motor Development

REVIEW

- What is the dynamic systems view?
- What are some reflexes that infants have?
- How do gross motor skills develop in infancy?
- How do fine motor skills develop in infancy?

REFLECT

- Which view of infant motor development do you prefer—the traditional maturational view or the dynamic systems view? Why?

3 SENSORY AND PERCEPTUAL DEVELOPMENT

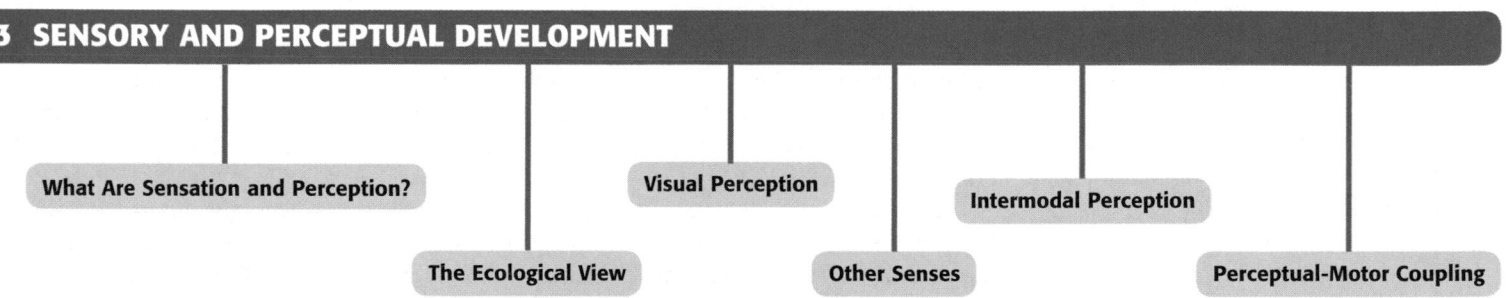

What Are Sensation and Perception?

The Ecological View

Visual Perception

Other Senses

Intermodal Perception

Perceptual-Motor Coupling

How do sensations and perceptions develop? Can a newborn see? If so, what can it perceive? What about the other senses—hearing, smell, taste, and touch? What are they like in the newborn, and how do they develop? Can an infant put together information from two modalities, such as sight and sound? These are among the intriguing questions that we will explore in this section.

What Are Sensation and Perception?

How does a newborn know that her mother's skin is soft rather than rough? How does a 5-year-old know what color his hair is? Infants and children "know" these things as a result of information that comes through the senses. Without vision, hearing, touch,

How would you use the Gibsons' ecological theory of perception and the concept of affordance to explain the role that perception is playing in this toddler's activity?

*T*he experiences of the first three years of life are almost entirely lost to us, and when we attempt to enter into a small child's world, we come as foreigners who have forgotten the landscape and no longer speak the native tongue.

—SELMA FRAIBERG
Developmentalist and Child Advocate, 20th Century

sensation The product of the interaction between information and the sensory receptors—the eyes, ears, tongue, nostrils, and skin.

perception The interpretation of what is sensed.

ecological view The view that perception functions to bring organisms in contact with the environment and to increase adaptation.

affordances Opportunities for interaction offered by objects that fit within our capabilities to perform functional activities.

taste, and smell, we would be isolated from the world; we would live in dark silence, a tasteless, colorless, feelingless void.

Sensation occurs when information interacts with sensory *receptors*—the eyes, ears, tongue, nostrils, and skin. The sensation of hearing occurs when waves of pulsating air are collected by the outer ear and transmitted through the bones of the inner ear to the auditory nerve. The sensation of vision occurs as rays of light contact the eyes, become focused on the retina, and are transmitted by the optic nerve to the visual centers of the brain.

Perception is the interpretation of what is sensed. The air waves that contact the ears might be interpreted as noise or as musical sounds, for example. The physical energy transmitted to the retina of the eye might be interpreted as a particular color, pattern, or shape, depending on how it is perceived.

The Ecological View

For the past several decades, much of the research on perceptual development in infancy has been guided by the ecological view of Eleanor and James J. Gibson (E. Gibson, 1969, 1989, 2001; J. Gibson, 1966, 1979). They argue that we do not have to take bits and pieces of data from sensations and build up representations of the world in our minds. Instead, our perceptual system can select from the rich information that the environment itself provides.

According to the Gibsons' **ecological view**, we directly perceive information that exists in the world around us. The view is called *ecological* "because it connects perceptual capabilities to information available in the world of the perceiver" (Kellman & Arterberry, 2006, p. 112). Thus, perception brings us into contact with the environment in order to interact with and adapt to it. Perception is designed for action. Perception gives people such information as when to duck, when to turn their bodies through a narrow passageway, and when to put their hands up to catch something.

In the Gibsons' view, objects have **affordances**, which are opportunities for interaction offered by objects that fit within our capabilities to perform activities. A pot may afford you something to cook with, and it may afford a toddler something to bang. Adults typically know when a chair is appropriate for sitting, when a surface is safe for walking, or when an object is within reach. We directly and accurately perceive these affordances by sensing information from the environment—the light or sound reflecting from the surfaces of the world—and from our own bodies through muscle receptors, joint receptors, and skin receptors, for example.

An important developmental question is, What affordances can infants or children detect and use? In one study, for example, when babies who could walk were faced with a squishy waterbed, they stopped and explored it, then chose to crawl rather than walk across it (Gibson & others, 1987). They combined perception and action to adapt to the demands of the task.

Similarly, as we described earlier in the section on motor development, infants who were just learning to crawl or just learning to walk were less cautious when confronted with a steep slope than experienced crawlers or walkers were (Adolph, 1997; Adolph & Joh, 2007, 2008). The more experienced crawlers and walkers perceived that a slope *affords* the possibility for not only faster locomotion but also for falling. Again, infants coupled perception and action to make a decision about what do in their environment. Through perceptual development, children become more efficient at discovering and using affordances.

Studying the infant's perception has not been an easy task. The *Research in Life-Span Development* interlude describes some of the ingenious ways researchers study the infant's perception.

Research in Life-Span Development
Studying the Newborn's Perception

The creature has poor motor coordination and can move itself only with great difficulty. Although it cries when uncomfortable, it uses few other vocalizations. In fact, it sleeps most of the time, about 16 to 17 hours a day. You are curious about this creature and want to know more about what it can do. You think to yourself, "I wonder if it can see. How could I find out?"

You obviously have a communication problem with the creature. You must devise a way that will allow the creature to "tell" you that it can see. While examining the creature one day, you make an interesting discovery. When you move an object horizontally in front of the creature, its eyes follow the object's movement.

The creature's head movement suggests that it has at least some vision. In case you haven't already guessed, the creature you have been reading about is the human infant, and the role you played is that of a researcher interested in devising techniques to learn about the infant's visual perception. After years of work, scientists have developed research methods and tools sophisticated enough to examine the subtle abilities of infants and to interpret their complex actions (Bendersky & Sullivan, 2007).

Visual Preference Method

Robert Fantz (1963) was a pioneer in this effort. Fantz made an important discovery that advanced the ability of researchers to investigate infants' visual perception: Infants look at different things for different lengths of time. Fantz placed infants in a "looking chamber," which had two visual displays on the ceiling above the infant's head. An experimenter viewed the infant's eyes by looking through a peephole. If the infant was fixating on one of the displays, the experimenter could see the display's reflection in the infant's eyes. This allowed the experimenter to determine how long the infant looked at each display. Fantz (1963) found that infants only 2 days old look longer at patterned stimuli, such as faces and concentric circles, than at red, white, or yellow discs. Infants 2 to 3 weeks old preferred to look at patterns—a face, a piece of printed matter, or a bull's-eye—longer than at red, yellow, or white discs (see Figure 4.17). Fantz's research method—studying whether infants can distinguish one stimulus from another by measuring the length of time they attend to different stimuli—is referred to as the **visual preference method**.

visual preference method A method used to determine whether infants can distinguish one stimulus from another by measuring the length of time they attend to different stimuli.

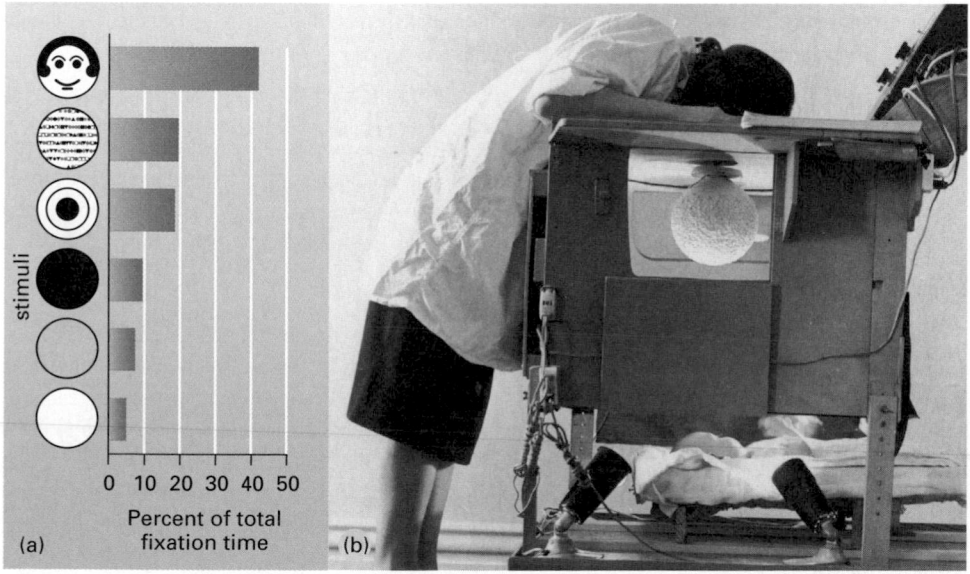

(a) Percent of total fixation time (b)

FIGURE 4.17 Fantz' Experiment on Infants' Visual Perception. (*a*) Infants 2 to 3 weeks old preferred to look at some stimuli more than others. In Fantz' experiment, infants preferred to look at patterns rather than at color or brightness. For example, they looked longer at a face, a piece of printed matter, or a bull's-eye than at red, yellow, or white discs. (*b*) Fantz used a "looking chamber" to study infants' perception of stimuli.

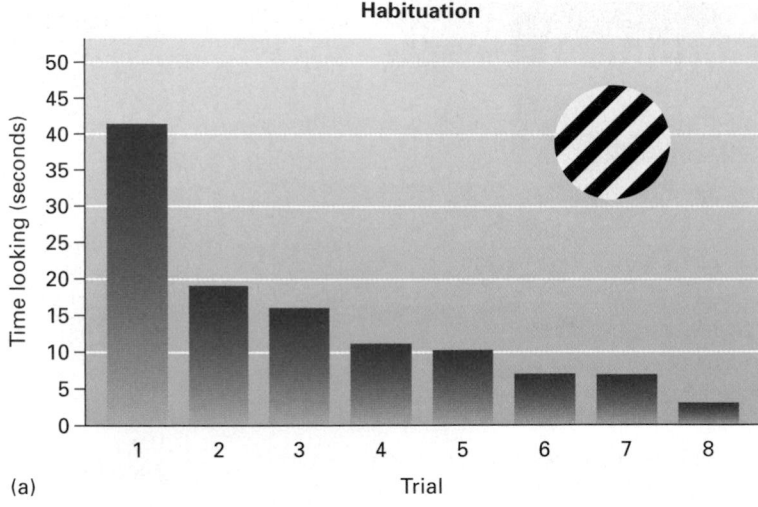

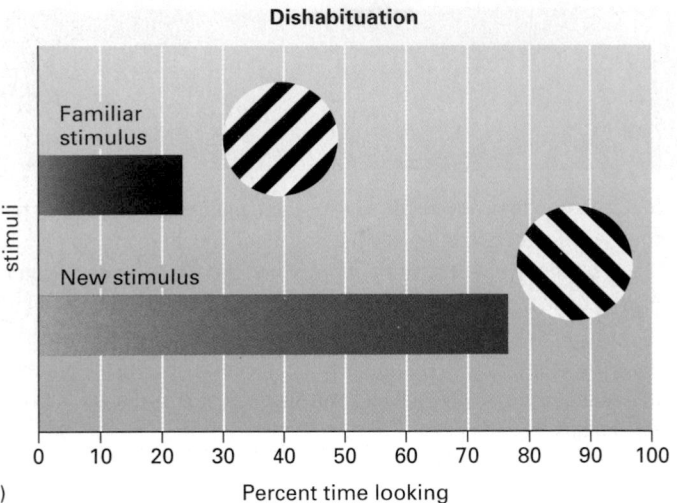

FIGURE 4.18 Habituation and Dishabituation. In the first part of one study, 7-hour-old newborns were shown the stimulus in (*a*). As indicated, the newborns looked at it an average of 41 seconds when it was first presented to them (Slater, Morison, & Somers, 1988). Over seven more presentations of the stimulus, they looked at it less and less. In the second part of the study, infants were presented with both the familiar stimulus to which they had just become habituated to (*a*) and a new stimulus (shown in *b*, which was rotated 90 degrees). The newborns looked at the new stimulus three times as much as the familiar stimulus.

Habituation and Dishabituation

Another way that researchers have studied infant perception is to present a stimulus (such as a sight or a sound) a number of times. If the infant decreases its response to the stimulus after several presentations, it indicates that the infant is no longer interested in looking at the stimulus. If the researcher now presents a new stimulus, the infant's response will recover—indicating the infant could discriminate between the old and new stimulus (Snyder & Torrence, 2008).

Habituation is the name given to decreased responsiveness to a stimulus after repeated presentations of the stimulus. **Dishabituation** is the recovery of a habituated response after a change in stimulation. Newborn infants can habituate to repeated sights, sounds, smells, or touches (Rovee-Collier, 2004). Among the measures researchers use in habituation studies are sucking behavior (sucking stops when the young infant attends to a novel object), heart and respiration rates, and the length of time the infant looks at an object. Figure 4.18 shows the results of one study of habituation and dishabituation with newborns (Slater, Morison, & Somers, 1988).

High-Amplitude Sucking

To assess an infant's attention to sound, researchers often use a method called *high-amplitude sucking*. In this method, infants are given a nonnutritive nipple to suck, and the nipple is connected to "a sound generating system. Each suck causes a noise to be generated and the infant learns quickly that sucking brings about this noise. At first, babies suck frequently, so the noise occurs often. Then, gradually, they lose interest in hearing repetitions of the same noise and begin to suck less frequently. At this point, the experimenter changes the sound that is being generated. If the babies renew vigorous sucking, we infer that they have discriminated the sound change and are sucking more because they want to hear the interesting new sound" (Menn & Stoel-Gammon, 2005, p. 71).

The Orienting Response and Tracking

A technique that can be used to determine if an infant can see or hear is the *orienting response*, which involves turning one's head toward a sight or sound. Another technique, *tracking*, consists of eye movements that follow (*track*) a moving object and can be used to evaluate an infant's early visual ability, or a startle response can be used to determine an infant's reaction to a noise (Bendersky & Sullivan, 2007).

Equipment

Technology can facilitate the use of most methods for investigating the infant's perceptual abilities. Videotape equipment allows researchers to investigate elusive behaviors. High-speed computers make it possible to perform complex data analysis in minutes. Other equipment records respiration, heart rate, body movement, visual fixation, and sucking behavior, which provide clues to what the infant is perceiving. For example, some researchers use equipment that detects if a change in infants' respiration follows a change in the pitch of a sound. If so, it suggests that the infants heard the pitch change. Thus, scientists have become ingenious at assessing the development of infants, discovering ways to "interview" them even though they cannot yet talk.

habituation Decreased responsiveness to a stimulus after repeated presentations of the stimulus.

dishabituation Recovery of a habituated response after a change in stimulation.

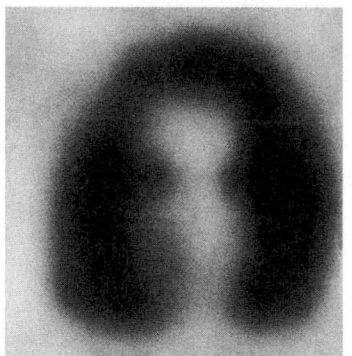 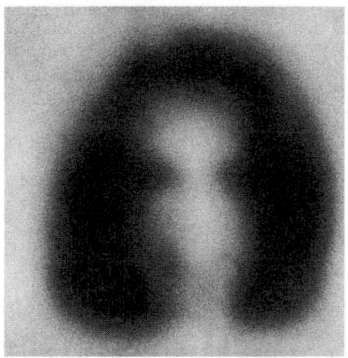 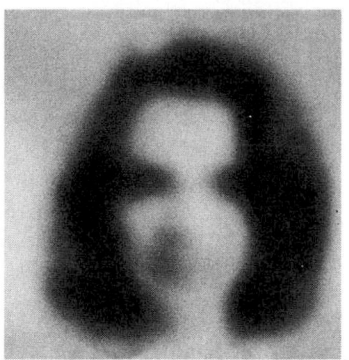 

FIGURE 4.19 Visual Acuity During the First Months of Life. The four photographs represent a computer estimation of what a picture of a face looks like to a 1-month-old, 2-month-old, 3-month-old, and 1-year-old (which approximates that of an adult).

Visual Perception

What do newborns see? How does visual perception develop in infancy?

Visual Acuity and Human Faces   Psychologist William James (1890/1950) called the newborn's perceptual world a "blooming, buzzing confusion." More than a century later, we can safely say that he was wrong (Slater, Field, & Hernandez-Reif, 2007). Even the newborn perceives a world with some order. That world, however, is far different from the one perceived by the toddler or the adult.

Just how well can infants see? At birth, the nerves and muscles and lens of the eye are still developing. As a result, newborns cannot see small things that are far away. The newborn's vision is estimated to be 20/240 on the well-known Snellen chart used for eye examinations, which means that a newborn can see at 20 feet what a normal adult can see at 240 feet (Aslin & Lathrop, 2008). In other words, an object 20 feet away is only as clear to the newborn as it would be if it were 240 feet away from an adult with normal vision (20/20). By 6 months of age, though, on *average* vision is 20/40 (Aslin & Lathrop, 2008).

Infants show an interest in human faces soon after birth (Slater, Field, & Hernandez-Reif, 2007). Figure 4.19 shows a computer estimation of what a picture of a face looks like to an infant at different ages from a distance of about 6 inches. Infants spend more time looking at their mother's face than a stranger's face as early as 12 hours after being born (Bushnell, 2003). By 3 months of age, infants match voices to faces, distinguish between male and female faces, and discriminate between faces of their own ethnic group and those of other ethnic groups (Kelly & others, 2005, 2007; Pascalls & Kelly, 2008).

Even very young infants soon change the way they gather information from the visual world, including human faces (Aslin & Lathrop, 2008). By using a special mirror arrangement, researchers projected an image of human faces in front of infants' eyes so that the infants' eye movements could be photographed (Maurer & Salapatek, 1976). As Figure 4.20 shows, the 2-month-old scans much more of the face than the 1-month-old, and the 2-month-old spends more time examining the internal details of the face. Thus, the 2-month-old gains more information about the world than the 1-month-old.

Also, as we discussed in the *Research in Life-Span Development* interlude, young infants can perceive certain patterns. With the help of his "looking chamber," Robert Fantz (1963) revealed that even 2- to 3-week-old infants prefer to look at patterned displays rather than nonpatterned displays. For example, they prefer to look at a normal human face rather than one with scrambled features, and prefer to look at a bull's-eye target or black-and-white stripes rather than a plain circle.

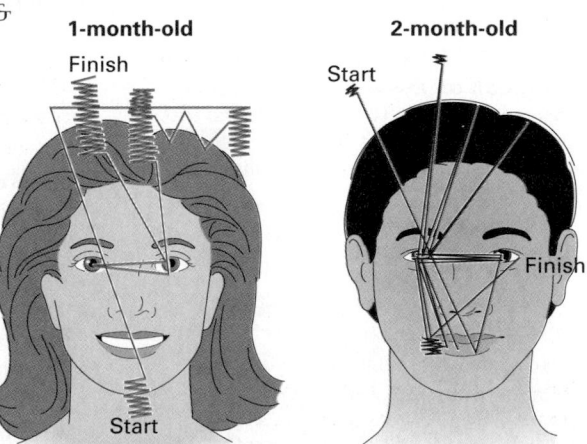

FIGURE 4.20 How 1- and 2-Month-Old Infants Scan the Human Face

Color Vision   The infant's color vision also improves (Kellman & Arterberry, 2006). By 8 weeks, and possibly by even 4 weeks, infants can discriminate some colors (Kelly, Borchert, & Teller, 1997). By 4 months of age, they have color preferences that mirror adults' in some cases, preferring saturated colors such as royal blue over pale blue, for example (Bornstein, 1975). In part, these changes in vision reflect maturation. Experience, however, is also necessary for vision to develop normally. For example, one study found that experience is necessary for normal color vision to develop (Sugita, 2004).

Perceptual Constancy   Some perceptual accomplishments are especially intriguing because they indicate that the infant's perception goes beyond the information provided by the senses (Arterberry, 2008; Slater, Field, & Hernandez-Reif, 2007). This is the case in *perceptual constancy*, in which sensory stimulation is changing but perception of the physical world remains constant. If infants did not develop perceptual constancy, each time they saw an object at a different distance or in a different orientation, they would perceive it as a different object. Thus, the development of perceptual constancy allows infants to perceive their world as stable. Two types of perceptual constancy are size constancy and shape constancy.

Size constancy is the recognition that an object remains the same even though the retinal image of the object changes as you move toward or away from the object. The farther away from us an object is, the smaller its image is on our eyes. Thus, the size of an object on the retina is not sufficient to tell us its actual size. For example, you perceive a bicycle standing right in front of you as smaller than the car parked across the street, even though the bicycle casts a larger image on your eyes than the car does. When you move away from the bicycle, you do not perceive it to be shrinking even though its image on your retinas shrinks; you perceive its size as constant.

But what about babies? Do they have size constancy? Researchers have found that babies as young as 3 months of age show size constancy (Bower, 1966; Day & McKenzie, 1973). However, at 3 months of age, this ability is not full-blown. It continues to develop until 10 or 11 years of age (Kellman & Banks, 1998).

Shape constancy is the recognition that an object remains the same shape even though its orientation to us changes. Look around the room you are in right now. You likely see objects of varying shapes, such as tables and chairs. If you get up and walk around the room, you will see these objects from different sides and angles. Even though your retinal image of the objects changes as you walk and look, you will still perceive the objects as the same shape.

Do babies have shape constancy? As with size constancy, researchers have found that babies as young as 3 months of age have shape constancy (Bower, 1966; Day & McKenzie, 1973). Three-month-old infants, however, do not have shape constancy for irregularly shaped objects, such as tilted planes (Cook & Birch, 1984).

FIGURE 4.21 Examining Infants' Depth Perception on the Visual Cliff. Eleanor Gibson and Richard Walk (1960) found that most infants would not crawl out on the glass, which indicated that they had depth perception.

size constancy The recognition that an object remains the same even though the retinal image of the object changes as you move toward or away from the object.

shape constancy The recognition that an object's shape remains the same even though its orientation to us changes.

Depth Perception   Decades ago, the inspiration for what would become a classic experiment came to Eleanor Gibson as she was eating a picnic lunch on the edge of the Grand Canyon. She wondered whether an infant looking over the canyon's rim would perceive the dangerous dropoff and back up. She also was worried that her own two young children would play too close to the canyon's edge and fall off. Might infants even have perceive depth?

To investigate this question, Eleanor Gibson and Richard Walk (1960) constructed a miniature cliff with a dropoff covered by glass in their laboratory. They placed infants on the edge of this visual cliff and had their mothers coax them to crawl onto the glass (see Figure 4.21). Most infants would not crawl out on the glass, choosing instead to remain on the shallow side, an indication that they could perceive depth.

The 6- to 12-month-old infants in the visual cliff experiment had extensive visual experience. Do younger infants without this experience still perceive depth? Since younger infants do not crawl, this question is difficult to answer. Two- to 4-month-old infants show differences in heart rate when they are placed directly on the deep side of the visual cliff instead of on the shallow side (Campos, Langer, & Krowitz, 1970). However, these differences might mean that young infants respond to differences in some visual characteristics of the deep and shallow cliffs, with no actual knowledge of depth. Although researchers do not know exactly how early in life infants can perceive depth, we do know that infants develop the ability to use binocular cues to depth by about 3 to 4 months of age.

Researchers also are interested in fine-detail depth perception, which is called *stereoacuity*. A study using random-dot TV patterns showed that stereoacuity did not improve from 6 to 12 months of age but improved rapidly after 1 year of age (Takai & others, 2005).

Nature, Nurture, and the Development of Infants' Visual Perception   There has been a longstanding interest in how strongly infants' visual perception is influenced by nature or nurture (Arterberry, 2008). A recent analysis concluded that much of vision develops from innate (nature) foundations and that the basic foundation of many visual abilities can be detected at birth, whereas others unfold maturationally (Kellman & Arterberry, 2006). Environmental experiences (nurture) likely refine or calibrate many visual functions, and they may be the driving force behind some functions.

Other Senses

Other sensory systems besides vision also develop during infancy. We will explore development in hearing, touch and pain, smell, and taste.

Hearing   During the last two months of pregnancy, as the fetus nestles in its mother's womb, it can hear sounds such as the mother's voice, music, and so on (Kisilevsky & others, 2003, 2004; Morokuma & others, 2008). Two psychologists wanted to find out if a fetus that heard Dr. Seuss' classic story *The Cat in the Hat* while still in the mother's womb would prefer hearing the story after birth (DeCasper & Spence, 1986). During the last months of pregnancy, sixteen women read *The Cat in the Hat* to their fetuses. Then shortly after they were born, the mothers read either *The Cat in the Hat* or a story with a different rhyme and pace, *The King, the Mice and the Cheese* (which was not read to them during prenatal development). The infants sucked on a nipple in a different way when the mothers read the two stories, suggesting that the infants recognized the pattern and tone of *The Cat in the Hat* (see Figure 4.22). This study illustrates not only that a fetus can hear but also that it has a remarkable ability to learn even before birth.

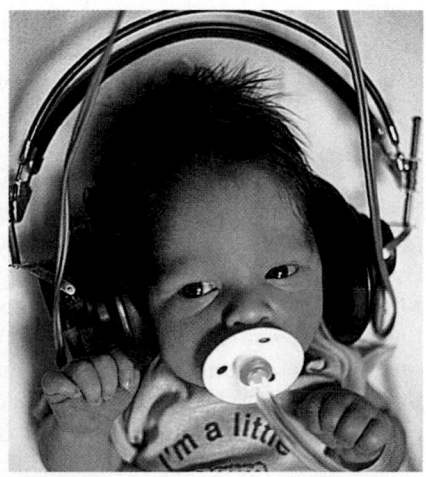

(a)   (b)

FIGURE 4.22 Hearing in the Womb. (*a*) Pregnant mothers read *The Cat in the Hat* to their fetuses during the last few months of pregnancy. (*b*) When they were born, the babies preferred listening to a recording of their mothers reading *The Cat in the Hat,* as evidenced by their sucking on a nipple that produced this recording, rather than another story, *The King, the Mice and the Cheese.*

The fetus can also recognize the mother's voice, as a recent study demonstrated (Kisilevsky & others, 2004). Sixty term fetuses (mean gestational age, 38.4 weeks) were exposed to a tape recording either of their mother or of a female stranger reading a passage. The sounds of the tape were delivered through a loudspeaker held just above the mother's abdomen. Fetal heart rate increased in response to the mother's voice but decreased in response to the stranger's voice.

What kind of changes in hearing take place during infancy? They involve perception of a sound's loudness, pitch, and localization:

- *Loudness.* Immediately after birth, infants cannot hear soft sounds quite as well as adults can; a stimulus must be louder to be heard by a newborn than by an adult (Trehub & others, 1991). For example, an adult can hear a whisper from about 4 to 5 feet away, but a newborn requires that sounds be closer to a normal conversational level to be heard at that distance.

- *Pitch.* Infants are also less sensitive to the pitch of a sound than adults are. *Pitch* is the perception of the frequency of a sound. A soprano voice sounds high pitched, a bass voice low pitched. Infants are less sensitive to low-pitched sounds and are more likely to hear high-pitched sounds (Aslin, Jusczyk, & Pisoni, 1998). By 2 years of age, infants have considerably improved their ability to distinguish sounds with different pitches.

- *Localization.* Even newborns can determine the general location from where a sound is coming, but by 6 months of age, they are more proficient at *localizing* sounds or detecting their origins. Their ability to localize sounds continues to improve in the second year (Saffran, Werker, & Warner, 2006).

Touch and Pain   Do newborns respond to touch? Can they feel pain?

Newborns do respond to touch. A touch to the cheek produces a turning of the head; a touch to the lips produces sucking movements.

Newborns can also feel pain (Field & Hernandez-Reif, 2008; Gunnar & Quevado, 2007). If and when you have a son and consider whether he should be circumcised, the issue of an infant's pain perception probably will become important to you. Circumcision is usually performed on young boys about the third day after birth. Will your young son experience pain if he is circumcised when he is 3 days old? An investigation by Megan Gunnar and her colleagues (1987) found that newborn infant males cried intensely during circumcision. The circumcised infant also displays amazing resiliency. Within several minutes after the surgery, they can nurse and interact in a normal manner with their mothers. And, if allowed to, the newly circumcised newborn drifts into a deep sleep, which seems to serve as a coping mechanism.

For many years, doctors performed operations on newborns without anesthesia. This practice was accepted because of the dangers of anesthesia and because of the supposition that newborns do not feel pain. As researchers demonstrated that newborns can feel pain, the practice of operating on newborns without anesthesia is being challenged. Anesthesia now is used in some circumcisions (Taddio, 2008).

The important ability to connect information about vision with information about touch is evident during infancy. Coordination of vision and touch has been well documented in 6-month-olds (Rose, 1990) and in one study was demonstrated in 2- to 3-month-olds (Steri, 1987).

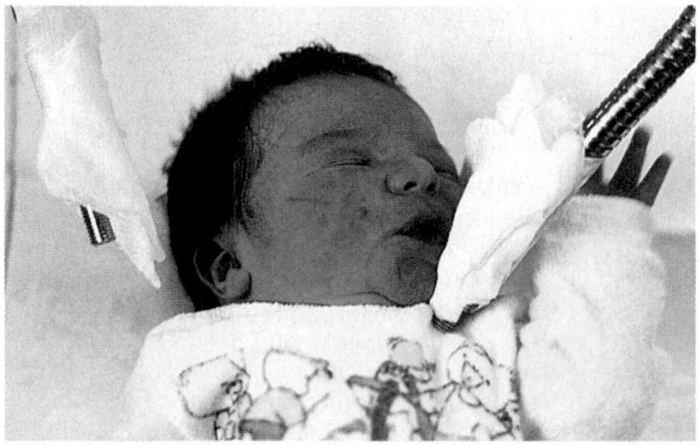

FIGURE 4.23 Newborns' Preference for the Smell of Their Mother's Breast Pad. In the experiment by MacFarlane (1975), 6-day-old infants preferred to smell their mother's breast pad rather than a clean one that had never been used, but 2-day-old infants did not show the preference, indicating that this odor preference requires several days of experience to develop.

Smell   Newborns can differentiate odors (Doty & Shah, 2008). The expressions on their faces seem to indicate that they like the way vanilla and strawberry smell but do not like the way rotten eggs and fish smell (Steiner, 1979). In one investigation, 6-day-old infants who were breast fed showed a clear preference for smelling their mother's breast pad rather than a clean breast pad (MacFarlane, 1975) (see Figure 4.23). However, when they were 2 days old, they did not show this preference, indicating that they require several days of experience to recognize this odor.

Taste   Sensitivity to taste might be present even before birth (Doty & Shah, 2008). When saccharin was added to the amniotic fluid of a near-term fetus, swallowing increased (Windle, 1940). In one study, even at only 2 hours of age, babies made different facial expressions when they tasted sweet, sour, and bitter solutions (Rosenstein & Oster, 1988) (see Figure 4.24). At about 4 months of age, infants begin to prefer salty tastes, which as newborns they had found to be aversive (Harris, Thomas, & Booth, 1990).

Intermodal Perception

Imagine yourself playing basketball or tennis. You are experiencing many visual inputs: the ball coming and going, other players moving around, and so on. However, you are experiencing many auditory inputs as well: the sound of the ball bouncing or being hit, the grunts and groans, and so on. There is good correspondence between much of the visual and auditory information: When you see the ball bounce, you hear a bouncing sound; when a player stretches to hit a ball, you hear a groan. When you look at and listen to what is going on, you do not experience just the sounds or just the sights—you put all these things together. You experience a unitary episode. This is **intermodal perception**, which involves integrating information from two or more sensory modalities, such as vision and hearing.

Early, exploratory forms of intermodal perception exist even in newborns (Bahrick & Hollich, 2008; Sann & Streri, 2007). For example, newborns turn their eyes and their head toward the sound of a voice or rattle when the sound is maintained for several seconds (Clifton & others, 1981), but the newborn can localize a sound and look at an object only in a crude way (Bechtold, Bushnell, & Salapatek, 1979). These early forms of intermodal perception become sharpened with experience in the first year of life (Hollich, Newman, & Jusczyk, 2005). In one study, infants as young as $3\frac{1}{2}$ months old looked more at their mother when they also heard her voice and longer at their father when they also heard his voice (Spelke & Owsley, 1979). Thus even young infants can coordinate visual-auditory information involving people.

Can young infants put vision and sound together as precisely as adults do? In the first six months, infants have difficulty connecting sensory input from different modes, but in the second half of the first year they show an increased ability to make this connection mentally.

Thus, babies are born into the world with some innate abilities to perceive relations among sensory modalities, but their intermodal abilities improve considerably through experience (Banks, 2005). As with all aspects of development, in perceptual development, nature and nurture interact and cooperate (Banks, 2005).

Perceptual-Motor Coupling

As we come to the end of this chapter, we return to the important theme of perceptual-motor coupling. The distinction between perceiving and doing has been a time-honored tradition in psychology. However, a number of experts on perceptual and motor development question whether this distinction makes sense (Adolph & Joh, 2007, 2008; Thelen & Smith, 2006). The main thrust of research in Esther Thelen's dynamic systems approach is to explore how people assemble motor behaviors for perceiving and acting. The main theme of the ecological approach of Eleanor and James J. Gibson is to discover how perception guides action. Action can guide perception, and perception can guide action. Only by moving one's eyes, head, hands, and arms and by moving from one location to another can an individual fully experience his or her environment and learn how to adapt to it. Perception and action are coupled.

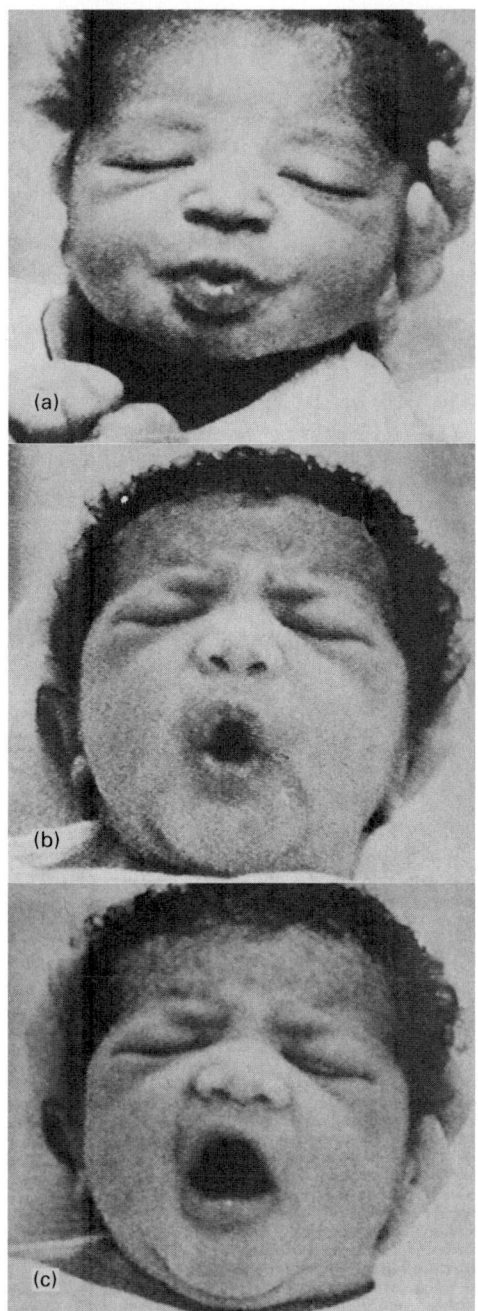

FIGURE 4.24 Newborns' Facial Responses to Basic Tastes. Facial expressions elicited by (a) a sweet solution, (b) a sour solution, and (c) a bitter solution.

intermodal perception The ability to relate and integrate information from two or more sensory modalities, such as vision and hearing.

Babies, for example, continually coordinate their movements with perceptual information to learn how to maintain balance, reach for objects in space, and move across various surfaces and terrains (Adolph & Joh, 2007, 2008; Thelen & Smith, 2006). They are motivated to move by what they perceive. Consider the sight of an attractive toy across the room. In this situation, infants must perceive the current state of their bodies and learn how to use their limbs to reach the toy. Although their movements at first are awkward and uncoordinated, babies soon learn to select patterns that are appropriate for reaching their goals.

Equally important is the other part of the perception-action coupling. That is, action educates perception (Adolph & Joh, 2007, 2008; Smith & Breazeal, 2007; Thelen & Smith, 2006). For example, watching an object while exploring it manually helps infants to discriminate its texture, size, and hardness. Locomoting in the environment teaches babies about how objects and people look from different perspectives, or whether surfaces will support their weight. Individuals perceive in order to move and move in order to perceive. Perceptual and motor development do not occur in isolation from each other but instead are coupled.

How are perception and action coupled in infants' development?

The infant is by no means as helpless as it looks and is quite capable of some very complex and important actions.

—HERB PICK
Contemporary Developmental Psychologist, University of Minnesota

Review and Reflect: Learning Goal 3

3 **Summarize the Course of Sensory and Perceptual Development in Infancy**

REVIEW

- What are sensation and perception?
- What is the ecological view of perception?
- How does visual perception develop in infancy?
- How do hearing, touch and pain, smell, and taste develop in infancy?
- What is intermodal perception?
- How is perceptual-motor development coupled?

REFLECT

- How much sensory stimulation should caregivers provide for infants? A little? A lot? Could an infant be given too much sensory stimulation? Explain.

Physical Development in Infancy

1 PHYSICAL GROWTH AND DEVELOPMENT IN INFANCY: DISCUSS PHYSICAL GROWTH AND DEVELOPMENT IN INFANCY

Patterns of Growth

- The cephalocaudal pattern is the sequence in which growth proceeds from top to bottom. The proximodistal pattern is the sequence in which growth starts at the center of the body and moves toward the extremities.

Height and Weight

- The average North American newborn is 20 inches long and weighs $7\frac{1}{2}$ pounds. Infants grow about 1 inch per month in the first year and nearly triple their weight by their first birthday. The rate of growth slows in the second year.

The Brain

- One of the most dramatic changes in the brain in the first two years of life is dendritic spreading, which increases the connections between neurons. Myelination, which speeds the conduction of nerve impulses, continues through infancy and even into adolescence. The cerebral cortex has two hemispheres (left and right). Lateralization refers to specialization of function in one hemisphere or the other. Early experiences play an important role in brain development. Neural connections are formed early in an infant's life. Before birth, genes mainly direct neurons to different locations. After birth, the inflowing stream of sights, sounds, smells, touches, language, and eye contact help shape the brain's neural connections, as does stimulation from caregivers and others.

Sleep

- Newborns usually sleep 16 to 17 hours a day. By 4 months of age, many American infants approach adultlike sleeping patterns. REM sleep—during which dreaming occurs—is present more in early infancy than in childhood and adulthood. Sleeping arrangements for infants vary across cultures. In America, infants are more likely to sleep alone than in many other cultures. Some experts believe shared sleeping can lead to sudden infant death syndrome (SIDS), a condition that occurs when a sleeping infant suddenly stops breathing and dies without an apparent cause.

Nutrition

- Infants need to consume about 50 calories per day for each pound they weigh. The growing consensus is that in most instances breast feeding is superior to bottle feeding for both the infant and the mother, although the correlational nature of studies must be considered. Severe infant malnutrition is still prevalent in many parts of the world. A special concern in impoverished countries is early weaning from breast milk and the misuse and hygiene problems associated with bottle feeding in these countries.

2 MOTOR DEVELOPMENT: DESCRIBE INFANTS' MOTOR DEVELOPMENT

The Dynamic Systems View

- Thelen's dynamic systems theory seeks to explain how motor behaviors are assembled for perceiving and acting. Perception and action are coupled. According to this theory, motor skills are the result of many converging factors, such as the development of the nervous system, the body's physical properties and its movement possibilities, the goal the child is motivated to reach, and environmental support for the skill. In the dynamic systems view, motor development is far more complex than the result of a genetic blueprint.

Reflexes

- Reflexes—automatic movements—govern the newborn's behavior. They include the sucking, rooting, and Moro reflexes. The rooting and Moro reflexes disappear after three to four months. Permanent reflexes include coughing and blinking. For infants, sucking is an especially important reflex because it provides a means of obtaining nutrition.

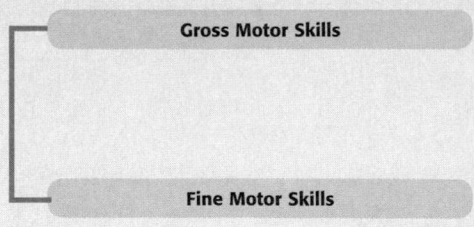

Gross Motor Skills

- Gross motor skills involve large-muscle activities. Key skills developed during infancy include control of posture and walking. Although infants usually learn to walk by their first birthday, the neural pathways that allow walking begin to form earlier. The age at which infants reach milestones in the development of gross motor skills may vary by as much as two to four months, especially for milestones in late infancy.

Fine Motor Skills

- Fine motor skills involve finely tuned movements. The onset of reaching and grasping marks a significant accomplishment, and this becomes more refined during the first two years of life.

3   SENSORY AND PERCEPTUAL DEVELOPMENT: SUMMARIZE THE COURSE OF SENSORY AND PERCEPTUAL DEVELOPMENT IN INFANCY

What Are Sensation and Perception?

- Sensation occurs when information interacts with sensory receptors. Perception is the interpretation of sensation.

The Ecological View

- Created by the Gibsons, the ecological view states that we directly perceive information that exists in the world around us. Perception brings people in contact with the environment to interact with and adapt to it. Affordances provide opportunities for interaction offered by objects that fit within our capabilities to perform activities.

Visual Perception

- Researchers have developed a number of methods to assess the infant's perception, including the visual preference method (which Fantz used to determine young infants' interest in looking at patterned over nonpatterned displays), habituation and dishabituation, and tracking. The infant's visual acuity increases dramatically in the first year of life. Infants' color vision improves as they develop. Young infants systematically scan human faces. By 3 months of age, infants show size and shape constancy. In Gibson and Walk's classic study, infants as young as 6 months of age had depth perception. Much of vision develops from biological foundations, but environmental experiences can contribute to the development of visual perception.

Other Senses

- The fetus can hear several weeks prior to birth. Immediately after birth, newborns can hear, but their sensory threshold is higher than that of adults. Developmental changes in the perception of loudness, pitch, and localization of sound occur during infancy. Newborns can respond to touch and feel pain. Newborns can differentiate odors, and sensitivity to taste may be present before birth.

Intermodal Perception

- Early, exploratory forms of intermodal perception—the ability to relate and integrate information from two or more sensory modalities—are present in newborns and become sharpened over the first year of life.

Perceptual-Motor Coupling

- Perception and action are often not isolated but rather are coupled. Individuals perceive in order to move and move in order to perceive.

KEY TERMS

KEY PEOPLE

Charles Nelson 116
Ernesto Pollitt 125
T. Berry Brazelton 126

Esther Thelen 127
Karen Adolph 130

Eleanor and James J. Gibson 134
Robert Fantz 135

William James 137
Richard Walk 138

E-LEARNING TOOLS

To help you master the material in this chapter, visit the Online Learning Center for *Life-Span Development*, twelfth edition, at **www.mhhe.com/santrockld12**.

Self-Assessment

Connect to **www.mhhe.com/santrockld12** to examine your understanding of physical development in infancy by completing the self-assessment, *My Beliefs About Nurturing a Baby's Physical Development*.

Taking It to the Net

Connect to **www.mhhe.com/santrockld12** to research the answers to these questions:

1. Beginning in the 1990s, a number of products were marketed to parents based on widely publicized research findings about how certain kinds of music could influence a child's cognitive development (popularly known as the "Mozart Effect"). Ben is a marketing manager for a company that publishes these products. He feels it's his responsibility to understand how these claims can be supported by what we currently know about child cognitive development. He would like to promote a CD recording of Mozart designed to be played in the nursery without making a glib causal connection between listening to a certain kind of music and a child's intelligence. How might Ben qualify the claims his company makes for the CD?

2. Huy grew up in a traditional Chinese family, where co-sleeping until adolescence was the norm. He sees no problem with allowing his infant daughter to sleep with him and his wife. His wife, Lori, who was born and raised in the United States, is concerned that allowing the baby to sleep in their bed places her at risk for SIDS. Is co-sleeping a significant risk factor for SIDS? What else can Huy and Lori do to reduce the risk?

3. Marianne has landed a part-time job as a nanny for Jack, a 2-month old boy. What can Marianne expect to see in terms of the child's sensory and motor development as she observes and interacts with Jack over the next six months?

Video Clips

The Online Learning Center includes two videos for Chapter 4. The first video is called "Nutritional Benefits of Breast Feeding." Is breast feeding better for the infant than bottle feeding? In this segment, a dietician details some of the benefits of breast feeding. The second video is called "Gross Motor Ability at 1 Year." A profile of 1-year-old Cindy illustrates some of the advances in gross motor skills that have occurred during the first year of life.

Health and Well-Being, Parenting, and Education Exercises

Build your decision-making skills by trying your hand at the health and well-being, parenting, and education exercises. Connect to **www.mhhe.com/santrockld12** to research the answers and complete the exercises.

5

I wish I could travel down by the road that crosses the baby's mind where reason makes kites of her laws and flies them. . . .

—RABINDRANATH TAGORE
Bengali Poet, Essayist, 20th Century

LEARNING GOALS

◆ Summarize and evaluate Piaget's theory of infant development.

◆ Describe how infants learn, remember, and conceptualize.

◆ Discuss infant assessment measures and the prediction of intelligence.

◆ Describe the nature of language and how it develops in infancy.

COGNITIVE DEVELOPMENT IN INFANCY

CHAPTER OUTLINE

Images of Life-Span Development
The Stories of Laurent, Lucienne, and Jacqueline

Jean Piaget, the famous Swiss psychologist, was a meticulous observer of his three children—Laurent, Lucienne, and Jacqueline. His books on cognitive development are filled with these observations. Here are a few of Piaget's observations of his children in infancy (Piaget, 1952):

- At 21 days of age, "Laurent found his thumb after three attempts: prolonged sucking begins each time. But, once he has been placed on his back, he does not know how to coordinate the movement of the arms with that of the mouth and his hands draw back even when his lips are seeking them" (p. 27).

- "During the third month, thumb sucking becomes less important to Laurent because of new visual and auditory interests. But, when he cries, his thumb goes to the rescue."

- Toward the end of Lucienne's fourth month, while she is lying in her crib, Piaget hangs a doll above her feet. Lucienne thrusts her feet at the doll and makes it move. "Afterward, she looks at her motionless foot for a second, then recommences. There is no visual control of her foot, for the movements are the same when Lucienne only looks at the doll or when I place the doll over her head. On the other hand, the tactile control of the foot is apparent: after the first shakes, Lucienne makes slow foot movements as though to grasp and explore" (p. 159).

- At 11 months, "Jacqueline is seated and shakes a little bell. She then pauses abruptly in order to delicately place the bell in front of her right foot; then she kicks hard. Unable to recapture it, she grasps a ball which she then places at the same spot in order to give it another kick" (p. 225).

- At 1 year, 2 months, "Jacqueline holds in her hands an object which is new to her: a round, flat box which she turns all over, shakes, [and] rubs against the bassinet. . . . She lets it go and tries to pick it up. But she only succeeds in touching it with her index finger, without grasping it. She nevertheless makes an attempt and presses on the edge. The box then tilts up and falls again" (p. 273). Jacqueline shows an interest in this result and studies the fallen box.

- At 1 year, 8 months, "Jacqueline arrives at a closed door with a blade of grass in each hand. She stretches out her right hand toward the [door] knob but sees that she cannot turn it without letting go of the grass. She puts the grass on the floor, opens the door, picks up the grass again, and enters. But when she wants to leave the room, things become complicated. She puts the grass on the floor and grasps the doorknob. But then she perceives that in pulling the door toward her she will simultaneously chase away the grass which she placed between the door and the threshold. She therefore picks it up in order to put it outside the door's zone of movement" (p. 339).

For Piaget, these observations reflect important changes in the infant's cognitive development. Piaget maintained that infants go through six substages as they progress in less than two short years from Laurent's thumb sucking to Jacqueline's problem solving.

PREVIEW

Piaget's descriptions of infants are just the starting point for our exploration of cognitive development. Excitement and enthusiasm about the study of infant cognition have been fueled by an interest in what newborns and infants know, by continued fascination about innate and learned factors in the infant's cognitive development, and by controversies about whether infants construct their knowledge (Piaget's view) or know their world more directly. In this chapter, we will study not only Piaget's theory of infant development but also learning, remembering, and conceptualizing by infants; individual differences; and language development.

1   PIAGET'S THEORY OF INFANT DEVELOPMENT

Cognitive Processes   **The Sensorimotor Stage**   **Evaluating Piaget's Sensorimotor Stage**

Poet Nora Perry asks, "Who knows the thoughts of a child?" As much as anyone, Piaget knew. Through careful observations of his own three children—Laurent, Lucienne, and Jacqueline—and observations of and interviews with other children, Piaget changed perceptions of the way children think about the world.

Piaget's theory is a general, unifying story of how biology and experience sculpt cognitive development. Piaget thought that, just as our physical bodies have structures that enable us to adapt to the world, we build mental structures that help us to adapt to the world. *Adaptation* involves adjusting to new environmental demands. Piaget stressed that children actively construct their own cognitive worlds; information is not just poured into their minds from the environment. He sought to discover how children at different points in their development think about the world and how systematic changes in their thinking occur.

Cognitive Processes

What processes do children use as they construct their knowledge of the world? Piaget developed several concepts to answer this question; especially important are schemes, assimilation, accommodation, organization, equilibrium, and equilibration.

Schemes   As the infant or child seeks to construct an understanding of the world, said Piaget (1954), the developing brain creates **schemes**. These are actions or mental representations that organize knowledge. In Piaget's theory, behavioral schemes (physical activities) characterize infancy, and mental schemes (cognitive activities) develop in childhood (Lamb, Bornstein, & Teti, 2002). A baby's schemes are structured by simple actions that can be performed on objects such as sucking, looking, and grasping. Older children have schemes that include strategies and plans for solving problems. For example, in the descriptions at the opening of this chapter, Laurent displayed a scheme for sucking; Jacqueline displayed a problem-solving scheme when she was able to open the door without losing her blade of grass. By the time we have reached adulthood, we have constructed an enormous number of diverse schemes, ranging from driving a car to balancing a budget to the concept of fairness.

In Piaget's view, what is a scheme? What schemes might this young infant be displaying?

schemes In Piaget's theory, actions or mental representations that organize knowledge.

*W*e are born capable of learning.

—Jean-Jacques Rousseau
Swiss-Born French Philosopher, 18th Century

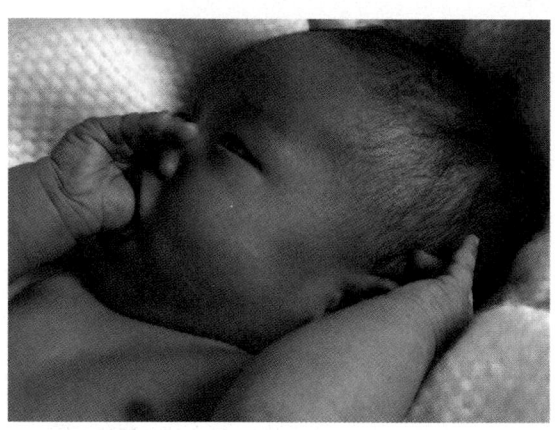

How might assimilation and accomodation be involved in infants' sucking?

assimilation Piagetian concept of using existing schemes to deal with new information or experiences.

accommodation Piagetian concept of adjusting schemes to fit new information and experiences.

organization Piaget's concept of grouping isolated behaviors and thoughts into a higher-order, more smoothly functioning cognitive system.

equilibration A mechanism that Piaget proposed to explain how children shift from one stage of thought to the next.

sensorimotor stage The first of Piaget's stages, which lasts from birth to about 2 years of age; infants construct an understanding of the world by coordinating sensory experiences with motoric actions.

Assimilation and Accommodation   To explain how children use and adapt their schemes, Piaget offered two concepts: assimilation and accommodation. **Assimilation** occurs when children use their existing schemes to deal with new information or experiences. **Accommodation** occurs when children adjust their schemes to take new information and experiences into account.

Think about a toddler who has learned the word *car* to identify the family's car. The toddler might call all moving vehicles on roads "cars," including motorcycles and trucks; the child has assimilated these objects to his or her existing scheme. But the child soon learns that motorcycles and trucks are not cars and fine-tunes the category to exclude motorcycles and trucks, accommodating the scheme.

Assimilation and accommodation operate even in very young infants. Newborns reflexively suck everything that touches their lips; they assimilate all sorts of objects into their sucking scheme. By sucking different objects, they learn about their taste, texture, shape, and so on. After several months of experience, though, they construct their understanding of the world differently. Some objects, such as fingers and the mother's breast, can be sucked, and others, such as fuzzy blankets, should not be sucked. In other words, they accommodate their sucking scheme.

Organization   To make sense out of their world, said Piaget, children cognitively organize their experiences. **Organization** in Piaget's theory is the grouping of isolated behaviors and thoughts into a higher-order system. Continual refinement of this organization is an inherent part of development. A boy who has only a vague idea about how to use a hammer may also have a vague idea about how to use other tools. After learning how to use each one, he relates these uses, organizing his knowledge.

Equilibration and Stages of Development   Assimilation and accommodation always take the child to a higher ground, according to Piaget. In trying to understand the world, the child inevitably experiences cognitive conflict, or *disequilibrium*. That is, the child is constantly faced with counterexamples to his or her existing schemes and with inconsistencies. For example, if a child believes that pouring water from a short and wide container into a tall and narrow container changes the amount of water, then the child might be puzzled by where the "extra" water came from and whether there is actually more water to drink. The puzzle creates disequilibrium; for Piaget, an internal search for equilibrium creates motivation for change. The child assimilates and accommodates, adjusting old schemes, developing new schemes, and organizing and reorganizing the old and new schemes. Eventually, the organization is fundamentally different from the old organization; it is a new way of thinking.

In short, according to Piaget, children constantly assimilate and accommodate as they seek equilibrium. There is considerable movement between states of cognitive equilibrium and disequilibrium as assimilation and accommodation work in concert to produce cognitive change. **Equilibration** is the name Piaget gave to this mechanism by which children shift from one stage of thought to the next.

The result of these processes, according to Piaget, is that individuals go through four stages of development. A different way of understanding the world makes one stage more advanced than another. Cognition is *qualitatively* different in one stage compared with another. In other words, the way children reason at one stage is different from the way they reason at another stage. Here our focus is on Piaget's stage of infant cognitive development. In later chapters, when we study cognitive development in early childhood, middle and late childhood, and adolescence (Chapters 7, 9, and 11) we will explore the last three Piagetian stages.

The Sensorimotor Stage

The **sensorimotor stage** lasts from birth to about 2 years of age. In this stage, infants construct an understanding of the world by coordinating sensory experiences (such as

Substage	Age	Description	Example
1 Simple reflexes	Birth to 1 month	Coordination of sensation and action through reflexive behaviors.	Rooting, sucking, and grasping reflexes; newborns suck reflexively when their lips are touched.
2 First habits and primary circular reactions	1 to 4 months	Coordination of sensation and two types of schemes: habits (reflex) and primary circular reactions (reproduction of an event that initially occurred by chance). Main focus is still on the infant's body.	Repeating a body sensation first experienced by chance (sucking thumb, for example); then infants might accommodate actions by sucking their thumb differently from how they suck on a nipple.
3 Secondary circular reactions	4 to 8 months	Infants become more object-oriented, moving beyond self-preoccupation; repeat actions that bring interesting or pleasurable results.	An infant coos to make a person stay near; as the person starts to leave, the infant coos again.
4 Coordination of secondary circular reactions	8 to 12 months	Coordination of vision and touch—hand-eye coordination; coordination of schemes and intentionality.	Infant manipulates a stick in order to bring an attractive toy within reach.
5 Tertiary circular reactions, novelty, and curiosity	12 to 18 months	Infants become intrigued by the many properties of objects and by the many things they can make happen to objects; they experiment with new behavior.	A block can be made to fall, spin, hit another object, and slide across the ground.
6 Internalization of schemes	18 to 24 months	Infants develop the ability to use primitive symbols and form enduring mental representations.	An infant who has never thrown a temper tantrum before sees a playmate throw a tantrum; the infant retains a memory of the event, then throws one himself the next day.

FIGURE 5.1 Piaget's Six Substages of Sensorimotor Development

seeing and hearing) with physical, motoric actions—hence the term "sensorimotor." At the beginning of this stage, newborns have little more than reflexes with which to work. At the end of the sensorimotor stage, 2-year-olds can produce complex sensorimotor patterns and use primitive symbols. We first will summarize Piaget's descriptions of how infants develop. Later we will consider criticisms of his view.

Substages   Piaget divided the sensorimotor stage into six substages: (1) simple reflexes; (2) first habits and primary circular reactions; (3) secondary circular reactions; (4) coordination of secondary circular reactions; (5) tertiary circular reactions, novelty, and curiosity; and (6) internalization of schemes (see Figure 5.1).

Simple reflexes, the first sensorimotor substage, corresponds to the first month after birth. In this substage, sensation and action are coordinated primarily through reflexive behaviors, such as rooting and sucking. Soon the infant produces behaviors that resemble reflexes in the absence of the usual stimulus for the reflex. For example, a newborn will suck a nipple or bottle only when it is placed directly in the baby's mouth or touched to the lips. But soon the infant might suck when a bottle or nipple is only nearby. Even in the first month of life, the infant is initiating action and actively structuring experiences.

First habits and primary circular reactions is the second sensorimotor substage, which develops between 1 and 4 months of age. In this substage, the infant coordinates sensation and two types of schemes: habits and primary circular reactions. A *habit* is a scheme based on a reflex that has become completely separated from its eliciting stimulus. For example, infants in substage 1 suck when bottles are put to their lips or when they see a bottle. Infants in substage 2 might suck even when no bottle is present. A *circular reaction* is a repetitive action.

A **primary circular reaction** is a scheme based on the attempt to reproduce an event that initially occurred by chance. For example, suppose an infant accidentally

simple reflexes Piaget's first sensorimotor substage, which corresponds to the first month after birth. In this substage, sensation and action are coordinated primarily through reflexive behaviors.

first habits and primary circular reactions Piaget's second sensorimotor substage, which develops between 1 and 4 months of age. In this substage, the infant coordinates sensation and two types of schemes: habits and primary circular reactions.

primary circular reaction A scheme based on the attempt to reproduce an event that initially occurred by chance.

This 17-month-old is in Piaget's stage of tertiary circular reactions. *What might the infant do to suggest that she is in this stage?*

secondary circular reactions Piaget's third sensorimotor substage, which develops between 4 and 8 months of age. In this substage, the infant becomes more object-oriented, moving beyond preoccupation with the self.

coordination of secondary circular reactions Piaget's fourth sensorimotor substage, which develops between 8 and 12 months of age. Actions become more outwardly directed, and infants coordinate schemes and act with intentionality.

tertiary circular reactions, novelty, and curiosity Piaget's fifth sensorimotor substage, which develops between 12 and 18 months of age. In this substage, infants become intrigued by the many properties of objects and by the many things that they can make happen to objects.

internalization of schemes Piaget's sixth and final sensorimotor substage, which develops between 18 and 24 months of age. In this substage, the infant develops the ability to use primitive symbols.

object permanence The Piagetian term for understanding that objects and events continue to exist, even when they cannot directly be seen, heard, or touched.

sucks his fingers when they are placed near his mouth. Later, he searches for his fingers to suck them again, but the fingers do not cooperate because the infant cannot coordinate visual and manual actions.

Habits and circular reactions are stereotyped—that is, the infant repeats them the same way each time. During this substage, the infant's own body remains the infant's center of attention. There is no outward pull by environmental events.

Secondary circular reactions is the third sensorimotor substage, which develops between 4 and 8 months of age. In this substage, the infant becomes more object-oriented, moving beyond preoccupation with the self. The infant's schemes are not intentional or goal-directed, but they are repeated because of their consequences. By chance, an infant might shake a rattle. The infant repeats this action for the sake of its fascination. This is a *secondary circular reaction:* an action repeated because of its consequences. The infant also imitates some simple actions, such as the baby talk or burbling of adults, and some physical gestures. However, the baby imitates only actions that he or she is already able to produce.

Coordination of secondary circular reactions is Piaget's fourth sensorimotor substage, which develops between 8 and 12 months of age. To progress into this substage the infant must coordinate vision and touch, hand and eye. Actions become more outwardly directed. Significant changes during this substage involve the coordination of schemes and intentionality. Infants readily combine and recombine previously learned schemes in a coordinated way. They might look at an object and grasp it simultaneously, or they might visually inspect a toy, such as a rattle, and finger it simultaneously, exploring it tactilely. Actions are even more outwardly directed than before. Related to this coordination is the second achievement—the presence of intentionality. For example, infants might manipulate a stick in order to bring a desired toy within reach or they might knock over one block to reach and play with another one. Similarly, when 11-month-old Jacqueline, as described in the chapter opening, placed the ball in front of her and kicked it, she was demonstrating intentionality.

Tertiary circular reactions, novelty, and curiosity is Piaget's fifth sensorimotor substage, which develops between 12 and 18 months of age. In this substage, infants become intrigued by the many properties of objects and by the many things that they can make happen to objects. A block can be made to fall, spin, hit another object, and slide across the ground. *Tertiary circular reactions* are schemes in which the infant purposely explores new possibilities with objects, continually doing new things to them and exploring the results. Piaget says that this stage marks the starting point for human curiosity and interest in novelty.

Internalization of schemes is Piaget's sixth and final sensorimotor substage, which develops between 18 and 24 months of age. In this substage, the infant develops the ability to use primitive symbols. For Piaget, a *symbol* is an internalized sensory image or word that represents an event. Primitive symbols permit the infant to think about concrete events without directly acting them out or perceiving them. Moreover, symbols allow the infant to manipulate and transform the represented events in simple ways. In a favorite Piagetian example, Piaget's young daughter saw a matchbox being opened and closed. Later, she mimicked the event by opening and closing her mouth. This was an obvious expression of her image of the event.

Object Permanence Imagine how chaotic and unpredictable your life would be if you could not distinguish between yourself and your world. This is what the life of a newborn must be like, according to Piaget. There is no differentiation between the self and world; objects have no separate, permanent existence.

By the end of the sensorimotor period, objects are both separate from the self and permanent. **Object permanence** is the understanding that objects continue to exist even when they cannot be seen, heard, or touched. Acquiring the sense of object permanence is one of the infant's most important accomplishments, according to Piaget.

How could anyone know whether an infant had a sense of object permanence or not? The principal way that object permanence is studied is by watching an infant's reaction when an interesting object disappears (see Figure 5.2). If infants search for the object, it is assumed that they believe it continues to exist.

Object permanence is just one of the basic concepts about the physical world developed by babies. To Piaget, children, even infants, are much like little scientists, examining the world to see how it works. The *Research in Life-Span Development* interlude that follows describes some of the ways in which adult scientists try to discover what these "baby scientists" are finding out about the world.

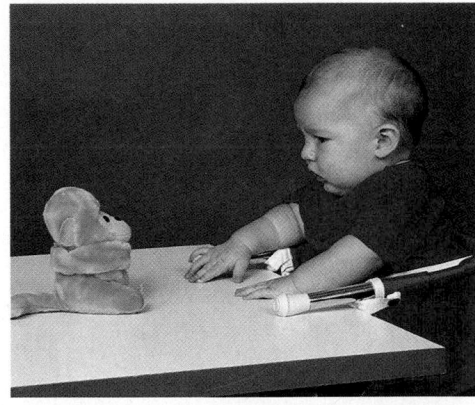

Research in Life-Span Development
Object Permanence and Causality

Two accomplishments of infants that Piaget examined were the development of object permanence and the child's understanding of causality. Let's examine two research studies that address these topics.

In both studies, Renée Baillargeon and her colleagues used a research method that involves *violation of expectations*. In this method, infants see an event happen as it normally would. Then, the event is changed, often in a way that creates a physically impossible event. If infants look longer at the changed event, that indicates they are surprised by it. In other words, the infants' reaction is interpreted to indicate that the infant had certain expectations about the world that were violated.

In one study focused on object permanence, researchers showed infants a toy car that moved down an inclined track, disappeared behind a screen, and then reemerged at the other end, still on the track (Baillargeon & DeVos, 1991) (see Figure 5.3) (*a*). After this sequence was repeated several times, something different occurred: A toy mouse was placed *behind* the tracks but was hidden by the screen while the car rolled by (*b*). This was the "possible" event. Then, the researchers created an "impossible event": The toy mouse was placed *on* the tracks but was secretly removed after the screen was lowered so that the car seemed to go through the mouse (*c*). In this study, infants as young as $3\frac{1}{2}$ months of age looked longer at the impossible event than at the possible event, indicating that they were surprised by it. Their surprise suggested that they remembered not only that the toy mouse still existed (object permanence) but its location.

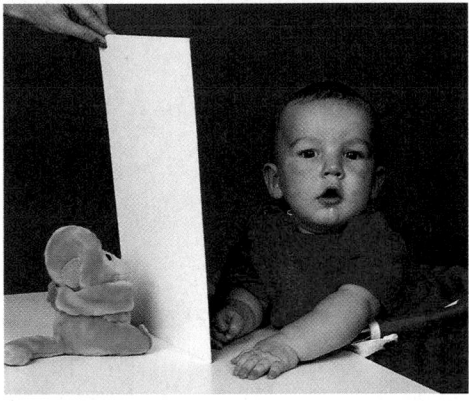

FIGURE 5.2 Object Permanence.
Piaget argued that object permanence is one of infancy's landmark cognitive accomplishments. For this 5-month-old boy, "out-of-sight" is literally out of mind. The infant looks at the toy monkey (*top*), but, when his view of the toy is blocked (*bottom*), he does not search for it. Several months later, he will search for the hidden toy monkey, reflecting the presence of object permanence.

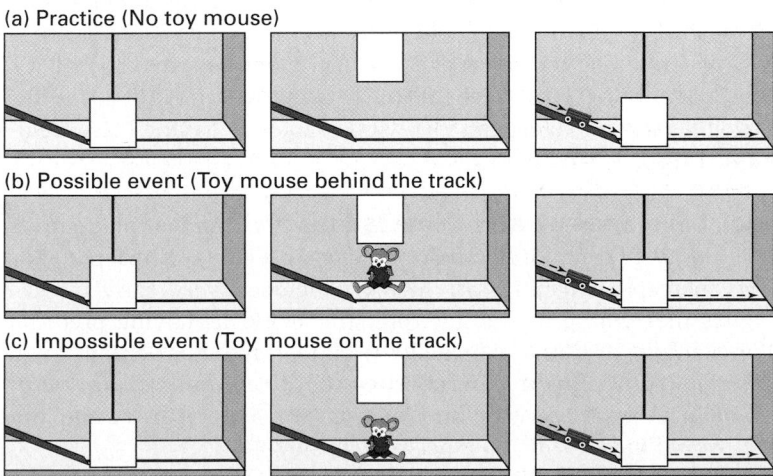

(a) Practice (No toy mouse)

(b) Possible event (Toy mouse behind the track)

(c) Impossible event (Toy mouse on the track)

FIGURE 5.3   Using the Violation of Expectations Method to Study Object Permanence in Infants. If infants looked longer at (*c*) than at (*b*), researchers reasoned that the impossible event in (*c*) violated the infants' expectations and that they remembered that the toy mouse existed.

Another study focused on the infant's understanding of causality (Kotovsky & Baillargeon, 1994). In this research, a cylinder rolls down a ramp and hits a toy bug at the bottom of the ramp. By $5\frac{1}{2}$ and $6\frac{1}{2}$ months of age, after infants have seen how far the bug will be pushed by a medium-sized cylinder, their reactions indicate that they understand that the bug will roll farther if it is hit by a large cylinder than if it is hit by a small cylinder. Thus, by the middle of the first year of life these infants understood that the size of a moving object determines how far it will move a stationary object that it collides with.

The research findings discussed in this interlude and other research indicate that infants develop object permanence earlier than Piaget proposed. Indeed, as you will see in the next section, a major theme of infant cognitive development today is that infants are more cognitively competent than Piaget envisioned.

Evaluating Piaget's Sensorimotor Stage

Piaget opened up a new way of looking at infants with his view that their main task is to coordinate their sensory impressions with their motor activity. However, the infant's cognitive world is not as neatly packaged as Piaget portrayed it, and some of Piaget's explanations for the cause of change are debated. In the past several decades, sophisticated experimental techniques have been devised to study infants, and there have been a large number of research studies on infant development. Much of the new research suggests that Piaget's view of sensorimotor development needs to be modified (Carlson & Zelazo, 2008; Meltzoff, 2007; Vallotton & Fischer, 2008).

The A-not-B Error One modification concerns Piaget's claim that certain processes are crucial in transitions from one stage to the next. The data do not always support his explanations. For example, in Piaget's theory, an important feature in the progression into substage 4, *coordination of secondary circular reactions*, is an infant's inclination to search for a hidden object in a familiar location rather than to look for the object in a new location. For example, if a toy is hidden twice, initially at location A and subsequently at location B, 8- to 12-month-old infants search correctly at location A initially. But when the toy is subsequently hidden at location B, they make the mistake of continuing to search for it at location A. **A-not-B error** (also called $A\overline{B}$ error) is the term used to describe this common mistake. Older infants are less likely to make the A-not-B error because their concept of object permanence is more complete.

Researchers have found, however, that the A-not-B error does not show up consistently (Sophian, 1985). The evidence indicates that A-not-B errors are sensitive to the delay between hiding the object at B and the infant's attempt to find it (Diamond, 1985). Thus, the A-not-B error might be due to a failure in memory. Another explanation is that infants tend to repeat a previous motor behavior (Clearfield & others, 2006; Smith, 1999).

Perceptual Development and Expectations A number of theorists, such as Eleanor Gibson (2001) and Elizabeth Spelke (1991; Spelke & Kinzler, 2007a, b), argue that infants' perceptual abilities are highly developed very early in development. Spelke argues that young infants interpret the world as having predictable occurrences. For example, in Chapter 4 we discussed research that demonstrated the presence of intermodal perception—the ability to coordinate information from two more sensory modalities, such as vision and hearing—by $3\frac{1}{2}$ months of age, much earlier than Piaget would have predicted (Spelke & Owsley, 1979).

Research also suggests that infants develop the ability to understand how the world works at a very early age (Gopnik & Schultz, 2007; Meltzoff, 2007). For example, by the time they are 3 months of age, infants develop expectations about future events. Marshall Haith and his colleagues (Canfield & Haith, 1991; Haith, Hazen, &

A-not-B error Also called A$\overline{B}$ error, this occurs when infants make the mistake of selecting the familiar hiding place (A) rather than the new hiding place (B) as they progress into substage 4 in Piaget's sensorimotor stage.

Goodman, 1988) presented pictures to infants in either a regular alternating sequence (such as left, right, left, right) or an unpredictable sequence (such as right, right, left, right). When the sequence was predictable, the 3-month-old infants began to anticipate the location of the picture, looking at the side on which it was expected to appear. However, younger infants did not develop expectations about where a picture would be presented.

What kinds of expectations do infants form? Are we born expecting the world to obey basic physical laws, such as gravity, or when do we learn about how the world works? Experiments by Elizabeth Spelke (1991, 2000; Spelke & Hespos, 2001) have addressed these questions. She placed babies before a puppet stage and showed them a series of actions that are unexpected if you know how the physical world works—for example, one ball seemed to roll through a solid barrier, another seemed to leap between two platforms, and a third appeared to hang in midair (Spelke, 1979). Spelke measured and compared the babies' looking times for unexpected and expected actions. She concluded that, by 4 months of age, even though infants do not yet have the ability to talk about objects, move around objects, manipulate objects, or even see objects with high resolution, they expect objects to be solid and continuous. However, at 4 months of age, infants do not expect an object to obey gravitational constraints (Spelke & others, 1992). Similarly, research by Renée Baillargeon and her colleagues (1995, 2004) documents that infants as young as 3 to 4 months expect objects to be *substantial* (in the sense that other objects cannot move through them) and *permanent* (in the sense that objects continue to exist when they are hidden).

In sum, researchers conclude that infants see objects as bounded, unitary, solid, and separate from their background, possibly at birth or shortly thereafter, but definitely by 3 to 4 months of age, much earlier than Piaget envisioned. Young infants still have much to learn about objects, but the world appears both stable and orderly to them.

However, some critics, such as Andrew Meltzoff (2008; Meltzoff & Moore, 1998), argue that Spelke's and Baillargeon's research relies on how long infants look at unexpected events and thus assess infants' *perceptual expectations* about where and when objects will reappear rather than tapping their *knowledge* about where the objects are when they are out of sight. Meltzoff points out that whether infants act on their perception is an important aspect of assessing object permanence and states that it does not appear that young infants can act on the information. Thus, Meltzoff (2008) concludes that whether longer looking time is a valid measure of object permanence and how early infants develop object permanence remains controversial.

By 6 to 8 months, infants have learned to perceive gravity and support—that an object hanging on the end of a table should fall, that ball-bearings will travel farther when rolled down a longer rather than a shorter ramp, and that cup handles will not fall when attached to a cup (Slater, Field, & Hernandez-Reif, 2007). As infants develop, their experiences and actions on objects help them to understand physical laws (Bremner, 2007).

Many researchers conclude that Piaget wasn't specific enough about how infants learn about their world and that infants are more competent than Piaget thought (Bremner, 2007; Spelke & Kinzler, 2007a, b). As they have examined the specific ways that infants learn, the field of infant cognition has become very specialized. There are many researchers working on different questions, with no general theory emerging that can connect all of the different findings (Nelson, 1999). Their theories often are local theories, focused on specific research questions, rather than grand theories like Piaget's (Kuhn, 1998). If there is a unifying theme, it is that investigators in infant development seek to understand more precisely how developmental changes in cognition take place and the big issue of nature and nurture (Spelke & Kinzler, 2007b).

A 4-month-old in Elizabeth Spelke's infant perception laboratory is tested to determine if she knows that an object in motion will not stop in midair. Spelke concluded that at 4 months babies don't expect objects like these balls to obey gravitational constraints, but that they do expect objects to be solid and continuous. Research by Spelke, Renee Baillargeon, and others suggest that infants develop an ability to understand how the world works earlier than Piaget envisioned. However, critics such as Andrew Meltzoff fault their research and conclude there is still controversy about how early some infant cognitive accomplishments occur.

What revisions in Piaget's theory of sensorimotor development do contemporary researchers conclude need to be made?

1 **Summarize and Evaluate Piaget's Theory of Infant Development**

REVIEW

- What cognitive processes are important in Piaget's theory?
- What are some characteristics of Piaget's stage of sensorimotor development?
- What are some contributions and criticisms of Piaget's sensorimotor stage?

REFLECT

- What are some implications of Piaget's theory of infant development for parenting?

2 LEARNING, REMEMBERING, AND CONCEPTUALIZING

| Conditioning | Attention | Memory | Imitation | Concept Formation and Categorization |

When Piaget hung a doll above 4-month-old Lucienne's feet, as described in the chapter opening, would she remember the doll? If Piaget had rewarded her for moving the doll with her foot, would that have affected Lucienne's behavior? If he had showed her how to shake the doll's hand, could she have imitated him? If he had showed her a different doll, could she have formed the concept of a "doll"?

Questions like these might be examined by researchers taking the behavioral and social cognitive or information-processing approaches introduced in Chapter 1. In contrast to Piaget's theory, these approaches do not describe infant development in terms of stages. Instead, they document gradual changes in the infant's ability to understand and process information about the world. In this section, we explore what researchers using these approaches can tell us about how infants learn, remember, and conceptualize.

Conditioning

In Chapter 1, we described Skinner's operant conditioning (in which the consequences of a behavior produce changes in the probability of the behavior's occurrence). Infants can learn through both types of conditioning. For example, if an infant's behavior is followed by a rewarding stimulus, the behavior is likely to recur.

Operant conditioning has been especially helpful to researchers in their efforts to determine what infants perceive (Watanabe & Taga, 2006). For example, infants will suck faster on a nipple when the sucking behavior is followed by a visual display, music, or a human voice (Rovee-Collier, 1987, 2007).

Carolyn Rovee-Collier (1987) has also demonstrated how infants can retain information from the experience of being conditioned. In a characteristic experiment, she places a 2½-month-old baby in a crib under an elaborate mobile (see Figure 5.4). She then ties one end of a ribbon to the baby's ankle and the other end to the mobile. Subsequently, she observes that the baby kicks and makes the mobile move. The movement of the mobile is the reinforcing stimulus (which increases the baby's kicking behavior) in this experiment. Weeks later, the baby is returned to the crib, but its foot is not tied to the mobile. The baby kicks, which suggests it has retained the information that if it kicks a leg, the mobile will move.

FIGURE 5.4 The Technique Used in Rovee-Collier's Investigation of Infant Memory. In Rovee-Collier's experiment, operant conditioning was used to demonstrate that infants as young as 2½ months of age can retain information from the experience of being conditioned. *What did infants recall in Rovee-Collier's experiment?*

Attention

Attention, the focusing of mental resources on select information, improves cognitive processing on many tasks. Even newborns can detect a contour and fix their attention on it. Older infants scan patterns more thoroughly. By 4 months, infants can selectively attend to an object. In adults, when individuals orient their attention to an object or event, the parietal lobes in the cerebral cortex are involved (Posner, 2003). It is likely that the parietal lobes are active when infants orient their attention, although research has not yet documented this. (Figure 4.4 in the previous chapter illustrates the location of the parietal lobes in the brain.)

Attention in the first year of life is dominated by an *orienting/investigative process* (Posner & Rothbart, 2007). This process involves directing attention to potentially important locations in the environment (that is, *where*) and recognizing objects and their features (such as color and form) (that is, *what*) (Courage & Richards, 2008). From 3 to 9 months of age, infants can deploy their attention more flexibly and quickly. Another important type of attention is *sustained attention*, also referred to as *focused attention* (Courage & Richards, 2008). New stimuli typically elicit an orienting response followed by sustained attention. It is sustained attention that allows infants to learn about and remember characteristics of a stimulus as it becomes familiar. Researchers have found that infants as young as 3 months of age engage in 5 to 10 seconds of sustained attention. From this age through the second year, the length of sustained attention increases (Courage & Richards, 2008).

Habituation and Dishabituation   Closely linked with attention are the processes of habituation and dishabituation that we discussed in Chapter 4. If you say the same word or show the same toy to a baby several times in a row, the baby usually pays less attention to it each time. This is *habituation*—decreased responsiveness to a stimulus after repeated presentations of the stimulus. *Dishabituation* is the increase in responsiveness after a change in stimulation. Chapter 4 described some of the measures that researchers use to study whether habituation is occurring, such as sucking behavior (sucking stops when an infant attends to a novel object), heart rates, and the length of time the infant looks at an object.

Infants' attention is strongly governed by novelty and habituation (Courage & Richards, 2008; Snyder & Torrence, 2008). When an object becomes familiar, attention becomes shorter, making infants more vulnerable to distraction (Oakes, Kannass, & Shaddy, 2002). One study found that 10-month-olds were more distractible than 26-month-olds (Ruff & Capozzoli, 2003). Another study revealed that infants who were labeled "short lookers" because of the brief time they focused attention had better memory at 1 year of age than were "long lookers," who had more sustained attention (Courage, Howe, & Squires, 2004).

Researchers study habituation to determine the extent to which infants can see, hear, smell, taste, and experience touch (Slater, Field, & Hernandez-Reif, 2007). Studies of habituation can also indicate whether infants recognize something they have previously experienced. Habituation provides a measure of an infant's maturity and well-being. Infants who have brain damage do not habituate well.

Knowing about habituation and dishabituation can help parents interact effectively with infants. Infants respond to changes in stimulation. Wise parents sense when an infant shows an interest and realize that they may have to repeat something many times for the infant to process information. But if the stimulation is repeated often, the infant stops responding to the parent. In parent-infant interaction, it is important for parents to do novel things and to repeat them often until the infant stops responding. The parent stops or changes behaviors when the infant redirects his or her attention (Rosenblith, 1992).

Joint Attention   Another aspect of attention that is an important aspect of infant development is **joint attention**, in which individuals focus on the same object or event. Joint attention requires (1) an ability to track another's behavior, such as following the

attention The focusing of mental resources on select information.

joint attention Occurs when individuals focus on the same object and an ability to track another's behavior is present, one individual directs another's attention, and reciprocal interaction is present.

FIGURE 5.5 Gaze Following in Infancy.
Researcher Rechele Brooks shifts her eyes from the infant to a toy in the foreground (*a*). The infant then follows her eye movement to the toy (*b*). Brooks and colleague Andrew Meltzoff (2005) found that infants begin to engage in this kind of behavior called "gaze following" at 10 to 11 months of age. *Why might gaze following be an important accomplishment for an infant?*

(a)

(b)

A mother and her infant daughter engaging in joint attention. *What about this photograph tells you that joint attention is occurring? Why is joint attention an important aspect of infant development?*

gaze of someone; (2) one person directing another's attention, and (3) reciprocal interaction (Butterworth, 2004). Early in infancy, joint attention usually involves a caregiver pointing or using words to direct an infant's attention. Emerging forms of joint attention occur at about 7 to 8 months, but it is not until toward the end of the first year that joint attention skills are frequently observed (Heimann & others, 2006; Meltzoff & Brooks, 2006). In a study conducted by Rechele Brooks and Andrew Meltzoff (2005), at 10 to 11 months of age infants first began engaging in "gaze following," looking where another person has just looked (see Figure 5.5). And by their first birthday, infants have begun to direct adults' to objects that capture their interest (Heimann & others, 2006).

Joint attention plays important roles in many aspects of infant development and considerably increases infants' ability to learn from other people (Striano, Reid, & Hoehl, 2006). Nowhere is this more apparent than in observations of interchanges between caregivers and infants as infants are learning language (Meltzoff & Brooks, 2009). When caregivers and infants frequently engage in joint attention, infants say their first word earlier and develop a larger vocabulary (Carpenter, Nagell, & Tomasello, 1998; Flom & Pick, 2003). In one study, infants' initiation of joint attention was linked to their receptive and expressive language at 3 years of age (Ulvund & Smith, 1996). Later in the chapter in our discussion of language, we will further discuss joint attention and the infant's language development.

Memory

Memory involves the retention of information over time. Attention plays an important role in memory as part of a process called *encoding*, which is the process by which information gets into memory. What can infants remember, when?

Some researchers such as Rovee-Collier (2008) have concluded that infants as young as 2 to 6 months of age can remember some experiences through $1\frac{1}{2}$ to 2 years of age. However, critics such as Jean Mandler (2004), a leading expert on infant cognition, argue that the infants in Rovee-Collier's experiments are displaying only implicit memory. **Implicit memory** refers to memory without conscious recollection—memories of skills and routine procedures that are performed automatically. In contrast, **explicit memory** refers to the conscious memory of facts and experiences.

When people think about memory, they are usually referring to explicit memory. Most researchers find that babies do not show explicit memory until the second half of the first year (Bauer, 2007, 2008; Bauer & others, 2003). Then, explicit memory improves substantially during the second year of life (Bauer, 2007, 2008; Carver & Bauer, 2001). In one longitudinal study, infants were assessed several times during their second year (Bauer & others, 2000). Older infants showed more accurate memory and required fewer prompts to demonstrate their memory than younger infants.

What changes in the brain are linked to infants' memory development? From about 6 to 12 months of age, the maturation of the hippocampus and the surrounding cerebral

memory A central feature of cognitive development, pertaining to all situations in which an individual retains information over time.

implicit memory Memory without conscious recollection; involves skills and routine procedures that are automatically performed.

explicit memory Memory of facts and experiences that individuals consciously know and can state.

cortex, especially the frontal lobes, make the emergence of explicit memory possible (Nelson, Thomas, & de Haan, 2006) (see Figure 5.6). Explicit memory continues to improve in the second year, as these brain structures further mature and connections between them increase. Less is known about the areas of the brain involved in implicit memory in infancy.

Let's examine another aspect of memory. Do you remember your third birthday party? Probably not. Most adults can remember little if anything from the first three years of their life. This is called *infantile* or *childhood amnesia.* The few reported adult memories of life at age 2 or 3 are at best very sketchy (Newcombe, 2008). Elementary school children also do not remember much of their early child years (Lie & Newcombe, 1999).

What is the cause of infantile amnesia? One reason older children and adults have difficulty recalling events from their infant and early child years is that during these early years the prefrontal lobes of the brain are immature; this area of the brain is believed to play an important role in storing memories for events (Boyer & Diamond, 1992).

In sum, most of young infants' conscious memories appear to be rather fragile and short-lived, although their implicit memory of perceptual-motor actions can be substantial (Bauer, 2007, 2008; Mandler, 2004). By the end of the second year, long-term memory is more substantial and reliable (Bauer, 2007, 2008).

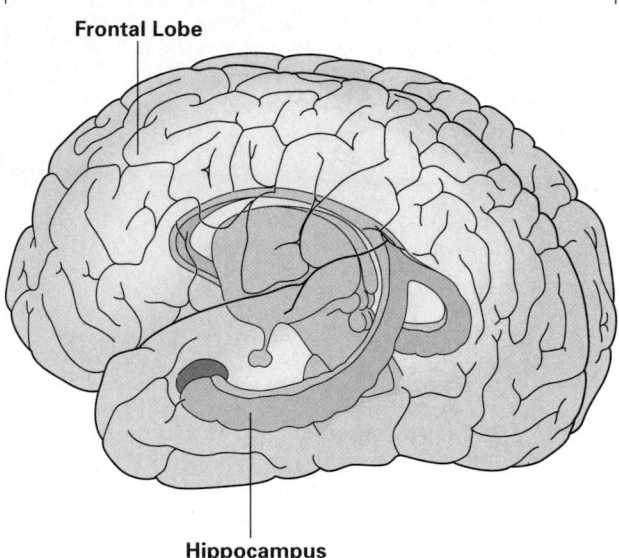

FIGURE 5.6 Key Brain Structures Involved in Explicit Memory Development in Infancy

Imitation

Can infants imitate someone else's emotional expressions? If an adult smiles, will the baby follow with a smile? If an adult protrudes her lower lip, wrinkles her forehead, and frowns, will the baby show a sad face?

Infant development researcher Andrew Meltzoff (2004, 2005, 2007; Meltzoff & Moore, 1999; Meltzoff & Williamson, 2008) has conducted numerous studies of infants' imitative abilities. He sees infants' imitative abilities as biologically based, because infants can imitate a facial expression within the first few days after birth. He also emphasizes that the infant's imitative abilities do not resemble a hardwired response but rather involve flexibility and adaptability. In Meltzoff's observations of infants across the first 72 hours of life, the infants gradually displayed more complete imitation of an adult's facial expression, such as protruding the tongue or opening the mouth wide (see Figure 5.7).

Meltzoff (2007) concludes that infants don't blindly imitate everything they see and often make creative errors. He also argues that beginning at birth there is an interplay between learning by observing and learning by doing (Piaget emphasized learning by doing).

Not all experts on infant development accept Meltzoff's conclusions that newborns are capable of imitation. Some say that these babies were engaging in little more than automatic responses to a stimulus.

Meltzoff (2005) also has studied **deferred imitation**, which occurs after a time delay of hours or days. Piaget held that deferred imitation doesn't occur until about 18 months of age. Meltzoff's research suggested that it occurs much earlier. In one study, Meltzoff (1988) demonstrated that 9-month-old infants could imitate actions—such as pushing a recessed button in a box, which produced a beeping sound—that they had seen performed 24 hours earlier. Also, in a recent study, engagement in deferred imitation at 9 months of age was a strong predictor of more extensive production of communicative gestures at 14 months of age (Heimann & others, 2006). Two of the most common infant gestures are (1) extending arm to show caregiver something the infant is holding, and (2) pointing with the arm and index finger extended at some interesting object or event.

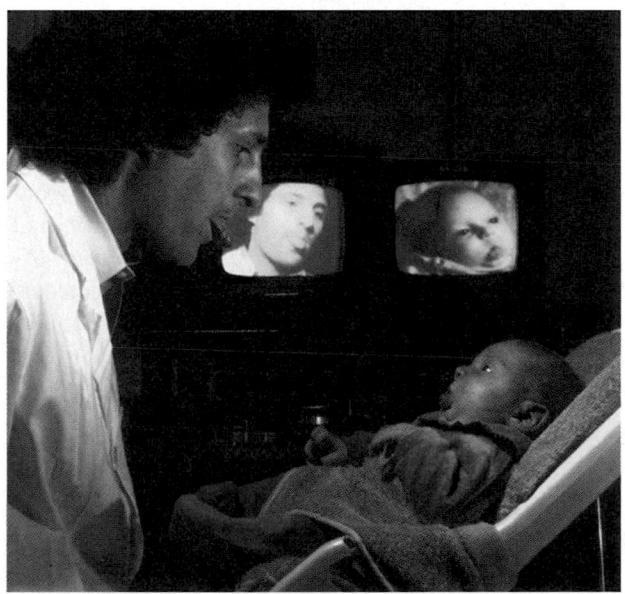

FIGURE 5.7 Infant Imitation. Infant development researcher Andrew Meltzoff protrudes his tongue in an attempt to get the infant to imitate his behavior. *How do Meltzoff's findings about imitation compare with Piaget's descriptions of infants' abilities?*

deferred imitation Imitation that occurs after a delay of hours or days.

FIGURE 5.8 Categorization in 9- to 11-Month-Olds. These are the stimuli used in the study that indicated 9- to 11-month-old infants categorized birds as animals and airplanes as vehicles even though the objects were perceptually similar (Mandler & McDonough, 1993).

*I*nfants are creating concepts and organizing their world into conceptual domains that will form the backbone of their thought throughout life.

—JEAN MANDLER
Contemporary Psychologist, University of California-San Diego

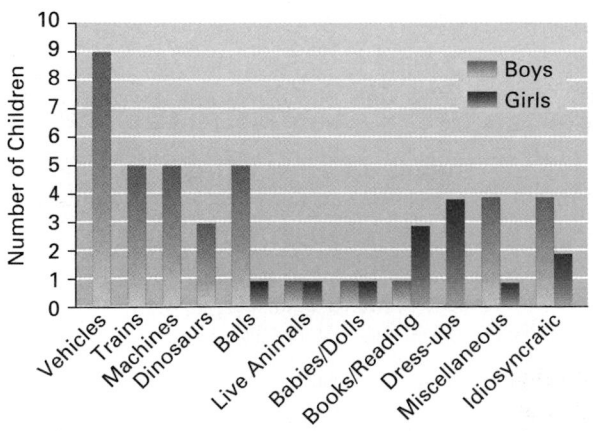

FIGURE 5.9 Categorization of Boys' and Girls' Intense Interests

Concept Formation and Categorization

Along with attention, memory, and imitation, concepts are key aspects of infants' cognitive development (Oakes, 2008; Quinn, Bhatt, & Hayden, 2008). To understand what concepts are, we first have to define *categories*: they group objects, events, and characteristics on the basis of common properties. *Concepts* are ideas about what categories represent, or said another way, the sort of thing we think category members are. Concepts and categories help us to simplify and summarize information. Without concepts, you would see each object and event as unique; you would not be able to make any generalizations.

Do infants have concepts? Yes, they do, although we do not know just how early concept formation begins (Booth, 2006; Mandler, 2004; Oakes, 2008; Quinn, 2007).

Using habituation experiments like those described earlier in the chapter, some researchers have found that infants as young as 3 months of age can group together objects with similar appearances (Quinn, 2007; Quinn, Bhatt, & Hayden, 2008). This research capitalizes on the knowledge that infants are more likely to look at a novel object than a familiar object. For example, in a characteristic study, young infants are shown a series of photographs of different types of cats in pairs (Quinn & Eimas, 1996). As they are shown more pictures of cats, they habituate to the animals, looking at them less and less. Then, after seeing a series of cats paired in photographs, when they are shown a photograph of a cat paired with a photogaph of a dog, they look longer at the dog, indicating an ability to group together objects characterized by similar properties.

Jean Mandler (2004) argues that these early categorizations are best described as *perceptual categorization*. That is, the categorizations are based on similar perceptual features of objects, such as size, color, and movement, as well as parts of objects, such as legs for animals. Mandler (2004) concludes that it is not until about 7 to 9 months of age that infants form *conceptual* categories rather than just making perceptual discriminations between different categories. In one study of 9- to 11-month-olds, infants classified birds as animals and airplanes as vehicles even though the objects were perceptually similar—airplanes and birds with their wings spread (Mandler & McDonough, 1993) (see Figure 5.8).

Further advances in categorization occur in the second year of life (Booth, 2006). Many infants' "first concepts are broad and global in nature, such as 'animal' or 'indoor thing.' Gradually, over the first two years these broad concepts become more differentiated into concepts such as 'land animal,' then 'dog,' or to 'furniture,' then 'chair'" (Mandler, 2006, p. 1). Also in the second year, infants often categorize objects on the basis of their shape (Landau, Smith, & Jones, 1998).

Do some very young children develop an intense, passionate interest in a particular category of objects or activities? A recent study confirmed that they do (DeLoache, Simcock, & Macari, 2007). A striking finding was the large gender difference in categories with an extreme intense interest in particular categories stronger for boys than girls. Categorization of boys' intense interests focused on vehicles, trains, machines, dinosaurs, and balls; girls' intense interests were more likely to involve dress-ups and books/reading (see Figure 5.9). When your author's grandson Alex was 18 to 24 months old, he already had developed an intense, passionate interest in the category of vehicles. For example, at this age, he categorized vehicles into such subcategories as cars, trucks, earth-moving equipment, and buses. In addition to common classifications of cars into police cars, jeeps, taxis, and such, and trucks into firetrucks, dump trucks, and the like, his categorical knowledge of earth-moving equipment included bulldozers and excavators, and he categorized buses into school buses, London buses, and funky Malta buses (retro buses on the island of Malta). Later, at 2 to 3 years of age, Alex developed an intense, passionate interest in categorizing dinosaurs.

In sum, the infant's advances in processing information—through attention, memory, imitation, and concept formation—is much richer, more gradual and less stage-like, and occurs earlier than was envisioned by earlier theorists, such as Piaget. As leading infant researcher Jean Mandler (2004) concluded, "The human infant shows a remarkable degree of learning power and complexity in what is being learned and in the way it is represented" (p. 304).

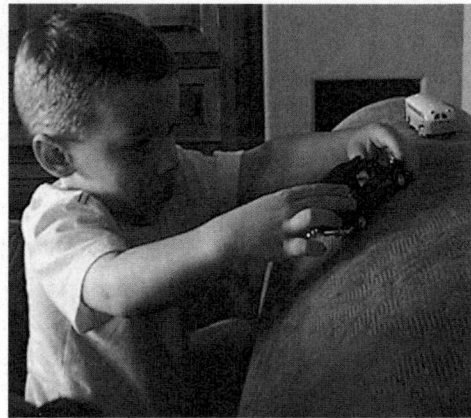

The author's grandson Alex at 2 years of age showing his intense, passionate interest in the category of vehicles while playing with a London taxi and a funky Malta bus.

Review and Reflect: Learning Goal 2

 Describe How Infants Learn, Remember, and Conceptualize

REVIEW

- How do infants learn through conditioning?
- What is attention? What characterizes attention in infants?
- To what extent can infants remember?
- How is imitation involved in infant learning?
- When do infants develop concepts, and how does concept formation change during infancy?

REFLECT

- If a friend told you that she remembers being abused by her parents when she was 2 years old, would you believe her? Explain your answer.

3 INDIVIDUAL DIFFERENCES AND ASSESSMENT

Measures of Infant Development

Predicting Intelligence

So far, we have discussed how the cognitive development of infants generally progresses. We have emphasized what is typical of the largest number of infants or the average infant, but the results obtained for *most* infants do not apply to *all* infants. It is advantageous to know whether an infant is developing at a slow, normal, or advanced pace during the course of infancy. If an infant advances at an especially slow rate, then some form of enrichment may be necessary. If an infant develops at an advanced pace, parents may be advised to provide toys that stimulate cognitive growth in slightly older infants. How is an infant's cognitive development assessed?

Measures of Infant Development

Individual differences in infant cognitive development have been studied primarily through the use of developmental scales or infant intelligence tests. For example, in Chapter 3 we discussed the Brazelton Neonatal Behavioral Assessment Scale (NBAS) and the Neonatal Intensive Care Unit Network Neurobehavioral Scale (NNNS), which are used to evaluate newborns. To read about the work of one infant assessment specialist, see the *Careers in Life-Span Development* profile.

Careers in Life-Span Development

Toosje Thyssen Van Beveren, Infant Assessment Specialist

Toosje Thyssen Van Beveren is a developmental psychologist at the University of Texas Medical Center in Dallas. She has a master's degree in child clinical psychology and a Ph.D. in human development. Currently, Van Beveren is involved in a 12-week program called New Connections, which is a comprehensive intervention for young children who were affected by substance abuse prenatally and for their caregivers.

In the New Connections program, Van Beveren assesses infants' developmental status and progress. She might refer the infants to a speech, physical, or occupational therapist and monitor the infants' services and progress. Van Beveren trains the program staff and encourages them to use the exercises she recommends. She also discusses the child's problems with the primary caregivers, suggests activities, and assists them in enrolling infants in appropriate programs.

During her graduate work at the University of Texas at Dallas, Van Beveren was author John Santrock's teaching assistant in his undergraduate course on life-span development for four years. As a teaching assistant, she attended classes, graded exams, counseled students, and

occasionally gave lectures. Each semester, Van Beveren returns to give a lecture on prenatal development and infancy. She also teaches part-time in the psychology department at UT–Dallas. In Van Beveren's words, "My days are busy and full. The work is often challenging. There are some disappointments but mostly the work is enormously gratifying."

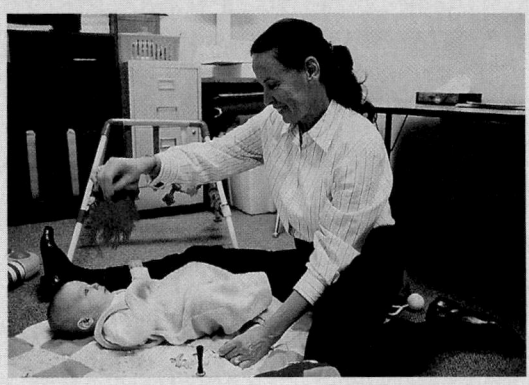

Toosje Thyssen Van Beveren conducting an infant assessment.

---

developmental quotient (DQ) An overall score that combines subscores in motor, language, adaptive, and personal-social domains in the Gesell assessment of infants.

Bayley Scales of Infant Development Scales developed by Nancy Bayley that are widely used in the assessment of infant development. The current version has three components: a mental scale, a motor scale, and an infant behavior profile.

The most important early contributor to the testing of infants was Arnold Gesell (1934). He developed a measure that helped sort out potentially normal babies from abnormal ones. This was especially useful to adoption agencies, which had large numbers of babies awaiting placement. Gesell's examination was used widely for many years and still is frequently employed by pediatricians to distinguish normal and abnormal infants. The current version of the Gesell test has four categories of behavior: motor, language, adaptive, and personal-social. The **developmental quotient (DQ)** combines subscores in these categories to provide an overall score.

The widely used **Bayley Scales of Infant Development** were developed by Nancy Bayley (1969) in order to assess infant behavior and predict later development. The current version, Bayley-III, has five scales: cognitive, language, motor, socioemotional, and adaptive (Bayley, 2005). The first three scales are administered directly to the infant while the latter two are questionnaires given to the caregiver. The Bayley-III also is more appropriate for use in clinical settings than the two previous editions (Lennon & others, 2008).

How should a 6-month-old perform on the Bayley mental scale? The 6-month-old infant should be able to vocalize pleasure and displeasure, persistently search for objects that are just out of immediate reach, and approach a mirror that is placed in front of the infant by the examiner. By 12 months of age, the infant should be able to inhibit behavior when commanded to do so, imitate words the examiner says (such as *Mama*), and respond to simple requests (such as "Take a drink").

The explosion of interest in infant development has produced many new measures, especially tasks that evaluate the ways infants process information (Rose, Feldman, & Wallace, 1992). The Fagan Test of Infant Intelligence is increasingly being used (Fagan, 1992). This test focuses on the infant's ability to process information in such ways as encoding the attributes of objects, detecting similarities and differences between objects, forming mental representations, and retrieving these representations. For example, it uses the amount of time babies look at a new object compared with the amount of time they spend looking at a familiar object to esti-mate their intelligence.

Predicting Intelligence

The infant-testing movement grew out of the tradition of IQ testing. However, IQ tests of older children pay more attention to verbal ability. Tests for infants contain far more items related to perceptual-motor development and include measures of social interaction.

Overall scores on such tests as the Gesell and the Bayley scales do not correlate highly with IQ scores obtained later in childhood. This is not surprising because the components tested in infancy are not the same as the components tested by IQ tests.

Unlike the Gesell and Bayley scales, the Fagan test is correlated with measures of intel-ligence in older children. In fact, evidence is accumulating that measures of habituation and dishabituation are linked to intelligence in childhood and adolescence (Kavsek, 2004; Sigman, Cohen, & Beckwith, 2000). It is important, however, not to go too far and think that connections between cognitive development in early infancy and later cognitive de-velopment are so strong that no discontinuity takes place. Some important changes in cognitive development occur after infancy, changes that we will describe in later chapters.

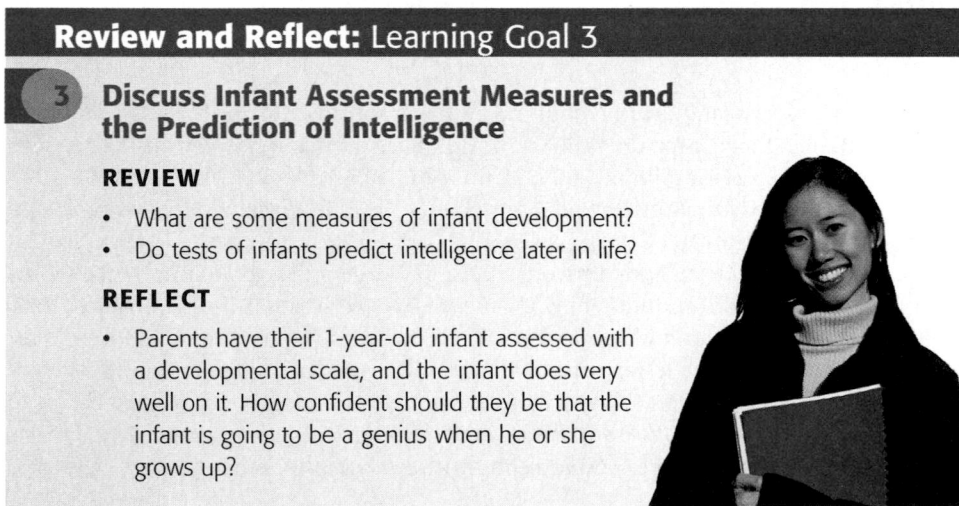

Review and Reflect: Learning Goal 3

3 **Discuss Infant Assessment Measures and the Prediction of Intelligence**

REVIEW

- What are some measures of infant development?
- Do tests of infants predict intelligence later in life?

REFLECT

- Parents have their 1-year-old infant assessed with a developmental scale, and the infant does very well on it. How confident should they be that the infant is going to be a genius when he or she grows up?

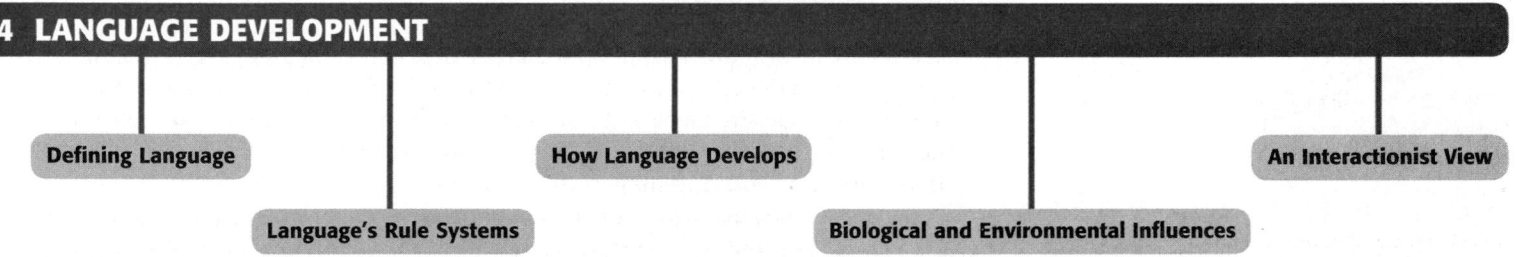

4 LANGUAGE DEVELOPMENT

Defining Language

Language's Rule Systems

How Language Develops

Biological and Environmental Influences

An Interactionist View

In 1799, a nude boy was observed running through the woods in France. The boy was captured when he was 11 years old. He was called the Wild Boy of Aveyron and was believed to have lived in the woods alone for six years (Lane, 1976). When found, he made no effort to communicate. He never learned to communicate effectively. Sadly, a modern-day wild child named Genie was discovered in Los Angeles in 1970. Despite intensive intervention, Genie has never acquired more than a primitive form of lan-guage. Both cases—the Wild Boy of Aveyron and Genie—raise questions about the biological and environmental determinants of language, topics that we also will exam-ine later in the chapter. First, though, we need to define language.

Defining Language

Language is a form of communication—whether spoken, written, or signed—that is based on a system of symbols. Language consists of the words used by a community and the rules for varying and combining them.

Think how important language is in our everyday lives. We need language to speak with others, listen to others, read, and write. Our language enables us to describe past events in detail and to plan for the future. Language lets us pass down information from one generation to the next and create a rich cultural heritage.

All human languages have some common characteristics (Berko Gleason, 2009; Goldin-Meadow, 2008). These include infinite generativity and organizational rules. **Infinite generativity** is the ability to produce an endless number of meaningful sentences using a finite set of words and rules. Rules describe the way language works (Berko Gleason, 2009). Let's explore what these rules involve.

Language's Rule Systems

When nineteenth-century American writer Ralph Waldo Emerson said, "The world was built in order, and the atoms march in tune," he must have had language in mind. Language is highly ordered and organized (Berko Gleason, 2005; Bohannon & Bonvillian, 2009). The organization involves five systems of rules: phonology, morphology, syntax, semantics, and pragmatics.

Phonology　Every language is made up of basic sounds. **Phonology** is the sound system of the language, including the sounds that are used and how they may be combined (Menn & Stoel-Gammon, 2009; Panneton, McIlreavey, & Bhullar, 2008). For example, English has the initial consonant cluster *spr* as in *spring*, but no words begin with the cluster *rsp*.

Phonology provides a basis for constructing a large and expandable set of words out of two or three dozen phonemes. A *phoneme* is the basic unit of sound in a language; it is the smallest unit of sound that affects meaning. For example, in English the sound represented by the letter *p*, as in the words *pot* and *spot*, is a phoneme. The /p/ sound is slightly different in the two words, but this variation is not distinguished in English, and therefore the /p/ sound is a single phoneme. In some languages, such as Hindi, the variations of the /p/ sound represent separate phonemes.

Morphology　**Morphology** refers to the units of meaning involved in word formation. A *morpheme* is a minimal unit of meaning; it is a word or a part of a word that cannot be broken into smaller meaningful parts. Every word in the English language is made up of one or more morphemes. Some words consist of a single morpheme (for example, *help*), whereas others are made up of more than one morpheme (for example, *helper* has two morphemes, *help* + *er*, with the morpheme *–er* meaning "one who," in this case "one who helps"). Thus, not all morphemes are words by themselves; for example, *pre-, -tion,* and *–ing* are morphemes.

Just as the rules that govern phonology describe the sound sequences that can occur in a language, the rules of morphology describe the way meaningful units (morphemes) can be combined in words (Lieven, 2008; Tager-Flusberg & Zukowski, 2009). Morphemes have many jobs in grammar, such as marking tense (for example, she walks versus she walked) and number (she walks versus they walk).

Syntax　**Syntax** involves the way words are combined to form acceptable phrases and sentences (Tager-Flusberg & Zukowski, 2009). If someone says to you, "Bob slugged Tom" or "Bob was slugged by Tom," you know who did the slugging and who was slugged in each case because you have a syntactic understanding of these sentence structures. You also understand that the sentence, "You didn't stay, did you?" is a grammatical sentence, but that "You didn't stay, didn't you? is unacceptable and ambiguous.

language A form of communication, whether spoken, written, or signed, that is based on a system of symbols.

infinite generativity The ability to produce an endless number of meaningful sentences using a finite set of words and rules.

phonology The sound system of the language, including the sounds that are used and how they may be combined.

morphology Units of meaning involved in word formation.

syntax The ways words are combined to form acceptable phrases and sentences.

FRANK & ERNEST: Thaves/Dist. by Newspaper Enterprise Association, Inc.

If you learn another language, English syntax will not get you very far. For example, in English an adjective usually precedes a noun (as in *blue sky*), whereas in Spanish the adjective usually follows the noun *(cielo azul)*. Despite the differences in their syntactic structures, however, syntactic systems in all the world's languages have some common ground (Naigles & Swensen, 2007). For example, no language we know of permits sentences like the following one:

The mouse the cat the farmer chased killed ate the cheese.

It appears that language users cannot process subjects and objects arranged in too complex a fashion in a sentence.

Semantics   **Semantics** refers to the meaning of words and sentences. Every word has a set of semantic features, which are required attributes related to meaning. *Girl* and *women*, for example, share many semantic features, but they differ semantically in regard to age.

Words have semantic restrictions on how they can be used in sentences (Bhagwat & Casaloa, 2008; Pan & Uccelli, 2009). The sentence *The bicycle talked the boy into buying a candy bar* is syntactically correct but semantically incorrect. The sentence violates our semantic knowledge that bicycles don't talk.

Pragmatics   A final set of language rules involves **pragmatics**, the appropriate use of language in different contexts. Pragmatics covers a lot of territory Aktar & Herold, 2008; Bryant, 2009. When you take turns speaking in a discussion or use a question to convey a command ("Why is it so noisy in here?" What is this, Grand Central Station?"), you are demonstrating knowledge of pragmatics. You also apply the pragmatics of English when you use polite language in appropriate situations (for example, when talking to one's teacher) or tell stories that are interesting, jokes that are funny, and lies that convince. In each of these cases, you are demonstrating that you understand the rules of your culture for adjusting language to suit the context.

At this point, we have discussed five important rule systems involved in language. An overview of these rule systems is presented in Figure 5.10.

How Language Develops

According to an ancient historian, in the thirteenth century, the Emperor of Germany, Frederick II, had a cruel idea. He wanted to know what language children would speak if no one talked to them. He selected several newborns and threatened their caregivers with death if they ever talked to the infants. Frederick never found out what language the children spoke because they all died. Today, we are still curious about infants' development of language, although our experiments and observations are, to say the least, far more humane than the evil Frederick's.

Whatever language they learn, infants all over the world follow a similar path in language development. What are some key milestones in this development?

semantics The meaning of words and sentences.

pragmatics The appropriate use of language in different contexts.

Rule System	Description	Examples
Phonology	The sound system of a language. A phoneme is the smallest sound unit in a language.	The word *chat* has three phonemes or sounds: /ch/ /ā/ /t/. An example of phonological rule in the English language is while the phoneme /r/ can follow the phonemes /t/ or /d/ in an English consonant cluster (such as *track* or *drab*), the phoneme /l/ cannot follow these letters.
Morphology	The system of meaningful units involved in word formation.	The smallest sound units that have a meaning are called morphemes, or meaning units. The word *girl* is one morpheme, or meaning unit; it cannot be broken down any further and still have meaning. When the suffix *s* is added, the word becomes *girls* and has two morphemes because the *s* changed the meaning of the word, indicating that there is more than one girl.
Syntax	The system that involves the way words are combined to form acceptable phrases and sentences.	Word order is very important in determining meaning in the English language. For example, the sentence "Sebastian pushed the bike" has a different meaning than "The bike pushed Sebastian."
Semantics	The system that involves the meaning of words and sentences.	Knowing the meaning of individual words—that is, vocabulary. For example, semantics includes knowing the meaning of such words as *orange*, *transportation*, and *intelligent*.
Pragmatics	The system of using appropriate conversation and knowledge of how to effectively use language in context.	An example is using polite language in appropriate situations, such as being mannerly when talking with one's teacher. Taking turns in a conversation involves pragmatics.

FIGURE 5.10 The Rule Systems of Language

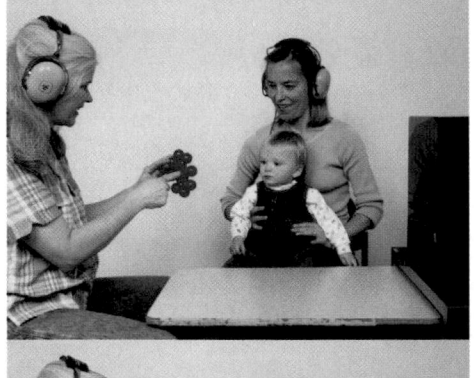

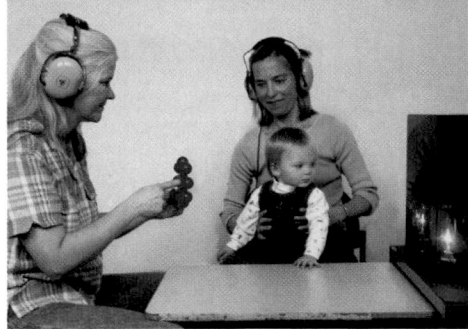

FIGURE 5.11 From Universal Linguist to Language-Specific Listener. In Patricia Kuhl's research laboratory babies listen to tape-recorded voices that repeat syllables. When the sounds of the syllables change, the babies quickly learn to look at the bear. Using this technique, Kuhl has demonstrated that babies are universal linguists until about 6 months of age, but in the next six months become language-specific listeners. *Does Kuhl's research give support to the view that either "nature" or "nurture" is the source of language acquisition?*

Recognizing Language Sounds   Long before they begin to learn words, infants can make fine distinctions among the sounds of the language (Sebastian-Galles, 2007). In Patricia Kuhl's (1993, 2000, 2007, 2009; Kuhl & others, 2006) research, phonemes from languages all over the world are piped through a speaker for infants to hear (see Figure 5.11). A box with a toy bear in it is placed where the infant can see it. A string of identical syllables is played; then the syllables are changed (for example, *ba ba ba ba*, and then *pa pa pa pa*). If the infant turns its head when the syllables change, the box lights up and the bear dances and drums, rewarding the infant for noticing the change.

Kuhl's (2007) research has demonstrated that from birth up to about 6 months of age, infants are "citizens of the world": they recognize when sounds change most of the time, no matter what language the syllables come from. But over the next six months, infants get even better at perceiving the changes in sounds from their "own" language, the one their parents speak, and gradually lose the ability to recognize differences that are not important in their own language.

Infants must fish out individual words from the nonstop stream of sound that makes up ordinary speech (Jusczyk, 2000). To do so, they must find the boundaries between words, which is very difficult for infants because adults don't pause between words when they speak. Still, infants begin to detect word boundaries by 8 months of age. For example, in one study, 8-month-old infants listened to recorded stories that contained unusual words, such as *hornbill* and *python* (Jusczyk & Hohne, 1997). Two weeks later, the researchers tested the infants with two lists of words, one made up of words in the stories, the other of new, unusual words that did not appear in the stories. The infants listened to the familiar words for a second longer, on average, than to new words.

Babbling and Other Vocalizations   Long before infants speak recognizable words, they produce a number of vocalizations (Jaswal & Fernald, 2007; Sachs, 2009). The functions of these early vocalizations are to practice making sounds, to communicate, and to attract attention (Lock, 2004). Babies' sounds go through this sequence during the first year:

- *Crying.* Babies cry even at birth. Crying can signal distress, but as we will discuss in Chapter 6, there are different types of cries that signal different things.

- *Cooing.* Babies first coo at about 2 to 4 months (Menn & Stoel-Gannon, 2009). These are gurgling sounds that are made in the back of the throat and usually express pleasure during interaction with the caregiver.

- *Babbling.* In the middle of the first year, babies babble—that is, they produce strings of consonant-vowel combinations, such as "ba, ba, ba, ba."

Gestures   Infants start using gestures, such as showing and pointing, at about 8 to 12 months of age. They may wave bye-bye, nod to mean "yes," show an empty cup to want more milk, and point to a dog to draw attention to it. Some early gestures are symbolic, as when an infant smacks her lips to indicate food/drink. Pointing is considered by language experts as an important index of the social aspects of language, and its follows this developmental sequence: from point-ing without checking on adult gaze to pointing while looking back and forth between an object and the adult. Lack of pointing is a significant indicator of problems in the infant's communication system. For example, failure to engage in pointing characterizes many autistic children.

First Words   Children understand their first words earlier than they speak them (Pan & Uccelli, 2009). As early as 5 months of age, infants recognize their name when someone says it. On the average, infants understand about 50 words at about 13 months, but they can't say this many words until about 18 months (Menyuk, Liebergott, & Schultz, 1995). Thus, in infancy *receptive vocabulary* (words the child under-stands) considerably exceeds *spoken vocabulary* (words the child uses).

A child's first words include those that name important people (*dada*), familiar animals (*kitty*), vehicles (*car*), toys (*ball*), food (*milk*), body parts (*eye*), clothes (*hat*), household items (*clock*), and greeting terms (*bye*). These were the first words of babies 50 years ago. They are the first words of babies today. Children often express various intentions with their single words, so that "cookie" might mean, "That's a cookie" or "I want a cookie."

The infant's spoken vocabulary rapidly increases once the first word is spoken (Pan & Uccelli, 2009). The average 18-month-old can speak about 50 words, but by the age of 2 years can speak about 200 words. This rapid increase in vocabulary that begins at ap-proximately 18 months is called the *vocabulary spurt* (Bloom, Lifter, & Broughton, 1985).

Like the timing of a child's first word, the timing of the vocabulary spurt varies (Lieven, 2008). Figure 5.12 shows the range for these two language milestones in 14 children. On average, these children said their first word at 13 months and had a vo-cabulary spurt at 19 months. However, the ages for the first word of individual children varied from 10 to 17 months and for their vocabulary spurt from 13 to 25 months.

Children sometimes overextend or underextend the meanings of the words they use (Woodward & Markman, 1998). *Overextension* is the tendency to apply a word to objects that are inappropriate for the word's meaning. For example, children at first may say *"dada"* not only for "father" but also for other men, strangers, or boys. With time, overextensions decrease and eventually disappear. *Underextension* is the ten-dency to apply a word too narrowly; it occurs when children fail to use a word to name a relevant event or object. For example, a child might use the word *boy* to describe a 5-year-old neighbor but not apply the word to a male infant or to a 9 year-old male.

Two-Word Utterances   By the time children are 18 to 24 months of age, they usu-ally utter two-word utterances. To convey meaning with just two words, the child relies heavily on gesture, tone, and context. The wealth of meaning children can com-municate with a two-word utterance includes the following (Slobin, 1972):

- Identification: "See doggie."
- Location: "Book there."

What characterizes the infant's early word learning?

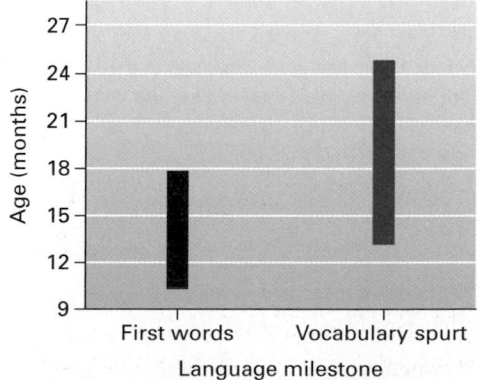

FIGURE 5.12 Variation in Language Milestones. *What are some possible explana-tions for variations in the timing of these mile-stones?*

Around the world, most young children learn to speak in two-word utterances, at about 18 to 24 months of age. *What are some examples of these two-word utterances?*

Typical Age	Language Milestones
Birth	Crying
2 to 4 months	Cooing begins
5 months	Understands first word
6 months	Babbling begins
7 to 11 months	Change from universal linguist to language-specific listener
8 to 12 months	Use gestures, such as showing and pointing Comprehension of words appears
13 months	First word spoken
18 months	Vocabulary spurt starts
18 to 24 months	Uses two-word utterances Rapid expansion of understanding of words

FIGURE 5.13 Some Language Milestones in Infancy. Despite great variations in the language input received by infants, around the world they follow a similar path in learning to speak.

telegraphic speech The use of short and precise words without grammatical markers such as articles, auxiliary verbs, and other connectives.

Broca's area An area in the brain's left frontal lobe involved in speech production.

Wernicke's area An area of the brain's left hemisphere that is involved in language comprehension.

aphasia A loss or impairment of language ability caused by brain damage.

- Repetition: "More milk."
- Nonexistence: "All gone thing."
- Negation: "Not wolf."
- Possession: "My candy."
- Attribution: "Big car."
- Agent-action: "Mama walk."
- Action-direct object: "Hit you."
- Action-indirect object: "Give Papa."
- Action-instrument: "Cut knife."
- Question: "Where ball?"

These examples are from children whose first language is English, German, Russian, Finnish, Turkish, or Samoan.

Notice that the two-word utterances omit many parts of speech and are remarkably succinct. In fact, in every language, a child's first combinations of words have this economical quality; they are telegraphic. **Telegraphic speech** is the use of short and precise words without grammatical markers such as articles, auxiliary verbs, and other connectives. Telegraphic speech is not limited to two words. "Mommy give ice cream" and "Mommy give Tommy ice cream" also are examples of telegraphic speech.

Biological and Environmental Influences

We have discussed a number of language milestones in infancy; Figure 5.13 summarizes the approximate time at which infants typically reach these milestones. But what makes this amazing development possible? Everyone who uses language in some way "knows" its rules and has the ability to create an infinite number of words and sentences. Where does this knowledge come from? Is it the product of biology? Is language learned and influenced by experiences?

Biological Influences   The ability to speak and understand language requires a certain vocal apparatus as well as a nervous system with certain capabilities. The nervous system and vocal apparatus of humanity's predecessors changed over hundreds of thousands or millions of years. With advances in the nervous system and vocal structures, *Homo sapiens* went beyond the grunting and shrieking of other animals to develop speech. Although estimates vary, many experts believe that humans acquired language about 100,000 years ago, which in evolutionary time, represents a very recent acquisition. It gave humans an enormous edge over other animals and increased the chances of human survival.

In the wild, chimps communicate through calls, gestures, and expressions, which evolutionary psychologists believe might be the roots of true language. *How strong is biology's role in language?*

Some language scholars view the remarkable similarities in how children acquire language all over the world as strong evidence that language has a biological basis. There is evidence that particular regions of the brain are predisposed to be used for language (Opitz & Friederici, 2007; Skipper & others, 2007). Two regions involved in language were first discovered in studies of brain-damaged individuals: **Broca's area**, an area in the left frontal lobe of the brain involved in producing words, and **Wernicke's area**, a region of the brain's left hemisphere involved in language comprehension (see Figure 5.14). Damage to either of these areas produces types of **aphasia**, which is a loss or impairment of language processing. Individuals with damage to Broca's area have difficulty producing words correctly; individuals with damage to Wernicke's area have poor comprehension and often produce fluent but incomprehensible speech.

Linguist Noam Chomsky (1957) proposed that humans are biologically prewired to learn language at a certain time and in a certain way. He said that children are born into the world with a **language acquisition device (LAD)**, a biological endowment that enables the child to detect certain features and rules of language, including phonology, syntax, and semantics. Children are prepared by nature with the ability to detect the sounds of language, for example, and follow rules such as how to form plurals and ask questions.

Chomsky's LAD is a theoretical construct, not a physical part of the brain. Is there evidence for the existence of a LAD? Supporters of the LAD concept cite the uniformity of language milestones across languages and cultures, evidence that children create language even in the absence of well-formed input, and biological substrates of language But as we will see, critics argue that even if infants have something like a LAD, it cannot explain the whole story of language acquisition.

Environmental Influences

Decades ago, behaviorists opposed Chomsky's hypothesis and argued that language represents nothing more than chains of responses acquired through reinforcement (Skinner, 1957). A baby happens to babble "Ma-ma"; Mama rewards the baby with hugs and smiles; the baby says "Mama" more and more. Bit by bit, said the behaviorists, the baby's language is built up. According to behaviorists, language is a complex learned skill, much like playing the piano or dancing.

The behaviorist view of language learning has several problems. First, it does not explain how people create novel sentences—sentences that people have never heard or spoken before. Second, children learn the syntax of their native language even if they are not reinforced for doing so. Social psychologist Roger Brown (1973) spent long hours observing parents and their young children. He found that parents did not directly or explicitly reward or correct the syntax of most children's utterances. That is, parents did not say "good," "correct," "right," "wrong," and so on. Also, parents did not offer direct corrections such as, "You should say two shoes, not two shoe." However, as we will see shortly, many parents do expand on their young children's grammatically incorrect utterances and recast many of those that have grammatical errors (Bonvillian, 2005).

The behavioral view is no longer considered a viable explanation of how children acquire language. But a great deal of research describes ways in which children's environmental experiences influence their language skills (Gathercole & Hoff, 2007). Many language experts argue that a child's experiences, the particular language to be learned, and the context in which learning takes place can strongly influence language acquisition (Goldfield & Snow, 2009; Tomasello, 2006).

Language is not learned in a social vacuum. Most children are bathed in language from a very early age (Tomasello, 2006). The Wild Boy of Aveyron, who never learned to communicate effectively, had lived in social isolation for years. The support and involvement of caregivers and teachers greatly facilitate a child's language learning (Snow & Yang, 2006). For example, one study found that when mothers immediately smiled and touched their 8-month-old infants after they babbled, the infants subsequently made more complex speechlike sounds than when mothers responded to their infants in a random manner (Goldstein, King, & West, 2003) (see Figure 5.15).

Michael Tomasello (2003, 2006) stresses that young children are intensely interested in their social world and that early in their development they can understand the intentions of other people. His *interaction view* of language emphasizes that children learn language in specific contexts. For example, when a toddler and a father are jointly focused on a book, the father might say, "See the birdie." In this case, even a toddler understands that the father intends to name something and knows to look in the direction of the pointing. Through this kind of joint attention, early in their development children are able to use their social skills to acquire language (Meltzoff & Brooks, 2009; Tomasello, Carpenter, & Liszkowski, 2007). For example, one recent study revealed that joint attention at 12 and 18 months predicted language skills at 24 months of age (Mundy & others, 2007).

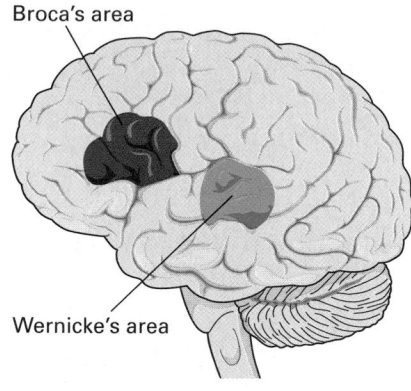

FIGURE 5.14 Broca's Area and Wernicke's Area. Broca's area is located in the frontal lobe of the brain's left hemisphere, and it is involved in the control of speech. Wernicke's area is a portion of the left hemisphere's temporal lobe that is involved in understanding language. *How does the role of these areas of the brain relate to lateralization, which was discussed in Chapter 3?*

FIGURE 5.15 Social Interaction and Babbling. One study focused on two groups of mothers and their 8-month-old infants (Goldstein, King, & West, 2003). One group of mothers was instructed to smile and touch their infants immediately after the babies cooed and babbled; the other group was also told to smile and touch their infants but in a random manner, unconnected to sounds the infants made. The infants whose mothers immediately responded in positive ways to their babbling subsequently made more complex, speechlike sounds, such as "da" and "gu." The research setting for this study, which underscores how important caregivers are in the early development of language, is shown above.

language acquisition device (LAD) Chomsky's term that describes a biological endowment that enables the child to detect the features and rules of language, including phonology, syntax, and semantics.

In particular, researchers have found that the child's vocabulary development is linked to the family's socioeconomic status and the type of talk that parents direct to their children. To read about these links, see the *Diversity in Life-Span Development* interlude that follows.

Diversity in Life-Span Development
Language Environment, Poverty, and Language Development

What characteristics of a family make a difference to a child's language development? Socioeconomic status has been linked with how much parents talk to their children and with young children's vocabulary. Betty Hart and Todd Risley (1995) observed the language environments of children whose parents were professionals and children whose parents were on welfare. Compared with the professional parents, the parents on welfare talked much less to their young children, talked less about past events, and provided less elaboration. As indicated in Figure 5.16, the children of the professional parents had a much larger vocabulary at 36 months of age than the children of the welfare parents.

Other research has linked how much mothers speak to their infants and the infants' vocabularies. For example, in one study by Janellen Huttenlocher and her colleagues (1991), infants whose mothers spoke more often to them had markedly higher vocabularies. By the second birthday, vocabulary differences were substantial.

However, a recent study of 1- to 3-year-old children living in low-income families found that the sheer amount of maternal talk was not the best predictor of a child's vocabulary growth (Pan & others, 2005). Rather, it was maternal language and literacy skills that were positively related to the children's vocabulary development. For example, when mothers used a more diverse vocabulary when talking with their children, their children's vocabulary benefited, but their children's vocabulary was not related to the total amount of their talkativeness with their children. Also, mothers who frequently

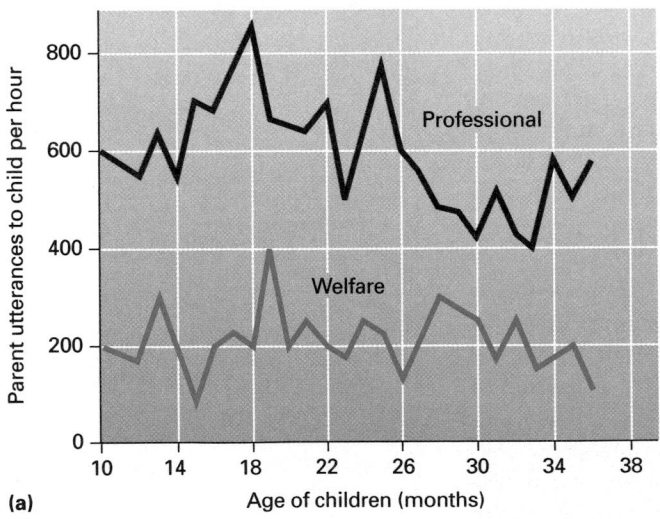

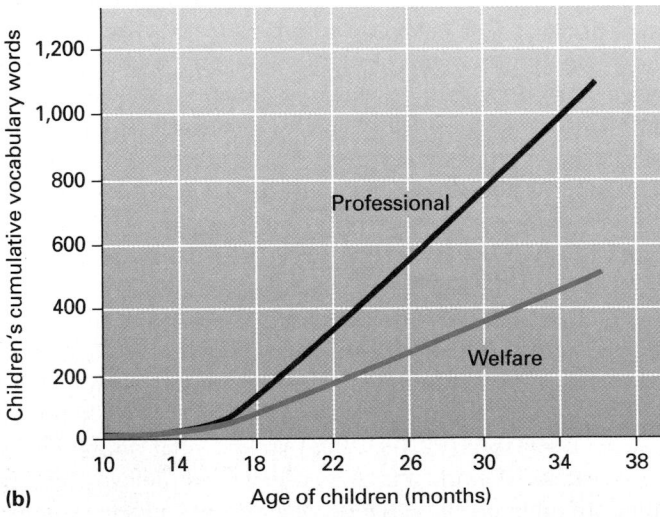

FIGURE 5.16 Language Input in Professional and Welfare Families and Young Children's Vocabulary Development. (*a*) In this study (Hart & Resley, 1995), parents from professional families talked with their young children more than parents from welfare families. (*b*) All of the children learned to talk, but children from professional families developed vocabularies that were twice as large as those from welfare families. Thus, by the time children go to preschool, they already have experienced considerable differences in language input in their families and developed different levels of vocabulary that are linked to their socioeconomic context. *Does this study indicate that poverty caused deficiencies in vocabulary development?*

used pointing gestures had children with a greater vocabulary. Pointing usually occurs in concert with speech, and it may enhance the meaning of mothers' verbal input to their children.

These research studies and others (NICHD Early Child Care Research Network, 2005) demonstrate the importan t effect that early speech input and poverty can have on the development of a child's language skills.

One intriguing component of the young child's linguistic environment is **child-directed speech**, language spoken in a higher pitch than normal with simple words and sentences (Soderstrom, 2007; Zangl & Mills, 2007). It is hard to use child-directed speech when not in the presence of a baby. As soon as you start talking to a baby, though, you shift into child-directed speech. Much of this is automatic and something most parents are not aware they are doing. Even 4-year-olds speak in simpler ways to 2-year-olds than to their 4-year-old friends. Child-directed speech has the important function of capturing the infant's attention and maintaining communication (Jaswal & Fernald, 2007).

Adults often use strategies other than child-directed speech to enhance the child's acquisition of language, including recasting, expanding, and labeling:

- *Recasting* is rephrasing something the child has said, perhaps turning it into a question or restating the child's immature utterance in the form of a fully grammatical sentence. For example, if the child says, "The dog was barking," the adult can respond by asking, "When was the dog barking?" Effective recasting lets the child indicate an interest and then elaborates on that interest.

- *Expanding* is restating, in a linguistically sophisticated form, what a child has said. For example, a child says, "Doggie eat," and the parent replies, "Yes, the doggie is eating."

- *Labeling* is identifying the names of objects. Young children are forever being asked to identify the names of objects. Roger Brown (1958) called this "the original word game" and claimed that much of a child's early vocabulary is motivated by this adult pressure to identify the words associated with objects.

Parents use these strategies naturally and in meaningful conversations. Parents do not (and should not) use any deliberate method to teach their children to talk, even for children who are slow in learning language. Children usually benefit when parents guide their children's discovery of language rather than overloading them with language; "following in order to lead" helps a child learn language. If children are not ready to take in some information, they are likely to tell you (perhaps by turning away). Thus, giving the child more information is not always better.

Remember, the encouragement of language development, not drill and practice, is the key. Language development is not a simple matter of imitation and reinforcement. To read further about ways that parents can facilitate children's language development, see the *Applications in Life-Span Development* interlude.

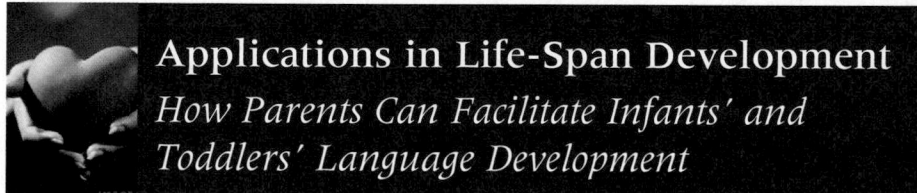

Applications in Life-Span Development
How Parents Can Facilitate Infants' and Toddlers' Language Development

In *Growing Up with Language*, linguist Naomi Baron (1992) provided ideas to help parents facilitate their child's language development. A summary of her ideas follows:

Infants

- *Be an active Conversational partner.* Initiate conversation with the infant. If the infant is in a daylong child-care program, ensure that the baby receives adequate language stimulation from adults.

child-directed speech Language spoken in a higher pitch than normal with simple words and sentences.

It is a good idea for parents to begin talking to their babies at the start. The best language teaching occurs when the talking is begun before the infant becomes capable of intelligible speech. *What are some other guidelines for parents to follow in helping their infants and toddlers develop their language?*

- *Talk as if the infant understands what you are saying.* Parents can generate self-fulfilling prophecies by addressing their young children as if they understand what is being said. The process may take four to five years, but children gradually rise to match the language model presented to them.

- *Use a language style with which you feel comfortable.* Don't worry about how you sound to other adults when you talk with your child. Your affect, not your content, is more important when talking with an infant. Use whatever type of baby talk with which you feel comfortable.

Toddlers

- *Continue to be an active conversational partner.* Engaging toddlers in conversation, even one-sided conversation, is the most important thing a parent can do to nourish a child linguistically.

- *Remember to listen.* Since toddlers' speech is often slow and laborious, parents are often tempted to supply words and thoughts for them. Be patient and let toddlers express themselves, no matter how painstaking the process is or how great a hurry you are in.

- *Use a language style with which you are comfortable, but consider ways of expanding your child's language abilities and horizons.* For example, using long sentences need not be problematic. Use rhymes. Ask questions that encourage answers other than "Yes" and "No." Actively repeat, expand, and recast the child's utterances. Introduce new topics. And use humor in your conversation.

- *Adjust to your child's idiosyncrasies instead of working against them.* Many toddlers have difficulty pronouncing words and making themselves understood. Whenever possible, make toddlers feel that they are being understood.

- *Avoid sexual stereotypes.* Don't let the toddler's sex determine your amount or style of conversation. Many American mothers are more linguistically supportive of girls than of boys, and many fathers talk less with their children than mothers do. Cognitively enriching initiatives from both mothers and fathers benefit both boys and girls.

- *Resist making normative comparisons.* Be aware of the ages at which your child reaches specific milestones (such as the first word, first 50 words), but do not measure this development rigidly against that of other children. Such social comparisons can bring about unnecessary anxiety.

An Interactionist View

If language acquisition depended only on biology, then the Wild Boy of Aveyron and Genie (discussed earlier in the chapter) should have talked without difficulty. A child's experiences influence language acquisition. But we have seen that language does have strong biological foundations. No matter how much you converse with a dog, it won't learn to talk. In contrast, children are biologically prepared to learn language. Children all over the world acquire language milestones at about the same time and in about the same order.

Environmental influences are also very important in development competence in language (Berko Gleason, 2009; Goldfield & Snow, 2009). Children whose parents provide them with a rich verbal environment show many positive benefits. Parents who pay attention to what their children are trying to say, expand their children's utterances, read to them, and label things in the environment, are providing valuable benefits for them (Berko Gleason, 2005).

An interactionist view emphasizes that both biology and experience contribute to language development. How much of the language is biologically determined, and how much depends on interaction with others is a subject of debate among linguists and psychologists (Hoff & Shatz, 2007). However, all agree that both biological capacity and relevant experience are necessary (Gathercole & Hoff, 2007; Tomasello, Carpenter, & Liskowski, 2007).

Review and Reflect: Learning Goal 4

 Describe the Nature of Language and How It Develops in Infancy

REVIEW

- What is language?
- What are language's rule systems?
- How does language develop in infancy?
- What are some biological and environmental influences on language?
- To what extent do biological and environmental influences interact to produce language development?

REFLECT

- Would it be a good idea for parents to hold large flash cards of words in front of their infant to help the infant learn language? Why or why not? What do you think Piaget would say about this activity?

Reach Your Learning Goals

Cognitive Development in Infancy

1 PIAGET'S THEORY OF INFANT DEVELOPMENT: SUMMARIZE AND EVALUATE PIAGET'S THEORY OF INFANT DEVELOPMENT

Cognitive Processes

- In Piaget's theory, children actively construct their own cognitive worlds, building mental structures to adapt to their world. Schemes are actions or mental representations that organize knowledge. Behavioral schemes (physical activities) characterize infancy, whereas mental schemes (cognitive activities) develop in childhood. Assimilation occurs when children use their existing schemes to deal with new information; accommodation refers to children's adjustment of their schemes in the face of new information. Through organization, children group isolated behaviors into a higher-order, more smoothly functioning cognitive system. Equilibration is a mechanism Piaget proposed to explain how children shift from one cognitive stage to the next. As children experience cognitive conflict in trying to understand the world, they use assimilation and accommodation to obtain equilibrium. The result is a new stage of thought. According to Piaget, there are four qualitatively different stages of thought.

The Sensorimotor Stage

- In sensorimotor thought, the first of Piaget's four stages, the infant organizes and coordinates sensations with physical movements. The stage lasts from birth to about 2 years of age. Sensorimotor thought has six substages: simple reflexes; first habits and primary circular reactions; secondary circular reactions; coordination of secondary circular reactions; tertiary circular reactions, novelty, and curiosity; and internalization of schemes. One key accomplishment of this stage is object permanence, the ability to understand that objects continue to exist even though the infant is no longer observing them. Another aspect involves infants' understanding of cause and effect.

Evaluating Piaget's Sensorimotor Stage

- Piaget opened up a whole new way of looking at infant development in terms of coordinating sensory input with motoric actions. In the past decades, revisions of Piaget's view have been proposed based on research. For example, researchers have found that a stable and differentiated perceptual world is established earlier than Piaget envisioned, and infants begin to develop concepts as well.

2 LEARNING, REMEMBERING, AND CONCEPTUALIZING: DESCRIBE HOW INFANTS LEARN, REMEMBER, AND CONCEPTUALIZE

Conditioning

- Both classical and operant conditioning occur in infants. Operant conditioning techniques have especially been useful to researchers in demonstrating infants' perception and retention of information about perceptual-motor actions.

Attention

- Attention is the focusing of mental resources on select information, and in infancy attention is closely linked with habituation. In the first year much of attention is of the orienting/investigate type, but sustained attention also becomes important. Habituation is the repeated presentation of the same stimulus, causing reduced attention to the stimulus. If a different stimulus is presented, and the infant pays increased attention to it, dishabituation is occurring. Joint attention plays an important role in infant development, especially in the infant's acquisition of language.

Memory

- Memory is the retention of information over time. Infants as young as 2 to 6 months of age can retain information about perceptual-motor actions. However, many experts argue that what we commonly think of as memory (consciously remembering the past) does not occur until the second half of the first year of life. By the end of the second year, long-term memory is more substantial and reliable. The hippocampus and frontal lobes of the brain are involved in development of explicit memory in infancy. The phenomenon of not being able to remember events that occurred before the age of 3—known as infantile or childhood amnesia—may be due to the immaturity of the prefrontal lobes of the brain at that age.

Imitation

- Meltzoff has shown that newborns can match their behaviors (such as protruding their tongue) to a model. His research also shows that deferred imitation occurs as early as 9 months of age.

Concept Formation and Categorization

- Mandler argues that it is not until about 7 to 9 months of age that infants form conceptual categories, although we do not know precisely when concept formation begins. Infants' first concepts are broad. Over the first two years of life, these broad concepts gradually become more differentiated.

3 INDIVIDUAL DIFFERENCES AND ASSESSMENT: DISCUSS INFANT ASSESSMENT MEASURES AND THE PREDICTION OF INTELLIGENCE

Measures of Infant Development

- Gesell's scale is still widely used by pediatricians to distinguish normal and abnormal infants; it provides a developmental quotient (DQ). The Bayley Scales of Infant Development, developed by Nancy Bayley, continue to be widely used today to assess infant development. The current version, the Bayley-III, consists of five scales: cognitive, language, motor, socioemotional, and adaptive. Increasingly used, the Fagan Test of Infant Intelligence assesses how effectively the infant processes information.

Predicting Intelligence

- Developmental scales for infants grew out of the tradition of IQ testing of older children. These scales are less verbal than IQ tests. Global scores on the Gesell and Bayley scales are not good predictors of childhood intelligence. However, measures of information processing such as speed of habituation and degree of dishabituation do correlate with intelligence later in childhood. There is both continuity and discontinuity between infant cognitive development and cognitive development later in childhood.

4 LANGUAGE DEVELOPMENT: DESCRIBE THE NATURE OF LANGUAGE AND HOW IT DEVELOPS IN INFANCY

Defining Language

- Language is a form of communication, whether spontaneous, written, or signed, that is based on a system of symbols. Language consists of all the words used by a community and the rules for varying and combining them. It is marked by infinite generativity.

Language's Rule Systems

- Phonology is the sound system of the language, including the sounds that are used and how they may be combined. Morphology refers to the units of meaning involved in word formation. Syntax is the way words are combined to form acceptable phrases and sentences. Semantics involves the meaning of words and sentences. Pragmatics is the appropriate use of language in different contexts.

How Language Develops

- Among the milestones in infant language development are crying (birth), cooing (1 to 2 months), babbling (6 months), making the transition from universal linguist to language-specific listener (7 to 11 months), using gestures (8 to 12 months), comprehension of words (8 to 12 months), first word spoken (13 months), vocabulary spurt (18 months), rapid expansion of understanding words (18 to 24 months), and two-word utterances (18 to 24 months).

Biological and Environmental Influences

- In evolution, language clearly gave humans an enormous advantage over other animals and increased their chance of survival. Broca's area and Wernicke's are important locations for language processing in the brain's left hemisphere. Chomsky argues that children are born with the ability to detect basic features and rules of language. In

175

other words, they are biologically prepared to learn language with a prewired language acquisition device (LAD). The behavioral view—that children acquire language as a result of reinforcement—has not been supported. Adults help children acquire language through child-directed speech, recasting, expanding, and labeling. Environmental influences are demonstrated by differences in the language development of children as a consequence of being exposed to different language environments in the home. Parents should talk extensively with an infant, especially about what the baby is attending to.

An Interactionist View

• Today, most language researchers believe that children everywhere arrive in the world with special social and linguistic capacities that make language acquisition not just likely, but inevitable for virtually all children. How much of the language is biologically determined, and how much depends on interaction with others, is a subject of debate among linguists and psychologists. However, all agree that both biological capacity and relevant experience are necessary.

KEY TERMS

schemes 149
assimilation 150
accommodation 150
organization 150
equilibration 150
sensorimotor stage 150
simple reflexes 151
first habits and primary
   circular reactions 151
primary circular reaction 151
secondary circular
   reactions 152

coordination of secondary
   circular reactions 152
tertiary circular reactions,
   novelty, and curiosity 152
internalization of
   schemes 152
object permanence 152
A-not-B error 154
attention 157
joint attention 157
memory 158
implicit memory 158

explicit memory 158
deferred imitation 159
developmental quotient
   (DQ) 162
Bayley Scales of Infant
   Development 162
language 164
infinite generativity 164
phonology 164
morphology 164
syntax 164
semantics 165

pragmatics 165
telegraphic speech 168
Broca's area 168
Wernicke's area 168
aphasia 168
language acquisition device
   (LAD) 169
child-directed speech 171

KEY PEOPLE

Jean Piaget 148
Renée Baillargeon 153
Eleanor Gibson 154
Elizabeth Spelke 154

Carolyn Rovee-Collier 156
Andrew Meltzoff 158
Jean Mandler 158
Arnold Gesell 162

Nancy Bayley 162
Patricia Kuhl 166
Noam Chomsky 169
Roger Brown 169

Michael Tomasello 169
Betty Hart and Todd Risley 170
Janellen Huttenlocher 170
Naomi Baron 171

E-LEARNING TOOLS

To help you master the material in this chapter, visit the Online Learning Center for *Life-Span Development*, twelfth edition, at **www.mhhe.com/santrockld12**.

Self-Assessment

Connect to **www.mhhe.com/santrockld12** to examine your understanding of cognitive development in infancy by completing the self-assessment, *My Beliefs About Nurturing a Baby's Mind*.

Taking It to the Net

Connect to **www.mhhe.com/santrockld12** to research the answers to these questions:

1. Toby must make a 15-minute class presentation on an important theorist who has significantly contributed to our understanding of human development. If Toby were to select Piaget, what types of information (written, spoken, visual) should he include in this presentation to his class?

2. Veronica works in an infant child-care center that serves mothers who are participating in a welfare-to-work program, advising the mothers about nutrition. What do these mothers need to know about the effect of poor nutrition on their child's cognitive development?

3. Taye is worried that his 1-year-old cousin, Matthew, whom he often babysits, is not on track with his language development as compared with his niece, Rita. By this age, what are some of the language-related milestones or tasks than an average child usually has achieved?

Video Clips

The Online Learning Center includes two videos for Chapter 5. The first video is called "Brain and Infant Cognition." Researchers discuss some of the central issues in the continuing debate over innate versus learned factors in the infant's cognitive development. The second video is called "Language Ability at 2 Years." A profile of 2-year-old Abby and her communication with her mother offers a snapshot of language development at the two-year mark.

Health and Well-Being, Parenting, and Education Exercises

Build your decision-making skills by trying your hand at the health and well-being, parenting, and education exercises. Connect to **www.mhhe.com/santrockld12** to research the answers and complete the exercises.

6

We never know the love of our parents until we have become parents.

—HENRY WARD BEECHER
American Writer, 19th Century

LEARNING GOALS

◆ Discuss the development of emotions and personality in infancy.

◆ Describe social orientation/ understanding and the development of attachment in infancy.

◆ Explain how social contexts influence the infant's development.

SOCIOEMOTIONAL DEVELOPMENT IN INFANCY

CHAPTER OUTLINE

1 **EMOTIONAL AND PERSONALITY DEVELOPMENT**
Emotional Development
Temperament
Personality Development

2 **SOCIAL ORIENTATION/UNDERSTANDING AND ATTACHMENT**
Social Orientation/Understanding
Attachment and Its Development
Individual Differences in Attachment
Caregiving Styles and Attachment

3 **SOCIAL CONTEXTS**
The Family
Child Care

Images of Life-Span Development
The Story of Darius' Fathering

An increasing number of fathers are staying home to care for their children (Rochelen & others, 2007; Wong & Rochlen, 2008). Consider 17-month-old Darius. On weekdays, Darius' father, a writer, cares for him during the day while his mother works full-time as a landscape architect. Darius' father is doing a great job of caring for him. Darius' father keeps Darius nearby while he is writing and spends lots of time talking to him and playing with him. From their interactions, it is clear that they genuinely enjoy each other.

Last month, Darius began spending one day a week at a child-care center. His parents carefully selected the center after observing a number of centers and interviewing teachers and center directors. His parents placed him in the center one day a week because they wanted Darius to get some experience with peers and to give his father some time out from his caregiving.

Darius' father looks to the future and imagines the Little League games Darius will play in and the many other activities he can enjoy with Darius. Remembering how little time his own father spent with him, he is dedicated to making sure that Darius has an involved, nurturing experience with his father.

When Darius' mother comes home in the evening, she spends considerable time with him. Darius shows a positive attachment to both his mother and his father.

Many fathers are spending more time with their infants today than in the past.

PREVIEW

In Chapters 4 and 5, you read about how the infant perceives, learns, and remembers. Infants also are socioemotional beings, capable of displaying emotions and initiating social interaction with people close to them. The main topics that we will explore in this chapter are emotional and personality development, social understanding and attachment, and the social contexts of the family and child care.

1 EMOTIONAL AND PERSONALITY DEVELOPMENT

Emotional Development	Temperament	Personality Development

Anyone who has been around infants for even a brief time detects that they are emotional beings. Not only do infants express emotions, but they also vary in their temperament. Some are shy and others are outgoing. Some are active and others much less so. In this section, we will explore these and other aspects of emotional and personality development in infants.

Emotional Development

Imagine your life without emotion. Emotion is the color and music of life, as well as the tie that binds people together. How do psychologists define and classify emotions, and why are they important to development? How do emotions develop during the first two years of life?

What Are Emotions?   For our purposes, we will define **emotion** as feeling, or affect, that occurs when a person is in a state or an interaction that is important to him or her, especially to his or her well-being (Campos, 2005). Psychologists classify the broad range of emotions in many ways, but almost all classifications designate an emotion as either positive or negative (Barrett & others, 2007). Positive emotions include enthusiasm, joy, and love. Negative emotions include anxiety, anger, guilt, and sadness.

Biological and Environmental Influences   Emotions are influenced both by biological foundations and by a person's experience. Biology's importance to emotion is also apparent in the changes in a baby's emotional capacities (Bell & Wolfe, 2007). Certain regions of the brain that develop early in life (such as the brain stem, hippocampus, and amygdala) play a role in distress, excitement, and rage, and even infants display these emotions (Buss & Goldsmith, 2007). But, as we discuss later in the chapter, infants only gradually develop the ability to regulate their emotions, and this ability seems tied to the gradual maturation of the frontal regions of the cerebral cortex (discussed in Chapter 4) that can exert control over other areas of the brain (Thompson & Goodvin, 2007).

These biological factors, however, are only part of the story of emotion. Emotions serve important functions in our relationships (Perez & Gauvain, 2007). As we discuss later in this section, emotions are the first language with which parents and infants communicate. Emotion-linked interchanges, as when Darius cries and his father sensitively responds, provide the foundation for the infant's developing attachment to the parent.

Social relationships, in turn, provide the setting for the development of a rich variety of emotions (Brownell & Kopp, 2007; Thompson, 2009a). When toddlers hear their parents quarreling, they often react with distress and inhibit their play. Well-functioning families make each other laugh and may develop a light mood to defuse conflicts. Biological evolution has endowed human beings to be *emotional*, but embeddedness in relationships and culture with others provides diversity in emotional experiences (Perez & Gauvain, 2007; Thompson & Virmani, 2009). For example, researchers have found that East Asian infants display less frequent and less positive and negative emotions than non-Latino White infants (Camras & others, 1998; Cole & Tan, 2007). Throughout childhood, East Asian parents encourage their children to show emotional reserve rather than emotional expressivity (Chen & others, 1998; Cole & Tan, 2007). Further, Japanese parents try to prevent their children from experiencing negative emotions, whereas non-Latino White mothers are more likely to respond after their children become distressed and then help them cope (Cole & Tan, 2007; Rothbaum & Trommsdorff, 2007).

Early Emotions   Leading expert on infant emotional development, Michael Lewis (2007) distinguishes between primary emotions and self-conscious emotions. **Primary emotions** are emotions that are present in humans and other animals; these emotions appear in the first six months of the human infant's development. Primary emotions include surprise, interest, joy, anger, sadness, fear, and disgust (see Figure 6.1 for infants' facial expressions of some of these early emotions). In Lewis' classification,

How do Japanese mothers handle their infants' and children's emotional development differently than non-Latino White mothers?

Blossoms are scattered by the wind
And the wind cares nothing, but
The blossoms of the heart
No wind can touch.

—**Yoshida Kenko**
Buddhist Monk, 14th Century

emotion Feeling, or affect, that occurs when a person is in a state or interaction that is important to him or her. Emotion is characterized by behavior that reflects (expresses) the pleasantness or unpleasantness of the state a person is in or the transactions being experienced.

primary emotions Emotions that are present in humans and other animals and emerge early in life; examples are joy, anger, sadness, fear, and disgust.

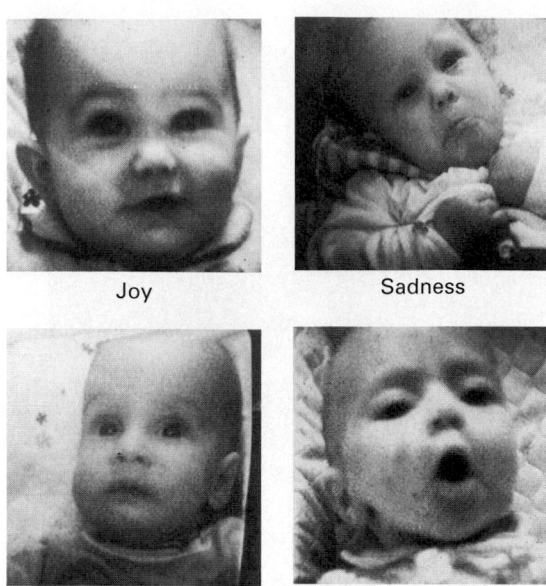

Joy   Sadness

Fear   Surprise

FIGURE 6.1 Expression of Different Emotions in Infants

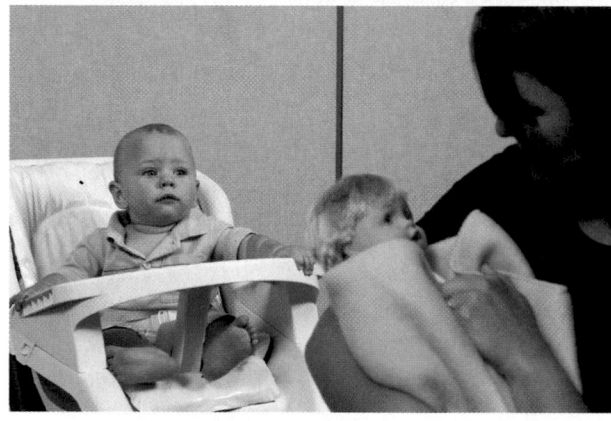

FIGURE 6.2 Research Setting for Sybil Hart's Attempt to Assess the Early Development of Jealousy. An infant becomes distressed when his mother gives attention to a lifelike baby doll. *What are some possible interpretations of the infant's distress?*

self-conscious emotions require self-awareness that involves consciousness and a sense of "me." Self-conscious emotions include jealousy, empathy, embarrassment, pride, shame, and guilt, most of these occurring for the first time at some point in the second half of the first year through the second year. Some experts on emotion call self-conscious emotions such as embarrassment, shame, guilt, and pride *other-conscious emotions* because they involve the emotional reactions of others when they are generated (Saarni & others, 2006). For example, approval from parents is linked to toddlers beginning to show pride when they successfully complete a task.

Researchers such as Joseph Campos (2005) and Michael Lewis (2007) debate how early in the infant and toddler years the emotions that we have described first appear and their sequence. As an indication of the controversy regarding when certain emotions first are displayed by infants, consider jealousy. Some researchers argue that jealousy does not emerge until approximately 18 months of age (Lewis, 2007), whereas others emphasize that it is displayed much earlier (Draghi-Lorenz, 2007; Draghi-Lorenz, Reddy, & Costall, 2001). Consider a research study in which 6-month-old infants observed their mothers either giving attention to a lifelike baby doll (hugging or gently rocking it, for example) or to a book (Hart & Carrington, 2002). When mothers directed their attention to the doll, the infants were more likely to display negative emotions, such as anger and sadness, which may have indicated their jealousy (see Figure 6.2). On the other hand, their expressions of anger and sadness may have reflected frustration in not being able to have the novel doll to play with. Debate about the onset of an emotion such as jealousy illustrates the complexity and difficulty in indexing early emotions.

Emotional Expression and Social Relationships Emotional expressions are involved in infants' first relationships. The ability of infants to communicate emotions permits coordinated interactions with their caregivers and the beginning of an emotional bond between them (Thomann & Carter, 2008; Thompson, 2009b). Not only do parents change their emotional expressions in response to infants' emotional expressions, but infants also modify their emotional expressions in response to their parents' emotional expressions. In other words, these interactions are mutually regulated. Because of this coordination, the interactions are described as *reciprocal,* or *synchronous,* when all is going well. Sensitive, responsive parents help their infants grow emotionally, whether the infants respond in distressed or happy ways (Thompson & Newton, 2009).

Cries and smiles are two emotional expressions that infants display when interacting with parents. These are babies' first forms of emotional communication.

---

self-conscious emotions Emotions that require self-awareness, especially consciousness and a sense of "me"; examples include jealousy, empathy, and embarrassment.

basic cry A rhythmic pattern usually consisting of a cry, a briefer silence, a shorter inspiratory whistle that is higher pitched than the main cry, and then a brief rest before the next cry.

anger cry A variation of the basic cry, with more excess air forced through the vocal cords.

Crying Crying is the most important mechanism newborns have for communicating with their world. The first cry verifies that the baby's lungs have filled with air. Cries also may provide information about the health of the newborn's central nervous system. Newborns even tend to respond with cries and negative facial expressions when they hear other newborns cry (Dondi, Simion, & Caltran, 1999).

Babies have at least three types of cries:

- **Basic cry.** A rhythmic pattern that usually consists of a cry, followed by a briefer silence, then a shorter whistle that is somewhat higher in pitch than the main cry, then another brief rest before the next cry. Some infancy experts believe that hunger is one of the conditions that incites the basic cry.

- **Anger cry.** A variation of the basic cry in which more excess air is forced through the vocal cords.

- **Pain cry.** A sudden long, initial loud cry followed by breath holding; no preliminary moaning is present. The pain cry is stimulated by a high-intensity stimulus.

Most adults can determine whether an infant's cries signify anger or pain (Zeskind, 2009; Zeskind, Klein, & Marshall, 1992). Parents can distinguish the cries of their own baby better than those of another baby.

What are some different types of cries?

Smiling The power of the infant's smiles was appropriately captured by British theorist John Bowlby (1969): "Can we doubt that the more and better an infant smiles the better he is loved and cared for? It is fortunate for their survival that babies are so designed by nature that they beguile and enslave mothers." Two types of smiling can be distinguished in infants:

- **Reflexive smile.** A smile that does not occur in response to external stimuli and appears during the first month after birth, usually during sleep.

- **Social smile.** A smile that occurs in response to an external stimulus, typically a face in the case of the young infant. Social smiling occurs as early as 2 months of age.

Daniel Messinger (2008) recently described the developmental course of infant smiling. From 2 to 6 months after birth, infants' social smiling increases considerably, both in self-initiated smiles and smiles in response to others' smiles. At 6 to 12 months, smiles that couple what is called the Duchenne marker (eye constriction) and mouth opening occur in the midst of highly enjoyable interactions and play with parents (see Figure 6.3). In the second year, smiling continues to occur in such positive circumstances with parents, and in many cases an increase in smiling occurs when interacting with peers. Also in the second year, toddlers become increasingly aware of the social meaning of smiles, especially in their relationship with parents.

FIGURE 6.3 A 6-Month-Old's Strong Smile.
This strong smile reflects the Duchenne marker (eye constriction) and mouth opening.

Fear One of a baby's earliest emotions is fear, which typically first appears at about 6 months of age and peaks at about 18 months. However, abused and neglected infants can show fear as early as 3 months (Campos, 2005). Researchers have found that infant fear is linked to guilt, empathy, and low aggression at 6 to 7 years of age (Rothbart, 2007).

The most frequent expression of an infant's fear involves **stranger anxiety**, in which an infant shows a fear and wariness of strangers. Stranger anxiety usually emerges gradually. It first appears at about 6 months of age in the form of wary reactions. By age 9 months, the fear of strangers is often more intense, reaching a peak toward the end of the first year of life, then decreasing thereafter (Scher & Harel, 2008).

Not all infants show distress when they encounter a stranger. Besides individual variations, whether an infant shows stranger anxiety also depends on the social context and the characteristics of the stranger.

Infants show less stranger anxiety when they are in familiar settings. For example, in one study, 10-month-olds showed little stranger anxiety when they met a stranger in their own home but much greater fear when they encountered a stranger in a research laboratory (Sroufe, Waters, & Matas, 1974). Thus, it appears that, when infants feel secure, they are less likely to show stranger anxiety.

Who the stranger is and how the stranger behaves also influence stranger anxiety in infants. Infants are less fearful of child strangers than adult strangers. They also are less fearful of friendly, outgoing, smiling strangers than of passive, unsmiling strangers (Bretherton, Stolberg, & Kreye, 1981).

In addition to stranger anxiety, infants experience fear of being separated from their caregivers. The result is **separation protest**—crying when the caregiver leaves.

pain cry A sudden appearance of a long, initial loud cry without preliminary moaning, followed by breath holding.

reflexive smile A smile that does not occur in response to external stimuli. It happens during the month after birth, usually during sleep.

social smile A smile in response to an external stimulus, which, early in development, typically is a face.

stranger anxiety An infant's fear and wariness of strangers; it tends to appear in the second half of the first year of life.

separation protest An infant's distressed crying when the caregiver leaves.

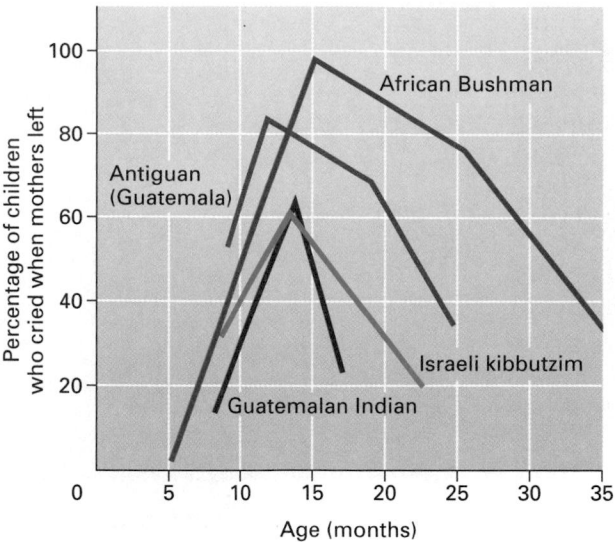

FIGURE 6.4 Separation Protest in Four Cultures. Note that separation protest peaked at about the same time in all four cultures in this study (13 to 15 months of age) (Kagan, Kearsley, & Zelazo, 1978). However, a higher percentage (100 percent) of infants in an African Bushman culture engaged in separation protest compared to only about 60 percent of infants in Guatemalan Indian and Israeli kibbutzim cultures. *What might explain the fact that separation protest peaks at about the same time in these cultures?*
Reprinted by permission of the publisher from *Infancy: Its Place in Human Development* by Jerome Kagan, Richard B. Kearsley, and Philip R. Zelazo, p. 107, Cambridge, Mass.: Harvard University Press. Copyright © 1978 by the President and Fellows of Harvard College.

Separation protest is initially displayed by infants at approximately 7 to 8 months and peaks at about 15 months among U.S. infants (Kagan, 2008). In fact, one study found that separation protest peaked at about 13 to 15 months in four different cultures (Kagan, Kearsley, & Zelazo, 1978). As indicated in Figure 6.4, the percentage of infants who engaged in separation protest varied across cultures, but the infants reached a peak of protest at about the same age—just before the middle of the second year of life.

Emotional Regulation and Coping   During the first year of life, the infant gradually develops an ability to inhibit, or minimize, the intensity and duration of emotional reactions (Calkins, 2007; Kopp, 2008). From early in infancy, babies put their thumbs in their mouths to soothe themselves. But at first, infants mainly depend on caregivers to help them soothe their emotions, as when a caregiver rocks an infant to sleep, sings lullabyes to the infant, gently strokes the infant, and so on.

The caregivers' actions influence the infant's neurobiological regulation of emotions (Thompson, Meyers, & Jochem, 2008). By soothing the infant, caregivers help infants to modulate their emotion and reduce the level of stress hormones (Gunnar & Quevedo, 2007). Many developmentalists stress that it is a good strategy for a caregiver to soothe an infant before the infant gets into an intense, agitated, uncontrolled state (McElwain & Booth-LaForce, 2006).

Later in infancy, when they become aroused, infants sometimes redirect their attention or distract themselves in order to reduce their arousal. By 2 years of age, toddlers can use language to define their feeling states and the context that is upsetting them (Kopp, 2008). A toddler might say, "Feel bad. Dog scare." This type of communication may help caregivers to help the child in regulating emotion.

Contexts can influence emotional regulation (Thompson & Goodvin, 2007). Infants are often affected by fatigue, hunger, time of day, which people are around them, and where they are. Infants must learn to adapt to different contexts that require emotional regulation. Further, new demands appear as the infant becomes older and parents modify their expectations. For example, a parent may take it in stride if a 6-month-old infant screams in a restaurant but may react very differently if a $1\frac{1}{2}$-year-old starts screaming.

To soothe or not to soothe—should a crying baby be given attention and soothed, or does this spoil the infant? Many years ago, the behaviorist John Watson (1928) argued that parents spend too much time responding to infant crying. As a consequence, he said, parents reward crying and increase its incidence. More recently, behaviorist Jacob Gewirtz (1977) found that a caregiver's quick, soothing response to crying increased crying. In contrast, infancy experts Mary Ainsworth (1979) and John Bowlby (1989) stress that you can't respond too much to infant crying in the first year of life. They believe that a quick, comforting response to the infant's cries is an important ingredient in the development of a strong bond between the infant and caregiver. In one of Ainsworth's studies, infants whose mothers responded quickly when they cried at 3 months of age cried less later in the first year of life (Bell & Ainsworth, 1972).

Controversy still characterizes the question of whether or how parents should respond to an infant's cries (Lewis & Ramsay, 1999). However, developmentalists increasingly argue that an infant cannot be spoiled in the first year of life, which suggests that parents should soothe a crying infant. This reaction should help infants develop a sense of trust and secure attachment to the caregiver.

Another technique for calming young infants is *swaddling*, which involves wrapping a young baby in a blanket. Swaddling is popular in many Middle Eastern countries and in the Navajo nation in the United States (Whiting, 1981). However,

Should a baby be given attention and soothed, or does this spoil the infant? Should the infant's age, the type of cry, and the circumstances be considered?

in the United States swaddling has generally been unpopular because it restricts freedom of movement and is thought to make babies passive (Saarni & others, 2006). Nonetheless, an increasing number of pediatricians recommend swaddling. A recent research review concluded that swaddled infants arouse less and sleep longer (van Sleuwen & others, 2007). In one study, newborns with brain injuries were randomly assigned to a swaddling condition (wrapping the baby in a blanket) or a massage therapy condition (Ohgi & others, 2004). Swaddling reduced the infants' crying more than the massage therapy.

Pediatricians and nurses who recommend swaddling stress that it stops the baby's uncontrolled arm and leg movements that can lead to frenzied crying (Huang & others, 2004). They also recommend tucking the baby tightly in the blanket so it does not become loose and become wrapped around the baby's face. An excellent book on how to calm a crying baby, including specific instructions on swaddling, is *The Happiest Baby on the Block* (Karp, 2002).

Temperament

Do you get upset a lot? Does it take much to get you angry, or to make you laugh? Even at birth, babies seem to have different emotional styles. One infant is cheerful and happy much of the time; another baby seems to cry constantly. These tendencies reflect **temperament**, which is an individual's behavioral style and characteristic way of responding.

Describing and Classifying Temperament   How would you describe your temperament or the temperament of a friend? Researchers have described and classified the temperament of individuals in different ways (Kagan, 2009; Rothbart, 2009). Here we will examine three of those ways.

Chess and Thomas' Classification   Psychiatrists Alexander Chess and Stella Thomas (Chess & Thomas, 1977; Thomas & Chess, 1991) identified three basic types, or clusters, of temperament:

- An **easy child** is generally in a positive mood, quickly establishes regular routines in infancy, and adapts easily to new experiences.
- A **difficult child** reacts negatively and cries frequently, engages in irregular daily routines, and is slow to accept change.
- A **slow-to-warm-up child** has a low activity level, is somewhat negative, and displays a low intensity of mood.

In their longitudinal investigation, Chess and Thomas found that 40 percent of the children they studied could be classified as easy, 10 percent as difficult, and 15 percent as slow to warm up. Notice that 35 percent did not fit any of the three patterns. Researchers have found that these three basic clusters of temperament are moderately stable across the childhood years.

Kagan's Behavioral Inhibition   Another way of classifying temperament focuses on the differences between a shy, subdued, timid child and a sociable, extraverted, bold child (Asendorph, 2008). Jerome Kagan (2002, 2009; Kagan & others, 2007) regards shyness with strangers (peers or adults) as one feature of a broad temperament category called *inhibition to the unfamiliar*. Inhibited children react to many aspects of unfamiliarity with initial avoidance, distress, or subdued affect, beginning about 7 to 9 months of age.

Kagan has found that inhibition shows considerable stability from infancy through early childhood. One study classified toddlers into extremely inhibited, extremely uninhibited, and intermediate groups (Pfeifer & others, 2002). Follow-up assessments occurred at 4 and 7 years of age. Continuity was demonstrated for both inhibition and

"Oh, he's cute, all right, but he's got the temperament of a car alarm."
Copyright © The New Yorker Collection 1999 Barbara Smaller from cartoonbank.com.
All Rights Reserved.

temperament An individual's behavioral style and characteristic way of emotionally responding.

easy child A child who is generally in a positive mood, quickly establishes regular routines in infancy, and adapts easily to new experiences.

difficult child A child who tends to react negatively and cry frequently, engages in irregular daily routines, and is slow to accept change.

slow-to-warm-up child A child who has a low activity level, is somewhat negative, and displays a low intensity of mood.

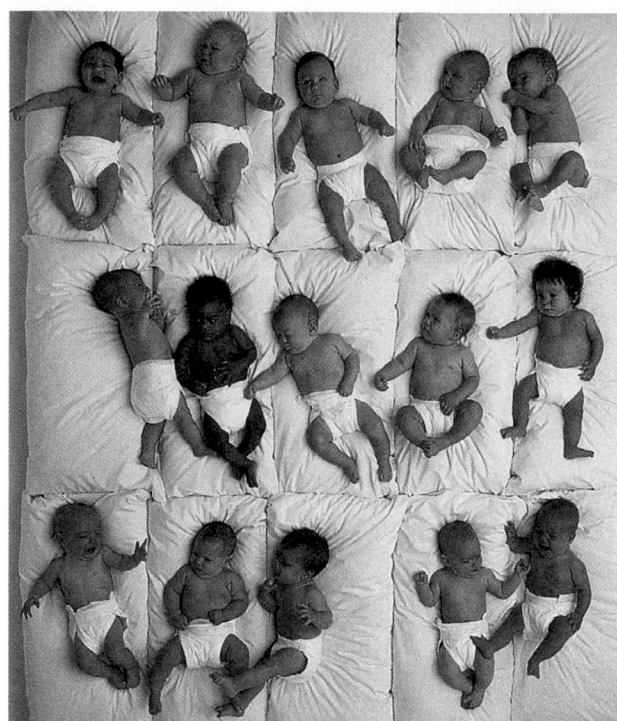

What are some ways that developmentalists have classified infants' temperaments? Which classification makes the most sense to you, based on your observations of infants?

lack of inhibition, although a substantial number of the inhibited children moved into the intermediate groups at 7 years of age.

Rothbart and Bates' Classification New classifications of temperament continue to be forged. Mary Rothbart and John Bates (2006) argue that three broad dimensions best represent what researchers have found to characterize the structure of temperament: extraversion/surgency, negative affectivity, and effortful control (self-regulation):

- *Extraversion/surgency* includes "positive anticipation, impulsivity, activity level, and sensation seeking" (Rothbart, 2004, p. 495). Kagan's uninhibited children fit into this category.

- *Negative affectivity* includes "fear, frustration, sadness, and discomfort" (Rothbart, 2004, p. 495). These children are easily distressed; they may fret and cry often. Kagan's inhibited children fit this category.

- *Effortful control (self-regulation)* includes "attentional focusing and shifting, inhibitory control, perceptual sensitivity, and low-intensity pleasure" (Rothbart, 2004, p. 495). Infants who are high on effortful control show an ability to keep their arousal from getting too high and have strategies for soothing themselves. By contrast, children low on effortful control are often unable to control their arousal; they become easily agitated and intensely emotional.

In Rothbart's (2004, p. 497) view, "early theoretical models of temperament stressed the way we are moved by our positive and negative emotions or level of arousal, with our actions driven by these tendencies." The more recent emphasis on effortful control, however, advocates that individuals can engage in a more cognitive, flexible approach to stressful circumstances.

Rothbart and Maria Gartstein (2008, p. 323) recently described the following developmental changes in temperament during infancy. During early infancy, smiling and laughter are emerging as part of the positive affectivity dimension of temperament. Also, by 2 months of age, infants show anger and frustration when their actions don't produce an interesting outcome. During this time, infants often are susceptible to distress and overstimulation. From 4 to 12 months of age, fear and irritability become more differentiated with inhibition (fear) increasingly linked to new and unpredictable experiences. Not all temperament characteristics are in place by the first birthday. Positive emotionality becomes more stable later in infancy, and the characteristics of extraversion/surgency can be determined in the toddler period. Improved attention skills in the toddler and preschool years are related to an increase in effortful control, which serves as a foundation for improved self-regulation.

Biological Foundations and Experience
How does a child acquire a certain temperament? Kagan (2002) argues that children inherit a physiology that biases them to have a particular type of temperament. However, through experience they may learn to modify their temperament to some degree. For example, children may inherit a physiology that biases them to be fearful and inhibited, but they learn to reduce their fear and inhibition to some degree.

Biological Influences Physiological characteristics have been linked with different temperaments (Rothbart & Bates, 2006). In particular, an inhibited temperament is associated with a unique physiological pattern that includes high and stable heart rate, high level of the hormone cortisol, and high activity in the right frontal lobe of the brain (Kagan, 2008). This pattern may be tied to the excitability of the amygdala, a structure of the brain that plays an important role in fear and inhibition. An inhibited temperament or negative affectivity may also be linked to low levels of the neurotransmitter serotonin, which may increase an individual's vulnerability to fear and frustration (Kramer, 1993).

What is heredity's role in the biological foundations of temperament? Twin and adoption studies suggest that heredity has a moderate influence on differences in temperament within a group of people (Buss & Goldsmith, 2007). The contemporary view is that temperament is a biologically based but evolving aspect of behavior; it evolves as the child's experiences are incorporated into a network of self-perceptions and behavioral preferences that characterize the child's personality (Thompson & Goodvin, 2007).

Gender, Culture, and Temperament   Gender may be an important factor shaping the context that influences the fate of temperament. Parents might react differently to an infant's temperament depending on whether the baby is a boy or a girl. For example, in one study, mothers were more responsive to the crying of irritable girls than to the crying of irritable boys (Crockenberg, 1986).

Similarly, the reaction to an infant's temperament may depend in part on culture (Cole & Tan, 2007; Perez & Gauvain, 2007). For example, an active temperament might be valued in some cultures (such as the United States) but not in other cultures (such as China). Indeed, children's temperament can vary across cultures (Putnam, Sanson, & Rothbart, 2002). Behavioral inhibition is more highly valued in China than in North America, and researchers have found that Chinese children are more inhibited than Canadian infants (Chen & others, 1998). The cultural differences in temperament were linked to parent attitude and behaviors. Canadian mothers of inhibited 2-year-olds were less accepting of their infants' inhibited temperament, whereas Chinese mothers were more accepting.

In short, many aspects of a child's environment can encourage or discourage the persistence of temperament characteristics (Bates & Pettit, 2007; Rothbart & Sheese, 2007). One useful way of thinking about these relationships applies the concept of goodness of fit, which we examine next.

An infant's temperament can vary across cultures. *What do parents need to know about a child's temperament?*

Goodness of Fit and Parenting

Goodness of fit refers to the match between a child's temperament and the environmental demands the child must cope with (Schoppe-Sullivan & others, 2007; Thompson, Meyer, & Jochem, 2008). Suppose Jason is an active toddler who is made to sit still for long periods of time and Jack is a slow-to-warm-up toddler who is abruptly pushed into new situations on a regular basis. Both Jason and Jack face a lack of fit between their temperament and environmental demands. Lack of fit can produce adjustment problems (Rothbart & Bates, 2006).

Some temperament characteristics pose more parenting challenges than others, at least in modern Western societies (Rothbart, 2009). When children are prone to distress, as exhibited by frequent crying and irritability, their parents may eventually respond by ignoring the child's distress or trying to force the child to "behave." In one research study, though, extra support and training for mothers of distress-prone infants improved the quality of mother-infant interaction (van den Boom, 1989). The training led the mothers to alter their demands on the child, improving the fit between the child and the environment.

Many parents don't become believers in temperament's importance until the birth of their second child. They viewed their first child's behavior as a result of how they treated the child. But then they find that some strategies that worked with their first child are not as effective with the second child. Some problems experienced with the first child (such as those involved in feeding, sleeping, and coping with strangers) do not exist with the second child, but new problems arise. Such experiences strongly suggest that children differ from each other very early in life, and that these differences have important implications for parent-child interaction (Rothbart & Putnam, 2002). To read further about some positive strategies for parenting that take into account the child's temperament, see the *Applications in Life-Span Development* interlude.

goodness of fit Refers to the match between a child's temperament and the environmental demands with which the child must cope.

Applications in Life-Span Development
Parenting and the Child's Temperament

What are the implications of temperamental variations for parenting? Although answers to this question necessarily are speculative, these conclusions regarding the best parenting strategies to use in relation to children's temperament were reached by temperament experts Ann Sanson and Mary Rothbart (1995):

- *Attention to and respect for individuality.* Good parenting involves sensitivity to the child's individual characteristics. A goal might be accomplished in one way with one child and in another way with another child, depending on the child's temperament.

- *Structuring the child's environment.* Crowded, noisy environments can pose greater problems for some children (such as a "difficult child") than others (such as an "easy child"). We might also expect that a fearful, withdrawing child would benefit from slower entry into new contexts.

- *The "difficult child" and packaged parenting programs.* Programs for parents often focus on dealing with children who have "difficult" temperaments. In some cases, "difficult child" refers to Thomas and Chess' description of a child who reacts negatively, cries frequently, engages in irregular daily routines, and is slow to accept change. In others, the concept might be used to describe a child who is irritable, displays anger frequently, does not follow directions well, or some other negative characteristic. Acknowledging that some children are harder than others to parent is often helpful, and advice on how to handle particular difficult characteristics can be useful. However, whether a particular characteristic is difficult depends on its fit with the environment. To label a child "difficult" has the danger of becoming a self-fulfilling prophecy. If a child is identified as "difficult," people may treat the child in a way that actually elicits "difficult" behavior. One recent study did find that having access to experiences that encourage coping and build self-regulatory skills was beneficial to children with a difficult temperament (Bradley & Corwyn, 2008).

Too often, we pigeonhole children into categories without examining the context (Rothbart & Bates, 2006; Saarni, 2002). Nonetheless, caregivers need to take children's temperament into account. Research does not yet allow for many highly specific recommendations, but, in general, caregivers should (1) be sensitive to the individual characteristics of the child, (2) be flexible in responding to these characteristics, and (3) avoid applying negative labels to the child.

Personality Development

Emotions and temperament form key aspects of *personality*, the enduring personal characteristics of individuals. Let's now examine characteristics that often are thought of as central to personality development during infancy: trust and the development of self and independence.

Trust   According to Erik Erikson (1968), the first year of life is characterized by the trust-versus-mistrust stage of development. Following a life of regularity, warmth, and protection in the mother's womb, the infant faces a world that is less secure. Erikson proposed that infants learn trust when they are cared for in a consistent, warm manner. If the infant is not well fed and kept warm on a consistent basis, a sense of mistrust is likely to develop.

Trust versus mistrust is not resolved once and for all in the first year of life. It arises again at each successive stage of development, which can have positive or negative outcomes. For example, children who leave infancy with a sense of trust can still have their sense of mistrust activated at a later stage, perhaps if their parents are separated or divorced under conflicting circumstances.

The Developing Sense of Self   Real or imagined, the sense of self is a strong motivating force in life. When does the individual begin to sense a separate existence from others?

According to leading expert Ross Thompson (2007), studying the self in infancy is difficult mainly because infants cannot tell us how they experience themselves. Infants cannot verbally express their views of the self. They also cannot understand complex instructions from researchers.

One ingenious strategy to test infants' visual self-recognition is the use of a mirror technique, in which an infant's mother first puts a dot of rouge on the infant's nose. Then an observer watches to see how often the infant touches its nose. Next, the infant is placed in front of a mirror, and observers detect whether nose touching increases. Why does this matter? The idea is that increased nose touching indicates that the infant recognizes the self in the mirror and is trying to touch or rub off the rouge because the rouge violates the infant's view of the self. Increased touching indicates that the infant realizes that it is the self in the mirror but that something is not right since the real self does not have a dot of rouge on it.

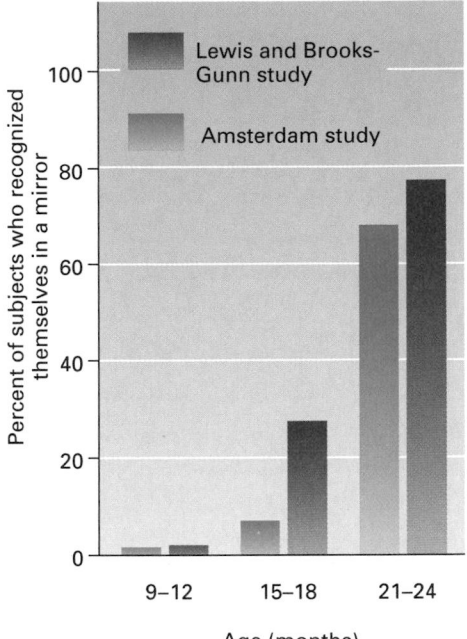

Figure 6.5 displays the results of two investigations that used the mirror technique. The researchers found that before they were 1 year old, infants did not recognize themselves in the mirror (Amsterdam, 1968; Lewis & Brooks-Gunn, 1979). Signs of self-recognition began to appear among some infants when they were 15 to 18 months old. By the time they were 2 years old, most children recognized themselves in the mirror. In sum, infants begin to develop a self-understanding called self-recognition at approximately 18 months of age (Hart & Karmel, 1996; Lewis, 2005).

Late in the second year and early in the third year, toddlers show other emerging forms of self-awareness that reflect a sense of "me" (Laible & Thompson, 2007). For example, they refer to themselves such as by saying "me big"; they label their internal experiences such as emotions; they monitor themselves as when a toddler says, "do it myself"; and say that things are theirs (Bates, 1990; Fasig, 2000).

FIGURE 6.5 The Development of Self-Recognition in Infancy. The graph shows the findings of two studies in which infants less than 1 year of age did not recognize themselves in the mirror. A slight increase in the percentage of infant self-recognition occurred around 15 to 18 months of age. By 2 years of age, a majority of children recognized themselves. *Why do researchers study whether infants recognize themselves in a mirror?*

Independence   Not only does the infant develop a sense of self in the second year of life, but independence also becomes a more central theme in the infant's life (Keller, 2007; Mangelsdorf & Wong, 2008). The theories of Margaret Mahler and Erik Erikson have important implications for both self-development and independence. Mahler (1979) argues that the child goes through a separation and then an individuation process. *Separation* involves the infant's movement away from the mother. *Individuation* involves the development of self.

Erikson (1968), like Mahler, stressed that independence is an important issue in the second year of life. Erikson describes the second stage of development as the stage of autonomy versus shame and doubt. Autonomy builds as the infant's mental and motor abilities develop. At this point in development, not only can infants walk, but they can also climb, open and close, drop, push and pull, and hold and let go. Infants feel pride in these new accomplishments and want to do everything themselves, whether the activity is flushing a toilet, pulling the wrapping off a package, or deciding what to eat. It is important for parents to recognize the motivation of toddlers to do what they are capable of doing at their own pace. Then they can learn to control their muscles and their impulses themselves. But when caregivers are impatient and do for toddlers what they are capable of doing themselves, shame and doubt develop. Every parent has rushed a child from time to time. It is only when parents consistently overprotect toddlers or criticize accidents (wetting, soiling, spilling, or breaking, for example) that children develop an excessive sense of shame and doubt about their ability to control themselves and their world. As we discuss in later chapters, Erikson emphasized that the stage of autonomy versus shame and doubt has important implications for the individual's future development.

Erikson believed that autonomy versus shame and doubt is the key developmental theme of the toddler years. *What are some good strategies for parents to use with their toddlers?*

Review and Reflect: Learning Goal 1

 Discuss the Development of Emotions and Personality in Infancy

REVIEW

- What are emotions? What is the nature of an infant's emotions, and how do they change?
- What is temperament, and how does it develop in infancy?
- What are some important aspects of personality in infancy, and how do they develop?

REFLECT

- How would you describe your temperament? Does it fit one of Chess and Thomas' three styles—easy, slow to warm up, or difficult? If you have siblings, is your temperament similar or different from theirs?

2 SOCIAL ORIENTATION/UNDERSTANDING AND ATTACHMENT

Social Orientation/Understanding

Attachment and Its Development

Individual Differences in Attachment

Caregiving Styles and Attachment

A mother and her baby engaging in face-to-face play. *At what age does face-to-face play usually begin, and when does it typically start decreasing in frequency?*

So far, we have discussed how emotions and emotional competence change as children develop. We have also examined the role of emotional style; in effect, we have seen how emotions set the tone of our experiences in life. But emotions also write the lyrics because they are at the core of our relationships with others.

Social Orientation/Understanding

As socioemotional beings, infants show a strong interest in the social world and are motivated to orient to it and understand it. In earlier chapters, we described many of the biological and cognitive foundations that contribute to the infant's development of social orientation and understanding. We will call attention to relevant biological and cognitive factors as we explore social orientation; locomotion; intention, goal-directed behavior, and cooperation; and social referencing. Discussing biological, cognitive, and social processes together reminds us of an important aspect of development that was pointed out in Chapter 1: These processes are intricately intertwined (Diamond, 2007).

Social Orientation   From early in their development, infants are captivated by the social world. As we discussed in our coverage of infant perception in Chapter 4, young infants stare intently at faces and are attuned to the sounds of human voices, especially their caregiver's (Ramsay-Rennels & Langlois, 2007). Later, they become adept at interpreting the meaning of facial expressions.

Face-to-face play often begins to characterize caregiver-infant interactions when the infant is about 2 to 3 months of age. The focused social interaction of face-to-face play may include vocalizations, touch, and gestures (Leppanen & others, 2007). Such play is part of many mothers' motivation to create a positive emotional state in their infants (Laible & Thompson, 2007; Thompson, 2009a).

In part because of such positive social interchanges between caregivers and infants, by 2 to 3 months of age, infants respond differently to people than objects, showing more positive emotion to people than to inanimate objects, such as puppets (Legerstee, 1997). At this age, most infants expect people to react positively when the infants initiate a behavior, such as a smile or a vocalization. This finding has been discovered using a method called the *still-face paradigm*, in which the caregiver alternates between engaging in face-to-face interaction with the infant and remaining still and unresponsive. As early as 2 to 3 months of age, infants show more withdrawal, negative emotions, and self-directed behavior when their caregivers are still and unresponsive (Adamson & Frick, 2003). The frequency of face-to-face play decreases after 7 months of age as infants become more mobile (Thompson, 2006).

Infants also learn about the social world through contexts other than face-to-face play with a caregiver (Thompson, 2009b; Thompson & Newton, 2009). Even though infants as young as 6 months of age show an interest in each other, their interaction with peers increases considerably in the last half of the second year. Between 18 to 24 months of age, children markedly increase their imitative and reciprocal play, such as imitating nonverbal actions like jumping and running (Eckerman & Whitehead, 1999). One recent study involved presenting 1- and 2-year-olds with a simple cooperative task that consisted of pulling a lever to get an attractive toy (Brownell, & Ramani, & Zerwas, 2006) (see Figure 6.6). Any coordinated actions of the 1-year-olds appeared to be more coincidental rather than cooperative, whereas the 2-year-olds' behavior was characterized as more active cooperation to reach a goal. As increasing numbers of U.S. infants experience child care outside the home, they are spending more time in social play with other peers (Field, 2007). Later in the chapter, we will further discuss child care.

FIGURE 6.6 The Cooperation Task. The cooperation task consisted of two handles on a box, atop which was an animated musical toy, surreptitiously activated by remote control when both handles were pulled. The handles were placed far enough apart that one child could not pull both handles. The experimenter demonstrated the task, saying, "Watch! If you pull the handles, the doggie will sing" (Brownell, Ramani, & Zerwas, 2006).

Locomotion   Recall from earlier in the chapter how important independence is for infants, especially in the second year of life. As infants develop the ability to crawl, walk, and run, they are able to explore and expand their social world. These newly developed self-produced locomotor skills allow the infant to independently initiate social interchanges on a more frequent basis (Laible & Thompson, 2007; Thompson, 2006). Remember from Chapter 4 that the development of these gross motor skills is the result of a number of factors including the development of the nervous system, the goal the infant is motivated to reach, and environmental support for the skill (Adolph, 2008; Adolph & Joh, 2008).

Locomotion is also important for its motivational implications (Thompson, 2008). Once infants have the ability to move in goal-directed pursuits, the reward from these pursuits leads to further efforts to explore and develop skills.

Intention, Goal-Directed Behavior, and Cooperation   Perceiving people as engaging in intentional and goal-directed behavior is an important social cognitive accomplishment, and this initially occurs toward the end of the first year (Laible & Thompson, 2007; Thompson, 2006). Joint attention and gaze following help the infant to understand that other people have intentions (Meltzoff, 2007; Tomasello & Carpenter, 2007). Recall from Chapter 5 that *joint attention* occurs when the caregiver and infant focus on the same object or event. We indicated that emerging aspects of joint attention occur at about 7 to 8 months, but at about 10 to 11 months of age joint attention intensifies and infants begin to follow the caregiver's gaze. By their first birthday, infants have begun to direct the caregiver's attention to objects that capture their interest (Heimann & others, 2006).

In the study on cooperating to reach a goal that was discussed earlier, 1- and 2-year-olds also were assessed with two social understanding tasks, observation of children's behavior in a joint attention task, and the parents' perceptions of the language the children use about the self and others (Brownell, Ramani, & Zerwas, 2006). Those with

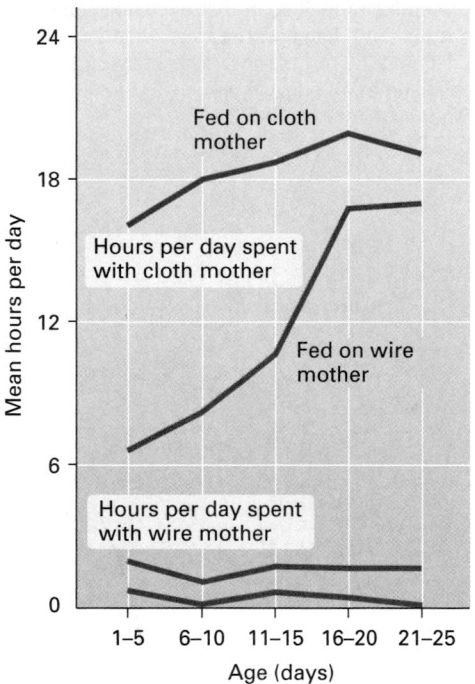

FIGURE 6.7 Contact Time with Wire and Cloth Surrogate Mothers. Regardless of whether the infant monkeys were fed by a wire or a cloth mother, they overwhelmingly preferred to spend contact time with the cloth mother. *How do these results compare with what Freud's theory and Erikson's theory would predict about human infants?*

social referencing "Reading" emotional cues in others to help determine how to act in a particular situation.

attachment A close emotional bond between two people.

more advanced social understanding were more likely to cooperate. To cooperate, the children had to connect their own intentions with the peer's intentions and put this understanding to use in interacting with the peer to reach a goal. Further, a recent study revealed that initiating and responding to joint attention at 12 months of age were linked to being socially competent (for example, not aggressive or defiant, showing empathy, and engaging in sustained attention) at 30 months of age (Vaughan & others, 2007).

Social Referencing   Another important social cognitive accomplishment in infancy is developing the ability to "read" the emotions of other people. **Social referencing** is the term used to describe "reading" emotional cues in others to help determine how to act in a particular situation. The development of social referencing helps infants to interpret ambiguous situations more accurately, as when they encounter a stranger and need to know whether to fear the person (de Rosnay & others, 2006; Thompson, 2006). By the end of the first year, a mother's facial expression—either smiling or fearful—influences whether an infant will explore an unfamiliar environment.

Infants become better at social referencing in the second year of life. At this age, they tend to "check" with their mother before they act; they look at her to see if she is happy, angry, or fearful. For example, in one study, 14- to 22-month-old infants were more likely to look at their mother's face as a source of information for how to act in a situation than were 6 to 9-month-old infants (Walden, 1991).

Infants' Social Sophistication and Insight   In sum, researchers are discovering that infants are more socially sophisticated and insightful at younger ages than previously envisioned (Hamlin, Hallinan, & Woodward, 2008; Thompson, 2008, 2009a, b). This sophistication and insight is reflected in infants' perceptions of others' actions as intentionally motivated and goal-directed (Brune & Woodward, 2007) and their motivation to share and participate in that intentionality by their first birthday (Tomasello & Carpenter, 2007). The more advanced social cognitive skills of infants could be expected to influence their understanding and awareness of attachment to a caregiver.

Attachment and Its Development

A small curly-haired girl named Danielle, age 11 months, begins to whimper. After a few seconds, she begins to wail. Soon her mother comes into the room, and Danielle's crying ceases. Quickly, Danielle crawls over to where her mother is seated and reaches out to be held. Danielle has just demonstrated attachment to her mother. **Attachment** is a close emotional bond between two people.

There is no shortage of theories about infant attachment. Three theorists discussed in Chapter 1—Freud, Erikson, and Bowlby—proposed influential views.

Freud emphasized that infants become attached to the person or object that provides oral satisfaction. For most infants, this is the mother, since she is most likely to feed the infant. Is feeding as important as Freud thought? A classic study by Harry Harlow (1958) reveals that the answer is no (see Figure 6.7).

Harlow removed infant monkeys from their mothers at birth; for six months they were reared by surrogate (substitute) "mothers." One surrogate mother was made of wire, the other of cloth. Half of the infant monkeys were fed by the wire mother, half by the cloth mother. Periodically, the amount of time the infant monkeys spent with either the wire or the cloth mother was computed. Regardless of which mother fed them, the infant monkeys spent far more time with the cloth mother. Even if the wire mother, but not the cloth mother, provided nourishment, the infant monkeys spent more time with the cloth mother And when Harlow frightened the monkeys, those "raised" by the cloth mother ran to the mother and clung to it; those raised by the wire mother did not. Whether the mother provided comfort seemed to determine whether the monkeys associated the mother with security. This study clearly demonstrated that feeding is not the crucial element in the attachment process and that contact comfort is important.

Physical comfort also plays a role in Erik Erikson's (1968) view of the infant's development. Recall Erikson's proposal that the first year of life represents the stage of trust versus mistrust. Physical comfort and sensitive care, according to Erikson (1968), are key to establishing a basic trust in infants. The infant's sense of trust, in turn, is the foundation for attachment and sets the stage for a lifelong expectation that the world will be a good and pleasant place to be.

The ethological perspective of British psychiatrist John Bowlby (1969, 1989) also stresses the importance of attachment in the first year of life and the responsiveness of the caregiver. Bowlby maintains both infants and their primary caregivers are biologically predisposed to form attachments. He argues that the newborn is biologically equipped to elicit attachment behavior. The baby cries, clings, coos, and smiles. Later, the infant crawls, walks, and follows the mother. The immediate result is to keep the primary caregiver nearby; the long-term effect is to increase the infant's chances of survival (Thompson, 2006).

Attachment does not emerge suddenly but rather develops in a series of phases, moving from a baby's general preference for human beings to a partnership with primary caregivers. Following are four such phases based on Bowlby's conceptualization of attachment (Schaffer, 1996):

- *Phase 1: From birth to 2 months.* Infants instinctively direct their attachment to human figures. Strangers, siblings, and parents are equally likely to elicit smiling or crying from the infant.

- *Phase 2: From 2 to 7 months.* Attachment becomes focused on one figure, usually the primary caregiver, as the baby gradually learns to distinguish familiar from unfamiliar people.

- *Phase 3: From 7 to 24 months.* Specific attachments develop. With increased locomotor skills, babies actively seek contact with regular caregivers, such as the mother or father.

- *Phase 4: From 24 months on.* Children become aware of others' feelings, goals, and plans and begin to take these into account in forming their own actions.

Researchers' recent findings that infants are more socially sophisticated and insightful than previously envisioned suggests that some of the characteristics of Bowlby's phase 4, such as understanding the goals and intentions of the attachment figure, appear to be developing in phase 3 as attachment security is taking shape (Thompson, 2008).

Bowlby argued that infants develop an *internal working model* of attachment, a simple mental model of the caregiver, their relationship, and the self as deserving of nurturant care. The infant's internal working model of attachment with the caregiver influences the infant's and later the child's subsequent responses to other people (Bretherton & Munholland, 2009; Posada, 2008). The internal model of attachment also has played a pivotal role in the discovery of links between attachment and subsequent emotion understanding, conscious development, and self-concept (Thompson, 2006).

In sum, attachment emerges from the social cognitive advances that allow infants to develop expectations for the caregiver's behavior and to determine the affective quality of their relationship (Laible & Thompson, 2007; Thompson, 2006, 2009b). These social cognitive advances include recognizing the caregiver's face, voice, and other features, as well as developing an internal working model of expecting the caregiver to provide pleasure in social interaction and relief from distress.

Individual Differences in Attachment

Although attachment to a caregiver intensifies midway through the first year, isn't it likely that that quality of babies' attachment experiences varies? Mary Ainsworth (1979) thought so. Ainsworth created the **Strange Situation**, an observational measure of infant attachment in which the infant experiences a series of introductions, separations, and reunions with the caregiver and an adult stranger in a prescribed order. In using the Strange Situation, researchers hope that their observations will provide information about the infant's motivation to be near the caregiver and the degree to which the caregiver's presence provides the infant with security and confidence.

Strange Situation An observational measure of infant attachment that requires the infant to move through a series of introductions, separations, and reunions with the caregiver and an adult stranger in a prescribed order.

What is the nature of secure and insecure attachment?

Based on how babies respond in the Strange Situation, they are described as being securely attached or insecurely attached (in one of three ways) to the caregiver:

- **Securely attached babies** use the caregiver as a secure base from which to explore the environment. When in the presence of their caregiver, securely attached infants explore the room and examine toys that have been placed in it. When the caregiver departs, securely attached infants might mildly protest, and when the caregiver returns these infants reestablish positive interaction with her, perhaps by smiling or climbing on her lap. Subsequently, they often resume playing with the toys in the room.

- **Insecure avoidant babies** show insecurity by avoiding the caregiver. In the Strange Situation, these babies engage in little interaction with the caregiver, are not distressed when she leaves the room, usually do not reestablish contact with on her return, and may even turn their back on her. If contact is established, the infant usually leans away or looks away.

- **Insecure resistant babies** often cling to the caregiver and then resist her by fighting against the closeness, perhaps by kicking or pushing away. In the Strange Situation, these babies often cling anxiously to the caregiver and don't explore the playroom. When the caregiver leaves, they often cry loudly and push away if she tries to comfort them on her return.

- **Insecure disorganized babies** are disorganized and disoriented. In the Strange Situation, these babies might appear dazed, confused, and fearful. To be classified as disorganized, babies must show strong patterns of avoidance and resistance or display certain specified behaviors, such as extreme fearfulness around the caregiver.

Evaluating the Strange Situation   Does the Strange Situation capture important differences among infants? As a measure of attachment, it may be culturally biased. For example, German and Japanese babies often show different patterns of attachment than American infants. As illustrated in Figure 6.8, German infants are more likely to show an avoidant attachment pattern and Japanese infants are less likely to display this pattern than U.S. infants (van IJzendoorn & Kroonenberg, 1988). The avoidant pattern in German babies likely occurs because their caregivers encourage them to be independent (Grossmann & others, 1985). Also as shown in Figure 6.7, Japanese babies are more likely than American babies to be categorized as resistant. This may have more to do with the Strange Situation as a measure of attachment than with attachment insecurity itself. Japanese mothers rarely let anyone unfamiliar with their babies care for them. Thus, the Strange Situation might create considerably more stress for Japanese infants than for American infants, who are more accustomed to separation from their mothers (Miyake, Chen, & Campos, 1985). Even though there are cultural variations in attachment classification, the most frequent classification in every culture studied so far is secure attachment (Thompson, 2006; van IJzendoorn & Kroonenberg, 1988).

Some critics stress that behavior in the Strange Situation—like other laboratory assessments—might not indicate what infants do in a natural environment. But researchers have found that infants' behaviors in the Strange Situation are closely related to how they behave at home in response to separation and reunion with their mothers (Pederson & Moran, 1996). Thus, many infant researchers believe the Strange Situation continues to show merit as a measure of infant attachment.

Interpreting Differences in Attachment   Do individual differences in attachment matter? Ainsworth argues that secure attachment in the first year of life provides an important foundation for psychological development later in life. The securely attached infant moves freely away from the mother but keeps track of where she is through periodic glances. The securely attached infant responds positively to being picked up by others and, when put back down, freely moves away to play. An insecurely attached infant, by contrast, avoids the mother or is ambivalent toward her, fears strangers, and is upset by minor, everyday separations.

securely attached babies Babies that use the caregiver as a secure base from which to explore the environment.

insecure avoidant babies Babies that show insecurity by avoiding the caregiver.

insecure resistant babies Babies that often cling to the caregiver, then resist her by fighting against the closeness, perhaps by kicking or pushing away.

insecure disorganized babies Babies that show insecurity by being disorganized and disoriented.

If early attachment to a caregiver is important, it should relate to a child's social behavior later in development. For some children, early attachments seem to foreshadow later functioning (Cassidy, 2009; Egeland, 2009). In the extensive longitudinal study conducted by Alan Sroufe and his colleagues (2005a, b), early secure attachment (assessed by the Strange Situation at 12 and 18 months) was linked with positive emotional health, high self-esteem, self-confidence, and socially competent interaction with peers, teachers, camp counselors, and romantic partners through adolescence. Another study revealed that being classified as insecure resistant in infancy was a negative predictor of cognitive development in elementary school (O'Connor & McCartney, 2007).

For some children, though, there is less continuity (Thompson & Goodvin, 2007). Not all research reveals the power of infant attachment to predict subsequent development. In one longitudinal study, attachment classification in infancy did not predict attachment classification at 18 years of age (Lewis, Feiring, & Rosenthal, 2000). In this study, the best predictor of an insecure attachment classification at 18 was the occurrence of parental divorce in the intervening years. Consistently positive caregiving over a number of years is likely an important factor in connecting early attachment and the child's functioning later in development. Indeed, researchers have found that early secure attachment *and* subsequent experiences, especially maternal care and life stresses, are linked with children's later behavior and adjustment (Belsky & Pasco Fearon, 2002; Thompson, 2006).

Some developmentalists conclude that too much emphasis has been placed on the attachment bond in infancy (Newcombe, 2007). Jerome Kagan (1987, 2002), for example, points out that infants are highly resilient and adaptive; he argues that they are evolutionarily equipped to stay on a positive developmental course, even in the face of wide variations in parenting. Kagan and others stress that genetic characteristics and temperament play more important roles in a child's social competence than the attachment theorists, such as Bowlby and Ainsworth, are willing to acknowledge (Bakermans-Kranenburg & others, 2007; Chaudhuri & Williams, 1999). For example, if some infants inherit a low tolerance for stress, this, rather than an insecure attachment bond, may be responsible for an inability to get along with peers.

Another criticism of attachment theory is that it ignores the diversity of socializing agents and contexts that exists in an infant's world. A culture's value system can influence the nature of attachment (Grossman & Grossman, 2009; van IJzendoorn & Sagi-Schwartz, 2009). In some cultures, infants show attachments to many people. Among the Hausa (who live in Nigeria), both grandmothers and siblings provide a significant amount of care for infants (Harkness & Super, 1995). Infants in agricultural societies tend to form attachments to older siblings, who are assigned a major responsibility for younger siblings' care. Researchers recognize the importance of competent, nurturant caregivers in an infant's development (Parke & Buriel, 2006). At issue, though, is whether or not secure attachment, especially to a single caregiver, is critical (Lamb, 2005; Thompson, 2006).

Despite such criticisms, there is ample evidence that security of attachment is important to development (Posada, 2008; Thompson, 2009b). Secure attachment in infancy is important because it reflects a positive parent-infant relationship and provides the foundation that supports healthy socioemotional development in the years that follow.

Caregiving Styles and Attachment

Is the style of caregiving linked with the quality of the infant's attachment? Securely attached babies have caregivers who are sensitive to their signals and are consistently available to respond to their infants' needs (Juffer & others, 2007; Main, 2000). These caregivers often let their babies have an active part in determining the onset and pacing of interaction in the first year of life.

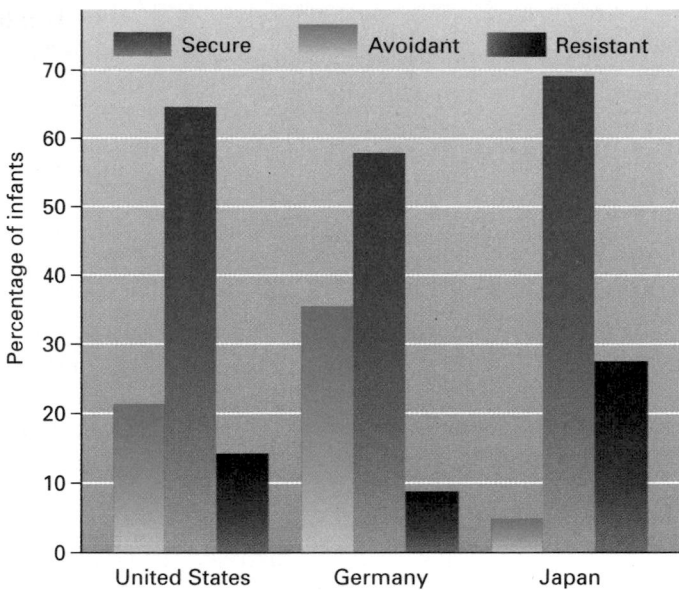

FIGURE 6.8 Cross-Cultural Comparison of Attachment. In one study, infant attachment in three countries—the United States, Germany, and Japan—was measured in the Ainsworth Strange Situation (van IJzendoorn & Kroonenberg, 1988). The dominant attachment pattern in all three countries was secure attachment. However, German infants were more avoidant and Japanese infants were less avoidant and more resistant than U.S. infants. *What are some explanations for differences in how German, Japanese, and American infants respond to the Strange Situation?*

In the Hausa culture, siblings and grandmothers provide a significant amount of care for infants. *How might these variations in care affect attachment?*

How do the caregivers of insecurely attached babies interact with them? Caregivers of avoidant babies tend to be unavailable or rejecting (Bakermans-Kranenburg & others, 2007). They often don't respond to their babies' signals and have little physical contact with them. When they do interact with their babies, they may behave in an angry and irritable way. Caregivers of resistant babies tend to be inconsistent; sometimes they respond to their babies' needs, and sometimes they don't. In general, they tend not to be very affectionate with their babies and show little synchrony when interacting with them. Caregivers of disorganized babies often neglect or physically abuse them (Benoit, 2009; Toth, 2009). In some cases, these caregivers are depressed (Thompson, 2008).

Review and Reflect: Learning Goal 2

 2 Describe Social Orientation/Understanding and the Development of Attachment in Infancy

REVIEW

- How do infants orient to the social world?
- What is attachment, and how is it conceptualized?
- What are some individual variations in attachment? What are some criticisms of attachment theory?
- How are caregiving styles related to attachment?

REFLECT

- How might the infant's temperament be related to way in which attachment is classified? Look at the temperament categories we described, and reflect on how these might be more likely to show up in infants in some attachment categories than others.

3 SOCIAL CONTEXTS

The Family   **Child Care**

Children socialize parents just as parents socialize children.

Now that we have explored the infant's emotional and personality development and attachment, let's examine the social contexts in which these occur. We will begin by studying a number of aspects of the family and then turn to a social context in which infants increasingly spend time—child care.

The Family

The family can be thought of as a constellation of subsystems—a complex whole made up of interrelated, interacting parts—defined in terms of generation, gender, and role. Each family member participates in several subsystems (Fiese & Winter, 2008; Parke & others, 2008). The father and child represent one subsystem, the mother and father another; the mother-father-child represent yet another; and so on.

These subsystems have reciprocal influences on each other (Belsky, 2009a), as Figure 6.9 highlights. For example, Jay Belsky (1981) emphasizes that marital relations, parenting, and infant behavior and development can have both direct and indirect effects on each other. An example of a direct effect is the influence of the parents' behavior on the child. An indirect effect is how the relationship between the spouses mediates the way a parent acts toward the child (Hsu, 2004). For example, marital conflict might reduce the efficiency of parenting, in which case marital conflict would indirectly affect the child's behavior. The simple fact that two people are becoming parents may have profound effects of their relationship.

The Transition to Parenthood   When people become parents through pregnancy, adoption, or stepparenting, they face disequilibrium and must adapt. Parents want to develop a strong attachment with their infant, but they still want to maintain strong attachments to their spouse and friends, and possibly continue their careers. Parents ask themselves how this new being will change their lives. A baby places new restrictions on partners; no longer will they be able to rush out to a movie on a moment's notice, and money may not be readily available for vacations and other luxuries. Dual-career parents ask, "Will it harm the baby to place her in child care? Will we be able to find responsible babysitters?"

In a longitudinal investigation of couples from late pregnancy until $3\frac{1}{2}$ years after the baby was born, couples enjoyed more positive marital relations before the baby was born than after (Cowan & Cowan, 2000; Cowan & others, 2005). Still, almost one-third showed an increase in marital satisfaction. Some couples said that the baby had both brought them closer together and moved them farther apart; being parents enhanced their sense of themselves and gave them a new, more stable identity as a couple. Babies opened men up to a concern with intimate relationships, and the demands of juggling work and family roles stimulated women to manage family tasks more efficiently and pay attention to their own personal growth.

The Bringing Home Baby project is a workshop for new parents that emphasizes strengthening the couples' relationship, understanding and becoming acquainted with the baby, resolving conflict, and developing parenting skills. Evaluations of the project revealed that parents who participated improved in their ability to work together as parents, fathers were more involved with their baby and sensitive to the baby's behavior, mothers had a lower incidence of postpartum depression symptoms, and their baby showed better overall development than participants in a control group (Gottman, Shapiro, & Parthemer, 2004; Shapiro & Gottman, 2005).

Reciprocal Socialization   For many years, socialization between parents and children was viewed as a one-way process: Children were considered to be the products of their parents' socialization techniques. However, parent-child interaction is reciprocal (Fiese & Winter, 2008; Thompson & Newton, 2009). **Reciprocal socialization** is socialization that is bidirectional. That is, children socialize parents just as parents socialize children. For example, the interaction of mothers and their infants is like a dance or a dialogue in which successive actions of the partners are closely coordinated. This coordinated dance or dialogue can assume the form of mutual synchrony in which each person's behavior depends on the partner's previous behavior. Or it can be reciprocal in the sense that actions of the partners are matched, as when one partner imitates the other or when there is mutual smiling.

When reciprocal socialization has been studied in infancy, mutual gaze, or eye contact, plays an important role in early social interaction. In one investigation, the mother and infant engaged in a variety of behaviors while they looked at each other. By contrast, when they looked away from each other, the rate of such behaviors dropped considerably (Stern & others, 1977). In sum, the behaviors of mothers and infants involve substantial interconnection, mutual regulation, and synchronization (Moreno, Posada, & Goldyn, 2006). A recent study revealed that *parent-infant synchrony*—the temporal coordination of social behavior—played an important role in children's development (Feldman, 2007). In this study, parent-infant synchrony at 3 and 9 months of age were positively linked to children's self-regulation from 2 to 6 years of age.

An important form of reciprocal socialization is **scaffolding**, in which parents time interactions in such a way that the infant experiences turn-taking with the parents. Scaffolding involves parental behavior that supports children's efforts, allowing them to

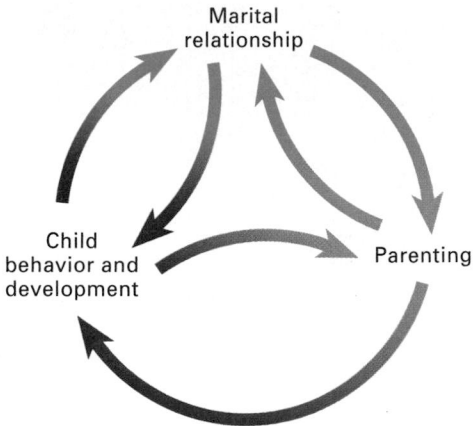

FIGURE 6.9 Interaction Between Children and Their Parents: Direct and Indirect Effects

What kinds of adaptations do new parents need to make?

reciprocal socialization Socialization that is bidirectional; children socialize parents, just as parents socialize children.

scaffolding Parents time interactions so that infants experience turn-taking with the parents.

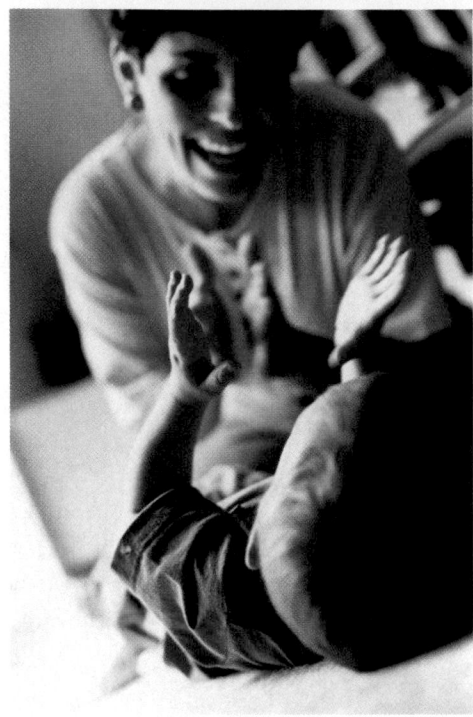

Caregivers often play games such as peek-a-boo and pat-a-cake. *How is scaffolding involved in these games?*

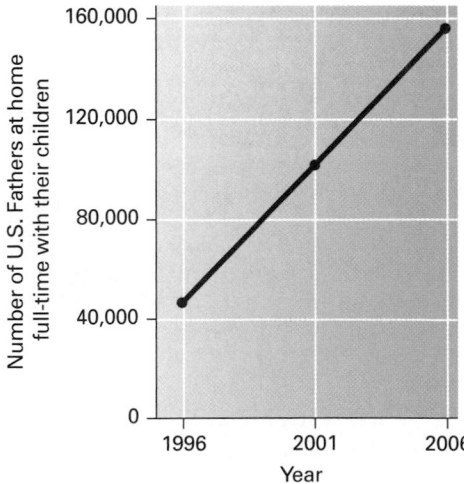

FIGURE 6.10 The Increase in the Number of U.S. Fathers Staying at Home Full-Time with Their Children

be more skillful than they would be if they were to rely only on their own abilities (Field, 2007). In using scaffolding, caregivers provide a positive, reciprocal framework in which they and their children interact. For example, in the game peek-a-boo, the mother initially covers the baby. Then she removes the cover and registers "surprise" at the infant's reappearance. As infants become more skilled at peek-a-boo, pat-a-cake, and so on, there are other caregiver games that exemplify scaffolding and turn-taking sequences. In one study, infants who had more extensive scaffolding experiences with their parents (especially in the form of turn-taking) were more likely to engage in turn-taking when they interacted with their peers (Vandell & Wilson, 1988). Engaging in turn-taking and games like peek-a-boo reflect the development of joint attention by the caregiver and infant, which we discussed in Chapter 6 (Tomasello & Carpenter, 2007).

Maternal and Paternal Caregiving An increasing number of U.S. fathers stay home full-time with their children (Wong & Rochlen, 2008). As indicated in Figure 6.10, there was a 300-plus percent increase in stay-at-home fathers in the United States from 1996 to 2006. A large portion of the full-time fathers have career-focused wives who provide the main family income. A recent study revealed that the stay-at-home fathers were as satisfied with their marriage as traditional parents, although they indicated that they missed their daily life in the workplace (Rochlen & others, 2008). In this study, the stay-at-home fathers reported that they tended to be ostracized when they took their children to playgrounds and often were excluded from parent groups.

Can fathers take care of infants as competently as mothers can? Observations of fathers and their infants suggest that fathers have the ability to act as sensitively and responsively as mothers with their infants (Parke, 2004; Parke & Buriel, 2006). Perhaps the caregiving behavior of male humans resembles that of other male primates, who show notoriously low interest in their offspring. However, when forced to live with infants whose female caregivers are absent, the males can competently rear the infants. Remember, however, that although fathers can be active, nurturant, involved caregivers with their infants, many do not choose to follow this pattern (Lamb, 2000).

Do fathers behave differently toward infants than mothers do? Maternal interactions usually center on child-care activities—feeding, changing diapers, bathing. Paternal interactions are more likely to include play (Parke, 2004; Parke & Buriel, 2006). Fathers engage in more rough-and-tumble play. They bounce infants, throw them up in the air, tickle them, and so on (Lamb, 2000). Mothers do play with infants, but their play is less physical and arousing than that of fathers.

In one study, fathers were interviewed about their caregiving responsibilities when their children were 6, 15, 24, and 36 months of age (NICHD Early Child Care Research Network, 2000). Some of the fathers were videotaped while playing with their children at 6 and 36 months. Fathers were more involved in caregiving—bathing, feeding, dressing the child, taking the child to child care, and so on—when they worked fewer hours and mothers worked more hours, when mothers and fathers were younger, when mothers reported greater marital intimacy, and when the children were boys.

Child Care

How do most fathers and mothers interact differently with infants?

Many U.S. children today experience multiple caregivers. Most do not have a parent staying home to care for them; instead, the children have some type of care provided by others—"child care." Many parents worry that child care will reduce their infants' emotional attachment to them, retard the infants' cognitive development, fail to teach them how to control anger, and allow them to be unduly influenced by their peers. How extensive is child care? Are the worries of these parents justified?

Parental Leave   Today far more young children are in child care than at any other time in history. About 2 million children in the United States currently receive formal, licensed child care, and uncounted millions of children are cared for by unlicensed babysitters. In part, these numbers reflect the fact that U.S. adults cannot receive paid leave from their jobs to care for their young children. However, as described in the *Diversity in Life-Span Development* interlude, many countries provide extensive parental leave policies.

Diversity in Life-Span Development
Child-Care Policies Around the World

Child-care policies around the world vary in elgibility criteria, leave duration, benefit level, and the extent to which parents take advantage of the policies (Lero, 2009; Tolani & Brooks-Gunn, 2008). There are five types of parental leave from employment (Kammerman, 1989, 2000a, b, 2009):

- *Maternity leave.* In some countries the pre-birth leave is compulsory as is a 6- to 10-week leave following birth.

- *Paternity leave.* This is usually much briefer than maternity leave. It may be especially important when a second child is born and the first child requires care.

- *Parental leave.* This gender-neutral leave usually follows a maternity leave and allows either women or men to share the leave policy or choose which of them will use it. In 1998, the European Union mandated a three-month parental leave.

- *Child-rearing leave.* In some countries, this is a supplement to a maternity leave or a variation on a parental leave. A child-rearing leave is usually longer than a maternity leave and is typically paid at a much lower level.

- *Family leave.* This covers reasons other than the birth of a new baby and can allow time off from employment to care for an ill child or other family members, time to accompany a child to school for the first time, or time to visit a child's school.

Europe led the way in creating new standards of parental leave: The European Union (EU) mandated a paid 14-week maternity leave in 1992. In most European countries today, working parents on leave receive from 70 percent of the worker's prior wage to the full wage and paid leave averages about 16 weeks (Tolani & Brooks-Gunn, 2008). The United States currently allows up to 12 weeks of unpaid leave for caring for a newborn.

Most countries restrict eligible benefits to women employed for a minimum time prior to child birth (Belsky, 2009b; Howes, 2009; Owen, 2009; Tolani & Brooks-Gunn, 2008). In Denmark, even unemployed mothers are eligible for extended parental leave related to childbirth. In Germany child-rearing leave is available to almost all parents. The Nordic countries (Denmark, Norway, and Sweden) have extensive gender-equity family leave policies for childbirth that emphasize the contributions of both women and men (Tolani & Brooks-Gunn, 2008). For example, in Sweden, parents can take an 18-month job-protected parental leave with benefits allowed to be shared by parents and applied to full-time or part-time work.

How are child-care policies in many European countries, such as Sweden, different than those in the United States?

Variations in Child Care   Because the United States does not have a policy of paid leave for child care, child care in the United States has become a major national concern (Tolani & Brooks-Gunn, 2008). Many factors influence the effects of child care, including the age of the child, the type of child care, and the quality of the program.

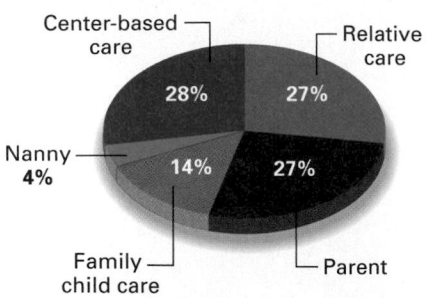

FIGURE 6.11 Primary Care Arrangements in the United States for Children Under 5 Years of Age with Employed Mothers

The type of child care varies extensively (Ahnert & Lamb, 2009; McCartney, 2009). Child care is provided in large centers with elaborate facilities and in private homes. Some child-care centers are commercial operations; others are nonprofit centers run by churches, civic groups, and employers. Some child-care providers are professionals; others are mothers who want to earn extra money. Figure 6.11 presents the primary care arrangements for children under 5 years of age with employed mothers (Clarke-Stewart & Miner, 2008).

Child-care quality makes a difference. What constitutes a high-quality child-care program for infants? In high-quality child care (Clarke-Stewart & Miner, 2008, p. 273):

> Caregivers encourage the children to be actively engaged in a variety of activities, have frequent, positive interactions that include smiling, touching, holding, and speaking at the child's eye level, respond properly to the child's questions or requests, and encourage children to talk about their experiences, feelings, and ideas.

High-quality child care also involves providing children with a safe environment, access to age-appropriate toys and participation in age-appropriate activities, and a low caregiver-child ratio that allows caregivers to spend considerable time with children on an individual basis.

Children are more likely to experience poor-quality child care if they come from families with few resources (psychological, social, and economic) (Cabrera, Hutchens, & Peters, 2006; McCartney, 2009). Many researchers have examined the role of poverty in the quality of child care (Giannarelli, Sonenstein, & Stagner, 2006). One study found that extensive child care was harmful to low-income children only when the care was of low quality (Votruba-Drzal, Coley, & Chase-Lansdale, 2004). Even if the child was in child care more than 45 hours a week, high-quality care was linked with fewer internalizing problems (anxiety, for example) and externalizing problems (aggressive and destructive behaviors, for example). A recent study revealed that children from low-income families benefited in terms of school readiness and language development when their parents selected higher-quality child care (McCartney & others, 2007).

To read about one individual who provides quality child care to individuals from impoverished backgrounds, see the *Careers in Life-Span Development* profile. In the *Research in Life-Span Development* interlude that follows, you can read about an ongoing national study of child care and its effects.

Careers in Life-Span Development

Rashmi Nakhre, Child-Care Director

Rashmi Nakhre has two master's degrees—one in psychology the other in child development—and is director of the Hattie Daniels Day Care Center in Wilson, North Carolina. Nakhre received the Distinguished Woman of North Carolina Award for 1999–2000.

Nakhre first worked at the child-care center soon after she arrived in the United States 25 years ago. She says that she took the job initially because she needed the money but "ended up falling in love with my job." Nakhre has turned the Wilson, North Carolina, child-care center into a model for other centers. The center almost closed several years after she began working there because of financial difficulties. Nakhre played a major role in raising funds not only to keep it open but to improve it. The center provides quality child care for the children of many Latino migrant workers.

Rashmi Nakhre, child-care director, working with some of the children at her center.

Research in Life-Span Development
A National Longitudinal Study of Child Care

In 1991, the National Institute of Child Health and Human Development (NICHD) began a comprehensive, longitudinal study of child-care experiences. Data were collected on a diverse sample of almost 1,400 children and their families at 10 locations across the United States over a period of seven years. Researchers used multiple methods (trained observers, interviews, questionnaires, and testing) and they measured many facets of children's development, including physical health, cognitive development, and socioemotional development. Following are some of the results (NICHD Early Child Care Research Network, 2001, 2002, 2003, 2004, 2005, 2006).

- *Patterns of use.* Many families placed their infants in child care very soon after the child's birth, and there was considerable instability in the child-care arrangements. By 4 months of age, nearly three-fourths of the infants had entered some form of nonmaternal child care. Almost half of the infants were cared for by a relative when they first entered care; only 12 percent were enrolled in child-care centers. Socioeconomic factors were linked to the amount and type of care. For example, mothers with higher incomes and families that were more dependent on the mother's income placed their infants in child care at an earlier age. Mothers who believed that maternal employment has positive effects on children were more likely than other mothers to place their infant in nonmaternal care for more hours. Low-income families were more likely than more affluent families to use child care, but infants from low-income families who were in child care averaged as many hours as other income groups. In the preschool years, mothers who were single, those with more education, and families with higher incomes used more hours of center care than other families. Minority families and mothers with less education used more hours of care by relatives.

- *Quality of care.* Evaluations of quality of care were based on such characteristics as group size, child-adult ratio, physical environment, caregiver characteristics (such as formal education, specialized training, and child-care experience), and caregiver behavior (such as sensitivity to children). An alarming conclusion is that a majority of the child care in the first three years of life was of unacceptable low quality. Positive caregiving by nonparents in child-care settings was infrequent—only 12 percent of the children studied experienced positive nonparental child care (such as positive talk, lack of detachment and flat affect, and language stimulation)! Further, infants from low-income families experienced lower quality of child care than infants from higher-income families. When quality of caregivers' care was high, children performed better on cognitive and language tasks, were more cooperative with their mothers during play, showed more positive and skilled interaction with peers, and had fewer behavior problems. Caregiver training and good child-staff ratios were linked with higher cognitive and social competence when children were 54 months of age. Using data collected as part of the NICHD early child care longitudinal study, a recent analysis indicated that higher-quality early child care, especially at 27 months of age, was linked to children's higher vocabulary scores in the fifth grade (Belsky & others, 2007).

Higher-quality child care was also related to higher-quality mother-child interaction among the families that used nonmaternal care. Further, poor-quality care was related to an increase of insecure attachment to the mother among infants who were 15 months of age, but only when the mother was low in sensitivity and responsiveness. However, child-care quality was not linked to attachment security at 36 months of age.

- *Amount of child care.* The quantity of child care predicted some child outcomes. When children spent extensive amounts of time in child care beginning in infancy, they experienced less sensitive interactions with their mother, showed more behavior problems, and had higher rates of illness (Vandell, 2004). Many of these comparisons involved children in child care for less than 30 hours a week versus those in child care for more than

What are some important findings from the national longitudinal study of child care conducted by the National Institute of Child Health and Human Development?

45 hours a week. In general, though, when children spent 30 hours or more per week in child care, their development was less than optimal (Ramey, 2005).

- *Family and parenting influences.* The influence of families and parenting was not weakened by extensive child care. Parents played a significant role in helping children to regulate their emotions. Especially important parenting influences were being sensitive to children's needs, being involved with children, and cognitively stimulating them.

What are some strategies parents can follow in regard to child care? Child-care expert Kathleen McCartney (2003, p. 4) offered this advice:

- *Recognize that the quality of your parenting is a key factor in your child's development.*

- *Monitor your child's development.* "Parents should observe for themselves whether their children seem to be having behavior problems." They need to talk with child-care providers and pediatrician about their child's behavior.

- *Take some time to find the best child care.* Observe different child-care facilities and be certain that you like what you see. "Quality child care costs money, and not all parents can afford the child care they want. However, state subsidies, and other programs like Head Start, are available for families in need."

Review and Reflect: Learning Goal 3

 Explain How Social Contexts Influence the Infant's Development

REVIEW

- What are some important family processes in infant development?
- How does child care influence infant development?

REFLECT

- Imagine that a friend of yours is getting ready to put her baby in child care. What advice would you give to her? Do you think she should stay home with the baby? Why or why not? What type of child care would you recommend?

Socioemotional Development in Infancy

1 EMOTIONAL AND PERSONALITY DEVELOPMENT: DISCUSS THE DEVELOPMENT OF EMOTIONS AND PERSONALITY IN INFANCY

Emotional Development

- Emotion is feeling, or affect, that occurs when a person is in a state or an interaction that is important to him or her. The broad range of emotions includes enthusiasm, joy, and love (positive emotions) and anxiety, anger, and sadness (negative emotions). Psychologists stress that emotions, especially facial expressions of emotions, have a biological foundation. Biological evolution endowed humans to be emotional, but embeddedness in culture and relationships provides diversity in emotional experiences. Emotions are the first language with which parents and infants communicate and play key roles in parent-child relationships. Infants display a number of emotions early in their development, although researchers debate the onset and sequence of these emotions. Lewis distinguishes between primary emotions and self-conscious emotions. Crying is the most important mechanism newborns have for communicating with their world. Babies have at least three types of cries—basic, anger, and pain cries. Controversy swirls about whether babies should be soothed when they cry, although increasingly experts recommend immediately responding in a caring way in the first year. Social smiling occurs as early as 2 months of age. Two fears that infants develop are stranger anxiety and separation from a caregiver (which is reflected in separation protest). As infants develop, it is important for them to engage in emotional regulation.

Temperament

- Temperament is an individual's behavioral style and characteristic way of emotional responding. Chess and Thomas classified infants as (1) easy, (2) difficult, or (3) slow to warm up. Kagan proposed that inhibition to the unfamiliar is an important temperament category. Rothbart and Bates' view of temperament emphasizes this classification: (1) extraversion/surgency, (2) negative affectivity, and (3) effortful control (self-regulation). Physiological characteristics are associated with different temperaments. Children inherit a physiology that biases them to have a particular type of temperament, but through experience they learn to modify their temperament style to some degree. Goodness of fit refers to the match between a child's temperament and the environmental demands the child must cope with. Goodness of fit can be an important aspect of a child's adjustment. Although research evidence is sketchy at this point in time, some general recommendations are that caregivers should (1) be sensitive to the individual characteristics of the child, (2) be flexible in responding to these characteristics, and (3) avoid negative labeling of the child.

Personality Development

- Erikson argued that an infant's first year is characterized by the stage of trust versus mistrust. The infant begins to develop a self-understanding called self-recognition at about 18 months of age. Independence becomes a central theme in the second year of life. Mahler argues that the infant separates herself from her mother and then develops individuation. Erikson stressed that the second year of life is characterized by the stage of autonomy versus shame and doubt.

2 SOCIAL ORIENTATION/UNDERSTANDING AND ATTACHMENT: DESCRIBE SOCIAL ORIENTATION/UNDERSTANDING AND THE DEVELOPMENT OF ATTACHMENT IN INFANCY

Social Orientation/Understanding

- Infants show a strong interest in the social world and are motivated to understand it. Infants orient to the social world early in their development. Face-to-face play with a caregiver begins to occur at about 2 to 3 months of age. Newly developed self-produced locomotion skills significantly expand the infant's ability to initiate social interchanges and explore their social world more independently. Perceiving people as engaging in intentional and goal-directed behavior is an important social cognitive accomplishment and this occurs toward the end of the first year. Social referencing increases in the second year of life.

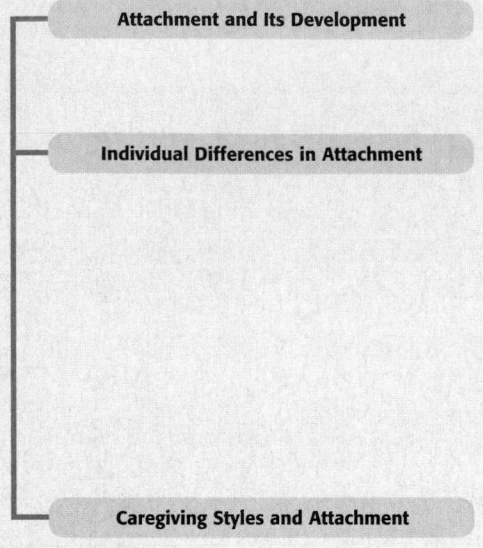

- Attachment is a close emotional bond between two people. In infancy, contact comfort and trust are important in the development of attachment. Bowlby's ethological theory stresses that the caregiver and the infant are biologically predisposed to form an attachment. Attachment develops in four phases during infancy.

- Securely attached babies use the caregiver, usually the mother, as a secure base from which to explore the environment. Three types of insecure attachment are avoidant, resistant, and disorganized. Ainsworth created the Strange Situation, an observational measure of attachment. Ainsworth points out that secure attachment in the first year of life provides an important foundation for psychological development later in life. The strength of the link between early attachment and later development has varied somewhat across studies. Some critics argue that attachment theorists have not given adequate attention to genetics and temperament. Other critics stress that they have not adequately taken into account the diversity of social agents and contexts. Cultural variations in attachment have been found, but in all cultures studied to date secure attachment is the most common classification.

- Caregivers of secure babies are sensitive to the babies' signals and are consistently available to meet their needs. Caregivers of avoidant babies tend to be unavailable or rejecting. Caregivers of resistant babies tend to be inconsistently available to their babies and usually are not very affectionate. Caregivers of disorganized babies often neglect or physically abuse their babies.

3 SOCIAL CONTEXTS: EXPLAIN HOW SOCIAL CONTEXTS INFLUENCE THE INFANT'S DEVELOPMENT

The Family

- The transition to parenthood requires considerable adaptation and adjustment on the part of parents. Children socialize parents just as parents socialize children. Parent-infant synchrony and scaffolding are important aspects of reciprocal socialization. Belsky's model describes direct and indirect effects. The mother's primary role when interacting with the infant is caregiving; the father's is playful interaction.

Child Care

- More U.S. children are in child care now than at any earlier point in history. The quality of child care is uneven, and child care remains a controversial topic. Quality child care can be achieved and seems to have few adverse effects on children. In the NICHD child-care study, infants from low-income families were more likely to receive the lowest quality of care. Also, higher quality of child care was linked with fewer child problems.

KEY TERMS

emotion 181
primary emotions 181
self-conscious emotions 182
basic cry 182
anger cry 182
pain cry 183
reflexive smile 183

social smile 183
stranger anxiety 183
separation protest 183
temperament 185
easy child 185
difficult child 185
slow-to-warm-up child 185

goodness of fit 187
social referencing 192
attachment 192
Strange Situation 193
securely attached babies 194
insecure avoidant
   babies 194

insecure resistant babies 194
insecure disorganized
   babies 194
reciprocal socialization 197
scaffolding 197

KEY PEOPLE

Michael Lewis 181
Joseph Campos 182
John Watson 184
Jacob Gewirtz 184
Mary Ainsworth 184

John Bowlby 184
Alexander Chess and Stella
   Thomas 185
Jerome Kagan 185

Mary Rothbart and John
   Bates 186
Erik Erikson 188
Ross Thompson 188

Margaret Mahler 189
Harry Harlow 192
Jay Belsky 196
Kathleen McCartney 202

E-LEARNING TOOLS

To help you master the material in this chapter, visit the Online Learning Center for *Life-Span Development*, twelfth edition, at **www.mhhe.com/santrockld12**.

Self-Assessment

Connect to **www.mhhe.com/santrockld12** to examine your understanding of infant emotions and socialization by completing the self-assessment, *My Beliefs About Nurturing a Baby's Socioemotional Development*.

Taking It to the Net

Connect to **www.mhhe.com/santrockld12** to research the answers to these questions:

1. Catherine is conducting a class for new parents at a local clinic. What advice should Catherine give the parents about how parenting practices can affect a child's inborn temperament?

2. Justin read about a new concept known as "attachment parenting." What is it, and how can parents engage in it? Do you think it is a good idea? What specifically can parents do to help ensure that their children develop secure attachment?

Video Clips

The Online Learning Center, includes two videos for Chapter 6. The first video is called "Attachment Theory." This segment reviews the three main theories of infant attachment. In an interview, one researcher argues that attachment theory led to a revolution in developmental psychology. The second video is called "Quality Child-Care Indicators." More children are placed in child care today than at any other time in history. This segment addresses some of the common anxieties about possible long-term effects of formal child care.

Health and Well-Being, Parenting, and Education Exercises

Build your decision-making skills by trying your hand at the health and well-being, parenting, and education exercises. Connect to **www.mhhe.com/santrockld12** to research the answers and complete the exercises.

EARLY CHILDHOOD

You are troubled at seeing him spend his early years doing nothing. What! Is it nothing to be happy? Is it nothing to skip, to play, to run about all day long? Never in his life will he be so busy as now.

—JEAN-JACQUES ROUSSEAU
Swiss-Born French Philosopher, 18th Century

In early childhood, our greatest untold poem was being only 4 years old. We skipped and ran and played all the sun long, never in our lives so busy, busy being something we had not quite grasped yet. Who knew our thoughts, which we worked up into small mythologies all our own? Our thoughts and images and drawings took wings. The blossoms of our heart, no wind could touch. Our small world widened as we discovered new refuges and new people. When we said; "I," we meant something totally unique, not to be confused with any other. Section 4 consists of two chapters: "Physical and Cognitive Development in Early Childhood" (Chapter 7) and "Socioemotional Development in Early Childhood" (Chapter 8).

7

*The greatest person
ever known
Is one all poets have
outgrown;
The poetry, innate
and untold,
Of being only four
years old.*

—CHRISTOPHER MORLEY
American Novelist, 20th Century

LEARNING GOALS

◆ Identify physical changes in early childhood.

◆ Describe three views of the cognitive changes that occur in early childhood.

◆ Summarize how language develops in early childhood.

◆ Evaluate different approaches to early childhood education.

PHYSICAL AND COGNITIVE DEVELOPMENT IN EARLY CHILDHOOD

CHAPTER OUTLINE

1 PHYSICAL CHANGES

Body Growth and Change

Motor Development

Nutrition

Illness and Death

2 COGNITIVE CHANGES

Piaget's Preoperational Stage

Vygotsky's Theory

Information Processing

3 LANGUAGE DEVELOPMENT

Understanding Phonology and Morphology

Changes in Syntax and Semantics

Advances in Pragmatics

Young Children's Literacy

4 EARLY CHILDHOOD EDUCATION

Variations in Early Childhood Education

Education for Young Children Who Are Disadvantaged

Controversies in Early Childhood Education

Images of Life-Span Development
Reggio Emilia's Children

The Reggio Emilia approach is an educational program for young children that was developed in the northern Italian city of Reggio Emilia. Children of single parents and children with disabilities have priority in admission; other children are admitted according to a scale of needs. Parents pay on a sliding scale based on income.

The children are encouraged to learn by investigating and exploring topics that interest them. A wide range of stimulating media and materials is available for children to use as they learn music, movement, drawing, painting, sculpting, collages, puppets and disguises, and photography, for example (Strong-Wilson & Ellis, 2007).

In this program, children often explore topics in a group, which fosters a sense of community, respect for diversity, and a collaborative approach to problem solving (Hyson, Copple, & Jones, 2006). Two co-teachers are present to serve as guides for children. The Reggio Emilia teachers consider a project as an adventure, which can start from an adult's suggestion, from a child's idea, or from an event, such as a snowfall or something else unexpected. Every project is based on what the children say and do. The teachers allow children enough time to think and craft a project.

At the core of the Reggio Emilia approach is the image of children who are competent and have rights, especially the right to outstanding care and education. Parent participation is considered essential, and cooperation is a major theme in the schools. Many early childhood education experts believe the Reggio Emilia approach provides a supportive, stimulating context in which children are motivated to explore their world in a competent and confident manner (New, 2005, 2007).

A Reggio Emilia classroom in which young children explore topics that interest them.

PREVIEW

Parents and educators who clearly understand how young children develop can play an active role in creating programs that foster their natural interest in learning, rather than stifling it. In this chapter, we will explore the physical, cognitive, and language changes that typically occur as the toddler develops into the preschooler, and then examine different approaches to early childhood education.

1 PHYSICAL CHANGES

Body Growth and Change · Motor Development · Nutrition · Illness and Death

Remember from Chapter 4 that an infant's growth in the first year is rapid and follows cephalocaudal and proximodistal patterns. Around their first birthday, most infants begin to walk. During an infant's second year, the growth rate begins to slow down, but both gross and fine motor skills progress rapidly. The infant develops a sense of mastery through increased proficiency in walking and running. Improvement in fine motor skills—such as being able to turn the pages of a book one at a time—also contributes to the infant's sense of mastery in the second year. The growth rate continues to slow down in early childhood. Otherwise, we would be a species of giants.

Body Growth and Change

Growth in height and weight is the obvious physical change that characterizes early childhood. Unseen changes in the brain and nervous system are no less significant in preparing children for advances in cognition and language.

Height and Weight   The average child grows $2\frac{1}{2}$ inches in height and gains between 5 and 7 pounds a year during early childhood. As the preschool child grows older, the percentage of increase in height and weight decreases with each additional year. Girls are only slightly smaller and lighter than boys during these years, a difference that continues until puberty. During the preschool years, both boys and girls slim down as the trunks of their bodies lengthen. Although their heads are still somewhat large for their bodies, by the end of the preschool years most children have lost their top-heavy look. Body fat also shows a slow, steady decline during the preschool years. The chubby baby often looks much leaner by the end of early childhood. Girls have more fatty tissue than boys; boys have more muscle tissue.

Growth patterns vary individually. Think back to your preschool years. This was probably the first time you noticed that some children were taller than you, some shorter; some were fatter, some thinner; some were stronger, some weaker. Much of the variation was due to heredity, but environmental experiences were also involved. A review of the height and weight of children around the world concluded that the two most important contributors to height differences are ethnic origin and nutrition (Meredith, 1978). The urban, middle-socioeconomic-status, and firstborn children were taller than rural, lower-socioeconomic-status, and later-born children. In the United States, African American children are taller than White children.

The Brain   One of the most important physical developments during early childhood is the continuing development of the brain and nervous system (Edin & others, 2007; Nelson, 2009). Although the brain continues to grow in early childhood, it does not grow as rapidly as in infancy. By the time children reach 3 years of age, the brain is three-quarters of its adult size. By age 6, the brain has reached about 95 percent of its adult volume (Lenroot & Giedd, 2006). Thus, the brain of a 5-year-old is nearly the size it will be when the child reaches adulthood, but as we will see in later chapters, the development that occurs inside the brain continues through the remaining childhood and adolescent years.

Some of the brain's interior changes involve increases in dendritic connections as well as **myelination**, in which nerve cells are covered and insulated with a layer of fat cells (see Figure 7.1). Myelination has the effect of increasing the speed and efficiency of information traveling through the nervous system (Fair & Schalaggar, 2008). Myelination is important in the development of a number of children's abilities (de Haan & Martinos, 2008). For example, myelination in the areas of the brain related to hand-eye coordination is not complete until about 4 years of age.

Researchers also have discovered that children's brains undergo dramatic anatomical changes between the ages of 3 and 15 (Thompson & others, 2000). By repeatedly

The bodies of 5-year-olds and 2-year-olds are different. Notice that the 5-year-old not only is taller and weighs more, but also has a longer trunk and legs than the 2-year-old. *Can you think of some other physical differences between 2- and 5-year-olds?*

Myelin Sheath   Axon

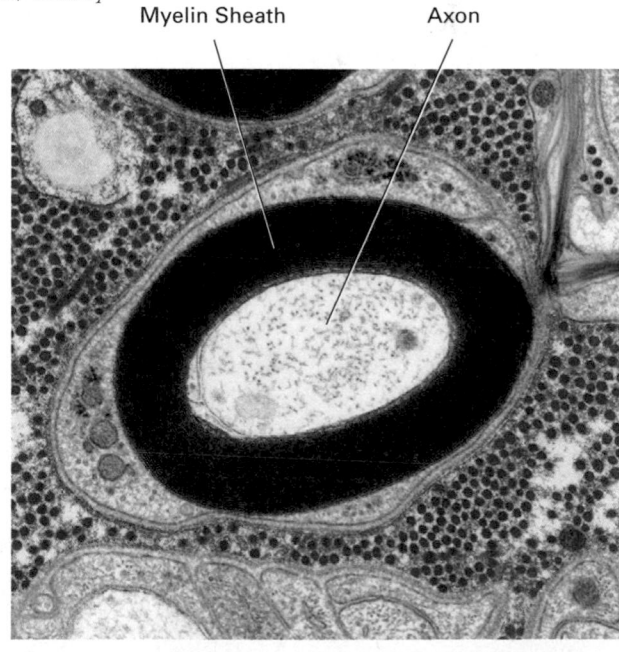

FIGURE 7.1 A Myelinated Nerve Fiber. The myelin sheath, shown in brown, encases the axon (white). This image was produced by an electron microscope that magnified the nerve fiber 12,000 times. *What role does myelination play in the brain's development and children's cognition?*

myelination The process by which the nerve cells are covered and insulated with a layer of fat cells, which increases the speed at which information travels through the nervous system.

obtaining brain scans of the same children for up to four years, they found that the children's brains experience rapid, distinct spurts of growth. The amount of brain material in some areas can nearly double within as little as a year, followed by a drastic loss of tissue as unneeded cells are purged and the brain continues to reorganize itself. The scientists found that the overall size of the brain did not show dramatic growth in the 3- to 15-year age range. However, what did dramatically change were local patterns within the brain. Researchers have found that from 3 to 6 years of age the most rapid growth takes place in the frontal lobe areas involved in planning and organizing new actions, and in maintaining attention to tasks.

Motor Development

Running as fast as you can, falling down, getting right back up and running just as fast as you can . . . building towers with blocks . . . scribbling . . . cutting paper with scissors; during your preschool years, you probably developed the ability to perform all of these activities.

Gross Motor Skills   The preschool child no longer has to make an effort simply to stay upright and to move around. As children move their legs with more confidence and carry themselves more purposefully, moving around in the environment becomes more automatic.

At 3 years of age, children enjoy simple movements, such as hopping, jumping, and running back and forth, just for the sheer delight of performing these activities. They take considerable pride in showing how they can run across a room and jump all of 6 inches. The run-and-jump will win no Olympic gold medals, but for the 3-year-old the activity is a source of considerable pride and accomplishment.

At 4 years of age, children are still enjoying the same kind of activities, but they have become more adventurous. They scramble over low jungle gyms as they display their athletic prowess.

At 5 years of age, children are even more adventuresome than when they were 4. It is not unusual for self-assured 5-year-olds to perform hair-raising stunts on practically any climbing object. Five-year-olds run hard and enjoy races with each other and their parents.

Fine Motor Skills   At 3 years of age, although children have had the ability to pick up the tiniest objects between their thumb and forefinger for some time, they are still somewhat clumsy at it. Three-year-olds can build surprisingly high block towers, each block placed with intense concentration but often not in a completely straight line. When 3-year-olds play with a simple jigsaw puzzle, they are rather rough in placing the pieces. Even when they recognize the hole a piece fits into, they are not very precise in positioning the piece. They often try to force the piece in the hole or pat it vigorously.

By 4 years of age, children's fine motor coordination has improved substantially and become much more precise. Sometimes 4-year-old children have trouble building high towers with blocks because, in their desire to place each of the blocks perfectly, they may upset those already stacked. By age 5, children's fine motor coordination has improved further. Hand, arm, and body all move together under better command of the eye. Mere towers no longer interest the 5-year-old, who now wants to build a house or a church, complete with steeple, though adults might still need to be told what each finished project is meant to be.

Nutrition

Eating habits are important aspects of development during early childhood (Black & Hurley, 2009; Schiff, 2009; Wardlaw & Smith, 2009). What children eat affects their skeletal growth, body shape, and susceptibility to disease.

How do gross motor skills change in early childhood?

Overweight Young Children   Being overweight has become a serious health problem in early childhood, and many parents do not recognize that their children are overweight. (Bolling & Daniels, 2008; Reilly, 2009; Wabitsch, 2009). For example, one recent study of parents with 2- to 17-year-old children found that few parents of overweight children perceived their children to be too heavy and were not worried about the children's weight (Eckstein & others, 2006).

Young children's eating behavior is strongly influenced by their caregivers' behavior (Black & Hurley, 2007, 2009; Ventura & others, 2009). Young children's eating behavior improves when caregivers eat with children on a predictable schedule, model eating healthy food, make mealtimes pleasant occasions, and engage in certain feeding styles. Distractions from television, family arguments, and competing activities should be minimized so children can focus on eating. A sensitive/responsive caregiver feeding style, in which the caregiver is nurturant, provides clear information about what is expected, and appropriately responds to children's cues, is recommended (Black & Hurley, 2007, 2009). Forceful and restrictive caregiver behaviors are not recommended. For example, a restrictive feeding style is linked to children being overweight (Black & Lozoff, 2008).

What are some trends in the eating habits and weight of young children?

The Centers for Disease Control and Prevention (2008) has categories for obesity, overweight, and at risk for being overweight. These categories are determined by body mass index (BMI), which is computed by a formula that takes into account height and weight. Only children and adolescents at or above the 97th percentile are classified as obese; those at or above the 95th percentile as overweight; and those at or above the 85th percentile as at risk for being overweight.

The percentages of young children who are overweight or at risk for being overweight in the United States has increased dramatically in recent decades, and the percentages are likely to grow unless changes occur in children's lifestyles (Ebbeling & Ludwig, 2008). A recent study revealed that in 2003 to 2006, 11 percent of U.S. 2- to 19-year-olds were obese, 16 percent were overweight, and 38 percent were at risk for being overweight (Ogden, Carroll, & Flegal, 2008). The good news from this large-scale study is that the percentages in these categories have started to level off rather than increase, as they had been doing in the last several decades.

The risk for overweight young children of continuing to be overweight when they become older was documented in another recent study (Nader & others, 2006). The body mass index of more than 1,000 children was obtained from their health records at seven different times from 2 to 12 years of age. Eighty percent of the children who were at risk for being overweight at 3 years of age were also at risk for being overweight or were overweight at 12 years of age. A recent study of 3-year-old children in low-income, urban families revealed that young Latino children were twice as likely to be overweight as African American and non-Latino White young children (Kimbro, Brooks-Gunn, & McLanahan, 2006).

One comparison of 34 countries revealed that the United States had the second highest rate of child obesity (Janssen & others, 2005). Childhood obesity contributes to a number of health problems in young children (Pinto & others, 2007). For example, physicians are now seeing type 2 (adult-onset) diabetes (a condition directly linked with obesity and a low level of fitness) in children as young as 5 years of age (Danne & Becker, 2007).

Routine physical activity should be a daily occurrence for young children (Robbins, Powers, & Burgess, 2008). The child's life should be centered around activities, not meals.

- Preschool children's physical activity was enhanced by family members engaging in sports together and by parents' perception that it was safe for their children to play outside (Beets & Foley, 2008).

- Preschool children's physical activity varied greatly across different child-care centers (Bower & others, 2008). Active opportunities, presence of fixed and portable play equipment, and physical activity training were linked to preschool children's higher physical activity in the centers.

- Incorporation of a "move and learn" physical activity curriculum increased the activity level of 3- to 5-year-old children in a half-day preschool program (Trost, Fees, & Dzewaltowski, 2008).

To read about a research study focused on the importance of activities in young children's lives, see the *Research in Life-Span Development* interlude.

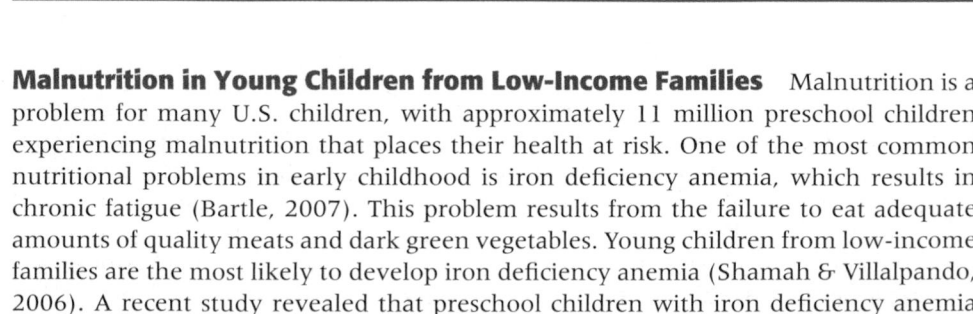

Research in Life-Span Development
Physical Activity in Young Children Attending Preschools

One study examined the activity level of 281 3- to 5-year-olds in nine preschools (Pate & others, 2004). The preschool children wore accelerometers, a small activity monitor, for four to five hours a day. Height and weight assessments of the children were made to calculate their body mass index (BMI).

Guidelines recommend that preschool children engage in two hours of physical activity per day, divided into one hour of structured activity and one hour of unstructured free-play (National Association for Sport and Physical Education, 2002). In this study, the young children participated in an average of 7.7 minutes per hour of moderate to vigorous activity, usually in a block of time when they were outside. Over the course of eight hours of a preschool day, these children would get approximately one hour of moderate and vigorous physical activity, only about 50 percent of the amount recommended. The researchers concluded that young children are unlikely to engage in another hour per day of moderate and vigorous physical activity outside their eight hours spent in preschool and thus are not getting adequate opportunities for physical activity.

Gender and age differences characterized the preschool children's physical activity. Boys were more likely to engage in moderate or vigorous physical activity than girls. Four- and five-year-old children were more likely to be sedentary than three-year-old children.

The young children's physical activity also varied according to the particular preschool they attended. The time that they participated in moderate and vigorous physical activity ranged from 4.4 to 10.2 minutes per hour across the nine preschools. Thus, the policies and practices of particular preschools influence the extent to which children engage in physical activity. The researchers concluded that young children need more vigorous play and organized activities. Unfortunately, there is a trend toward reducing time for physical activity, especially eliminating recess, in U.S. elementary schools that is trickling down to kindergarten and preschool programs. This decrease is part of a larger trend that involves narrowing early childhood programs to focus on academic learning and moving away from more comprehensive programs that focus on the whole child (Hyson, 2007). We will discuss this topic further later in this chapter.

How much physical activity should preschool children engage in per day?

Malnutrition in Young Children from Low-Income Families   Malnutrition is a problem for many U.S. children, with approximately 11 million preschool children experiencing malnutrition that places their health at risk. One of the most common nutritional problems in early childhood is iron deficiency anemia, which results in chronic fatigue (Bartle, 2007). This problem results from the failure to eat adequate amounts of quality meats and dark green vegetables. Young children from low-income families are the most likely to develop iron deficiency anemia (Shamah & Villalpando, 2006). A recent study revealed that preschool children with iron deficiency anemia were slower to display positive affect and touch novel toys for the first time than their nonanemic counterparts (Lozoff & others, 2007).

Many children in low-income families do not get essential amounts of iron, vitamins, or protein (Bryce & others, 2008; Cunningham-Sabo & others, 2008). A recent study revealed that young children who had lower intakes of fresh fruits and vegetables cooked in olive oil and higher intakes of canned fruit and vegetables, and processed salad dressing, were more likely to come from lower-income, less-educated families than higher-income, more-educated families (Sausenthaler & others, 2007). In part, to address this problem in the United States, the Special Supplemental Nutrition Program for Women, Infants, and Children (WIC) serves approximately 7,500,000 participants in the United States. Positive influences on young children's nutrition and health have been found for participants in WIC (Herman & others, 2008). For example, one study found that participating in WIC was linked with a lower risk for being overweight in young Mexican American children (Melgar-Quinonez & Kaiser, 2004). Another study revealed that WIC children who were anemic improved the most when they did not eat snacks and dried fruits (Swanson & others, 2007).

Illness and Death

What are the greatest risks to the health of young children in the United States? How pervasive is death among young children around the world?

The United States   Young children's active and exploratory nature, coupled with being unaware of danger in many instances, often puts them in situations in which they are at risk for injuries (Boles & Robert, 2008; Schwebel, 2008). In the United States, motor vehicle accidents are the leading cause of death in young children, followed by cancer and cardiovascular disease (National Vital Statistics Report, 2004) (see Figure 7.2). In addition to motor vehicle accidents, other accidental deaths in children involve drowning, falls, burns, and poisoning (Bessey & others, 2006).

Children's safety is influenced not only by their own skills and safety behaviors but also by characteristics of their family and home, school and peers, and the community's actions (Snowdon & others, 2008; Tinsley, 2003). Figure 7.3 describes steps that can be taken in each of these contexts to enhance children's safety and prevent injury (Sleet & Mercy, 2003).

Parental smoking is another major danger to children (Martinez-Donate & others, 2007). Estimates indicate that approximately 22 percent of children and adolescents in the United States are exposed to tobacco smoke in the home. An increasing number of studies reach the conclusion that children are at risk for health problems when they live in homes in which a parent smokes (Carlsen & Carlsen, 2008). Children exposed to tobacco smoke in the home are more likely to develop wheezing symptoms and asthma than children in nonsmoking homes (Herrmann, King, & Weitzman, 2008).

Another concern is the poor health status of many young children from low-income families in the United States (Larson & others, 2008; Ruel & others, 2008). Children in poverty face a higher risk for lead poisoning than children living in higher-socioeconomic conditions (Canfield & Jusko, 2008). An estimated 3 million U.S. children under 6 years of age are thought to be at risk for lead poisoning (Moya, Bearer, & Etzel, 2004).

The State of Illness and Health of the World's Children   Poverty in the United States is dwarfed by poverty in developing countries around the world. Each year UNICEF produces a report entitled *The State of the World's Children*. In a recent report, UNICEF (2006) concluded that the under-5 mortality rate is the result of a wide range of factors, including the nutritional health and health knowledge of mothers, the level of immunization, dehydration, availability of maternal and child health services, income and food availability in the family, availability of clean water and safe sanitation, and the overall safety of the child's environment.

The devastating effects on the health of young children occur in countries where poverty rates are high (UNICEF, 2008). The poor are the majority in nearly one of every five nations in the world. They often experience lives of hunger, malnutrition, illness, inadequate access to health care, unsafe water, and a lack of protection from harm (Amuna & Zotor, 2008; Bhutta & others, 2008).

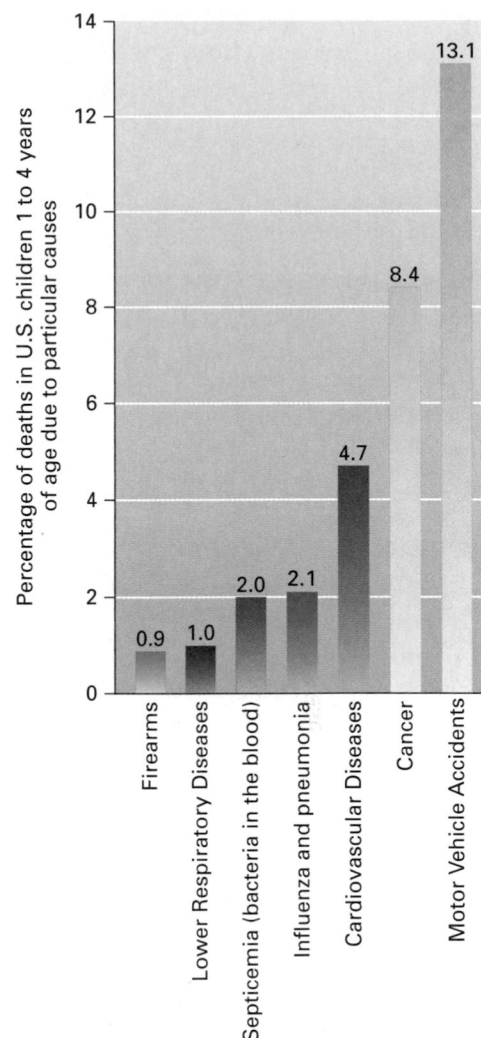

FIGURE 7.2 Main Causes of Death in Children 1 through 4 Years of Age. These figures show the percentage of deaths in U.S. children 1 to 4 years of age due to particular causes in 2002 (National Vital Statistics Reports, 2004).

Individual

Development of social skills and ability to regulate emotions

Impulse control (such as not darting out into a street to retrieve a ball)

Frequent use of personal protection (such as bike helmets and safety seats)

Family/Home

High awareness and knowledge of child management and parenting skills

Frequent parent protective behaviors (such as use of child safety seats)

Presence of home safety equipment (such as smoke alarms and cabinet locks)

School/Peers

Promotion of home/school partnerships

Absence of playground hazards

Injury prevention and safety promotion policies and programs

Community

Availability of positive activities for children and their parents

Active surveillance of environmental hazards

Effective prevention policies in place (such as pool fencing)

FIGURE 7.3 Characteristics That Enhance Young Children's Safety. In each context of a child's life, steps can be taken to create conditions that enhance the child's safety and reduce the likelihood of injury. *How are the contexts listed in the figure related to Bronfenbrenner's theory (described in Chapter 1)?*

Many children in impoverished countries die before reaching the age of 5 from dehydration and malnutrition brought about by diarrhea. *What are some of the other main causes of death in young children around the world?*

In the last decade, there has been a dramatic increase in the number of young children who have died because of HIV/AIDS transmitted to them by their parents (UNICEF, 2008). Deaths in young children due to HIV/AIDS especially occur in countries with high rates of poverty and low levels of education (Boeving & Forsyth, 2008). For example, the uneducated are four times more likely to believe that there is no way to avoid AIDS and three times more likely to be unaware that the virus can be transmitted from mother to child (UNICEF, 2006).

Many of the deaths of young children around the world can be prevented by a reduction in poverty and improvements in nutrition, sanitation, education, and health services (UNICEF, 2006, 2007, 2008).

Review and Reflect: Learning Goal 1

 Identify Physical Changes in Early Childhood

REVIEW

- How does the body grow and change during early childhood?
- What changes take place in motor development during early childhood?
- What role does nutrition play in early childhood?
- What are some major causes of illness and death among young children in the United States and around the world?

REFLECT

- What were your eating habits as a young child? In what ways are they similar or different to your current eating habits? Were your early eating habits a forerunner of whether or not you have weight problems today?

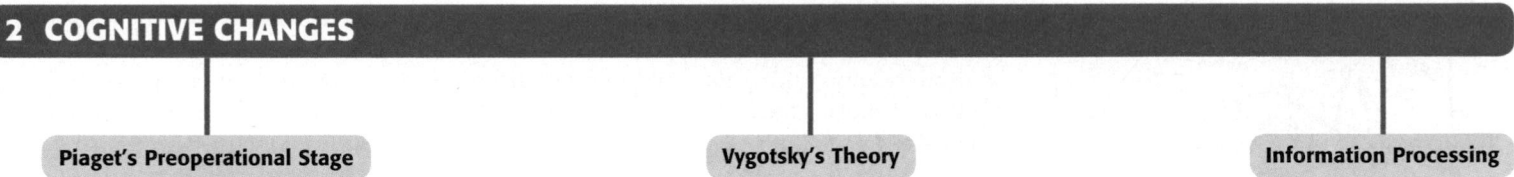

2 COGNITIVE CHANGES

Piaget's Preoperational Stage   **Vygotsky's Theory**   **Information Processing**

The cognitive world of the preschool child is creative, free, and fanciful. Preschool children's imaginations work overtime, and their mental grasp of the world improves. Our coverage of cognitive development in early childhood focuses on three theories: Piaget's, Vygotsky's, and information processing.

Piaget's Preoperational Stage

Remember from Chapter 6 that during Piaget's first stage of development, the senso-rimotor stage, the infant progresses in the ability to organize and coordinate sensations and perceptions with physical movements and actions. The **preoperational stage**, which lasts from approximately 2 to 7 years of age, is the second Piagetian stage. In this stage, children begin to represent the world with words, images, and drawings. They form stable concepts and begin to reason. At the same time, the young child's cognitive world is dominated by egocentrism and magical beliefs.

Because Piaget called this stage "preoperational," it might sound like an unimportant waiting period. Not so. However, the label *preoperational* emphasizes that the child does not yet perform **operations**, which are reversible mental actions; they allow children to do mentally what before they could do only physically. Mentally adding and subtracting numbers are examples of operations. *Preoperational thought* is the beginning of the ability to reconstruct in thought what has been established in behavior. It can be divided into two substages: the symbolic function substage and the intuitive thought substage.

The Symbolic Function Substage   The **symbolic function substage** is the first substage of preoperational thought, occurring roughly between the ages of 2 and 4. In this substage, the young child gains the ability to mentally represent an object that is not present. This ability vastly expands the child's mental world (Carlson & Zelazo, 2008). Young children use scribble designs to represent people, houses, cars, clouds, and so on; they begin to use language and engage in pretend play. However, although young children make distinct progress during this substage, their thought still has important limitations, two of which are egocentrism and animism.

Egocentrism is the inability to distinguish between one's own perspective and someone else's perspective. Piaget and Barbel Inhelder (1969) initially studied young children's egocentrism by devising the three mountains task (see Figure 7.4). The child walks around the model of the mountains and becomes familiar with what the mountains look like from different perspectives, and she can see that there are different objects on

preoperational stage Piaget's second stage, lasting from about 2 to 7 years of age, during which children begin to represent the world with words, images, and drawings and symbolic thought goes beyond simple connections of sensory information and physical action; stable concepts are formed, mental reasoning emerges, egocentrism is present, and magical beliefs are constructed.

operations In Piaget's theory, these are reversible mental actions that allow children to do mentally what they formerly did physically.

symbolic function substage Piaget's first substage of preoperational thought, in which the child gains the ability to mentally represent an object that is not present (between about 2 and 4 years of age).

egocentrism The inability to distinguish between one's own perspective and someone else's (salient feature of the first substage of preoperational thought).

FIGURE 7.4 The Three Mountains Task. View 1 shows the child's perspective from where he or she is sitting. View 2 is an example of one of the photographs the child would be shown, along with other photographs taken from different perspectives. It shows what the mountains look like to a person sitting at spot B. When asked what a view of the mountains looks like from position B, the preoperational child selects a photograph taken from location A, the child's view at the time. A child who thinks in a preoperational way cannot take the perspective of a person sitting at another spot.

Model of Mountains

Child seated here

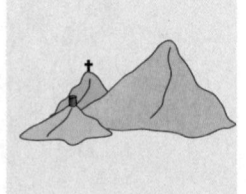

Photo 1
(View from A)

Photo 2
(View from B)

Photo 3
(View from C)

Photo 4
(View from D)

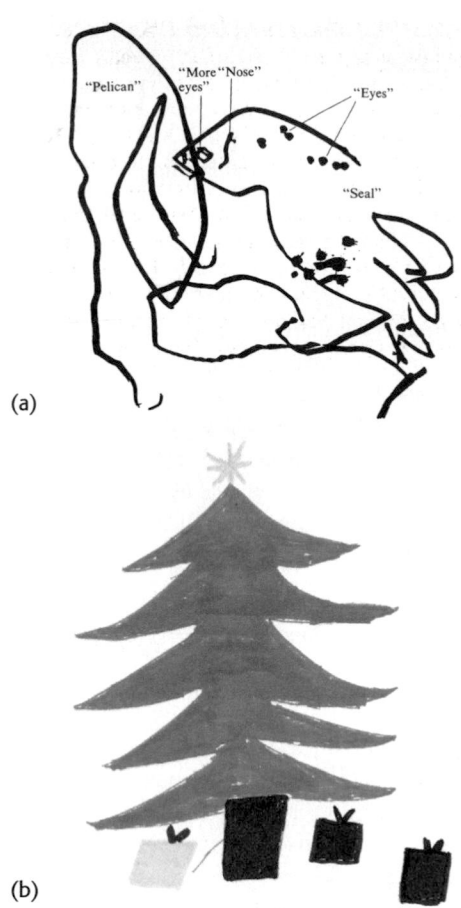

(a)

(b)

FIGURE 7.5 The Symbolic Drawings of Young Children. (*a*) A 3½-year-old's symbolic drawing. Halfway into his drawing, the 3½-year-old artist said it was a "pelican kissing a seal." (*b*) This 11-year-old's drawing is neater and more realistic but also less inventive.

the mountains. The child is then seated on one side of the table on which the mountains are placed. The experimenter moves a doll to different locations around the table, at each location asking the child to select from a series of photos the one photo that most accurately reflects the view that the doll is seeing. Children in the preoperational stage often pick their own view rather than the doll's view. Preschool children frequently show the ability to take another's perspective on some tasks but not others.

Animism, another limitation of preoperational thought, is the belief that inanimate objects have lifelike qualities and are capable of action. A young child might show animism by saying, "That tree pushed the leaf off, and it fell down," or "The sidewalk made me mad; it made me fall down." A young child who uses animism fails to distinguish the appropriate occasions for using human and nonhuman perspectives.

Possibly because young children are not very concerned about reality, their drawings are fanciful and inventive. Suns are blue, skies are yellow, and cars float on clouds in their symbolic, imaginative world. One 3½-year-old looked at a scribble he had just drawn and described it as a pelican kissing a seal (see Figure 7.5a). The symbolism is simple but strong, like abstractions found in some modern art. Twentieth-century Spanish artist Pablo Picasso commented, "I used to draw like Raphael but it has taken me a lifetime to draw like young children." In the elementary school years, a child's drawings become more realistic, neat, and precise (see Figure 7.5b). Suns are yellow, skies are blue, and cars travel on roads (Winner, 1986).

The Intuitive Thought Substage The **intuitive thought substage** is the second substage of preoperational thought, occurring between approximately 4 and 7 years of age. In this substage, children begin to use primitive reasoning and want to know the answers to all sorts of questions. Consider 4-year-old Tommy, who is at the beginning of the intuitive thought substage. Although he is starting to develop his own ideas about the world he lives in, his ideas are still simple, and he is not very good at thinking things out. He has difficulty understanding events that he knows are taking place but which he cannot see. His fantasized thoughts bear little resemblance to reality. He cannot yet answer the question "What if?" in any reliable way. For example, he has only a vague idea of what would happen if a car were to hit him. He also has difficulty negotiating traffic because he cannot do the mental calculations necessary to estimate whether an approaching car will hit him when he crosses the road.

By the age of 5, children have just about exhausted the adults around them with "why" questions. The child's questions signal the emergence of interest in reasoning and in figuring out why things are the way they are. Following are some samples of the questions children ask during the questioning period of 4 to 6 years of age (Elkind, 1976): "What makes you grow up?" "Who was the mother when everybody was a baby?" "Why do leaves fall?" "Why does the sun shine?"

Piaget called this substage *intuitive* because young children seem so sure about their knowledge and understanding yet are unaware of how they know what they know. That is, they know something but know it without the use of rational thinking.

Centration and the Limits of Preoperational Thought One limitation of preoperational thought is **centration**, a centering of attention on one characteristic to the exclusion of all others. Centration is most clearly evidenced in young children's lack of **conservation**, the awareness that

"I still don't have all the answers, but I'm beginning to ask the right questions."
© The New Yorker Collection, 1989, Lee Lorenz from cartoonbank.com. All Rights Reserved.

animism The belief that inanimate objects have lifelike qualities and are capable of action.

intuitive thought substage Piaget's second substage of preoperational thought, in which children begin to use primitive reasoning and want to know the answers to all sorts of questions (between 4 and 7 years of age).

centration The focusing of attention on one characteristic to the exclusion of all others.

conservation In Piaget's theory, awareness that altering an object's or a substance's appearance does not change its basic properties.

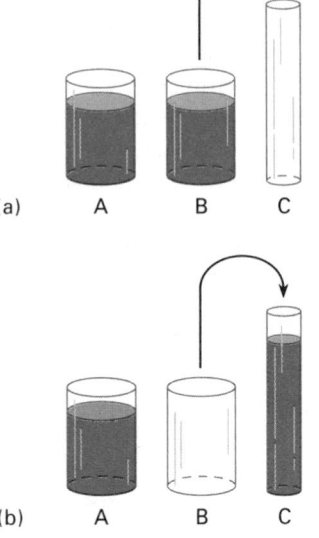

(a) A   B   C

(b) A   B   C

FIGURE 7.6 Piaget's Conservation Task.
The beaker test is a well-known Piagetian test to determine whether a child can think operationally—that is, can mentally reverse actions and show conservation of the substance. (*a*) Two identical beakers are presented to the child. Then the experimenter pours the liquid from B into C, which is taller and thinner than A or B. (*b*) The child is asked if these beakers (A and C) have the same amount of liquid. The preoperational child says "no." When asked to point to the beaker that has more liquid, the preoperational child points to the tall, thin beaker.

altering an object's or a substance's appearance does not change its basic properties. For example, to adults, it is obvious that a certain amount of liquid stays the same, regardless of a container's shape. But this is not at all obvious to young children. Instead, they are struck by the height of the liquid in the container; they focus on that characteristic to the exclusion of others.

The situation that Piaget devised to study conservation is his most famous task. In the conservation task, children are presented with two identical beakers, each filled to the same level with liquid (see Figure 7.6). They are asked if these beakers have the same amount of liquid, and they usually say yes. Then the liquid from one beaker is poured into a third beaker, which is taller and thinner than the first two. The children are then asked if the amount of liquid in the tall, thin beaker is equal to that which remains in one of the original beakers. Children who are less than 7 or 8 years old usually say no and justify their answers in terms of the differing height or width of the beakers. Older children usually answer yes and justify their answers appropriately ("If you poured the water back, the amount would still be the same").

In Piaget's theory, failing the conservation-of-liquid task is a sign that children are at the preoperational stage of cognitive development. The failure demonstrates not only centration but also an inability to mentally reverse actions. For example, in the conservation of matter example shown in Figure 7.7, preoperational children say that

FIGURE 7.7 Some Dimensions of Conservation: Number, Matter, and Length.
What characteristics of preoperational thought do children demonstrate when they fail these conservation tasks?

Type of Conservation	Initial Presentation	Manipulation	Preoperational Child's Answer
Number	Two identical rows of objects are shown to the child, who agrees they have the same number.	One row is lengthened and the child is asked whether one row now has more objects.	Yes, the longer row.
Matter	Two identical balls of clay are shown to the child. The child agrees that they are equal.	The experimenter changes the shape of one of the balls and asks the child whether they still contain equal amounts of clay.	No, the longer one has more.
Length	Two sticks are aligned in front of the child. The child agrees that they are the same length.	The experimenter moves one stick to the right, then asks the child if they are equal in length.	No, the one on the top is longer.

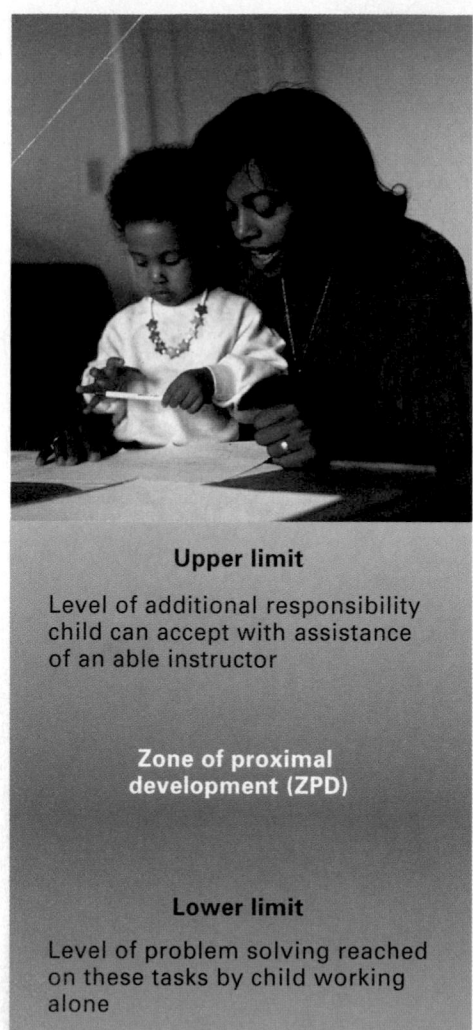

Upper limit

Level of additional responsibility child can accept with assistance of an able instructor

Zone of proximal development (ZPD)

Lower limit

Level of problem solving reached on these tasks by child working alone

FIGURE 7.8 Vygotsky's Zone of Proximal Development. Vygotsky's zone of proximal development has a lower limit and an upper limit. Tasks in the ZPD are too difficult for the child to perform alone. They require assistance from an adult or a more-skilled child. As children experience the verbal instruction or demonstration, they organize the information in their existing mental structures, so they can eventually perform the skill or task alone.

zone of proximal development (ZPD) Vygotsky's term for tasks too difficult for children to master alone but that can be mastered with the assistance of adults or more-skilled children.

the longer shape has more clay because they assume that "longer is more." Preoperational children cannot mentally reverse the clay-rolling process to see that the amount of clay is the same in both the shorter ball shape and the longer stick shape.

In addition to failing to conserve volume, preoperational children also fail to conserve number, matter, length, and area. However, children often vary in their performance on different conservation tasks. Thus, a child might be able to conserve volume but not number.

Some developmentalists disagree with Piaget's estimate of when children's conservation skills emerge. For example, Rochel Gelman (1969) showed that when the child's attention to relevant aspects of the conservation task is improved, the child is more likely to conserve. Gelman has also demonstrated that attentional training on one dimension, such as number, improves the preschool child's performance on another dimension, such as mass. Thus, Gelman argues that conservation appears earlier than Piaget thought and that attention is especially important in explaining conservation.

Vygotsky's Theory

Piaget's theory is a major developmental theory. Another developmental theory that focuses on children's cognition is Vygotsky's theory. Like Piaget, Vygotsky (1962) emphasized that children actively construct their knowledge and understanding. In Piaget's theory, children develop ways of thinking and understanding by their actions and interactions with the physical world. In Vygotsky's theory, children are more often described as social creatures than in Piaget's theory. They develop their ways of thinking and understanding primarily through social interaction. Their cognitive development depends on the tools provided by society, and their minds are shaped by the cultural context in which they live (Cole & Gajdamaschko, 2007; Holzman, 2009).

We briefly described Vygotsky's theory in Chapter 1. Here we take a closer look at his ideas about how children learn and his view of the role of language in cognitive development.

The Zone of Proximal Development   Vygotsky's belief in the importance of social influences, especially instruction, on children's cognitive development is reflected in his concept of the zone of proximal development. **Zone of proximal development (ZPD)** is Vygotsky's term for the range of tasks that are too difficult for the child to master alone but that can be learned with guidance and assistance of adults or more-skilled children. Thus, the lower limit of the ZPD is the level of skill reached by the child working independently. The upper limit is the level of additional responsibility the child can accept with the assistance of an able instructor (see Figure 7.8). The ZPD captures the child's cognitive skills that are in the process of maturing and can be accomplished only with the assistance of a more-skilled person (Alvarez & del Rio, 2007; Gauvain & Perez, 2007). Vygotsky (1962) called these the "buds" or "flowers" of development, to distinguish them from the "fruits" of development, which the child already can accomplish independently.

Scaffolding   Closely linked to the idea of the ZPD is the concept of scaffolding. *Scaffolding* means changing the level of support. Over the course of a teaching session, a more-skilled person (a teacher or advanced peer) adjusts the amount of guidance to fit the child's current performance (Daniels, 2007; de Vries, 2005). When the student is learning a new task, the skilled person may use direct instruction. As the student's competence increases, less guidance is given.

Dialogue is an important tool of scaffolding in the zone of proximal development (Tappan, 1998). Vygotsky viewed children as having rich but unsystematic, disorganized, and spontaneous concepts. In a dialogue, these concepts meet with the skilled helper's more systematic, logical, and rational concepts. As a result, the child's concepts become more systematic, logical, and rational. For example, a dialogue might take place between a teacher and a child when the teacher uses scaffolding to help a child understand a concept like "transportation."

Language and Thought   The use of dialogue as a tool for scaffolding is only one example of the important role of language in a child's development. According to Vygotsky, children use speech not only for social communication, but also to help them solve tasks. Vygotsky (1962) further believed that young children use language to plan, guide, and monitor their behavior. This use of language for self-regulation is called *private speech*. For Piaget private speech is egocentric and immature, but for Vygotsky it is an important tool of thought during the early childhood years (John-Steiner, 2007; Wertsch, 2007).

Vygotsky said that language and thought initially develop independently of each other and then merge. He emphasized that all mental functions have external, or social, origins. Children must use language to communicate with others before they can focus inward on their own thoughts. Children also must communicate externally and use language for a long period of time before they can make the transition from external to internal speech. This transition period occurs between 3 and 7 years of age and involves talking to oneself. After a while, the self-talk becomes second nature to children, and they can act without verbalizing. When this occurs, children have internalized their egocentric speech in the form of *inner speech*, which becomes their thoughts.

Lev Vygotsky (1896–1934), shown here with his daughter, reasoned that children's cognitive development is advanced through social interaction with more-skilled individuals embedded in a sociocultural backdrop. *How is Vygotsky's theory different from Piaget's?*

Vygotsky reasoned that children who use a lot of private speech are more socially competent than those who don't. He argued that private speech represents an early transition in becoming more socially communicative. For Vygotsky, when young children talk to themselves, they are using language to govern their behavior and guide themselves. For example, a child working on a puzzle might say to herself, "Which pieces should I put together first? I'll try those green ones first. Now I need some blue ones. No, that blue one doesn't fit there. I'll try it over here."

Piaget maintained that self-talk is egocentric and reflects immaturity. However, researchers have found support for Vygotsky's view that private speech plays a positive role in children's development (Winsler, Carlton, & Barry, 2000). Researchers have found that children use private speech more when tasks are difficult, following errors, and when they are not sure how to proceed (Berk, 1994). They also have revealed that children who use private speech are more attentive and improve their performance more than children who do not use private speech (Berk & Spuhl, 1995).

Teaching Strategies   Vygotsky's theory has been embraced by many teachers and has been successfully applied to education (Daniels, 2007; Holzman, 2009). Here are some ways Vygotsky's theory can be incorporated in classrooms:

1. *Assess the child's ZPD.* Like Piaget, Vygotsky did not suggest that formal, standardized tests are the best way to assess children's learning. Rather, Vygotsky argued that assessment should focus on determining the child's zone of proximal development. The skilled helper presents the child with tasks of varying difficulty to determine the best level at which to begin instruction.

2. *Use the child's ZPD in teaching.* Teaching should begin toward the zone's upper limit, so that the child can reach the goal with help and move to a higher level of skill and knowledge. Offer just enough assistance. You might ask, "What can I do to help you?" Or simply observe the child's intentions and attempts and provide support when needed. When the child hesitates, offer encouragement. And encourage the child to practice the skill. You may watch and appreciate the child's practice or offer support when the child forgets what to do.

How can Vygotsky's ideas be applied to educating children?

3. *Use more-skilled peers as teachers.* Remember that it is not just adults who are important in helping children learn. Children also benefit from the support and guidance of more-skilled children (John-Steiner, 2007).

4. *Monitor and encourage children's use of private speech.* Be aware of the developmental change from externally talking to oneself when solving a problem during the preschool years to privately talking to oneself in the early elementary school years. In the elementary school years, encourage children to internalize and self-regulate their talk to themselves.

5. *Place instruction in a meaningful context.* Educators today are moving away from abstract presentations of material, instead providing students with opportunities to experience learning in real-world settings. For example, instead of just memorizing math formulas, students work on math problems with real-world implications.

6. *Transform the classroom with Vygotskian ideas.* What does a Vygotskian classroom look like? The Kamehameha Elementary Education Program (KEEP) is based on Vygotsky's theory (Tharp, 1994). The ZPD is the key element of instruction in this program. Children might read a story and then interpret its meaning. Many of the learning activities take place in small groups. All children spend at least 20 minutes each morning in a setting called "Center One." In this context, scaffolding is used to improve children's literary skills. The instructor asks questions, responds to students' queries, and builds on the ideas that students generate. Thousands of children from low-income families have attended KEEP public schools—in Hawaii, on an Arizona Navajo Indian reservation, and in Los Angeles. Compared with a control group of non-KEEP children, the KEEP children participated more actively in classroom discussion, were more attentive in class, and had higher reading achievement (Tharp & Gallimore, 1988).

The *Applications in Life-Span Development* interlude further explores the implications of Vygotsky's theory for children's education.

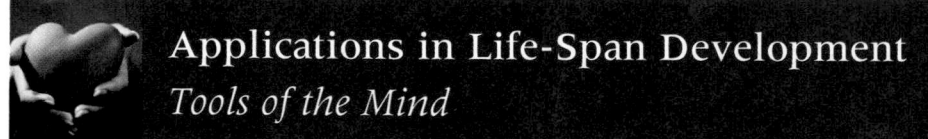

Applications in Life-Span Development
Tools of the Mind

Tools of the Mind is an early childhood education curriculum that emphasizes children's development of self-regulation and the cognitive foundations of literacy (Hyson, Copple, & Jones, 2006). The curriculum was created by Elena Bodrova and Deborah Leong (2007) and has been implemented in more than 200 classrooms. Most of the children in the Tools of the Mind programs are at risk because of their living circumstances, which in many instances involve poverty and other difficult conditions such as being homeless and having parents with drug problems.

Tools of the Mind is grounded in Vygotsky's (1962) theory with special attention given to cultural tools and developing self-regulation, the zone of proximal development, scaffolding, private speech, shared activity, and play as important activity. In a Tools of the Mind classroom, dramatic play has a central role. Teachers guide children in creating themes that are based on the children's interests, such as treasure hunt, store, hospital, and restaurant. Teachers also incorporate field trips, visitor presentations, videos, and books in the development of children's play. They also help children develop a play plan, which increases the maturity of their play. Play plans describe what the children expect to do in the play period, including the imaginary context, roles, and props to be used. The play plans increase the quality of their play and self-regulation.

Scaffolding writing is another important theme in the Tools of the Mind classroom. Teachers guide children in planning their own message by drawing a line to stand for each word the child says. Children then repeat the message, pointing to each line as they say the word. Then, the child writes on the lines, trying to represent each word with some letters or symbols. Figure 7.9 shows how the scaffolding writing process improved a 5-year-old child's writing over the course of two months.

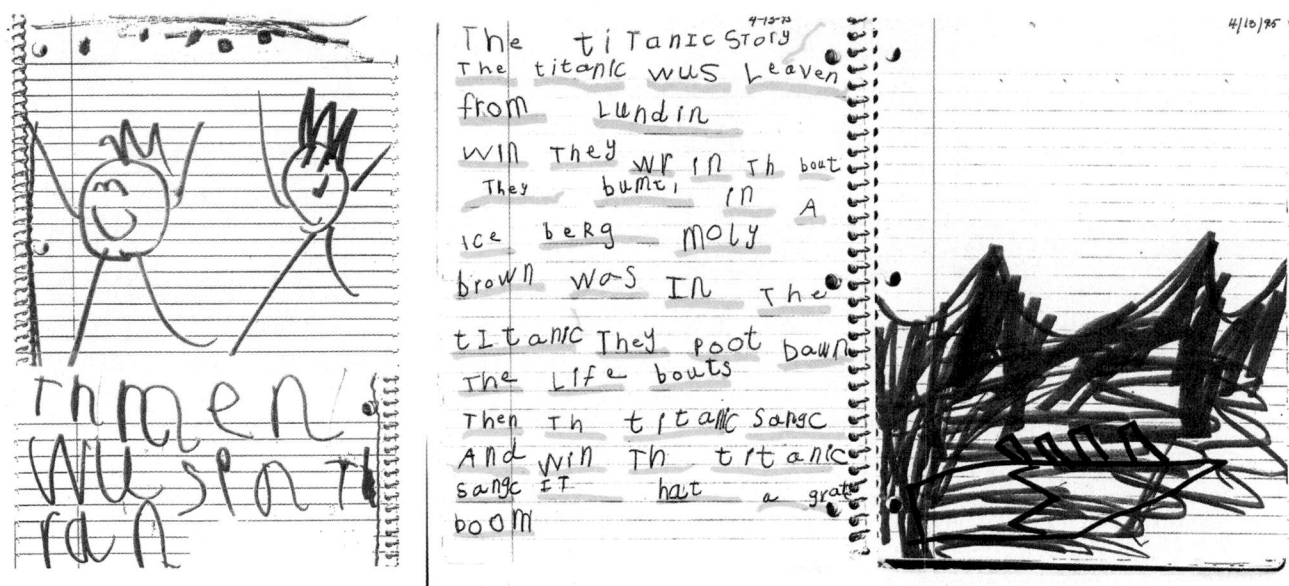

(a) Five-year-old Aaron's independent journal writing prior to using the scaffolded writing technique.

(b) Aaron's journal two months after using the scaffolded writing technique.

FIGURE 7.9 Writing Progress of a 5-Year-Old Boy Over Two Months Using the Scaffolding Writing Process in Tools of the Mind

Research assessments of children's writing in Tools of the Mind classrooms revealed that they have more advanced writing skills than children in other early childhood programs (Bodrova & Leong, 2007) (see Figure 7.9). For example, they write more complex messages, use more words, spell more accurately, show better letter recognition, and have a better understanding of the concept of a sentence.

Evaluating Vygotsky's Theory   Even though their theories were proposed at about the same time, most of the world learned about Vygotsky's theory later than they learned about Piaget's theory, so Vygotsky's theory has not yet been evaluated as thoroughly. Vygotsky's view of the importance of sociocultural influences on children's development fits with the current belief that it is important to evaluate the contextual factors in learning (Gauvain & Perez, 2007).

We already have mentioned several comparisons of Vygotsky's and Piaget's theories, such as Vygotsky's emphasis on the importance of inner speech in development and Piaget's view that such speech is immature. Although both theories are constructivist, Vygotsky's is a **social constructivist approach**, which emphasizes the social contexts of learning and the construction of knowledge through social interaction.

In moving from Piaget to Vygotsky, the conceptual shift is from the individual to collaboration, social interaction, and sociocultural activity (Halford, 2008). The endpoint of cognitive development for Piaget is formal operational thought. For Vygotsky, the endpoint can differ depending on which skills are considered to be the most important in a particular culture. For Piaget, children construct knowledge by transforming, organizing, and reorganizing previous knowledge. For Vygotsky, children construct knowledge through social interaction (Rogoff & others, 2007). The implication of Piaget's theory for teaching is that children need support to explore their world and discover knowledge. The main implication of Vygotsky's theory for teaching is that students need many opportunities to learn with the teacher and more-skilled peers. In both Piaget's and Vygotsky's theories, teachers serve as facilitators and guides, rather than as directors and molders of learning. Figure 7.10 compares Vygotsky's and Piaget's theories.

social constructivist approach An approach that emphasizes the social contexts of learning and that knowledge is mutually built and constructed. Vygotsky's theory reflects this approach.

	Vygotsky	Piaget
Sociocultural Context	Strong emphasis	Little emphasis
Constructivism	Social constructivist	Cognitive constructivist
Stages	No general stages of development proposed	Strong emphasis on stages (sensorimotor, preoperational, concrete operational, and formal operational)
Key Processes	Zone of proximal development, language, dialogue, tools of the culture	Schema, assimilation, accommodation, operations, conservation, classification
Role of Language	A major role; language plays a powerful role in shaping thought	Language has a minimal role; cognition primarily directs language
View on Education	Education plays a central role, helping children learn the tools of the culture	Education merely refines the child's cognitive skills that have already emerged
Teaching Implications	Teacher is a facilitator and guide, not a director; establish many opportunities for children to learn with the teacher and more-skilled peers	Also views teacher as a facilitator and guide, not a director; provide support for children to explore their world and discover knowledge

FIGURE 7.10 Comparison of Vygotsky's and Piaget's Theories

Criticisms of Vygotsky's theory also have surfaced (Karpov, 2006). Some critics point out that Vygotsky was not specific enough about age-related changes (Gauvain, 2008). Another criticism focuses on Vygotsky not adequately describing how changes in socioemotional capabilities contribute to cognitive development (Gauvain, 2008). Yet another criticism is that he overemphasized the role of language in thinking. Also, his emphasis on collaboration and guidance has potential pitfalls. Might facilitators be too helpful in some cases, as when a parent becomes too overbearing and controlling? Further, some children might become lazy and expect help when they might have done something on their own.

Information Processing

Piaget's and Vygotsky's theories provided important ideas about how young children think and how their thinking changes. More recently, the information-processing approach has generated research that illuminates how children process information during the preschool years. What are the limitations and advances in the young child's ability to pay attention to the environment, to remember, to develop strategies and solve problems, and to understand their own mental processes and those of others?

What are some advances in children's attention in early childhood?

Attention Recall that in Chapter 5 we defined *attention* as the focusing of mental resources on select information. The child's ability to pay attention improves significantly during the preschool years (Posner & Rothbart, 2007). Toddlers wander around, shift attention from one activity to another, and seem to spend little time focused on any one object or event. By comparison, the preschool child might be observed watching television for a half hour. One study videotaped young children in their homes (Anderson & others, 1985). In 99 families who were observed for 4,672 hours, visual attention to television dramatically increased during the preschool years.

Young children especially make advances in two aspects of attention—executive attention and sustained (Courage & Richards, 2008; Rothbart & Gartstein, 2008).

Executive attention involves action planning, allocating attention to goals, error detection and compensation, monitoring progress on tasks, and dealing with novel or difficult circumstances. **Sustained attention** is focused and extended engagement with an object, task, event, or other aspect of the environment.

Mary Rothbart and Maria Gartstein (2008, p. 332) recently described why advances in executive and sustained attention are so important in early childhood:

> The development of the . . . executive attention system supports the rapid increases in effortful control in the toddler and preschool years. Increases in attention are due, in part, to advances in comprehension and language development. As children are better able to understand their environment, this increased appreciation of their surroundings helps them to sustain attention for longer periods of time.

In at least two ways, however, the preschool child's control of attention is still deficient:

- *Salient versus relevant dimensions.* Preschool children are likely to pay attention to stimuli that stand out, or are *salient,* even when those stimuli are not relevant to solving a problem or performing a task. For example, if a flashy, attractive clown presents the directions for solving a problem, preschool children are likely to pay more attention to the clown than to the directions. After the age of 6 or 7, children attend more efficiently to the dimensions of the task that are relevant, such as the directions for solving a problem. This change reflects a shift to cognitive control of attention, so that children act less impulsively and reflect more.

- *Planfulness.* When experimenters ask children to judge whether two complex pictures are the same, preschool children tend to use a haphazard comparison strategy, not examining all of the details before making a judgment. By comparison, elementary school age children are more likely to systematically compare the details across the pictures, one detail at a time (Vurpillot, 1968) (see Figure 7.11).

In Central European countries, such as Hungary, kindergarten children participate in exercises designed to improve their attention (Mills & Mills, 2000; Posner & Rothbart, 2007). For example, in one eye-contact exercise, the teacher sits in the center of a circle of children and each child is required to catch the teacher's eye before being permitted to leave the group. In other exercises created to improve attention, teachers have children participate in stop-go activities during which they have to listen for a specific signal, such as as drumbeat or an exact number of rhythmic beats, before stopping the activity.

Preschool children's ability to control and sustain their attention is related to school readiness (Posner & Rothbart, 2007). For example, a study of more than 1,000 children revealed that their ability to sustain their attention at 54 months of age was linked to their school readiness (which included achievement and language skills) (NICHD Early Child Care Research Network, 2005).

Memory *Memory*—the retention of information over time—is a central process in children's cognitive development. In Chapter 5, we saw that most of an infant's memories are fragile and, for the most part, short-lived—except for the memory of perceptual-motor actions, which can be substantial (Mandler, 2004). Thus, we saw that to understand the infant's capacity to remember we need to distinguish *implicit memory* from *explicit memory.* Explicit memory, however, itself comes in many forms. One distinction occurs between relatively permanent or *long-term memory* and short-term memory.

Short-Term Memory In **short-term memory**, individuals retain information for up to 30 seconds if there is no rehearsal of the information. Using rehearsal (repeating information after it has been presented), we can keep information in short-term memory for a much longer period. One method of assessing short-term memory is the

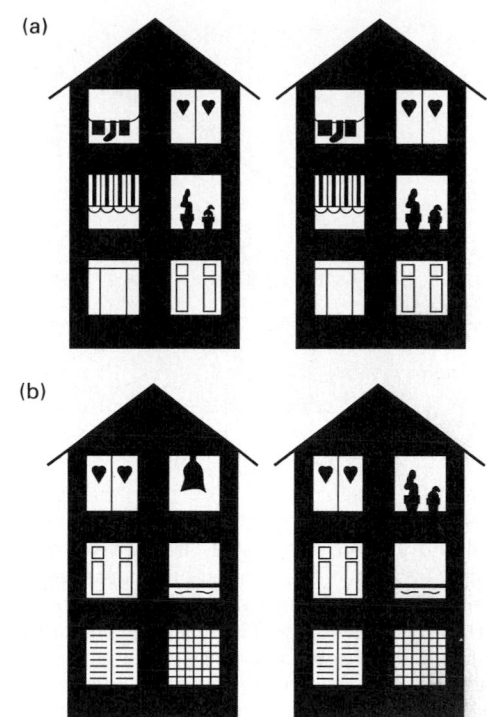

(a)

(b)

FIGURE 7.11 The Planfulness of Attention. In one study, children were given pairs of houses to examine, like the ones shown here (Vurpillot, 1968). For three pairs of houses, what was in the windows was identical (*a*). For the other three pairs, the windows had different items in them (*b*). By filming the reflection in the children's eyes, it could be determined what they were looking at, how long they looked, and the sequence of their eye movements. Children under 6 examined only a fragmentary portion of each display and made their judgments on the basis of insufficient information. By contrast, older children scanned the windows in more detailed ways and were more accurate in their judgments of which windows were identical.

executive attention Involves action planning, allocating attention to goals, error detection and compensation, monitoring progress on tasks, and dealing with novel or difficult circumstances.

sustained attention Focused and extended engagement with an object, task, event, or other aspect of the environment.

short-term memory The memory component in which individuals retain information for up to 30 seconds, assuming there is no rehearsal of the information.

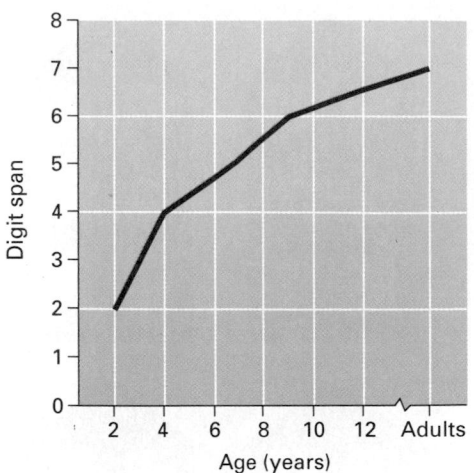

FIGURE 7.12 Developmental Changes in Memory Span. In one study, from 2 years of age to 7 years of age children's memory span increased about 3 digits to 5 digits (Dempster, 1981). Between 7 and 13 years of age, memory span had increased on average only another 1½ digits, to 7 digits. *What factors might contribute to the increase in memory span during childhood?*

memory-span task. You hear a short list of stimuli—usually digits—presented at a rapid pace (one per second, for example). Then you are asked to repeat the digits.

Research with the memory-span task suggests that short-term memory increases during early childhood. For example, in one investigation, memory span increased from about 2 digits in 2- to 3-year-old children to about 5 digits in 7-year-old children, yet between 7 and 13 years of age memory span increased only by 1½ digits (Dempster, 1981) (see Figure 7.12). Keep in mind, though, that memory span varies from one individual to another.

Why does memory span change with age? Rehearsal of information is important; older children rehearse the digits more than younger children. Speed and efficiency of processing information are important, too, especially the speed with which memory items can be identified (Schneider, 2004).

The speed-of-processing explanation highlights a key point in the information-processing perspective: The speed with which a child processes information is an important aspect of the child's cognitive abilities, and there is abundant evidence that the speed with which many cognitive tasks are completed improves dramatically across the childhood years (Kail, 2007; Mabbott & others, 2006).

How Accurate Are Young Children's Long-Term Memories?   While the toddlers' short-term memory span increases during the early childhood years, their memory also becomes more accurate. Young children can remember a great deal of information if they are given appropriate cues and prompts. Increasingly, young children are even being allowed to testify in court, especially if they are the only witnesses to abuse, a crime, and so forth. Several factors can influence the accuracy of a young child's memory (Bruck & Ceci, 1999):

- *There are age differences in children's susceptibility to suggestion.* Preschoolers are the most suggestible age group in comparison with older children and adults (Pipe, 2008). For example, preschool children are more susceptible to believing misleading or incorrect information given after an event (Ghetti & Alexander, 2004). Despite these age differences, there is still concern about the reaction of older children when they are subjected to suggestive interviews (Poole & Lindsay, 1996).

- *There are individual differences in susceptibility.* Some preschoolers are highly resistant to interviewers' suggestions, whereas others immediately succumb to the slightest suggestion. A research review found that the following noncognitive factors were linked to being at risk for suggestibility: low self-concept, low support from parents, and mothers' insecure attachment in romantic relationships (Bruck & Melnyk, 2004).

- *Interviewing techniques can produce substantial distortions in children's reports about highly salient events.* Children are suggestible not just about peripheral details but also about the central aspects of an event (Bruck, Ceci, & Hembrooke, 1998). In some cases, children's false reports can be tinged with sexual connotations. In laboratory studies, young children have made false claims about "silly events" that involved body contact (such as "Did the nurse lick your knee?" or "Did she blow in your ear?"). A significant number of preschool children have falsely reported that someone touched their private parts, kissed them, and hugged them, when these events clearly did not happen in the research. Nonetheless, young children are capable of recalling much that is relevant about an event (Fivush, 1993). When young children do accurately recall information about an event, the interviewer often has a neutral tone, there is limited use of misleading questions, and there is an absence of any motivation for the child to make a false report (Bruck & Ceci, 1999).

Four-year-old Jennifer Royal was the only eyewitness to one of her playmates' being shot to death. She was allowed to testify in open court and the clarity of her statements helped to convict the gunman. *What are some issues involved in whether young children should be allowed to testify in court?*

In sum, whether a young child's eyewitness testimony is accurate or not may depend on a number of factors such as the type, number, and intensity of the suggestive techniques the child has experienced. It appears that the reliability of young children's reports has as much to do with the skills and motivation of the interviewer as with any natural limitations on young children's memory (Bruck, Ceci, & Principe, 2006).

Strategies and Problem Solving   In Chapter 1, we mentioned that information-processing theory emphasizes the importance of using good strategies. **Strategies** consist of deliberate mental activities to improve the processing of information (Bjorklund, 2008; Pressley, 2007). For example, rehearsing information and organizing it are two typical strategies that older children and adults use to remember more effectively. For the most part, young children do not use rehearsal and organization to remember (Miller & Seier, 1994).

During early childhood, the relatively stimulus-driven toddler is transformed into a child capable of flexible, goal-directed problem solving (Zelazo & Müller, 2004; Zelazo & others, 2003). For example, 3- to 4-year-olds cannot understand that a single stimulus can be described in incompatible ways from two different perspectives (Perner & others, 2002). Consider a problem in which children must sort stimuli using the rule of *color.* In the course of the color sorting, a child may describe a red rabbit as "a *red one*" to solve the problem. However, in a subsequent task, the child may need to discover a rule that describes the rabbit as just "a *rabbit*" to solve the problem. If 3- to 4-year-olds fail to understand that it is possible to provide multiple descriptions of the same stimulus, they persist in describing the stimulus as "a red rabbit." Researchers have found that at about 4 years of age, children acquire the concept of perspectives, which allows them to appreciate that a single stimulus can be described in two different ways (Frye, 1999).

Some developmental psychologists use their training in areas such as cognitive development to pursue careers in applied areas. To read about the work of Helen Schwe, an individual who followed this path, see the *Careers in Life-Span Development* interlude.

strategies Deliberate mental activities to improve the processing of information.

Careers in Life-Span Development

Helen Schwe, Developmental Psychologist and Toy Designer

Helen Schwe obtained a Ph.D. from Stanford University in developmental psychology but she now spends her days talking with computer engineers and designing "smart" toys for children. Smart toys are designed to improve children's problem-solving and symbolic thinking skills.

When she was a graduate student, Schwe worked part-time for Hasbro toys, testing its children's software on preschoolers. Her first job after graduate school was with Zowie entertainment, which was subsequently bought by LEGO. According to Schwe, "Even in a toy's most primitive stage of development, . . . you see children's creativity in responding to challenges, their satisfaction when a problem is solved or simply their delight when they are having fun" (p. 50). In addition to conducting experiments and focus groups at different stages of a toy's development, Schwe also assesses the age-appropriateness of a toy. Most of her current work focuses on 3- to 5-year-old children. (Source: Schlegel, 2000, pp. 50–51).

Helen Schwe, a developmental psychologist, with some of the "smart" toys she designed.

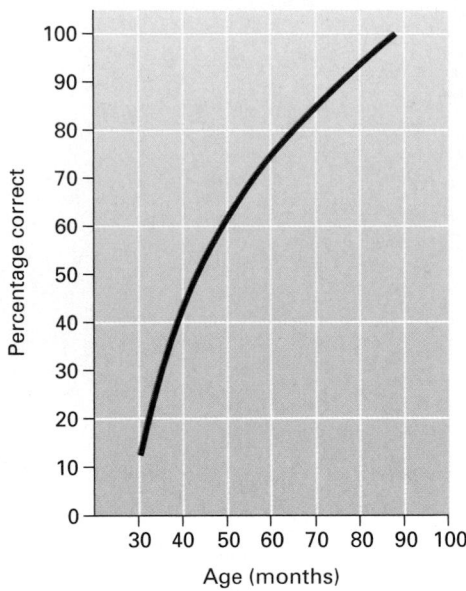

FIGURE 7.13 Developmental Changes in False-Belief Performance. False-belief performance–the child's understanding that a person has a false belief that contradicts reality–dramatically increases from 2½ years of age through the middle of the elementary school years. In a summary of the results of many studies, 2½-year-olds gave incorrect responses about 80 percent of the time (Wellman, Cross, & Watson, 2001). At 3 years, 8 months, they were correct about 50 percent of the time, and after that, gave increasingly correct responses.

The Child's Theory of Mind   Even young children are curious about the nature of the human mind. They have a **theory of mind**, which refers to awareness of one's own mental processes and the mental processes of others. Studies of theory of mind view the child as "a thinker who is trying to explain, predict, and understand people's thoughts, feelings, and utterances" (Harris, 2006, p. 847). Researchers are increasingly discovering that children's theory of mind is linked to cognitive processes. For example, a recent study revealed that infants' attention to intentional actions was linked to 4-year-olds' theory of mind (Wellman & others, 2008). And another recent study found that theory of mind competence at age 3 is related to a higher level of metamemory at age 5 (Lockl & Schneider, 2007).

Developmental Changes   Children's theory of mind changes as they develop through childhood (Astington & Dack, 2008; Doherty, 2008; Flavell, 2004). Some changes occur quite early in development, as we see next.

From 18 months to 3 years of age, children begin to understand three mental states:

- *Perceptions.* By 2 years of age, children recognize that another person will see what's in front of her own eyes instead of what's in front of the child's eyes (Lempers, Flavell, & Flavell, 1977), and by 3 years of age, they realize that looking leads to knowing what's inside a container (Pratt & Bryant, 1990).

- *Emotions.* The child can distinguish between positive (for example, happy) and negative (sad, for example) emotions. A child might say, "Tommy feels bad."

- *Desires.* All humans have some sort of desires. But when do children begin to recognize that someone else's desires may different from their own? Toddlers recognize that if people want something, they will try to get it. For instance, a child might say, "I want my mommy."

Two- to three-year-olds understand the way that desires are related to actions and to simple emotions. For example, they understand that people will search for what they want and that if they obtain it, they are likely to feel happy, but if they don't they will keep searching for it and are likely to feel sad or angry (Wellman & Woolley, 1990). Children also refer to desires earlier and more frequently than they refer to cognitive states such as thinking and knowing (Bartsch & Wellman, 1995).

One of the landmark developments in understanding others' desires is recognizing that someone else may have different desires from one's own (Astington & Dack, 2008; Doherty, 2008). Eighteen-month-olds understand that their own food preferences may not match the preferences of others—they will give an adult the food to which she says "Yummy!" even if the food is something that the infants detest (Repacholi & Gopnik, 1997). As they get older, they can verbalize that they themselves do not like something but an adult might (Flavell, & others, 1992).

Between the ages of 3 to 5, children come to understand that the mind can represent objects and events accurately or inaccurately. The realization that people can have *false beliefs*—beliefs that are not true—develops in a majority of children by the time they are 5 years old (Wellman, Cross, & Watson, 2001) (see Figure 7.13). This point is often described as a pivotal one in understanding the mind—recognizing that beliefs are not just mapped directly into the mind from the surrounding world, but also that different people can have different, and sometimes incorrect, beliefs (Liu & others, 2008). In a classic false-belief task, young children were shown a Band-Aids box and asked what was inside (Jenkins & Astington, 1996). To the children's surprise, the box actually contained pencils. When asked what a child who had never seen the box would think was inside, 3-year-olds typically responded, "Pencils." However, the 4- and 5-year-olds, grinning at the anticipation of the false

theory of mind Refers to the awareness of one's own mental processes and the mental processes of others.

beliefs of other children who had not seen what was inside the box, were more likely to say "Band-Aids."

In a similar task, children are told a story about Sally and Anne: Sally places a toy in a basket and then leaves the room (see Figure 7.14). In her absence, Anne takes the toy from the basket and places it in a box. Children are asked where Sally will look for the toy when she returns. The major finding is that 3-year-olds tend to fail false-belief tasks, saying that Sally will look in the box (even though Sally could not know that the toy has moved to this new location). Four-year-olds and older children tend to pass the task, correctly saying that Sally will have a "false belief"—she will think the object is in the basket, even though that belief is now false. The conclusion from these studies is that children younger than 4 years old do not understand that it is possible to have a false belief.

However, there are many reasons to question the focus on this one supposedly pivotal moment in the development of a theory of mind. For example, the false-belief task is a complicated one that involves a number of factors such as the characters in the story and all of their individual actions (Bloom & German, 2000). Children also have to disregard their own knowledge in making predictions about what others would think, which is difficult for young children (Birch & Bloom, 2003).

Another important issue is that there is more to understanding the minds of others than this false-belief task would indicate. Indeed, there are signs of understanding the minds of others before children pass the false-belief task (Bloom & German, 2000). Recent research revealed that 15-month-old infants may expect that people will try to find objects based on where they last saw the objects, not where the objects are now, suggesting some sort of primitive understanding of false belief (Onishi & Baillergeon, 2005). And in general this kind of task has only two possible outcomes: knowledge or ignorance (Miller, 2000). Someone either has the right information to make a judgment of the contents of a box, or someone does not. Even $2\frac{1}{2}$-year-olds can recognize when someone is ignorant of information: Toddlers gesture toward a toy placed on a top shelf far more often if their parent was not present when the toy was hidden than if the parent had been in the room (O'Neill, 1996). There is much more to understanding knowledge in the minds of others than understanding that others may be ignorant or knowledgeable of a certain fact. So while passing the false-belief task is important, there is much development in understanding the mind both earlier and later in development.

One example of a limitation in 3- to 5-year-olds' understanding of the mind is how they think about thinking. Preschoolers often underestimate when mental activity is likely occurring. For example, they sometimes think that a person who is sitting quietly or reading is not actually thinking very much (Flavell, Green, & Flavell, 1995). Their understanding of their own thinking is also limited. One study revealed that even 5-year-olds have difficulty reporting their thoughts (Flavell, Green, & Flavell, 1995). Children were asked to think quietly about the room in their home where they kept their toothbrushes. Shortly after this, many children denied they had been thinking at all and failed to mention either a toothbrush or a bathroom. In another study, when 5-year-olds were asked to try to have no thoughts at all for about 20 seconds, they reported that they were successful at doing this (Flavell, Green, & Flavell, 2000). By contrast, most of the 8-year-olds said they engaged in mental activity during the 20 seconds and reported specific thoughts.

It is only beyond the preschool years—at approximately 5 to 7 years of age—that children have a deepening appreciation of the mind itself rather than just an understanding of mental states. For example, they begin to recognize that people's behaviors do not necessarily reflect their thoughts and feelings (Flavell, Green, & Flavell, 1993). Not until middle and late childhood do children see the mind as an active constructor of knowledge or processing center (Flavell, Green, & Flavell, 1998) and move from understanding that beliefs can be false to realizing that the same event can be open to multiple interpretations (Carpendale & Chandler, 1996).

Sally   Anne

FIGURE 7.14 The Sally and Anne False-Belief Task. In the false-belief task, the skit above in which Sally has a basket and Anne has a box is shown to children. Sally places a toy in her basket and then leaves. While Sally is gone and can't watch, Anne removes the toy from Sally's basket and places it in her box. Sally then comes back and the children are asked where they think Sally will look for her toy. Children are said to "pass" the false-belief task if they understand that Sally looks in her basket first before realizing the toy isn't there.

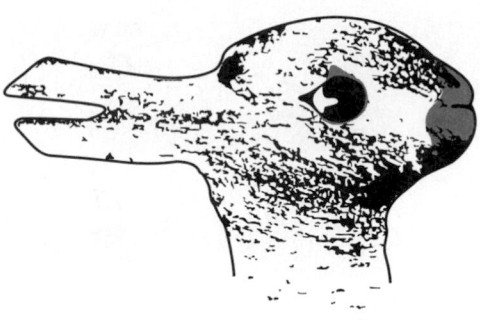

FIGURE 7.15 Ambiguous Line Drawing

For example, in one study, children saw an ambiguous line drawing (for example, a drawing that could be seen as either a duck or a rabbit); one puppet told the child she believed the drawing was a duck while another puppet told the child he believed the drawing was a rabbit (see Figure 7.15). Before the age of 7, children said that there was one right answer, and it was not okay for both puppets to have different opinions.

Five- and six-year olds understand that human sources may have different experiences, but they still think there is an objective truth (Kuhn, Cheney, & Weinstock, 2000). They reason that if others have misinformation or misunderstand something, they must be inaccurately perceiving reality. By age 7, children are able to recognize that reality is not directly knowable, that knowledge is subjective, and that people may have different interpretations of the same event due to differing interpretive processes (Mills, 2007).

While most research on children's theory of mind focuses on children around or before their preschool years, at 7 years of age and beyond there are important developments in the ability to understand the beliefs and thoughts of others. Although understanding that people may have different interpretations is important, it is also important to recognize that some interpretations and beliefs may still be evaluated on the basis of the merits of arguments and evidence (Kuhn, Cheney, & Weinstock, 2000). In early adolescence, children begin to understand that people can have ambivalent feelings (Flavell & Miller, 1998; Whitesell & Harter, 1989). They start to recognize that the same person can feel both happy and sad about the same event. They also engage in more recursive thinking: thinking about what other people are thinking about.

Individual Differences   As in other developmental research, there are individual differences in when children reach certain milestones in their theory of mind. For example, preschoolers who have more siblings perform better on theory of mind tasks than preschoolers with fewer siblings, especially if they have older siblings (McAlister & Peterson, 2007). Children who talk with their parents about feelings frequently as 2-year-olds show better performance on theory of mind tasks (Ruffman, Slade, & Crowe, 2002), as do children who frequently engage in pretend play (Harris, 2000). Children who are deaf but have hearing parents perform more poorly on theory of mind tasks than deaf children raised by deaf parents, presumably because they have fewer opportunities to engage in communication with their parents about mental states (Courtin, 2000).

Executive function, which describes several functions (such as inhibition and planning) that are important for flexible, future-oriented behavior, also may be connected to theory of mind development (Doherty, 2008). For example, in one executive function task, children are asked to say the word "night" when they see a picture of a sun, and the word "day" when they see a picture of a moon and stars. Children who perform better at executive function tasks seem also to have a better understanding of theory of mind (Sabbagh & others, 2006).

There may also be some gender differences in talking about the mind. Parents tend to discuss emotions more with their daughters than with their sons, and that could influence children's understanding of other people's feelings and desires (Adams & others, 1995). Some researchers have suggested that females understand false beliefs slightly earlier than males, but other individual differences (such as overall language ability) may be more important in developing a more advanced understanding of theory of mind (Charman, Ruffman, & Clements, 2002).

Theory of Mind and Autism   Another individual difference in understanding the mind involves autism (Doherty, 2008; Tager-Flusberg, 2007). Approximately 1 in 150 children is estimated to have some sort of autism spectrum disorder (Centers for Disease

Control and Prevention, 2007). Autism can usually be diagnosed by the age of 3 years, and sometimes earlier. Children with autism show a number of behaviors different from children their age, including deficits in social interaction and communication as well as repetitive behaviors or interests. They often show indifference toward others, in many instances preferring to be alone and showing more interest in objects than people. It now is accepted that autism is linked to genetic and brain abnormalities (Iacoboni & Dapretto, 2006).

Children and adults with autism have difficulty in social interactions, often described as huge deficits in theory of mind. These deficits are generally greater than deficits in children the same mental age with mental retardation (Baron-Cohen, 1995). Researchers have found that autistic children have difficulty in developing a theory of mind, especially in understanding others' beliefs and emotions (Harris, 2006). Although children with autism tend to do poorly reasoning in false-belief tasks (Peterson, 2005), they can perform much better on reasoning tasks requiring an understanding of physical causality.

However, it is important to consider individual variations in autistic children and particular aspects of theory of mind (Harris, 2006). Autistic children are not a homogeneous group and some have less severe social and communication problems than others. Thus, it is not surprising that children who have less severe forms of autism do better than those who have more severe forms of the disorder on some theory of mind tasks. For example, higher-functioning autistic children show reasonable progress in understanding others' desires (Harris, 2006). A further important consideration in thinking about autism and theory of mind is that autistic children's difficulty in understanding others' beliefs and emotions might not be due solely to theory of mind deficits but to other aspects of cognition such as problems in focusing attention or some general intellectual impairment (Renner, Grofer Klinger, & Klinger, 2006). Some recent theories of autism suggest that weaknesses in executive functioning may relate to the problems those with autism have on theory of mind tasks. Other theories have pointed out that typically developing individuals process information by extracting the big picture, whereas those with autism process information in a very detailed, almost obsessive way. It may be that in autism, a number of different but related deficits lead to the social cognitive deficits (Rajendran & Mitchell, 2007).

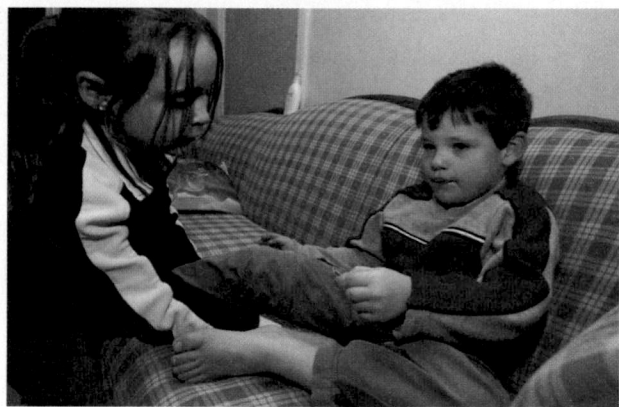

This boy sitting on the sofa is autistic. *What are some characteristics of autistic children? What are some deficits in autistic children's theory of mind?*

Review and Reflect: Learning Goal 2

 Describe Three Views of the Cognitive Changes That Occur in Early Childhood

REVIEW

- What characterizes Piaget's stage of preoperational thought?
- What does Vygotsky's theory suggest about how preschool children construct knowledge?
- What are some important ways in which information processing changes during early childhood? What characterizes children's theory of mind?

REFLECT

- Should children be taught concepts such as conservation? Explain.

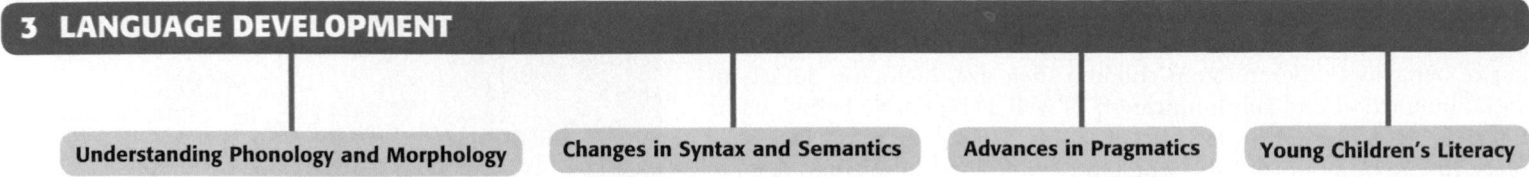

3 LANGUAGE DEVELOPMENT

Understanding Phonology and Morphology | Changes in Syntax and Semantics | Advances in Pragmatics | Young Children's Literacy

Toddlers move rather quickly from producing two-word utterances to creating three-, four-, and five-word combinations. Between 2 and 3 years of age, they begin the transition from saying simple sentences that express a single proposition to saying complex sentences.

As young children learn the special features of their own language, there are extensive regularities in how they acquire that particular language (Berko Gleason, 2009). For example, all children learn the prepositions *on* and *in* before other prepositions. Children learning other languages, such as Russian or Chinese, also acquire the particular features of those languages in a consistent order.

Understanding Phonology and Morphology

During the preschool years, most children gradually become more sensitive to the sounds of spoken words and become increasingly capable of producing all the sounds of their language (National Research Council, 1999). By the time, children are 3 years of age, they can produce all the vowel sounds and most of the consonant sounds (Menn & Stoel-Gammon, 2009).

Young children can even produce complex consonant clusters such as *str-* and *-mpt-*. They notice rhymes, enjoy poems, make up silly names for things by substituting one sound for another (such as *bubblegum, bubblebum, bubbleyum*), and clap along with each syllable in a phrase.

By the time children move beyond two-word utterances, they demonstrate a knowledge of morphology rules (Tager-Flusberg & Zukowski, 2009). Children begin using the plural and possessive forms of nouns (such as *dogs* and *dog's*). They put appropriate endings on verbs (such as *-s* when the subject is third-person singular and *-ed* for the past tense). They use prepositions (such as *in* and *on*), articles (such as *a* and *the*), and various forms of the verb *to be* (such as "I *was* going to the store"). Some of the best evidence for changes in children's use of morphological rules occurs in their overgeneralization of the rules, as when a preschool child say "foots" instead of "feet," or "goed" instead of "went."

In a classic experiment that was designed to study children's knowledge of morphological rules, such as how to make a plural, Jean Berko (1958) presented preschool children and first-grade children with cards such as the one shown in Figure 7.16. Children were asked to look at the card while the experimenter read aloud the words on the card. Then the children were asked to supply the missing word. This might sound easy, but Berko was interested in the children's ability to apply the appropriate morphological rule, in this case to say "wugs" with the *z* sound that indicates the plural.

Although the children's answers were not perfect, they were much better than chance. What makes Berko's study impressive is that most of the words were made up for the experiment. Thus, the children could not base their responses on remembering past instances of hearing the words. Because they could make the plurals or past tenses of words they had never heard before, this was proof that they knew the morphological rules.

This is a wug.

Now there is another one. There are two of them. There are two _____ .

FIGURE 7.16 Stimuli in Berko's Study of Young Children's Understanding of Morphological Rules. In Jean Berko's (1958) study, young children were presented cards, such as this one with a "wug" on it. Then the children were asked to supply the missing word; in supplying the missing word, they had to say it correctly too. "Wugs" is the correct response here.

Changes in Syntax and Semantics

Preschool children also learn and apply rules of syntax (Lieven, 2008; Tager-Flusberg & Zukowski, 2009). They show a growing mastery of complex rules for how words should be ordered. Consider *wh-* questions, such as "Where is Daddy going?" or "What is that boy doing?" To ask these questions properly, the child must know two important differences between *wh-* questions and affirmative statements (for instance, "Daddy is going to work" and "That boy is waiting on the school bus"). First, a *wh-* word must be added at the beginning of the sentence. Second, the auxiliary verb must be inverted—that is, exchanged with the subject of the sentence. Young children learn quite early where to put the *wh-* word, but they take much longer to learn the auxiliary-inversion rule. Thus, preschool children might ask, "Where Daddy is going?" and "What that boy is doing?"

Gains in semantics also characterize early childhood. Vocabulary development is dramatic (Lieven, 2008; Pan & Uccelli, 2009). Some experts have concluded that between 18 months and 6 years of age, young children learn about one new word every waking hour (Gelman & Kalish, 2006)! By the time they enter first grade, it is estimated that children know about 14,000 words (Clark, 1993).

Advances in Pragmatics

Changes in pragmatics also characterize young children's language development (Bryant, 2009). A 6-year-old is simply a much better conversationalist than a 2-year-old is. What are some of the improvements in pragmatics during the preschool years?

Young children begin to engage in extended discourse (Akhtar & Herold, 2008, p. 581). For example, they learn culturally specific rules of conversation and politeness, and become sensitive to the need to adapt their speech in different settings. Their developing linguistic skills and increasing ability to take the perspective of others contribute to their generation of more competent narratives.

As children get older, they become increasingly able to talk about things that are not here (grandma's house, for example) and not now (what happened to them yesterday or might happen tomorrow, for example). A preschool child can tell you what she wants for lunch tomorrow, something that would not have been possible at the two-word stage of language development.

Around 4 to 5 years of age, children learn to change their speech style to suit the situation. For example, even 4-year-old children speak differently to a 2-year-old than to a same-aged peer; they use shorter

What characterizes young children's advances in pragmatics?

sentences with the 2-year-old. They also speak differently to an adult than to a same-aged peer, using more polite and formal language with the adult (Shatz & Gelman, 1973).

Young Children's Literacy

The concern about the ability of U.S. children to read and write has led to a careful examination of preschool and kindergarten children's experiences, with the hope that a positive orientation toward reading and writing can be developed early in life (McGee & Richgels, 2008; Soderman & Farrell, 2008). Parents and teachers need to provide young children a supportive environment for them to develop literacy skills (Tamis-LeMonda & Rodriquez, 2009). Children should be active participants and be immersed in a wide range of interesting listening, talking, writing, and reading experiences.

Anna Mudd began writing stories when she was 4 years old. Above is her story, "The devl and the babe goste," which she wrote as a 6-year-old. The story includes poetic images, sophisticated syntax, and vocabulary that reflect advances in language development. *What are some guidelines parents and teachers can follow in helping young children develop literacy skills?*

Instruction should be built on what children already know about oral language, reading, and writing. Further, early precursors of literacy and academic success include language skills, phonological and syntactic knowledge, letter identification, and conceptual knowledge about print and its conventions and functions (Jalongo, 2007; Otto, 2008). A longitudinal study found that phonological awareness, letter name and sound knowledge, and naming speed in kindergarten were linked to reading success in the first and second grade (Schattschneider & others, 2004). In another longitudinal study, the number of letters children knew in kindergarten was highly correlated (.52) with their reading achievement in high school (Stevenson & Newman, 1986).

The advances in language that take place in early childhood lay the foundation for later development in the elementary school years, which we will discuss in Chapter 9.

Review and Reflect: Learning Goal 3

3 **Summarize How Language Develops in Early Childhood**

REVIEW

- How do phonology and morphology change during early childhood?
- What characterizes young children's understanding of syntax and semantics in early childhood?
- What advances in pragmatics occur in early childhood?
- What are some effective ways to guide young children's literacy?

REFLECT

- How are nature and nurture likely to be involved in the dramatic increase in a young child's spoken vocabulary?

4 EARLY CHILDHOOD EDUCATION

Variations in Early Childhood Education

Education for Young Children Who Are Disadvantaged

Controversies in Early Childhood Education

To the teachers at a Reggio Emilia program (described in the chapter opening), preschool children are active learners, exploring the world with their peers, constructing their knowledge of the world in collaboration with their community, aided but not directed by the teachers. In many ways, the Reggio Emilia approach applies ideas consistent with the views of Piaget and Vygotsky discussed in this chapter. Does it matter to the children? How do other early education programs treat children, and how do the children fare? Our exploration of early childhood education focuses on variations in programs, education for young children who are disadvantaged, and some controversies in early childhood education.

Variations in Early Childhood Education

Attending preschool is rapidly becoming the norm for U.S. children. In 2002, 43 states funded pre-kindergarten programs, and 55 percent of U.S. 3- and 4-year-old children attended center-based programs (NAEYC, 2005). Many other 3- and 4-year-old children attend private preschool programs.

There are many variations in the way young children are educated (Schweinhart, 2009; Driscoll & Nagel, 2008). The foundation of early childhood education has been the child-centered kindergarten.

What are some characteristics of the child-centered kindergarten?

The Child-Centered Kindergarten
Nurturing is a key aspect of the **child-centered kindergarten**, which emphasizes the education of whole child and concern for his or her physical, cognitive, and socioemotional development (Follari, 2007). Instruction is organized around the child's needs, interests, and learning styles. Emphasis is on the process of learning, rather than what is learned (Morrison, 2008). The child-centered kindergarten honors three principles: Each child follows a unique developmental pattern; young children learn best through firsthand experiences with people and materials; and play is extremely important in the child's total development. *Experimenting, exploring, discovering, trying out, restructuring, speaking,* and *listening* are frequent activities in excellent kindergarten programs. Such programs are closely attuned to the developmental status of 4- and 5-year-old children.

The Montessori Approach
Montessori schools are patterned after the educational philosophy of Maria Montessori (1870–1952), an Italian physician-turned-educator, who crafted a revolutionary approach to young children's education at the beginning of the twentieth century. Her work began in Rome with a group of children who were mentally retarded. She was successful in teaching them to read, write, and pass examinations designed for normal children. Some time later, she turned her attention to poor children from the slums of Rome and had similar success in teaching them. Her approach has since been adopted extensively in private nursery schools in the United States.

Larry Page and Sergey Brin, founders of the highly successful Internet search engine, Google, recently said that their early years at Montessori schools were a major factor in their success (International Montessori Council, 2006). During an interview with Barbara Walters, they said they learned how to be self-directed and self-starters at Montessori (ABC News, 2005). They commented that Montessori experiences encouraged them to think for themselves and allowed them the freedom to develop their own interests.

The **Montessori approach** is a philosophy of education in which children are given considerable freedom and spontaneity in choosing activities. They are allowed to move from one activity to another as they desire. The teacher acts as a facilitator rather than a director. The teacher shows the child how to perform intellectual activities, demonstrates interesting ways to explore curriculum materials, and offers help when the child requests it. "By encouraging children to make decisions from an early age, Montessori programs seek to develop self-regulated problem solvers who can make choices and manage their time effectively" (Hyson, Copple, & Jones, 2006, p. 14). The number of Montessori schools in the United States has expanded dramatically in recent years, from one school in 1959 to 355 schools in 1970 to approximately 4,000 in 2005 (Whitescarver, 2006).

Some developmentalists favor the Montessori approach, but others believe that it neglects children's social development (Chattin-McNichols, 1992). For example, while Montessori fosters independence and the development of cognitive skills, it deemphasizes verbal interaction between the teacher and child and peer interaction. Montessori's critics also argue that it restricts imaginative play and that its heavy

child-centered kindergarten Education that involves the whole child by considering both the child's physical, cognitive, and socioemotional development and the child's needs, interests, and learning styles.

Montessori approach An educational philosophy in which children are given considerable freedom and spontaneity in choosing activities and are allowed to move from one activity to another as they desire.

	Developmentally Appropriate	Developmentally Inappropriate
Teaching to enhance development and learning	Teachers plan and prepare a learning environment that fosters children's initiative, active exploration of material, and sustained engagement with other children, adults, and activities.	The environment is disorderly with little structure.
	In selecting materials, teachers consider children's developmental levels and cultural backgrounds.	The organization of the environment limits children's interaction with other children.
	Teachers maintain a safe, healthy environment and carefully supervise children.	Teachers don't adequately monitor children. Learning materials are mainly drill-and-practice, workbook-type activities rather than interesting and engaging activities.
	Teachers give children opportunities to plan and select many of their program activities from a variety of learning areas and projects.	The program provides few or no opportunities for children to make choices. Children spend too much time sitting and being quiet. Children do a lot of paper-and-pencil seatwork.
	Teachers encourage children's language and communication skills.	Teachers don't provide adequate time for children to develop concepts and skills.
	Teaching strategies involve observing and interacting with children to determine what each child is capable of doing.	Too many activities are uninteresting and unchallenging, or so difficult, that they diminish children's intrinsic motivation to learn.
	Teachers support children's play and child-chosen activities. They also provide many opportunities for children to plan, think about, reflect on, and discuss their own experiences.	Teachers spend too much time providing negative feedback and punishment.

FIGURE 7.17 Examples of NAEYC Guidelines for Appropriate and Inappropriate Practices for 3- Through 5-Year-Olds That Involve Teaching to Enhance Development and Learning

reliance on self-corrective materials may not adequately allow for creativity and for a variety of learning styles (Goffin & Wilson, 2001).

Developmentally Appropriate and Inappropriate Education Many educators and psychologists conclude that preschool and young elementary school children learn best through active, hands-on teaching methods such as games and dramatic play. They know that children develop at varying rates and that schools need to allow for these individual differences. They also argue that schools should focus on improving children's socioemotional development, as well as their cognitive development (Brewer, 2007; Kostelnik, Soderman, & Whiren, 2007). Educators refer to this type of schooling as **developmentally appropriate practice**, which is based on knowledge of the typical development of children within an age span (age-appropriateness), as well as the uniqueness of the child (individual-appropriateness). In contrast, developmentally inappropriate practice for young children relies on abstract paper-and-pencil activities presented to large groups. Figure 7.17 provides examples of developmentally appropriate and inappropriate practices (NAEYC, 1997).

One study compared 182 children from five developmentally appropriate kindergarten classrooms (with hands-on activities and integrated curriculum tailored to meet age group, cultural, and individual learning styles) and five developmentally inappropriate kindergarten classrooms (which had an academic, direct instruction emphasis with extensive use of workbooks/worksheets, seatwork, and rote drill/practice activities) in a Louisiana school system (Hart & others, 2003). Children from the two types of classrooms did not differ in pre-kindergarten readiness, and the classrooms were balanced in terms of sex and socioeconomic status. Teacher ratings of child behavior and scores on the California Achievement Test were obtained through the third grade. Children taught in developmentally inappropriate classrooms had slower growth in vocabulary, math application, and math computation.

However, not all studies show significant positive benefits for developmentally appropriate education (Hyson, 2007). Among the reasons it is difficult to generalize about research on developmentally appropriate education is that individual programs often vary, and developmentally appropriate education is an evolving concept. Recent changes in the concept have given more attention to sociocultural

developmentally appropriate practice Education that focuses on the typical developmental patterns of children (age-appropriateness) and the uniqueness of each child (individual-appropriateness).

factors, the teacher's active involvement and implementation of systematic intentions, as well as how strong academic skills should be emphasized and how they should be taught.

Education for Young Children Who Are Disadvantaged

For many years, U.S. children from low-income families did not receive any education before they entered the first grade. Often, they began first grade already several steps behind their classmates in their readiness to learn. In the summer of 1965, the federal government began an effort to break the cycle of poverty and poor education for young children in the United States through **Project Head Start**. It is a compensatory program designed to provide children from low-income families the opportunity to acquire the skills and experiences important for success in school. After almost half a century, Head Start continues to be the largest federally funded program for U.S. children with almost 1 million U.S. children enrolled annually (Hagen & Lamb-Parker, 2008).

Head Start programs are not all created equal (Hustedt & Barnett, 2009). One estimate is that 40 percent of the 1,400 Head Start programs are of questionable quality (Zigler & Styfco, 1994). More attention needs to be given to developing consistently high-quality Head Start programs (Chambers, Cheung, & Slavin, 2006). One individual who is strongly motivated to make Head Start a valuable learning experience for young children from disadvantaged backgrounds is Yolanda Garcia. To read about her work, see the *Careers in Life-Span Development* profile.

Project Head Start A government-funded program that is designed to provide children from low-income families the opportunity to acquire the skills and experiences important for school success.

Careers in Life-Span Development

Yolanda Garcia, Director of Children's Services/Head Start

Yolanda Garcia has been the Director of the Children's Services Department for the Santa Clara, California, County Office of Education since 1980. As director, she is responsible for managing child development programs for 2,500 3- to 5-year-old children in 127 classrooms. Her training includes two master's degrees, one in public policy and child welfare from the University of Chicago and another in education administration from San Jose State University.

Garcia has served on many national advisory committees that have resulted in improvements in the staffing of Head Start programs. Most notably, she served on the Head Start Quality Committee that recommended the development of Early Head Start and revised performance standards for Head Start programs. Garcia currently is a member of the American Academy of Science Committee on the Integration of Science and Early Childhood Education.

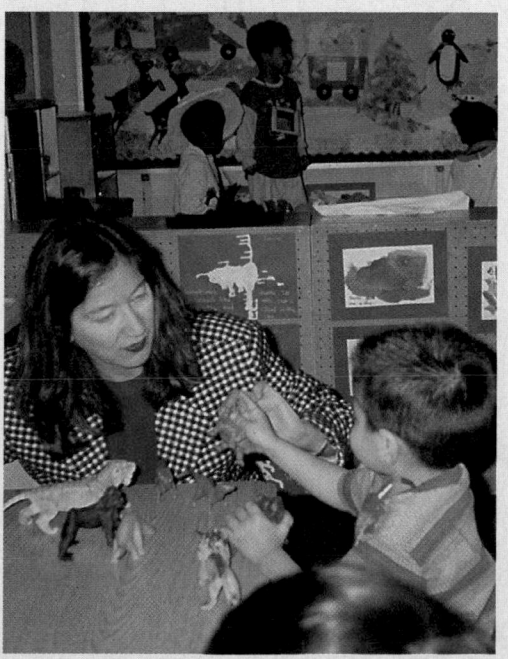

Yolanda Garcia, Director of Children's Services/ Head Start, working with some Head Start children in Santa Clara, California.

Evaluations support the positive influence of quality early childhood programs on both the cognitive and social worlds of disadvantaged young children (Currie, 2009; Ryan, Fauth, & Brooks-Gunn, 2006; Zigler, 2009). One high-quality early childhood education program (although not a Head Start program) is the Perry Preschool program in Ypsilanti, Michigan, a two-year preschool program that includes weekly home visits from program personnel. In analyses of the long-term effects of the program, adults who had been in the Perry Preschool program were compared with a control group of adults from the same background who did not receive the enriched early childhood education (Schweinhart & others, 2005; Weikert, 1993). Those who had been in the Perry Preschool program had fewer teen pregnancies and higher high school graduation rates, and at age 40 more were in the workforce, owned their own homes, had a savings account, and had fewer arrests.

Controversies in Early Childhood Education

Two current controversies in early childhood education involve (1) what the curriculum for early childhood education should be (Hyson, 2007), and (2) whether preschool education should be universal in the United States (Zigler, Gilliam, & Jones, 2006).

Regarding the curriculum controversy, on one side are those who advocate a child-centered, constructivist approach much like that emphasized by the NAEYC along the lines of developmentally appropriate practice. On the other side are those who advocate an academic, direct instruction approach.

In reality, many high-quality early childhood education programs include both academic and constructivist approaches. Many education experts like Lilian Katz (1999), though, worry about academic approaches that place too much pressure on young children to achieve and don't provide any opportunities to actively construct knowledge. Competent early childhood programs also should focus on cognitive development *and* socioemotional development, not exclusively on cognitive development (Kagan & Kauerz, 2009; Kagan & Scott-Little, 2004; NAEYC, 2002).

Another early childhood education controversy focuses on whether preschool education should be instituted for all U.S. 4-year-old children. Edward Zigler and his colleagues (2006) recently argued that the United States should have universal preschool education. They emphasize that quality preschools prepare children for school readiness and academic success. Zigler and his colleagues (2006) cite research that shows quality preschool programs increase the likelihood that once children go to elementary and secondary school they will be less likely to be retained in a grade or drop out of school. They also point to analyses indicating that universal preschool would bring considerable cost savings on the order of billions of dollars because of a diminished need for remedial and justice services (Karoly & Bigelow, 2005).

Critics of universal preschool education argue that the gains attributed to preschool and kindergarten education are often overstated. They especially stress that research has not proven that nondisadvantaged children improve as a result of attending a preschool. Thus, the critics say it is more important to improve preschool education for young children who are disadvantaged rather than funding preschool education for all 4-year-old children. Some critics, especially homeschooling advocates, emphasize that young children should be educated by their parents, not by schools. Thus, controversy continues to characterize whether universal preschool education should be implemented.

In Japan and many developing countries, some of the goals of early childhood education are quite different from those of American programs. To read about the differences, see the *Diversity in Life-Span Development* interlude.

What is the curriculum controversy in early childhood education?

Diversity in Life-Span Development

Early Childhood Education in Japan and Developing Countries

As in America, there is diversity in Japanese early childhood education. Some Japanese kindergartens have specific aims, such as early musical training or the practice of Montessori strategies. In large cities, some kindergartens are attached to universities that have elementary and secondary schools. In most Japanese preschools, however, little emphasis is put on academic instruction.

In one study, 300 Japanese and 210 American preschool teachers, child development specialists, and parents were asked about various aspects of early childhood education (Tobin, Wu, & Davidson, 1989). Only 2 percent of the Japanese respondents listed "to give children a good start academically" as one of their top three reasons for a society to have preschools. In contrast, over half the American respondents chose this as one of their top three choices. Japanese schools do not teach reading, writing, and mathematics but rather skills like persistence, concentration, and the ability to function as a member of a group. The vast majority of young Japanese children are taught to read at home by their parents.

In the comparison of Japanese and American parents, more than 60 percent of the Japanese parents said that the purpose of preschool is to give children experience being a member of the group compared with slightly more than 20 percent of the U.S. parents (Tobin, Wu, & Davidson, 1989) (see Figure 7.18). Lessons in living and working together grow naturally out of the Japanese culture. In many Japanese kindergartens, children wear the same uniforms, including caps, which are of different colors to indicate the classrooms to which they belong. They have identical sets of equipment, kept in identical drawers and shelves. This is not intended to turn the young children into robots, as some Americans have observed, but to impress on them that other people, just like themselves, have needs and desires that are equally important (Hendry, 1995).

Japan is a highly advanced industrialized country. What about developing countries—how do they compare to the United States in educating young children? The wide range of programs and emphasis on the education of the whole child—physically, cognitively, and socioemotionally—that characterizes U.S. early childhood does not exist in many developing countries (Roopnarine & Metindogan, 2006). Economic pressures and parents' belief that education should be academically rigorous have produced teacher-centered rather child-centered early childhood education programs in most developing countries. Among the countries in which this type of early childhood education has been observed are Jamaica, China, Thailand, Kenya, and Turkey. In these countries, young children are usually given few choices and are educated in highly structured settings. Emphasis is on learning academic skills through rote memory and recitation (Lin, Johnson, & Johnson, 2003). Programs in Mexico, Singapore, Korea, and Hong Kong have been observed to be closer to those in the United States in their emphasis on curriculum flexibility and play-based methods (Cisneros-Cohernour & others, 2000).

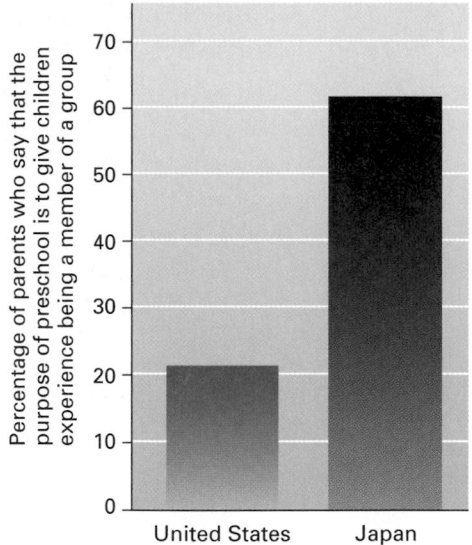

FIGURE 7.18 Comparison of Japanese and U.S. Parents' Views on the Purpose of Preschool

What characterizes early childhood education in Japan?

A kindergarten class in Kingston, Jamaica. *What characterizes kindergarten in many developing countries like Jamaica?*

Review and Reflect: Learning Goal 4

 Evaluate Different Approaches to Early Childhood Education

REVIEW

• What are some variations in early childhood education?
• What are the main efforts to educate young children who are disadvantaged?
• What are two controversies about early childhood education?

REFLECT

• Might preschool be more beneficial to children from middle-income than low-income families? Why?

Physical and Cognitive Development in Early Childhood

1 PHYSICAL CHANGES: IDENTIFY PHYSICAL CHANGES IN EARLY CHILDHOOD

Body Growth and Change

- The average child grows $2\frac{1}{2}$ inches in height and gains between 5 and 7 pounds a year during early childhood. Growth patterns vary individually, though. Some of the brain's interior changes in early childhood are due to myelination. From 3 to 6 years of age, the most rapid growth in the brain occurs in the frontal lobes.

Motor Development

- Gross motor skills increase dramatically during early childhood. Children become increasingly adventuresome as their gross motor skills improve. Fine motor skills also improve substantially during early childhood.

Nutrition

- Too many young children in the United States are being raised on diets that are too high in fat. The child's life should be centered on activities, not meals. Other nutritional concerns include malnutrition in early childhood and the inadequate diets of many children living in poverty.

Illness and Death

- In recent decades, vaccines have virtually eradicated many diseases that once resulted in the deaths of many young children. The disorders still most likely to be fatal for young children in the United States are cancer and cardiovascular disease, but accidents are the leading cause of death in young children. A special concern is the poor health status of many young children in low-income families. There has been a dramatic increase in HIV/AIDS in young children in developing countries in the last decade.

2 COGNITIVE CHANGES: DESCRIBE THREE VIEWS OF THE COGNITIVE CHANGES THAT OCCUR IN EARLY CHILDHOOD

Piaget's Preoperational Stage

- According to Piaget, in the preoperational stage children cannot yet perform operations, which are reversible mental actions, but they begin to represent the world with symbols, to form stable concepts, and to reason. During the symbolic function substage, which occurs between about 2 and 4 years of age, children begin to mentally represent an object that is not present, but their thought is limited by egocentrism and animism. During the intuitive thought substage, which stretches from about 4 to 7 years of age, children begin to reason and to bombard adults with questions. Thought at this substage is called intuitive because children seem so sure about their knowledge yet are unaware of how they know what they know. Centration and a lack of conservation also characterize the preoperational stage.

Vygotsky's Theory

- Vygotsky's theory represents a social constructivist approach to development. According to Vygotsky, children construct knowledge through social interaction, and they use language not only to communicate with others but also to plan, guide, and monitor their own behavior and to help them solve problems. His theory suggests that adults should assess and use the child's zone of proximal development (ZPD), which is the range of tasks that are too difficult for children to master alone but which can be learned with the guidance and assistance of adults or more-skilled children. The theory also suggests that adults and peers should teach through scaffolding, which involves changing the level of support over the course of a teaching session, with the more-skilled person adjusting guidance to fit the student's current performance level.

Information Processing

- The child's ability to attend to stimuli dramatically improves during early childhood. Advances in executive attention and sustained attention are especially important in early childhood, but the young child still attends to the salient rather than the relevant features of a task. Significant improvement in short-term memory occurs during early childhood. With good prompts, young children's long-term memories can be accurate, although young children can be led into developing false memories. Young children usually don't use strategies to remember, but they can learn rather simple, goal-directed problem-solving. Young children are curious about the human mind, and this has been studied under the topic of theory of mind. A number of developmental changes characterize children's theory of mind, including those involved in false beliefs. Individual variations also are involved in theory mind. For example, autistic children have difficulty in developing a theory of mind.

3   LANGUAGE DEVELOPMENT: SUMMARIZE HOW LANGUAGE DEVELOPS IN EARLY CHILDHOOD

Understanding Phonology and Morphology

Changes in Syntax and Semantics

Advances in Pragmatics

Young Children's Literacy

- Young children increase their grasp of language's rule systems. In terms of phonology, most young children become more sensitive to the sounds of spoken language. Berko's classic experiment demonstrated that young children understand morphological rules.

- Preschool children learn and apply rules of syntax and how words should be ordered. In terms of semantics, vocabulary development increases dramatically during early childhood.

- Young children's conversational skills improve, they increase their sensitivity to the needs of others in conversation, and they learn to change their speech style to suit the situation.

- Parents and teachers need to provide young children a supportive environment for them to develop literacy skills. Children should be active participants and be immersed in a wide range of interesting listening, talking, writing, and reading experiences.

4   EARLY CHILDHOOD EDUCATION: EVALUATE DIFFERENT APPROACHES TO EARLY CHILDHOOD EDUCATION

Variations in Early Childhood Education

Education for Young Children Who Are Disadvantaged

Controversies in Early Childhood Education

- The child-centered kindergarten emphasizes the education of the whole child, with particular attention to individual variation, the process of learning, and the importance of play in development. The Montessori approach allows children to choose from a range of activities while teachers serve as facilitators. Developmentally appropriate practice (illustrated by the Reggio Emilia approach) focuses on the typical patterns of children (age-appropriateness) and the uniqueness of each child (individual-appropriateness). Such practice contrasts with developmentally inappropriate practice, which ignores the concrete, hands-on approach to learning.

- The U.S. government has tried to break the poverty cycle with programs such as Head Start. Model programs have been shown to have positive effects on children who live in poverty.

- Controversy characterizes early childhood education curricula. On the one side are the child-centered, constructivist advocates, on the other are those who advocate an instructivist, academic approach. Another controversy focuses on whether preschool education matters. Some parents can educate young children as effectively as a school does; however, most parents do not have the skills, time, and commitment to do so.

KEY TERMS

myelination 211	animism 218	social constructivist	child-centered
preoperational	intuitive thought	approach 223	kindergarten 235
stage 217	substage 218	executive attention 225	Montessori approach 235
operations 217	centration 218	sustained attention 225	developmentally
symbolic function	conservation 218	short-term memory 225	appropriate practice 236
substage 217	zone of proximal	strategies 227	Project Head Start 237
egocentrism 217	development (ZPD) 220	theory of mind 228	

KEY PEOPLE

Jean Piaget 217	Rochel Gelman 220	Mary Rothbart and Maria	Jean Berko 232
Barbel Inhelder 217	Lev Vygotsky 220	Gartstein 225	Maria Montessori 235

E-LEARNING TOOLS

To help you master the material in this chapter, visit the Online Learning Center for *Life-Span Development*, twelfth edition, at **www.mhhe.com/santrockld12**.

Self-Assessment

Connect to **www.mhhe.com/santrockld12** to examine your understanding of cognitive development in early childhood by completing the self-assessment, *What I Think Is Important in Early Childhood Education*.

Taking It to the Net

Connect to **www.mhhe.com/santrockld12** to research the answers to these questions:

1. A child's grasp of elementary physics (conservation laws, for example) normally improves during Piaget's preoperational stage. Many adults, however, nevertheless retain a set of incorrect assumptions about motion and matter—what psychologists sometimes refer to as "intuitive physics." Julien is 5 years old. When asked to describe the trajectory a chess piece would follow as it spun off a revolving circular table, Julien answers that it would follow a curved trajectory (an answer inconsistent with Newton's first law of motion). What other misconceptions about the physical world might Julien be likely to retain past the age of 10?

2. Beyonce, who is working in a prosecutor's office for her senior internship, has been asked to write a memo on the suggestibility of child witnesses and how likely a jury is to believe a child's testimony in court cases. How can she find information for the memo that provides research-based facts as well as guidelines for dealing with child witnesses that will be helpful for the prosecutors?

Video Clips

The Online Learning Center includes a video for Chapter 7 called "Children and Nutrition." Diet and physical activity, as this segment demonstrates, are important aspects of a healthy lifestyle. These lifestyle choices begin in early childhood.

Health and Well-Being, Parenting, and Education Exercises

Build your decision-making skills by trying your hand at the health and well-being, parenting, and education exercises. Connect to **www.mhhe.com/santrockld12** to research the answers and complete the exercises.

8

Let us play, for it is yet day
And we cannot go to sleep;
Besides, in the sky the little birds fly
And the hills are all covered with sheep.

—WILLIAM BLAKE
English Poet, 19th Century

LEARNING GOALS

◆ Discuss emotional and personality development in early childhood.

◆ Explain how families can influence young children's development.

◆ Describe the roles of peers, play, and television in young children's development.

SOCIOEMOTIONAL DEVELOPMENT IN EARLY CHILDHOOD

CHAPTER OUTLINE

Images of Life-Span Development
Craig Lesley's Complicated Early Emotional and Social Life

In his memoir *Burning Fence: A Western Memoir of Fatherhood,* award-winning novelist Craig Lesley describes one memory from his early childhood:

> Lifting me high above his head, my father placed me in the crotch of the Bing cherry tree growing beside my mother's parents' house in The Dalles. A little frightened at the dizzying height, I pressed my palms into the tree's rough, peeling bark. My father stood close, reassuring. I could see his olive skin, dazzling smile, and sharp-creased army uniform.
>
> "Rudell, don't let him fall." My mother watched, her arms held out halfway, as if to catch me. . . .
>
> The cherries were ripe and robins flittered through the green leaves, pecking at the Bings. Tipping my head back I could see blue sky beyond the extended branches.
>
> "That's enough. Bring him down now." My mother's arms reached out farther.
>
> Laughing, my father grabbed me under the arms, twirled me around, and plunked me into the grass. I wobbled a little. Imprinted on my palms was the pattern of the tree bark, and I brushed off the little bark pieces on my dungarees.
>
> In a moment, my grandmother gave me a small glass of lemonade. . . .
>
> This first childhood memory of my father remains etched in my mind. . . .
>
> When I grew older, I realized that my father had never lifted me into the cherry tree. After Rudell left, I never saw him until I was fifteen. My grandfather had put me in the tree. Still, the memory of my father lifting me into the tree persists. Even today, I remain half-convinced by the details, the press of bark against my palms, the taste of lemonade, the texture of my father's serge uniform. Apparently, my mind has cross-wired the photographs of my handsome father in his army uniform with the logical reality that my grandfather set me in the crotch of the tree.
>
> Why can I remember the event so vividly? I guess because I wanted so much for my father to be there. I have no easy answers. (Lesley, 2005, pp. 8–10)

Like millions of children, Lesley experienced a family torn by divorce; he would also experience abuse by a stepfather. When his father left, Lesley was an infant, but even as a preschooler, he felt his father's absence. Once he planned to win a gift for his father so that his grandmother "could take it to him and then he'd come to see me" (Lesley, 2005, p. 16). In just a few years, the infant had become a child with a complicated emotional and social life.

PREVIEW

In early childhood, children's emotional lives and personalities develop in significant ways, and their small worlds widen. In addition to the continuing influence of family relationships, peers take on a more significant role in children's development, and play fills the days of many young children's lives.

1 EMOTIONAL AND PERSONALITY DEVELOPMENT

The Self   Emotional Development   Moral Development   Gender

Many changes characterize young children's socioemotional development in early childhood. Their developing minds and social experiences produce remarkable advances in the development of their self, emotional maturity, moral understanding, and gender awareness.

The Self

We learned in Chapter 6 that during the second year of life children make considerable progress in self-recognition. In the early childhood years, young children develop in many ways that enable them to enhance their self-understanding.

Initiative Versus Guilt In Chapter 1, you read about Erik Erikson (1968) eight developmental stages that are encountered during certain time periods in the human life span. As you learned in Chapter 6, Erikson's first stage, trust versus mistrust, describes what he considers to be the main developmental task of infancy. Erikson's psychosocial stage associated with early childhood is *initiative versus guilt.* By now, children have become convinced that they are persons of their own; during early childhood, they begin to discover what kind of person they will become. They identify intensely with their parents, who most of the time appear to them to be powerful and beautiful, although often unreasonable, disagreeable, and sometimes even dangerous. During early childhood, children use their perceptual, motor, cognitive, and language skills to make things happen. They have a surplus of energy that permits them to forget failures quickly and to approach new areas that seem desirable—even if dangerous—with undiminished zest and some increased sense of direction. On their own *initiative,* then, children at this stage exuberantly move out into a wider social world.

The great governor of initiative is *conscience.* Their initiative and enthusiasm may bring them not only rewards but also guilt, which lowers self-esteem.

Self-Understanding and Understanding Others Recent research studies have revealed that young children are more psychologically aware—of themselves and others—than used to be thought (Laible & Thompson, 2007; Mueller & others, 2008). This increased psychological awareness reflects young children's expanding psychological sophistication.

Self-Understanding In Erikson's portrait of early childhood, the young child clearly has begun to develop **self-understanding**, which is the representation of self, the substance and content of self-conceptions (Harter, 2006). Though not the whole of personal identity, self-understanding provides its rational underpinnings. Mainly through interviews, researchers have probed children's conceptions of many aspects of self-understanding.

As we saw in Chapter 6, "Socioemotional Development in Infancy," early self-understanding involves self-recognition. In early childhood, young children think that the self can be described by many material characteristics, such as size, shape, and color. They distinguish themselves from others through many physical and material attributes. Says 4-year-old Sandra, "I'm different from Jennifer because I have brown hair and she has blond hair." Says 4-year-old Ralph, "I am different from Hank because I am taller and I am different from my sister because I have a bicycle." Physical

self-understanding The child's cognitive representation of self, the substance and content of the child's self-conceptions.

Young children are more psychologically aware of themselves and others than used to be thought. Some children are better than others at understanding people's feelings and desires—and, to some degree, these individual differences are influenced by conversations caregivers have with young children about feelings and desires.

activities are also a central component of the self in early childhood (Keller, Ford, & Meacham, 1978). For example, preschool children often describe themselves in terms of activities such as play. In sum, in early childhood, children often provide self-descriptions that involve body attributes, material possessions, and physical activities.

Although young children mainly describe themselves in terms of concrete, observable features and action tendencies, at about 4 to 5 years of age, as they hear others use psychological trait and emotion terms, they begin to include these in their own self-descriptions (Marsh, Ellis, & Craven, 2002). Thus, in a self-description, a 4-year-old might say, "I'm not scared. I'm always happy."

Young children's self-descriptions are typically unrealistically positive, as reflected in the comment of this 4-year-old who says he is always happy, which he is not (Harter, 2006). This occurs because they don't yet distinguish between their desired competence and their actual competence, tend to confuse ability and effort (thinking that differences in ability can be changed as easily as can differences in effort), don't engage in spontaneous social comparison of their abilities with those of others, and tend to compare their present abilities with what they could do at an earlier age (by which they usually look quite good). Perhaps as adults we should all be so optimistic about our abilities (Thompson, 2008).

Understanding Others   Children also make advances in their understanding of others in early childhood (Bibok, Carpendale, & Lewis, 2008; Gelman, Heyman, Legare, 2007). As we saw in Chapter 7, "Physical and Cognitive Development in Early Childhood," young children's theory of mind includes understanding that other people have emotions and desires. And at about 4 to 5 years, children not only start describing themselves in terms of psychological traits, but they also begin to perceive others in terms of psychological traits. Thus, a 4-year-old might say, "My teacher is nice."

Something important for children to develop is an understanding that people don't always give accurate reports of their beliefs (Gee & Heyman, 2007). Researchers have found that even 4-year-olds understand that people may make statements that aren't true to obtain what they want or to avoid trouble (Lee & others, 2002). For example, one recent study revealed that 4- and 5-year-olds were increasingly skeptical of another child's claim to be sick when the children were informed that the child was motivated to avoid having to go to camp (Gee & Heyman, 2007). Another recent study found that at 3 years of age, children mistrusted people who made a single error, but it wasn't until 4 years of age that children took into account the relative frequency of errors informants made when deciding whom to trust (Pasquini & others, 2007).

Individual differences characterize young children's social understanding (Laible & Thompson, 2007). Some young children are better than others at understanding what people are feeling and what they desire, for example. To some degree, these individual differences are linked to conversations caregivers have with young children about other people's feelings and desires, and children's opportunities to observe others talking about people's feelings and desires. For example, a mother might say to her 3-year-old, "You should think about Raphael's feelings next time before you hit him."

Emotional Development

The young child's growing awareness of self is linked to the ability to feel an expanding range of emotions. Young children, like adults, experience many emotions during the course of a day. Their emotional development in early childhood allows them to try to make sense of other people's emotional reactions and to begin to control their own emotions.

Self-Conscious Emotions Recall from Chapter 6 that even young infants experience emotions such as joy and fear, but to experience *self-conscious emotions,* children must be able to refer to themselves and be aware of themselves as distinct from others (Lewis, 2007). Pride, shame, embarrassment, and guilt are examples of self-conscious emotions. Self-conscious emotions do not appear to develop until self-awareness appears around 18 months of age.

During the early childhood years, emotions such as pride and guilt become more common. They are especially influenced by parents' responses to children's behavior. For example, a young child may experience shame when a parent says, "You should feel bad about biting your sister."

Young Children's Emotion Language and Understanding of Emotion Among the most important changes in emotional development in early childhood are an increased understanding of emotion and an increased ability to talk about one's own and others' emotions (Kuebli, 1994). Between 2 and 4 years of age, children considerably increase the number of terms they use to describe emotions (Ridgeway, Waters, & Kuczaj, 1985). During this time, they are also learning about the causes and consequences of feelings (Denham, Bassett, & Wyatt, 2007).

When they are 4 to 5 years of age, children show an increased ability to reflect on emotions. They also begin to understand that the same event can elicit different feelings in different people. Moreover, they show a growing awareness that they need to manage their emotions to meet social standards (Bruce, Olen, & Jensen, 1999).

Emotion Regulation As we saw in Chapter 6, "Socioemotional Development in Infancy," emotion regulation is an important aspect of development (Saarni & others, 2006). Emotion regulation especially plays a key role in children's ability to manage the demands and conflicts they face in interacting with others (Denham, Bassett, & Wyatt, 2007).

Emotion-Coaching and Emotion-Dismissing Parents Parents can play an important role in helping young children regulate their emotions (Klimes-Dougan & Zeman, 2007; Stocker & others, 2007). Depending on how they talk with their children about emotion, parents can be described as taking an *emotion-coaching* or an *emotion-dismissing* approach (Gottman, 2008). The distinction between these approaches is most evident in the way the parent deals with the child's negative emotions (anger, frustration, sadness, and so on). *Emotion-coaching parents* monitor their children's emotions, view their children's negative emotions as opportunities for teaching, assist them in labeling emotions, and coach them in how to deal effectively with emotions. In contrast, *emotion-dismissing parents* view their role as to deny, ignore, or change negative emotions. Researchers have observed that emotion-coaching parents interact with their children in a less rejecting manner, use more scaffolding and praise, and are more nurturant than are emotion-dismissing parents (Gottman & DeClaire, 1997). Moreover, the children of emotion-coaching parents were better at soothing themselves when they got upset, more effective in regulating their negative affect, focused their attention better, and had fewer behavior problems than the children of emotion-dismissing parents. A recent study revealed that having emotion-dismissing parents is linked with children's poor emotion regulation (Lunkenheimer, Shields, & Cortina, 2007).

Regulation of Emotion and Peer Relations Emotions play a strong role in determining the success of a child's peer relationships (Saarni & others, 2006). Specifically, the

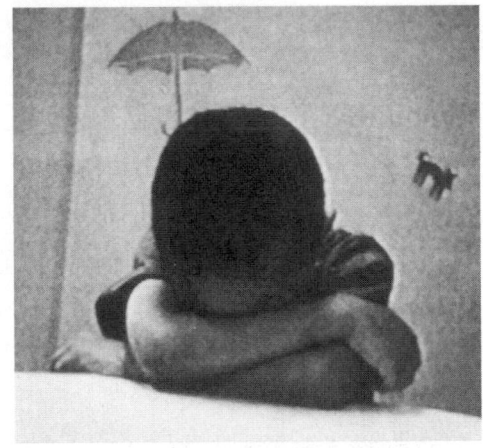

A young child expressing the emotion of shame. *Why is shame called a "self-conscious emotion"?*

An emotion-coaching parent. *What are some differences in emotion-coaching and emotion-dismissing parents?*

What role does emotion regulation play in peer relations?

> *What is moral is what you feel good after and what is immoral is what you feel bad after.*
>
> —Ernest Hemingway
> *American Author, 20th Century*

moral development Development that involves thoughts, feelings, and behaviors regarding rules and conventions about what people should do in their interactions with other people.

heteronomous morality The first stage of moral development in Piaget's theory, occurring from approximately 4 to 7 years of age. Justice and rules are conceived of as unchangeable properties of the world, removed from the control of people.

autonomous morality In Piaget's theory, displayed by older children (about 10 years of age and older). The child becomes aware that rules and laws are created by people and that, in judging an action, one should consider the actor's intentions as well as the consequences.

ability to modulate one's emotions is an important skill that benefits children in their relationships with peers. Moody and emotionally negative children are more likely to experience rejection by their peers, whereas emotionally positive children are more popular (Stocker & Dunn, 1990).

Moral Development

Unlike a crying infant, a screaming 5-year-old is likely to be thought responsible for making a fuss. The parents may worry about whether the 5-year-old is a "bad" child. Although there are some who view children as innately good, many developmentalists believe that just as parents help their children become good readers, musicians, or athletes, parents must nurture goodness and help their children develop morally. **Moral development** involves the development of thoughts, feelings, and behaviors regarding rules and conventions about what people should do in their interactions with other people. Major developmental theories have focused on different aspects of moral development.

Moral Feelings   Feelings of anxiety and guilt are central to the account of moral development provided by Freud's psychoanalytic theory (introduced in Chapter 1). According to Freud, to reduce anxiety, avoid punishment, and maintain parental affection, children identify with parents, internalizing their standards of right and wrong, and thus form the *superego*, the moral element of personality.

Freud's ideas are not backed by research, but guilt certainly can motivate moral behavior. Other emotions, however, also contribute to the child's moral development, including positive feelings. One important example is *empathy*, which is responding to another person's feelings with an emotion that echoes the other's feelings (Eisenberg, Fabes, & Spinrad, 2006).

Infants have the capacity for some purely empathic responses, but empathy often requires the ability to discern another's inner psychological states, or what is called *perspective taking*. Learning how to identify a wide range of emotional states in others and to anticipate what kinds of action will improve another person's emotional state help to advance children's moral development (Johansson, 2006).

Moral Reasoning   Interest in how children think about moral issues was stimulated by Piaget (1932), who extensively observed and interviewed children from the ages of 4 through 12. Piaget watched children play marbles to learn how they used and thought about the game's rules. He also asked children about ethical issues—theft, lies, punishment, and justice, for example. Piaget concluded that children go through two distinct stages in how they think about morality.

- From about 4 to 7 years of age, children display **heteronomous morality**, the first stage of moral development in Piaget's theory. Children think of justice and rules as unchangeable properties of the world, removed from the control of people.

- From 7 to 10 years of age, children are in a transition showing some features of the first stage of moral reasoning and some stages of the second stage, autonomous morality.

- From about 10 years of age and older, children show **autonomous morality**. They become aware that rules and laws are created by people, and in judging an action, they consider the actor's intentions as well as the consequences.

Because young children are heteronomous moralists, they judge the rightness or goodness of behavior by considering its consequences, not the intentions of the actor. For example, to the heteronomous moralist, breaking twelve cups accidentally is worse than breaking one cup intentionally. As children develop into moral autonomists, intentions become more important than consequences.

The heteronomous thinker also believes that rules are unchangeable and are handed down by all-powerful authorities. When Piaget suggested to young children that they use new rules in a game of marbles, they resisted. By contrast, older children—moral autonomists—accept change and recognize that rules are merely convenient conventions, subject to change.

The heteronomous thinker also believes in **immanent justice**, the concept that if a rule is broken, punishment will be meted out immediately. The young child believes that a violation is connected automatically to its punishment. Thus, young children often look around worriedly after doing something wrong, expecting inevitable punishment. Immanent justice also implies that if something unfortunate happens to someone, the person must have transgressed earlier. Older children, who are moral autonomists, recognize that punishment occurs only if someone witnesses the wrongdoing and that, even then, punishment is not inevitable.

How do these changes in moral reasoning occur? Piaget argued that, as children develop, they become more sophisticated in thinking about social matters, especially about the possibilities and conditions of cooperation. Piaget reasoned that this social understanding comes about through the mutual give-and-take of peer relations. In the peer group, where others have power and status similar to the child's, plans are negotiated and coordinated, and disagreements are reasoned about and eventually settled. Parent-child relations, in which parents have the power and children do not, are less likely to advance moral reasoning, because rules are often handed down in an authoritarian way.

How is this child's moral thinking likely to be different about stealing a cookie depending on whether he is in Piaget's heteronomous or autonomous stage?

Moral Behavior   The behavioral and social cognitive approach, initially described in Chapter 1, focuses on moral behavior rather than moral reasoning (Bugental & Grusec, 2006). It holds that the processes of reinforcement, punishment, and imitation explain the development of moral behavior. When children are rewarded for behavior that is consistent with laws and social conventions, they are likely to repeat that behavior. When models who behave morally are provided, children are likely to adopt their actions. And, when children are punished for immoral behavior, those behaviors are likely to be reduced or eliminated. However, because punishment may have adverse side effects, as discussed later in this chapter, it needs to be used judiciously and cautiously.

If a 4-year-old boy has been rewarded by his mother for telling the truth when he breaks a glass at home, does that mean that he is likely to tell the truth to his preschool teacher when he knocks over a vase and breaks it? Not necessarily; the situation influences behavior. More than a half century ago, a comprehensive study of thousands of children in many situations—at home, at school, and at church, for example—found that the totally honest child was virtually nonexistent; so was the child who cheated in all situations (Hartshorne & May, 1928–1930). Behavioral and social cognitive researchers emphasize that what children do in one situation is often only weakly related to what they do in other situations. A child might cheat in class but not in a game; a child might steal a piece of candy when alone but not steal it when others are present.

Social cognitive theorists also stress that the ability to resist temptation is closely tied to the development of self-control (Mischel, 2004). To achieve this self-control, children must learn to delay gratification. According to social cognitive theorists, cognitive factors are important in the child's development of self-control (Bandura, 2007a, b).

Conscience   **Conscience** refers to an internal regulation of standards of right and wrong that involves an integration of all three components of moral development we have described so far—moral thought, feeling, and behavior (Kochanska & Aksan, 2007). Reflecting the presence of a conscience in young children, researchers have found that young children are aware of right and wrong, have the capacity to show empathy toward others, experience guilt, indicate discomfort following a transgression, and are sensitive to violating rules (Kochanska & Aksan, 2007).

immanent justice The concept that, if a rule is broken, punishment will be meted out immediately.

conscience An internal regulation of standards of right and wrong that involves an integration of moral thought, feeling, and behavior.

A major interest in young children's conscience focuses on the children's relationship with their caregivers. Especially important in this regard is the emergence of the young children's willingness to embrace the values of their parents that flows from a positive, close relationship (Kochanska & Aksan, 2007). For example, children who are securely attached are more likely to internalize their parents' values and rules (Laible & Thompson, 2007). In the next section, we further examine the important role of parents in young children's development, with much of this discussion providing more detailed information about how parents influence the development of a child's conscience.

Parenting and Young Children's Moral Development Both Piaget and Lawrence Kohlberg held that parents do not provide unique or essential inputs to children's moral development. Parents, in their view, are responsible for providing role-taking opportunities and cognitive conflict, but peers play the primary role in moral development. Research reveals that both parents and peers contribute to children's moral maturity (Hastings, Utendale, & Sullivan, 2007).

In Ross Thompson's (2006; Laible & Thompson, 2007) view, young children are moral apprentices, striving to understand what is moral. They can be assisted in this quest by the "sensitive guidance of adult mentors in the home who provide lessons about morality in everyday experiences" (Thompson, Meyer, & McGinley, 2006, p. 290). Among the most important aspects of the relationship between parents and children that contribute to children's moral development are relational quality, parental discipline, proactive strategies, and conversational dialogue.

Parent-child relationships introduce children to the mutual obligations of close relationships (Kochanska & others, 2008; Thompson, Meyer, & Jochem, 2008). Parents' obligations include engaging in positive caregiving and guiding children to become competent human beings. Children's obligations include responding appropriately to parents' initiatives and maintaining a positive relationship with parents. Also, secure attachment may play an important role in children's moral development. A secure attachment can place the child on a positive path for internalizing parents' socializing goals and family values (Kochanska & others, 2004). And a recent study revealed that an early mutually responsive orientation between parents and their infant and a decrease in parents' use of power assertion in disciplining a young child were linked to an increase in the child's internalization and self-regulation (Kochanska & others, 2008).

An important parenting strategy is to proactively avert potential misbehavior by children before it takes place (Thompson, Meyer, & McGinley, 2006). With younger children, being proactive means using diversion, such as distracting their attention or moving them to alternative activities. With older children, being proactive may involve talking with them about values that the parents deem important. Transmitting these values can help older children and adolescents to resist the temptations that inevitably emerge in such contexts as peer relations and the media that can be outside the scope of direct parental monitoring.

Conversations related to moral development can benefit children whether they occur as part of a discipline encounter or outside the encounter in the everyday stream of parent-child interaction (Thompson, Meyer, & McGinley, 2006). The conversations can be planned or spontaneous and can focus on topics such as past events (for example, a child's prior misbehavior or positive moral conduct), shared future events (for example, going somewhere that may involve a temptation and requires positive moral behavior), and immediate events (for example, talking with the child about a sibling's tantrums).

What are some aspects of relationships between parents and children that contribute to children's moral development?

Gender

Recall from Chapter 1 that *gender* refers to the social and psychological dimensions of being male or female, and even preschool children display many of these dimensions.

Gender identity is the sense of being male or female, which most children acquire by the time they are 3 years old. **Gender roles** are sets of expectations that prescribe how females or males should think, act, and feel. During the preschool years, most children increasingly act in ways that match their culture's gender roles.

How is gender influenced by biology? By children's social experiences? By cognitive factors?

Biological Influences   Biology clearly plays a role in gender development. Among the possible biological influences are chromosomes, hormones, and evolution.

Chromosomes and Hormones   Biologists have learned a great deal about how sex differences develop. Recall that humans normally have 46 chromosomes arranged in pairs (see Chapter 2). The 23rd pair consists of a combination of X and Y chromosomes, usually two X chromosomes in a female and an X and a Y in a male. In the first few weeks of gestation, however, female and male embryos look alike.

Males start to differ from females when genes on the Y chromosome in the male embryo trigger the development of testes rather than ovaries; the testes secrete copious amounts of the class of hormones known as androgens, which lead to the development of male sex organs. Low levels of androgens in the female embryo allow the normal development of female sex organs.

Thus, hormones play a key role in the development of sex differences (Lippa, 2005). The two main classes of sex hormones are estrogens and androgens, which are secreted by the *gonads* (ovaries in females, testes in males). *Estrogens,* such as estradiol, influence the development of female physical sex characteristics. *Androgens,* such as testosterone, promote the development of male physical sex characteristics.

The Evolutionary Psychology View   How might physical differences between the sexes give rise to psychological differences between males and females? Evolutionary psychology (introduced in Chapter 2) offers one answer. According to evolutionary psychology, adaptation during human evolution produced psychological differences between males and females (Buss, 2007, 2008). Because of their differing roles in reproduction, males and females faced differing pressures when the human species was evolving. In particular, because having multiple sexual liaisons improves the likelihood that males will pass on their genes, natural selection favored males who adopted short-term mating strategies. These are strategies that allow a male to win the competition with other males for sexual access to females. Therefore, say evolutionary psychologists, males evolved dispositions that favor violence, competition, and risk taking.

In contrast, according to evolutionary psychologists, females' contributions to the gene pool were improved when they secured resources that ensured that their offspring would survive (Geher & Miller, 2007). As a consequence, natural selection favored females who devoted effort to parenting and chose successful, ambitious mates who could provide their offspring with resources and protection.

Critics of evolutionary psychology argue that its hypotheses are backed by speculations about prehistory, not evidence, and that in any event people are not locked into behavior that was adaptive in the evolutionary past. Critics also claim that the evolutionary view pays little attention to cultural and individual variations in gender differences (Matlin, 2008; Smith, 2007).

Social Influences   Many social scientists do not locate the cause of psychological gender differences in biological dispositions. Rather, they argue that these differences are due to social experiences. Explanations for how gender differences come about through experience include both social and cognitive theories.

gender identity The sense of being male or female, which most children acquire by the time they are 3 years old.

gender role A set of expectations that prescribes how females or males should think, act, and feel.

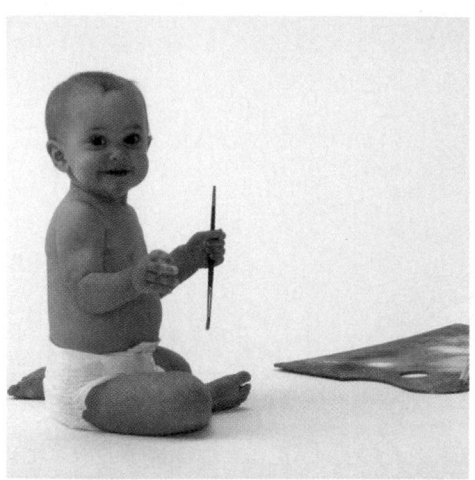

First imagine that this is a photograph of a baby girl. *What expectations would you have for her?* Then imagine that this is a photograph of a baby boy. *What expectations would you have for him?*

Social Theories of Gender Three main social theories of gender have been proposed—social role theory, psychoanalytic theory, and social cognitive theory. Alice Eagly (2001; 2009) proposed **social role theory**, which states that gender differences result from the contrasting roles of women and men. In most cultures around the world, women have less power and status than men, and they control fewer resources (UNICEF, 2008). Compared with men, women perform more domestic work, spend fewer hours in paid employment, receive lower pay, and are more thinly represented in the highest levels of organizations. In Eagly's view, as women adapted to roles with less power and less status in society, they showed more cooperative, less dominant profiles than men. Thus, the social hierarchy and division of labor are important causes of gender differences in power, assertiveness, and nurture.

The **psychoanalytic theory of gender** stems from Freud's view that the preschool child develops a sexual attraction to the opposite-sex parent. This is the process known as the Oedipus (for boys) or Electra (for girls) complex. At 5 or 6 years of age, the child renounces this attraction because of anxious feelings. Subsequently, the child identifies with the same-sex parent, unconsciously adopting the same-sex parent's characteristics. However, developmentalists have observed that gender development does not proceed as Freud proposed. Children become gender-typed much earlier than 5 or 6 years of age, and they become masculine or feminine even when the same-sex parent is not present in the family.

The social cognitive approach discussed in Chapter 2 provides an alternative explanation of how children develop gender-typed behavior. According to the **social cognitive theory of gender**, children's gender development occurs through observing and imitating what other people say and do, and through being rewarded and punished for gender-appropriate and gender-inappropriate behavior (Bussey & Bandura, 1999). From birth onward, males and females are treated differently. When infants and toddlers show gender differences, adults tend to reward them. Parents often use rewards and punishments to teach their daughters to be feminine ("Karen, you are being a good girl when you play gently with your doll") and their sons to be masculine ("Keith, a boy as big as you is not supposed to cry"). Parents, however, are only one of many sources through which children learn gender roles (Blakemore, Berenbaum, & Liben, 2009). Culture, schools, peers, the media, and other family members also provide gender role models. For example, children also learn about gender from observing other adults in the neighborhood and on television (Bugental & Grusec, 2006). As children get older, peers become increasingly important. Let's take a closer look at the influence of parents and peers.

Parental Influences Parents, by action and by example, influence their children's gender development (Leaper & Friedman, 2007; Keenan, 2009). Both mothers and fathers are psychologically important to their children's gender development (Grusec & Davidov, 2007). Cultures around the world, however, tend to give mothers and fathers different roles (Kagitcibasi, 2007). A recent research review provided these conclusions (Bronstein, 2006):

- *Mothers' socialization strategies.* In many cultures, mothers socialize their daughters to be more obedient and responsible than their sons. They also place more restrictions on daughters' autonomy.

- *Fathers' socialization strategies.* Fathers show more attention to sons than daughters, engage in more activities with sons, and put forth more effort to promote sons' intellectual development.

Thus, according to Bronstein (2006, pp. 269–270), "Despite an increased awareness in the United States and other Western cultures of the detrimental effects of gender stereotyping, many parents continue to foster behaviors and perceptions that are consonant with traditional gender role norms."

social role theory A theory that gender differences result from the contrasting roles of men and women.

psychoanalytic theory of gender A theory deriving from Freud's view that the preschool child develops a sexual attraction to the opposite-sex parent, by approximately 5 or 6 years of age renounces this attraction because of anxious feelings, and subsequently identifies with the same-sex parent, unconsciously adopting the same-sex parent's characteristics.

social cognitive theory of gender A theory that emphasizes that children's gender development occurs through the observation and imitation of gender behavior and through the rewards and punishments children experience for gender-appropriate and gender-inappropriate behavior.

Peer Influences Parents provide the earliest discrimination of gender roles, but before long, peers join the process of responding to and modeling masculine and feminine behavior. In fact, peers become so important to gender development that the playground has been called "gender school" (Luria & Herzog, 1985).

Peers extensively reward and punish gender behavior (Leaper & Friedman, 2007). For example, when children play in ways that the culture says are sex-appropriate, their peers tend to reward them. But peers often reject children who act in a manner that is considered more characteristic of the other gender (Matlin, 2008). A little girl who brings a doll to the park may find herself surrounded by new friends; a little boy might be jeered. However, there is greater pressure for boys to conform to a traditional male role than for girls to conform to a traditional female role (Fagot, Rogers, & Leinbach, 2000). For example, a preschool girl who wants to wear boys' clothing receives considerably more approval than a boy who wants to wear a dress. The very term "tomboy" implies broad social acceptance of girls' adopting traditional male behaviors.

Gender molds important aspects of peer relations. It influences the composition of children's groups, the size of groups, and interactions within a group (Maccoby, 1998, 2002):

- *Gender composition of children's groups.* Around the age of 3, children already show a preference to spend time with same-sex playmates. From 4 to 12 years of age, this preference for playing in same-sex groups increases, and during the elementary school years children spend a large majority of their free time with children of their own sex (see Figure 8.1).

- *Group size.* From about 5 years of age onward, boys are more likely to associate together in larger clusters than girls are. Boys are also more likely to participate in organized group games than girls are. In one study, same-sex groups of six children were permitted to use play materials in any way they wished (Benenson, Apostolaris, & Parnass, 1997). Girls were more likely than boys to play in dyads or triads, while boys were more likely to interact in larger groups and seek to attain a group goal.

- *Interaction in same-sex groups.* Boys are more likely than girls to engage in rough-and-tumble play, competition, conflict, ego displays, risk taking, and seeking dominance. By contrast, girls are more likely to engage in "collaborative discourse," in which they talk and act in a more reciprocal manner.

Cognitive Influences

Observation, imitation, rewards and punishment—these are the mechanisms by which gender develops according to social cognitive theory. Interactions between the child and the social environment are the main keys to gender development in this view. Some critics who adopt a cognitive approach argue that this explanation pays too little attention to the child's own mind and understanding, and portrays the child as passively acquiring gender roles (Martin & Ruble, 2004).

One influential cognitive theory is **gender schema theory**, which states that gender-typing emerges as children gradually develop gender schemas of what is gender-appropriate and gender-inappropriate in their culture (Ruble, Martin, & Berenbaum, 2006; Zosuls, Lurye, & Ruble, 2008). A *schema* is a cognitive structure, a network of associations that guide an individual's perceptions. A *gender schema* organizes the world in terms of female and male. Children are internally motivated to perceive the world and to act in accordance with their developing schemas. Bit by bit, children pick up what is gender-appropriate and gender-inappropriate in their culture, and develop gender schemas that shape how they perceive the world and what they remember (Blakemore, Berenbaum, & Liben, 2009). Children are motivated to act in ways that conform with these gender schemas. Thus, gender schemas fuel gender-typing.

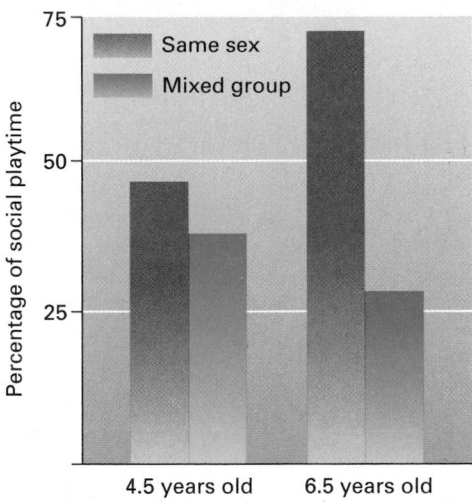

FIGURE 8.1 Developmental Changes in Percentage of Time Spent in Same-Sex and Mixed-Group Settings. Observations of children show that they are more likely to play in same-sex than mixed-sex groups. This tendency increases between 4 and 6 years of age.

gender schema theory The theory that gender-typing emerges as children develop gender schemas of their culture's gender-appropriate and gender-inappropriate behavior.

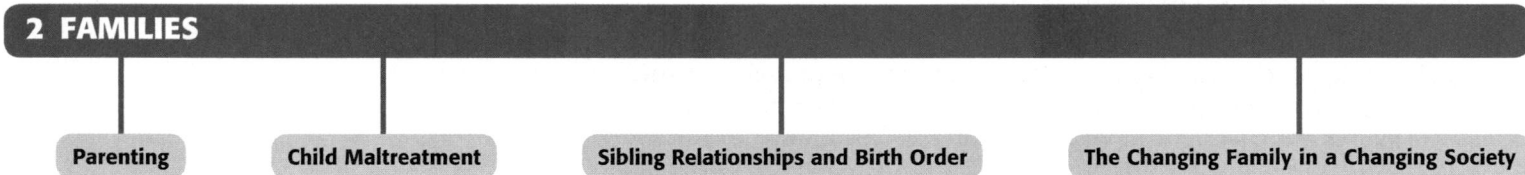

2 FAMILIES

Parenting   **Child Maltreatment**   **Sibling Relationships and Birth Order**   **The Changing Family in a Changing Society**

Attachment to a caregiver is a key social relationship during infancy, but we saw in Chapter 6 that some experts maintain that secure attachment and the infant years have been overdramatized as determinants of life-span development. Social and emotional development is also shaped by other relationships and by temperament, contexts, and social experiences in the early childhood years and later. In this section, we will discuss social relationships of early childhood beyond attachment. We will explore the different types of parenting, sibling relationships, and variations in family structures.

Parenting

A few years ago, there was considerable interest in Mozart CDs that were marketed with the promise that playing them would enrich infants' and young children's

Calvin and Hobbes

CALVIN & HOBBES, Copyright © 1991 and 1993 by Watterson. Distributed by Universal Press Syndicate. Reprinted with permission. All Rights Reserved.

brains. Some of the parents who bought them probably thought, "I don't have enough time to spend with my children so I'll just play these intellectual CDs and then they won't need me as much." Similarly, one-minute bedtime stories are being marketed for parents to read to their children (Walsh, 2000). There are one-minute bedtime bear books, puppy books, and so on. Parents who buy them know it is good for them to read with their children, but they don't want to spend a lot of time doing it. Behind the popularity of these products is an unfortunate theme which suggests that parenting can be done quickly, with little or no inconvenience (Sroufe, 2000).

What is wrong with these quick-fix approaches to parenting? Good parenting takes time and effort (Goodnow, 2009). You can't do it in a minute here and a minute there. You can't do it with CDs.

Of course, it's not just the quantity of time parents spend with children that is important for children's development—the quality of the parenting is clearly important (Bornstein & Zlotnik, 2008; Grusac, 2009; Landry, 2009). To understand variations in parenting, let's consider the styles parents use when they interact with their children, how they discipline their children, and coparenting.

Baumrind's Parenting Styles
Diana Baumrind (1971) argues parents should be neither punitive nor aloof. Rather, they should develop rules for their children and be affectionate with them. She has described four types of parenting styles:

- **Authoritarian parenting** is a restrictive, punitive style in which parents exhort the child to follow their directions and respect their work and effort. The authoritarian parent places firm limits and controls on the child and allows little verbal exchange. For example, an authoritarian parent might say, "You do it my way or else." Authoritarian parents also might spank the child frequently, enforce rules rigidly but not explain them, and show rage toward the child. Children of authoritarian parents are often unhappy, fearful, and anxious about comparing themselves with others, fail to initiate activity, and have weak communication skills. Sons of authoritarian parents may behave aggressively (Hart & others, 2003).

- **Authoritative parenting** encourages children to be independent but still places limits and controls on their actions. Extensive verbal give-and-take is allowed, and parents are warm and nurturant toward the child. An authoritative parent might put his arm around the child in a comforting way and say, "You know you should not have done that. Let's talk about how you can handle the situation better next time." Authoritative parents show pleasure and support in response to children's constructive behavior. They also expect mature, independent, and age-appropriate behavior by children. Children whose parents are authoritative are often cheerful, self-controlled and self-reliant, and achievement-oriented; they tend to maintain friendly relations with peers, cooperate with adults, and cope well with stress.

- **Neglectful parenting** is a style in which the parent is very uninvolved in the child's life. Children whose parents are neglectful develop the sense that other aspects of the parents' lives are more important than they are. These children tend to be socially incompetent. Many have poor self-control and don't handle independence well. They frequently have low self-esteem, are immature, and may be alienated from the family. In adolescence, they may show patterns of truancy and delinquency.

- **Indulgent parenting** is a style in which parents are highly involved with their children but place few demands or controls on them. Such parents let their children do what they want. The result is that the children never learn to control their own behavior and always expect to get their way. Some parents deliberately rear their children in this way because they believe the combination

*P*arenting is a very important profession, but no test of fitness for it is ever imposed in the interest of children.

—GEORGE BERNARD SHAW
Irish Playwright, 20th Century

authoritarian parenting A restrictive, punitive style in which parents exhort the child to follow their directions and to respect work and effort. The authoritarian parent places firm limits and controls on the child and allows little verbal exchange. Authoritarian parenting is associated with childern's social incompetence.

authoritative parenting A parenting style in which parents encourage their children to be independent but still place limits and controls on their actions. Extensive verbal give-and-take is allowed, and parents are warm and nurturant toward the child. Authoritative parenting is associated with children's social competence.

neglectful parenting A style of parenting in which the parent is very uninvolved in the child's life; it is associated with children's social incompetence, especially a lack of self-control.

indulgent parenting A style of parenting in which parents are highly involved with their children but place few demands or controls on them. Indulgent parenting is associated with children's social incompetence, especially a lack of self-control.

	Accepting, responsive	Rejecting, unresponsive
Demanding, controlling	Authoritative	Authoritarian
Undemanding, uncontrolling	Indulgent	Neglectful

FIGURE 8.2 Classification of Parenting Styles. The four types of parenting styles (authoritative, authoritarian, indulgent, and neglectful) involve the dimensions of acceptance and responsiveness, on the one hand, and demand and control on the other. For example, authoritative parenting involves being both accepting/responsive and demanding/controlling.

of warm involvement and few restraints will produce a creative, confident child. However, children whose parents are indulgent rarely learn respect for others and have difficulty controlling their behavior. They might be domineering, egocentric, noncompliant, and have difficulties in peer relations.

These four classifications of parenting involve combinations of acceptance and responsiveness on the one hand and demand and control on the other (Maccoby & Martin, 1983). How these dimensions combine to produce authoritarian, authoritative, neglectful, and indulgent parenting is shown in Figure 8.2.

Parenting Styles in Context Do the benefits of authoritative parenting transcend the boundaries of ethnicity, socioeconomic status (SES), and household composition? Although occasional exceptions have been found, evidence linking authoritative parenting with competence on the part of the child occurs in research across a wide range of ethnic groups, social strata, cultures, and family structures (Steinberg & Silk, 2002).

Nonetheless, researchers have found that in some ethnic groups, aspects of the authoritarian style may be associated with more positive child outcomes than Baumrind predicts (Parke & Buriel, 2006). Elements of the authoritarian style may take on different meanings and have different effects depending on the context.

For example, Asian American parents often continue aspects of traditional Asian child-rearing practices that have sometimes been described as authoritarian. The parents exert considerable control over their children's lives. However, Ruth Chao (2001, 2005, 2007; Chao & Tseng, 2002) argues that the style of parenting used by many Asian American parents is distinct from the domineering control of the authoritarian style. Instead, Chao argues that the control reflects concern and involvement in their children's lives and is best conceptualized as a type of training. The high academic achievement of Asian American children may be a consequence of their "training" parents (Stevenson & Zusho, 2002).

An emphasis on requiring respect and obedience is also associated with the authoritarian style, but in Latino child rearing this focus may be positive rather than punitive. Rather than suppressing the child's development, it may encourage the development of a different type of self. Latino child-rearing practices encourage the development of a self and identity that is embedded in the family and requires respect and obedience (Harwood & others, 2002). Furthermore, many Latino families have several generations living together and helping each other (Zinn & Wells, 2000). In these circumstances, emphasizing respect and obedience by children may be part of maintaining a harmonious home and may be important in the formation of the child's identity.

Even physical punishment, another characteristics of the authoritarian style, may have varying effects in different contexts. African American parents are more likely than non-Latino White parents to use physical punishment (Deater-Deckard & Dodge, 1997). However, the use of physical punishment has been linked with increased externalized child problems (such as acting out and high levels of aggression) in non-Latino White families but not in African American families. One explanation of this finding points to the need for African American parents to enforce rules in the dangerous environments in which they are more likely to live (Harrison-Hale, McLoyd, & Smedley, 2004). In this context, requiring obedience to parental authority may be an adaptive strategy to keep children from engaging in antisocial behavior that can have serious consequences for the victim or the perpetrator. As we see next, though, overall, the use of physical punishment in disciplining children raises many concerns.

Punishment   For centuries, corporal (physical) punishment, such as spanking, has been considered a necessary and even desirable method of disciplining children. Use of corporal punishment is legal in every state in America. A national survey of U.S. parents with 3- and 4-year-old children found that 26 percent of parents reported spanking their children frequently, and 67 percent of the parents reported yelling at their children frequently (Regalado & others, 2004). A cross-cultural comparison found that individuals in the United States and Canada were among those with the most favorable attitudes toward corporal punishment and were the most likely to remember it being used by their parents (Curran & others, 2001) (see Figure 8.3).

An increasing number of studies have examined the outcomes of physically punishing children, although those that have been conducted are correlational. Clearly, it would be highly unethical to randomly assign parents to either spank or not spank their children in an experimental study. Recall that cause and effect cannot be determined in a correlational study. In one correlational study, spanking by parents was linked with children's antisocial behavior, including cheating, telling lies, being mean to others, bullying, getting into fights, and being disobedient (Strauss, Sugarman, & Giles-Sims, 1997).

A research review concluded that corporal punishment by parents is associated with higher levels of immediate compliance and aggression by the children (Gershoff, 2002). The review also found that corporal punishment is associated with lower levels of moral internalization and mental health (Gershoff, 2002). One study revealed that children whose parents hit or slapped them in the prior two weeks showed more emotional and adjustment problems than children who had not been hit or slapped by parents in the same time frame (Aucoin, Frick, & Bodin, 2006). A recent study also found a link between the use of physical punishment by parents and children's negative behavioral adjustment at 36 months and in the first grade (Mulvaney & Mebert, 2007). Another recent study also discovered that a history of harsh physical discipline was linked to adolescent depression and externalized problems, such as juvenile delinquency (Bender & others, 2007).

Some critics, though, argue that the research evidence is not yet sound enough to warrant a blanket injunction against corporal punishment, especially mild corporal punishment (Kazdin & Benjet, 2003).

What are some reasons for avoiding spanking or similar punishments? The reasons include:

- When adults punish a child by yelling, screaming, or spanking, they are presenting children with out-of-control models for handling stressful situations. Children may imitate this aggressive, out-of-control behavior (Sim & Ong, 2005).

- Punishment can instill fear, rage, or avoidance. For example, spanking the child may cause the child to avoid being around the parent and to fear the parent.

- Punishment tells children what not to do rather what to do. Children should be given feedback, such as "Why don't you try this?"

- Punishment can be abusive. Parents might unintentionally become so aroused when they are punishing the child that they become abusive (Durrant, 2008).

Most child psychologists recommend handling misbehavior by reasoning with the child, especially explaining the consequences of

According to Ruth Chao, what type of parenting style do many Asian American parents use?

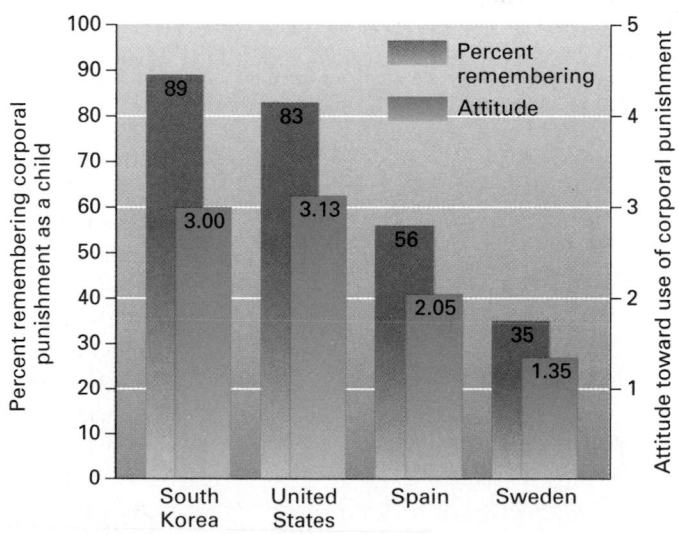

FIGURE 8.3   Corporal Punishment in Different Countries. A 5-point scale was used to assess attitudes toward corporal punishment with scores closer to 1 indicating an attitude against its use and scores closer to 5 suggesting an attitude favoring its use. *Why are studies of corporal punishment correlational studies, and how does that affect their usefulness?*

How do most child psychologists recommend handling a child's misbehavior?

the child's actions for others. *Time out,* in which the child is removed from a setting that offers positive reinforcement, can also be effective. For example, when the child has misbehaved, a parent might take away TV viewing for a specified time.

In Chapter 6, we described the family as a system and discussed possible links between marital relationships and parenting practices. To read about a family systems study involving marital conflict and the use of physical punishment, see the *Research in Life-Span Development* interlude.

Research in Life-Span Development
Marital Conflict, Individual Hostility, and the Use of Physical Punishment

A longitudinal study assessed couples across the transition to parenting to investigate possible links between marital conflict, individual adult hostility, and the use of physical punishment with young children (Kanoy & others, 2003). Before the birth of the first child, the level of marital conflict was observed in a marital problem-solving discussion; answers to questionnaires regarding individual characteristics were also obtained. Thus, these characteristics of the couples were not influenced by characteristics of the child. When the children were 2 and 5 years old, the couples were interviewed about the frequency and intensity of their physical punishment of the children. At both ages, the parents' level of marital conflict was again observed in a marital problem-solving discussion.

The researchers found that both hostility and marital conflict were linked with the use of physical punishment. Individuals with high rates of hostility on the prenatal measures used more frequent and more severe physical punishment with their children. The same was evident for marital conflict—when marital conflict was high, both mothers and fathers were more likely to use physical punishment in disciplining their young children.

If parents who have a greater likelihood of using physical punishment can be identified in prenatal classes, these families could be encouraged to use other forms of discipline before they get into a pattern of physically punishing their children.

Coparenting   The relationship between marital conflict and the use of punishment highlights the importance of *coparenting,* which is the support that parents provide one another in jointly raising a child. Poor coordination between parents, undermining of the other parent, lack of cooperation and warmth, and disconnection by one parent are conditions that place children at risk for problems (McHale, 2007; McHale & Sullivan, 2008; Schoppe-Sullivan & others, 2007). For example, in one study, 4-year-old children from families characterized by low levels of mutuality and support in coparenting were more likely than their classmates to show difficulties in social adjustment on the playground (McHale, Johnson, & Sinclair, 1999). By contrast, parental cooperation and warmth are linked with children's prosocial behavior and competence in peer relations.

Parents who do not spend enough time with their children or who have problems in child rearing can benefit from counseling and therapy. To read about the work of marriage and family counselor Darla Botkin, see the *Careers in Life-Span Development* profile.

Child Maltreatment

Unfortunately, punishment sometimes leads to the abuse of infants and children (Newton & Vandeven, 2008). In 2002, approximately 906,000 U.S. children were found to be victims of child abuse (U.S. Department of Health and Human Services, 2005). Eighty-four percent of these children were abused by a parent or parents. Laws in many states now require physicians and teachers to report suspected cases of child abuse, yet many cases go unreported, especially those of battered infants.

Child maltreatment involves grossly inadequate and destructive aspects of parenting.

—**Dante Cicchetti**
Contemporary Developmental Psychologist, University of Minnesota.

Careers in Life-Span Development

Darla Botkin, Marriage and Family Therapist

Darla Botkin is a marriage and family therapist who teaches, conducts research, and engages in marriage and family therapy. She is on the faculty of the University of Kentucky. Botkin obtained a bachelor's degree in elementary education with a concentration in special education and then went on to receive a master's degree in early childhood education. She spent the next six years working with children and their families in a variety of settings, including child care, elementary school, and Head Start. These experiences led Botkin to recognize the interdependence of the developmental settings that children and their parents experience (such as home, school, and work). She returned to graduate school and obtained a Ph.D. in family studies from the University of Tennessee. She then became a faculty member in the Family Studies program at the University of Kentucky. Completing further coursework and clinical training in marriage and family therapy, she became certified as a marriage and family therapist.

Botkin's current interests include working with young children in family therapy, gender and ethnic issues in family therapy, and the role of spirituality in family wellness.

Darla Botkin (*left*), conducting a family therapy session.

Whereas the public and many professionals use the term *child abuse* to refer to both abuse and neglect, developmentalists increasingly use the term *child maltreatment* (Pollak, 2009; Toth & Cicchetti, 2009). This term does not have quite the emotional impact of the term *abuse* and acknowledges that maltreatment includes diverse conditions.

Types of Child Maltreatment The four main types of child maltreatment are physical abuse, child neglect, sexual abuse, and emotional abuse (National Clearinghouse on Child Abuse and Neglect, 2004):

- *Physical abuse* is characterized by the infliction of physical injury as result of punching, beating, kicking, biting, burning, shaking, or otherwise harming a child. The parent or other person may not have intended to hurt the child; the injury may have resulted from excessive physical punishment.

- *Child neglect* is characterized by failure to provide for the child's basic needs. Neglect can be physical (abandonment, for example), educational (allowing chronic truancy, for example), or emotional (marked inattention to the child's needs, for example). Child neglect is by far the most common form of child maltreatment. In every country where relevant data have been collected, neglect occurs up to three times as often as abuse (Benoit, Coolbear, & Crawford, 2008).

- *Sexual abuse* includes fondling a child's genitals, intercourse, incest, rape, sodomy, exhibitionism, and commercial exploitation through prostitution or the production of pornographic materials (Johnson, 2008).

- *Emotional abuse (psychological/verbal abuse/mental injury)* includes acts or omissions by parents or other caregivers that have caused, or could cause, serious behavioral, cognitive, or emotional problems.

Children at a shelter for domestic violence in Tel Aviv, Israel.

This print ad was created by Prevent Child Abuse America to make people aware of its national blue wristband campaign. The campaign's goal is to educate people about child abuse prevention and encourage them to support the organization.

Source: Prevent Child Abuse America

Although any of these forms of child maltreatment may be found separately, they often occur in combination. Emotional abuse is almost always present when other forms are identified.

The Context of Abuse No single factor causes child maltreatment (Toth & Cicchetti, 2009). A combination of factors, including the culture, family, and developmental characteristics of the child, likely contribute to child maltreatment (Dumont, Widom, & Czaja, 2007; Jaffe & others, 2007).

The extensive violence that takes place in American culture is reflected in the occurrence of violence in the family (Durrant, 2008; Kitzman, 2009). A regular diet of violence appears on television screens, and parents often resort to power assertion as a disciplinary technique. In China, where physical punishment is rarely used to discipline children, the incidence of child abuse is reported to be very low.

The family itself is obviously a key part of the context of abuse (MacMillan, 2009). The interactions of all family members need to be considered, regardless of who performs the violent acts against the child (Kim & Cicchetti, 2006). For example, even though the father may be the one who physically abuses the child, the behavior of the mother, the child, and siblings also should be evaluated. A mother who conveniently goes shopping whenever the father is angry with the child, or siblings who tease the child for "deserving" a beating, may contribute to the abuse.

Were parents who abuse children abused by their own parents? About one-third of parents who were abused themselves when they were young go on to abuse their own children (Cicchetti & Toth, 2006). Thus, some, but not a majority, of parents are involved in an intergenerational transmission of abuse (Dixon, Browne, & Hamilton-Giachritsis, 2005). Mothers who break out of the intergenerational transmission of abuse often report having had at least one warm, caring adult in their background; have a close, positive marital relationship; and have received therapy (Egeland, Jacobvitz, & Sroufe, 1988).

Developmental Consequences of Abuse Among the consequences of child maltreatment in childhood and adolescence are poor emotion regulation, attachment problems, problems in peer relations, difficulty in adapting to school, and other psychological problems such as depression and delinquency (Toth & Cicchetti, 2009; Oates, 2009). As shown in Figure 8.4, maltreated young children in foster care were more likely to show abnormal stress hormone levels than middle-SES young children living with their birth family (Gunnar & Fisher, 2006). In this study, the abnormal stress hormone levels were mainly present in the foster children who were neglected, best described as "institutional neglect" (Fisher, 2005). Abuse also may have this effect on young children (Gunnar & Fisher, 2006). Later, during the adult years, individuals who were maltreated as children often have difficulty in establishing and maintaining healthy intimate relationships (Minzenberg, Poole, & Vinogradov, 2006). As adults, maltreated children are also at higher risk for violent behavior toward other adults—especially dating partners and marital partners—as well as for substance abuse, anxiety, and depression (Mass, Herrenkohl, & Sousa, 2008; Stewart, Livingston, & Dennsison, 2008).

What can be done to prevent or reduce the incidence of child maltreatment? In one study of maltreating mothers and their 1-year-olds, two treatments were effective in reducing child maltreatment: (1) home visitation that emphasized improved parenting, coping with stress, and increasing support for the mother; and (2) parent-infant psychotherapy that focused on improving maternal-infant attachment (Cicchetti, Toth, & Rogosch, 2005).

Sibling Relationships and Birth Order

How do developmentalists characterize sibling relationships? How extensively does birth order influence behavior?

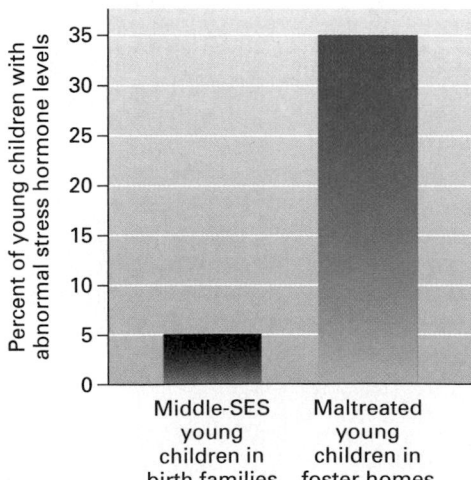

FIGURE 8.4 Abnormal Stress Hormone Levels in Young Children in Different Types of Rearing Conditions

Sibling Relationships Approximately 80 percent of American children have one or more siblings—that is, sisters and brothers (Dunn, 2007). Any of you who have grown up with siblings probably have a rich memory of aggressive, hostile interchanges. Siblings in the presence of each other when they are 2 to 4 years of age, on average, have a conflict once every 10 minutes and then the conflicts go down somewhat from 5 to 7 years of age (Kramer, 2006). What do parents do when they encounter sibings having a verbal or physical confrontation? One study revealed that they do one of three things: (1) intervene and try to help them resolve the conflict, (2) admonish or threaten them, or (3) do nothing at all (Kramer & Perozynski, 1999). Of interest is that in families with two siblings 2 to 5 years of age, the most frequent parental reaction is do nothing at all.

Laurie Kramer (2006), who conducted a number of research studies on siblings, says that not intervening and letting sibling conflict escalate is not a good strategy. She developed a program titled, "More Fun with Sisters and Brothers," that teaches 4- to 8-year-old siblings social skills for developing positive interactions (Kramer & Radey, 1997). Among the social skills taught in the program are how to appropriately initiate play, how to accept and refuse invitations to play, perspective taking, how to deal with angry feelings, and how to manage conflict. A recent study of 5- to 10-year-old sibings and their parents found that training parents to mediate sibling disputes increased children's understanding of conflicts and reduced sibling conflict (Smith & Ross, 2007).

However, conflict is only one of the many dimensions of sibling relations (Howe & Recchia, 2008, 2009). Sibling relations include helping, sharing, teaching, fighting, and playing, and siblings can act as emotional supports, rivals, and communication partners (Pomery & others, 2005).

Judy Dunn (2007), a leading expert on sibling relationships, recently described three important characteristics of sibling relationships:

- *Emotional quality of the relationship.* Both intensive positive and negative emotions are often expressed by siblings toward each other. Many children and adolescents have mixed feelings toward their siblings.

- *Familiarity and intimacy of the relationship.* Siblings typically know each other very well, and this intimacy suggests that they can either provide support or tease and undermine each other, depending on the situation.

- *Variation in sibling relationships.* Some siblings describe their relationships more positively than others. Thus, there is considerable variation in sibling relationships. We just indicated that many siblings have mixed feelings about each other, but some children and adolescents mainly describe their sibling in warm, affectionate ways, whereas others primarily talk about how irritating and mean a sibling is.

Birth Order Whether a child has older or younger siblings has been linked to development of certain personality characteristics. For example, a recent review concluded that "firstborns are the most intelligent, achieving, and conscientious, while later-borns are the most rebellious, liberal, and agreeable" (Paulhus, 2008, p. 210). Compared with later-born children, firstborn children have also been described as more adult-oriented, helpful, conforming, and self-controlled. However, when such birth-order differences are reported, they often are small.

What characterizes children's sibling relationships?

What accounts for such differences related to birth order? Proposed explanations usually point to variations in interactions with parents and siblings associated with being in a particular position in the family. This is especially true in the case of the firstborn child (Teti, 2001). The oldest child is the only one who does not have to share parental love and affection with other siblings—until another sibling comes along. An infant requires more attention than an older child; this means that the firstborn sibling receives less attention after the newborn arrives. Does this result in conflict between parents and the firstborn? In one research study, mothers became more negative, coercive, and restraining and played less with the firstborn following the birth of a second child (Dunn & Kendrick, 1982).

The one-child family is becoming much more common in China because of the strong motivation to limit the population growth in the People's Republic of China. The policy is still relatively new, and its effects on children have not been fully examined. *In general, though, what have researchers found the only child to be like?*

What is the only child like? The popular conception is that the only child is a "spoiled brat," with such undesirable characteristics as dependency, lack of self-control, and self-centered behavior. But researchers present a more positive portrayal of the only child. Only children often are achievement-oriented and display a desirable personality, especially in comparison with later-borns and children from large families (Falbo & Poston, 1993; Jiao, Ji, & Jing, 1996).

So far, our discussion suggests that birth order might be a strong predictor of behavior. However, an increasing number of family researchers stress that when all of the factors that influence behavior are considered, birth order itself shows limited ability to predict behavior. Think about some of the other important factors in children's lives that influence their behavior beyond birth order. They include heredity, models of competency or incompetency that parents present to children on a daily basis, peer influences, school influences, socioeconomic factors, sociohistorical factors, and cultural variations. When someone says firstborns are always like this but last-borns are always like that, the person is making overly simplistic statements that do not adequately take into account the complexity of influences on a child's development.

The Changing Family in a Changing Society

Beyond variations in the number of siblings, the families that children experience differ in many important ways. The number of children growing up in single-parent families is staggering. As shown in Figure 8.5, the United States has one of the highest percentage of single-parent families in the world. Among two-parent families, there are those in which both parents work, or have divorced parents who have remarried, or gay or lesbian parents. Differences in culture and socioeconomic status (SES) also influence families. How do these variations in families affect children?

Working Parents   More than one of every two U.S. mothers with a child under the age of 5 is in the labor force; more than two of every three with a child from 6 to 17 years of age is. Maternal employment is a part of modern life, but its effects are still debated.

Work can produce positive and negative effects on parenting (Goldberg & Lucas-Thompson, 2008). Recent research indicates that what matters for children's development is the nature of the parents' work rather than whether one or both parents works outside the home (Clarke-Stewart, 2006; Goldberg & Lucas-Thompson, 2008). Ann Crouter (2006) recently described how parents bring their experiences at work into their homes. She concluded that parents who have poor working conditions, such as long hours, overtime work, stressful work, and lack of autonomy at work, are likely to be more irritable at home and engage in less effective parenting than their counterparts who have better work conditions in their jobs. A consistent finding is the children

FIGURE 8.5 Single-Parent Families in Different Countries

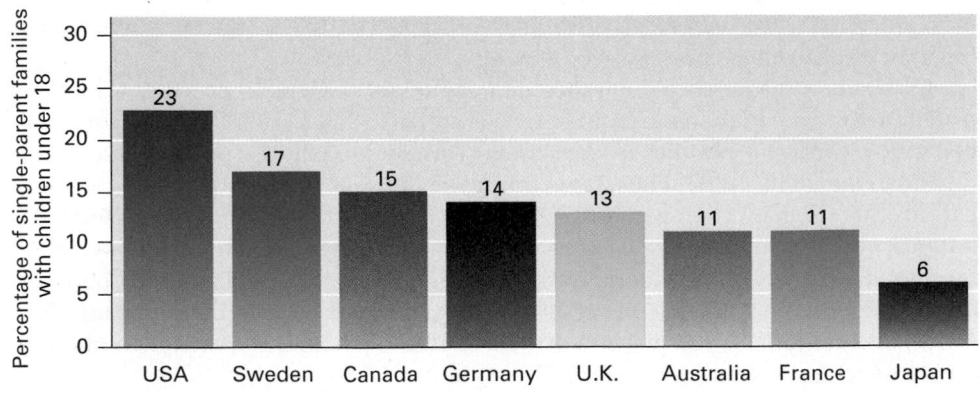

(especially girls) of working mothers engage in less gender stereotyping and have more egalitarian views of gender (Goldberg & Lucas-Thompson, 2008).

Children in Divorced Families   Divorce rates changed rather dramatically in the United States and many countries around the world in the late twentieth century (Amato & Irving, 2006). The U.S. divorce rate increased dramatically in the 1960s and 1970s but has declined since the 1980s. However, the divorce rate in the United States is still much higher than in most other countries.

It is estimated that 40 percent of children born to married parents in the United States will experience their parents' divorce (Hetherington & Stanley-Hagan, 2002). Let's examine some important questions about children in divorced families.

Are children better adjusted in intact, never-divorced families than in divorced families? Most researchers agree that children from divorced families show poorer adjustment than their counterparts in nondivorced families (Hetherington, 2006; Wallerstein, 2008) (see Figure 8.6). Those who have experienced multiple divorces are at greater risk. Children in divorced families are more likely than children in nondivorced families to have academic problems, to show externalized problems (such as acting out and delinquency) and internalized problems (such as anxiety and depression), to be less socially responsible, to have less competent intimate relationships, to drop out of school, to become sexually active at an early age, to take drugs, to associate with antisocial peers, to have low self-esteem, and to be less securely attached as young adults (Conger & Chao, 1996). One recent study revealed that when individuals experienced the divorce of their parents in childhood and adolescence, it was linked to having unstable romantic or marital relationships and low levels of education in adulthood (Amato, 2006). Nonetheless, keep in mind that a majority of children in divorced families do not have significant adjustment problems (Ahrons, 2007). One study found that 20 years after their parents had divorced when they were children, approximately 80 percent of adults concluded that their parents' decision to divorce was a wise one (Ahrons, 2004).

Should parents stay together for the sake of the children? Whether parents should stay in an unhappy or conflicted marriage for the sake of their children is one of the most commonly asked questions about divorce (Hetherington, 2006). If the stresses and disruptions in family relationships associated with an unhappy, conflictual marriage that erode the well-being of children are reduced by the move to a divorced, single-parent family, divorce can be advantageous. However, if the diminished resources and increased risks associated with divorce also are accompanied by inept parenting and sustained or increased conflict, not only between the divorced couple but also among the parents, children, and siblings, the best choice for the children would be for an unhappy marriage to be retained (Hetherington & Stanley-Hagan, 2002). It is difficult to determine how these "ifs" will play out when parents either remain together in an acrimonious marriage or become divorced.

Note that marital conflict may have negative consequences for children in the context of marriage or divorce (Cox & others, 2008). A longitudinal study revealed that conflict in nondivorced families was associated with emotional problems in children (Amato, 2006). Indeed, many of the problems children from divorced homes experience begin during the predivorce period, a time when parents are often in active conflict with each other. Thus, when children from divorced homes show problems, the problems may not be due only to the divorce, but also to the marital conflict that led to it (Thompson, 2008).

How much do family processes matter in divorced families? Family processes matter a great deal (Kelly, 2007; Wallerstein, 2008). When divorced parents' relationship with each other is harmonious, and when they use authoritative parenting, the adjustment of children improves (Hetherington, 2006). A number of researchers have shown that a disequilibrium, which includes diminished parenting skills, occurs in the year following the divorce but that, by two years after the divorce, restabilization has occurred and parenting skills have improved (Hetherington, 1989).

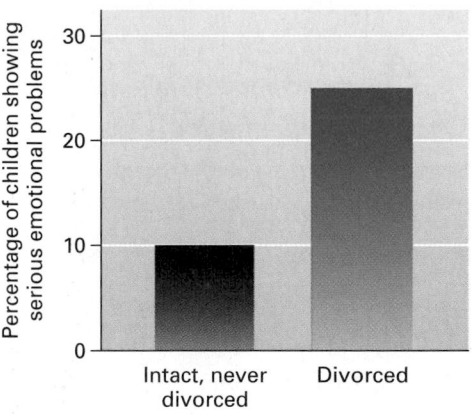

FIGURE 8.6 Divorce and Children's Emotional Problems. In Hetherington's research, 25 percent of children from divorced families showed serious emotional problems compared with only 10 percent of children from intact, never-divorced families. However, keep in mind that a substantial majority (75 percent) of the children from divorced families did not show serious emotional problems.

What concerns are involved in whether parents should stay together for the sake of the children or become divorced?

As marriage has become a more optional, less permanent institution in contemporary America, children and adolescents are encountering stresses and adaptive challenges associated with their parents' marital transitions.

—E. Mavis Hetherington
Contemporary Psychologist, University of Virginia

What factors influence an individual child's vulnerability to suffering negative consequences as a result of living in a divorced family? Among the factors involved in the child's risk and vulnerability are the child's adjustment prior to the divorce, as well as the child's personality and temperament, gender, and custody situation (Hetherington, 2006). Children whose parents later divorce show poorer adjustment before the breakup (Amato & Booth, 1996). Children who are socially mature and responsible, who show few behavioral problems, and who have an easy temperament are better able to cope with their parents' divorce. Children with a difficult temperament often have problems in coping with their parents' divorce (Hetherington, 2000).

Earlier studies reported gender differences in response to divorce, with divorce being more negative for girls than boys in mother-custody families. However, more recent studies have shown that gender differences are less pronounced and consistent than was previously believed. Some of the inconsistency may be due to the increase in father custody, joint custody, and increased involvement of noncustodial fathers, especially in their sons' lives (Palmer, 2004). An analysis of studies found that children in joint-custody families were better adjusted than children in sole-custody families (Bauserman, 2002). Some studies have shown that boys adjust better in father-custody families, girls in mother-custody families, whereas other studies have not (Maccoby & Mnookin, 1992; Santrock & Warshak, 1979).

What role does socioeconomic status play in the lives of children in divorced families? Custodial mothers experience the loss of about one-fourth to one-half of their predivorce income, in comparison with a loss of only one-tenth by custodial fathers (Emery, 1994). This income loss for divorced mothers is accompanied by increased workloads, high rates of job instability, and residential moves to less desirable neighborhoods with inferior schools (Sayer, 2006).

In sum, many factors are involved in determining how divorce influences a child's development (Hetherington, 2006). To read about some strategies for helping children cope with the divorce of their parents, see the *Applications in Life-Span Development* interlude.

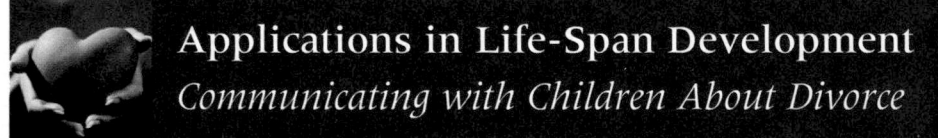

Applications in Life-Span Development
Communicating with Children About Divorce

Ellen Galinsky and Judy David (1988) developed a number of guidelines for communicating with children about divorce.

- ***Explain the separation.*** As soon as daily activities in the home make it obvious that one parent is leaving, tell the children. If possible, both parents should be present when children are told about the separation to come. The reasons for the separation are very difficult for young children to understand. No matter what parents tell children, children can find reasons to argue against the separation. It is extremely important for parents to tell the children who will take care of them and to describe the specific arrangements for seeing the other parent.

- ***Explain that the separation is not the child's fault.*** Young children often believe their parents' separation or divorce is their own fault. Therefore, it is important to tell children that they are not the cause of the separation. Parents need to repeat this a number of times.

- ***Explain that it may take time to feel better.*** Tell young children that it's normal to not feel good about what is happening and that many other children feel this way when their parents become separated. It is also okay for divorced parents to share some of their emotions with children, by saying something like "I'm having a hard time since the separation just like you, but I know it's going to get better after a while." Such statements are best kept brief and should not criticize the other parent.

- ***Keep the door open for further discussion.*** Tell your children to come to you anytime they want to talk about the separation. It is healthy for children to express their pent-up emotions in discussions with their parents and to learn that the parents are willing to listen to their feelings and fears.

- ***Provide as much continuity as possible.*** The less children's worlds are disrupted by the separation, the easier their transition to a single-parent family will be. This means maintaining the rules already in place as much as possible. Children need parents who care enough to not only give them warmth and nurturance but also set reasonable limits.

- ***Provide support for your children and yourself.*** After a divorce or separation, parents are as important to children as before the divorce or separation. Divorced parents need to provide children with as much support as possible. Parents function best when other people are available to give them support as adults and as parents. Divorced parents can find people who provide practical help and with whom they can talk about their problems.

Gay Male and Lesbian Parents   Increasingly, gay male and lesbian couples are creating families that include children. Approximately 20 percent of lesbians and 10 percent of gay men are parents (Patterson, 2004). There may be more than 1 million gay and lesbian parents in the United States today.

Like heterosexual couples, gay male and lesbian parents vary greatly. They may be single or they may have same gender partners. Many lesbian mothers and gay fathers are noncustodial parents because they lost custody of their children to heterosexual spouses after a divorce.

Most children of gay and lesbian parents were born in a heterosexual relationship that ended in a divorce—in most cases, it was probably a relationship in which one or both parents only later identified themselves as gay male or lesbian. In other cases, lesbians and gay men became parents as a result of donor insemination and surrogates, or through adoption.

Parenthood among lesbians and gay men is controversial. Opponents claim that being raised by gay male or lesbian parents harms the child's development. But researchers have found few differences between children growing up with lesbian mothers or gay fathers on the one hand, and children growing up with heterosexual parents on the other (Patterson, 2004; Patterson & Hastings, 2007). For example, children growing up in gay male or lesbian families are just as popular with their peers, and no differences are found in the adjustment and mental health of children living in these families when they are compared with children in heterosexual families (Hyde, 2007). Contrary to the once-popular expectation that being raised by a gay male or lesbian parent would result in the child growing up to be gay or lesbian, in fact the overwhelming majority of children from gay or lesbian families have a heterosexual orientation (Tasker & Golombok, 1997).

What are the research findings regarding the development and psychological well-being of children raised by gay male and lesbian couples?

Cultural, Ethnic, and Socioeconomic Variations   Parenting can be influenced by culture, ethnicity, and socioeconomic status. Recall from Bronfenbrenner's ecological theory (see Chapter 1) that a number of social contexts influence the child's development. In Bronfenbrenner's theory, culture, ethnicity, and socioeconomic status are classified as part of the macrosystem because they represent broader, societal contexts.

Cross-Cultural Studies   Different cultures often give different answers to such basic questions as what the father's role in the family should be, what support systems are available to families, and how children should be disciplined (Fiese & Winter, 2008). There are important cross-cultural variations in parenting (Kagitcibasi, 2007). In some cultures (such as Arab countries, mentioned earlier in this chapter), authoritarian parenting is widespread.

What are some characteristics of families within different ethnic groups?

Cultural change, brought about by such factors as increasingly frequent international travel, the Internet and electronic communications, and economic globalization, is coming to families in many countries around the world. There are trends toward greater family mobility, migration to urban areas, separation as some family members work in cities or countries far from their homes, smaller families, fewer extended-family households, and increases in maternal employment (Brown & Larson, 2002). These trends can change the resources that are available to children. For example, when several generations no longer live close by, children may lose support and guidance from grandparents, aunts, and uncles. On the positive side, smaller families may produce more openness and communication between parents and children.

Ethnicity Families within different ethnic groups in the United States differ in their typical size, structure, composition, reliance on kinships networks, and levels of income and education (Hernandez, Denton, & Maccartney, 2007; Liu & others, 2009). Large and extended families are more common among minority groups than among the White majority. For example, 19 percent of Latino families have three or more children, compared with 14 percent of African American and 10 percent of White families. African American and Latino children interact more with grandparents, aunts, uncles, cousins, and more-distant relatives than do White children.

Single-parent families are more common among African Americans and Latinos than among White Americans (Coltrane & others, 2008; Harris & Graham, 2007). In comparison with two-parent households, single parents often have more limited resources of time, money, and energy (Barajas, Phillipsen, & Brooks-Gunn, 2008; Wilson, 2008). Ethnic minority parents also are less educated and more likely to live in low-income circumstances than their White counterparts. Still, many impoverished ethnic minority families manage to find ways to raise competent children (Hattery & Smith, 2007).

Of course, individual families vary, and how ethnic minority families deal with stress depends on many factors (Wong, Kinzie, & Kinzie, 2009). Whether the parents are native-born or immigrants, how long the family has been in this country, their socioeconomic status, and their national origin all make a difference (Fuligni & Fuligni, 2007; Parke & others, 2008). The characteristics of the family's social context also influence its adaptation. What are the attitudes toward the family's ethnic group within its neighborhood or city? Can the family's children attend good schools? Are there community groups that welcome people from the family's ethnic group? Do members of the family's ethnic group form community groups of their own? To read further about ethnic minority parenting, see the *Diversity in Life-Span Development* interlude.

Diversity in Life-Span Development
Acculturation and Ethnic Minority Parenting

Ethnic minority children and their parents "are expected to transcend their own cultural background and to incorporate aspects of the dominant culture" into children's development. They undergo varying degrees of *acculturation*, which refers to cultural changes that occur when one culture comes in contact with another. Asian American parents, for example, may feel pressed to modify the traditional training style of parental control discussed earlier as they encounter the more permissive parenting typical of the dominant culture.

The level of family acculturation can affect parenting style by influencing expectations for children's development, parent-child interactions, and the role of the extended family (Ishii-Kuntz,

2004; Martinez & Halgunseth, 2004). For example, in one study, the level of acculturation and maternal education were the strongest predictors of maternal-infant interaction patterns in Latino families (Perez-Febles, 1992).

The family's level of acculturation also influences important decisions about child care and early childhood education (Bradley & McKelvey, 2007). For example, "an African American mother might prefer to leave her children with extended family while she is at work because the kinship network is seen as a natural way to cope with maternal absence. This well-intentioned, culturally appropriate decision might, however, put the child at an educational and social disadvantage relative to other children of similar age who have the benefit of important preschool experiences that may ease the transition into early school years." Less acculturated and more acculturated family members may disagree about the appropriateness of various caregiving practices, possibly creating conflict or confusion.

The opportunities for acculturation that young children experience depend mainly on their parents and extended family. If they send the children to a child-care center, school, church, or other community setting, the children are likely to learn about the values and behaviors of the dominant culture, and they may be expected to adapt to that culture's norms. Thus, Latino children raised in a traditional family in which the family's good is considered more important than the individual's interests may attend a preschool in which children are rewarded for asserting themselves. Chinese American children whose traditional parents value behavioral inhibition (as discussed in Chapter 6) may be rewarded outside the home for being active and emotionally expressive. Over time, the differences in the level of acculturation experienced by children and by their parents and extended family may grow. (Source: Garcia, Coll & Pachter, 2002, pp. 7–8)

How is acculturation involved in ethnic minority parenting?

Socioeconomic Status Low-income families have less access to resources than higher-income families (Leon-Guerrero, 2009; Philipsen, Johnson, & Brooks-Gunn, 2009). The differential in access to resources includes nutrition, health care, protection from danger, and enriching educational and socialization opportunities, such as tutoring and lessons in various activities. These differences are compounded in low-income families characterized by long-term poverty (Conger & Conger, 2008; Gupta, Thornton, & Huston, 2008).

In America and most Western cultures, differences have been found in child rearing among different socioeconomic-status (SES) groups (Hoff, Laursen, & Tardif, 2002, p. 246):

- "Lower-SES parents (1) are more concerned that their children conform to society's expectations, (2) create a home atmosphere in which it is clear that parents have authority over children," (3) use physical punishment more in disciplining their children, and (4) are more directive and less conversational with their children.

- "Higher-SES parents (1) are more concerned with developing children's initiative" and delay of gratification, "(2) create a home atmosphere in which children are more nearly equal participants and in which rules are discussed as opposed to being laid down" in an authoritarian manner, (3) are less likely to use physical punishment, and (4) "are less directive and more conversational" with their children.

Parents in different socioeconomic groups also tend to think differently about education (Huston & Ripke, 2006). Middle- and upper-income parents more often think of education as something that should be mutually encouraged by parents and teachers. By contrast, low-income parents are more likely to view education as the teacher's job. Thus, increased school-family linkages especially can benefit students from low-income families.

Review and Reflect: Learning Goal 2

2 **Explain How Families Can Influence Young Children's Development**

REVIEW

- What are the four main parenting styles, and what aspects of parenting are linked with young children's development?
- What are the types and consequences of child maltreatment?
- How are sibling relationships and birth order related to young children's development?
- How is young children's development affected by having two wage-earning parents, having divorced parents, and being part of a particular cultural, ethnic, and socioeconomic group?

REFLECT

- Which style or styles of parenting did your mother and father use in rearing you? What effects do you think their parenting styles have had on your development?

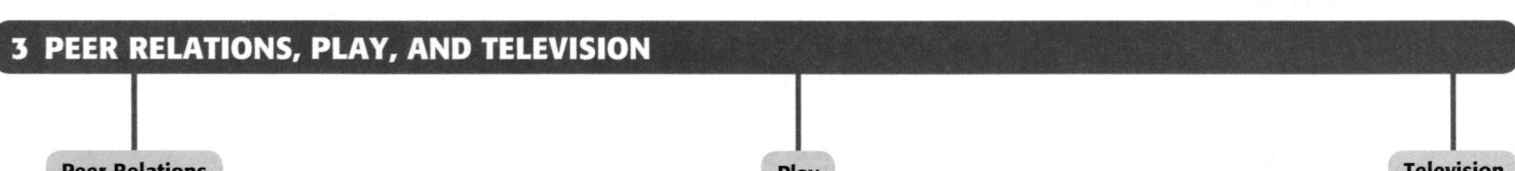

3 PEER RELATIONS, PLAY, AND TELEVISION

Peer Relations   **Play**   **Television**

What are some characteristics of peer relations in early childhood?

The family is an important social context for children's development. However, children's development also is strongly influenced by what goes on in other social contexts, such as in peer groups and when children are playing or watching television.

Peer Relations

As children grow older, they spend an increasing amount of time with their *peers*—children of about the same age or maturity level.

What are the functions of a child's peer group? One of its most important functions is to provide a source of information and comparison about the world outside the family. Children receive feedback about their abilities from their peer group. Children evaluate what they do in terms of whether it is better than, as good as, or worse than what other children do. It is hard to make these judgments at home because siblings are usually older or younger.

Good peer relations can be necessary for normal socioemotional development (Howes, 2008; Prinstein & Dodge, 2008). Special concerns focus on children who are withdrawn and aggressive (Bukowski, Brendgen, & Vitaro, 2007). Withdrawn children who are rejected by peers or are victimized and feel lonely are at risk for depression. Children who are aggressive with their peers are at risk for developing a number of problems, including delinquency and dropping out of school (Dishion, Piehler, & Myers, 2008; Dodge, Coie, & Lynam, 2006).

Recall from our discussion of gender that by about the age of 3, children already prefer to spend time with same-sex rather than opposite-sex playmates, and this preference increases in early childhood. During these same years the frequency of peer interaction, both positive and negative, picks up considerably (Hartup, 1983). Although aggressive interaction and rough-and-tumble play increase, the proportion of aggressive exchanges, compared with friendly exchanges, decreases. Many preschool children spend considerable time in peer interaction just conversing with playmates about such matters as "negotiating roles and rules in play, arguing, and agreeing" (Rubin, Bukowski, & Parker, 2006). We will have much more to say about peer relations in Chapter 10, "Socioemotional Development in Middle and Late Childhood."

Play

An extensive amount of peer interaction during childhood involves play, but social play is only one type of play. *Play* is a pleasurable activity that is engaged in for its own sake, and its functions and forms vary.

Play's Functions   Play is essential to the young child's health (Sutterby & Frost, 2006). Theorists have focused on different aspects of play and highlighted a long list of functions.

According to Freud and Erikson, play helps the child master anxieties and conflicts. Because tensions are relieved in play, the child can cope with life's problems. Play permits the child to work off excess physical energy and to release pent-up tensions. Therapists use *play therapy* both to allow the child to work off frustrations and to analyze the child's conflicts and ways of coping with them (Malchiodi, 2008; Sanders, 2008). Children may feel less threatened and be more likely to express their true feelings in the context of play.

Play also is an important context for cognitive development (Roskos & Christie, 2007; Sawyer & DeZutter, 2007). Piaget (1962) maintained that play advances children's cognitive development. At the same time, he said that children's cognitive development *constrains* the way they play. Play permits children to practice their competencies and acquired skills in a relaxed, pleasurable way. Piaget thought that cognitive structures need to be exercised, and play provides the perfect setting for this exercise. For example, children who have just learned to add or multiply begin to play with numbers in different ways as they perfect these operations, laughing as they do so.

Vygotsky (1962) also considered play to be an excellent setting for cognitive development. He was especially interested in the symbolic and make-believe aspects of play, as when a child substitutes a stick for a horse and rides the stick as if it were a horse. For young children, the imaginary situation is real. Parents should encourage such imaginary play, because it advances the child's cognitive development, especially creative thought.

Daniel Berlyne (1960) described play as exciting and pleasurable in itself because it satisfies our exploratory drive. This drive involves curiosity and a desire for information about something new or unusual. Play is a means whereby children can safely explore and seek out new information. Play encourages exploratory behavior by offering children the possibilities of novelty, complexity, uncertainty, surprise, and incongruity.

Types of Play   The contemporary perspective on play emphasizes both the cognitive and the social aspects of play (Neuman, 2007; Sumaroka & Bornstein, 2008). Among the most widely studied types of children's play today are sensorimotor and practice play, pretense/symbolic play, social play, constructive play, and games (Bergen, 1988).

Sensorimotor and Practice Play   **Sensorimotor play** is behavior by infants to derive pleasure from exercising their sensorimotor schemes. The development of sensorimotor play follows Piaget's description of sensorimotor thought, which we discussed in Chapter 4. Infants initially engage in exploratory and playful visual and motor

And that park grew up with me; that small world widened as I learned its secrets and boundaries, as I discovered new refuges in its woods and jungles: hidden homes and lairs for the multitudes of imagination, for cowboys and Indians. . . . I used to dawdle on half holidays along the bent and Devonfacing seashore, hoping for gold watches or the skull of a sheep or a message in a bottle to be washed up with the tide.

—**DYLAN THOMAS**
Welsh Poet, 20th Century

sensorimotor play Behavior engaged in by infants to derive pleasure from exercising their existing sensorimotor schemas.

What are some different theories about the role of play in children's development?

transactions in the second quarter of the first year of life. For example, at 9 months of age, infants begin to select novel objects for exploration and play, especially responsive objects, such as toys that make noise or bounce. At 12 months of age, infants enjoy making things work and exploring cause and effect.

Practice play involves the repetition of behavior when new skills are being learned or when physical or mental mastery and coordination of skills are required for games or sports. Sensorimotor play, which often involves practice play, is primarily confined to infancy, whereas practice play can be engaged in throughout life. During the preschool years, children often engage in practice play. Although practice play declines in the elementary school years, practice play activities such as running, jumping, sliding, twirling, and throwing balls or other objects are frequently observed on the playgrounds at elementary schools.

A preschool "superhero" at play.

practice play Play that involves repetition of behavior when new skills are being learned or when physical or mental mastery and coordination of skills are required for games or sports.

pretense/symbolic play Play in which the child transforms the physical environment into a symbol.

social play Play that involves social interactions with peers.

Pretense/Symbolic Play **Pretense/symbolic play** occurs when the child transforms the physical environment into a symbol. Between 9 and 30 months of age, children increase their use of objects in symbolic play. They learn to transform objects—substituting them for other objects and acting toward them as if they were these other objects (Kavanaugh, 2006). For example, a preschool child treats a table as if it were a car and says, "I'm fixing the car," as he grabs a leg of the table.

Many experts on play consider the preschool years the "golden age" of symbolic/pretense play that is dramatic or sociodramatic in nature (Fein, 1986). This type of make-believe play often appears at about 18 months of age and reaches a peak at 4 to 5 years of age, then gradually declines.

Some child psychologists conclude that pretend play is an important aspect of young children's development and often reflects advances in their cognitive development, especially as an indication of symbolic understanding. For example, Catherine Garvey (2000) and Angeline Lillard (2006) emphasize that hidden in young children's pretend play narratives are remarkable capacities for role-taking, balancing of social roles, metacognition (thinking about thinking), testing of the reality-pretense distinction, and numerous nonegocentric capacities that reveal the remarkable cognitive skills of young children.

Social Play **Social play** is play that involves interaction with peers, and it is the focus of Parten's classification. Social play increases dramatically during the preschool years.

Constructive Play   **Constructive play** combines sensorimotor/practice play with symbolic representation. Constructive play occurs when children engage in the self-regulated creation of a product or a solution. Constructive play increases in the preschool years as symbolic play increases and sensorimotor play decreases. Constructive play is also a frequent form of play in the elementary school years, both in and out of the classroom.

Games   **Games** are activities that are engaged in for pleasure and have rules. Often they involve competition. Preschool children may begin to participate in social games that involve simple rules of reciprocity and turn-taking. However, games take on a much stronger role in the lives of elementary school children. In one study, the highest incidence of game playing occurred between 10 and 12 years of age (Eiferman, 1971). After age 12, games decline in popularity (Bergen, 1988).

Television

Few developments in society in the second half of the twentieth century had a greater impact on children than television (Brooks-Gunn & Donahue, 2008; Murray & Murray, 2008; Pecora). Although it is only one of the many types of mass media that affect children's behavior, television is the most influential. The persuasive capabilities of television are staggering (Comstock & Scharrer, 2006).

   Many children spend more time in front of the television set than they do with their parents. Just how much television do young children watch? Surveys vary, with the figures ranging from an average of two to four hours a day (Roberts & Foehr, 2008). Compared with their counterparts in other developed countries, children in the United States watch television for considerably longer periods. Television can have a negative influence on children by making them passive learners, distracting them from doing homework, teaching them stereotypes, providing them with violent models of aggression, and presenting them with unrealistic views of the world (Dubow, Huesmann, & Greenwood, 2007; Murray, 2007). However, television can have a positive influence on children's development by presenting motivating educational programs, increasing their information about the world beyond their immediate environment, and providing models of prosocial behavior (Bryant, 2007; Wilson, 2008).

"Mrs. Horton, could you stop by school today?"
Copyright © Martha Campbell.

Effects of Television on Children's Aggression   The extent to which children are exposed to violence and aggression on television raises special concern (Murray & Murray, 2008; Wilson, 2008). For example, Saturday morning cartoon shows average more than 25 violent acts per hour. In one experiment, preschool children were randomly assigned to one of two groups: One group watched television shows taken directly from violent Saturday morning cartoons on 11 days; the second group watched television cartoon shows with all of the violence removed (Steur, Applefield, & Smith, 1971). The children were then observed during play at their preschool. The preschool children who had seen the TV cartoon shows with violence kicked, choked, and pushed their playmates more than did the preschool children who watched nonviolent TV cartoon shows. Because the children were randomly assigned to the two conditions (TV cartoons with violence versus nonviolent TV cartoons), we can conclude that exposure to TV violence *caused* the increased aggression in the children in this investigation.

   Other research has found links between watching television violence as a child and acting aggressively years later. For example, in one study, exposure to media violence at 6 to 10 years of age was linked with young adult aggressive behavior (Huesmann & others, 2003). In another study, long-term exposure to television violence was significantly related to the likelihood of aggression in 1,565 12- to 17-year-old boys (Belson, 1978). Boys who watched the most aggression on television were the most likely to commit a violent crime, swear, be aggressive in sports, threaten violence

constructive play Play that combines sensorimotor and repetitive activity with symbolic representation of ideas. Constructive play occurs when children engage in self-regulated creation or construction of a product or a solution.

games Activities engaged in for pleasure that include rules and often competition with one or more individuals.

How is television violence linked to children's aggression?

toward another boy, write slogans on walls, or break windows. These studies are *correlational*, so we can conclude from them that television violence is *associated with* aggressive behavior.

In addition to television violence, there is increased concern about children who play violent video games, especially those that are highly realistic (Escobar-Chaves & Anderson, 2008). Children can become so deeply immersed in some electronic games that they experience an altered state of consciousness in which rational thought is suspended and arousing aggressive scripts are learned (Roberts, Henrikson, & Foehr, 2004). The direct rewards that players receive ("winning points") for their actions may also enhance the influence of video games.

Correlational studies indicate that children who extensively play violent electronic games are more aggressive than their counterparts who spend less time playing the games or do not play them at all (Cohen, 1995). Experiments have not yet been conducted to demonstrate increased aggression subsequent to playing violent video games, although a recent analysis of research studies concluded that playing violent video games is linked to aggression in both males and females (Anderson, Gentile, & Buckley, 2007; Carnagey, Anderson, & Bushman, 2007).

Effects of Television on Children's Prosocial Behavior   Television also can teach children that it is better to behave in positive, prosocial ways than in negative, antisocial ways (Bryant, 2007). In an early study, Aimee Leifer (1973) selected episodes from the television show *Sesame Street* that reflected positive social interchanges which taught children how to use their social skills. For example, in one interchange, two men were fighting over the amount of space available to them; they gradually began to cooperate and to share the space. Children who watched these episodes copied these behaviors, and in later social situations they applied the prosocial lessons they had learned.

Review and Reflect: Learning Goal 3

3   **Describe the Roles of Peers, Play, and Television in Young Children's Development**

REVIEW

- How do peers affect young children's development?
- What are some theories and types of play?
- How does television influence young children's development?

REFLECT

- What guidelines would you recommend to parents to help them to make television a more positive influence on their children's development? Consider factors such as the child's age, the child's activities other than TV, the parents' patterns of interaction with the children, and types of TV shows.

Socioemotional Development in Early Childhood

1 EMOTIONAL AND PERSONALITY DEVELOPMENT: DISCUSS EMOTIONAL AND PERSONALITY DEVELOPMENT IN EARLY CHILDHOOD

The Self

- In Erikson's theory, early childhood is a period when development involves resolving the conflict of initiative versus guilt. The toddler's rudimentary self-understanding develops into the preschooler's representation of the self in terms of body parts, material possessions, and physical activities. At about 4 to 5 years of age, children also begin to use traitlike self-descriptions. Young children display more sophisticated self-understanding and understanding of others than previously thought.

Emotional Development

- Young children's range of emotions expands during early childhood as they increasingly experience self-conscious emotions such as pride, shame, and guilt. Between 2 and 4 years old, children use an increasing number of terms to describe emotion and learn more about the causes and consequences of feelings. At 4 to 5 years of age, children show an increased ability to reflect on emotions and understand that a single event can elicit different emotions in different people. They also show a growing awareness of the need to manage emotions to meet social standards. Emotion-coaching parents have children who engage in more effective self-regulation of their emotions than do emotion-dismissing parents. Emotional regulation plays an important role in successful peer relations.

Moral Development

- Moral development involves thoughts, feelings, and actions regarding rules and regulations about what people should do in their interactions with others. Freud's psychoanalytic theory emphasizes the importance of feelings in the development of the superego, the moral branch of personality. Positive emotions, such as empathy, also contribute to the child's moral development. Piaget analyzed moral reasoning and concluded that children from about 4 to 7 years of age display heteronomous morality, judging behavior by its consequences. According to behavioral and social cognitive theorists, moral behavior develops as a result of reinforcement, punishment and imitation, and there is considerable situational variability in moral behavior. Conscience refers to an internal regulation of standards of right and wrong that involves an integration of moral thought, feeling, and behavior. Young children's conscience emerges out of relationships with parents. Parents influence young children's moral development through the quality of parent-child relationships, being proactive in helping children avert misbehavior, and by engaging children in conversational dialogue about moral issues.

Gender

- Gender refers to the social and psychological dimensions of being male or female. Gender identity is acquired by 3 years of age for most children. A gender role is a set of expectations that prescribes how females or males should think, act, and feel. Biological influences on gender development include chromosomes and hormones. However, biology is not completely destiny in gender development; children's socialization experiences matter a great deal. Social role theory, psychoanalytic theory, and social cognitive theory emphasize various aspects of social experiences in the development of gender characteristics. Parents influence children's gender development, and peers are especially adept at rewarding gender-appropriate behavior. Gender schema theory emphasizes the role of cognition in gender development.

2 FAMILIES: EXPLAIN HOW FAMILIES CAN INFLUENCE YOUNG CHILDREN'S DEVELOPMENT

Parenting

- Authoritarian, authoritative, neglectful, and indulgent are four main parenting styles. Authoritative parenting is the most widely used style around the world and is the style most often associated with children's social competence. However, ethnic variations in parenting styles suggest that in Asian American families, some aspects of control may benefit children. Physical punishment is widely used by U.S. parents, but there are a number of reasons why it is not a good choice. Coparenting has positive effects on children's development.

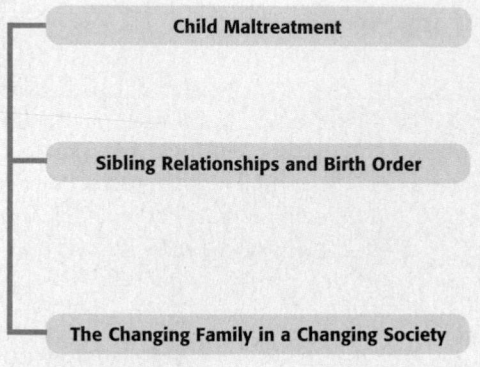

Child Maltreatment

Sibling Relationships and Birth Order

The Changing Family in a Changing Society

- Child maltreatment may take the form of physical abuse, child neglect, sexual abuse, and emotional abuse. Child maltreatment places the child at risk for academic, emotional, and social problems. Adults who suffered child maltreatment are also vulnerable to a range of problems.

- Siblings interact with each other in positive and negative ways. Birth order is related in certain ways to personality characteristics—for example, firstborns are more adult-oriented and self-controlled but have more guilt, anxiety, and difficulty coping with stress. Only children often are achievement-oriented. By itself, however, birth order it is not a good predictor of behavior.

- In general, having both parents employed full-time outside the home has not been shown to have negative effects on children. However, the nature of parents' work can affect their parenting quality. Divorce can have negative effects on children's adjustment, but so can an acrimonious relationship between parents who stay together for their children's sake. If divorced parents develop a harmonious relationship and practice authoritative parenting, children's adjustment improves. Researchers have found few differences between children growing up in gay male or lesbian families and children growing up in heterosexual families. Cultures vary on a number of issues regarding families. African American and Latino children are more likely than White American children to live in single-parent families and larger families and to have extended family connections. Low-income families have less access to resources than higher-income families. Lower-SES parents create a home atmosphere that involves more authority and physical punishment with children than higher-SES parents. Higher-SES parents are more concerned about developing children's initiative and delay of gratification.

3 PEER RELATIONS, PLAY, AND TELEVISION: DESCRIBE THE ROLES OF PEERS, PLAY, AND TELEVISION IN YOUNG CHILDREN'S DEVELOPMENT

Peer Relations

Play

Television

- Peers are powerful socialization agents. Peers provide a source of information and comparison about the world outside the family.

- Play's functions include affiliation with peers, tension release, advances in cognitive development, exploration, and provision of a safe haven. The contemporary perspective on play emphasizes both the cognitive and the social aspects of play. Among the most widely studied types of children's play are sensorimotor play, practice play, pretense/symbolic play, social play, constructive play, and games.

- Television can have both negative influences (such as turning children into passive learners and presenting them with aggressive models) and positive influences (such as providing models of prosocial behavior) on children's development. TV violence is not the only cause of children's aggression, but it can induce aggression. Prosocial behavior on TV can teach children positive behavior.

KEY TERMS

self-understanding 247
moral development 250
heteronomous morality 250
autonomous morality 250
immanent justice 251
conscience 251
gender identity 253

gender role 253
social role theory 254
psychoanalytic theory of gender 254
social cognitive theory of gender 254
gender schema theory 255

authoritarian parenting 257
authoritative parenting 257
neglectful parenting 257
indulgent parenting 257
sensorimotor play 271

practice play 272
pretense/symbolic play 272
social play 272
constructive play 273
games 273

KEY PEOPLE

Erik Erikson 247
Jean Piaget 250
Sigmund Freud 250

Lawrence Kohlberg 252
Ross Thompson 252
Diana Baumrind 257

Ruth Chao 258
Laurie Kramer 263
Judy Dunn 263

Ann Crouter 264
Lev Vygotsky 271
Daniel Berlyne 271

E-LEARNING TOOLS

To help you master the material in this chapter, visit the Online Learning Center for *Life-Span Development*, twelfth edition, at **www.mhhe.com/santrockld12**.

Self-Assessment

Connect to **www.mhhe.com/santrockld12** to examine your beliefs about caring for young children by completing the self-assessment, *My Parenting Style*.

Taking It to the Net

Connect to **www.mhhe.com/santrockld12** to research the answers to these questions:

1. Doris and Ken are in the process of getting a divorce. Both of them want full custody of their two children: Kevin, age 10, and Chrissie, age 3. Although the divorce process has been very stressful for both of them, Doris and Ken share concerns about the effects their divorce might have on their children. What immediate effects can they expect, especially given the custody battle? How might Kevin's reactions differ from Chrissie's? What might the long-term effects of the divorce be on their children?

2. Karen's mother is concerned about how best to help her daughter, Teresa, whose husband has abandoned her and their 5-year-old son. What are some of the challenges that Teresa may have to face, and how can her mother help her through this difficult time?

3. Jonathan and Diedre want to shield their children from the violence on television, but they are not sure how to go about it—other than by not allowing any television viewing at all. What recommendations does the APA have for parents?

Video Clips

The Online Learning Center includes two videos for Chapter 8. The first video is called "When a Second Baby Comes Along." Are there patterns among the personality traits of firstborn siblings? A researcher discusses the significance of birth order and offers some practical advice about preparing a child for a new brother or sister. The second video is called "Cultural Variations in Father's Role." A son will typically speak of his father as a role model, but the actual role that fathers play in their sons' and daughters' development continues to be a subject of research. This segment looks at some of that research.

Health and Well-Being, Parenting, and Education Exercises

Build your decision-making skills by trying your hand at the health and well-being, parenting, and education exercises. Connect to **www.mhhe.com/santrockld12** to research the answers and complete the exercises.

SECTION FIVE

MIDDLE AND LATE CHILDHOOD

Every forward step we take we leave some phantom of ourselves behind.

—John Lancaster Spalding
American Educator, 19th Century

In middle and late childhood, children are on a different plane, belonging to a generation and feeling all their own. It is the wisdom of the human life span that at no time are children more ready to learn than during the period of expansive imagination at the end of early childhood. Children develop a sense of wanting to make things—and not just to make them, but to make them well and even perfectly. They seek to know and to understand. They are remarkable for their intelligence and for their curiosity. Their parents continue to be important influences in their lives, but their growth also is shaped by peers and friends. They don't think much about the future or about the past, but they enjoy the present moment. Section 5 consists of two chapters: "Physical and Cognitive Development in Middle and Late Childhood" (Chapter 9) and "Socioemotional Development in Middle and Late Childhood" (Chapter 10).

9

> *The thirst to know
> and understand. . . .
> These are the good in
> life's rich hand.*
>
> —Sir William Watson
> *English Poet, 20th Century*

LEARNING GOALS

- ◆ Describe physical changes and health in middle and late childhood.

- ◆ Identify children with different types of disabilities and issues in educating them.

- ◆ Explain cognitive changes in middle and late childhood.

- ◆ Discuss language development in middle and late childhood.

PHYSICAL AND COGNITIVE DEVELOPMENT IN MIDDLE AND LATE CHILDHOOD

CHAPTER OUTLINE

Images of Life-Span Development
The Story of Angie and Her Weight

The following comments are by Angie, an elementary-school-aged girl:

> When I was eight years old, I weighed 125 pounds. My clothes were the size that large teenage girls wear. I hated my body and my classmates teased me all the time. I was so overweight and out of shape that when I took a P.E. class my face would get red and I had trouble breathing. I was jealous of the kids who played sports and weren't overweight like I was.
>
> I'm nine years old now and I've lost 30 pounds. I'm much happier and proud of myself. How did I lose the weight? My mom said she had finally decided enough was enough. She took me to a pediatrician who specializes in helping children lose weight and keep it off. The pediatrician counseled my mom about my eating and exercise habits, then had us join a group that he had created for overweight children and their parents. My mom and I go to the group once a week and we've now been participating in the program for six months. I no longer eat fast food meals and my mom is cooking more healthy meals. Now that I've lost weight, exercise is not as hard for me and I don't get teased by the kids at school. My mom's pretty happy too because she's lost 15 pounds herself since we've been in the counseling program.

Not all overweight children are as successful as Angie at reducing their weight. Indeed, being overweight or obese in childhood has become a major national concern in the United States. Later in the chapter, we will further explore being overweight and obese in childhood, including obesity's causes and outcomes.

PREVIEW

During the middle and late childhood years, children grow taller, heavier, and stronger. They become more adept at using their physical skills, and they develop new cognitive skills. This chapter is about physical and cognitive development in middle and late childhood. To begin, we will explore some changes in physical development.

---

1 PHYSICAL CHANGES AND HEALTH

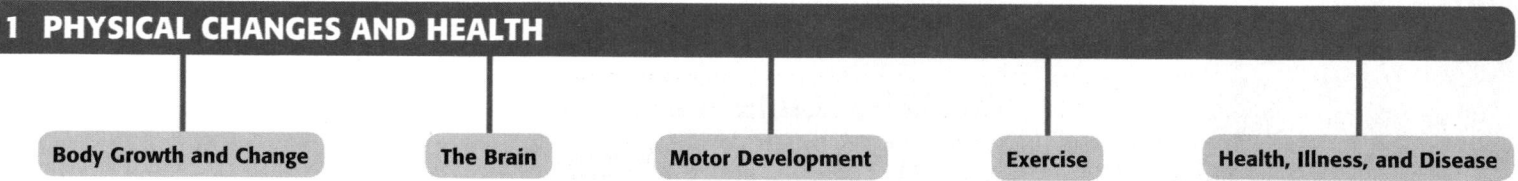

Body Growth and Change | The Brain | Motor Development | Exercise | Health, Illness, and Disease

Continued change characterizes children's bodies during middle and late childhood, and their motor skills improve. As children move through the elementary school years, they gain greater control over their bodies and can sit and attend for longer periods of time. Regular exercise is one key to making these years a time of healthy growth and development.

Body Growth and Change

The period of middle and late childhood involves slow, consistent growth. This is a period of calm before the rapid growth spurt of adolescence. During the elementary school years, children grow an average of 2 to 3 inches a year until, at the age of 11, the average girl is 4 feet, 10¼ inches tall, and the average boy is 4 feet, 9 inches tall. During the middle and late childhood years, children gain about 5 to 7 pounds a year. The weight increase is due mainly to increases in the size of the skeletal and muscular systems, as well as the size of some body organs.

Proportional changes are among the most pronounced physical changes in middle and late childhood. Head circumference and waist circumference decrease in relation to body height (Kliegman & others, 2007). A less noticeable physical change is that bones continue to ossify during middle and late childhood but yield to pressure and pull more than mature bones.

Muscle mass and strength gradually increase during these years as "baby fat" decreases. The loose movements and knock-knees of early childhood give way to improved muscle tone. Thanks to both heredity and to exercise, children double their strength capabilities during these years. Because of their greater number of muscle cells, boys are usually stronger than girls.

The Brain

The development of brain-imaging techniques, such as magnetic resonance imaging (MRI), has led to an increase in research on changes in the brain during middle and late childhood, and how these brain changes are linked to improvements in cognitive development (Toga, Thompson, & Sowell, 2006). Total brain volume stabilizes by the end of middle and late childhood, but significant changes in various structures and regions of the brain continue to occur. In particular, the brain pathways and circuitry involving the prefrontal cortex, the highest level in the brain, continue to increase in middle and late childhood (Durston & Casey, 2006) (see Figure 9.1). These advances in the prefrontal cortex are linked to children's improved attention, reasoning, and cognitive control (Anderson, Jacobs, & Harvey, 2005).

Changes also occur in the thickness of the cerebral cortex (cortical thickness) in middle and late childhood (Toga, Thompson, & Sowell, 2006). One study used brain scans to assess cortical thickness in 5- to 11-year-old children (Sowell & others, 2004). Cortical thickening across a two-year time period was observed in the temporal and frontal lobe areas that function in language, which may reflect improvements in language abilities such as reading. Figure 4.4 in Chapter 4 shows the locations of the temporal and frontal lobes in the brain.

As children develop, activation of some brain areas increase while others decrease (Dowker, 2006). One shift in activation that occurs as children develop is from diffuse, larger areas to more focal, smaller areas (Turkeltaub & others, 2003). This shift is characterized by synaptic pruning, in which areas of the brain not being used lose synaptic connections and those being used show an increase in connections. In a recent study, researchers found less diffusion and more focal activation in the prefrontal cortex from 7 to 30 years of age (Durston & others, 2006). The activation change was accompanied by increased efficiency in cognitive performance, especially in *cognitive control*, which involves flexible and effective control in a number of areas. These areas include controlling attention, reducing interfering thoughts, inhibiting motor actions, and being flexible in switching between competing choices (Munkata, 2006).

Motor Development

During middle and late childhood, children's motor skills become much smoother and more coordinated than they were in early childhood. For example, only one child in a thousand can hit a tennis ball over the net at the age of 3, yet by the age of 10 or 11 most children can learn to play the sport. Running, climbing, skipping rope, swimming, bicycle riding, and skating are just a few of the many physical skills elementary school children can master. In gross motor skills involving large muscle activity, boys usually outperform girls.

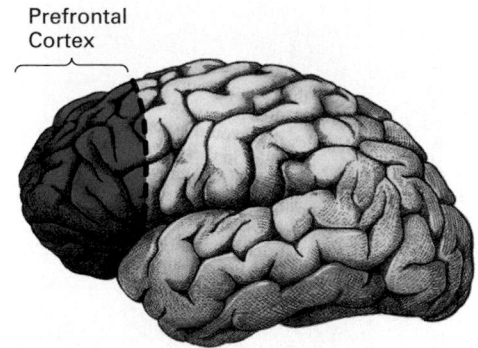

Prefrontal Cortex

FIGURE 9.1 The Prefrontal Cortex. The brain pathways and circuitry involving the prefrontal cortex (shaded in purple) show significant advances in development during middle and late childhood. *What cognitive processes are these changes in the prefrontal cortex linked to?*

*E*very forward step we take we leave some phantom of ourselves behind.

—JOHN LANCASTER SPALDING
American Educator, 19th Century

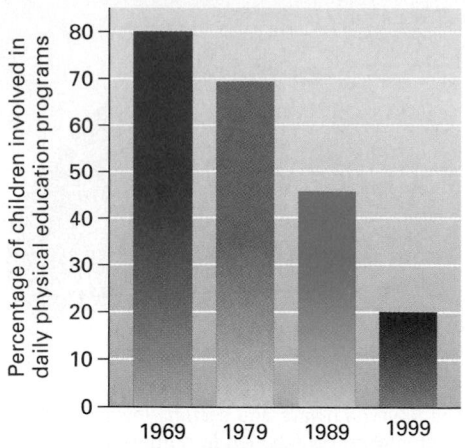

FIGURE 9.2 Percentage of Children Involved in Daily Physical Education Programs in the United States from 1969 to 1999. There has been a dramatic drop in the percentage of children participating in daily physical education programs in the United States, from 80 percent in 1969 to only 20 percent in 1999.

Increased myelination of the central nervous system is reflected in the improvement of fine motor skills during middle and late childhood. Children can more adroitly use their hands as tools. Six-year-olds can hammer, paste, tie shoes, and fasten clothes. By 7 years of age, children's hands have become steadier. At this age, children prefer a pencil to a crayon for printing, and reversal of letters is less common. Printing becomes smaller. At 8 to 10 years of age, the hands can be used independently with more ease and precision. Fine motor coordination develops to the point at which children can write rather than print words. Cursive letter size becomes smaller and more even. At 10 to 12 years of age, children begin to show manipulative skills similar to the abilities of adults. They can master the complex, intricate, and rapid movements needed to produce fine-quality crafts or to play a difficult piece on a musical instrument. Girls usually outperform boys in their use of fine motor skills.

Exercise

Elementary school children are far from physical maturity, so they need to be active (Floriani & Kennedy, 2008; Rink, 2009). They become more fatigued by long periods of sitting than by running, jumping, or bicycling. Physical action, such as batting a ball, skipping rope, or balancing on a beam, is essential for these children to refine their developing skills. It is becoming increasingly clear that exercise plays an important role in children's growth and development (Corbin & others, 2008; Fahey, Insel, & Roth, 2009).

Are U.S. children getting enough exercise? In one historical comparison, the percentage of children involved in daily P.E. programs in schools decreased from 80 percent in 1969 to 20 percent in 1999 (Health Management Resources, 2001) (see Figure 9.2). Educators and policy makers in many other countries around the world, including China, Finland, and Great Britain, have become very concerned about the sedentary lifestyles of many children in their countries (Fogelholm, 2008; Liu & others, 2008).

Television watching is linked with low activity and obesity in children (Gable, Chang, & Krull, 2007; Wells & others, 2008). A related concern is the dramatic increase in computer use by children. Researchers have found that the total time that children and adolescents spend in front of a television or computer screen places them at risk for reduced activity and being overweight (Lajunen & others, 2007; te Velde & others, 2007). One recent study revealed that children who watched two or more hours of TV a day were less likely to participate in organized physical activities and less likely to have two more servings of a fruit a day than their counterparts who watched less than two hours of TV a day (Salmon, Campbell, & Crawford, 2006). A longitudinal study also found that a higher incidence of watching TV in childhood and adolescence was linked with being overweight, being less physically fit, and having higher cholesterol levels at 26 years of age (Hancox, Milne, & Poulton, 2004).

Increasing children's exercise levels have positive outcomes (Beets & Foley, 2008; Corbin & others, 2008). For example, a recent study also revealed that a high-intensity resistance training program decreased children's body fat and increased their muscle strength (Benson, Torode, & Fiatarone Singh, 2008). Another recent study found that 45 minutes of moderate physical activity and 15 minutes of vigorous physical activity daily were related to decreased odds of children being overweight (Wittmeier, Mollard, & Kriellaars, 2008). And recent research has shown that aerobic exercise was linked to increases in an important cognitive activity—planning—in overweight 9-year-old children (Davis & others, 2007).

Here are some ways to get children to exercise more:

- Offer more physical activity programs run by volunteers at school facilities.
- Improve physical fitness activities in schools.
- Have children plan community and school activities that really interest them.
- Encourage families to focus more on physical activity, and encourage parents to exercise more. A recent study revealed that when 9- to 13-year-olds had free time they were more likely to engage in physical activity when they felt safe,

What are some good strategies for increasing children's exercise?

had a number of places to be active, and had parents who participated in physical activities with them (Heitzler & others, 2006).

Health, Illness, and Disease

For the most part, middle and late childhood is a time of excellent health. Disease and death are less prevalent at this time than during other periods in childhood and in adolescence.

Accidents and Injuries   Injuries are the leading cause of death during middle and late childhood, and the most common cause of severe injury and death in this period is motor vehicle accidents, either as a pedestrian or as a passenger (Wilson & Hockenberry, 2008). The use of safety-belt restraints greatly reduces the severity of motor vehicle injuries. Other serious injuries involve bicycles, skateboards, roller skates, and other sports equipment.

Most accidents occur in or near the child's home or school. The most effective prevention strategy is to educate the child about proper use of equipment and the hazards of risk taking (Betz & Sowden, 2008). Safety helmets, protective eye and mouth shields, and protective padding are recommended for children who engage in active sports (Briem & others, 2004).

As we saw in Chapter 7, "Physical and Cognitive Development in Early Childhood," caregivers play a key role in preventing childhood injuries. A recent study in four developing countries (Ethiopia, Peru, Vietnam, and India) revealed that depression in caregivers was consistently linked to children's risk of injury for all types of injury assessed (burns, serious falls, broken bones, and near-fatal injury) (Howe, Huttly, & Abramsky, 2006).

Cancer   Cancer is the second leading cause of death in U.S. children 5 to 14 years of age. One in every 330 children in the United States develops cancer before the age of 19. The incidence of cancer in children has slightly increased in recent years (National Cancer Institute, 2008a).

Child cancers mainly attack the white blood cells (leukemia), brain, bone, lymph system, muscles, kidneys, and nervous system. All are characterized by an uncontrolled proliferation of abnormal cells (Hijiya & others, 2007). As indicated in Figure 9.3, the most common cancer in children is leukemia, a cancer in which bone marrow manufactures an abundance of abnormal white blood cells, which crowd out normal cells, making the child susceptible to bruising and infection (Rubnitz & others, 2006).

Because of advancements in cancer treatment, children with cancer are surviving longer (National Cancer Institute, 2008b). For example, in the 1960s, less than 5 percent of children with an acute form of leukemia survived for more than five years; today, approximately 25 percent of these children survive for five years or more.

Cardiovascular Disease   Cardiovascular disease is uncommon in children. Nonetheless, environmental experiences and behavior in the childhood years can sow the seeds for cardiovascular disease in adulthood. Many elementary-school-aged children already possess one or more of the risk factors for cardiovascular disease, such as hypertension and obesity (Beilin & Huang, 2008; Urbina, 2008). A recent study revealed that high blood pressure goes undiagnosed in 75 percent of children with the disease (Hansen, Gunn, & Kaelber, 2007). Another study found that high blood pressure was most likely to be present in Latino children (25 percent) and least characteristic of Asian American children (14 percent) (Sorof & others, 2004).

Child life specialists are among the health professionals who work to make the lives of children with diseases such as cancer and cardiovascular disease less stressful. To read about the work of child life specialist Sharon McCleod, see the *Careers in Life-Span Development* profile.

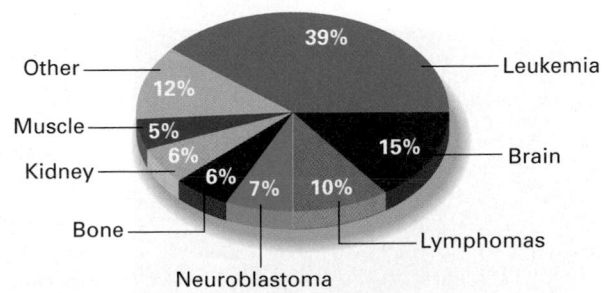

FIGURE 9.3 Types of Cancer in Children. Cancers in children have a different profile from adult cancers, which attack mainly the lungs, colon, breast, prostate, and pancreas.

Careers in Life-Span Development

Sharon McLeod, Child Life Specialist

Sharon McLeod is a child life specialist who is clinical director of the Child Life and Recreational Therapy Department at the Children's Hospital Medical Center in Cincinnati.

Under McLeod's direction, the goals of the Child Life Department are to promote children's optimal growth and development, reduce the stress of health-care experiences, and provide support to child patients and their families. These goals are accomplished through therapeutic play and developmentally appropriate activities, educating and psychologically preparing children for medical procedures, and serving as a resource for parents and other professionals regarding children's development and health-care issues.

McLeod says that human growth and development provides the foundation for her profession of child life specialist. She also describes her best times as a student when she conducted fieldwork, had an internship, and experienced hands-on theories and concepts she learned in her courses.

Sharon McLeod, child life specialist, working with a child at Children's Hospital Medical Center in Cincinnati.

What are some concerns about children's cardiovascular health and obesity?

Overweight Children Being overweight is an increasing health problem (Li & others, 2007; Price & Gwin, 2008). Recall from Chapter 7, "Physical and Cognitive Development in Early Childhood," that being overweight is defined in terms of body mass index (BMI), which is computed by a formula that takes into account height and weight—children at or above the 97th percentile are included in the obesity category, at or above the 95th percentile in the overweight category, and children at or above the 85th percentile are described as at risk for being overweight (Centers for Disease Control and Prevention, 2007). Over the last three decades, the percentage of U.S. children who are at risk for being overweight has doubled from 15 percent in the 1970s to almost 30 percent today, and the percentage of children who are overweight has tripled during this time frame (Paxson & others, 2006). Recently, however, the increase in child obesity began to level off. A large-scale U.S. study revealed that using the criteria for obesity just stated, child obesity increased from 7 percent to 11 percent from 1980 to 1994 but was essentially the same from 2002 (16 percent) to 2006 (17 percent) (Odgen, Carroll, & Flegal, 2008). Still, the levels of child obesity, overweight, and risk for being overweight are still far too high (Ebbeling & Ludwig, 2008). For example, researchers have found that being overweight as a child is a risk factor for being obese as an adult, and as we will see shortly, there are many other negative consequences for being overweight as a child (Janssen & others, 2004). Also, note that girls are more likely than boys to be overweight, and this gender difference occurs in many countries (Holmback & others, 2007; Sweeting, 2008).

What are the causes for the increase in obesity? Changes in diet are one suspect. From the late 1970s through the late 1990s, key dietary shifts took place among U.S. children as young as 2 years of age through the adult years: greater away-from-home consumption, large increases in total calories from salty snacks, soft drinks, and pizza; and large decreases in calories from low- and medium-fat milk and medium- and high-fat beef and pork (Nielsen, Siega-Riz, & Popkin, 2002). Children's total caloric intake also increased.

The increase in overweight children in recent decades is cause for great concern because being overweight raises the risk for many medical and psychological problems (Freedman & others, 2007). Overweight children are at risk for developing pulmonary problems, such as sleep apnea (which involves upper-airway obstruction), and hip problems (Tauman & Gozal, 2006). Diabetes, hypertension (high blood pressure), and elevated blood cholesterol levels also are common in children who are overweight (Plachta-Danielzik & others, 2008; Vohr & Boney, 2008). Once considered rare, hypertension in children has become increasingly common in overweight children (Thompson & others, 2007). A recent study found that children with a high body mass index and waist circumference are at risk for *metabolic syndrome*—a constellation of factors, including obesity, high blood pressure, and type 2 diabetes— placing individuals at risk for developing cardiovascular disease in adulthood (Sun & others, 2008). Overweight children with cardiovascular problems are more likely to come from low-socioeconomic-status families than higher-status ones (Longo-Mbenza, Lukoki, & M'Buyamba-Kabangu, 2007). Social and psychological consequences of being overweight in childhood include low self-esteem, depression, and some exclusion of obese children from peer groups (Datar & Sturm, 2004; Gibson & others, 2008). A recent study also revealed that obese children were perceived as less attractive, more tired, and more socially withdrawn than nonobese peers (Zeller, Reiter-Purtill, & Ramey, 2008).

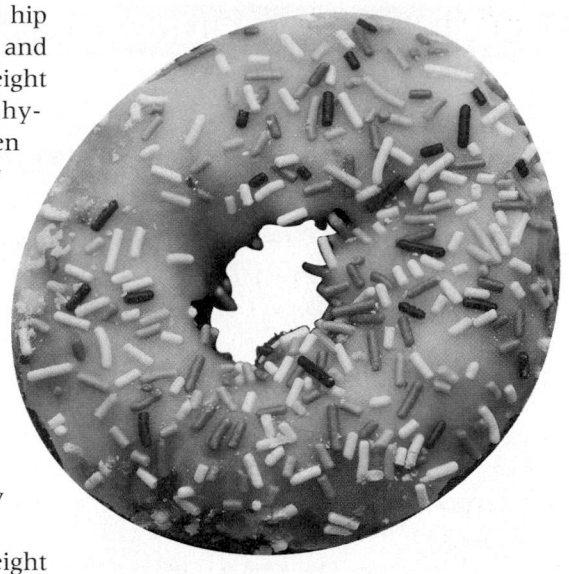

Parents play an important role in preventing children from becoming overweight and helping them lose weight if they become overweight (Wofford, 2008). They can encourage healthy eating habits in children by eating more family meals together, making healthy foods available, and not keeping sugar-sweetened beverages and other unhealthy foods in the home. They also can help reduce the likelihood their children will become overweight by reducing children's TV time, getting children involved in sports and other physical activities, and being healthy, physically active models themselves (Salmon, Campbell, & Crawford, 2006). A recent study revealed that Latino parents who monitored what their children ate had children who ate healthier foods and exercised more than their counterparts whose eating habits were not monitored (Arrendondo & others, 2006). As we learned in Angie's story at the beginning of the chapter, a combination of behavioral modification, parental involvement, and a structured program can effectively help overweight children (De Santis-Moniaci & Altshuler, 2007; Robbins, Power, & Burgess, 2008).

What can parents do to prevent their children from being overweight or obese?

Review and Reflect: Learning Goal 1

 Describe Physical Changes and Health in Middle and Late Childhood

REVIEW

- What are some changes in body growth and proportion in middle and late childhood?
- What characterizes the development of the brain in middle and late childhood?
- How do children's motor skills develop in middle and late childhood?
- What role does exercise play in children's lives?
- What are some characteristics of health, illness, and disease in middle and late childhood?

REFLECT

- One way that children get exercise is to play a sport. What might be some positive and negative aspects of parental involvement in children's sports? Should some parents be discouraged from coaching their children in sports or watching their children play in sports? Explain.

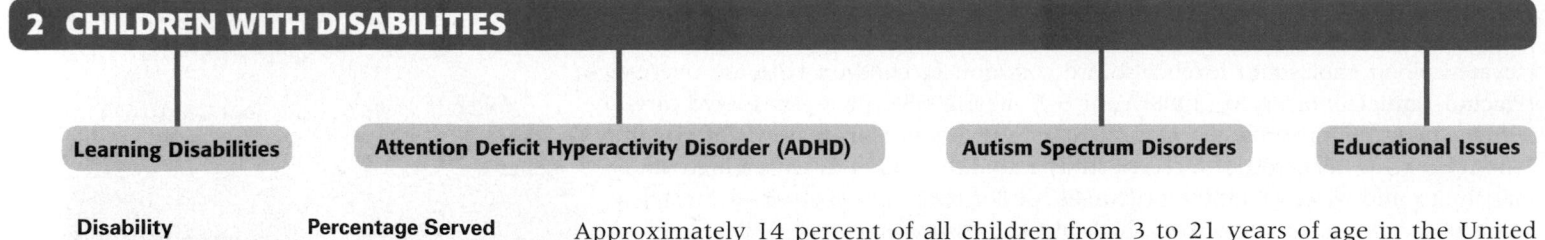

2 CHILDREN WITH DISABILITIES

| Learning Disabilities | Attention Deficit Hyperactivity Disorder (ADHD) | Autism Spectrum Disorders | Educational Issues |

Disability	Percentage Served
Specific learning disabilities	5.6
Speech or language impairments	3.0
Mental retardation	1.1
Emotional disturbance	1.0

FIGURE 9.4 The Four Highest Percentages of Students with a Disability Served by a Federal Program in 2005–2006 as a Percentage of Total School Enrollment (National Center for Education Statistics, 2007)

Approximately 14 percent of all children from 3 to 21 years of age in the United States receive special education or related services (National Center for Education Statistics, 2007). Figure 9.4 shows the four largest groups of students with a disability who were served by federal programs in the 2005–2006 school year (National Center for Education Statistics, 2007). As indicated in Figure 9.4, students with a learning disability were by far the largest group of students with a disability to be given special education, followed by children with speech or language impairments, mental retardation, and emotional disturbance.

Learning Disabilities

The U.S. government created a definition of learning disabilities in 1997 and then reauthorized the definition with a few minor changes in 2004. Following is a description of the government's definition of what determined whether a child should be classified as having a learning disability. A child with a **learning disability** has difficulty in learning that involves understanding or using spoken or written language, and the difficulty can appear in listening, thinking, reading, writing, and spelling. A learning disability also may involve difficulty in doing mathematics. To be classified as a learning disability, the learning problem is not primarily the result of visual, hearing, or motor disabilities; mental retardation; emotional disorders; or due to environmental, cultural, or economic disadvantage.

A recent national survey revealed that 8 percent of U.S. children have a learning disability (Bloom & Dey, 2006). About three times as many boys as girls are classified as having a learning disability. Among the explanations for this gender difference are a greater biological vulnerability among boys and *referral bias*. That is, boys are more likely to be referred by teachers for treatment because of troublesome behavior.

Diagnosing whether a child has a learning disability is often a difficult task (Bender, 2008; Fritschmann & Solari, 2008). Because federal guidelines are just that—guidelines—it is up to each state, or in some cases school systems within a state, to determine how to define and implement diagnosis of learning disabilities. The same child might be diagnosed as having a learning disability in one school system and receive services but not be diagnosed and not receive services in another school system. In such cases, parents sometimes will move—either to obtain or avoid the diagnosis.

Approximately 80 percent of children with a learning disability have a reading problem (Shaywitz, Gruen, & Shaywitz, 2007). **Dyslexia** is a category reserved for individuals who have a severe impairment in their ability to read and spell (Harley, 2008; Reid & others, 2009).

The precise causes of learning disabilities have not yet been determined (Bender, 2008; Hallahan, Kauffman, & Pullen, 2009). However, some possible causes have been proposed. Learning disabilities tends to run in families with one parent having a disability such as dyslexia, although the specific genetic transmission of learning disabilities has not been discovered (Petrill & others, 2006). Some leading researchers argue that some reading disabilities are likely due to genetics but that a majority are the result of environmental influences (Shaywitz, Morris & Shaywitz, 2008).

Researchers also use brain-imaging techniques, such as magnetic resonance imaging, to reveal any regions of the brain that might be involved in learning

learning disability Describes a child who has difficulty in learning that involves understanding or using spoken or written language, and the difficulty can appear in listening, thinking, reading, writing, and spelling. A learning disability also may involve difficulty in doing mathematics. To be classified as a learning disability, the learning problem is not primarily the result of visual, hearing, or motor disabilities; mental retardation; emotional disorders; or due to environmental, cultural, or economic disadvantage.

dyslexia A category of learning disabilities involving a severe impairment in the ability to read and spell.

disabilities (Shaywitz, Lyon, & Shaywitz, 2006) (see Figure 9.5). This research indicates that it is unlikely learning disabilities reside in a single, specific brain location. More likely, learning disabilities are due to problems in integrating information from multiple brain regions or subtle difficulties in brain structures and functions.

Interventions with children who have a learning disabilty often focus on improving reading ability (Bender, 2008; Lyytinen & Erskine, 2009). Intensive instruction over a period of time by a competent teacher can help many children (Berninger, 2006). For example, a recent brain-imaging study of 15 children with severe reading difficulties, who had not shown adequate progress in response to reading instruction in the first grade, were given an intensive eight weeks of instruction in phonological decoding skills and then another intensive eight weeks of word recognition skills (Simos & others, 2007). Significant improvement in a majority of the children's reading skills and changes in brain regions involved in reading occurred as a result of the intensive instruction.

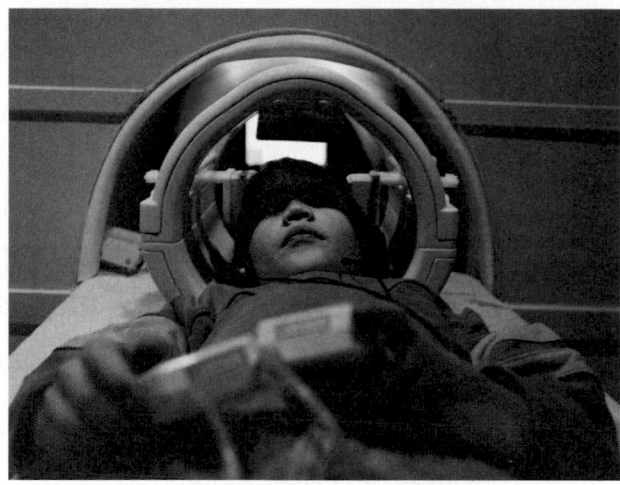

FIGURE 9.5 Brain Scans and Learning Disabilities. An increasing number of studies are using MRI brain scans to examine the brain pathways involved in learning disabilities. Shown here is 9-year-old Patrick Price, who has dyslexia. Patrick is going through an MRI scanner disguised by drapes to look like a child-friendly castle. Inside the scanner, children must lie virtually motionless as words and symbols flash on a screen, and they are asked to identify them by clicking different buttons.

Attention Deficit Hyperactivity Disorder (ADHD)

Attention deficit hyperactivity disorder (ADHD) is a disability in which children consistently show one or more of these characteristics over a period of time: (1) inattention, (2) hyperactivity, and (3) impulsivity. Children who are inattentive have such difficulty focusing on any one thing that they may get bored with a task after only a few minutes—or even seconds. Children who are hyperactive show high levels of physical activity, seeming to be almost constantly in motion. Children who are impulsive have difficulty curbing their reactions; they do not do a good job of thinking before they act. Depending on the characteristics that children with ADHD display, they can be diagnosed as (1) ADHD with predominantly inattention, (2) ADHD with predominantly hyperactivity/impulsivity, or (3) ADHD with both inattention and hyperactivity/impulsivity.

The number of children diagnosed and treated for ADHD has increased substantially in recent decades, by some estimates doubling in the 1990s. The disorder occurs as much as four to nine times more in boys than in girls. There is controversy, however, about the increased diagnosis of ADHD (Zentall, 2006; Taylor, Smiley, & Richards, 2009). Some experts attribute the increase mainly to heightened awareness of the disorder. Others are concerned that many children are being incorrectly diagnosed.

Definitive causes of ADHD have not been found. However, a number of causes have been proposed (Biederman, 2007). Some children likely inherit a tendency to develop ADHD from their parents (Goos, Ezzatian, & Schachar, 2007). Other children likely develop ADHD because of damage to their brain during prenatal or postnatal development (Banerjee, Middleton, & Faraone, 2007). Among early possible contributors to ADHD are cigarette and alcohol exposure during prenatal development and low birth weight (Greydanus, Pratt, & Patel, 2007).

As with learning disabilities, the development of brain-imaging techniques is leading to a better understanding of ADHD (Shaw & others, 2007). A recent study revealed that peak thickness of the cerebral cortex occurred three years later (10.5 years) in children with ADHD than in children without ADHD (peak at 7.5 years) (Shaw & others, 2007). The delay was more prominent in the prefrontal regions of the brain that especially are important in attention and planning (see Figure 9.6).

Stimulant medication such as Ritalin or Adderall (which has fewer side effects than Ritalin) is effective in improving the attention of many children with ADHD, but it usually does not improve their attention to the same level as children who do

Many children with ADHD show impulsive behavior, such as this child who is jumping out of his seat and throwing a paper airplane at other children. *How would you handle this situation if you were a teacher and this were to happen in your classroom?*

attention deficit hyperactivity disorder (ADHD) A disability in which children consistently show one or more of the following characteristics: (1) inattention, (2) hyperactivity, and (3) impulsivity.

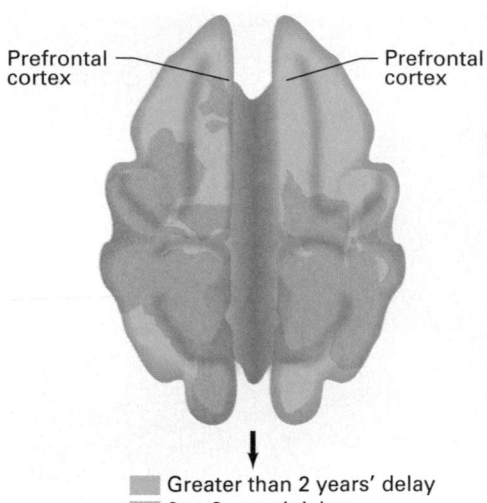

Prefrontal cortex   Prefrontal cortex

■ Greater than 2 years' delay
■ 0 to 2 years' delay

FIGURE 9.6 Regions of the Brain in Which Children with ADHD Had a Delayed Peak in the Thickness of the Cerebral Cortex. *Note:* The greatest delays occurred in the prefrontal cortex.

What characterizes autism spectrum disorders?

autism spectrum disorders (ASD) Also called pervasive developmental disorders, they range from the severe disorder labeled autistic disorder to the milder disorder called Asperger syndrome. Children with these disorders are characterized by problems in social interaction, verbal and nonverbal communication, and repetitive behaviors.

autistic disorder A severe autism spectrum disorder that has its onset in the first three years of life and includes deficiencies in social relationships, abnormalities in communication, and restricted, repetitive, and stereotyped patterns of behavior.

Asperger syndrome A relatively mild autism spectrum disorder in which the child has relatively good verbal language, milder nonverbal language problems, and a restricted range of interests and relationships.

not have ADHD (Pliszka, 2007). Researchers have often found that a combination of medication (such as Ritalin) and behavior management improves the behavior of children with ADHD better than medication alone or behavior management alone, although not in all cases (Jensen & others, 2007). Other drugs, such as the stimulant called mixed amphetamine salts extended release (MAS XR) and the nonstimulant Strattera (atomoxetine), are currently being studied in the treatment of children with ADHD, and early findings involving these drugs are promising (Bhatara & Aparasu, 2007; Faraone, 2007).

Critics argue that many physicians are too quick to prescribe stimulants for children with milder forms of ADHD (Marcovitch, 2004). Also, in 2006, the U.S. government issued a warning about the cardiovascular risks of stimulant medication to treat ADHD.

Recent studies have also focused on the possibility that exercise might reduce ADHD (Tantillo & others, 2006). Some mental health experts now recommend that children with ADHD exercise several times a day and speculate that the increase in rates of ADHD have coincided with the decline in U.S. children's exercise (Ratey, 2006).

Autism Spectrum Disorders

Autism spectrum disorders (ASD), also called pervasive developmental disorders, range from the severe disorder labeled *autistic disorder* to the milder disorder called *Asperger syndrome*. Autism spectrum disorders are characterized by problems in social interaction, problems in verbal and nonverbal communication, and repetitive behaviors (Boucher, 2009; Hall, 2009; Simpson & LaCava, 2008). Children with these disorders may also show atypical responses to sensory experiences (National Institute of Mental Health, 2008). Autism spectrum disorders can often be detected in children as early as 1 to 3 years of age (Chapman, 2009).

Autistic disorder is a severe developmental autism spectrum disorder that has its onset in the first three years of life and includes deficiencies in social relationships, abnormalities in communication, and restricted, repetitive, and stereotyped patterns of behavior. Estimates indicate that approximately two to five of every 10,000 young children in the United States have autistic disorder. Boys are about four times more likely to have an autistic disorder than girls.

Asperger syndrome is a relatively mild autism spectrum disorder in which the child has relatively good verbal language, milder nonverbal language problems, and a restricted range of interests and relationships (Bennett & others, 2007). Children with Asperger syndrome often engage in obsessive repetitive routines and preoccupations with a particular subject (South, Ozonoff, & McMahon, 2005). For example, a child may be obsessed with baseball scores or railroad timetables.

What causes the autism spectrum disorders? The current consensus is that autism is a brain dysfunction with abnormalities in brain structure and neurotransmitters (Lainhart, 2006). Genetic factors likely play a role in the development of the autism spectrum disorders (Katzov, 2007). A recent study revealed that mutations—missing or duplicated pieces of DNA on chromosome 16 can raise a child's risk of developing autism 100-fold (Weiss & others, 2008). Estimates are that approximately 1 million U.S. children have an autistic disorder, so about 10,000 have this genetic mutation. There is no evidence that family socialization causes autism (Rutter & Schopler, 1987). Mental retardation is present in some children with autism; others show average or above-average intelligence (McCarthy, 2007).

Children with autism benefit from a well-structured classroom, individualized instruction, and small-group instruction (Pueschel & others, 1995). As with children who are mentally retarded, behavior modification techniques are sometimes effective in helping autistic children learn (Hall, 2009).

Educational Issues

Until the 1970s most U.S. public schools either refused enrollment to children with disabilities or inadequately served them. This changed in 1975, when *Public Law 94-142*, the Education for All Handicapped Children Act, required that all students with disabilities be given a free, appropriate public education. In 1990, Public Law 94-142 was recast as the *Individuals with Disabilities Education Act* (IDEA). IDEA was amended in 1997 and then reauthorized in 2004 and renamed the Individuals with Disabilities Education Improvement Act (Rosenberg, Westling, & McLeskey, 2008).

IDEA spells out broad mandates for services to children with disabilities of all kinds (Gargiulo, 2009; Smith & others, 2008). These services include evaluation and eligibility determination, appropriate education and an individualized education plan (IEP), and education in the least restrictive environment (LRE).

An **individualized education plan (IEP)** is a written statement that spells out a program that is specifically tailored for the student with a disability (Friend, 2008). The **least restrictive environment (LRE)** is a setting that is as similar as possible to the one in which children who do not have a disability are educated. This provision of the IDEA has given a legal basis to efforts to educate children with a disability in the regular classroom (Bryant, Smith, & Bryant, 2008). The term **inclusion** describes educating a child with special education needs full-time in the regular classroom (Hick & Thomas, 2009; Rosenberg, Westling, & McLeskey, 2008). Figure 9.7 indicates that in a recent school year that slightly more than 50 percent of U.S. students with a disability spent more than 80 percent of their school day in a general classroom.

A major aspect of the 2004 reauthorization of IDEA involved aligning it with the government's No Child Left Behind (NCLB) legislation, which mandates general assessments of educational progress that include students with disabilities. This alignment includes requiring most students with disabilities "to take standard tests of academic achievement and to achieve at a level equal to that of students without disabilities. Whether this expectation is reasonable is an open question" (Hallahan & Kauffman, 2006, pp. 28–29).

Many legal changes regarding children with disabilities have been extremely positive (Carter, Prater, & Dyches, 2009; Turnbull, Huerta, & Stowe, 2009). Compared with several decades ago, far more children today are receiving competent, specialized services. For many children, inclusion in the regular classroom, with modifications or supplemental services, is appropriate (Smith & others, 2008). However, some leading experts on special education argue that in some cases the effort to educate children with disabilities in the regular classroom has become too extreme. For example, James Kauffman and his colleagues (Kauffman & Hallahan, 2005; Kauffman, McGee, & Brigham, 2004) state that inclusion too often has meant making accommodations in the regular classroom that do not always benefit children with disabilities. They advocate a more individualized approach that does not always involve full inclusion but allows options such as special education outside the regular classroom. Kauffman and his colleagues (2004, p. 620) acknowledge that children with disabilities "*do* need the services of specially trained professionals" and "*do* sometimes need altered curricula or adaptations to make their learning possible." However, "we sell students with disabilities short when we pretend that they are not different from typical students. We make the same error when we pretend that they must *not* be expected to put forth extra effort if they are to learn to do some things—or learn to do something in a different way." Like general education, special education should challenge students with disabilities "to become all they can be."

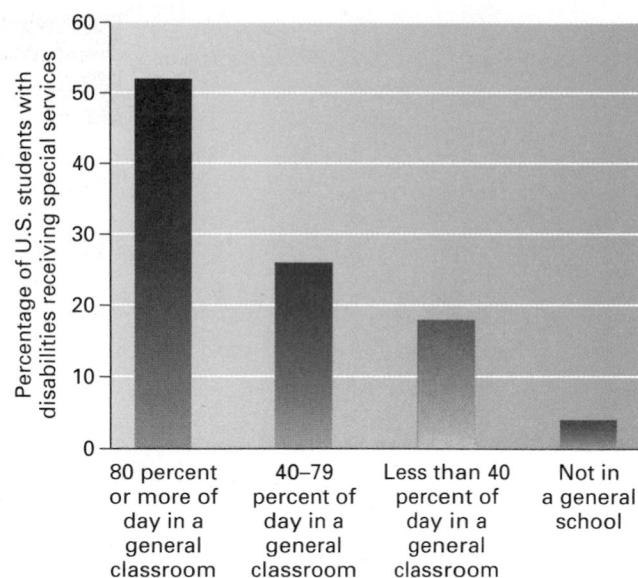

FIGURE 9.7 Percentage of U.S. Students with Disabilities 6 to 21 Years of Age Receiving Special Services in the General Classroom (Data for 2004–2005 School Year; National Center for Education Statistics, 2007)

IDEA mandates free, appropriate education for all children. *What services does IDEA mandate for children with disabilities?*

individualized education plan (IEP) A written statement that spells out a program specifically tailored to a child with a disability.

least restrictive environment (LRE) A setting that is as similar as possible to the one in which children who do not have a disability are educated.

inclusion Educating a child with special education needs full-time in the regular classroom.

Review and Reflect: Learning Goal 2

 Identify Children with Different Types of Disabilities and Issues in Educating Them

REVIEW

- Who are children with disabilities? What characterizes children with learning disabilities?
- How would you describe children with attention deficit hyperactivity disorder?
- What are autism spectrum disorders, what are they caused by, and how are they characterized?
- What are some issues in educating children with disabilities?

REFLECT

- Think back on your own schooling and how children with learning disabilities or ADHD either were or were not diagnosed. Were you aware of such individuals in your classes? Were they helped by specialists? You may know one or more individuals with a learning disability or ADHD. Ask them about their educational experiences and whether they think schools could have done a better job of helping them.

---

3 COGNITIVE CHANGES

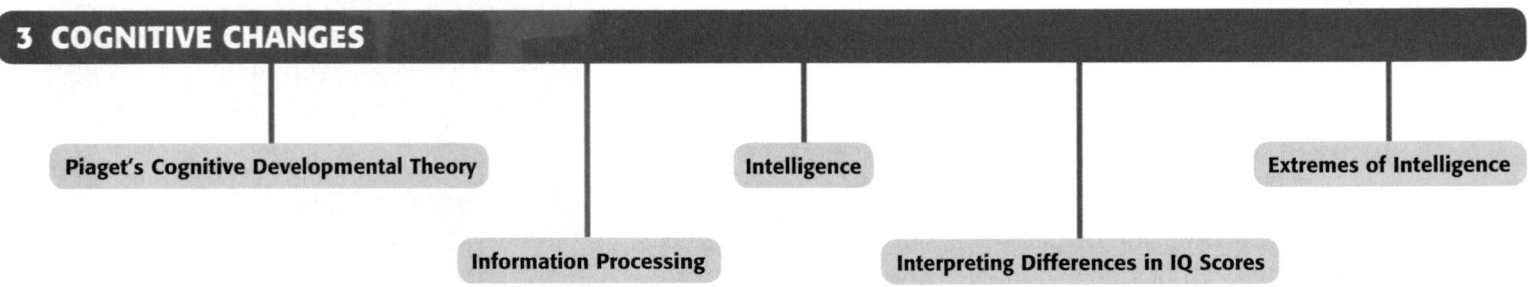

| Piaget's Cognitive Developmental Theory | | Intelligence | | Extremes of Intelligence |
| Information Processing | | | Interpreting Differences in IQ Scores | |

Do children enter a new stage of cognitive development in middle and late childhood? How do children process information in this age period? What is the nature of children's intelligence? Let's explore these questions.

Piaget's Cognitive Developmental Theory

According to Piaget (1952), the preschool child's thought is preoperational. Preschool children can form stable concepts, and they have begun to reason, but their thinking is flawed by egocentrism and magical belief systems. As we discussed in Chapter 7, however, Piaget may have underestimated the cognitive skills of preschool children. Some researchers argue that under the right conditions, young children may display abilities that are characteristic of Piaget's next stage of cognitive development, the stage of concrete operational thought (Gelman, 1969). Here we will cover the characteristics of concrete operational thought and evaluate Piaget's portrait of this stage.

The Concrete Operational Stage   Piaget proposed that the *concrete operational stage* lasts from approximately 7 to 11 years of age. In this stage, children can perform concrete operations, and they can reason logically as long as reasoning can be applied to specific or concrete examples. Remember that *operations* are mental actions that are reversible, and *concrete operations* are operations that are applied to real, concrete objects.

The conservation tasks described in Chapter 7 indicate whether children are capable of concrete operations. For example, recall that in one task involving conservation of matter, the child is presented with two identical balls of clay. The experimenter rolls one

> *W*e owe to Piaget the present field of cognitive development with its image of the developing child, who through its own active and creative commerce with its environment, builds an orderly succession of cognitive structures enroute to intellectual maturity.
>
> **—JOHN FLAVELL**
> *Contemporary Developmental Psychologist, Stanford University*

ball into a long, thin shape; the other remains in its original ball shape. The child is then asked if there is more clay in the ball or in the long, thin piece of clay. By the time children reach the age of 7 or 8, most answer that the amount of clay is the same. To answer this problem correctly, children have to imagine the clay rolling back into a ball. This type of imagination involves a reversible mental action applied to a real, concrete object. Concrete operations allow the child to consider several characteristics rather than focus on a single property of an object. In the clay example, the preoperational child is likely to focus on height *or* width. The concrete operational child coordinates information about both dimensions.

What other abilities are characteristic of children who have reached the concrete operational stage? One important skill is the ability to classify or divide things into different sets or subsets and to consider their interrelationships. Consider the family tree of four generations that is shown in Figure 9.8 (Furth & Wachs, 1975). This family tree suggests that the grandfather (A) has three children (B, C, and D), each of whom has two children (E through J), and that one of these children (J) has three children (K, L, and M). A child who comprehends the classification system can move up and down a level, across a level, and up and down and across within the system. The concrete operational child understands that person J can at the same time be father, brother, and grandson, for example.

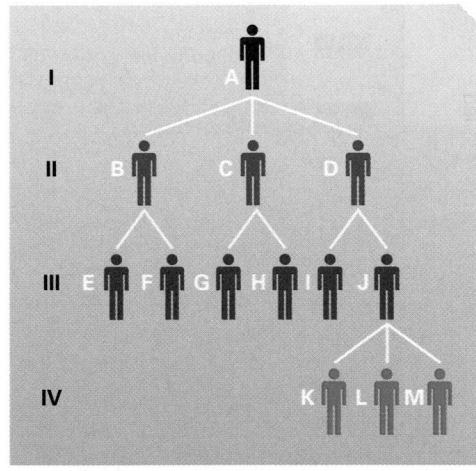

FIGURE 9.8 Classification: An Important Ability in Concrete Operational Thought. A family tree of four generations (*I to IV*): The preoperational child has trouble classifying the members of the four generations; the concrete operational child can classify the members vertically, horizontally, and obliquely (up and down and across). For example, the concrete operational child understands that a family member can be a son, a brother, and a father, all at the same time.

Children who have reached the concrete operational stage are also capable of **seriation**, which is the ability to order stimuli along a quantitative dimension (such as length). To see if students can serialize, a teacher might haphazardly place eight sticks of different lengths on a table. The teacher then asks the students to order the sticks by length. Many young children end up with two or three small groups of "big" sticks or "little" sticks, rather than a correct ordering of all eight sticks. Another mistaken strategy they use is to evenly line up the tops of the sticks but ignore the bottoms. The concrete operational thinker simultaneously understands that each stick must be longer than the one that precedes it and shorter than the one that follows it.

Another aspect of reasoning about the relations between classes is **transitivity**, which is the ability to logically combine relations to understand certain conclusions. In this case, consider three sticks (A, B, and C) of differing lengths. A is the longest, B is intermediate in length, and C is the shortest. Does the child understand that if A is longer than B and B is longer than C, then A is longer than C? In Piaget's theory, concrete operational thinkers do; preoperational thinkers do not.

Evaluating Piaget's Concrete Operational Stage Has Piaget's portrait of the concrete operational child stood the test of research? According to Piaget, various aspects of a stage should emerge at the same time. In fact, however, some concrete operational abilities do not appear in synchrony. For example, children do not learn to conserve at the same time they learn to cross-classify.

Furthermore, education and culture exert stronger influences on children's development than Piaget reasoned (Gauvain & Perez, 2007). Some preoperational children can be trained to reason at a concrete operational stage. And the age at which children acquire conservation skills is related to how much practice their culture provides in these skills. Among Wolof children in the West African nation of Senegal, for example, only 50 percent of the 10- to 13-year-olds understood the principle of conservation (Greenfield, 1966). Comparable studies among cultures in central Australia, New Guinea (an island north of Australia), the Amazon jungle region of Brazil, and rural Sardinia (an island off the coast of Italy) yielded similar results (Dasen, 1977).

Thus, although Piaget was a giant in the field of developmental psychology, his conclusions about the concrete operational stage have been challenged. In Chapter 11, after examining the final stage in his theory of cognitive development, we will further evaluate Piaget's contributions and the criticisms of his theory.

Neo-Piagetians argue that Piaget got some things right but that his theory needs considerable revision. They give more emphasis to how children use attention,

An outstanding teacher, and education in the logic of science and mathematics, are important cultural experiences that promote the development of operational thought. *Might Piaget have underestimated the roles of culture and schooling in children's cognitive development?*

seriation The concrete operation that involves ordering stimuli along a quantitative dimension (such as length).

transitivity The ability to logically combine relations to understand certain conclusions.

neo-Piagetians Developmentalists who argue that Piaget got some things right but that his theory needs considerable revision. They have elaborated on Piaget's theory, giving more emphasis to information-processing, strategies, and precise cognitive steps.

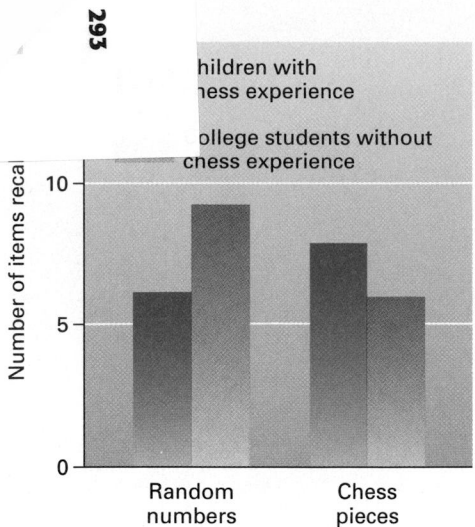

FIGURE 9.9 **The Role of Expertise in Memory.** Notice that when 10- to 11-year-old children and college students were asked to remember a string of random numbers that had been presented to them, the college students fared better. However, the 10- to 11-year-olds who had experience playing chess ("experts") had better memory for the location of chess pieces on a chess board than college students with no chess experience ("novices") (Chi, 1978).

memory, and strategies to process information (Case & Mueller, 2001). They especially believe that a more accurate portrayal of children's thinking requires attention to children's strategies, the speed at which children process information, the particular task involved, and the division of problems into smaller, more precise steps (Morra & others, 2008). These are issues addressed by the information-processing approach, and we discuss some of them later in this chapter.

Another alternative comes from Vygotsky. As we discussed in Chapter 7, Vygotksy, like Piaget, held that children construct their knowledge of the world. But Vygotsky did not propose stages of cognitive development, and he emphasized the importance of social interaction, the social contexts of learning, and the child's use of language to plan, guide, and monitor behavior (Cole & Gajdamaschko, 2007; Daniels, 2007).

Information Processing

If instead of analyzing the type of thinking that children display we examine how they handle information during middle and late childhood, what do we find? During these years, most children dramatically improve their ability to sustain and control attention. As we discussed in Chapter 7, they pay more attention to task-relevant stimuli than to salient stimuli. Other changes in information processing during middle and late childhood involve memory, thinking, and metacognition.

Memory   In Chapter 7, we concluded that short-term memory increases considerably during early childhood but after the age of 7 does not show as much increase. **Long-term memory**, a relatively permanent and unlimited type of memory, increases with age during middle and late childhood. In part, improvements in memory reflect children's increased knowledge and their increased use of strategies.

Knowledge and Expertise   Much of the research on the role of knowledge in memory has compared experts and novices (Ericcson & others, 2006). *Experts* have acquired extensive knowledge about a particular content area; this knowledge influences what they notice and how they organize, represent, and interpret information. This in turn affects their ability to remember, reason, and solve problems. When individuals have expertise about a particular subject, their memory also tends to be good regarding material related to that subject.

For example, one study found that 10- and 11-year-olds who were experienced chess players ("experts") were able to remember more information about chess pieces than college students who were not chess players ("novices") (Chi, 1978) (see Figure 9.9). In contrast, when the college students were presented with other stimuli, they were able to remember them better than the children were. Thus, the children's expertise in chess gave them superior memories, but only in chess.

There are developmental changes in expertise. Older children usually have more expertise about a subject than younger children do, which can contribute to their better memory for the subject.

Strategies   If we know anything at all about long-term memory, it is that long-term memory depends on the learning activities individuals engage in when learning and remembering information (Pressley & others, 2007). Recall from Chapter 7 that *strategies* consist of deliberate mental activities to improve the processing of information. They do not occur automatically but require effort and work. Two important strategies are creating mental images and elaborating on information (Murray, 2007).

Mental imagery can help even young school children to remember pictures. However, for remembering verbal information, mental imagery works better for older children than for younger children (Schneider, 2004). In one study, 20 sentences were presented to first- through sixth-grade children to remember—such as "The angry bird shouted at the white dog" and "The policeman painted the circus tent

long-term memory A relatively permanent type of memory that holds huge amounts of information for a long period of time.

on a windy day" (Pressley & others, 1987). Children were randomly assigned either to an imagery condition in which they were told to make a picture in their head for each sentence or to a control condition in which they were told just to try hard. The instructions to form images helped older elementary school children (grades 4 through 6) but did not help the younger elementary school children (grades 1 through 3).

Elaboration is an important strategy that involves engaging in more extensive processing of information. When individuals engage in elaboration, their memory benefits (Kellogg, 2007). Thinking of examples and referencing one's self are good ways to elaborate information. Thinking about personal associations with information makes the information more meaningful and helps children to remember it.

The use of elaboration changes developmentally (Pressley & McCormick, 2007). Adolescents are more likely to use elaboration spontaneously than children. Elementary school children can be taught to use elaboration strategies on a learning task, but they will be less likely than adolescents to use the strategies on other learning tasks in the future. Nonetheless, verbal elaboration can be an effective strategy for processing information even for young elementary school children.

Fuzzy Trace Theory Might something other than knowledge and strategies be responsible for the improvement in memory during the elementary school years? Charles Brainerd and Valerie Reyna (1993; Reyna, 2004; Reyna & Brainerd, 1995) argue that fuzzy traces account for much of this improvement. Their **fuzzy trace theory** states that memory is best understood by considering two types of memory representations: (1) verbatim memory trace, and (2) gist. The *verbatim memory trace* consists of the precise details of the information, whereas *gist* refers to the central idea of the information. When gist is used, fuzzy traces are built up. Although individuals of all ages extract gist, young children tend to store and retrieve verbatim traces. At some point during the early elementary school years, children begin to use gist more and, according to the theory, this contributes to the improved memory and reasoning of older children because fuzzy traces are more enduring and less likely to be forgotten than verbatim traces.

Thinking Three important aspects of thinking are being able to think critically, creatively, and scientifically.

Critical Thinking Currently, there is considerable interest among psychologists and educators in critical thinking (Halpern, 2007; Sternberg, Roediger, & Halpern, 2007). **Critical thinking** involves thinking reflectively and productively, and evaluating evidence. In this book, the second part of the Review and Reflect sections of each chapter challenges you to think critically about a topic or an issue related to the discussion.

Jacqueline and Martin Brooks (2001) lament that few schools really teach students to think critically and develop a deep understanding of concepts. Deep understanding occurs when students are stimulated to rethink previously held ideas. In Brooks and Brooks' view, schools spend too much time getting students to give a single correct answer in an imitative way, rather than encouraging them to expand their thinking by coming up with new ideas and rethinking earlier conclusions. They observe that too often teachers ask students to recite, define, describe, state, and list, rather than to analyze, infer, connect, synthesize, criticize, create, evaluate, think, and rethink. Many successful students complete their assignments, do well on tests and get good grades, yet they don't ever learn to think critically and deeply. They think superficially, staying on the surface of problems rather than stretching their minds and becoming deeply engaged in meaningful thinking.

Creative Thinking Cognitively competent children not only think critically, but also creatively (Rickards, Moger, & Runco, 2009). **Creative thinking** is the ability to think in novel and unusual ways and to come up with unique solutions to problems. Thus, intelligence and creativity are not the same thing. This difference was recognized by

"For God's sake, think! Why is he being so nice to you?"
Copyright © The New Yorker Collection 1998 Sam Gross from cartoonbank.com. All Rights Reserved.

elaboration An important strategy that involves engaging in more extensive processing of information.

fuzzy trace theory States that memory is best understood by considering two types of memory representations: (1) verbatim memory trace, and (2) gist. In this theory, older children's better memory is attributed to the fuzzy traces created by extracting the gist of information.

critical thinking Thinking reflectively and productively, as well as evaluating the evidence.

creative thinking The ability to think in novel and unusual ways and to come up with unique solutions to problems.

What do you mean, "What is it?" It's the spontaneous, unfettered expression of a young mind not yet bound by the restraints of narrative or pictorial representation.
Science Cartoons Plus. Used with permission.

J. P. Guilford (1967), who distinguished between **convergent thinking**, which produces one correct answer and characterizes the kind of thinking that is required on conventional tests of intelligence, and **divergent thinking**, which produces many different answers to the same question and characterizes creativity. For example, a typical item on a conventional intelligence test is "How many quarters will you get in return for 60 dimes?" In contrast, the following question has many possible answers: "What image comes to mind when you hear the phrase 'sitting alone in a dark room' or 'some unique uses for a paper clip'?"

It is important to recognize that children will show more creativity in some domains than others (Rickards, Moger, & Runco, 2009; Sternberg, 2009d). A child who shows creative thinking skills in mathematics may not exhibit these skills in art, for example.

An important goal is to help children become more creative. The following *Applications in Life-Span Development* interlude examines some recommendations for ways to accomplish this goal.

Applications in Life-Span Development
Strategies for Increasing Children's Creative Thinking

Here are strategies for increasing children's creative thinking.

Encourage Brainstorming

Brainstorming is a technique in which people are encouraged to come up with creative ideas in a group, play off each other's ideas, and say practically whatever comes to mind that seems relevant to a particular issue. Participants are usually told to hold off from criticizing others' ideas at least until the end of the brainstorming session.

Provide Environments That Stimulate Creativity

Some environments nourish creativity, others inhibit it (Piggot, 2007). Parents and teachers who encourage creativity often rely on children's natural curiosity. They provide exercises and activities that stimulate children to find insightful solutions to problems, rather than ask a lot of questions that require rote answers (Beghetto & Kaufman, 2009). Teachers also encourage creativity by taking students on field trips to locations where creativity is valued. Howard Gardner (1993) emphasizes that science, discovery, and children's museums offer rich opportunities to stimulate creativity.

Don't Overcontrol Students

Teresa Amabile (1993) says that telling children exactly how to do things leaves them feeling that originality is a mistake and exploration is a waste of time. If, instead of dictating which activities they should engage in, you let children select their interests, and you support their inclinations, you will be less likely to destroy their natural curiosity.

Encourage Internal Motivation

Excessive use of prizes, such as gold stars, money, or toys, can stifle creativity by undermining the intrinsic pleasure students derive from creative activities. Creative children's motivation is the satisfaction generated by the work itself. Competition for prizes and formal evaluations often undermine intrinsic motivation and creativity (Amabile & Hennesey, 1992). However, this is not to rule out material rewards altogether.

Build Children's Confidence

To expand children's creativity, encourage children to believe in their own ability to create something innovative and worthwhile. Building children's confidence in their creative skills aligns with Bandura's (2008, 2009) concept of *self-efficacy*, the belief that one can master a situation and produce positive outcomes.

convergent thinking Thinking that produces one correct answer and is characteristic of the kind of thinking tested by standardized intelligence tests.

divergent thinking Thinking that produces many answers to the same question and is characteristic of creativity.

brainstorming A technique in which individuals are encouraged to come up with creative ideas in a group, play off each other's ideas, and say practically whatever comes to mind.

Guide Children to Be Persistent and Delay Gratification

Most highly successful creative products take years to develop. Most creative individuals work on ideas and projects for months and years without being rewarded for their efforts (Sternberg & Williams, 1996). Children don't become experts at sports, music, or art overnight. It usually takes many years working at something to become an expert at it; so it is with being a creative thinker who produces a unique, worthwhile product.

Encourage Children to Take Intellectual Risks

Creative individuals take intellectual risks and seek to discover or invent something never before discovered or invented (Sternberg & Williams, 1996). They risk spending extensive time on an idea or project that may not work. Creative people are not afraid of failing or getting something wrong (Beghetto & Kaufman, 2009).

Introduce Children to Creative People

Teachers can invite creative people to their classrooms and ask them to describe what helps them become creative or to demonstrate their creative skills. A writer, poet, musician, scientist, and many others can bring their props and productions to the class, turning it into a theater for stimulating students' creativity.

What are some good strategies for guiding children in thinking more creatively?

Scientific Thinking   Like scientists, children ask fundamental questions about reality and seek answers to problems that seem utterly trivial or unanswerable to other people (such as, Why is the sky blue?). Do children generate hypotheses, perform experiments, and reach conclusions about their data in ways resembling those of scientists?

Scientific reasoning often is aimed at identifying causal relations. Like scientists, children place a great deal of emphasis on causal mechanisms. Their understanding of how events are caused weighs more heavily in their causal inferences than even such strong influences as whether the cause happened immediately before the effect.

There also are important differences between the reasoning of children and the reasoning of scientists. Children are more influenced by happenstance events than by an overall pattern, and children tend to maintain their old theories regardless of the evidence (Kuhn, Schauble, & Garcia-Mila, 1992). Children might go through mental gymnastics trying to reconcile seemingly contradictory new information with their existing beliefs. For example, after learning about the solar system, children sometimes conclude that there are two earths, the seemingly flat world in which they live and the round ball floating in space that their teacher described.

Children also have difficulty designing experiments that can distinguish among alternative causes. Instead, they tend to bias the experiments in favor of whatever hypothesis they began with. Sometimes they see the results as supporting their original hypothesis even when the results directly contradict it (Schauble & others, 1996). Thus, although there are important similarities between children and scientists, in their basic curiosity and in the kinds of questions they ask, there are also important differences in the degree to which they can separate theory and evidence and in their ability to design conclusive experiments (Lehrer & Schauble, 2006).

Too often, the skills scientists use, such as careful observation, graphing, self-regulatory thinking, and knowing when and how to apply one's knowledge to solve problems, are not routinely taught in schools. Children have many concepts that are incompatible with science and reality. Good teachers perceive and understand a child's underlying scientific concepts, then use the concepts as a scaffold for learning (Magnusson & Palinscar, 2005). Effective science teaching helps children distinguish between fruitful errors and misconceptions, and detect plainly wrong ideas that need to be replaced by more accurate conceptions (Bybee, Powell, & Trowbridge, 2007).

Elementary school science teacher, Luis Recalde, holds up a seaweed specimen in one of the hands-on, high-interest learning contexts he creates for students. Recalde, a fourth- and fifth-grade science teacher at Vincent E. Mauro Elementary School, in New Haven, Connecticut, uses every opportunity to make science fascinating and motivating for students to learn. Recalde infuses hands-on science experiences with energy and enthusiasm. To help students get a better sense of what it is like to be a scientist, he brings lab coats to the classroom for students to wear. He holds science fair workshops for teachers and often gives up his vacation time to help students with science projects.

Cognitive developmentalist John Flavell (*left*) is a pioneer in providing insights about children's thinking. Among his many contributions are creating the field of metacognition and conducting numerous studies in this area, including metamemory and theory of mind studies.

What are some developmental changes in metacognition?

Many science teachers help their students construct their knowledge of science through discovery and hands-on laboratory investigations (Victor, Kellough, & Tai, 2008). Constructivist teaching emphasizes that children have to build their own scientific knowledge and understanding. Keep in mind, though, that it is important that students not be left completely on their own to construct scientific knowledge independent of *science content*. Students' inquiry should be guided (Moyer, Hackett, & Everett, 2007). It is important for teachers—at a minimum—initially to scaffold students' science learning, extensively monitor their progress, and ensure that they are learning science content. Thus, in pursuing science investigations, students need to learn inquiry skills *and* science content (Gallagher, 2007).

How might experiences in families, economic conditions, and culture be linked to children's science achievement? A recent study of more than 107,000 students in 41 countries examined this question (Chiu, 2007). Students had higher science achievement scores when their schools had more resources, when they lived in two-parent families, experienced more family involvement, lived with fewer siblings, lived in wealthier countries, or lived in countries with more equal distribution of household income.

Metacognition   One expert in children's thinking, Deanna Kuhn (1999), argues that to help students become better thinkers, schools should pay more attention to helping students develop skills that entail knowing about their own (and others') knowing. In other words, schools should do more to develop **metacognition**, which is cognition about cognition, or knowing about knowing (Flavell, 2004).

The majority of developmental studies classified as "metacognitive" have focused on *metamemory*, or knowledge about memory. This includes general knowledge about memory, such as knowing that recognition tests are easier than recall tests. It also encompasses knowledge about one's own memory, such as a student's ability to monitor whether she has studied enough for a test that is coming up next week.

Young children do have some general knowledge about memory. By 5 or 6 years of age, children usually already know that familiar items are easier to learn than unfamiliar ones, that short lists are easier than long ones, that recognition is easier than recall, and that forgetting is more likely to occur over time (Lyon & Flavell, 1993). However, in other ways young children's metamemory is limited. They don't understand that related items are easier to remember than unrelated ones and that remembering the gist of a story is easier than remembering information verbatim (Kreutzer, Leonard, & Flavell, 1975). By the fifth grade, students understand that gist recall is easier than verbatim recall.

Young children also have only limited knowledge about their own memory. They have an inflated opinion of their memory abilities. For example, in one study a majority of young children predicted that they would be able to recall all 10 items on a list of 10 items. When tested for this, none of the young children managed this feat (Flavell, Friedrichs, & Hoyt, 1970). As they move through the elementary school years, children give more realistic evaluations of their memory skills (Schneider & Pressley, 1997).

In addition to metamemory, metacognition includes knowledge about strategies. In the view of Michael Pressley (2003, 2007), the key to education is helping students learn a rich repertoire of strategies that result in solutions to problems. Good thinkers routinely use strategies and effective planning to solve problems. Good thinkers also know when and where to use strategies. Understanding when and where to use strategies often results from monitoring the learning situation (Pressley & McCormick, 2007).

Pressley and his colleagues (Pressley & others, 2001, 2003, 2004, 2007) spent considerable time in recent years observing strategy instruction by teachers and strategy use by students in elementary and secondary school classrooms. They conclude that strategy instruction is far less complete and intense than what students need in order to learn how to use strategies effectively. They argue that education needs to be

metacognition Cognition about cognition, or knowing about knowing.

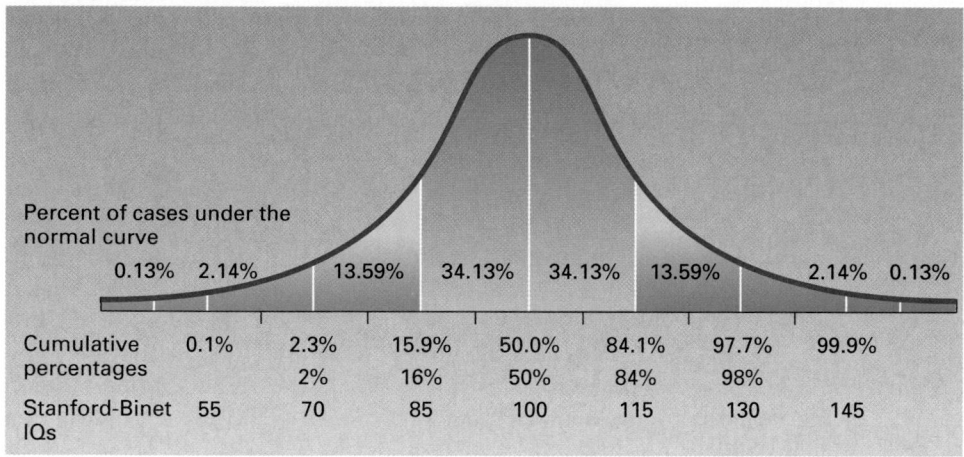

Percent of cases under the normal curve								
0.13%	2.14%	13.59%	34.13%	34.13%	13.59%	2.14%	0.13%	
Cumulative percentages	0.1%	2.3%	15.9%	50.0%	84.1%	97.7%	99.9%	
		2%	16%	50%	84%	98%		
Stanford-Binet IQs	55	70	85	100	115	130	145	

FIGURE 9.10 The Normal Curve and Stanford Binet IQ Scores. The distribution of IQ scores approximates a normal curve. Most of the population falls in the middle range of scores. Notice that extremely high and extremely low scores are very rare. Slightly more than two-thirds of the scores fall between 85 and 115. Only about 1 in 50 individuals has an IQ of more than 130, and only about 1 in 50 individuals has an IQ of less than 70.

restructured so that students are provided with more opportunities to become competent strategic learners.

Intelligence

How can intelligence be defined? **Intelligence** is the ability to solve problems and to adapt and learn from experiences. But even this broad definition doesn't satisfy everyone. As you will see shortly, Robert Sternberg (2008a, b, 2009a, b) proposes that practical know-how should be considered part of intelligence. In his view, intelligence involves weighing options carefully and acting judiciously, as well as developing strategies to improve shortcomings. Also, a definition of intelligence based on a theory such as Vygotsky's, which we discussed in Chapter 7, would have to include the ability to use the tools of the culture with help from more-skilled individuals. Because intelligence is such an abstract, broad concept, it is not surprising that there are so many different ways to define it.

Interest in intelligence has often focused on individual differences and assessment. **Individual differences** are the stable, consistent ways in which people are different from each other. We can talk about individual differences in personality or any other domain, but it is in the domain of intelligence that the most attention has been directed at individual differences. For example, an intelligence test purports to inform us about whether a student can reason better than others who have taken the test. Let's go back in history and see what the first intelligence test was like.

The Binet Tests In 1904, the French Ministry of Education asked psychologist Alfred Binet to devise a method of identifying children who were unable to learn in school. School officials wanted to reduce crowding by placing students who did not benefit from regular classroom teaching in special schools. Binet and his student Theophile Simon developed an intelligence test to meet this request. The test is called the 1905 Scale. It consisted of 30 questions on topics ranging from the ability to touch one's ear to the ability to draw designs from memory and define abstract concepts.

Binet developed the concept of **mental age (MA)**, an individual's level of mental development relative to others. Not much later, in 1912, William Stern created the concept of **intelligence quotient (IQ)**, a person's mental age divided by chronological age (CA), multiplied by 100. That is: $IQ = MA/CA \times 100$. If mental age is the same as chronological age, then the person's IQ is 100. If mental age is above chronological age, then IQ is more than 100. If mental age is below chronological age, then IQ is less than 100.

The Binet test has been revised many times to incorporate advances in the understanding of intelligence and intelligence tests. These revisions are called the *Stanford-Binet tests* (Stanford University is where the revisions have been done). By administering the test to large numbers of people of different ages (from preschool through late adulthood) from different backgrounds, researchers have found that scores on the Stanford-Binet approximate a normal distribution (see Figure 9.10). A **normal distribution** is

intelligence Problem-solving skills and the ability to learn from and adapt to the experiences of everyday life.

individual differences The stable, consistent ways in which people are different from each other.

mental age (MA) Binet's measure of an individual's level of mental development, compared with that of others.

intelligence quotient (IQ) A person's mental age divided by chronological age, multiplied by 100.

normal distribution A symmetrical distribution with most scores falling in the middle of the possible range of scores and a few scores appearing toward the extremes of the range.

...es

A child must think logically and abstractly to answer a number of questions about how things might be similar.

Example: "In what way are a lion and a tiger alike?"

Comprehension

This subscale is designed to measure an individual's judgment and common sense.

Example: "What is the advantage of keeping money in a bank?"

Nonverbal Subscales

Block Design

A child must assemble a set of multicolored blocks to match designs that the examiner shows. Visual-motor coordination, perceptual organization, and the ability to visualize spatially are assessed.

Example: "Use the four blocks on the left to make the pattern on the right."

FIGURE 9.11 Sample Subscales of the Wechsler Intelligence Scale for Children–Fourth Edition (WISC-IV). The Wechsler includes 11 subscales, 6 verbal and 5 nonverbal. Three of the subscales are shown here. Simulated items similar to those found in the *Wechsler Intelligence Scale for Children–Fourth Edition.* Copyright © 2003 by Harcourt Assessment, Inc. Reproduced by permission. All rights reserved. "Wechsler Intelligence Scale for Children" and "WISC" are trademarks of Harcourt Assessment, Inc. registered in the United States of America and/or other jurisdictions.

"You're wise, but you lack tree smarts."

triarchic theory of intelligence Sternberg's theory that intelligence consists of analytical intelligence, creative intelligence, and practical intelligence.

Robert J. Sternberg, who developed the triarchic theory of intelligence.

symmetrical, with a majority of the scores falling in the middle of the possible range of scores and few scores appearing toward the extremes of the range.

The Wechsler Scales   Another set of tests widely used to assess students' intelligence is called the *Wechsler scales,* developed by psychologist David Wechsler. They include the Wechsler Preschool and Primary Scale of Intelligence–Third Edition (WPPSI-III) to test children from the ages of 2 years 6 months to 7 years 3 months of age; the Wechsler Intelligence Scale for Children–Fourth Edition (WISC-IV) for children and adolescents 6 to 16 years of age; and the Wechsler Adult Intelligence Scale–Third Edition (WAIS-III).

The Wechsler scales not only provide an overall IQ score, but they also yield several composite indexes (for example, the Verbal Comprehension Index, the Working Memory Index, and the Processing Speed Index) that allow the examiner to quickly determine the areas in which the child is strong or weak. Three of the Wechsler subscales are shown in Figure 9.11.

Types of Intelligence   Is it more appropriate to think of a child's intelligence as a general ability or as a number of specific abilities? Robert Sternberg and Howard Gardner have proposed influential theories oriented to this second viewpoint.

Sternberg's Triarchic Theory   Robert J. Sternberg (1986, 2004, 2007a, b, 2008a, b, 2009a, b) developed the **triarchic theory of intelligence**, which states that intelligence comes in three forms: (1) *analytical intelligence,* which refers to the ability to analyze, judge, evaluate, compare, and contrast; (2) *creative intelligence,* which consists of the ability to create, design, invent, originate, and imagine; and (3) *practical intelligence,* which involves the ability to use, apply, implement, and put ideas into practice.

Sternberg (2002c; Sternberg & others, 2007) says that children with different triarchic patterns "look different" in school. Students with high analytic ability tend to be favored in conventional schooling. They often do well under direct instruction, in which the teacher lectures and gives students objective tests. They often are considered to be "smart" students who get good grades, show up in high-level tracks, do well on traditional tests of intelligence and the SAT, and later get admitted to competitive colleges.

In contrast, children who are high in creative intelligence often are not on the top rung of their class. Many teachers have specific expectations about how assignments should be done, and creatively intelligent students may not conform to those expectations. Instead of giving conformist answers, they give unique answers, for which they might get reprimanded or marked down. No teacher wants to discourage creativity, but Sternberg stresses that too often a teacher's desire to improve students' knowledge supresses creative thinking.

Like children high in creative intelligence, children who are practically intelligent often do not relate well to the demands of school. However, many of these children do well outside of the classroom's walls. They may have excellent social skills and good common sense. As adults, some become successful managers, entrepreneurs, or politicians in spite of having undistinguished school records.

Gardner's Eight Frames of Mind   Howard Gardner (1983, 1993, 2002) suggests there are eight types of intelligence, or "frames of mind." These are described here, with examples of the types of vocations in which they are reflected as strengths (Campbell, Campbell, & Dickinson, 2004):

- *Verbal:* The ability to think in words and use language to express meaning. Occupations: Authors, journalists, speakers.
- *Mathematical:* The ability to carry out mathematical operations. Occupations: Scientists, engineers, accountants.
- *Spatial:* The ability to think three-dimensionally. Occupations: Architects, artists, sailors.
- *Bodily-kinesthetic:* The ability to manipulate objects and be physically adept. Occupations: Surgeons, craftspeople, dancers, athletes.
- *Musical:* A sensitivity to pitch, melody, rhythm, and tone. Occupations: Composers, musicians, and sensitive listeners.
- *Interpersonal:* The ability to understand and interact effectively with others. Occupations: Successful teachers, mental health professionals.
- *Intrapersonal:* The ability to understand oneself. Occupations: Theologians, psychologists.
- *Naturalist:* The ability to observe patterns in nature and understand natural and human-made systems. Occupations: Farmers, botanists, ecologists, landscapers.

According to Gardner, everyone has all of these intelligences to varying degrees. As a result, we prefer to learn and process information in different ways. People learn best when they can do so in a way that uses their stronger intelligences.

Howard Gardner, here working with a young child, developed the view that intelligence comes in the forms of these eight kinds of skills: verbal, mathematical, spatial, bodily-kinesthetic, musical, intrapersonal, interpersonal, and naturalist.

Evaluating the Multiple-Intelligence Approaches   Sternberg's and Gardner's approaches have much to offer. They have stimulated teachers to think more broadly about what makes up children's competencies. And they have motivated educators to develop programs that instruct students in multiple domains. These approaches have also contributed to interest in assessing intelligence and classroom learning in innovative ways, such as by evaluating student portfolios (Moran & Gardner, 2006, 2007).

Still, doubts about multiple-intelligences approaches persist. A number of psychologists think that the multiple-intelligence views have taken the concept of specific intelligences too far (Jensen, 2008; Johnson, te Nijenhuis, & Bouchard, 2008). Some argue that a research base to support the three intelligences of Sternberg or the eight intelligences of Gardner has not yet emerged. One expert on intelligence, Nathan Brody (2007), observes that people who excel at one type of intellectual task are likely to excel in others. Thus, individuals who do well at memorizing lists of digits are also likely to be good at solving verbal problems and spatial layout problems. If musical skill reflects a distinct type of intelligence, ask other critics, why not label the skills of outstanding chess players, prizefighters, painters, and poets as types of intelligence?

The argument between those who support the concept of general intelligence and those who advocate the multiple-intelligences view is ongoing (Brody, 2007; Horn, 2007; Sternberg, 2008a, b, 2009a, b). Sternberg (2007a, b) actually accepts that there is a general intelligence for the kinds of analytical tasks that traditional IQ tests assess but thinks that the range of tasks those tests measure is far too narrow.

Children in the Key School form "pods," in which they pursue activities of special interest to them. Every day, each child can choose from activities that draw on Gardner's eight frames of mind. The school has pods that range from gardening to architecture to gliding to dancing.

Culture and Intelligence   Differences in conceptions of intelligence occur not only among psychologists but also among cultures. What is viewed as intelligent in one culture may not be thought of as intelligent in another (Cole, 2006). For example, people in Western cultures tend to view

"You can't build a hut, you don't know how to find edible roots and you know nothing about predicting the weather. In other words, you do terribly on our I.Q. test."
Copyright © 1992 by Sidney Harris. Reprinted with permission.

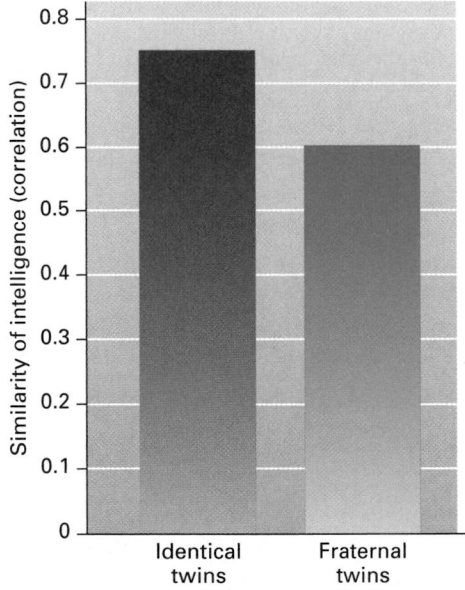

FIGURE 9.12 Correlation Between Intelligence Test Scores and Twin Status. The graph represents a summary of research findings that have compared the intelligence test scores of identical and fraternal twins. An approximate .15 difference has been found with a higher correlation for identical twins (.75) and a lower correlation for fraternal twins (.60).

heritability The fraction of variance in a population that is attributed to genetics and is computed using correlational techniques.

intelligence in terms of reasoning and thinking skills, whereas people in Eastern cultures see intelligence as a way for members of a community to engage successfully in in social roles (Nisbett, 2003). One study found that Taiwanese Chinese conceptions of intelligence emphasize understanding and relating to others, including when to show and when not to show one's intelligence (Yang & Sternberg, 1997).

Interpreting Differences in IQ Scores

The IQ scores that result from tests such as the Stanford-Binet and Wechsler scales provide information about children's mental abilities. However, interpreting what performance on an intelligence test means is debated (Campbell, 2007; Plomin, DeFries, & Fulker, 2007; Sternberg, 2009a, b).

The Influence of Genetics How strong is the effect of genetics on intelligence? The concept of heritability attempts to tease apart the effects of heredity and environment in a population. **Heritability** is the fraction of the variance in a population that is attributed to genetics. The heritability index is computed using correlational techniques, which we first discussed in Chapter 1. Thus, 1.00 is the highest degree of heritability that is hypothetically possible, and correlations of .70 and above suggest a strong genetic influence. A committee of respected researchers convened by the American Psychological Association concluded that by late adolescence, the heritability of intelligence is about .75, which reflects a strong genetic influence (Neisser & others, 1996).

Most research on heredity and environment does not include environments that differ radically. Thus, it is not surprising that many genetic studies show environment to be a fairly weak influence on intelligence (Fraser, 1995).

The heritability index has several flaws. It is only as good as the data entered into its analysis and the interpretations made from it (Sternberg, Kaufman, & Grigorenko, 2008). The data are virtually all from traditional IQ tests, which some experts think are not always the best indicator of intelligence (Sternberg, 2008a, b). Also, the heritability index assumes that we can treat genetic and environmental influences as factors that can be separated, with each part contributing a distinct amount of influence. As we discussed in Chapter 2, genes and the environment interact: Genes always exist in an environment and the environment shapes their activity.

One strategy for examining the role of heredity in intelligence is to compare the IQs of identical and fraternal twins, which we initially discussed in Chapter 2. Recall that identical twins have exactly the same genetic makeup but fraternal twins do not. If intelligence is genetically determined, say some investigators, identical twins' IQs should be more similar than the intelligence of fraternal twins. A research review of many studies found that the difference in the average correlation of intelligence between identical and fraternal twins was 15, a relatively low correlation (Grigorenko, 2000) (see Figure 9.12).

Today, most researchers agree that genetics and environment interact to influence intelligence (Gottlieb, 2007; Preiss & Sternberg, 2009; Sternberg, 2009a, b). For most people, this means that modifications in environment can change their IQ scores considerably. Although genetic endowment may always influence a person's intellectual ability, the environmental influences and opportunities we provide children and adults do make a difference (Campbell, 2007; Sternberg, 2009a, b).

Environmental Influences In Chapter 5 we described one study that demonstrated the influence of parents on cognitive abilities. Researchers went into homes and observed how extensively parents from welfare and middle-income professional families talked and communicated with their young children (Hart & Risley, 1995). They found that the middle-income professional parents were much more likely to communicate with their young children than the welfare parents were. How much the parents communicated with their children in the first three years of their lives was correlated with the children's Stanford-Binet IQ scores at age 3. The more parents communicated with their children, the higher the children's IQs were.

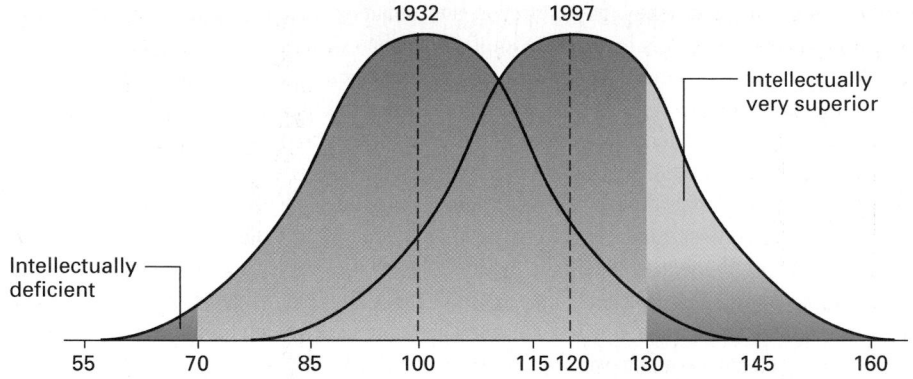

FIGURE 9.13 Increasing IQ Scores from 1932 to 1997. As measured by the Stanford-Binet intelligence test, American children seem to be getting smarter. Scores of a group tested in 1932 fell along a bell-shaped curve with half below 100 and half above. Studies show that if children took that same test today, half would score above 120 on the 1932 scale. Very few of them would score in the "intellectually deficient" end, on the left side, and about one-fourth would rank in the "very superior" range.

Schooling also influences intelligence (Gustafsson, 2007). The biggest effects have been found when large groups of children have been deprived of formal education for an extended period, resulting in lower intelligence (Ceci & Gilstrap, 2000). Another possible effect of education can be seen in rapidly increasing IQ test scores around the world (Flynn, 1999, 2007). IQ scores have been increasing so fast that a high percentage of people regarded as having average intelligence at the turn of the century would be considered below average in intelligence today (see Figure 9.13). If a representative sample of people today took the Stanford-Binet test version used in 1932, about 25 percent would be defined as having very superior intelligence, a label usually accorded to fewer than 3 percent of the population. Because the increase has taken place in a relatively short time, it can't be due to heredity, but rather may be due to increasing levels of education attained by a much greater percentage of the world's population, or to other environmental factors such as the explosion of information to which people are exposed. The worldwide increase in intelligence test scores that has occurred over a short time frame has been called the *Flynn effect* after the researcher who discovered it, James Flynn.

Researchers are increasingly concerned about improving the early environment of children who are at risk for impoverished intelligence (Barajas, Philipsen, & Brooks-Gunn, 2008). For various reasons, many low-income parents have difficulty providing an intellectually stimulating environment for their children. Programs that educate parents to be more sensitive caregivers and better teachers, as well as support services such as quality child-care programs, can make a difference in a child's intellectual development (Coltrane & others, 2008). Thus the efforts to counteract a deprived early environment's effect on intelligence emphasize prevention rather than remediation.

A review of the research on early interventions concluded that (1) high-quality child-care center-based interventions are associated with increases in children's intelligence and school achievement; (2) the interventions are most successful with poor children and children whose parents have little education; (3) the positive benefits continue through adolescence, but are not as strong as in early childhood or the beginning of elementary school; and (4) the programs that continue into middle and late childhood have the best long-term results (Brooks-Gunn, 2003). To read further about environmental influences on intelligence, see the *Research in Life-Span Development* interlude.

 ## Research in Life-Span Development
The Abecedarian Project

Each morning a young mother waited with her child for the bus that would take the child to school. The child was only 2 months old, and "school" was an experimental program at the University of North Carolina at Chapel Hill. There the child experienced a number of interventions designed to improve her intellectual development—everything from bright objects dangled in front of her eyes while she was a baby to language instruction and counting activities when she was a toddler (Wickelgren, 1999). The child's mother had an IQ of 40 and could not read signs or determine how much change she should receive from a cashier. Her grandmother had a similarly low IQ.

Today, at age 20, the child's IQ measures 80 points higher than her mother's did when the child was 2 months old. Not everyone agrees that IQ can be affected this extensively, but environment can make a substantial difference in a child's intelligence. As behavior geneticist Robert Plomin (1999) says, even something that is highly heritable (like intelligence) may be malleable through interventions.

The child we just described was part of the Abecedarian Intervention program at the University of North Carolina at Chapel Hill conducted by Craig Ramey and his associates (Ramey & Campbell, 1984; Ramey & Ramey, 1998; Ramey, Ramey, & Lanzi, 2001). They randomly assigned 111 young children from low-income, poorly educated families to either an intervention group, which received full-time, year-round child care along with medical and social work services, or to a control group, which received medical and social benefits but no child care. The child-care program included gamelike learning activities aimed at improving language, motor, social, and cognitive skills.

The success of the program in improving IQ was evident by the time the children were 3 years old. At that age, the experimental group showed normal IQs averaging 101, a 17-point advantage over the control group. Recent follow-up results suggest that the effects are long-lasting. More than a decade later at age 15, children from the intervention group still maintained an IQ advantage of 5 points over the control-group children (97.7 to 92.6) (Campbell & others, 2001; Ramey, Ramey, & Lanzi, 2001). They also did better on standardized tests of reading and math, and were less likely to be held back a year in school. Also, the greatest IQ gains were made by the children whose mothers had especially low IQs—below 70. At age 15, these children showed a 10-point IQ advantage over a group of children whose mothers' IQs were below 70 but did not experience the child-care intervention.

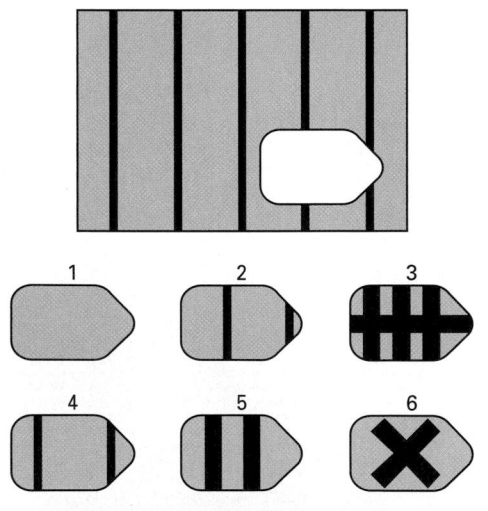

FIGURE 9.14 Sample Item from the Raven's Progressive Matrices Test.
Individuals are presented with a matrix arrangement of symbols, such as the one at the top of this figure, and must then complete the matrix by selecting the appropriate missing symbol from a group of symbols, such as the ones at the bottom. Simulated item similar to those found in the *Raven's Progressive Matrices.* Copyright © 1998 by Harcourt Assessment, Inc. Reproduced with permission. All rights reserved.

culture-fair tests Tests of intelligence that are designed to be free of cultural bias.

Group Differences   On the average, African American schoolchildren in the United States score 10 to 15 points lower on standardized intelligence tests than White American schoolchildren do (Brody, 2000). Children from Latino families also score lower than White children. These are *average scores,* however; there is significant overlap in the distribution of scores. About 15 to 25 percent of African American schoolchildren score higher than half of White schoolchildren do, and many White schoolchildren score lower than most African American schoolchildren.

As African Americans have gained social, economic, and educational opportunities, the gap between African Americans and Whites on standardized intelligence tests has begun to narrow (Ogbu & Stern, 2001). This gap especially narrows in college, where African American and White students often experience more similar environments than in the elementary and high school years (Myerson & others, 1998). Also, when children from disadvantaged African American families are adopted into more-advantaged middle-socioeconomic-status families, their scores on intelligence tests more closely resemble national averages for middle-socioeconomic-status children than for lower-socioeconomic-status children (Scarr & Weinberg, 1983).

Creating Culture-Fair Tests   **Culture-fair tests** are tests of intelligence that are intended to be free of cultural bias. Two types of culture-fair tests have been devised. The first includes items that are familiar to children from all socioeconomic and ethnic backgrounds, or items that at least are familiar to the children taking the test. For example, a child might be asked how a bird and a dog are different, on the assumption that all children have been exposed to birds and dogs. The second type of culture-fair test has no verbal questions. Figure 9.14 shows a sample question from the Raven's Progressive Matrices Test. Even though tests such as the Raven's Progressive Matrices are designed to be culture-fair, people with more education still score higher on them than do those with less education.

Why is it so hard to create culture-fair tests? Most tests tend to reflect what the dominant culture thinks is important (Shiraev & Levy, 2007). If tests have time limits, that will bias the test against groups not concerned with time. If languages differ, the same words might have different meanings for different language groups. Even pictures can produce bias because some cultures have less experience with drawings and photographs (Anastasi & Urbina, 1996). Within the same culture, different subgroups could have different attitudes, values, and motivation, and this could affect their performance on intelligence tests. Items that ask why buildings should be made of brick are biased against children who have little or no experience with brick houses. Questions about railroads, furnaces, snow, distances between cities, and so on can be biased against groups who have less experience than others with these contexts. Recall, too, that cultures define what is intelligent differently. Because of such difficulties in creating culture-fair tests, Robert Sternberg and his colleagues (Sternberg, 2009e; Sternberg & Grigorenko, 2008; Zhang & Sternberg, 2008) conclude that there are no culture-fair tests, only *culture-reduced tests.*

Using Intelligence Tests   Psychological tests are tools. Like all tools, their effectiveness depends on the knowledge, skill, and integrity of the user. A hammer can be used to build a beautiful kitchen cabinet, or it can be used as a weapon of assault. Like a hammer, psychological tests can be used for positive purposes, or they can be badly abused. Here are some cautions about IQ that can help you avoid the pitfalls of using information about a child's intelligence in negative ways:

- *Avoid stereotyping and expectations.* A special concern is that the scores on an IQ test easily can lead to stereotypes and expectations about students. Sweeping generalizations are too often made on the basis of an IQ score. An IQ test should always be considered a measure of current performance. It is not a measure of fixed potential. Maturational changes and enriched environmental experiences can advance a student's intelligence.

- *Know that IQ is not a sole indicator of competence.* Another concern about IQ tests occurs when they are used as the main or sole assessment of competence. A high IQ is not the ultimate human value. As we have seen in this chapter, it is important to consider not only students' intellectual competence in such areas as verbal skills but also their creative and practical skills.

- *Use caution in interpreting an overall IQ score.* In evaluating a child's intelligence, it is wiser to think of intelligence as consisting of a number of domains. Keep in mind the different types of intelligence described by Sternberg and Gardner. Remember that, by considering the different domains of intelligence, you can find that every child has at least one or more strengths.

Extremes of Intelligence

Intelligence tests have been used to discover indications of mental retardation or intellectual giftedness, the extremes of intelligence. At times, intelligence tests have been misused for this purpose. Keeping in mind the theme that an intelligence test should not be used as the sole indicator of mental retardation or giftedness, we will explore the nature of these intellectual extremes.

Mental Retardation   **Mental retardation** is a condition of limited mental ability in which an individual has a low IQ, usually below 70 on a traditional intelligence test, and has difficulty adapting to everyday life. About 5 million Americans fit this definition of mental retardation.

There are several classifications of mental retardation (Hodapp & Dykens, 2006). About 89 percent of the mentally retarded fall into the mild category, with IQs of 55 to 70; most of them are able to live independently as adults and work at a variety of jobs. About 6 percent are classified as moderately retarded, with IQs of 40 to 54; these people can attain a second-grade level of skills and may be able to support themselves as adults through some types of labor. About 3.5 percent of the mentally retarded are

A child with Down syndrome. *What causes a child to develop Down syndrome? In which major classification of mental retardation does the condition fall?*

mental retardation A condition of limited mental ability in which an individual has a low IQ, usually below 70 on a traditional test of intelligence, and has difficulty adapting to everyday life.

At 2 years of age, art prodigy Alexandra Nechita colored in coloring books for hours and also took up pen and ink. She had no interest in dolls or friends. By age 5 she was using watercolors. Once she started school, she would start painting as soon as she got home. At the age of 8, in 1994, she saw the first public exhibit of her work. In succeeding years, working quickly and impulsively on canvases as large as 5 feet by 9 feet, she has completed hundreds of paintings, some of which sell for close to $100,000 apiece. As a teenager, she continues to paint—relentlessly and passionately. It is, she says, what she loves to do. *What are some characteristics of children who are gifted?*

organic retardation Mental retardation that is caused by a genetic disorder or brain damage.

cultural-familial retardation Retardation that is characterized by no evidence of organic brain damage, but the individual's IQ is generally between 50 and 70.

gifted Having above-average intelligence (an IQ of 130 or higher) and/or superior talent for something.

in the severe category, with IQs of 25 to 39; these individuals learn to talk and accomplish very simple tasks but require extensive supervision. Less than 1 percent have IQs below 25; they fall into the profoundly mentally retarded classification and need constant supervision.

Mental retardation can have an organic cause, or it can be social and cultural in origin:

- **Organic retardation** is mental retardation that is caused by a genetic disorder or by brain damage; the word *organic* refers to the tissues or organs of the body, indicating physical damage. Most people who suffer from organic retardation have IQs that range between 0 and 50. However, children with Down syndrome have an average IQ of approximately 50. As discussed in Chapter 2, Down syndrome is caused by an extra copy of chromosome 21.

- **Cultural-familial retardation** is a mental deficit in which no evidence of organic brain damage can be found; individuals' IQs generally range from 50 to 70. Psychologists suspect that such mental deficits result from the normal variation that distributes people along the range of intelligence scores combined with growing up in a below-average intellectual environment.

Giftedness There have always been people whose abilities and accomplishments outshine others'—the whiz kid in class, the star athlete, the natural musician. People who are **gifted** have above-average intelligence (an IQ of 130 or higher) and/or superior talent for something. When it comes to programs for the gifted, most school systems select children who have intellectual superiority and academic aptitude, whereas children who are talented in the visual and performing arts (arts, drama, dance), athletics, or other special aptitudes tend to be overlooked (Clark, 2008; Karnes & Stephens, 2008).

What are the characteristics of children who are gifted? Despite speculation that giftedness is linked with having a mental disorder, no relation between giftedness and mental disorder has been found. Similarly, the idea that gifted children are maladjusted is a myth, as Lewis Terman (1925) found when he conducted an extensive study of 1,500 children whose Stanford-Binet IQs averaged 150. The children in Terman's study were socially well adjusted, and many went on to become successful doctors, lawyers, professors, and scientists. Studies support the conclusion that gifted people tend to be more mature than others, have fewer emotional problems than others, and grow up in a positive family climate (Davidson, 2000).

Ellen Winner (1996) described three criteria that characterize gifted children, whether in art, music, or academic domains:

1. *Precocity.* Gifted children are precocious. They begin to master an area earlier than their peers. Learning in their domain is more effortless for them than for ordinary children. In most instances, these gifted children are precocious because they have an inborn high ability in a particular domain or domains.

2. *Marching to their own drummer.* Gifted children learn in a qualitatively different way than ordinary children. One way that they march to a different drummer is that they need minimal help, or scaffolding, from adults to learn. In many instances, they resist any kind of explicit instruction. They often make discoveries on their own and solve problems in unique ways.

3. *A passion to master.* Gifted children are driven to understand the domain in which they have high ability. They display an intense, obsessive interest and an ability to focus. They motivate themselves, says Winner, and do not need to be "pushed" by their parents.

Is giftedness a product of heredity or environment? Likely both. Individuals who are gifted recall that they had signs of high ability in a particular area at a very young age, prior to or at the beginning of formal training (Howe & others, 1995). This suggests the importance of innate ability in giftedness. However, researchers have also found that individuals with world-class status in the arts, mathematics, science, and sports all report strong family support and years of training and practice (Bloom, 1985). Deliberate practice is an important characteristic of individuals who become experts in a particular domain (Balchin, Hymer, & Matthews, 2009; Sternberg, 2009f). For example, in one study, the best musicians engaged in twice as much deliberate practice over their lives as did the least successful ones (Ericsson, Krampe, & Tesch-Romer, 1993).

An increasing number of experts argue that the education of children who are gifted in the United States requires a significant overhaul (Sternberg, 2009f; Webb & others, 2007). Some educators conclude that the inadequate education of children who are gifted has been compounded by the federal government's No Child Left Behind policy that seeks to raise the achievement level of students who are not doing well in school at the expense of enriching the education of children who are gifted (Clark, 2008; Cloud, 2007). Ellen Winner (1996, 2006) argues that too often children who are gifted are socially isolated and underchallenged in the classroom. It is not unusual for them to be ostracized and labeled "nerds" or "geeks." A child who is truly gifted often is the only such child in the room who does not have the opportunity to learn with students of like ability. Many eminent adults report that school was a negative experience for them, that they were bored and sometimes knew more than their teachers (Bloom, 1985). Winner believes that American education will benefit when standards are raised for all children. When some children are still underchallenged, she recommends that they be allowed to attend advanced classes in their domain of exceptional ability such as allowing some especially precocious middle school students to take college classes in their area of expertise. For example, Bill Gates, founder of Microsoft, took college math classes and hacked a computer security system at 13; Yo-Yo Ma, famous cellist, graduated from high school at 15 and attended Juilliard School of Music in New York City.

A young Bill Gates, founder of Microsoft and now the world's richest person. Like many highly gifted students, Gates was not especially fond of school. He hacked a computer security system when he was 13, and as a high school student, he was allowed to take some college math classes. He dropped out of Harvard University and began developing a plan for what was to become Microsoft Corporation. *What are some ways that schools can enrich the education of such highly talented students as Gates to make it a more challenging, interesting, and meaningful experience?*

Review and Reflect: Learning Goal 3

3 Explain Cognitive Changes in Middle and Late Childhood

REVIEW

- What characterizes Piaget's stage of concrete operational thought? What are some contributions and criticisms of Piaget?
- How do children process information in the middle and late childhood years?
- What is intelligence, and how is it assessed?
- What determines individual and group differences in IQ scores?
- What are the key characteristics of mental retardation and giftedness?

REFLECT

- A CD-ROM, *Children's IQ and Achievement Test*, now lets parents test their child's IQ and how well the child is performing in relation to their grade in school. What might be some problems with parents giving their children an IQ test?

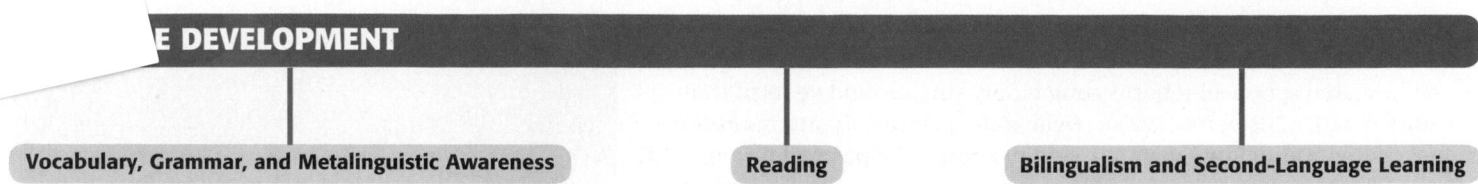

E DEVELOPMENT

Vocabulary, Grammar, and Metalinguistic Awareness   Reading   Bilingualism and Second-Language Learning

Children gain new skills as they enter school that make it possible to learn to read and write: These include increased use of language to talk about things that are not physically present, learning what a word is, and learning how to recognize and talk about sounds (Berko Gleason, 2003). They also learn the *alphabetic principle,* that the letters of the alphabet represent sounds of the language.

Vocabulary, Grammar, and Metalinguistic Awareness

During middle and late childhood, changes occur in the way children's mental vocabulary is organized. When asked to say the first word that comes to mind when they hear a word, preschool children typically provide a word that often follows the word in a sentence. For example, when asked to respond to *dog* the young child may say "barks," or to the word *eat* respond with "lunch." At about 7 years of age, children begin to respond with a word that is the same part of speech as the stimulus word. For example, a child may now respond to the word *dog* with "cat" or "horse." To *eat*, they now might say "drink." This is evidence that children now have begun to categorize their vocabulary by parts of speech (Berko Gleason, 2003).

The process of categorizing becomes easier as children increase their vocabulary. Children's vocabulary increases from an average of about 14,000 words at age 6 to an average of about 40,000 words by age 11.

Children make similar advances in grammar (Lust, 2007, 2009). During the elementary school years, children's improvement in logical reasoning and analytical skills helps them understand such constructions as the appropriate use of comparatives *(shorter, deeper)* and subjectives ("If you were president . . ."). During the elementary school years, children become increasingly able to understand and use complex grammar, such as the following sentence: *The boy who kissed his mother wore a hat.* They also learn to use language in a more connected way, producing connected discourse. They become able to relate sentences to one another to produce descriptions, definitions, and narratives that make sense. Children must be able to do these things orally before they can be expected to deal with them in written assignments.

These advances in vocabulary and grammar during the elementary school years are accompanied by the development of **metalinguistic awareness**, which is knowledge about language, such as knowing what a preposition is or the ability to discuss the sounds of a language. Metalinguistic awareness allows children "to think about their language, understand what words are, and even define them" (Berko Gleason, 2005, p. 4). It improves considerably during the elementary school years (Pan & Uccelli, 2009). Defining words becomes a regular part of classroom discourse, and children increase their knowledge of syntax as they study and talk about the components of sentences such as subjects and verbs (Meltzi & Ely, 2009).

Children also make progress in understanding how to use language in culturally appropriate ways—pragmatics (Levinson, 2009). By the time they enter adolescence, most children know the rules for the use of language in everyday contexts—that is, what is appropriate and inappropriate to say.

Reading

Before learning to read, children learn to use language to talk about things that are not present; they learn what a word is; and they learn how to recognize sounds and talk about them (Berko Gleason, 2003). Children who begin elementary school with a robust vocabulary have an advantage when it comes to learning to read (Paris & Paris,

What are the main approaches to teaching children how to read?

metalinguistic awareness Refers to knowledge about language, such as knowing what a preposition is or the ability to discuss the sounds of a language.

2006). For example, a recent study revealed that a good vocabulary was linked with high reading comprehension in second-grade students (Berninger & Abbott, 2005). A fluent vocabulary helps readers access word meaning effortlessly.

How should children be taught to read? Currently, debate focuses on the whole-language approach versus the phonics approach (Reutzel & Cooter, 2009; Vacca & others, 2009).

The **whole-language approach** stresses that reading instruction should parallel children's natural language learning. In some whole-language classes, beginning readers are taught to recognize whole words or even entire sentences, and to use the context of what they are reading to guess at the meaning of words. Reading materials that support the whole-language approach are whole and meaningful—that is, children are given material in its complete form, such as stories and poems, so that they learn to understand language's communicative function. Reading is connected with listening and writing skills. Although there are variations in whole-language programs, most share the premise that reading should be integrated with other skills and subjects, such as science and social studies, and that it should focus on real-world material. Thus, a class might read newspapers, magazines, or books, and then write about and discuss them.

In contrast, the **phonics approach** emphasizes that reading instruction should teach basic rules for translating written symbols into sounds. Early phonics-centered reading instruction should involve simplified materials. Only after children have learned correspondence rules that relate spoken phonemes to the alphabet letters that are used to represent them should they be given complex reading materials, such as books and poems (Cunningham, 2009; Rasinski & Padak, 2008).

Which approach is better? Research suggests that children can benefit from both approaches, but instruction in phonics needs to be emphasized (Meltzi & Ely, 2009). An increasing number of experts in the field of reading now conclude that direct instruction in phonics is a key aspect of learning to read (Cunningham & Hall, 2009; Mayer, 2008).

Bilingualism and Second-Language Learning

Are there sensitive periods in learning a second language? That is, if individuals want to learn a second language, how important is the age at which they begin to learn it? For many years, it was claimed that if individuals did not learn a second language prior to puberty they would never reach native-language learners' proficiency in the second language (Johnson & Newport, 1991). However, recent research indicates a more complex conclusion: Sensitive periods likely vary across different language systems. (Thomas & Johnson, 2008). Thus, for late language learners, such as adolescents and adults, new vocabulary is easier to learn than new sounds or new grammar (Neville, 2006; Werker & Tees, 2005). For example, children's ability to pronounce words with a nativelike accent in a second language typically decreases with age, with an especially sharp drop occurring after the age of about 10 to 12. Also, adults tend to learn a second language faster than children, but their final level of second-language attainment is not as high as children's. And the way children and adults learn a second language differs somewhat. Compared with adults, children are less sensitive to feedback, less likely to use explicit strategies, and more likely to learn a second language from large amounts of input (Thomas & Johnson, 2008).

Students in the United States are far behind their counterparts in many developed countries in learning a second language. For example, in Russia, schools have 10 grades, called *forms*, which roughly correspond to the 12 grades in American schools. Russian children begin school at age 7 and begin learning English in the third form. Because of this emphasis on teaching English, most Russian citizens under the age of 40 today are able to speak at least some English. The United States is the only technologically advanced Western nation that does not have a national foreign language requirement at the high school level, even for students in rigorous academic programs.

U.S. students who do not learn a second language may be missing more than the chance to acquire a skill (Garcia, 2008). *Bilingualism*—the ability to speak two languages—has a positive effect on children's cognitive development (Gibbons & Ng, 2004). Children who are fluent in two languages perform better than their single-language counterparts

whole-language approach An approach to reading instruction based on the idea that instruction should parallel children's natural language learning. Reading materials should be whole and meaningful.

phonics approach The idea that reading instruction should teach the basic rules for translating written symbols into sounds.

on tests of control of attention, concept formation, analytical reasoning, cognitive flexibility, and cognitive complexity (Bialystok, 1999, 2001, 2007, 2009). They also are more conscious of the structure of spoken and written language and better at noticing errors of grammar and meaning, skills that benefit their reading ability (Bialystok, 1993, 1997).

In the United States, many immigrant children go from being monolingual in their home language to bilingual in that language and in English, only to end up monolingual speakers of English. This is called *subtractive bilingualism,* and it can have negative effects on children, who often become ashamed of their home language.

A current controversy related to bilingualism involves bilingual education (Pena, & Bedore, 2009; Quiocho, & Ulanoff, 2009). To read about this controversy, see the *Diversity in Life-Span Development* interlude.

Diversity in Life-Span Development
Bilingual Education

A current controversy related to bilingualism involves the millions of U.S. children who come from homes in which English is not the primary language (Gonzalez, 2009; Lessow-Hurley, 2009). What is the best way to teach these children?

For the last two decades, the preferred strategy has been *bilingual education,* which teaches academic subjects to immigrant children in their native language while slowly teaching English (Horwitz, 2008; Peregoy & Boyle, 2009). Advocates of bilingual education programs argue that if children who do not know English are taught only in English, they will fall behind in academic subjects. How, they ask, can 7-year-olds learn arithmetic or history taught only in English when they do not speak the language?

Some critics of bilingual programs argue that too often it is thought that immigrant children need only one year of bilingual education. However, in general it takes immigrant children approximately three to five years to develop speaking proficiency and seven years to develop reading proficiency in English (Hakuta, Butler, & Witt, 2000). Also, immigrant children of course vary in their ability to learn English (Diaz-Rico, 2008; Eschevarria, Vogt, & Short, 2008). Children who come from lower socioeconomic backgrounds have more difficulty than those from higher socioeconomic backgrounds (Hakuta, 2001). Thus, especially for immigrant children from low socioeconomic backgrounds, more years of bilingual education may be needed than they currently are receiving.

Critics who oppose bilingual education argue that as a result of these programs, the children of immigrants are not learning English, which puts them at a permanent disadvantage in U.S. society. California, Arizona, and Massachusetts have significantly reduced the number of bilingual education programs. Some states continue to endorse bilingual education, but the emphasis that test scores be reported separately for English-language learners (students whose main language is not English) in the No Child Left Behind state assessments has shifted attention to literacy in English (Rivera & Collum, 2006; Snow & Yang, 2006).

What have researchers found regarding outcomes of bilingual education programs? Drawing conclusions about the effectiveness of bilingual education programs is difficult because of variations across programs in the number of years they are in effect, type of instruction, qualities of schooling other than bilingual education, teachers, children, and other factors. Further, no effectively conducted experiments that compare bilingual education with English-only education in the United States have been conducted (Snow & Yang, 2006). Some experts have concluded that the quality of instruction is more important in determining outcomes than the language in which it is delivered (Lesaux & Siegel, 2003).

Research supports bilingual education in that (1) children have difficulty learning a subject when it is taught in a language they do not understand, and (2) when both languages are integrated in the classroom, children learn the second language more

A first- and second-grade bilingual English-Cantonese teacher instructing students in Chinese in Oakland, California. *What have researchers found about the effectiveness of bilingual education?*

readily and participate more actively (Gonzales, Yawkey, & Minaya-Rowe, 2006; Hakuta, 2000, 2001, 2005). However, many of the research results report only modest rather than strong support for bilingual education, and some supporters of bilingual education now acknowledge that English-only instruction can produce positive outcomes for English-language learners (Lesaux & Siegel, 2003).

Review and Reflect: Learning Goal 4

 Discuss Language Development in Middle and Late Childhood

REVIEW

- What are some changes in vocabulary and grammar in the middle and late childhood years?
- What controversy characterizes how to teach children to read?
- What is bilingual education? What issues are involved in bilingual education?

REFLECT

- What are some of the key considerations in using a balanced approach to teaching reading?

Reach Your Learning Goals

Physical and Cognitive Development in Middle and Late Childhood

1 PHYSICAL CHANGES AND HEALTH: DESCRIBE PHYSICAL CHANGES AND HEALTH IN MIDDLE AND LATE CHILDHOOD

Body Growth and Change

- The period of middle and late childhood involves slow, consistent growth. During this period, children grow an average of 2 to 3 inches a year. Muscle mass and strength gradually increase. Among the most pronounced changes in body growth and proportion are decreases in head circumference and waist circumference in relation to body height.

The Brain

- Changes in the brain in middle and late childhood included advances in functioning in the prefrontal cortex, which are reflected in improved attention, reasoning, and cognitive control. During middle and late childhood, less diffusion and more focal activation occurs in the prefrontal cortex, a change that is associated with an increase in cognitive control.

Motor Development

- During the middle and late childhood years, motor development becomes much smoother and more coordinated. Children gain greater control over their bodies and can sit and attend for longer periods of time. However, their lives should be activity-oriented and very active. Increased myelination of the central nervous system is reflected in improved motor skills. Improved fine motor skills appear in the form of handwriting development. Boys are usually better at gross motor skills, girls at fine motor skills.

Exercise

- Most American children do not get nearly enough exercise. Parents play an especially important role in guiding children to increase their exercise. Heavy television and computer use are linked to lower activity levels in children.

Health, Illness, and Disease

- For the most part, middle and late childhood is a time of excellent health. The most common cause of severe injury and death in childhood is motor vehicle accidents, with most occurring at or near the child's home or school. Cancer is the second leading cause of death in children (after accidents). Leukemia is the most common childhood cancer. Cardiovascular disease is uncommon in children but the precursors to adult cardiovascular disease are often already apparent in children. Obesity in children poses serious health risks. The increase in the prevalence of obesity among children is linked to poor diet, inadequate exercise, and poor eating habits.

2 CHILDREN WITH DISABILITIES: IDENTIFY CHILDREN WITH DIFFERENT TYPES OF DISABILITIES AND ISSUES IN EDUCATING THEM

Learning Disabilities

- Approximately 14 percent of U.S. children from 3 to 21 years of age receive special education or related services. A child with a learning disability has difficulty in learning that involves understanding or using spoken or written language and the difficulty can appear in listening, thinking, reading, writing, and spelling. A learning disability also may involve difficulty in doing mathematics. To be classified as a learning disability, the learning problem is not primarily the result of visual, hearing, or motor disabilities; mental retardation; emotional disorders; or due to environmental, cultural, or economic disadvantage. Dyslexia is a category of learning disabilities that involves a severe impairment in the ability to read and spell.

Attention Deficit Hyperactivity Disorder (ADHD)

- Attention deficit hyperactivity disorder (ADHD) is a disability in which individuals consistently show problems in one or more of these areas: (1) inattention, (2) hyperactivity, and (3) impulsivity. ADHD has been increasingly diagnosed.

| **Autism Spectrum Disorders** | • Autism spectrum disorders (ASD), also called pervasive developmental disorders, range from autistic disorder, a severe developmental disorder, to Asperger syndrome, a relatively mild autism spectrum disorder. The current consensus is that autism is a brain dysfunction with abnormalities in brain structure and neurotransmitters. Children with autism spectrum disorders are characterized by problems in social interaction, verbal and nonverbal communication, and repetitive behaviors. |

| **Educational Issues** | • In 1975, Public Law 94-142, the Education for All Handicapped Children Act, required that all children with disabilities be given a free, appropriate public education. This law was renamed the Individuals with Disabilities Education Act (IDEA) in 1990 and updated in 2004. IDEA includes requirements that children with disabilities receive an individual education plan (IEP), which is a written plan that spells out a program tailored to the child, and that they be educated in the least restrictive environment (LRE), which is a setting that is as similar as possible to the one in which children without disabilities are educated. The term inclusion means educating children with disabilities full-time in the regular classroom. |

3 COGNITIVE CHANGES: EXPLAIN COGNITIVE CHANGES IN MIDDLE AND LATE CHILDHOOD

Piaget's Cognitive Developmental Theory

• Piaget said that the stage of concrete operational thought characterizes children from about 7 to 11 years of age. During this stage, children are capable of concrete operations, conservation, classification, seriation, and transitivity. Critics argue that some abilities emerge earlier than Piaget thought, that elements of a stage do not appear at the same time, and that education and culture have more influence on development than Piaget predicted. Neo-Piagetians place more emphasis on how children process information, strategies, speed of information processing, and the division of cognitive problems into more precise steps.

Information Processing

• Long-term memory increases in middle and late childhood. Knowledge and expertise influence memory. Strategies, such as imagery and elaboration, can be used by children to improve their memory. Fuzzy trace theory has been proposed to explain developmental changes in memory. Critical thinking involves thinking reflectively and productively, as well as evaluating the evidence. A special concern is the lack of emphasis on critical thinking in many schools. Creative thinking is the ability to think in novel and unusual ways and to come up with unique solutions to problems. Guilford distinguished between convergent and divergent thinking. A number of strategies can be used to encourage children's creative thinking, including brainstorming. Children think like scientists in some ways, but in others they don't. Metacognition is knowing about knowing. Most metacognitive studies have focused on metamemory. Pressley views the key to education as helping students learn a rich repertoire of strategies.

Intelligence

• Intelligence consists of problem-solving skills and the ability to adapt to and learn from life's everyday experiences. Interest in intelligence often focuses on individual differences and assessment. Widely used intelligence tests today include the Stanford-Binet tests and Wechsler scales. Results on these tests may be reported in terms of an overall IQ or in terms of performance on specific areas of the tests. Sternberg proposed that intelligence comes in three main forms: analytical, creative, and practical. Gardner proposes that there are eight types of intelligence: verbal, math, spatial, bodily-kinesthetic, interpersonal skills, intrapersonal skills, musical skills, and naturalist skills. The multiple-intelligence approaches have expanded our conception of intelligence, but critics argue that the research base for these approaches is not well established.

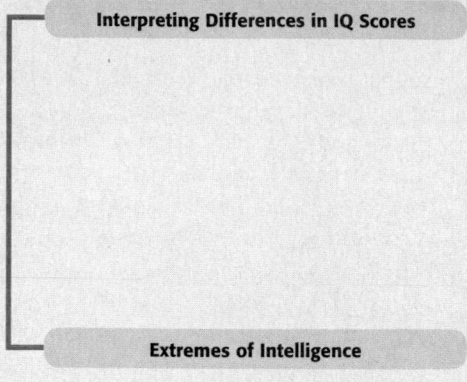

Interpreting Differences in IQ Scores

- IQ scores are influenced by both genetics and characteristics of the environment. Studies of heritability indicate that genetics has a strong influence on the variance in IQ scores within a population, but environmental changes can alter the IQ scores of most people considerably. Parents, home environments, schools, and intervention programs can influence these scores. Intelligence test scores have risen considerably around the world in recent decades—called the Flynn effect—and this supports the role of environment in intelligence. Group differences in IQ scores may reflect many influences, including cultural bias. Tests may be biased against certain groups because they are not familiar with a standard form of English, with the content tested, or with the testing situation. Tests are likely to reflect the values and experience of the dominant culture.

Extremes of Intelligence

- Mental retardation involves low IQ and problems in adapting to everyday life. One classification of mental retardation distinguishes organic and cultural-familial retardation. A child who is gifted has above-average intelligence and/or superior talent for something. Terman contributed to our understanding that gifted children are not more maladjusted than nongifted children. Three characteristics of gifted children are precocity, individuality, and a passion to master a domain. Critics argue that gifted children have been miseducated.

4   LANGUAGE DEVELOPMENT: DISCUSS LANGUAGE DEVELOPMENT IN MIDDLE AND LATE CHILDHOOD

Vocabulary, Grammar, and Metalinguistic Awareness

- Children become more analytical and logical in their approach to words and grammar. In terms of grammar, children now better understand comparatives and subjectives. They become increasingly able to use complex grammar and produce narratives that make sense. Improvements in metalinguistic awareness—knowledge about language—are evident during the elementary school years as children increasingly define words, increase their knowledge of syntax, and understand better how to use language in culturally appropriate ways.

Reading

- A current debate in reading focuses on the phonics approach versus the whole-language approach. The phonics approach advocates phonetics instruction and giving children simplified materials. The whole-language approach stresses that reading instruction should parallel children's natural language learning and giving children whole-language materials, such as books and poems.

Bilingualism and Second-Language Learning

- Recent research indicates a complex conclusion about whether there are sensitive periods in learning a second language. Bilingual education aims to teach academic subjects to immigrant children in their native languages while gradually adding English instruction. Researchers have found that bilingualism does not interfere with performance in either language.

KEY TERMS

KEY PEOPLE

James Kauffman 291
Jean Piaget 292
Charles Brainerd and Valerie
   Reyna 295
Jacqueline and Martin
   Brooks 295

J. P. Guilford 296
Teresa Amabile 296
Deanna Kuhn 298
Michael Pressley 298
Alfred Binet 299
Theophile Simon 299

David Wechsler 300
Robert J. Sternberg 300
Howard Gardner 301
Nathan Brody 301
James Flynn 303
Craig Ramey 304

Lewis Terman 306
Ellen Winner 307

E-LEARNING TOOLS

To help you master the material in this chapter, visit the Online Learning Center for *Life-Span Development,* twelfth edition, at **www.mhhe.com/santrockld12**.

Self-Assessment

Connect to **www.mhhe.com/santrockld12** to learn more about various kinds of intelligence by completing the self-assessments, *Evaluating Myself on Gardner's Eight Types of Intelligence* and *How Emotionally Intelligent Am I?*

Taking It to the Net

Connect to **www.mhhe.com/santrockld12** to research the answers to these questions:

1. Clarice and Henry's daughter Emma is in second grade. Emma's teacher recently told Clarice and Henry that Emma has been showing signs of ADHD in the classroom. These symptoms seem to occur only while Emma is at school. What should Clarice and Henry do to confirm the diagnosis before Ritalin or similar drugs are prescribed?

2. Noah's parents are upset to hear that their fourth-grader may have dyslexia. Noah's father voices to his son's teacher his concern that people will think Noah is slow. What should Noah's teacher inform these parents about the nature and causes of dyslexia?

Video Clips

The Online Learning Center includes a video for Chapter 9 called "Interactivity: Sensorimotor Neural Circuits." One of the more noticeable developments of the middle and late childhood years is a refinement of motor skills. This segment looks at how different children achieve this new level of physical coordination.

Health and Well-Being, Parenting, and Education Exercises

Build your decision-making skills by trying your hand at the health and well-being, parenting, and education exercises. Connect to **www.mhhe.com/santrockld12** to research the answers and complete the exercises.

10

Children are busy becoming something they have not quite grasped yet, something which keeps changing.

—ALASTAIR REID
American Poet, 20th Century

LEARNING GOALS

◆ Discuss emotional and personality development in middle and late childhood.

◆ Describe developmental changes in parent-child relationships, parents as managers, and societal changes in families.

◆ Identify changes in peer relationships in middle and late childhood.

◆ Characterize contemporary approaches to student learning and sociocultural aspects of schooling and achievement.

SOCIOEMOTIONAL DEVELOPMENT IN MIDDLE AND LATE CHILDHOOD

CHAPTER OUTLINE

1 EMOTIONAL AND PERSONALITY DEVELOPMENT

The Self

Emotional Development

Moral Development

Gender

2 FAMILIES

Developmental Changes in Parent-Child Relationships

Parents as Managers

Stepfamilies

3 PEERS

Developmental Changes

Peer Status

Social Cognition

Bullying

Friends

4 SCHOOLS

Contemporary Approaches to Student Learning

Socioeconomic Status and Ethnicity

Cross-Cultural Comparisons of Achievement

Images of Life-Span Development
The South Bronx

In *The Shame of the Nation,* Jonathan Kozol (2005) described his visits to 60 U.S. schools in urban low-income areas in 11 states. He saw many schools in which the minority population was 80 to 90 percent. Kozol observed numerous inequities—unkempt classrooms, hallways, and restrooms; inadequate textbooks and supplies; and lack of resources. He also saw teachers mainly instructing students to memorize material by rote, especially as preparation for mandated tests, rather than stimulating them to engage in higher-level thinking. Kozol also frequently observed teachers using threatening disciplinary tactics to control the classroom.

However, some teachers Kozol observed were effective in educating children in these undesirable conditions. At P.S. 30 in the South Bronx, Mr. Bedrock teaches fifth grade. One student in his class, Serafina, recently lost her mother to AIDS. When author Jonathan Kozol visited the class, he was told that two other children had taken the role of "allies in the child's struggle for emotional survival" (Kozol, 2005, p. 291). Textbooks are in short supply for the class, and the social studies text is so out of date it claims that Ronald Reagan is the country's president. But Mr. Bedrock told Kozol that it's a "wonderful" class this year. About their teacher, 56-year-old Mr. Bedrock, one student said, "'He's getting old, . . . but we love him anyway'" (p. 292). Kozol found the students orderly, interested, and engaged.

What are some of the challenges faced by children growing up in the South Bronx?

PREVIEW

The years of middle and late childhood bring many changes to children's social and emotional lives. Transformations in their relationships with parents and peers occur, and schooling takes on a more academic flavor. The development of their self-conceptions, moral reasoning, and moral behavior is also significant.

1 EMOTIONAL AND PERSONALITY DEVELOPMENT

The Self   **Emotional Development**   **Moral Development**   **Gender**

In this section, we will explore how the self continues to develop during middle and late childhood and the emotional changes that take place during these years. We will also discuss children's moral development and many aspects of the role that gender plays in their development in middle and late childhood.

The Self

What is the nature of the child's self-understanding, understanding of others, and self-esteem during the elementary school years? What role do self-efficacy and self-regulation play in children's achievement?

The Development of Self-Understanding In middle and late childhood, especially from 8 to 11 years of age, children increasingly describe themselves with psychological characteristics and traits in contrast to the more concrete self-descriptions of younger children. Older children are more likely to describe themselves as "*popular, nice, helpful, mean, smart,* and *dumb*" (Harter, 2006, p. 526).

In addition, during the elementary school years, children become more likely to recognize social aspects of the self (Harter, 2006). They include references to social groups in their self-descriptions, such as referring to themselves as Girl Scouts, as Catholics, or as someone who has two close friends (Livesly & Bromley, 1973).

Children's self-understanding in the elementary school years also includes increasing reference to social comparison (Harter, 2006). At this point in development, children are more likely to distinguish themselves from others in comparative rather than in absolute terms. That is, elementary-school-age children are no longer as likely to think about what they do or do not do, but are more likely to think about what they can do in comparison with others.

Consider a series of studies in which Diane Ruble (1983) investigated children's use of social comparison in their self-evaluations. Children were given a difficult task and then offered feedback on their performance, as well as information about the performances of other children their age. The children were then asked for self-evaluations. Children younger than 7 made virtually no reference to the information about other children's performances. However, many children older than 7 included socially comparative information in their self-descriptions.

In sum, in middle and late childhood, self-description increasingly involves psychological and social characteristics, including social comparison.

Understanding Others In Chapter 8, we described the advances and limitations of young children's understanding of others. In middle and late childhood, children show an increase in **perspective taking**, the ability to assume other people's perspectives and understand their thoughts and feelings. In Robert Selman's (1980) view, at about 6 to 8 years of age, children begin to understand that others may have a perspective because some people have more access to information. Then, he says, in the next several years, children become aware that each individual is aware of the other's perspective and that putting one's self in the other's place is a way of judging the other person's intentions, purposes, and actions.

What are some changes in children's understanding of others in middle and late childhood?

Perspective taking is especially thought to be important in whether children develop prosocial or antisocial attitudes and behavior. In terms of prosocial behavior, taking another's perspective improves children's likelihood of understanding and sympathizing with others when they are distressed or in need (Eisenberg, Fabes, & Spinrad, 2006). In terms of antisocial behavior, some researchers have found that children who have a low level of perspective-taking skills engage in more antisocial behavior than children at higher levels (Chandler, 1973).

In middle and late childhood, children also become more skeptical of others' claims. In Chapter 8, we indicated that even 4-year-old children show some skepticism of others' claims. In middle and late childhood, children become increasingly skeptical of some sources of information about psychological traits. For example, in one study, 10- to 11-year-olds were more likely to reject other children's self-reports that they were *smart* and *honest* than were 6- to 7-year-olds (Heyman & Legare, 2005). The more psychologically sophisticated 10- to 11-year-olds also showed a better understanding that others' self-reports may involve socially desirable tendencies than the 6- to 7-year-olds. In a recent cross-cultural comparison of 6- to 11-year-olds from the United States and China, older children showed increased skepticism of others' self-reports concerning value-laden traits, such as *honest, smart,* and *nice,* but did not show increased skepticism about less value-laden characteristics such as *outgoing, likes salty food,* and *likes the color red* (Heyman, Fu, & Lee, 2007).

perspective taking The ability to assume other people's perspectives and understand their thoughts and feelings.

Older Chinese children were more likely to expect others to show modesty when talking about themselves than were their U.S. counterparts.

Self-Esteem and Self-Concept   High self-esteem and a positive self-concept are important characteristics of children's well-being (Harter, 2006). Investigators sometimes use the terms *self-esteem* and *self-concept* interchangeably or do not precisely define them, but there is a meaningful difference between them. **Self-esteem** refers to global evaluations of the self; it is also called *self-worth* or *self-image*. For example, a child may perceive that she is not merely a person but a *good* person. **Self-concept** refers to domain-specific evaluations of the self. Children can make self-evaluations in many domains of their lives—academic, athletic, appearance, and so on. In sum, *self-esteem* refers to global self-evaluations, *self-concept* to domain-specific evaluations.

Self-esteem reflects perceptions that do not always match reality (Baumeister & others, 2003). A child's self-esteem might reflect a belief about whether he or she is intelligent and attractive, for example, but that belief is not necessarily accurate. Thus, high self-esteem may refer to accurate, justified perceptions of one's worth as a person and one's successes and accomplishments but it can also refer to an arrogant, grandiose, unwarranted sense of superiority over others (Krueger, Vohs, & Baumeister, 2008). In the same manner, low self-esteem may reflect either an accurate perception of one's shortcomings or a distorted, even pathological insecurity and inferiority.

Variations in self-esteem have been linked with many aspects of children's development. However, much of the research is *correlational* rather than *experimental*. Recall from Chapter 1 that correlation does not equal causation. Thus, if a correlational study finds an association between children's low self-esteem and low academic achievement, low academic achievement could cause the low self-esteem as much as low self-esteem causes low academic achievement.

In fact, there are only moderate correlations between school performance and self-esteem, and these correlations do not suggest that high self-esteem produces better school performance (Baumeister & others, 2003). Efforts to increase students' self-esteem have not always led to improved school performance (Davies & Brember, 1999).

Children with high self-esteem have greater initiative, but this can produce positive or negative outcomes (Baumeister & others, 2003). High-self-esteem children are prone to both prosocial and antisocial actions (Krueger, Vohs, & Baumeister, 2008). A recent study revealed that over time aggressive children with high self-esteem increasingly valued the rewards that aggression can bring and belittled their victims (Menon & others, 2007).

In addition, a current concern is that too many of today's children grow up receiving praise for mediocre or even poor performance and as a consequence have inflated self-esteem (Graham, 2005; Stipek, 2005). They may have difficulty handling competition and criticism. This theme is vividly captured by the title of a book, *Dumbing Down Our Kids: Why American Children Feel Good About Themselves But Can't Read, Write, or Add* (Sykes, 1995).

What are some good strategies for effectively increasing children's self-esteem? See the *Applications in Life-Span Development* interlude for some answers to this question.

What are some issues involved in understanding children's self-esteem in school?

 # Applications in Life-Span Development
Increasing Children's Self-Esteem

Four ways children's self-esteem can be improved include identifying the causes of low self-esteem, providing emotional support and social approval, helping children achieve, and helping children cope (Bednar, Wells, & Peterson, 1995; Harter, 2006).

- *Identify the causes of low self-esteem.* Intervention should target the causes of low self-esteem. Children have the highest self-esteem when they perform competently in domains that are important to them. Therefore, children should be encouraged to identify and value

---

self-esteem The global evaluative dimension of the self. Self-esteem is also referred to as self-worth or self-image.

self-concept Domain-specific evaluations of the self.

areas of competence. These areas might include academic skills, athletic skills, physical attractiveness, and social acceptance.

- *Provide emotional support and social approval.* Some children with low self-esteem come from conflicted families or conditions in which they experienced abuse or neglect—situations in which support was not available. In some cases, alternative sources of support can be arranged either informally through the encouragement of a teacher, a coach, or another significant adult, or more formally, through programs such as Big Brothers and Big Sisters.

- *Help children achieve.* Achievement also can improve children's self-esteem. For example, the straightforward teaching of real skills to children often results in increased achievement and, thus, in enhanced self-esteem. Children develop higher self-esteem because they know the important tasks that will achieve their goals, and they have performed them or similar behaviors in the past.

- *Help children cope.* Self-esteem is often increased when children face a problem and try to cope with it, rather than avoid it. If coping rather than avoidance prevails, children often face problems realistically, honestly, and nondefensively. This produces favorable self-evaluative thoughts, which lead to the self-generated approval that raises self-esteem.

How can parents help children develop higher self-esteem?

Self-Efficacy   **Self-efficacy** is the belief that one can master a situation and produce favorable outcomes. Albert Bandura (2001, 2007a, b, 2008, 2009), whose social cognitive theory we described in Chapter 1, states that self-efficacy is a critical factor in whether or not students achieve. Self-efficacy is the belief that "I can"; helplessness is the belief that "I cannot." Students with high self-efficacy endorse such statements as "I know that I will be able to learn the material in this class" and "I expect to be able to do well at this activity."

Dale Schunk (2008; Schunk, Pintrich, & Meece, 2008) has applied the concept of self-efficacy to many aspects of students' achievement. In his view, self-efficacy influences a student's choice of activities. Students with low self-efficacy for learning may avoid many learning tasks, especially those that are challenging. By contrast, high-self-efficacy counterparts eagerly work at learning tasks (Schunk, 2008). Students with high self-efficacy are more likely to expend effort and persist longer at a learning task than students with low self-efficacy.

Self-Regulation   One of the most important aspects of the self in middle and late childhood is the increased capacity for self-regulation. This increased capacity is characterized by deliberate efforts to manage one's behavior, emotions, and thoughts, leading to increased social competence and achievement (Laible & Thompson, 2007; Thompson, 2009a).

The increased capacity in self-regulation is linked to developmental advances in the brain's prefrontal cortex, which was discussed in Chapter 9, "Physical and Cognitive Development in Middle and Late Childhood." Recall our discussion there of the increased focal activation in the prefrontal cortex that is linked to improved in cognitive control, which includes self-regulation (Durston & others, 2006).

What characterizes Erikson's stage of industry versus inferiority?

Industry versus Inferiority   In Chapter 1, we described Erik Erikson's (1968) eight stages of human development. His fourth stage, industry versus inferiority, appears during middle and late childhood. The term *industry* expresses a dominant theme of this period: Children become interested in how things are made and how they work. When children are encouraged in their efforts to make, build, and work—whether building a model airplane, constructing a tree house, fixing a bicycle, solving an addition problem, or cooking—their sense of industry increases. However, parents who see their children's efforts at making things as "mischief" or "making a mess" encourage children's development of a sense of inferiority.

self-efficacy The belief that one can master a situation and produce favorable outcomes.

Children's social worlds beyond their families also contribute to a sense of industry. School becomes especially important in this regard. Consider children who are slightly below average in intelligence. They are too bright to be in special classes but not bright enough to be in gifted classes. They fail frequently in their academic efforts, developing a sense of inferiority. By contrast, consider children whose sense of industry is derogated at home. A series of sensitive and committed teachers may revitalize their sense of industry (Elkind, 1970).

Emotional Development

In Chapter 8, we saw that preschoolers become more adept at talking about their own and others' emotions. They also show a growing awareness of the need to control and manage their emotions to meet social standards. In middle and late childhood, children further develop their understanding and self-regulation of emotion (Saarni & others, 2006).

What are some changes in emotion during the middle and late childhood years?

Developmental Changes   Developmental changes in emotions during the middle and late childhood years include the following (Denham, Bassett, & Wyatt, 2007; Kuebli, 1994; Thompson & Goodvin, 2005):

- *Improved emotional understanding.* For example, children in elementary school develop an increased ability to understand such complex emotions as pride and shame. These emotions become less tied to the reactions of other people; they become more self-generated and integrated with a sense of personal responsibility.

- *Increased understanding that more than one emotion can be experienced in a particular situation.* A third-grader, for example, may realize that achieving something might involve both anxiety and joy.

- *Increased tendency to be aware of the events leading to emotional reactions.* A fourth-grader may become aware that her sadness today is influenced by her friend moving to another town last week.

- *Ability to suppress or conceal negative emotional reactions.* A fifth-grader has learned to tone down his anger better than he used to when one of his classmates irritates him.

- *The use of self-initiated strategies for redirecting feelings.* In the elementary school years, children become more reflective about their emotional lives and increasingly use strategies to control their emotions. They become more effective at cognitively managing their emotions, such as soothing oneself after an upset.

- *A capacity for genuine empathy.* For example, a fourth-grader feels sympathy for a distressed person and experiences vicariously the sadness the distressed person is feeling.

Coping with Stress   An important aspect of children's emotional lives is learning how to cope with stress (Taylor & Stanton, 2007). As children get older, they more accurately appraise a stressful situation and determine how much control they have over it. Older children generate more coping alternatives to stressful conditions and use more cognitive coping strategies (Saarni & others, 2006). They are better than younger children at intentionally shifting their thoughts to something that is less stressful; and at reframing, or changing one's perception of a stressful situation. For example, a younger child may be very disappointed that a teacher did not say hello when the child arrived in the classroom. An older child may reframe the situation and think, "My teacher may have been busy with other things and just forgot to say hello."

By 10 years of age, most children are able to use these cognitive strategies to cope with stress (Saarni, 1999). However, in families that have not been supportive and are characterized by turmoil or trauma, children may be so overwhelmed by stress that they do not use such strategies (Klingman, 2006).

The terrorist attacks on the World Trade Center in New York City and the Pentagon in Washington, D.C., on September 11, 2001, and hurricanes Katrina and Rita in September 2005, raised special concerns about how to help children cope with such stressful events (Osofsky, 2007). Researchers have offered some recommendations for parents, teachers, and other adults caring for children (Gurwitch & others, 2001, pp. 4–11):

- Reassure children (numerous times, if necessary) of their safety and security.

- Allow children to retell events and be patient in listening to them.

- Encourage children to talk about any disturbing or confusing feelings, reassuring them that such feelings are normal after a stressful event.

- Protect children from reexposure to frightening situations and reminders of the trauma—for example, by limiting discussion of the event in front of the children.

- Help children make sense of what happened, keeping in mind that children may misunderstand what took place. For example, young children "may blame themselves, believe things happened that did not happen, believe that terrorists are in the school, etc. Gently help children develop a realistic understanding of the event" (p. 10).

Traumatic events may cause individuals to think about the moral aspects of life. Hopelessness and despair may short-circuit moral development when a child is confronted by the violence of war zones and impoverished inner cities (Nader, 2001). Let's further explore children's moral development.

What are some effective strategies to help children cope with traumatic events, such as the terrorist attacks on the United States on 9/11/2001 and hurricane Katrina in September, 2005?

Moral Development

Remember from Chapter 8 our description of Piaget's view of moral development. Piaget proposed that younger children are characterized by heteronomous morality—but that, by 10 years of age, they have moved into a higher stage called autonomous morality. According to Piaget, older children consider the intentions of the individual, believe that rules are subject to change, and are aware that punishment does not always follow wrongdoing.

A second major perspective on moral development was proposed by Lawrence Kohlberg (1958, 1986). Piaget's cognitive stages of development serve as the underpinnings for Kohlberg's theory, but Kohlberg suggested that there are six stages of moral development. These stages, he argued, are universal. Development from one stage to another, said Kohlberg, is fostered by opportunities to take the perspective of others and to experience conflict between one's current stage of moral thinking and the reasoning of someone at a higher stage.

Kohlberg arrived at his view after 20 years of using a unique interview with children. In the interview, children are presented with a series of stories in which characters face moral dilemmas. The following is the most popular Kohlberg dilemma:

> In Europe a woman was near death from a special kind of cancer. There was one drug that the doctors thought might save her. It was a form of radium that a druggist in the same town had recently discovered. The drug was expensive to make, but the druggist was charging ten times what the drug cost him to make. He paid $200 for the radium and charged $2,000 for a small dose of the drug. The sick woman's husband, Heinz, went to everyone he knew to borrow the money, but he could only get together $1,000 which is half of what it cost. He told the druggist that his wife was dying and asked him to sell it cheaper or let him pay later. But the druggist said, "No, I discovered the drug, and I am going to make money from it." So Heinz got desperate and broke into the man's store to steal the drug for his wife. (Kohlberg, 1969, p. 379)

This story is one of 11 that Kohlberg devised to investigate the nature of moral thought. After reading the story, the interviewee answers a series of questions about the moral dilemma. Should Heinz have stolen the drug? Was stealing it right or wrong? Why? Is it a husband's duty to steal the drug for his wife if he can get it no

Lawrence Kohlberg, the architect of a provocative cognitive developmental theory of moral development. *What is the nature of his theory?*

LEVEL 1 Preconventional Level No Internalization	LEVEL 2 Conventional Level Intermediate Internalization	LEVEL 3 Postconventional Level Full Internalization
Stage 1 Heteronomous Morality *Children obey because adults tell them to obey. People base their moral decisions on fear of punishment.* **Stage 2** Individualism, Purpose, and Exchange *Individuals pursue their own interests but let others do the same. What is right involves equal exchange.*	**Stage 3** Mutual Interpersonal Expectations, Relationships, and Interpersonal Conformity *Individuals value trust, caring, and loyalty to others as a basis for moral judgments.* **Stage 4** Social System Morality *Moral judgments are based on understanding of the social order, law, justice, and duty.*	**Stage 5** Social Contract or Utility and Individual Rights *Individuals reason that values, rights, and principles undergird or transcend the law.* **Stage 6** Universal Ethical Principles *The person has developed moral judgments that are based on universal human rights. When faced with a dilemma between law and conscience, a personal, individualized conscience is followed.*

FIGURE 10.1 Kohlberg's Three Levels and Six Stages of Moral Development. Kohlberg argued that people everywhere develop their moral reasoning by passing through these age–based stages. *Where does Kohlberg's theory stand on the nature-nurture and continuity-discontinuity issues discussed in Chapter 1?*

other way? Would a good husband steal? Did the druggist have the right to charge that much when there was no law setting a limit on the price? Why or why not?

The Kohlberg Stages   Based on the answers interviewees gave for this and other moral dilemmas, Kohlberg described three levels of moral thinking, each of which is characterized by two stages (see Figure 10.1).

Preconventional reasoning is the lowest level of moral reasoning, said Kohlberg. At this level, good and bad are interpreted in terms of external rewards and punishments.

- *Stage 1.* **Heteronomous morality** is the first stage of preconventional reasoning. At this stage, moral thinking is tied to punishment. For example, children think that they must obey because they fear punishment for disobedience.
- *Stage 2.* **Individualism, instrumental purpose, and exchange** is the second stage of preconventional reasoning. At this stage, individuals reason that pursuing their own interests is the right thing to do but they let others do the same. Thus, they think that what is right involves an equal exchange. They reason that if they are nice to others, others will be nice to them in return.

Conventional reasoning is the second, or intermediate, level in Kohlberg's theory of moral development. At this level, individuals apply certain standards, but they are the standards set by others, such as parents or the government.

- *Stage 3.* **Mutual interpersonal expectations, relationships, and interpersonal conformity** is Kohlberg's third stage of moral development. At this stage, individuals value trust, caring, and loyalty to others as a basis of moral judgments. Children and adolescents often adopt their parents' moral standards at this stage, seeking to be thought of by their parents as a "good girl" or a "good boy."
- *Stage 4.* **Social systems morality** is the fourth stage in Kohlberg's theory of moral development. At this stage, moral judgments are based on understanding the social order, law, justice, and duty. For example, adolescents may reason that in order for a community to work effectively, it needs to be protected by laws that are adhered to by its members.

preconventional reasoning The lowest level in Kohlberg's theory of moral development. The individual's moral reasoning is controlled primarily by external rewards and punishment.

heteronomous morality Kohlberg's first stage of preconventional reasoning in which moral thinking is tied to punishment.

individualism, instrumental purpose, and exchange Kohlberg's second stage of preconventional reasoning. At this stage, individuals pursue their own interests but also let others do the same.

conventional reasoning The second, or intermediate, level in Kohlberg's theory of moral development. At this level, individuals abide by certain standards but they are the standards of others such as parents or the laws of society.

mutual interpersonal expectations, relationships, and interpersonal conformity Kohlberg's third stage of moral development. At this stage, individuals value trust, caring, and loyalty to others as a basis of moral judgments.

social systems morality The fourth stage in Kohlberg's theory of moral development. Moral judgments are based on understanding the social order, law, justice, and duty.

Postconventional reasoning is the highest level in Kohlberg's theory of moral development. At this level, the individual recognizes alternative moral courses, explores the options, and then decides on a personal moral code.

- *Stage 5.* **Social contract or utility and individual rights** is the fifth Kohlberg stage. At this stage, individuals reason that values, rights, and principles undergird or transcend the law. A person evaluates the validity of actual laws, and social systems can be examined in terms of the degree to which they preserve and protect fundamental human rights and values.

- *Stage 6.* **Universal ethical principles** is the sixth and highest stage in Kohlberg's theory of moral development. At this stage, the person has developed a moral standard based on universal human rights. When faced with a conflict between law and conscience, the person reasons that conscience should be followed, even though the decision might bring risk.

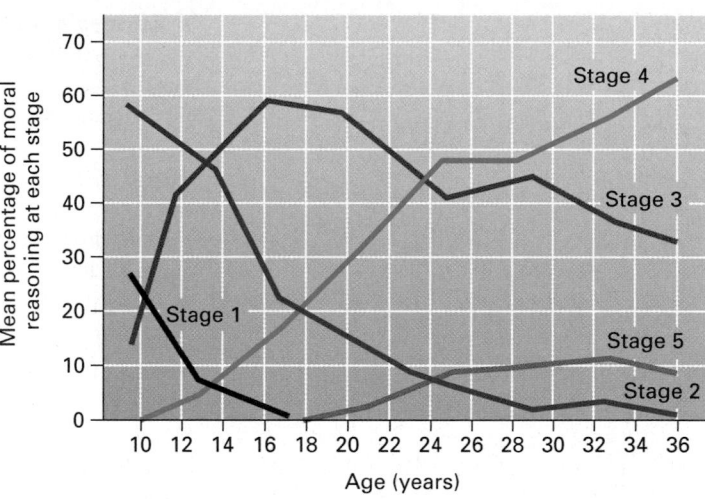

FIGURE 10.2 Age and the Percentage of Individuals at Each Kohlberg Stage. In one longitudinal study of males from 10 to 36 years of age, at age 10 most moral reasoning was at stage 2 (Colby & others, 1983). At 16 to 18 years of age, stage 3 became the most frequent type of moral reasoning, and it was not until the mid-twenties that stage 4 became the most frequent. Stage 5 did not appear until 20 to 22 years of age, and it never characterized more than 10 percent of the individuals. In this study, the moral stages appeared somewhat later than Kohlberg envisioned and stage 6 was absent. *Do you think it matters that all of the participants in this study were males? Why or why not?*

Kohlberg maintained that these levels and stages occur in a sequence and are age-related: Before age 9, most children use level 1, preconventional reasoning based on external rewards and punishments, when they consider moral choices. By early adolescence, their moral reasoning is increasingly based on the application of standards set by others. Most adolescents reason at stage 3, with some signs of stages 2 and 4. By early adulthood, a small number of individuals reason in postconventional ways.

What evidence supports this description of development? A 20-year longitudinal investigation found that use of stages 1 and 2 decreased with age (Colby & others, 1983) (see Figure 10.2). Stage 4, which did not appear at all in the moral reasoning of 10-year-olds, was reflected in the moral thinking of 62 percent of the 36-year-olds. Stage 5 did not appear until age 20 to 22 and never characterized more than 10 percent of the individuals.

Thus, the moral stages appeared somewhat later than Kohlberg initially envisioned, and reasoning at the higher stages, especially stage 6, was rare. Although stage 6 has been removed from the Kohlberg moral judgment scoring manual, it still is considered to be theoretically important in the Kohlberg scheme of moral development.

Influences on the Kohlberg Stages   What factors influence movement through Kohlberg' stages? Although moral reasoning at each stage presupposes a certain level of cognitive development, Kohlberg argued that advances in children's cognitive development did not ensure development of moral reasoning. Instead, moral reasoning also reflects children's experiences in dealing with moral questions and moral conflict.

Several investigators have tried to advance individuals' levels of moral development by having a model present arguments that reflect moral thinking one stage above the individuals' established levels. This approach applies the concepts of equilibrium and conflict that Piaget used to explain cognitive development. By presenting arguments slightly beyond the children' level of moral reasoning, the researchers created a disequilibrium that motivated the children to restructure their moral thought. The upshot of studies using this approach is that virtually any plus-stage discussion, for any length of time, seems to promote more advanced moral reasoning (Walker, 1982).

Kohlberg emphasized that peer interaction and perspective taking are critical aspects of the social stimulation that challenges children to change their moral reasoning. Whereas adults characteristically impose rules and regulations on children, the give-and-take among peers gives children an opportunity to take the perspective of another person and to generate rules democratically. Kohlberg stressed that in principle, encounters with any peers can produce perspective-taking opportunities that may advance a child's moral reasoning. A recent research review of cross-cultural studies involving Kohlberg's theory revealed strong support for a link between perspective-taking skills and more advanced moral judgments (Gibbs & others, 2007).

postconventional reasoning The highest level in Kohlberg's theory of moral development. At this level, the individual recognizes alternative moral courses, explores the options, and then decides on a personal moral code.

social contract or utility and individual rights The fifth Kohlberg stage. At this stage, individuals reason that values, rights, and principles undergird or transcend the law.

universal ethical principles The sixth and highest stage in Kohlberg's theory of moral development. Individuals develop a moral standard based on universal human rights.

Kohlberg's Critics Kohlberg's theory provoked debate, research, and criticism (Narvaez & Lapsley, 2008, 2009; Power & others, 2008). Key criticisms involve the link between moral thought and moral behavior, the roles of culture and the family in moral development, and the significance of concern for others.

Moral Thought and Moral Behavior Kohlberg's theory has been criticized for placing too much emphasis on moral thought and not enough emphasis on moral behavior (Walker, 2004). Moral reasons can sometimes be a shelter for immoral behavior. Corrupt CEOs and politicians endorse the loftiest of moral virtues in public before their own behavior is exposed. Whatever the latest public scandal, you will probably find that the culprits displayed virtuous thoughts but engaged in immoral behavior. No one wants a nation of cheaters and thieves who can reason at the postconventional level. The cheaters and thieves may know what is right yet still do what is wrong. Heinous actions can be cloaked in a mantle of moral virtue.

The mantle of virtue is not necessarily a ruse; it is often taken on sincerely. Social cognitive theorist Albert Bandura (1999, 2002) argues that people usually do not engage in harmful conduct until they have justified the morality of their actions to themselves. Immoral conduct is made personally and socially acceptable by portraying it as serving socially worthy or moral purposes or even as doing God's will. Bandura provides the examples of Islamic extremists who mount jihad (holy war) against what they see as a tyrannical, decadent people seeking to enslave the Islamic world and antiabortion activists who bomb abortion clinics or murder doctors in order to discourage abortions.

This 14-year-old boy in Nepal is thought to be the sixth holiest Buddhist in the world. In one study of 20 adolescent male Buddhist monks in Nepal, the issue of justice, a basic theme in Kohlberg's theory, was not a central focus in the monks' moral views (Huebner & Garrod, 1993). Also, the monks' concerns about prevention of suffering and the importance of compassion are not captured in Kohlberg's theory.

Culture and Moral Reasoning Kohlberg emphasized that his stages of moral reasoning are universal, but some critics claim his theory is culturally biased (Miller, 2007; Wainryb, 2006). Both Kohlberg and his critics may be partially correct. One review of forty-five studies in twenty-seven cultures around the world, mostly non-European, provided support for the universality of Kohlberg's first four stages (Snarey, 1987). Individuals in diverse cultures developed through these four stages in sequence as Kohlberg predicted. A more recent research revealed support for the qualitative shift from Stage 2 to Stage 3 across cultures (Gibbs & others, 2007). Stages 5 and 6, however, have not been found in all cultures (Gibbs & others, 2007; Snarey, 1987). Furthermore, Kohlberg's scoring system does not recognize the higher-level moral reasoning of certain cultures and thus that moral reasoning is more culture-specific that Kohlberg envisioned (Snarey, 1987).

In sum, although Kohlberg's approach does capture much of the moral reasoning voiced in various cultures around the world, his approach misses or misconstrues some important moral concepts in particular cultures (Miller, 2007; Wainryb, 2006).

Families and Moral Development Kohlberg argued that family processes are essentially unimportant in children's moral development. As noted earlier, he argued that parent-child relationships usually provide children with little opportunity for give-and-take or perspective taking. Rather, Kohlberg said that such opportunities are more likely to be provided by children's peer relations.

Did Kohlberg underestimate the contribution of family relationships to moral development? A number of developmentalists emphasize that *inductive discipline*, which uses reasoning and focuses children's attention on the consequences of their actions for others, positively influences moral development (Hoffman, 1970). They also stress that parents' moral values influence children's developing moral thoughts (Laible & Thompson, 2007). Nonetheless, most developmentalists agree with Kohlberg, and Piaget, that peers play an important role in the development of moral reasoning.

Gender and the Care Perspective The most publicized criticism of Kohlberg's theory has come from Carol Gilligan (1982, 1992, 1996), who argues that Kohlberg's theory reflects a gender bias. According to Gilligan, Kohlberg's theory is based on a male norm that puts abstract principles above relationships and concern for others and sees the individual as standing alone and independently making moral decisions. It puts justice at the heart of morality. In contrast to Kohlberg's **justice perspective**, Gilligan argues for a **care perspective**, which is a moral perspective that views people in terms of their connectedness with others and emphasizes interpersonal communication, relationships with others, and concern for others. According to Gilligan, Kohlberg greatly underplayed the care perspective, perhaps because he was a male, because most of his research was with males rather than females, and because he used male responses as a model for his theory.

In extensive interviews with girls from 6 to 18 years of age, Gilligan and her colleagues found that girls consistently interpret moral dilemmas in terms of human relationships and base these interpretations on listening and watching other people (Gilligan, 1992; Gilligan & others, 2003). However, a meta-analysis (a statistical analysis that combines the results of many different studies) casts doubt on Gilligan's claim of substantial gender differences in moral judgment (Jaffe & Hyde, 2000). In this study, overall, only a small sex difference in care-based reasoning favored females, but this sex difference was greater in adolescence than childhood. When differences occurred, they were better explained by the nature of the dilemma than by gender (for example, both males and females tended to use care-based reasoning to deal with interpersonal dilemmas and justice reasoning to handle societal dilemmas). In sum, experts have now concluded that there is no evidence to support Gilligan's claim that Kohlberg downplayed females' moral thinking (Hyde, 2005, 2007a, b; Hyde & Lindberg, 2007; Walker, 2006).

Other research, though, has revealed differences in how boys and girls tend to interpret some aspects of moral situations (Eisenberg, Fabes, & Spinrad, 2006). In support of this idea, one study found that females rated prosocial dilemmas (those emphasizing altruism and helping) as more significant than males did (Wark & Krebs, 2000). Another study revealed that young adolescent girls used more care-based reasoning about dating dilemmas than did boys (Weisz & Black, 2002).

Social Conventional Reasoning Some theorists and researchers argue that Kohlberg did not adequately distinguish between moral reasoning and social conventional reasoning (Smetana, 2006; Turiel, 2006). **Social conventional reasoning** focuses on conventional rules that have been established by social consensus in order to control behavior and maintain the social system. The rules themselves are arbitrary, such as using a fork at meals and raising your hand in class before speaking.

In contrast, moral reasoning focuses on ethical issues and rules of morality. Unlike conventional rules, moral rules are not arbitrary. They are obligatory, widely accepted, and somewhat impersonal (Turiel, 2006). Rules pertaining to lying, cheating, stealing, and physically harming another person are moral rules because violation of these rules affronts ethical standards that exist apart from social consensus and convention. Moral judgments involve concepts of justice, whereas social conventional judgments are concepts of social organization.

Prosocial Behavior Whereas Kohlberg's and Gilligan's theories have focused primarily on the development of moral reasoning, the study of prosocial moral behavior has placed more emphasis on the behavioral aspects of moral development (Hastings, Utendale, & Sullivan, 2007). Children engage in both immoral antisocial acts such as lying and cheating and prosocial moral behavior such as showing empathy or acting altruistically (Carlo, 2006). Even during the preschool years, children may care for others or comfort others in distress, but prosocial behavior occurs more often in adolescence than in childhood (Eisenberg & Morris, 2004).

William Damon (1988) described how sharing develops. During their first years, when children share, it is usually not for reasons of empathy but for the fun of the social play ritual or out of imitation. Then, at about 4 years of age, a combination of empathic awareness and adult encouragement produces a sense of obligation on the

Carol Gilligan *(center)* is shown with some of the students she has interviewed about the importance of relationships in a female's development. *What is Gilligan's view of moral development?*

justice perspective A moral perspective that focuses on the rights of the individual; individuals independently make moral decisions.

care perspective The moral perspective of Carol Gilligan, which views people in terms of their connectedness with others and emphasizes interpersonal communication, relationships with others, and concern for others.

social conventional reasoning Thoughts about social consensus and convention, in contrast to moral reasoning, which stresses ethical issues.

How does children's sharing change from the preschool to the elementary school years?

part of the child to share with others. Most 4-year-olds are not selfless saints, however. Children believe they have an obligation to share but do not necessarily think they should be as generous to others as they are to themselves.

Children's sharing comes to reflect a more complex sense of what is just and right during middle and late childhood. By the start of the elementary school years, children begin to express objective ideas about fairness (Eisenberg, Fabes, & Spinrad, 2006). It is common to hear 6-year-old children use the word *fair* as synonymous with equal or same. By the mid to late elementary school years, children believe that equity instead sometimes means that people with special merit or special needs deserve special treatment.

Missing from the factors that guide children's sharing is one that many adults might expect to be the most influential: the motivation to obey adult authority figures. Surprisingly, a number of studies have shown that adult authority has only a small influence on children's sharing (Eisenberg, 1982). Parental advice and prodding certainly foster standards of sharing, but the give-and-take of peer requests and arguments provides the most immediate stimulation of sharing.

Moral Personality   Beyond the development of moral reasoning and specific moral feelings and prosocial behaviors, do children also develop a pattern of moral characteristics that is distinctively their own? In other words, do children develop a *moral personality*, and if so, what are its components? Researchers have focused attention on three possible components: (1) moral identity, (2) moral character, and (3) moral exemplars:

- *Moral identity.* Individuals have a moral identity when moral notions and moral commitments are central to their lives. They construct the self with reference to moral categories. Violating their moral commitment would place the integrity of their self at risk.

- *Moral character.* A person with moral character has the willpower, desires, and integrity to stand up to pressure, overcome distractions and disappointments, and behave morally. A person of good moral character displays moral virtues such as "honesty, truthfulness, and trustworthiness, as well as those of care, compassion, thoughtfulness, and considerateness. Other salient traits revolve around virtues of dependability, loyalty, and conscientiousness" (Walker, 2002, p. 74).

- *Moral exemplars.* Moral exemplars are people who have lived exemplary moral lives. Their moral personality, identity, character, and set of virtues reflect moral excellence and commitment.

In sum, moral development is a multifaceted, complex concept. Included in this complexity are their thoughts, feelings, behaviors, and personality.

Gender

Gilligan's claim that Kohlberg's theory of moral development reflects gender bias reminds us of the pervasive influence of gender on development. Long before elementary school, boys and girls show preferences for different toys and activities. As we discussed in Chapter 8, preschool children display a gender identity and gender-typed behavior that reflects biological, cognitive, and social influences. Here we will examine gender stereotypes, gender similarities and differences, and gender-role classification.

Gender Stereotypes   According to the old ditty, boys are made of "frogs and snails" and girls are made of "sugar and spice and all that is nice." In the past, a well-adjusted boy was supposed to be independent, aggressive, and powerful. A well-adjusted girl was supposed to be dependent, nurturant, and uninterested in power. The masculine characteristics were considered to be healthy and good by society; the feminine characteristics were considered undesirable. These notions reflect **gender stereotypes**, which are broad categories that reflect general impressions and beliefs about females and males.

Recent research has found that gender stereotypes are, to a great extent, still present in today's world, both in the lives of children and adults (Hyde, 2005, 2007a, b;

*W*hat are little boys made of?
Frogs and snails
And puppy-dogs' tails.
What are little girls made of?
Sugar and spice
And all that's nice.

—J. O. HALLIWELL
English Author, 19th Century

gender stereotypes Broad categories that reflect our impressions and beliefs about females and males.

Hyde & Lindberg, 2007; Ruble, Martin, & Berenbaum, 2006). A recent study revealed that children's gender stereotyping increased from preschool through the fifth grade (Miller & others, 2007). In this study, preschoolers tended to stereotype dolls and appearance as characteristic of girls' interests and toys and behaviors (such as action heroes and hitting) as the province of boys (Miller & others, 2007). During middle and late childhood, children expanded the range and extent of their gender stereotyping in such areas as occupations, sports, and school tasks. Researchers also have found that boys' gender stereotypes are more rigid than girls' (Ruble, Martin, & Berenbaum, 2006).

Gender Similarities and Differences   What is the reality behind gender stereotypes? Let's examine some of the similarities and differences between the sexes, keeping in mind that (1) the differences are averages—not all females versus all males; (2) even when differences are reported, there is considerable overlap between the sexes; and (3) the differences may be due primarily to biological factors, sociocultural factors, or both. First, we will examine physical similarities and differences, and then we will turn to cognitive and socioemotional similarities and differences.

Physical Development   Women have about twice the body fat of men, most concentrated around breasts and hips. In males, fat is more likely to go to the abdomen. On the average, males grow to be 10 percent taller than females. Other physical differences are less obvious. From conception on, females have a longer life expectancy than males, and females are less likely than males to develop physical or mental disorders. Males have twice the risk of coronary disease as females.

Differences in hormones contribute to many of these physical differences between the sexes. Recall that androgens such as testosterone are male sex hormones and estrogens are female sex hormones, although both males and females produce androgens and estrogens. Male hormones promote the growth of long bones; female hormones stop such growth at puberty. Estrogen strengthens the immune system, making females more resistant to infection, for example. Female hormones also signal the liver to produce more "good" cholesterol, which makes females' blood vessels more elastic than males'. In contrast, testosterone triggers the production of low-density lipoprotein, which clogs blood vessels. Higher levels of stress hormones cause faster clotting in males, but also higher blood pressure than in females.

Does gender matter when it comes to brain structure and function? Human brains are much alike, whether the brain belongs to a male or a female (Halpern, 2006; Halpern & others, 2007). However, researchers have found some differences in the brains of males and females (Hofer & others, 2007a, b). Among the differences that have been discovered are:

- Female brains are smaller than male brains, but female brains have more folds; the larger folds (called convolutions) allow more surface brain tissue within the skulls of females than males (Luders & others, 2004).

- One part of the hypothalamus responsible for sexual behavior is larger in men than women (Swaab & others, 2001).

- Portions of the corpus callosum—the band of tissues through which the brains' two hemispheres communicate—is larger in females than males (Le Vay, 1991).

- An area of the parietal lobe that functions in visuospatial skills is larger in males than females (Frederikse & others, 2000).

- The areas of the brain involved in emotional expression show more metabolic activity in females than males (Gur & others, 1995).

Cognitive Development   In a classic review of gender differences, Eleanor Maccoby and Carol Jacklin (1974) concluded that males have better math and visuospatial skills (the kinds of skills an architect needs to design a building's angles and dimensions), whereas females have better verbal abilities. Subsequently, Maccoby (1987) revised her conclusion about several gender dimensions. She said that the accumulation of

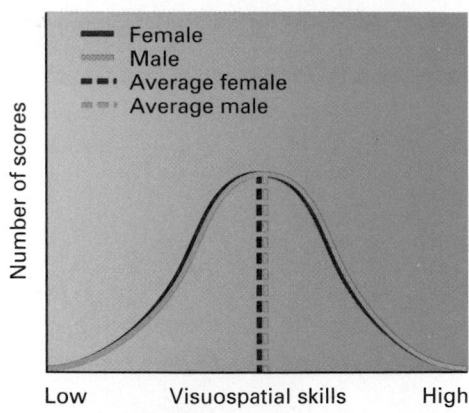

FIGURE 10.3 Visuospatial Skills of Males and Females. Notice that, although an average male's visuospatial skills are higher than an average female's, scores for the two sexes almost entirely overlap. Not all males have better visuospatial skills than all females—the overlap indicates that, although the average male score is higher, many females outperform most males on such tasks.

"So according to the stereotype, you can put two and two together, but I can read the handwriting on the wall."
© Joel Pett. All rights reserved.

research evidence now suggests that verbal differences between females and males have virtually disappeared but that the math and visuospatial differences still exist. For example, despite equal participation in the National Geography Bee, in most years all 10 finalists are boys (Liben, 1995). Also, a recent research review revealed that boys have better visuospatial skills than girls (Halpern & others, 2007).

Some experts in gender, such as Janet Shibley Hyde (2005, 2007a, b; Hyde & others, 2008), suggest that the cognitive differences between females and males have been exaggerated. For example, there is considerable overlap in the distributions of female and male scores on math and visuospatial tasks (see Figure 10.3).

In the most recent National Assessment of Educational Progress (2005, 2007), girls scored significantly higher than boys in literacy skills, although boys scored slightly higher than girls in math and science skills. For example, in reading skills, 41 percent of girls reached the proficient level (compared with 29 percent of boys), and in writing skills, 32 percent of girls were proficient (compared with 16 percent of boys). In math, 25 percent of males were proficient (compared with 21 percent of females), and in science, 21 percent of males were proficient (compared with 16 percent of females). Clearly, both U.S. boys and girls have room to make considerable improvement in their academic skills.

Socioemotional Development   Three areas of socioemotional development in which gender similarities and differences have been studied extensively are aggression, emotion, and prosocial behavior.

One of the most consistent gender differences is that boys are more physically aggressive than girls are (Baillargeon & others, 2007; Tremblay, 2009). The difference occurs in all cultures and appears very early in children's development (White, 2001). The physical aggression difference is especially pronounced when children are provoked. Both biological and environmental factors have been proposed to account for gender differences in aggression. Biological factors include heredity and hormones. Environmental factors include cultural expectations, adult and peer models, and social agents that reward aggression in boys and punish aggression in girls.

Although boys are consistently more physically aggressive than girls, might girls show as much or more verbal aggression, such as yelling, than boys? When verbal aggression is examined, gender differences often disappear; sometimes, though, verbal aggression is more pronounced in girls (Eagly & Steffen, 1986).

Recently, increased interest has been shown in *relational aggression,* which involves harming someone by manipulating a relationship (Crick, Ostrov, & Werner, 2006). Relational aggression includes such behaviors as trying to make others dislike a certain individual by spreading malicious rumors about the person (Underwood, 2004). Researchers have found mixed results regarding gender and relational aggression, with some studies showing girls engaging in more relational aggression and others revealing no differences between boys and girls (Young, Boye, & Nelson, 2006). One consistency in findings is that relational aggression comprises a greater percentage of girls' overall aggression than is the case for boys (Putallaz & others, 2007).

Are there gender differences in emotion? Beginning in the elementary school years, boys are more likely to hide their negative emotions, such as sadness, and girls are less likely to express disappointment that might hurt others' feelings (Eisenberg, Martin, & Fabes, 1996). Beginning in early adolescence, girls say they experience more sadness, shame, and guilt, and report more intense emotions, while boys are more likely to deny that they experience these emotions (Ruble, Martin, & Berenbaum, 2006). Males usually show less self-regulation of emotion than females, and this low self-control can translate into behavioral problems (Eisenberg, Spinrad, & Smith, 2004). In one study, children's low self-regulation was linked with greater aggression, the teasing of others, overreaction to frustration, low cooperation, and inability to delay gratification (Block & Block, 1980).

What gender differences characterize aggression?

The following items are from the Bem Sex-Role Inventory. When taking the BSRI, a person is asked to indicate on a 7-point scale how well each of the 60 characteristics describes herself or himself. The scale ranges from 1 (never or almost never true) to 7 (always or almost always true).

FIGURE 10.4 The Bem Sex-Role Inventory

Examples of masculine items	Examples of feminine items
Defends open beliefs	Does not use harsh language
Forceful	Affectionate
Willing to take risks	Loves children
Dominant	Understanding
Aggressive	Gentle

Scoring: The items are scored on independent dimensions of masculinity and femininity as well as androgyny and undifferentiate classifications.

Are there gender differences in prosocial behavior? Females view themselves as more prosocial and empathic (Eisenberg & Morris, 2004). Across childhood and adolescence, females engage in more prosocial behavior (Hastings, Utendale, & Sullivan, 2007). The biggest gender difference occurs for kind and considerate behavior with a smaller difference in sharing.

Earlier in the chapter, we discussed Carol Gilligan's theory that many females are more sensitive about relationships and have better relationship skills than males do. In Chapter 14, "Socioemotional Development in Early Adulthood," we will further explore this area of gender.

Gender-Role Classification   Not long ago, it was accepted that boys should grow up to be masculine and girls to be feminine. In the 1970s, however, as both females and males became dissatisfied with the burdens imposed by their stereotypic roles, alternatives to femininity and masculinity were proposed. Instead of describing masculinity and femininity as a continuum in which more of one means less of the other, it was proposed that individuals could have both masculine and feminine traits.

This thinking led to the development of the concept of **androgyny**, the presence of positive masculine and feminine characteristics in the same person (Bem, 1977; Spence & Helmreich, 1978). The androgynous boy might be assertive (masculine) and nurturant (feminine). The androgynous girl might be powerful (masculine) and sensitive to others' feelings (feminine). Measures have been developed to assess androgyny (see Figure 10.4).

Gender experts, such as Sandra Bem, argue that androgynous individuals are more flexible, competent, and mentally healthy than their masculine or feminine counterparts. To some degree, though, which gender-role classification is best depends on the context involved. For example, in close relationships, feminine and androgynous orientations might be more desirable. One study found that girls and individuals high in femininity showed a stronger interest in caring than did boys and individuals high in masculinity (Karniol, Groz, & Schorr, 2003). However, masculine and androgynous orientations might be more desirable in traditional academic and work settings because of the achievement demands in these contexts.

Despite talk about the "sensitive male," William Pollack (1999) argues that little has been done to change traditional ways of raising boys. He says that the "boy code" tells boys that they should show little if any emotion and should act tough. Boys learn the boy code in many contexts—sandboxes, playgrounds, schoolrooms, camps, hangouts. The result, according to Pollack, is a "national crisis of boyhood." Pollack and others suggest that boys would benefit from being socialized to express their anxieties and concerns and to better regulate their aggression.

Gender in Context   Both the concept of androgeny and gender stereotypes talk about people in terms of personality traits such as "aggressive" or "caring." However,

androgyny The presence of positive masculine and feminine characteristics in the same individual.

In China, females and males are usually socialized to behave, feel, and think differently. The old patriarchal traditions of male supremacy have not been completely uprooted. Chinese women still make considerably less money than Chinese men do, and, in rural China (such as here in the Lixian Village of Sichuan) male supremacy still governs many women's lives.

which traits people display may vary with the situation (Leaper & Friedman, 2007). Thus, the nature and extent of gender differences may depend on the context (Blakemore, Berenbaum, & Liben, 2009).

Consider helping behavior. The stereotype is that females are better than males at helping. But it depends on the situation. Females are more likely than males to volunteer their time to help children with personal problems and to engage in caregiving behavior. However, in situations in which males feel a sense of competence and that involve danger, males are more likely than females to help (Eagly & Crowley, 1986). For example, a male is more likely than a female to stop and help a person stranded by the roadside with a flat tire. Indeed, one study documented that males are more likely to help when the context is masculine in nature (MacGeorge, 2003).

"She is emotional; he is not"—that is the master emotional stereotype. However, like differences in helping behavior, emotional differences in males and females depend on the particular emotion involved and the context in which it is displayed (Shields, 1991). Males are more likely to show anger toward strangers, especially male strangers, when they feel they have been challenged. Males also are more likely to turn their anger into aggressive action. Emotional differences between females and males often show up in contexts that highlight social roles and relationships. For example, females are more likely to discuss emotions in terms of relationships, and they are more likely to express fear and sadness.

The importance of considering gender in context is nowhere more apparent than when examining what is culturally prescribed behavior for females and males in different countries around the world (Matlin, 2008). Although there has been greater acceptance of androgyny and similarities in male and female behavior in the United States, in many countries gender roles have remained gender-specific. For example, in many Middle Eastern countries, the division of labor between males and females is dramatic. Males are socialized and schooled to work in the public sphere, females in the private world of home and child rearing. For example, in Iran, the dominant view is that the man's duty is to provide for his family and the woman's is to care for her family and household. China also has been a male-dominant culture. Although women have made some strides in China, especially in urban areas, the male role is still dominant. Most males in China do not accept androgynous behavior and gender equity.

Review and Reflect: Learning Goal 1

1 **Discuss Emotional and Personality Development in Middle and Late Childhood**

REVIEW

- What changes take place in the self during the middle and late childhood years?
- How does emotion change during middle and late childhood?
- What is Kohlberg's theory of moral development, and how has it been criticized? How does prosocial behavior develop during the middle and late childhood years?
- What are gender stereotypes, and what some important gender differences?

REFLECT

- A young man who had been sentenced to serve 10 years for selling a small amount of marijuana walked away from a prison camp six months after he was sent there. He is now in his fifties and has been a model citizen. Should he be sent back to prison? Why or why not? At which Kohlberg stage should your response be placed?

2 FAMILIES

| Developmental Changes in Parent-Child Relationships | Parents as Managers | Stepfamilies |

Our discussion of parenting and families in this section focuses on how parent-child interactions typically change in middle and late childhood, the importance of parents being effective managers of children's lives, and how children are affected by living with stepparents.

Developmental Changes in Parent-Child Relationships

As children move into the middle and late childhood years, parents spend considerably less time with them. In one study, parents spent less than half as much time with their children aged 5 to 12 in caregiving, instruction, reading, talking, and playing as when the children were younger (Hill & Stafford, 1980). Although parents spend less time with their children in middle and late childhood than in early childhood, parents continue to be extremely important in their children's lives. In a recent analysis of the contributions of parents in middle and late childhood, the following conclusion was reached: "Parents serve as gatekeepers and provide scaffolding as children assume more responsibility for themselves and . . . regulate their own lives" (Huston & Ripke, 2006, p. 422).

Parents especially play an important role in supporting and stimulating children's academic achievement in middle and late childhood (Gupta, Thorton, & Huston, 2008; Huston & Ripke, 2006). The value parents place on education can mean the difference in whether children do well in school. Parents not only influence children's in-school achievement, but they also make decision about children's out-of-school activities. Whether children participate in such activities as sports, music, and other activities is heavily influenced by the extent to which parents sign up children for such activities and encourage their participation (Simpkins & others, 2006).

Elementary school children tend to receive less physical discipline than they did as preschoolers. Instead of spanking or coercive holding, their parents are more likely to use deprivation of privileges, appeals to the child's self-esteem, comments designed to increase the child's sense of guilt, and statements that the child is responsible for his or her actions.

During middle and late childhood, some control is transferred from parent to child. The process is gradual, and it produces *coregulation* rather than control by either the child or the parent alone. Parents continue to exercise general supervision and control, while children are allowed to engage in moment-to-moment self-regulation. The major shift to autonomy does not occur until about the age of 12 or later. A key developmental task as children move toward autonomy is learning to relate to adults outside the family on a regular basis—adults who interact with the child much differently than parents, such as teachers.

Parents as Managers

Parents can play important roles as managers of children's opportunities, as monitors of their behavior, and as social initiators and arrangers (Parke & Buriel, 2006). Mothers are more likely than fathers to engage in a managerial role in parenting.

Researchers have found that family management practices are positively related to students' grades and self-responsibility, and negatively to school-related problems (Eccles, 2007; Taylor & Lopez, 2005). Among the most important family management practices in this regard are maintaining a structured and organized family environment, such as establishing routines for homework, chores, bedtime,

What are some changes in the focus of parent-child relationships in middle and late childhood?

and so on, and effectively monitoring the child's behavior. A recent research review of family functioning in African American students' academic achievement found that when African American parents monitored their son's academic achievement by ensuring that homework was completed, restricted time spent on nonproductive distractions (such as video games and TV), and participated in a consistent, positive dialogue with teachers and school officials, their son's academic achievement benefited (Mandara, 2006).

Stepfamilies

Not only has divorce become commonplace in the United States, so has getting remarried (Hetherington, 2006). It takes time for parents to marry, have children, get divorced, and then remarry. Consequently, there are far more elementary and secondary school children than infant or preschool children living in stepfamilies.

The number of remarriages involving children has grown steadily in recent years. Also, divorces occur at a 10 percent higher rate in remarriages than in first marriages (Cherlin & Furstenberg, 1994). About half of all children whose parents divorce will have a stepparent within four years of the separation.

Remarried parents face some unique tasks. The couple must define and strengthen their marriage and at the same time renegotiate the biological parent-child relationships and establish stepparent-stepchild and stepsibling relationships (Coleman, Ganong, & Fine, 2004). The complex histories and multiple relationships make adjustment difficult in a stepfamily (Hetherington & Stanley-Hagan, 2002). Only one-third of stepfamily couples stay remarried.

In some cases, the stepfamily may have been preceded by the death of a spouse. However, by far the largest number of stepfamilies are preceded by divorce rather than death (Pasley & Moorefield, 2004). Three common types of stepfamily structure are (1) stepfather, (2) stepmother, and (3) blended or complex. In stepfather families, the mother typically had custody of the children and remarried, introducing a stepfather into her children's lives. In stepmother families, the father usually had custody and remarried, introducing a stepmother into his children's lives. In a blended or complex stepfamily, both parents bring children from previous marriages to live in the newly formed stepfamily.

In E. Mavis Hetherington's (2006) most recent longitudinal analyses, children and adolescents who had been in a simple stepfamily (stepfather or stepmother) for a number of years were adjusting better than in the early years of the remarried family and were functioning well in comparison to children and adolescents in conflicted nondivorced families and children and adolescents in complex (blended) stepfamilies. More than 75 percent of the adolescents in long-established simple stepfamilies described their relationships with their stepparents as "close" or "very close." Hetherington (2006) concluded that in long-established simple stepfamilies adolescents seem to eventually benefit from the presence of a stepparent and the resources provided by the stepparent.

Children often have better relationships with their custodial parents (mothers in stepfather families, fathers in stepmother families) than with stepparents (Santrock, Sitterle, & Warshak, 1988). Also, children in simple families (stepmother, stepfather) often show better adjustment than their counterparts in complex (blended) families (Hetherington & Kelly, 2002).

As in divorced families, children in stepfamilies show more adjustment problems than children in nondivorced families (Hetherington & Kelly, 2002). The adjustment problems are similar to those found among children of divorced parents—academic problems and lower self-esteem, for example (Anderson & others, 1999). However, it is important to recognize that a majority of children in stepfamilies do not have problems. In one analysis, 25 percent of children from stepfamilies showed adjustment problems compared to 10 percent in intact, never-divorced families (Hetherington & Kelly, 2002).

How does living in a stepfamily influence a child's development?

Adolescence is an especially difficult time for the formation of a stepfamily (Anderson & others, 1999). This may occur because becoming part of a stepfamily exacerbates normal adolescent concerns about identity, sexuality, and autonomy.

Review and Reflect: Learning Goal 2

 2 **Describe Developmental Changes in Parent-Child Relationships, Parents as Managers, and Societal Changes in Families**

REVIEW

- What changes characterize parent-child relationships in middle and late childhood?
- How can parents be effective managers of children's lives?
- How does being in a stepfamily influence children's development?

REFLECT

- What was your relationship with your parents like when you were in elementary school? How do you think it influenced your development?

3 PEERS

| Developmental Changes | Peer Status | Social Cognition | Bullying | Friends |

Having positive relationships with peers is especially important in middle and late childhood (Bukowski, Laursen, & Rubin, 2009; Rubin, Fredstrom & Bowker, 2008). Engaging in positive interactions with peers, resolving conflicts with peers in nonaggressive ways, and having quality friendships in middle and late childhood not only have positive outcomes at this time in children's lives, but also are linked to more positive relationship outcomes in adolescence and adulthood (Huston & Ripke, 2006). For example, in one longitudinal study, being popular with peers and engaging in low levels of aggression at 8 years of age were related to higher levels of occupational status at 48 years of age (Huesmann & others, 2006). Another study found that peer competence (a composite measure that included social contact with peers, popularity with peers, friendship, and social skills) in middle and late childhood was linked to having better relationships with coworkers in early adulthood (Collins & van Dulmen, 2006).

Developmental Changes

As children enter the elementary school years, reciprocity becomes especially important in peer interchanges. Researchers estimate that the percentage of time spent in social interaction with peers increases from approximately 10 percent at 2 years of age to more than 30 percent in middle and late childhood (Rubin, Bukowski, & Parker, 2006). In one early study, a typical day in elementary school included approximately 300 episodes with peers (Barker & Wright, 1951). As children move through middle and late childhood, the size of their peer group increases, and peer interaction is less closely supervised by adults (Rubin, Bukowski, & Parker, 2006). Until about 12 years of age, children's preference for same-sex peer groups increases.

Peer Status

Which children are likely to be popular with their peers and which ones are disliked? Developmentalists address this and similar questions by examining *sociometric status*, a term that describes the extent to which children are liked or disliked by their peer group (Ladd, Herald, & Andrews, 2006). Sociometric status is typically assessed by asking children to rate how much they like or dislike each of their classmates. Or it may be assessed by asking children to nominate the children they like the most and those they like the least.

Developmentalists have distinguished five peer statuses (Wentzel & Asher, 1995):

What are some statuses that children have with their peers?

- **Popular children** are frequently nominated as a best friend and are rarely disliked by their peers.

- **Average children** receive an average number of both positive and negative nominations from their peers.

- **Neglected children** are infrequently nominated as a best friend but are not disliked by their peers.

- **Rejected children** are infrequently nominated as someone's best friend and are actively disliked by their peers

- **Controversial children** are frequently nominated both as someone's best friend and as being disliked.

Popular children have a number of social skills that contribute to their being well liked. They give out reinforcements, listen carefully, maintain open lines of communication with peers, are happy, control their negative emotions, act like themselves, show enthusiasm and concern for others, and are self-confident without being conceited (Hartup, 1983; Rubin, Bukowski, & Parker, 1998).

Neglected children engage in low rates of interaction with their peers and are often described as shy by peers. The goal of many training programs for neglected children is to help them attract attention from their peers in positive ways and to hold that attention by asking questions, by listening in a warm and friendly way, and by saying things about themselves that relate to the peers' interests. They also are taught to enter groups more effectively.

Rejected children often have more serious adjustment problems than those who are neglected (Bukowski, Brendgen, & Vitaro, 2007; Dishion, Piehler, & Myers, 2008). One study found that in kindergarten, children who were rejected by their peers were less likely to engage in classroom participation, more likely to express a desire to avoid school, and more likely to report being lonely than children who were accepted by their peers (Buhs & Ladd, 2001). The combination of being rejected by peers and being aggressive forecasts problems. Another study evaluated 112 fifth-grade boys over a period of seven years until the end of high school (Kupersmidt & Coie, 1990). The best predictor of whether rejected children would engage in delinquent behavior or drop out of school later during adolescence was aggression toward peers in elementary school.

John Coie (2004, pp. 252–253) provided three reasons why aggressive peer-rejected boys have problems in social relationships:

- "First, the rejected, aggressive boys are more impulsive and have problems sustaining attention. As a result, they are more likely to be disruptive of ongoing activities in the classroom and in focused group play.

- Second, rejected, aggressive boys are more emotionally reactive. They are aroused to anger more easily and probably have more difficulty calming down once aroused. Because of this they are more prone to become angry at peers and attack them verbally and physically. . . .

- Third, rejected children have fewer social skills in making friends and maintaining positive relationships with peers."

popular children Children who are frequently nominated as a best friend and are rarely disliked by their peers.

average children Children who receive an average number of both positive and negative nominations from peers.

neglected children Children who are infrequently nominated as a best friend but are not disliked by their peers.

rejected children Children who are infrequently nominated as a best friend and are actively disliked by their peers.

controversial children Children who are frequently nominated both as someone's best friend and as being disliked.

Not all rejected children are aggressive (Bukowski, Brendgen, & Vitaro, 2007). Although aggression and its related characteristics of impulsiveness and disruptiveness underlie rejection about half the time, approximately 10 to 20 percent of rejected children are shy.

How can rejected children be trained to interact more effectively with their peers? Rejected children may be taught to more accurately assess whether the intentions of their peers are negative (Bierman, 2004). They may be asked to engage in role playing or to discuss hypothetical situations involving negative encounters with peers, such as when a peer cuts into a line ahead of them. In some programs, children are shown videotapes of appropriate peer interaction and asked to draw lessons from what they have seen (Ladd, Buhs, & Troop, 2004).

One social-skills intervention program was successful in increasing social acceptance and self-esteem and decreasing depression and anxiety in peer-rejected children (DeRosier, & Marcus, 2005). Students participated in the program once a week (50 to 60 minutes) for eight weeks. The program included instruction in how to manage emotions, how to improve prosocial skills, how to become better communicators, and how to compromise and negotiate.

Social Cognition

A boy accidentally trips and knocks another boy's soft drink out of his hand. That boy misinterprets the encounter as hostile, which leads him to retaliate aggressively against the boy who tripped. Through repeated encounters of this kind, the aggressive boy's classmates come to perceive him as habitually acting in inappropriate ways.

This encounter demonstrates the importance of *social cognition*—thoughts about social matters, such as the aggressive boy's interpretation of an encounter as hostile and his classmates' perception of his behavior as inappropriate (Gauvain & Perez, 2007; Gibbons, Pomery, & Gerrard, 2008). Children's social cognition about their peers becomes increasingly important for understanding peer relationships in middle and late childhood. Of special interest are the ways in which children process information about peer relations and their social knowledge (Bukowski, Laursen, & Rubin, 2009; Dodge, Coie, & Lynam, 2006).

Kenneth Dodge (1983) argues that children go through five steps in processing information about their social world. They decode social cues, interpret, search for a response, select an optimal response, and enact. Dodge has found that aggressive boys are more likely to perceive another child's actions as hostile when the child's intention is ambiguous. And, when aggressive boys search for cues to determine a peer's intention, they respond more rapidly, less efficiently, and less reflectively than do nonaggressive children. These are among the social cognitive factors believed to be involved in children's conflicts.

Social knowledge also is involved in children's ability to get along with peers. They need to know what goals to pursue in poorly defined or ambiguous situations, how to initiate and maintain a social bond, and what scripts to follow to get other children to be their friends. For example, as part of the script for getting friends, it helps to know that saying nice things, regardless of what the peer does or says, will make the peer like the child more.

Bullying

Significant numbers of students are victimized by bullies (Juvonen & Galvin, 2008; Peskin & others, 2007). In a national survey of more than 15,000 sixth- through tenth-grade students, nearly one of every three students said that they had experienced occasional or frequent involvement as a victim or perpetrator in bullying (Nansel & others, 2001). In this study, bullying was defined as verbal or physical behavior intended to disturb someone less powerful. As shown in Figure 10.5, being belittled about looks or speech was the most frequent type of bullying. A recent study revealed

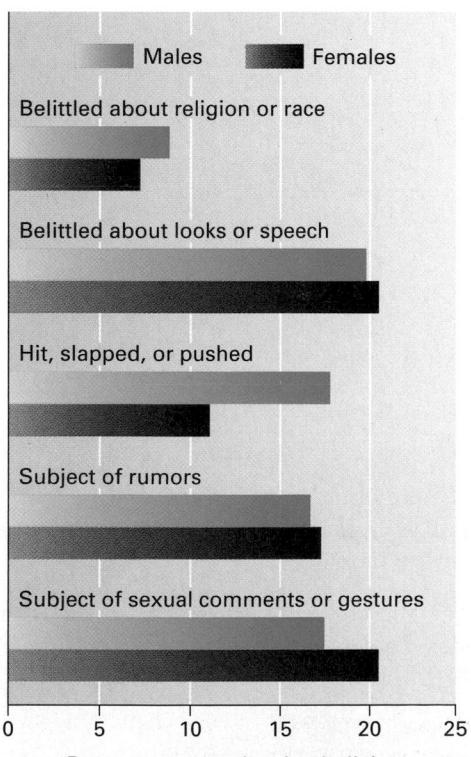

FIGURE 10.5 Bullying Behaviors Among U.S. Youth. This graph shows the type of bullying most often experienced by U.S. youth. The percentages reflect the extent to which bullied students said that they had experienced a particular type of bullying. In terms of gender, note that when they were bullied, boys were more likely to be hit, slapped, or pushed than girls were.

that bullying decreased as students went from the fall of the sixth grade (20 percent were bullied extensively) through the spring of the eighth grade (6 percent were bullied extensively) (Nylund & others, 2007).

Who is likely to be bullied? In the study just described, boys and younger middle school students were most likely to be affected (Nansel & others, 2001). Children who said they were bullied reported more loneliness and difficulty in making friends, while those who did the bullying were more likely to have low grades and to smoke and drink alcohol. Researchers have found that anxious, socially withdrawn, and aggressive children are often the victims of bullying (Hanish & Guerra, 2004). Anxious and socially withdrawn children may be victimized because they are nonthreatening and unlikely to retaliate if bullied, whereas aggressive children may be the targets of bullying because their behavior is irritating to bullies (Rubin, Bukowski, & Parker, 2006).

What are the outcomes of bullying? A recent study indicated that bullies and their victims in adolescence were more likely to experience depression and engage in suicide ideation and attempt suicide than their counterparts who were not involved in bullying (Brunstein Klomek & others, 2007). Another recent study revealed that bullies, victims, or those who were both bullies and victims had more health problems (such as headaches, dizziness, sleep problems, and anxiety) than their counterparts who were not involved in bullying (Srabstein & others, 2006). To read further about bullying, see the *Research in Life-Span Development* interlude.

Research in Life-Span Development
Aggressive Victims, Passive Victims, and Bullies

One study examined the extent to which aggressive victims (who provoke their peers and respond to threats or attacks with reactive aggression), passive victims (who submit to aggressors' demands), and bullies (who act aggressively toward their peers but are rarely attacked in return) showed different developmental pathways (Hanish & Guerra, 2004). The children were assessed initially in the fourth grade and then again in the sixth grade.

Peer sociometric ratings were used to identify children as aggressive victims, passive victims, bullies, uninvolved, and average. Each child received a booklet containing randomized lists (separated by gender) of the names of all children in the class. The children were asked to mark all peers' names that were applicable to certain questions. The questions included items that assessed aggression and victimization, such as "Who starts a fight over nothing?" and "Who are the children who are getting picked on?"

The results indicated that "aggressive victims became less prevalent and passive victims and bullies became more prevalent with age. Although it was common for aggressive victims and bullies to move from one group to the other across time, there was little overlap with the passive victim group" (p. 17).

What are some characteristics of bullying? What are some strategies to reduce bullying?

How can bullying be reduced? A recent research review revealed mixed results for school-based intervention (Vreeman & Carroll, 2007). School-based interventions vary greatly, ranging from involving the whole school in an antibullying campaign to individualized social skills training. Following are two of the most promising bullying intervention programs and where you can obtain information about them:

- *Olweus Bullying Prevention.* Created by Dan Olweus, this program focuses on 6- to 5-year-olds, with the goal of decreasing opportunities and rewards for bullying. School staff are instructed in ways to improve peer relations and make schools safer. When properly implemented, the program reduces bullying by 30 to 70 percent (Ericson, 2001; Olweus, 2003). Information on how to implement the program can be obtained from the Center for the Prevention of Violence at the University of Colorado: www.colorado.edu/espv/blueprints.

- *Steps to Respect.* This bullying program consists of three steps: (1) establishing a school-wide approach, such as creating antibullying policies and determining consequences for bullying; (2) training staff and parents to deal with bullying; and (3) teaching students to recognize, not tolerate, and handle bullying. In this third step, teachers provide skills training, such as how to be assertive, and information about bullying to students in grades 3 through 6. The skills training by teachers occurs over a 12- to 14-week period. A recent study found that Steps to Respect was successful in reducing bullying and argumentativeness in third- through sixth-grade students (Frey & others, 2005). For more information about Step to Respect consult this Web site: www.cfchildren.org/

Friends

Like adult friendships, children's friendships are typically characterized by similarity. Throughout childhood, friends are more similar than dissimilar in terms of age, sex, race, and many other factors. Friends often have similar attitudes toward school, similar educational aspirations, and closely aligned achievement orientations.

Why are children's friendships important? Willard Hartup (1983, 1996; Hartup & Abecassis, 2004) has studied peer relations and friendship for more than three decades. He recently concluded that friends can be cognitive and emotional resources from childhood through old age. Friends can foster self-esteem and a sense of well-being.

More specifically, children's friendships can serve six functions (Gottman & Parker, 1987):

- *Companionship.* Friendship provides children with a familiar partner and play-mate, someone who is willing to spend time with them and join in collaborative activities.

- *Stimulation.* Friendship provides children with interesting information, excitement, and amusement.

- *Physical support.* Friendship provides time, resources, and assistance.

- *Ego support.* Friendship provides the expectation of support, encouragement, and feedback, which helps children maintain an impression of themselves as competent, attractive, and worthwhile individuals.

- *Social comparison.* Friendship provides information about where the child stands vis-à-vis others and whether the child is doing okay.

- *Affection and intimacy.* Friendship provides children with a warm, close, trusting relationship with another individual. **Intimacy in friendships** is characterized by self-disclosure and the sharing of private thoughts. Research reveals that intimate friendships may not appear until early adolescence (Berndt & Perry, 1990).

Although having friends can be a developmental advantage, not all friendships are alike (Bagwell, 2004). People differ in the company they keep—that is, who their friends are. Developmental advantages occur when children have friends who are socially skilled and supportive. However, it is not developmentally advantageous to have coercive and conflict-ridden friendships (Rubin, Fredstrom, & Bowker, 2008).

The importance of friendship was underscored in a two-year longitudinal study (Wentzel, Barry, & Caldwell, 2004). Sixth-grade students who did not have a friend engaged in less prosocial behavior (cooperation, sharing, helping others), had lower grades, and were more emotionally distressed (depression, low well-being) than their counterparts who had one or more friends. Two years later, in the eighth grade, the students who did not have a friend in the sixth grade were still more emotionally distressed.

What are some functions of friendship?

intimacy in friendships Self-disclosure and the sharing of private thoughts.

Review and Reflect: Learning Goal 3

3 **Identify Changes in Peer Relationships in Middle and Late Childhood**

REVIEW

- What developmental changes characterize peer relations in middle and late childhood?
- How does children's peer status influence their development?
- How is social cognition involved in children's peer relations?
- What is the nature of bullying?
- What are children's friendships like?

REFLECT

- If you were a school principal, what would you do to reduce bullying in your school?

4 SCHOOLS

| Contemporary Approaches to Student Learning | Socioeconomic Status and Ethnicity | Cross-Cultural Comparisons of Achievement |

Is this classroom more likely constructivist or direct instruction? Explain.

constructivist approach A learner-centered approach that emphasizes the importance of individuals actively constructing their knowledge and understanding with guidance from the teacher.

For most children, entering the first grade signals new obligations. They develop new relationships and develop new standards by which to judge themselves. School provides children with a rich source of new ideas to shape their sense of self (Powell, 2009). They will spend many years in schools as members of small societies in which there are tasks to be accomplished, people to be socialized and socialized by, and rules that define and limit behavior, feelings, and attitudes. By the time students graduate from high school, they have spent 12,000 hours in the classroom.

Contemporary Approaches to Student Learning

Controversy swirls about the best way to teach children and how to hold schools and teachers accountable for whether children are learning (Armstrong, Henson, & Savage, 2009; Kellough & Carjuzaa, 2009; Stiggins, 2008).

Constructivist and Direct Instruction Approaches   The **constructivist approach** is a learner-centered approach that emphasizes the importance of individuals actively constructing their knowledge and understanding with guidance from the teacher. In the constructivist view, teachers should not attempt to simply pour information into children's minds. Rather, children should be encouraged to explore their world, discover knowledge, reflect, and think critically with careful monitoring and meaningful guidance from the teacher (Morrison, 2008). The constructivist belief is that for too long in American education children have been required to sit still, be passive learners, and rotely memorize irrelevant as well as relevant information (Silberman, 2006).

Today, constructivism may include an emphasis on collaboration—children working with each other in their efforts to know and understand (Bodrova & Leong, 2007).

A teacher with a constructivist instructional philosophy would not have children memorize information rotely but would give them opportunities to meaningfully construct the knowledge and understand the material while guiding their learning (Kafai, 2006).

By contrast, the **direct instruction approach** is a structured, teacher-centered approach that is characterized by teacher direction and control, high teacher expectations for students' progress, maximum time spent by students on academic tasks, and efforts by the teacher to keep negative affect to a minimum. An important goal in the direct instruction approach is maximizing student learning time.

Advocates of the constructivist approach argue that the direct instruction approach turns children into passive learners and does not adequately challenge them to think in critical and creative ways (Eby, Herrell, & Jordan, 2009). The direct instruction enthusiasts say that the constructivist approaches do not give enough attention to the content of a discipline, such as history or science. They also believe that the constructivist approaches are too relativistic and vague.

Some experts in educational psychology believe that many effective teachers use both a constructivist *and* a direct instruction approach rather than either exclusively (Bransford & others, 2006). Further, some circumstances may call more for a constructivist approach, others for a direction instruction approach. For example, experts increasingly recommend an explicit, intellectually engaging direct instruction approach when teaching students with a reading or a writing disability (Berninger, 2006).

Accountability   Since the 1990s, the U.S. public and governments at every level have demanded increased accountability from schools. One result was the spread of state-mandated tests to measure just what students had or had not learned (Gronlund & Waugh, 2009; McNergney & McNergney, 2009). Many states identified objectives for students in their state and created tests to measure whether students were meeting those objectives. This approach became national policy in 2002 when the No Child Left Behind (NCLB) legislation was signed into law.

Advocates argue that statewide standardized testing will have a number of positive effects. These include improved student performance; more time teaching the subjects that are tested; high expectations for all students; identification of poorly performing schools, teachers, and administrators; and improved confidence in schools as test scores rise.

Critics argue that the NCLB legislation is doing more harm than good (Noddings, 2007; Sadker, Sadker, & Zittleman, 2008). One criticism stresses that using a single test as the sole indicator of students' progress and competence presents a very narrow view of students' skills (Lewis, 2007). This criticism is similar to the one leveled at IQ tests, which we described in Chapter 8. To assess student progress and achievement, many psychologists and educators emphasize that a number of measures should be used, including tests, quizzes, projects, portfolios, classroom observations, and so on. Also, the tests used as part of NCLB don't measure creativity, motivation, persistence, flexible thinking, and social skills (Stiggins, 2008). Critics point out that teachers end up spending far too much class time "teaching to the test" by drilling students and having them memorize isolated facts at the expense of teaching that focuses on thinking skills, which students need for success in life (Pressley, 2007). Also, recall from Chapter 9 that some individuals are concerned that in the era of No Child Left Behind policy there is a neglect of students who are gifted in the effort to raise the achievement level of students who are not doing well (Clark, 2008; Cloud, 2007).

Consider also the following: Each state is allowed to have different criteria for what constitutes passing or failing grades on tests designated for NCLB inclusion. An analysis of NCLB data indicated that almost every fourth-grade student in Mississippi knows how to read but only half of Masschusetts' students do (Birman &

What are some issues involved in the No Child Left Behind legislation?

direct instruction approach A structured, teacher-centered approach that is characterized by teacher direction and control, mastery of academic skills, high expectations for students' progress, maximum time spent on learning tasks, and efforts to keep negative affect to a minimum.

others, 2007). Clearly, Mississippi's standards for passing the reading test are far below those of Massachusetts. In the recent analysis of state-by-state comparisons, many states have taken the safe route and kept the standard for passing low. Thus, while one of NCLB's goals was to raise standards for achievement in U.S. schools, apparently allowing states to set their own standards likely has lowered achievement standards.

Consider also that one goal of NCLB is to close the ethnic achievement gap that characterizes lower achievement by African American and Latino students and higher achievement by Asian American and non-Latino White students. However, leading expert Linda Darling-Hammond (2007) recently concluded that NCLB has failed to reach this goal. She criticizes NCLB for inappropriate assessment of English-language learners and students with special needs, strong incentives to exclude low-achieving students from school to achieve test score targets, and the continued shortage of highly qualified teachers in high-need schools.

Despite such criticisms, the U.S. Department of Education is committed to implementing No Child Left Behind, and schools are making accommodations to meet the requirement of this law. Indeed, most educators support the importance of high expectations and high standards of excellence for students and teachers. At issue, however, is whether the tests and procedures mandated by NCLB are the best ones for achieving these high standards (Sadker, Sadker, & Zittleman, 2008; Yell & Dragow, 2009).

Socioeconomic Status and Ethnicity

Children from low-income, ethnic minority backgrounds have more difficulties in school than do their middle-socioeconomic-status, White counterparts. Why? Critics argue that schools have not done a good job of educating low-income, ethnic minority students to overcome the barriers to their achievement (Banks, 2008; Gollnic & Chinn, 2009). Let's further explore the roles of socioeconomic status and ethnicity in schools.

Jill Nakamura, teaching in her first-grade classroom. Jill Nakamura teaches at a school located in a high-poverty area. She visits students at home early in the school year in an effort to connect with them and develop a partnership with their parents. "She holds a daily after school club for students reading below grade level . . .; those who don't want to attend must call parents to tell them. In one school year (2004), she "raised the percent of students reading at or above grade level from 29 percent to 76 percent" (Briggs, 2004, p. 6D).

The Education of Students from Low-Income Backgrounds

Many children in poverty face problems that present barriers to their learning (Ballentine & Hammock, 2009; Coltrane & others, 2008; Wilson, 2008). They might have parents who don't set high educational standards for them, who are incapable of reading to them, and who don't have enough money to pay for educational materials and experiences, such as books and trips to zoos and museums. They might be malnourished and live in areas where crime and violence are a way of life (Barajas, Philipsen, & Brooks-Gunn, 2008).

Compared with schools in higher-income areas, schools in low-income areas are more likely to have more students with low achievement test scores, low graduation rates, and small percentages of students going to college; they are more likely to have young teachers with less experience; and they are more likely to encourage rote learning (Spring, 2008). Too few schools in low-income neighborhoods provide students with environments that are conducive to learning (Tozer, Senese, & Violas, 2006). Many of the schools' buildings and classrooms are old and crumbling. These are the types of undesirable conditions Jonathan Kozol (2005) observed in many inner-city schools, including the South Bronx in New York City, as described at the beginning of the chapter. To read about ways to improve the schools and families of children living in poverty, see the *Diversity in Life-Span Development* interlude.

Diversity in Life-Span Development
Improving Resources for Schools and Families in Impoverished Areas

The schools that children from impoverished backgrounds attend often have fewer resources than schools in higher-income neighborhoods (Liu & Hernandez, 2008). In low-income areas, schools are more likely to be staffed by young teachers with less experience than schools in higher-income neighborhoods (Liu & Hernandez, 2008). Schools in low-income areas also are more likely to encourage rote learning, whereas schools in higher-income areas are more likely to work with children to improve their thinking skills (Spring, 2008). In sum, far too many schools in low-income neighborhoods provide students with environments that are not conducive to effective learning (Hutson, 2008; Rowley, Kurtz-Costas, & Cooper, 2009).

Might intervention with families of children living in poverty improve children's school performance? In a recent experimental study, Aletha Huston and her colleagues (2006; Gupta, Thornton, & Huston, 2007) evaluated the effects of New Hope—a program designed to increase parental employment and reduce family poverty—on adolescent development. They randomly assigned families with 6- to 10-year-old children living in poverty to the New Hope program and a control group. New Hope offered adults living in poverty who were employed 30 or more hours a week benefits that were designed to increase family income (a wage supplement which ensured that net income increased as parents earned more) and provide work supports through subsidized child care (for any child under age 13) and health insurance. Management services were provided to New Hope participants to assist them in job searches and other needs. The New Hope program was available to the experimental group families for three years (until the children were 9 to 13 years old). Five years after the program began and two years after it had ended, the program's effects on the children were examined when they were 11 to 16 years old. Compared with adolescents in the control group, New Hope adolescents were more competent at reading, had better school performance, were less likely to be in special education classes, had more positive social skills, and were more likely to be in formal after-school arrangements. New Hope parents reported better psychological well-being and a greater sense of self-efficacy in managing their adolescents than control parents did.

Ethnicity in Schools More than one-third of all African American and almost one-third of all Latino students attend schools in the 47 largest city school districts in the United States, compared with only 5 percent of all White and 22 percent of all Asian American students. Many of these inner-city schools are still segregated, are grossly underfunded, and do not provide adequate opportunities for children to learn effectively. Thus, the effects of SES and the effects of ethnicity are often intertwined (Healey, 2009).

Even outside of inner-city schools, school segregation remains a factor in U.S. education (Gollnick & Chinn, 2009; Nieto & Bode, 2008). Almost one-third of all African American and Latino students attend schools in which 90 percent or more of the students are from minority groups (Banks, 2008).

The school experiences of students from different ethnic groups vary considerably (Koppelman & Goodheart, 2008; Taylor & Whittaker, 2009). African American and Latino students are much less likely than non-Latino White or Asian American students to be enrolled in academic, college preparatory programs and are much more likely to be enrolled in remedial and special education programs. Asian American students are far more likely than other ethnic minority groups to take advanced math and science courses in high school. African American students are twice as likely as Latinos, Native Americans, or Whites to be suspended from school.

In *The Shame of a Nation,* Jonathan Kozol (2005) criticized the inadequate quality and lack of resources in many U.S. schools, especially those in the poverty areas of inner cities, that have high concentrations of ethnic minority children. Kozol praises teachers like Angela Lively (*above*), who keeps a box of shoes in her Indianapolis classroom for students in need.

Some experts say that a form of institutional racism permeates many American schools by which teachers accept a low level of performance from children of color (Ogbu & Stern, 2001; Spencer, 1999). American anthropologist John Ogbu (1989) proposed that ethnic minority students are placed in a position of subordination and exploitation in the American educational system. He believes that students of color, especially African Americans and Latinos, have inferior educational opportunities, are exposed to teachers and school administrators who have low academic expectations for them, and encounter negative stereotypes (Ogbu & Stern, 2001). In one study of middle schools in predominantly Latino areas of Miami, Latino and White teachers rated African American students as having more behavioral problems than African American teachers rated the same students as having (Zimmerman & others, 1995).

Following are some strategies for improving relationships among ethnically diverse students:

What are some features of a jigsaw classroom?

- *Turn the class into a jigsaw classroom.* When Eliot Aronson was a professor at the University of Texas at Austin, the school system contacted him for ideas on how to reduce the increasing racial tension in classrooms. Aronson (1986) developed the concept of "jigsaw classroom," in which students from different cultural backgrounds are placed in a cooperative group in which they have to construct different parts of a project to reach a common goal. Aronson used the term *jigsaw* because he saw the technique as much like a group of students cooperating to put different pieces together to complete a jigsaw puzzle. How might this work? Team sports, drama productions, and music performances are examples of contexts in which students participate cooperatively to reach a common goal; however, the jigsaw technique also lends itself to group science projects, history reports, and other learning experiences with a variety of subject matter.

- *Encourage students to have positive personal contact with diverse other students.* Mere contact does not do the job of improving relationships with diverse others. For example, busing ethnic minority students to predominantly White schools, or vice versa, has not reduced prejudice or improved interethnic relations. What matters is what happens after children get to school. Especially beneficial in improving interethnic relations is sharing one's worries, successes, failures, coping strategies, interests, and other personal information with people of other ethnicities. When this happens, people tend to look at others as individuals rather than as members of a homogeneous group.

- *Reduce bias.* Teachers can reduce bias by displaying images of children from diverse ethnic and cultural groups, selecting play materials and classroom activities that encourage cultural understanding, helping students resist stereotyping, and working with parents to reduce children's exposure to bias and prejudice at home.

- *View the school and community as a team.* James Comer (1988, 2004, 2006) advocates a community, team approach as the best way to educate children. Three important aspects of the Comer Project for Change are (1) a governance and management team that develops a comprehensive school plan, assessment strategy, and staff development plan; (2) a mental health or school support team; and (3) a parent's program. Comer believes that the entire school community should have a cooperative rather than an adversarial attitude. The Comer program is currently operating in more than 600 schools in 26 states. Read further about James Comer's work in the *Careers in Life-Span Development* profile.

- *Be a competent cultural mediator.* Teachers can play a powerful role as cultural mediators by being sensitive to biased content in materials and classroom interactions, learning more about different ethnic groups, being sensitive to children's ethnic attitudes, viewing students of color positively, and thinking of positive ways to get parents of color more involved as partners with teachers in educating children (Manning & Baruth, 2009; Taylor & Whittaker, 2009).

Careers in Life-Span Development

James Comer, Child Psychiatrist

James Comer grew up in a low-income neighborhood in East Chicago, Indiana, and credits his parents with leaving no doubt about the importance of education. He obtained a BA degree from Indiana University. He went on to obtain a medical degree from Howard University College of Medicine, a Master of Public Health degree from the University of Michigan School of Public Health, and psychiatry training at the Yale University School of Medicine's Child Study Center. He currently is the Maurice Falk professor of Child Psychiatry at the Yale University Child Study Center and an associate dean at the Yale University Medical School. During his years at Yale, Comer has concentrated his career on promoting a focus on child development as a way of improving schools. His efforts in support of healthy development of young people are known internationally.

Comer is, perhaps, best known for the founding of the School Development Program in 1968, which promotes the collaboration of parents, educators, and community to improve social, emotional, and academic outcomes for children.

James Comer (*left*) is shown with some of the inner-city African American children who attend a school that became a better learning environment because of Comer's intervention.

Cross-Cultural Comparisons of Achievement

American children are more achievement-oriented than their counterparts in many countries. However, the relatively poor performance of American children in math and science in comparison with their counterparts in some other countries, especially Asian countries, has been highly publicized in recent decades. In 2003, fourth-grade students in five countries (Singapore, Chinese Taipei, Japan, Hong Kong, and England) had higher math scores than U.S. students, who had higher math scores than students in 19 countries (Gonzales & others, 2004). In science comparisons, fourth-graders in 11 countries (highest scores were for Singapore, Hong Kong, Japan, and Chinese Taipei) had higher scores than their U.S. counterparts, who had higher scores than fourth-graders in 13 countries.

Harold Stevenson and his colleagues (Stevenson, 1995, 2000; Stevenson & Hofer,1999; Stevenson & others, 1990; Stevenson & Zusko, 2002) have completed five cross-cultural comparisons of students in the United States, China, Taiwan, and Japan. In these studies, Asian students consistently outperform American students in mathematics. And, the longer the students are in school, the wider the gap becomes between Asian and American students—the lowest difference is in the first grade, the highest in the eleventh grade (the highest grade studied).

To learn more about the reasons for these large cross-cultural differences, Stevenson and his colleagues spent thousands of hours observing in classrooms, as well as interviewing and surveying teachers, students, and parents. They found that the Asian teachers spent more of their time teaching math than did the American teachers. For example, more than one-fourth of total classroom time in the first grade was spent on math instruction in Japan, compared with only one-tenth of the time in the U.S. first-grade classrooms. Moreover, the Asian students were in school an average of 240 days a year, compared with 178 days in the United States.

Differences were also found between the Asian and American parents. American parents were more likely to believe that their children's math achievement was due to innate ability, whereas the Asian parents were more likely to say that their children's math achievement was the consequence of effort and training (see Figure 10.6).

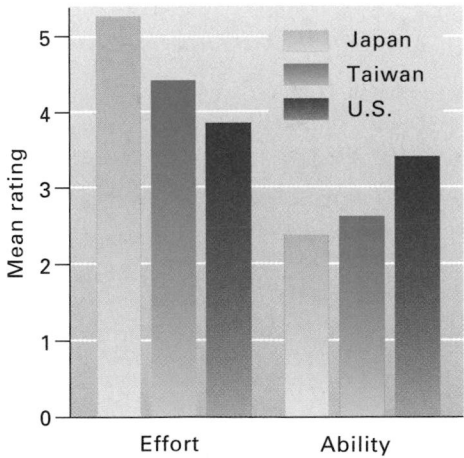

FIGURE 10.6 Mothers' Beliefs About the Factors Responsible for Children's Math Achievement in Three Countries. In one study, mothers in Japan and Taiwan were more likely to believe that their children's math achievement was due to effort rather than innate ability, while U.S. mothers were more likely to believe their children's math achievement was due to innate ability (Stevenson, Lee, & Stigler, 1986). If parents believe that their children's math achievement is due to innate ability and their children are not doing well in math, the implication is that they are less likely to think their children will benefit from putting forth more effort.

Marva Collins, challenging a child to achieve.

Related to the differences in Asian and U.S. parents involving explanations of effort and ability, Carol Dweck (2006) described the importance of children's **mindset**, which she defines as the cognitive view individuals develop for themselves. She concludes that individuals have one of two mindsets: (1) *fixed mindset,* in which they believe that their qualities are carved in stone and cannot change; or (2) *growth mindset,* in which they believe their qualities can change and improve through their effort.

Dweck (2006) argued that individuals' mindsets influence whether they will be optimistic or pessimistic, what their goals will be and how hard they will strive to reach those goals, and their achievement. Dweck says that mindsets begin to be shaped in childhood as children interact with parents, teachers, and coaches, who themselves have either a fixed mindset or a growth mindset. She described the growth mindset of Chicago second-grade teacher Marva Collins, a masterful teacher. Collins' goal is to change apathetic, fixed-mindset children into growth-mindset children. On the first day of school, she tells her students, many of whom are repeating the second grade,

> I know most of you can't spell your name. You don't know the alphabet, you don't know how to read, you don't know homonyms or how to syllabicate. I promise you that you will. None of you has ever failed. School may have failed you. Well, goodbye to failure, children. Welcome to success. You will read hard books in here and understand what you read. You will write every day. . . . But you must help me to help you. If you don't give anything, don't expect anything. Success is not coming to you, you must come to it. (Dweck, 2006, pp. 188–189)

Marva Collins' second-grade students usually have to start off with the lowest level of reader available, but by the end of the school year, most of the students are reading at the fifth-grade level.

Returning to Stevenson's research, the American parents also had much lower expectations for their children's education and achievement than did the Asian parents. In Stevenson's view, the change that is needed most in U.S. education is higher expectations for achievement. Other experts, such as Phylis Blumenfeld, Jacquelynne Eccles, and Joyce Epstein (Blumenfeld, Kempler, & Krajcik, 2006; Eccles, 2007; Epstein, 2007) conclude that high achievement standards, as well as teacher concern for individual children, engaging children in meaningful and interesting learning tasks, and positive connections between schools and families, are key aspects of improving U.S. children's academic achievement.

> . . . *K*eep the growth mindset in your thoughts. Then, when you bump up against obstacles, you can turn to it . . . showing you a path into the future.
>
> —CAROL DWECK
> *Contemporary Psychologist, Stanford University*

mindset The cognitive view, either fixed or growth, that individuals develop for themselves.

Review and Reflect: Learning Goal 4

 4   **Characterize Contemporary Approaches to Student Learning and Sociocultural Aspects of Schooling and Achievement**

REVIEW

- What are two major contemporary issues in educating children?
- How do socioeconomic status and ethnicity influence schooling?
- What are some cross-cultural comparisons of achievement?

REFLECT

- Should the United States be worried about the low performance of its students in mathematics and science in comparison to Asian students? Are Americans' expectations for students too low?

Reach Your Learning Goals

Socioemotional Development in Middle and Late Childhood

---

1 EMOTIONAL AND PERSONALITY DEVELOPMENT: DISCUSS EMOTIONAL AND PERSONALITY DEVELOPMENT IN MIDDLE AND LATE CHILDHOOD

The Self

- In middle and late childhood, self-understanding increasingly involves social and psychological characteristics, including social comparison. Children increase their perspective taking in middle and late childhood, and their social understanding shows increasing psychological sophistication as well. Self-concept refers to domain-specific evaluations of the self. Self-esteem refers to global evaluations of the self and is also referred to as self-worth or self-image. Self-esteem is only moderately related to school performance but is more strongly linked to initiative. Four ways to increase self-esteem are to (1) identify the causes of low self-esteem, (2) provide emotional support and social approval, (3) help children achieve, and (4) help children cope. Self-efficacy is the belief that one can master a situation and produce positive outcomes. Bandura believes that self-efficacy is a critical factor in whether students will achieve. Schunk argues that self-efficacy influences a student's choice of tasks, with low-efficacy students avoiding many learning tasks. Erikson's fourth stage of development, industry versus inferiority, characterizes the middle and late childhood years.

Emotional Development

- Developmental changes in emotion include increased understanding of complex emotions such as pride and shame, detecting that more than one emotion can be experienced in a particular situation, taking into account the circumstances that led up to an emotional reaction, improvements in the ability to suppress and conceal negative emotions, and using self-initiated strategies to redirect feelings. As children get older, they use a greater variety of coping strategies and more cognitive strategies.

Moral Development

- Kohlberg argued that moral development consists of three levels—preconventional, conventional, and postconventional—and six stages (two at each level). Kohlberg maintained that these stages were age-related. Influences on movement through the stages include cognitive development, imitation and cognitive conflict, peer relations, and perspective taking. Criticisms of Kohlberg's theory have been made, especially by Gilligan, who advocates a stronger care perspective. Other criticisms focus on the inadequacy of moral reasoning to predict moral behavior, culture and family influences, and the distinction between moral reasoning and social conventional reasoning. Prosocial behavior involves positive moral behaviors such as sharing. Most sharing in the first three years is not done for empathy, but at about 4 years of age empathy contributes to sharing. By the start of the elementary school years, children express objective ideas about fairness. By the mid- to late elementary school years, children believe equity can mean that others with special needs/merit deserve special treatment. Recently, there has been a surge of interest in moral personality.

Gender

- Gender stereotypes are widespread around the world. A number of physical differences exist between males and females. Some experts argue that cognitive differences between males and females have been exaggerated. In terms of socioemotional differences, males are more physically aggressive than females, whereas females regulate their emotions better and engage in more prosocial behavior than males. Gender-role classification focuses on how masculine, feminine, or androgynous individuals are. Androgyny means having both positive feminine and masculine characteristics. It is important to think about gender in terms of context.

2 FAMILIES: DESCRIBE DEVELOPMENTAL CHANGES IN PARENT-CHILD RELATIONSHIPS, PARENTS AS MANAGERS, AND SOCIETAL CHANGES IN FAMILIES

Developmental Changes in Parent-Child Relationships

Parents as Managers

Stepfamilies

- Parents spend less time with children during middle and late childhood than in early childhood. Parents especially play an important role in supporting and stimulating chidren's academic achievement. Discipline changes and control is more coregulatory.

- Parents have important roles as managers of children's opportunities, as monitors of their behavior, and social initiators and arrangers. Mothers are more likely to function in these parental management roles than fathers.

- As in divorced families, children living in stepparent families have more adjustment problems than their counterparts in nondivorced families. However, a majority of children in stepfamilies do not have adjustment problems. Children in complex (blended) stepfamilies have more problems than children in simple stepfamilies or nondivorced families.

3 PEERS: IDENTIFY CHANGES IN PEER RELATIONSHIPS IN MIDDLE AND LATE CHILDHOOD

Developmental Changes

Peer Status

Social Cognition

Bullying

Friends

- Among the developmental changes in peer relations in middle and late childhood are increased preference for same-sex groups, an increase in time spent in peer interaction and the size of the peer group, and less supervision of the peer group by adults.

- Popular children are frequently nominated as a best friend and are rarely disliked by their peers. Average children receive an average number of both positive and negative nominations from their peers. Neglected children are infrequently nominated as a best friend but are not disliked by their peers. Rejected children are infrequently nominated as a best friend and are actively disliked by their peers. Controversial children are frequently nominated both as a best friend and as being disliked by peers. Rejected children are especially at risk for a number of problems.

- Social information-processing skills and social knowledge are two important dimensions of social cognition in peer relations.

- Significant numbers of children are bullied, and this can result in short-term and long-term negative effects for both the victims and bullies.

- Like adult friends, children who are friends tend to be similar to each other. Children's friendships serve six functions: companionship, stimulation, physical support, ego support, social comparison, and intimacy/affection.

4 SCHOOLS: CHARACTERIZE CONTEMPORARY APPROACHES TO STUDENT LEARNING AND SOCIOCULTURAL ASPECTS OF SCHOOLING AND ACHIEVEMENT

Contemporary Approaches to Student Learning

Socioeconomic Status and Ethnicity

Cross-Cultural Comparisons of Achievement

- Two contemporary issues involve whether it is best to educate students by using a constructivist approach (a learner-centered approach) or a direct instruction approach (a teacher-centered approach) and how to hold teachers accountable for whether children are learning. In the United States, standardized testing of elementary schools students has been mandated by both many state governments and by the No Child Left Behind federal legislation. Numerous criticisms of NCLB have been made.

- Children in poverty face many barriers to learning at school as well as at home. The effects of SES and ethnicity on schools are intertwined as many U.S. schools are segregated. Low expectations for ethnic minority children represent one of the barriers to their learning.

- American children are more achievement-oriented than children in many countries, but perform more poorly in math and science than many children in Asian countries, such as China, Taiwan, and Japan.

KEY TERMS

perspective taking 319
self-esteem 320
self-concept 320
self-efficacy 321
preconventional
   reasoning 324
heteronomous morality 324
individualism, instrumental
   purpose, and
   exchange 324

conventional reasoning 324
mutual interpersonal
   expectations, relationships,
   and interpersonal
   conformity 324
social systems morality 324
postconventional
   reasoning 325
social contract or utility and
   individual rights 325

universal ethical
   principles 325
justice perspective 327
care perspective 327
social conventional
   reasoning 327
gender stereotypes 328
androgyny 331
popular children 336
average children 336

neglected children 336
rejected children 336
controversial children 336
intimacy in friendships 339
constructivist approach 340
direct instruction
   approach 341
mindset 346

KEY PEOPLE

Jonathan Kozol 318
Diane Ruble 319
Albert Bandura 321
Dale Schunk 321
Erik Erikson 321
Lawrence Kohlberg 323

Carol Gilligan 326
William Damon 327
Eleanor Maccoby 329
Carol Jacklin 329
Janet Shibley Hyde 330
Sandra Bem 331

William Pollack 331
E. Mavis Hetherington 334
John Coie 336
Kenneth Dodge 337
Dan Olweus 338
Willard Hartup 339

Linda Darling-Hammond 342
John Ogbu 344
Eliot Aronson 344
James Comer 345
Harold Stevenson 345
Carol Dweck 346

E-LEARNING TOOLS

To help you master the material in this chapter, visit the Online Learning Center for *Life-Span Development*, twelfth edition, at **www.mhhe.com/santrockld12**.

Self-Assessment

Connect to **www.mhhe.com/santrockld12** to reflect on your childhood by completing the self-assessment, *My Socioemotional Development as a Child*.

Taking It to the Net

Connect to **www.mhhe.com/santrockld12** to research the answers to these questions:

1. Ling, a third-grade teacher, overheard a talk-show discussion on emotional intelligence. She has seen several books on the subject in the local library but was unaware of its impact on learning. What is emotional intelligence, and how can Ling and her students' parents facilitate this type of development in children?

2. Frank is researching the latest information on bullying after his younger brother told him of his recent experiences with bullies at his junior high school. What information is available on the prevalence of bullying, the makeup of the children who bully, and why this type of behavior is increasing?

3. Dimitri is a high school English teacher. He has heard about the controversy between direct instruction and constructivist points of view, and he would like to try out both approaches in his classroom. How might Dimitri conduct his class differently according to each paradigm?

Video Clips

The Online Learning Center includes two videos for Chapter 10. The first video is called "Characteristics of Children Who Bully." How are bullies made? What causal factors distinguish those who are likely to bully from those likely to be bullied? This segment explores the power dynamics of childhood bullying. The second video is called "Schools and Public Policy." The transition to middle school can be a major paradigm shift for the student. In this segment, Dr. Jacquelynne Eccles describes how her study of the social parameters of middle school has led to changes in public policy.

Health and Well-Being, Parenting, and Education Exercises

Build your decision-making skills by trying your hand at the health and well-being, parenting, and education exercises. Connect to **www.mhhe.com/santrockld12** to research the answers and complete the exercises.

ADOLESCENCE

*In no order of things is
adolescence the simple
time of life.*

—JEAN ERSKINE STEWART
American Writer, 20th Century

Adolescents try on one face after another, seeking to find a

face of their own. Their generation of young people is the

fragile cable by which the best and the worst of their parents'

generation is transmitted to the present. In the end, there are

only two lasting bequests parents can leave youth—one being

roots, the other wings. Section 6 contains two chapters:

"Physical and Cognitive Development in Adolescence"

(Chapter 11) and "Socioemotional Development in

Adolescence" (Chapter 12).

11

In youth, we clothe ourselves with rainbows, and go brave as the zodiac.

—Ralph Waldo Emerson
American Poet, 19th Century

LEARNING GOALS

◆ Discuss the nature of adolescence.

◆ Describe the changes involved in puberty as well as changes in the brain and sexuality during adolescence.

◆ Identify adolescent problems related related to health, substance use and abuse, and eating disorders.

◆ Explain cognitive changes in adolescence.

◆ Summarize some key aspects of how schools influence adolescent development.

PHYSICAL AND COGNITIVE DEVELOPMENT IN ADOLESCENCE

CHAPTER OUTLINE

1

THE NATURE OF ADOLESCENCE

2

PHYSICAL CHANGES
Puberty

The Brain

Adolescent Sexuality

3

ISSUES IN ADOLESCENT HEALTH
Adolescent Health

Substance Use and Abuse

Eating Disorders

4

ADOLESCENT COGNITION
Piaget's Theory

Adolescent Egocentrism

Information Processing

5

SCHOOLS
The Transition to Middle or Junior High School

Effective Schools for Young Adolescents

High School

Service Learning

Images of Life-Span Development
Latisha, Arnie, and Katie

Fifteen-year-old Latisha developed a drinking problem, and recently she was kicked off the cheerleading squad for missing practice so often—but that didn't stop her drinking. She and her friends began skipping school regularly so they could drink. Fourteen-year-old Arnie is a juvenile delinquent. Last week he stole a TV set, struck his mother and bloodied her face, broke out some streetlights in the neighborhood, and threatened a boy with a wrench and hammer.

Twelve-year-old Katie, more than just about anything else, wanted a playground in her town. She knew that the other kids also wanted one, so she put together a group that generated funding ideas for the playground. They presented their ideas to the town council. Her group got more youth involved, and they raised money by selling candy and sandwiches door-to-door. The playground became a reality, a place where, as Katie says, "People have picnics and make friends." Katie's advice: "You won't get anywhere if you don't try."

Adolescents like Latisha and Arnie are the ones we hear about the most. But there are many adolescents like Katie who contribute in positive ways to their communitiy and competently make the transition through adolescence. Indeed, for most adolescents, adolescence is not a time of rebellion, crisis, pathology, and deviance. A far more accurate vision of adolescence is that it is a time of evaluation, decision making, commitment, and carving out a place in the world. Most of the problems of today's youth are not with the youth themselves. What adolescents need is access to a range of legitimate opportunities and to long-term support from adults who care deeply about them (Crosnoe & Trinitapoli, 2008; Lerner, Boyd, & Du, 2008).

> **PREVIEW**
>
> **Adolescence is a transitional period in the human life span, linking childhood and adulthood. We begin the chapter by examining some general characteristics of adolescence followed by coverage of major physical changes and health issues of adolescence. Then we describe the significant cognitive changes that characterize adolescence and various aspects of schools for adolescents.**

1 THE NATURE OF ADOLESCENCE

As in development during childhood, genetic/biological and environmental/social factors influence adolescent development. During their childhood years of development, adolescents experienced thousands of hours of interactions with parents, peers, and teachers, but now they face dramatic biological changes, new experiences, and new developmental tasks. Relationships with parents take a different form, moments with peers become more intimate, and dating occurs for the first time, as do sexual exploration and possibly intercourse. The adolescent's thoughts are more abstract and idealistic. Biological changes trigger a heightened interest in body image. Adolescence has both continuity and discontinuity with childhood.

There is a long history of worrying about how adolescents will "turn out." In 1904, G. Stanley Hall proposed the "storm-and-stress" view that adolescence is a

Growing up has never been easy. However, adolescence is not best viewed as a time of rebellion, crisis, pathology, and deviance. A far more accurate vision of adolescence describes it as a time of evaluation, of decision making, of commitment, and of carving out a place in the world. Most of the problems of today's youth are not with the youth themselves. What adolescents need is access to a range of legitimate opportunities and to long-term support from adults who deeply care about them. *What might be some examples of such support and caring?*

turbulent time charged with conflict and mood swings. However, when Daniel Offer and his colleagues (1988) studied the self-images of adolescents in the United States, Australia, Bangladesh, Hungary, Israel, Italy, Japan, Taiwan, Turkey, and West Germany, at least 73 percent of the adolescents displayed a healthy self-image. Although there were differences among them, the adolescents were happy most of the time, they enjoyed life, they perceived themselves as able to exercise self-control, they valued work and school, they felt confident about their sexual selves, they expressed positive feelings toward their families, and they felt they had the capability to cope with life's stresses: not exactly a storm-and-stress portrayal of adolescence.

Public attitudes about adolescence emerge from a combination of personal experience and media portrayals, neither of which produce an objective picture of how normal adolescents develop (Feldman & Elliott, 1990). Some of the readiness to assume the worst about adolescents likely involves the short memories of adults. Many adults measure their current perceptions of adolescents by their memories of their own adolescence. Adults may portray today's adolescents as more troubled, less respectful, more self-centered, more assertive, and more adventurous than they were.

However, in matters of taste and manners, the young people of every generation have seemed unnervingly radical and different from adults—different in how they look, in how they behave, in the music they enjoy, in their hairstyles, and in the clothing they choose. It is an enormous error, though, to confuse adolescents' enthusiasm for trying on new identities and enjoying moderate amounts of outrageous behavior with hostility toward parental and societal standards. Acting out and boundary testing are time-honored ways in which adolescents move toward accepting, rather than rejecting, parental values.

Most adolescents negotiate the lengthy path to adult maturity successfully, but too large a group does not (Lerner, Boyd, & Du, 2008). Ethnic, cultural, gender, socioeconomic, age, and lifestyle differences influence the actual life trajectory of every adolescent (Patterson & Hastings, 2007). Different portrayals of adolescence emerge, depending on the particular group of adolescents being described (Balsano & others, 2008). Today's adolescents are exposed to a complex menu of lifestyle options through the media, and many face the temptations of drug use and sexual activity at increasingly young ages. Too many adolescents are not provided with adequate opportunities and support to become competent adults (Eccles, Brown, & Templeton, 2008).

Review and Reflect: Learning Goal 1

 Discuss the Nature of Adolescence

REVIEW

• What characterizes adolescent development?

REFLECT

• How much have adolescents changed or stayed the same over the last 30 to 40 years?

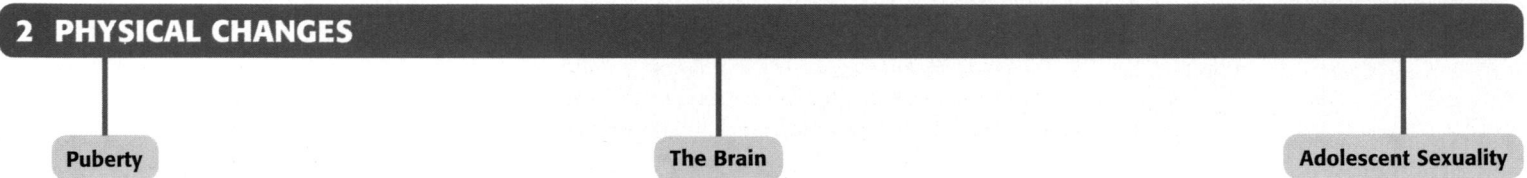

2 PHYSICAL CHANGES

Puberty **The Brain** **Adolescent Sexuality**

One father remarked that the problem with his teenage son was not that he grew, but that he did not know when to stop growing. As we will see, there is considerable variation in the timing of the adolescent growth spurt. In addition to pubertal changes, other physical changes we will explore involve sexuality and the brain.

Puberty

Puberty is not the same as adolescence. For most of us, puberty ends long before adolescence does, although puberty is the most important marker of the beginning of adolescence. **Puberty** is a period of rapid physical maturation involving hormonal and bodily changes that occurs primarily during early adolescence. Puberty is not a single, sudden event. We know whether a young boy or girl is going through puberty, but pinpointing puberty's beginning and end is difficult. Among the most noticeable changes are signs of sexual maturation and increases in height and weight.

Sexual Maturation, Height, and Weight Think back to the onset of your puberty. Of the striking changes that were taking place in your body, what was the

ZITS By Jerry Scott and Jim Borgman

ZITS © ZITS Partnership. King Features Syndicate.

puberty A period of rapid physical involving hormonal and bodily changes that occurs mainly during early adolescence.

first to occur? Researchers have found that male pubertal characteristics typically develop in this order: increase in penis and testicle size, appearance of straight pubic hair, minor voice change, first ejaculation (which usually occurs through masturbation or a wet dream), appearance of kinky pubic hair, onset of maximum growth in height and weight, growth of hair in armpits, more detectable voice changes, and, finally, growth of facial hair.

What is the order of appearance of physical changes in females? First, either the breasts enlarge or pubic hair appears. Later, hair appears in the armpits. As these changes occur, the female grows in height and her hips become wider than her shoulders. **Menarche**—a girl's first menstruation—comes rather late in the pubertal cycle. Initially, her menstrual cycles may be highly irregular. For the first several years, she may not ovulate every menstrual cycle; some girls do not ovulate at all until a year or two after menstruation begins. No voice changes comparable to those in pubertal males occur in pubertal females. By the end of puberty, the female's breasts have become more fully rounded.

Marked weight gains coincide with the onset of puberty (Jasik, C. B., & Lustig, 2008). During early adolescence, girls tend to outweigh boys, but by about age 14 boys begin to surpass girls. Similarly, at the beginning of the adolescent period, girls tend to be as tall as or taller than boys of their age, but by the end of the middle school years most boys have caught up or, in many cases, surpassed girls in height.

As indicated in Figure 11.1, the growth spurt occurs approximately two years earlier for girls than for boys. The mean age at the beginning of the growth spurt in girls is 9; for boys, it is 11. The peak rate of pubertal change occurs at $11\frac{1}{2}$ years for girls and $13\frac{1}{2}$ years for boys. During their growth spurt, girls increase in height about $3\frac{1}{2}$ inches per year, boys about 4 inches. Boys and girls who are shorter or taller than their peers before adolescence are likely to remain so during adolescence; however, as much as 30 percent of an individual's height in late adolescence is unexplained by his or her height in the elementary school years.

Hormonal Changes   Behind the first whisker in boys and the widening of hips in girls is a flood of **hormones**, powerful chemical substances secreted by the endocrine glands and carried through the body by the bloodstream. The endocrine system's role in puberty involves the interaction of the hypothalamus, the pituitary gland, and the gonads. The **hypothalamus** is a structure in the brain that is involved with eating and sex. The **pituitary gland** is an important endocrine gland that controls growth and regulates other glands; among these, the **gonads**—the testes in males, the ovaries in females—are particularly important in giving rise to pubertal changes in the body.

How do the gonads, or sex glands, work? The pituitary sends a signal via *gonadotropins* (hormones that stimulate the testes or ovaries) to the appropriate gland to manufacture hormones. These hormones give rise to such changes as the production of sperm in males and menstruation and the release of eggs from the ovaries in females. The pituitary gland, through interaction with the hypothalamus, detects when the optimal level of hormones is reached and responds and maintains it with additional gonadotropin secretion (Yoo & others, 2006).

Not only does the pituitary gland release gonadotropins that stimulate the testes and ovaries, but through interaction with the hypothalamus the pituitary gland also secretes hormones that either directly lead to growth and skeletal maturation or that produce growth effects through interaction with the thyroid gland, located at the base of the throat.

The concentrations of certain hormones increase dramatically during adolescence (Herbison & others, 2008). *Testosterone* is a hormone associated in boys with the development of genitals, an increase in height, and a change in voice. *Estradiol* is a type of estrogen; in girls it is associated with breast, uterine, and skeletal development. In one study,

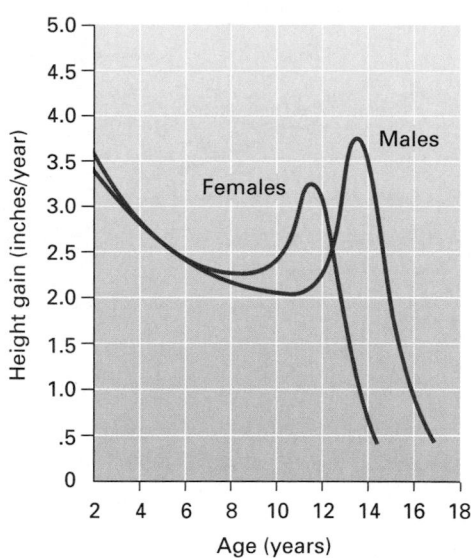

FIGURE 11.1 Pubertal Growth Spurt. On the average, the peak of the growth spurt during puberty occurs 2 years earlier for girls ($11\frac{1}{2}$) than for boys ($13\frac{1}{2}$). *How are hormones related to the growth spurt and to the difference between the average height of adolescent boys and girls?*

What are some of the differences in the ways girls and boys experience pubertal growth?

menarche A girl's first menstruation.

hormones Powerful chemical substances secreted by the endocrine glands and carried through the body by the bloodstream.

hypothalamus A structure in the brain that monitors eating and sex.

pituitary gland An important endocrine gland that controls growth and regulates other glands, including the gonads.

gonads The sex glands—the testes in males and the ovaries in females.

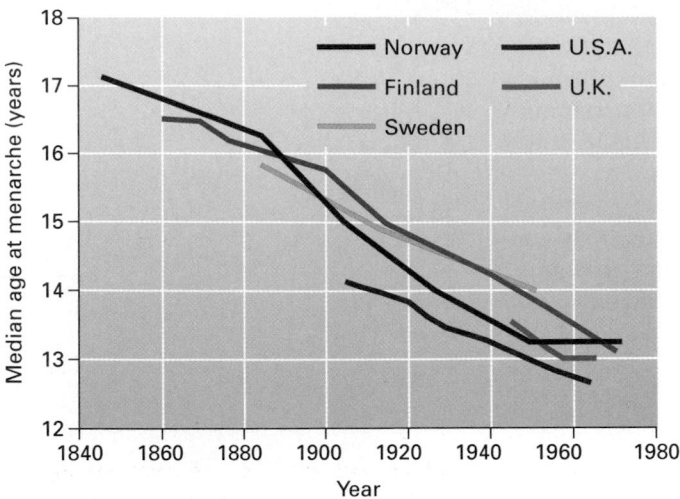

FIGURE 11.2 Median Ages at Menarche in Selected Northern European Countries and the United States from 1845 to 1969. Notice the steep decline in the age at which girls experienced menarche in four northern European countries and the United States from 1845 to 1969. Recently the age at which girls experience menarche has been leveling off.

Adolescents show a strong preoccupation with their changing bodies and develop images of what their bodies are like. *Why might adolescent males have more positive body images than adolescent females?*

testosterone levels increased eighteenfold in boys but only twofold in girls during puberty; estradiol increased eightfold in girls but only twofold in boys (Nottelmann & others, 1987). Thus, both testosterone and estradiol are present in the hormonal makeup of both boys and girls, but testosterone dominates in male pubertal development, estradiol in female pubertal development (Richmond & Rogol, 2007).

The same influx of hormones that grows hair on a male's chest and increases the fatty tissue in a female's breasts may also contribute to psychological development in adolescence (DeRose & Brooks-Gunn, 2008; Vermeersch & others, 2008). In one study of boys and girls ranging in age from 9 to 14, a higher concentration of testosterone was present in boys who rated themselves as more socially competent (Nottelmann & others, 1987). However, hormonal effects by themselves do not account for adolescent development (Dorn & others, 2006; Graber, 2008). For example, in one study, social factors were much better predictors of young adolescent girls' depression and anger than hormonal factors (Brooks-Gunn & Warren, 1989). Behavior and moods also can affect hormones (DeRose & Brooks-Gunn, 2008). Stress, eating patterns, exercise, sexual activity, tension, and depression can activate or suppress various aspects of the hormonal system (Foster & Brooks-Gunn, 2008; Sontag & others, 2008). In sum, the hormone-behavior link is complex.

Timing and Variations in Puberty   In the United States—where children mature up to a year earlier than children in European countries—the average age of menarche has declined significantly since the mid-nineteenth century (see Figure 11.2). Fortunately, however, we are unlikely to see pubescent toddlers, since what has happened in the past century is likely the result of improved nutrition and health.

Why do the changes of puberty occur when they do, and how can variations in their timing be explained? The basic genetic program for puberty is wired into the species (Divall & Radovick, 2008), but nutrition, health, and other environmental factors also affect puberty's timing and makeup (Hermann-Giddens, 2006, 2007; Ji & Chen, 2008; McDowell, Brody, & Hughes, 2007).

For most boys, the pubertal sequence may begin as early as age 10 or as late as $13\frac{1}{2}$, and may end as early as age 13 or as late as 17. Thus the normal range is wide enough that, given two boys of the same chronological age, one might complete the pubertal sequence before the other one has begun it. For girls, menarche is considered within the normal range if it appears between the ages of 9 and 15.

Body Image   One psychological aspect of physical change in puberty is certain: Adolescents are preoccupied with their bodies and develop images of what their bodies are like (Allen & others, 2008; Jones, Bain & King, 2008). Preoccupation with body image is strong throughout adolescence, but it is especially acute during early adolescence, a time when adolescents are more dissatisfied with their bodies than in late adolescence (Graber & Brooks-Gunn, 2002).

Gender differences characterize adolescents' perceptions of their bodies. In general, girls are less happy with their bodies and have more negative body images than boys throughout puberty (Bearman & others, 2006). As pubertal change proceeds, girls often become more dissatisfied with their bodies, probably because their body fat increases. In contrast, boys become more satisfied as they move through puberty, probably because their muscle mass increases (Bearman & others, 2006). Here is a sampling of recent research on body image in adolescence:

• *Appearance.* Adolescent males who evaluated their appearance more positively and who said appearance was very important to them were more likely to engage in risky sexy behavior, whereas adolescent females who evaluated their appearance more positively were less likely to engage in risky behavior (Gillen, Lefkowitz, & Shearer, 2006).

- *Physical and mental health problems.* A longitudinal study of more than 2,500 adolescents found that lower body satisfaction placed them at risk for poorer overall health (Neumark-Sztainer & others, 2006). Another study indicated that 12- to 17-year-old female patients in psychiatric hospitals who had a negative body image were more depressed, anxiety-prone, and suicidal than same-aged female patients who were less concerned about their body image (Dyl & others, 2006).

- *Best and worst aspects of being a boy or a girl.* The negative aspects of puberty for girls appeared in a recent study that explored 400 middle school boys' and girls' perceptions of the best and worst aspects of being a boy or a girl (Zittleman, 2006). In the views of the middle school students, at the top of the list of the worst things about being a girl was the biology of being female, which included such matters as childbirth, PMS, periods, and breast cancer. The middle school students said that aspects of discipline (such as getting into trouble and being blamed more than girls even when they were not at fault) are the worst things about being a boy. However, another aspect of physical development was at the top of the students' list of the best things about being a girl—appearance (which included choosing clothes, hair styles, and beauty treatments). Students said the best thing about being a boy was playing sports.

Body art, such as tattoos and body piercing, is increasing in adolescence and emerging adulthood. *Why do youth engage in such body modification?*

Although we have described gender differences in the body images of adolescents, emphasizing that girls tend to have more negative body images than boys, keep in mind that there is considerable variation with many adolescent girls having positive body images and many adolescent boys having negative body images. Further, a recent research review revealed an increase in body satisfaction for non-Latino White adolescent girls but not for African American adolescent girls (Grabe & Hyde, 2006).

Body Art An increasing number of adolescents are obtaining tattoos and getting parts of their body pierced (Mayers & Chiffriller, 2008). Many of these youth engage in such body modification to be different, to stamp their identity as unique. In one study of adolescents, 60 percent of the students with tattoos had academic grades of As and Bs (Armstrong, 1995). In this study, the average age at which the adolescents got their first tattoo was 14 years of age. Some studies indicate that tattoos and body piercings are markers for risk taking in adolescence (Deschesnes, Fines, & Demers, 2006). A recent study revealed that having multiple body piercings is especially a marker for risk-taking behavior (Suris & others, 2007). However, other researchers argue that body art is increasingly used to express individuality and self-expression rather than rebellion (Armstrong & others, 2004).

Early and Late Maturation Some of you entered puberty early, others late, and still others right on time. Adolescents who mature earlier or later than their peers perceive themselves differently (Costello & others, 2007). In the Berkeley Longitudinal Study some years ago, early-maturing boys perceived themselves more positively and had more successful peer relations than did their late-maturing counterparts (Jones, 1965). When the late-maturing boys were in their thirties, however, they had developed a stronger sense of identity than the early-maturing boys had (Peskin, 1967). This may have occurred because the late-maturing boys had more time to explore life's options, or because the early-maturing boys continued to focus on their advantageous physical status instead of on career development and achievement. More recent research confirms, though, that at least during adolescence it is advantageous to be an early-maturing rather than a late-maturing boy (Graber, Brooks-Gunn, & Warren, 2006).

For girls, early and late maturation have been linked with body image. In the sixth grade, early-maturing girls show greater satisfaction with their figures than do late-maturing girls, but by the tenth grade late-maturing girls are more satisfied (Simmons & Blyth, 1987) (see Figure 11.3). One possible reason for this is that in late

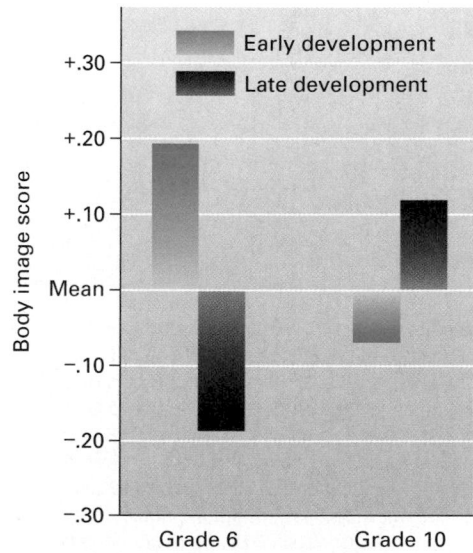

FIGURE 11.3 Early- and Late-Maturing Adolescent Girls' Perceptions of Body Image in Early and Late Adolescence. The sixth-grade girls in this study had positive body images scores if they were early-maturers but negative body image scores if they were late-maturers (Simmons & Blyth, 1987). Positive body image scores indicated satisfaction with their figures. By the tenth grade, however, it was the late-maturers who had positive body image scores.

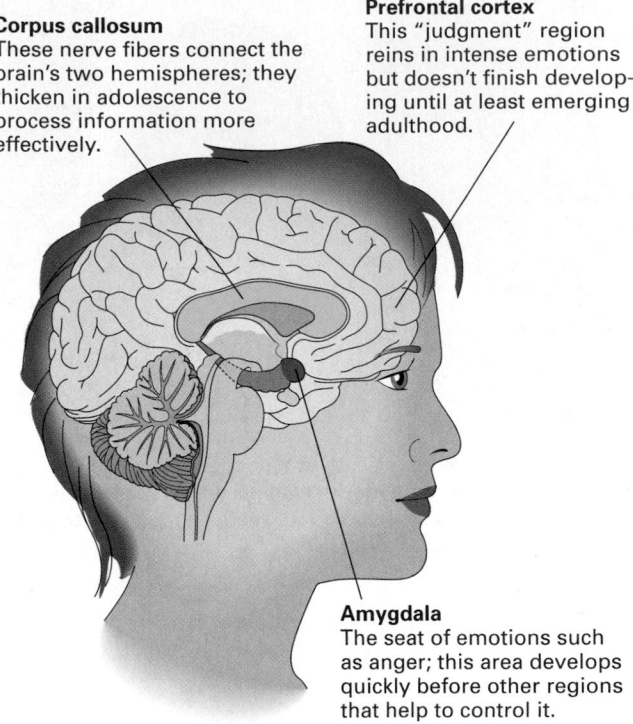

Corpus callosum
These nerve fibers connect the brain's two hemispheres; they thicken in adolescence to process information more effectively.

Prefrontal cortex
This "judgment" region reins in intense emotions but doesn't finish developing until at least emerging adulthood.

Amygdala
The seat of emotions such as anger; this area develops quickly before other regions that help to control it.

FIGURE 11.4 Changes in the Adolescent Brain

Lee Malvo was 17 years old, when he and John Muhammad, an adult, went on a sniper spree in 2002, terrorizing the Washington, D.C., area and killing ten people. A 2005 U.S. Supreme Court ruling stated that individuals who are 18 years of age and under, like Malvo, cannot be given the death penalty. *Are there implications for what scientists are learning about the adolescent's brain for legal decisions, such as the death penalty?*

corpus callosum The location where fibers connect the brain's left and right hemispheres

amygdala The region of the brain that is the seat of emotions.

adolescence early-maturing girls are shorter and stockier, whereas late-maturing girls are taller and thinner. Thus, late-maturing girls in late adolescence have bodies that more closely approximate the current American ideal of feminine beauty—tall and thin.

An increasing number of researchers have found that early maturation increases girls' vulnerability to a number of problems (Biehl, Natsuaki, & Ge, 2007; Mendle, Turkheimer, & Emery, 2007). Early-maturing girls are more likely to smoke, drink, be depressed, have an eating disorder, struggle for earlier independence from their parents, and have older friends; and their bodies are likely to elicit responses from males that lead to earlier dating and earlier sexual experiences (Wiesner & Ittel, 2002). For example, a recent study revealed that early maturing girls were more likely to try cigarettes and alcohol without their parents' knowledge (Westling & others, 2008).

The Brain

Along with the rest of the body, the brain is changing during adolescence, but the study of adolescent brain development is in its infancy. As advances in technology take place, significant strides will also likely be made in charting developmental changes in the adolescent brain (Giedd, 2008; McAnarney, 2008; Steinberg, 2009). What do we know now?

Using fMRI brain scans, scientists have recently discovered that adolescents' brains undergo significant structural changes (Casey, Getz, & Galvan, 2008; Toga, Thompson, & Sowell, 2006). The **corpus callosum**, where fibers connect the brain's left and right hemispheres, thickens in adolescence, and this improves adolescents' ability to process information (Giedd & others, 2006). We described advances in the development of the *prefrontal cortex*—the highest level of the frontal lobes involved in reasoning, decision making, and self-control—in Chapters 8 and 10. However, the prefrontal cortex doesn't finish maturing until the emerging adult years, approximately 18 to 25 years of age, or later, but the **amygdala**—the seat of emotions such as anger—matures earlier than the prefrontal cortex. Figure 11.4 shows the locations of the corpus callosum, prefrontal cortex, and amygdala.

Leading researcher Charles Nelson (2003) points out that although adolescents are capable of very strong emotions their prefrontal cortex hasn't adequately developed to the point at which they can control these passions. It is as if their brain doesn't have the brakes to slow down their emotions. Or consider this interpretation of the development of emotion and cognition in adolescents: "early activation of strong 'turbo-charged' feelings with a relatively un-skilled set of 'driving skills' or cognitive abilities to modulate strong emotions and motivations" (Dahl, 2004, p. 18).

Of course, a major issue is which comes first, biological changes in the brain or experiences that stimulate these changes? (Lerner, Boyd, & Du, 2008). Consider a recent study in which the prefrontal cortex thickened and more brain connections formed when adolescents resisted peer pressure (Paus & others, 2008). Scientists have yet to determine whether the brain changes come first or whether the brain changes are the result of experiences with peers, parents, and others. Once again, we encounter the nature/nurture issue that is so prominent in examining development through the life span.

Are there implications of what we now know about changes in the adolescent's brain for taking drugs and the legal system? According to leading expert Jay Giedd (2007, pp. 1-2D), "Biology doesn't make teens rebellious or have purple hair or take drugs. It does not mean you are going to do drugs, but it gives you more of a chance to do that." Also, can the recent brain research we have just discussed be used to argue that because the adolescent's brain, especially the higher-level prefrontal cortex, is still developing, adolescents should not be given a death penalty? Leading expert Elizabeth Sowell (2004) says that scientists can't just do brain scans on adolescents and decide if they should be tried as adults. In 2005, the death penalty for adolescents (under the age of 18) was prohibited by the U.S. Supreme Court, but it still continues to be debated (Ash, 2006).

Adolescent Sexuality

Not only are adolescents characterized by substantial changes in physical growth and the development of the brain, but adolescence also is a bridge between the asexual child and the sexual adult (Kelly, 2008; Strong & others, 2008). Adolescence is a time of sexual exploration and experimentation, of sexual fantasies and realities, of incorporating sexuality into one's identity. Adolescents have an almost insatiable curiosity about sexuality. They are concerned about whether they are sexually attractive, how to do sex, and what the future holds for their sexual lives. Although most adolescents experience times of vulnerability and confusion, the majority will eventually develop a mature sexual identity.

Every society gives some attention to adolescent sexuality. In some societies, adults clamp down and protect adolescent females from males by chaperoning them; other societies promote very early marriage. Then there are societies that allow some sexual experimentation.

In the United States; the sexual culture is widely available to adolescents. They learn a great deal about sex from television, videos, magazines, the lyrics of popular music, and Web sites (Epstein & Ward, 2008; Hyde & Price, 2007).

How might watching sex on television be linked to adolescents' behavior? One study of 1,762 12- to 17-year-olds found that watching more sexually explicit TV shows was linked with an increased likelihood of initiating sexual intercourse in the next 12 months (Collins & others, 2004). Adolescents in the highest 10 percent of viewing sexually explicit TV shows were twice as likely to engage in sexual intercourse as those in the lowest 10 percent. The results held regardless of whether the TV programs involved actual sexual behavior or just talk about sex. Another recent study revealed that more frequent viewing and stronger identification with popular TV characters were related to greater levels of sexual activity in one's peers (Ward & Friedman, 2006).

Developing a Sexual Identity   Mastering emerging sexual feelings and forming a sense of sexual identity is a multifaceted and lengthy process. It involves learning to manage sexual feelings (such as sexual arousal and attraction), developing new forms of intimacy, and learning the skills to regulate sexual behavior to avoid undesirable consequences.

An adolescent's sexual identity involves activities, interests, styles of behavior, and an indication of sexual orientation (whether an individual has same-sex or other-sex attractions) (Buzwell & Rosenthal, 1996). For example, some adolescents have a high anxiety level about sex, others a low level. Some adolescents are strongly aroused sexually, others less so. Some adolescents are very active sexually, others not at all. Some adolescents are sexually inactive in response to their strong religious upbringing; others go to church regularly, yet their religious training does not inhibit their sexual activity (Thorton & Camburn, 1989).

It is commonly believed that most gay males and lesbians quietly struggle with same-sex attractions in childhood, do not engage in heterosexual dating, and gradually recognize that they are a gay male or a lesbian in mid to late adolescence (Savin-Williams & Diamond, 2004). Many youth do follow this developmental pathway, but others do not (Bos & others, 2008; Diamond, 2008). For example, many youth have no recollection of early same-sex attractions and experience a more abrupt sense of their same-sex attraction in late adolescence (Savin-Williams, 2006). Researchers also have found that the majority of adolescents with same-sex attractions also experience some degree of other-sex attractions (Garofalo & others, 1999). Even though some adolescents who are attracted to individuals of their same sex fall in love with these individuals, others claim that their same-sex attractions are purely physical (Savin-Williams, 2006, 2008a, b).

Sex is virtually everywhere in the American culture and is used to sell just about everything. *What evidence is cited in the text to indicate that messages from the media influence adolescents' attitudes or behavior?*

*S*exual arousal emerges as a new phenomenon in adolescence and it is important to view sexuality as a normal aspect of adolescent development.

—**Shirley Feldman**
Contemporary Psychologist, Stanford University

What characterizes same-sex attractions in adolescence?

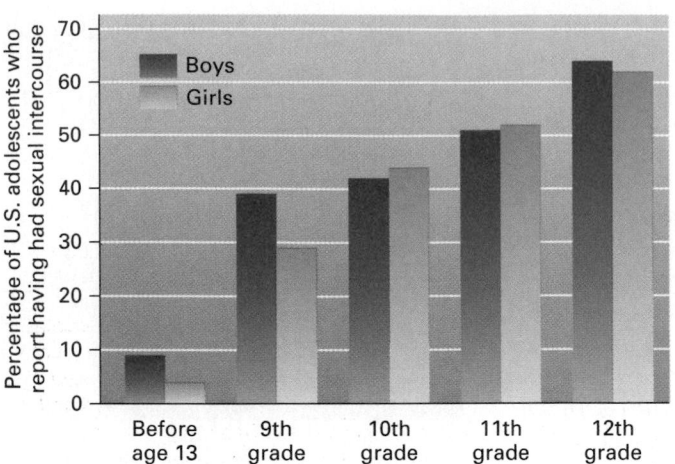

FIGURE 11.5 Timing of Sexual Intercourse in U.S. Adolescents

What are some risks for early initiation of sexual intercourse?

In sum, gay male and lesbian youth have diverse patterns of initial attraction, often have bisexual attractions, and may have physical or emotional attraction to same-sex individuals but do not always fall in love with them (Diamond, 2008; Savin-Williams & Cohen, 2007; Savin-Williams & Ream, 2007). In Chapter 13, "Physical and Cognitive Development in Early Adulthood," we will further explore same-sex and heterosexual attraction.

The Timing of Adolescent Sexual Behaviors The timing of sexual initiation varies by country as well as by gender and other socioeconomic characteristics (Eaton & others, 2008). In one cross-cultural study, among females, the proportion having first intercourse by age 17 ranged from 72 percent in Mali to 47 percent in the United States and 45 percent in Tanzania (Singh & others, 2000). The percentage of males who had their first intercourse by age 17 ranged from 76 percent in Jamaica to 64 percent in the United States and 63 percent in Brazil. Within the United States, male, African American, and inner-city adolescents report being the most sexually active, whereas Asian American adolescents have the most restrictive sexual timetable (Feldman, Turner, & Araujo, 1999).

A recent national survey revealed that 63 percent of twelfth-graders (64 percent of males, 62 percent of females) reported that they had experienced sexual intercourse compared with 34 percent of ninth-graders (39 percent of males, 29 percent of females) (MMWR, 2006) (see Figure 11.5. By age 20, 77 percent of U.S. youth have engaged in sexual intercourse (Dworkin & Santelli, 2007).

Many adolescents are not emotionally prepared to handle sexual experiences, especially in early adolescence. Early sexual activity is linked with risky behaviors such as drug use, delinquency, and school-related problems (Armour & Haynie, 2007; Dryfoos & Barkin, 2006). In a longitudinal study from 10 to 12 years of age to 25 years of age, early sexual intercourse and affiliation with deviant peers were linked to substance use disorders in emerging adulthood (Cornelius & others, 2007). A recent study revealed that not feeling close to their parents, having low self-esteem, and watching television extensively were linked to adolescents being sexually active at 15 years of age (Hyde & Price, 2007). And a recent research review found that earlier onset of sexual intercourse was linked to living with other than two biological parents and a lower level of parental monitoring (Zimmer-Gembeck & Helfand, 2008).

There has been a dramatic increase in oral sex during adolescence (Bersamin & others, 2006; Brewster & Harker Tillman, 2008). In a national survey, 55 percent of U.S. 15- to 19-year-old boys and 54 percent of girls said they had engaged in oral sex (National Center for Health Statistics, 2002). In the survey, more than 20 percent of the adolescents who had not had sexual intercourse had engaged in oral sex. A recent study found that adolescents who engaged in oral sex were older, had engaged in heavy drinking in the past month, perceived their peers to be sexually active, and thought their friends would approve of their sexual activity more than adolescents who had not engaged in oral sex (Bersamin & others, 2006). What is especially worrisome about the increase in oral sex during adolescence is how casually many engage in the practice. It appears that for many adolescents oral sex is a recreational activity practiced outside of an intimate, caring relationship (Walsh & Bennett, 2004). One reason for the increase in oral sex during adolescence is the belief that oral sex is not really sex, so technically those who engage in oral sex but not sexual intercourse consider themselves technically still to be virgins. Another reason for the increase is the perception that oral sex is likely to be safer and less likely to result in sexually transmitted infections than sexual intercourse. Thus, many adolescents appear to be unaware of the health risks linked to oral sex, such as the possibility of contracting infections such as HIV.

Contraceptive Use Sexual activity carries with it considerable risks if appropriate safeguards are not taken (Carroll, 2007; Strong & others, 2008). Youth encounter two kinds of risks: unintended unwanted pregnancy and sexually transmitted infections. Both of these risks can be reduced significantly if contraception is used.

The good news is that adolescents are increasing their use of contraceptives (Frost, Darroch, & Ramez, 2008; Santelli & others, 2007). For example, a recent large-scale study revealed a substantial increase in the use of a contraceptive (61.5 percent in 2007 compared with 46.2 percent in 1991) by U.S. high school students during the last time they had sexual intercourse (among students who were sexually active (Centers for Disease Control and Prevention, 2008).

Although adolescent contraceptive use is increasing, many sexually active adolescents still do not use contraceptives, or they use them inconsistently (Holocombe & others, 2008). A recent study of female adolescents living in low-income circumstances revealed that those who inconsistently used contraceptives were more likely to have a desire to become pregnant, have less frequent communication with their partners about contraceptive use, and have a greater number of life sexual partners than their counterparts who consistently used contraceptives (Davies & others, 2006).

Sexually Transmitted Infections   Some forms of contraception, such as birth control pills or implants, do not protect against sexually transmitted infections, or STIs. **Sexually transmitted infections (STIs)** are contracted primarily through sexual contact, including oral-genital and anal-genital contact. Every year more than 3 million American adolescents (about one-fourth of those who are sexually experienced) acquire an STI (Centers for Disease Control and Prevention, 2006). In a single act of unprotected sex with an infected partner, a teenage girl has a 1 percent risk of getting HIV, a 30 percent risk of acquiring genital herpes, and a 50 percent chance of contracting gonorrhea (Glei, 1999). Yet another very widespread STI is chlamydia. In Chapter 13, we will describe these and other sexually transmitted infections.

Adolescent Pregnancy   In cross-cultural comparisons, the United States continues to have one of the highest adolescent pregnancy and childbearing rates in the industrialized world, despite a considerable decline in the 1990s (Centers for Disease Control and Prevention, 2002). As Figure 11.6 shows, the U.S. adolescent pregnancy rate is five times as high as in Sweden. This dramatic difference exists in spite of the fact that U.S. adolescents are no more sexually active than their counterparts in the Sweden.

Despite the negative comparisons of the United States with many other developed countries, there are encouraging trends in U.S. adolescent pregnancy rates (Santelli & others, 2007). In 2004, births to adolescent girls fell to a record low (Child Trends, 2006). The rate of births to adolescent girls has dropped 30 percent since 1991. Reasons for these declines include increased contraceptive use and fear of sexually transmitted infections such as AIDS.

Outcomes   Adolescent pregnancy creates health risks for both the baby and the mother. Infants born to adolescent mothers are more likely to have low birth weights— a prominent factor in infant mortality—as well as neurological problems and childhood illness (Chedraui, 2008). Adolescent mothers often drop out of school. Although many adolescent mothers resume their education later in life, they generally never catch up economically with women who postpone childbearing until their twenties. One longitudinal study found that the children of women who had their first birth during their teens had lower achievement test scores and more behavioral problems than did children whose mothers had their first birth as adults (Hofferth & Reid, 2002).

Though the consequences of America's high adolescent pregnancy rate are cause for great concern, it often is not pregnancy alone that leads to negative consequences for an adolescent mother and her offspring (Oxford & others, 2006). Adolescent mothers are more likely to come from low-SES backgrounds (Crosby & Holtgrave, 2006). Many adolescent mothers also were not good students before they became pregnant (Malamitsi-Puchner & Boutsikou, 2006). However, not every adolescent female who

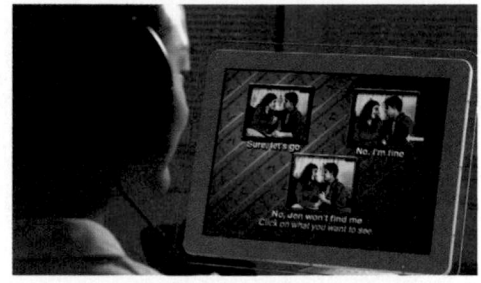

Psychologists are exploring ways to encourage adolescents to make less risky sexual decisions. Here an adolescent participates in an interactive video session developed by Julie Downs and her colleagues at the Department of Social and Decision Making Sciences at Carnegie Mellon University. The videos help adolescents evaluate their responses and decisions in high-risk sexual contexts.

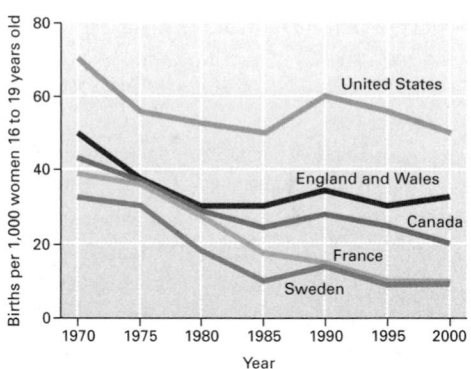

FIGURE 11.6 Cross-Cultural Comparisons of Adolescent Pregnancy Rates. Pregnancy rates among U.S. adolescents are among the highest in the industrialized world (Centers for Disease Control and Prevention, 2002).

Sexually transmitted infections (STIs) Infections that are contracted primarily through sexual contact, including oral-genital and anal-genital contact.

bears a child lives a life of poverty and low achievement. Thus, although adolescent pregnancy is a high-risk circumstance, and adolescents who do not become pregnant generally fare better than those who do, some adolescent mothers do well in school and have positive outcomes (Leadbeater & Way, 2000).

Serious, extensive efforts are needed to help pregnant adolescents and young mothers enhance their educational and occupational opportunities (Key & others, 2008). Adolescent mothers also need help in obtaining competent child care and in planning for the future (Jumping-Eagle & others, 2008).

All adolescents can benefit from age-appropriate family-life education (Weyman, 2003). Family and consumer science educators teach life skills, such as effective decision making, to adolescents. To read about the work of one family and consumer science educator, see the *Careers in Life-Span Development* profile. And to learn more about ways to reduce adolescent pregnancy, see the *Applications in Life-Span Development* interlude.

Careers in Life-Span Development

Lynn Blankenship, Family and Consumer Science Educator

Lynn Blankenship is a family and consumer science educator. She has an undergraduate degree in this area from the University of Arizona. She has taught for more than 20 years, the last 14 at Tucson High Magnet School.

Blankenship was awarded the Tucson Federation of Teachers Educator of the Year Award for 1999–2000 and the Arizona Teacher of the Year in 1999.

Blankenship especially enjoys teaching life skills to adolescents. One of her favorite activities is having students care for an automated baby that imitates the needs of real babies. She says that this program has a profound impact on students because the baby must be cared for around the clock for the duration of the assignment. Blankenship also coordinates real-world work experiences and training for students in several child-care facilities in the Tucson area.

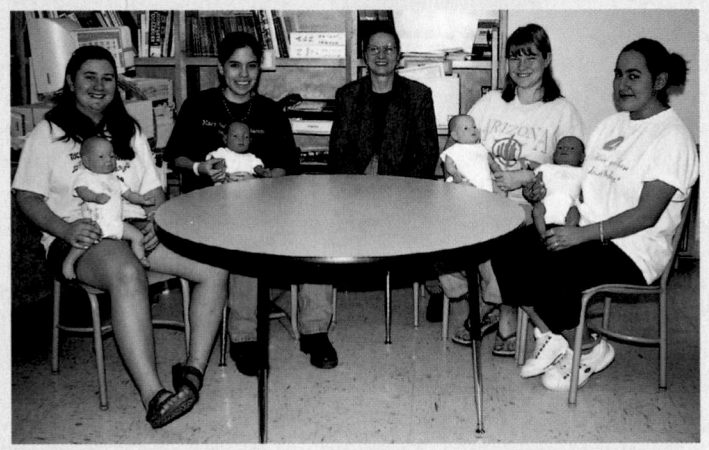

Lynn Blankenship (*center*) teaching life skills to students.

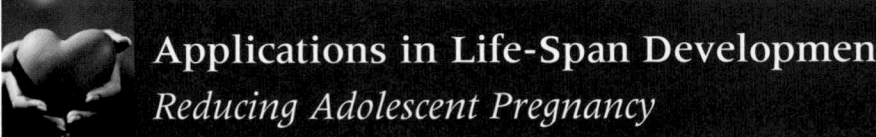

Applications in Life-Span Development
Reducing Adolescent Pregnancy

One strategy for reducing adolescent pregnancy, called the Teen Outreach Program (TOP), focuses on engaging adolescents in volunteer community service and stimulates discussions that help adolescents appreciate the lessons they learn through volunteerism. In one study, 695 adolescents in grades 9 to 12 were randomly assigned to either a Teen Outreach group or a control group (Allen & others, 1997). They were assessed at both program entry and at program exit nine months later. The rate of pregnancy was substantially lower for the Teen Outreach adolescents. These adolescents also had a lower rate of school failure and academic suspension.

Girls, Inc., has four programs that are intended to increase adolescent girls' motivation to avoid pregnancy until they are mature enough to make responsible decisions about motherhood (Roth & others, 1998). Growing Together, a series of five two-hour workshops for mothers and adolescents, and Will Power/Won't Power, a series of six two-hour sessions that focus on assertiveness training,

These are not adolescent mothers, but rather adolescents who are participating in the Teen Outreach Program (TOP), which engages adolescents in volunteer community service. These adolescent girls are serving as volunteers in a child-care center for crack babies. Researchers have found that such volunteer experiences can reduce the rate of adolescent pregnancy.

are for 12- to 14-year-old girls. For older adolescent girls, Taking Care of Business provides nine sessions that emphasize career planning as well as information about sexuality, reproduction, and contraception. Health Bridge coordinates health and education services—girls can participate in this program as one of their club activities. Girls who participated in these programs were less likely to get pregnant than girls who did not participate (Girls, Inc., 1991).

Currently, a major controversy in sex education is whether schools should have an abstinence-only program or a program that emphasizes contraceptive knowledge (Cabezon & others, 2005). Two recent research reviews found that abstinence-only programs do not delay the initiation of sexual intercourse and do not reduce HIV risk behaviors (Kirby, Laris, & Rolleir, 2007; Underhill, Montgomery, & Operario, 2007). Further, a recent study revealed that adolescents who experienced comprehensive sex education were less likely to report adolescent pregnancies than those who were given abstinence-only sex education or no education (Kohler, Manhart, & Lafferty, 2008). A number of leading experts on adolescent sexuality conclude that sex education programs which emphasize contraceptive knowledge do not increase the incidence of sexual intercourse and are more likely to reduce the risk of adolescent pregnancy and sexually transmitted infections than abstinence-only programs (Alan Guttmacher Institute, 2007; Constantine, 2008; Eisenberg & others, 2008; Dworkin & Santelli, 2007; Hyde & DeLamater, 2008).

Review and Reflect: Learning Goal 2

 Describe the Changes Involved in Puberty as Well as Changes in the Brain and Sexuality During Adolescence

REVIEW

- What are some key aspects of puberty?
- What changes typically occur in the brain during adolescence?
- What are some important aspects of sexuality in adolescence?

REFLECT

- Did you experience puberty early or late? How did this timing affect your development?

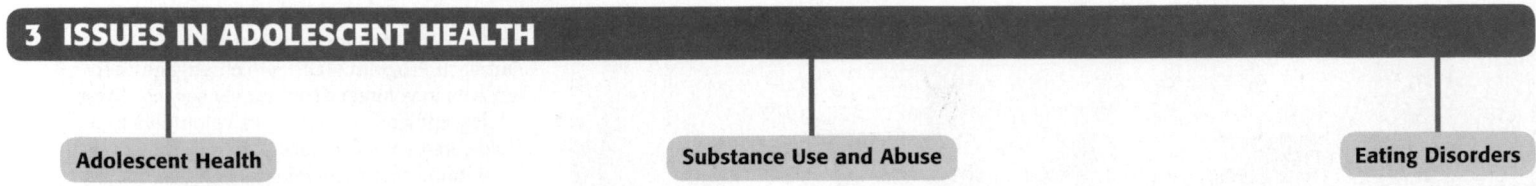

3 ISSUES IN ADOLESCENT HEALTH

Adolescent Health   **Substance Use and Abuse**   **Eating Disorders**

Many health experts argue that whether adolescents are healthy depends primarily on their own behavior. To improve adolescent health, adults should aim to (1) increase adolescents' health-enhancing behaviors, such as eating nutritiously, exercising, wearing seat belts, and getting adequate sleep; and (2) reduce adolescents' health-compromising behaviors, such as drug abuse, violence, unprotected sexual intercourse, and dangerous driving.

Adolescent Health

Adolescence is a critical juncture in the adoption of behaviors that are relevant to health (Park & others, 2008; Sirard & Barr-Anderson, 2008). Many of the behaviors that are linked to poor health habits and early death in adults begin during adolescence. Conversely, the early formation of healthy behavior patterns, such as regular exercise and a preference for foods low in fat and cholesterol, not only has immediate health benefits but helps in adulthood to delay or prevent disability and mortality from heart disease, stroke, diabetes, and cancer (Schiff, 2009).

Nutrition and Exercise Concerns are growing about adolescents' nutrition and exercise (Robbins, Powers, & Burgess, 2008; Sabiston & Crocker, 2008). The percentage of overweight U.S.12- to 19-year-olds increased from 11 to 17 percent for from the early 1990s through 2004 (Eaton & others, 2006). The negative outcomes of being overweight in adolescence were revealed in a recent study that found 62 percent of the male and 73 percent of the female adolescents in the 85th to 94th percentile of body mass index (BMI) became obese adults (Wang & others, 2008). In this study, of those at the 95th percentile and higher for BMI, 80 percent of the male and 92 percent of the female adolescents became obese adults. Other research also indicates increases in being overweight during adolescence in European countries (Irwin, 2004). In a comparison of adolescents in 28 countries, U.S. adolescents ate more junk food than adolescents in most other countries (World Health Organization, 2000). U.S. adolescents were more likely to eat fried foods and less likely to eat fruits and vegetables than adolescents in most other countries studied. U.S. adolescents are decreasing their intake of fruits and vegetables. The National Youth Risk Survey found that U.S. high school students decreased their intake of fruits and vegetables from 1999 through 2005 (MMWR, 2006).

In a cross-cultural study, just two-thirds of U.S. adolescents exercised at least twice a week, compared with 80 percent or more of adolescents in Ireland, Austria, Germany, and the Slovak Republic (World Health Organization, 2000). U.S. boys and girls become less active as they reach and progress through adolescence (Merrick & others, 2005). A study of more than 3,000 U.S. adolescents found that 34 percent were in the lowest fitness category (Carnethon, Gulati, & Greenland, 2005). Another study revealed that physical fitness in adolescence was linked to physical fitness in adulthood (Mikkelsson & others, 2006). Also, a recent study of non-Latino White girls found that higher physical activity at 9 and 11 years of age predicted higher self-esteem at 11 and 13 years of age (Schmalz & others, 2007).

Gender and ethnic differences in exercise participation rates are noteworthy, and they reflect the trend of decreasing exercise from early through late adolescence (Eaton & others, 2008). A recent study revealed that approximately 40 percent of female and 57 percent of male adolescents met U.S. guidelines for physical activity (Butcher & others, 2008). A recent study found that Latino and African American 7- to 14-year-olds had lower aerobic fitness levels than their non-Latino White counterparts (Shaibi, Ball, & Goran, 2006). Also, as indicated in Figure 11.7, in the National

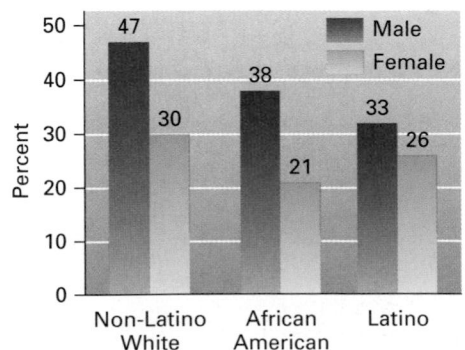

FIGURE 11.7 Exercise Rates of U.S. High School Students: Gender and Ethnicity. *Note:* Data are for high school students who were physically active doing any kind of physical activity that increased their heart rate and made them breathe hard some of the time for a total of at least 60 minutes/day on five or more of the seven days preceding the survey.

Youth Risk Survey, non-Latino White boys exercised the most, African American girls the least (MMWR, 2006).

Sleep Patterns Like nutrition and exercise, sleep is an important influence on well-being. Might changing sleep patterns in adolescence contribute to adolescents' health-compromising behaviors? Recently there has been a surge of interest in adolescent sleep patterns (Liu & others, 2008; Loessi & others, 2008).

The National Sleep Foundation (2006) conducted a U.S. survey of 1,602 caregivers and their 11- to 17-year-olds. Forty-five percent of the adolescents got inadequate sleep on school nights (less than eight hours). Older adolescents (ninth- to twelfth-graders) got markedly less sleep on school nights than younger adolescents (sixth- to eighth-graders)—62 percent of the older adolescents got inadequate sleep compared to 21 percent of the younger adolescents. Adolescents who got inadequate sleep (eight hours or less) on school nights were more likely to feel more tired or sleepy, more cranky and irritable, fall asleep in school, be in a depressed mood, and drink caffeinated beverages than their counterparts who got optimal sleep (nine or more hours). In another recent study of 750 14- to 15-year-olds, getting less sleep at night was linked to higher levels of anxiety, depression, and fatigue the next day (Fuligni & Hardway, 2006).

Many adolescents stay up later at night and sleep longer in the morning than they did when they were children, and this changing timetable has physiological underpinnings (Yang & others, 2005). These findings have implications for the hours during which adolescents learn most effectively in school (Hansen & others, 2005).

Mary Carskadon and her colleagues (2004, 2005, 2006; Jenni & Carskadon, 2007; Tarokh & Carskadon, 2008) have conducted a number of research studies on adolescent sleep patterns. They found that when given the opportunity adolescents will sleep an average of 9 hours and 25 minutes a night. Most get considerably less than nine hours of sleep, especially during the week. This shortfall creates a sleep deficit, which adolescents often attempt to make up on the weekend. The researchers also found that older adolescents tend to be more sleepy during the day than younger adolescents. They theorized that this sleepiness was not due to academic work or social pressures. Rather, their research suggests that adolescents' biological clocks undergo a shift as they get older, delaying their period of wakefulness by about one hour. A delay in the nightly release of the sleep-inducing hormone melatonin, which is produced in the brain's pineal gland, seems to underlie this shift. Melatonin is secreted at about 9:30 P.M. in younger adolescents and approximately an hour later in older adolescents.

Carskadon has suggested that early school starting times may cause grogginess, inattention in class, and poor performance on tests. Based on her research, school officials in Edina, Minnesota, decided to start classes at 8:30 A.M. rather than the usual 7:25 A.M. Since then there have been fewer referrals for discipline problems, and the number of students who report being ill or depressed has decreased. The school system reports that test scores have improved for high school students, but not for middle school students. This finding supports Carskadon's suspicion that early start times are likely to be more stressful for older than for younger adolescents.

Leading Causes of Death in Adolescence The three leading causes of death in adolescence are accidents, homicide, and suicide. More than half of all deaths in adolescents ages 10 to 19 are due to accidents, and most of those, especially among older adolescents, involve motor vehicles. Risky driving habits, such as speeding, tailgating, and driving under the influence of alcohol or other drugs, may be more important causes of these accidents than is lack of driving experience. In about 50 percent of the motor vehicle fatalities involving an adolescent, the driver has a blood alcohol level of 0.10 percent, twice the level needed to be "under the influence" in some states. A high rate of intoxication is also often present in adolescents who die as pedestrians or while using recreational vehicles.

In Mary Carskadon's sleep laboratory at Brown University, an adolescent girl's brain activity is being monitored. Carskadon (2005) says that in the morning, sleep-deprived adolescents' "brains are telling them its night time . . . and the rest of the world is saying it's time to go to school" (p. 19).

A makeshift memorial for Mehlville High School student Megan Landholt stands on Lemay Ferry Road in South St. Louis County, MO, Friday, March 7, 2003. Car crashes resulting in eight teenage deaths in South St. Louis County in the past year and a half led police to hold a meeting at Oakville Senior High School to talk about ways to reduce fatalities.

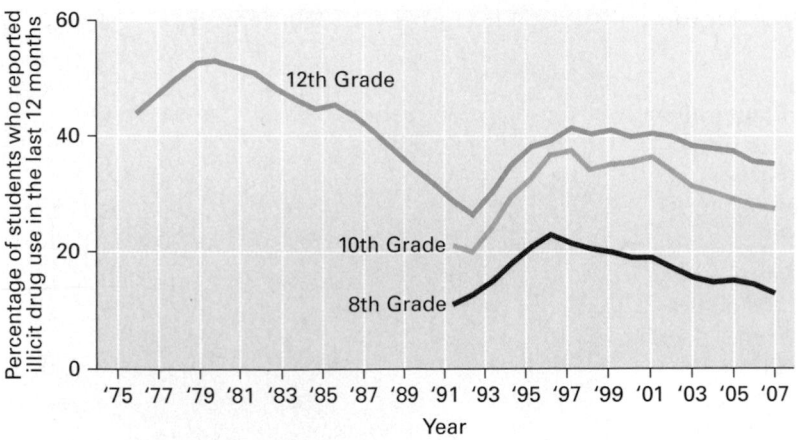

FIGURE 11.8 Trends in Drug Use by U.S. Eighth-, Tenth-, and Twelfth-Grade Students. This graph shows the percentage of U.S. eighth-, tenth-, and twelfth-grade students who reported having taken an illicit drug in the last 12 months from 1991 to 2007, for eighth- and tenth-graders, and from 1975 to 2007, for twelfth-graders (Johnston & others, 2008).

Homicide is the second leading cause of death in adolescence (National Center for Health Statistics, 2006), especially among African American male adolescents. The adolescent suicide rate has tripled since the 1950s. Suicide accounts for 6 percent of the deaths in the 10-to-14 age group and 12 percent of deaths in the 15-to-19 age group. We will discuss suicide further in Chapter 12.

Substance Use and Abuse

Each year since 1975, Lloyd Johnston and his colleagues at the Institute of Social Research at the University of Michigan have monitored the drug use of America's high school seniors in a wide range of public and private high schools. Since 1991, they also have surveyed drug use by eighth- and tenth-graders. In 2007, the University of Michigan study, called the Monitoring the Future Study, surveyed 50,000 students in nearly 400 secondary schools.

According to this study, the proportions of eighth-, tenth-, and twelfth-grade U.S. students who used any illicit drug declined in the late 1990s and first years of the twenty-first century (Johnston & others, 2008) (see Figure 11.8). Nonetheless, even with the recent decline in use, the United States still has one of the highest rates of adolescent drug use of any industrialized nation. For example, one study revealed that a higher percentage of U.S. adolescents have used an illicit drug than adolescents in most European countries (Hibell & others, 2004).

How extensive is alcohol use by U.S. adolescents? Sizeable declines in adolescence alcohol use have occurred in recent years (Johnston & others, 2008). The percentage of U.S. eighth-graders saying that they had any alcohol to drink in the past 30 days fell from a 1996 high of 26 percent to 16 percent in 2007. The 30-day prevalence fell among tenth-graders from 39 percent in 2001 to 33 percent in 2007 and among high school seniors from 72 percent in 1980 to 44 percent in 2007. Binge drinking (defined in the University of Michigan surveys as having five or more drinks in a row in the last two weeks) by high school seniors declined from 41 percent in 1980 to 29 percent in 2007. Binge drinking by eighth- and tenth-graders also has dropped in recent years. A consistent sex difference occurs in binge drinking, with males engaging in this more than females.

Cigarette smoking among U.S. adolescents peaked in 1996 and 1997 and has gradually declined since then (Johnston & others, 2008). Following peak use in 1996, smoking rates for U.S. eighth-graders have fallen by 50 percent. In 2007, the percentages of adolescents who said they smoked cigarettes in the last 30 days were 22 percent (twelfth grade), 14 percent (tenth grade), and 7 percent (eighth grade).

Cigarette smoking (in which the active drug is nicotine) is one of the most serious yet preventable health problems. Smoking is likely to begin in grades 7 through 9, although sizable portions of youth are still establishing regular smoking habits during high school and college. Risk factors for becoming a regular smoker in adolescence include having a friend who smoked, a weak academic orientation, and low parental support (Tucker, Ellickson, & Klein, 2003).

An alarming recent trend is use of prescription painkillers by adolescents (Forrester, 2007). A 2004 survey revealed that 18 percent of U.S. adolescents had used Vicodin at some point in their lifetime, and 10 percent had used Oxycontin (Partnership for a Drug-Free America, 2005). These drugs fall into the general class of drugs called narcotics, and they are highly addictive. In this recent national survey, 9 percent of adolescents said they had abused cough medications to intentionally get high. Adolescents cite the medicine cabinets of their parents or of friends' parents as the main source for their prescription painkillers (Johnston & others, 2008).

The Roles of Development, Parents, and Peers A special concern involves adolescents who begin to use drugs early in adolescence or even in childhood (King

& Chassin, 2007). A recent study revealed that individuals who began drinking alcohol before 14 years of age were more likely to become alcohol dependent than their counterparts who began drinking alcohol at 21 years of age or older (Hingson, Heeren, & Winter, 2006). A longitudinal study of individuals from 8 to 42 years of age also found that early onset of drinking was linked to increased risk of heavy drinking in middle age (Pitkanen, Lyyra, & Pulkkinen, 2005)

Parents, peers, social support, and educational success can play important roles in preventing adolescent drug abuse. Positive relationships with parents and others can reduce adolescents' drug use (Wood & others, 2004). In one study, parental control and monitoring were linked with a lower incidence of problem behavior by adolescents, including substance abuse (Fletcher, Steinberg, & Williams-Wheeler, 2004). A recent study also revealed that adolescents who averaged having less than two family dinners a week were more likely to drink alcohol, smoke cigarettes, and abuse prescription drugs than their adolescent counterparts who averaged five or more family dinners a week (CASA, 2007). Another recent study of more than 5,000 middle school students revealed that having friends in their school's social network and having fewer friends who use substances were related to a lower level of substance use (Ennett & others, 2006). Researchers also recently have found that educational success—getting good grades, not dropping out of school, being connected to their school—has a protective role in reducing adolescents' drug use (Bachman & others, 2008). To read about a program created to reduce adolescent drinking and smoking, see the *Research in Life-Span Development* interlude.

What are some factors that contribute to whether adolescents drink heavily?

Research in Life-Span Development
Evaluation of a Family Program Designed to Reduce Drinking and Smoking in Young Adolescents

Few experimental studies have been conducted to determine if family programs can reduce drinking and smoking in young adolescents. In one recent experimental study, 1,326 families with 12- to 14-year-old adolescents living throughout the United States were interviewed (Bauman & others, 2002). After the baseline interviews, participants were randomly assigned either to go through the Family Matters program (experimental group) or to not experience the program (control group) (Bauman & others, 2002).

The families assigned to the Family Matters program received four mailings of booklets. Each mailing was followed by a telephone call from a health educator to "encourage participation by all family members, answer any questions, and record information" (Bauman & others, 2002, pp. 36–37). The first booklet focused on the negative consequences of adolescent substance abuse to the family. The second emphasized "supervision, support, communication skills, attachment, time spent together, educational achievement, conflict reduction, and how well adolescence is understood." The third booklet asked parents to "list things that they do that might inadvertently encourage their child's use of tobacco or alcohol, identify rules that might influence the child's use, and consider ways to monitor use. Then adult family members and the child meet to agree upon rules and sanctions related to adolescent use." Booklet four deals with what "the child can do to resist peer and media pressures for use."

Two follow-up interviews with the parents and adolescents were conducted three months and one year after the experimental group completed the program. Adolescents in the Family Matters program reported lower alcohol and cigarette use both at three months and again one year after the program had been completed. Figure 11.9 shows the results for alcohol.

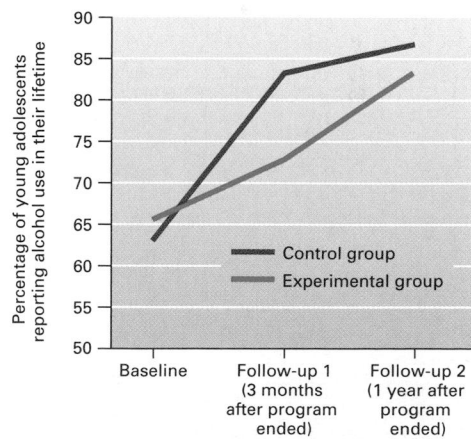

FIGURE 11.9 Young Adolescents' Reports of Alcohol Use in the Family Matters Program. Note that at baseline (before the program started) the young adolescents in the Family Matters program (experimental group) and their counterparts who did not go through the program (control group) reported approximately the same lifetime use of alcohol (slightly higher use by the experimental group). However, three months after the program ended, the experimental group reported lower alcohol use, and this reduction was still present one year after the program ended, although at a reduced level.

Anorexia nervosa has become an increasing problem for adolescent girls and young adult women. *What are some possible causes of anorexia nervosa?*

Eating Disorders

Eating disorders have become increasingly common among adolescents (Kirsch & others, 2007; Stice & others, 2007). Here are some research findings involving adolescent eating disorders:

- *Body image.* In general, adolescencets were dissatisfied with their bodies, with males desiring to increase their upper body and females wanting to decrease the overall size of their body (Ata, Ludden, & Lally, 2007). In this study, low self-esteem and social support, weight-related teasing, and pressure to lose weight were linked to adolescents' negative body image. In another study, girls who felt negatively about their bodies in early adolescence were more likely to develop eating disorders, two years later, than their counterparts who did not feel negatively about their bodies (Attie & Brooks-Gunn, 1989).

- *Parenting.* Adolescents who reported observing more healthy eating patterns and exercise by their parents had more healthy eating patterns and exercised more themselves (Pakpreo & others, 2005). Negative parent-adolescent relationships were linked with increased dieting by girls over a one-year period (Archibald, Graber, & Brooks-Gunn, 1999).

- *Sexual activity.* Girls who were both sexually active with their boyfriends and in pubertal transition were the most likely to be dieting or engaging in disordered eating patterns (Cauffman, 1994).

- *Role models and the media.* Girls who were highly motivated to look like same-sex figures in the media were more likely than their peers to become very concerned about their weight (Field & others, 2001). Watching commercials with idealized thin female images increased adolescent girls' dissatisfaction with their bodies (Hargreaves & Tiggemann, 2004). A recent study of adolescent girls revealed that frequently reading magazine articles about dieting and weight loss was linked with unhealthy weight-control behaviors such as fasting, skipping meals, and smoking more cigarettes five years later (van den Berg & others, 2007).

Let's now examine two eating problems—anorexia nervosa and bulimia nervosa. Researchers consistently have discovered that the onset of anorexia nervosa and bulimia nervosa occurs in adolescence and that their onset in adulthood is rare (Striegel-Moore & Bulik, 2007). They also have found that eating disorders, including anorexia nervosa and bulimia nervosa, are far more likely to characterize females than males (Hoek, 2006).

Anorexia Nervosa   Although most U.S. girls have been on a diet at some point, slightly less than 1 percent ever develop anorexia nervosa. **Anorexia nervosa** is an eating disorder that involves the relentless pursuit of thinness through starvation. It is a serious disorder that can lead to death. Three main characteristics apply to people suffering from anorexia nervosa: (1) weight less than 85 percent of what is considered normal for their age and height; (2) an intense fear of gaining weight that does not decrease with weight loss; and (3) a distorted image of their body shape (Rigaud & others, 2007). Even when they are extremely thin, they see themselves as too fat. They never think they are thin enough, especially in the abdomen, buttocks, and thighs. They usually weigh themselves frequently, often take their body measurements, and gaze critically at themselves in mirrors.

Anorexia nervosa typically begins in the early to middle adolescent years, often following an episode of dieting and some type of life stress. It is about 10 times more likely to occur in females than males. When anorexia nervosa does occur in males, the symptoms and other characteristics (such as a distorted body image and family conflict) are usually similar to those reported by females who have the disorder (Ariceli & others, 2005).

Most anorexics are non-Latino White adolescent or young adult females from well-educated, middle- and upper-income families and are competitive and high-achieving

anorexia nervosa An eating disorder that involves the relentless pursuit of thinness through starvation.

(Schmidt, 2003). They set high standards, become stressed about not being able to reach the standards, and are intensely concerned about how others perceive them. Unable to meet these high expectations, they turn to something they can control: their weight. Offspring of mothers with anorexia nervosa are at risk for becoming anorexic themselves (Striegel-Moore & Bulik, 2007). Problems in family functioning are increasingly being found to be linked to the appearance of anorexia nervosa in adolescent girls (Benninghoven & others, 2007), and a recent research review indicated that family therapy is often the most effective treatment of adolescent girls with anorexia nervosa (Bulik & others, 2007).

The fashion image in U.S. culture contributes to the incidence of anorexia nervosa (Striegel-Moore & Bulik, 2007). The media portray thin as beautiful in their choice of fashion models, who many adolescent girls strive to emulate. And many adolescent girls who strive to be thin hang out together. A recent study of adolescent girls revealed that friends often share similar body image and eating problems (Hutchinson & Rapee, 2007). In this study, an individual girl's dieting and extreme weight-loss behavior could be predicted from her friends' dieting and extreme weight-loss behavior.

Bulimia Nervosa Whereas anorexics control their eating by restricting it, most bulimics cannot. **Bulimia nervosa** is an eating disorder in which the individual consistently follows a binge-and-purge pattern. The bulimic goes on an eating binge and then purges by self-inducing vomiting or using a laxative. Although many people binge and purge occasionally and some experiment with it, a person is considered to have a serious bulimic disorder only if the episodes occur at least twice a week for three months.

As with anorexics, most bulimics are preoccupied with food, have a strong fear of becoming overweight, are depressed or anxious, and have a distorted body image. A recent study revealed that bulimics overvalued their body weight and shape, and this overvaluation was linked to higher depression and lower self-esteem (Hrabosky & others, 2007). Unlike anorexics, people who binge and purge typically fall within a normal weight range, which makes bulimia more difficult to detect.

Approximately 1 to 2 percent of U.S. women are estimated to develop bulimia nervosa, and about 90 percent of bulimics are women. Bulimia nervosa typically begins in late adolescence or early adulthood. Many women who develop bulimia nervosa were somewhat overweight before the onset of the disorder, and the binge eating often began during an episode of dieting. As with anorexia nervosa, about 70 percent of individuals who develop bulimia nervosa eventually recover from the disorder (Agras & others, 2004).

Review and Reflect: Learning Goal 3

 Identify Adolescent Problems Related to Health, Substance Use and Abuse, and Eating Disorders

REVIEW

- What are key concerns about the health of adolescents?
- What are some characteristics of adolescents' substance use and abuse?
- What are the characteristics of the major eating disorders?

REFLECT

- What do you think should be done to reduce the use of drugs by adolescents?

bulimia nervosa An eating disorder in which the individual consistently follows a binge-and-purge pattern.

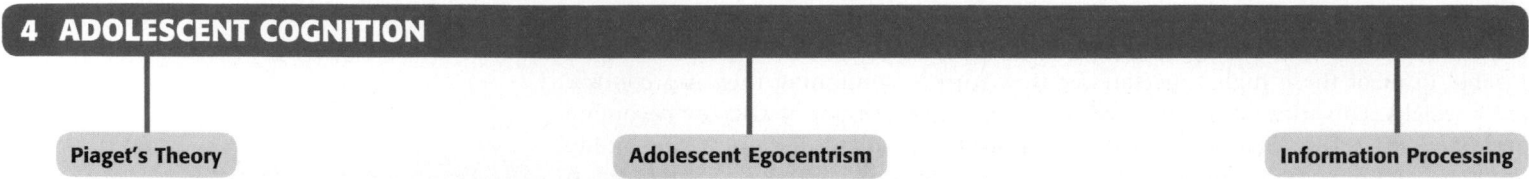

4 ADOLESCENT COGNITION

| Piaget's Theory | Adolescent Egocentrism | Information Processing |

Might adolescents' ability to reason hypothetically and to evaluate what is ideal versus what is real lead them to engage in demonstrations, such as this protest related to better ethnic relations? What other causes might be attractive to adolescents' newfound cognitive abilities of hypothetical-deductive reasoning and idealistic thinking?

> T*he thoughts of youth are long, long thoughts.*
>
> —HENRY WADSWORTH LONGFELLOW
> *American Poet, 19th Century*

hypothetical-deductive reasoning Piaget's formal operational concept that adolescents have the cognitive ability to develop hypotheses, or best guesses, about ways to solve problems, such as an algebraic equation.

Adolescents' developing power of thought opens up new cognitive and social horizons. Let's examine what their developing power of thought is like, beginning with Piaget's theory (1952).

Piaget's Theory

As we discussed in Chapter 9, Piaget proposed that around 7 years of age children enter the *concrete operational stage* of cognitive development. They can reason logically about concrete events and objects, and they make gains in the ability to classify objects and to reason about the relationships between classes of objects. Around age 11, according to Piaget, the fourth and final stage of cognitive development, the formal operational stage, begins.

The Formal Operational Stage What are the characteristics of the formal operational stage? Formal operational thought is more abstract than concrete operational thought. Adolescents are no longer limited to actual, concrete experiences as anchors for thought. They can conjure up make-believe situations, abstract propositions, and events that are purely hypothetical, and can try to reason logically about them.

The abstract quality of thinking during the formal operational stage is evident in the adolescent's verbal problem-solving ability. Whereas the concrete operational thinker needs to see the concrete elements A, B, and C to be able to make the logical inference that if A = B and B = C, then A = C, the formal operational thinker can solve this problem merely through verbal presentation.

Another indication of the abstract quality of adolescents' thought is their increased tendency to think about thought itself. One adolescent commented, "I began thinking about why I was thinking what I was. Then I began thinking about why I was thinking about what I was thinking about what I was." If this sounds abstract, it is, and it characterizes the adolescent's enhanced focus on thought and its abstract qualities.

Accompanying the abstract nature of formal operational thought is thought full of idealism and possibilities, especially during the beginning of the formal operational stage, when assimilation dominates. Adolescents engage in extended speculation about ideal characteristics—qualities they desire in themselves and in others. Such thoughts often lead adolescents to compare themselves with others in regard to such ideal standards. And their thoughts are often fantasy flights into future possibilities.

At the same time that adolescents think more abstractly and idealistically, they also think more logically. Children are likely to solve problems through trial and error; adolescents begin to think more as a scientist thinks, devising plans to solve problems and systematically testing solutions. This type of problem solving requires **hypothetical-deductive reasoning**, which involves creating a hypothesis and deducing its implications, which provides ways to test the hypothesis. Thus, formal operational thinkers develop hypotheses about ways to solve problems and then systematically deduce the best path to follow to solve the problem.

Evaluating Piaget's Theory Researchers have challenged some of Piaget's ideas on the formal operational stage (Byrnes, 2008). Among their findings is that there is much more individual variation than Piaget envisioned: Only about one in three young adolescents is a formal operational thinker, and many American adults never become formal operational thinkers; neither do many adults in other cultures.

Furthermore, education in the logic of science and mathematics promotes the development of formal operational thinking. This point recalls a criticism of Piaget's theory that we discussed in Chapter 9: Culture and education exert stronger influences on cognitive development than Piaget maintained (Rogoff & others, 2007).

Piaget's theory of cognitive development has been challenged on other points as well (Bauer, 2007, 2008). As we noted in Chapter 9, Piaget conceived of stages as unitary structures of thought, with various aspects of a stage emerging at the same time. However, most contemporary developmentalists agree that cognitive development is not as stage-like as Piaget thought (Kellman & Arterberry, 2006). Furthermore, children can be trained to reason at a higher cognitive stage, and some cognitive abilities emerge earlier than Piaget thought (Scholnick, 2008). For example, even 2-year-olds are nonegocentric in some contexts. When they realize that another person will not see an object, they investigate whether the person is blindfolded or looking in a different direction. Some understanding of the conservation of number has been demonstrated as early as age 3, although Piaget did not think it emerged until 7. Other cognitive abilities can emerge later than Piaget thought (Byrnes, 2008). As we just noted, many adolescents still think in concrete operational ways or are just beginning to master formal operations, and even many adults are not formal operational thinkers.

Despite these challenges to Piaget's ideas, we owe him a tremendous debt (Carpendale, Muller, & Bibok, 2008). Piaget was the founder of the present field of cognitive development, and he developed a long list of masterful concepts of enduring power and fascination: assimilation, accommodation, object permanence, egocentrism, conservation, and others. Psychologists also owe him the current vision of children as active, constructive thinkers. And they have a debt to him for creating a theory that generated a huge volume of research on children's cognitive development.

Piaget also was a genius when it came to observing children. His careful observations demonstrated inventive ways to discover how children act on and adapt to their world. He also showed us how children need to make their experiences fit their schemes yet simultaneously adapt their schemes to experience. Piaget also revealed how cognitive change is likely to occur if the context is structured to allow gradual movement to the next higher level. Concepts do not emerge suddenly, full-blown, but instead develop through a series of partial accomplishments that lead to increasingly comprehensive understanding (Gelman & Kalish, 2006).

Adolescent Egocentrism

Adolescent egocentrism is the heightened self-consciousness of adolescents. David Elkind (1976) points out that adolescent egocentrism has two key components—the imaginary audience and personal fable. The **imaginary audience** is adolescents' belief that others are as interested in them as they themselves are, as well as attention-getting behavior—attempts to be noticed, visible, and "on stage." For example, an eighth-grade boy might walk into the classroom and think that all eyes are riveted on his spotty complexion. Adolescents sense that they are "on stage" in early adolescence, believing they are the main actors and all others are the audience.

According to Elkind, the **personal fable** is the part of adolescent egocentrism involving a sense of uniqueness and invincibility (or invulnerability). For example, 13-year-old Adrienne says this about herself: "No one understands me, particularly my parents. They have no idea of what I am feeling." Adolescents' sense of personal uniqueness makes them feel that no one can understand how they really feel. As part of their effort to retain a sense of personal uniqueness, adolescents might craft a story about the self that is filled with fantasy, immersing themselves in a world that is far removed from reality. Personal fables frequently show up in adolescent diaries.

Adolescents also often show a sense of invincibility or invulnerability. For example, during a conversation with a girl her same age, 14-year-old Margaret says, "Are you kidding? I won't get pregnant." This sense of invincibility may also lead them to believe that they themselves are invulnerable to dangers and catastrophes (such as deadly car wrecks) that happen to other people. As a result, some adolescents engage in risky

Many adolescent girls spend long hours in front of the mirror, depleting cans of hairspray, tubes of lipstick, and jars of cosmetics. *How might this behavior be related to changes in adolescent cognitive and physical development?*

adolescent egocentrism The heightened self-consciousness of adolescents.

imaginary audience Involves adolescents' belief that others are as interested in them as they themselves are, as well as attention-getting behavior motivated by a desire to be noticed, visible, and "on stage."

personal fable The part of adolescent egocentrism that involves an adolescent's sense of uniqueness and invincibility (or invulnerability).

behaviors such as drag racing, drug use, suicide, and having sexual intercourse without using contraceptives or barriers against STIs (Alberts, Elkind, & Ginsberg, 2007).

A recent study of sixth- through twelfth-graders examined whether aspects of the personal fable were linked to various aspects of adolescent adjustment (Aalsma, Lapsley, & Flannery, 2006). A sense of invincibility or invulnerability was linked to engaging in risky behaviors, such as smoking cigarettes, drinking alcohol, and delinquency, whereas a sense of personal uniqueness was related to depression and suicidal thoughts.

Information Processing

According to Deanna Kuhn (Kuhn & Franklin, 2006), the most important cognitive change in adolescence is improvement in *executive functioning*, which involves higher-order cognitive activities such as reasoning, making decisions, monitoring thinking critically, and monitoring one's cognitive progress. Improvements in executive functioning permit more effective learning and an improved ability to determine how attention will be allocated, to make decisions, and to engage in critical thinking.

Decision Making   Adolescence is a time of increased decision making—which friends to choose, which person to date, whether to have sex, buy a car, go to college, and so on (Keating, 2007; Rivers, Reyna, & Mills, 2008; Sunstein, 2008). How competent are adolescents at making decisions? Older adolescents are described as more competent than younger adolescents, who in turn are more competent than children (Keating, 1990). Compared with children, young adolescents are more likely to generate different options, examine a situation from a variety of perspectives, anticipate the consequences of decisions, and consider the credibility of sources.

However, older adolescents' decision-making skills are far from perfect, as are adults' (Klaczynski, 2005). Being able to make competent decisions does not guarantee that one will make them in everyday life, where breadth of experience often comes into play (Keating, 1990). As an example, driver-training courses improve adolescents' cognitive and motor skills to levels equal to, or sometimes superior to, those of adults. However, driver training has not been effective in reducing adolescents' high rate of traffic accidents, although recently researchers have found that implementing a graduated driver licensing (GDL) program can reduce crash and fatality rates for adolescent drivers (Keating, 2007). GDR components include a learner's holding period, practice driving certification, night driving restriction, and passenger restriction.

Most people make better decisions when they are calm rather than emotionally aroused. That may especially be true for adolescents, who have a tendency to be emotionally intense. The same adolescent who makes a wise decision when calm may make an unwise decision when emotionally aroused (Giedd, 2008; Steinberg, 2009). In the heat of the moment, emotions may overwhelm decision-making ability.

The social context plays a key role in adolescent decision making. For example, adolescents' willingness to make risky decisions is more likely to occur in contexts where substances and other temptations are readily available (Gerrard & others, 2008; Reyna & Rivers, 2008). Recent research reveals that the presence of peers in risk-taking situations increases the likelihood that adolescents will make risky decisions (Steinberg, 2008). In one study of risk taking involving a simulated driving task, the presence of peers increased an adolescent's decision to engage in risky driving by 50 percent but had no effect on adults (Gardner & Steinberg, 2005). One view is that the presence of peers activates the brain's reward system, especially dopamine pathways (Steinberg, 2008).

Adolescents need more opportunities to practice and discuss realistic decision making. Many real-world decisions on matters such as sex, drugs, and daredevil driving occur in an atmosphere

What are some of the decisions adolescents have to make? What characterizes their decision making?

of stress that includes time constraints and emotional involvement. One strategy for improving adolescent decision making is to provide more opportunities for them to engage in role playing and peer group problem solving.

Critical Thinking   Adolescence is an important transitional period in the development of critical thinking (Keating, 1990). In one study of fifth-, eighth-, and eleventh-graders, critical thinking increased with age but still occurred in only 43 percent of even the eleventh-graders, and many adolescents showed self-serving biases in their reasoning (Klaczynski & Narasimham, 1998).

If fundamental skills (such as literacy and math skills) are not developed during childhood, critical-thinking skills are unlikely to mature in adolescence. For the subset of adolescents who lack such fundamental skills, potential gains in adolescent thinking are unlikely. For other adolescents, however, cognitive changes that allow improved critical thinking in adolescence include the following: (1) increased speed, automaticity, and capacity of information processing, which free cognitive resources for other purposes; (2) more breadth of content knowledge in a variety of domains; (3) increased ability to construct new combinations of knowledge; and (4) a greater range and more spontaneous use of strategies or procedures for applying or obtaining knowledge, such as planning, considering alternatives, and cognitive monitoring.

> *The error of youth is to believe that intelligence is a substitute for experience, while the error of age is to believe that experience is a substitute for intelligence.*
>
> —LYMAN BRYSON
> *American Author, 20th Century*

Review and Reflect: Learning Goal 4

 4 **Explain Cognitive Changes in Adolescence**

REVIEW

- What is Piaget's theory of adolescent cognitive development?
- What is adolescent egocentrism?
- What are some important aspects of information processing in adolescence?

REFLECT

- Using Piaget's theory of cognitive development as a guide, suppose an 8-year-old and a 16-year-old are watching a political convention on television. How might their perceptions of the proceedings differ? What Piagetian concepts would these perceptions reflect?

---

5 SCHOOLS

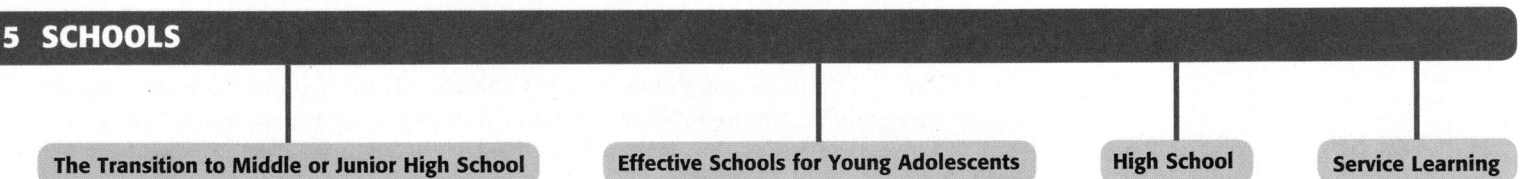

| The Transition to Middle or Junior High School | Effective Schools for Young Adolescents | High School | Service Learning |

What is the transition from elementary to middle or junior high school like? What are the characteristics of effective schools for adolescents? How can adolescents benefit from service learning?

The Transition to Middle or Junior High School

The first year of middle school or junior high school can be difficult for many students (Anderman & Mueller, 2009; Cook & others, 2008). For example, in one study of the transition from sixth grade in an elementary school to the seventh grade in a junior high school, adolescents' perceptions of the quality of their school life plunged in the seventh grade

The transition from elementary to middle or junior high school occurs at the same time as a number of other developmental changes. *What are some of these other developmental changes?*

(Hirsch & Rapkin, 1987). Compared with their earlier feelings as sixth-graders, the seventh-graders were less satisfied with school, were less committed to school, and liked their teachers less. The drop in school satisfaction occurred regardless of how academically successful the students were.

The transition to middle or junior high school takes place at a time when many changes—in the individual, in the family, and in school—are occurring simultaneously. These changes include puberty and related concerns about body image; the emergence of at least some aspects of formal operational thought, including accompanying changes in social cognition; increased responsibility and decreased dependency on parents; change to a larger, more impersonal school structure; change from one teacher to many teachers and from a small, homogeneous set of peers to a larger, more heterogeneous set of peers; and an increased focus on achievement and performance. Moreover, when students make the transition to middle or junior high school, they experience the **top-dog phenomenon**, moving from being the oldest, biggest, and most powerful students in the elementary school to being the youngest, smallest, and least powerful students in the middle or junior high school.

There can also be positive aspects to the transition to middle or junior high school. Students are more likely to feel grown up, have more subjects from which to select, have more opportunities to spend time with peers and locate compatible friends, and enjoy increased independence from direct parental monitoring. They also may be more challenged intellectually by academic work.

Effective Schools for Young Adolescents

Educators and psychologists worry that junior high and middle schools have become watered-down versions of high schools, mimicking their curricular and extracurricular schedules. Critics argue that these schools should offer activities that reflect a wide range of individual differences in biological and psychological development among young adolescents. In 1989 the Carnegie Corporation issued an extremely negative evaluation of our nation's middle schools. It concluded that most young adolescents attended massive, impersonal schools; were taught from irrelevant curricula; trusted few adults in school; and lacked access to health care and counseling. It recommended that the nation should develop smaller "communities" or "houses" to lessen the impersonal nature of large middle schools, have lower student-to-counselor ratios (10 to 1 instead of several-hundred-to-1), involve parents and community leaders in schools, develop new curricula, have teachers team teach in more flexibly designed curriculum blocks that integrate several disciplines, boost students' health and fitness with more in-school programs, and help students who need public health care to get it. Twenty years later, experts are still finding that middle schools throughout the nation need a major redesign if they are to be effective in educating adolescents (Eccles, 2007).

High School

Just as there are concerns about U.S. middle school education, so are there concerns about U.S. high school education. Critics stress that in many high schools expectations for success and standards for learning are too low. Critics also argue that too often high schools foster passivity and that schools should create a variety of pathways for students to achieve an identity. Many students graduate from high school with inadequate reading, writing, and mathematical skills—including many who go on to college and have to enroll in remediation classes there. Other students drop out of high school and do not have skills that will allow them to obtain decent jobs, much less to be informed citizens.

In the last half of the twentieth century and the first several years of the twenty-first century, U.S. high school dropout rates declined (National Center for Education

top-dog phenomenon The circumstance of moving from the top position in elementary school to the lowest position in middle or junior high school.

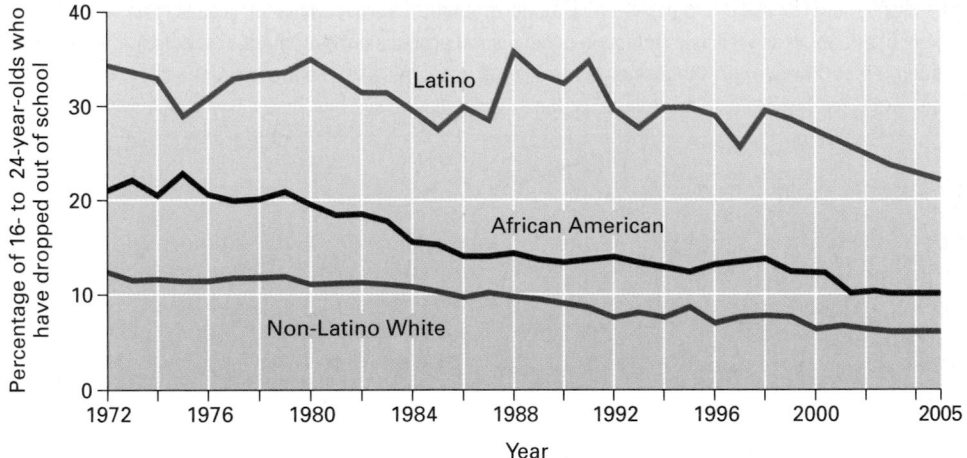

FIGURE 11.10 Trends in High School Dropout Rates. From 1972 through 2005, the school dropout rate for Latinos remained very high (22 percent of 16- to 24-year-olds in 2005). The African American dropout rate was still higher (10 percent) than the White non-Latino rate (6 percent) in 2005. (*Source:* National Center for Education Statistics, 2007.)

Statistics, 2007) (see Figure 11.10). In the 1940s, more than half of U.S. 16- to 24-year-olds had dropped out of school; by 2005, this figure had decreased to 8 percent. The dropout rate of Latino adolescents remains high, although it is decreasing in the twenty-first century. The highest dropout rate in the United States, though, likely occurs for Native American youth—less than 50 percent finish their high school education.

Students drop out of school for many reasons. In one study, almost 50 percent of the dropouts cited school-related reasons for leaving school, such as not liking school or being expelled or suspended (Rumberger, 1983). Twenty percent of the dropouts (but 40 percent of the Latino students) cited economic reasons for leaving school. One-third of the female students dropped out for personal reasons such as pregnancy or marriage.

According to a research review, the most effective programs to discourage dropping out of high school provide early reading programs, tutoring, counseling, and mentoring (Lehr & others, 2003). They also emphasize the creation of caring environments and relationships, use block scheduling, and offer community-service opportunities.

Clearly, then, early detection of children's school-related difficulties and getting children engaged with school in positive ways are important strategies for reducing the dropout rate. Also, recently the Bill and Melinda Gates Foundation (2008) funded efforts to reduce the dropout rate in schools where dropout rates are high. One strategy that is being emphasized in the Gates' funding is keeping students at risk for dropping out of school with the same teachers through their high school years. The hope is that the teachers will get to know these students much better, their relationship with the students will improve, and they will be able to monitor and guide the students toward graduating from high school. One program that has been very effective in reducing school dropout rates is described in the following *Diversity in Life-Span Development* interlude.

Diversity in Life-Span Development
"I Have a Dream" Program

These adolescents participate in the "I Have a Dream" (IHAD) Program, a comprehensive, long-term dropout prevention program that has been very successful. *What are some other strategies for reducing high school dropout rates?*

"I Have a Dream" (IHAD) is an innovative comprehensive, long-term dropout prevention program administered by the National "I Have a Dream" Foundation in New York. Since the National IHAD Foundation was created in 1986, it has grown to number over 180 projects in 64 cities and 27 states, serving more than 13,500 children ("I Have a Dream" Foundation, 2008). Local IHAD projects around the country "adopt" entire grades (usually the third or fourth) from public elementary schools, or corresponding age cohorts from public housing developments. These children—"Dreamers"—are then provided with a program of academic, social, cultural, and recreational activities throughout their elementary, middle school, and high school years.

Evaluations of IHAD programs have found dramatic improvements in grades, test scores, and school attendance, as well as a reduction of behavioral problems of Dreamers. For example, in Portland, Oregon, twice as many Dreamers as control-group students had reached a math standard, and the Dreamers were less likely to be referred to the juvenile justice system (Davis, Hyatt, & Arrasmith, 1998).

Service Learning

Service learning is a form of education that promotes social responsibility and service to the community. In service learning, adolescents engage in activities such as tutoring, helping older adults, working in a hospital, assisting at a child-care center, or cleaning up a vacant lot to make a play area. An important goal of service learning is for adolescents to become less self-centered and more strongly motivated to help others (Hart, Matsuba, & Atkins, 2008). Service learning is often more effective when two conditions are met (Nucci, 2006): (1) giving students some degree of choice in the service activities in which they participate, and (2) providing students opportunities to reflect about their participation.

Service learning takes education out into the community (Enfield & Collins, 2008; Nelson, J. A., & Eckstein, 2008). One eleventh-grade student worked as a reading tutor for students from low-income backgrounds with reading skills well below their grade levels. She commented that until she did the tutoring, she did not realize how many students had not experienced the same opportunities that she had when she was growing up. An especially rewarding moment was when one young girl told her, "I want to learn to read like you so I can go to college when I grow up." Thus, a key feature of service learning is that it not only benefits adolescents but also the recipients of their help.

Researchers have found that service learning benefits adolescents in a number of ways (Reinders & Youniss, 2006). These improvements in adolescent development related to service learning include higher grades in school, increased goal setting, higher self-esteem, an improved sense of being able to make a difference for others, and an increased likelihood that they will serve as volunteers in the future (Benson & others, 2006; Hart, Atkins, & Donnelly, 2006). A recent study of more than 4,000 high school students revealed that those who worked directly with individuals in need were better adjusted academically, and those who worked for organizations had better civic outcomes (Schmidt, Shumow, & Kackar, 2007). And another recent study found that adolescent girls participated in service learning more than adolescent boys (Webster & Worrell, 2008).

What are some of the positive effects of service learning?

Review and Reflect: Learning Goal 5

5 **Summarize Some Key Aspects of How Schools Influence Adolescent Development**

REVIEW

- What is the transition to middle or junior high school like?
- What are some characteristics of effective schools for young adolescents?
- What are some important things to know about high school dropouts and improving high schools?
- What is service learning, and how does it affect adolescent development?

REFLECT

- What was your middle or junior high school like? How did it measure up to the Carnegie Foundation's recommendations?

service learning A form of education that promotes social responsibility and service to the community.

Physical and Cognitive Development in Adolescence

1 THE NATURE OF ADOLESCENCE: DISCUSS THE NATURE OF ADOLESCENCE

- Many stereotypes of adolescents are too negative. Most adolescents today successfully negotiate the path from childhood to adulthood. However, too many of today's adolescents are not provided with adequate opportunities and support to become competent adults. It is important to view adolescents as a heterogeneous group because different portraits of adolescents emerge, depending on the particular set of adolescents being described.

2 PHYSICAL CHANGES: DESCRIBE THE CHANGES INVOLVED IN PUBERTY AS WELL AS CHANGES IN THE BRAIN AND SEXUALITY DURING ADOLESCENCE

Puberty

- Puberty is a period of rapid physical maturation involving hormonal and bodily changes that occurs primarily during early adolescence. Puberty's determinants include nutrition, health, and heredity. The endocrine system's influence on puberty involves an interaction of the hypothalamus, the pituitary gland, and the gonads (sex glands). The initial onset of the pubertal growth spurt occurs on the average at 9 years for girls and 11 for boys, reaching a peak change for girls at $11\frac{1}{2}$ and for boys at $13\frac{1}{2}$. Individual variation in pubertal changes is substantial. Adolescents show considerable interest in their body image, with girls having more negative body images than boys do. Adolescents increasingly have tattoos and body piercings (body art). For boys, early maturation brings benefits, at least during early adolescence. Early-maturing girls are vulnerable to a number of risks.

The Brain

- Changes in the brain during adolescence involve the thickening of the corpus callosum and a gap in maturation between the amygdala and the prefrontal cortex, which functions in reasoning and self-regulation.

Adolescent Sexuality

- Adolescence is a time of sexual exploration and sexual experimentation. Having sexual intercourse in early adolescence is associated with negative developmental outcomes. Contraceptive use by adolescents is increasing. About one in four sexually experienced adolescents acquire a sexually transmitted infection (STI). America's adolescent pregnancy rate is high but has been decreasing in recent years.

3 ISSUES IN ADOLESCENT HEALTH: IDENTIFY ADOLESCENT PROBLEMS RELATED TO HEALTH, SUBSTANCE USE AND ABUSE, AND EATING DISORDERS

Adolescent Health

- Adolescence is a critical juncture in health because many of the factors related to poor health habits and early death in the adult years begin during adolescence. Poor nutrition, lack of exercise, and inadequate sleep are concerns. The three leading causes of death in adolescence are accidents, homicide, and suicide.

Substance Use and Abuse

- Despite recent declines in use, the United States has one of the highest rate of adolescent illicit drug use of any industrialized nation. Alcohol abuse is a major adolescent problem, although its rate has been dropping in recent years, as has cigarette smoking. A recent concern is the increased use of prescription painkillers by adolescents. Parents, peers, social support, and educational success play important roles in whether adolescents take drugs.

Eating Disorders

- Eating disorders have increased in adolescence with a substantial increase in the percentage of adolescents who are overweight. Two eating disorders that may emerge in adolescence are anorexia nervosa and bulimia nervosa. Anorexia nervosa typically starts in the early to middle adolescent years, following a dieting episode, and involves the relentless pursuit of thinness through starvation. Bulimia nervosa involves a binge-and-purge pattern, but unlike anorexics, bulemics typically fall within a normal weight range.

4 ADOLESCENT COGNITION: EXPLAIN COGNITIVE CHANGES IN ADOLESCENCE

Piaget's Theory

- During the formal operational stage, Piaget's fourth stage of cognitive development, thought is more abstract, idealistic, and logical than during the concrete operational stage. However, many adolescents are not formal operational thinkers but are consolidating their concrete operational thought.

Adolescent Egocentrism

- Elkind describes adolescent egocentrism as the heightened self-consciousness of adolescents that consists of two parts: the imaginary audience and the personal fable.

Information Processing

- Changes in information processing in adolescence are mainly reflected in improved executive functioning, which includes advances in decision making and critical thinking.

5 SCHOOLS: SUMMARIZE SOME KEY ASPECTS OF HOW SCHOOLS INFLUENCE ADOLESCENT DEVELOPMENT

The Transition to Middle or Junior High School

- The transition to middle or junior high school coincides with many social, familial, and individual changes in the adolescent's life, and this transition is often stressful. One source of stress is the move from the top-dog position to the lowest position in school.

Effective Schools for Young Adolescents

- Some critics argue that a major redesign of U.S. middle schools is needed. Critics say that U.S. high schools foster passivity and do not develop students academic skills adequately. Characteristics of effective schools include having lower student-to-counselor ratios, involving parents and community leaders in schools, team teaching, and boosting students' health and fitness.

High School

- A number of strategies have been proposed for improving U.S. high schools, including higher expectations and better support. The overall high school dropout rate declined considerably in the last half of the twentieth century, but the dropout rates of Latino and Native American youth remain very high.

Service Learning

- Service learning, a form of education that promotes social responsibility and service to the community, is related to a number of positive benefits for adolescents such as higher grades, increased goal setting, and improved self-esteem.

KEY TERMS

puberty 356
menarche 357
hormones 357
hypothalamus 357
pituitary gland 357

gonads 357
corpus callosum 360
amygdala 360
sexually transmitted
    infections (STIs) 363

anorexia nervosa 370
bulimia nervosa 371
hypothetical-deductive
    reasoning 372
adolescent egocentrism 373

imaginary audience 373
personal fable 373
top-dog phenomenon 376
service learning 378

KEY PEOPLE

Lloyd Johnston 368   Jean Piaget 372   David Elkind 373   Deanna Kuhn 374

E-LEARNING TOOLS

To help you master the material in this chapter, visit the Online Learning Center for *Life-Span Development*, twelfth edition, at **www.mhhe.com/santrockld12**.

Self-Assessment

Connect to **www.mhhe.com/santrockld12** to reflect on your early teenage years by completing the self-assessment, *My Romantic and Sexual Involvement in Adolescence*.

Taking It to the Net

Connect to **www.mhhe.com/santrockld12** to research the answers to these questions:

1. Sharon wonders why so much of the talk about adolescent pregnancy focuses on the girl's motivation and behavior. She wonders: What about the guys? How do adolescent males become absentee fathers?

2. Miguel plans to take a comparative literature class. His uncle, a high school literature teacher, looks at the course syllabus and says it is made up of titles that "pander to adolescent angst." He tells Miguel about the "Werther Effect," named after *The Sorrows of Young Werther*, a novella by Johann Wolfgang von Goethe that provoked a wave of adolescent suicides across Europe in the late 1700s. What elements of a story like *Werther* would appeal to the sensibilities of a typical adolescent?

3. Emory is petitioning his public school administrative board to expand the school system's service learning program. What pedagogical advantages of service learning should he emphasize in his presentation?

Video Clips

The Online Learning Center includes two videos for Chapter 11. The first video is called "Sex Among Teens at Age 15." These informal interviews with 15-year-olds offer a snapshot of contemporary adolescent attitudes toward sex. The second video is called "Eating Disorders." Obesity, anorexia nervosa, and bulimia are described in this segment, which also addresses the question of why these problems have become so common among adolescents.

Health and Well-Being, Parenting, and Education Exercises

Build your decision-making skills by trying your hand at the health and well-being, parenting, and education exercises. Connect to **www.mhhe.com/santrockld12** to research the answers and complete the exercises.

12

In case you're worried about what's going to become of the younger generation, it's going to grow up and start worrying about the younger generation.

—Roger Allen
Contemporary American Writer

LEARNING GOALS

- ◆ Discuss changes in the self, identity, and religious/spiritual development in adolescence.

- ◆ Describe changes that take place in adolescents' relationships with their parents.

- ◆ Characterize the changes that occur in peer relations during adolescence.

- ◆ Explain how culture influences adolescent development.

- ◆ Identify adolescent problems in socioemotional development and strategies for helping adolescents with problems.

SOCIOEMOTIONAL DEVELOPMENT IN ADOLESCENCE

CHAPTER OUTLINE

Images of Life-Span Development
Jewel Cash, Teen Dynamo

Jewel Cash seated next to her mother participating in a crime watch meeting at a community center.

The mayor of the city says she is "everywhere." She recently persuaded the city's school committee to consider ending the practice of locking tardy students out of their classrooms. She also swayed a neighborhood group to support her proposal for a winter jobs program. According to one city councilman, "People are just impressed with the power of her arguments and the sophistication of the argument" (Silva, 2005, pp. B1, B4). She is Jewel E. Cash, and she is only 16 years old.

A junior at Boston Latin Academy, Jewel was raised in one of Boston's housing projects by her mother, a single parent. Today she is a member of the Boston Student Advisory Council, mentors children, volunteers at a women's shelter, manages and dances in two troupes, and is a member of a neighborhood watch group—among other activities. Jewel is far from typical, but her activities illustrate that cognitive and socioemotional development allows even adolescents to be capable, effective individuals.

PREVIEW

Significant changes characterize socioemotional development in adolescence. These changes include increased efforts to understand one's self and searching for an identity. Changes also occur in the social contexts of adolescents' lives, with transformations occurring in relationships with families and peers in cultural contexts. Adolescents also may develop socioemotional problems, such as delinquency and depression.

1 THE SELF, IDENTITY, AND RELIGIOUS/SPIRITUAL DEVELOPMENT

Self-Esteem   Identity   Religious and Spiritual Development

Jewel Cash told an interviewer from the *Boston Globe,* "I see a problem and I say, 'How can I make a difference?'. . . I can't take on the world, even though I can try. . . . I'm moving forward but I want to make sure I'm bringing people with me." (Silva, 2005, pp. B1, B4). Jewel's confidence and positive identity sound at least as impressive as her activities. This section examines how adolescents develop characteristics like these. How much did you understand yourself during adolescence, and how did you acquire the stamp of your identity? Is your identity still developing?

Self-Esteem

Recall from Chapter 10 that *self-esteem* is the overall way we evaluate ourselves. Controversy characterizes the extent to which self-esteem changes during adolescence and whether there are gender differences in adolescents' self-esteem (Harter, 2006). In one study, both boys and girls had particularly high self-esteem in childhood, but their self-esteem dropped considerably during adolescence (Robins & others, 2002). The self-esteem of girls declined more than the self-esteem of boys during adolescence in this study. Another study also found that the self-esteem of girls declined during early adolescence, but it found that the self-esteem of boys increased in early adolescence (Baldwin & Hoffman, 2002). In this study, high adolescent self-esteem was related to positive family relationships.

Does self-esteem in adolescence foreshadow adjustment and competence in adulthood? A New Zealand longitudinal study assessed self-esteem at 11, 13, and 15 years of age and adjustment and competence of the same individuals when they were 26 years old (Trzesniewski & others, 2006). The results revealed that adults characterized by poorer mental and physical health, worse economic prospects, and higher levels of criminal behavior were more likely to have low self-esteem in adolescence than their better adjusted, more competent adult counterparts.

Some critics argue that developmental changes and gender differences in self-esteem during adolescence have been exaggerated (Harter, 2002). For example, in one analysis of research studies on self-esteem in adolescence, it was concluded that girls have only slightly more negative self-esteem than do boys (Kling & others, 1999). Despite the differing results and interpretations, the self-esteem of girls is likely to decline at least somewhat during early adolescence.

Why would the self-esteem of girls decline during early adolescence? One explanation points to girls' negative body images during pubertal change. Another explanation involves the greater interest young adolescent girls take in social relationships and society's failure to reward that interest (Impett & others, 2008).

What are some important dimensions of identity?

Identity

Who am I? What am I all about? What am I going to do with my life? What is different about me? How can I make it on my own? These questions reflect the search for an identity. By far the most comprehensive and provocative theory of identity development is Erik Erikson's. In this section, we examine his views on identity. We also discuss contemporary research on how identity develops and how social contexts influence that development.

What Is Identity? Identity is a self-portrait composed of many pieces, including these:

- The career and work path the person wants to follow (vocational/career identity)
- Whether the person is conservative, liberal, or middle-of-the-road (political identity)
- The person's spiritual beliefs (religious identity)
- Whether the person is single, married, divorced, and so on (relationship identity)
- The extent to which the person is motivated to achieve and is intellectual (achievement, intellectual identity)
- Whether the person is heterosexual, homosexual, or bisexual (sexual identity)
- Which part of the world or country a person is from and how intensely the person identifies with his or her cultural heritage (cultural/ethnic identity)
- The kind of things a person likes to do, which can include sports, music, hobbies, and so on (interests)
- The individual's personality characteristics (such as being introverted or extraverted, anxious or calm, friendly or hostile, and so on) (personality)
- The individual's body image (physical identity)

Synthesizing the identity components can be a long and drawn-out process, with many negations and affirmations of various roles and faces. Identity development gets done in bits and pieces. Decisions are not made once and for all, but have to be made again and again. Identity development does not happen neatly, and it does not happen cataclysmically (Kroger, 2007; Orbe, 2008; Phinney, 2008).

> *"Who are you?" said the Caterpillar. Alice replied, rather shyly, "I–I hardly know, Sir, just at present— at least I know who I was when I got up this morning, but I must have changed several times since then."*
>
> —**Lewis Carroll**
> *English Writer, 19th Century*

Erikson's View   Questions about identity surface as common, virtually universal, concerns during adolescence. Some decisions made during adolescence might seem trivial: whom to date, whether or not to break up, which major to study, whether to study or play, whether or not to be politically active, and so on. Over the years of adolescence, however, such decisions begin to form the core of what the individual is all about as a human being—what is called his or her identity.

It was Erik Erikson (1950, 1968) who first understood how central questions about identity are to understanding adolescent development. That identity is now believed to be a key aspect of adolescent development is a result of Erikson's masterful thinking and analysis.

Erikson's theory was introduced in Chapter 1. Recall that his fifth developmental stage, which individuals experience during adolescence, is *identity versus identity confusion*. During this time, said Erikson, adolescents are faced with deciding who they are, what they are all about, and where they are going in life.

The search for an identity during adolescence is aided by a *psychosocial moratorium*, which is Erikson's term for the gap between childhood security and adult autonomy. During this period, society leaves adolescents relatively free of responsibilities and free to try out different identities. Adolescents in effect search their culture's identity files, experimenting with different roles and personalities. They may want to pursue one career one month (lawyer, for example) and another career the next month (doctor, actor, teacher, social worker, or astronaut, for example). They may dress neatly one day, sloppily the next. This experimentation is a deliberate effort on the part of adolescents to find out where they fit in the world. Most adolescents eventually discard undesirable roles.

Youth who successfully cope with conflicting identities emerge with a new sense of self that is both refreshing and acceptable. Adolescents who do not successfully resolve this identity crisis suffer what Erikson calls identity confusion. The confusion takes one of two courses: Individuals withdraw, isolating themselves from peers and family, or they immerse themselves in the world of peers and lose their identity in the crowd.

Developmental Changes   Although questions about identity may be especially important during adolescence, identity formation neither begins nor ends during these years. It begins with the appearance of attachment, the development of the sense of self, and the emergence of independence in infancy; the process reaches its final phase with a life review and integration in old age. What is important about identity development in adolescence, especially late adolescence, is that for the first time, physical development, cognitive development, and socioemotional development advance to the point at which the individual can sort through and synthesize childhood identities and identifications to construct a viable path toward adult maturity.

How do individual adolescents go about the process of forming an identity? Eriksonian researcher James Marcia (1980, 1994) reasons that Erikson's theory of identity development contains four *statuses* of identity, or ways of resolving the identity crisis: identity diffusion, identity foreclosure, identity moratorium, and identity achievement. What determines an individual's identity status? Marcia classifies individuals based on the existence or extent of their crisis or commitment (see Figure 12.1). **Crisis** is defined as a period of identity development during which the individual is exploring alternatives. Most researchers use the term *exploration* rather than crisis. **Commitment** is personal investment in identity.

crisis Marcia's term for a period of identity development during which the adolescent is exploring alternatives.

commitment Marcia's term for the part of identity development in which adolescents show a personal investment in identity.

FIGURE 12.1 Marcia's Four Statuses of Identity. According to Marcia, an individual's status in developing an identity can be described as identity diffusion, identity foreclosure, identity moratorium, or identity achievement. The status depends on the presence or absence of (1) a crisis or exploration of alternatives and (2) a commitment to an identity. *What is the identity status of most young adolescents?*

Position on Occupation and Ideology	Identity Status			
	Identity diffusion	Identity foreclosure	Identity moratorium	Identity achievement
Crisis	Absent	Absent	Present	Present
Commitment	Absent	Present	Absent	Present

The four statuses of identity are:

- **Identity diffusion**, the status of individuals who have not yet experienced a crisis or made any commitments. Not only are they undecided about occupational and ideological choices, they are also likely to show little interest in such matters.

- **Identity foreclosure** is the status of individuals who have made a commitment but not experienced a crisis. This occurs most often when parents hand down commitments to their adolescents, usually in an authoritarian way, before adolescents have had a chance to explore different approaches, ideologies, and vocations on their own.

- **Identity moratorium** is the status of individuals who are in the midst of a crisis but whose commitments are either absent or are only vaguely defined.

- **Identity achievement** is the status of individuals who have undergone a crisis and made a commitment.

How does identity change in emerging adulthood?

Emerging Adulthood and Beyond A consensus is developing that the key changes in identity are more likely to take place in emerging adulthood (18 to 25 years of age) or later than in adolescence (Kroger, 2007; Luyckx & others, 2008a, b). For example, Alan Waterman (1985, 1999) has found that from the years preceding high school through the last few years of college, the number of individuals who are identity achieved increases, whereas the number who are identity diffused decreases. College upperclassmen are more likely to be identity achieved than college freshmen or high school students. Many young adolescents, on the other hand, are identity diffused. These developmental changes are especially true for vocational choice. In terms of religious beliefs and political ideology, fewer college students reach the identity-achieved status; a substantial number are characterized by foreclosure and diffusion. Thus, the timing of identity development may depend on the particular dimension involved (Arehart & Smith, 1990).

One of emerging adulthood's themes is not having many social commitments, which gives individuals considerable independence in developing a life path (Arnett, 2006). James Cote (2006) argues that because of this freedom, developing a positive identity in emerging adulthood requires considerable self-discipline and planning. Without this self-discipline and planning, emerging adults are likely to drift and not follow any particular direction. Cote also stresses that emerging adults who obtain a higher education are more likely to be on a positive identity path. Those who don't obtain a higher education, he says, tend to experience frequent job changes, not because they are searching for an identity but rather because they are just trying to eke out a living in a society that rewards higher education.

Resolution of the identity issue during adolescence and emerging adulthood does not mean that identity will be stable through the remainder of life. Many individuals who develop positive identities follow what are called "MAMA" cycles; that is, their identity status changes from *moratorium* to *achievement* to *moratorium* to *achievement* (Marcia, 1994). These cycles may be repeated throughout life (Francis, Fraser, & Marcia, 1989). Marcia (2002) points out that the first identity is just that—it is not, and should not be expected to be, the final product.

In short, questions about identity come up throughout life. An individual who develops a healthy identity is flexible and adaptive, open to changes in society, in relationships, and in careers. This openness assures numerous reorganizations of identity throughout the individual's life.

Family Influences Parents are important figures in the adolescent's development of identity (Beyers & Goossens, 2008; Cooper, Behrens, & Trinh, 2008; Luyckx &

> *Once formed, an identity furnishes individuals with a historical sense of who they have been, a meaningful sense of who they are now, and a sense of who they might become in the future.*
>
> —**JAMES MARCIA**
> *Contemporary Psychologist,*
> *Simon Fraser University*

identity diffusion Marcia's term for the status of individuals who have not yet experienced a crisis (explored meaningful alternatives) or made any commitments.

identity foreclosure Marcia's term for the status of individuals who have made a commitment but have not experienced a crisis.

identity moratorium Marcia's term for the status of individuals who are in the midst of a crisis, but their commitments are either absent or vaguely defined.

identity achievement Marcia's term for the status of individuals who have undergone a crisis and have made a commitment.

How might parents influence the adolescent's identity development?

Michelle Chin, age 16: "Parents do not understand that teenagers need to find out who they are, which means a lot of experimenting, a lot of mood swings, a lot of emotions and awkwardness. Like any teenager, I am facing an identity crisis. I am still trying to figure out whether I am a Chinese American or an American with Asian eyes."

individuality Individuality consists of two dimensions: self-assertion (the ability to have and communicate a point of view) and separateness (the use of communication patterns to express how one is different from others).

connectedness Connectedness consists of two dimensions: mutuality (sensitivity to and respect for others' views) and permeability (openness to others' views).

ethnic identity An enduring, basic aspect of the self that includes a sense of membership in an ethnic group and the attitudes and feelings related to that membership.

others, 2007, 2008c; Schacter & Ventura, 2008). Researchers have found that a family atmosphere that promotes both individuality and connectedness are important in the adolescent's identity development (Cooper & Grotevant, 1989):

- **Individuality** consists of two dimensions: self-assertion (the ability to have and communicate a point of view) and separateness (the use of communication patterns to express how one is different from others).
- **Connectedness** also consists of two dimensions: mutuality, which involves sensitivity to and respect for others' views, and permeability, which involves openness to others' views.

In general, then, research indicates that identity formation is enhanced by family relationships that are both individuated, which encourages adolescents to develop their own point of view, and connected, which provides a secure base from which adolescents can explore their widening social worlds. When connectedness is strong and individuation weak, adolescents often have an identity foreclosure status. When connectedness is weak, adolescents often reveal identity confusion.

Ethnic Identity   Throughout the world, ethnic minority groups have struggled to maintain their ethnic identities while blending in with the dominant culture (Erikson, 1968). **Ethnic identity** is an enduring aspect of the self that includes a sense of membership in an ethnic group, along with the attitudes and feelings related to that membership. Thus, for adolescents from ethnic minority groups, the process of identity formation has an added dimension: the choice between two or more sources of identification—their own ethnic group and the mainstream, or dominant culture (Phinney & Ong, 2007). Many adolescents resolve this choice by developing a *bicultural identity*. That is, they identify in some ways with their ethnic group and in other ways with the majority culture (Phinney, 2006). One recent study of Mexican American and Asian American college students found that they identified both with the American mainstream culture and their culture of origin (Devos, 2006).

For ethnic minority individuals, adolescence and emerging adulthood are often special junctures in their development (Phinney, 2008; Syed & Azmitia, 2008; Umana-Taylor & others, 2008; Way & others, 2008). Although children are aware of some ethnic and cultural differences, individuals consciously confront their ethnicity for the first time in adolescence or emerging adulthood. Unlike children, adolescents and emerging adults have the ability to interpret ethnic and cultural information, to reflect on the past, and to speculate about the future.

The indicators of identity change often differ for each succeeding generation (Berry, 2007; Phinney & Ong, 2007). First-generation immigrants are likely to be secure in their identities and unlikely to change much; they may or may not develop a new identity. The degree to which they begin to feel "American" appears to be related to whether or not they learn English, develop social networks beyond their ethnic group, and become culturally competent in their new country. Second-generation immigrants are more likely to think of themselves as "American," possibly because citizenship is granted at birth. Their ethnic identity is likely to be linked to retention of their ethnic language and social networks. In the third and later generations, the issues become more complex. Historical, contextual, and political factors that are unrelated to acculturation may affect the extent to which members of this generation retain their ethnic identities. For non-European ethnic groups, racism and discrimination influence whether ethnic identity is retained.

Researchers are increasingly finding that a positive ethnic identity is linked to positive outcomes for ethnic minority adolescents (Umana-Taylor, 2006). For example, in one study ethnic identity was related to higher school engagement and lower aggression (Van Buren & Graham, 2003). And in a recent study, Navajo adolescents' affirmation and belonging to their ethnic heritage was linked to higher self-esteem, school connectedness, and social functioning (Jones & Galliher, 2007).

Many children and adolescents show an interest in religion, and many religious institutions created by adults (such as this Muslim school in Malaysia) are designed to introduce them to religious benefits and ensure that they will carry on a religious tradition.

Religious and Spiritual Development

In Chapter 11, we described the many positive benefits of service learning. A number of studies have found that that adolescents who are involved in religious institutions are more likely to engage in service learning than their counterparts who don't participate in religious institutions (Oser, Scarlett, & Bucher, 2006). Let's explore adolescents' concepts of religion and spirituality, as well as their religious and spiritual experiences.

Religious issues are important to many adolescents, but in the twenty-first century, a downtrend in religious interest among adolescents has occurred. In a national study of American freshmen, in 2007, 78 percent said they attended a religious service frequently or occasionally during their senior year in high school, down from a high of 85 percent in 1997 (Pryor & others, 2007).

A recent developmental study revealed that religiousness declined from 14 to 20 years of age in the United States (Koenig, McGue, & Iacono, 2008) (see Figure 12.2). In this study, religiousness was assessed with items such as frequency of prayer, frequency of discussing religious teachings, frequency of deciding moral actions for religious reasons, and the overall importance of religion in everyday life. As indicated in Figure 12.2, more change in religiousness occurred from 14 to 18 years of age than from 20 to 24 years of age. Also, attending religious services was highest at 14 years of age, declining from 14 to 18 years of age and increasing at 20 years of age. More change occurred in attending religious services than in religiousness.

Analysis of the World Values Survey of 18- to 24-year-olds revealed that emerging adults in less developed countries were more likely to be religious than their counterparts in more developed countries (Lippman & Keith, 2006). For example, emerging adults' reports of religion being very important in their lives ranged from a low of 0 in Japan to 93 percent in Nigeria, and belief in God ranged from a low of 40 percent in Sweden to a high of 100 percent in Pakistan.

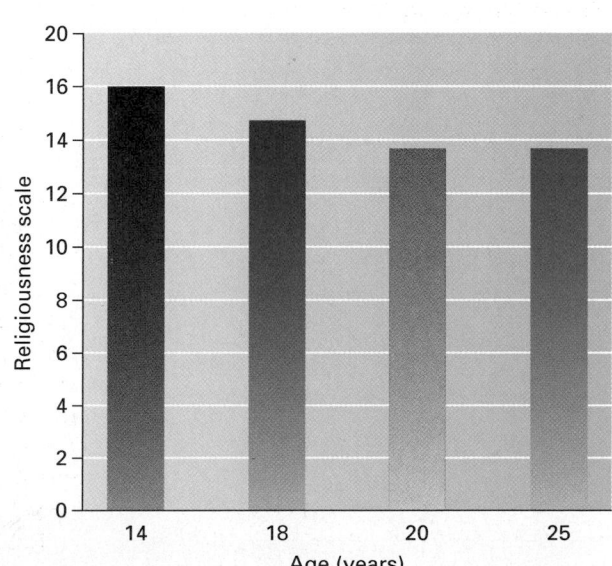

FIGURE 12.2 Developmental Changes in Reiligiousness from 14 to 25 Years of Age. *Note:* The religiousness scale ranged from 0 to 32 with higher scores indicating stronger religiousness.

What are some positive roles of religion in adolescents' lives?

Religion and Identity Development As we saw earlier in this chapter, identity development becomes a central focus of adolescence and emerging adulthood (Kroger, 2007). As part of their search for identity, adolescents and emerging adults begin to grapple in more sophisticated, logical ways with such questions as "Why am I on this planet?" "Is there really a God or higher spiritual being, or have I just been believing what my parents and the church imprinted in my mind?" "What really are my religious views?" A recent analysis of the link between identity and spirituality concluded that adolescence and adulthood can serve as gateways to a spiritual identity that "transcends, but not necessarily excludes, the assigned religious identity in childhood" (Templeton & Eccles, 2006, p. 261).

The Positive Role of Religion in Adolescents' Lives Researchers have found that various aspects of religion are linked with positive outcomes for adolescents (Benson, P. L., Roehlkepartain & Hong, 2008; Good, M. & Willoughby, 2008; Lerner, Roeser, & Phelps, 2008). Religion also plays a role in adolescents' health and whether they engage in problem behaviors (Cotton & others, 2006). For example, in a recent national random sample of more than 2,000 11- to 18-year-olds, those who were higher in religiosity were less likely to smoke, drink alcohol, use marijuana, not be truant from school, not engage in delinquent activities, and not be depressed than their low-religiosity counterparts (Sinha, Cnaan, & Gelles, 2007). A recent study of Indonesian Muslim 13-year-olds revealed that their religious involvement was linked to their social competence, including positive peer relations, academic achievement, emotional regulation, prosocial behavior, and self-esteem (French & others, 2008).

Many religious adolescents also internalize their religion's message about caring and concern for people (Ream & Savin-Williams, 2003). For example, in one survey, religious youth were almost three times as likely to engage in community service as nonreligious youth (Youniss, McLellan, & Yates, 1999).

Review and Reflect: Learning Goal 1

1 Discuss Changes in the Self, Identity, and Religious/Spiritual Development in Adolescence

REVIEW

- What are some changes in self-esteem that take place in adolescence?
- How does identity develop in adolescence?
- What characterizes religious and spiritual development in adolescence?

REFLECT

- Where are you in your identity development? Get out a sheet of paper and list each of the pieces of identity (vocational, political, religious, relationship achievement/intellectual, sexual, gender, cultural/ethnic, interest, personality, and physical) in a column on the left side of the paper. Then write the four identity statuses (diffused, foreclosed, moratorium, and achieved) across the top of the page. Next to each dimension of identity, place a check mark in the appropriate space that reflects your identity status for the particular aspect of identity. If you checked diffused or foreclosed for any of the dimensions, think about what you need to do to move on to a moratorium status in those areas.

2 FAMILIES

Autonomy and Attachment

Parent-Adolescent Conflict

Adolescence typically alters the relationship between parents and their children. Among the most important aspects of family relationships in adolescence are those that involve autonomy, attachment, and parent-adolescent conflict.

Autonomy and Attachment

With most adolescents, parents are likely to find themselves engaged in a delicate balancing act, weighing competing needs for autonomy and control, for independence and connection.

The Push for Autonomy
The typical adolescent's push for autonomy and responsibility puzzles and angers many parents. As parents see their teenager slipping from their grasp, they may have an urge to take stronger control. Heated emotional exchanges may ensue, with either side calling names, making threats, and doing whatever seems necessary to gain control. Parents may seem frustrated because they *expect* their teenager to heed their advice, to want to spend time with the family, and to grow up to do what is right. Most parents anticipate that their teenager will have some difficulty adjusting to the changes that adolescence brings, but few parents imagine and predict just how strong an adolescent's desires will be to spend time with peers or how intensely adolescents will want to show that it is they—not their parents—who are responsible for their successes and failures.

Adolescents' ability to attain autonomy and gain control over their behavior is acquired through appropriate adult reactions to their desire for control (Collins & Steinberg, 2006; Soenens & others, 2007). At the onset of adolescence, the average individual does not have the knowledge to make appropriate or mature decisions in all areas of life. As the adolescent pushes for autonomy, the wise adult relinquishes control in those areas where the adolescent can make reasonable decisions, but continues to guide the adolescent to make reasonable decisions in areas in which the adolescent's knowledge is more limited. Gradually, adolescents acquire the ability to make mature decisions on their own (Harold, Colarossi, & Mercier, 2007).

Gender differences characterize autonomy-granting in adolescence. Boys are given more independence than girls. In one study, this was especially true in U.S. families with a traditional gender-role orientation (Bumpus, Crouter, & McHale, 2001).

The Role of Attachment
Recall from Chapter 6 that one of the most widely discussed aspects of socioemotional development in infancy is secure attachment to caregivers. In the past decade, researchers have explored whether secure attachment also might be an important concept in adolescents' relationships with their parents (Furman, 2007; Zimmerman, 2007). For example, Joseph Allen and his colleagues (Allen, 2007; Allen & others, 2005, 2007) found that securely attached adolescents were less likely than those who were insecurely attached to engage in problem behaviors such as juvenile delinquency and drug abuse. A recent study also revealed that securely attached adolescents in the senior year of high school had a greater capacity for romantic intimacy four years later (Mayseless & Scharf, 2007).

Other research has examined possible links between secure attachment to parents and good relations with peers. Researchers have found that securely attached adolescents have better peer relations than their insecurely attached counterparts (Laible, Carlo, & Raffaeli, 2000). However, the correlations between adolescent-parent attachments

What are strategies parents can use to guide adolescents in effectively handling their increased motivation for autonomy?

*W*hen I was a boy of 14, my father was so ignorant I could hardly stand to have the man around. But when I got to be 21, I was astonished at how much he had learnt in 7 years.

—**Mark Twain**
American Writer and Humorist, 19th Century

Stacey Christensen, age 16: "I am lucky enough to have open communication with my parents. Whenever I am in need or just need to talk, my parents are there for me. My advice to parents is to let your teens grow at their own pace, be open with them so that you can be there for them. We need guidance, our parents need to help but not be too overwhelming."

Conflict with parents increases in early adolescence. *What is the nature of this conflict in a majority of American families?*

*I*t is not enough for parents to understand children. They must accord children the privilege of understanding them.

—MILTON SAPIRSTEIN
American Psychiatrist, 20th Century

and adolescent outcomes are moderate, indicating that the success or failure of parent-adolescent attachments does not necessarily guarantee success or failure in peer relationships.

Balancing Freedom and Control   We have seen that parents play very important roles in adolescent development (Collins & Steinberg, 2006). Although adolescents are moving toward independence, they still need to stay connected with families (Hair & others, 2008). For example, the National Longitudinal Study on Adolescent Health of more than 12,000 adolescents found that those who did not eat dinner with a parent five or more days a week had dramatically higher rates of smoking, drinking, marijuana use, getting into fights, and initiation of sexual activity (Council of Economic Advisors, 2000). In another study, parents who played an active role in monitoring and guiding their adolescents' development were more likely to have adolescents with positive peer relations and lower drug use than parents who had a less active role (Mounts, 2002).

Parent-Adolescent Conflict

Although parent-adolescent conflict increases in early adolescence, it does not reach the tumultuous proportions G. Stanley Hall envisioned at the beginning of the twentieth century (Eisenberg & others, 2008). Rather, much of the conflict involves the everyday events of family life, such as keeping a bedroom clean, dressing neatly, getting home by a certain time, and not talking forever on the phone. The conflicts rarely involve major dilemmas such as drugs or delinquency.

Conflict with parents often escalates during early adolescence, remains somewhat stable during the high school years, and then lessens as the adolescent reaches 17 to 20 years of age. Parent-adolescent relationships become more positive if adolescents go away to college than if they attend college while living at home (Sullivan & Sullivan, 1980).

The everyday conflicts that characterize parent-adolescent relationships may actually serve a positive developmental function. These minor disputes and negotiations facilitate the adolescent's transition from being dependent on parents to becoming an autonomous individual. For example, in one study, adolescents who expressed disagreement with their parents explored identity development more actively than did adolescents who did not express disagreement with their parents (Cooper & others, 1982). Recognizing that conflict and negotiation can serve a positive developmental function can tone down parental hostility.

The old model of parent-adolescent relationships suggested that as adolescents mature they detach themselves from parents and move into a world of autonomy apart from parents. The old model also suggested that parent-adolescent conflict is intense and stressful throughout adolescence. The new model emphasizes that parents serve as important attachment figures and support systems while adolescents explore a wider, more complex social world. The new model also emphasizes that, in most families, parent-adolescent conflict is moderate rather than severe and that the everyday negotiations and minor disputes not only are normal but also can serve the positive developmental function of helping the adolescent make the transition from childhood dependency to adult independence (see Figure 12.3).

Still, a high degree of conflict characterizes some parent-adolescent relationships. One estimate of the proportion of parents and adolescents who engage in prolonged, intense, repeated, unhealthy conflict is about one in five families (Montemayor, 1982). Although this figure represents a minority of adolescents, it indicates that 4 to 5 million American families encounter serious, highly stressful parent-adolescent conflict. And this prolonged, intense conflict is associated with various adolescent problems: movement out of the home, juvenile delinquency, school dropout, pregnancy and

Old Model	New Model
Autonomy, detachment from parents; parent and peer worlds are isolated	Attachment and autonomy; parents are important support systems and attachment figures; adolescent-parent and adolescent-peer worlds have some important connections
Intense, stressful conflict throughout adolescence; parent-adolescent relationships are filled with storm and stress on virtually a daily basis	Moderate parent-adolescent conflict is common and can serve a positive developmental function; conflict greater in early adolescence

FIGURE 12.3 Old and New Models of Parent-Adolescent Relationships

early marriage, membership in religious cults, and drug abuse (Brook & others, 1990; Crean, 2008). To read about some strategies for parenting adolescents, see the *Applications in Life-Span Development* interlude.

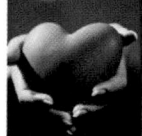

Applications in Life-Span Development
Strategies for Parenting Adolescents

Competent adolescent development is most likely when adolescents have parents who:

1. *Show them warmth and respect, and avoid the tendency to be too controlling or too permissive.*

2. *Demonstrate sustained interest in their lives.* Parents need to spend time with their adolescents and monitor their lives.

3. *Understand and adapt to their cognitive and socioemotional development.*

4. *Communicate expectations for high standards of conduct and achievement.*

5. *Display constructive ways of dealing with problems and conflict.* Moderate conflict is a normal part of the adolescent's desire for independence and search for an identity.

6. *Understand that adolescents don't become adults overnight.* Adolescence is a long journey.

Review and Reflect: Learning Goal 2

2 **Describe Changes That Take Place in Adolescents' Relationships with Their Parents**

REVIEW

- How do needs for autonomy and attachment develop in adolescence?
- What characterizes parent-adolescent conflict?

REFLECT

- How much autonomy did your parents give you in adolescence? Too much? Too little? How intense was your conflict with your parents during adolescence? What were the conflicts mainly about? Would you behave differently toward your own adolescents than your parents did with you? If so, how?

3 PEERS

What changes take place in friendship during the adolescent years?

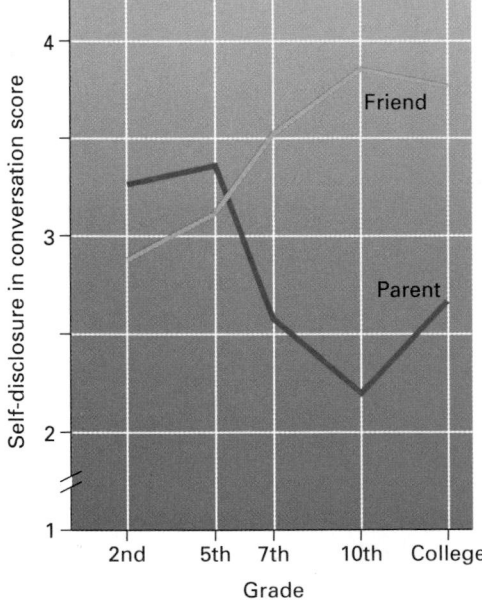

FIGURE 12.4 Developmental Changes in Self-Disclosing Conversations. Self-disclosing conversations with friends increased dramatically in adolescence while declining in an equally dramatic fashion with parents. However, self-disclosing conversations with parents began to pick up somewhat during the college years. The measure of self-disclosure involved a 5-point rating scale completed by the children and youth with a higher score representing greater self-disclosure. The data shown represent the means for each age group.

Peers play powerful roles in the lives of adolescents (Allen & Antonishak, 2008; Brown & others, 2008). When you think back to your own adolescent years, you probably recall many of your most enjoyable moments as experiences shared with peers. Peer relations undergo important changes in adolescence, including changes in friendships and in peer groups and the beginning of romantic relationships. In middle and late childhood, as we discussed in Chapter 10, the focus of peer relations is on being liked by classmates and being included in games or lunchroom conversations. Being overlooked or, worse yet, being rejected can have damaging effects on children's development that sometimes are carried forward to adolescence (Bukowski, Velasquez, & Brendgen, 2008).

Friendships

For most children, being popular with their peers is a strong motivator. Beginning in early adolescence, however, teenagers typically prefer to have a smaller number of friendships that are more intense and intimate than those of young children.

Harry Stack Sullivan (1953) was the most influential theorist to discuss the importance of adolescent friendships. In contrast to other psychoanalytic theorists who focused almost exclusively on parent-child relationships, Sullivan argued that friends are also important in shaping the development of children and adolescents. Everyone, said Sullivan, has basic social needs, such as the need for tenderness (secure attachment), playful companionship, social acceptance, intimacy, and sexual relations. Whether or not these needs are fulfilled largely determines our emotional well-being. For example, if the need for playful companionship goes unmet, then we become bored and depressed; if the need for social acceptance is not met, we suffer a lowered sense of self-worth.

During adolescence, said Sullivan, friends become increasingly important in meeting social needs. In particular, Sullivan argued that the need for intimacy intensifies during early adolescence, motivating teenagers to seek out close friends. If adolescents fail to forge such close friendships, they experience loneliness and a reduced sense of self-worth.

Many of Sullivan's ideas have withstood the test of time (Buhrmester, 2005). For example, adolescents report disclosing intimate and personal information to their friends more often than do younger children (Buhrmester, 1998) (see Figure 12.4). Adolescents also say they depend more on friends than on parents to satisfy their needs for companionship, reassurance of worth, and intimacy. The ups and downs of experiences with friends shape adolescents' well-being (Berndt, 2002).

The characteristics of friends have an important influence on adolescent development (Crosnoe & others, 2008; Rubin, Fredstrom, & Bowker, 2008). A recent study revealed that friends' grade-point average was an important positive attribute (Cook, Deng, & Morgano, 2007). Friends' grade-point average was a consistent predictor of positive school achievement and also was linked to a lower level of negative behavior in areas such as drug abuse and acting out.

Although most adolescents develop friendships with individuals who are close to their own age, some adolescents become best friends with younger or older individuals. Do older friends encourage adolescents to engage in delinquent behavior or early sexual behavior? Adolescents who interact with older youth do engage in these behaviors more frequently, but it is not known whether the older youth guide younger adolescents toward deviant behavior or whether the younger adolescents were already prone to deviant behavior before they developed the friendship with the older youth (Billy, Rodgers, & Udry, 1984). A recent study also revealed that over time, from the sixth through tenth grades, girls were more likely to have older male friends, which places some girls on a developmental trajectory for engaging in problem behavior (Poulin & Pedersen, 2007).

Peer Groups

How extensive is peer pressure in adolescence? What roles do cliques and crowds play in adolescents' lives? As we see next, researchers have found that the standards of peer groups and the influence of crowds and cliques become increasingly important during adolescence.

Most adolescents conform to the mainstream standards of their peers. However, the rebellious or anticonformist adolescent reacts counter to the mainstream peer group's expectations, deliberately moving away from the actions or beliefs this group advocates.

Peer Pressure
Young adolescents conform more to peer standards than children do. Around the eighth and ninth-grades, conformity to peers—especially to their antisocial standards—peaks (Leventhal, 1994). At this point, adolescents are most likely to go along with a peer to steal hubcaps off a car, draw graffiti on a wall, or steal cosmetics from a store counter. A recent study revealed that 14 to 18 years of age is an especially important time for developing the ability to stand up for what one believes and resist peer pressure to do otherwise (Steinberg & Monahan, 2007). One study also found that U.S. adolescents are more likely than Japanese adolescents to put pressure on their peers to resist parental influence (Rothbaum & others, 2000).

Cliques and Crowds
Cliques and crowds assume more important roles in the lives of adolescents than children (Brown & others, 2008). **Cliques** are small groups that range from 2 to about 12 individuals and average about 5 to 6 individuals. The clique members are usually of the same sex and about the same age.

Cliques can form because adolescents engage in similar activities, such as being in a club or on a sports team. Some cliques also form because of friendship. Several adolescents may form a clique because they have spent time with each other, share mutual interests, and enjoy each other's company. Not necessarily friends, they often develop a friendship if they stay in the clique. What do adolescents do in cliques? They share ideas and hang out together. Often they develop an in-group identity in which they believe that their clique is better than other cliques.

Crowds are larger than cliques and less personal. Adolescents are usually members of a crowd based on reputation, and they may or may not spend much time together. Many crowds are defined by the activities adolescents engage in (such as "jocks" who are good at sports or "druggies" who take drugs) (Brown & others, 2008). Reputation-based crowds often appear for the first time in early adolescence and usually become less prominent in late adolescence (Collins & Steinberg, 2006).

In one study, crowd membership was associated with adolescent self-esteem (Brown & Lohr, 1987). The crowds included jocks (athletically oriented), populars (well-known students who led social activities), normals (middle-of-the-road students who made up the masses), druggies or toughs (known for illicit drug use or other delinquent activities), and nobodies (low in social skills or intellectual abilities). The self-esteem of the jocks and the populars was highest, whereas that of the nobodies was lowest. One group of adolescents not in a crowd had self-esteem equivalent to that of the jocks and the populars; this group was the independents, who indicated that crowd membership was not important to them. Keep in mind that these data are correlational; self-esteem could increase an adolescent's probability of becoming a crowd member, just as crowd membership could increase the adolescent's self-esteem.

Dating and Romantic Relationships

Adolescents spend considerable time either dating or thinking about dating (Furman & Simon, 2008). Dating can be a form of recreation, a source of status, a setting for learning about close relationships, as well as a way of finding a mate.

> *T*eenagers are people who express a burning desire to be different by dressing exactly alike.
>
> **—Anonymous**

clique A small group that ranges from 2 to about 12 individuals, averaging about 5 to 6 individuals, and can form because adolescents engage in similar activities.

crowd A larger group structure than a clique, a crowd is usually formed based on reputation and members may or may not spend much time together.

What are dating relationships like in adolescence?

Developmental Changes in Dating and Romantic Relationships Can you remember confiding to a friend in middle school or junior high that you "liked" someone? Or what it was like when you first had an exclusive relationship with someone, "going out" with that person and only that person? One study found that 40 percent of the sixth-graders studied had announced that "I like" someone (Buhrmester, 2001). But it wasn't until the tenth grade that half of the adolescents had a romantic relationship that lasted two months or longer. By the twelfth grade, a quarter of the adolescents still had not had a romantic relationship that lasted two months or longer. Another study found that 35 percent of 15- to 16-year-olds and almost 60 percent of 17- and 18-year-olds had had dating relationships that endured for 11 months or longer (Carver, Joyner, & Udry, 2003).

In their early exploration of romantic relationships, today's adolescents often find comfort in numbers and begin hanging out together in mixed-sex groups (O'Sullivan & others, 2007). Sometimes they just hang out at someone's house or get organized enough to get someone to drive them to a mall or a movie. Or they may try *cyberdating*—"dating" over the Internet—as another alternative to traditional dating. Cyberdating is popular especially among middle school students. Of course, cyberdating can be dangerous since one does not know who is really at the other end of the computer link. By the time they reach high school and are able to drive, most adolescents are more interested in real-life dating.

The functions of dating and romantic relationships also tend to change over the course of adolescence. Young adolescents are likely to see romantic relationships, not as a way of fulfilling attachment or sexual needs, but as a context for exploring how attractive they are, how they should romantically interact with someone, and how all of this looks to the peer group (Brown, 1999).

Dating in Gay Male and Lesbian Youth Recently, researchers have begun to study romantic relationships in gay male and lesbian youth (Savin-Williams, 2007, 2008). Many sexual minority youth date other-sex peers, which can help them to clarify their sexual orientation or disguise it from others (Savin-Williams & Ream, 2007). Most gay male and lesbian youth have had some same-sex sexual experience, often with peers who are "experimenting," and then go on to a primarily heterosexual orientation (Savin-Williams & Cohen, 2007). In one study, gay male and lesbian youth rated the breakup of a current romance as their second most stressful problem, second only to disclosure of their sexual orientation to their parents (D'Augelli, 1991).

Sociocultural Contexts and Dating The sociocultural context exerts a powerful influence on adolescents' dating patterns. This influence may be seen in differences in dating patterns among ethnic groups within the United States. For example, one study found that Asian American adolescents were less likely to have been involved in a romantic relationship in the past 18 months than African American or Latino adolescents (Carver, Joyner, & Udry, 2003).

Values, religious beliefs, and traditions often dictate the age at which dating begins, how much freedom in dating is allowed, whether dates must be chaperoned by adults or parents, and the roles of males and females in dating. For example, Latino and Asian American cultures have more conservative standards regarding adolescent dating than does the Anglo-American culture. Dating may become a source of conflict within a family if the parents have immigrated from cultures in which dating begins at a late age, little freedom in dating is allowed, dates are chaperoned, and adolescent girl dating is especially restricted. When immigrant adolescents choose to adopt the ways of the dominant U.S. culture (such as unchaperoned dating), they often clash with parents and extended-family members who have more traditional values.

In one study, Latina young adults in the midwestern United States reflected on their experiences in dating during adolescence (Raffaeli & Ontai, 2004). They said that their parents placed strict boundaries on their romantic involvement. As a result, the young women said that their adolescent dating experiences were filled with tension and conflict. Over half of the Latinas engaged in "sneak dating" without their parents' knowledge.

What are some ethnic variations in dating during adolescence?

Dating and Adjustment   Researchers have linked dating and romantic relationships with various measures of how well adjusted adolescents are (Friedlander & others, 2007). Not surprisingly, one study of tenth-grade adolescents found that those who dated were more likely to be accepted by their peers and to be perceived as more physically attractive than those who did not date (Furman, Ho, & Low, 2005). Another study found that 14- to 19-year-old adolescents who were not involved in a romantic relationship had more social anxiety than their counterparts who were dating or romantically involved (La Greca & Harrison, 2005).

How is dating linked to adolescent adjustment?

But dating and romantic relationships at an unusually early age have been linked with several problems. For example, early dating and "going with" someone is associated with adolescent pregnancy and problems at home and school (Florsheim, Moore, & Edgington, 2003). In one study, girls' early romantic involvement was linked with lower grades, less active participation in class discussion, and school-related problems (Buhrmester, 2001). Even at the tenth-grade level, adolescents who dated had more externalized problems, such as delinquency, and engaged in substance use (as well as genital sexual behavior) more than their counterparts who did not date (Furman, Ho, & Low, 2005). A recent study of adolescent girls revealed that a higher frequency of dating was linked to having depressive symptoms and emotionally unavailable parents (Steinberg & Davila, 2008). Another recent study of adolescent girls found that those who engaged in co-rumination (excessive discussion of problems with friends) were more likely to be involved in a romantic relationship, and together co-rumination and romantic involvement predicted an increase in depressive symptoms (Starr & Davila, 2008).

Review and Reflect: Learning Goal 3

 Characterize the Changes That Occur in Peer Relations During Adolescence

REVIEW

- What changes take place in friendship during adolescence?
- What are adolescents' peer groups like?
- What is the nature of adolescent dating and romantic relationships?

REFLECT

- What were your peer relationships like during adolescence? What peer groups were you involved in? How did they influence your development? What were your dating and romantic relationships like in adolescence? If you could change anything about the way you experienced peer relations in adolescence, what would it be?

4 CULTURE AND ADOLESCENT DEVELOPMENT

Cross-Cultural Comparisons   **Ethnicity**

We live in an increasingly diverse world, one in which there is increasing contact between adolescents from different cultures and ethnic groups. In this section, we will explore these differences as they relate to adolescents. We will describe how adolescents in various cultures spend their time, and some of the rites of passage they undergo. We will also examine how ethnicity affects U.S. adolescents and their development.

Asian Indian adolescents in a marriage ceremony

Cross-Cultural Comparisons

What traditions remain for adolescents around the globe? What circumstances are changing adolescents' lives?

Traditions and Changes in Adolescence around the Globe   Consider some of the variations of adolescence around the world (Brown & Larson, 2002):

- Two-thirds of Asian Indian adolescents accept their parents' choice of a marital partner for them.
- In the Philippines, many female adolescents sacrifice their own futures by migrating to the city to earn money that they can send home to their families.
- In the Middle East, many adolescents are not allowed to interact with the other sex, even in school.
- Street youth in Kenya and other parts of the world learn to survive under highly stressful circumstances (Nsamenang, 2002). In some cases abandoned by their parents, they may engage in delinquency or prostitution to provide for their economic needs.
- Whereas individuals in the United States are marrying later than in past generations, youth in Russia are marrying earlier to legitimize sexual activity (Stetsenko, 2002).

Thus, depending on the culture being observed, adolescence may involve many different experiences (Strohmeier & Schmitt-Rodermund, 2008).

Some cultures have retained their traditions regarding adolescence, but rapid global change is altering the experience of adolescence in many places, presenting new opportunities and challenges to young people's health and well-being. Around the world, adolescents' experiences may differ.

Muslim school in Middle East with boys only

Health   Adolescent health and well-being have improved in some respects but not in others. Overall, fewer adolescents around the world die from infectious diseases and malnutrition now than in the past (UNICEF, 2008). However, a number of adolescent health-compromising behaviors (especially illicit drug use and unprotected sex) are increasing in frequency (Blum & Nelson-Mmari, 2004). Extensive increases in the rates of HIV in adolescents have occurred in many sub-Saharan countries (UNICEF, 2008).

Gender   Around the world, the experiences of male and female adolescents continue to be quite different (Brown & Larson, 2002). Except in a few regions, such as Japan, the Philippines, and Western countries, males have far greater access to educational opportunities than females (UNICEF, 2008). In many countries, adolescent females have less freedom than males to pursue a variety of careers and engage in various leisure activities. Gender differences in sexual expression are widespread, especially in India, Southeast Asia, Latin America, and Arab countries where there are far more restrictions on the sexual activity of adolescent females than on males. These gender differences do appear to be narrowing over time, however. In some countries, educational and career opportunities for women are expanding, and control over adolescent girls' romantic and sexual relationships is weakening.

Family   In some countries, adolescents grow up in closely knit families with extensive extended kin networks that retain a traditional way of life. For example, in Arab countries, "adolescents are taught strict codes of conduct and loyalty" (Brown & Larson, 2002, p. 6). However, in Western countries such as the United States, parenting is less authoritarian than in the past, and much larger numbers of adolescents are growing up in divorced families and stepfamilies.

In many countries around the world, current trends "include greater family mobility, migration to urban areas, family members working in distant cities or countries,

Street youth in Rio de Janeiro

smaller families, fewer extended-family households, and increases in mothers' employment" (Brown & Larson, 2002, p. 7). Unfortunately, many of these changes may reduce the ability of families to spend time with their adolescents.

Peers   Some cultures give peers a stronger role in adolescence than others (Brown & Larson, 2002; Brown & others, 2008). In most Western nations, peers figure prominently in adolescents' lives, in some cases taking on roles that are otherwise assumed by parents. Among street youth in South America, the peer network serves as a surrogate family that supports survival in dangerous and stressful settings. In other regions of the world, such as in Arab countries, peer relations are restricted, especially for girls (Booth, 2002).

In sum, adolescents' lives are characterized by a combination of change and tradition. Researchers have found both similarities and differences in the experiences of adolescents in different countries (Larson & Wilson, 2004). To read about how adolescents around the world spend their time, see the *Diversity in Life-Span Development* interlude.

Diversity in Life-Span Development
How Adolescents Around the World Spend Their Time

How do East Asian and U.S. adolescents spend their time differently?

Reed Larson, Suman Verma, and their colleagues (Larson, 2001; Larson & Verma, 1999; Watkins, Larson, & Sullivan, 2008) have examined how adolescents spend their time in work, play, and developmental activities such as school. U.S. adolescents spend about 60 percent as much time on schoolwork as East Asian adolescents do, which is mainly due to U.S. adolescents doing less homework (Larson & Verma, 1999).

What U.S. adolescents have in greater quantities than adolescents in other industrialized countries is discretionary time (Larson & Wilson, 2004). About 40 to 50 percent of U.S. adolescents' waking hours (not counting summer vacations) is spent in discretionary activities compared with 25 to 35 percent in East Asia and 35 to 45 percent in Europe. Whether this additional discretionary time is a liability or an asset for U.S. adolescents, of course, depends on how they use it.

According to Larson (2001), for optimal development, U.S. adolescents may have too much unstructured time because when adolescents are allowed to choose what they do with their time, they typically engage in unchallenging activities such as hanging out and watching TV. Although relaxation and social interaction are important aspects of adolescence, it seems unlikely that spending large numbers of hours per week in unchallenging activities fosters development. Structured voluntary activities may provide more promise for adolescent development than unstructured time, especially if adults give responsibility to adolescents, challenge them, and provide competent guidance in these activities (Larson & others, 2007; Watkins, Larson, & Sullivan, 2008).

Rites of Passage   Another variation in the experiences of adolescents in different cultures is whether the adolescents go through a rite of passage. Some societies have elaborate ceremonies that signal the adolescent's move to maturity and achievement of adult status (Kottak, 2004). A **rite of passage** is a ceremony or ritual that marks an individual's transition from one status to another. Most rites of passage focus on the transition to adult status. In some traditional cultures, rites of passage are the avenue through which adolescents gain access to sacred adult practices, to knowledge, and to sexuality. These rites often involve dramatic practices intended to facilitate the adolescent's separation from the immediate family, especially the mother. The transformation is usually characterized by some form of ritual death and rebirth, or by means of contact with the spiritual world. Bonds are forged between the adolescent and the adult instructors through shared rituals, hazards, and secrets to allow the adolescent to enter the adult world. This kind of ritual provides a forceful and discontinuous entry into the adult world at a time when the adolescent is perceived to be ready for the change.

These Congolese Kota boys painted their faces as part of a rite of passage to adulthood. *What rites of passage do American adolescents have?*

rite of passage A ceremony or ritual that marks an individual's transition from one status to another. Most rites of passage focus on the transition to adult status.

Consider the flowers of a garden: Though differing in kind, color, form, and shape, yet, in as much as they are refreshed by the waters of one spring, revived by the breath of one wind, invigorated by the rays of one sun, this diversity increases their charm and adds to their beauty. . . . How unpleasing to the eye if all the flowers and plants, the leaves and blossoms, the fruits, the branches, and the trees of that garden were all of the same shape and color! Diversity of hues, form, and shape enriches and adorns the garden and heightens its effect.

—ABDU'L BAHA
Persian Baha'i Religious Leader, 19th/20th Century

An especially rich tradition of rites of passage for adolescents has prevailed in African cultures, especially sub-Saharan Africa. Under the influence of Western industrialized culture, many of these rites are disappearing today, although they are still prevalent in locations where formal education is not readily available.

Do we have such rites of passage for American adolescents? We certainly do not have universal formal ceremonies that mark the passage from adolescence to adulthood. Certain religious and social groups do, however, have initiation ceremonies that indicate that an advance in maturity has been reached: the Jewish bar and bat mitzvah, the Catholic confirmation, and social debuts, for example. School graduation ceremonies come the closest to being culture-wide rites of passage in the United States. The high school graduation ceremony has become nearly universal for middle-class adolescents and increasing numbers of adolescents from low-income backgrounds.

Ethnicity

Earlier in this chapter, we explored the identity development of ethnic minority adolescents. Here we will further examine immigration and the relationship between ethnicity and socioeconomic status.

Immigration   Relatively high rates of immigration are contributing to the growth of ethnic minorities in the United States (Liu & others, 2008; Wong & others, 2008). Immigrants often experience stressors uncommon to or less prominent among longtime residents such as language barriers, dislocations and separations from support networks, changes in SES status, and the dual struggle to preserve identity and to acculturate.

The adjustment of immigrants to their new country may be complicated by the fact that both native-born Americans and immigrants may be torn between two values related to ethnic issues: assimilation and pluralism.

- **Assimilation** is the absorption of ethnic minority groups into the dominant group, which often means the loss of some or virtually all of the behavior and values of the ethnic group. Individuals who endorse assimilation usually advocate that ethnic minority groups become more American.

- **Pluralism** is the coexistence of distinct ethnic and cultural groups in the same society, each of which maintains its cultural differences.

Many of the families that have immigrated in recent decades to the United States, such as Mexican Americans and Asian Americans, come from collectivist cultures in which family obligation is strong (Fuligni & Fuligni, 2007). For adolescents this family obligation may take the form of assisting parents in their occupations and contributing to the family's welfare (Parke & Buriel, 2006). This often means helping out in jobs in construction, gardening, cleaning, or restaurants. In some cases, the long hours immigrant youth work in such jobs can be detrimental to their academic achievement.

assimilation The absorption of ethnic minority groups into the dominant group, which often involves the loss of some or virtually all of the behavior and values of the ethnic minority group.

pluralism The coexistence of distinct ethnic and cultural groups in the same society, each of which maintains its cultural differences.

Jason Leonard, age 15: "I want America to know that most of us black teens are not troubled people from broken homes and headed to jail. . . . In my relationships with my parents, we show respect for each other and we have values in our house. We have traditions we celebrate together, including Christmas and Kwanzaa."

Ethnicity and Socioeconomic Status   Much of the research on ethnic minority adolescents has failed to tease apart the influences of ethnicity and socioeconomic status. Ethnicity and socioeconomic status can interact in ways that exaggerate the influence of ethnicity because ethnic minority individuals are overrepresented in the lower socioeconomic levels of American society (Healey, 2008; Rowley, Kurtz-Costes, & Cooper, 2009). Consequently, researchers too often have given ethnic explanations for aspects of adolescent development that were largely due instead to socioeconomic status.

Not all ethnic minority families are poor. However, poverty contributes to the stressful life experiences of many ethnic minority adolescents (Leon-Guerrero, 2009). Thus, many ethnic minority adolescents experience a double disadvantage: (1) prejudice, discrimination, and bias because of their ethnic minority status; and (2) the stressful effects of poverty.

Although some ethnic minority youth have middle-income backgrounds, economic advantage does not entirely enable them to escape the prejudice, discrimination, and bias associated with being a member of an ethnic minority group (Banks, 2008; Harris & Graham, 2007). Even Japanese Americans, who are often characterized as a "model minority" because of their strong achievement orientation and family cohesiveness, still experience stress associated with ethnic minority status.

Recent studies provide insight into the discrimination experienced by ethnic minority adolescents. In one study, discrimination of seventh- to tenth-grade African American students was related to their lower level of psychological functioning, including perceived stress, symptoms of depression, and lower perceived well-being; more positive attitudes toward African American students by others were associated with more positive psychological functioning in the African American adolescents (Sellers & others, 2006). The most frequent type of racial hassles reported by the African American adolescents were being accused of something or treated suspiciously and being treated as if you were "stupid," being "talked down to" (see Figure 12.5). Also, in a study of Latino youth, discrimination was negatively linked, and social and parental support were positively related, to their academic success (DeGarmo & Martinez, 2006).

Type of Racial Hassle	Percent of Adolescents Who Reported the Racial Hassle in the Past Year
Being accused of something or treated suspiciously	71.0
Being treated as if you were "stupid," being "talked down to"	70.7
Others reacting to you as if they were afraid or intimidated	70.1
Being observed or followed while in public places	69.1
Being treated rudely or disrespectfully	56.4
Being ignored, overlooked, not given service	56.4
Others expecting your work to be inferior	54.1
Being insulted, called a name, or harassed	52.2

FIGURE 12.5 African-American Adolescents' Reports of Racial Hassles in the Past Year

---

Review and Reflect: Learning Goal 4

4 **Explain How Culture Influences Adolescent Development**

REVIEW

- What are some comparisons of adolescents in different cultures? How do adolescents around the world spend their time? What are rites of passage?
- How does ethnicity influence adolescent development?

REFLECT

- What is your ethnicity? Have you ever been stereotyped because of your ethnicity? How different is your identity from the mainstream culture?

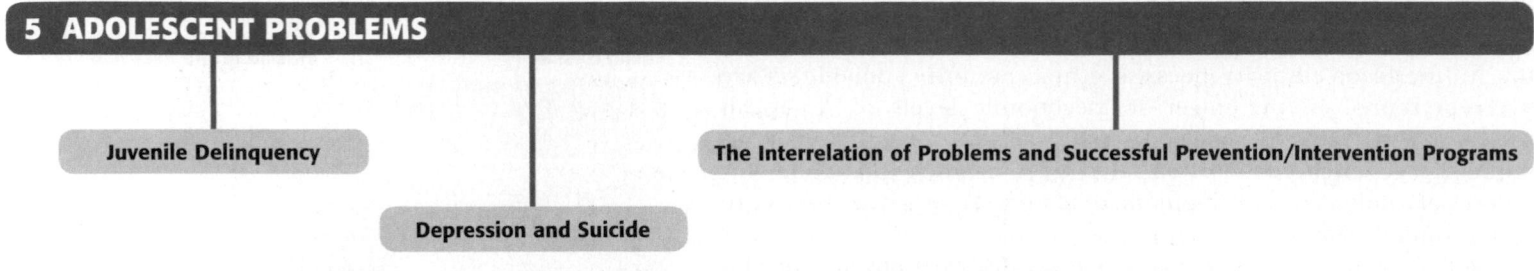

5 ADOLESCENT PROBLEMS

Juvenile Delinquency

Depression and Suicide

The Interrelation of Problems and Successful Prevention/Intervention Programs

In Chapter 11, we described several adolescent problems: substance abuse, sexually transmitted infections, and eating disorders. In this chapter, we will examine the problems of juvenile delinquency, depression, and suicide. We will also explore interrelationships among adolescent problems and how such problems can be prevented or remedied.

Juvenile Delinquency

The label **juvenile delinquent** is applied to an adolescent who breaks the law or engages in behavior that is considered illegal. Like other categories of disorders, juvenile delinquency is a broad concept; legal infractions range from littering to murder. Because the adolescent technically becomes a juvenile delinquent only after being judged guilty of a crime by a court of law, official records do not accurately reflect the number of illegal acts juvenile delinquents commit. Estimates of the number of juvenile delinquents in the United States are sketchy, but FBI statistics indicate that at least 2 percent of all youth are involved in juvenile court cases.

U.S. government statistics reveal that juvenile court caseloads for males were three times higher than for females in 2002 (National Center for Juvenile Justice, 2006). In the last two decades, however, there has been a greater increase in female delinquency than in male delinquency (National Center for Juvenile Justice, 2006). For both male and female delinquents, rates for property offenses are higher than for other rates of offenses (such as offenses against persons, drug offenses, and public order offenses). Arrests of adolescent males for delinquency still are much higher than for adolescent females.

Delinquency rates among minority groups and lower-socioeconomic-status youth are especially high in proportion to the overall population of these groups. However, such groups have less influence over the judicial decision-making process in the United States and, therefore, may be judged delinquent more readily than their White, middle-socioeconomic-status counterparts.

One issue in juvenile justice is whether an adolescent who commits a crime should be tried as an adult (Grimes, 2007). In one study, trying adolescent offenders as adults increased rather than reduced their crime rate (Myers, 1999). The study evaluated more than 500 violent youth in Pennsylvania, which has adopted a "get tough" policy. Although these 500 offenders had been given harsher punishment than a comparison group retained in juvenile court, they were more likely to be rearrested—and rearrested more quickly—for new offenses once they were returned to the community. This suggests that the price of short-term public safety attained by prosecuting juveniles as adults might increase the number of criminal offenses over the long run.

A distinction is made between early-onset—before age 11—and late-onset—after 11—antisocial behavior. Early-onset antisocial behavior is associated with more negative developmental outcomes than late-onset antisocial behavior (Schulenberg & Zarrett, 2006). Early-onset antisocial behavior is more likely to persist into emerging adulthood and is associated with more mental health and relationship problems (Loeber & others, 2007).

juvenile delinquent An adolescent who breaks the law or engages in behavior that is considered illegal.

Causes of Delinquency   What causes delinquency? Many causes have been proposed, including heredity, identity problems, community influences, and family experiences. Erik Erikson (1968), for example, points out that adolescents whose development has restricted them from acceptable social roles or made them feel that they cannot measure up to the demands placed on them may choose a negative identity. Adolescents with a negative identity may find support for their delinquent image among peers, reinforcing the negative identity. For Erikson, delinquency is an attempt to establish an identity, although a negative one.

Although delinquency is less exclusively a phenomenon of lower socioeconomic status than it was in the past, some characteristics of lower-class culture might promote delinquency. The norms of many lower-SES peer groups and gangs are antisocial, or counterproductive, to the goals and norms of society at large. Getting into and staying out of trouble are prominent features of life for some adolescents in low-income neighborhoods (Flannery & others, 2003). Being "tough" and "masculine" are high-status traits for lower-SES boys, and these traits are often measured by the adolescent's success in performing and getting away with delinquent acts. Furthermore, adolescents in communities with high crime rates observe many models who engage in criminal activities (Loeber & others, 2007). These communities may be characterized by poverty, unemployment, and feelings of alienation toward the middle class (Byrnes & others, 2007). Quality schooling, educational funding, and organized neighborhood activities may be lacking in these communities (Molnar & others, 2007).

What are some factors that are linked to whether adolescents engage in delinquent acts?

Certain characteristics of family support systems are also associated with delinquency (Cavell & others, 2007; Feinberg & others, 2007). Parents of delinquents are less skilled in discouraging antisocial behavior and in encouraging skilled behavior than are parents of nondelinquents. Parental monitoring of adolescents is especially important in determining whether an adolescent becomes a delinquent (Laird & others, 2008). For example, a recent study revealed that maternal monitoring was linked to a lower incidence of delinquency in Latino girls (Loukas, Suizzo, & Prelow, 2007). Family discord and inconsistent and inappropriate discipline are also associated with delinquency (Bor, McGee, & Fagan, 2004). A recent study revealed that being physically abused in the first five years of life was linked to a greater risk of delinquency in adolescence (Lansford & others, 2007). And an increasing number of studies have found that siblings can have a strong influence on delinquency (Bank, Burraston, & Snyder, 2004). In one study, high levels of hostile sibling relationships and older sibling delinquency were linked with younger sibling delinquency in both brother and sister pairs (Slomkowski & others, 2001). Finally, having delinquent peers greatly increases the risk of becoming delinquent (Bukowski, Brendgen, & Vitaro, 2007). For example, a recent study found that peer rejection and having deviant friends at 7 to 13 years of age were linked with increased delinquency at 14 to 15 years of age (Vitaro, Pedersen, & Brendgen, 2007). Also, another recent study revealed that association with deviant peers was linked to a higher incidence of delinquency in male African American adolescents (Bowman, Prelow, & Weaver, 2007).

Cognitive factors, such as low self-control, low intelligence, and lack of sustained attention, also were implicated in delinquency. For example, a recent study revealed that low-IQ serious delinquents were characterized by low self-control (Koolhof & others, 2007). Another recent study found that at age 16 nondelinquents were more likely to have a higher verbal IQ and engage in sustained attention than delinquents (Loeber & others, 2007).

One individual whose goal is to help at-risk adolescents, such as juvenile delinquents, cope more effectively with their lives is Rodney Hammond. Read about his work in the *Careers in Life-Span Development* profile.

Common parenting weaknesses in the families of antisocial boys include a lack of supervision, poor disciplining skills, limited problem-solving abilities, and a tendency to be uncommunicative with sons.

—Gerald Patterson
Contemporary American Psychologist, University of Oregon

Careers in Life-Span Development

Rodney Hammond, Health Psychologist

Rodney Hammond described his college experiences:

> When I started as an undergraduate at the University of Illinois, Champaign-Urbana, I hadn't decided on my major. But to help finance my education, I took a part-time job in a child development research program sponsored by the psychology department. There, I observed inner-city children in settings designed to enhance their learning. I saw firsthand the contribution psychology can make, and I knew I wanted to be a psychologist. (American Psychological Association, 2003, p. 26).

Rodney Hammond went on to obtain a doctorate in school and community psychology with a focus on children's development. For a number of years, he trained clinical psychologists at Wright State University in Ohio and directed a program to reduce violence in ethnic minority youth. There, he and his associates taught at-risk youth how to use social skills to effectively manage conflict and to recognize situations that could lead to violence. Today, Hammond is Director of Violence Prevention at the Centers for Disease Control and Prevention in Atlanta. Hammond says that if you are interested in people and problem solving, psychology is a wonderful way to put these together.

Rodney Hammond, counseling an adolescent girl about the risks of adolescence and how to effectively cope with them.

Depression and Suicide

What is the nature of depression in adolescence? What causes an adolescent to commit suicide?

Depression Depression is more likely to occur in adolescence than in childhood and more likely to occur in adulthood than adolescence. Researchers have found a linear increase in major depressive disorder from 15 to 22 years of age (Kessler & Walters, 1998). However, an early onset of a mood disorder, such as major depressive disorder in adolescence, is linked with more negative outcomes than a late onset of a mood disorder (Schulenberg & Zarrett, 2006). For example, the early onset is associated with further recurrences of depression and with an increased risk of being diagnosed with an anxiety disorder, substance abuse, eating disorder, suicide attempt, and unemployment at a future point in development (Graber, 2004).

Further, adolescent girls and emerging adult women consistently have higher rates of depression than their male counterparts (Frydenberg, 2007; Nolen-Hoeksema, 2007). Among the reasons for this gender difference are that females tend to ruminate in their depressed mood and amplify it; females' self-images, especially their body images, are more negative than males'; females face more discrimination than males do; and puberty occurs earlier for girls than for boys. As a result girls experience a piling up of changes and life experiences in the middle school years that can increase depression.

Certain family factors place adolescents at risk for developing depression. These include having a depressed parent, emotionally unavailable parents, parents who have high marital conflict, and parents with financial problems. For example, a recent study revealed that parent-adolescent conflict and low parental support were linked to adolescent depression (Sheeber & others, 2007). Another recent study found that being in a two-parent family structure and feeling connected to parents, peers, and school were protective factors associated with a lower incidence of depressed mood during adolescence (Costello & others, 2008).

Poor peer relationships also are associated with adolescent depression (Kistner & others, 2006). Not having a close relationship with a best friend, having less contact with friends, and experiencing peer rejection all increase depressive tendencies in adolescents. Problems in adolescent romantic relationships can also trigger depression, especially for girls (Davila & Steinberg, 2006).

Friendship often provide social support. However, a recent study of third- through ninth-graders revealed that one aspect of social support in friendship may have costs as well as benefits (Rose, Carlson, & Waller, 2007). In the study, girls' co-rumination (as reflected in excessively discussing problems) predicted not only an increase in positive friendship quality but also an increase in further co-rumination as well as an increase in depressive and anxiety symptoms. However, for boys, co-rumination predicted only an increase in positive friendship quality but not an increase in depressive and anxiety symptoms. One implication of the research is that some girls who are vulnerable to developing internalized problems may go undetected because they have supportive friendships.

What type of treatment is most likely to reduce depression in adolescence? A recent study revealed that depressed adolescents recovered faster when they took an antidepressant and received cognitive behavior therapy that involved improving their coping skills than when they took only an antidepressant or received only cognitive behavior therapy (The TADS Team, 2007). However, a safety concern has emerged with regard to taking antidepressants such as Prozac, and in 2004 the U.S. Food and Drug Administration assigned warnings to such drugs stating that they slightly increase the risk of suicidal behavior in adolescents. In the study just described, 15 percent of depressed adolescents who took Prozac only had suicidal thoughts or attempted suicide compared with only 6 percent receiving cognitive behavior therapy alone and 8 percent receiving Prozac plus cognitive behavior therapy.

What are some characteristics of adolescents who become depressed? What are some factors that are linked with suicide attempts by adolescents?

Suicide   Suicide behavior is rare in childhood but escalates in adolescence and then increases further in emerging adulthood (Park & others, 2006). Suicide is the third-leading cause of death in 10- to 19-year-olds today in the United States (National Center for Health Statistics, 2007). After increasing to high levels in the 1990s, suicide rates in adolescents have declined in recent years (Gould & others, 2003). In 2004, 4,214 U.S. individuals from 15 to 24 years of age committed suicide (Minino, Heron, & Smith, 2006). Emerging adults have triple the rate of suicide as adolescents (Park & others, 2006).

Although a suicide threat should always be taken seriously, far more adolescents contemplate or attempt it unsuccessfully than actually commit it (Miranda & others, 2008). In a national study, in 2005, 17 percent of U.S. high school students said that they had seriously considered or attempted suicide in the last 12 months (Eaton & others, 2006). As shown in Figure 12.6, this percentage has declined since 1991. In the national survey, in 2005, 2.3 percent reported a suicide attempt that resulted in an injury, poisoning, or drug overdose that had been treated by a doctor. Females were more likely to attempt suicide than males, but males were more likely to succeed in committing suicide. Males use more lethal means, such as guns, in their suicide attempts, whereas adolescent females are more likely to cut their wrists or take an overdose of sleeping pills—methods less likely to result in death.

One issue focuses on whether lesbian and gay male adolescents are especially vulnerable to suicide. In one study of 12,000 adolescents, approximately 15 percent of lesbian and gay male youth said that they had attempted suicide compared with 7 percent of heterosexual youth (Russell & Joyner, 2001). However, Richard Savin-Williams (2001) found that

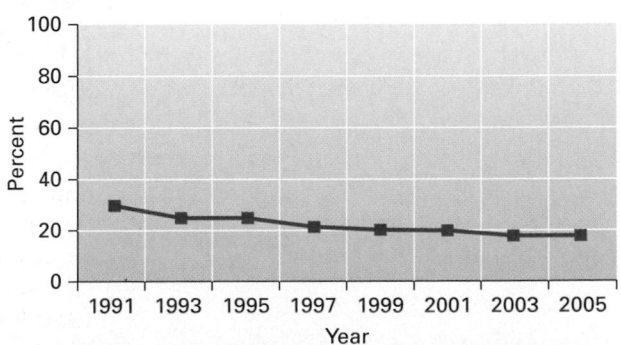

FIGURE 12.6 Percentage of U.S. Ninth- to Twelfth-Grade Students Who Seriously Considered Attempting Suicide in the Previous 12 Months from 1991 to 2005

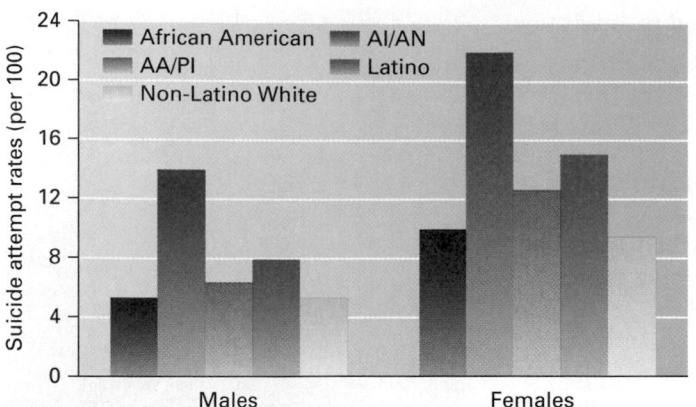

FIGURE 12.7 Suicide Attempts by U.S. Adolescents from Different Ethnic Groups. *Note:* Data shown are for one-year rates of self-reported suicide attempts. AI/AN = American Indian/Alaska Native; AA/PI = Asian/American/Pacific Islander.

lesbian and gay male adolescents were only slightly more likely than heterosexual adolescents to attempt suicide. He argues that most studies have exaggerated the suicide rates for lesbian and gay male adolescents because they survey only the most disturbed youth who are attending support groups or hanging out at shelters for lesbian and gay male youth.

Distal, or earlier, experiences often are involved in suicide attempts as well. The adolescent may have a long-standing history of family instability and unhappiness. Just as a lack of affection and emotional support, high control, and pressure for achievement by parents during childhood are related to adolescent depression, such combinations of family experiences also are likely to show up as distal factors in adolescents' suicide attempts.

Adolescents' peer relations also are linked to suicide attempts. A recent research review revealed that prior suicide attempts by member of an adolescent's social groups were linked to the probability the adolescent also would attempt suicide (de Leo & Heller, 2008). Adolescents who attempt suicide may lack supportive friendships. One study found that social isolation was linked with suicide attempts in adolescent girls (Bearman & Moody, 2004).

Cultural contexts also are linked to suicide attempts and adolescent suicide attempts vary across ethnic groups in the United States. As indicated in Figure 12.7, more than 20 percent of American Indian/Alaska Native (AI/AN) female adolescents reported that they had attempted suicide in the previous year, and suicide accounts for almost 20 percent of AI/AN deaths in 15- to 19-year-olds (Goldston & others, 2008). As indicated in Figure 12.7, African American and non-Latino White males reported the lowest incidence of suicide attempts. A major risk factor in the high rate of suicide attempts by AI/AN adolescents is their elevated rate of alcohol abuse.

Just as genetic factors are associated with depression, they also are associated with suicide (Kapornai & Vetro, 2008). The closer a person's genetic relationship to someone who has committed suicide, the more likely that person is to also commit suicide.

What is the psychological profile of the suicidal adolescent? Suicidal adolescents often have depressive symptoms (Ash, 2008). Although not all depressed adolescents are suicidal, depression is the most frequently cited factor associated with adolescent suicide (Bethell & Rhoades, 2008). A sense of hopelessness, low self-esteem, and high self-blame are also associated with adolescent suicide (O'Donnell & others, 2004). A recent study found that perception of being a burden on others and thwarted belongingness were linked to suicidal thoughts (Van Orden & others, 2008). A recent study also revealed that overweight middle school students were more likely to think about, plan, and attempt suicide than their counterparts who were not overweight (Whetstone, Morrissey, & Cummings, 2007). And another recent study found that preteen alcohol use was linked to suicide attempts in adolescence (Swahn, Bossarte, & Sullivent, 2008).

The Interrelation of Problems and Successful Prevention/ Intervention Programs

We have described some of the major adolescent problems in this chapter and in Chapter 11: substance abuse; juvenile delinquency; school-related problems, such as dropping out of school; adolescent pregnancy and sexually transmitted infections; eating disorders; depression; and suicide.

The four problems that affect the most adolescents are (1) drug abuse, (2) juvenile delinquency, (3) sexual problems, and (4) school-related problems (Dryfoos, 1990; Dryfoos & Barkin, 2006). The adolescents most at risk have more than one of these problems. Researchers are increasingly finding that problem behaviors in adolescence are interrelated (Mason, Hitchings, & Spoth, 2007; Thompson, Ho, & Kingree, 2007). For example, heavy substance abuse is related to early sexual activity, lower grades, dropping out of school, and delinquency (Caminis & others, 2007). Early initiation of sexual activity is associated with the use of cigarettes and alcohol, the use of marijuana and other illicit drugs, lower grades, dropping out of school, and delinquency. Delinquency is related to early sexual activity, early pregnancy, substance abuse, and dropping out of school (D'Amico & others, 2008; Doherty, Green, & Ensminger, 2008). As many as 10 percent of adolescents in the United States have been estimated to engage in all four of these problem behaviors (for example, adolescents who have dropped out of school, are behind in their grade level, are users of heavy drugs, regularly use cigarettes and marijuana, and are sexually active but do not use contraception). In 1990, it was estimated that another 15 percent of high-risk youth engage in two or three of the four main problem behaviors (Dryfoos, 1990). Recently, this figure was increased increased to 20 percent of all U.S. adolescents (Dryfoos & Barkin, 2006).

A review of the programs that have been successful in preventing or reducing adolescent problems found these common components (Dryfoos, 1990; Dryfoos & Barkin, 2006):

1. *Intensive individualized attention.* In successful programs, high-risk adolescents are attached to a responsible adult, who gives the adolescent attention and deals with the adolescent's specific needs. This theme occurs in a number of programs. In a successful substance-abuse program, a student assistance counselor is available full-time for individual counseling and referral for treatment.

2. *Community-wide multiagency collaborative approaches.* The basic philosophy of community-wide programs is that a number of different programs and services have to be in place. In one successful substance-abuse program, a community-wide health promotion campaign has been implemented that uses local media and community education, in concert with a substance-abuse curriculum in the schools.

3. *Early identification and intervention.* Reaching younger children and their families before children develop problems, or at the beginning of their problems, is a successful strategy (Aber & others, 2006). One preschool program serves as an excellent model for the prevention of delinquency, pregnancy, substance abuse, and dropping out of school. Operated by the High/Scope Foundation in Ypsilanti, Michigan, the Perry Preschool has had a long-term positive impact on its students. This enrichment program, directed by David Weikart, serves disadvantaged African American children. They attend a high-quality two-year preschool program and receive weekly home visits from program personnel. Based on official police records, by age 19, individuals who had attended the Perry Preschool program were less likely to have been arrested and reported fewer adult offenses than a control group did. The Perry Preschool students also were less likely to drop out of school, and teachers rated their social behavior as more competent than that of a control group who had not received the enriched preschool experience (High/Scope Resource, 2005). To read further about an extensive intervention program, see the *Research in Life-Span Development* interlude.

How are problems interrelated in adolescence? Which components of programs have been successful in preventing or reducing adolescent problems?

Research in Life-Span Development
Fast Track

Fast Track is an intervention that attempts to lower the risk of juvenile delinquency and other problems (The Conduct Problems Prevention Research Group, 2007; Dodge & the Conduct Problems Prevention Research Group, 2007; Lochman & the Conduct Problems Prevention Research Group, 2007; Slough & others, 2008). Schools in four areas (Durham, North Carolina; Nashville, Tennessee;

Seattle, Washington; and rural central Pennsylvania) were identified as high risk based on neigh-borhood crime and poverty data. Researchers screened more than 9,000 kindergarten children in the four schools and randomly assigned 891 of the highest-risk and moderate-risk children to intervention or control groups. The average age of the children when the intervention began was 6.5 years of age.

The 10-year intervention consisted of parent behavior management training, child social cognitive skills training, reading tutoring, home visitations, mentoring, and a revised classroom curriculum that was designed to increase socioemotional competence and decrease aggres-sion. Outcomes were assessed in the third, sixth, and ninth grades for conduct disorder (multiple instances of behaviors such as truancy, running away, fire setting, cruelty to animals, breaking and entering, and excessive fighting across a six-month period), oppositional defiant disorder (an ongoing pattern of disobedient, hostile, and defiant behavior toward authority figures), attention deficit hyperactivity disorder (as described in Chapter 9, being characterized by one or more of these characteristics over a period of time: inattention, hyperactivity, and impulsivity), any exter-nalizing disorder (presence of any of the three disorders previously described), and self-reported antisocial behavior (a list of 34 behaviors, such as skipping school, stealing, and attacking some-one with an intent to hurt them).

The extensive intervention was successful only for children and adolescents who were identified as the highest risk in kindergarten, lowering their incidence of conduct disorder, atten-tion deficit hyperactivity disorder, any externalized disorder, and antisocial behavior. Positive outcomes for the intervention occurred as early as the third grade and continued through the ninth grade. For example, in the ninth grade the intervention reduced the likelihood that the highest-risk kindergarten children would develop conduct disorder by 75 percent, attention deficit hyperactiv-ity disorder by 53 percent, and any externalized disorder by 43 percent.

Review and Reflect: Learning Goal 5

5 **Identify Adolescent Problems in Socioemotional Development and Strategies for Helping Adolescents with Problems**

REVIEW

- What is juvenile delinquency? What causes it?
- What is the nature of depression and suicide in adolescence?
- How are adolescent problems interrelated? What are some components of successful prevention/ intervention programs for adolescents?

REFLECT

- Are the consequences of risk taking in adolescence today more serious than in the past? If so, why?

Socioemotional Development in Adolescence

1 THE SELF, IDENTITY, AND RELIGIOUS/SPIRITUAL DEVELOPMENT: CHANGES IN ADOLESCENCE

Self-Esteem

- Some researchers have found that self-esteem declines in early adolescence for both boys and girls, but the drop for girls is greater. Other researchers caution that these declines are often exaggerated and actually are small.

Identity

- Identity development is complex and is done in bits and pieces. Erikson argues that identity versus identity confusion is the fifth stage of the human life span, which individuals experience during adolescence. A psychosocial moratorium during adolescence allows the personality and role experimentation that are important aspects of identity development. James Marcia proposed four identity statuses—identity diffusion, foreclosure, moratorium, and achievement—that are based on crisis (exploration) and commitment. Increasingly, experts argue the main changes in identity occur in emerging adulthood rather than adolescence. Individuals often follow *moratorium-achievement-moratorium-achievement* (MAMA) cycles in their lives. Parents are important figures in adolescents' identity development. Identity development is facilitated by family relations that promote both individuality and connectedness. Throughout the world, ethnic minority groups have struggled to maintain their identities while blending into the majority culture.

Religious and Spiritual Development

- Many adolescents show an interest in religious and spiritual development. As part of their search for identity, many adolescents and emerging adults begin to grapple with more complex aspects of religion. Various aspects of religion are linked with positive outcomes in adolescent development.

2 FAMILIES: DESCRIBE CHANGES THAT TAKE PLACE IN ADOLESCENTS' RELATIONSHIPS WITH THEIR PARENTS

Autonomy and Attachment

- Many parents have a difficult time handling the adolescent's push for autonomy, even though the push is one of the hallmarks of adolescence. Adolescents do not simply move into a world isolated from parents; attachment to parents increases the probability that an adolescent will be socially competent.

Parent-Adolescent Conflict

- Parent-adolescent conflict increases in adolescence. The conflict is usually moderate rather than severe, and the increased conflict may serve the positive developmental function of promoting autonomy and identity. A subset of adolescents experiences high parent-adolescent conflict, which is linked with negative outcomes.

3 PEERS: CHARACTERIZE THE CHANGES THAT OCCUR IN PEER RELATIONS DURING ADOLESCENCE

Friendships

- Harry Stack Sullivan was the most influential theorist to discuss the importance of adolescent friendships. He argued that there is a dramatic increase in the psychological importance and intimacy of close friends in early adolescence. Friends became increasingly important in meeting social need.

Peer Groups

- Children groups are less formal and less heterogeneous than adolescent groups. The pressure to conform to peers is strong during adolescence, especially during the eighth and ninth grades. Cliques and crowds assume more importance in the lives of adolescents than in the lives of children. Membership in certain crowds—especially jocks and populars—is associated with increased self-esteem. Independents also show high self-esteem.

Dating and Romantic Relationships

- Dating can have many functions. Younger adolescents often begin to hang out together in mixed-sex groups. Many gay male and lesbian youth date other-sex peers, which can help them to clarify their sexual orientation or disguise it from others. Culture can exert a powerful influence on adolescent dating. Dating shows mixed connections with adjustment during adolescence. Early dating is linked with developmental problems.

4   CULTURE AND ADOLESCENT DEVELOPMENT: EXPLAIN HOW CULTURE INFLUENCES ADOLESCENT DEVELOPMENT

Cross-Cultural Comparisons

- There are both similarities and differences in adolescents across different countries. In some countries, traditions are being continued in the socialization of adolescents, whereas in others, substantial changes in the experiences of adolescents are taking place. Adolescents often fill their time with different activities, depending on the culture in which they live. A rite of passage is a ceremony or ritual that marks an individual's transition from one status to another, especially into adulthood. In primitive cultures, rites of passage are often well defined. In contemporary America, rites of passage to adulthood are ill-defined.

Ethnicity

- Many of the families that have immigrated in recent decades to the United States come from collectivist cultures in which there is a strong sense of family obligation. Much of the research on ethnic minority adolescents has not teased apart the influences of ethnicity and socioeconomic status. Because of this failure, too often researchers have given ethnic explanations for characteristics that were largely due to socioeconomic factors. Although not all ethnic minority families are poor, poverty contributes to the stress of many ethnic minority adolescents.

5   ADOLESCENT PROBLEMS: IDENTIFY ADOLESCENT PROBLEMS IN SOCIOEMOTIONAL DEVELOPMENT AND STRATEGIES FOR HELPING ADOLESCENTS WITH PROBLEMS

Juvenile Delinquency

- A juvenile delinquent is an adolescent who breaks the law or engages in conduct that is considered illegal. Heredity, identity problems, community influences, and family experiences have been proposed as causes of juvenile delinquency.

Depression and Suicide

- Adolescents and emerging adults have a higher rate of depression than children. Female adolescents and emerging adults are more likely to have mood and depressive disorders than their male counterparts. Adolescent suicide is the third leading cause of death in U.S. adolescents. Both proximal (recent) and distal (earlier) factors are likely involved in suicide's causes.

The Interrelation of Problems and Successful Prevention/Intervention Programs

- Researchers are increasingly finding that problem behaviors in adolescence are interrelated, and at-risk adolescents have one or more of these problems: (1) drug abuse, (2) juvenile delinquency, (3) sexual problems, and (4) school-related problems. Dryfoos found a number of common components in successful programs designed to prevent or reduce adolescent problems: They provide individual attention to high-risk adolescents, they develop community-wide intervention, and they include early identification and intervention.

KEY TERMS

crisis 386
commitment 386
identity diffusion 387
identity foreclosure 387

identity moratorium 387
identity achievement 387
individuality 388
connectedness 388

ethnic identity 388
clique 395
crowd 395
rite of passage 399

assimilation 400
pluralism 400
juvenile delinquent 402

KEY PEOPLE

Erik Erikson 386   James Marcia 386   Alan Waterman 387   Harry Stack Sullivan 394

E-LEARNING TOOLS

To help you master the material in this chapter, visit the Online Learning Center for *Life-Span Development,* twelfth edition, at **www.mhhe.com/ santrockld12**.

Self-Assessment

Connect to **www.mhhe.com/santrockld12** to reflect on your feelings and your early teenage years by completing these self-assessments: *My Self-Esteem, How Much Did My Parents Monitor My Behavior in Adolescence?* and *Am I Depressed?*

Taking It to the Net

Connect to **www.mhhe.com/santrockld12** to research the answers to these questions:

1. Shelley's mother is Euro-American and her father is Japanese. Many people who do not know her have a hard time identifying her ethnic background, and she is continually asked, "What are you?" There are several other minority students at her school, although few of them openly identify themselves as biracial or multiracial. Shelley is now in the process of figuring out who she is. What are some of the challenges biracial or multiracial adolescents face? How might their identity development progress?

2. Fourteen-year-old Denise, an only child, and her mother, Doris, always had a great relationship—until recently. Now it seems that they are constantly arguing. Doris is trying to understand what is going on with her daughter. How can she tell if Denise's behavior is normal for a 14-year-old?

3. The local school board wants to try to prevent violent and tragic incidents like those in Littleton, Colorado, and Springfield, Oregon. It has asked its principals and teachers to study an APA publication that identifies warning signs of violence and suggests interventions. What will they learn from it, and how can they try to prevent similar situations in their school district?

Video Clips

The Online Learning Center includes two videos for Chapter 12. The first is called "Adolescent Self-Esteem." In this segment, Dr. Susan Harter examines the connection between self-concept and self-esteem and the way adolescents form attitudes about themselves. The second video is called "Girls and Body Image." Interviews with 14-year-old girls, about their emerging image of themselves as female, test the validity of the so-called "gender intensification hypothesis."

Health and Well-Being, Parenting, and Education Exercises

Build your decision-making skills by trying your hand at the health and well-being, parenting, and education exercises. Connect to **www.mhhe.com/santrockld12** to research the answers and complete the exercises.

EARLY ADULTHOOD

*How many roads must a
man walk down before
you call him a man?*

—BOB DYLAN
American Folk Singer, 20th Century

Early adulthood is a time for work and a time for love,
sometimes leaving little time for anything else. For some of
us, finding our place in adult society and committing to a more
stable life take longer than we imagine. We still ask ourselves
who we are and wonder if it isn't enough just to be. Our
dreams continue and our thoughts are bold, but at some point
we become more pragmatic. Sex and love are powerful
passions in our lives—at time angels of light, at others fiends
of torment. And we possibly will never know the love of our
parents until we become parents ourselves. Section 7
contains two chapters: "Physical and Cognitive Development
in Early Adulthood" (Chapter 13) and "Socioemotional
Development in Early Adulthood" (Chapter 14).

13

Whatever you, can do, or dream you can, begin it. Boldness has genius, power, and magic.

—JOHANN WOLFGANG VON GOETHE
German Playwright and Novelist, 19th Century

LEARNING GOALS

◆ Describe the transition from adolescence to adulthood.

◆ Identify the changes in physical development in young adults.

◆ Discuss sexuality in young adults.

◆ Characterize cognitive changes in early adulthood.

◆ Explain the key dimensions of careers and work in early adulthood.

PHYSICAL AND COGNITIVE DEVELOPMENT IN EARLY ADULTHOOD

CHAPTER OUTLINE

Images of Life-Span Development
Dave Eggers, Pursuing a Career in the Face of Stress

He was a senior in college when both of his parents died of cancer within five weeks of each other. What would he do? He and his 8-year-old brother left Chicago to live in California, where his older sister was entering law school. Dave would take care of his younger brother, but he needed a job. That first summer, he took a class in furniture painting; then he worked for a geological surveying company, re-creating maps on a computer. Soon, though, he did something very different: With friends from high school, Dave Eggers started *Might,* a satirical magazine for twenty-somethings. It was an edgy, highly acclaimed publication, but not a moneymaker. After a few years, Eggers had to shut down the magazine, and he abandoned California for New York.

This does not sound like a promising start for a career. But within a decade after his parents' death, Eggers had not only raised his young brother but had also founded a quarterly journal and Web site, *McSweeney's,* and had written a best-seller, *A Heartbreaking Work of Staggering Genius*, which received the National Book Critics Circle Award and was nominated for a Pulitzer Prize. It is a slightly fictionalized account of Eggers' life as he helped care for his dying mother, raised his brother, and searched for his own place in the world. Despite the pain of his loss and the responsibility for his brother, Eggers quickly built a record of achievement as a young adult.

Dave Eggers, talented and insightful author.

PREVIEW

In this chapter, we will explore many aspects of physical and cognitive development in early adulthood. These include some of the areas that were so important in Dave Eggers' life, such as maximizing his creative talents and pursuing a career. We also will explore changes in physical development, sexuality, and cognitive development. We will begin where we left off in Section 6, "Adolescence," and address the transition from adolescence to adulthood, a time during which Dave Eggers displayed resilience in the face of intense stress.

1 THE TRANSITION FROM ADOLESCENCE TO ADULTHOOD

Becoming an Adult

The Transition from High School to College

When does an adolescent become an adult? In Chapter 11, we saw that it is not easy to tell when a girl or a boy enters adolescence. The task of determining when an individual becomes an adult is more difficult.

Becoming an Adult

For most individuals, becoming an adult involves a lengthy transition period. Recently, the transition from adolescence to adulthood has been referred to as

emerging adulthood, which occurs from approximately 18 to 25 years of age (Arnett, 2006, 2007). Experimentation and exploration characterize the emerging adult. At this point in their development, many individuals are still exploring which career path they want to follow, what they want their identity to be, and which lifestyle they want to adopt (for example, single, cohabiting, or married).

Key Features Jeffrey Arnett (2006) recently concluded that five key features characterize emerging adulthood:

- *Identity exploration, especially in love and work.* Emerging adulthood is the time during which key changes in identity take place for many individuals (Cote, 2006; Kroger, 2007)

- *Instability.* Residential changes peak during early adulthood, a time during which there also is often instability in love, work, and education.

- *Self-focused.* According to Arnett (2006, p. 10), emerging adults "are self-focused in the sense that they have little in the way of social obligations, little in the way of duties and commitments to others, which leaves them with a great deal of autonomy in running their own lives."

- *Feeling in-between.* Many emerging adults don't consider themselves adolescents or full-fledged adults.

- *The age of possibilities, a time when individuals have an opportunity to transform their lives.* Arnett (2006) describes two ways in which emerging adulthood is the age of possibilities: (1) many emerging adults are optimistic about their future; and (2) for emerging adults who have experienced difficult times while growing up, emerging adulthood presents an opportunity to direct their lives in a more positive direction (Schulenberg & Zarrett, 2006).

Consider the changing life of Michael Maddaus (Broderick, 2003; Masten, Obradovic, & Burt, 2006). Growing up as a child and adolescent in Minneapolis, his mother drank heavily and his stepfather abused him. He coped by spending increasing time on the streets, being arrested more than 20 times for his delinquency, frequently being placed in detention centers, and rarely going to school. At 17, he joined the Navy and the experience helped him to gain self-discipline and hope. After his brief stint in the Navy, he completed a GED and began taking community college classes. However, he continued to have some setbacks with drugs and alcohol. A defining moment as an emerging adult came when he delivered furniture to a surgeon's home. The surgeon became interested in helping Michael, and his mentorship led to Michael volunteering at a rehabilitation center, then to a job with a neurosurgeon. Eventually, he obtained his undergraduate degree, went to medical school, got married, and started a family. Today, Michael Maddaus is a successful surgeon. One of his most gratifying volunteer activities is telling his story to troubled youth.

In a longitudinal study, Ann Masten and her colleagues (2006) found that emerging adults who became competent after experiencing difficulties while growing up were more intelligent, experienced higher parenting quality, and were less likely to grow up in poverty or low-income circumstances than their counterparts who did not become competent as emerging adults. A further analysis focused on individuals who were still showing maladaptive patterns in emerging adulthood but had gotten their lives together by the time they were in the late twenties and early thirties. The three characteristics shared by these "late-bloomers" were support by adults, being planful, and showing positive aspects of autonomy. In some cases, . . . "military service, marriage and romantic relationships, higher education, religion affiliations, and work opportunities may provide turning-point opportunities for changing the life course during emerging adulthood" (Masten, Obradovic, & Burt, 2006, p. 179).

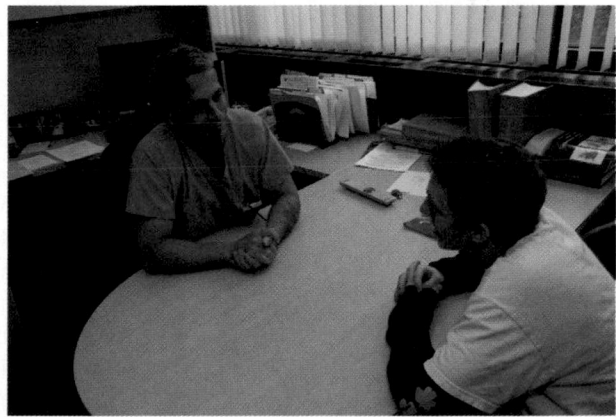

Dr. Michael Maddaus, counseling a troubled youth.

emerging adulthood The transition from adolescence to adulthood (approximately 18 to 25 years of age) that involves experimentation and exploration.

Markers of Becoming an Adult   In the United States, the most widely recognized marker of entry into adulthood is holding a more or less permanent, full-time job, which usually happens when an individual finishes school—high school for some, college for others, graduate or professional school for still others. However, other criteria are far from clear. Economic independence is one marker of adult status, but achieving it is often a long process. College graduates are increasingly returning to live with their parents as they attempt to establish themselves economically. A longitudinal study found that at age 25 only slightly more than half of the participants were fully financially independent of their family of origin (Cohen & others, 2003). The most dramatic findings in this study, though, involved the extensive variability in the individual trajectories of adult roles across ten years from 17 to 27 years of age; many of the participants moved back and forth between increasing and decreasing economic dependency.

Other studies show us that taking responsibility for oneself is likely an important marker of adult status for many individuals. In one study, more than 70 percent of college students said that being an adult means accepting responsibility for the consequences of one's actions, deciding on one's own beliefs and values, and establishing a relationship with parents as an equal adult (Arnett, 1995). And in a recent study, both parents and college students agreed that taking responsibility for one's actions and developing emotional control are important aspects of becoming an adult (Nelson & others, 2007). However, parents and college students didn't always agree on other aspects of what it takes to become an adult. For example, parents were more likely than college students to emphasize that not getting drunk and driving safely are important aspects of becoming an adult.

What we have said about the markers of adult status mainly characterize individuals in industrialized societies, especially Americans. Are the criteria for adulthood the same in developing countries as they are in the United States? In developing countries, marriage is more often a significant marker for entry into adulthood, and this usually occurs much earlier than the adulthood markers in the United States (Arnett, 2004).

The new freedoms and responsibilities of emerging adulthood represent major changes in individuals' lives. Keep in mind, though, that considerable continuity still glues adolescence and adulthood together. For example, a longitudinal study found that religious views and behaviors of emerging adults were especially stable and that their attitudes toward drugs were stable to a lesser degree (Bachman & others, 2002).

What determines an individual's well-being in the transition to adulthood? In a review of research, three types of assets were especially important to well-being during this transition: intellectual (academic success, ability to plan, and good decision-making skills); psychological (mental health, mastery motivation, confidence in one's competence, identity, values, and community contributions); and social (connectedness to others through friendship and positive peer relations) (Eccles & Goodman, 2002). In one study of individuals from 18 to 26 years of age, succeeding rather than stalling in developmental tasks such as work, romantic involvement, and citizenship was linked to a positive trajectory of well-being (Schulenberg, Bryant, & O'Malley, 2004).

The transition from high school to college often involves positive as well as negative features. In college, students are likely to feel grown up, be able to spend more time with peers, have more opportunities to explore different lifestyles and values, and enjoy greater freedom from parental monitoring. However, college involves a larger, more impersonal school structure and an increased focus on achievement and its assessment. *What was your transition to college like?*

The Transition from High School to College

For many individuals in developed countries, going from high school to college is an important aspect of the transition to adulthood. Just as the transition from elementary school to middle or junior high school involves change and possible stress, so does the transition from high school to college. The two transitions have many parallels. Going from being a senior in high school to being a freshman in college replays the top-dog phenomenon of transferring from the oldest and most powerful group of students to the youngest and least powerful group of students that occurred earlier as adolescence began. For many students, the transition from high school to college involves movement to a larger, more impersonal school structure; interaction with peers from more diverse geographical and sometimes more diverse ethnic backgrounds; and increased focus on achievement and its assessment. And like the transition from elementary to middle or junior high school, the transition from high school to college can involve positive features. Students are more likely to feel grown up, have more subjects from which to select, have more time to spend with peers, have more opportunities to explore different lifestyles and values, enjoy greater independence from parental monitoring, and be challenged intellectually by academic work (Santrock & Halonen, 2008).

Today's college students experience more stress and are more depressed than in the past, according to a national study of more than 300,000 freshmen at more than 500 colleges and universities (Pryor & others, 2007). And a recent national survey conducted by the American College Health Association (2008) of more than 90,000 students on 177 campuses revealed that feeling things are hopeless, feeling overwhelmed with all they have to do, feeling mentally exhausted, feeling sad, and feeling depressed are not uncommon in college students. Figure 13.1 indicates the percentage of students who had these feelings and how many times a year they experienced them.

In one study, the academic circumstances creating the most stress for students were tests and finals, grades and competition, professors and class environment, too many demands, papers and essay exams, career and future success, and studying (Murphy, 1996). The personal circumstances that caused the most stress for students were intimate relationships, finances, parental conflicts and expectations, and roommate conflicts.

Most college campuses have a counseling center with access to mental health professionals who can help you to learn effective ways to cope with stress. Counselors can provide good information about coping with stress and academic matters. To read about the work of college counselor Grace Leaf, see the *Careers in Life-Span Development* profile.

Mental Health Difficulty	1–4 Times	5–8 Times	9 or More Times
Felt things were hopeless	39	11	13
Felt overwhelmed all I had to do	32	25	36
Felt mentally exhausted	32	24	35
Felt so depressed it was difficult to function	28	7	10
Seriously contemplated suicide	8	1	1
Attempted suicide	1.2	.2	.2

FIGURE 13.1 College Students' Mental Health Difficulties in the Past Year. *Note: Figure shows the percentage of college students who responded to the question: "Within the last school year, how many times have you . . . ?*

Careers in Life-Span Development

Grace Leaf, College/Career Counselor

Grace Leaf is a counselor at Spokane Community College in Washington. She has a master's degree in educational leadership and is working toward a doctoral degree in educational leadership at Gonzaga University in Washington. Her job involves teaching orientation for international students, conducting individual and group advising, and doing individual and group career planning. Leaf tries to connect students with goals and values and help them design an educational program that fits their needs and visions.

Grace Leaf, counseling college students at Spokane Community College about careers.

Review and Reflect: Learning Goal 1

1 **Describe the Transition from Adolescence to Adulthood**

REVIEW

- What is the nature of emerging adulthood? What are two main criteria for becoming an adult?
- What is the transition from high school to college like?

REFLECT

- What do you think is the most important criterion for becoming an adult? Does it make sense to describe becoming an adult in terms of "emerging adulthood" over a period of years, or is there a specific age at which someone becomes an adult? Explain.

2 PHYSICAL DEVELOPMENT

| Physical Performance and Development | Health | Eating and Weight | Regular Exercise | Substance Abuse |

As we learn more about healthy lifestyles and how they contribute to a longer life span, emerging and young adults are increasingly interested in learning about physical performance, health, nutrition, exercise, and addiction.

Physical Performance and Development

Most of us reach our peak physical performance before the age of 30, often between the ages of 19 and 26. This peak of physical performance occurs not only for the average young adult, but for outstanding athletes as well. Even though athletes as a group keep getting better than their predecessors—running faster, jumping higher, and lifting more weight—the age at which they reach their peak performance has remained virtually the same (Schultz & Curnow, 1988).

Different types of athletes, however, reach their peak performances at different ages. Most swimmers and gymnasts peak in their late teens. Golfers and marathon runners tend to peak in their late twenties. In other areas of athletics, peak performance is often in the early to mid-twenties.

Not only do we reach our peak in physical performance during early adulthood, but it is also during this age period that we begin to decline in physical performance. Muscle tone and strength usually begin to show signs of decline around the age of 30. Sagging chins and protruding abdomens also may begin to appear for the first time. The lessening of physical abilities is a common complaint among the just-turned thirties. Sensory systems show little change in early adulthood, but the lens of the eye loses some of its elasticity and becomes less able to change shape and focus on near objects. Hearing peaks in adolescence, remains constant in the first part of early adulthood, and then begins to decline in the last part of early adulthood. And in the mid- to late twenties, the body's fatty tissue increases.

Health

Emerging adults have more than twice the mortality rate of adolescents (Park & others, 2006) (see Figure 13.2). As indicated in Figure

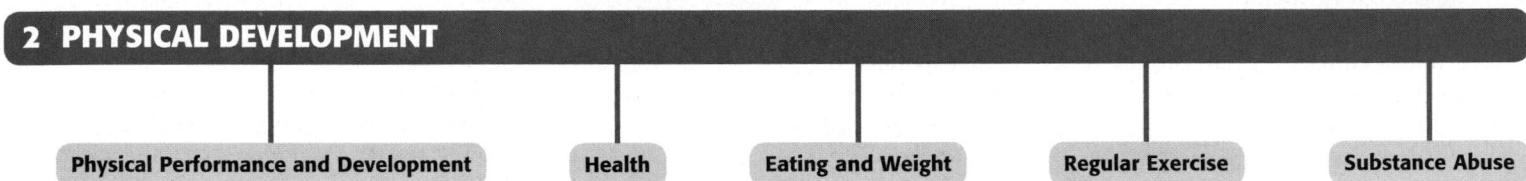

FIGURE 13.2 Mortality Rates of U.S. Adolescents and Emerging Adults

Legend:
- Other
- Suicide
- Homicide
- Unintentional Injury

Y-axis: Deaths per 100,000

Ages 12–17: Males 47.1, Females 24.3
Ages 18–24: Males 137.0, Females 49.3

13.2, males are mainly responsible for the higher mortality rate of emerging adults.

Although emerging adults have a higher death rate than adolescents, emerging adults have few chronic health problems, and they have fewer colds and respiratory problems than when they were children (Rimsza & Kirk, 2005). Although most college students know what it takes to prevent illness and promote health, they don't fare very well when it comes to applying this information to themselves (Murphy-Hoefer, Alder, & Higbee, 2004).

A longitudinal study revealed that most bad health habits engaged in during adolescence increased in emerging adulthood (Harris & others, 2006). Inactivity, diet, obesity, substance use, reproductive health care, and health-care access worsened in emerging adulthood. For example, when they were 12 to 18 years of age, only 5 percent reported no weekly exercise, but when they became 19 to 26 years of age, 46 percent said they did not exercise during a week.

In emerging and early adulthood, few individuals stop to think about how their personal lifestyles will affect their health later in their adult lives. As emerging adults, many of us develop a pattern of not eating breakfast, not eating regular meals, and relying on snacks as our main food source during the day, eating excessively to the point where we exceed the normal weight for our age, smoking moderately or excessively, drinking moderately or excessively, failing to exercise, and getting by with only a few hours of sleep at night (Cousineau, Goldstein, & Franco, 2005). These lifestyles are associated with poor health, which in turn impacts life satisfaction. In the Berkeley Longitudinal Study—in which individuals were evaluated over a period of 40 years—physical health at age 30 predicted life satisfaction at age 70, more so for men than for women (Mussen, Honzik, & Eichorn, 1982).

The health profile of emerging and young adults can be improved by reducing the incidence of certain health-impairing lifestyles, such as overeating, and by engaging in health-improving lifestyles that include good eating habits, exercising regularly, and not abusing drugs (Robbins, Powers, & Burgess, 2008; Teague & others, 2009).

Why might it be easy to develop bad health habits in early adulthood?

Eating and Weight

In Chapters 7 and 9, we discussed aspects of overweight children's lives, and in Chapter 11 we examined the eating disorders of anorexia nervosa and bulimia nervosa in adolescence. Now, we will turn our attention to obesity and the extensive preoccupation that many young adults have with dieting.

Obesity Obesity is a serious and pervasive health problem for many individuals (Corbin & others, 2008; Hahn, Payne, & Lucas, 2009). As shown in Figure 13.3, the prevalence of obesity in U.S. adults 20 years of age and older increased from 19 percent in 1997 to slightly above 25 percent in 2005 (Centers for Disease Control and Prevention, 2006). In this survey, obesity was defined as having a body mass index (which takes into account height and weight) of 30 or more. In the survey, 22 percent of U.S. adults 20 to 39 years of age were classified as obese in 2005. A recent study of more than 168,000 adults in 63 countries revealed that worldwide 40 percent of the men and 30 percent of the women were overweight and 24 percent of the men and 27 percent of the women were obese (Balkau & others, 2007).

Obesity is linked to increased risk of hypertension, diabetes, and cardiovascular disease (Hahn, Payne, & Lucas, 2008). For individuals who are 30 percent overweight, the probability of dying in middle adulthood increases by about 40 percent.

What factors are involved in obesity? The possible culprits include heredity, leptin, set point, and metabolism and environmental factors and gender.

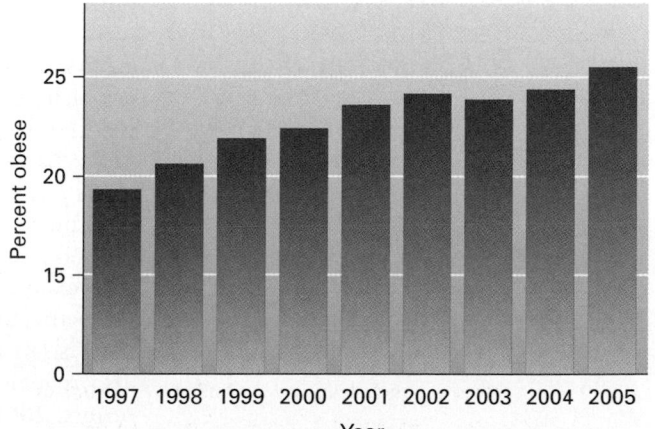

FIGURE 13.3 Prevalence of Obesity Among Adults Aged 20 Years and Over: United States, 1997–2005

Heredity   Until recently, the genetic component of obesity had been underestimated by scientists (Jamshidi & others, 2007). Some individuals do inherit a tendency to be overweight. Researchers have documented that animals can be inbred to have a propensity for obesity (Liu & others, 2005). Further, identical human twins have similar weights, even when they are reared apart (Collaku & others, 2004).

Leptin   *Leptin* (from the Greek word *leptos,* which means "thin") is a protein that is involved in satiety (the condition of being full to satisfaction) and released by fat cells, resulting in decreased food intake and increased energy expenditure. Leptin acts as an antiobesity hormone (Jasik & Lustig, 2009). In humans, leptin concentrations have been linked with weight, percentage of body fat, weight loss in a single diet episode, and cumulative percentage of weight loss (de Luis & others, 2007). Some scientists are interested in the possibility that leptin might help obese individuals lose weight.

Set Point   The amount of stored fat in your body is an important factor in your *set point,* the weight you maintain when you make no effort to gain or lose weight. Fat is stored in what are called adipose cells. When these cells are filled, you do not get hungry. When people gain weight—because of genetic predisposition, childhood eating patterns, or adult overeating—the number of their fat cells increases, and they might not be able to get rid of them. A normal-weight individual has 30 to 40 billion fat cells. An obese individual has 80 to 120 billion fat cells. Some scientists have proposed that these fat cells can shrink but might not go away.

Environmental Factors   Environmental factors play an important role in obesity (Wardlaw & Smith, 2009). The human genome has not changed markedly in the last century, yet obesity has noticeably increased (Li & others, 2007). The obesity rate has doubled in the United States since 1900. This dramatic increase in obesity likely is due to greater availability of food (especially food high in fat), energy-saving devices, and declining physical activity. One study found that in 2000, U.S. women ate 335 calories more a day and men 168 more a day than they did in the early 1970s (National Center for Health Statistics, 2004).

Sociocultural factors are involved in obesity, which is six times more prevalent among women with low incomes than among women with high incomes. Americans also are more obese than Europeans and people in many other areas of the world (Williams, 2005).

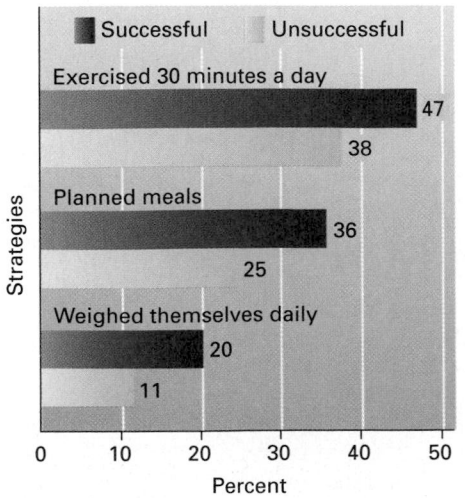

How effective are diet programs?

FIGURE 13.4 Comparison of Strategies in Successful and Unsuccessful Dieters

Dieting   Ironically, while obesity is on the rise, dieting has become an obsession with many Americans (Schiff, 2009). Although many Americans regularly embark on a diet, few are successful in keeping weight off long term. A recent research review of the long-term outcomes of calorie-restricting diets revealed that overall one-third to two-thirds of dieters regain more weight than they lost on their diets (Mann & others, 2007). However, some individuals do lose weight and maintain the loss (Applebaum, 2008; Herman, Van Strien, & Polivy, 2008). How often this occurs and whether some diet programs work better than others are still open questions.

What we do know about losing weight is that the most effective programs include exercise (Fahey, Insel, & Roth, 2009; Wardlaw & Hampl, 2007). Exercise not only burns up calories, but continues to elevate the person's metabolic rate for several hours *after* exercising. A recent study of approximately 2,000 U.S. adults found that exercising 30 minutes a day, planning meals, and weighing themselves daily were the main strategies used by successful dieters compared with unsuccessful dieters (Kruger, Blanck, & Gillespe, 2006) (see Figure 13.4). Another recent study also revealed that daily weigh-ins are linked to maintaining weight loss (Wing & others, 2007).

Even when diets do produce weight loss, they can place the dieter at risk for other health problems (Cunningham & Hyson, 2006). One main concern focuses on weight cycling—yo-yo dieting—in which the person is in a recurring cycle of weight loss and weight gain (Janacek & others, 2005). Also, liquid diets and other very low calorie strategies are linked with gallbladder damage.

With these problems in mind, when overweight people diet and maintain their weight loss, they do become less depressed and reduce their risk for a number of health-impairing disorders (Daubenmeir & others, 2007; Mensah & Brown, 2007).

Regular Exercise

One of the main reasons that health experts want people to exercise is that it helps to prevent diseases, such as heart disease and diabetes (Anspaugh, Hamrick, & Rosato, 2009; Hoeger & Hoeger, 2008). Many health experts recommend that young adults engage in 30 minutes or more of aerobic exercise a day, preferably every day. **Aerobic exercise** is sustained exercise—jogging, swimming, or cycling, for example—that stimulates heart and lung activity. Most health experts recommend that you raise your heart rate to at least 60 percent of your maximum heart rate. Only about one-fifth of adults, however, are active at these recommended levels of physical activity.

Researchers have found that exercise benefits not only physical health, but mental health as well. In particular, exercise improves self-concept and reduces anxiety and depression (Brenes & others, 2007). Meta-analyses have shown that exercise can be as effective in reducing depression as psychotherapy (Richardson & others, 2005). One study of more than 600 adults found that exercise was associated with positive mental health and obesity was linked to poor mental health (Rohrer, Pierce, & Blackburn, 2005).

Research on the benefits of exercise suggests that both moderate and intense activities produce important physical and psychological gains (Gostic, 2005). Some people enjoy rigorous, intense exercise. Others enjoy more moderate exercise routines. The enjoyment and pleasure we derive from exercise added to its aerobic benefits make exercise one of life's most important activities (Insel & Roth, 2008). To read about ways to incorporate regular exercise into your life, see the *Applications in Life-Span Development* interlude.

What are some strategies for incorporating exercise into your life?

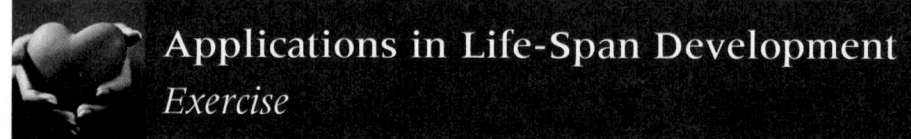

Applications in Life-Span Development
Exercise

Here are some helpful strategies for building exercise into your life:

- *Reduce TV time.* Heavy TV viewing is linked to poor health and obesity (Duvigneaud & others, 2007). Replace some of your TV time with exercise.

- *Chart your progress.* Systematically recording your exercise workouts will help you to chart your progress. This strategy is especially helpful over the long term.

- *Get rid of excuses.* People make up all kinds of excuses for not exercising. A typical excuse is, "I don't have enough time." You likely do have enough time.

- *Imagine the alternative.* Ask yourself whether you are too busy to take care of your own health. What will your life be like if you lose your health?

- *Learn more about exercise.* The more you know about exercise, the more you are likely to start an exercise program and continue it.

aerobic exercise Sustained exercise (such as jogging, swimming, or cycling) that stimulates heart and lung activity.

Substance Abuse

In Chapter 11, we explored substance abuse in adolescence. Fortunately, by the time individuals reach their mid-twenties, many have reduced their use of alcohol and drugs. That is the conclusion reached by Jerald Bachman and his colleagues (2002) in a longitudinal analysis of more than 38,000 individuals who were evaluated from the time they were high school seniors through their twenties. Recent national studies indicate that individuals who don't go to college are more likely to take drugs than college students and college-educated adults, except for one substance—alcohol, which college students are more likely to use (Johnston & others, 2007). Also, as in adolescence, male college students and young adults are more likely to take drugs than their female counterparts (Johnston & others, 2007).

Let's take a closer look at use of alcohol and nicotine by young adults and at the nature of **addiction**, which is a behavior pattern characterized by an overwhelming involvement with a drug and securing its supply.

Alcohol   Let's examine two problems associated with drinking: binge drinking and alcoholism.

Binge Drinking   Heavy binge drinking often increases in college, and it can take its toll on students (Kinney, 2009; Wu & others, 2007). Chronic binge drinking is more common among college men than women and students living away from home, especially in fraternity houses (Schulenberg & others, 2000).

In a national survey of drinking patterns on 140 campuses, almost half of the binge drinkers reported problems that included (Wechsler & others, 1994) missing classes, physical injuries, troubles with police, and having unprotected sex. For example, binge-drinking college students were 11 times more likely to fall behind in school, 10 times more likely to drive after drinking, and twice as likely to have unprotected sex than college students who did not binge drink. Also, one recent study found that after an evening of binge drinking memory retrieval was significantly impaired during the alcohol hangover the next morning (Verster & others, 2003).

A special concern is the increase in binge drinking by females during emerging adulthood. One study found a 125 percent increase in binge drinking at all-women colleges from 1993 through 2001 (Wechsler & others, 2002).

When does binge drinking peak during development? A longitudinal study revealed that binge drinking peaks at about 21 to 22 years of age and then declines through the remainder of the twenties (Bachman & others, 2002) (see Figure 13.5).

Alcoholism   *Alcoholism* is a disorder that involves long-term, repeated, uncontrolled, compulsive, and excessive use of alcoholic beverages and that impairs the drinker's health and social relationships. One in nine individuals who drink continues the path to alcoholism.

What kinds of problems are associated with binge drinking in college?

FIGURE 13.5 Binge Drinking in the Adolescence–Early Adulthood Transition. Note that the percentage of individuals engaging in binge drinking peaked at 21 or 22 years of age and then began to gradually decline through the remainder of the twenties. Binge drinking was defined as having five or more alcoholic drinks in a row in the past two weeks.

addiction A pattern of behavior characterized by an overwhelming involvement with using a drug and securing its supply.

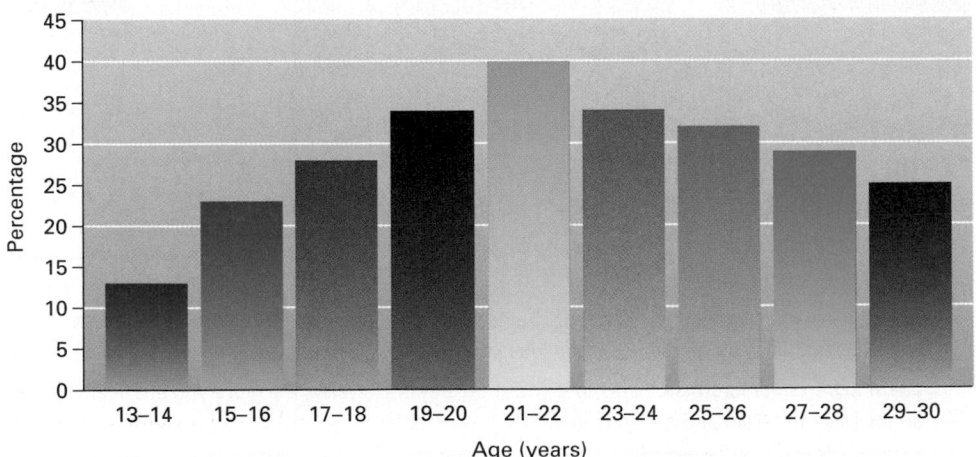

Those who do are disproportionately related to alcoholics (Redgrave & others, 2007). Family studies consistently reveal a high frequency of alcoholism in the first-degree relatives of alcoholics (Conway, Swendsen, & Merikangas, 2003). Indeed, researchers have found that heredity likely plays a role in alcoholism, although the precise hereditary mechanism has not been found (Miles & Williams, 2007). An estimated 50 to 60 percent of individuals who become alcoholics are believed to have a genetic predisposition for it.

Although studies reveal a genetic influence on alcoholism, they also show that environmental factors play a role (Ksir, Hart, & Ray, 2008). For example, family studies indicate that many individuals who suffer from alcoholism do not have close relatives who are addicted to alcohol (Martin & Sher, 1994). The large cultural variations in alcohol use mentioned earlier also underscore the environment's role in alcoholism.

About one-third of alcoholics recover whether or not they are ever in a treatment program. This figure was found in a long-term study of 700 individuals over 50 years and has consistently been found by other researchers as well (Vaillant, 1992). There is a "one-third rule" for alcoholism: by age 65, one-third are dead or in terrible shape, one-third are abstinent or drinking socially, and one-third are still trying to beat their addiction. A positive outcome and recovery from alcoholism are predicted by certain factors: (1) a strong negative experience related to drinking, such as a serious medical emergency or condition; (2) finding a substitute dependency to compete with alcohol abuse, such as meditation, exercise, or overeating (which of course has its own negative health consequences); (3) having new social supports (such as a concerned, helpful employer or a new marriage); and (4) joining an inspirational group, such as a religious organization or Alcoholics Anonymous (Vaillant, 1992).

Cigarette Smoking and Nicotine
Converging evidence from a number of studies underscores the dangers of smoking or being around those who do (Akhter & others, 2007). For example, smoking is linked to 30 percent of cancer deaths, 21 percent of heart disease deaths, and 82 percent of chronic pulmonary disease deaths. Secondhand smoke is implicated in as many as 9,000 lung cancer deaths a year. Children of smokers are at special risk for respiratory and middle-ear diseases (Wallace-Bell, 2003).

Fewer people smoke today than in the past, and almost half of all living adults who ever smoked have quit. In the United States, the prevalence of smoking in men has dropped from 42 percent in 1965 to 21 percent today (Centers for Disease Control and Prevention, 2006). However, more than 50 million Americans still smoke cigarettes today. And cigar smoking and tobacco chewing, with risks similar to those of cigarette smoking, have increased. National studies of college students indicate that the peak rate in current smoking occurred in 1999 (31 percent of students), declined moderately to 24 percent in 2005, and then dropped substantially in 2006 to 19 percent (Johnston & others, 2007). Among young adults 19 to 28 years of age, there has been only a slight drop in the percentage of current smokers in the last decade (30 percent in 1996 to 27 percent in 2006) (Johnston & others, 2007).

Most adult smokers would like to quit, but their addiction to nicotine often makes quitting a challenge. Nicotine, the active drug in cigarettes, is a stimulant that increases the smoker's energy and alertness, a pleasurable and reinforcing experience. Nicotine also stimulates neurotransmitters that have a calming or pain-reducing effect.

Four main methods are used to help smokers overcome their addiction to nicotine: (1) using a substitute source of nicotine, such as nicotine gum and the nicotine patch; (2) taking an antidepressant such as Zyban; (3) controlling stimuli associated with smoking—for example, sensitizing the smoker to social cues that are linked to smoking, such as a social drink; and (4) going "cold turkey," that is, simply stopping smoking without making any major changes in their lifestyle. Lighter smokers usually have more success with going "cold turkey" than heavy smokers.

Studies indicate that when people do stop smoking, their risk of cancer is reduced. For example, a recent study revealed a decrease in lung cancer death after smoking cessation (Wakai & others, 2007). In this study, earlier cessation of smoking resulted in a lower rate of lung cancer.

What are some of the factors that contribute to whether individuals become alcoholics?

"There's no shooting—we just make you keep smoking."

"there's no shooting—we just make you keep smoking."

Review and Reflect: Learning Goal 2

 Identify the Changes in Physical Development in Young Adults

REVIEW

- How does physical performance peak and then slow down in early adulthood?
- What characterizes health in emerging and early adulthood?
- What are some important things to know about eating and weight?
- What are the benefits of exercise?
- How extensive is substance abuse in young adults? What effects does it have on their lives?

REFLECT

- To discourage smoking, many governments now levy heavy taxes on cigarettes because of their negative health effects. Would you recommend that the U.S. government levy similar heavy taxes on fatty foods because of their negative health effects? Explain.

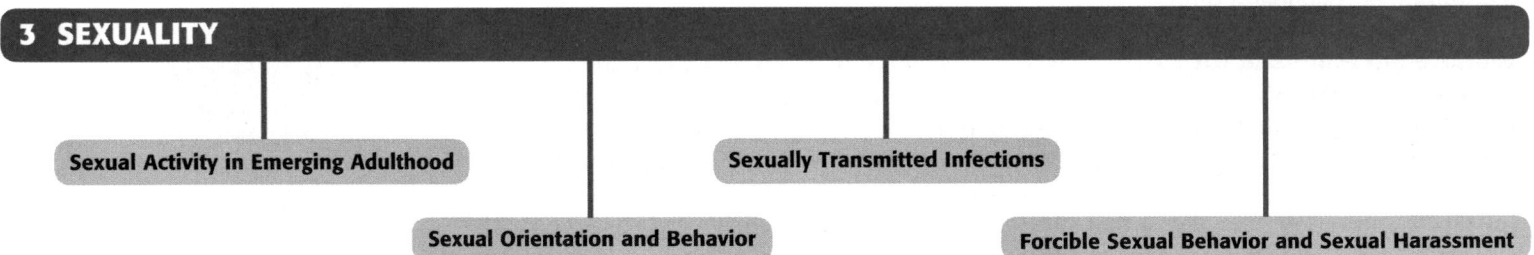

3 SEXUALITY

Sexual Activity in Emerging Adulthood

Sexual Orientation and Behavior

Sexually Transmitted Infections

Forcible Sexual Behavior and Sexual Harassment

We do not need sex for everyday survival the way we need food and water, but we do need it for the survival of the species. In Chapter 9, we looked at how adolescents develop a sexual identity and become sexually active. What happens to their sexuality in adulthood? Let's examine the sexual activity of Americans and their sexual orientation, as well as some of the problems that can be associated with sexual activity.

Sexual Activity in Emerging Adulthood

At the beginning of emerging adulthood (age 18), surveys indicate that slightly more than 60 percent of individuals have experienced sexual intercourse, but by the end of emerging adulthood (age 25), most individuals have had sexual intercourse (Lefkowitz & Gillen, 2006). Also, the average age of marriage in the United States is currently 27 for males and 26 for females (Popenoe & Whitehead, 2006). Thus, emerging adulthood is a time frame during which most individuals are "both sexually active and unmarried" (Lefkowitz & Gillen, 2006, p. 235).

Patterns of heterosexual behavior for males and females in emerging adulthood include the following (Lefkowitz & Gillen, 2006):

- Males have more casual sexual partners, and females report being more selective about their choice of a sexual partner.
- Approximately 60 percent of emerging adults have had sexual intercourse with only one individual in the past year, but compared with young adults in their late twenties and thirties, emerging adults are more likely to have had sexual intercourse with two or more individuals.

- Although emerging adults have sexual intercourse with more individuals than young adults, they have sex less frequently. Approximately 25 percent of emerging adults report having sexual intercourse only a couple of times a year or not at all (Michael & others, 1994).

- Casual sex is more common in emerging adulthood than in young adulthood. One study indicated that 30 percent of emerging adults said they had "hooked up" with someone and had sexual intercourse during college (Paul, McManus, & Hayes, 2000).

Sexual Orientation and Behavior

Obtaining accurate information about such a private activity as sexual behavior is not easy. The best information we currently have comes from what is often referred to as the 1994 Sex in America survey. In this well-designed, comprehensive study of American adults' sexual patterns, Robert Michael and his colleagues (1994) interviewed more than 3,000 people from 18 to 59 years of age who were randomly selected, a sharp contrast from earlier samples that were based on unrepresentative groups of volunteers.

Heterosexual Attitudes and Behavior   Here are some of the key findings from the 1994 Sex in America survey:

- Americans tend to fall into three categories: One-third have sex twice a week or more, one-third a few times a month, and one-third a few times a year or not at all.

- Married (and cohabiting) couples have sex more often than noncohabiting couples (see Figure 13.6).

- Most Americans do not engage in kinky sexual acts. When asked about their favorite sexual acts, the vast majority (96 percent) said that vaginal sex was "very" or "somewhat" appealing. Oral sex was in third place, after an activity that many have not labeled a sexual act—watching a partner undress.

- Adultery is clearly the exception rather than the rule. Nearly 75 percent of the married men and 85 percent of the married women indicated that they have never been unfaithful.

- Men think about sex far more than women do—54 percent of the men said they think about it every day or several times a day, whereas 67 percent of the women said they think about it only a few times a week or a few times a month.

In sum, one of the most powerful messages in the 1994 survey was that Americans' sexual lives are more conservative than previously believed. Although 17 percent of the men and 3 percent of the women said they have had sex with at least 21 partners, the overall impression from the survey was that sexual behavior is ruled by marriage and monogamy for most Americans.

Sources of Sexual Orientation   In the Sex in America survey, 2.7 percent of the men and 1.3 percent of the women reported that they had had same-sex relations in the past year (Michael & others, 1994). Why are some individuals lesbian, gay, or bisexual (LGB) and others heterosexual? Speculation about this question has been extensive (Crooks & Baur, 2008).

Until the end of the nineteenth century, it was generally believed that people were either heterosexual or homosexual. Today, it is more accepted to view sexual orientation, not as an either/or proposition, but as a continuum from exclusive male-female relations to exclusive same-sex relations (Strong & others, 2008). Some individuals are also *bisexual,* being sexually attracted to people of both sexes.

All people, regardless of their sexual orientation, have similar physiological responses during sexual arousal and seem to be aroused by the same types of tactile

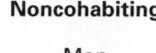
Noncohabiting

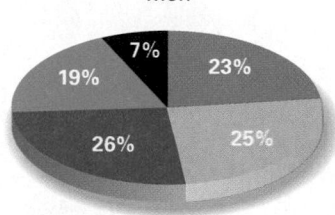
Men

Women

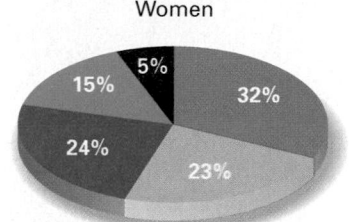
Cohabiting (married)

Men

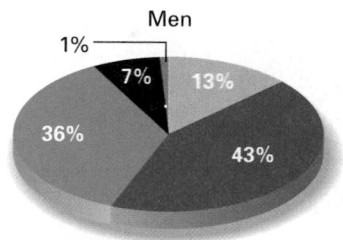

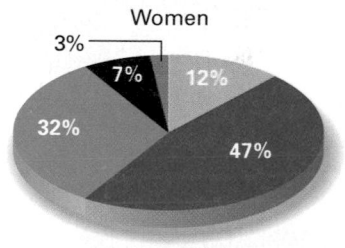
Women

Never

A few times a year

A few times a month

2–3 times a week

4 or more times a week

FIGURE 13.6 The Sex in America Survey. The percentages show noncohabiting and cohabiting (married) males' and female's responses to the question "How often have you had sex in the past year?" in a 1994 survey (Michael & others, 1994). *What was one feature of the Sex in America survey that made it superior to most surveys of sexual behavior?*

What likely determines an individual's sexual preference?

stimulation. Investigators typically find no differences between LGBs and heterosexuals in a wide range of attitudes, behaviors, and adjustments (Peplau & Fingerhut, 2007). One review did find a higher prevalence of mental disorders in lesbians, gay men, and bisexuals than in heterosexuals and concluded that the difference was due to the stress associated with minority status involving stigma, prejudice, and discrimination (Meyer, 2003). Homosexuality once was classified as a mental disorder, but both the American Psychiatric Association and the American Psychological Association discontinued this classification as a mental disorder in the 1970s.

Recently, researchers have explored the possible biological basis of same-sex relations. The results of hormone studies have been inconsistent. If gay males are given male sex hormones (androgens), their sexual orientation doesn't change. Their sexual desire merely increases. A very early prenatal critical period might influence sexual orientation (James, 2005). In the second to fifth months after conception, exposure of the fetus to hormone levels characteristic of females might cause the individual (male or female) to become attracted to males (Ellis & Ames, 1987). If this critical-period hypothesis turns out to be correct, it would explain why clinicians have found that sexual orientation is difficult, if not impossible, to modify.

With regard to anatomical structures, neuroscientist Simon LeVay (1991) found that an area of the hypothalamus that governs sexual behavior is twice as large (about the size of a grain of sand) in heterosexual males as in gay males. This area was found to be about the same size in gay males and heterosexual females. Critics of this research point out that many of the gay males in the study had AIDS and suggest that their brains could have been altered by the disease.

An individual's sexual orientation—same-sex, heterosexual, or bisexual—is most likely determined by a combination of genetic, hormonal, cognitive, and environmental factors (Baldwin & Baldwin, 1998). Most experts on same-sex relations point out that no one factor alone causes sexual orientation and that the relative weight of each factor can vary from one individual to the next.

Attitudes and Behavior of Lesbians and Gay Males   Many gender differences that appear in heterosexual relationships occur in same-sex relationships (Savin-Williams, 2008; Savin-Williams & Ream, 2007). For example, like heterosexual women, lesbians have fewer sexual partners than gay men, and lesbians have less permissive attitudes about casual sex outside a primary relationship than gay men (Peplau & Fingerhut, 2007). In a recent study that compared same-sex couples with opposite-sex dating, engaged, and married dyads, no differences were found in attachment security (Roisman & others, 2008). In this study, one difference between dyads was that lesbians were the most effective at working together in positive ways during laboratory observations.

How can lesbians and gay males adapt to a world in which they are a minority? According to psychologist Laura Brown (1989), lesbians and gay males experience life as a minority in a dominant, majority culture. For lesbians and gay men, developing a *bicultural identity* creates new ways of defining themselves. Brown maintains that lesbians and gay males adapt best when they don't define themselves in polarities, such as trying to live in an encapsulated lesbian or gay male world completely divorced from the majority culture or completely accepting the dictates and bias of the majority culture. Balancing the demands of the two cultures—the minority lesbian/gay male culture and the majority heterosexual culture—can often lead to more effective coping for lesbians and gay males, says Brown.

A special concern involving sexual minority individuals are the hate crimes and stigma-related experiences they encounter. In a recent study, approximately 20 percent of sexual minority adults reported that they had experienced a person or property crime related to their sexual orientation, about 50 percent said they had experienced verbal harassment, and more than 10 percent said they had encountered employment or housing discrimination (Herek, 2008).

STI	Description/cause	Incidence	Treatment
Gonorrhea	Commonly called the "drip" or "clap." Caused by the bacterium *Neisseria gonorrhoeae*. Spread by contact between infected moist membranes (genital, oral-genital, or anal-genital) of two individuals. Characterized by discharge from penis or vagina and painful urination. Can lead to infertility.	500,000 cases annually in U.S.	Penicillin, other antibiotics
Syphilis	Caused by the bacterium *Treponema pallidum*. Characterized by the appearance of a sore where syphilis entered the body. The sore can be on the external genitals, vagina, or anus. Later, a skin rash breaks out on palms of hands and bottom of feet. If not treated, can eventually lead to paralysis or even death.	100,000 cases annually in U.S.	Penicillin
Chlamydia	A common STI named for the bacterium *Chlamydia trachomatis*, an organism that spreads by sexual contact and infects the genital organs of both sexes. A special concern is that females with chlamydia may become infertile. It is recommended that adolescent and young adult females have an annual screening for this STI.	About 3 million people in U.S. annually.	Antibiotics
Genital herpes	Caused by a family of viruses with different strains. Involves an eruption of sores and blisters. Spread by sexual contact.	One of five U.S. adults	No known cure but antiviral medications can shorten outbreaks
AIDS	Caused by a virus, the human immunodeficiency virus (HIV), which destroys the body's immune system. Semen and blood are the main vehicles of transmission. Common symptoms include fevers, night sweats, weight loss, chronic fatigue, and swollen lymph nodes.	More than 300,000 cumulative cases of HIV virus in U.S. 25–34-year-olds; epidemic incidence in sub-Saharan countries	New treatments have slowed the progression from HIV to AIDS; no cure
Genital warts	Caused by the human papillomavirus, which does not always produce symptoms. Usually appear as small, hard painless bumps in the vaginal area, or around the anus. Very contagious. Certain high-risk types of this virus cause cervical cancer and other genital cancers. May recur despite treatment. A new HPV preventive vaccine, Gardasil, has benn approved for Girls and Women 9–26 years of age.	About 5.5 million new cases annually; considered the most common STI in the U.S.	A topical drug, freezing, or surgery

FIGURE 13.7 Sexually Transmitted Infections

Sexually Transmitted Infections

Sexually transmitted infections (STIs) are diseases that are primarily contracted through sex—intercourse as well as oral-genital and anal-genital sex. STIs affect about one of every six U.S. adults (National Center for Health Statistics, 2007). Among the most prevalent STIs are bacterial infections (such as gonorrhea, syphilis, and chlamydia), and STIs caused by viruses—genital herpes, genital warts, and HIV, which can lead to AIDS. Figure 13.7 describes several sexually transmitted infections.

No single STI has had a greater impact on sexual behavior, or created more public fear in the last several decades, than infection with the human immunodeficiency virus (HIV) (Strong & others, 2008). HIV is a sexually transmitted infection that destroys the body's immune system. Once infected with HIV, the virus breaks down and overpowers the immune system, which leads to acquired immune deficiency syndrome (AIDS). An individual sick with AIDS has such a weakened immune system that a common cold can be life-threatening.

As of January 1, 2005, 310,000 cases of AIDS in 25- to 34-year-olds had been reported in the United States, with about 80 percent of these being males and almost half intravenous (IV) drug users (Centers for Disease Control and Prevention, 2008). Because of education and the development of more effective drug treatments, deaths due to HIV/AIDS have begun to decline in the United States (National Center for Health Statistics, 2007).

Globally, the total number of individuals with HIV reached 39.5 million in 2006 (UNAIDS, 2006). The greatest concern about HIV/AIDS is in sub-Saharan Africa, where it has reached epidemic proportions, with 24.7 million individuals infected with HIV in 2006 (UNAIDS, 2006). To put this in perspective, a total of approximately

sexually transmitted infections (STIs) Diseases that are contracted primarily through sex.

What are some good strategies for protecting against HIV and other sexually transmitted infections? How effectively have you practiced these strategies?

982,000 cases of AIDS had been reported to the Centers for Disease Control and Prevention (2008) through 2006 in the United States.

To protect yourself, just asking a date about his or her sexual behavior does not guarantee protection from HIV and other sexually transmitted infections. For example, in one investigation, 655 college students were asked to answer questions about lying and sexual behavior (Cochran & Mays, 1990). Of the 422 respondents who said they were sexually active, 34 percent of the men and 10 percent of the women said they had lied so their partner would have sex with them. Much higher percentages—47 percent of the men and 60 percent of the women—said they had been lied to by a potential sexual partner. When asked what aspects of their past they would be most likely to lie about, more than 40 percent of the men and women said they would understate the number of their sexual partners. Twenty percent of the men, but only 4 percent of the women, said they would lie about their results from an HIV blood test.

What are some good strategies for protecting against HIV and other sexually transmitted infections? They include:

- *Knowing your and your partner's risk status.* Anyone who has had previous sexual activity with another person might have contracted an STI without being aware of it. Spend time getting to know a prospective partner before you have sex. Use this time to inform the other person of your STI status and inquire about your partner's. Remember that many people lie about their STI status.

- *Obtaining medical examinations.* Many experts recommend that couples who want to begin a sexual relationship should have a medical checkup to rule out STIs before they engage in sex. If cost is an issue, contact your campus health service or a public health clinic.

- *Having protected, not unprotected, sex.* When correctly used, latex condoms help to prevent many STIs from being transmitted. Condoms are most effective in preventing gonorrhea, syphilis, chlamydia, and HIV. They are less effective against the spread of herpes.

- *Not having sex with multiple partners.* One of the best predictors of getting an STI is having sex with multiple partners. Having more than one sex partner elevates the likelihood that you will encounter an infected partner.

Forcible Sexual Behavior and Sexual Harassment

Too often, sex involves the exercise of power (Clark & Carroll, 2008). Here we will briefly look at three of the problems that may result: two types of rape and sexual harassment.

Rape   **Rape** is forcible sexual intercourse with a person who does not give consent. Legal definitions of rape differ from state to state. For example, in some states, husbands are not prohibited from forcing their wives to have intercourse, although this has been challenged in several of those states.

Because victims may be reluctant to suffer the consequences of reporting rape, the actual incidence is not easily determined (Carroll, 2007). Rape occurs most often in large cities, where it has been reported that 8 of every 10,000 women 12 years and older are raped each year. Nearly 200,000 rapes are reported each year in the United States. Although most victims of rape are women, rape of men does occur (McLean, Balding, & White, 2005). Men in prisons are especially vulnerable to rape, usually by heterosexual males who use rape as a means of establishing their dominance and power.

Why does rape of women occur so often in the United States? Among the causes given are that males are socialized to be sexually aggressive, to regard women as inferior beings, and to view their own pleasure as the most important objective in sexual relations (Beech, Ward, & Fisher, 2006). Researchers have found that male rapists share the following characteristics: aggression enhances their sense of power or masculinity; they are angry at women in general; and they want to hurt and humiliate their victims (Strong & others, 2008).

Rape is a traumatic experience for the victims and those close to them (Gannon & others, 2008; Kilmartin & Allison, 2007). Victims initially feel shock and numbness and often are acutely disorganized. Some show their distress through words and tears, others

rape Forcible sexual intercourse with a person who does not consent to it.

internalize their suffering. As victims strive to get their lives back to normal, they may experience depression, fear, anxiety, and increased substance use for months or years (Herrera & others, 2006). Sexual dysfunctions, such as reduced sexual desire and an inability to reach orgasm, occur in 50 percent of female rape victims (Sprei & Courtois, 1988). Many victims make changes in their lives—such as moving to a new apartment or refusing to go out at night. Recovery depends on the victim's coping abilities, psychological adjustments prior to the assault, and social support (White & Frabutt, 2006). Parents, partner, and others close to the victim can provide important support for recovery, as can mental health professionals.

An increasing concern is **date or acquaintance rape**, which is coercive sexual activity directed at someone with whom the victim is at least casually acquainted (Clark & Carroll, 2008; Wolitzky-Taylor & others, 2008). By some estimates, one in three adolescent girls will be involved in a controlling, abusive relationship before she graduates from high school, and two-thirds of college freshman women report having been date raped or having experienced an attempted date rape at least once (Watts & Zimmerman, 2002). About two-thirds of college men admit that they fondle women against their will, and half admit to forcing sexual activity. To read further about rape on college campuses, see the *Research in Life-Span Development* interlude.

Research in Life-Span Development
Campus Sexual Assault

A major study that focused on campus sexual assault involved a phone survey of 4,446 women attending two- or four-year colleges (Fisher, Cullen, & Turner, 2000). Sexual victimization was measured in a two-stage process. First, a series of screening questions were asked to determine if the respondent had experienced an act that might possibly be a victimization. Second, if the respondent answered "yes," the respondent was asked detailed questions about the incident, such as the type of unwanted contact and the means of coercion. In addition, respondents were asked about other aspects of their lives, including their lifestyles, routine activities, living arrangements, and prior sexual victimization.

Slightly less than 3 percent said that they either had experienced a rape or an attempted rape during the academic year. About 1 of 10 college women said that they had experienced rape in their lifetime. Unwanted or uninvited sexual contacts were widespread, with more than one-third of the college women reporting these incidents. As shown in Figure 13.8, in this study, most women (about 9 of 10) knew the person who sexually victimized them. Most of the women attempted to take protective actions against their assailants but were then reluctant to report the victimization to the police for a number of reasons (such as embarrassment, not clearly understanding the legal definition of rape, or not wanting to define someone they knew who victimized them as a rapist). Several factors were associated with sexual victimization: living on campus, being unmarried, getting drunk frequently, and experiencing prior sexual victimization. The majority of rapes occurred in living quarters.

In addition, this research examined a form of sexual victimization that has been studied infrequently: stalking. Thirteen percent of the female students said they had been stalked since the school year began. As with other sexual victimizations, 80 percent knew their stalkers, who most often were boyfriends (42 percent) or classmates (24 percent). Stalking incidents lasted an average of 60 days.

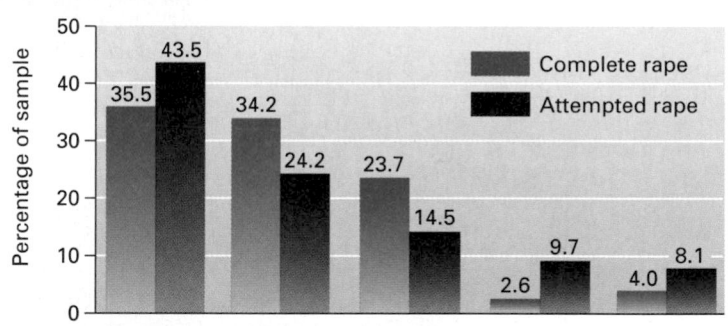

FIGURE 13.8 Relationship Between Victim and Offender in Completed and Attempted Rapes of College Women. In a recent phone survey of college women, slighty less than 3 percent of the women said they had experienced a rape or attempted rape during the academic year (Fisher, Cullen, & Turner, 2000). The percentages shown here indicate the relationship between the victim and the offender. *What were some possible advantages and disadvantages of using a phone survey rather than face-to-face interviews to conduct this study?*

Sexual Harassment Sexual harassment is a manifestation of power of one person over another. It takes many forms—from inappropriate sexual remarks and physical contact (patting, brushing against one's body) to blatant propositions and sexual assaults (Leaper & Brown, 2008; Mitchell, Koien, & Crow, 2008). Millions of women experience sexual

date or acquaintance rape Coercive sexual activity directed at someone with whom the perpetrator is at least casually acquainted.

harassment each year in work and educational settings. Sexual harassment of men by women also occurs but to a far lesser extent than sexual harassment of women by men.

In a recent survey of 2,000 college women, 62 percent reported that they had experienced sexual harassment while attending college (American Association of University Women, 2006). Most of the college women said that the sexual harassment involved noncontact forms such as crude jokes, remarks, and gestures. However, almost one-third said that the sexual harassment was physical in nature. A recent study of almost 1,500 college women revealed that when they had been sexually harassed they reported an increase in psychological distress, greater physical illness, and an increase in disordered eating (Huerta & others, 2006).

Sexual harassment can result in serious psychological consequences for the victim. Sexual harassment is a manifestation of power of one person over another. The elimination of such exploitation requires the development of work and academic environments that provide equal opportunities to develop a career and obtain education in a climate free of sexual harassment (Das, 2008; Rospenda, Richman, & Shannon, 2008).

Review and Reflect: Learning Goal 3

 Discuss Sexuality in Young Adults

REVIEW

- What characterizes the sexual activity of emerging adults?
- What is the nature of heterosexuality and same-sex sexual orientation?
- What are sexually transmitted infections? What are some important things to know about AIDS?
- What is rape? Date or acquaintance rape? What are the effects of forcible sexual behavior and sexual harassment?

REFLECT

- What can be done to reduce forcible sexual behavior and sexual harassment?

4 COGNITIVE DEVELOPMENT

Cognitive Stages   Creativity

Are there changes in cognitive performance during these years? To explore the nature of cognition in early adulthood, we will focus on issues related to cognitive stages and creative thinking.

Cognitive Stages

Are young adults more advanced in their thinking than adolescents are? Let's examine what Piaget and others have said about this intriguing question.

Piaget's View   Piaget concluded that an adolescent and an adult think qualitatively in the same way. That is, Piaget argued that at approximately 11 to 15 years of age, adolescents enter the formal operational stage, which is characterized by more logical, abstract, and idealistic thinking than the concrete operational thinking of 7- to 11-year-olds. Piaget did stress that young adults are more *quantitatively* advanced in their thinking in the sense that they have more knowledge than adolescents. He also reasoned, as do information-processing psychologists, that adults especially increase their knowledge in a specific area, such as a physicist's understanding of physics or a financial analyst's knowledge about finance. According to Piaget, however, formal operational thought is the final stage in cognitive development, and it characterizes adults as well as adolescents.

Some developmentalists theorize it is not until adulthood that many individuals consolidate their formal operational thinking. That is, they may begin to plan and hypothesize about intellectual problems in adolescence, but they become more systematic and sophisticated at this as young adults. Nonetheless, even many adults do not think in formal operational ways at all (Keating, 2004).

Realistic and Pragmatic Thinking   Some developmentalists propose that as young adults move into the world of work, their way of thinking does change. One idea is that as they face the constraints of reality, which work promotes, their idealism decreases (Labouvie-Vief, 1986).

A related change in thinking was proposed that concludes it is unlikely that adults go beyond the powerful methods of scientific thinking characteristic of the formal operational stage (Schaie & Willis, 2000). However, adults do progress beyond adolescents in their use of intellect. For example, in early adulthood individuals often switch from acquiring knowledge to applying knowledge as they pursue success in their work (Schaie & Willis, 2000).

Reflective and Relativistic Thinking   William Perry (1999) also described changes in cognition that take place in early adulthood. He said that adolescents often view the world in terms of polarities—right/wrong, we/they, or good/bad. As youth age into adulthood, they gradually move away from this type of absolutist thinking as they become aware of the diverse opinions and multiple perspectives of others. Thus, in Perry's view, the absolutist, dualistic thinking of adolescence gives way to the reflective, relativistic thinking of adulthood. Other developmentalists also observe that reflective thinking is an important indicator of cognitive change in young adults (Fischer & Bidell, 2006).

Expanding on Perry's view, Gisela Labouvie-Vief (2006) recently proposed that the increasing complexity of cultures in the past century has generated a greater need for more reflective, complex thinking that takes into account the changing nature of knowledge and challenges. She also emphasizes that the key aspects of cognitive development in emerging adulthood include deciding on a particular worldview, recognizing that the worldview is subjective, and understanding that diverse worldviews should be acknowledged. In her perspective, considerable individual variation characterizes the thinking of emerging adults, with the highest level of thinking attained by only some. She argues that the level of education emerging adults achieve especially influences how likely they will maximize their cognitive potential.

Is There a Fifth, Postformal Stage?   Some theorists have pieced together cognitive changes in young adults and proposed a new stage of cognitive development, **postformal thought**, which is qualitatively different from Piaget's formal operational thought (Sinnott, 2003). Postformal thought involves understanding that the correct answer to a problem requires reflective thinking and can vary from one situation to another, and that the search for truth is often an ongoing, never-ending process (Kitchener, King, & Deluca, 2006). Postformal thought also includes the belief that solutions to problems need to be realistic and that emotion and subjective factors can influence thinking.

What is postformal thought like in practice? As young adults engage in more reflective judgment when solving problems, they might think deeply about many aspects of politics, their career and work, relationships, and other areas of life (Labouvie-Vief & Diehl, 1999). They might understand that what might be the best solution to a problem at work (with a coworker or boss) might not be the best solution at home (with a romantic partner). Many young adults also become more skeptical about there being a single truth and often are not willing to accept an answer as final. They also often recognize that thinking can't just be abstract but rather has to be realistic

What are some ways that young adults might think differently than adolescents?

postformal thought A form of thought that is qualitatively different from Piaget's formal operational thought. It involves understanding that the correct answer to a problem can require reflective thinking, that the correct answer can vary from one situation to another, and that the search for truth is often an ongoing, never-ending process. It also involves the belief that solutions to problems need to be realistic and that emotion and subjective factors can influence thinking.

and pragmatic. And many young adults understand that emotions can play a role in thinking—for example, that they are likely to think more clearly when they are in a calm and collected state than when they are angry and highly aroused.

How strong is the evidence for a fifth, postformal stage of cognitive development? Researchers have found that young adults are more likely to engage in this postformal thinking than adolescents are (Commons & Bresette, 2006). But critics argue that research has yet to document that postformal thought is a qualitatively more advanced stage than formal operational thought.

Creativity

Early adulthood is a time of great creativity for some people. At the age of 30, Thomas Edison invented the phonograph, Hans Christian Andersen wrote his first volume of fairy tales, and Mozart composed *The Marriage of Figaro*. One early study of creativity found that individuals' most creative products were generated in their thirties and that 80 percent of the most important creative contributions were completed by age 50 (Lehman, 1960).

More recently, researchers have found that creativity does peak in adulthood and then decline, but that the peak often occurs in the forties. However, qualifying any conclusion about age and creative accomplishments are (1) the magnitude of the decline in productivity, (2) contrasts across creative domains, and (3) individual differences in lifetime output (Simonton, 1996).

Even though a decline in creative contributions is often found in the fifties and later, the decline is not as great as commonly thought. An impressive array of creative accomplishments occur in late adulthood. One of the most remarkable examples of creative accomplishment in late adulthood can be found in the life of Henri Chevreul. After a distinguished career as a physicist, Chevreul switched fields in his nineties to become a pioneer in gerontological research. He published his last research paper just a year prior to his death at the age of 103!

Any consideration of decline in creativity with age requires consideration of the field of creativity involved. In such fields as philosophy and history, older adults often show as much creativity as when they were in their thirties and forties. By contrast, in such fields as lyric poetry, abstract math, and theoretical physics, the peak of creativity is often reached in the twenties or thirties.

There also is extensive individual variation in the lifetime output of creative individuals. Typically, the most productive creators in any field are far more prolific than their least productive counterparts. The contrast is so extreme that the top 10 percent of creative producers frequently account for 50 percent of the creative output in a particular field. For instance, only 16 composers account for half of the music regularly performed in the classical repertoire.

Can you make yourself more creative? In Chapter 9, "Physical and Cognitive Development in Middle and Late Childhood," we presented some strategies for stimulating creative thinking in children, and these strategies can also be used by adults. Other strategies for becoming more creative have been suggested by Mihaly Csikszentmihalyi (pronounced ME-high CHICK-sent-me-high-ee).

Csikszentmihalyi (1995) interviewed 90 leading figures in art, business, government, education, and science to learn how creativity works. He discovered that creative people regularly experience a state he calls *flow,* a heightened state of pleasure experienced when we are engaged in mental and physical challenges that absorb us. Csikszentmihalyi (2000) points out that everyone is capable of achieving flow. Based on his interviews with some of the most creative people in the world, the first step toward a more creative life is cultivating your curiosity and interest. How can you do this?

- *Try to be surprised by something every day.* Maybe it is something you see, hear, or read about. Become absorbed in a lecture or a book. Be open to what the world is telling you. Life is a stream of experiences. Swim widely and deeply in it, and your life will be richer.

- *Try to surprise at least one person every day.* In a lot of things you do, you have to be predictable and patterned. Do something different for a change. Ask a question

Mihaly Csikszentmihalyi, in the setting where he gets his most creative ideas. *When and where do you get your most creative thoughts?*

you normally would not ask. Invite someone to go to a show or a museum you never have visited.

- *Write down each day what surprised you and how you surprised others.* Most creative people keep a diary, notes, or lab records to ensure that their experience is not fleeting or forgotten. Start with a specific task. Each evening record the most surprising event that occurred that day and your most surprising action. After a few days, reread your notes and reflect on your past experiences. After a few weeks, you might see a pattern of interest emerging in your notes, one that might suggest an area you can explore in greater depth.

- *When something sparks your interest, follow it.* Usually when something captures your attention, it is short-lived—an idea, a song, a flower. Too often we are too busy to explore the idea, song, or flower further. Or we think these areas are none of our business because we are not experts about them. Yet the world is our business. We can't know which part of it is best suited to our interests until we make a serious effort to learn as much about as many aspects of it as possible.

- *Wake up in the morning with a specific goal to look forward to.* Creative people wake up eager to start the day. Why? Not necessarily because they are cheerful, enthusiastic types but because they know that there is something meaningful to accomplish each day, and they can't wait to get started.

- *Spend time in settings that stimulate your creativity.* In Csikszentmihalyi's (1995) research, he gave people an electronic pager and beeped them randomly at different times of the day. When he asked them how they felt, they reported the highest levels of creativity when walking, driving, or swimming. I (your author) do my most creative thinking when I'm jogging. These activities are semiautomatic in that they take a certain amount of attention while leaving some time free to make connections among ideas. Another setting in which highly creative people report coming up with novel ideas is the sort of half-asleep, half-awake state we are in when we are deeply relaxed or barely awake.

Review and Reflect: Learning Goal 4

4 **Characterize Cognitive Changes in Early Adulthood**

REVIEW

- What changes in cognitive development in young adults have been proposed?
- Does creativity decline in adulthood? How can people lead more creative lives?

REFLECT

- What do you think are the most important cognitive changes that take place in young adults?

5 CAREERS AND WORK

Developmental Changes   **Monitoring the Occupational Outlook**   **The Impact of Work**

Earning a living, choosing an occupation, establishing a career, and developing in a career—these are important themes of early adulthood. What are some of the factors that go into choosing a job or career, and how does work typically affect the lives of young adults?

"Your son has made a career choice, Mildred. He's going to win the lottery and travel a lot."
© 2004. Reprinted courtesy of Bunny Hoest and Parade Magazine.

Developmental Changes

Many children have idealistic fantasies about what they want to be when they grow up. For example, many young children want to be superheroes, sports stars, or movie stars. In the high school years, they often have begun to think about careers on a somewhat less idealistic basis. In their late teens and early twenties, their career decision making has usually turned more serious as they explore different career possibilities and zero in on the career they want to enter. In college, this often means choosing a major or specialization that is designed to lead to work in a particular field. By their early and mid-twenties, many individuals have completed their education or training and started to enter a full-time occupation. From the mid-twenties through the remainder of early adulthood, individuals often seek to establish their emerging career in a particular field. They may work hard to move up the career ladder and improve their financial standing.

Monitoring the Occupational Outlook

As you explore the type of work you are likely to enjoy and in which you can succeed, it is important to be knowledgeable about different fields and companies. Occupations may have many job openings one year but few in another year as economic conditions change. Thus, it is critical to keep up with the occupational outlook in various fields. An excellent source for doing this is the U.S. government's *Occupational Outlook Handbook, 2008–2009* (2008) which is revised every two years.

According to the 2008–2009 handbook, service industries, especially education and health services, and professional and business services, are projected to account for the most new jobs in the next decade. Projected job growth varies widely by education requirements. Jobs that require a college degree are expected to grow the fastest. Most of the highest-paying occupations require a college degree.

The Impact of Work

Work defines people in fundamental ways (Blustein, 2008; Fouad & Bynner, 2008). It is an important influence on their financial standing, housing, the way they spend their time, where they live, their friendships, and their health. Some people define their identity through their work. Work also creates a structure and rhythm to life that is often missed when individuals do not work for an extended period. When unable to work, many individuals experience emotional distress and low self-esteem.

Most individuals spend about one-third of their lives at work. In one survey, 35 percent of Americans worked 40 hours a week, but 18 percent worked 51 hours or more per week (Center for Survey Research at the University of Connecticut, 2000). Only 10 percent worked less than 30 hours a week.

An important consideration regarding work is how stressful it is. A recent national survey of U.S. adults revealed that 55 percent indicated they were less productive because of stress (American Psychological Association, 2007). In this study, 52 percent reported that they considered or made a career decision, such as looking for a new job, declining a promotion, or quitting a job, because of stress in the workplace (American Psychological Association, 2007). In this survey, main sources of stress included low salaries (44 percent), lack of advancement opportunities (42 percent), uncertain job expectations (40 percent), and long hours (39 percent).

Many adults have changing expectations about work, yet employers often aren't meeting their expectations (Moen, 2007; Orrange, 2007). For example, current policies and practices were designed for a single breadwinner (male) workforce and an industrial economy, making these policies and practices out of step with a workforce of women and men, and of single parent and dual earners. Many workers today want flexibility and greater control over the time and timing of their work, and yet most employers offer little flexibility, even though policies like flextime may be "on the books."

Work During College   Eighty percent of U.S. undergraduate college students worked during the 1999–2000 academic year (National Center for Education Statistics, 2002). Forty-eight percent of undergraduates identified themselves mainly as students working to meet school expenses and 32 percent as employees who decided to enroll in school. Undergraduate students who identified themselves as working to meet expenses worked an average of 26 hours per week; those who considered themselves to be employees worked an average of 40 hours per week.

Working can pay or help offset some costs of schooling, but working also can restrict students' opportunities to learn. For those who identified themselves primarily as students, one recent national study found that as the number of hours worked per week increased, their grades suffered (National Center for Education Statistics, 2002) (see Figure 13.9). Other research found that as the number of hours college students work increased, the more likely they were to drop out of college (National Center for Education Statistics, 2002). Thus, college students need to carefully examine whether the number of hours they work is having a negative impact on their college success.

Of course, jobs also can contribute to your education. More than 1,000 colleges in the United States offer *cooperative (co-op) programs*, which are paid apprenticeships in a field that you are interested in pursuing. (You may not be permitted to participate in a co-op program until your junior year.) Other useful opportunities for working while going to college include internships and part-time or summer jobs relevant to your field of study. In a national survey of employers, almost 60 percent said their entry-level college hires had co-op or internship experience (Collins, 1996). Participating in these work experiences can be a key factor in whether you land the job you want when you graduate.

Unemployment   Unemployment produces stress regardless of whether the job loss is temporary, cyclical, or permanent. Researchers have found that unemployment is related to physical problems (such as heart attack and stroke), mental problems (such as depression and anxiety), marital difficulties, and homicide (Gallo & others, 2006). A 15-year longitudinal study of more than 24,000 adults found that life satisfaction dropped considerably following unemployment and increased after becoming reemployed but did not completely return to the life satisfaction level previous to being unemployed (Lucas & others, 2004). A recent study also revealed that immune system functioning declined with unemployment and increased with new employment (Cohen & others, 2007).

Stress comes not only from a loss of income and the resulting financial hardships but also from decreased self-esteem. Individuals who cope best with unemployment have financial resources to rely on, often savings or the earnings of other family members. The support of understanding, adaptable family members also helps individuals cope with unemployment. Job counseling and self-help groups can provide practical advice on job searching, résumés, and interviewing skills, and also give emotional support.

Dual-Earner Couples   Dual-earner couples may have particular problems finding a balance between work and the rest of life (Pitt-Catsouphes, Kossek, & Sweet, 2006). If both partners are working, who cleans up the house or calls the repairman or takes care of the other endless details involved in maintaining a home? If the couple has children, who is responsible for being sure that the children get to school or to piano practice, who writes the notes to approve field trips or meets the teacher or makes the dental appointments?

Although single-earner married families still make up a sizable minority of families, the two-earner couple has increased considerably in the last three decades (Barnett, 2001). As more U.S. women worked outside the home, the division of responsibility for work and family changed. Recent research suggests that (Barnett, 2001; Barnett & others, 2001):

- *U.S. husbands are taking increased responsibility for maintaining the home.* Although husbands are doing more housework, they still don't do as much as wives do.

What are some characteristics of work settings linked with employees' stress?

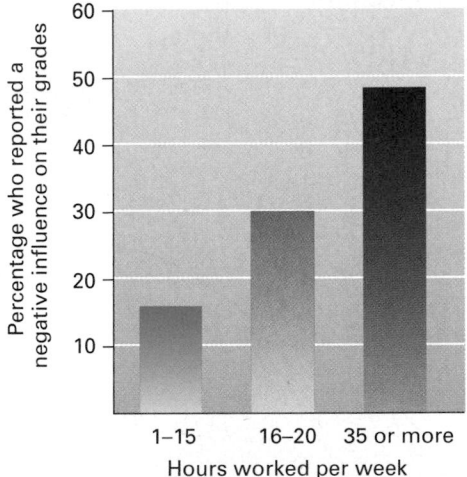

FIGURE 13.9 The Relation of Hours Worked Per Week in College to Grades. Among students working to pay for school expenses, 16 percent of those working 1 to 15 hours per week reported that working negatively influenced their grades (National Center for Education Statistics, 2002). Thirty percent of college students who worked 16 to 20 hours a week said the same, as did 48 percent who worked 35 hours or more per week.

- *U.S. women are taking increased responsibility for breadwinning.* In about one-third of two-earner couples, wives earn as much as or more than their husbands.

- *U.S. men are showing greater interest in their families and parenting.* Young adult men are reporting that family is at least as important to them as work.

In the *Diversity in Life-Span Development* interlude, we further explore gender and work by examining gender in the workplace. Ethnic diversity in the workplace also is discussed in the interlude.

Diversity in Life-Span Development
Diversity in the Workplace

The workplace is becoming increasingly diverse [*Occupational Outlook Handbook, 2008–2009,* (2008)]. Whereas at one time few women were employed outside the home, in developed countries women have increasingly entered the labor force (UNICEF, 2007, 2008). In 2004, in the United States, men made up 53.6 percent of the labor force, women 46.4 percent (*Occupational Outlook Handbook, 2006–2007* [2006]). In the United States, more than one-fourth of all lawyers, physicians, computer scientists, and chemists today are females.

Ethnic diversity also is increasing in the workplace in every developed country except France. In the United States, between 1980 and 2004, the percentage of Latinos and Asian Americans more than doubled in the workplace, a trend that is expected to continue (*Occupational Outlook Handbook, 2006–2007* [2006]; U.S. Bureau of Labor Statistics, 2005). Latinos are projected to constitute a larger percentage of the labor force than African Americans by 2014, growing from 12 percent to 15 percent (*Occupational Outlook Handbook, 2006–2007* [2006]). Asian Americans will continue to be the fastest growing of the labor force groups. The increasing diversity in the workplace requires a sensitivity to cultural differences, and the cultural values that workers bring to a job need to be recognized and appreciated (Fassinger, 2008).

Despite the increasing diversity in the workplace, women and ethnic minorities experience difficulty in breaking through the *glass ceiling.* This invisible barrier to career advancement prevents women and ethnic minorities from holding managerial or executive jobs regardless of their accomplishments and merits.

How has the diversity of the workplace changed in recent years?

Review and Reflect: Learning Goal 5

5 **Explain the Key Dimensions of Careers and Work in Early Adulthood**

REVIEW

- What are some developmental changes in careers and work?
- Which areas are likely to offer the greatest increase in jobs in the next decade?
- What are some important things to know about work?

REFLECT

- What careers do you want to pursue? How much education will they take? What are some changes in men's roles in home and family matters in the last 40 years?

Reach Your Learning Goals

Physical and Cognitive Development in Early Adulthood

1 THE TRANSITION FROM ADOLESCENCE TO ADULTHOOD: DESCRIBE THE TRANSITION FROM ADOLESCENCE TO ADULTHOOD

Becoming an Adult

- Emerging adulthood is the term now given to the transition from adolescence to adulthood. Its age range is about 18 to 25 years of age, and it is characterized by experimentation and exploration. There is both continuity and change in the transition from adolescence to adulthood. Two criteria for adult status are economic independence and taking responsibility for the consequences of one's actions.

The Transition from High School to College

- The transition from high school to college can involve both positive and negative features. Although students may feel more grown up and be intellectually challenged by academic work, for many the transition involves a focus on the stressful move from being the oldest and most powerful group of students to being the youngest and least powerful group. U.S. college students today report experiencing more stress and are more depressed than college students of the 1980s.

2 PHYSICAL DEVELOPMENT: IDENTIFY THE CHANGES IN PHYSICAL DEVELOPMENT IN YOUNG ADULTS

Physical Performance and Development

- Peak physical performance is often reached between 19 and 26 years of age. Toward the latter part of early adulthood, a detectable slowdown in physical performance is apparent for most individuals.

Health

- Emerging adults have more than twice the mortality rate of adolescents, with males being mainly responsible for the increase. Despite their higher mortality rate, emerging adults in general have few chronic health problems. Many emerging adults develop bad health habits that can affect their health later in life.

Eating and Weight

- Obesity is a serious problem, with about 25 percent of Americans overweight enough to be at increased health risk. Heredity, leptin, set point, and environmental factors are involved in obesity. Most diets don't work long term. For those that do, exercise is usually an important component.

Regular Exercise

- Both moderate and intense exercise produce important physical and psychological gains.

Substance Abuse

- By the mid-twenties, a reduction in alcohol and drug use often takes place. Binge drinking among college students is still a major concern and can cause students to miss classes, have trouble with police, and have unprotected sex. Alcoholism is a disorder that impairs an individual's health and social relationships. Fewer young adults are smoking cigarettes, and a number of strategies, such as nicotine substitutes, have shown some success in getting smokers to quit.

3 SEXUALITY: DISCUSS SEXUALITY IN YOUNG ADULTS

Sexual Activity in Emerging Adulthood

- Emerging adulthood is a time during which most individuals are sexually active and become married. Emerging adults have sexual intercourse with more individuals than young adults, but they have sex less frequently. Also, casual sex is more common in emerging adulthood than early adulthood.

Sexual Orientation and Behavior

Sexually Transmitted Infections

Forcible Sexual Behavior and Sexual Harassment

- In the 1994 Sex in America survey, American adults' sexual lives were portrayed as more conservative than in earlier surveys. An individual's sexual preference likely is the result of a combination of genetic, hormonal, cognitive, and environmental factors.

- Also called STIs, sexually transmitted infections are contracted primarily through sexual contact. The STI that has received the most attention in the last several decades is infection with HIV, which can lead to AIDS (acquired immune deficiency syndrome). A person with AIDS has a weakened immune system—even a cold can be life-threatening.

- Rape is forcible sexual intercourse with a person who does not give consent. Date or acquaintance rape involves coercive sexual activity directed at someone with whom the victim is at least casually acquainted. Sexual harassment occurs when one person uses his or her power over another individual in a sexual manner, which can result in serious psychological consequences for the victim.

4 COGNITIVE DEVELOPMENT: CHARACTERIZE COGNITIVE CHANGES IN EARLY ADULTHOOD

Cognitive Stages

Creativity

- Formal operational thought, entered at about age 11 to 15, is Piaget's final cognitive stage. According to Piaget, although adults are quantitatively more knowledgeable than adolescents, adults do not enter a new, qualitatively different stage. Some experts argue that the idealism of Piaget's formal operational stage declines in young adults, and is replaced by more realistic, pragmatic thinking. Some propose that differences like these constitute a qualitatively different, fifth cognitive stage, called postformal thought.

- Creativity peaks in adulthood, often in the forties, and then declines. However, there is extensive individual variation in lifetime creative output. Csikszentmihalyi proposed that the first step toward living a creative life is to cultivate curiosity and interest.

5 CAREERS AND WORK: EXPLAIN THE KEY DIMENSIONS OF CAREERS AND WORK IN EARLY ADULTHOOD

Developmental Changes

Monitoring the Occupational Outlook

The Impact of Work

- Many young children have idealistic fantasies about a career. In the late teens and early twenties, their career thinking has usually turned more serious. By their early to mid-twenties, many individuals have completed their education or training and started in a career. In the remainder of early adulthood, they seek to establish their emerging career and start moving up the career ladder.

- Jobs that require a college education will be the fastest growing and highest paying in the United States. in the next decade, especially education and health services, and business and professional services.

- Work defines people in fundamental ways and is a key aspect of their identity. Most individuals spend about one-third of their adult life at work. Eighty percent of U.S. college students work while going to college. Working during college can have positive or negative outcomes. Unemployment produces stress regardless of whether the job loss is temporary, cyclical, or permanent. The increasing number of women who work in careers outside the home has led to new work-related issues. Because of dual-earner households, there has been a considerable increase in the time men spend in household work and child care. The U.S. workplace has become increasingly diverse.

KEY TERMS

emerging adulthood 417
aerobic exercise 423
addiction 424

sexually transmitted
  infections (STIs) 429
rape 430

date or acquaintance
  rape 431
postformal thought 433

KEY PEOPLE

Jeffrey Arnett 417
Ann Masten 417
Jerald Bachman 424

Robert Michael 427
Simon LeVay 428
Laura Brown 428

Jean Piaget 432
William Perry 433
Gisela Labouvie-Vief 433

Mihaly Csikszentmihalyi 434

E-LEARNING TOOLS

To help you master the material in this chapter, visit the Online Learning Center for *Life-Span Development*, twelfth edition, at **www.mhhe.com/santrockld12**.

Self-Assessment

Connect to **www.mhhe.com/santrockld12** to examine some topics that are important to young adults by completing the self-assessments, *How Much Do I Know About STDs?*, *Matching My Personality Type to Careers*, and *My Career Goals*.

Taking It to the Net

Connect to **www.mhhe.com/santrockld12** to research the answers to these questions:

1. Brian is a college senior who just turned 21. Brian's mother and grandfather both suffered from alcoholism; he has painful memories of his mother's out-of-control drinking when he was a child. Now that he is of legal drinking age, Brian would like to drink recreationally and sensibly, but he is concerned that he may have a psychological or genetic tendency toward alcohol abuse. What are some warning signs of a predisposition toward alcoholism? What precautions should Brian take to ensure that he remains a responsible drinker?

2. Nanette is working part-time in her college human resources office. She has been asked to start gathering information for a sexual harassment information booklet. What are the essential characteristics of sexual harassment, and how should she communicate how the signs are identified?

3. Lisa is a 28-year-old graphic designer who lost her job in the dot-com industry after working only two years at a design agency. She has been forced to work as a freelance designer for the past three years, without health benefits or job security, and she is beginning to despair of finding a full-time job in her field. How are unemployment and lack of job security linked to depression? How might Lisa's experience have been different if she had found herself unemployed at the age of 50?

Video Clips

The Online Learning Center includes a video for Chapter 13 called "On Being a Working Mom." The working parents profiled in this segment offer two perspectives on the problem of maintaining the proper balance between work and the rest of life.

Health and Well-Being, Parenting, and Education Exercises

Build your decision-making skills by trying your hand at the health and well-being, parenting, and education exercises. Connect to **www.mhhe.com/santrockld12** to research the answers and complete the exercises.

14

Love is a canvas furnished by nature and embroidered by imagination.

—VOLTAIRE
French Essayist, 18th Century

LEARNING GOALS

◆ Describe stability and change in temperament, and summarize adult attachment styles.

◆ Identify some key aspects of attraction, love, and close relationships.

◆ Characterize adult life styles.

◆ Discuss making marriages work, parenting, and divorce.

◆ Summarize the role of gender in relationships.

SOCIOEMOTIONAL DEVELOPMENT IN EARLY ADULTHOOD

CHAPTER OUTLINE

443

Images of Life-Span Development
Gwenna and Greg: Her Pursuit and His Lack of Commitment

Commitment is an important issue in a romantic relationship for most individuals. Consider Gwenna, who decides that it is time to have a talk with Greg about his commitment to their relationship (Lerner, 1989, pp. 44–45):

> She shared her perspective on both the strengths and weaknesses of their relationship and what her hopes were for the future. She asked Greg to do the same. Unlike earlier conversations, this one was conducted without her pursuing him, pressuring him, or diagnosing his problems with women. At the same time, she asked Greg some clear questions, which exposed his vagueness.
>
> "How will you know when you are ready to make a commitment? What specifically would you need to change or be different than it is today?"
>
> "I don't know," was Greg's response. When questioned further, the best he could come up with was that he'd just feel it.
>
> "How much more time do you need to make a decision one way or another?"
>
> "I'm not sure," Greg replied. "Maybe a couple of years, but I really can't answer a question like that. I can't predict my feelings."
>
> And so it went.
>
> Gwenna really loved this man, but two years (and maybe longer) was longer than she could comfortably wait. So, after much thought, she told Greg that she would wait till fall (about ten months), but that she would move on if he couldn't commit himself to marriage by then. She was open about her wish to marry and have a family with him, but she was equally clear that her first priority was a mutually committed relationship. If Greg was not at that point by fall, then she would end the relationship—painful though it would be.
>
> During the waiting period, Gwenna was able to not pursue him and not get distant or otherwise reactive to his expressions of ambivalence and doubt. In this way she gave Greg emotional space to struggle with his dilemma and the relationship had its best chance of succeeding. Her bottom-line position ("a decision by fall") was not a threat or an attempt to rope Greg in, but rather, a clear statement of what was acceptable to her.
>
> When fall arrived, Greg told Gwenna he needed another six months to make up his mind. Gwenna deliberated a while and decided she could live with that. But when the six months were up, Greg was uncertain and asked for more time. It was then that Gwenna took the painful but ultimately empowering step of ending their relationship.

PREVIEW

Love is of central importance in each of our lives, as it is in Gwenna and Greg's lives. Shortly, we will discuss the many faces of love, as well as marriage and the family, the diversity of adult lifestyles, and the role of gender in relationships. To begin, though, we will return to an issue we initially raised in Chapter 1: stability and change.

1 STABILITY AND CHANGE FROM CHILDHOOD TO ADULTHOOD

Temperament   **Attachment**

For adults, socioemotional development revolves around adaptively integrating our emotional experiences into enjoyable relationships with others on a daily basis (Thompson & Goodvin, 2005). Young adults like Gwenna and Greg face choices and challenges in adopting lifestyles that will be emotionally satisfying, predictable, and manageable for them. They do not come to these tasks as blank slates, but do their decisions and actions simply reflect the persons they had already become when they were 5 years old or 10 years old or 20 years old?

Current research shows that the first 20 years of life are not meaningless in predicting an adult's socioemotional life (Caspi & Shiner, 2006). And there is also every reason to believe that experiences in the early adult years are important in determining what the individual is like later in adulthood. A common finding is that the smaller the time intervals over which we measure socioemotional characteristics, the more similar an individual will look from one measurement to the next. Thus, if we measure an individual's self-concept at the age of 20 and then again at the age of 30, we will probably find more stability than if we measured the individual's self-concept at the age of 10 and then again at the age of 30.

In trying to understand the young adult's socioemotional development, it would be misleading to look at an adult's life only in the present tense, ignoring the unfolding of social relationships and emotions. So, too, it would be a mistake to search only through a 30-year-old's first 5 to 10 years of life in trying to understand why he or she is having difficulty in a close relationship.

Temperament

How stable is temperament? Recall that *temperament* is an individual's behavioral style and characteristic emotional responses. In early adulthood, most individuals show fewer emotional mood swings than they did in adolescence, and they become more responsible and engage in less risk-taking behavior (Caspi, 1998). Along with these signs of a general change in temperament, researchers also find links between some dimensions of childhood temperament and adult personality. For example, in one longitudinal study, children who were highly active at age 4 were likely to be very outgoing at age 23 (Franz, 1996).

Are other aspects of temperament in childhood linked with adjustment in adulthood? In Chapter 4, we saw that researchers have proposed various ways of describing and classifying types and dimensions of personality. Research has linked several of these types and dimensions during childhood with characteristics of adult personality. For example:

- *Easy and difficult temperaments (two categories in Chess and Thomas' classification of types of temperament).* Here is what we know based on the few longitudinal studies that have been conducted on this topic (Caspi, 1998). In one longitudinal study, children who had an easy temperament at 3 to 5 years of age were likely to be well adjusted as young adults (Chess & Thomas, 1987). In contrast, many children who had a difficult temperament at 3 to 5 years of age were not well adjusted as young adults. Also, other researchers have found that boys with a difficult temperament in childhood are less likely as adults to continue their formal education, whereas girls with a difficult temperament in childhood are more likely to experience marital conflict as adults (Wachs, 2000).

To what extent is temperament in childhood linked to temperament in adulthood?

- *Inhibition, a characteristic studied extensively by Jerome Kagan* (2008). Individuals who had an inhibited temperament in childhood are less likely than other adults to be assertive or experience social support, and more likely to delay entering a stable job track (Wachs, 2000).

- *Ability to control one's emotions (a dimension in Mary Rothbart and John Bates' analysis of temperament).* In one longitudinal study, when 3-year-old children showed good control of their emotions and were resilient in the face of stress, they were likely to continue to handle emotions effectively as adults (Block, 1993). By contrast, when 3-year-olds had low emotional control and were not very resilient, they were likely to show problems in these areas as young adults.

In sum, these studies reveal some continuity between certain aspects of temperament in childhood and adjustment in early adulthood. However, keep in mind that these connections between childhood temperament and adult adjustment are based on only a small number of studies, and more research is needed to verify these linkages. Indeed, Theodore Wachs (1994, 2000) proposed ways that linkages between temperament in childhood and personality in adulthood might vary depending on the intervening contexts in individuals' experience. For example, Figure 14.1 describes contexts in which an infant who displayed an inhibited temperament might develop a relatively sociable adult personality. As discussed in Chapter 6, many aspects of the environment—including gender, culture, parenting, and goodness of fit generally—may influence the persistence of aspects of a child's temperament through life.

Attachment

Like temperament, attachment appears during infancy and plays an important part in socioemotional development (Cassidy, 2009; Weinfield & others, 2009). We discussed its role in infancy and adolescence (see Chapters 6 and 12). How do these earlier patterns of attachment and adults' attachment styles influence the lives of adults?

Although relationships with romantic partners differ from those with parents, romantic partners fulfill some of the same needs for adults as parents do for their children (Mikulincer & Shaver, 2007, 2009). Recall from Chapter 6 that *securely attached* infants are defined as those who use the caregiver as a secure base from which to explore the environment. Similarly, adults may count on their romantic partners to be a secure base to which they can return and obtain comfort and security in stressful times (Feeney, 2009; Zeifman & Hazan, 2009).

FIGURE 14.1 Temperament in Childhood, Personality in Adulthood, and Intervening Contexts. Varying experiences with caregivers, the physical environment, peers, and schools can modify links between temperament in childhood and personality in adulthood. The example given here is for inhibition.

Initial Temperament Trait: Inhibition

	Child A	Child B
Intervening Context		
Caregivers	Caregivers (parents) who are sensitive and accepting, and let child set his or her own pace.	Caregivers who use inappropriate "low-level control" and attempt to force the child into new situations.
Physical Environment	Presence of "stimulus shelters" or "defensible spaces" that the children can retreat to when there is too much stimulation.	Child continually encounters noisy, chaotic environments that allow no escape from stimulation.
Peers	Peer groups with other inhibited children with common interests, so the child feels accepted.	Peer groups consist of athletic extroverts, so the child feels rejected.
Schools	School is "undermanned," so inhibited children are more likely to be tolerated and feel they can make a contribution.	School is "overmanned," so inhibited children are less likely to be tolerated and more likely to feel undervalued.
Personality Outcomes		
	As an adult, individual is closer to extraversion (outgoing, sociable) and is emotionally stable.	As an adult, individual is closer to introversion and has more emotional problems.

Do adult attachment patterns with partners reflect childhood attachment patterns with parents? In a retrospective study, Cindy Hazan and Philip Shaver (1987) revealed that young adults who were securely attached in their romantic relationships were more likely to describe their early relationship with their parents as securely attached. In a longitudinal study, infants who were securely attached at 1 year of age were securely attached 20 years later in their adult romantic relationships (Steele & others, 1998). However, in another longitudinal study, links between early attachment styles and later attachment styles were lessened by stressful and disruptive experiences, such as the death of a parent or instability of caregiving (Lewis, Feiring, & Rosenthal, 2000).

Hazan and Shaver (1987, p. 515) measured attachment styles using the following brief assessment:

Read each paragraph and then place a check mark next to the description that best describes you:

_____ 1.   I find it relatively easy to get close to others and I am comfortable depending on them and having them depend on me. I don't worry about being abandoned or about someone getting too close to me.

_____ 2.   I am somewhat uncomfortable being close to others. I find it difficult to trust them completely and to allow myself to depend on them. I get nervous when anyone gets too close to me and it bothers me when someone tries to be more intimate with me than I feel comfortable with.

_____ 3.   I find that others are reluctant to get as close as I would like. I often worry that my partner doesn't really love me or won't want to stay with me. I want to get very close to my partner, and this sometimes scares people away.

These items correspond to three attachment styles—secure attachment (option 1 above) and two insecure attachment styles (avoidant—option 2 above, and anxious—option 3 above):

- **Secure attachment style**. Securely attached adults have positive views of relationships, find it easy to get close to others, and are not overly concerned with or stressed out about their romantic relationships. These adults tend to enjoy sexuality in the context of a committed relationship and are less likely than others to have one-night stands.

- **Avoidant attachment style**. Avoidant individuals are hestitant about getting involved in romantic relationships and once in a relationship tend to distance themselves from their partner.

- **Anxious attachment style**. These individuals demand closeness, are less trusting, and are more emotional, jealous, and possessive.

The majority of adults (about 60 to 80 percent) describe themselves as securely attached, and not surprisingly adults prefer having a securely attached partner (Shaver & Mikulincer, 2007; Zeifman & Hazan, 2009).

Researchers are studying links between adults' current attachment styles and many aspects of their lives (Feeney, 2009; Feeney & Monin, 2009; Mikulincer & Shaver, 2009). For example, securely attached adults are more satisfied with their close relationships than insecurely attached adults, and the relationships of securely attached adults are more likely to be characterized by trust, commitment, and longevity (Feeney, 2009; Feeney & Collins, 2007). Securely attached adults also are more likely than insecurely attached adults to provide support when they are distressed and more likely to give support when their partner is distressed (Rholes & Simpson, 2007). Also, one study found that adults with avoidant and anxious attachment styles were more likely to be depressed than securely attached adults (Hankin, Kassel, & Abela, 2005). Another study revealed that women with anxious or avoidant attachment styles and men with an avoidant attachment style were more likely to have unwanted but consensual sexual experiences than securely attached adults (Gentzler & Kerns, 2004). And a recent study of young women revealed a link between having an avoidant attachment pattern and a lower incidence of female orgasm (Cohen & Belsky, 2008).

What are some key dimensions of attachment in adulthood, and how are they related to relationship patterns and well-being?

secure attachment style An attachment style that describes adults who have positive views of relationships, find it easy to get close to others, and are not overly concerned or stressed out about their romantic relationships.

avoidant attachment style An attachment style that describes adults who are hesitant about getting involved in romantic relationships and once in a relationship tend to distance themselves from their partner.

anxious attachment style An attachment style that describes adults who demand closeness, are less trusting, and are more emotional, jealous, and possessive.

A recent research review and conceptualization of attachment by leading experts Mario Mikulincer and Phillip Shaver (2007) concluded the following about the benefits of secure attachment. Individuals who are securely attached have a well-integrated sense of self-acceptance, self-esteem, and self-efficacy. They have the ability to control their emotions, are optimistic, and are resilient. Facing stress and adversity, they activate cognitive representations of security, are mindful of what is happening around them, and mobilize effective coping strategies.

Mikulincer and Shaver's (2007) review also concluded that attachment insecurity places couples at risk for relationship problems. For example, when an anxious individual is paired with an avoidant individual, the anxious partner's needs and demands frustrate the avoidant partner's preference for distance in the relationship; the avoidant partner's need for distance causes stress for the anxious partner's need for closeness. The result: Both partners are unhappy in the relationship and the anxious-avoidant pairing can produce abuse or violence when a partner criticizes or tries to change the other's behavior. Researchers also have found that when both partners have an anxious attachment pattern, the pairing usually produces dissatisfaction with the marriage and can lead to a mutual attack and retreat in the relationship (Feeney, 2009). When both partners have an anxious attachment style, they feel misunderstood and rejected, excessively dwell on their own insecurities, and seek to control the other's behavior (Mikulincer & Shaver, 2007, 2009).

If you have an insecure attachment style, are you stuck with it and does it doom you to have problematic relationships? Attachment categories are somewhat stable in adulthood but adults do have the capacity to change their attachment thinking and behavior. It also is important to note that although attachment insecurities are linked to relationship problems, attachment style makes only a moderate-size contribution to relationship functioning and that other factors contribute to relationship satisfaction and success (Mikulincer & Shaver, 2007, 2009). Later in the chapter, we will discuss such factors in our coverage of marital relationships.

Review and Reflect: Learning Goal 1

 Describe Stability and Change in Temperament, and Summarize Adult Attachment Styles

REVIEW

- How stable is temperament from childhood to adulthood?
- What attachment styles characterize adults, and how are they linked to relationship outcomes?

REFLECT

- What is your attachment style? How do you think it affects your relationships?

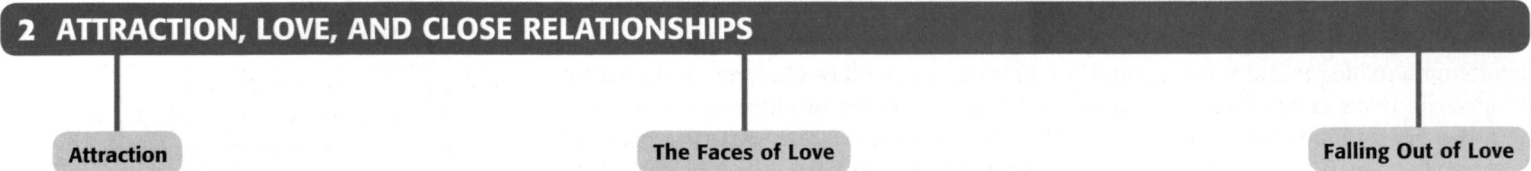

2 ATTRACTION, LOVE, AND CLOSE RELATIONSHIPS

| Attraction | The Faces of Love | Falling Out of Love |

These are the themes of our exploration of close relationships: how they get started in the first place, the faces of love, and falling out of love.

DILBERT © Scott Adams/Dist. by United Feature Syndicate, Inc.

Attraction

What attracts people like Gwenna and Greg to each other and motivates them to spend more time with each other? How important are personality traits and physical attraction in determining the relationships we form?

Familiarity and Similarity   Familiarity may breed contempt, as the old saying goes, but social psychologists have found that familiarity is a necessary condition for a close relationship to develop. For the most part, friends and lovers are people who have been around each other for a long time; they may have grown up together, gone to high school or college together, worked together, or gone to the same social events (Brehm, 2002).

Another old saying, "Birds of a feather flock together," also helps to explain attraction. Overall, our friends and lovers are much more like us than unlike us (Berscheid, 2000). Friends and lovers tend to have similar attitudes, values, lifestyles, and physical attractiveness. For some characteristics, though, opposites may attract. An introvert may wish to be with an extravert, or someone with little money may wish to associate with someone who is wealthy, for example.

Why are people attracted to others who have similar attitudes, values, and lifestyles? **Consensual validation** is one reason. Our own attitudes and values are supported when someone else's attitudes and values are similar to ours—their attitudes and values validate ours. Another reason that similarity matters is that people tend to shy away from the unknown. We often prefer to be around people whose attitudes and values we can predict. And similarity implies that we will enjoy doing things with another person who likes the same things and has similar attitudes.

Physical Attractiveness   As important as familiarity and similarity may be, they do not explain the spark that often ignites a romantic relationship: physical attractiveness.

How important is physical attractiveness in relationships? Psychologists do not consider the link between physical beauty and attraction to be as clear-cut as many advertising agencies would like us to believe. For example, psychologists have determined that heterosexual men and women differ on the importance of good looks when they seek an intimate partner. Women tend to rate as most important such traits as considerateness, honesty, dependability, kindness, understanding, and earning prospects; men prefer good looks, cooking skills, and frugality (Buss & Barnes, 1986; Eastwick & Finkel, 2008).

Complicating research about the role of physical attraction is changing standards of what is deemed attractive. The criteria for beauty can differ, not just across cultures, but over time within cultures as well (Lamb & others, 1993). In the 1950s, the ideal of female beauty in the United States was typified by the well-rounded figure of Marilyn Monroe. Today, Monroe's 135-pound, 5-foot, 5-inch physique might be regarded as a bit overweight. The current ideal physique for both men and women is neither pleasingly plump nor extremely slender.

consensual validation An explanation of why individuals are attracted to people who are similar to them. Our own attitudes and behavior are supported and validated when someone else's attitudes and behavior are similar to our own.

The force of similarity also operates at a physical level. We usually seek out someone at our own level of attractiveness in physical characteristics as well as social attributes we addressed previously. Research validates the **matching hypothesis**, which states that, although we may prefer a more attractive person in the abstract, in the real world we end up choosing someone who is close to our own level of attractiveness (Kalick & Hamilton, 1986). However, a recent study revealed that the matching hypothesis did not hold up for couples once they became married (McNulty, Karney, & Neff, 2008). In the first six months of the marriage, the only link between levels of attractiveness and various aspects of the marital relationship was that attractive husbands were less satisfied. Also, rather than similarity, it was the difference between marital partners' attractiveness that best predicted their behavior toward each other: Both spouses behaved more positively when the wife was more attractive and behaved more negatively when the husband was more attractive. Thus, although matched attractiveness plays a powerful role early in relationships it may have less influence in marriage.

The Faces of Love

Once we are initially attracted to another person, other opportunities exist that may deepen the relationship to love. Love refers to a vast and complex territory of human behavior, spanning a range of relationships that includes friendship, romantic love, affectionate love, and consummate love (Berscheid, 1988). In most of these types of love, one recurring theme is intimacy (Weis & Sternberg, 2008).

Intimacy   Self-disclosure and the sharing of private thoughts are hallmarks of intimacy. As we discussed in Chapter 12, adolescents have an increased need for intimacy. At the same time, they are engaged in the essential tasks of developing an identity and establishing their independence from their parents. Juggling the competing demands of intimacy, identity, and independence also becomes a central task of adulthood.

*W*e are what we love.

—**Erik Erikson**
Danish-Born American Psychoanalyst and Author, 20th Century

Erikson's Stage: Intimacy Versus Isolation   Recall from our discussion in Chapter 10 that Erik Erikson (1968) argues that identity versus identity confusion—pursuing who we are, what we are all about, and where we are going in life—is the most important issue to be negotiated in adolescence. In early adulthood, according to Erikson, after individuals are well on their way to establishing stable and successful identities, they enter the sixth developmental stage, which is intimacy versus isolation. Erikson describes intimacy as finding oneself while losing oneself in another person, and it requires a commitment to another person. If a person fails to develop an intimate relationship in early adulthood, according to Erikson, isolation results.

An inability to develop meaningful relationships with others can harm an individual's personality. It may lead individuals to repudiate, ignore, or attack those who frustrate them. Such circumstances account for the shallow, almost pathetic attempts of youth to merge themselves with a leader. Many youth want to be apprentices or disciples of leaders and adults who will shelter them from the harm of the "outgroup" world. If this fails—and Erikson points out that it must—sooner or later the individuals recoil into a self-search to discover where they went wrong. This introspection sometimes leads to painful depression and isolation. It also may contribute to a mistrust of others.

matching hypothesis States that although we prefer a more attractive person in the abstract, in the real world we end up choosing someone who is close to our own level.

Intimacy and Independence   Development in early adulthood often involves balancing intimacy and commitment on the one hand, and independence and freedom on the other. At the same time as individuals are trying to establish an identity, they face the challenges of increasing their independence from their parents, developing an intimate relationship with another individual, and continuing their friendship commitments. They also face the task of making decisions for themselves without always relying on what others say or do.

The extent to which young adults develop autonomy has important implications for them. For example, young adults who have not sufficiently moved away from parental ties may have difficulty in both interpersonal relationships and a career.

The balance between intimacy and commitment, on the one hand, and independence and freedom, on the other, is delicate. Some individuals are able to experience a healthy independence and freedom along with an intimate relationship. Keep in mind that intimacy and commitment, and independence and freedom, are not just concerns of early adulthood. They are important themes of development that are worked and reworked throughout the adult years.

Friendship   Increasingly researchers are finding that friendship plays an important role in development throughout the human life span (Rawlins, 2009). As we saw in Chapter 8, friendship can serve many functions—such as companionship, intimacy/affection, support, and a source of self-esteem. In some cases, friends can provide a better buffer from stress and be a better source of emotional support than family members. This might be because friends choose each other, whereas family ties are obligatory. Individuals often select a friend in terms of such criteria as loyalty, trustworthiness, and support. Thus, it is not surprising that in times of stress individuals turn to their friends for emotional support (Fehr, 2000).

As with children, adult friends usually come from the same age group. For many individuals, friendships formed in the twenties often continue through the twenties and into the thirties, although some new friends may be made in the thirties and some lost because of moving or other circumstances.

Gender Differences in Friendships   As in the childhood years, there are gender differences in adult friendship (Lauer & Lauer, 2007). Compared with men, women have more close friends and their friendships involve more self-disclosure and exchange of mutual support (Dow & Wood, 2006). Women are more likely to listen at length to what a friend has to say and be sympathetic, and women have been labeled as "talking companions" because talk is so central to their relationship (Gouldner & Strong, 1987). Women's friendships tend to be characterized not only by depth but also by breadth: Women share many aspects of their experiences, thoughts, and feelings (Wood, 2001).

When female friends get together, they like to talk, but male friends are more likely to engage in activities, especially outdoors. Thus, the adult male pattern of friendship often involves keeping one's distance while sharing useful information. Men are less likely than women to talk about their weaknesses with their friends, and men want practical solutions to their problems rather than sympathy (Tannen, 1990). Also, adult male friendships are more competitive than those of women (Wood, 2001). For example, male friends disagree with each other more.

Friendships Between Women and Men   What about female-male friendship? Cross-gender friendships are more common among adults than among elementary school children, but not as common as same-gender friendships in adulthood (Fehr, 2000). Cross-gender friendships can provide both opportunities and problems (Rawlins, 2009). The opportunities involve learning more about common feelings and interests and shared characteristics, as well as acquiring knowledge and understanding of beliefs and activities that historically have been typical of one gender.

Problems can arise in cross-gender friendships because of different expectations. For example, a woman might expect sympathy from a male friend but might receive a proposed solution rather than a shoulder to cry on (Tannen, 1990). Another problem that can plague an adult cross-gender friendship is unclear sexual boundaries, which can produce tension and confusion (Swain, 1992).

How is adult friendship different among female friends, male friends, and cross-gender friends?

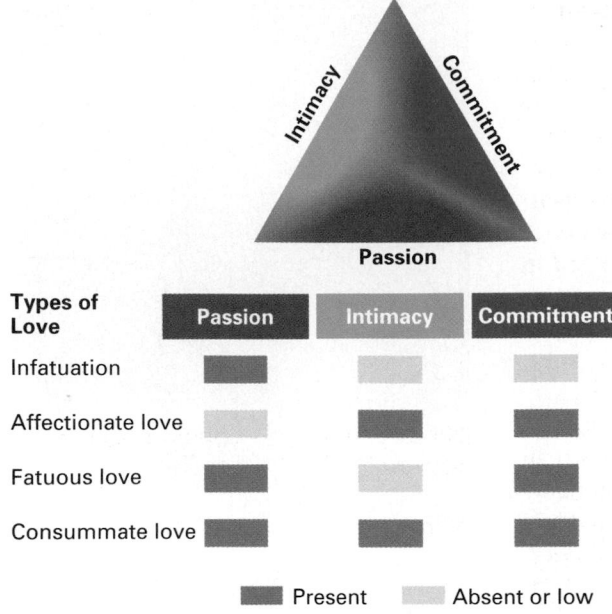

FIGURE 14.2 Sternberg's Triangle of Love. Sternberg identified three types of love: passion, intimacy, and commitment. Various combinations of these result in infatuation, affectionate love, fatuous love, and consummate love.

Romantic Love   Some friendships evolve into **romantic love**, which is also called passionate love, or eros. Romantic love has strong components of sexuality and infatuation, and it often predominates in the early part of a love relationship (Regan, 2008).

A complex intermingling of different emotions goes into romantic love—including such emotions as passion fear, anger, sexual desire, joy, and jealousy (Regan, 2008). Well-known love researcher Ellen Berscheid (1988) says that sexual desire is the most important ingredient of romantic love. Obviously, some of these emotions are a source of anguish (Daley & Hammen, 2002), which can lead to other issues such as depression. One study found that a relationship between romantic lovers was more likely than a relationship between friends to be a cause of depression (Berscheid & Fei, 1977).

Affectionate Love   Love is more than just passion. **Affectionate love**, also called *companionate love,* is the type of love that occurs when someone desires to have the other person near and has a deep, caring affection for the person.

The early stages of love have more romantic love ingredients—but as love matures, passion tends to give way to affection (Berscheid & Reis, 1998; Harvey & Weber, 2002). Phillip Shaver (1986) proposed a developmental model of love in which the initial phase of romantic love is fueled by a mixture of sexual attraction and gratification, a reduced sense of loneliness, uncertainty about the security of developing another attachment, and excitement from exploring the novelty of another human being. With time, he says, sexual attraction wanes, attachment anxieties either lessen or produce conflict and withdrawal, novelty is replaced with familiarity, and lovers either find themselves securely attached in a deeply caring relationship or distressed—feeling bored, disappointed, lonely, or hostile, for example. In the latter case, one or both partners may eventually end the relationship and then move on to another relationship.

Consummate Love   So far we have discussed two forms of love: romantic (or passionate) and affectionate (or companionate). According to Robert J. Sternberg (1988), these are not the only forms of love. Sternberg proposed a triarchic theory of love in which love can be thought of as a triangle with three main dimensions—passion, intimacy, and commitment. Passion, as described earlier in the romantic love section, is physical and sexual attraction to another. Intimacy relates to the emotional feelings of warmth, closeness, and sharing in a relationship. Commitment is the cognitive appraisal of the relationship and the intent to maintain the relationship even in the face of problems.

In Sternberg's theory, the strongest, fullest form of love is *consummate love,* which involves all three dimensions (see Figure 14.2). If passion is the only ingredient in a relationship (with intimacy and commitment low or absent), we are merely *infatuated.* An affair or a fling in which there is little intimacy and even less commitment is an example. A relationship marked by intimacy and commitment but low or lacking in passion is called *affectionate love,* a pattern often found among couples who have been married for many years. If passion and commitment are present but intimacy is not, Sternberg calls the relationship *fatuous love,* as when one person worships another from a distance. But if couples share all three dimensions—passion, intimacy, and commitment—they experience consummate love.

Falling Out of Love

The collapse of a close relationship may feel tragic. In the long run, however, as was the case for Gwenna, our happiness and personal development may benefit from getting over being in love and ending a close relationship.

romantic love Also called passionate love, or eros, romantic love has strong sexual and infatuation components and often predominates in the early period of a love relationship.

affectionate love In this type of love, also called companionate love, an individual desires to have the other person near and has a deep, caring affection for the other person.

In particular, ending a close relationship may be wise if you are obsessed with a person who repeatedly betrays your trust; if you are involved with someone who is draining you emotionally or financially or both; or if you are desperately in love with someone who does not return your feelings.

Being in love when love is not returned can lead to depression, obsessive thoughts, sexual dysfunction, inability to work effectively, difficulty in making new friends, and self-condemnation. When involved in unrequited love, thinking clearly in such relationships is often difficult, because our thoughts are so colored by arousing emotions.

Some people get taken advantage of in relationships (Metts & Cupach, 2007; Tafoya & Spitzberg, 2007). For example, without either person realizing it, a relationship can evolve in a way that creates dominant and submissive roles. Detecting this pattern is an important step toward learning either to reconstruct the relationship or to end it if the problems cannot be worked out. To read further about breakups of romantic relationships, see the *Research in Life-Span Development* interlude.

What are some negative aspects of being in love when love is not returned?

Research in Life-Span Development
Personal Growth Following a Romantic Relationship Breakup

Studies of romantic breakups have mainly focused on their negative aspects (Kato, 2005; Kurdek, 1997). Few studies have examined the possibility that a romantic breakup might lead to positive changes.

One study assessed the personal growth that can follow the breakup of a romantic relationship (Tashiro & Frazier, 2003). The participants were 92 undergraduate students who had experienced a relationship breakup in the past nine months. They were asked to describe "what positive changes, if any, have happened as a result of your breakup that might serve to improve your future romantic relationships" (p. 118).

Self-reported positive growth was common following a romantic breakup. Changes were categorized in terms of person, relational, and environmental changes. The most commonly reported types of growth were person changes, which included feeling stronger and more self-confident, more independent, and better off emotionally. Relational positive changes included gaining relational wisdom, and environmental positive changes included having better friendships because of the breakup. Figure 14.3 provides examples of these positive changes. Women reported more positive growth than did men.

Change category	Exemplars of frequently mentioned responses
Person positives	1. "I am more self-confident." 2. "Through breaking up I found I could handle more on my own." 3. "I didn't always have to be the strong one, it's okay to cry or be upset without having to take care of him."
Relational positives	1. "Better communication." 2. "I learned many relationship skills that I can apply in the future (for example, the importance of saying you're sorry)." 3. "I know not to jump into a relationship too quickly."
Environmental positives	1. "I rely on my friends more. I forgot how important friends are when I was with him." 2. "Concentrate on school more: I can put so much more time and effort toward school." 3. "I believe friends' and family's opinions count—will seek them out in future relationships."

FIGURE 14.3 Examples of Positive Changes in the Aftermath of a Romantic Breakup

Review and Reflect: Learning Goal 2

2 **Identify Some Key Aspects of Attraction, Love, and Close Relationships**

REVIEW

- What attracts someone to another person?
- What are some different types of love?
- What characterizes falling out of love?

REFLECT

- If you were to give someone advice about love, what would it be?

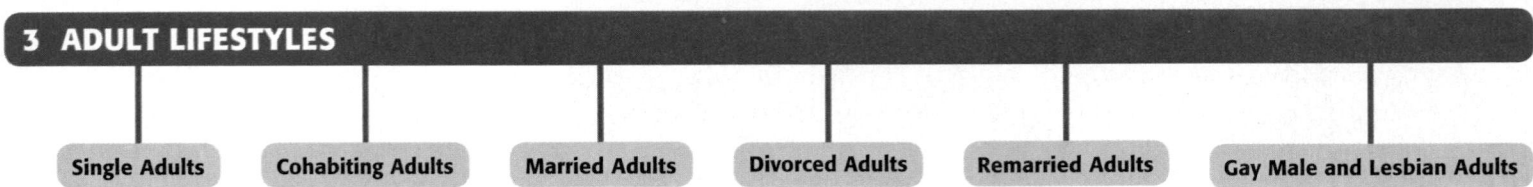

3 ADULT LIFESTYLES

Single Adults **Cohabiting Adults** **Married Adults** **Divorced Adults** **Remarried Adults** **Gay Male and Lesbian Adults**

Should I get married? If I wait any longer, will it be too late? Will I get left out? Should I stay single or is it too lonely a life? Do I want to have children? How will it affect my marriage? These are questions that many young adults pose to themselves as they consider their lifestyle options.

Adults today choose many lifestyles and form many types of families (Benokraitis, 2008). One of the most striking social changes in recent decades is the decreased stigma attached to people who do not maintain what were long considered conventional families. They may choose to live alone, cohabit, marry, divorce, remarry, or live with someone of the same sex. Let's explore each of these lifestyles and how they affect adults.

Single Adults

Over a 30-year period, a dramatic rise in the percentage of single adults has occurred. From 2000 to 2006, there was a significant increase in single adults in the United States from 20 to 29 years of age (U.S. Census Bureau, 2006). In 2000, 64 percent of men in this age range said they were single, but by 2006 the percentage had increased to 73 percent, while the comparable percentages for women were 53 percent in 2000 and 62 percent in 2006.

Even when singles enjoy their lifestyles and are highly competent individuals, they often are stereotyped (Schwartz & Scott, 2007). Stereotypes associated with being single range from the "swinging single" to the "desperately lonely, suicidal" single. Of course, most single adults are somewhere between these extremes. Common problems of single adults may include forming intimate relationships with other adults, confronting loneliness, and finding a niche in a society that is marriage-oriented. Advantages of being single include having time to make decisions about one's life course, time to develop personal resources to meet goals, freedom to make autonomous decisions and pursue one's own schedule and interests, opportunities to explore new places and try out new things, and privacy.

Once adults reach the age of 30, there can be increasing pressure to settle down and get married. This is when many single adults make a conscious decision to marry or to remain single. A recent national survey revealed that a higher percentage of singles (58 percent) reported they experienced extreme stress in the past month than married (52 percent) and divorced individuals (48 percent) (American Psychological Association, 2007).

Cohabiting Adults

Cohabitation refers to living together in a sexual relationship without being married. Cohabitation has undergone considerable changes in recent years (Casper & Bianchi, 2007; Cherlin, 2007; Popenoe, 2008) (see Figure 14.4). The percentage of U.S. couples who cohabit before marriage has increased from approximately 11 percent in 1970 to almost 60 percent at the beginning of the twenty-first century (Bumpass & Lu, 2000). Cohabiting rates are even higher in some countries—in Sweden, cohabitation before marriage is virtually universal.

A number of couples view their cohabitation not as a precursor to marriage but as an ongoing lifestyle. These couples do not want the official aspects of marriage. In the United States, cohabiting arrangements tend to be short-lived, with one-third lasting less than a year (Hyde & DeLamater, 2008). Less than 1 out of 10 lasts five years. Of course, it is easier to dissolve a cohabitation relationship than to divorce.

Do cohabiting relationships differ from marriage in ways other than the legal aspects? Relationships between cohabiting men and women tend to be more equal than those between husbands and wives (Wineberg, 1994).

Although cohabitation offers some advantages, it also can produce some problems (Meier & Allen, 2008; Trask & Koivur, 2007). Disapproval by parents and other family members can place emotional strain on the cohabiting couple. Some cohabiting couples have difficulty owning property jointly. Legal rights on the dissolution of the relationship are less certain than in a divorce.

If a couple lives together before they marry, does cohabiting help or harm their chances of later having a stable and happy marriage? Some researchers have found no differences in marital quality between individuals who earlier cohabited and those who did not (Watson & DeMeo, 1987). Other researchers have found lower rates of marital satisfaction and higher rates of divorce in couples who lived together before getting married (Whitehead & Popenoe, 2003). A longitudinal study found that the timing of cohabitation is a key factor in marital outcomes (Kline & others, 2004). Couples who cohabitated before they became engaged were at greater risk for poor marital outcomes than those who cohabited only after becoming engaged. Further, a recent study revealed that postdivorce cohabitation of any type (with the future spouse or with someone else) was linked with a lower level of remarital happiness (Xu, Hudspeth, & Bartkowski, 2006).

In sum, researchers have found either that cohabitation leads to no differences or that cohabitation is not good for a marriage. What might explain the finding that cohabiting is linked with divorce more than not cohabiting? The most frequently given explanation is that the less traditional lifestyle of cohabitation may attract less conventional individuals who are not great believers in marriage in the first place (Whitehead & Popenoe, 2003). An alternative explanation is that the experience of cohabiting changes people's attitudes and habits in ways that increase their likelihood of divorce (Solot & Miller, 2002). And one study revealed that those who cohabit prior to marriage have worse problem-solving skills in marriage than their counterparts who did not cohabit (Cohan & Kleinbaum, 2002).

Married Adults

Until about 1930, stable marriage was widely accepted as the endpoint of adult development. In the last 60 years, however, personal fulfillment both inside and outside marriage has emerged as a goal that competes with marital stability (Skolnick, 2007). The changing norm of male-female equality in marriage has produced marital relationships that are more fragile and intense than they were earlier in the twentieth century.

Marital Trends In recent years, marriage rates in the United States have

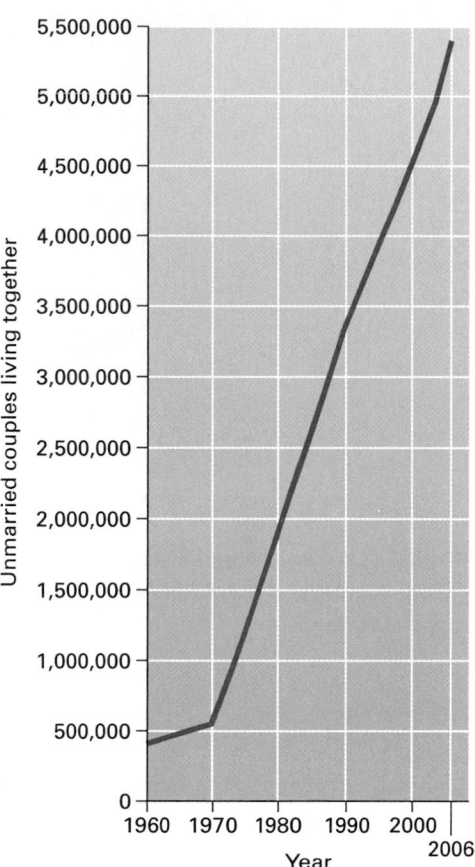

FIGURE 14.4 The Increase in Cohabitation in the United States. Since 1970, there has been a dramatic increase in the number of unmarried adults living together in the United States.

What are some potential advantages and disadvantages of cohabitation?

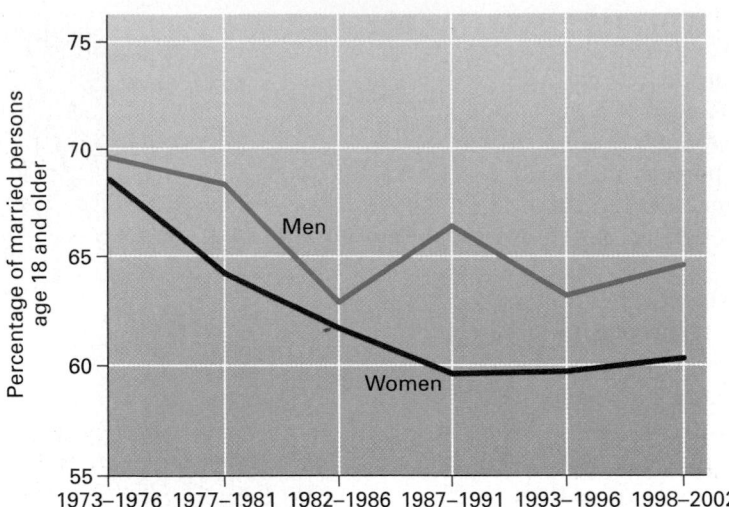

FIGURE 14.5 Percentage of Married Persons Age 18 and Older Above with "Very Happy" Marriages

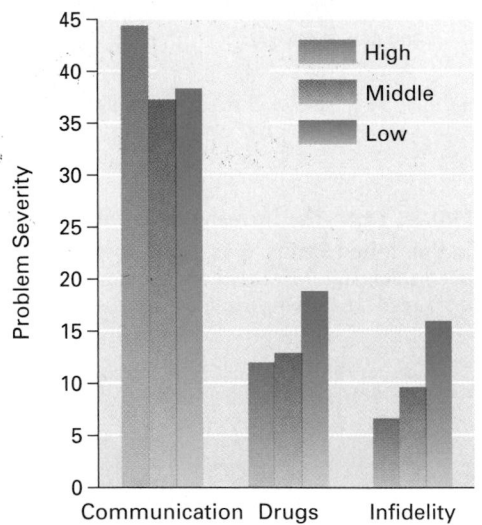

FIGURE 14.6 Severity of Specific Relationship Problems in Low-, Middle-, and High-Income Households. (above) *Why do you think communication was rated the most severe relationship problems in high-income households?*

declined. More adults are remaining single longer today. In 2005, the U.S. average age for a first marriage climbed to just over 27 years for men and 26 years for women, higher than at any point in history (U.S. Census Bureau, 2006). In addition, the increase in cohabitation and a slight decline in the percentage of divorced individuals who remarry contributed to the decline in marriage rates in the United States (Popenoe, 2007).

Despite the decline in marriage rates, approximately 85 percent of Americans are expected to marry at some point in their lives (Popenoe, 2007). If women and men are going to marry, virtually all enter into a first-time marriage by the time they are 45 years of age (Popenoe & Whitehead, 2005).

Is there a best age to get married? Marriages in adolescence are more likely to end in divorce than marriages in adulthood (Furstenberg, 2007). One survey revealed that getting married in the United States between 23 and 27 years of age resulted in a lower likelihood of becoming divorced (Glenn, 2005). However, overall, researchers have not been able to pin down a specific age or age span of several years in adulthood for getting married that is most likely to result in a successful marriage (Furstenberg, 2007).

How happy are people who do marry? The average duration of a marriage in the United States is currently just over nine years As indicated in Figure 14.5, the percentage of married individuals in the United States who said their marriages were "very happy" declined from the 1970s through the early 1990s, but recently has begun to increase (Popenoe & Whitehead, 2005). Notice in Figure 14.5 that men consistently report being happier in their marriage than women.

Social Contexts Contexts within a culture and across cultures are powerful influences on marriage (Karney & Bradbury, 2005). A U.S. study found that although communication was rated as a relatively severe problem regardless of household income, it was rated most severe in high-income households (Karney, Garvan, & Thomas, 2003) (see Figure 14.6). By contrast, drugs and infidelity were rated as more severe problems in low-income households.

Many aspects of marriage vary across cultures. For example, as part of China's efforts to control population growth, a 1981 law sets the minimum age for marriage at 22 years for males, 20 for females. More information about marriage in different cultures appears in the *Diversity in Life-Span Development* interlude.

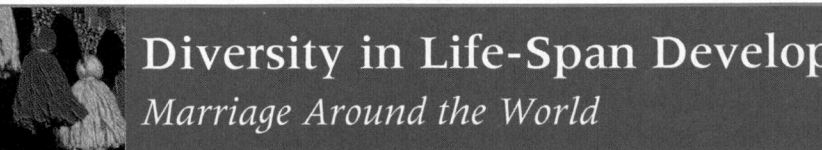

Diversity in Life-Span Development
Marriage Around the World

The traits that people look for in a marriage partner vary around the world. In one large-scale study of 9,474 adults from 37 cultures on six continents and five islands, people varied most regarding how much they valued chastity—desiring a marital partner with no previous experience in sexual intercourse (Buss & others, 1990). Chastity was the most important characteristic in selecting a marital partner in China, India, Indonesia, Iran, Taiwan, and the Palestinian Arab culture. Adults from Ireland and Japan placed moderate importance on chastity. In contrast, adults in Sweden, Finland, Norway, the Netherlands, and Germany generally said that chastity was not important in selecting a marital partner.

Domesticity is also valued in some cultures and not in others. In this study, adults from the Zulu culture in South Africa, Estonia, and Colombia placed a high value on housekeeping skills in their marital preference. By contrast, adults in the United States, Canada, and all Western European countries except Spain said that housekeeping skill was not an important trait in their partner.

(a)

(b)

(c)

Religion plays an important role in marriage in many cultures. For example, Islam stresses the honor of the male and the purity of the female. It also emphasizes the woman's role in childbearing, child rearing, educating children, and instilling the Islamic faith in their children. In India, more than 70 percent of marriages continue to be arranged. However, as more women have entered the workforce in India and moved from rural areas to cities, these Indian women increasingly resist an arranged marriage.

International comparisons of marriage also reveal that individuals in Scandinavian countries marry later than Americans, whereas their counterparts in Eastern Europe marry earlier (Bianchi & Spani, 1986). In Denmark, for example, almost 80 percent of the women and 90 percent of the men aged 20 to 24 have never been married. In Hungary, less than 40 percent of the women and 70 percent of the men the same age have never been married. In Scandinavian countries, cohabitation is popular among young adults; however, most Scandinavians eventually marry (Popenoe, 2007). In Sweden, on average women delay marriage until they are 31, men until they are 33. Some countries, such as Hungary, encourage early marriage and childbearing to offset declines in the population. Like Scandinavian countries, Japan has a high proportion of unmarried young people. However, rather than cohabiting as the Scandinavians do, unmarried Japanese young adults live at home longer with their parents before marrying.

(*a*) In Scandinavian countries, cohabitation is popular; only a small percentage of 20- to 24-year-olds are married. (*b*) Islam stresses male honor and female purity. (*c*) Japanese young adults live at home longer with their parents before marrying than young adults in most countries.

Premarital Education An increasing number of emerging and young adults are obtaining premarital education that provides information about relationships (Busby & others, 2007; Duncan, Holman, & Yang, 2007). Might premarital education improve the quality of a marriage and possibly reduce the chances that the marriage will end in a divorce? Researchers have found that it can (Carroll & Doherty, 2003). For example, a recent survey of more than 3,000 adults revealed that premarital education was linked to a higher level of marital satisfaction and commitment to a spouse, a lower level of destructive marital conflict, and a 31 percent lower likelihood of divorce (Stanley & others, 2006). The premarital education programs in the study ranged from several hours to 20 hours with a median of 8 hours. It is recommended that premarital education begin approximately six months to a year before the wedding.

The Benefits of a Good Marriage Are there any benefits to having a good marriage? There are. Individuals who are happily married live longer, healthier lives than either divorced individuals or those who are unhappily married (Karasu, 2007; Wilson & Smallwood, 2008). A recent study assessed 94,000 Japanese, 40 to 79 years of age, on two occasions: at the beginning of the study and approximately 10-years later (Ikeda & others, 2007). Compared with never-married individuals, those who were married had a lower risk of dying in the 10-year period. In another study, women in happy marriages had lower levels of biological and cardiovascular risk factors—such as blood pressure, cholesterol levels, and body mass index—and lower levels of depression, anxiety, and anger than women in unhappy marriages (Gallo & others, 2003). And a recent study indicated that the longer women were married, the less likely they were to develop a chronic health condition and the longer that men were married, the lower their risk was of developing a disease (Dupre & Meadows, 2007).

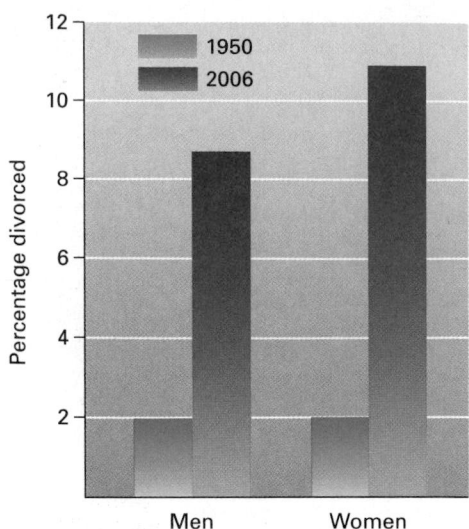

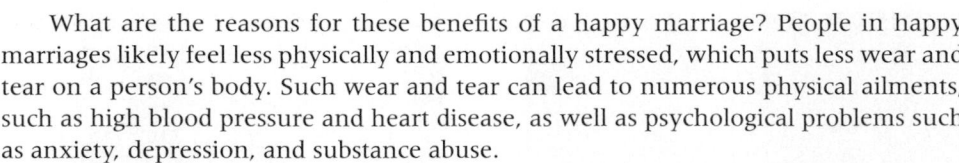

FIGURE 14.7 Percentage of Divorced U.S. Men and Women: 1950 and 2006. *Why do you think more women are divorced than men?*

What are the reasons for these benefits of a happy marriage? People in happy marriages likely feel less physically and emotionally stressed, which puts less wear and tear on a person's body. Such wear and tear can lead to numerous physical ailments, such as high blood pressure and heart disease, as well as psychological problems such as anxiety, depression, and substance abuse.

There is increasing evidence that stressful events of many types reduce the immune system's capabilities, rendering the person vulnerable to disease and infection. One study compared unhappily and happily married individuals and found that unhappily married individuals had immune systems that were not functioning as effectively as those of happily married individuals (Kiecolt-Glaser & Glaser, 1988). An unhappy marriage increases an individual's risk of getting sick by approximately one-third and can even shorten a person's life by an average of four years (Gove, Style, & Hughes, 1990).

Divorced Adults

Divorce has become epidemic in the United States (Ahrons, 2007; Coontz, 2007). The number of divorced adults rose from 2 percent of the adult population in 1950 to 3 percent in 1970 to 10 percent in 2002. Figure 14.7 shows the percentage of divorced men and women in the United States in 1950 and 2006 (U.S. Census Bureau, 2006). The divorce rate was increasing annually by 10 percent, but has been declining since the 1980s (Amato, 2006; Hernandez, 2007).

Although divorce has increased for all socioeconomic groups, those in some groups have a higher incidence of divorce. Youthful marriage, low educational level, low income, not having a religious affiliation, having parents who are divorced, and having a baby before marriage are factors that are associated with increases in divorce (Popenoe, 2007; Rodriques, Hall, & Fincham, 2006).

Earlier, we indicated that researchers have not been able to pin down a specific age that is the best time to marry so that the marriage is unlikely to end in a divorce. However, if a divorce is going to occur, it usually takes place early in a marriage; most occur in the fifth to tenth year of marriage (National Center for Health Statistics, 2000) (see Figure 14.8). This timing may reflect an effort by partners in troubled marriages to stay in the marriage and try to work things out. If after several years these efforts don't improve the relationship, they may then seek a divorce.

Both partners experience challenges after a marriage dissolves (Amato, 2006; Feeney & Monin, 2009). Both divorced women and divorced men complain of loneliness, diminished self-esteem, anxiety about the unknowns in their lives, and difficulty in forming satisfactory new intimate relationships (Hetherington, 2006). A recent study revealed that following marital dissolution, both men and women were more likely to experience an episode of depression than individuals who remained with a spouse over a two-year period (Rotermann, 2007).

Despite all of these stresses and challenges, many people do cope effectively with divorce. Later in this chapter, we consider the varied paths people take after a divorce and suggested strategies for coping.

Remarried Adults

On average, divorced adults remarry within four years after their divorce, with men remarrying sooner than women. Stepfamilies come in many sizes and forms (Anderson & Sabatelli, 2007). The custodial and noncustodial parents and stepparent all might have been married and divorced, in some cases more than once. These parents might have residential children from prior marriages and a large network of grandparents and other relatives. Researchers have found that remarried adults are more likely to have higher levels of depressive symptoms than adults in intact, never-divorced families (Barrett & Turner, 2005).

Why do remarried adults find it so difficult to stay remarried? For one thing, many remarry not for love but for financial reasons, for help

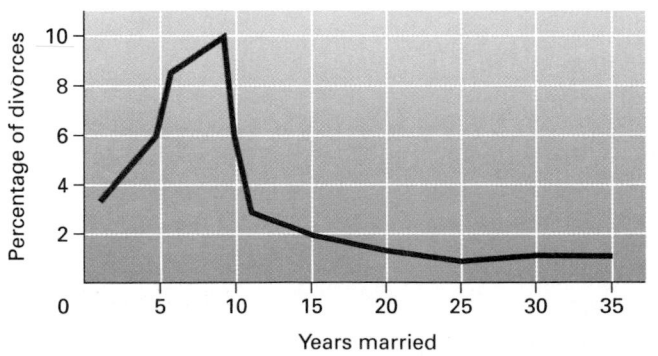

FIGURE 14.8 The Divorce Rate in Relation to Number of Years Married. Shown here is the percentage of divorces as a function of how long couples have been married. Notice that most divorces occur in the early years of marriage, peaking in the fifth to tenth years of marriage.

in rearing children, and to reduce loneliness. They also might carry into the stepfamily negative patterns that produced failure in an earlier marriage. Remarried couples also experience more stress in rearing children than parents in never-divorced families (Ganong, Coleman, & Hans, 2006).

Gay Male and Lesbian Adults

The legal and social context of marriage creates barriers to breaking up that do not usually exist for same-sex partners (Green & Mitchell, 2009; Weston, 2007). But in other ways, researchers have found that gay and lesbian relationships are similar—in their satisfactions, loves, joys, and conflicts—to heterosexual relationships (Mohr, 2009; Peplau & Fingerhut, 2007). For example, like heterosexual couples, gay and lesbian couples need to find the balance of romantic love, affection, autonomy, and equality that is acceptable to both partners (Kurdek, 2006). An increasing number of gay and lesbian couples are creating families that include children (see Figure 14.9).

There are a number of misconceptions about gay male and lesbian couples (Kurdek, 2007; Peplau & Fingerhut, 2007). Contrary to stereotypes, one partner is masculine and the other feminine in only a small percentage of gay male and lesbian couples. Only a small segment of the gay male population have a large number of sexual partners, and this is uncommon among lesbians. Furthermore, researchers have found that gay male and lesbian couples prefer long-term, committed relationships (Peplau & Fingerhut, 2007). About half of committed gay male couples do have an open relationship that allows the possibility of sex (but not affectionate love) outside of the relationship. Lesbian couples usually do not have this open relationship.

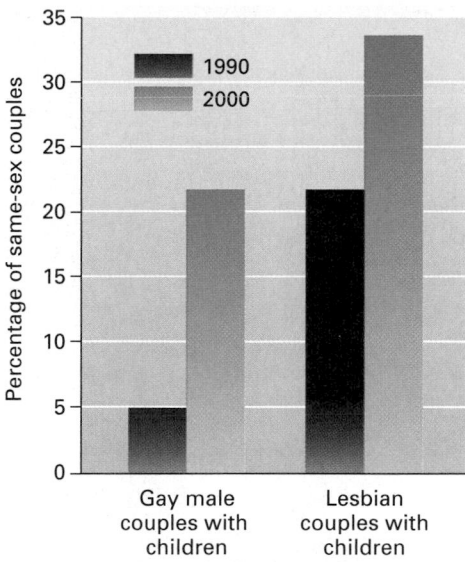

FIGURE 14.9 Percentage of Gay Male and Lesbian Couples with Children: 1990 and 2000. *Why do you think more lesbian couples have children than gay male couples?*

Review and Reflect: Learning Goal 3

3 **Characterize Adult Lifestyles**

REVIEW

- What are characteristics of the lives of single adults?
- What are key features of the lives of cohabiting adults?
- What are current marital trends?
- How does divorce affect adults?
- What are the lives of remarried parents like?
- How are gay male and lesbian couples like or unlike heterosexual couples?

REFLECT

- Which type of lifestyle are you living today? What do you think are the advantages and disadvantages of this lifestyle for you? If you could have a different lifestyle, which one would it be? Why?

4 MARRIAGE AND THE FAMILY

Making Marriage Work **Becoming a Parent** **Dealing with Divorce**

Whatever lifestyles young adults choose, they will bring certain challenges. Because many choose the lifestyle of marriage, we'll consider some of the challenges in marriage and how to make it work. We also examine some challenges in parenting and trends in childbearing. Given the statistics about divorce rates in previous section, we'll then consider how to deal with divorce.

John Gottman

*U*nlike most approaches to helping couples, mine is based on knowing what makes marriages succeed rather than fail.

—JOHN GOTTMAN
Contemporary Psychologist,
University of Washington

What makes marriages work? What are the benefits of having a good marriage?

Making Marriage Work

John Gottman (1994, 2006; Gottman & Gottman, 2009; Gottman, Gottman, & Declaire, 2006) has been studying married couples' lives since the early 1970s. He uses many methods to analyze what makes marriages work. Gottman interviews couples about the history of their marriage, their philosophy about marriage, and how they view their parents' marriages. He videotapes them talking to each other about how their day went and evaluates what they say about the good and bad times of their marriages. Gottman also uses physiological measures to measure their heart rate, blood flow, blood pressure, and immune functioning moment by moment. He also checks back in with the couples every year to see how their marriage is faring. Gottman's research represents the most extensive assessment of marital relationships available. Currently he and his colleagues are following 700 couples in seven studies.

Gottman argues that it is important to realize that love is not something magical and that through knowledge and effort couples can improve their relationship. In his research, Gottman has found that seven main principles determine whether a marriage will work:

- *Establishing love maps.* Individuals in successful marriages have personal insights and detailed maps of each other's life and world. They aren't psychological strangers. In good marriages, partners are willing to share their feelings with each other. They use these "love maps" to express not only their understanding of each other but also their fondness and admiration.

- *Nurturing fondness and admiration.* In successful marriages, partners sing each other's praises. More than 90 percent of the time, when couples put a positive spin on their marriage's history, the marriage is likely to have a positive future.

- *Turning toward each other instead of away.* In good marriages, spouses are adept at turning toward each other regularly. They see each other as friends. This friendship doesn't keep arguments from occurring, but it can prevent differences from overwhelming the relationship. In these good marriages, spouses respect each other and appreciate each other's point of view despite disagreements.

- *Letting your partner influence you.* Bad marriages often involve one spouse who is unwilling to share power with the other. Although power-mongering is more common in husbands, some wives also show this trait. A willingness to share power and to respect the other person's view is a prerequisite to compromising. A recent study revealed that equality in decision making was one of the main factors that predicted positive marriage quality (Amato & others, 2007).

- *Solving solvable conflicts.* Two types of problems occur in marriage: (1) perpetual and (2) solvable. Perpetual problems are the type that do not go away and may include differences about whether to have children and how often to have sex. Solvable problems can be worked out and may include such things as not helping each other reduce daily stresses and not being verbally affectionate. Unfortunately, more than two-thirds of marital problems fall into the perpetual category. Fortunately, marital therapists have found that couples often don't have to solve their perpetual problems for the marriage to work.

  Work, stress, in-laws, money, sex, housework, a new baby: These are among the typical areas of marital conflict, even in happy marriages. When there is conflict in these areas, it usually means that a husband and wife have different ideas about either the importance of the tasks involved or how they should be accomplished. If the conflict creates a perpetual problem, no amount of problem-solving expertise will fix it. The tension will decrease only when both partners feel comfortable living with the ongoing difference. However, when the issue is solvable, the challenge is to find the right strategy for dealing with it.

  In his research, Gottman has found that to resolve conflicts, couples should start out with a soft rather than a harsh approach, try to make and receive "repair attempts," regulate their emotions, compromise, and be tolerant of each other's faults. Conflict resolution is not about one person making changes, it is about negotiating and accommodating each other.

- *Overcoming gridlock.* One partner wants the other to attend church, the other is an atheist. One partner is a homebody, the other wants to go out and socialize a lot. Such problems often produce gridlock. Gottman believes the key to ending gridlock is not to solve the problem, but to move from gridlock to dialogue and be patient.

- *Creating shared meaning.* The more partners can speak candidly and respectfully with each other, the more likely it is that they will create shared meaning in their marriage. This also includes sharing goals with one's spouse and working together to achieve each other's goals.

In addition to Gottman's view, other experts on marriage argue that such factors as forgiveness and commitment are important aspects of a successful marriage (Fincham, Stanley, & Beach, 2007). These factors function as self-repair processes in healthy relationships. For example, spouses may have a heated argument that has the potential to harm their relationship (Amato, 2007). After calming down, they may forgive each other and repair the damage. Also, spouses who have a strong commitment to each other may in times of conflict sacrifice their personal self-interest for the benefit of the marriage. Commitment especially becomes important when a couple is not happily married and can help them get through hard times with the hope that the future will involve more positive changes in the relationship.

For remarried couples, strategies for coping with the stress of living in a stepfamily include these (Visher & Visher, 1989):

- *Have realistic expectations.* Allow time for loving relationships to develop, and look at the complexity of the stepfamily as a challenge to overcome.

- *Develop new positive relationships within the family.* Create new traditions and ways of dealing with difficult circumstances. Allocation of time is especially important because so many people are involved. The remarried couple needs to allot time alone for each other.

Becoming a Parent

For many young adults, parental roles are well planned, coordinated with other roles in life, and developed with the individual's economic situation in mind. For others, the discovery that they are about to become parents is a startling surprise. In either event, the prospective parents may have mixed emotions and romantic illusions about having a child.

Parenting Myths and Reality   The needs and expectations of parents have stimulated many myths about parenting (DeGenova & Rice, 2008). These parenting myths include:

- The birth of a child will save a failing marriage.

- As a possession or extension of the parent, the child will think, feel, and behave like the parents did in their childhood.

- Having a child gives the parents a "second chance" to achieve what they should have achieved.

- Parenting is an instinct and requires no training.

Parenting requires a number of interpersonal skills and imposes emotional demands, yet there is little in the way of formal education for this task. Most parents learn parenting practices from their own parents—some they accept, some they discard. Unfortunately, when methods of parents are passed on from one generation to the next, both desirable and undesirable practices are perpetuated. Adding to reality of the task of parenting, husbands and wives may bring different parenting practices to the marriage.

What are some parenting myths?

We never know the love of our parents until we have become parents.

—HENRY WARD BEECHER
American Clergyman, 19th Century

The parents, then, may struggle with each other about which is a better practice to interact with a child.

Parent educators seek to help individuals to become better parents. To read about the work of one parent educator, see the *Careers in Life-Span Development* profile.

Careers in Life-Span Development

Janis Keyser, Parent Educator

Janis Keyser is a parent educator and teaches in the Department of Early Childhood Education at Cabrillo College in California. In addition to teaching college classes and conducting parenting workshops, she also has coauthored a book with Laura Davis (1997). *Becoming the Parent You Want to Be: A Source-Book of Strategies for the First Five Years.*

Keyser also writes as an expert on the iVillage Web site (www. parentsplace.com). And she also co-authors a nationally syndicated parenting column, "Growing Up, Growing Together." She is the mother of three, stepmother of five, grandmother of twelve, and great-grandmother of six.

Janis Keyser (*right*), conducting a parenting workshop.

Trends in Childbearing   Like marriage, the age at which individuals have children has been increasing. In 2005, the average age at which women gave birth for the first time was a record high 25.2 years of age, up from 21 years of age in 2001 (Joint Economics Committee, 2007).

As birth control has become common practice, many individuals consciously choose when they will have children and how many children they will rear. The number of one-child families is increasing, for example, and U.S. women overall are having fewer children. These childbearing trends are creating several trends:

- By giving birth to fewer children and reducing the demands of child care, women free up a significant portion of their life spans for other endeavors.

- Men are apt to invest a greater amount of time in fathering.

- Parental care is often supplemented by institutional care (child care, for example).

As a result of their increased time in the workplace, are mothers spending less time in caring for their children? A recent study reported on time allocation by parents from 1965 to 2000 (Bianchi, Robinson, & Milkie, 2006). The results indicated that fathers are increasing their participation in household chores, with mothers reducing their housework but not their child care. Parents now keep time with children high through effective time management and multitasking, spending more of their leisure time with children than in the past and curtailing time with spouse, extended family, and friends.

As more women show an increased interest in developing a career, they are not only marrying later, but also having fewer children and having them later in life. What are some of the advantages of having children early or late? Some of the advantages of having children early (in the twenties) are that the parents are likely to have more physical energy (for example, they can cope better with such matters as getting up in the middle of the night with infants and waiting up until adolescents come home at night); the mother is likely to have fewer medical problems with pregnancy and childbirth; and the parents may be less likely to build up expectations for their children, as do many couples who have waited many years to have children.

There are also advantages to having children later (in the thirties): The parents will have had more time to consider their goals in life, such as what they want from their family and career roles; the parents will be more mature and will be able to benefit from their life experiences to engage in more competent parenting; and the parents will be better established in their careers and have more income for child-rearing expenses.

In earlier times, motherhood and making a home for her family was considered a full-time occupation and the natural occupation for women. Nurturing children and having a career were thought to be incompatible. We have come to recognize that the balance between caring and achieving, nurturing and working—although difficult to manage—can be accomplished. But as more and more U.S. women moved into the workplace and delayed childbirth in recent years, popular magazines and books began warning women that they would regret this delay and risked ending up childless (Hewlett, 2002). They argue that many high-achieving women will ultimately be happier if they have a child in their twenties or thirties. Critics argue that the optimal age for motherhood depends on the individual and that many women become mothers after they are 35 years of age.

What are some pathways adults follow after they divorce?

Dealing with Divorce

If a marriage doesn't work, what happens after divorce? Psychologically, one of the most common characteristics of divorced adults is difficulty in trusting someone else in a romantic relationship. Following a divorce, though, people's lives can take diverse turns (Tashiro, Frazier, & Berman, 2006). In E. Mavis Hetherington's research, men and women took six common pathways in exiting divorce (Hetherington & Kelly, 2002, pp. 98–108):

- *The enhancers.* Accounting for 20 percent of the divorced group, most were females who "grew more competent, well-adjusted, and self-fulfilled" following their divorce (p. 98). They were competent in multiple areas of life, showed a remarkable ability to bounce back from stressful circumstances, and create something meaningful out of problems.

- *The good-enoughs.* The largest group of divorced individuals, they were described as average people coping with divorce. They showed some strengths and some weaknesses, some successes and some failures. When they experienced a problem, they tried to solve it. Many of them attended night classes, found new friends, developed active social lives, and were motivated to get higher-paying jobs. However, they were not as good at planning and were less persistent than the enhancers. Good-enough women usually married men who educationally and economically were similar to their first husbands, often going into a new marriage that was not much of an improvement over the first one.

- *The seekers.* These individuals were motivated to find new mates as soon as possible. "At one year post-divorce, 40 percent of the men and 38 percent of women had been classified as seekers. But as people found new partners or remarried, or became more secure or satisfied in their single life, this category shrank and came to be predominated by men" (p. 102).

- *The libertines.* People in this category often spent more time in singles bars and had more casual sex than their counterparts in the other divorce categories. However, by the end of the first year postdivorce, they often grew disillusioned with their sensation-seeking lifestyle and wanted a stable relationship.

- *The competent loners.* These individuals, which made up only about 10 percent of the divorced group, were "well-adjusted, self-sufficient, and socially skilled." They had a successful career, an active social life, and a wide range of interests. However, "unlike enhancers, competent loners had little interest in sharing their lives with anyone else" (p. 105).

- *The defeated.* Some of these individuals had problems before their divorce, and these problems increased after the breakup when "the added stress of a failed marriage was more than they could handle. Others had difficulty coping because divorce cost them a spouse who had supported them, or in the case of a drinking problem, restricted them" (p. 106).

To read about some guidelines for coping and adapting in the aftermath of divorce, see the *Applications in Life-Span Development* interlude.

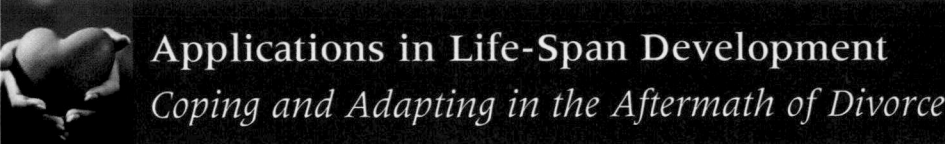

Applications in Life-Span Development
Coping and Adapting in the Aftermath of Divorce

Hetherington recommends these strategies for divorced adults (Hetherington & Kelly, 2002):

- Think of divorce as a chance to grow personally and to develop more positive relationships.

- Make decisions carefully. The consequences of your decision making regarding work, lovers, and children may last a lifetime.

- Focus more on the future than the past. Think about what is most important for you going forward in your life, set some challenging goals, and plan how to reach them.

- Use your strengths and resources to cope with difficulties.

- Don't expect to be successful and happy in everything you do. "The road to a more satisfying life is bumpy and will have many detours" (p. 109).

- Remember that "you are never trapped by one pathway. Most of those who were categorized as defeated immediately after divorce gradually moved on to a better life, but moving onward usually requires some effort" (p. 109).

Review and Reflect: Learning Goal 4

 4   **Discuss Making Marriages Work, Parenting, and Divorce**

REVIEW

- What makes a marriage work?
- What are some current trends in childbearing?
- What paths do people take after a divorce?

REFLECT

- What do you predict will be some major changes in families by the end of the twenty-first century?

5 GENDER, RELATIONSHIPS, AND SELF-DEVELOPMENT

| Gender and Communication | Women's Development | Men's Development |

Stereotypes about differences in men's and women's attitudes toward communication and about differences in how they communicate with each other have spawned countless cartoons and jokes. Are the supposed differences real? In this section, we will explore the answer to this question and also consider some aspects of both the woman's role and the man's role in relationships.

Gender and Communication

When Deborah Tannen (1990) analyzed the talk of women and men, she found that many wives complain about their husbands that "He doesn't listen to me anymore" and "He doesn't talk to me anymore." Lack of communication, though high on women's lists of reasons for divorce, is mentioned much less often by men.

Communication problems between men and women may come in part from differences in their preferred ways of communicating (Gamble & Gamble, 2008). Tannen distinguishes two ways of communications: rapport talk and report talk. **Rapport talk** is the language of conversation; it is a way of establishing connections and negotiating relationships. **Report talk** is talk that is designed to give information, which includes public speaking. According to Tannen, women enjoy rapport talk more than report talk, and men's lack of interest in rapport talk bothers many women. In contrast, men prefer to engage in report talk. Men hold center stage through such verbal performances as telling stories and jokes. They learn to use talk as a way of getting and keeping attention.

How extensive are the gender differences in communication? Research has yielded somewhat mixed results. Several studies do reveal some gender differences (Anderson, 2006). One study of a sampling of students' e-mails found that people could guess the writer's gender two-thirds of the time (Thompson & Murachver, 2001). Another study revealed that women make 63 percent of phone calls and when talking to another woman stay on the phone longer (7.2 minutes) than men do when talking with other men (4.6 minutes) (Smoreda & Licoppe, 2000). However, meta-analyses suggest that overall gender differences in communication are small for both children and adults (Hyde, 2005, 2007; Leaper & Smith, 2004). Further, a recent analysis revealed no gender differences in the average number of total words spoken by seven different samples of college men and women over 17 waking hours (Mehl & others, 2007).

A thorough recent study documented some gender differences in specific aspects of communication (Newman & others, 2008). In this study, women used words more for discussing people and what they were doing, as well as for communicating internal processes to others, including expression of doubts. By contrast, men used words more for external events, objects, and processes, including occupation, money, sports, and swearing. Contrary to popular stereotypes, men and women could not be distinguished in their reference to sexuality and anger. Thus, while gender similarity likely characterizes communication in general, as just indicated, there do seem to be some gender differences in certain aspects of communication.

*U*nderstanding the other's ways of talking is a giant leap across the communication gap between women and men, and a giant step toward opening lines of communication.

—DEBORAH TANNEN
Contemporary Sociologist, Georgetown University

"You have no idea how nice it is to have someone to talk to."
Copyright © 1994 by Don Orehek.

Women's Development

Tannen's analysis of women's preference for rapport talk suggests that women place a high value on relationships and focus on nurturing their connections with others. This view echoes some ideas of Jean Baker Miller (1986), who has been an important voice in stimulating the examination of psychological issues from a female perspective. Miller argues that when researchers examine what women have been doing in life, a large part of it is active participation in the development of others. In Miller's view, women often try to interact with others in ways that will foster the other person's development along many dimensions—emotionally, intellectually, and socially.

Most experts believe it is important for women to not only maintain their competency in relationships but to be self-motivated, too (Hyde, 2007; Matlin, 2008). As Harriet Lerner (1989) concludes in her book *The Dance of Intimacy,* it is important for women to bring to their relationships nothing less than a strong, assertive, independent, and authentic self. She emphasizes that competent relationships are those in which the separate "I-ness" of both persons can be appreciated and enhanced while still staying emotionally connected to each other.

In sum, Miller, Tannen, and other gender experts such as Carol Gilligan, whose ideas you read about in Chapter 10, believe that women are more relationship-oriented than men—and that this relationship orientation should be prized as a skill

rapport talk The language of conversation; it is a way of establishing connections and negotiating relationships.

report talk Talk that is designed to give information and includes public speaking.

How might men be able to reconstruct their masculinity in positive ways?

in our culture more than it currently is. Critics of this view of gender differences in relationships contend that it is too stereotypical (Dindia, 2006; Hyde, 2007). They argue that there is greater individual variation in the relationship styles of men and women than this view acknowledges.

Men's Development

The male of the species—what is he really like? What are his concerns? According to Joseph Pleck's (1995) *role-strain view,* male roles are contradictory and inconsistent. Men not only experience stress when they violate men's roles, they also are harmed when they do act in accord with men's roles. Here are some of the areas where men's roles can cause considerable strain (Levant, 2002):

• *Health.* Men live 5 years less than women do. They have higher rates of stress-related disorders, alcoholism, car accidents, and suicide. Men are more likely than women to be the victims of homicide. In sum, the male role is hazardous to men's health.

• *Male-female relationships.* Too often, the male role involves expectations that men should be dominant, powerful, and aggressive and should control women. "Real men," according to many traditional definitions of masculinity, look at women in terms of their bodies, not their minds and feelings, have little interest in rapport talk and relationships, and do not consider women equal to men in work or many other aspects of life. Thus the traditional view of the male role encourages men to disparage women, be violent toward women, and refuse to have equal relationships with women.

• *Male-male relationships.* Too many men have had too little interaction with their fathers, especially fathers who are positive role models. Nurturing and being sensitive to others have been considered aspects of the female role, not the male role. And the male role emphasizes competition rather than cooperation. All of these aspects of the male role have left men with inadequate positive, emotional connections with other males.

To reconstruct their masculinity in more positive ways, Ron Levant (2002) suggests that every man should (1) reexamine his beliefs about manhood, (2) separate out the valuable aspects of the male role, and (3) get rid of those parts of the masculine role that are destructive. All of this involves becoming more "emotionally intelligent"—that is, becoming more emotionally self-aware, managing emotions more effectively, reading emotions better (one's own emotions and others'), and being motivated to improve close relationships.

Review and Reflect: Learning Goal 5

 5 Summarize the Role of Gender in Relationships

REVIEW

• What are some differences in how men and women communicate?
• What are some important aspects of the woman's role in relationships?
• What are some important aspects of the man's role in relationships?

REFLECT

• If you are female, what would you change about the way men function in relationships? If you are male, what would you change about the way women function in relationships?

Socioemotional Development in Early Adulthood

1 STABILITY AND CHANGE FROM CHILDHOOD TO ADULTHOOD: DESCRIBE STABILITY AND CHANGE IN TEMPERAMENT, AND SUMMARIZE ADULT ATTACHMENT STYLES

Temperament

- Links between childhood temperament and adult personality can vary, depending on contexts in an individual's experience. A high activity level in early childhood is linked with being an outgoing young adult. Young adults show fewer mood swings, are more responsible, and engage in less risk taking than adolescents. In some cases, certain dimensions of temperament in childhood are linked with adjustment problems in early adulthood.

Attachment

- Three adult attachment styles are secure attachment, avoidant attachment, and anxious attachment. Attachment styles in early adulthood are linked with a number of relationship patterns and developmental outcomes. For example, securely attached adults often show more positive relationship patterns than insecurely attached adults. Also, adults with avoidant and anxious attachment styles tend to be more depressed and have more relationship problems than securely attached adults.

2 ATTRACTION, LOVE, AND CLOSE RELATIONSHIPS: IDENTIFY SOME KEY ASPECTS OF ATTRACTION, LOVE, AND CLOSE RELATIONSHIPS

Attraction

- Familiarity precedes a close relationship. We like to associate with people who are similar to us. The principles of consensual validation and matching can explain this. Similarity in personality attributes may be especially important in a relationship's success. The criteria for physical attractiveness vary across cultures and historical time.

The Faces of Love

- The different types of love include friendship, romantic love, affectionate love, and consummate love. Friendship plays an important role in adult development, especially in terms of emotional support. Romantic love, also called passionate love, includes passion, sexuality, and a mixture of emotions, not all of which are positive. Affectionate love, also called companionate love, usually becomes more important as relationships mature. Shaver proposed a developmental model of love and Sternberg a triarchic model of love (passion, intimacy, and commitment).

Falling Out of Love

- The collapse of a close relationship can be traumatic, but for some individuals it results in happiness and personal development. For most individuals, falling out of love is painful and emotionally intense.

3 ADULT LIFESTYLES: CHARACTERIZE ADULT LIFESTYLES

Single Adults

- Being single has become an increasingly prominent lifestyle. Autonomy is one of its advantages. Intimacy, loneliness, and finding a positive identity in a marriage-oriented society are challenges faced by single adults.

Cohabiting Adults

- Cohabitation is an increasingly popular lifestyle. Cohabitation does not lead to greater marital happiness but rather to no differences or to differences that suggest that cohabitation is not good for a marriage.

Married Adults

- The age at which individuals marry in the United States is increasing. Despite a decline in marriage rates, a large percentage of Americans still marry. The benefits of marriage include better physical and mental health and a longer life.

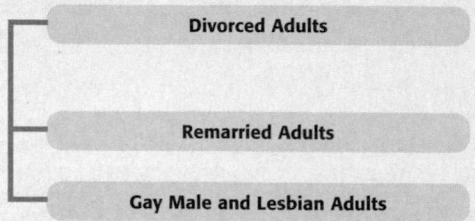

Divorced Adults	• The U.S. divorce rate increased dramatically in the twentieth century but began to decline in the 1980s. Divorce is complex and emotional. Both divorced men and women can experience loneliness, anxiety, and difficulty in forming new relationships.
Remarried Adults	• Stepfamilies are complex and adjustment is difficult. Remarried adults are more prone to experience depression than adults in never-divorced families.
Gay Male and Lesbian Adults	• One of the most striking findings about gay male and lesbian couples is how similar their relationships are to heterosexual couples' relationships.

4 MARRIAGE AND THE FAMILY: DISCUSS MAKING MARRIAGES WORK, PARENTING, AND DIVORCE

Making Marriage Work	• Gottman's research indicates that in marriages that work couples establish love maps, nurture fondness and admiration, turn toward each other, accept the influence of the partner, solve solvable conflicts, overcome gridlock, and create shared meaning.
Becoming a Parent	• Families are becoming smaller, and many women are delaying childbirth until they have become well established in a career. There are some advantages to having children earlier in adulthood, and some advantages to having them later.
Dealing with Divorce	• Hetherington identified six pathways taken by people after divorce: enhancers, good-enoughs, seekers, libertines, competent loners, and the defeated. About 20 percent became better adjusted and more competent after the divorce.

5 GENDER, RELATIONSHIPS, AND SELF-DEVELOPMENT: SUMMARIZE THE ROLE OF GENDER IN RELATIONSHIPS

Gender and Communication	• Tannen distinguishes between rapport talk, which many women prefer, and report talk, which many men prefer. Meta-analyses have found small gender differences in overall communication, but recent research suggests some gender differences in specific aspects of communication, such as the way men and women use words.
Women's Development	• Some gender experts contend that women are more relationship-oriented than men and that their interactions focus on fostering the development of other people. Critics argue that there is more individual variation in women's and men's relationship styles than this view acknowledges. Many experts believe that it is important for females to retain their competence and interest in relationships, but also to direct more effort into self-development.
Men's Development	• The traditional male role involves considerable strain, which takes a toll on men's health. The role also discourages interest in relationships, equal relationships with women, and positive emotional connections with other men.

KEY TERMS

secure attachment style 447
avoidant attachment
  style 447

anxious attachment
  style 447
consensual validation 449

matching hypothesis 450
romantic love 452
affectionate love 452

rapport talk 465
report talk 465

KEY PEOPLE

Theodore Wachs 446
Cindy Hazan 447
Phillip Shaver 447
Mario Mikulincer 448

Erik Erikson 450
Ellen Berscheid 452
Phillip Shaver 452
Robert J. Sternberg 452

John Gottman 460
E. Mavis Hetherington 463
Deborah Tannen 465
Jean Baker Miller 465

Harriet Lerner 465
Joseph Pleck 466

E-LEARNING TOOLS

To help you master the material in this chapter, visit the Online Learning Center for *Life-Span Development,* twelfth edition, at **www.mhhe.com/santrockld12**.

Self-Assessment

Connect to **www.mhhe.com/santrockld12** to learn more about falling in love and finding a mate by completing the self-assessments, *What Is My Love Like?*, *The Characteristics I Desire in a Potential Mate,* and *My Attitudes Towards Women.*

Taking It to the Net

Connect to **www.mhhe.com/santrockld12** to research the answers to these questions:

1. Yolanda, who is divorced with two young children, is contemplating a marriage proposal from her boyfriend Dana, also divorced with one young child. She is concerned about the potential issues that may arise from this union. What should Yolanda consider before making this decision about her future?

2. Kelly, at 29 years old, is surprised to hear about two close friends from college, both of whom are getting divorced after only a few years of marriage. One of these friends, April, tells her that "starter marriages" are happening more and more frequently. Is April correct about a growing trend of divorces before the age of 30 and, if so, what might be some of the factors behind this trend?

3. Rochelle and her boyfriend Mark are both 18 years old and are attending college. Rochelle would like to drop out of school to get married and have children, arguing that she can finish college and pursue a career later on. What are some of the advantages and disadvantages of this plan, as compared with waiting to have children until she and her husband-to-be have finished college and established themselves in careers?

Video Clips

The Online Learning Center includes two videos for Chapter 14. The first is called "Falling in Love." Are there patterns in the process of falling in love that apply generally? When does romantic love lead to companionate love? One couple offer themselves as a case study. The second video is called "Choosing Not to Cohabitate." This segment explores some of the motives for cohabitation (for example, living together out of wedlock), as well as some of the advantages and disadvantages of this life choice.

Health and Well-Being, Parenting, and Education Exercises

Build your decision-making skills by trying your hand at the health and well-being, parenting, and education exercises. Connect to **www.mhhe.com/santrockld12** to research the answers and complete the exercises.

MIDDLE ADULTHOOD

*Generations will depend
on the ability of every
procreating individual to
face his children.*

—Erik Erikson
American Psychologist, 20th Century

In middle adulthood, what we have been forms what we will be.

For some of us, middle age is such a foggy place, a time when

we need to discover what we are running from and to and why.

We compare our life with what we vowed to make it. In middle

age, more time stretches before us, and some evaluations,

however reluctant, have to be made. As the young-old polarity

greets us with a special force, we need to join the daring youth

with the discipline of age in a way that does justice to both. As

middle-aged adults, we come to sense that the generations of

living things pass in a short while and, like runners, hand on the

torch of life. Section 8 consists of two chapters: "Physical and

Cognitive Development in Middle Adulthood" (Chapter 15) and

"Socioemotional Development in Middle Adulthood" (Chapter 16).

15

When more time stretches before one, some assessments, however reluctantly and incompletely, begin to be made.

—JAMES BALDWIN
American Novelist, 20th Century

LEARNING GOALS

◆ Explain how midlife is changing, and define middle adulthood.

◆ Discuss physical changes in middle adulthood.

◆ Identify cognitive changes in middle adulthood.

◆ Characterize career development, work, and leisure in middle adulthood.

◆ Explain the roles of religion and meaning in life during middle adulthood.

PHYSICAL AND COGNITIVE DEVELOPMENT IN MIDDLE ADULTHOOD

CHAPTER OUTLINE

Images of Life-Span Development
Time Perspectives

Our perception of time depends on where we are in the life span. We are more concerned about time at some points in life than others (Schroots, 2007). Jim Croce's song "Time in a Bottle" reflects a time perspective that develops in the adult years:

> If I could save Time in a bottle
> The first thing that I'd like to do
> Is to save every day
> Til Eternity passes away
> Just to spend them with you . . .
> But there never seems to be enough time
> To do the things you want to do
> Once you find them
> I've looked around enough to know
> That you're the one I want to go
> Through time with
> —Jim Croce, "Time in a Bottle"

Jim Croce's song connects time with love and the hope of going through time with someone we love. Love and intimacy are important themes of adult development. So is time. Middle-aged adults begin to look back to where they have been, reflecting on what they have done with the time they have had. They look toward the future more in terms of how much time remains to accomplish what they hope to do with their lives.

PREVIEW

When young adults look forward in time to what their lives might be like as middle-aged adults, too often they anticipate that things will go downhill. However, like all periods of the human life span, for most individuals there usually are positive and negative features of middle age. In this first chapter on middle adulthood, we will discuss physical changes; cognitive changes; changes in careers, work, and leisure; as well as the importance of religion and meaning in life during middle adulthood. To begin, though, we will explore how middle age is changing.

---

1 THE NATURE OF MIDDLE ADULTHOOD

Changing Midlife   **Defining Middle Adulthood**

Is midlife experienced the same way today as it was 100 years ago? How can middle adulthood be defined, and what are some of its main characteristics?

Changing Midlife

Many of today's 50-year-olds are in better shape, more alert, and more productive than their 40-year-old counterparts from a generation or two earlier. As more people lead healthier lifestyles and medical discoveries help to stave off the aging process, the boundaries of middle age are being pushed upward. It looks like middle age is starting later and lasting longer for increasing numbers of active, healthy, and productive people. A current saying is "60 is the new 40," implying that many 60-year-olds today are living a life that is as active, productive, and healthy as earlier generations did in their forties. One study found that almost half of the individuals 65 to 69 years of age considered themselves middle-aged (National Council on Aging, 2000), and another study found a similar pattern: Half of the 60- to 75-year-olds viewed themselves as being middle-aged (Lachman, Maier, & Budner, 2000). Also, some individuals consider the upper boundary of midlife as the age at which they make the transition from work to retirement.

How is midlife changing?

When Carl Jung studied midlife transitions early in the twentieth century, he referred to midlife as the afternoon of life (Jung, 1933). Midlife serves as an important preparation for late adulthood, "the evening of life" (Lachman, 2004, p. 306). But "midlife" came much earlier in Jung's time. In 1900 the average life expectancy was only 47 years of age; only 3 percent of the population lived past 65. Today, the average life expectancy is 78, and 12 percent of the U.S. population is older than 65. As a much greater percentage of the population lives to an older age, the midpoint of life and what constitutes middle age or middle adulthood are getting harder to pin down (Staudinger & Bluck, 2001).

Compared with previous decades and centuries, an increasing percentage of the population is made up of middle-aged and older adults (Uhlenberg & Dannefer, 2007). In the past, the age structure of the population could be represented by a pyramid, with the largest percentage of the population in the childhood years. Today, the percentages of people at different ages in the life span are more similar, creating what is called the "rectangularization" of the age distribution (a vertical rectangle) (Willis & Martin, 2005). The rectangularization has been created by health advances that promote longevity, low fertility rates, and the aging of the baby-boom cohort (Moen, 2007).

Defining Middle Adulthood

Though the age boundaries are not set in stone, we will consider **middle adulthood** as the developmental period that begins at approximately 40 to 45 years of age and extends to about 60 to 65 years of age. For many people, middle adulthood is a time of declining physical skills and expanding responsibility; a period in which people become more conscious of the young-old polarity and the shrinking amount of time left in life; a point when individuals seek to transmit something meaningful to the next generation; and a time when people reach and maintain satisfaction in their careers. In sum, middle adulthood involves "balancing work and relationship responsibilities in the midst of the physical and psychological changes associated with aging" (Lachman, 2004, p. 305).

In midlife, as in other age periods, individuals make choices, selecting what to do, how to invest time and resources, and evaluating what aspects of their lives they need to change. In midlife, "a serious accident, loss, or illness" may be a "wake-up call" and produce "a major restructuring of time and a reassessment" of life's priorities (Lachman, 2004, p. 310). And with an absence of seniority protections, many middle-aged adults experience unexpected job loss and/or are strongly encouraged to take early retirement packages (Sweet, Moen, & Meiksins, 2007).

The concept of gains (growth) and losses (decline) is an important one in life-span development. An increasing number of experts conclude that middle adulthood is the age period in which gains and losses as well as biological and sociocultural factors balance each other (Baltes, Lindenberger, & Staudinger, 2006; Willis & Schaie, 2005). Although biological functioning declines in middle adulthood, sociocultural supports

middle adulthood The developmental period that begins at approximately 40 to 45 years of age and extends to about 60 to 65 years of age.

Middle age is a mix of new opportunities and expanding resources accompanied by declines in physical abilities.

—LOIS VERBRUGGE
University of Michigan

such as education, career, and relationships may peak in middle adulthood (Willis & Schaie, 2005). Thus, middle adulthood may be a unique developmental period in which growth and loss balance each other for many individuals.

Remember from our discussion in Chapter 1 that individuals not only have a chronological age, but also biological, psychological, and social ages. Some experts conclude that compared with earlier and later periods, middle age is influenced more by sociocultural factors (Dittmann-Kohli, 2005; Willis & Martin, 2005).

For many increasingly healthy adults, middle age is lasting longer. Indeed, an increasing number of experts on middle adulthood describe the age period of 55 to 65 as *late midlife* (Deeg, 2005). Compared with earlier midlife, late midlife is more likely to be characterized by "the death of a parent, the last child leaving the parental home, becoming a grandparent, the preparation for retirement, and in most cases actual retirement. Many people in this age range experience their first confrontation with health problems." (Deeg, 2005, p. 211). Overall, then, although gains and losses may balance each other in early midlife, losses may begin to dominate gains for many individuals in late midlife (Baltes, Lindenberger, & Staudinger, 2006).

Keep in mind, though, that midlife is characterized by individual variations (Perrig-Chiello & Perren, 2005). As life-span expert Gilbert Brim (1992) commented, middle adulthood is full of changes, twists, and turns; the path is not fixed. People move in and out of states of success and failure.

Review and Reflect: Learning Goal 1

 Explain How Midlife Is Changing, and Define Middle Adulthood

REVIEW

- How is middle age today different than in past generations?
- How is middle adulthood defined, and what are some of its characteristics?

REFLECT

- How do you think you will experience (are experiencing or have experienced) middle age differently from your parents or grandparents?

2 PHYSICAL DEVELOPMENT

| Physical Changes | Health and Disease | Mortality Rates | Sexuality |

What physical changes characterize middle adulthood? How healthy are middle-aged adults? What are the main causes of death in middle age? How sexually active are individual in middle adulthood?

Physical Changes

Unlike the rather dramatic physical changes that occur in early adolescence and the sometimes abrupt decline in old age, midlife physical changes are usually gradual

(Ebersole, Hess, & Luggen, 2004). One study found that self-ratings of physical health became more negative as individuals aged through the midlife period (Cleary, Zaborski, & Ayanian, 2004).

Although everyone experiences some physical change due to aging in the middle adulthood years, the rates of this aging vary considerably from one individual to another. Genetic makeup and lifestyle factors play important roles in whether chronic disease will appear and when. Middle age is a window through which we can glimpse later life while there is still time to engage in prevention and to influence some of the course of aging (Lachman, 2004). Let's now explore some of the physical changes of middle age.

Visible Signs   One of the most visible signs of physical changes in middle adulthood is physical appearance. The first outwardly noticeable signs of aging usually are apparent by the forties or fifties. The skin begins to wrinkle and sag because of a loss of fat and collagen in underlying tissues (Tsukahara & others, 2007). Small, localized areas of pigmentation in the skin produce aging spots, especially in areas that are exposed to sunlight, such as the hands and face (McCullough & Kelly, 2006). Hair becomes thinner and grayer due to a lower replacement rate and a decline in melanin production. Fingernails and toenails develop ridges and become thicker and more brittle.

Since a youthful appearance is stressed in many cultures, individuals whose hair is graying, whose skin is wrinkling, whose bodies are sagging, and whose teeth are yellowing strive to make themselves look younger. Undergoing cosmetic surgery, dyeing hair, purchasing wigs, enrolling in weight reduction programs, participating in exercise regimens, and taking heavy doses of vitamins are common in middle age. Baby boomers have shown a strong interest in plastic surgery and Botox, which may reflect their desire to take control of the aging process (De Boulle, 2007; Lachman & Firth, 2004).

Famous actor Sean Connery as a young adult in his twenties (*top*) and as a middle-aged adult in his fifties (*bottom*). *What are some of the most outwardly noticeable signs of aging in the middle adulthood years?*

Height and Weight   Individuals lose height in middle age, and many gain weight. On average, from 30 to 50 years of age, men lose about inch in height, then may lose another inch from 50 to 70 years of age (Hoyer & Roodin, 2003). The height loss for women can be as much as 2 inches from 25 to 75 years of age. Note that there are large variations in the extent to which individuals become shorter with aging. The decrease in height is due to bone loss in the vertebrae. On average, body fat accounts for about 10 percent of body weight in adolescence; it makes up 20 percent or more in middle age.

In a recent national survey, 29 percent of U.S. adults 40 to 59 years of age were classified as obese (Centers for Disease Control and Prevention, 2006). In Chapter 13, we saw that in this survey 22 percent of U.S. adults 20 to 39 years of age were classified as obese. Being overweight is a critical health problem in middle adulthood (Aldwin, Spiro, & Park, 2006). For example, obesity increases the probability that an individual will suffer a number of other ailments, among them hypertension (abnormally high blood pressure) diabetes, and digestive disorders (Brouwer & others, 2007). A recent large-scale study found that being overweight or obese in middle age increases an individual's risk of dying earlier (Adams & others, 2006). More than 500,000 50- to 71-year-olds completed surveys about their height and weight, and the researchers examined the participants' death records across a 10-year period. Those who were overweight (defined as a body mass index, which takes into account height and weight, of 25 or more) at 50 had a 20 to 40 percent higher risk of earlier death, whereas those who were obese (a body mass index of 30 or more) had a 100 to 200 percent higher risk of premature death.

Strength, Joints, and Bones   As we saw in Chapter 13, maximum physical strength often is attained in the twenties. The term *sarcopenia* is given to age-related loss of muscle mass and strength (Delmonico & others, 2007). The rate of muscle loss with age occurs at a rate of approximately 1 to 2 percent per year past the age of 50 (Marcell, 2003). A loss of strength especially occurs in the back and legs. Exercise can reduce the decline involved in sarcopenia (Johnston, De Lisio, & Parise, 2008; Melov & others, 2007).

Peak functioning of the body's joints also usually occurs in the twenties. The cushions for the movement of bones (such as tendons and ligaments) become less efficient

FIGURE 15.1 The Relation of Age and Gender to Cardiovascular Disease. Notice the sharp increase in cardiovascular disease in middle age.

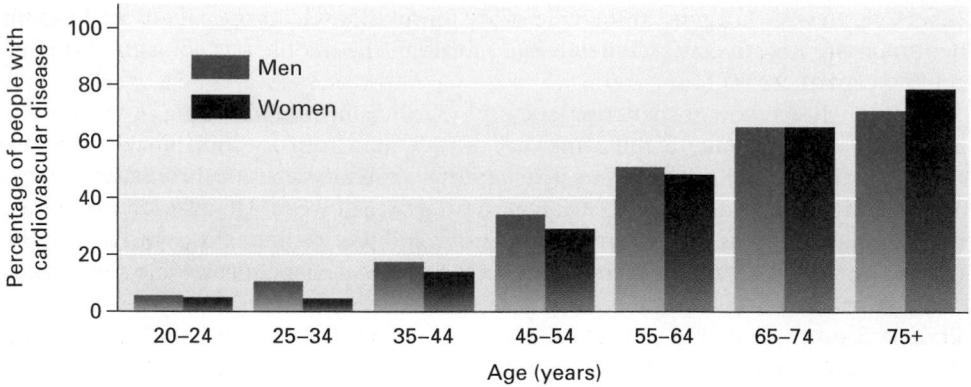

in the middle-adult years, a time when many individuals experience joint stiffness and more difficulty in movement.

Maximum bone density occurs by the mid- to late thirties, from which point there is a progressive loss of bone. The rate of this bone loss begins slowly but accelerates in the fifties (Ryan & Elahi, 2007). Women experience about twice the rate of bone loss as men. By the end of midlife, bones break more easily and heal more slowly (Gueldner & others, 2007).

Vision and Hearing *Accommodation* of the eye—the ability to focus and maintain an image on the retina—experiences its sharpest decline between 40 and 59 years of age. In particular, middle-aged individuals begin to have difficulty viewing close objects (Fozard & Gordon-Salant, 2001).

The eye's blood supply also diminishes, although usually not until the fifties or sixties. The reduced blood supply may decrease the visual field's size and account for an increase in the eye's blind spot. At 60 years of age, the retina receives only one-third as much light as it did at 20 years of age, much of which is due to a decrease in the size of the pupil (Scialfa & Kline, 2007).

Hearing also can start to decline by the age of 40. Auditory assessments indicate that hearing loss occurs in as many as 50 percent of individuals 50 years and older (Fowler & Leigh-Paffenroth, 2007). Sensitivity to high pitches usually declines first. The ability to hear low-pitched sounds does not seem to decline much in middle adulthood, though. Men usually lose their sensitivity to high-pitched sounds sooner than women do. However, this gender difference might be due to men's greater exposure to noise in occupations such as mining, automobile work, and so on (Kline & Scialfa, 1996).

Researchers are identifying new possibilities for improving the vision and hearing of people as they age (Cervino & others, 2007). One way this is being carried out is through better control of glare or background noise (Kim & others, 2007). Further, recent advances in hearing aids dramatically improve hearing for many individuals (Chia & others, 2007).

Cardiovascular System Midlife is the time when high blood pressure and high cholesterol "often take adults by surprise" (Lachman, 2004, p. 307). Indeed, the cardiovascular system changes in middle adulthood and, as indicated in Figure 15.1, cardiovascular disease increases considerably in middle age. Fatty deposits and scar tissue slowly accumulate in the linings of blood vessels, gradually reducing blood flow to various organs, including the heart and brain (Masoro, 2006).

The level of cholesterol in the blood increases through the adult years and in midlife begins to accumulate on the artery walls, increasing the risk of cardiovascular disease (Kurth & others, 2007). The type of cholesterol in the blood, however, influences its effect. Cholesterol comes in two forms: LDL (low-density lipoprotein) and HDL (high-density lipoprotein). LDL is often

Members of the Masai tribe in Kenya, Africa, can stay on a treadmill for a long time because of their active lives. Heart disease is extremely low in the Masai tribe, which also can be attributed to their energetic lifestyle.

referred to as "bad" cholesterol because when the level of LDL is too high, it sticks to the lining of blood vessels, which can lead to atherosclerosis (hardening of the arteries). HDL is often referred to as "good" cholesterol because when it is high and LDL is low, the risk of cardiovascular disease is lessened (Akerblom & others, 2008).

Blood pressure (hypertension), too, usually rises in the forties and fifties. At menopause, a woman's blood pressure rises sharply and usually remains above that of a man through life's later years (Alessandri & others, 2007; Rosano & others, 2007).

An increasing problem in middle and late adulthood is *metabolic syndrome*, a condition characterized by hypertension, obesity, and insulin resistance (You & others, 2008). Metabolic syndrome often leads to the development of diabetes and cardiovascular disease (Espinola-Klein & others, 2007; Reusch & Draznin, 2007). A recent study revealed that individuals who had metabolic syndrome had an increased risk for early death, especially when they had high blood pressure and high glucose combined with low HDL or high triglycerides (Hong & others, 2007).

Exercise, weight control, and a diet rich in fruits, vegetables, and whole grains can often help to stave off many cardiovascular problems in middle age (Church & others, 2007; Jae & others, 2007). For example, cholesterol levels are influenced by heredity, but LDL can be reduced and HDL increased by eating food that is low in saturated fat and cholesterol and by exercising regularly (Masley & others, 2008). Weight loss and exercise are strongly recommended in the treatment of metabolic syndrome (Dupuy & others, 2007). A recent study of 60-year-old men and women revealed a strong link between low levels of leisure time physical activity and the presence of metabolic syndrome (Halldin & others, 2007).

Although still the leading cause of death in adults, the good news is that deaths due to cardiovascular disease have actually been decreasing in the United States since the 1970s. Why the decrease? A recent research review provided some answers to this question: Quitting smoking, lowering blood pressure and cholesterol, and exercising saved an estimated 200,000-plus lives in the United States from 1998 to 2000 (Ford & others, 2007). However, over the same time frame, an increase in obesity and diabetes led to an estimated loss of almost 60,000 lives. The total estimated saved lives (approximately 150,000) by reducing risk factors for cardiovascular disease represented approximately the same number of saved lives as high-tech treatments such as vascular surgery.

To read further about the link between exercise and cardiovascular disease, see the *Research in Life-Span Development* interlude.

What characterizes metabolic syndrome?

Research in Life-Span Development
Fitness in Young Adults and Cardiovascular Health in Middle Age

One longitudinal study was the first large-scale observational study to examine the role of fitness on healthy young adults' development of risk factors for heart disease (Carnethon & others, 2003). Previous studies had focused on the relation between fitness and death from heart disease and stroke.

The study involved 4,487 men and women in four cities (Birmingham, Alabama; Chicago, Illinois; Minneapolis, Minnesota; and Oakland, California). Initial assessments were made when the participants were 18 to 30 years of age with follow-up assessments conducted 2, 5, 7, 10, and 15 years later. Cardiorespiratory fitness was measured with an exercise treadmill test, which consisted of up to nine two-minute stages of progressive difficulty.

Poor cardiorespiratory fitness in young men and women, determined by the duration of their treadmill exercise test, was associated with the risk of developing hypertension, diabetes, and metabolic syndrome in middle age. Improved fitness over seven years was related to a reduced risk of developing diabetes and metabolic syndrome.

How might physical fitness in early adulthood be linked to health in middle adulthood?

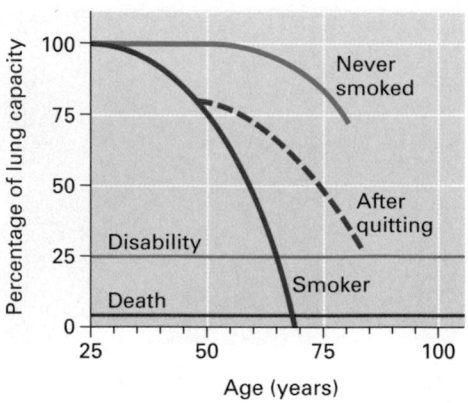

FIGURE 15.2 The Relation of Lung Capacity to Age and Cigarette Smoking. Lung capacity shows little change through middle age for individuals who have not smoked. However, smoking is linked with reduced lung capacity in middle-aged and older adults. When individuals stop smoking, their lung capacity becomes greater than those who continue to smoke, but not as great as the lung capacity of individuals who have never smoked.

Lungs There is little change in lung capacity through most of middle adulthood. However, at about the age of 55, the proteins in lung tissue become less elastic. This change, combined with a gradual stiffening of the chest wall, decreases the lungs' capacity to shuttle oxygen from the air people breathe to the blood in their veins. As shown in Figure 15.2, the lung capacity of individuals who are smokers drops precipitously in middle age, but if the individuals quit smoking, their lung capacity improves, although not to the level of individuals who have never smoked.

Sleep Some aspects of sleep become more problematic in middle age (Alessi, 2007; Campbell & Murphy, 2007). The total number of hours slept usually remains the same as in early adulthood, but beginning in the forties, wakeful periods are more frequent and there is less of the deepest type of sleep (stage 4). The amount of time spent lying awake in bed at night begins to increase in middle age, and this can produce a feeling of being less rested in the morning (Abbot, 2003). Sleep problems in middle-aged adults are more common in individuals who use a higher number of prescription and nonprescription drugs, are obese, have cardiovascular disease, or are depressed (Kaleth & others, 2007; Miller & Cappuccio, 2007).

Health and Disease

In middle adulthood, the frequency of accidents declines and individuals are less susceptible to colds and allergies than in childhood, adolescence, or early adulthood. Indeed, many individuals live through middle adulthood without having a disease or persistent health problem. However, disease and persistent health problems become more common in middle adulthood for other individuals (Spiro, 2001).

   Chronic disorders are characterized by a slow onset and a long duration. Chronic disorders are rare in early adulthood, increase in middle adulthood, and become common in late adulthood. Overall, arthritis is the leading chronic disorder in middle age, followed by hypertension, but the frequency of chronic disorders in middle age varies by gender. Men have a higher incidence of fatal chronic conditions (such as coronary heart disease, cancer, and stroke); women have a higher incidence of nonfatal ones (such as arthritis, varicose veins, and bursitis).

Stress and Disease Stress is increasingly being found to be a factor in disease (Kyrous & Tsigos, 2007). The cumulative effect of stress often takes a toll on the health of individuals by the time they reach middle age (Aldwin, Spiro, & Park, 2006). Stress is linked to disease through both the immune system and cardiovascular disease (Ah, Kang, & Carpenter, 2007).

The Immune System and Stress The immune system keeps us healthy by recognizing foreign materials such as bacteria, viruses, and tumors and then destroying them. Its machinery consists of billions of white blood cells located in the circulatory system. The number of white blood cells and their effectiveness in killing foreign viruses or bacteria are related to stress levels. When a person is under stress, viruses and bacteria are more likely to multiply and cause disease. One recent study in young and middle-aged adults revealed that persistently unemployed individuals had lower natural killer (NK) cell levels than their previously unemployed counterparts who became reemployed (Cohen & others, 2007). NK cells are a type of white blood cell that is more likely to be present in low-stress circumstances (see Figure 15.3).

   Immune system functioning decreases with normal aging (Weng, 2006). The term *immunosenescence* is used to describe the progressive decline of immune system function with aging (Shah & Ershler, 2007).

Stress and the Cardiovascular System Sometimes the link between stress and cardiovascular disease is indirect. For example, people who live in a chronically stressed condition are more likely to take up smoking, start overeating, and avoid exercising.

chronic disorders Disorders that are characterized by slow onset and long duration. They are rare in early adulthood, they increase during middle adulthood, and they become common in late adulthood.

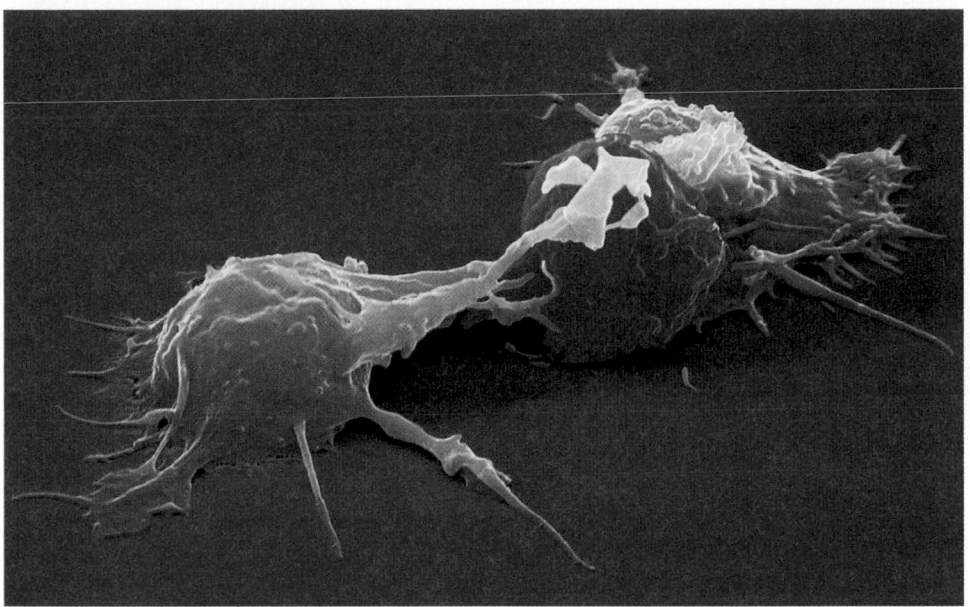

FIGURE 15.3 NK Cells and Cancer. Two natural killer (NK) cells (*yellow*) are shown attacking a leukemia cell (*red*). Notice the blisters that the leukemia cell has developed to defend itself. Nonetheless, the NK cells are surrounding the leukemia cell and are about to destroy it.

All of these stress-related behaviors are linked with the development of cardiovascular disease (Schneiderman & others, 2001). In addition, however, researchers have found that stress and negative emotions can affect the development and course of cardiovascular disease by altering underlying physiological processes (Das & O'Keefe, 2006).

You may have heard someone say something like "It's no wonder she died of a heart attack with all of the stress he put her through." But is it true that emotional stress can cause a person to have a heart attack? A clear link between emotional stress and having a heart attack has not been found, but chronic emotional stress is associated with high blood pressure, heart disease, and early death (Kiecolt-Glaser & others, 2002). And a recent study revealed that negative emotional events and anger at work were linked with the occurrence of acute coronary syndrome, a severe, sudden heart condition that has not yet developed into a heart attack (Lipovetsky & others, 2007). Apparently, the surge in adrenaline caused by severe emotional stress causes the blood to clot more rapidly, and blood clotting is a major factor in heart attacks (Fogoros, 2001).

Culture and Health Culture plays an important role in coronary disease. Cross-cultural psychologists maintain that studies of immigrants shed light on the role culture plays in health. When people migrate to another culture, their health practices are likely to change while their genetic predispositions to certain disorders remain constant (Ilola, 1990; Jorgensen, Borch-Johnsen, & Bjerregaard, 2006).

Consider the Ni-Hon-San Study (Nippon–Honolulu–San Francisco), an ongoing study of approximately 12,000 Japanese men in Hiroshima and Nagasaki (Japan), Honolulu, and San Francisco. In the study, the Japanese men living in Japan have had the lowest rate of coronary heart disease, those living in Honolulu have had an intermediate rate, and those living in San Francisco have had the highest rate. The Japanese men's cholesterol level, glucose level, and weight all increased as they migrated. Why? As the Japanese men migrated farther away from Japan, they acculturated, and their health practices, such as diet, changed. The Japanese men in California, for example, ate 40 percent more fat than the men in Japan.

Conversely, Japanese men in California have much lower rates of cerebrovascular disease (stroke) than Japanese men living in Japan. Businessmen in Japan tend to consume vast quantities of alcohol and to chain-smoke, both of which are high-risk

In the Ni-Hon-San Study, what health variations were found for Japanese men living in Japan (top), *Honolulu* (middle), *and San Francisco* (bottom)?

factors for stroke. Stroke was the leading cause of death in Japan until it was surpassed by cancer in 1981. However, death rates from stroke for Japanese American men are at the same level as those of White American men. Researchers suspect that this level is related to a change in behavior. That is, Japanese American men consume less alcohol and smoke less than their counterparts in Japan. To read more about cultural factors in health, see the *Diversity in Life-Span Development* interlude.

Diversity in Life-Span Development
Health Promotion in African Americans, Latinos, Asian Americans, and Native Americans

There are differences within ethnic groups as well as among them. This is just as true of health within ethnic groups as it is of, say, family structure. Asian Americans, for example, are strikingly varied in their national backgrounds, lifestyles, and health. They range from highly acculturated Japanese Americans, who may be well educated and have excellent access to health care, to the many Indo-Chinese refugees who have few economic resources and may be in poor health. The living conditions and lifestyles of individuals within an ethnic group are influenced by their socioeconomic status, immigrant status, social and language skills, occupational opportunities, and such social resources as the availability of meaningful support networks—all of which play a role in health (Whitfield, 2006).

Despite these variations within ethnic groups, it is useful to know about differences among ethnic groups (Kurian & Cardarelli, 2007; Lin & Pi-Sunyer, 2007). African Americans, for example, have an above-average rate of high blood pressure, and there is increasing evidence that diabetes occurs at an above-average rate among Latinos, making this disease a major health problem (Crane & Wallace, 2007). Also, Latinas are less likely than non-Latina Whites to obtain Pap test screening and have higher rates of cervical cancer (Byrd, Chavez, & Wilson, 2007).

Prejudice and racial segregation are the historical underpinnings for the chronic stress of discrimination and poverty that adversely affects the health of many African Americans (Shavers & Shavers, 2006). Support systems, such as an extended family network, may be especially important resources to improve the health of African Americans and help them cope with stress.

Prejudice and discrimination may also be significant stressors affecting the heath of immigrants from Puerto Rico, Mexico, and elsewhere in Latin America. Immigrants may also face cultural barriers to adequate health care, including a lack of financial resources and poor language skills, which often prevent effective doctor-patient communications. In addition, immigrants often are unfamiliar with how the medical system operates, confused about the need to see numerous people, and uncertain about why they have to wait so long for service (Snowden & Cheung, 1990).

Health-care professionals can increase their effectiveness with ethnic minority patients by improving their knowledge of patients' attitudes, beliefs, and folk practices regarding health and disease. Such information should be integrated into Western treatment rather than ignored at the risk of alienating patients.

Mortality Rates

Infectious disease was the main cause of death until the middle of the twentieth century. As infectious disease rates declined, and more individuals lived through middle age, chronic disorders increased. Chronic diseases are now the main causes of death for individuals in middle adulthood (Merrill & Verbrugge, 1999).

In middle age, many deaths are caused by a single, readily identifiable condition, whereas in old age, death is more likely to result from the combined effects of several chronic conditions (Gessert, Elliott, & Haller, 2003). Figure 15.4 shows the leading causes of death in middle age. Heart disease is the leading cause, followed by cancer and cerebrovascular disease (National Center for Health Statistics, 2006). In the first half of middle age, cancer claims more lives than heart disease; this is reversed in the second half. Men have higher mortality rates than women for all of the leading causes of death.

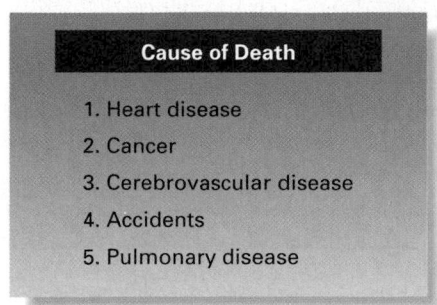

Cause of Death

1. Heart disease
2. Cancer
3. Cerebrovascular disease
4. Accidents
5. Pulmonary disease

FIGURE 15.4 Leading Causes of Death in Middle Adulthood

Sexuality

What kinds of changes characterize the sexuality of women and men as they go through middle age? **Climacteric** is a term that is used to describe the midlife transition in which fertility declines. Let's explore the substantial differences in the climacteric of women and men.

Menopause   Most of us know something about menopause. But is what we know accurate? What is menopause, when does it occur, and what are its side effects?

Menopause is the time in middle age, usually in the late forties or early fifties, when a woman's menstrual periods completely cease. The average age at which women have their last period is 51 (Wise, 2006). However, there is large variation in the age at which menopause occurs—from 39 to 59 years of age. Virtually all women are postmenopausal by 60 years of age (Gosden, 2007).

Recall from Chapter 11, "Physical and Cognitive Development in Adolescence," that the timing of *menarche*, a girl's first menstruation, significantly decreased in the twentieth century, occurring as much as four years earlier in some countries (Hermann-Giddens, 2007). Has there been a similar earlier onset in the occurrence of menopause? No, there hasn't been a similar earlier corresponding change in menopause, and there is little or no correlation between the onset of menarche and the onset of menopause (Gosden, 2007).

Perimenopause is the transitional period from normal menstrual periods to no menstrual periods at all, which often takes up to 10 years (De Franciscis & others, 2007). Perimenopause is most common in the forties but can occur in the thirties. A study of 30- to 50-year-old women found that depressed feelings, headaches, moodiness, and palpitations were the symptoms that women in perimenopause most frequently discussed with health-care providers (Lyndaker & Hulton, 2004).

Heredity and experience influence the onset of menopause (Gosden, 2007). Menopause is influenced by multiple genes. Menopause occurs one to two years earlier in women who smoke cigarettes on a regular basis because tobacco smoke and tar can damage ovaries (Gosden, 2007). A recent study revealed that menopause occurs later in women who exercise regularly (Santoro & others, 2007). And a recent eight-year longitudinal study of women in their forties and fifties found that walking regularly $1\frac{1}{2}$ hours a day five days a week was linked to fewer symptoms of anxiety and depression as women made the transition from having regular menstrual periods to menopause (Nelson & others, 2008).

Not only the timing but also the side effects of Menopause vary greatly (Shakhatreh & Mas'ad, 2006). In menopause, production of estrogen by the ovaries declines dramatically, and this decline produces uncomfortable symptoms in some women—"hot flashes," nausea, fatigue, and rapid heartbeat, for example (Cooper & others, 2008). Cross-cultural studies reveal wide variations in the menopause experience (Freeman & Sherif, 2007; Sievert, Obermeyer, & Saliba, 2007). For example, hot flashes are uncommon in Mayan women (Beyene, 1986). Asian women report fewer hot flashes than women in Western societies (Payer, 1991). It is difficult to determine the extent to which these cross-cultural variations are due to genetic, dietary, reproductive, or cultural factors.

In the United States, research based on small samples of women who go to physicians or therapists because they are having problems associated with menopause sometimes creates the impression that menopause is necessarily a traumatic event. In fact, in a large-scale study of Americans in midlife, just over 50 percent of middle-aged women reported having no hot flashes at all (Brim, 1999). Almost two-thirds of postmenopausal women said they were relieved that their periods had stopped. Only 1 percent said they felt "only regret" that they no longer had their period. Some menopausal women report depression and irritability, but in some instances these feelings are related to other circumstances such as becoming divorced, losing a job, caring for a sick parent, and so on (Gannon, 1998). Also, a recent study in Taiwan found no significant effect of menopausal transition on women's quality of life (Cheng & others, 2007). Another recent study revealed that menopausal symptoms increased in women who smoked cigarettes, drank alcohol, were currently using oral contraceptives, were depressed, and ate high-sugar-content foods (Sabia & others, 2008).

Researchers have found that almost 50 percent of Canadian and American women have occasional hot flashes, but only one in seven Japanese women do (Lock, 1998). *What factors might account for these variations?*

climacteric The midlife transition in which fertility declines.

menopause Cessation of a woman's menstrual periods, usually in the late forties or fifties.

In sum, menopause overall is not the negative experience for most women it was once thought to be. However, the loss of fertility is an important marker for women—it means that they have to make final decisions about having children (Wise, 2006). Women in their thirties who have never had children sometimes speak about being "up against the biological clock" because they cannot postpone choices about having children much longer.

Until recently, hormone replacement therapy was often prescribed as treatment for unpleasant side effects of menopause. *Hormone replacement therapy (HRT)* augments the declining levels of reproductive hormone production by the ovaries (Ekstrom, 2005). HRT can consist of various forms of estrogen, and usually a progestin. A study of HRT's effects was halted as evidence emerged that participants who were receiving HRT faced an increased risk of stroke (National Institutes of Health, 2004). Estrogen alone increased the risk of stroke by about the same amount as estrogen combined with progestin. Preliminary data also indicated a trend toward increased risk of dementia (deterioration of mental functioning) among those receiving HRT. On the positive side, the study found that estrogen lowered the risk of hip fractures and did not increase the risk of heart attacks or breast cancer.

The National Institutes of Health recommend that women with a uterus who are currently taking hormones should consult with their doctor to determine whether they should continue the treatment. If they are taking HRT for short-term relief of symptoms, the benefits may outweigh the risks (Schindler, 2006). However, the recent evidence of risks associated with HRT suggests that long-term hormone therapy should be seriously reevaluated (Warren, 2007). Because of the potential negative effects of HRT, many middle-aged women are seeking alternatives such as regular exercise, dietary supplements, herbal remedies, relaxation therapy, acupuncture, and nonsteroidal medications (Gosden, 2007; Writing Group for the British Menopause Council & others, 2008). For example, one recent study revealed that acupuncture and relaxation therapy reduced the number of hot flashes middle-aged women experienced (Zaborowska & others, 2007).

One likely positive benefit of estrogen therapy is that may help to protect against cognitive aging in women. A recent research review concluded that estrogen has protective effects on verbal memory and working memory when it is initiated soon after menopause begins—but when administered many years following menopause, there is no cognitive protection, and it even be harmful when initiated later (Sherwin, 2007).

Hormonal Changes in Middle-Aged Men

Do men go through anything like the menopause that women experience? That is, is there a male menopause? During middle adulthood, most men do not lose their capacity to father children, although there usually is a modest decline in their sexual hormone level and activity (Kohler & others, 2008). Men experience hormonal changes in their fifties and sixties, but nothing like the dramatic drop in estrogen that women experience (Leonard, 2004). Testosterone production begins to decline about 1 percent a year during middle adulthood, and sperm count usually shows a slow decline, although men do not lose their fertility in middle age (Harman, 2007). The gradual decline in men's testosterone levels in middle age can reduce their sexual drive (Stones & Stones, 2007).

A common development in middle-aged men is **erectile dysfunction**, the inability to adequately achieve and maintain an erection that results in satisfactory sexual performance (Sadeghi-Nejad, Seftel, & Munarriz, 2007). In a recent national study of U.S. men 40 years and older, 22 percent said they "sometimes" or "never" get or keep an erection adequate for sexual intercourse (Laumann & others, 2007). The percentage of men with erectile dysfunction increased the older they were and decreased if they engaged in regular exercise and had a college education.

Middle-aged men's erections are less full and less frequent, and require more stimulation to achieve them. Researchers once attributed these changes to psychological factors, but increasingly they find that as many as 75 percent of the erectile dysfunctions in middle-aged men stem from physiological problems. Smoking, diabetes, hypertension,

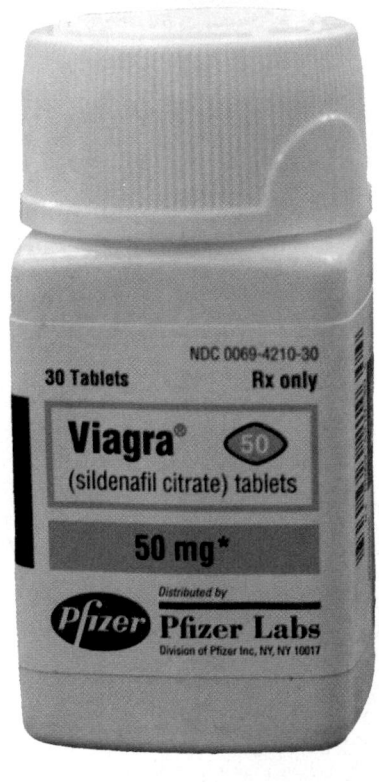

erectile dysfunction The inabilty to adequately achieve and maintain an erection that results in satisfactory sexual performance.

and elevated cholesterol levels are at fault in many erectile problems in middle-aged men (Laumann & others, 2007; Sadeghi-Nejad, Seftel, & Munarriz, 2007).

Treatment for men with erectile dysfunction has focused recently on the drug Viagra and on similar drugs that appeared after Viagra became popular, such as Levitra and Cialis (Kim, 2008). Viagra works by allowing increased blood flow into the penis, which produces an erection. Its success rate is in the range of 60 to 85 percent (Pavone & others, 2008). Studies continue to show that a high percentage of men who take Viagra for erectile dysfunction are highly satisfied with the effectiveness of the drug (Abdo & others, 2008; McCullough & others, 2008). Researchers also have found that Levitra and Cialis are as successful as Viagra in treating erectile dysfunction and have similar side effects (Rubio-Aurioles & others, 2008; Sharlip & others, 2008).

Sexual Attitudes and Behavior   Although the ability of men and women to function sexually shows little biological decline in middle adulthood, sexual activity usually occurs on a less frequent basis than in early adulthood (Stones & Stones, 2007). Figure 15.5 shows the age trends in frequency of sex from the Sex in America survey (described in Chapter 13). The frequency of having sex was greatest for individuals aged 25 to 29 years old (47 percent had sex twice a week or more) and dropped off for individuals in their fifties (23 percent of 50- to 59-year-old males said they had sex twice a week or more; only 14 percent of the females in this age group reported this frequency) (Michael & others, 1994). Note, though, that the Sex in America survey may underestimate the frequency of sexual activity of middle-aged adults because the data were collected prior to the widespread use of erectile dysfunction drugs such as Viagra. Other research indicates that middle-aged men want sex, think about it more, and masturbate more often than middle-aged women (Stones & Stones, 2007). For many other forms of sexual behavior, such as kissing and hugging, sexual touching, and oral sex, male and female middle-aged adults report similar frequency of engagement (Stones & Stones, 2007).

Living with a spouse or partner makes all the difference in whether people engage in sexual activity, especially for women over 40 years of age. In one study conducted by the MacArthur Foundation, 95 percent of women in their forties with partners said that they have been sexually active in the last six months, compared with only 53 percent of those without partners (Brim, 1999). By their fifties, 88 percent of women living with a partner have been sexually active in the last six months, but only 37 percent of those who are neither married nor living with someone say they have had sex in the last six months.

		Percentage engaging in sex			
Age groups	Not at all	A few times per year	A few times per month	2–3 times a week	4 or more times a week
Men					
18–24	15	21	24	28	12
25–29	7	15	31	36	11
30–39	8	15	37	23	6
40–49	9	18	40	27	6
50–59	11	22	43	20	3
Women					
18–24	11	16	2	9	12
25–29	5	10	38	37	10
30–39	9	16	6	33	6
40–49	15	16	44	20	5
50–59	30	22	35	12	2

FIGURE 15.5 The Sex in America Survey: Frequency of Sex at Different Points in Adult Development. *Why do you think the frequency of sex declines as men and women get older?*

Review and Reflect: Learning Goal 2

2 **Discuss Physical Changes in Middle Adulthood**

REVIEW

- What are some key physical changes in middle adulthood?
- How would you characterize health and disease in middle adulthood?
- What are the main causes of death in middle age?
- What are the sexual lives of middle-aged adults like?

REFLECT

- Were you surprised by any of the characteristics of the sexual lives of middle-aged adults? If so, which ones?

3 COGNITIVE DEVELOPMENT

Intelligence   **Information Processing**

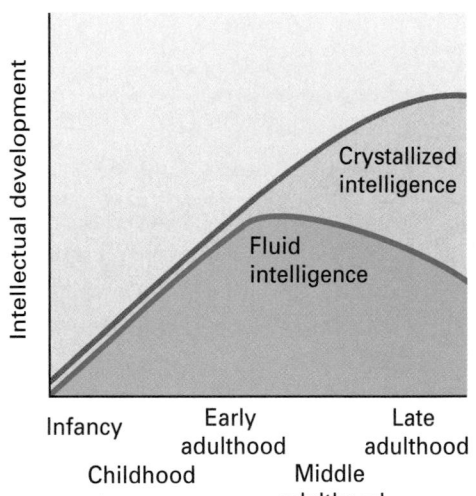

FIGURE 15.6 Fluid and Crystallized Intellectual Development Across the Life Span. According to Horn, crystallized intelligence (based on cumulative learning experiences) increases throughout the life span, but fluid intelligence (the ability to perceive and manipulate information) steadily declines from middle adulthood.

crystallized intelligence Accumulated information and verbal skills, which increase with in middle adulthood, according to Horn.

fluid intelligence The ability to reason abstractly, which begins to decline from middle adulthood on, according to Horn.

We have seen that middle-aged adults may not see as well, run as fast, or be as healthy as they were in their twenties and thirties. But what about their cognitive skills? Do they decline as we enter and move through middle adulthood? To answer this question, we will explore the possibility of cognitive changes in intelligence and information processing.

Intelligence

Our exploration of possible changes in intelligence in middle adulthood focuses on the concepts of fluid and crystallized intelligence, the Seattle Longitudinal Study, and cohort effects.

Fluid and Crystallized Intelligence John Horn argues that some abilities begin to decline in middle age while others increase (Horn & Donaldson, 1980). Horn maintains that **crystallized intelligence**, an individual's accumulated information and verbal skills, continues to increase in middle adulthood, whereas **fluid intelligence**, one's ability to reason abstractly, begins to decline in the middle adulthood years (see Figure 15.6).

Horn's data were collected in a cross-sectional manner. Remember from Chapter 1 that a cross-sectional study assesses individuals of different ages at the same point in time. For example, a cross-sectional study might assess the intelligence of different groups of 40-, 50-, and 60-year-olds in a single evaluation, such as in 1980. The 40-year-olds in the study would have been born in 1940 and the 60-year-olds in 1920—different eras that offered different economic and educational opportunities. The 60-year-olds likely had fewer educational opportunities as they grew up. Thus, if we find differences between 40- and 60-year-olds on intelligence tests when they are assessed cross-sectionally, these differences might be due to cohort effects related to educational differences rather than to age.

By contrast, remember from Chapter 1 that in a longitudinal study, the same individuals are studied over a period of time. Thus, a longitudinal study of intelligence in middle adulthood might consist of giving the same intelligence test to the same individuals when they are 40, 50, and 60 years of age. As we see next, whether data on intelligence are collected cross-sectionally or longitudinally can make a difference in what is found about changes in crystallized and fluid intelligence and about intellectual decline.

The Seattle Longitudinal Study The Seattle Longitudinal Study that involves extensive evaluation of intellectual abilities in the adulthood years was initiated by K. Warner Schaie (1994, 1996, 2005). Participants have been assessed in seven-year intervals since 1956: 1963, 1970, 1977, 1984, 1991, 1998, and 2005. Five hundred individuals initially were tested in 1956. New waves of participants are added periodically. The main focus in the Seattle Longitudinal Study has been on individual change and stability in intelligence, and the study is considered to be one of the most thorough examinations of how people develop and change as they go through the adulthood years.

The main mental abilities tested are:

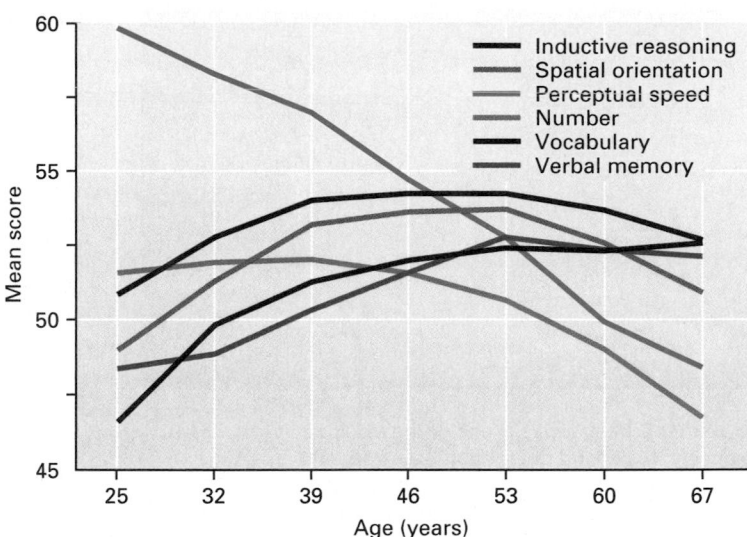

FIGURE 15.7 Longitudinal Changes in Six Intellectual Abilities from Age 25 to Age 67

- *Vocabulary* (ability to understand ideas expressed in words)

- *Verbal memory* (ability to encode and recall meaningful language units, such as a list of words)

- *Number* (ability to perform simple mathematical computations such as addition, subtraction, and multiplication)

- *Spatial orientation* (ability to visualize and mentally rotate stimuli in two- and three-dimensional space)

- *Inductive reasoning* (ability to recognize and understand patterns and relationships in a problem and use this understanding to solve other instances of the problem)

- *Perceptual speed* (ability to quickly and accurately make simple discriminations in visual stimuli)

As shown in Figure 15.7, the highest level of functioning for four of the six intellectual abilities occurred in the middle adulthood years (Willis & Schaie, 1999). For both women and men, peak performance on verbal ability, verbal memory, inductive reasoning, and spatial orientation was attained in middle age. For only two of the six abilities—number and perceptual speed—were there declines in middle age. Perceptual speed showed the earliest decline, actually beginning in early adulthood. Interestingly, in terms of John Horn's ideas that were discussed earlier, for the participants in the Seattle Longitudinal Study, middle age was a time of peak performance for some aspects of both crystallized intelligence (verbal ability) and fluid intelligence (spatial orientation and inductive reasoning).

When Schaie (1994) assessed intellectual abilities both cross-sectionally and longitudinally, he found decline more likely in the cross-sectional than in the longitudinal assessments. For example, as shown in Figure 15.8, when assessed cross-sectionally, inductive reasoning showed a consistent decline in the middle adulthood years. In contrast, when assessed longitudinally, inductive reasoning increased until toward the end of middle adulthood, when it began to show a slight decline. In Schaie's (2008) view, it is in middle adulthood, not early adulthood, that people reach a peak in their cognitive functioning for many intellectual skills.

In further analysis, Schaie (2007) recently examined generational differences in parents and their children over a seven-year time frame from 60 to 67 years of age. That is, parents were assessed when they were 60 to 67 years of age, then when their children reached 60 to 67 years of age, they also were assessed. Higher levels of cognitive functioning occurred for the second generation in inductive reasoning, verbal memory, and spatial orientation, whereas the first generation scored higher on number. Noteworthy was the finding that the parent generation showed cognitive decline from 60 to 67 years of age, but their offspring showed stability or modest increase in cognitive functioning across the same age range.

The results from Schaie's study that have been described so far focus on *average* cognitive stability or change for all participants across the middle adulthood years. Schaie and Sherry Willis (Schaie, 2005; Willis & Schaie, 2005) examined individual differences for

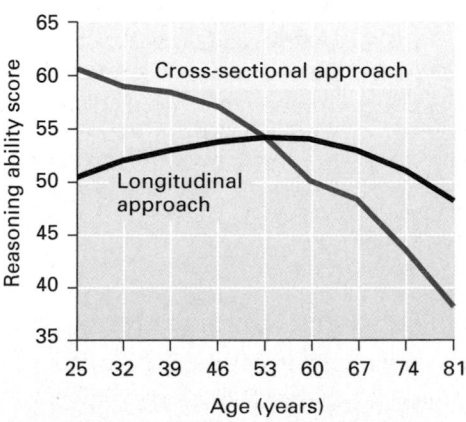

FIGURE 15.8 Cross-Sectional and Longitudinal Comparisons of Intellectual Change in Middle Adulthood. *Why do you think reasoning ability peaks during middle adulthood.*

K. Warner Schaie (*right*) is one of the leading pioneers in the field of life-span development. He is shown here with two older adults who are actively using their cognitive skills. Schaie's research represents one of the most thorough examinations of how individuals develop and change as they go through the adult years.

the participants in the Seattle study and found substantial individual variations. They classified participants as "decliners," "stable," and "gainers" for three categories—number ability, delayed recall (a verbal memory task), and word fluency—from 46 to 60 years of age. The largest percentage of decline (31 percent) or gain (16 percent) occurred for delayed recall; the largest percentage with stable scores (79 percent) occurred for numerical ability. Word fluency declined for 20 percent of the individuals from 46 to 60 years of age.

Might the individual variations in cognitive trajectories in midlife be linked to cognitive impairment in late adulthood? In Willis and Schaie's analysis, cognitively normal and impaired older adults did not differ on measures of vocabulary, spatial orientation, and numerical ability in middle adulthood. However, declines in memory (immediate recall and delayed recall), word fluency, and perceptual speed in middle adulthood were linked to neuropsychologists' ratings of the individuals' cognitive impairment in late adulthood.

Information Processing

As we saw in our discussion of theories of development (Chapter 1) and of cognitive development from infancy through adolescence (Chapters 5, 7, 9, and 11), the information-processing approach provides another way of examining cognitive abilities. Among the information-processing changes that take place in middle adulthood are those involved in speed of processing information, memory, expertise, and practical problem-solving skills.

Speed of Information Processing As we saw in Schaie's (1994, 1996) Seattle Longitudinal Study, perceptual speed begins declining in early adulthood and continues to decline in middle adulthood. A common way to assess speed of information is through a reaction-time task, in which individuals simply press a button as soon as they see a light appear (Hartley, 2006). Middle-aged adults are slower to push the button when the light appears than young adults are. However, keep in mind that the decline is not dramatic—under 1 second in most investigations.

A current interest focuses on possible causes for the decline in speed of processing information in adults (Salthouse, 2007). The causes may occur at different levels of analysis, such as cognitive ("maintaining goals, switching between tasks, or preserving internal representations despite distraction"), neuroanatomical ("changes in specific brain regions, such as the prefrontal cortex"), and neurochemical ("changes in neurotransmitter systems") such as dopamine (Hartley, 2006, p. 201).

Memory In Schaie's (1994, 1996) Seattle Longitudinal Study, verbal memory peaked in the fifties. However, in some other studies, verbal memory has shown a decline in middle age, especially when assessed in cross-sectional studies. For example, in several studies, when asked to remember lists of words, numbers, or meaningful prose, younger adults outperformed middle-aged adults (Salthouse & Skovronek, 1992). Although there still is some controversy about whether memory declines in the middle adulthood years, most experts conclude that it does decline (Hoyer & Verhaeghen, 2006). However, some experts argue that studies that have concluded there is a decline in memory during middle age often have compared young adults in their twenties with older middle-aged adults in their late fifties and even have included some individuals in their sixties (Schaie, 2000). In this view, memory decline either is nonexistent or minimal in the early part of middle age but does occur in the latter part of middle age or in late adulthood (Backman, Small, & Wahlin, 2001).

Aging and cognition expert Denise Park (2001) argues that starting in late middle age, more time is needed to learn new information. The slowdown in learning new information has been linked to changes in **working memory**, the mental "workbench" where individuals manipulate and assemble information when making decisions, solving problems, and comprehending written and spoken language (Baddeley,

working memory The mental "workbench" where individuals manipulate and assemble information when decision making problem solving and comprehending Language.

2000, 2007). In this view, in late middle age, working memory capacity—the amount of information that can be immediately retrieved and used—becomes more limited (Leonards, Ibanez, & Giannakopoulos, 2002). Think of this situation as an overcrowded desk with many items in disarray. As a result of the overcrowding and disarray, long-term memory becomes less reliable, more time is needed to enter new information into long-term storage, and more time is required to retrieve the information. Thus, Park concludes that much of the blame for declining memory in late middle age is a result of information overload that builds up as we go through the adult years.

Memory decline is more likely to occur when individuals don't use effective memory strategies, such as organization and imagery (Sugar, 2007). By organizing lists of phone numbers into different categories, or imagining the phone numbers as representing different objects around the house, many individuals can improve their memory in middle adulthood.

Expertise   Because it takes so long to attain, expertise often shows up more in the middle adulthood than in the early adulthood years (Kim & Hasher, 2005). Recall from Chapter 10 that *expertise* involves having extensive, highly organized knowledge and understanding of a particular domain. Developing expertise and becoming an "expert" in a field usually is the result of many years of experience, learning, and effort.

Strategies that distinguish experts from novices include these:

- Experts are more likely to rely on their accumulated experience to solve problems.
- Experts often process information automatically and analyze it more efficiently when solving a problem in their domain than novices do.
- Experts have better strategies and shortcuts to solving problems in their domain than novices do.
- Experts are more creative and flexible in solving problems in their domain than novices are.

Practical Problem Solving   Everyday problem solving is another important aspect of cognition (Blanchard-Fields & Mienaltowski, 2007). Nancy Denney (1986, 1990) observed circumstances such as how young and middle-aged adults handled a landlord who would not fix their stove and what they did if a bank failed to deposit a check. She found that the ability to solve such practical problems improved through the forties and fifties as individuals accumulated practical experience. However, since Denney's research other studies on everyday problem-solving and decision-making effectiveness across the adult years have been conducted (Blanchard-Fields & Mienaltowski, 2007). A recent meta-analysis of these studies indicated that everyday problem-solving and decision-making effectiveness remained stable in early and middle adulthood, then declined in late adulthood (Thornton & Dumke, 2005).

Stephen J. Hawking is a world-renowned expert in physics. Hawking authored the best-selling book, *A Brief History of Time.* Hawking has a neurological disorder that prevents him from walking or talking. He communicates with the aid of a voice-equipped computer. *What distinguishes experts from novices?*

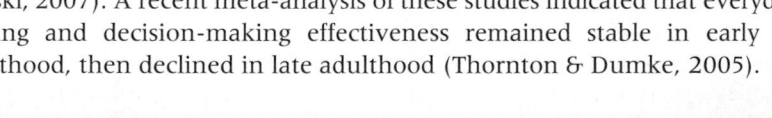

Review and Reflect: Learning Goal 3

3   **Identify Cognitive Changes in Middle Adulthood**

REVIEW

- How does intelligence develop in middle adulthood?
- What changes take place in processing information during middle age?

REFLECT

- What do you think are the most important cohort effects that can influence the development of intelligence in middle age? How are these likely to change in the future?

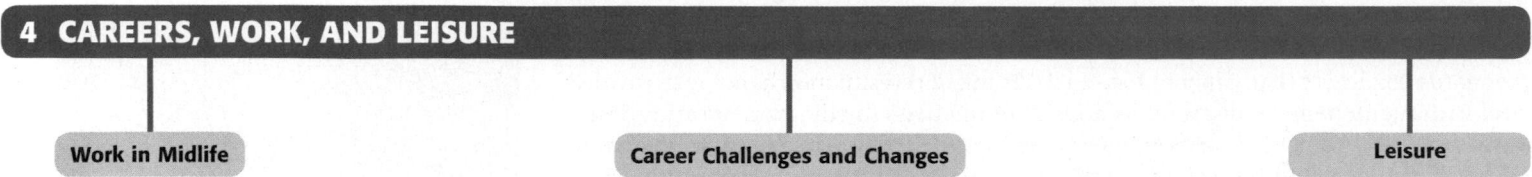

4 CAREERS, WORK, AND LEISURE

Work in Midlife   **Career Challenges and Changes**   **Leisure**

What are some issues that workers face in midlife? What role does leisure play in the lives of middle-aged adults?

Work in Midlife

The role of work, whether one works in a full-time career, a part-time job, as a volunteer, or a homemaker, is central during middle adulthood. Many middle-aged adults reach their peak in position and earnings. However, they also be saddled with multiple financial burdens from rent or mortgage, child care, medical bills, home repairs, college tuition, loans to family members, or bills from nursing homes.

In the United States, approximately 80 percent of individuals 40 to 59 years of age are employed. In the 51-to-59 age group, slightly less than 25 percent do not work. More than half of this age group say that a health condition or an impairment limits the type of paid work that they do (Sterns & Huyck, 2001).

For many people, midlife is a time of evaluation, assessment, and reflection in terms of the work they do and want to do in the future (Moen & Spencer, 2006). Among the work issues that some people face in midlife are recognizing limitations in career progress, deciding whether to change jobs or careers, deciding whether to rebalance family and work, and planning for retirement (Sterns & Huyck, 2001).

Couples increasingly have both spouses in the workforce who are expecting to retire. Historically retirement has been a male transition, but today far more more couples have to plan two retirements, his and hers (Moen & Altobelli, 2007; Moen, Kelly, & Magennis, 2008).

Career Challenges and Changes

The current middle-aged worker faces several important challenges in the twenty-first century (Cleveland & Shore, 2007). These include the globalization of work, rapid developments in information technologies, downsizing of organizations, early retirement, and concerns about pensions and health care.

Globalization has replaced what was once a primarily White male workforce with employees of different ethnic and national backgrounds. To improve profits, many companies are restructuring, downsizing, and outsourcing jobs. One of the outcomes of this is to offer incentives to middle-aged employees to retire early—in their fifties, or in some cases even forties, rather than their sixties.

HAGAR © King Features Syndicate.

The decline in defined-benefit pensions and increased uncertainty about the fate of health insurance are decreasing the sense of personal control for middle-aged workers. As a consequence, many are delaying retirement plans.

Some midlife career changes are self-motivated, others are the consequence of losing one's job (Moen & Spencer, 2006). Some individuals in middle age decide that they don't want to do the same work they have been doing for the rest of their lives (Hoyer & Roodin, 2003). One aspect of middle adulthood involves adjusting idealistic hopes to realistic possibilities in light of how much time individuals have before they retire and how fast they are reaching their occupational goals (Levinson, 1978). If individuals perceive that they are behind schedule, if their goals are unrealistic, they don't like the work they are doing, or their job has become too stressful, they could become motivated to change jobs.

Leisure

As adults, not only must we learn how to work well, but we also need to learn how to relax and enjoy leisure (Danigelis, 2007). **Leisure** refers to the pleasant times after work when individuals are free to pursue activities and interests of their own choosing—hobbies, sports, or reading, for example. In one analysis of research on what U.S. adults regret the most, not engaging in more leisure was one of the top six regrets (Roese & Summerville, 2005).

Leisure can be an especially important aspect of middle adulthood (Parkes, 2006). By middle adulthood, more money is available to many individuals, and there may be more free time and paid vacations. In short, midlife changes may produce expanded opportunities for leisure.

In one study, 12,338 men 35 to 57 years of age were assessed each year for five years regarding whether they took vacations or not (Gump & Matthews, 2000). Then, the researchers examined the medical and death records over nine years for men who lived for at least a year after the last vacation survey. Compared with those who never took vacations, men who went on annual vacations were 21 percent less likely to die over the nine years and 32 percent less likely to die of coronary heart disease.

Adults at midlife need to begin preparing psychologically for retirement. Constructive and fulfilling leisure activities in middle adulthood are an important part of this preparation (Danigelis, 2007). If an adult develops leisure activities that can be continued into retirement, the transition from work to retirement can be less stressful.

Sigmund Freud once commented that the two things adults need to do well to adapt to society's demands are to work and to love. To his list we add "to play." In our fast-paced society, it is all too easy to get caught up in the frenzied, hectic pace of our achievement-oriented work world and ignore leisure and play. *Imagine your life as a middle-aged adult. What would be the ideal mix of work and leisure? What leisure activities do you want to enjoy as a middle-aged adult?*

Review and Reflect: Learning Goal 4

 Characterize Career Development, Work, and Leisure in Middle Adulthood

REVIEW

- What are some issues that workers face in midlife?
- What career challenges and changes might people experience in middle adulthood?
- What characterizes leisure in middle age?

REFLECT

- What do you want your work life and leisure to be like in middle age? If you are middle-aged, what is your work life and leisure like? If you are an older adult, what were they like in middle age?

leisure The pleasant times after work when individuals are free to pursue activities and interests of their own choosing.

5 RELIGION AND MEANING IN LIFE

Religion and Adult Lives   **Religion and Health**   **Meaning in Life**

What role does religion play in our development as adults? Is meaning of life an important theme for many middle-aged adults?

What roles do religion and spirituality play in the lives of middle-aged adults?

Religion and Adult Lives

In the MacArthur Study of Midlife Development, more than 70 percent of U.S. middle-aged adults said they are religious and consider spirituality a major part of their lives (Brim, 1999).

In thinking about religion and adult development, it is important to consider the role of individual differences (McCullough & others, 2005). Religion is a powerful influence in some adults' lives, whereas it plays little or no role in others' lives (Myers, 2000). Further, the influence of religion in people's lives may change as they develop. In John Clausen's (1993) longitudinal investigation, some individuals who had been strongly religious in their early adult years became less so in middle age; others became more religious in middle age. In a longitudinal study of individuals from their early thirties through their late sixties/early seventies, a significant increase in spirituality occurred between late middle (mid-fifties/early sixties) and late adulthood (Wink & Dillon, 2002) (see Figure 15.9).

Women have consistently shown a stronger interest in religion than males have. In the longitudinal study just described, the spirituality of women increased more than men in the second half of life (Wink & Dillon, 2002).

Religion and Health

What might be some of the effects of religion on physical health? Some cults and religious sects encourage behaviors that are damaging to health such as ignoring sound medical advice (Williams & Sternthal, 2007). For individuals in the religious mainstream, however, there is generally either no link between religion and physical health or a positive effect (Koenig, 2007). Researchers have found that religious commitment helps to moderate blood pressure and hypertension, and that religious attendance is linked to a reduction in hypertension (Gillum & Ingram, 2007). Also, a number of studies have confirmed a positive association between religious participation and longevity (Oman & Thoresen, 2006). In the *Applications in Life-Span Development* interlude that follows, we explore links between religion and coping.

FIGURE 15.9 Level of Spirituality in Four Adult Age Periods. In a longitudinal study, the spirituality of individuals in four different adult age periods—early (thirties), middle (forties), late middle (mid-fifties/early sixties), and late (late sixties/early seventies) adulthood—was assessed (Wink & Dillon, 2002). Based on responses to open-ended questions in interviews, the spirituality of the individuals was coded on a 5-point scale with 5 being the highest level of spirituality and 1 the lowest.

Applications in Life-Span Development
Religion and Coping

What is the relation between religion and the ability to cope with stress? In a study of 850 medically ill patients admitted to an acute-care hospital, religious coping was related to low depression (Koenig & others, 1992). Religious coping is often beneficial during times of high stress (Koenig, 2001). For example, in one study, individuals were divided into those who were experiencing high stress and those with low stress (Manton, 1989). In the high-stress group, spiritual support was significantly related to low depression and high self-esteem. No such links were found in the low-stress group.

A recent interest in linking religion and coping focuses on **meaning-making coping**, which involves drawing on beliefs, values, and goals to change the meaning of a stressful situation, especially in times of chronic stress as when a loved one dies. In Crystal Park's (2005, 2007) view, individuals who are religious experience more disruption of their beliefs, values, and goals immediately after the death of a loved one than individuals who are not religious. Eventually, though, individuals who are religious often show better adjustment to the loss. Initially, religion is linked with more depressed feelings about a loved one's death. Over time, however, as religious individuals search for a type of meaning in their loss, the depressed feelings lessen. Thus, religion can serve as a meaning system through which bereaved individuals are able to reframe their loss and even find avenues of personal growth.

How is religion linked to the ability to cope with stress?

In sum, various dimensions of religiousness can help some individuals cope more effectively with their lives (Park, 2007). Religious counselors often advise people about mental health and coping. To read about the work of one religious counselor, see the *Careers in Life-Span Development* interlude.

Careers in Life-Span Development

Gabriel Dy-Liasco, Pastoral Counselor

Gabriel Dy-Lisasco is a pastoral counselor at the Pastoral Counseling and Consultation Centers of Greater Washington, D.C. He obtained his Ph.D. in pastoral counseling from Loyola College in Maryland and also has experience as a psychotherapist in such mental health settings as a substance-abuse program, military family center, psychiatric clinic, and community mental health center. As a pastoral counselor,

he works with adolescents and adults in the aspects of their lives that they show the most concern about—psychological, spiritual, or the interface of both. Having lived in Peru, Japan, and the Philippines, he brings considerable multicultural experience to the counseling setting, Dr. Dy-Liasco also is a professor in the Graduate School of Psychology and Counseling at Regent University in the Washington, D.C., area.

Meaning in Life

Austrian psychiatrist Viktor Frankl's mother, father, brother, and wife died in the concentration camps and gas chambers in Auschwitz, Poland. Frankl survived the concentration camp and went on to write about meaning in life. In his book, *Man's Search for Meaning,* Frankl (1984) emphasized each person's uniqueness and the finiteness of life. He argued that examining the finiteness of our existence and the certainty of death adds meaning to life. If life were not finite, said Frankl, we could spend our life doing just about whatever we please because time would continue forever.

Frankl said that the three most distinct human qualities are spirituality, freedom, and responsibility. Spirituality, in his view, does not have a religious underpinning. Rather, it refers to a human being's uniqueness—to spirit, philosophy, and mind. Frankl proposed that people need to ask themselves such questions as why they exist, what they want from life, and what the meaning of their life is.

It is in middle adulthood that individuals begin to be faced with death more often, especially the deaths of parents and other older relatives. Also faced with less time in

meaning-making coping Involves drawing on beliefs, values, and goals to change the meaning of a stressful situation, especially in times of chronic stress as when a loved one dies.

What characterizes the search for meaning in life?

their life, many individuals in middle age begin to ask and evaluate the questions that Frankl proposed. And as we indicated in the discussion of religion and coping, meaning-making coping is especially helpful in times of chronic stress and loss.

Roy Baumeister and Kathleen Vohs (2002, pp. 610–611) argue that the quest for a meaningful life can be understood in terms of four main needs for meaning that guide how people try to make sense of their lives:

- *Need for purpose.* "Present events draw meaning from their connection with future events." Purposes can be divided into (1) goals and (2) fulfillments. Life can be oriented toward a future anticipated state, such as living happily ever after or being in love.

- *Need for values.* This "can lend a sense of goodness or positive characterization of life and justify certain courses of action. Values enable people to decide whether certain acts are right or wrong." Frankl's (1984) view of meaning in life emphasized value as the main form of meaning that people need.

- *Need for a sense of efficacy.* This involves the "belief that one can make a difference. A life that had purposes and values but no efficacy would be tragic. The person might know what is desirable but could not do anything with that knowledge." With a sense of efficacy, people believe that they can control their environment, which has positive physical and mental health benefits (Bandura, 2007a, b).

- *Need for self-worth.* Most individuals want to be "good, worthy persons. Self-worth can be pursued individually, such as" finding out that one is very good at doing something, or collectively, as when people find self-esteem from belonging to a group or category of people.

Review and Reflect: Learning Goal 5

 Explain the Roles of Religion and Meaning in Life During Middle Adulthood

REVIEW

- What are some characteristics of religion in middle-aged individuals?
- How is religion linked to physical and mental health?
- What role does meaning in life play in middle adulthood?

REFLECT

- What are the most important aspects of meaning in life? Might the components of meaning in life vary depending on how old someone is? Explain.

Physical and Cognitive Development in Middle Adulthood

1 THE NATURE OF MIDDLE ADULTHOOD: EXPLAIN HOW MIDLIFE IS CHANGING, AND DEFINE MIDDLE ADULTHOOD

Changing Midlife

- As more people live to an older age, what we think of as middle age seems to be occurring later. A major reason developmentalists are beginning to study middle age is because of the dramatic increase in the number of individuals entering this period of the life span.

Defining Middle Adulthood

- Middle age involves extensive individual variation. With this variation in mind, we will consider middle adulthood to be entered at about 40 to 45 years of age and exited at approximately 60 to 65 years of age. Middle adulthood is the age period in which gains and losses as well as biological and sociocultural factors balance each other. Some experts conclude that sociocultural factors influence development in midlife more than biological factors.

2 PHYSICAL DEVELOPMENT: DISCUSS PHYSICAL CHANGES IN MIDDLE ADULTHOOD

Physical Changes

- The physical changes of midlife are usually gradual. Genetic and lifestyle factors play important roles in whether chronic diseases will appear and when. Among the physical changes of middle adulthood are outwardly noticeable changes in physical appearance (wrinkles, aging spots); height (decrease) and weight (increase); strength, joints, and bones; vision and hearing; cardiovascular system; lungs; and sleep.

Health and Disease

- In middle age, the frequency of accidents declines and individuals are less susceptible to colds and allergies. Chronic disorders rarely appear in early adulthood, increase in middle adulthood, and become more common in late adulthood. Arthritis is the leading chronic disorder in middle age, followed by hypertension. Men have more fatal chronic disorders, women more nonfatal ones in middle age. Immune system functioning declines with aging. Emotional stress likely is an important factor contributing to cardiovascular disease. People who live in a chronically stressed condition are likelier to smoke, overeat, and not exercise. All of these stress-related behaviors are linked with cardiovascular disease. Culture plays an important role in coronary disease.

Mortality Rates

- In middle age, the leading causes of death, in order, are heart disease, cancer, and cerebrovascular disease.

Sexuality

- Climacteric is the midlife transition in which fertility declines. The vast majority of women do not have serious physical or psychological problems related to menopause, which usually arrives in the late forties and early fifties, but menopause is an important marker because it signals the end of childbearing capability. Hormone replacement therapy (HRT) augments the declining levels of reproductive hormone production by the ovaries. HRT consists of various forms of estrogen, and usually progestin. Recent evidence of risks associated with HRT suggests that its long-term use should be seriously evaluated. Men do not experience an inability to father children in middle age, although their testosterone levels decline. A male menopause, like the dramatic decline in estrogen in women, does not occur. Sexual behavior occurs less frequently in middle adulthood than in early adulthood. Nonetheless, a majority of middle-aged adults show a moderate or strong interest in sex.

3   COGNITIVE DEVELOPMENT: IDENTIFY COGNITIVE CHANGES IN MIDDLE ADULTHOOD

Intelligence

- Horn argued that crystallized intelligence (accumulated information and verbal skills) continues to increase in middle adulthood, whereas fluid intelligence (ability to reason abstractly) begins to decline. Schaie and Willis found that longitudinal assessments of intellectual abilities are less likely than cross-sectional assessments to find declines in middle adulthood and are even more likely to find improvements. The highest level of four intellectual abilities (vocabulary, verbal memory, inductive reasoning, and spatial orientation) occurred in middle age. Recent analysis shows considerable individual variation in intellectual abilities across middle adulthood and indicates that variations in some abilities are more predictive of cognitive impairment in late adulthood than others.

Information Processing

- Speed of information processing, often assessed through reaction time, continues to decline in middle adulthood. Although Schaie found that verbal memory increased in middle age, some researchers have found that memory declines in middle age. Working memory declines in late middle age. Memory is more likely to decline in middle age when individuals don't use effective strategies. Expertise involves having an extensive, highly organized knowledge and an understanding of a particular domain. Expertise often increases in the middle adulthood years. Practical problem solving remains stable in the early and middle adulthood years but declines in late adulthood.

4   CAREERS, WORK, AND LEISURE: CHARACTERIZE CAREER DEVELOPMENT, WORK, AND LESIURE IN MIDDLE ADULTHOOD

Work in Midlife

- For many people, midlife is a time of reflection, assessment, and evaluation of their current work and what they plan to do in the future. One important issue is whether individuals will continue to do the type of work they presently do or change jobs or careers.

Career Challenges and Changes

- The current middle-aged worker faces such challenges as the globalization of work, rapid developments in information technologies, downsizing of organizations, early retirement, and concerns about pensions and health care. Midlife job or career changes can be self-motivated or forced on individuals.

Leisure

- We not only need to learn to work well, but we also need to learn to enjoy leisure. Midlife may be an especially important time for leisure because of the physical changes that occur and because of preparation for an active retirement.

5   RELIGION AND MEANING IN LIFE: EXPLAIN THE ROLES OF RELIGION AND MEANING IN LIFE DURING MIDDLE ADULTHOOD

Religion and Adult Lives

- Religion is an important dimension of many Americans' lives, as well as the lives of people around the world. Females show a stronger interest in religion than males do. It is important to consider individual differences in religious interest.

Religion and Health

- In some cases, religion can be negatively linked to physical health, as when cults or religious sects discourage individuals from obtaining medical care. In mainstream religions, religion usually shows either a positive association or no association with physical health. Religion can play an important role in coping for some individuals. Religion can help bereaved individuals reframe their loss and find avenues for personal growth.

Meaning in Life

- Frankl argues that examining the finiteness of our existence leads to exploration of meaning in life. Faced with the death of older relatives and less time to live themselves, many middle-aged individuals increasingly examine life's meaning. Baumeister and Vohs argue that a quest for a meaningful life involves four main needs: purpose, values, efficacy, and self-worth.

KEY TERMS

middle adulthood 475
chronic disorders 480
climacteric 483

menopause 483
erectile dysfunction 484
crystallized intelligence 486

fluid intelligence 486
working memory 488

leisure 491
meaning-making coping 493

KEY PEOPLE

Gilbert Brim 476
John Horn 486
K. Warner Schaie 487

Sherry Willis 487
Denise Park 488
Nancy Denney 489

John Clausen 492
Crystal Park 493
Victor Frankl 493

Roy Baumeister and Kathleen
Vohs 494

E-LEARNING TOOLS

To help you master the material in this chapter, visit the Online Learning Center for *Life-Span Development*, twelfth edition, at **www.mhhe.com/santrockld12**.

Self-Assessment

Connect to **www.mhhe.com/santrockld12** to reflect on philosophical issues by completing the self-assessments, *My Spiritual Well-Being* and *What Is My Purpose in Life?*

Taking It to the Net

Connect to **www.mhhe.com/santrockld12** to research the answers to these questions:

1. In their book, *Midlife Crisis at 30: How the Stakes Have Changed for a New Generation and What to Do About It* (Rodale Press, 2004), Lia Macko and Kerry Rubin describe how young professional women face a "midlife crisis." They claim that a woman's experience at age 30 today is analogous to what men have traditionally experienced at age 50. What changing factors would account for this alleged shift? Do you think Macko and Rubin overstate their case or oversimplify it at any point?

2. Advances in health and hygiene mean that Americans tend to live longer. What do we need to know about how to cultivate physical health and productivity in America's aging population?

3. Harry can't decide whether to go to theological seminary to study for the ministry or go to medical school. Recent polls indicate that his interests are not necessarily incompatible. What are people reporting about the role of religion in mental and physical health?

Health and Well-Being, Parenting, and Education Exercises

Build your decision-making skills by trying your hand at the health and well-being, parenting, and education exercises. Connect to **www.mhhe.com/santrockld12** to research the answers and complete the exercises.

16

*The generations of
living things pass in
a short time, and like
runners, hand on the
torch of life.*

—Lucretius
Roman Poet, 1st Century b.c.

LEARNING GOALS

◆ Describe personality theories and
   development in middle adulthood.

◆ Discuss stability and change
   in development during middle
   adulthood, including longitudinal
   studies.

◆ Identify some important aspects
   of close relationships in middle
   adulthood.

SOCIOEMOTIONAL DEVELOPMENT IN MIDDLE ADULTHOOD

CHAPTER OUTLINE

Images of Life-Span Development
Middle-Age Variations

Forty-five-year-old Sarah feels tired, depressed, and angry when she looks back on the way her life has gone. She became pregnant when she was 17 and married Ben, the baby's father. They stayed together for three years after their son was born, and then Ben left her for another woman. Sarah went to work as a salesclerk to make ends meet. Eight years later, she married Alan, who had two children of his own from a previous marriage. Sarah stopped working for several years to care for the children. Then, like Ben, Alan started going out on her. She found out about it from a friend. Nevertheless, Sarah stayed with Alan for another year. Finally he was gone so much that she could not take it anymore and decided to divorce him. Sarah went back to work again as a salesclerk; she has been in the same position for 16 years now. During those 16 years, she has dated a number of men, but the relationships never seemed to work out. Her son never finished high school and has drug problems. Her father just died last year, and Sarah is trying to help her mother financially, although she can barely pay her own bills. Sarah looks in the mirror and does not like what she sees. She sees her past as a shambles, and the future does not look rosy, either.

Forty-five-year-old Wanda feels energetic, happy, and satisfied. As a young woman, she graduated from college and worked for three years as a high school math teacher. She married Andy, who had just finished law school. One year later, they had their first child, Josh. Wanda stayed home with Josh for two years, and then returned to her job as a math teacher. Even during her pregnancy, Wanda stayed active and exercised regularly, playing tennis almost every day. After her pregnancy, she kept up her exercise habits. Wanda and Andy had another child, Wendy. Now, as they move into their middle-age years, their children are both off to college, and Wanda and Andy are enjoying spending more time with each other. Last weekend they visited Josh at his college, and the weekend before they visited Wendy at her college. Wanda continued working as a high school math teacher until six years ago. She had developed computer skills as part of her job and taken some computer courses at a nearby college, doubling up during the summer months. She resigned her math teaching job and took a job with a computer company, where she has already worked her way into management. Wanda looks in the mirror and likes what she sees. She sees her past as enjoyable, although not without hills and valleys, and she looks to the future with zest and enthusiasm.

PREVIEW

As with Sarah and Wanda, there are individual variations in the way people experience middle age. To begin the chapter, we will examine personality theories and development in middle age, including ideas about individual variation. Then we will turn our attention to how much individuals change or stay the same as they go through the adult years and finally explore a number of aspects of close relationships during the middle adulthood years.

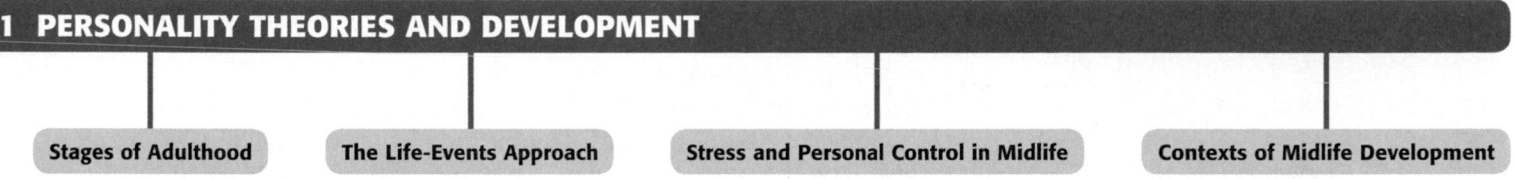

1 PERSONALITY THEORIES AND DEVELOPMENT

| Stages of Adulthood | The Life-Events Approach | Stress and Personal Control in Midlife | Contexts of Midlife Development |

What is the best way to conceptualize middle age? Is it a stage or a crisis? How extensively is middle age influenced by life events? Do middle-aged adults experience stress and personal control differently than young and older adults? Is personality linked with contexts such as the point in history in which individuals go through midlife, their culture, and their gender?

Stages of Adulthood

Adult stage theories have been plentiful, and they have contributed to the view that midlife brings a crisis in development. Two prominent theories that define stages of adult development are Erik Erikson's life-span view and Daniel Levinson's seasons of a man's life.

Erikson's Stage of Generativity versus Stagnation
Erikson (1968) proposed that middle-aged adults face a significant issue—generativity versus stagnation, which is the name Erikson gave to the seventh stage in his life-span theory. *Generativity* encompasses adults' desire to leave legacies of themselves to the next generation (Petersen, 2002). Through these legacies adults achieve a kind of immortality. By contrast, *stagnation* (sometimes called "self-absorption") develops when individuals sense that they have done nothing for the next generation.

Middle-aged adults can develop generativity in a number of ways (Kotre, 1984). Through biological generativity, adults have offspring. Through parental generativity, adults nurture and guide children. Through work generativity, adults develop skills that are passed down to others. And through cultural generativity, adults create, renovate, or conserve some aspect of culture that ultimately survives.

Through generativity, adults promote and guide the next generation by parenting, teaching, leading, and doing things that benefit the community (Petersen, 2006; Pratt & others, 2008a, b). One of the participants in a study of aging said: "From twenty to thirty I learned how to get along with my wife. From thirty to forty I learned how to be a success at my job, and at forty to fifty I worried less about myself and more about the children" (Vaillant, 2002, p. 114). Generative adults commit themselves to the continuation and improvement of society as a whole through their connection to the next generation. Generative adults develop a positive legacy of the self and then offer it as a gift to the next generation.

Does research support Erikson's theory that generativity is an important dimension of middle age? Yes, it does (Coleman & Podolskij, 2007; Gramling, 2007; Pratt & others, 2008a, b). One recent study revealed that parents' generativity was linked to young adult offsprings' successful development (Peterson, 2006). In this study, parents who were generative had young adult children who were conscientious and agreeable.

In another study, Carol Ryff (1984) examined the views of women and men at different ages and found that middle-aged adults especially were concerned about generativity. In yet another study, generative women with careers found gratification through work; generative women who had not worked in a career experienced gratification through parenting (Peterson & Stewart, 1996). And in a longitudinal study of Smith College women, generativity increased from the thirties through the fifties (Stewart, Ostrove, & Helson, 2001; Zucker, Ostrove, & Stewart, 2002) (see Figure 16.1).

One modification of Erikson's theory proposes that Erikson's three adult stages—involving intimacy (early adulthood), generativity (middle adulthood), and integrity

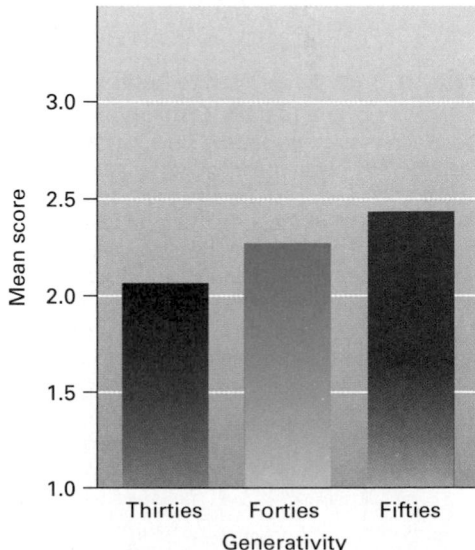

FIGURE 16.1 Changes in Generativity from the Thirties Through the Fifties. Generativity increased in Smith College women as they aged from their thirties through their fifties (Stewart, Ostrove, & Helson, 2001). The women rated themselves on a 3-point scale indicating the extent to which they thought the statements about generativity were descriptive of their lives. Higher scores reflect greater generativity.

Generativity

Feeling needed by people

Effort to ensure that young people get their chance to develop

Influence in my community or area of interest

A new level of productivity or effectiveness

Appreciation and awareness of older people

Having a wider perspective

Interest in things beyond my family

Identity certainty

A sense of being my own person

Excitement, turmoil, confusion about my impulses and potential (reversed)

Coming near the end of one road and not yet finding another (reversed)

Feeling my life is moving well

Searching for a sense of who I am (reversed)

Wishing I had a wider scope to my life (reversed)

Anxiety that I won't live up to opportunities (reversed)

Feeling secure and committed

FIGURE 16.2 Items Used to Assess Generativity and Identity Certainty. These items were used to assess generativity and identity certainty in the longitudinal study of Smith College women (Stewart, Ostrove, & Helson, 2001). In the assessment of identity certainty, five of the items involved reversed scoring. For example, if an individual scored high on the item "Searching for a sense of who I am," it was an indication of identity uncertainty rather than identity certainty.

Mid-life crises are greatly exaggerated in America.

—GEORGE VAILLANT

Contemporary Psychologist, Harvard University

(late adulthood)—are best viewed as developmental phases within identity. In this view, identity remains the central core of the self's development across all of the adult years (Whitbourne & Connolly, 1999).

Whether or not identity holds this central place in adult development, research does support its continuing importance during middle adulthood. For example, in one study, having a positive identity was linked with generativity in middle age (Vandewater, Ostrove, & Stewart, 1997). In the longitudinal study of Smith College women, identity certainty increased from the thirties through the fifties. Figure 16.2 describes the items that were used to assess generativity and identity certainty in the Smith College Study.

Levinson's Seasons of a Man's Life In *The Seasons of a Man's Life* (1978), clinical psychologist Daniel Levinson reported the results of extensive interviews with forty middle-aged men. The interviews were conducted with hourly workers, business executives, academic biologists, and novelists. Levinson bolstered his conclusions with information from the biographies of famous men and the development of memorable characters in literature. Although Levinson's major interest focused on midlife change, he described a number of stages and transitions during the period from 17 to 65 years of age, as shown in Figure 16.3. Levinson emphasizes that developmental tasks must be mastered at each stage.

At the end of one's teens, according to Levinson, a transition from dependence to independence should occur. This transition is marked by the formation of a dream— an image of the kind of life the youth wants to have, especially in terms of a career and marriage. Levinson sees the twenties as a *novice phase* of adult development. It is a time of reasonably free experimentation and of testing the dream in the real world. In early adulthood, the two major tasks to be mastered are exploring the possibilities for adult living and developing a stable life structure.

From about the ages of 28 to 33, the man goes through a transition period in which he must face the more serious question of determining his goals. During the thirties, he usually focuses on family and career development. In the later years of this period, he enters a phase of *Becoming One's Own Man* (or BOOM, as Levinson calls it). By age 40, he has reached a stable location in his career, has outgrown his earlier, more tenuous attempts at learning to become an adult, and now must look forward to the kind of life he will lead as a middle-aged adult.

According to Levinson, the transition to middle adulthood lasts about five years (ages 40 to 45) and requires the adult male to come to grips with four major conflicts that have existed in his life since adolescence: (1) being young versus being old, (2) being destructive versus being constructive, (3) being masculine versus being feminine, and (4) being attached to others versus being separated from them. Seventy to 80 percent of the men Levinson interviewed found the midlife transition tumultuous and psychologically painful, as many aspects of their lives came into question. According to Levinson, the success of the midlife transition rests on how effectively the individual reduces the polarities and accepts each of them as an integral part of his being.

Because Levinson interviewed middle-aged males, we can consider the data about middle adulthood more valid than the data about early adulthood. When individuals are asked to remember information about earlier parts of their lives, they may distort and forget things. The original Levinson data included no females, although Levinson (1996) reported that his stages, transitions, and the crisis of middle age hold for females as well as males. Levinson's work included no statistical analysis. However, the quality and quantity of the Levinson biographies make them outstanding examples of the clinical tradition.

How Pervasive Are Midlife Crises? Levinson (1978) views midlife as a crisis, arguing that the middle-aged adult is suspended between the past and the future, trying to cope with this gap that threatens life's continuity. George Vaillant (1977) has a different view. Vaillant's study—called the "Grant Study"—involved Harvard University men in their early thirties and in their late forties who initially had been interviewed as undergraduates. He concludes that just as adolescence is a time for detecting parental flaws and discovering the truth about childhood, the forties are a decade of reassessing and recording the truth about the adolescent and adulthood years. However, whereas Levinson sees midlife as a crisis, Vaillant maintains that only a minority of adults experience a midlife crisis:

> Just as pop psychologists have reveled in the not-so-common high drama of adolescent turmoil, also the popular press, sensing good copy, had made all too much of the mid-life crisis. The term mid-life crisis brings to mind some variation of the renegade minister who leaves behind four children and the congregation that loved him in order to drive off in a magenta Porsche with a 25-year-old striptease artiste. As with adolescent turmoil, mid-life crises are much rarer in community samples. (pp. 222–223)

Thus, for most people midlife is not a crisis. As we saw in Chapter 15, many cognitive skills, such as vocabulary, verbal memory, and inductive reasoning, peak in midlife, and many individuals reach the height of their career success in midlife. Further, in midlife, reports of general well-being and life satisfaction tend to be high (Martin, Grunendahl, & Martin, 2001).

Further, the following research studies all document that midlife is not characterized by pervasive crises:

- One study found that 26 percent of middle-aged U.S. adults said they had experienced a midlife crisis, but most attributed the crisis to negative life events rather than aging (Wethington, Kessler, & Pixley, 2004).

- A longitudinal study of more than 2,000 individuals found few midlife crises (McCrae & Costa, 1990; Siegler & Costa, 1999). In this study, the emotional instability of individuals did not significantly increase through their middle-aged years (see Figure 16.4).

- A study found that adults experienced a peak of personal control and power in middle age (Clark-Plaskie & Lachman, 1999).

- A study of individuals described as young (average age 19), middle-aged (average age 46), and older (average age 73) adults found that their ability to master their environment, autonomy, and personal relations improved during middle age (Keyes & Ryff, 1998) (see Figure 16.5).

Adult development experts are virtually unanimous in their belief that midlife crises have been exaggerated (Brim, Ryff, & Kessler, 2004; Lachman, 2004; Wethington, Kessler, & Pixley, 2004). In sum:

- The stage theories place too much emphasis on crises in development, especially midlife crises.

- There often is considerable individual variation in the way people experience the stages, a topic that we will turn to next.

Individual Variations Stage theories focus on the universals of adult personality development as they try to pin down stages that all individuals go through in their adult lives. These theories do not adequately address individual variations in adult development. One extensive study of a random sample of 500 men at midlife, for example, found extensive individual variation among men (Farrell & Rosenberg, 1981). In the individual variations view, middle-aged adults interpret, shape, alter, and give meaning to their lives (Arpanantikui, 2004).

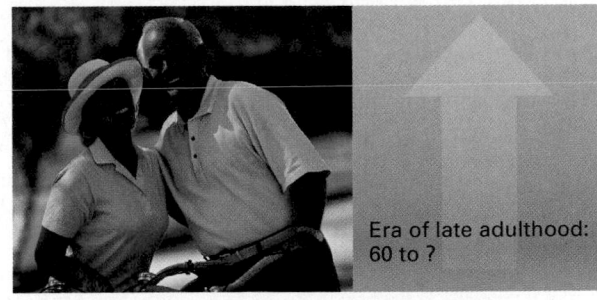

Era of late adulthood: 60 to ?

Late adult transition: Age 60 to 65

Culminating life structure for middle adulthood: 55 to 60

Age 50 transition: 50 to 55

Entry life structure for middle adulthood: 45 to 50

Middle adult transition: Age 40 to 45

Culminating life structure for early adulthood: 33 to 40

Age 30 transition: 28 to 33

Entry life structure for early adulthood: 22 to 28

Early adult transition: Age 17 to 22

FIGURE 16.3 Levinson's Periods of Adult Development (above). According to Levinson, adulthood for men has three main stages, which are surrounded by transition periods. Specific tasks and challenges are associated with each stage.

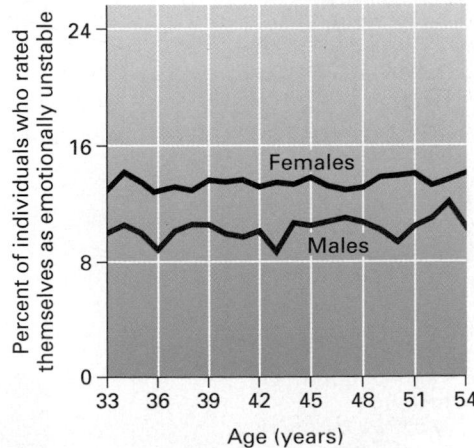

FIGURE 16.4 Emotional Instability and Age. In one longitudinal study, the emotional instability of individuals was assessed from age 33 to age 54 (McCrae & Costa, 1990). No significant increase in emotional instability occurred during the middle-aged years.

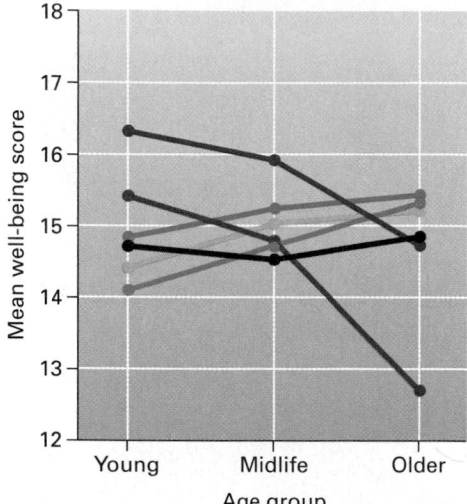

Dimensions of well-being
— Self-acceptance
— Purpose in life
— Positive relations
— Environmental mastery
— Personal growth
— Autonomy

FIGURE 16.5 Age and Well-Being (above). In one study, six dimensions of well-being (self-acceptance, positive relations, personal growth, purpose in life, environmental mastery, and autonomy) were assessed in three different age groups of individuals (young adults, middle-aged adults, and older adults) (Keyes & Ryff, 1998). An increase or little change in most of the dimensions of well-being occurred during middle adulthood.

Some individuals may experience a midlife crisis in some contexts of their lives but not others (Lachman, 2004). For example, turmoil and stress may characterize a person's life at work even while things are going smoothly at home.

Researchers have found that in one-third of the cases in which individuals have reported having a midlife crisis, the "crisis is triggered by life events such as a job loss, financial problems, or illness" (Lachman, 2004, p. 315). Let's now explore the role of life events in midlife development.

The Life-Events Approach

Age-related stages represent one major way to examine adult personality development. A second major way to conceptualize adult personality development is to focus on life events (Lorenz & others, 2006; Murray & Zautra, 2007). In the early version of the life-events approach, life events were viewed as taxing circumstances for individuals, forcing them to change their personality (Holmes & Rahe, 1967). Such events as the death of a spouse, divorce, marriage, and so on were believed to involve varying degrees of stress, and therefore likely to influence the individual's development.

Today's life-events approach is more sophisticated. In the **contemporary life-events approach**, how life events influence the individual's development depends not only on the life event itself but also on mediating factors (such as physical health and family supports), the individual's adaptation to the life event (such as appraisal of the threat and coping strategies), the life-stage context, and the sociohistorical context (see Figure 16.6). For example, if individuals are in poor health and have little family support, life events are likely to be more stressful. And a divorce may be more stressful after many years of marriage when adults are in their fifties than when they have only been married several years and are in their twenties (Chiriboga, 1982), indicating that the life-stage context of an event makes a difference. The sociohistorical context also makes a difference. For example, adults may be able to cope more effectively with divorce today than in the 1950s because divorce has become more commonplace and accepted in today's society. Whatever the context or mediating variables, however, one individual may perceive a life event as highly stressful, whereas another individual may perceive the same event as a challenge.

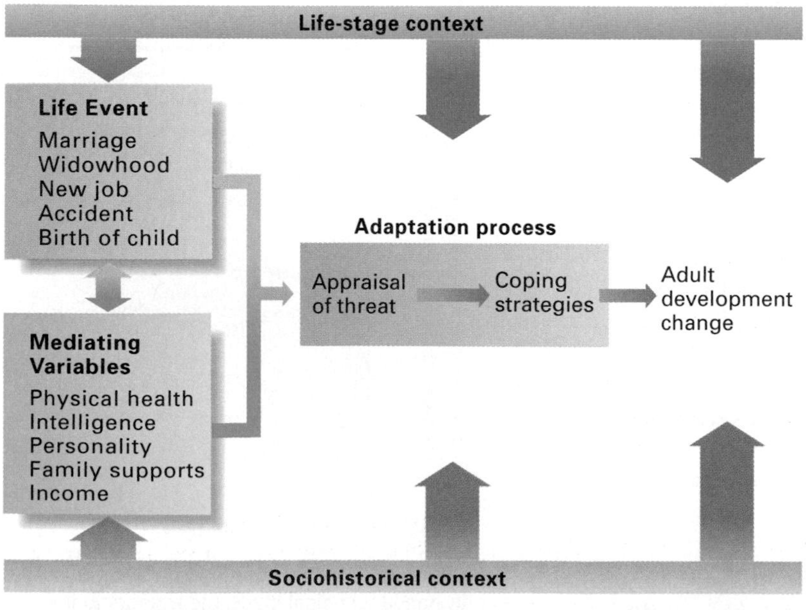

Though the life-events approach is a valuable addition to understanding adult development, like other approaches to adult development, it has its drawbacks. One of the most significant drawbacks is that the life-events approach places too much emphasis on change, not adequately recognizing the stability that, at least to some degree, characterizes adult development.

Another drawback of the life-events approach is that it may not be life's major events that are the primary sources of stress, but our daily experiences (Jacobs & others, 2006). Enduring a boring but tense job or marriage and living in poverty do not show up on scales of major life events. Yet the everyday pounding we take from these living conditions can add up to a highly stressful life and eventually illness.

Some psychologists conclude that we can gain greater insight into the source of life's stresses by focusing less on major events and more on daily hassles and daily uplifts (Baker, 2006; Neupert, Almeida, & Charles, 2007). One study found that the most frequent daily hassles of college students were wasting time, concerns about meeting high standards, and being lonely (Kanner & others, 1981). Among the most frequent uplifts of the college students were entertainment, getting along well with friends, and completing a task. In this

FIGURE 16.6 A Contemporary Life-Events Framework for Interpreting Adult Developmental Change. According to the contemporary life-events approach, the influence of a life event depends on the event itself, on mediating variables, on the life-stage and sociohistorical context, and on the individual's appraisal of the event and coping strategies.

Life-stage context

Life Event
Marriage
Widowhood
New job
Accident
Birth of child

Mediating Variables
Physical health
Intelligence
Personality
Family supports
Income

Adaptation process
Appraisal of threat → Coping strategies → Adult development change

Sociohistorical context

same study, the most frequent daily hassles of middle-aged adults were concerns about weight and the health of a family member, while their most frequent daily uplifts involved relating well with a spouse or lover, or a friend (see Figure 16.7). And the middle-aged adults were more likely than the college students to report that their daily hassles involved economic concerns (rising prices and taxes, for example). Critics of the daily hassles approach argue that some of the same problems involved with life-events scales occur when daily hassles are assessed (Dohrenwend & Shrout, 1985). For example, knowing about an adult's daily hassles tells us nothing about physical changes, about how the individual copes with hassles, or about how the individual perceives hassles.

Stress and Personal Control in Midlife

As we have seen, there is conclusive evidence that midlife is not a time when a majority of adults experience a tumultuous crisis, and when they do experience a midlife crisis it is often linked to stressful life events. Do middle-aged adults experience stress differently than young adults and older adults? One study using daily diaries over a one-week period found that both young and middle-aged adults had more days that were stressful and that were characterized by multiple stresses than older adults (Almeida & Horn, 2004). In this study, although young adults experienced daily stressors more frequently than middle-aged adults, middle-aged adults experienced more "overload" stressors that involved juggling too many activities at once. A recent study also revealed that middle-aged and older adults showed a smaller increase in psychological distress to interpersonal stressors than younger adults, and middle-aged adults were less physically reactive to work stressors than were younger adults (Neupert, Almeida, & Charles, 2007).

To what extent do middle-aged adults perceive that they can control what happens to them? Researchers have found that on average a sense of personal control decreases as adults become older (Lachman, 2006). In one study, approximately 80 percent of the young adults (25 to 39 years of age), 71 percent of the middle-aged adults (40 to 59 years of age), and 62 percent of the older adults (60 to 75 years of age) reported that they were often in control of their lives (Lachman & Firth, 2004). However, some aspects of personal control increase with age while others decrease (Lachman, 2006). For example, middle-aged adults feel they have a greater sense of control over their finances, work, and marriage than younger adults but less control over their sex life and their children (Lachman & Firth, 2004; Lachman & Weaver, 1998).

Contexts of Midlife Development

Both Sarah and Wanda, whose stories appeared at the opening to this chapter, are working mothers. In almost every other way, however, their lives could scarcely be more different. Why? Part of the answer might lie in the different contexts of their lives. The contemporary life-events approach (like Bronfenbrenner's theory, discussed in Chapter 1) highlights the importance of the complex setting of our lives—of everything from our income and family supports to our sociohistorical circumstances. Let's examine how three aspects of the contexts of life influence development during middle adulthood: historical contexts (cohort effects), gender, and culture.

Historical Contexts (Cohort Effects)   Some developmentalists argue that changing historical times and different social expectations influence how different cohorts—groups of individuals born in the same year or time period—move through the life span (Schaie, 2007). Bernice Neugarten (1986) argues that our values, attitudes, expectations, and behaviors are influenced by the period in which we live. For example, individuals born during the difficult times of the Great Depression may have a different outlook on life than those born during the optimistic 1950s, says Neugarten.

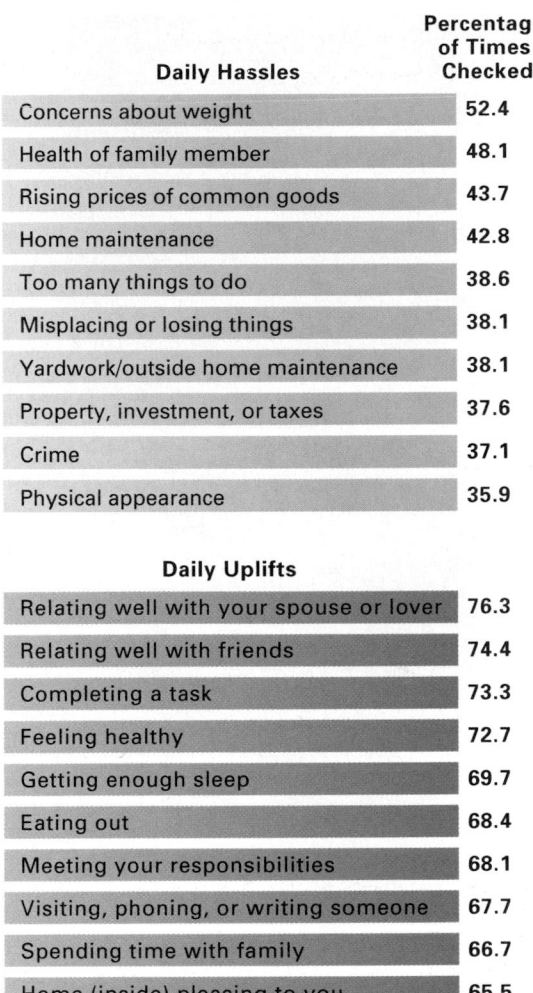

Daily Hassles	Percentage of Times Checked
Concerns about weight	52.4
Health of family member	48.1
Rising prices of common goods	43.7
Home maintenance	42.8
Too many things to do	38.6
Misplacing or losing things	38.1
Yardwork/outside home maintenance	38.1
Property, investment, or taxes	37.6
Crime	37.1
Physical appearance	35.9

Daily Uplifts	
Relating well with your spouse or lover	76.3
Relating well with friends	74.4
Completing a task	73.3
Feeling healthy	72.7
Getting enough sleep	69.7
Eating out	68.4
Meeting your responsibilities	68.1
Visiting, phoning, or writing someone	67.7
Spending time with family	66.7
Home (inside) pleasing to you	65.5

FIGURE 16.7 The Ten Most Frequent Daily Hassles and Uplifts of Middle-Aged Adults over a Nine-Month Period. *How do these hassles and uplifts compare with your own?*

contemporary life-events approach Emphasizes that how a life event influences the individual's development depends not only on the life event, but also on mediating factors, the individual's adaptation to the life event, the life-stage context, and the sociohistorical context.

Activity/event	Appropriate age range	Percent who agree (late '50s study)		Percent who agree (late '70s study)	
		Men	Women	Men	Women
Best age for a man to marry	20–25	80	90	42	42
Best age for a woman to marry	19–24	85	90	44	36
When most people should become grandparents	45–50	84	79	64	57
Best age for most people to finish school and go to work	20–22	86	82	36	38
When most men should be settled on a career	24–26	74	64	24	26
When most men hold their top jobs	45–50	71	58	38	31
When most people should be ready to retire	60–65	83	86	66	41
When a man has the most responsibilities	35–50	79	75	49	50
When a man accomplishes most	40–50	82	71	46	41
The prime of life for a man	35–50	86	80	59	66
When a woman has the most responsibilities	25–40	93	91	59	53
When a woman accomplishes most	30–45	94	92	57	48

FIGURE 16.8 Individuals' Conceptions of the Best Age for Major Life Events and Achievements: Late 1950s and Late 1970s. *What do you think is the best age to experience these major life events and accomplishments?*

Neugarten (1986) holds that the social environment of a particular age group can alter its **social clock**—the timetable according to which individuals are expected to accomplish life's tasks, such as getting married, having children, or establishing themselves in a career. Social clocks provide guides for our lives; individuals whose lives are not synchronized with these social clocks find life to be more stressful than those who are on schedule, says Neugarten. For example, the fact that Sarah's pregnancy occurred when she was a teenager probably increased the stressfulness of that pregnancy. Neugarten argues that today there is much less agreement than in the past on the right age or sequence for the occurrence of major life events such as having children or retiring. Indeed, one study found that, between the late 1950s and the late 1970s, there was a dramatic decline in adults' beliefs that there is a "best age" for major life events and achievements (Passuth, Maines, & Neugarten, 1984) (see Figure 16.8).

Trying to tease out universal truths and patterns about adult development from one birth cohort is complicated because the findings may not apply to another birth cohort. Most of the individuals studied by Levinson and Vaillant, for example, were born before and during the Great Depression. What was true for these individuals may not be true for the post–baby-boom generation as they approach the midlife transition. The midlife men in Levinson's and Vaillant's studies might have been burned out at a premature age rather than being representatives of a normal developmental pattern (Rossi, 1989).

Gender Contexts Critics say that the stage theories of adult development have a male bias (Deutsch, 1991). For example, the central focus of stage theories is on career choice and work achievement, which historically have dominated men's life choices and life chances more than women's. The stage theories do not adequately address women's concerns about relationships, interdependence, and caring (Gilligan, 1982).

social clock The timetable according to which individuals are expected to accomplish life's tasks, such as getting married, having children, or establishing themselves in a career.

The adult stage theories have also placed little importance on childbearing and child rearing. Women's family roles are complex and often have a higher salience in their lives than in men's lives. The role demands that women experience in balancing career and family are usually not experienced as intensely by men. And the type of stressors experienced by middle-aged women and men may differ. One study revealed that middle-aged women had more interpersonal stressors, whereas their male counterparts had more self-focused stressors (Almeida & Horn, 2004).

Many women who are now at midlife and beyond experienced a role shift in their late twenties, thirties, or beyond (Fodor & Franks, 1990). As they were engaging in traditional roles, the women's movement began and changed the lives of a substantial number of traditionally raised women and their families. Changes are still occurring for many midlife women (George, 2006; Moen & Spencer, 2006). Basic changes in social attitudes regarding labor force participation, families, and gender roles have begun to broaden the opportunities available for women in middle adulthood as well as other life-span periods (Moen & Wethington, 1999). The effects of these changes are the most far-reaching for the baby-boom cohort now moving through midlife. The employment patterns across the life span for women now in their middle adult years more closely resemble those of men than they did in the past (Contemporary Research Press, 1993).

Should midlife and the years beyond be feared by women as bringing the loss of youth and opportunity, a time of decline? Or is it a new prime of life, a time for renewal, for shedding preoccupations with a youthful appearance and body, and for seeking new challenges, valuing maturity, and enjoying change?

In one study, the early fifties were indeed a new prime of life for many women (Mitchell & Helson, 1990). In the sample of 700 women aged 26 to 80, women in their early fifties most often described their lives as "first-rate." Conditions that distinguished the lives of women in their early fifties from those of women in other age periods included more "empty nests," better health, higher income, and more concern for parents. Women in their early fifties showed confidence, involvement, security, and breadth of personality.

In sum, the view that midlife is a negative age period for women is stereotypical, as so many perceptions of age periods are (Aldwin & Levenson, 2001). Midlife is a diversified, heterogeneous period for women, just as it is for men.

Critics say the stage theories of adult development have a male bias by emphasizing career choice and achievement, and that they do not adequately address women's concerns about relationships, interdependence, and caring. The stage theories assume a normative sequence of development, but as women's roles have become more varied and complex, determining what is normative is difficult. *What kinds of changes have taken place in middle-aged women's lives in recent years?*

Cultural Contexts   In many cultures, especially nonindustrialized cultures, the concept of middle age is not very clear, or in some cases is absent. It is common in nonindustrialized societies to describe individuals as young or old, but not as middle-aged (Grambs, 1989). Some cultures have no words for "adolescent," "young adult," or "middle-aged adult."

Consider the Gusii culture, located south of the equator in the African country of Kenya. The Gusii divide the life course differently for females and males (LeVine, 1979): females: (1) infant, (2) uncircumcised girl, (3) circumcised girl, (4) married woman, and (5) female elder; males: (1) infant, (2) uncircumcised boy, (3) circumcised boy warrior, and (4) male elder. Thus, movement from one status to the next is due primarily to life events, not age, in the Gusii culture.

Although the Gusii do not have a clearly labeled midlife transition, some of the Gusii adults do reassess their lives around the age of 40. At this time, these Gusii adults examine their current status and the limited time they have remaining in their lives. Their physical strength is decreasing, and they know they cannot farm their land forever, so they seek spiritual powers by becoming ritual practitioners or healers. As in the American culture, however, a midlife crisis in the Gusii culture is the exception rather than the rule.

What is middle age like for women in other cultures? It depends on the modernity of the culture and the culture's view of gender roles (Dittmann-Kohli, 2005). Some anthropologists believe that when women become middle-aged in nonindustrialized societies they may experience certain advantages (Brown, 1985). First, they are often

Gusii dancers perform on habitat day in Nairobi, Kenya. Movement from one status to another in the Gusii culture is due primarily to life events, not age. The Gusii do not have a clearly labeled midlife transition.

freed from cumbersome restrictions that were placed on them when they were younger. For example, in middle age they enjoy greater geographical mobility. Child care has ceased or can be delegated, and domestic chores are reduced. They may venture forth from the village for commercial opportunities, visits to relatives living at a distance, and religious events. Second, with middle age a woman has the right to exercise authority over specified younger kin. Middle-aged women can extract labor from younger family members. The work of middle-aged women tends to be administrative, delegating tasks and making assignments to younger women. Middle-aged women also make important decisions for certain members of the younger generation: what a grandchild is to be named, who is ready to be initiated, and who is eligible to marry whom. A third major change brought on by middle age in nonindustrialized societies is eligibility for special statuses and the possibility that these provide recognition beyond the household. These statuses include the vocations of midwife, curer, holy woman, and matchmaker.

Even among industrialized cultures, the cultural context of middle-age development may differ in significant ways. Consider the social clock. In one study, Australian adults were asked the same questions about the best age for experiencing various life circumstances as Neugarten had asked American adults (Peterson, 1996). Compared with the Americans, the Australian adults advocated later ages for marriage and grandparenthood, a younger age for leaving school, and a broader age range for retiring.

Review and Reflect: Learning Goal 1

 Describe Personality Theories and Development in Middle Adulthood

REVIEW

- What are some theories of adult stages of development?
- What is the life-events approach?
- How do middle-aged adults experience stress and personal control differently than young and older adults?
- How do contexts influence midlife development?

REFLECT

- Which approach makes more sense to you—adult stage or life events? Or do you think both approaches should be considered in understanding an adult's development? Explain your answer.

2 STABILITY AND CHANGE

Longitudinal Studies

Conclusions

Sarah's adult life, described in the chapter opening, has followed a painful path. Were her sorrows inevitable as a result of how she learned to cope with problems earlier in life? Now middle-aged, is it possible for her to change her coping strategies or how she relates to other people? Recall from Chapter 1 that questions like these about stability and change are an important issue in life-span development.

Openness	**C**onscientiousness	**E**xtraversion	**A**greeableness	**N**euroticism (emotional stability)
• Imaginative or practical	• Organized or disorganized	• Sociable or retiring	• Softhearted or ruthless	• Calm or anxious
• Interested in variety or routine	• Careful or careless	• Fun-loving or somber	• Trusting or suspicious	• Secure or insecure
• Independent or conforming	• Disciplined or impulsive	• Affectionate or reserved	• Helpful or uncooperative	• Self-satisfied or self-pitying

FIGURE 16.9 The Big Five Factors of Personality. Each of the broad supertraits that encompasses more narrow traits and characteristics. Use the acronym OCEAN to remember the big five personality factors (openness, conscientiousness, extraversion, agreeableness, neuroticism).

Longitudinal Studies

We will examine four longitudinal studies to help us understand the extent to which there is stability or change in adult development: Costa and McCrae's Baltimore Study, the Berkeley Longitudinal Studies, Helson's Mills College Study, and Vaillant's studies.

Costa and McCrae's Baltimore Study   A major study of adult personality development continues to be conducted by Paul Costa and Robert McCrae (1998; McCrae & Costa, 2003, 2006). They focus on what are called the **Big Five factors of personality**, which are openness to experience, conscientiousness, extraversion, agreeableness, and neuroticism (emotional stability); they are described in Figure 16.9. (Notice that if you create an acronym from these factor names, you will get the word *OCEAN*.) A number of research studies point toward these factors as important dimensions of personality (Costa & McCrae, 1998; McCrae & Costa, 2003, 2006).

Using their five-factor personality test, Costa and McCrae (1995, 2000) studied approximately a thousand college-educated men and women ages 20 to 96, assessing the same individuals over many years. Data collection began in the 1950s to the mid-1960s and is ongoing. Costa and McCrae concluded that considerable stability occurs in the five personality factors—emotional stability, extraversion, openness, agreeableness, and conscientiousness. However, one study found that conscientiousness continued to develop in late adulthood (Roberts, Walton, & Bogg, 2005), and another study revealed that older adults were more conscientious and agreeable than middle-aged and younger adults (Allemand, Zimprich, & Hendriks, 2008).

A recent meta-analysis of personality stability and change organized according to the Big-Five framework included 87 longitudinal studies spanning 10 to 101 years of age (Roberts, Walton, & Viechtbauer, 2006):

- Results for extraversion were complex until it was subdivided into social dominance (assertiveness, dominance) and social vitality (talkativeness, sociability). Social dominance increased from adolescence through middle adulthood, whereas social vitality increased in adolescence and then decreased in early and late adulthood.

- Agreeableness and conscientiousness increased in early and middle adulthood.

- Neuroticism decreased in early adulthood.

- Openness to experience increased in adolescence and early adulthood and then decreased in late adulthood.

In general, personality traits changed most during early adulthood.

Berkeley Longitudinal Studies   In the Berkeley Longitudinal Studies, more than 500 children and their parents were initially studied in the late 1920s and early 1930s. The book *Present and Past in Middle Life* (Eichorn & others, 1981) profiles these individuals

Big Five factors of personality Emotional stability (neuroticism), extraversion, openness to experience, agreeableness, and conscientiousness.

Based on their study of middle-aged women, Ravenna Helson and her colleagues described the women as experiencing a midlife consciousness rather than a midlife crisis. *What were some other findings in the Mills College study?*

as they became middle-aged. The results from early adolescence through a portion of midlife did not support either extreme in the debate over whether personality is characterized by stability or change. Some characteristics were more stable than others, however. The most stable characteristics were the degree to which individuals were intellectually oriented, self-confident, and open to new experiences. The characteristics that changed the most included the extent to which the individuals were nurturant or hostile and whether or not they had good self-control.

John Clausen (1993), one of the researchers in the Berkeley Longitudinal Studies, stresses that too much attention has been given to discontinuities for all members of the human species, as exemplified in the adult stage theories. Rather, he considers that some people experience recurrent crises and change a great deal over the life course, whereas others have more stable, continuous lives and change far less.

Helson's Mills College Study   Another longitudinal investigation of adult personality development was conducted by Ravenna Helson and her colleagues (Helson, 1997; Helson & Wink, 1992; Stewart, Osgrove, & Helson, 2001). They initially studied 132 women who were seniors at Mills College in California in the late 1950s and then studied them again when they were in their thirties, forties, and fifties. Helson and her colleagues distinguished three main groups among the Mills women: family-oriented, career-oriented (whether or not they also wanted families), and those who followed neither path (women without children who pursued only low-level work).

Despite their different college profiles and their diverging life paths, the women in all three groups experienced some similar psychological changes over their adult years. Between the ages of 27 and the early forties, there was a shift toward less traditionally feminine attitudes, including greater dominance, greater interest in events outside the family, and more emotional stability. This may have been due to societal changes from the 1950s to the 1980s rather than to age changes. The women in the third group (women without children who pursued low-level work) changed less than those committed to career or family.

During their early forties, many of the women shared the concerns that stage theorists such as Levinson found in men: concern for young and old, introspectiveness, interest in roots, and awareness of limitations and death. However, the researchers in the Mills College Study concluded that rather than being in a midlife crisis, the women were experiencing *midlife consciousness.* The researchers also indicated that commitment to the tasks of early adulthood—whether to a career or family (or both)—helped women learn to control their impulses, develop interpersonal skills, become independent, and work hard to achieve goals. Women who did not commit themselves to one of these lifestyle patterns faced fewer challenges and did not develop as fully as the other women (Rosenfeld & Stark, 1987).

In the Mills College Study, some women moved toward becoming "pillars of society" in their early forties to early fifties. Menopause, caring for aging parents, and an empty nest were not associated with an increase in responsibility and self-control (Helson & Wink, 1992). The identity certainty and awareness of aging of the Mills College women increased from their thirties through their fifties (Stewart, Osgrove, & Helson, 2001).

George Vaillant's Studies   Longitudinal studies by George Vaillant help us examine a somewhat different question than the studies described so far: Does personality at middle age predict what a person's life will be like in late adulthood? Vaillant (2002) has conducted three longitudinal studies of adult development and aging: (1) a sample of 268 socially advantaged Harvard graduates born about 1920 (called the Grant Study); (2) a sample of 456 socially disadvantaged inner-city men born about 1930; and (3) a sample of 90 middle-SES, intellectually gifted women born about 1910. These individuals have been assessed numerous times (in most cases, every two years), beginning in the 1920s to 1940s and continuing today for those still living. The main assessments involve extensive interviews with the participants, their parents, and teachers.

Vaillant categorized 75- to 80-year-olds as "happy-well," "sad-sick," and "dead." He used data collected from these individuals when they were 50 years of age to predict which categories they were likely to end up in at 75 to 80 years of age. Alcohol abuse and smoking at age 50 were the best predictors of which individuals would be dead at 75 to 80 years of age. Other factors at age 50 were linked with being in the "happy-well" category at 75 to 80 years of age: getting regular exercise, avoiding being overweight, being well-educated, having a stable marriage, being future-oriented, being thankful and forgiving, empathizing with others, being active with other people, and having good coping skills.

Wealth and income at age 50 were not linked with being in the "happy-well" category at 75 to 80 years of age. Generativity in middle age (defined as "taking care of the next generation") was more strongly related than intimacy to whether individuals would have an enduring and happy marriage at 75 to 80 years of age (Vaillant, 2002).

The results for one of Vaillant's studies, the Grant Study of Harvard men, are shown in Figure 16.10. Note that when individuals at 50 years of age were not heavy smokers, did not abuse alcohol, had a stable marriage, exercised, maintained a normal weight, and had good coping skills, they were more likely to be alive and happy at 75 to 80 years of age.

Conclusions

What can be concluded about stability and change in personality development during the adult years? According to a recent research review by leading researchers Brent Roberts and Daniel Mroczek (2008), there is increasing evidence that personality traits continue to change during the adult years, even into late adulthood. However, in the recent meta-analysis of 92 longitudinal studies described earlier, the greatest change in personality traits occurred in early adulthood—from about 20 to 40 years of age (Roberts, Walton, & Viechbauer, 2006).

Thus, people show more stability in their personality when they reach midlife than when they were younger adults. These findings support what is called a *cumulative personality model* of personality development, which states that with time and age people become more adept at interacting with their environment in ways that promotes increased stability in personality (Caspi & Roberts, 2001).

This does not mean that change is absent throughout middle and late adulthood Ample evidence shows that social contexts, new experiences, and sociohistorical changes can affect personality development, but the changes in middle and late adulthood are usually not as great as in early adulthood (Mroczek, Spiro, & Griffin, 2006).

In general, changes in personality traits across adulthood also occur in a positive direction. Over time, "people become more confident, warm, responsible, and calm" (Roberts & Mroczek, 2008, p. 33). Such positive changes equate with becoming more socially mature.

In sum, recent research contradicts the old view that stability in personality begins to set in at about 30 years of age (Roberts & Mroczek, 2008; Roberts, Wood, & Caspi, 2008; Roberts & others, 2008a, b). Although there are some consistent developmental changes in the personality traits of large numbers of people, at the individual level, people can show unique patterns of personality traits—and these patterns often reflect life experiences related to themes of their particular developmental period (Roberts & Mroczek, 2008). For example, researchers have found that individuals who are in a stable marriage and a solid career track become more socially dominant, conscientious, and emotionally stable as they go through early adulthood (Roberts & Wood, 2006). And for some of these individuals, there is greater change in their personality traits than for other individuals (Roberts & Mroczek, 2008; Roberts & others, 2008a, b).

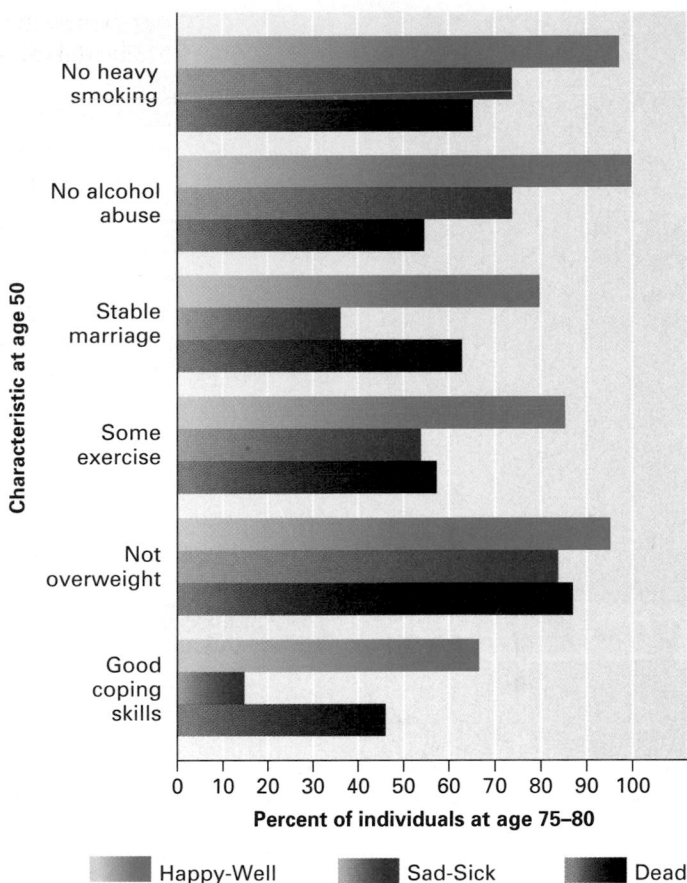

FIGURE 16.10 Links Between Characteristics at Age 50 and Health and Happiness at Age 75 to 80 (above). In a longitudinal study, the characteristics shown above at age 50 were related to whether individuals were happy-well, sad-sick, or dead at age 75 to 80 (Vaillant, 2002).

At age 55, actor Jack Nicholson said "I feel exactly the same as I've always felt: a slightly reined-in voracious beast." Nicholson felt his personality had not changed much. Some others might think they have changed more. *How much does personality change and how does it stay the same through adulthood?*

2 **Discuss Stability and Change in Development During Middle Adulthood, Including Longitudinal Studies**

REVIEW

• Identify four longitudinal studies and describe their results.
• What conclusions can be reached about stability and change in development during middle adulthood

REFLECT

• Why is it important to conduct longitudinal studies when investigating stability and change in development?

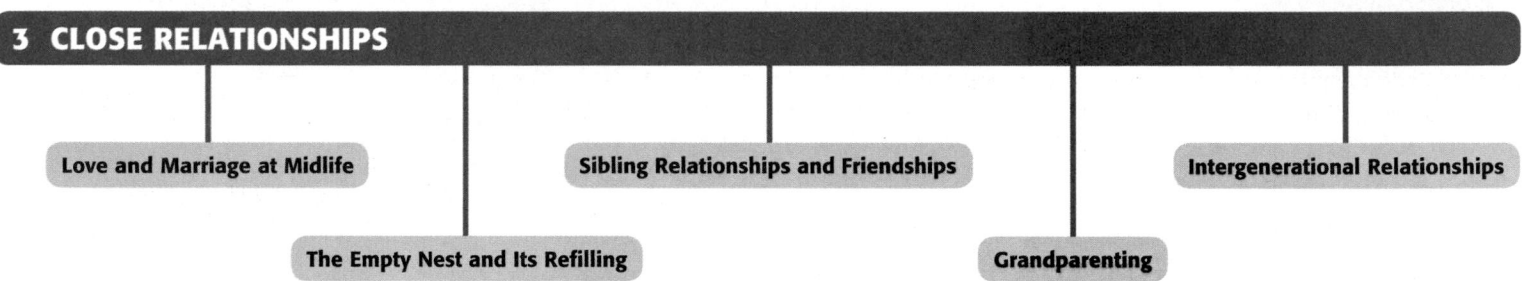

3 CLOSE RELATIONSHIPS

- Love and Marriage at Midlife
- The Empty Nest and Its Refilling
- Sibling Relationships and Friendships
- Grandparenting
- Intergenerational Relationships

There is a consensus among middle-aged **Americans** that a major component of well-being involves positive relationships with others, especially parents, spouse, and offspring (Lachman, 2004; Markus & others, 2004). To begin our examination of midlife relationships, let's explore love and marriage in middle-aged adults.

Love and Marriage at Midlife

What characterizes marriage in middle adulthood?

Remember from Chapter 14 that two major forms of love are romantic love and affectionate love. The fires of romantic love are strong in early adulthood. Affectionate, or companionate, love increases during middle adulthood. That is, physical attraction, romance, and passion are more important in new relationships, especially in early adulthood. Security, loyalty, and mutual emotional interest become more important as relationships mature, especially in middle adulthood.

Even some marriages that were difficult and rocky during early adulthood turn out to be better adjusted during middle adulthood. Although the partners may have lived through a great deal of turmoil, they eventually discover a deep and solid foundation on which to anchor their relationship. In middle adulthood, the partners may have fewer financial worries, less housework and chores, and more time with each other. Middle-aged partners are more likely to view their marriage as positive if they engage in mutual activities.

Most individuals in midlife who are married voice considerable satisfaction with being married. In a large-scale study of individuals in middle adulthood, 72 percent of those who were married said their marriage was either "excellent" or "very good" (Brim, 1999). Possibly by middle age, many of the worst marriages already have dissolved.

Divorce in middle adulthood may be more positive in some ways, more negative in others, than divorce in early adulthood. On the one hand, for mature individuals, the perils of divorce can be fewer and less intense than for younger individuals. They have more resources, and they can use this time as an opportunity to simplify their lives by disposing of possessions, such as a large home, which they no longer need. Their children are adults and may be able to cope with their parents' divorce more effectively. The partners may have gained a better understanding of themselves and may be searching for changes that could include the end to a poor marriage. One study found that women who initiated a divorce in midlife were characterized more by self-focused growth and optimism than women whose husbands initiated the divorce (Sakraida, 2005).

On the other hand, the emotional and time commitment to marriage that has existed for so many years may not be lightly given up. Many midlife individuals perceive a divorce as failing in the best years of their lives. The divorcer might see the situation as an escape from an untenable relationship, but the divorced partner usually sees it as betrayal, the ending of a relationship that had been built up over many years and that involved a great deal of commitment and trust. Also, divorce may lower the economic standing of some middle-aged and older women who have a limited number of options (Mitchell, 2007). These women may lack the necessary education, skills, and employment experience that enable them to maintain a standard of living that is as high as when they were married. In sum, divorce in midlife may have positive outcomes for some individuals and negative outcomes for others (Carr & Pudrovska, 2007).

A survey by AARP (2004) of 1,148 40- to 79-year-olds who were divorced at least once in their forties, fifties, or sixties found that staying married because of their children was by far the main reason many people took so long to become divorced. Despite the worry and stress involved in going through a divorce, three in four of the divorcees said they had made the right decision to dissolve their marriage and reported a positive outlook on life. Sixty-six percent of the divorced women said they initiated the divorce compared with only 41 percent of the divorced men. The divorced women were much more afraid of having financial problems (44 percent) than the divorced men (11 percent). Following are the main reasons the middle-aged and older adult women cited for their divorce: (1) verbal, physical, or emotional abuse (23 percent); (2) alcohol or drug abuse (18 percent); and (3) cheating (17 percent). The main reasons the middle-aged and older men cited for their divorce: (1) no obvious problems, just fell out of love (17 percent); (2) cheating (14 percent); and (3) different values, lifestyles (14 percent).

The Empty Nest and Its Refilling

An important event in a family is the launching of a child into adult life. Parents face new adjustments as a result of the child's absence. Students usually think that their parents suffer from their absence. In fact, parents who live vicariously through their children might experience the **empty nest syndrome**, which includes a decline in marital satisfaction after children leave the home. For most parents, however, marital satisfaction does not decline after children have left home but rather increases during the years after child rearing (Fingerman, 2006; Fingerman & Lang, 2004). With their children gone, marital partners have time to pursue career interests and more time for each other.

In today's uncertain economic climate, the refilling of the empty nest is becoming a common occurrence as adult children return to live at home after several years of college, after graduating from college, or to save money after taking a full-time job

What are some ways that divorce might be more positive or more negative in middle adulthood than in early adulthood?

empty nest syndrome A decrease in marital satisfaction after children leave home, because parents derive considerable satisfaction from their children.

Doonesbury

BY GARRY TRUDEAU

(Noriko, 2005). Young adults also may move back in with their parents after an unsuccessful career or a divorce. And some individuals don't leave home at all until their middle to late twenties because they cannot financially support themselves. Numerous labels have been applied to these young adults who return to their parents' homes to live, including "boomerang kids," and "B2B" (or Back-to-Bedroom) (Furman, 2005).

The middle generation has always provided support for the younger generation, even after the nest is bare. Through loans and monetary gifts for education, and through emotional support, the middle generation has helped the younger generation. Adult children appreciate the financial and emotional support their parents provide them at a time when they often feel considerable stress about their career, work, and lifestyle. And parents feel good that they can provide this support.

However, as with most family living arrangements, there are both pluses and minuses when adult children return to live at home. A common complaint voiced by both adult children and their parents is a loss of privacy. The adult children complain that their parents restrict their independence, cramp their sex lives, reduce their rock music listening, and treat them as children rather than adults. Parents often complain that their quiet home has become noisy, that they stay up late worrying when their adult children will come home, that meals are difficult to plan because of conflicting schedules, that their relationship as a married couple has been invaded, and that they have to shoulder too much responsibility for their adult children. In sum, when adult children return home to live, a disequilibrium in family life is created, which requires considerable adaptation on the part of parents and their adult children. To read about strategies that young adults and their parents can use to get along better, see the *Applications in Life-Span Development interlude.*

Applications in Life-Span Development
Strategies for Parents and Their Young Adult Children

When adult children ask to return home to live, parents and their adult children should agree on the conditions and expectations beforehand. For example, they might discuss and agree on whether young adults will pay rent, wash their own clothes, cook their own meals, do any household chores, pay their phone bills, come and go as they please, be sexually active or drink alcohol at home, and so on. If these conditions aren't negotiated at the beginning, conflict often results because the expectations of parents and young adult children will likely be violated.

Parents need to treat young adult children more like adults than children and let go of much of their parenting role. Parents should not interact with young adult children as if they are dependent children who need to be closely monitored and protected but rather as adults who are capable of responsible, mature behavior. Adult children have the right to choose how much they sleep and eat, how they dress, who they choose as friends and lovers, what career they pursue, and how they spend their money. However, if the young adult children act in ways that interfere with their parents' lifestyles, parents need to say so. The discussion should focus not on the young adult children's choices but on how their activities are unacceptable while living together in the same home.

Some parents don't let go of their young adult children when they should. They engage in "permaparenting," which can impede not only their adult children's movement toward independence and responsibility but also their own postparenting lives. "Helicopter parents" is another label used for parents who hover too closely in their effort to ensure that their children succeed in college and adult life (Paul, 2003). Although well intentioned, this intrusiveness by parents can slow the process by which their children become responsible adults.

When they move back home, young adult children need to think about how they will need to change their behavior to make the living arrangement work. Elina Furman (2005) provides some good recommendations in *Boomerang Nation: How to Survive Living with Your Parents . . . the Second*

What are some strategies that can help parents and their young adult children get along better?

Time Around. She recommends that when young adult children move back home they expect to make adjustments. And as recommended earlier, she urges young adults to sit down with their parents and negotiate the ground rules for living at home before they actually move back. Furman also recommends that young adults set a deadline for how long they will live at home and then stay focused on their goals (whether to save enough money to pay off their debts, save enough to start a business or buy their own home, finish graduate school, and so on). Too often young adults spend the money they save by moving home on such luxuries as spending binges, nights on the town, expensive clothes, and unnecessary travel, which only delay their ability to move out of their parents' home.

Sibling Relationships and Friendships

Sibling relationships persist over the entire life span for most adults (Dunn, 2007). Eighty-five percent of today's adults have at least one living sibling. Sibling relationships in adulthood may be extremely close, apathetic, or highly rivalrous. The majority of sibling relationships in adulthood are close (Cicirelli, 1991). Those siblings who are psychologically close to each other in adulthood tended to be that way in childhood. It is rare for sibling closeness to develop for the first time in adulthood (Dunn, 1984). A recent study revealed that adult siblings often provide practical and emotional support to each other (Voorpostel & Blieszner, 2008).

Friendships continue to be important in middle adulthood just as they were in early adulthood (Antonucci, 1989). It takes time to develop intimate friendships, so friendships that have endured over the adult years are often deeper than those that have just been formed in middle adulthood.

Grandparenting

Grandparents play important roles in the lives of many grandchildren (Oberlander, Black, & Starr, 2007). Many adults become grandparents for the first time during middle age. Researchers have consistently found that grandmothers have more contact with grandchildren than grandfathers (Watson, Randolph, & Lyons, 2005). Perhaps women tend to define their role as grandmothers as part of their responsibility for maintaining ties between family members across generations. Men may have fewer expectations about the grandfather role and see it as more voluntary.

Grandparent Roles and Styles   What is the meaning of the grandparent role? Three prominent meanings are attached to being a grandparent (Neugarten & Weinstein, 1964). For some older adults, being a grandparent is a source of biological reward and continuity. For others, being a grandparent is a source of emotional self-fulfillment, generating feelings of companionship and satisfaction that may have been missing in earlier adult-child relationships. And for yet others, being a grandparent is a remote role. A recent study revealed that grandparenting can provide a sense of purpose and a feeling of being valued during middle and late adulthood when generative needs are strong (Thiele & Whelan, 2008).

The grandparent role may have different functions in different families, in different ethnic groups and cultures, and in different situations (Watson, Randolph, & Lyons, 2005). For example, in one study of White, African American, and Mexican American grandparents and grandchildren, the Mexican American grandparents saw their grandchildren more frequently, provided more support for the grandchildren and their parents, and had more satisfying relationships with their grandchildren (Bengtsson, 1985). And in a study of three generations of families in Chicago, grandmothers had closer relationships with their children and grandchildren and gave more personal advice than grandfathers did (Hagestad, 1985).

The diversity of grandparenting also was apparent in an early investigation of how grandparents interacted with their grandchildren (Neugarten & Weinstein, 1964). Three styles were dominant—formal, fun-seeking, and distant. In the formal style, the grandparent performed what was considered to be a proper and prescribed role. These

What are some grandparents roles and styles?

grandparents showed a strong interest in their grandchildren, but were careful not to give child-rearing advice. In the fun-seeking style, the grandparent was informal and playful. Grandchildren were a source of leisure activity; mutual satisfaction was emphasized. A substantial portion of grandparents were distant figures. In the distant-figure style, the grandparent was benevolent but interaction was infrequent. Grandparents who were over the age of 65 were more likely to display a formal style of interaction; those under 65 were more likely to display a fun-seeking style.

The Changing Profile of Grandparents   An increasing number of U.S. grandchildren live with their grandparents (Ross & Aday, 2006). In 1980, 2.3 million grandchildren lived with their grandparents, but in 2005 that figure had reached 6.1 million (U.S. Census Bureau, 2006). Divorce, adolescent pregnancies, and drug use by parents are the main reasons that grandparents are thrust back into the "parenting" role they thought they had shed. One study of grandparents raising their grandchildren found that stress was linked with three conditions: younger grandparents, grandchildren with physical and psychological problems, and low family cohesion (Sands & Goldberg-Glen, 2000).

Less than 20 percent of grandparents whose grandchildren move in with them are 65 years old or older. Almost half of the grandchildren who move in with grandparents are raised by a single grandmother. These families are mainly African American (53 percent). When both grandparents are raising grandchildren, the families are overwhelmingly non-Latino White.

Grandparents who take in grandchildren are in better health, are better educated, are more likely to be working outside the home, and are younger than grandparents who move in with their children. According to the 2006 U.S. Census report, a majority of the grandparents living with their children contributed to the family income and provided child care while parents worked. Only about 10 percent of the grandparents who move in with their children and grandchildren are in poverty. Almost half of the grandparents who move in with their children are immigrants. Partly because women live longer than men, there are more grandmothers than grandfathers who live with their children. About 70 percent of the grandparents who move in with their children are grandmothers.

Might grandparents' health become worse when they care for grandchildren on an extensive basis? A recent study of more than 12,000 50- to 80-year-old grandparents found that any negative effects on grandparent health were the exception rather than the rule (Hughes & others, 2007).

In some cases, divorce may increase children's contact with grandparents, as when grandparents assume a stronger caregiving role; in others, a custodial parent may try to restrict grandparents' time with children. One recent study revealed that when children's relationships with their father deteriorated after a divorce, their relationships with their paternal grandparents were distant, negative, or nonexistent (Ahrons, 2007).

As divorce and remarriage have become more common, a special concern of grandparents is visitation privileges with their grandchildren (Kivnik & Sinclair, 2007). In the last two decades, more states have passed laws giving grandparents the right to petition a court for visitation privileges with their grandchildren, even if a parent objects. Whether such forced visitation rights for grandparents are in the child's best interest is still being debated.

Intergenerational Relationships

Family is important to most people. When 21,000 adults aged 40 to 79 in 21 countries were asked, "When you think of who you are, you think mainly of _____," 63 percent said "family," 9 percent said "religion," and 8 percent said "work" (HSBC Insurance, 2007). In this study, in all 21 countries, middle-aged and older adults expressed a strong feeling of responsibility between generations in their family, with the strongest intergenerational ties indicated in Saudi Arabia, India, and Turkey. More than 80 percent of the middle-aged and older adults reported that adults have a duty to care for their parents (and parents-in-law) in time of need later in life.

Adults in midlife play important roles in the lives of the young and the old (Ha & Ingersoll-Dayton, 2008; Pratt & others, 2008b; Wolff & Kasper, 2006). Middle-aged adults share their experience and transmit values to the younger generation (McAdams, 2001; Swartz, 2008). They may be launching children and experiencing the empty nest, adjusting to having grown children return home, or becoming grandparents. They also may be giving or receiving financial assistance, caring for a widowed or sick parent, or adapting to being the oldest generation after both parents have died (Silverstein, Gans, & Yang, 2006).

With each new generation, personality characteristics, attitudes, and values are replicated or changed (Bengtsson & Psouni, 2008; Brook & others, 2007). As older family members die, their biological, intellectual, emotional, and personal legacies are carried on in the next generation. Their children become the oldest generation and their grandchildren the second generation. As adult children become middle-aged, they often develop more positive perceptions of their parents (Field, 1999). In one study, conflicts between mothers and daughters decreased across the life course in both the United States and Japan (Akiyama & Antonucci, 1999).

For the most part, family members maintain considerable contact across generations (Miller-Day, 2004). However, a recent study found that married men and women have a lower incidence of intergenerational contact than never married or divorced individuals (Sarkisian & Gerstel, 2008). In this study, married adults were less likely to live with their parents, keep in touch, and give or receive emotional, financial, or practical help. Nonetheless, another recent study revealed that when young adults have children they are more likely to see their parents than if they don't have children (Bucx & others, 2008).

Both similarity and dissimilarity across generations are found. For example, similarity between parents and an adult child is most noticeable in religion and politics, least in gender roles, lifestyle, and work orientation.

What are the most common conflicts between parents and their adult children? In one study, they included communication and interaction style (such as "He is always yelling" and "She is too critical"), habits and lifestyle choices (such as sexual activity, living arrangements), child-rearing practices and values (such as decisions about having children, being permissive or controlling), politics, religion, and ideology (such as lack of religious involvement) (Clarke & others, 1999). In this study, there were generational differences in perceptions of the main conflicts between parents and adult children. Parents most often listed habits and lifestyle choices; adult children cited communication and interaction style.

The following studies provide further evidence of the importance of intergenerational relationships in development:

- In a New Zealand study of the child-rearing antecedents of intergenerational relations, supportive family environments and parenting in childhood (assessed when the children were 3 to 15 years of age) were linked with more positive relationships (in terms of contact, closeness, conflict, and reciprocal assistance) between the children and their middle-aged parents when the children were 26 years of age (Belsky & others, 2001).

- In another study, individuals who felt trusted by their parents in adolescence reported greater closeness to their parents in early adulthood (Jacobs & Tanner, 1999). Also in this study, daughters who had experienced long-term lack of trust during adolescence were more alienated from their parents as young adults than sons who had similar experiences.

- In another study, the motivation of adult children to provide social support to their older parents was linked with earlier family experiences (Silverstein & others, 2002). Children who spent more time in shared activities with their parents and were given more financial support by them earlier in their lives provided more support to their parents when they became older.

Middle-aged and older adults around the world show a strong sense of family responsibility. A recent study of middle-aged and older adults in 21 countries revealed the strongest intergenerational ties in Saudi Arabia.

In case you're worried about what's going to become of the younger generation, it's going to grow up and start worrying about the younger generation.

—ROGER ALLEN
American Writer, 20th Century

What is the nature of intergenerational relationships?

• In a recent study, divorce in the grandparent generation was linked to less education and marital conflict in the grandchild generation (Amato & Cheadle, 2005). These links were mediated by these characteristics of the middle generation: less education, increased marital conflict, and more tension in early parent-child relationships.

• In another recent study, evidence was found for the intergenerational transmission of conduct disorder across three generations, with the connection stronger for males than females (D'Onofrio & others, 2007)

Gender differences also characterize intergenerational relationships (Etaugh & Bridges, 2004; Nauck & Suckow, 2006). In one study, mothers and their daughters had much closer relationships during their adult years than mothers and sons, fathers and daughters, and fathers and sons (Rossi, 1989). Also in this study, married men were more involved with their wives' kin than with their own. And maternal grandmothers and maternal aunts were cited twice as often as their counterparts on the paternal side of the family as the most important or loved relative. Also, a recent study revealed that mothers' intergenerational ties were more influential for grandparent-grandchild relationships than fathers' (Monserud, 2008). To read further about intergenerational relationships between mothers and daughters, see the *Research in Life-Span Development* interlude.

Research in Life-Span Development
"We Had a Nice Little Chat": Mothers' and Daughters' Descriptions of Enjoyable Visits at Different Points in Adult Development

Although researchers have documented that mothers and daughters in adulthood generally have frequent contact and mutually positive feelings, little is known about what mothers and daughters like about their relationship. To examine this topic, Karen Fingerman (2000) studied 48 pairs of older adult mothers (mean age, 76 years) and their middle-aged daughters (mean age, 46 years), and 44 pairs of middle-aged mothers (mean age, 47 years) and their young adult daughters (mean age, 21 years). Interviewers asked participants (p. 98):

> Think about the last time you had a particularly enjoyable visit with your daughter/mother. By visit, I mean a time when you got together, went to the other's house (or your daughter came home from college), or talked on the phone. Tell a little about what went on. Please provide as much information as you can about the visit, what happened, and why it was particularly enjoyable.

Transcriptions of the visits were coded, and the results for the coded categories were as follows (Fingerman, 2000, pp. 100–102):

• *Investment and connection.* Mothers in both age groups were more invested in their relationship with their daughters than their daughters were with them.

• *Family.* Older mothers and daughters were more likely than younger pairs to describe the larger kin network, such as the daughter's children, siblings, father, husband, or the family in general. By contrast, younger pairs "were more likely to stick to their own relationship and to discuss situations in which the two of them had enjoyed a special event."

• *Nurturance.* "Young adult daughters and older adult mothers were more likely to report pleasure from having the other party help them in some way than were middle-aged women."

• *Interacting.* Younger mothers tended to focus on activities in which they enjoyed their daughters' emergence as young adults. "Younger daughters derived pleasure from having their mothers around as sounding boards, whereas older daughters" enjoyed the link to the past that their mothers represented.

- *Negative comments.* Mothers and daughters in the older pairs "were more likely to say something negative than were younger mothers and daughters," although these comments were still infrequent.

In sum, mothers' and daughters' perceptions of their visits reflected a combination of individual developmental needs. Although the focus of mothers' and daughters' relationships may change, in general, mothers were more invested in their daughters than the reverse throughout adulthood.

Middle-aged adults have been described as the "sandwich," "squeezed," or "overload" generation because of the responsibilities they have for their adolescent and young adult children on the one hand and their aging parents on the other (Etaugh & Bridges, 2004; Riley & Bowen, 2005). These simultaneous pressures from adolescents or young adult children and aging parents may contribute to stress in middle adulthood. Many middle-aged adults experience considerable stress when their parents become very ill and die. One survey found that when adults enter midlife, 41 percent have both parents alive but that 77 percent leave midlife with no parents alive (Bumpass & Aquilino, 1994).

When adults immigrate to another country, intergenerational stress may be increased. To read about the role of immigration and acculturation in intergenerational relationships among Mexican Americans, see the *Diversity in Life-Span Development* interlude.

Diversity in Life-Span Development
Intergenerational Relationships in Mexican American Families: The Effects of Immigration and Acculturation

In the last several decades, increasing numbers of Mexicans have immigrated to the United States, and their numbers are expected to increase. The pattern of immigration usually involves separation from the extended family (Crowley, Lichter, & Qian, 2006; Parra-Cardona & others, 2006). It may also involve separation of immediate family members, with the husband coming first and then later bringing his wife and children. Those initially isolated, especially the wife, experience considerable stress due to relocation and the absence of family and friends. Within several years, a social network is usually established in the ethnic neighborhood.

As soon as some stability in their lives is achieved, Mexican families may sponsor the immigration of extended family members, such as a maternal or paternal sister or mother who provides child care and enables the mother to go to work. In some cases, the older generation remains behind and joins their grown children in old age. The accessibility of Mexico facilitates visits to and from the native village for vacations or at a time of crisis, such as when an adolescent runs away from home.

Three levels of acculturation often exist within a Mexican American family (Falicov & Karrer, 1980). The mother and the grandparents may be at the beginning level, the father at an intermediate level, and the children at an advanced level. The discrepancies between acculturation levels can give rise to conflicting expectations within the family (Sarkisian, Gerena, & Gerstel, 2006). The immigrant parents' model of child rearing may be out of phase with the dominant culture's model, which may cause reverberations through the family's generations, as we discussed in earlier chapters. For example, the mother and grandparents may be especially resistant to the demands for autonomy and dating made by adolescent daughters, and so may the father (Wilkinson-Lee & others, 2006). And in recent years an increasing number of female youth leave their Mexican American homes to further their education, an event that is often stressful for families with strong ties to Mexican values.

As children leave home, parents begin to face their future as a middle-aged couple. This may be difficult for many Mexican American middle-aged couples because their value orientations have prepared them better for parenting than for relating as a married couple. Family therapists who work with Mexican Americans frequently report that a common pattern is psychological distance between the spouses and a type of emotional separation in midlife. The marital partners

What are three levels of acculturation that characterize many Mexican American families?

continue to live together and carry on their family duties but relate to each other only at a surface level. The younger generation of Mexican Americans may find it difficult to accept their parents' lifestyle, may question their marital arrangement, and may rebel against their value orientations. Despite the intergenerational stress that may be brought about by immigration and acculturation, the majority of Mexican American families maintain considerable contact across generations and continue to have a strong family orientation (Escandon, 2006).

Lillian Troll has conducted research on intergenerational relations and women's development in midlife. To read about her work, see the *Careers in Life-Span Development profile*.

Careers in Life-Span Development

Lillian Troll, Professor of Psychology and Life-Span Development and Researcher on Families and Aging Women

Lillian Troll has been a leading figure in the field of adult development and aging. She graduated from the University of Chicago with a joint major in psychology and premedicine. During World War II she dropped out of graduate school to work in Washington, where she helped develop the array of Army screening and achievement tests. After the war she became a suburban housewife and mother, following her husband's career moves from city to city. For a decade, the closest Troll came to a career in life-span development was founding a nursery school in New Jersey.

Many years later, after her divorce, Troll returned to the University of Chicago and, in 1967, completed a Ph.D. in life-span development. She then began teaching and conducting research on generations in the family and women's development, first at Wayne State University in Detroit and then, as a 60-year-old grandmother, at Rutgers University

Psychology Department. In 1986 she retired and moved to California, where she continued research at the University of California at San Francisco, by collaborating with Colleen Johnson on a longitudinal study of the "oldest-old" (people over 85).

Lillian Troll (*left*) with participants in a study of aging women.

Review and Reflect: Learning Goal 3

 Identify Some Important Aspects of Close Relationships in Middle Adulthood

REVIEW

- How can love and marriage at midlife be characterized?
- What is the empty nest? How has it been refilling?
- What are sibling relationships and friendships like in middle adulthood?
- What is the nature of grandparenting?
- What are relationships across generations like?

REFLECT

- Might there be distinctive phases of middle adulthood? Think about what you have read in this chapter and Chapter 15 and describe what these subphases might be. Would they be linked to age? If so, how?

Socioemotional Development in Middle Adulthood

1 PERSONALITY THEORIES AND DEVELOPMENT: DESCRIBE PERSONALITY THEORIES AND DEVELOPMENT IN MIDDLE ADULTHOOD

Stages of Adulthood

- Erikson says that the seventh stage of the human life span, generativity versus stagnation, occurs in middle adulthood. Four types of generativity are biological, parental, work, and cultural. In Levinson's theory, developmental tasks should be mastered at different points in development, and changes in middle age focus on four conflicts: being young versus being old, being destructive versus being constructive, being masculine versus being feminine, and being attached to others versus being separated from them. Levinson proposed that a majority of Americans, especially men, experience a midlife crisis. Research, though, indicates that midlife crises are not pervasive. There is considerable individual variation in development during the middle adulthood years.

The Life-Events Approach

- According to the early version of the life-events approach, life events produce taxing circumstances that create stress in people's lives. In the contemporary version of the life-events approach, how life events influence the individual's development depends not only on the life event but also on mediating factors, adaptation to the event, the life-stage context, and the sociohistorical context.

Stress and Personal Control in Midlife

- Researchers have found that young and middle-aged adults experience more stressful days, more multiple stressors, and more overload stressors than do older adults. On average, a sense of personal control decreases as adults become older—however, some aspects of personal control increase while others decrease.

Contexts of Midlife Development

- Neugarten argues that the social environment of a particular cohort can alter its social clock—the timetable according to which individuals are expected to accomplish life's tasks. Critics say that the adult stage theories are male biased because they place too much emphasis on achievement and careers and do not adequately address women's concerns about relationships. Midlife is a heterogeneous period for women, as it is for men. For some women, midlife is the prime of their lives. Many cultures do not have a clear concept of middle age. In many nonindustrialized societies, a woman's status improves in middle age.

2 STABILITY AND CHANGE: DISCUSS STABILITY AND CHANGE IN DEVELOPMENT DURING MIDDLE ADULTHOOD, INCLUDING LONGITUDINAL STUDIES

Longitudinal Studies

- In Costa and McCrae's Baltimore Study, the Big Five personality factors—openness to Experience, conscientiousness, extraversion, agreeableness, and neuroticism—showed considerable stability. However, a recent meta-analysis of the Big Five personality factors found increases and declines of specific factors across the adult years, with the most change occurring in early adulthood. In the Berkeley Longitudinal Studies, the extremes in the stability-change argument were not supported. The most stable characteristics were intellectual orientation, self-confidence, and openness to new experiences. The characteristics that changed the most were nurturance, hostility, and self-control. In Helson's Mills College Study of women, there was a shift toward less traditional feminine characteristics from age 27 to the early forties, but this might have been due to societal changes. In their early forties, women experienced many of the concerns that Levinson described for men. However, rather than a midlife crisis, this is best called midlife consciousness. George Vaillant's research revealed links between a number of characteristics at age 50 and health and well-being at 75 to 80 years of age.

Conclusions

- The cumulative personality model states that with time and age personality becomes more stable. Change in personality traits occurs more in early adulthood than middle and late adulthood, but a number of aspects of personality do continue to change after early adulthood. Change in personality traits across adulthood occurs in a positive direction, reflecting social maturity. At the individual level, changes in personality are often linked to life experiences related to a particular developmental period. Some people change more than others.

3   CLOSE RELATIONSHIPS: IDENTIFY SOME IMPORTANT ASPECTS OF CLOSE RELATIONSHIPS IN MIDDLE ADULTHOOD

Love and Marriage at Midlife

- Affectionate love increases in midlife, especially in marriages that have endured many years. A majority of middle-aged adults who are married say that their marriage is very good or excellent. Researchers recently have found that the perils of divorce in midlife can be few and less intense than for divorcing young adults.

The Empty Nest and Its Refilling

- Rather than decreasing marital satisfaction as once thought, the empty nest increases it for most parents. Following an unsuccessful career or a divorce, an increasing number of young adults are returning home to live with their parents. Some young adults do not leave until their middle to late twenties because they are unable to financially support themselves.

Sibling Relationships and Friendships

- Sibling relationships continue throughout life. Some are close, others are distant. Friendships continue to be important in middle age.

Grandparenting

- There are different grandparent roles and styles. Grandmothers spend more time with grandchildren than grandfathers, and the grandmother role involves greater expectations for maintaining ties across generations than the grandfather role. The profile of grandparents is changing, due to such factors as divorce and remarriage. An increasing number of U.S. grandchildren live with their grandparents.

Intergenerational Relationships

- Family members usually maintain contact across generations. Mothers and daughters have the closest relationships. The middle-aged generation, which has been called the "sandwich" or "squeezed" generation, plays an important role in linking generations.

KEY TERMS

contemporary life-events approach 505

social clock 506

Big Five factors of personality 509

empty nest syndrome 513

KEY PEOPLE

Erik Erikson 501
Carol Ryff 501
Daniel Levinson 502
George Vaillant 502

Bernice Neugarten 505
Paul Costa and Robert McCrae 509
John Clausen 510

Ravenna Helson 510
Brent Roberts and Daniel Mroczek 511
Karen Fingerman 518

E-LEARNING TOOLS

To help you master the material in this chapter, visit the Online Learning Center for *Life-Span Development*, twelfth edition, at **www.mhhe.com/santrockld12**.

Self-Assessment

Connect to **www.mhhe.com/santrockld12** to learn more about the stress-illness relationship, how extraverted or introverted you are, and how generative you are by completing the self-assessments, *Life Events and My Chance of Significant Illness in the Coming Year*, *Extraversion*, and *How Generative Am I?*

Taking It to the Net

Connect to **www.mhhe.com/santrockld12** to research the answers to this question:

What did psychologist Daniel Goleman find out about how Erik Erikson and his wife Joan dealt with Erikson's seventh developmental stage, generativity versus stagnation, in their own lives?

Video Clips

The Online Learning Center includes a video for Chapter 16 called "Balancing Work and Family." In this segment, a working mother describes her strategies for dealing with this challenge.

Health and Well-Being, Parenting, and Education Exercises

Build your decision-making skills by trying your hand at the health and well-being, parenting, and education exercises. Connect to **www.mhhe.com/santrockld12** to research the answers and complete the exercises.

LATE ADULTHOOD

To be seventy years young is sometimes far more cheerful and hopeful than to be forty years old.

—OLIVER WENDELL HOLMES, SR.
American Physician, 19th Century

The rhythm and meaning of human development eventually wend their way to late adulthood, when each of us stands alone at the heart of the earth and suddenly it is evening. We shed the leaves of youth and are stripped by the winds of time down to the truth. We learn that life is lived forward but understood backward. We trace the connection between the end and the beginning of life and try to figure out what this whole show is about before it is out. Ultimately, we come to know that we are what survives of us. Section 9 contains three chapters: "Physical Development in Late Adulthood (Chapter 17), "Cognitive Development in Late Adulthood" (Chapter 18), and "Socioemotional Development in Late Adulthood" (Chapter 19).

17

Each of us stands alone at the heart of the earth, pierced through by a ray of sunshine: And suddenly it is evening.

—SALVATORE QUASIMODO
Italian Poet, 20th Century

LEARNING GOALS

◆ Characterize longevity and the biological theories of aging.

◆ Describe how a person's brain and body change in late adulthood.

◆ Identify health problems in older adults and how they can be treated.

PHYSICAL DEVELOPMENT IN LATE ADULTHOOD

Images of Life-Span Development
Learning to Age Successfully

Jonathan Swift said, "No wise man ever wished to be younger." Without a doubt, a 70-year-old body does not work as well as it once did. It is also true that an individual's fear of aging is often greater than need be. As more individuals live to a ripe *and* active old age, our image of aging is changing. While on the average a 75-year-old's joints should be stiffening, people can practice not to be average. For example, a 75-year-old man might *choose* to train for and run a marathon; an 80-year-old woman whose capacity for work is undiminished might *choose* to make and sell children's toys.

Consider 85-year-old Sadie Halperin, who has been working out for 11 months at a rehabilitation center for the aged in Boston. She lifts weights and rides a stationary bike. She says that before she started working out, about everything she did—shopping, cooking, walking—was a major struggle. Sadie says she always felt wobbly and held on to a wall when she walked. Now she walks down the center of the hallways and reports that she feels wonderful. Initially she could lift only 15 pounds with both legs; now she lifts 30 pounds. At first she could bench-press only 20 pounds; now she bench-presses 50 pounds. Sadie's exercise routine has increased her muscle strength and helps her to battle osteoporosis by slowing the calcium loss from her bones, which can lead to deadly fractures (Ubell, 1992).

Eighty-five-year old Sadie Halperin doubled her strength in exercise after just 11 months. Before developing an exercise routine, she felt wobbly and often had to hold on to a wall when she walked. Now she walks down the middle of hallways and says she feels wonderful.

PREVIEW

The story of Sadie Halperin's physical development and well-being raises some truly fascinating questions about life-span development, which we will explore in this chapter. They include: Why do we age, and what, if anything, can we do to slow down the process? How long can we live? What chance do you have of living to be 100? How does the body change in old age? Can certain eating habits and exercise help us live longer?

1 LONGEVITY

| Life Expectancy and Life Span | The Young-Old, the Old-Old, and the Oldest-Old | Biological Theories of Aging |

In his eighties, Nobel-winning chemist Linus Pauling argued that vitamin C slows the aging process. Aging researcher Roy Walford fasted two days a week because he believed calorie restriction slows the aging process. What do we really know about longevity?

Life Expectancy and Life Span

We are no longer a youthful society. The proportion of individuals at different ages has become increasingly similar. Since the beginning of recorded history, **life span**,

life span The upper boundary of life, the maximum number of years an individual can live. The maximum life span of human beings is about 120 to 125 years of age.

the maximum number of years an individual can live, has remained at approximately 120 to 125 years of age. But since 1900, improvements in medicine, nutrition, exercise, and lifestyle have increased our life expectancy an average of 30 additional years.

Recall from Chapter 1 that **life expectancy** is the number of years that the average person born in a particular year will probably live. Sixty-five-year-olds in the United States today can expect to live an average of 18 more years (20 for females, 16 for males) (National Center for Health Statistics, 2006). The average life expectancy of individuals born today in the United States is 78.1 years (National Center for Health Statistics, 2008).

Differences in Life Expectancy How does the United States fare in life expectancy, compared with other countries around the world? We do considerably better than some, a little worse than some others. Japan has the highest life expectancy at birth today (81 years) (UNICEF, 2004). Differences in life expectancies across countries are due to such factors as health conditions and medical care throughout the life span.

Life expectancy also differs for various ethnic groups within the United States and for men and women. For example, the life expectancy of African Americans (73) in the United States is five years lower than the low expectancy for non-Latino Whites (78) (National Center for Health Statistics, 2008). Non-Latino White women have a life expectancy of 81, followed by African American women (77), non-Latino White men (76 years), and African American men (70 years) (Heron & others, 2008).

Today, the overall life expectancy for females is 80.7 years of age, for males 75.4 years of age (Heron & others, 2008). Beginning in the mid-thirties, females outnumber males; this gap widens during the remainder of the adult years. By the time adults are 75 years of age, more than 61 percent of the population is female; for those 85 and over, the figure is almost 70 percent female. Why can women expect to live longer than men? Social factors such as health attitudes, habits, lifestyles, and occupation are probably important (Land & Yang, 2006). For example, men are more likely than women to die from the leading causes of death in the United States, such as cancer of the respiratory system, motor vehicle accidents, cirrhosis of the liver, emphysema, and coronary heart disease (Yoshida & others, 2006). These causes of death are associated with lifestyle. For example, the sex difference in deaths due to lung cancer and emphysema occurs because men are heavier smokers than women.

The sex difference in longevity also is influenced by biological factors (Oksuzyan & others, 2008). In virtually all species, females outlive males. Women have more resistance to infections and degenerative diseases (Candore & others, 2006). For example, the female's estrogen production helps to protect her from arteriosclerosis (hardening of the arteries). And the additional X chromosome that women carry in comparison to men may be associated with the production of more antibodies to fight off disease.

What about yourself? What is the likelihood that you will live to be 100? To evaluate this possibility, see Figure 17.1.

Centenarians In industrialzed countries, the number of centenarians (individuals 100 years and older) is increasing at a rate of approximately 7 percent each year (Perls, 2007). In the United States, there were only 15,000 centenarians in 1980, a number that had risen to 77,000 in 2000, and it is projected that this number will reach more than 800,000 by 2050. It is estimated that there are 75 to 100 supercentenarians (individuals 110 years or older) in the United and about 300 to 450 worldwide (Perls, 2007).

Many people expect that "the older you get, the sicker you get." However, researchers are finding that is not true for some centenarians (Terry & others, 2008;

*T*o me old age is always fifteen years older than I am.

—**BERNARD BARUCH**
American Statesman, 20th Century

life expectancy The number of years that will probably be lived by the average person born in a particular year.

This test gives you a rough guide for predicting your longevity. The basic life expectancy for males is age 75, and for females it is 81. Write down your basic life expectancy. If you are in your fifties or sixties, you should add ten years to the basic figure because you have already proved yourself to be a durable individual. If you are over age 60 and active, you can even add another two years.

Life Expectancy

Decide how each item applies to you and add or subtract the appropriate number of years from your basic life expectancy.

1. Family history
___ Add five years if two or more of your grandparents lived to 80 or beyond.
___ Subtract four years if any parent, grandparent, sister, or brother died of a heart attack or stroke before 50.
___ Subtract two years if anyone died from these diseases before 60.
___ Subtract three years for each case of diabetes, thyroid disorder, breast cancer, cancer of the digestive system, asthma, or chronic bronchitis among parents or grandparents.

2. Marital status
___ If you are married, add four years.
___ If you are over 25 and not married, subtract one year for every unmarried decade.

3. Economic status
___ Add two years if your family income is over $60,000 per year.
___ Subtract three years if you have been poor for the greater part of your life.

4. Physique
___ Subtract one year for every 10 pounds you are overweight.
___ For each inch your girth measurement exceeds your chest measurement deduct two years.
___ Add three years if you are over 40 and not overweight.

5. Exercise
___ Add three years if you exercise regularly and moderately (jogging three times a week).
___ Add five years if you exercise regularly and vigorously (long-distance running three times a week).
___ Subtract three years if your job is sedentary.
___ Add three years if your job is active.

6. Alcohol
___ Add two years if you are a light drinker (one to three drinks a day).
___ Subtract five to ten years if you are a heavy drinker (more than four drinks per day).
___ Subtract one year if you are a teetotaler.

7. Smoking
___ Subtract eight years if you smoke two or more packs of cigarettes per day.
___ Subtract two years if you smoke one to two packs per day.
___ Subtract two years if you smoke less than one pack.
___ Subtract two years if you regularly smoke a pipe or cigars.

8. Disposition
___ Add two years if you are a reasoned, practical person.
___ Subtract two years if you are aggressive, intense, and competitive.
___ Add one to five years if you are basically happy and content with life.
___ Subtract one to five years if you are often unhappy, worried, and often feel guilty.

9. Education
___ Subtract two years if you have less than a high school education.
___ Add one year if you attended four years of school beyond high school.
___ Add three years if you attended five or more years beyond high school.

10. Environment
___ Add four years if you have lived most of your life in a rural environment.
___ Subtract two years if you have lived most of your life in an urban environment.

11. Sleep
___ Subtract five years if you sleep more than nine hours a day.

12. Temperature
___ Add two years if your home's thermostat is set at no more than 68 F.

13. Health care
___ Add three years if you have regular medical checkups and regular dental care.
___ Subtract two years if you are frequently ill.

___ **Your Life Expectancy Total**

FIGURE 17.1 Can You Live to Be 100?

Xie & others, 2008). One study of 400 centenarians found that 32 percent of the males and 15 percent of the females had never been diagnosed with common age-associated diseases such as heart disease, cancer, and stroke (Evert & others, 2003). Another study of 93 centenarians revealed that despite some physical limitations, they had a low rate of age-associated diseases and most had good mental health (Selim & others, 2005).

A disproportionate number of centenarians are women. However, although women are more likely to attain exceptional longevity than men, among centenarians men are more likely to be healthier than women (Terry & others, 2008). One explanation for this gender difference in centenarians' health is that to reach exceptional old age men may need to be in excellent health (Perls, 2007). By contrast, women may be more adaptive in living with illnesses when they are older and thus can reach an exceptional old age in spite of having a chronic disabilty.

Three participants in the New England Centenarian Study: (*Left*) Adelaide Kruger, age 101, watering her flowers; (*middle*) Waldo McBurney, age 104, active beekeeper, gardener, and runner who has earned five gold medals and set international records in track and field events in his age group; (*right*) Daphne Brann, age 110, voting in an election.

In the ongoing New England Centenarian Study, a majority of the centenarians have had difficult lives, such as surviving the Holocaust and living in extreme poverty as an immigrant to the United States (Perls, Lauerman, & Silver, 1999). What has contributed to their survival is their ability to cope successfully with stress.

What chance do you have of living to be 100? Genes play an important role in surviving to an extreme old age (Johnson & others, 2007; Kim, 2007). But there are also other factors at work such as family history, health (weight, diet, smoking, and exercise), education, personality, and lifestyle (Rudin & others, 2007). To further examine the factors that are involved in living to a very old age, read the following *Diversity in Life-Span Development* interlude.

Diversity in Life-Span Development
Living Longer in Okinawa

Individuals live longer on the Japanese island of Okinawa in the East China Sea than anywhere else in the world. In Okinawa, there are 34.7 centenarians for every 100,000 inhabitants, the highest ratio in the world. In comparison, the United States has about 10 centenarians for every 100,000 residents. The life expectancy in Okinawa is 81.2 years (86 for women, 78 for men), also highest in the world.

What is responsible for such longevity in Okinawa? Some possible explanations include (Willcox, Willcox, & Suzuki, 2002; Willcox & others, 2007, 2008):

- *Diet.* Okinawans eat very healthy food, heavy on grains, fish, and vegetables, light on meat, eggs, and dairy products. The risk of dying of cancer is far lower among Okinawans than among Japanese and Americans (see Figure 17.2). About 100,000 Okinawans moved to Brazil and quickly adopted the eating regimen of their new home, one heavy on red meat. The result: The life expectancy of the Brazilian Okinawans is now 17 years lower than Okinawa's 81 years!

- *Low-stress lifestyle.* The easygoing lifestyle in Okinawa more closely resembles that of a laid-back South Sea island than that of the high-stress world on the Japanese mainland.

- *Caring community.* Okinawans look out for each other and do not isolate or ignore their older adults. If older adults need help, they don't hesitate to ask a neighbor. Such support and caring is likely responsible for Okinawa having the lowest suicide rate among older women in East Asia, an area noted for its high suicide rate among older women.

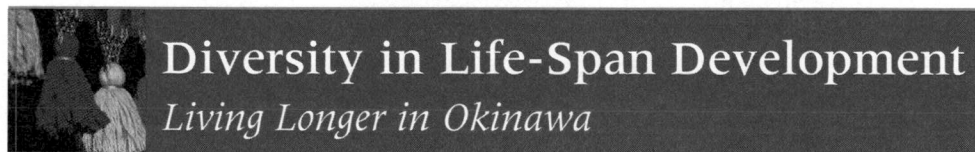

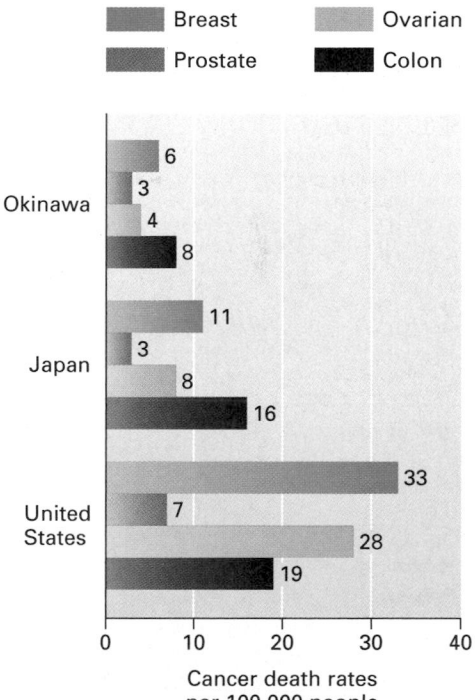

FIGURE 17.2 Risks of Dying from Cancer in Okinawa, Japan, and the United States. The risk of dying from different forms of cancer is lower in Okinawa than in the United States and Japan (Willcox, Willcox, & Suzuki, 2002). Okinawans eat lots of tofu and soy products, which are rich in flavonoids (believed to lower the risk of breast and prostate cancer). They also consume large amounts of fish, especially tuna, mackerel, and salmon, which reduce the risk of breast cancer.

Toshiko Taira, 80, weaves cloth from the fibers of banana trees on a loom in Okinawa. She, like many Okinawans, believes that such sense of purpose helps people to live longer.

- *Activity.* Many older adults in Okinawa are active, engaging in such activities as taking walks and working in their gardens. Many older Okinawans also continue working at their jobs.
- *Spirituality.* Many older adults in Okinawa find a sense of purpose in spiritual matters. Prayer is commonplace and believed to ease the mind of stress and problems.

The Young-Old, the Old-Old, and the Oldest-Old

Do you want to live to be 100, or 90? As we discussed in Chapter 1, these ages are part of late adulthood, which begins in the sixties and extends to approximately 120 to 125 years of age. This is the longest span of any period of human development—50 to 60 years. Some developmentalists distinguish between the *young-old* (65 to 74 years of age) and the *old-old*, or *old age* (75 years and older) (Charness & Bosman, 1992). Yet others distinguish the *oldest-old* (85 years and older) from younger older adults (65 to 84 years age) (Baltes & Smith, 2003).

An increased interest in successful aging is producing a portrayal of the oldest-old that is more optimistic than past stereotypes (Zubenko & others, 2007). Interventions such as cataract surgery and a variety of rehabilitation strategies are improving the functioning of the oldest-old. And there is cause for optimism in the development of new regimens of prevention and intervention, such as engaging in regular exercise (Senchina & Kohut, 2007; Timmerman & Volpe, 2008).

Many experts on aging prefer to talk about such categories as the young-old, old-old, and oldest-old in terms of *function* rather than age. Remember from Chapter 1 that we described age not only in terms of chronological age, but also in terms of biological age, psychological age, and social age. Thus, in terms of *functional age*—the person's actual ability to function—an 85-year-old might well be more biologically and psychologically fit than a 65-year-old.

Still, there are some significant differences between adults in their sixties or seventies and adults who are 85 and older (Baltes, Lindenberger, & Staudinger, 2006). As we discussed in Chapter 1, Paul Baltes and his colleagues (Baltes, 2003; Scheibe, Freund, & Baltes, 2007) argue that the oldest-old (85 and over) face a number of problems, including sizable losses in cognitive potential and ability to learn; an increase in chronic stress; a sizable prevalence of physical and mental disabilities; high levels of frailty; increased loneliness; and the difficulty of dying at older ages with dignity. He contrasts the problems of the oldest-old with the increase in successful aging of adults in their sixties and seventies. Compared with the oldest-old, the young-old have a substantial potential for physical and cognitive fitness, higher levels of emotional well-being, and more effective strategies for mastering the gains and losses of old age.

The oldest-old today are mostly female, and the majority of these women are widowed and live alone, if not institutionalized. The majority also are hospitalized at some time in the last years of life, and the majority die alone in a hospital or institution. Their needs, capacities, and resources are often different from those of older adults in their sixties and seventies (Scheibe, Freund, & Baltes, 2007).

Despite the negative portrait of the oldest-old by Baltes and his colleagues, they are a heterogeneous, diversified group. In the New England Centenarian Study, 15 percent of the individuals 100 years and older were living independently at home, 35 percent with a family or in assisted living, and 50 percent in nursing homes (Perls, 2007).

A significant number the oldest-old have cognitive impairments, but many do not. Almost one-fourth of the oldest-old are institutionalized, and many report some limitation of activity or difficulties in caring for themselves. However, more than three-fourths are not institutionalized. The majority of older adults aged 80 and over continue to live in the community. More than one-third of older adults 80 and over who live in the community report that their health is excellent or good; 40 percent say that they have no activity limitation (Suzman & others, 1992).

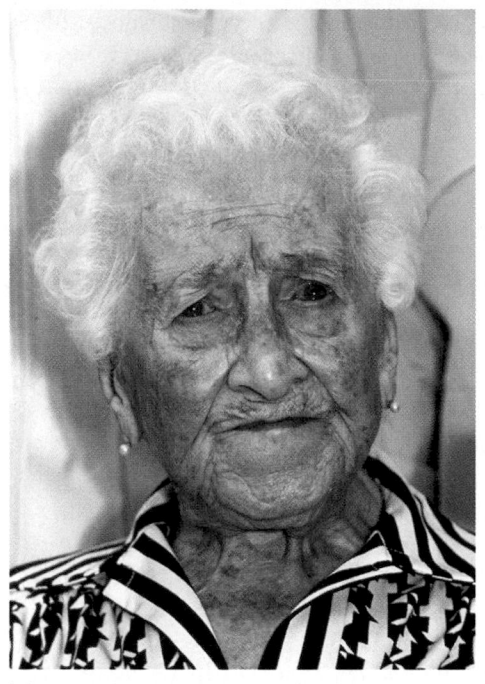

(a)

(b)

(*a*) Frenchwoman Jeanne Louise Calment, who recently died at the age of 122. Greater ages have been claimed, but scientists say the maximum human life span is about 120 to 125. (*b*) Heredity is an important component of how long we will live. For example, in Figure 17.1, you were able to add five years to your life expectancy if two or more of your grandparents lived to 80 or beyond. And if you were born a female, you start out with a basic life expectancy that is six years more than if you were born a male. The three sisters shown here are all in their eighties.

Less than 50 percent of U.S. 85- to 89-year-olds have a disability (Siegler, Bosworth, & Poon, 2003); a substantial subgroup of the oldest-old are robust and active. The oldest-old who have aged successfully have often been unnoticed and unstudied.

Biological Theories of Aging

Even if we stay remarkably healthy, we begin to age at some point. In fact, some life-span experts argue that biological aging begins at birth (Schaie, 2000). What are the biological explanations of aging? Intriguing explanations of why we age are provided by four biological theories: cellular clock theory, free-radical theory, mitochondrial theory, and hormonal stress theory.

Cellular Clock Theory   **Cellular clock theory** is Leonard Hayflick's (1977) theory that cells can divide a maximum of about 75 to 80 times and that, as we age, our cells become less capable of dividing. Hayflick found that cells extracted from adults in their fifties to seventies divided fewer than 75 to 80 times. Based on the ways cells divide, Hayflick places the upper limit of the human life-span potential at about 120 to 125 years of age.

In the last decade, scientists have tried to fill in a gap in cellular clock theory (Snyder, 2008; Zhao & others, 2008). Hayflick did not know why cells die. The answer may lie at the tips of chromosomes, at *telomeres,* which are DNA sequences that cap chromosomes (Shay & Wright, 2007). Each time a cell divides, the telomeres become shorter and shorter (see Figure 17.3). After about 70 or 80 replications, the telomeres are dramatically reduced, and the cell no longer can reproduce.

Injecting the enzyme *telomerase* into human cells grown in the laboratory can substantially extend the life of the cells beyond the approximately 70 to 80 normal

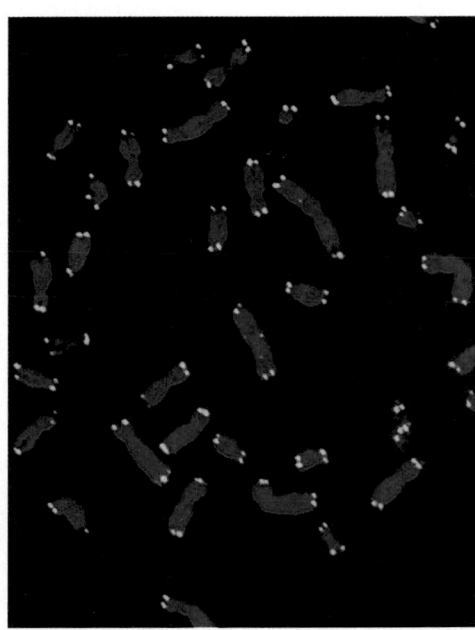

FIGURE 17.3 Telomeres and Aging. The photograph shows actual telomeres lighting up the tips of chromosomes.

cellular clock theory Leonard Hayflick's theory that the maximum number of times that human cells can divide is about 75 to 80. As we age, our cells have less capability to divide.

FIGURE 17.4 Mitochondria. This color-coded illustration of a typical cell shows mitochondria in green. The illustration also includes the nucleus (pink) with its DNA (brown). *What are ways that changes in mitochondria might be involved in aging?*

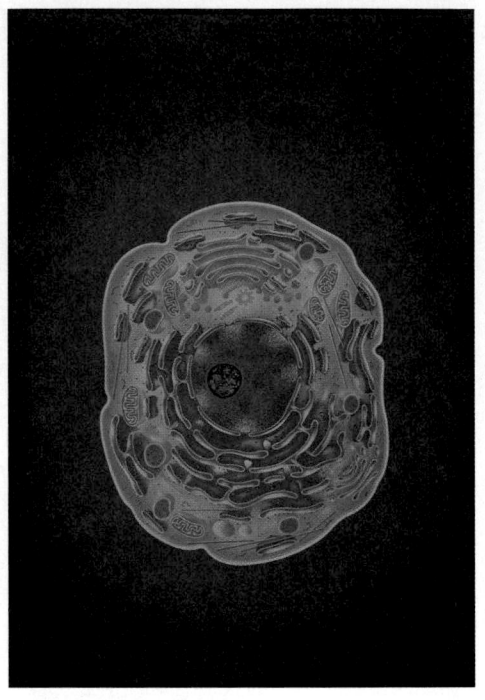

cell divisions (Aubert & Lansdorp, 2008; Shay & Wright, 2006, 2007). However, telomerase is present in approximately 85 percent of cancerous cells and thus may not produce healthy life extension of cells (Fakhoury, Nimmo, & Autexier, 2007). To capitalize on the high presence of telomerase in cancerous cells, researchers currently investigating gene therapies that inhibit telomerase and lead to the death of cancerous cells while keeping healthy cells alive (Baird, 2007; Chen, Yang, & Zhang, 2008).

Free-Radical Theory A second microbiological theory of aging is **free-radical theory**, which states that people age because when cells metabolize energy, the by-products include unstable oxygen molecules known as *free radicals* (Chehab & others, 2008). The free radicals ricochet around the cells, damaging DNA and other cellular structures (Laurent & others, 2008). The damage can lead to a range of disorders, including cancer and arthritis (Katakura, 2006). Overeating is linked with an increase in free radicals, and researchers recently have found that calorie restriction—a diet restricted in calories although adequate in proteins, vitamins, and minerals—reduces the oxidative damage created by free radicals (Keijer & van Schothorst, 2008). And a recent study revealed a greater concentration of free radicals in 20- to 80-year-old smokers than nonsmokers (Reddy Thavanati & others, 2008).

Mitochondrial Theory There is increasing interest in the role that *mitochondria*—tiny bodies within cells that supply essential energy for function, growth, and repair—might play in aging (Boveris & Navarro, 2008) (see Figure 17.4). **Mitochondrial theory** states that aging is due to the decay of mitochondria. It appears that this decay is primarily due to oxidative damage and loss of critical micronutrients supplied by the cell (Druzhyna, Wilson, & Ledoux, 2008).

How does this damage and loss of nutrients occur? Among the by-products of mitochondrial energy production are the free radicals we just described. According to the mitochondrial theory, the damage caused by free radicals initiates a self-perpetuating cycle in which oxidative damage impairs mitochondrial function, which results in the generation of even greater amounts of free radicals. The result is that over time, the affected mitochondria become so inefficient that they cannot generate enough energy to meet cellular needs (Lee & Wei, 2007). One recent study found that exercise in older adults increased mitochondrial activity in their cells (Menshikova & others, 2006). The researchers concluded that the increased mitochondrial activity might lead to an increase in mitochondria.

Defects in mitochondria are linked with cardiovascular disease, neurodegenerative diseases such as dementia, and decline in liver functioning (Amstrong, 2007; Kim, Wei, & Sowers, 2008). Mitochondria likey play important roles in neuronal plasticity (Mattson, 2007). However, it is not known whether the defects in mitochondria cause aging or are merely accompaniments of the aging process.

Hormonal Stress Theory The three theories—cellular clock, free radical, and mitochondrial—of aging that we have discussed so far attempt to explain aging at the cellular level. In contrast, **hormonal stress theory** argues that aging in the body's

free-radical theory A microbiological theory of aging that states that people age because inside their cells normal metabolism produces unstable oxygen molecules known as free radicals. These molecules ricochet around inside cells, damaging DNA and other cellular structures.

mitochondrial theory The theory that aging is caused by the decay of mitochondria, tiny cellular bodies that supply energy for function, growth, and repair.

hormonal stress theory The theory that aging in the body's hormonal system can lower resistance to stress and increase the likelihood of disease.

hormonal system can lower resistance to stress and increase the likelihood of disease (Finch & Seeman, 1999).

Normally, when people experience stressors, the body responds by releasing certain hormones. As people age, the hormones stimulated by stress remain at elevated levels longer than when people were younger (Brown-Borg, 2007; Simm & others, 2008). These prolonged, elevated levels of stress-related hormones are associated with increased risks for many diseases, including cardiovascular disease, cancer, diabetes, and hypertension (Magri & others, 2006).

Recently, a variation of hormonal stress theory has emphasized the contribution of a decline in immune system functioning with aging (Larbi & others, 2008). Aging contributes to immune system deficits that give rise to infectious diseases in older adults (Suvas, 2008). The extended duration of stress and diminished restorative processes in older adults may accelerate the effects of aging on immunity.

Which of these biological theories best explains aging? That question has not yet been answered. It might turn out that all of these biological processes contribute to aging.

Review and Reflect: Learning Goal 1

1 Characterize Longevity and the Biological Theories of Aging

REVIEW

- What is the difference between life span and life expectancy? What characterizes centenarians? What sex differences exist in longevity?
- How can the differences between the young-old, old-old, and oldest-old be summarized?
- What are the four main biological theories of aging?

REFLECT

- If we could increase the maximum human life span, would this be beneficial? If so, to whom?

2 THE COURSE OF PHYSICAL DEVELOPMENT IN LATE ADULTHOOD

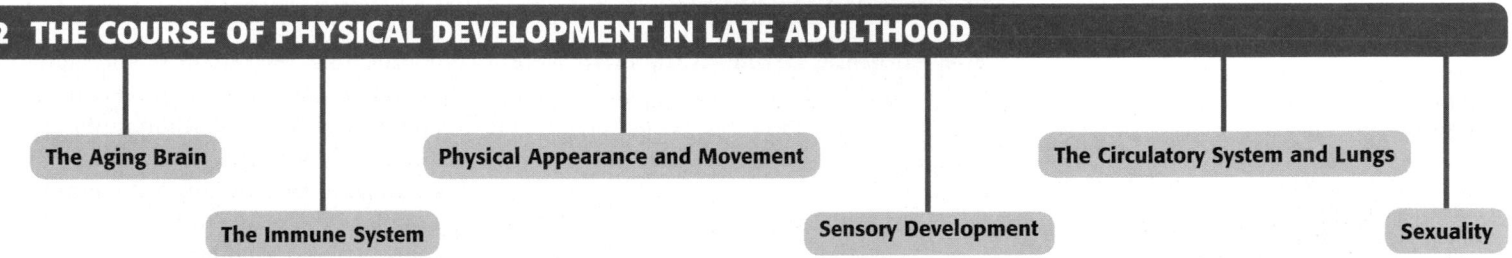

The Aging Brain

The Immune System

Physical Appearance and Movement

Sensory Development

The Circulatory System and Lungs

Sexuality

Physical decline is inevitable if we manage to live to an old age, but the timing of problems related to aging is not uniform. One analysis involved the MacArthur Research Network on Successful Aging Study, a three-site longitudinal study of successful aging in women and men 70 to 79 years of age. In this study, physical performance (such as walking efficiency, maintaining balance, and repeatedly standing up and sitting down) did decline with age, but there was considerable individual variation (Seeman & others, 1994). Healthy, higher-income participants performed better than older adults in poor health from low-income backgrounds. A majority of the older adults also maintained their physical performance over a three-year period in their seventies, and some even improved their performance during this time.

The physical decline that accompanies aging usually occurs slowly, and sometimes even lost function can be restored. We'll examine the main physical changes behind the losses of late adulthood.

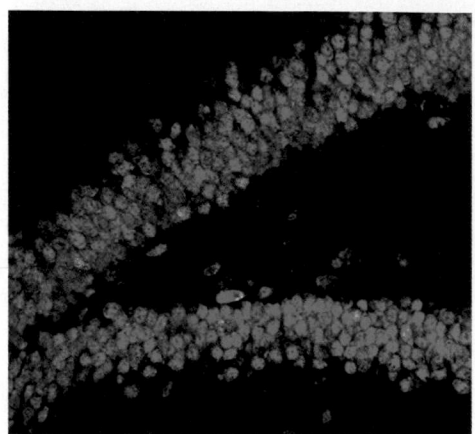

Exercise

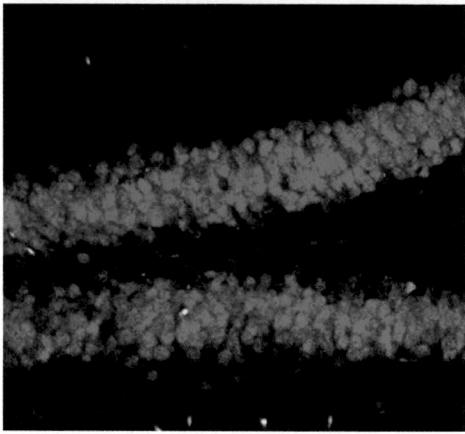

Enriched Environment

FIGURE 17.5 Generating New Nerve Cells in Adult Mice. Researchers have found that exercise (running) and an enriched environment (a larger cage and many toys) can cause brain cells to divide and form new brain cells (Kempermann, van Praag, & Gage, 2000). Cells were labeled with a chemical marker that becomes integrated into the DNA of dividing cells (red). Four weeks later, they were also labeled to mark neurons (nerve cells). As shown here, both the running mice and the mice in an enriched environment had many cells that were still dividing (red) and others that had differentiated into new nerve cells (orange).

neurogenesis The generation of new neurons.

The Aging Brain

How does the brain change during late adulthood? Does it retain plasticity?

The Shrinking, Slowing Brain On average, the brain loses 5 to 10 percent of its weight between the ages of 20 and 90. Brain volume also decreases (Bondare, 2007). One study found that the volume of the brain was 15 percent less in older adults than younger adults (Shan & others, 2005). Scientists are not sure why these changes occur but believe they might result from a decrease in dendrites, damage to the myelin sheath that covers axons, or simply the death of brain cells.

Some areas shrink more than others. The prefrontal cortex is one area that shrinks with aging, and recent research has linked this shrinkage with a decrease in working memory and other cognitive activities in older adults (Pardo & others, 2007).

A general slowing of function in the brain and spinal cord begins in middle adulthood and accelerates in late adulthood (Birren, 2002). Both physical coordination and intellectual performance are affected. For example, after age 70, many adults no longer show a knee jerk, and by age 90 most reflexes are much slower (Spence, 1989). The slowing of the brain can impair the performance of older adults on intelligence tests and various cognitive tasks, especially those that are timed (Birren, Woods, & Williams, 1980). For example, one recent neuroimaging study revealed that older adults were more likely to be characterized by slower processing in the prefrontal cortex during retrieval of information on a cognitive task than were younger adults (Rypma, Eldreth, & Rebbechi, 2007).

Aging has also been linked to a reduction in the production of some neurotransmitters, including acetylcholine, dopamine, and gamma-aminobutyric acid (GABA) (Dickstein & others, 2007; McNeil & others, 2007). Some researchers conclude that reductions in acetylcholine may be responsible for small declines in memory functioning and even with the severe memory loss associated with Alzheimer disease, which we discuss in Chapter 18 (Holzgrabe & others, 2007). Normal age-related reductions in dopamine may cause problems in planning and carrying out motor activities (Erixon-Lindroth & others, 2005). Severe reductions in the production of dopamine have been linked with age-related diseases characterized by a loss of motor control, such as Parkinson disease (Hauser & Zesiewicz, 2007). GABA helps to control the preciseness of the signal sent from one neuron to another, decreasing "noise," and its production decreases with aging (Yuan, 2008).

The Adapting Brain If the brain were a computer, this description of the aging brain might lead you to think that it could not do much of anything. However, unlike a computer, the brain has remarkable repair capability (Grady, 2008; Hillman, Erickson, & Kramer, 2008). Even in late adulthood, the brain loses only a portion of its ability to function, and the activities older adults engage in can influence the brain's development (Erickson & others, 2007). For example, in a recent fMRI study, six months of aerobic exercise increased the brain volume of older adults (Colcombe & others, 2006).

Can adults, even aging adults, generate new neurons? Researchers have found that **neurogenesis**, the generation of new neurons, does occur in lower mammalian species, such as mice (Sun & Bartke, 2007). Also, research indicates that exercise and an enriched, complex environment can generate new brain cells in mice and that stress reduces their survival rate (Mora, Segovia, & del Arco, 2007; Pereira & others, 2007; Thomas, Hotsenpiller, & Peterson, 2007) (see Figure 17.5). It also is now accepted that neurogenesis can occur in humans (Libert, Cohen, & Guarente, 2008). However, researchers have documented neurogenesis in only two brain regions: the hippocampus, which is involved in memory, and the olfactory bulb, which is involved in smell (Gould, 2007; Verret & others, 2007). It also is not known what functions these new brain cells perform, and at this point researchers have documented that they last for only several weeks (Nelson, 2006). Researchers currently are studying factors that might inhibit and promote neurogenesis, including various drugs, stress, and exercise (Chen & others, 2007; Mora & others, 2007). They also are examining how the grafting of neural stem cells to various regions of the brain, such as the hippocampus, might increase neurogenesis (Hattiangady & others, 2007).

Dendritic growth can occur in human adults, possibly even in older adults (Eliasieh, Liets, & Chalupa, 2007). Recall from Chapter 4, "Physical Development in Infancy," that dendrites are the receiving portion of the neuron. One study compared the brains of adults at various ages (Coleman, 1986). From the forties through the seventies, the growth of dendrites increased. However, in people in their nineties, dendritic growth no longer occurred. This dendritic growth might compensate for the possible loss of neurons through the seventies but not in the nineties. Lack of dendritic growth in older adults could be due to a lack of environmental stimulation and activity. Further research is needed to clarify what changes characterize dendrites during aging.

Stanley Rapaport (1994), chief of the neurosciences laboratory at the National Institute on Aging, demonstrated another way in which the aging brain can adapt. He compared the brains of younger and older people engaged in the same tasks. The older brains had rewired themselves to compensate for losses. If one neuron was not up to the job, neighboring neurons helped to pick up the slack. Rapaport concluded that as brains age, they can shift responsibilities for a given task from one region to another.

Changes in lateralization may provide one type of adaptation in aging adults (Cabeza, 2002). Recall that lateralization is the specialization of function in one hemisphere of the brain or the other. Using neuroimaging techniques, researchers found that brain activity in the prefrontal cortex is lateralized less in older adults than in younger adults when they are engaging in cognitive tasks (Cabeza, 2002; Rossi & others, 2005). For example, Figure 17.6 shows that when younger adults are given the task of recognizing words they have previously seen, they process the information primarily in the right hemisphere; older adults are more likely to use both hemispheres (Madden & others, 1999). The decrease in lateralization in older adults might play a compensatory role in the aging brain. That is, using both hemispheres may improve the cognitive functioning of older adults.

Of course, there are individual differences in how the brain changes in older adults. Consider highly successful businessman 80-year-old T. Boone Pickens, who continues to lead a highly active lifestyle, regularly exercising and engaging in cognitively complex work. Undergoing a recent fMRI in cognitive neuroscientist Denise Park's laboratory, when Pickens was presented various cognitive tasks, instead of showing both hemispheres being active, Pickens' left hemisphere was still dominant, just as the case with most younger adults (Helman, 2008). Indeed, as the cognitive tasks became more complex, the more Pickens used the left hemisphere of his brain (see Figure 17.7). To read further about aging and the brain, see the *Research in Life-Span Development* interlude.

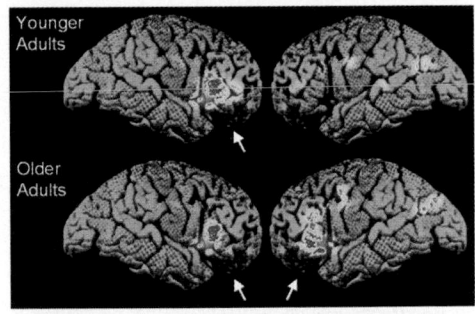

FIGURE 17.6 The Decrease in Brain Lateralization in Older Adults. Younger adults primarily used the right prefrontal region of the brain (*top left photo*) during a recall memory task, whereas older adults used both the left and right prefrontal regions (*bottom two photos*).

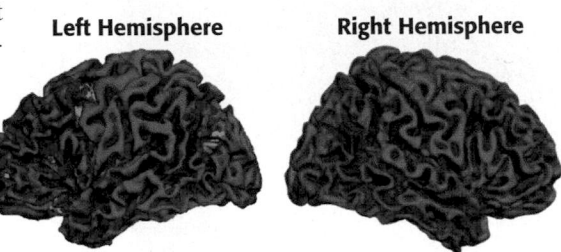

Left Hemisphere   Right Hemisphere

FIGURE 17.7 Individual Differences in Hemispheric Specialization in Older Adults. On tough questions—such as "Are 'zombie' and 'unicorn' living or nonliving?"—the red patches indicate that 80-year-old T. Boone Pickens (above, holding a model of the brain) was relying mainly on the left hemisphere of his brain to make a decision. Most older adults show a stronger bilateral activation, using both hemispheres more equally than Pickens, whose lateralization was more characteristic of younger adults.

Research in Life-Span Development
The Nun Study

The Nun Study, directed by David Snowdon, is an intriguing ongoing investigation of aging in 678 nuns, many of whom are from a convent in Mankato, Minnesota (Grossi & others, 2007; Snowdon, 2003; Tyas & others, 2007). Each of the 678 nuns agreed to participate in annual assessments of their cognitive and physical functioning. They also agreed to donate their brains for scientific research when they die, and they are the largest group of brain donors in the world. Examination of the nuns' donated brains, as well as others', has led neuroscientists to believe that the brain has a remarkable

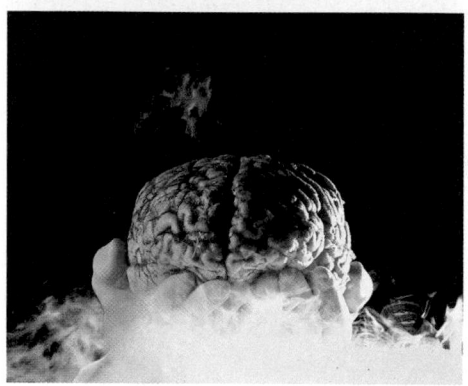

Top: Sister Marcella Zachman (*left*) finally stopped teaching at age 97. Now, at 99, she helps ailing nuns exercise their brains by quizzing them on vocabulary or playing a card game called Skip-Bo, at which she deliberately loses. Sister Mary Esther Boor (*right*), also 99 years of age, is a former teacher who stays alert by doing puzzles and volunteering to work the front desk. *Below:* A technician holds the brain of a deceased Mankato nun. The nuns donate their brains for research that explores the effects of stimulation on brain growth.

Percentage of total weight

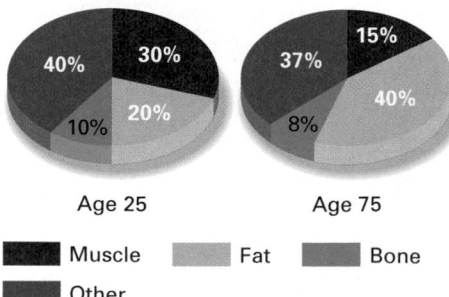

FIGURE 17.8 Changes in Body Composition of Bone, Muscle, and Fat from 25 to 75 Years of Age. Notice the decrease in bone and muscle and the increase in fat from 25 to 75 years of age.

capacity to change and grow, even in old age. The Sisters of Notre Dame in Mankato lead an intellectually challenging life, and brain researchers believe this contributes to their quality of life as older adults and possibly to their longevity.

Findings from the Nun Study so far include:

- Idea density, a measure of linguistic ability assessed early in the adult years (age 22), was linked with higher brain weight, fewer incidences of mild cognitive impairment, and fewer characteristics of Alzheimer disease in 75- to 95-year-old nuns (Riley & others, 2005).

- Positive emotions early in adulthood were linked to longevity (Danner, Snowdon, & Friesen, 2001). Handwritten autobiographies from 180 nuns, composed when they were 22 years of age, were scored for emotional content. The nuns whose early writings had higher scores for positive emotional content were more likely to still be alive at 75 to 95 years of age than their counterparts whose early writings were characterized by negative emotional content.

- Sisters who had taught for most of their lives showed more moderate declines in intellectual skills than those who had spent most of their lives in service-based tasks, which supports the notion that stimulating the brain with intellectual activity keeps neurons healthy and alive (Snowdon, 2002).

This and other research provides hope that scientists will discover ways to tap into the brain's capacity to adapt in order to prevent and treat brain diseases (Dobrossy & Dunnett, 2005). For example, scientists might learn more effective ways to help older adults recover from strokes. Even when areas of the brain are permanently damaged by stroke, new message routes can be created to get around the blockage or to resume the function of that area, indicating that the brain does adapt.

The Immune System

Decline in the functioning of the body's immune system with aging is well documented (Larbi & others, 2008, Suvas, 2008). As we indicated earlier in our discussion of hormonal stress theory, the extended duration of stress and diminished restorative processes in older adults may accelerate the effects of aging on immunity (Colonna-Romano & others, 2008). Also, malnutrition involving low levels of protein is linked to a decrease in T cells that destroy infected cells and hence to deterioration in the immune system (Virts, Phillips, & Thoman, 2006). Exercise can improve immune system functioning (Phillips, Burns, & Lord, 2007). Because of the decline in the functioning of the immune system that accompanies aging, vaccination against influenza is especially important in older adults (Kumar & Burns, 2008).

Physical Appearance and Movement

In late adulthood, the changes in physical appearance that began occurring during middle age (as discussed in Chapter 15) become more pronounced (McCarter, 2006). Wrinkles and age spots are the most noticeable changes.

We also get shorter when we get older. As we saw in Chapter 15, both men and women become shorter in late adulthood because of bone loss in their vertebrae (Hoyer & Roodin, 2003).

Our weight usually drops after we reach 60 years of age. This likely occurs because we lose muscle, which also gives our bodies a "sagging" look (Harridge & Saltin, 2007). Figure 17.8 shows the decline in percentage of muscle and bone from age 25 to age 75, and the corresponding increase in the percentage of fat.

Older adults move more slowly than young adults, and this slowing occurs for movements with a wide range of difficulty (Rossit & Harvey, 2008; Vernazza-Martin & others, 2008) (see Figure 17.9). Even when they perform everyday tasks such as reaching and grasping, moving from one place to another, and continuous movement, older adults tend to move more slowly than when they were young

(Mollenkopf, 2007; Woollacott, 2007). Adequate mobility is an important aspect of maintaining an independent and active lifestyle in late adulthood (Baezner & others, 2008; Callisaya & others, 2008). One recent study of the functional ability of noninstitutionalized individuals 70 years of age and older revealed that over an eight-year period, the most deterioration occurred in their mobility (Holstein & others, 2007). The good news is that regular walking decreases the onset of physical disability in older adults (Newman & others, 2006). Also, in a recent study, 70- to 89-year-olds at risk for mobility disability were randomly assigned to 12 months of either physical activity or a successful aging educational intervention (Rejeski & others, 2008). Older adults who engaged in physical activity showed more mobility gains than those in the educational intervention. And another recent study revealed that a higher level of physical activity and a lower level of adiposity (fatness) were linked to lower mobility restrictions in older adults (Koster & others, 2008). Also, exercise and appropriate weight lifting can help to reduce the decrease in muscle mass and improve the older person's body appearance (Der Ananian & Prohaska, 2007). We will have more to say about the benefits of exercise later in this chapter.

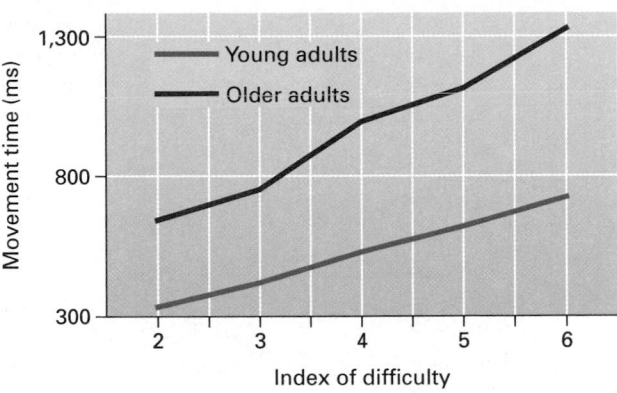

FIGURE 17.9 Movement and Aging. Older adults take longer to move than young adults, and this occurs across a range of movement difficulty (Ketcham & Stelmach, 2001).

Sensory Development

Seeing, hearing, and other aspects of sensory functioning are linked with our ability to perform everyday activities. This link was documented in a study of more than 500 adults, 70 to 102 years of age, in which sensory acuity, especially in vision, was related to whether and how well older adults bathed and groomed themselves, completed household chores, engaged in intellectual activities, and watched TV (Marsiske, Klumb, & Baltes, 1997). How do vision, hearing, taste, smell, touch, and pain change in late adulthood?

Vision   With aging, visual acuity, color vision, and depth perception decline. Several diseases of the eye also may emerge in aging adults.

Visual Acuity   In late adulthood, the decline in vision that began for most adults in early or middle adulthood becomes more pronounced (Berger & Porell, 2008; Ferrer-Blasco & others, 2008). Night driving is especially difficult, to some extent because tolerance for glare diminishes (Stutts, 2007). *Dark adaptation* is slower, meaning that older individuals take longer to recover their vision when going from a well-lighted room to semidarkness. The area of the visual field becomes smaller, suggesting that the intensity of a stimulus in the peripheral area of the visual field needs to be increased if the stimulus is to be seen. Events taking place away from the center of the visual field might not be detected (Stutts, 2007).

This visual decline often can be traced to a reduction in the quality or intensity of light reaching the retina. At 60 years of age, the retina receives only about one-third as much light as it did at 20 years of age (Scialfa & Kline, 2007). In extreme old age, these changes might be accompanied by degenerative changes in the retina, causing severe difficulty in seeing. Large-print books and magnifiers might be needed in such cases.

An extensive study of visual changes in adults found that the age of older adults was a significant factor in how extensively their visual functioning differed from that of younger adults (Brabyn & others, 2001). Beyond 75, and more so beyond age 85, older adults showed significantly worse performance on a number of visual tasks when compared with young adults and older adults in their sixties and early seventies. The greatest decline in visual perception beyond 75, and especially beyond 85, involved glare. The older adults, especially those 85 and older, fared much

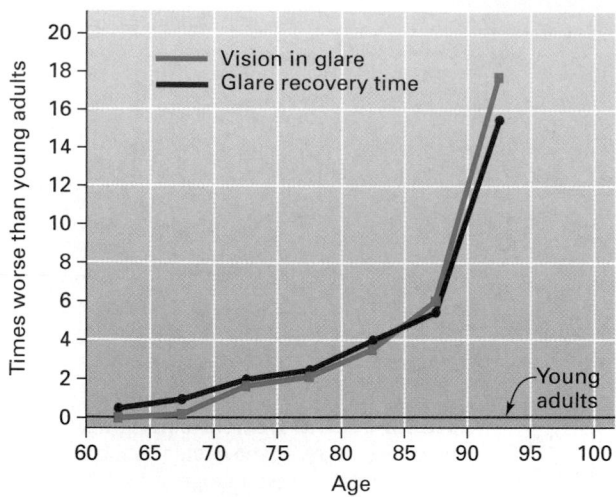

FIGURE 17.10 Rates of Decline in Visual Functioning Related to Glare in Adults of Different Ages. Older adults, especially those 85 and older, fare much worse than younger adults in being able to see clearly when glare is present, and their recovery from glare is much slower. These data were collected from a random sample of community-dwelling older adults living in Marin County, California. For each age, the factor by which the group's median performance was worse than normative values for young adults is shown.

FIGURE 17.11 Macular Degeneration. This simulation of the effect of macular degeneration shows how individuals with this eye disease can see their peripheral field of vision but can't clearly see what is in their central visual field.

cataracts Involve a thickening of the lens of the eye that causes vision to become cloudy, opaque, and distorted.

glaucoma Damage to the optic nerve because of the pressure created by a buildup of fluid in the eye.

macular degeneration A disease that involves deterioration of the macula of the retina, which corresponds to the focal center of the visual field.

worse in being able to see clearly when glare was present, and they took much longer to recover from glare than younger adults (see Figure 17.10). For example, whereas young adults recover vision following glare in less than 10 seconds, 50 percent of 90-year-olds have not recovered vision after 1.5 minutes.

Color Vision Color vision also may decline with age in older adults as a result of the yellowing of the lens of the eye (Scialfa & Kline, 2007). This decline is most likely to occur in the green-blue-violet part of the color spectrum. As a result, older adults may have trouble accurately matching closely related colors such as navy socks and black socks.

Depth Perception As with many areas of perception, depth perception changes little after infancy until adults become older. Depth perception typically declines in late adulthood, which can make it difficult for the older adult to determine how close or far away or how high or low something is (Norman & others, 2006). A decline in depth perception can make steps or street curbs difficult to manage.

A decrease in contrast sensitivity is one factor that diminishes the older adult's ability to perceive depth (Stutts, 2007). Light-dark contrast is produced by the amount of light reflected by surfaces (a light object is brighter than a dark object). The difference in contrast makes objects that contrast with the background easier to see. Compared with younger adults, older adults need sharper contrasts and sharper edges around an object to differentiate it from its background.

Diseases of the Eye Three diseases that can impair the vision of older adults are cataracts, glaucoma, and macular degeneration:

- **Cataracts** involve a thickening of the lens of the eye that causes vision to become cloudy, opaque, and distorted (Sugimoto, Kuze, & Uji, 2008). By age 70, approximately 30 percent of individuals experience a partial loss of vision due to cataracts. Initially, cataracts can be treated by glasses; if they worsen, a simple surgical procedure can remove them (Muskesh & others, 2006).

- **Glaucoma** involves damage to the optic nerve because of the pressure created by a buildup of fluid in the eye (Lacey, Cate, & Broadway, 2008). Approximately 1 percent of individuals in their seventies and 10 percent of those in their nineties have glaucoma, which can be treated with eyedrops. If left untreated, glaucoma can ultimately destroy a person's vision (Friedman & others, 2008).

- **Macular degeneration** is a disease that involves deterioration of the *macula* of the retina, which corresponds to the focal center of the visual field. Individuals with macular degeneration may have relatively normal peripheral vision but be unable to see clearly what is right in front of them (Redmond & White, 2008) (see Figure 17.11). It affects 1 in 25 individuals from 66 to 74 years of age and 1 in 6 of those 75 years old and older. A recent study revealed that cigarette smoking is a contributing factor in macular degeneration (Schmidt & others, 2006). If the disease is detected early, it can be treated with laser surgery (Cook, Patel, & Tufail, 2008). However, macular degeneration is difficult to treat and thus a leading cause of blindness in older adults (Gohel & others, 2008).

Hearing For hearing as for vision, the age of older adults is important in determining the degree of decline (Stenklev, Vik, & Laukli, 2004) (see Figure 17.12). The decline in

Perceptual System	Young-Old (65 to 74 years)	Old-Old (75 years and older)
Vision	There is a loss of acuity even with corrective lenses. Less transmission of light occurs through the retina (half as much as in young adults). Greater susceptibility to glare occurs. Color discrimination ability decreases.	There is a significant loss of visual acuity and color discrimination, and a decrease in the size of the perceived visual field. In late old age, people are at significant risk for visual dysfunction from cataracts and glaucoma.
Hearing	There is a significant loss of hearing at high frequencies and some loss at middle frequencies. These losses can be helped by a hearing aid. There is greater susceptibility to masking of what is heard by noise.	There is a significant loss at high and middle frequencies. A hearing aid is more likely to be needed than in young-old age.

FIGURE 17.12 Vision and Hearing Decline in the Young-Old and the Old-Old

vision and hearing is much greater in individuals 75 years and older than in individuals 65 to 74 years of age (Charness & Bosman, 1992).

Hearing impairment usually does not become much of an impediment until late adulthood (Fozard & Gordon-Salant, 2001). Only 19 percent of individuals from 45 to 54 years of age experience some type of hearing problem, but for those 75 to 79, the figure reaches 75 percent (Harris, 1975). It has been estimated that 15 percent of the population over the age of 65 is legally deaf, usually due to degeneration of the *cochlea,* the primary neural receptor for hearing in the inner ear (Frisina & Walton, 2006).

Older adults often don't recognize that they have a hearing problem, deny that they have one, or accept it as a part of growing old (Fowler & Leigh-Paffenroth, 2007). Older women are more likely to seek treatment for their hearing problem than older men (Fowler & Leigh-Paffenroth, 2007).

Two devices can be used to minimize the problems linked to hearing loss in older adults: (1) hearing aids that amplify sound to reduce middle ear–based conductive hearing loss, and (2) cochlear implants that restore some hearing following neurosensory hearing loss (Pauley & others, 2008). Currently, researchers are exploring the use of stem cells as an alternative to the use of cochlear implants (Pauley & others, 2008).

Smell and Taste   Most older adults lose some of their sense of smell or taste, or both (Roberts & Rosenberg, 2006). These losses often begin around 60 years of age (Hawkes, 2006). Researchers have found that older adults show a greater decline in their sense of smell than in their taste (Schiffman, 2007). Smell and taste decline less in healthy older adults than in their less healthy counterparts.

Reductions in the ability to smell and taste can reduce enjoyment of food and life satisfaction (Rolls & Drewnowski, 2007). Also, a decline in the sense of smell can reduce the ability to detect smoke from a fire. If elderly individuals need to be encouraged to eat more, compounds that stimulate the olfactory nerve are sometimes added to food. However, many older adults compensate for their diminished taste and smell by eating sweeter, spicier, and saltier foods, which can lead to eating more low-nutrient, highly seasoned "junk food" (Hoyer & Roodin, 2003). Further, a recent study of 19 to 39, 40 to 59, and 60-year-old and older adults revealed that although adults' ability to detect a smell declined as they got older, the perceived pleasantness of a smell increased in the older group (Markovic & others, 2007).

Touch and Pain   Changes in touch and pain are also associated with aging (Deshpande & others, 2008; Harkins & Scott, 2007). One study found that, with aging, individuals could detect touch less in the lower extremities (ankles, knees, and so on) than in the upper extremities (wrists, shoulders, and so on) (Corso, 1977). For most older adults, a decline in touch sensitivity is not problematic (Hoyer & Roodin, 2003).

Researchers have found that most older adults show a reduction in their sense of smell and taste. However, a recent study revealed that the perceived pleasantness of a smell increased in older adults (Markovic & others, 2007).

Older adults are less sensitive to pain and suffer from it less than younger adults (Harkins, Price, & Martinelli, 1986). Although decreased sensitivity to pain can help older adults cope with disease and injury, it can also mask injury and illness that need to be treated.

The Circulatory System and Lungs

Cardiovascular disorders increase in late adulthood (Tulenko, Lapotofsky, & Mason, 2007; Yamasue & others, 2008). In one analysis, 57 percent of 80-year-old-men and 60 percent of 81-year-old women had hypertension, and 32 percent of the men and 31 percent of the women had experienced a stroke (Aronow, 2007).

Today, most experts on aging even recommend that consistent blood pressures above 120/80 should be treated to reduce the risk of heart attack, stroke, or kidney disease (Kagiyama & others, 2008; Krakoff, 2008). A rise in blood pressure with age can be linked with illness, obesity, anxiety, stiffening of blood vessels, or lack of exercise (Ferinni & Ferinni, 2008). The longer any of these factors persist, the worse the individual's blood pressure gets (Hawkins & Dunn, 2006).

Lung capacity drops 40 percent between the ages of 20 and 80, even without disease (Fozard, 1992). Lungs lose elasticity, the chest shrinks, and the diaphragm weakens (Cherniack & Cherniack, 2007). The good news, though, is that older adults can improve lung functioning with diaphragm-strengthening exercises. Severe impairments in lung functioning and death can result from smoking (Whincup & others, 2006).

Sexuality

In the absence of two circumstances—disease and the belief that old people are or should be asexual—sexuality can be lifelong. Aging, however, does induce some changes in human sexual performance, more so in the male than in the female (Bauman, 2008).

Orgasm becomes less frequent in males with age, occurring in every second to third attempt rather than every time. More direct stimulation usually is needed to produce an erection. From 65 to 80 years of age, approximately one out of four men have serious problems getting and/or keeping erections, and after 80 years of age the percentage rises to one out of two men (Butler & Lewis, 2002).

A recent interview study of more than 3,000 adults 57 to 85 years of age revealed that many older adults are sexually active as long as they are healthy (Lindau & others, 2007). Sexual activity did decline through the later years of life: 73 percent of 57- to 64-year-olds, 53 percent of 65- to 74-year-olds, and 26 percent 75- to 85-year-olds reported that they were sexually active. Even in the sexually active oldest group (75 to 85), more than 50 percent said they still have sex at least two to three times a month. Fifty-eight percent of sexually active 65- to 74-year-olds and 31 percent of 75- to 85-year-olds said they engage in oral sex. As with middle-aged and younger adults, older adults who did not have a partner were far less likely to be sexually active than those who had a partner. For older adults with a partner who reported not having sex, the main reason was poor health, especially the male partner's physical health.

As indicated in Figure 17.13, sexual activity with a partner declined from the last part of middle adulthood through late adulthood, with a lower rate of sexual activity with a partner for women than men. Indeed, a challenge for a sexually interested older woman is not having a partner. At 70 years of age, approximately 70 percent of women don't have a partner compared with only about 35 percent of men. Many older women's husbands have died, and many older men are with younger women.

Various therapies for older adults who report sexual difficulties have been effective (Malatesta, 2007). In one study, sex education—which consisted largely of simply giving

What are some characteristics of sexuality in older adults? How does sexuality change as older adults go through the late adulthood period?

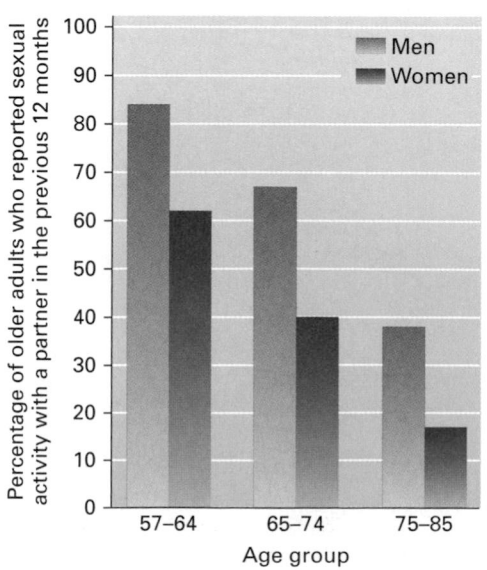

FIGURE 17.13 Sexual Activity in Older Adults with a Partner

sexual information—led to increased sexual interest, knowledge, and activity in older adults (White & Catania, 1981). Even when intercourse is impaired by infirmity, other relationship needs persist, among them closeness, sensuality, and being valued as a man or a woman (Brock & Jennings, 2007; Hurd Clarke, 2006). We discuss these needs in Chapter 19.

Review and Reflect: Learning Goal 2

 2 Describe How a Person's Brain and Body Change in Late Adulthood

REVIEW

• How much plasticity and adaptability does the aging brain have?
• How does the immune system change with aging?
• What changes in physical appearance and movement characterize late adulthood?
• How do vision, hearing, smell and taste, touch, and sensitivity to pain change in older adults?
• How does the circulatory system change in older adults? How do the lungs change in older adults?
• What is the nature of sexuality in late adulthood?

REFLECT

• If you could interview the Mankato nuns, what questions would you want to ask them?

3 HEALTH

Health Problems — **Substance Abuse** — **Exercise, Nutrition, and Weight** — **Health Treatment**

How healthy are older adults? What types of health problems do they have, and what can be done to maintain or improve their health and ability to function in everyday life?

Health Problems

As we age, the probability increases that we will have some disease or illness (Ferrucci & Koh, 2007). The majority of adults still alive at 80 years of age or older are likely to have some type of impairment. Chronic diseases (those with a slow onset and a long duration) are rare in early adulthood, increase in middle adulthood, and become more common in late adulthood (Kane, 2007). As indicated in Figure 17.14, 84 percent of U.S. adults 65 years of age and older have one or more chronic conditions, and 62 percent have two more chronic conditions (Partnership for Solutions, 2002).

As shown in Figure 17.15, arthritis is the most common chronic disorder in late adulthood, followed by hypertension. Older women have a higher incidence of arthritis and hypertension and are more likely to have visual problems, but are less likely to have hearing problems, than older men are.

Although adults over the age of 65 often have a physical impairment, many of them can still carry on their everyday activities or work. Chronic conditions

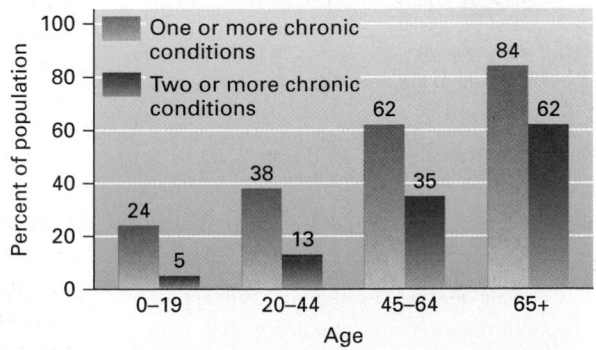

FIGURE 17.14 Percent of U.S. Population with Chronic Conditions Across Age Groups

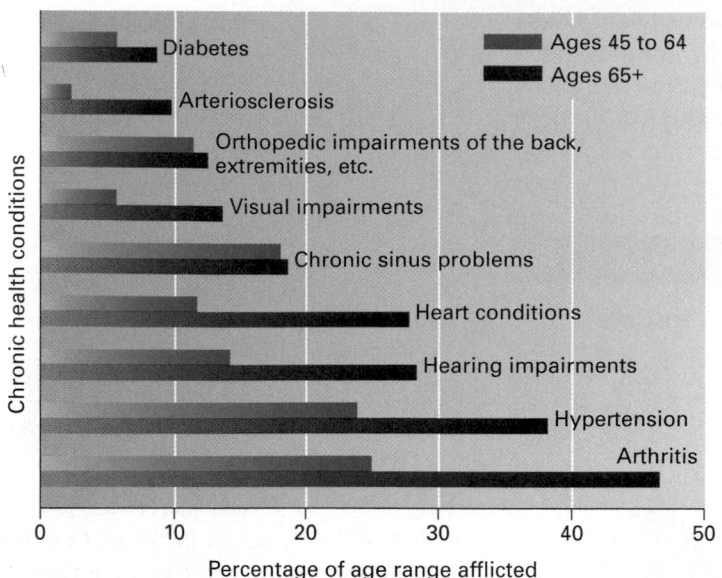

FIGURE 17.15 The Most Prevalent Chronic Conditions in Middle and Late Adulthood

What characterizes osteoporosis? What are factors that contribute to the development of osteoporosis?

arthritis Inflammation of the joints that is accompanied by pain, stiffness, and movement problems; especially common in older adults.

osteoporosis A chronic condition that involves an extensive loss of bone tissue and is the main reason many older adults walk with a marked stoop. Women are especially vulnerable to osteoporosis.

associated with the greatest limitation on work are heart conditions (52 percent), diabetes (34 percent), asthma (27 percent), and arthritis (27 percent). Conflict in relationships has been linked with greater decline in older adults with diabetes or hypertension (Seeman & Chen, 2002). Low income is also strongly related to health problems in late adulthood (Ferraro, 2006). Approximately three times as many poor as nonpoor older adults report that their activities are limited by chronic disorders.

Causes of Death in Older Adults Nearly three-fourths of all older adults die of heart disease, cancer, or cerebrovascular disease (stroke). Chronic lung diseases, pneumonia and influenza, and diabetes round out the six leading causes of death among older adults. If cancer, the second leading cause of death in older adults, were completely eliminated, the average life expectancy would rise by only one to two years. However, if all cardiovascular and kidney diseases were eradicated, the average life expectancy of older adults would increase by approximately 10 years. This increase in longevity is already under way as the number of strokes among older adults has declined considerably in the last several decades. The decline in strokes is due to improved treatment of high blood pressure, a decrease in smoking, better diet, and an increase in exercise.

Ethnicity is linked with the death rates of older adults (National Center for Health Statistics, 2008). Among ethnic groups in the United States, African Americans have high death rates for stroke, heart disease, lung cancer, and female breast cancer. Asian Americans and Latinos have low death rates for these diseases. In the last decade, death rates for most diseases in African Americans, Latinos, and Asian Americans have decreased. However, death rates for most diseases still remain high for African Americans (National Center for Health Statistics, 2008).

Arthritis **Arthritis** is an inflammation of the joints accompanied by pain, stiffness, and movement problems. Arthritis is especially common in older adults (Walji & Badley, 2007). This disorder can affect hips, knees, ankles, fingers, and vertebrae. Individuals with arthritis often experience pain and stiffness, as well as problems in moving about and performing routine daily activities. There is no known cure for arthritis. However, the symptoms of arthritis can be reduced by drugs, such as aspirin, range-of-motion exercises for the afflicted joints, weight reduction, and, in extreme cases, replacement of the crippled joint with a prosthesis (Spinetti & others, 2007). Recent studies also document the benefits of exercise in older adults with arthritis (Bulthius & others, 2007; Metsios & others, 2008).

Osteoporosis Normal aging brings some loss of bone tissue, but in some instances loss of bone tissue can become severe. **Osteoporosis** involves an extensive loss of bone tissue. Osteoporosis is the main reason many older adults walk with a marked stoop. Women are especially vulnerable to osteoporosis, the leading cause of broken bones in women (Iacono, 2007). Approximately 80 percent of osteoporosis cases in the United States occur in females, 20 percent in males. Almost two-thirds of all women over the age of 60 are affected by osteoporosis. It is more common in non-Latina White, thin, and small-framed women.

Osteoporosis is related to deficiencies in calcium, vitamin D, estrogen, and lack of exercise (Lin & Lane, 2008). To prevent osteoporosis, young and middle-aged women should eat foods rich in calcium (such as dairy products, broccoli, turnip greens, and kale), get more exercise, and avoid smoking (Cashman, 2008; Lanham-New, 2008). Drugs such as Fosamax can be used to reduce the risk of osteoporosis (Suzuki & others, 2008). Aging women should also get bone density checks (Hourigan & others, 2008).

A program of regular exercise has the potential to reduce osteoporosis (Hongo & others, 2007; Schwab & Klein, 2008).

Accidents   Accidents are the seventh leading cause of death among older adults. Injuries resulting from a fall at home or during a traffic accident in which an older adult is a driver or an older pedestrian is hit by a vehicle are common (Aschkenasy & Rothenhaus, 2006). Falls are the leading cause of injury deaths among adults who are 65 years and older (National Center for Health Statistics, 2008). Each year, approximately 200,000 adults over the age of 65 (most of them women) fracture a hip in a fall. Half of these older adults die within 12 months, frequently from pneumonia. Because healing and recuperation are slower in older adults, an accident that is only a temporary setback for a younger person may result in long-term hospital or home care for an older adult. In one study, an exercise program reduced the risk of falls in elderly adults (Province & others, 1995). In another study, Tai Chi, a form of balance training, improved the coordination of older adults in challenging conditions (Wong & others, 2001).

Substance Abuse

In many cases, older adults are taking multiple medications, which can increase the risks associated with consuming alcohol or other drugs. For example, when combined with tranquilizers or sedatives, alcohol use can impair breathing, produce excessive sedation, and be fatal.

How extensive is substance abuse in older adults? A national survey found that binge drinking (having five or more drinks in one day) declines through the late adulthood years (National Center for Health Statistics, 2002) (see Figure 17.16). Indeed, a majority (58 percent) of U.S. adults 65 years and older completely abstain from alcohol, an increase from 38 percent of 45- to 64-year-olds. These declines are usually attributed to an increase in illness and disease (Aldwin, Spiro, & Park, 2006).

Despite these declines in alcohol use, the Substance Abuse and Mental Health Services Administration (2002) has identified substance abuse among older adults as the "invisible epidemic" in the United States. The belief is that substance abuse often goes undetected in older adults, and there is concern about older adults who not only abuse illicit drugs but prescription drugs as well (Segal, 2007). Too often, screening questionnaires are not appropriate for older adults, and the consequences of alcohol abuse—such as depression, inadequate nutrition, congestive heart failure, and frequent falls—may erroneously be attributed to other medical or psychological conditions (Hoyer & Roodin, 2003). Because of the dramatic increase in the number of older adults anticipated over the twenty-first century, substance abuse is likely to characterize an increasing number of older adults (Atkinson, Ryan, & Turner, 2001).

Late-onset alcoholism is the label used to describe the onset of alcoholism after the age of 65. Late-onset alcoholism is often related to loneliness, loss of a spouse, or a disabling condition.

Recent studies have revealed a protective effect of moderate alcohol use in older adults (Strandberg & others, 2007). One study revealed better physical and mental health, and increased longevity in older adults who drank moderately compared with those who drank heavily or did not drink at all (Rozzini, Ranhoff, & Trabucchi, 2007). The explanation of moderate drinking's benefits involve better physical and mental performance, being more open to social contacts, and being able to assert mastery over one's life.

Researchers have especially found that moderate drinking of red wine is linked to better health and increased longevity (Kaur & others, 2007). Explanation of the benefits of red wine center on its connection to lowering stress and reduced risk of coronary

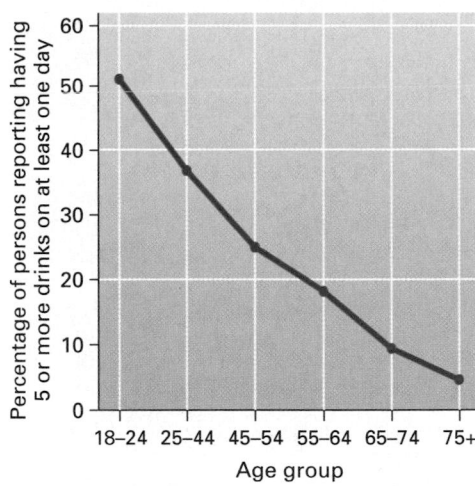

FIGURE 17.16 Age and the Consumption of Five or More Drinks on at Least One Day in the United States. The graph shows the considerable decline in having five or more drinks on at least one day as people get older (National Center for Health Statistics, 2002).

How many of us older persons have really been prepared for the second half of life, for old age, and eternity?

—Carl Jung
Swiss Psychoanalyst, 20th Century

What might explain the finding that drinking red wine in moderation is linked to better health and increased longevity?

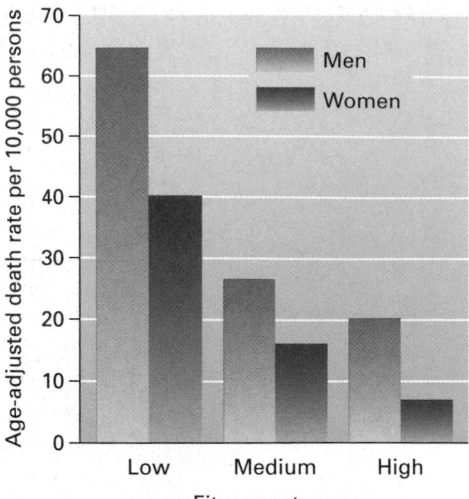

FIGURE 17.17 Physical Fitness and Mortality. In this study of middle-aged and older adults, being moderately fit or highly fit meant that individuals were less likely to die over a period of eight years than their low-fitness (sedentary) counterparts (Blair & others, 1989)

All we know about older adults indicates that they are healthier and happier the more active they are. Several decades ago, it was believed that older adults should be more passive and inactive to be well adjusted and satisfied with life. In today's world, we believe that while older adults may be in the evening of their life span, they are not meant to live out their remaining years passively.

heart disease. A chemical in red wine—resveratrol—has been hypothesized to play a key role in red wine's health benefits, although consistent evidence for this link have yet to be found (Putics & others, 2008). Scientists are exploring how resveratrol, as well as calorie restriction, increase SIRT1, an enzyme that is involved in DNA repair and aging (Pallas & others, 2008).

Exercise, Nutrition, and Weight

Can exercise slow the aging process? Can eating a nutritious but calorie-reduced diet increase longevity? Let's examine how exercise, nutrition, and weight might influence how healthily we age.

Exercise Although we may be in the evening of our lives in late adulthood, we are not meant to live out our remaining years passively. Everything we know about older adults suggests they are healthier and happier the more active they are.

In one study, exercise literally meant a difference in life or death for middle-aged and older adults. More than 10,000 men and women were divided into categories of low fitness, medium fitness, and high fitness (Blair & others, 1989). Then they were studied over a period of eight years. As shown in Figure 17.17, sedentary participants (low fitness) were more than twice as likely to die during the eight-year time span of the study than those who were moderately fit and more than three times as likely to die as those who were highly fit. The positive effects of being physically fit occurred for both men and women in this study. Further, a recent study revealed that 60-year-old and older adults who were in the lowest fifth in terms of physical fitness as determined by a treadmill test were four times more likely to die over a 12-year period than their counterparts who were in the top fifth of physical fitness (Sui & others, 2007). Also, in this study, older adults who were physically fit but overweight had a lower mortality risk over the 12 years than their normal-weight counterparts who were low in fitness (Sui & others, 2007). And a longitudinal study found that men who exercised regularly at 72 years of age had a 30 percent higher probability of still being alive at 90 years of age than their sedentary counterparts (Yates & others, 2008).

Gerontologists increasingly recommend strength training in addition to aerobic activity and stretching for older adults (Suetta & others, 2008). The average person's lean body mass declines with age—about 6.6 pounds of lean muscle are lost each decade during the adult years. The rate of loss accelerates after age 45. Weight lifting can preserve and possibly increase muscle mass in older adults (Johnston, De Lisio, & Parise, 2008). One study found that strength training alone or combined aerobic and strength training were more effective than aerobic training alone in improving older adults' muscle strength (Haykowsky & others, 2005). In another study, it also reduced depression in older adults (Singh, Clements, & Fiatarone, 1997). A review of 62 research studies concluded that strength training can improve muscle strength and some aspects of functional limitation, such as gait speed, in older adults (Latham & others, 2004).

Exercise is an excellent way to maintain health (Deeny & others, 2008; Temple & others, 2008). The current recommended level of aerboic activity for adults 60 years of age and older is 30 minutes of moderately intense activity, such as brisk walking or riding a stationary bicycle, five or more days a week, and strength training on two or more days a week (Der Ananian & Prohaska, 2007). Flexibility and balance exercises also are recommended.

Researchers continue to document the positive effects of exercise in older adults (Henwood, Riek, & Taaffe, 2008; Kramer & Erickson, 2007). Exercise helps people to live independent lives with dignity in late adulthood (Yates & others, 2008). At 80, 90, and even 100 years of age, exercise can help prevent older adults from falling down or even being institutionalized. Being physically fit means being able to do the things you want to do, whether you are young or old. More about research on exercise's positive benefits for health is shown in Figure 17.18.

Researchers who study exercise and aging have discovered the following:

- *Exercise is linked to increased longevity.* In a longitudinal study of Chinese women, those who exercised regularly were less likely to die over approximately a six-year time period (Matthews & others, 2007). In one analysis, energy expenditure by older adults during exercise that burns up at least 1,000 calories a week was estimated to increase life expectancy by about 30 percent, while burning up 2,000 calories a week in exercise was estimated to increase life expectancy by about 50 percent (Lee & Skerrett, 2001).

- *Exercise is related to prevention of common chronic diseases.* Exercise can reduce the risk of developing cardiovascular disease, type 2 diabetes, osteoporosis, stroke, and breast cancer (Sagiv & others, 2007; Weil, 2008).

- *Exercise is associated with improvement in the treatment of many diseases.* When exercise is used as part of the treatment, individuals with these diseases show improvement in symptoms: arthritis, pulmonary disease, congestive heart failure, coronary artery disease, hypertension, type 2 diabetes, obesity, and Alzheimer disease (O'Rourke & Hashimoto, 2007; Rizvi, 2007; Sumic & others, 2007).

- *Exercise improves older adults' cellular functioning.* Researchers increasingly are finding that exercise improves cellular functioning in older adults (Boveris & Navarro, 2008). For example, a recent study revealed that telomere length was greater in leukocytes (white blood cells) when older adults had a higher level of physical activity during leisure time (Cherkas & others, 2008).

- *Exercise can optimize body composition and reduce the decline in motor skills as aging occurs.* Exercise can increase muscle mass and bone mass, as well as decrease bone fragility (Iacono, 2007; Melov & others, 2007). Also, a recent study of more than 850 older adults revealed that one additional hour of physical activity per week was associated with an approximate 5 percent decrease in motor functioning over an eight-year time period (Buchman & others, 2007).

- *Exercise reduces the likelihood that older adults will develop mental health problems and can be effective in the treatment of mental health problems.* For example, exercise reduces the likelihood that older adults will develop depression and can be effective in treating depression in older adults (Brenes & others, 2007; Lindwell & others, 2007).

- *Exercise is linked to improved brain and cognitive functioning in older adults.* As we saw earlier in the chapter, exercise increases brain volume in older adults (Kramer & Erickson, 2007). However, the effects of exercise on the older adults' brain may not occur independently of other lifestyle factors such as diet and participation in social activities (Kramer & Erickson, 2007). There is some indication, though, that excerise may reverse the harmful effects of a high-saturated-fat diet (Mattson, 2000). Also, older adults who exercise process information more effectively than older adults who don't exercise (Deeny & others, 2008; Lindwall, Rennemark, & Berggren, 2008).

Despite the extensive documentation of exercise's power to improve older adults' health and quality of life, a recent national survey revealed that older adults have increased their exercise levels only slightly in recent years (Centers for Disease Control and Prevention, 2008) (see Figure 17.19). Possible explanations of older adults' failure to substantially increase their exercise focus on such factors as chronic illnesses, life crises (such as a spouse's death) that disrupt exercise schedules, embarrassment at being around others who are in better shape (especially if they haven't exercised much

FIGURE 17.18 The Jogging Hog Experiment. Jogging hogs reveal the dramatic effects of exercise on health. In one investigation, a group of hogs was trained to run approximately 100 miles per week (Bloor & White, 1983). Then, the researchers narrowed the arteries that supplied blood to the hogs' hearts. The hearts of the jogging hogs developed extensive alternate pathways for blood supply, and 42 percent of the threatened heart tissue was salvaged compared with only 17 percent in a control group of nonjogging hogs.

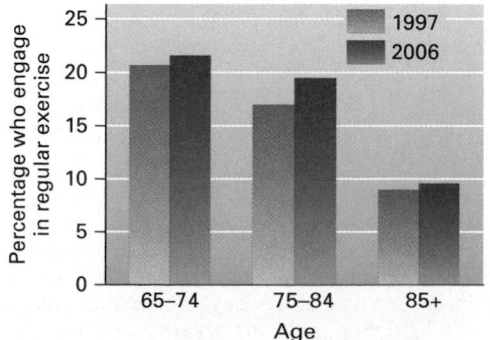

FIGURE 17.19 Regular Exercise by U.S. Older Adults: 1997 to 2006

earlier in life), and the "why bother?" factor (not believing that exercise will improve their lives much) (Painter, 2008). But as we have seen, it is never too late to begin exercising, and older adults can significantly benefit from regular exercise. We will further discuss the influence of exercise on older adults' cognitive functioning in Chapter 18.

Nutrition and Weight   Two aspects of undernutrition in older adults especially interest researchers: (1) vitamin and mineral deficiency, and (2) the role of calorie restriction in improving health and extending life.

Some older adults engage in dietary restriction that is harmful to their health, especially when they do not get adequate vitamins and minerals. One change in eating behavior in older adults is decreased snacking between meals, which may contribute to harmful weight loss, especially in women (Morley, 2003). Among the strategies for increasing weight gain in these women are the use of taste enhancers and of calorie supplements between meals.

Seventeenth-century English philosopher and essayist Francis Bacon was the first author to recommend scientific evaluation of diet and longevity. He advocated a frugal diet. Does a restricted intake of food increase longevity, or could it possibly even extend the human life span?

Scientists have accumulated considerable evidence that calorie restriction (CR) in laboratory animals (in most cases rats) can increase the animals' life span (Huffman & others, 2008; Wei & others, 2008). Animals fed diets restricted in calories, although adequate in protein, vitamins, and minerals, live as much as 40 percent longer than animals given unlimited access to food (Jolly, 2005). And chronic problems such as kidney disease appear at a later age (Fernandez, 2008; Larson-Meyer, & others, 2008). CR also delays biochemical alterations such as the age-related rise in cholesterol and triglycerides observed in both humans and animals (Fontana, 2008). And recent research indicates that CR may provide neuroprotection for an aging central nervous system (Ingram, Young, & Mattison, 2007; Newton & others, 2007) (see Figure 17.20).

No one knows for certain how CR works to increase the life span of animals (Anderson & Weindruch, 2007). Some scientists argue that it might lower the level of free radicals and reduce oxidative stress in cells (Lopez-Lluch

FIGURE 17.20 Calorie Restriction in Monkeys. Shown here are two male monkeys at the Wisconsin Primate Research Center. Both are 24 years old. The monkey in the photograph on the right was raised on a calorie-restricted diet, while the monkey in the left photograph was raised on a normal diet. Notice that the monkey on the calorie-restricted diet looks younger; he also has lower glucose and insulin levels. The monkey raised on a normal diet has higher triglycerides and more oxidative damage to his cells.

& others, 2006). For example, one study found that calorie restriction slowed the age-related increase in oxidative stress (Ward & others, 2005). Others argue that calorie restriction might trigger a state of emergency called "survival mode" in which the body eliminates all unnecessary functions to focus only on staying alive. This survival mode likely is the result of evolution in which calorie restriction allowed animals to survive periods of famine, and thus the genes remain in the genomes of animal and human species today (Chen & Guarente, 2007).

Whether similar very low-calorie diets can stretch the human life span is not known (Mattison & others, 2007). In some instances, the animals in these studies ate 40 percent less than normal. In humans, a typical level of calorie restriction involves a 30 percent decrease, which translates into about 1,120 calories a day for the average woman and 1,540 for the average man.

Leaner men do live longer, healthier lives. In one study of 19,297 Harvard alumni, those weighing the least were less likely to die over the past three decades (Lee & others, 1993).

The Controversy over Vitamins and Aging   For years, most experts on aging and health argued that a balanced diet was all that was needed for successful aging; vitamin supplements were not recommended. However, recent research suggests the possibility that some vitamin supplements—mainly a group called "antioxidants," which includes vitamin C, vitamin E, and beta-carotene—help to slow the aging process and improve the health of older adults.

The theory is that antioxidants counteract the cell damage caused by free radicals, which are produced both by the body's own metabolism and by environmental factors such as smoking, pollution, and bad chemicals in the diet (Flora, 2007; Li & Schellhorn, 2007). When free radicals cause damage (oxidation) in one cell, a chain reaction of damage follows. Antioxidants act much like a fire extinguisher, helping to neutralize free-radical activity.

Some research studies find links between the antioxidant vitamins and health (Marko & others, 2007). One study linked low blood vitamin C concentration in older adults with an earlier incidence of death (Fletcher, Breeze, & Shetty, 2003). Another study found that people who took vitamin E supplements for two years significantly reduced their risk of heart disease—by up to 40 percent (Rimm & others, 1993). However, a recent analysis of 19 studies of vitamin E revealed that middle-aged and older adults who took 200 IU of vitamin E or more a day were more likely to die than their counterparts who did not take vitamin E (Miller & others, 2005). The researchers concluded that most individuals get enough vitamin E in their diet and should not take vitamin E supplements. They argue that vitamin E in low doses may be a powerful antioxidant but in higher doses may increase oxidative damage.

There is no evidence that antioxidants can increase the human life span, but some aging and health experts conclude that vitamin C and beta-carotene can reduce a person's risk of becoming frail and sick in the later adult years (Korantzopoulos & others, 2007). However, there are still a lot of blanks and uncertainties in what we know. That is, we don't know which vitamins should be taken, how large a dose should be taken, what the restraints are, and so on. Critics also argue that the key experimental studies documenting the effectiveness of the vitamins in slowing the aging process have not been conducted. The studies in this area thus far have been so-called population studies that are correlational rather than experimental in nature. Other factors—such as exercise, better health practices, and good nutritional habits—might be responsible for the positive findings about vitamins and aging rather than vitamins per se. Also, the free-radical theory is a theory and not a fact, and is only one of a number of theories about why we age.

Possible links between vitamins and cognitive performance in older adults also have been the focus of increased research attention. For example, a recent study revealed that individuals 65 years of age and older who took higher levels of antioxidant vitamins had less cognitive decline than their counterparts who took lower levels (Wengreen & others, 2007). Some studies have found that taking B vitamins, especially folate, B_6, and B_{12}, is positively related to cognitive performance in older adults (Feng & others, 2006; Calvaresi & Bryan, 2001). However, other studies indicate that taking B vitamins and other supplemental vitamins have no effect on the cognitive functioning of older adults (McNeill & others, 2007).

Health Treatment

The increase in the aging population is predicted to dramatically escalate health-care costs over the foreseeable future. As older adults live longer, disease management programs will need to be expanded to handle the chronic disorders of older adults (Garrett & Martini, 2007). The increasing health services demand created by the expanding population of older adults is likely to bring shortages of many types of health-care professionals, including geriatric nurses, doctors, and health-care aides (Curtin, 2007; Moore, 2007).

What is the quality of health treatment that older adults in the United States receive? A study of older adults with health problems revealed that they receive the recommended medical care they need only half the time (Wenger & others, 2003). The researchers examined the medical records of 372 frail older adults who had been treated by two managed-care organizations over the course of one year. Then they documented the medical care each patient received and judged it using standard indicators of quality. For example, many older adults with an unsteady gait don't get the help they need, such as physical therapy to improve their walking ability. Clearly, the quality of health treatment older adults receive needs to be significantly improved (Gatz, 2006).

Geriatric nurses can be especially helpful in treating the health-care problems of older adults. To read about the work of one geriatric nurse, see the *Careers in Life-Span Development* profile.

Careers in Life-Span Development

Sarah Kagan, Geriatric Nurse

Sarah Kagan is a professor of nursing at the University of Pennsylvania School of Nursing. She provides nursing consultation to patients, their families, nurses, and physicians on the complex needs of older adults related to their hospitalization. She also consults on research and the management of patients who have head and neck cancers. Kagan also teaches in the undergraduate nursing program, where she directs the course Nursing Care in the Older Adult. In 2003, she was awarded a MacArthur Fellowship for her work in the field of nursing.

In Kagan's own words:

> I'm lucky to be doing what I love—caring for older adults and families—and learning from them so that I can share this knowledge and develop or investigate better ways of caring. My special interests in the care of older adults who have cancer allow me the intimate privilege of being with patients at the best and worst times of their lives. That intimacy acts as a beacon—it reminds me of the value I and nursing as a profession contribute to society and the rewards offered in return (Kagan, 2008, p. 1).

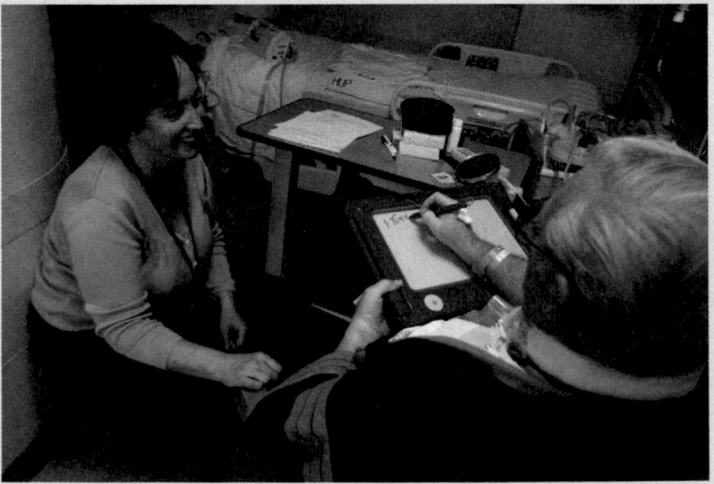

Sarah Kagan with a patient.

About 3 percent of adults 65 years of age and older in the United States reside in a nursing home at any point in time. However, as older adults age, their probability of being in a nursing home or other extended-care facility increases. Twenty-three percent of adults 85 years of age and older live in nursing homes or other extended-care facilities. What is the quality of nursing homes and extended-care facilities for older adults? What is the relationship between older adults and health-care providers?

The quality of nursing homes and other extended-care facilities for older adults varies enormously and is a source of continuing national concern (Kurrle, 2006). More than one-third are seriously deficient, failing federally mandated inspections because they do not meet the minimum standards for physicians, pharmacists, and various rehabilitation specialists (such as occupational and physical therapists). Further concerns focus on the patient's right to privacy, access to medical information, safety, and life-style freedom within the individual's range of mental and physical capabilities. There is an increasing demand for home health-care workers because of the increasing population of older adults and their preference to stay out of nursing homes (Moos, 2007).

Because of the inadequate quality of many nursing homes and the escalating costs for nursing home care, many specialists in the health problems of the aged conclude that home health care, day-care centers, and preventive medicine clinics are good alternatives (Castle, 2001). They are potentially less expensive than hospitals and nursing homes. They also are less likely to engender the feelings of depersonalization and dependency that occur so often in residents of institutions (Greene & others, 1995). One recent study found that older adults in a community-based long-term care program performed better on cognitive tasks and were less depressed than their counterparts in an institutional-based long-term care facility (Marek & others, 2005).

In a classic study, Judith Rodin and Ellen Langer (1977) found that an important factor related to health, and even survival, in a nursing home is the patient's feelings of control and self-determination. A group of elderly nursing home residents were encouraged to make more day-to-day choices and thus feel they had more responsibility for control over their lives. They began to decide such matters as what they ate, when their visitors could come, what movies they saw, and who could come to their rooms. A similar group in the same nursing home was told by the administrator how caring the nursing home was and how much the staff wanted to help, but these residents were given no opportunity to take more control over their lives. Eighteen months later, the residents given responsibility and control were more alert and active, and said they were happier, than the residents who were only encouraged to feel that the staff would try to satisfy their needs. And the "responsible" or "self-control" group had significantly better improvement in their health than did the "dependent" group. Even more important was the finding that after 18 months only half as many nursing home residents in the "responsibility" group had died as in the "dependent" group (see Figure 17.21). Perceived control over one's environment, then, can literally be a matter of life or death.

In another research study, Rodin (1983) measured stress-related hormones in several groups of nursing home residents. Then she taught the residents coping skills to help them deal better with day-to-day problems. They were taught how to say no when they did not want something, without worrying whether they would offend someone. They were given assertiveness training and learned time-management skills. After the training, the nursing home residents had greatly reduced levels of cortisol (a hormone closely related to stress that has been implicated in a number of diseases). The cortisol levels of the assertiveness-training residents remained lower, even after 18 months. Further, these nursing home residents were healthier and had a reduced need for medication, compared with residents who had not been taught the coping skills.

Rodin's research shows that simply giving nursing home residents options for control and teaching them coping skills can change their behavior and improve their health. To read further about health-care providers and older adults, see the *Applications in Life-Span Development* interlude.

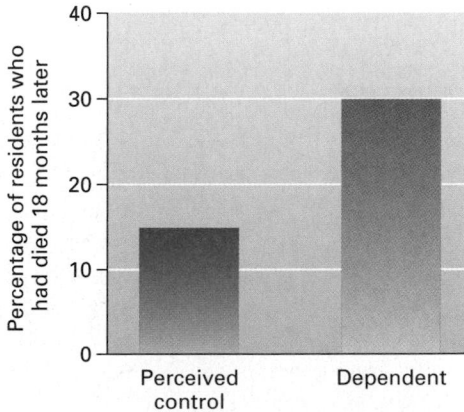

FIGURE 17.21 Perceived Control and Mortality. In the study by Rodin and Langer (1977), nursing home residents who were encouraged to feel more in control of their lives were more likely to be alive 18 months later than those who were treated to feel more dependent on the nursing home staff.

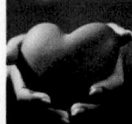

Applications in Life-Span Development
Health-Care Providers and Older Adults

The attitudes of both the health-care provider and the older adult are important aspects of the older adult's health care (Aud & others, 2006). Unfortunately, health-care providers too often share society's stereotypes and negative attitudes toward older adults (Reyna, Goodwin, & Ferrari, 2007). In a health-care setting, these attitudes can take the form of avoidance, dislike, and begrudged tolerance rather than positive, hopeful treatment. Health-care personnel are more likely to be interested in treating younger persons, who more often have acute problems with a higher prognosis for successful recovery. They often are less motivated to treat older persons, who are more likely to have chronic problems with a lower prognosis for successful recovery.

Not only are physicians less responsive to older patients, but older patients often take a less active role in medical encounters with health-care personnel than do younger patients. Older adults should be encouraged to take a more active role in their own health care.

Mathilde Spett (*right*), who is 91 years old, injured herself in a fall but recently graduated from a walker to a cane and learned how to stay on a better diet with the help of home-care aide, Marilyn Ferguson (*left*). The demand for home-care aides is predicted to increase dramatically in the next several decades because of the likely doubling of the 65-year and older population and older adults' preference for remaining out of nursing homes (Moos, 2007). Not only is it important to significantly increase the number of health-care professionals to treat older adults, it is also very important that they not harbor negative stereotypes of older adults and that they show very positive attitudes toward them.

Review and Reflect: Learning Goal 2

3 **Identify Health Problems in Older Adults and How They Can Be Treated**

REVIEW

- What are some common health problems in older adults? What are the main causes of death in older adults?
- What characterizes substance abuse in late adulthood?
- How do exercise, nutrition, and weight influence development in late adulthood?
- What are some options and issues in the health treatment of older adults?

REFLECT

- What changes in your lifestyle now might help you age more successfully when you become an older adult?

Physical Development in Late Adulthood

1   LONGEVITY: CHARACTERIZE LONGEVITY AND THE BIOLOGICAL THEORIES OF AGING

Life Expectancy and Life Span

- Life expectancy refers to the number of years that will probably be lived by an average person born in a particular year. Life span is the maximum number of years an individual can live. Life expectancy has dramatically increased; life span has not. An increasing number of individuals live to be 100 or older genetics health, and coping well with stress can contribute to becoming a centenarians. On the average, females live about six years longer than males do. The sex difference is likely due to biological and social factors.

The Young-Old, the Old-Old, and the Oldest-Old

- In terms of chronological age, the young-old have been described as being 65 to 74 years of age, the old-old as 75 years and older, and the oldest-old as 85 years and older. Many experts on aging prefer to describe the young-old, old-old, and oldest-old in terms of functional age rather than chronological age. This view accounts for the fact that some 85-year-olds are more biologically and psychologically fit than some 65-year-olds. However, those 85 and older face significant problems, whereas those in their sixties and seventies are experiencing an increase in successful aging.

Biological Theories of Aging

- Four biological theories are cellular clock theory, free-radical theory, mitochondrial theory, and hormonal stress theory. Hayflick proposed the cellular clock theory, which states that cells can divide a maximum of about 75 to 80 times, and that as we age, our cells become less capable of dividing. Telomeres are likely involved in explaining why cells lose their capacity to divide. According to free-radical theory, people age because unstable oxygen molecules called free radicals are produced in the cells and damage cellular structures. According to mitochondrial theory, aging is due to the decay of mitochondria, tiny cellular bodies that supply energy for function, growth, and repair. According to hormonal stress theory, aging in the body's hormonal system can lower resilience to stress and increase the likelihood of disease.

2   THE COURSE OF PHYSICAL DEVELOPMENT IN LATE ADULTHOOD: DESCRIBE HOW A PERSON'S BRAIN AND BODY CHANGE IN LATE ADULTHOOD

The Aging Brain

- The brain loses weight and volume with age, and there is a general slowing of function in the central nervous system that begins in middle adulthood and increases in late adulthood. However, researchers have recently found that older adults can generate new neurons and, at least through the seventies, new dendrites. The aging brain retains considerable plasticity and adaptiveness. For example, it may compensate for losses in some regions of the brain by shifting responsibilities to other regions. A decrease in lateralization may reflect this kind of compensation, or it may reflect an age-related decline in the specialization of function.

The Immune System

- Decline in immune system functioning with aging is well documented. Exercise can improve immune system functioning.

Physical Appearance and Movement

- The most obvious signs of aging are wrinkled skin and age spots on the skin. People get shorter as they age, and their weight often decreases after age 60 because of loss of muscle. The movement of older adults slows across a wide range of movement tasks.

Sensory Development

- Declines in visual acuity, color vision, and depth perception usually occur with age, especially after age 75. The yellowing of the eye's lens with age reduces color differentiation. The ability to see the periphery of a visual field also declines in older adults. Significant declines in visual functioning related to glare characterize adults 75 years and older and even more so for those 85 and older. Three diseases that can impair the vision of older adults are cataracts, glaucoma, and macular degeneration. Hearing decline can begin in middle age but usually does not become much of an impediment until late adulthood. Hearing aids (for conductive hearing loss) and cochlear implants (for neurosensory hearing loss) can diminish hearing problems for many older adults. Smell and taste can decline, although the decline is minimal in healthy older adults. Changes in touch sensitivity are associated with aging, although this does not present a problem for most older adults. Sensitivity to pain decreases in late adulthood.

The Circulatory System and Lungs

- Cardiovascular disorders increase in late adulthood. Consistent high blood pressure should be treated to reduce the risk of stroke, heart attack, and kidney disease. Lung capacity does drop with age, but older adults can improve lung functioning with diaphragm-strengthening exercises.

Sexuality

- Aging in late adulthood does include some changes in sexual performance, more for males than females. Nonetheless, there are no known age limits to sexual activity.

3 HEALTH: IDENTIFY HEALTH PROBLEMS IN OLDER ADULTS AND HOW THEY CAN BE TREATED

Health Problems

- As we age, our probability of disease or illness increases. Chronic disorders are rare in early adulthood, increase in middle adulthood, and become more common in late adulthood. The most common chronic disorder in late adulthood is arthritis. Nearly three-fourths of older adults die of heart disease, cancer, or stroke. Osteoporosis is the main reason many older adults walk with a stoop; women are especially vulnerable. Accidents are usually more debilitating to older than to younger adults.

Substance Abuse

- Alcohol use and abuse declines in older adults, although this is more difficult to detect in older adults than in younger adults.

Exercise, Nutrition, and Weight

- The physical benefits of exercise have clearly been demonstrated in older adults. Aerobic exercise and weight lifting are both recommended if the adults are physically capable of them. There is concern about older adults who do not get adequate vitamins and minerals, especially women. Calorie restriction in animals can increase the animals' life span, but whether this works with humans is not known. In humans, being overweight is associated with an increased mortality rate. Most nutritional experts recommend a well-balanced, low-fat diet for older adults, but do not recommend an extremely low-calorie diet. Controversy surrounds the question of whether vitamin supplements—especially the antioxidants vitamin C, vitamin E, and beta-carotene—can slow the aging process and improve older adults' health. Recent research has found a link between taking B vitamins and positive cognitive performance in older adults.

Health Treatment

- Although only 3 percent of adults over 65 reside in nursing homes, 23 percent of adults 85 and over do. The quality of nursing homes varies enormously. Alternatives to nursing homes are being proposed. Simply giving nursing home residents options for control and teaching coping skills can change their behavior and improve their health. The attitudes of both the health-care provider and the older adult patient are important aspects of the older adult's health care. Too often health-care personnel share society's negative view of older adults.

KEY TERMS

life span 528
life expectancy 529
cellular clock theory 533

free-radical theory 534
mitochondrial theory 534
hormonal stress theory 534

neurogenesis 536
cataracts 540
glaucoma 540

macular degeneration 540
arthritis 544
osteoporosis 544

KEY PEOPLE

Leonard Hayflick 533   Stanley Rapaport 537   Judith Rodin 551   Ellen Langer 551

E-LEARNING TOOLS

To help you master the material in this chapter, visit the the Online Learning Center for *Life-Span Development*, twelfth edition, at **www.mhhe.com/santrockld12**.

Self-Assessment

Connect to **www.mhhe.com/santrockld12** to reflect on what aging means to you by completing the self-assessment, *My Beliefs About Aging*.

Taking It to the Net

Connect to **www.mhhe.com/santrockld12** to research the answers to these questions:

1. Do you think you will live to be 100? Investigate your chances of becoming a centenarian by reading the results from an ongoing Harvard University Medical School study.

2. Seventy-year-old Jack knows that regular exercise is important to maintain a healthy heart. But what are the other benefits to staying active, and how much exercising should Jack do?

3. Patty's 85-year-old mother, who lives with her and her family, has begun eating less and less. She tells Patty, "Eating is no fun anymore. I can't taste anything." What can Patty do to make meals more appealing for her mother?

Video Clips

The Online Learning Center includes a video for Chapter 17 called "Human Development: Cognitive Functioning in Centenarians." Do mental faculties invariably diminish as one gets older? Or is the brain, as Dr. Marjorie Silver claims in this segment, a muscle that requires regular exercise?

Health and Well-Being, Parenting, and Education Exercises

Build your decision-making skills by trying your hand at the health and well-being, parenting, and education exercises. Connect to **www.mhhe.com/santrockld12** to research the answers and complete the exercises.

18

The night hath not yet come: We are not quite cut off from labor by the failing of light; some work remains for us to do and dare.

—Henry Wadsworth Longfellow
American Poet, 19th Century

LEARNING GOALS

◆ Describe the cognitive functioning of older adults.

◆ Characterize changes in language in older adults.

◆ Discuss aging and adaptations to work and retirement.

◆ Describe mental health problems in older adults.

◆ Explain the role of religion in the lives of older adults.

COGNITIVE DEVELOPMENT IN LATE ADULTHOOD

Images of Life-Span Development
Lily Hearst and Sister Mary, Active Minds

Throughout her life, Lily Hearst has pursued a range of interests including the arts, music, science, and politics. She has a degree in music and reads and speaks three languages. Now, at 101 years old, she lives independently and exercises every day. She reads *The Wall Street Journal* daily, teaches piano, and plays in a classical trio at the North Berkeley Senior Center [in Berkeley, California].

Lily keeps a strict daily routine that begins at seven o'clock, when she gets out of bed, exercises, and fixes her own breakfast. At nine she goes to the pool and swims eight laps. A friend drives her to the senior center where she attends classes, reads, watches movies, and plays piano. Lily keeps track of her life with a date book, writing down engagements and other things she needs to remember. She takes pride in the fact that she is never late for an appointment (Exploratorium, 2004, pp. 1–2).

Another centenarian, Sister Mary, was a participant in the Nun Study, which we described in Chapter 17. She died in 1993 at 101 years of age. Even at 100, Sister Mary continued to score high on measures of cognitive skills (Snowdon, 1997). She loved to read and late in her life was often observed looking through a magnifying glass as she read books, magazines, and newspapers.

PREVIEW

Lily Hearst and Sister Mary led very active cognitive lives as older adults. Just how well older adults can and do function cognitively is an important question we will explore in this chapter. We also will examine the important topics of language development, work and retirement, mental health, and religion.

1 COGNITIVE FUNCTIONING IN OLDER ADULTS

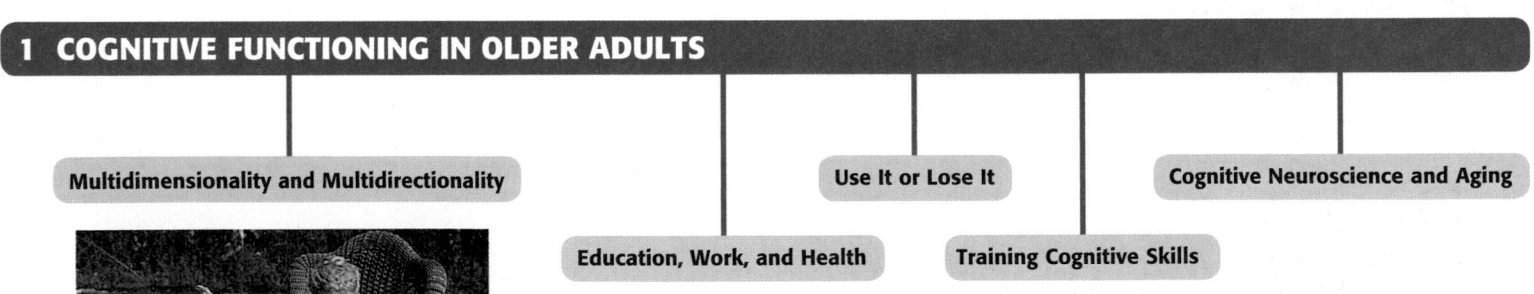

Multidimensionality and Multidirectionality

Education, Work, and Health

Use It or Lose It

Training Cognitive Skills

Cognitive Neuroscience and Aging

Grandma Moses, known in her time as the "grand old lady of American art," took up painting at the age of 76 and continued to paint past her hundredth birthday.

At age 76, Anna Mary Robertson Moses, better known as Grandma Moses, took up painting and became internationally famous, staging fifteen one-woman shows throughout Europe. At age 89, Arthur Rubinstein gave one of his best performances at New York's Carnegie Hall. When Pablo Casals was 95, a reporter asked him, "Mr. Casals, you are the greatest cellist who ever lived. Why do you still practice six hours a day?" Mr. Casals replied, "Because I feel like I am making progress" (Canfield & Hansen, 1995).

Multidimensionality and Multidirectionality

In thinking about the nature of cognitive change in adulthood, it is important to consider that cognition is a multidimensional concept. It is also important to consider that although some dimensions of cognition might decline as we age, others might remain stable or even improve (Bucur & Madden, 2007).

Cognitive Mechanics and Cognitive Pragmatics   Paul Baltes (2003; Baltes, Lindenberger, & Staudinger, 2006) clarified the distinction between those aspects of the aging mind that show decline and those that remain stable or even improve:

- **Cognitive mechanics** are the "hardware" of the mind and reflect the neurophysiological architecture of the brain developed through evolution. Cognitive mechanics consist of these components: speed and accuracy of the processes involved in sensory input, attention, visual and motor memory, discrimination, comparison, and categorization. Because of the strong influence of biology, heredity, and health on cognitive mechanics, their decline with aging is likely. Some researchers conclude that the decline in cognitive mechanics may begin as soon as early midlife (Li & others, 2004).

- **Cognitive pragmatics** are the culture-based "software programs" of the mind. Cognitive pragmatics include reading and writing skills, language comprehension, educational qualifications, professional skills, and also the type of knowledge about the self and life skills that help us to master or cope with life. Because of the strong influence of culture on cognitive pragmatics, their improvement into old age is possible. Thus, although cognitive mechanics may decline in old age, cognitive pragmatics may actually improve, at least until individuals become very old (see Figure 18.1).

The distinction between cognitive mechanics and cognitive pragmatics is similar to the one between fluid (mechanics) and crystallized (pragmatics) intelligence that was described in Chapter 15. Indeed, the similarity is so strong that some experts now use these terms to describe cognitive aging patterns: *fluid mechanics* and *crystallized pragmatics* (Lovden & Lindenberger, 2007).

A cross-sectional life-span study of age differences in five cognitive abilities found support for the concepts of fluid mechanics and crystallized pragmatics (Li & others, 2004). As shown in Figure 18.2, older adults scored lower than their younger counterparts on three measures of fluid mechanics (episodic memory, perceptual speed, and reasoning) but no age differences were found on a measure of crystallized pragmatics (verbal knowledge).

What factors are most likely to contribute to the decline in fluid mechanics in late adulthood? Among the most likely candidates are processing speed, working memory capacity, and suppressing irrelevant information (inhibition) (Lovden & Lindenberger, 2007).

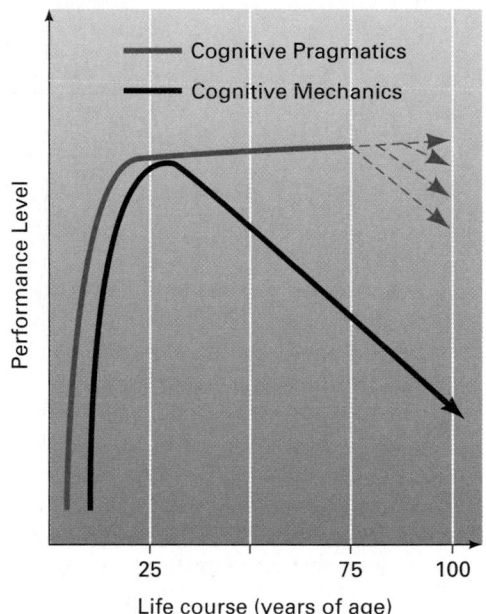

FIGURE 18.1 Theorized Age Changes in Cognitive Mechanics and Cognitive Pragmatics. Baltes argues that cognitive mechanics decline during aging, whereas cognitive pragmatics do not, at least for many people until they become very old. Cognitive mechanics have a biological/genetic foundation; cognitive pragmatics have an experiential/cultural foundation. The broken lines from 75 to 100 years of age indicate possible individual variations in cognitive pragmatics.

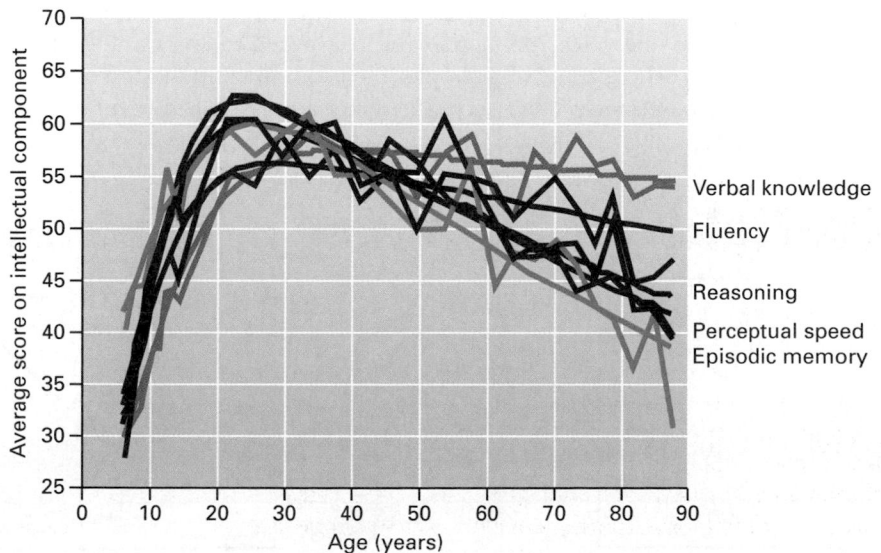

FIGURE 18.2 Changes in Intellectual Components Across the Life Span

cognitive mechanics The "hardware" of the mind, reflecting the neurophysiological architecture of the brain as developed through evolution. Cognitive mechanics involve the speed and accuracy of the processes involving sensory input, visual and motor memory, discrimination, comparison, and categorization.

cognitive pragmatics The culture-based "software programs" of the mind. Cognitive pragmatics include reading and writing skills, language comprehension, educational qualifications, professional skills, and also the type of knowledge about the self and life skills that help us to master or cope with life.

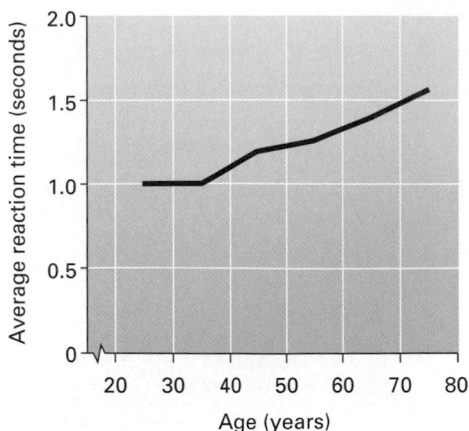

FIGURE 18.3 The Relation of Age to Reaction Time. In one study, the average reaction time began to slow in the forties, and this decline accelerated in the sixties and seventies (Salthouse, 1994). The task used to assess reaction time required individuals to match numbers with symbols on a computer screen.

Now that we have examined the distinction between fluid mechanics and crystallized pragmatics, let's explore some of the more specific cognitive processes that reflect these two general domains, beginning with this aspect of cognitive mechanics: speed of processing.

Speed of Processing It is now well accepted that the speed of processing information declines in late adulthood (Bucur & Madden, 2007). Figure 18.3 illustrates this decline.

Although speed of processing information slows down in late adulthood, there is considerable individual variation in this ability (Hartley, 2006). Accumulated knowledge may compensate to some degree for slower processing speed in older adults. For example, one recent study found that knowledge was more important on a memory task for older adults than younger adults and that older adults may rely on age-related increases in knowledge to partially compensate for a decline in processing speed (Hedden, Lautenschlager, & Park, 2005).

The decline in processing speed in older adults is likely due to a decline in functioning of the brain and central nervous system (Fabiani & others, 2006). Health and exercise may influence how much decline in processing speed occurs (Gerrotsen & others, 2003). One study found that following six months of aerobic exercise older adults showed improvement on reaction time tasks (Kramer & others, 1999).

The importance of processing speed was underscored in two recent studies:

- Across a 16-year period, the cognitive skills of older adults in four domains were assessed: processing speed, memory, verbal ability, and spatial ability (Finkel & others, 2007). A decline in processing speed was a lead indicator of subsequent decline in memory and spatial ability, but not verbal ability.

- The survival of 56-year-olds was monitored until the age of 70 (Deary & Der, 2005). A link between IQ and mortality was present, but after the reaction time of the study's participants was examined, the association of IQ and mortality disappeared. This suggests that slower processing of information might be responsible for the association of lower IQ and mortality.

Attention Changes in attention are important aspects of cognitive aging (Kramer & Madden, 2008; Stine-Morrow, 2007). Three aspects of attention that have been investigated in older adults are selective attention, divided attention, and sustained attention:

- **Selective attention** is focusing on a specific aspect of experience that is relevant while ignoring others that are irrelevant. An example of selective attention is the ability to focus on one voice among many in a crowded room or a noisy restaurant. Another is making a decision about which stimuli to attend to when making a left turn at an intersection. Generally, older adults are less adept at selective attention than younger adults are (Brown, McKenzie, & Doan, 2005; Bucur &

selective attention Focusing on a specific aspect of experience that is relevant while ignoring others that are irrelevant.

Garfield ® by Jim Davis

Madden, 2007). However, on simple tasks involving a search for a feature, such as determining whether a target item is present on a computer screen, age differences are minimal when individuals are given sufficient practice.

- **Divided attention** involves concentrating on more than one activity at the same time. When the two competing tasks are reasonably easy, age differences among adults are minimal or nonexistent. However, the more difficult the competing tasks are, the less effectively older adults divide attention than younger adults (Bucur & Madden, 2007; Maciokas & Crognale, 2003). In one study, the ability to engage in a conversation while simultaneously driving a simulator through highway traffic (in an experimental laboratory) was examined in 17- to 25-year-olds, 26- to 49-year-olds, and 50- to 80-year-olds (McKnight & McKnight, 1993). A nondistraction control condition also was included. Overall, the participants performed more poorly in the divided attention condition than in the nondistraction control condition. Also, the older adults (50 to 80 years old) performed worse in the divided attention condition than the younger two groups but not in the control condition. Thus, placing more demands on the attention of the older adults led them to perform more poorly on the driving task.

- **Sustained attention** is the state of readiness to detect and respond to small changes occurring at random times in the environment. Sometimes sustained attention is referred to as *vigilance*. On tests of simple vigilance, older adults usually perform as well as younger adults, but on complex vigilance tasks older adults' performance usually drops (Bucur & Madden, 2007). For example, a recent study revealed that older adults showed less effective decision making on a complex laboratory task that required sustained attention than did younger adults (Isella & others, 2008).

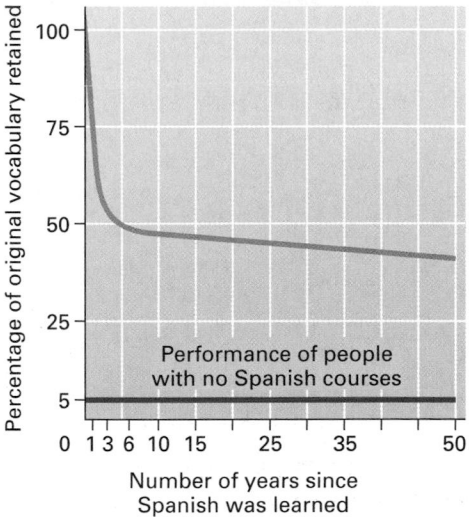

FIGURE 18.4 Memory for Spanish as a Function of Age Since Spanish Was Learned. An initial steep drop over about a three-year period in remembering the vocabulary learned in Spanish classes occurred. However, there was little dropoff in memory for Spanish vocabulary from three years after taking Spanish classes to 50 years after taking them. Even 50 years after taking Spanish classes, individuals still remembered almost 50 percent of the vocabulary.

Memory   Let's examine a research study that addresses how we remember as we age. Non-Latino adults of various ages in the United States were studied to determine how much Spanish they remembered from classes they had taken in high school or college (Bahrick, 1984). The individuals chosen for the study had used Spanish very little since they initially learned it in high school or college. Not surprisingly, the young adults who had taken Spanish within the last three years remembered Spanish best. After that, the deterioration in memory was gradual (see Figure 18.4). For example, older adults who had studied Spanish 50 years earlier remembered about 80 percent of what young adults did who had studied it in the last three years! The most important factor in the adults' memory of Spanish was not how long ago they studied it but how well they initially learned it—those who got an A in Spanish 50 years earlier remembered more Spanish than adults who got a C when taking Spanish only one year earlier.

Memory does change during aging, but not all memory changes with age in the same way (Smith, 2007). The main dimensions of memory and aging that have been studied include episodic memory; semantic memory; cognitive resources (such as working memory and perceptual speed); explicit and implicit memory; source memory; prospective memory; memory beliefs; and noncognitive factors such as health, education, and socioeconomic factors (Smith, 1996).

Episodic Memory   **Episodic memory** is the retention of information about the where and when of life's happenings. For example, what was it like when your younger sister or brother was born, what happened to you on your first date, what were you doing when you heard that airplanes had struck the World Trade Center, and what did you eat for breakfast this morning?

Younger adults have better episodic memory than older adults have (Bucur & Madden, 2007). A recent study of 18- to 94-year-olds revealed that increased age was linked to increased difficulty in retrieving episodic information, facts, and events (Siedlecki, 2007).

divided attention Concentrating on more than one activity at the same time.

sustained attention The state of readiness to detect and respond to small changes occurring at random times in the environment.

episodic memory The retention of information about the where and when of life's happenings.

Autobiographical memory is the personal recollection of events and facts. Autobiographical memories are stored as episodic memories (Daselaar & others, 2008). A robust finding in autobiographical memory is called the *reminiscence bump*, in which adults remember more events from the second and third decades of their lives than from other decades (Bernstein & Rubin, 2002). The "bump" is found more for positive than negative life events. A recent study revealed that the "bump" was characterized not only by positive life events but also by high perceived control over the event and high perceived influence of the event on one's later development (Gluck & Bluck, 2007).

Semantic Memory   **Semantic memory** is a person's knowledge about the world. It includes a person's fields of expertise, such as knowledge of chess for a skilled chess player; general academic knowledge of the sort learned in school, such as knowledge of geometry; and "everyday knowledge" about the meanings of words, famous individuals, important places, and common things, such as what day is Valentine's Day. Semantic memory appears to be independent of an individual's personal identity with the past. For example, you can access a fact—such as "Lima is the capital of Peru"—and not have the foggiest idea of when and where you learned it.

Does semantic memory decline during aging? Among the tasks that researchers often use to assess semantic memory are vocabulary, general knowledge, and word identification (Bucur & Madden, 2007). Older adults do often take longer to retrieve semantic information, but usually they can ultimately retrieve it. For the most part, episodic memory declines more in older adults than semantic memory (Hoyer & Verhaeghen, 2006).

Although many aspects of semantic memory are reasonably well preserved in late adulthood, a common memory problem for older adults is the *tip-of-the-tongue (TOT) phenomenon*, in which individuals can't quite retrieve familiar information but have the feeling that they should be able to retrieve it (Bucur & Madden, 2007). Researchers have found that older adults are more likely to be experience TOT states than younger adults (Bucur & Madden, 2007).

Cognitive Resources: Working Memory and Perceptual Speed   One view of memory suggests that a limited number of cognitive resources can be devoted to any cognitive task. Two important cognitive resource mechanisms are working memory and perceptual speed. Recall from Chapter 15 that *working memory* is closely linked to short-term memory but places more emphasis on memory as a place for mental work. Working memory is like a mental "workbench" that allows individuals to manipulate and assemble information when making decisions, solving problems, and comprehending written and spoken language (Baddeley, 2006, 2007a, b). Researchers have found declines in working memory during the late adulthood years (Blank, Nijhoit, & Spiess, 2007; Cook & others, 2007; Towse, 2008).

Perceptual speed is another cognitive resource that has been studied by researchers on aging (Dixon & others, 2007). Perceptual speed is the ability to perform simple perceptual-motor tasks such as deciding whether pairs of two-digit or two-letter strings are the same or different or determining the time required to step on the brakes when the car directly ahead stops. Perceptual speed shows considerable decline in late adulthood, and it is strongly linked with decline in working memory (Bopp & Verhaeghen, 2007). A recent study revealed that trial-to-trial variability in perceptual speed on a reaction time task signaled impending decline in cognitive performance in older adults (Lovden & others, 2007).

Explicit and Implicit Memory   Researchers also have found that aging is linked with changes in explicit memory (Hoyer & Verhaeghen, 2006). **Explicit memory** is memory of facts and experiences that individuals consciously know and can state. Explicit memory also is sometimes called *declarative memory*. Examples of explicit memory include being at a grocery store and remembering what you wanted to buy, being able to name the capital of Illinois, or recounting the events of a movie you have seen. **Implicit memory** is memory without conscious recollection; it involves skills and

semantic memory A person's knowledge about the world—including a person's fields of expertise, general academic knowledge of the sort learned in school, and "everyday knowledge."

explicit memory Memory of facts and experiences that individuals consciously know and can state.

implicit memory Memory without conscious recollection; involves skills and routine procedures that are automatically performed.

routine procedures that are automatically performed. Examples of implicit memory include driving a car, swinging a golf club, or typing on a computer keyboard, without having to consciously think about it.

Implicit memory is less likely to be adversely affected by aging than explicit memory (Kessels, Boekhorst, & Postma, 2005). Thus, older adults are more likely to forget what items they wanted to buy at a grocery store (unless they write them down on a list and take it with them) than they are to forget how to drive a car. Their perceptual speed might be slower in driving the car, but they remember how to do it.

In Chapter 1, we described research by Lynn Hasher and her colleagues (2001) indicating that the explicit memory of evening-type younger adults was better when tested in the P.M., whereas the explicit memory of morning-type older adults was better when it was tested in the A.M. A recent study replicated that finding but also examined a possible link between implicit memory and time of day testing (May, Hasher, & Foong, 2005). For implicit memory, morning-type older adults and evening-type young adults performed better at off-peak times (morning for young adults, evening for older adults).

Source Memory   **Source memory** is the ability to remember where one learned something. Failures of source memory increase with age in the adult years, and they can create awkward situations, as when an older adult forgets who told a joke and retells it to the source (Dodson, Bawa, & Slotnick, 2007; Roediger & Geraci, 2007).

One study found that awareness of character can compensate for the age declines in source memory (Rahal, May, & Hasher, 2002). In a typical memory source study, before playing a tape, participants listen to a series of statements spoken by either a male or a female voice. At the end, participants read the statements and say which voice spoke to them. The researchers added this twist to their study. Before playing the tape, some of the older adults were told that one voice belonged to a saintly person who never told a lie and that the other person was a dishonest cad. As in past studies, the older adults had difficulty in remembering which voice spoke which given line. However, those who were told about the trustworthiness of the speakers more accurately judged whether a given statement was likely to be true or false, suggesting that older adults can remember information about a source when it is important to them.

Lynn Hasher (2003, p. 1301), one of the researchers who conducted the memory source study just described, argues that age differences are substantial when individuals are asked "for a piece of information that just doesn't matter much. But if you ask for information that is important, old people do every bit as well as young adults . . . young people have mental resources to burn. As people get older, they get more selective in how they use their resources."

Prospective Memory   **Prospective memory** involves remembering to do something in the future, such as remembering to take your medicine or remembering to do an errand. Although some researchers have found a decline in prospective memory with age, a number of studies show that whether there is a decline is complex and depends on such factors as the nature of the task and what is being assessed (Einstein & McDaniel, 2005; Marsh & others, 2007; Park & others, 2007; Rendell & others, 2007). For example, age-related deficits occur more often in time-based (such as remembering to call someone next Friday) than in event-based (remembering to tell your friend to read a particular book the next time you see her) prospective memory tasks.

Beliefs, Expectations, and Feelings   Some studies have found that older adults' beliefs and expectancies about memory play a role in their actual memory (Zanardo, De Beni, & Moe, 2006). It matters what people tell themselves about their ability to remember. Older adults' positive or negative beliefs or expectancies about their memory skills are related to their actual memory performance (Hess & Hinson, 2006). Recall from the *Research in Life-Span Development* interlude in Chapter 1 our description of a study in which older adults were randomly assigned to read one of two mock newspaper articles at the beginning of a testing situation (Hess & others, 2003). One described the declines in memory that characterize aging; the other emphasized research

source memory The ability to remember where one learned something.

prospective memory Involves remembering to do something in the future.

on the preservation of memory skills in older adults. The older adults who read the pessimistic account of memory and aging remembered 20 to 30 percent fewer words than people who read about the ability to maintain memory in old age.

Attitudes and feelings also matter (Reese & Cherry, 2004). One study found that individuals with low anxiety about their memory skills and high self-efficacy regarding their use of memory in everyday contexts had better memory performance than their high-anxiety/low-self-efficacy counterparts (McDougall & others, 1999).

Noncognitive Factors   Health, education, and socioeconomic status (SES) can influence an older adult's performance on memory tasks (Czernochowski, Fabiani, & Friedman, 2007; Schaie, 2008; Yaffe & others, 2007). Although such noncognitive factors as good health are associated with less memory decline in older adults, they do not eliminate memory decline.

One criticism of research on memory and aging is that it has relied primarily on laboratory tests of memory. The argument is that such tasks are contrived and do not represent the everyday cognitive tasks performed by older adults. If researchers used more everyday life memory tasks, would memory decline be found in older adults? A number of researchers have found that using more familiar tasks reduces age decrements in memory but does not eliminate them. Younger adults are better than older adults at remembering faces, routes through town, grocery items, and performed activities. In one study, younger adults (20 to 40 years old) remembered news content in print, audio, and TV format better than older adults did (60 to 80 years old) (Frieske & Park, 1999).

Conclusions About Memory and Aging   Some, but not all, aspects of memory decline in older adults (Smith, 2007). The decline occurs primarily in episodic and working memory, not in semantic memory or implicit memory. A decline in perceptual speed is associated with memory decline. Successful aging does not mean eliminating memory decline, but reducing it and adapting to it (van Hooren & others, 2007). As we will see later in this chapter, older adults can use certain strategies to reduce memory decline.

Wisdom   Does wisdom, like good wine, improve with age? What is this thing we call "wisdom"? **Wisdom** is expert knowledge about the practical aspects of life that permits excellent judgment about important matters. This practical knowledge involves exceptional insight into human development and life matters, good judgment, and an understanding of how to cope with difficult life problems. Thus, wisdom, more than standard conceptions of intelligence, focuses on life's pragmatic concerns and human conditions (Staudinger & Dorner, 2007).

In regard to wisdom, research by Baltes and his colleagues (Baltes & Kunzmann, 2007; Scheibe, Freund, & Baltes, 2007; Scheibe, Kuntzmann, & Baltes, 2007) has found that:

- High levels of wisdom are rare. Few people, including older adults, attain a high level of wisdom. That only a small percentage of adults show wisdom supports the contention that it requires experience, practice, or complex skills.

- The time frame of late adolescence and early adulthood is the main age window for wisdom to emerge (Staudinger & Dorner, 2007). No further advances in wisdom have been found for middle-aged and older adults beyond the level they attained as young adults.

- Factors other than age are critical for wisdom to develop to a high level. For example, certain life experiences, such as being trained and working in a field concerned with difficult life problems and having wisdom-enhancing mentors, contribute to higher levels of wisdom. Also, people higher in wisdom have values that are more likely to consider the welfare of others rather than their own happiness.

- Personality-related factors, such as openness to experience, generativity, and creativity, are better predictors of wisdom than cognitive factors such as intelligence.

Older adults might not be as quick with their thoughts or behavior as younger people, but wisdom may be an entirely different matter. This older woman shares the wisdom of her experience with a classroom of children. *How is wisdom described by life-span developmentalists?*

wisdom Expert knowledge about the practical aspects of life that permits excellent judgment about important matters.

Robert J. Sternberg (2003, 2008), whose triarchic theory of intelligence we described in Chapter 8, argues that wisdom is linked to both practical and academic intelligence. In his view, academic intelligence is a necessary but in many cases insufficient requirement for wisdom. Practical knowledge about the realities of life also is needed for wisdom. For Sternberg, balance between self-interest, the interests of others, and contexts produces a common good. Thus, wise individuals don't just look out for themselves—they also need to consider others' needs and perspectives, as well as the particular context involved. Sternberg assesses wisdom by presenting problems to individuals that require solutions which highlight various intrapersonal, interpersonal, and contextual interests. He also emphasizes that such aspects of wisdom should be taught in schools (Sternberg, 2008; Sternberg, Jarvin, & Reznitskaya, 2008). Sternberg's emphasis on using knowledge for the common good in a manner that addresses competing interests is what mainly differentiates it from Baltes and his colleagues' view of wisdom.

Education, Work, and Health

Education, work, and health are three important influences on the cognitive functioning of older adults. They are also three of the most important factors involved in understanding why cohort effects need to be taken into account in studying the cognitive functioning of older adults. Indeed cohort effects are very important to consider in the study of cognitive aging. For example, a recent study of two cohorts tested 16 years apart revealed that at age 74, the average performance on a wide range of cognitive tasks for older adults from the more recent cohort was equal to those of the older adults from the earlier cohort when they were 15 years younger (Zelinski & Kennison, 2007).

Education   Successive generations in America's twentieth century were better educated. Not only were today's older adults more likely to go to college when they were young adults than were their parents or grandparents, but more older adults are returning to college today to further their education than in past generations. Educational experiences are positively correlated with scores on intelligence tests and information-processing tasks, such as memory (Fritsch & others, 2007; Schaie, 2008). A recent study revealed that higher cognitive ability in 79-year-olds was linked to more years of education (Gow & others, 2008).

Older adults might seek more education for a number of reasons (Manheimer, 2007). They might want to better understand the nature of their aging. They might want to learn more about the social and technological changes that have produced dramatic changes in their lives. They might want to discover relevant knowledge and to learn relevant skills to cope with societal and job demands in later life. They might recognize that they need further education to remain competitive and stay in the workforce. And older adults may seek more education to enhance their self-discovery and the leisure activities that will enable them to make a smoother adjustment to retirement.

Work   Successive generations have also had work experiences that include a stronger emphasis on cognitively oriented labor (Elias & Wagster, 2007). Our great-grandfathers and grandfathers were more likely to be manual laborers than were our fathers, who are more likely to be involved in cognitively oriented occupations. As the industrial society continues to be replaced by the information society, younger generations will have more experience in jobs that require considerable cognitive investment. The increased emphasis on complex information processing in jobs likely enhances an individual's intellectual abilities (Schaie & Elder, 2006; Schooler, 2007).

In one study, substantive complex work was linked with higher intellectual functioning in older adults (Schooler, Mulatu, & Oates, 1999). This research is consistent with findings in a wide range of disciplines, including animal-based neurobiology

It is always in season for the old to learn.

—Aeschylus
Greek Playwright, 5th Century B.C.

How are education, work, and health linked to cognitive functioning in older adults?

studies, which strongly suggest that exposure to complex environments increases intellectual functioning throughout the life course (Kempermann, Kuhn, & Gage, 1997).

Health   Successive generations have also been healthier in late adulthood as better treatments for a variety of illnesses (such as hypertension) have been developed. Many of these illnesses have a negative impact on intellectual performance (Schaie & Elder, 2006). Hypertension has been linked to lower cognitive performance in a number of studies, not only in older adults but also in young and middle-aged adults (Vicario & others, 2005). Thus, some of the decline in intellectual performance found for older adults is likely due to health-related factors rather than to age per se.

K. Warner Schaie (1994) concluded that although some diseases—such as hypertension and diabetes—are linked to cognitive dropoffs, they do not directly cause mental decline. Rather, the lifestyles of the individuals with the diseases might be the culprits. For example, overeating, inactivity, and stress are related to both physical and mental decline (Lee & others, 2007). And researchers have found age-related cognitive decline in adults with mood disorders, such as depression (Chodosh & others, 2007; Gualtieri & Johnson, 2008).

A number of research studies have found that lifestyle and exercise are linked to improved cognitive functioning (Kramer & Erickson, 2007; Sumic & others, 2007). Here are the results of two of these studies:

- Community-dwelling women 65 years of age and older did not have cognitive impairment or physical limitations when they were initially assessed (Yaffe & others, 2001). Six to eight years later, the women with higher physical activity when they were initially assessed were less likely to experience cognitive decline.

- One hundred twenty-four individuals 60 to 75 years of age whose primary activity was sitting around the house were tested for their level of aerobic endurance and their level of cognitive functioning (Kramer & others, 1999). Cognitive functioning was assessed by tasks on working memory, planning, and scheduling. Half the group was randomly assigned to engage in yoga-type stretching activities, and the other half was randomly assigned to start walking three times a week. After six months, the walkers averaged a mile in 16 minutes, a minute faster than at the beginning, and the stretchers had become more flexible. When their cognitive functioning was retested after six months, the walkers scored up to 25 percent higher on the cognitive tests than the stretchers did.

Other researchers have found that aerobic exercise is related to improved memory and reasoning (Kramer & Erickson, 2007; Clarkson-Smith & Hartley, 1989). Walking or any other aerobic exercise appears to get blood and oxygen pumping to the brain, which can help people think more clearly (Studenski & others, 2006).

Two recent studies documented that the mental health of older adults can also influence their cognitive functioning. A recent study also revealed that depressive symptoms predicted cognitive decline in older adults (Chodosh & others, 2007). And a six-year longitudinal study found that higher levels of anxiety and depression assessed at the beginning of the study were linked to poorer memory functioning six years later (van Hooren & others, 2005).

A final aspect of health that is important to consider in cognitive functioning in older adults is *terminal decline*. This concept emphasizes that changes in cognitive functioning may be linked more to distance from death or cognition-related pathology than distance from birth (Lovden & Lindenberger, 2007).

Use It or Lose It

Changes in cognitive activity patterns might result in disuse and consequent atrophy of cognitive skills. This concept is captured in the concept of "use it or lose it." The mental activities that likely benefit the maintenance of cognitive skills in older adults are activities such as reading books, doing crossword puzzles, and going to lectures and concerts. Use it or lose it also is a significant component of the engagement model of cognitive optimization that emphasizes how intellectual and social engagement can buffer age-related declines in intellectual development (Park & others, 2007; Stine-Morrow, 2007). The following studies support the use it or lose it concept and the engagement model of cognitive optimization:

- In an analysis of participants in the Victoria Longitudinal Study, when middle-aged and older adults participated in intellectually engaging activities it served to buffer them against cognitive decline (Hultsch & others, 1999). Recent analyses of the participants in this study revealed that engagement in cognitively complex activities was linked to faster and more consistent processing speed (Bielak & others, 2007).

- In a longitudinal study of 801 Catholic priests 65 years and older, those who regularly read books, did crossword puzzles, or otherwise exercised their minds were 47 percent less likely to develop Alzheimer disease than the priests who rarely engaged in these activities (Wilson & others, 2002). Shortly, we will have much more to say about Alzheimer disease.

- A recent study revealed that reading daily was linked to reduced mortality in men in their seventies (Jacobs & others, 2008).

The Young@Heart chorus—whose average age is 80—performing. Young@Heart became a hit documentary in 2008. The documentary displays the singing talents, energy, and optimism of a remarkable group of older adults, who clearly are on the "use it" side of "use it or lose it."

Training Cognitive Skills

If older adults are losing cognitive skills, can they be retrained? An increasing number of research studies indicate that they can to a degree (Boron, Willis, & Schaie, 2007; Craik & others, 2007; Levine & others, 2007; Luo, Hendriks, & Craik, 2007; Winocur & others, 2007). Two key conclusions can be derived from research in this area: (1) training can improve the cognitive skills of many older adults; but (2) there is some loss in plasticity in late adulthood, especially in the oldest-old, 85 years and older (Baltes, Lindenberger, & Staudinger, 2006).

In an extensive recent study by Sherry Willis and her colleagues (2006), older adults were randomly assigned to one of four groups: those training in (1) reasoning, (2) memory, and (3) speed of processing; and (4) a control group that received no training. Each type of training showed an immediate effect in its domain—reasoning training improved reasoning, memory training improved memory, and speed of processing training improved speed of processing. However, the training effects did not transfer across cognitive domains, such that speed of processing training did not benefit the older adults' memory or reasoning, for example. The older adults who were given reasoning training did have less difficulty in the activities of daily living than a control group who did not receive this training. The activities of daily living that were assessed included how independently the older adults were able to prepare meals, do housework, do finances, go shopping, and engage in health maintenance. Each intervention maintained its effects on the specific targeted ability across the five years of the study. However, neither memory nor speed of processing training benefited the older adults' activities of daily living.

Another recent study had older adults participate in a 20-week activity called Senior Odyssey, a team-based program involving creative problem solving that is derived from the Odyssey of the Mind program for children and emerging adults (Stine-Morrow & others, 2007). In a field experiment, compared with a control group who did not experience Senior Odyssey, the Senior Odyssey participants showed improved processing speed, somewhat improved creative thinking, and increased mindfulness. *Mindfulness* involves generating new ideas, being open to new information, and being aware of multiple perspectives (Langer, 2000, 2007).

Another recent study trained older adults to increase their processing speed (Ball, Edwards, & Ross, 2007). As a result of the training, older adults increased their processing speed and the gain was maintained for two years. The benefits of the processing

What characterizes the "use it or lose it" concept of cognitive aging?

To what extent can training improve the cognitive functioning of older adults?

speed training translated into improvements in everyday activities, such as safer driving performance.

As we discussed earlier in the chapter, researchers are also finding that improving the physical fitness of older adults can improve their cognitive functioning (Kramer & Erickson, 2007). A research review revealed that aerobic fitness training improved the planning, scheduling, working memory, resistance to distraction, and processing involving multiple tasks in older adults (Colcombe & Kramer, 2003).

In sum, the cognitive vitality of older adults can be improved through cognitive and physical fitness training (Kramer & Erickson, 2007; Park & others, 2007; Siegler & others, 2008). However, benefits have not been observed in all studies (Salthouse, 2006). Further research is needed to determine more precisely which cognitive improvements occur through cognitive and physical fitness training in older adults (Stine-Morrow, 2007).

Cognitive Neuroscience and Aging

On several occasions in this chapter and in Chapter 17, we indicated that certain regions of the brain are involved in links between aging and cognitive functioning. In this section, we further explore the substantial increase in interest in the brain's role in aging and cognitive functioning. The field of *cognitive neuroscience* has emerged as the major discipline that studies links between brain and cognitive functioning (Grady, 2008; Hillman, Erickson, & Kramer, 2008). This field especially relies on brain-imaging techniques, such as fMRI (functional magnetic resonance imaging) and PET, to reveal the areas of the brain that are activated when individuals are engaging in certain cognitive activities (Hayes & Cabeza, 2008; Miller & others, 2008). For example, as an older adult is asked to encode and then retrieve verbal materials or images of scenes, the older adult's brain activity will be monitored by an fMRI brain scan.

Changes in the brain can influence cognitive functioning, and changes in cognitive functioning can influence the brain (Grady, 2008). For example, aging of the brain's prefrontal cortex may produce a decline in working memory (Smith, 2007). And when older adults do not regularly use their working memory (recall the section on "use it or lose it"), neural connections in the prefrontal lobe may atrophy. Further, cognitive interventions that activate older adults' working memory may increase these neural connections.

Although in its infancy as a field, the cognitive neuroscience of aging is beginning to uncover some important links between aging, the brain, and cognitive functioning. These include:

- Neural circuits in specific regions of the brain's prefrontal cortex decline, and this decline is linked to poorer performance by older adults on complex reasoning tasks, working memory, and episodic memory tasks (Daselaar & Cabeza, 2008; Grady, 2008).

- Recall from Chapter 17 that older adults are more likely than younger adults to use both hemispheres of the brain to compensate for aging declines in attention, memory, and language (Dennis & Cabeza, 2008; Grady, 2008).

- Functioning of the hippocampus declines less than the functioning of the frontal lobes in older adults, but further indication of possible compensation for memory decline in aging was found in a recent study of increased activation of the frontal lobes to possibly compensate for declining activation of the hippocampus (Gutchess & others, 2005).

- Patterns of neural differences with age are larger for retrieval than encoding (Park & Gutchess, 2005).

- Compared with younger adults, older adults show greater activity in the frontal and parietal regions while they are engaging in tasks that require cognitive control processes such as attention (Grady, 2008).

- An increasing number of cognitive and fitness-training studies include brain-imaging techniques such as fMRI to assess the results of such training on brain functioning (Kramer & Erickson, 2007; Hillman, Erickson, & Kramer, 2008). In one study, older adults who walked one hour a day three days a week for six months showed increased volume in the frontal and temporal lobes of the brain (Colcombe & others, 2006).

We are likely to see increased effort to uncover links between aging, the brain, and cognitive functioning in the next several decades.

Review and Reflect: Learning Goal 1

 Describe the Cognitive Functioning of Older Adults

REVIEW

- How is cognition multidimensional and multidirectional in older adults? What changes in cognitive processes take place in aging adults?
- How do education, work, and health affect cognition in aging adults?
- What is the concept of "use it or lose it"?
- To what extent can older adults' cognitive skills be trained?
- What characterizes the cognitive neuroscience of aging?

REFLECT

- Can you think of older adults who have made significant contributions in late adulthood other than those we mentioned in the chapter? Spend some time reading about these individuals, and evaluate how their intellectual interests contributed to their life satisfaction as older adults.

2 LANGUAGE DEVELOPMENT

Most research on language development has focused on infancy and childhood. It is generally thought that for most of adulthood individuals maintain their language skills (Thornton & Light, 2006). The vocabulary of individuals often continues to increase throughout most of the adult years, at least until late adulthood (Willis & Schaie, 2005). Many older adults maintain or improve their word knowledge and word meaning (Burke & Shafto, 2004).

In late adulthood, however, some decrements in language may appear (Obler, 2009; Stine-Morrow, 2007). Among the most common language-related complaints reported by older adults are difficulty in retrieving words to use in conversation and understanding spoken language in certain contexts (Clark-Cotton, Williams, & Goral, 2007). This often involves the *tip-of-the-tongue phenomenon*, in which individuals are confident that they can remember something but just can't quite seem to retrieve it from memory, which we discussed earlier in the section on memory and aging (Thornton & Light, 2006). Older adults also report that in less than ideal listening conditions they can have difficulty in understanding speech. This difficulty is most likely to occur when speech is rapid, competing stimuli are present (a noisy room, for example), and when they can't see their conversation partner (in a telephone conversation, for example). The difficulty in understanding speech may be due to hearing loss (Gordon-Salant & others,

What are some differences in the way older and younger adults communicate?

2006). In general, though, most language skills decline little among older adults if they are healthy (Clark-Cotton, Williams, & Goral, 2007).

Some aspects of the phonological skills of older adults are different than those of younger adults (Clark-Cotton, Williams, & Goral, 2007). Older adults' speech is typically lower in volume, slower, less precisely articulated, and less fluent (more pauses, fillers, repetition, and corrections). Despite these age differences, most older adults' speech skills are adequate for everyday communication.

Researchers have found conflicting information about changes in *discourse* (extended verbal expression in speech or writing) with aging. "Some [researchers] have reported increased elaborateness, whereas others have reported less varied and less complex syntax" (Obler, 2005, p. 468). One aspect of discourse where age differences have been found involves retelling a story or giving instructions for completing a task. When engaging in this type of discourse, older adults are more likely than younger adults to omit key elements creating discourse that is less fluent and more difficult to follow (Clark-Cotton, Williams, & Goral, 2007).

Nonlanguage factors may be responsible for some of the decline in language skills that do occur in older adults (Obler, 2009). Slower information-processing speed and a decline in working memory, especially in being able to keep information in mind while processing, likely contribute to lowered language efficiency in older adults (Stine-Morrow, 2007).

Language does change among individuals with Alzheimer disease, which we will discuss later in the chapter (Goral, Clark-Cotton, & Albert, 2007; Obler, 2009). Word-finding/generating difficulties are one of the earliest symptoms of Alzheimer disease, but most individuals with Alzheimer disease retain much of their ability to produce well-formed sentences until the late stages of the disease. Nonetheless, they do make more grammatical errors than older adults without Alzheimer disease.

Review and Reflect: Learning Goal 2

2 **Characterize Changes in Language in Older Adults**

REVIEW

*   How can changes in the language development of older adults be described?

REFLECT

*   Imagine that you are a researcher who is going to study the tip-of-the-tongue phenomenon in older adults. What type of task would you use to study this phenomenon?

---

3 WORK AND RETIREMENT

Work   **Retirement in the United States and Other Countries**   **Adjustment to Retirement**

What percentage of older adults continue to work? How productive are they? Who adjusts best to retirement? What is the changing pattern of retirement in the United States and around the world? These are some of the questions we now examine.

Work

In the beginning of the twenty-first century, the percentage of men over the age of 65 who continue to work full-time is less than at the beginning of the twentieth century. The decline from 1900 to 2000 has been as much as 70 percent.

An important change in older adults' work patterns is the increase in part-time work (Hardy, 2006). The percentage of older adults who work part-time has steadily increased since the 1960s. Aging and work expert James House (1998) concluded that many middle-aged workers would like to do less paid work, whereas many older adults would like to do more.

Some individuals maintain their productivity throughout their lives (Cleveland & Shore, 2007). Some of these older workers work as many or more hours than younger workers. In the National Longitudinal Survey of Older Men, good health, a strong psychological commitment to work, and a distaste for retirement were the most important characteristics related to continued employment into old age (seventies and eighties) (Parnes & Sommers, 1994). The probability of employment also was positively correlated with educational attainment and being married to a working wife.

Especially important to think about is the large cohort of baby boomers—78 million people who will begin to reach traditional retirement age in 2010. Because this cohort is so large, we are likely to see increasing numbers of older adults continue to work (Hart, 2007). The aging of the U.S. workforce will continue to at least until 2034, when the largest of the baby-boom cohorts reaches 70 (Manton & others, 2007).

Cognitive ability is one of the best predictors of job performance in older adults. And older workers have lower rates of absenteeism, fewer accidents, and increased job satisfaction, compared with their younger counterparts (Warr, 2004). This means that the older worker can be of considerable value to a company, above and beyond the older worker's cognitive competence. Changes in federal law now allow individuals over the age of 65 to continue working (Shore & Goldberg, 2005). Also, remember from our discussion earlier in the chapter that substantively complex work is linked with a higher level of intellectual functioning (Schooler, 2007). This likely is a reciprocal relation—that is, individuals with higher cognitive ability likely continue to work as older adults, and when they work in substantively complex jobs, this likely enhances their intellectual functioning.

An increasing number of middle-aged and older adults are embarking on a second or a third career (Moen & Spencer, 2006). In some cases, this is an entirely different type of work or a continuation of previous work but at a reduced level. Many older adults also participate in unpaid work—as a volunteer or as an active participant in a voluntary association. These options afford older adults opportunities for productive activity, social interaction, and a positive identity.

Significant numbers of retirees only partially retire, moving to part-time employment by either reducing the number of hours they work on their career jobs or by taking on new (and frequently lower-paying) jobs (Hardy, 2006; Taylor, 2007). Self-employed men are especially likely to continue paid employment, either on the same job or on a new job.

In summary, age affects many aspects of work (Charness, Czaja, & Sharit, 2007; Cleveland & Lim, 2007; Cleveland & Shore, 2007). Nonetheless, many studies of work and aging—such as evaluation of hiring and performance—reveal inconsistent results. Important contextual factors, such as age composition of departments or applicant pools, occupations, and jobs, all affect decisions about older workers. It also is important to recognize that ageist stereotypes of workers and of tasks can limit older workers' career opportunities and can encourage early retirement or other forms of downsizing that adversely affect older workers (Cleveland & Shore, 2007; Finkelstein & Farrell, 2007). For example, one recent study found that extensive negative stereotyping of older adults was involved in not hiring them (Gringart, Helmes, & Speelman, 2005). Also, employers' attributes of negative ageist stereotyping often focus on trainability, adaptability, creativity, and interest in new technology (Scialfa & Fernie, 2006).

Ninety-two-year-old Russell "Bob" Harrell (*right*) puts in 12-hour days at Sieco Consulting Engineers in Columbus, Indiana. A highway and bridge engineer, he designs and plans roads. James Rice (age 48), a vice president of client services at Sieco, says that "Bob" wants to learn something new every day and that he has learned many life lessons from being around him Harrell says he is not planning on retiring. *What are some variations in work and retirement in older adults?*

Retirement in the United States and Other Countries

At what age do most people retire in the United States? Do many people return to the workforce at some point after they have retired? What is retirement like in other countries?

The option to retire is a late-twentieth-century phenomenon in the United States (Atchley, 2007). It exists largely thanks to the implementation in 1935 of the Social Security system, which gives benefits to older workers when they retire. On the average, today's workers will spend 10 to 15 percent of their lives in retirement. A recent survey revealed that as baby boomers move into their sixties, they expect to delay retirement longer than their parents or grandparents (Frey, 2007).

In the past, when most people reached an accepted retirement age, such as some point in their sixties, retirement meant a one-way exit from full-time work to full-time leisure (Atchley, 2007). Leading expert Phyllis Moen (2007) recently described how to-day, when people reach their sixties, the life path they follow is less clear: (1) some individuals don't retire, continuing in their career jobs; (2) some retire from their career work and then take up a new and different job; (3) some retire from career jobs but do volunteer work; (4) some retire from a postretirement job and go on to yet another job; (5) some move in and out of the workforce, so they never really have a "career" job from which they retire; (6) some individuals who are in poor health move to a disability status and eventually into retirement; and (7) some who are laid off define it as "retirement."

Approximately 7 million retired Americans return to work after they have retired (Putnam Investments, 2006). When retired adults return to the labor force, it occurs on average four years after retirement (Hardy, 2006). In many instances, the jobs pay much less than their preretirement jobs. In one study of older adults who returned to work, approximately two-thirds said they were happy they had done so, whereas about one-third indicated they were forced to go back to work to meet financial needs (Putnam Investments, 2006).

Just as the life path after individuals reach retirement age may be varied, so are the reasons for working. For example, some older adults who reach retirement age work for financial reasons, others to stay busy, and yet others to "give back" (Moen, 2007). To read about work and retirement in different countries, see the *Diversity in Life-Span Development* interlude.

Diversity in Life-Span Development
Work and Retirement Around the World

A recent large-scale study of 21,000 individuals aged 40 to 79 in 21 countries examined patterns of work and retirement (HSBC Insurance, 2007). On average, 33 percent of individuals in their sixties and 11 percent in their seventies were still in some kind of paid employment. In this study, 19 percent of those in their seventies in the United States were still working, but only 1 percent of older adults in their seventies in France were still working. As indicated in Figure 18.5, a substantial percentage of individuals expect to continue working as long as possible before retiring (HSBC Insurance, 2007).

In the recent study of work and retirement in 21 countries, Japanese retirees missed the work slightly more than they expected and the money considerably less than they expected (HSBC Insurance, 2007). U.S. retirees missed both the work and the money slightly less than they expected. German retirees were the least likely to miss the work, Turkish and Chinese retirees the most likely to miss it. Regarding the money, Japanese and Chinese retirees were the least likely to miss it, Turkish retirees the most likely to miss it.

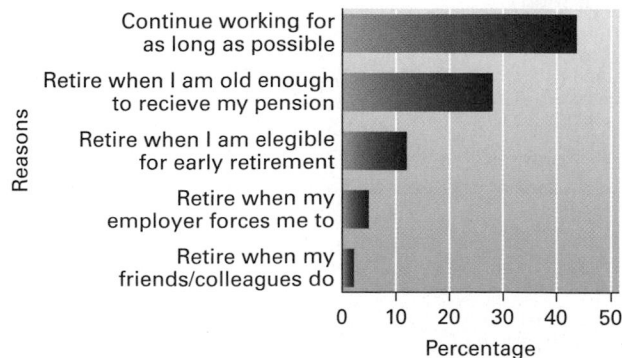

FIGURE 18.5 Reasons Given by People Regarding When They Expect to Retire from Work

Early retirement policies were introduced by many companies in the 1970s and 1980s, with an intent to make room for younger workers. However, in the recent survey, there was some indication that an increasing number of adults are beginning to reject the early retirement option as they hear about people who retired and then regretted it. In the 21 country study, on average only 12 percent of individuals in their forties and fifties expected to take early retirement, whereas 16 percent in their sixties and seventies had taken early retirement. Only in Germany, South Korea, and Hong Kong did a higher percentage of individuals expect earlier retirement than in the past.

In the recent cross-national study, to what extent did Japanese retirees miss the work and the money in comparison to U.S. retirees?

Adjustment to Retirement

Retirement is a process, not an event (Moen, 2007). Much of the research on retirement has been cross-sectional rather than longitudinal and has focused on men rather than women. One study found that men had higher morale when they had retired within the last two years compared with men who had been retired for longer periods of time (Kim & Moen, 2002). A recent study revealed that retired married and remarried women reported being more satisfied with their lives and in better health than retired women who were widowed, separated, divorced, or had never been married (Price & Joo, 2005). Another recent study indicated that women spend less time planning for retirement than men do (Jacobs-Lawson, Hershey, & Neukam, 2005).

Older adults who adjust best to retirement are healthy, have adequate income, are active, are better educated, have an extended social network including both friends and family, and usually were satisfied with their lives before they retired (Raymo & Sweeney, 2006). Older adults with inadequate income and poor health, and who must adjust to other stress that occurs at the same time as retirement, such as the death of a spouse, have the most difficult time adjusting to retirement (Reichstadt & others, 2007). A recent study also found that individuals who had difficulty in adjusting to retirement had a strong attachment to work, including full-time jobs and a long work history, lack of control over the transition to retirement, and low self-efficacy (van Solinge & Henkens, 2005).

The U.S. retirement system is in transition. Following are the results of a 2007 survey on retirement (Helman, VanDerhei, & Copeland, 2007): Half of the workers were not confident about their pension benefits; many workers count on benefits that won't be there when they retire; workers often don't heed advice about retirement even when they are provided the advice; workers overestimate long-term care coverage; most workers' savings are modest; and many workers know little about the social security income they will receive when they retire.

Flexibility is also a key factor in whether individuals adjust well to retirement (Baehr & Barnett, 2007). When people retire, they no longer have the structured environment they had when they were working, so they need to be flexible and discover and pursue their own interests (Eisdorfer, 1996). Cultivating interests and friends unrelated to work improves adaptation to retirement (Zarit & Knight, 1996).

Planning and then successfully carrying out the plan is an important aspect of adjusting well in retirement. A special concern in retirement planning involves women, who are likely to live longer than men and more likely to live alone (less likely to remarry and more likely to be widowed) (Moen, 2007).

Individuals who view retirement planning only in terms of finances don't adapt as well to retirement as those who have a more balanced retirement plan (Birren, 1996). It is important not only to plan financially for retirement, but to consider other areas of your life as well (Sener, Terzioglu, & Karabulet, 2007). In addition to financial planning, questions individuals need to ask about retirement include: What am I going to do with my leisure time? What am I going to do to stay active? What am I going to do socially? What am I going to do to keep my mind active?

In addition to financial planning, what are some other aspects of retirement planning that need to be carried out?

Review and Reflect: Learning Goal 3

 Discuss Aging and Adaptations to Work and Retirement

REVIEW

- What characterizes the work of older adults?
- Compare retirement in the United States with other countries.
- How can individuals adjust effectively to retirement?

REFLECT

- At what age would you like to retire? Or would you prefer to continue working as an older adult as long as you are healthy? At what age did your father and/or mother retire? How well did they adjust to retirement? Explain.

4 MENTAL HEALTH

| Depression | Dementia, Alzheimer Disease, and Other Afflictions | Fear of Victimization, Crime, and Elder Maltreatment |

Although a substantial portion of the population can now look forward to a longer life, that life may unfortunately be hampered by a mental disorder in old age. This prospect is both troubling to the individual and costly to society. Mental disorders make individuals increasingly dependent on the help and care of others. The cost of mental health disorders in older adults is estimated at more than $40 billion per year in the United States. More important than the loss in dollars, though, is the loss of human potential and the suffering. Although mental disorders in older adults are a major concern, older adults do not have a higher incidence of mental disorders than younger adults do (Busse & Blazer, 1996).

Depression

Major depression is a mood disorder in which the individual is deeply unhappy, demoralized, self-derogatory, and bored. The person does not feel well, loses stamina easily, has a poor appetite, and is listless and unmotivated. Major depression has been called the "common cold" of mental disorders. Researchers have found that depressive symptoms vary from less frequent to no more frequent in late adulthood than in middle adulthood (Hybels & Blazer, 2004). However, it is anticipated that the number of older adults with depression will increase as the current large cohort of baby boomers moves through late adulthood (Parmalee, 2007). A recent large-scale study of U.S. women 65 years of age and older revealed that 5.9 percent currently had depression and 12.3 percent had a diagnosis of depression of some point in their lifetime (McGuire & others, 2008).

One study found that the lower frequency of depressive symptoms in older adults compared with middle-aged adults was linked to fewer economic hardships, fewer negative social interchanges, and increased religiosity (Schieman, van Gundy, & Taylor, 2004). Other research indicates that older adults who engage in regular exercise, expecially aerobic exercise, are less likely to be depressed, whereas those who are in poor health and experiencing pain are more likely to be depressed (Kostka & Praczko, 2007; Lindwall & others, 2007; Mavandadi & others, 2007). Depressive symptoms

major depression A mood disorder in which the individual is deeply unhappy, demoralized, self-derogatory, and bored. The person does not feel well, loses stamina easily, has poor appetite, and is listless and unmotivated. Major depression is so widespread that it has been called the "common cold" of mental disorders.

increase in the oldest-old (85 years and older), and this increase is associated with a higher percentage of women in the group, more physical disability, more cognitive impairment, and lower socioeconomic status (Hybels & Blazer, 2004).

In the child, adolescent, and early adulthood years, females show greater depression than males do (Nolen-Hoeksema, 2007). Does this gender difference hold for middle-aged and older adults? A longitudinal study found greater depression in women than men at 50 and 60 years of age, but not at 80 years of age (Barefoot & others, 2001). Men showed increases in depressive symptoms from 60 to 80, but women did not. In this cohort, men may have undergone more profound role shifts after 60 years of age because they were more likely than women to have retired from active involvement in the work world. Thus, the absence of a gender difference in depression in older adults may be cohort-specific and may not hold as women who have entered the workforce in greater numbers are assessed in late adulthood.

Among the most common predictors of depression in older adults are earlier depressive symptoms, poor health, disability, loss events such as the death of a spouse, and low social support (Lee & Park, 2008; Wrosch & others, 2007). In one longitudinal study, widows showed elevated depressive symptoms up to two years following the death of a spouse (Turvey & others, 1999). In another study, depressive symptoms were higher in U.S. older adults who lived alone, especially immigrants (Wilmoth & Chen, 2003). However, good social support and being socially integrated in the community helped to buffer the effects of declining health on depression in these individuals (Hybels & Blazer, 2004).

Depression is a treatable condition, not only in young adults but in older adults as well (Lakey & others, 2008; Snowden, Steinman, & Frederick, 2008). Unfortunately, as many as 80 percent of older adults with depressive symptoms receive no treatment at all. Combinations of medications and psychotherapy produce significant improvement in almost four out of five older adults with depression (Koenig & Blazer, 1996).

Major depression can result not only in sadness, but also in suicidal tendencies (Hasche & Morrow-Howell, 2007; McLaren & others, 2007). Nearly 25 percent of individuals who commit suicide in the United States are 65 years of age or older (Church, Siegel, & Fowler, 1988). The older adult most likely to commit suicide is a male who lives alone, has lost his spouse, and is experiencing failing health (Ruckenhauser, Yazdani & Ravaglia, 2007).

What characterizes depression in older adults?

Dementia, Alzheimer Disease, and Other Afflictions

Among the most debilitating of mental disorders in older adults are the dementias (Jellinger & Atterns, 2007). In recent years, extensive attention has been focused on the most common dementia, Alzheimer disease. Other afflictions common in older adults are multi-infarct dementia and Parkinson disease.

Dementia   **Dementia** is a global term for any neurological disorder in which the primary symptoms involve a deterioration of mental functioning. Individuals with dementia often lose the ability to care for themselves and can lose the ability to recognize familiar surroundings and people (including family members) (Lovheim & others, 2008; Ouldred & Bryant, 2008). It is estimated that 20 percent of individuals over the age of 80 have dementia. Dementia is a broad category, and it is important that every effort is made to narrow the older adult's disorder and determine a specific cause of the deteriorating mental functioning (Whitehouse, 2007a).

Alzheimer Disease   One form of dementia is **Alzheimer disease**—a progressive, irreversible brain disorder that is characterized by a gradual deterioration of memory, reasoning, language, and eventually, physical function. In 2005, 4.5 million adults in the United States had Alzheimer disease, and it is estimated that at least 25 million adults worldwide have the disease (Alzheimer's Disease International, 2008). It is predicted that Alzheimer disease could triple in the next 50 years, as increasing numbers of people live to older ages. Because of the increasing prevalence of Alzheimer disease,

dementia A global term for any neurological disorder in which the primary symptoms involve a deterioration of mental functioning.

Alzheimer disease A progressive, irreversible brain disorder characterized by a gradual deterioration of memory, reasoning, language, and eventually physical function.

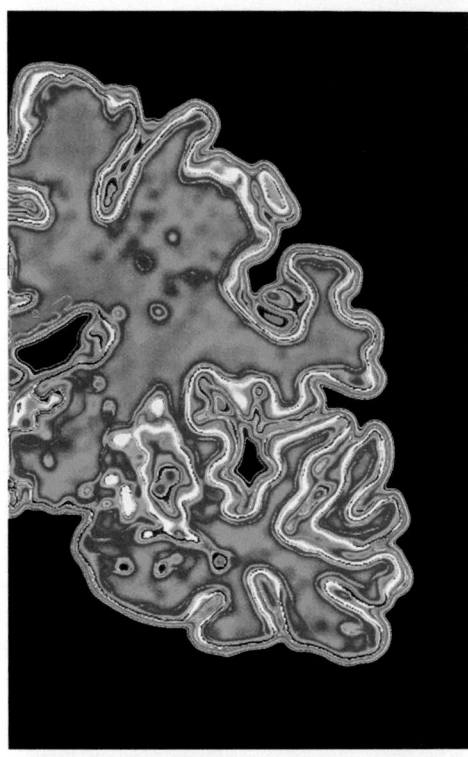

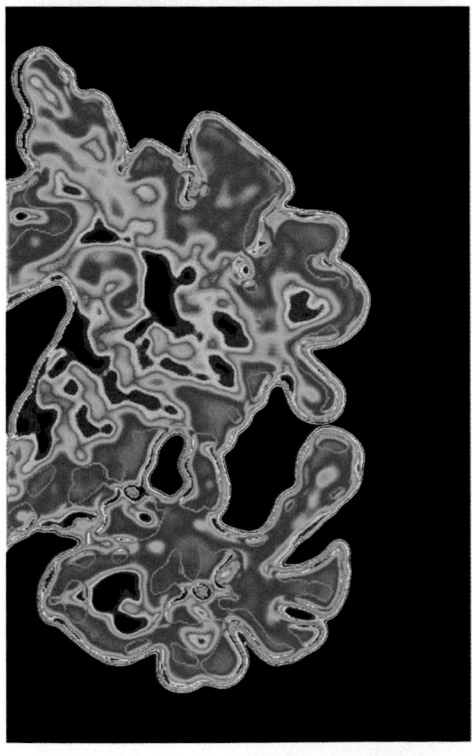

FIGURE 18.6 Two Brains: Normal Aging and Alzheimer Disease. The top computer graphic shows a slice of a normal aging brain, the bottom photograph a slice of a brain ravaged by Alzheimer disease. Notice the deterioration and shrinking in the Alzheimer disease brain.

researchers have stepped up their efforts to discover the causes of the disease and find more effective ways to treat it (Patterson & others, 2008).

Because of differences in onset, Alzheimer also is now described as *early-onset* (initially occurring in individuals younger than 65 years of age) or *late-onset* (which has its initial onset in individuals 65 years of age and older). Early-onset Alzheimer disease is rare (about 10 percent of all cases) and generally affects people 30 to 60 years of age.

Alzheimer disease involves a deficiency in the important brain messenger chemical acetylcholine, which plays an important role in memory (Amenta & Tayebati, 2008). Also, as Alzheimer disease progresses, the brain shrinks and deteriorates (see Figure 18.6). The deterioration of the brain in Alzheimer disease is characterized by the formation of *amyloid plaques* (dense deposits of protein that accumulate in the blood vessels) and *neurofibrillary tangles* (twisted fibers that build up in neurons) (Postina, 2008). Researchers are especially seeking ways to interrupt the progress of amyloid plaques and neurofibrillary tangles in Alzheimer patients (Nathalie & Jean-Noel, 2008; Nordberg, 2008).

Although scientists are not certain what causes Alzheimer disease, age is an important risk factor, and genes also likely play an important role (Bird, 2008; Vasudevaraju & others, 2008). The number of individuals with Alzheimer disease doubles every five years after the age of 65. A gene called *apolipoprotein E (apoE)*, which is linked to increasing presence of plaques and tangles in the brain, could play a role in as many as one-third of the cases of Alzheimer disease (Wang & Deng, 2008; Waring & Rosenberg, 2008). A recent study of almost 12,000 pairs of twins in Sweden found that identical twins were both more likely to develop Alzheimer disease than fraternal twins, suggesting a genetic influence on the disease (Gatz & others, 2006). And another recent study revealed that the presence of the *apoE* gene lowers the age of onset of Alzheimer disease (Sando & others, 2008).

Although individuals with a family history of Alzheimer disease are at greater risk, the disease is complex and likely caused by a number of factors, including lifestyles (Andel & others, 2008; Hooijmans & Kiliaan, 2008). For many years, scientists have known that a healthy diet, exercise, and weight control can lower the risk of cardiovascular disease. Now, they are finding that these healthy lifestyle factors may also lower the risk of Alzheimer disease. Researchers have revealed older adults with Alzheimer disease are more likely to also have cardiovascular disease than individuals who do not have Alzheimer disease (Cole & Vassar, 2008). Autopsies show that brains with the telltale signs of tangles and plaques of Alzheimer patients are three times more common in individuals with cardiovascular disease (Sparks & others, 1990). Recently, more cardiac risk factors have been implicated in Alzheimer disease—obesity, smoking, atherosclerosis, and high cholesterol (Almeida & others, 2008; Gazdzinski & others, 2008; Luchsinger, 2008).

As with many problems associated with aging, exercise may also reduce the risk of Alzheimer disease (Middleton & others, 2007). One study of more than 2,000 men 71 to 93 years of age revealed that those who walked less than one-fourth of a mile a day were almost twice as likely to develop Alzheimer disease as their male counterparts who walked more than two miles a day (Abbott & others, 2004).

Early Detection and Alzheimer Disease *Mild cognitive impairment (MCI)* represents a transitional state between the cognitive changes of normal aging and very early Alzheimer disease and other dementias (Peterson & Negash, 2008; Ries & others, 2008). MCI is increasingly recognized as a risk factor for Alzheimer disease (Bombois & others, 2008).

Deficits in episodic memory appear to be an especially important early indication of risk for subsequent development of Alzheimer disease (Belleville & others, 2008; Guarch & others, 2008). Also, special brain scans, such as fMRI, can detect changes in the brain that are fairly typical of early Alzheimer disease even before symptoms develop (Barrio & others, 2008).

Drug Treatment of Alzheimer Disease Several drugs called cholinerase inhibitors have been approved by the U.S. Food and Drug Administration to treat Alzheimer disease. Three of these drugs are now widely used to treat Alzheimer disease: donepezil (Aricept), rivastigmine (Exelon), and galantamine (Razadyne). They are designed to improve memory and other cognitive functions by increasing levels of acetylcholine in the brain (Choi & others, 2008). The drugs have been effective in slowing down the progression of Alzheimer symptoms in mild to moderate stages of the disease, but they have not been approved for advanced stages of Alzheimer disease. One recent study revealed that the three cholinerase inhibitors improved cognitive functioning in individuals with Alzheimer disease for as long as four to five years (Bullock & Dengiz, 2005). In 2003, memantine (Namenda) was approved for use in treating moderate to severe Alzheimer disease, and it works differently than the cholinerase inhibitors. Memantine is in the class of drugs called NMDA antagonists and it regulates the information-processing activities of the neurotransmitter glutamate (Shah & others, 2008). Researchers have found that memantine improves cognitive and behavioral functioning in individuals with moderate to severe Alzheimer disease (Farlow, Miller, & Pejovic, 2008). Researchers are beginning to study how combinations of drugs might further reduce Alzheimer symptoms. One recent review found that memantine combined with donepezil improved cognitive and behavioral functioning in individuals with moderate or severe Alzheimer disease (Xiong & Doraiswamy, 2005). Keep in mind, though, that the drugs used to treat Alzheimer disease only slow the downward progression of the disease; they do not treat its cause (Carcabelos, 2008).

Former president Ronald Reagan was diagnosed with Alzheimer disease at age 83.

Caring for Individuals with Alzheimer Disease A special concern is caring for Alzheimer patients (Cooper & others, 2008; Yaari & Corey-Bloom, 2007). Health-care professionals believe that the family can be an important support system for the Alzheimer patient, but this support can have costs for the family, who can become emotionally and physically drained by the extensive care required for a person with Alzheimer disease (Vellone & others, 2008). For example, depression has been reported in 50 percent of family caregivers for Alzheimer patients (Redinbaugh, MacCallum, & Kiecolt-Glaser, 1995). A recent meta-analysis found that female caregivers reported providing more caregiving hours, higher levels of burden and depression, as well as lower levels of well-being and physical health, than male caregivers (Pinquart & Sorensen, 2006).

Respite care (services that provide temporary relief for those who are caring for individuals with disabilities, illnesses, or the elderly) has been developed to help people who have to meet the day-to-day needs of Alzheimer patients. This type of care provides an important break away from the burden of providing chronic care (Yaari & Corey-Bloom, 2007). To read further about individuals who care for Alzheimer patients, see the *Research in Life-Span Development* interlude.

Research in Life-Span Development
The Stress of Caring for an Alzheimer Patient at Home

Researchers have recently found that the stress of caring for an Alzheimer patient at home can prematurely age the immune system, putting caregivers at risk for developing age-related diseases (Graham, Christian, & Kiecolt-Glaser, 2006; Mausbach & others, 2007). In one study, 119 older adults who were caring for a spouse with Alzheimer disease or another form of dementia (which can require up to 100 hours a week of time) were compared with 106 older adults who did not have to care for a chronically ill spouse (Kiecolt-Glaser & others, 2003). The age of the older adults upon entry into the study ranged from 55 to 89, with an average of 70.

Periodically during the six-year study, blood samples were taken and the levels of a naturally produced immune chemical called interleukin-6, or IL-6, were measured. IL-6 increases with age and can place people at risk for a number of illnesses, including cardiovascular disease, type 2 diabetes, frailty, and certain cancers. The researchers found that the levels of IL-6 increased four times as fast in the Alzheimer caregivers as in the older adults who did not have to care for a critically ill spouse (see Figure 18.7).

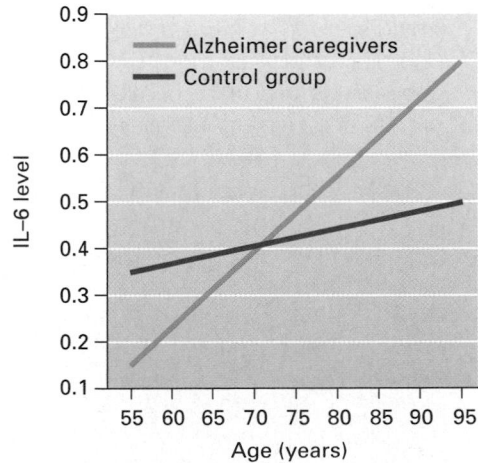

FIGURE 18.7 Comparison of IL-6 Levels in Alzheimer Caregivers and a Control Group of Noncaregivers. Notice that IL-6 (an immune chemical that places individuals at risk for a number of diseases) increased for both the Alzheimer caregivers and the control group of noncaregivers. However, also note that IL-6 increased significantly more in the Alzheimer caregivers. A higher score for IL-6 reflects a higher level of the immune chemical.

Each time IL-6 was assessed by drawing blood, the participants also completed a 10-item perceived stress scale to assess the extent they perceived their daily life during the prior week as "unpredictable, uncontrollable, and overloading" (Kiecolt-Glaser & others, 2003, p. 9091). Participants rated each item from 0 (never) to 4 (very often). Alzheimer caregivers reported greater stress than the noncaregiver controls across each of the six annual assessments.

There are many career opportunities for working with individuals who have Alzheimer disease. To read about the work of a director of an Alzheimer association, see the *Careers in Life-Span Development* profile.

Careers in Life-Span Development

Jan Weaver, Director of the Alzheimer's Association of Dallas

Dr. Jan Weaver joined the Alzheimer's Association, Greater Dallas Chapter, as director of services and education in 1999. Prior to that time, she served as associate director of education for the Texas Institute for Research and Education on Aging and director of the National Academy for Teaching and Learning About Aging at the University of North Texas. As a gerontologist, Weaver plans and develops services and educational programs that address patterns of human development related to aging. Among the services of the Alzheimer's Association that Weaver supervises are a resource center and helpline, a family assistance program, a care program, support groups, referral and information, educational conferences, and community seminars.

Weaver recognizes that people of all ages should have an informed and balanced view of older adults that helps them perceive aging as a process of growth and fulfillment rather than a process of decline and

dependency. Weaver earned her Ph.D. in sociology, with an emphasis in gerontology, from the University of North Texas in 1996.

Jan Weaver giving a lecture on Alzheimer disease.

Multi-Infarct Dementia **Multi-infarct dementia** involves a sporadic and progressive loss of intellectual functioning caused by repeated temporary obstruction of blood flow in cerebral arteries (Charlton & others 2006). The result is a series of mini-strokes. The term *infarct* refers to the temporary obstruction of blood vessels. It is estimated that 15 to 25 percent of dementias involve the vascular impairment of multi-infarct dementia.

Multi-infarct dementia is more common among men with a history of high blood pressure. The clinical picture of multi-infarct dementia is different than for Alzheimer disease—many patients recover from multi-infarct dementia, whereas Alzheimer disease shows a progressive deterioration. The symptoms of multi-infarct dementia include confusion, slurring of speech, writing impairment, and numbness on one side of the face, arm, or leg (Hoyer & Roodin, 2003). However, after each occurrence, there usually is a rather quick recovery, although each succeeding occurrence is usually more damaging. Approximately 35 to 50 percent of individuals who have these transient attacks will have a major stroke within five years unless the underlying problems

multi-infarct dementia Sporadic and progressive loss of intellectual functioning caused by repeated temporary obstruction of blood flow in cerebral arteries.

are treated. Especially recommended for these individuals are exercise, improved diet, and appropriate drugs, which can slow or stop the progression of the underlying vascular disease.

Parkinson Disease Another type of dementia is **Parkinson disease**, a chronic, progressive disease characterized by muscle tremors, slowing of movement, and partial facial paralysis. Parkinson disease is triggered by degeneration of dopamine-producing neurons in the brain (Daadi, 2008). Dopamine is a neurotransmitter that is necessary for normal brain functioning. Why these neurons degenerate is not known.

The main treatment for Parkinson disease involves administering drugs that enhance the effect of dopamine (dopamine agonists) in the disease's earlier stages and later administering the drug L-dopa, which is converted by the brain into dopamine (Stowe & others, 2008; Yamamoto & Schapira, 2008). However, it is difficult to determine the correct level of dosage of L-dopa, and it loses its efficacy over time. Another treatment for advanced Parkinson disease is deep brain stimulation (DBS), which involves implantation of electrodes within the brain (Ellrichmann, Harati, & Müller, 2008). The electrodes are then stimulated by a pacemaker-like device. Stem cell transplantation offers hope for the future in treating Parkinson disease (Newman & Bakay, 2008; Wang & others, 2008). Two factors that are associated with a lower risk of developing Parkinson disease are taking ibuprofen and drinking coffee (Chand & Litvan, 2007).

Fear of Victimization, Crime, and Elder Maltreatment

Some of the physical decline and limitations that characterize development in late adulthood contribute to a sense of vulnerability and fear among older adults (Gray & Acierno, 2002). For some older adults, the fear of crime may become a deterrent to travel, attendance at social events, and the pursuit of an active lifestyle. Almost one-fourth of older adults say they have a basic fear of being the victim of a crime. However, in reality, possibly because of the precautions they take, older adults are less likely than younger adults to be the victim of a crime. However, the crimes committed against older adults are likely to be serious offenses, such as armed robbery (Cohn & Harlow, 1993). Older adults are also victims of nonviolent crimes such as fraud, vandalism, purse snatching, and harassment (Fulmer, Guadagno, & Bolton, 2004). Estimates of the incidence of crimes against older adults may be low because older adults may not report crimes, fearing retribution from criminals or believing the criminal justice system cannot help them.

How often does elder abuse occur? A recent research review indicated that 6 percent of older adults reported experiencing significant abuse in the last month (Cooper, Selwood, & Livingston, 2008). In this study, 16 percent of home health-care staff admitted to significant psychological abuse of older adults. Elder maltreatment may be perpetuated by anyone, but it is primarily carried out by family members (MacDonald, 2007). As with child maltreatment, elder maltreatment can involve neglect, psychological abuse, or physical abuse. Older adults are most often abused by their spouses. A special concern is the burden older women carry in facing possible physical violence. In the research review just described, 5.6 percent of older adult couples said they had experienced physical violence in their relationship in the last month.

Older adults also can experience *institutional abuse*, which involves mistreatment of older adults living in facilities such as nursing homes, hospitals, or long-term care (MacDonald, 2007). Institutional abuse of older adults include the staff engaging in rough handling, hitting, or slapping patients, inappropriate treatment, and psychological abuse, such as social isolation and threats.

Muhammad Ali, one of the world's leading sports figures, has Parkinson disease.

Parkinson disease A chronic, progressive disease characterized by muscle tremors, slowing of movement, and partial facial paralysis.

Maltreated older adults, as well as older adults who are depressed, have a dementia, or another mental disorder may need mental health treatment. To read about this topic, see the *Applications in Life-Span Development* interlude.

Applications in Life-Span Development
Meeting the Mental Health Needs of Older Adults

Margaret Gatz (*right*) has been a crusader for better mental health treatment of older adults. She believes that mental health professionals need to be encouraged to include more older adults in their client lists and that we need to better educate the elderly about how they can benefit from therapy. *What are some common mechanisms of change that can be used to improve the mental health of older adults?*

Older adults receive disproportionately fewer mental health services (Knight & Lee, 2007; Knight & others, 2006). One estimate is that only 2.7 percent of all clinical services provided by psychologists go to older adults, although individuals aged 65 and over make up more than 11 percent of the population. Psychotherapy can be expensive. Although reduced fees and sometimes no fee can be arranged in public hospitals for older adults from low-income backgrounds, many older adults who need psychotherapy do not get it (Knight & Lee, 2007). It has been said that psychotherapists like to work with young, attractive, verbal, intelligent, and successful clients (called YAVISes) rather than those who are quiet, ugly, old, institutionalized, and different (called QUOIDs). Psychotherapists have been accused of failing to see older adults because they perceive that older adults have a poor prognosis for therapy success, they do not feel they have adequate training to treat older adults, who may have special problems requiring special treatment, and they may have stereotypes that label older adults as low-status and unworthy recipients of treatment (Virnig & others, 2004).

How can we better meet the mental health needs of older adults? First, psychologists must be encouraged to include more older adults in their client lists, and older adults must be convinced that they can benefit from therapy. Second, we must make mental health care affordable. For example, Medicare continues to fall short of providing many mental health services for older adults, especially those in need of long-term care (Knight & Lee, 2007).

Review and Reflect: Learning Goal 4

 4 **Describe Mental Health Problems in Older Adults**

REVIEW

- What is the nature of depression in older adults?
- What are dementia, Alzheimer disease, and other afflictions like in older adults?
- How extensive is fear of victimization, crime, and maltreatment in older adults?

REFLECT

- Older adults do not have more mental health problems than younger adults do, although many people perceive that older adults have more mental problems. What might account for this misperception?

5 RELIGION

In Chapter 15, we described religion and meaning in life with a special focus on middle age, including links between religion and health. Here we will continue our exploration of religion by describing its importance in the lives of many older adults.

In many societies around the world, older adults are the spiritual leaders in their churches and communities. For example, in the Catholic Church, more popes have been elected in their eighties than in any other 10-year period of the human life span.

The religious patterns of older adults have increasingly been studied (Benjamins & Finlayson, 2007; McFadden, 2007). A recent study revealed that African American and Caribbean Black older adults reported higher levels of religious participation, religious coping, and spirituality than non-Latino White older adults (Taylor, Chatters, & Jackson, 2007). One recent study of rural older adults found that their spirituality/religiousness was linked to a lower incidence of depression (Yoon & Lee, 2007).

Is religion related to a sense of well-being and life satisfaction in old age? In one study it was. Interviews were conducted with 1,500 U.S. White and African American individuals 66 years of age and older (Krause, 2003). Older adults who derived a sense of meaning in life from religion had higher levels of life satisfaction, self-esteem, and optimism. Also, older African American adults were more likely to find meaning in religion than their White counterparts. In another study, religious practices—such as prayer and scripture reading—and religious feelings were associated with a sense of well-being, especially for women and individuals over 75 years of age (Koenig, Smiley, & Gonzales, 1988). In one study of low-income Latinos in San Diego, a strong religious orientation was associated with better health (Cupertino & Haan, 1999). And in two recent studies, across an eight-year period, Mexican Americans aged 65 and older had slower rates of cognitive decline and a 32 percent reduction in risk of mortality compared with their counterparts who never attended church (Hill & others, 2005, 2006). Further, another recent study revealed that religious attendance at least weekly was linked to a lower risk of mortality (Gillum & others, 2008).

Religion can provide some important psychological needs in older adults, helping them face impending death, find and maintain a sense of meaningfulness and significance in life, and accept the inevitable losses of old age (Daaleman, Perera, & Studenski, 2004). In one study, although church attendance decreased in older adults in their last year of life, their feelings of religiousness and the strength or comfort they received from religion were either stable or increased (Idler, Kasl, & Hays, 2001). Socially, the religious community can provide a number of functions for older adults, such as social activities, social support, and the opportunity to assume teaching and leadership roles. Older adults can become deacons, elders, or religion teachers, assuming leadership roles they might have been unable to take on before they retired (Cox & Hammonds, 1988).

Might praying or meditating actually be associated with longevity? In one study, they were (McCullough & others, 2000). Nearly 4,000 women and men 65 years and older, mostly Christians, were asked about their health and whether they prayed or meditated. Those who said they rarely or never prayed had about a 50 percent greater risk of dying during the six-year study compared with those who prayed or meditated at least once a month. In this study, the researchers controlled for many factors known to place people at risk for dying, such as smoking, drinking, and social isolation. It is possible that prayer and meditation lower the incidence of death in older adults because they reduce stress and dampen the body's production of stress hormones such as adrenaline. A decrease in stress hormones is linked with a number of health benefits, including a stronger immune system (McCullough & others, 2000).

During late adulthood, many individuals increasingly engage in prayer. *How might this be linked with longevity?*

Review and Reflect: Learning Goal 5

 Explain the Role of Religion in the Lives of Older Adults

REVIEW

• What are some characteristics of religion in older adults?

REFLECT

• Do you think you will become more or less religious as an older adult? Explain.

Cognitive Development in Late Adulthood

1 COGNITIVE FUNCTIONING IN OLDER ADULTS: DESCRIBE THE COGNITIVE FUNCTIONING OF OLDER ADULTS

Multidimensionality and Multidirectionality

- Baltes emphasizes a distinction between cognitive mechanics (the "hardware" of the mind, reflecting the neurophysiological architecture, including the brain) and cognitive pragmatics (the culture-based "software" of the mind). Cognitive mechanics are more likely to decline in older adults than are cognitive pragmatics. Recently, the terms fluid mechanics and crystallized pragmatics have been used to describe cognitive mechanics and cognitive pragmatics, respectively. Researchers have found that the speed of processing information declines in late adulthood. Some changes in attention take place in adulthood. In selective attention, older adults fare more poorly than younger adults in general, but when tasks are simple and sufficient practice is given, age differences are minimal. Likewise, for divided attention, on simple tasks, adult age differences are minimal, but on difficult tasks older adults do worse than younger adults. Older adults perform as well as younger adults on measures of sustained attention. Younger adults have better episodic memory than older adults. Regarding semantic memory, older adults have more difficulty retrieving semantic information, but they usually can eventually retrieve it. Researchers have found declines in working memory and perceptual speed in older adults. Older adults are more likely to show declines in explicit than in implicit memory. Prospective memory involves remembering what to do in the future, and the relation of prospective memory to aging is complex. An increasing number of studies are finding that people's beliefs about memory play an important role in their memory performance. Noncognitive factors such as health, education, and socioeconomic status are linked with memory in older adults. Wisdom is expert knowledge about the practical aspects of life that permits excellent judgment about important matters. Baltes and his colleagues have found that high levels of wisdom are rare, the time frame of late adolescence and early adolescence is the main window for wisdom to emerge, factors other than age are critical for wisdom to develop, and personality-related factors are better predictors of wisdom than cognitive factors such as intelligence. Sternberg argues that wisdom involves both academic and practical aspects of intelligence. His balance theory emphasizes making competent decisions that take into account self-interest, the interests of others, and contexts to produce a common good.

Education, Work, and Health

- Successive generations of Americans have been better educated. Education is positively correlated with scores on intelligence tests. Older adults may return to education for a number of reasons. Successive generations have had work experiences that include a stronger emphasis on cognitively oriented labor. The increased emphasis on information processing in jobs likely enhances an individual's intellectual abilities. Poor health is related to decreased intellectual performance in late adulthood. Exercise and lifestyle are linked to improved cognitive functioning in older adults.

Use It or Lose It

- Researchers are finding that older adults who engage in cognitive activities, especially challenging ones, have higher cognitive functioning that those who don't use their cognitive skills.

Training Cognitive Skills

- There are two main conclusions that can be derived from research on training cognitive skills in older adults: (1) training can improve the cognitive skills of many older adults, but (2) there is some loss in plasticity in late adulthood.

Cognitive Neuroscience and Aging

- There has been considerable recent interest in the cognitive neuroscience of aging that focuses on links between aging, the brain, and cognitive functioning. This field especially relies on fMRI and PET scans to assess brain functioning while individuals are engaging in cognitive tasks. One of the most consistent findings in this field is a decline in the functioning of specific regions in the prefrontal cortex in older adults and links between this decline and poorer performance on complex reasoning, working memory, and episodic memory tasks.

---

2 LANGUAGE DEVELOPMENT: CHARACTERIZE CHANGES IN LANGUAGE IN OLDER ADULTS

- For many individuals, knowledge of words and word meanings continues unchanged or may even improve late adulthood. However, some decline in language skills may occur in retrieving words for use in conversation, understanding speech, phonological skills, and some aspects of discourse. These changes in language skills in older adults likely occur as a consequence of declines in hearing or memory, speed of processing information, or as a result of disease.

---

3 WORK AND RETIREMENT: DISCUSS AGING AND ADAPTATIONS TO WORK AND RETIREMENT

Work

- Today, the percentage of men over 65 who continue to work full-time is less than at the beginning of the twentieth century. An important change in older adults' work patterns is the increase in part-time work. Some individuals continue a life of strong work productivity throughout late adulthood.

Retirement in the United States and Other Countries

- A retirement option for older workers is a late-twentieth-century phenomenon in the United States. In one study, only 1 percent of French individuals in their seventies were working compared with 19 percent of U.S. individuals. German retirees were the least likely to miss working.

Adjustment to Retirement

- The pathways individuals follow when they reach retirment age today are less clear than in the past. Individuals who are healthy, have adequate income, are active, are better educated, have an extended social network of friends and family, and are satisfied with their lives before they retire adjust best to retirement.

---

4 MENTAL HEALTH: DESCRIBE MENTAL HEALTH PROBLEMS IN OLDER ADULTS

Depression

- Major depression has been called the "common cold" of mental disorders. However, a majority of older adults with depressive symptoms never receive mental health treatment.

Dementia, Alzheimer Disease, and Other Afflictions

- Dementia is a global term for any neurological disorder in which the primary symptoms involve a deterioration of mental functioning. Alzheimer disease is by far the most common dementia. This progressive, irreversible disorder is characterized by gradual deterioration of memory, reasoning, language, and eventually physical functioning. Special efforts are being made to discover the causes of Alzheimer disease and effective treatments for it. The increase in amyloid plaques and neurofibrillary tangles in Alzheimer patients may hold important keys to improving our understanding of the disease. Alzheimer disease involves a predictable, progressive decline, characterized by a deficiency in acetylcholine that affects memory. Also, in Alzheimer disease, the brain shrinks and deteriorates as plaques and tangles form. An important concern is caring for Alzheimer patients and the burdens this places on caregivers. In addition to Alzheimer disease, other types of dementia are multi-infarct dementia and Parkinson disease.

Fear of Victimization, Crime, and Elder Maltreatment

- Some of the physical decline and limitations that characterize development in late adulthood contribute to a sense of vulnerability and fear among older adults. Almost one-fourth of older adults say they have a basic fear of being the victim of a crime. Older women are more likely than older men to be victimized or abused.

5   RELIGION: EXPLAIN THE ROLE OF RELIGION IN THE LIVES OF OLDER ADULTS

- Many older adults are spiritual leaders in their church and community. Religious interest increases in old age and is related to a sense of well-being in the elderly.

KEY TERMS

cognitive mechanics 559
cognitive pragmatics 559
selective attention 560
divided attention 561
sustained attention 561

episodic memory 561
semantic memory 562
explicit memory 562
implicit memory 562
source memory 563

prospective memory 563
wisdom 564
major depression 574
dementia 575
Alzheimer disease 575

multi-infarct dementia 578
Parkinson disease 579

KEY PEOPLE

Paul Baltes 559
Lynn Hasher 563

Robert J. Sternberg 565
K. Warner Schaie 566

Sherry Willis 567

Phyllis Moen 572

E-LEARNING TOOLS

To help you master the material in this chapter, visit the the Online Learning Center for *Life-Span Development,* twelfth edition, at **www.mhhe.com/santrockld12**.

Self-Assessment

Connect to **www.mhhe.com/santrockld12** to reflect on aging and the workplace by completing the self-assessment, *My Perception of Older Workers.*

Taking It to the Net

Connect to **www.mhhe.com/santrockld12** to research the answers to these questions:

1. Jasper's 66-year-old father thinks he was passed over for a promotion because of his age. How can Jasper investigate whether his father has a legal claim against his company based on age discrimination. What rights do older workers have in their jobs?

2. Angela is interested in finding out more about how the causes, the nature, and the treatment of depression change over the life span. Her Aunt Sadie has become very depressed as she has gotten older, and Angela worries that her aunt might harm herself. What can Angela find out about the extent of depression in the

elderly population and why depression often goes undiagnosed, as well as the causes and the best treatment for depression?

3. Juan's grandfather has just been diagnosed with Alzheimer disease. What do Juan and his family members need to know about caring for his grandfather's physical needs? What legal and financial issues may need to be considered by Juan's family to help them better deal with this situation?

Video Clips

The Online Learning Center includes a video for Chapter 18 called "Retirement." Today's adults are among the first generation able to conceive of retirement as an *option.* This segment considers the psychological factors, rather than the purely economic motives, involved in the decision to retire or continue working.

Health and Well-Being, Parenting, and Education Exercises

Build your decision-making skills by trying your hand at the health and well-being, parenting, and education exercises. Connect to **www.mhhe.com/santrockld12** to research the answers and complete the exercises.

19

I am the family face;
Flesh perishes,
I live on,
Projecting trait and trace
Through time to times
anon,
And leaping from place
to place
Over oblivion.

—THOMAS HARDY
English Novelist and Poet,
19th Century

LEARNING GOALS

◆ Discuss four theories of
   socioemotional development and
   aging.

◆ Describe links between personality
   and mortality, and identify changes
   in the self and society in late
   adulthood.

◆ Characterize the families and
   social relationships of aging adults.

◆ Summarize how ethnicity, gender,
   and culture are linked with aging.

◆ Explain how to age successfully.

SOCIOEMOTIONAL DEVELOPMENT IN LATE ADULTHOOD

CHAPTER OUTLINE

Images of Life-Span Development
Bob Cousy

Bob Cousy was a star player on Boston Celtics teams that won numerous National Basketball Association championships. In recognition of his athletic accomplishments, Cousy was honored by ESPN as one of the top 100 athletes of the twentieth century. After he retired from basketball, he became a college basketball coach and then into his seventies was a broadcaster of Boston Celtics basketball games. Now in his eighties, Cousy has retired from broadcasting but continues to play golf and tennis on a regular basis. He has a number of positive social relationships, including a marriage of more than 50 years, children and grandchildren, and many friends.

As is the case with many famous people, their awards usually reveal little about their personal lives and contributions. Two situations exemplify his humanitarian efforts to help others (McClellan, 2004). When Cousy played for the Boston Celtics, his African American teammate, Chuck Cooper, was refused a room on a road trip because of his race. Cousy expressed anger to his coach about the situation and then accompanied an appreciative Cooper on a train back to Boston. In a second situation, "Today the Bob Cousy Humanitarian Fund honors individuals who have given their lives to using the game of basketball as a medium to help others" (p. 4). The Humanitarian Fund reflects Cousy's motivation to care for others, be appreciative and give something back, and make the world less self-centered.

Bob Cousy, as a Boston Celtics star when he was a young adult (*left*) and as an older adult (*right*). *What are some changes he has made in his life as an older adult?*

PREVIEW

Bob Cousy's life as an older adult reflects some of the themes of socioemotional development in older adults that we will discuss in this chapter. These include the important role that being active plays in life satisfaction, adapting to changing skills, and the positive role of close relationships with friends and family in an emotionally fulfilling life.

---

1 THEORIES OF SOCIOEMOTIONAL DEVELOPMENT

Erikson's Theory	Activity Theory	Socioemotional Selectivity Theory	Selective Optimization with Compensation Theory

We will explore four main theories of socioemotional development that focus on late adulthood: Erikson's theory, activity theory, socioemotional selectivity theory, and selective optimization with compensation theory.

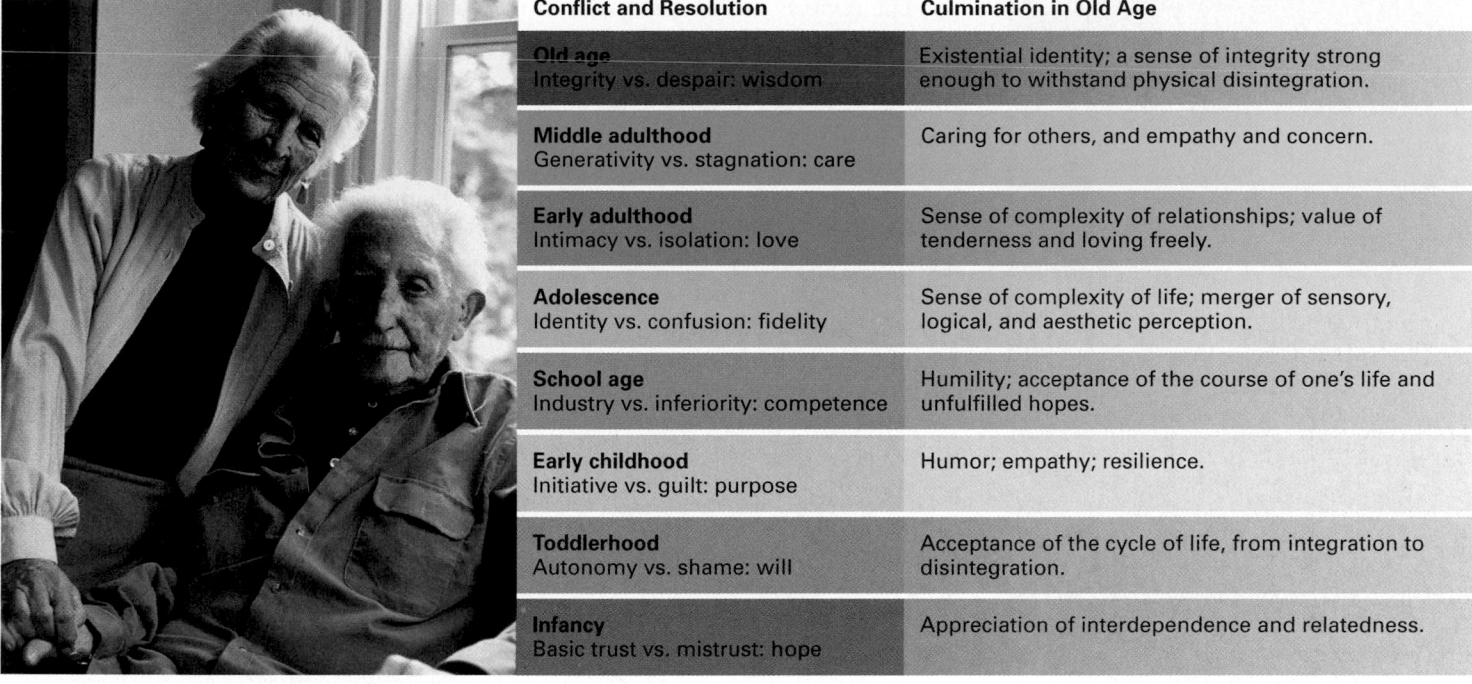

Conflict and Resolution	Culmination in Old Age
Old age Integrity vs. despair: wisdom	Existential identity; a sense of integrity strong enough to withstand physical disintegration.
Middle adulthood Generativity vs. stagnation: care	Caring for others, and empathy and concern.
Early adulthood Intimacy vs. isolation: love	Sense of complexity of relationships; value of tenderness and loving freely.
Adolescence Identity vs. confusion: fidelity	Sense of complexity of life; merger of sensory, logical, and aesthetic perception.
School age Industry vs. inferiority: competence	Humility; acceptance of the course of one's life and unfulfilled hopes.
Early childhood Initiative vs. guilt: purpose	Humor; empathy; resilience.
Toddlerhood Autonomy vs. shame: will	Acceptance of the cycle of life, from integration to disintegration.
Infancy Basic trust vs. mistrust: hope	Appreciation of interdependence and relatedness.

Erikson's Theory

We initially described Erik Erikson's (1968) eight stages of the human life span in Chapter 1, and as we explored different periods of development in this book, we examined the stages in more detail. Here we will discuss his final stage.

Integrity versus Despair   **Integrity versus despair** is Erikson's eighth and final stage of development, which individuals experience during late adulthood. This stage involves reflecting on the past and either piecing together a positive review or concluding that one's life has not been well spent. Through many different routes, the older adult may have developed a positive outlook in each of the preceding periods. If so, retrospective glances and reminiscences will reveal a picture of a life well spent, and the older adult will be satisfied (integrity). But if the older adult resolved one or more of the earlier stages in a negative way (being socially isolated in early adulthood or stagnated in middle adulthood, for example), retrospective glances about the total worth of his or her life might be negative (despair). Figure 19.1 portrays how positive resolutions of Erikson's eight stages can culminate in wisdom and integrity for older adults.

Life Review   Life review is prominent in Erikson's final stage of integrity versus despair. Life review involves looking back at one's life experiences, evaluating them, interpreting them, and often reinterpreting them. A leading expert on aging, Robert Butler, recently provided this perspective on life review: ". . . there are chances for pain, anger, guilt, and grief, but there are also opportunities for resolution and celebration, for affirmation and hope, for reconciliation and personal growth" (Butler, 2007, p. 72).

Butler (2007) states that the life review is set in motion by looking forward to death. Sometimes the life review proceeds quietly; at other times it is intense, requiring considerable work to achieve some sense of personality integration. The life review may be observed initially in stray and insignificant thoughts about oneself and one's life history. These thoughts may continue to emerge in brief intermittent spurts or become essentially continuous. One 76-year-old man commented, "My life is in the back of my mind. It can't be any other way. Thoughts of the past play on me. Sometimes I play with them, encouraging and savoring them; at other times I dismiss them."

FIGURE 19.1 Erikson's View of How Positive Resolution of the Eight Stages of the Human Life Span Can Culminate in Wisdom and Integrity in Old Age. In Erikson's view, each stage of life is associated with a particular psychosocial conflict and a particular resolution. In this chart, Erikson describes how the issue from each of the earlier stages can mature into the many facets of integrity and wisdom in old age. At left, Erikson is shown with his wife Joan, an artist.

integrity versus despair Erikson's eighth and final stage of development, which individuals experience in late adulthood. This involves reflecting on the past and either piecing together a positive review or concluding that one's life has not been well spent.

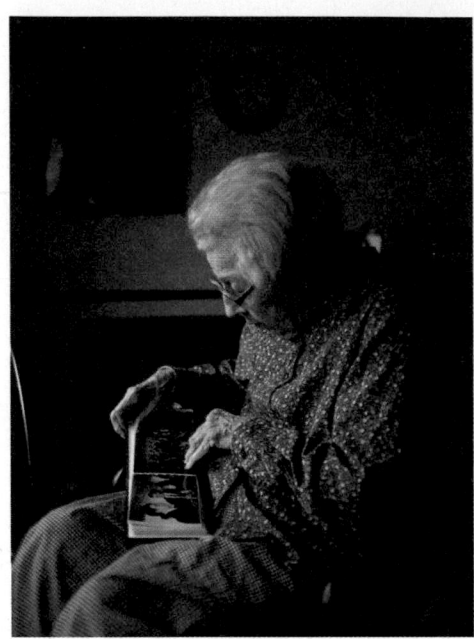

What characterizes a life review in late adulthood?

Should adults stay active or become more disengaged as they become older? Explain.

activity theory The theory that the more active and involved older adults are, the more likely they are to be satisfied with their lives.

Life reviews can include sociocultural dimensions, such as culture, ethnicity, and gender. Life reviews also can include interpersonal, relationship dimensions, including sharing and intimacy with family members or a friend (Cappeliez & O'Rourke, 2006). And life reviews can include personal dimensions, which might involve the creation and discovery of meaning and coherence. These personal dimensions might unfold in such a way that the pieces do or don't make sense to the older adult. In the final analysis, each person's life review is to some degree unique.

As the past marches in review, the older adult surveys it, observes it, and reflects on it (Haber, 2007). Reconsideration of previous experiences and their meaning occurs, often with revision or expanded understanding taking place. This reorganization of the past may provide a more valid picture for the individual, providing new and significant meaning to one's life (Stinson & Kirk, 2006). It may also help prepare the individual for death, in the process reducing fear (Cappeliez, O'Rourke, & Chaudhury, 2005).

One aspect of life review involves identifying and reflecting on not only the positive aspects of one's life but also on regrets as part of developing a mature wisdom and self-understanding (King & Hicks, 2007). A recent study examined reminiscence in German and Dutch adults from 40 to 85 years of age, focusing on what individuals regretted the most in their lives (Timmer, Westerhof, & Dittmann-Kohli, 2005). Regrets involved four major themes: (1) mistakes and bad decisions, (2) hard times, (3) social relationships, and (4) missed educational opportunities. The hope is that by examining not only the positive aspects of one's life, but also what an individual has regretted doing, a more accurate vision of the complexity of one's life and possibly increased life satisfaction will be attained (King & Hicks, 2007).

Some clinicians use *reminiscence therapy* with their older clients. Reminiscence therapy involves discussing past activities and experiences with another individual or group. The therapy may include the use of photographs, familiar items, and video/audio recordings. Researchers have found that reminiscence therapy improves the mood of older adults (Haight & Haight, 2007; Wang, 2007).

Activity Theory

Activity theory states that the more active and involved older adults are, the more likely they are to be satisfied with their lives. Researchers have found strong support for activity theory, beginning in the 1960s and continuing into the twenty-first century (Neugarten, Havighurst, & Tobin, 1968; Riebe & others, 2005). These researchers have found that when older adults are active, energetic, and productive, they age more successfully and are happier than if they disengage from society.

One large-scale longitudinal study of older adults in Manitoba, Canada, examined the relation between everyday activities and indicators of successful aging, namely, well-being, functioning, and mortality, over a six-year period (Menec, 2003). Participants were asked to fill out a 21-item activities checklist to indicate their participation in each of the activities within the past week. The activities were grouped into three categories: social activities (visiting family or relatives, for example), productive activities (volunteer work, doing light housework/gardening, for example), and solitary activities (collecting hobbies, for example). Well-being was assessed by asking participants how happy they were on a 5-point scale ranging from 1 = happy and interested in life to 5 = so unhappy that life is not worthwhile. Function was evaluated in terms of whether cognitive impairment or physical difficulties were present. Mortality (whether participants were dead or alive) was determined by examining data from the Office of Vital Statistics. The results indicated that greater overall activity (but especially social and productive activity) was related to happiness, better functioning, and a lower mortality rate.

Activity theory suggests that many individuals will achieve greater life satisfaction if they continue their middle-adulthood roles into late adulthood. If these roles are stripped from them (as in early retirement), it is important for them to find substitute roles that keep them active and involved.

Socioemotional Selectivity Theory

Socioemotional selectivity theory states that older adults become more selective about their social networks. Because they place a high value on emotional satisfaction, older adults spend more time with familiar individuals with whom they have had rewarding relationships. Developed by Laura Carstensen (1998, 2006, 2008), this theory states that older adults deliberately withdraw from social contact with individuals peripheral to their lives while they maintain or increase contact with close friends and family members with whom they have had enjoyable relationships. This selective narrowing of social interaction maximizes positive emotional experiences and minimizes emotional risks as individuals become older.

Socioemotional selectivity theory challenges the stereotype that the majority of older adults are in emotional despair because of their social isolation (Carstensen, 2008; Charles & Carstensen, 2007). Rather, older adults consciously choose to decrease the total number of their social contacts in favor of spending increasing time in emotionally rewarding moments with friends and family. That is, they systematically hone their social networks so that available social partners satisfy their emotional needs.

Is there research evidence to support life-span differences in the composition of social networks? Researchers have found that older adults have far smaller social networks than younger adults (Carstensen, 2006, 2008). In one study of individuals 69 to 104 years of age, the oldest participants had fewer peripheral social contacts than the relatively younger participants but about the same number of close emotional relationships (Lang & Carstensen, 1994). And a recent study revealed that compared with younger adults, older adults reported more intense positive emotions with family members, less intense positive emotions with new friends, and equally intense positive emotions with established friends (Charles & Piazza, 2007).

Socioemotional selectivity theory also focuses on the types of goals that individuals are motivated to achieve (Carstensen, Mikels, & Mather, 2006; Charles & Carstensen, 2007). It states that two important classes of goals are (1) knowledge-related and (2) emotional. This theory emphasizes that the trajectory of motivation for knowledge-related goals starts relatively high in the early years of life, peaking in adolescence and early adulthood, and then declining in middle and late adulthood (see Figure 19.2). The emotion trajectory is high during infancy and early childhood, declines from middle childhood through early adulthood, and increases in middle and late adulthood.

One of the main reasons given for these changing trajectories in knowledge-related and emotion-related goals involves the perception of time (Carstensen, 2006). When time is perceived as open-ended, as it is when individuals are younger, people are more strongly motivated to pursue information, even at the cost of emotional satisfaction. But as older adults perceive that they have less time left in their lives, they are motivated to spend more time pursuing emotional satisfaction.

Researchers have found that across diverse samples (Norwegians, Catholic nuns, African Americans, Chinese Americans, and European Americans) older adults report better control of their emotions and fewer negative emotions than younger adults (Mroczek, 2001). For example, one recent study revealed that older adults said they experience less intense negative emotions with family members, established friends, and new friends than younger adults reported (Charles & Piazza, 2007). Consider also these two recent studies: In one study, older adults socialized more frequently with their neighbors than middle-aged adults did (Cornwell, Laumann, & Schumm, 2008); in the other study, older adults described their own emotions and the emotions of others more positively than younger adults did (Lockenhoff, Costa, & Lane, 2008). Yet other recent studies have

Laura Carstensen (*right*), in a caring relationship with an older woman. Her theory of socioemotional selectivity is gaining recognition as an important theory.

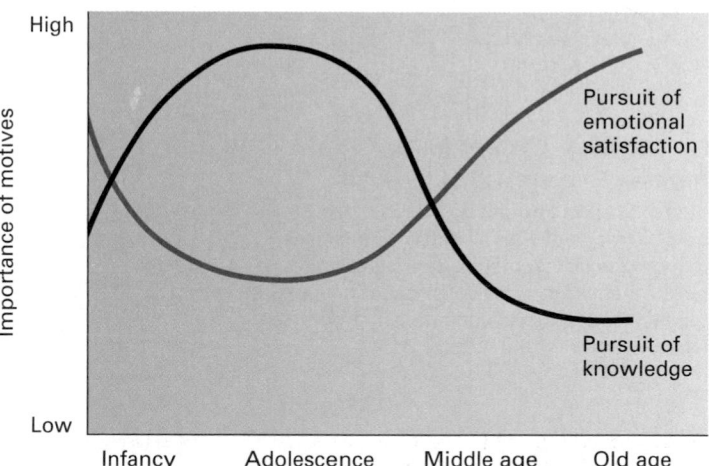

FIGURE 19.2 Idealized Model of Socioemotional Selectivity Through the Life Span. In Carstensen's theory of socioemotional selectivity, the motivation to reach knowledge-related and emotion-related goals changes across the life span.

socioemotional selectivity theory The theory that older adults become more selective about their social networks. Because they place a high value on emotional satisfaction, older adults often spend more time with familiar individuals with whom they have had rewarding relationships.

found that older adults are more inclined to engage in passive emotion self-regulation strategies (distracting oneself from the problem and suppressing feelings, for example) and are less inclined to express anger in dealing with interpersonal problems than younger adults are (Blanchard-Fields & Coats, 2007; Coats & Blanchard-Fields, 2008).

Thus, compared with younger adults, the feelings of older adults mellow (Schmidt & Schulz, 2007). Emotional life is on a more even keel with fewer highs and lows. It may be that although older adults have less extreme joy, they have more contentment, especially when they are connected in positive ways with friends and family. To read further about how emotion changes across the life span, see the *Research in Life-Span Development* interlude.

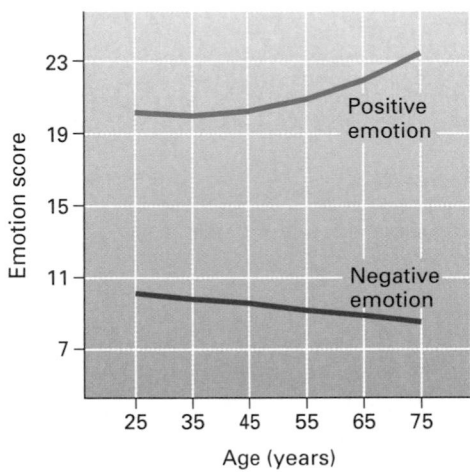

FIGURE 19.3 Changes in Positive and Negative Emotion Across the Adult Years. Positive and negative scores had a possible range of 6 to 30 with higher scores reflecting positive emotion and lower scores negative emotion. Positive emotion increased in the middle adulthood and late adulthood years while negative emotion declined.

Research in Life-Span Development
Changes in Emotion Across Adulthood

One study examined how emotion changes across the adulthood years in 2,727 persons from 25 to 74 years of age in the United States (Mroczek & Kolarz, 1998). Participants completed a survey that assessed the frequency of their positive and negative emotions over a 30-day time frame. Two six-item scales were created, one for positive emotion, the other for negative emotion. Participants rated each of the following items from 1 = none of the time to 5 = all of the time:

Positive Affect

1. Cheerful
2. In good spirits
3. Extremely happy
4. Calm or peaceful
5. Satisfied
6. Full of life

Negative Affect

1. So sad nothing could cheer you up
2. Nervous
3. Restless or fidgety
4. Hopeless
5. That everything was an effort
6. Worthless

Thus, scores could range from 6 to 30 for positive affect and for negative affect.

The results were that older adults reported experiencing more positive emotion and less negative emotion than younger adults, and the increase in positive emotion with age in adults increased at an accelerating rate (see Figure 19.3). In sum, researchers have found that the emotional life of older adults is more positive than once believed (Carstensen, 1998; Mroczek, 2001).

Selective Optimization with Compensation Theory

Selective optimization with compensation theory states that successful aging is linked with three main factors: selection, optimization, and compensation (SOC). The theory describes how people can produce new resources and allocate them effectively to the tasks they want to master (Riediger, Li, & Lindenberger, 2006). *Selection* is based on the concept that older adults have a reduced capacity and loss of functioning, which require a reduction in performance in most life domains. *Optimization* suggests that it is possible to maintain performance in some areas through continued practice and the use of new technologies. *Compensation* becomes relevant when life tasks require a level of capacity beyond the current level of the older adult's performance potential. Older adults especially need to compensate in circumstances with high mental or physical demands, such as when thinking about and memorizing new material very fast, reacting quickly when driving a car, or running fast. When older adults develop an illness, the need for compensation is obvious.

Selective optimization with compensation theory was proposed by Paul Baltes and his colleagues (Baltes, 2003; Baltes, Lindenberger, & Staudinger, 2006; Riediger, Li, & Lindenberger, 2006). They describe the life of the late Arthur Rubinstein to

selective optimization with compensation theory The theory that successful aging is related to three main factors: selection, optimization, and compensation.

illustrate their theory. When he was interviewed at 80 years of age, Rubinstein said that three factors were responsible for his ability to maintain his status as an admired concert pianist into old age. First, he mastered the weakness of old age by reducing the scope of his performances and playing fewer pieces (which reflects selection). Second, he spent more time at practice than earlier in his life (which reflects optimization). Third, he used special strategies, such as slowing down before fast segments, thus creating the image of faster playing (which reflects compensation).

The process of selective optimization with compensation is likely to be effective whenever people pursue successful outcomes. What makes SOC attractive to aging researchers is that it makes explicit how individuals can manage and adapt to losses. By using SOC, they can continue to live satisfying lives, although in a more restrictive manner. Loss is a common dimension of old age, although there are wide variations in the nature of the losses involved. Because of this individual variation, the specific form of selection, optimization, and compensation will likely vary, depending on the person's life history, pattern of interests, values, health, skills, and resources. To read about some strategies for effectively engaging in selective optimization with compensation, see the *Applications in Life-Span Development* interlude.

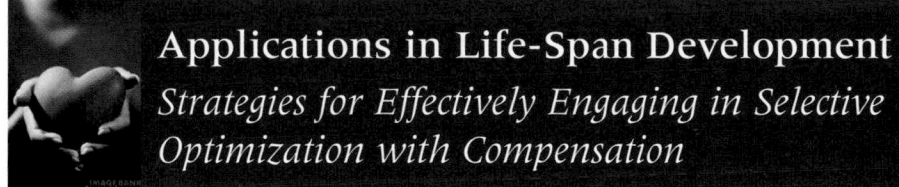

Applications in Life-Span Development
Strategies for Effectively Engaging in Selective Optimization with Compensation

What are some good strategies that aging adults can engage in to attain selective optimization with compensation? According to Paul Baltes and his colleagues (Baltes, Lindenberger, & Staudinger, 2006; Freund & Baltes, 2002), these strategies are likely to be effective:

Selection Strategies

- Focus on the most important goal at a particular time.
- Think about what you want in life and commit yourself to one or two major goals.
- To reach a particular goal, you may need to abandon other goals.

Optimization Strategies

- Keep working on what you have planned until you are successful.
- Persevere and keep trying until you reach your goal.
- When you want to achieve something, you may need to be patient until the right moment arrives.

Compensation Strategies

- When things don't go the way they used to, search for other ways to achieve what you want.
- If things don't go well for you, be willing to let others help you.
- When things don't go as well as in the past, keep trying other ways until you can achieve results that are similar to what you accomplished earlier in your life.

In Baltes' view (2003; Baltes, Lindenberger, & Staudinger, 2006), the selection of domains and life priorities is an important aspect of development. Life goals and priorities likely vary across the life course for most people. For many individuals, it is not just the sheer attainment of goals, but rather the attainment of *meaningful* goals, that makes life satisfying.

A cross-sectional study by Ursula Staudinger (1996) assessed the personal life investments of 25- to 105-year-olds (see Figure 19.4). From 25 to 34 years of age, participants said that they personally invested more time in work, friends, family, and independence, in that order. From 35 to 54 and 55 to 65 years of age, family became more important

25 to 34 Years	35 to 54 Years	55 to 65 Years	70 to 84 Years	85 to105 Years
Work	Family	Family	Family	Health
Friends	Work	Health	Health	Family
Family	Friends	Friends	Cognitive fitness	Thinking about life
Independence	Cognitive fitness	Cognitive fitness	Friends	Cognitive fitness

FIGURE 19.4 Degree of Personal Life Investment at Different Points in Life. Shown here are the top four domains of personal life investment at different points in life. The highest degree of investment is listed at the top (for example, work was the highest personal investment from 25 to 34 years of age, family from 35 to 84, and health from 85 to 105).

than friends to them in terms of their personal investment. Little changed in the rank ordering of persons 70 to 84 years old, but for participants 85 to 105 years old, health became the most important personal investment. Thinking about life showed up for the first time on the most important list for those who were 85 to 105 years old.

One point to note about the study just described is the demarcation of late adulthood into the subcategories of 70 to 84 and 85 to 105 years of age. This fits with our comments on a number of occasions in this book that researchers increasingly recognize the importance of comparing older adults of different ages rather than studying them as one age group.

Review and Reflect: Learning Goal 1

1 **Discuss Four Theories of Socioemotional Development and Aging**

REVIEW

*   What is Erikson's theory of late adulthood?
*   What is activity theory?
*   What is socioemotional selectivity theory?
*   What is selective optimization with compensation theory?

REFLECT

*   Which of the four theories best describes the lives of older adults you know? Explain.

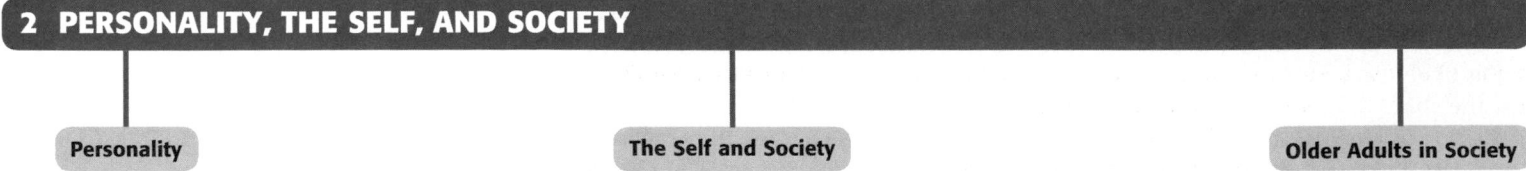

2 PERSONALITY, THE SELF, AND SOCIETY

Personality   **The Self and Society**   **Older Adults in Society**

Some personality traits change in late adulthood? Is personality linked to mortality in older adults? Do self-perceptions and self-control change in late adulthood? How are older adults perceived and treated by society?

Personality

Researchers have found that several of the Big Five factors of personality continue to change in late adulthood. For example, in one study, conscientiousness continued to develop in late adulthood (Roberts, Walton, & Bogg, 2005), and in another study, older adults were more conscientious and agreeable than middle-aged and younger adults (Allemand, Zimprich, & Hendriks, 2008).

Might certain personality traits be related to how long older adults live? Researchers have found that some personality traits are associated with the mortality of older adults (Martin, Friedman, & Schwartz, 2007; Mroczek & Spiro, 2007; Schmidt & Schulz, 2007).

We described the Big Five factors of personality in Chapter 16, "Socioemotional Development in Middle Adulthood." A longitudinal study of more than 1,200 individuals across seven decades revealed that the Big Five personality factor of conscientiousness predicted higher mortality risk from childhood through late adulthood (Martin, Friedman, & Schwartz, 2007). Another study found that two of the Big Five factors were linked to older adults' mortality in one study, with low conscientiousness and high neuroticism predicting earlier death (Wilson & others, 2004). And in a 12-year longitudinal study of older men, a high average level of neuroticism and an increasing level of neuroticism were linked to lower survival (Mroczek & Spiro, 2007).

Affect and outlook on life are also linked to mortality in older adults (Mroczek, Spiro, & Griffin, 2006). Older adults characterized by negative affect don't live as long as those who display more positive affect, and optimistic older adults who have a positive outlook on life live longer than their counterparts who are more pessimistic and have a negative outlook on life (Levy & others, 2002).

The Self and Society

Our exploration of the self focuses on changes in self-esteem, possible selves, self-acceptance, and self control. In Chapter 12, we described how self-esteem drops in adolescence, especially for girls. How does self-esteem change in the adult years?

Self-Esteem   In the cross-sectional study of self-esteem described in Chapter 12, a very large, diverse sample of 326,641 individuals from 9 to 90 were assessed (Robins & others, 2002). About two-thirds of the participants were from the United States. The individuals were asked to respond to the item "I have high self-esteem" on the following 5-point scale:

1	2	3	4	5
Strongly Disagree				Strongly Agree

Self-esteem increased in the twenties, leveled off in the thirties and forties, rose considerably in the fifties and sixties, and then dropped significantly in the seventies and eighties (see Figure 19.5). Through most of the adult years, the self-esteem of males was higher than the self-esteem of females. However, in the seventies and eighties, the self-esteem of males and females converged.

Why might self-esteem decline in older adults? Explanations include deteriorating physical health and negative societal attitudes toward older adults, although these factors were not examined in the large-scale study just described. Researchers have found that in late adulthood, being widowed, institutionalized, or physically impaired, having a low religious commitment, and experiencing a decline in health are linked to low self-esteem (Giarrusso & Bengtson, 2007).

Is self-esteem more stable at some points in the life span than at others? A recent meta-analysis revealed that self-esteem was the least stable in early childhood (Trzesniewski, Donnellan, & Robins, 2003). One reason for this may be that young children don't completely understand the questions they are asked about their self-esteem but rather provide responses based on their current mood. The stability of self-esteem increased in late adolescence and early adulthood. By late adolescence, individuals are

FIGURE 19.5 Self-Esteem Across the Life Span. One cross-sectional study found that self-esteem was high in childhood, dropped in adolescence, increased through early and middle adulthood, then dropped in the seventies and eighties (Robins & others, 2002). More than 300,000 individuals were asked the extent to which they have high self-esteem on a 5-point scale, with 5 being "Strongly Agree" and 1 being "Strongly Disagree."

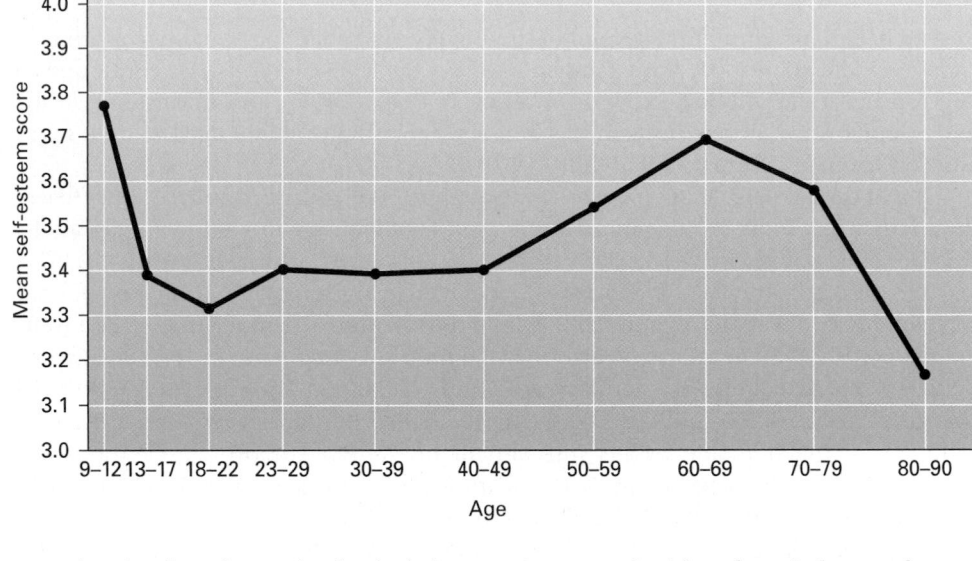

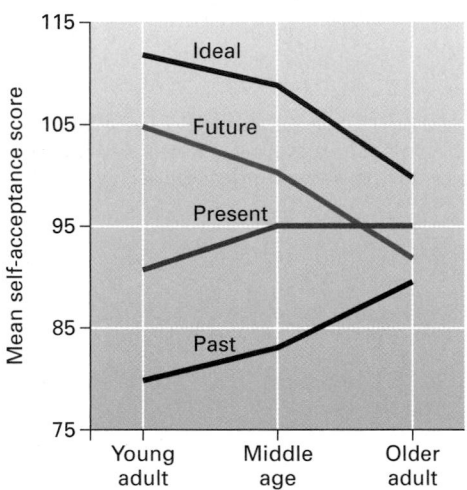

FIGURE 19.6 Changes in Self-Acceptance Across the Adult Years. Acceptance of ideal and future selves decreases with age, acceptance of past selves increases with age, and acceptance of present selves increases slightly in middle age and then levels off.

possible selves What individuals might become, what they would like to become, and what they are afraid of becoming.

experiencing less dramatic physical changes (compared with pubertal change, for example) and are able to better engage in self-control that likely contributed to the increase in stability of self-esteem. The stability of self-esteem decreased in late adulthood, a time during which dramatic life changes and shifting social circumstances (such as death of a loved one and deteriorating health) may occur.

Possible Selves **Possible selves** are what individuals might become, what they would like to become, and what they are afraid of becoming (Hoppmann & Smith, 2007; Markus & Nurius, 1987). One recent study of older adults (mean age of 81) revealed that hope-related activities had more positive effect and a higher probability of survival over a 10-year period (Hoppmann & others, 2007). Also in this study, hoped-for selves were linked to more likely participation in these domains. Another study of older adults 70 to 100-plus years found that over time 72 percent of the older adults added new domains of hope and 53 percent added new fears (Smith & Freund, 2002).

Self-Acceptance Another aspect of the self that changes across the adult years is self-acceptance. In one study, the self-acceptance of individuals at different points in adult development depended on whether they were describing their past, present, future, or ideal selves (Ryff, 1991). As shown in Figure 19.6, young and middle-aged adults showed greater acceptance of their ideal and future selves than their present and past selves. However, in older adults there was little difference in acceptance of various selves because of decreased acceptance of ideal and future selves and increased acceptance of past selves.

Self-Control Although older adults are aware of age-related losses, most still effectively maintain a sense of self-control. A recent survey across a range of 21 developed and developing countries revealed that a majority of adults in their sixties and seventies reported being in control of their lives (HSBC Insurance, 2007). In developed countries such as Denmark, the United States, and Great Britain, adults in their sixties and seventies said they had more control over their their lives than their counterparts in their forties and fifties. Older adults in Denmark reported the highest self-control.

The negative effects of age-typical problems, such as a decline in physical and cognitive skills and an increase in illness, may be buffered by a flexible, accommodating control style. Researchers have found that *accommodating control strategies* (changing one's goals to fit a given circumstance) increase in importance, and *assimilative control strategies* (changing a situation to meet one's goals) decrease in importance beginning in middle adulthood (Brandstädter & Renner, 1990).

However, it is important to consider not just general self-control but how people self-regulate their behavior in specific areas of their lives. One study examined individuals from 13 to 90 years of age. For the oldest group (60 to 90 years of age), self-control was lowest in the physical domain; for the youngest group (13 to 18 years of age), it was lowest in the social domain (Bradley & Webb, 1976). Other researchers have found a decline in perceived self-control in cognitive functioning in older adults (Bertrand & Lachman, 2003).

Older Adults in Society

Does society negatively stereotype older adults? What are some social policy issues in an aging society?

Stereotyping Older Adults Social participation by older adults is often discouraged by **ageism**, which is prejudice against others because of their age, especially prejudice against older adults (Hess, 2006; Nelson, 2007). They are often perceived as incapable of thinking clearly, learning new things, enjoying sex, contributing to the community, or holding responsible jobs. Many older adults face painful discrimination and might be too polite and timid to attack it. Because of their age, older adults might not be hired for new jobs or might be eased out of old ones; they might be shunned socially; and they might be edged out of their family life.

The personal consequences of negative stereotyping about aging can be serious (Norris, Pratt, & Hebblewaite, 2007; Roberts, 2008). A physician (60 years old himself) recently told an 80-year-old: "Well, of course, you are tired. You just need to slow down. Don't try to do so much. After all you are very old." Many older adults accept this type of advice even though it is rooted in age stereotyping rather than medical records. Further, a recent longitudinal study of adults 70 years of age and older revealed that the older adults who had more negative aging stereotypes at the beginning of the study were more likely to experience hearing decline three years later (Levy, Slade, & Gill, 2006).

Ageism is widespread (Barnes & others, 2008; Tang, 2008). One study found that men were more likely to negatively stereotype older adults than were women (Rupp, Vodanovich, & Crede, 2005). Research indicates that the most frequent form is disrespect for older adults, followed by assumptions about ailments or frailty caused by age (Palmore, 2004). However, the increased number of adults living to an older age has led to active efforts to improve society's image of older adults, obtain better living conditions for older adults, and gain political clout.

Policy Issues in an Aging Society The aging society and older persons' status in this society raise policy issues about the well-being of older adults. These include the status of the economy, the provision of health care, supports for families who care for older adults, and generational inequity, each of which we consider in turn (Neugarten, 1988).

Status of the Economy An important issue involving the economy and aging is the concern that our economy cannot bear the burden of so many older persons, who by reason of their age alone are usually consumers rather than producers. However, not all persons 65 and over are nonworkers, and not all persons 18 to 64 are workers. And considerably more individuals in the 55-to-64 age group are in the workforce—three out of five men—than a decade ago. Thus, it is incorrect to simply describe older adults as consumers and younger adults as producers.

Health Care An aging society also brings with it various problems involving health care (Browne & Braun, 2008; Kane, 2007). Escalating health-care costs are currently causing considerable concern (Williams, 2008). One factor that contributes to the surge in health costs is the increasing number of older adults (Rice & Fineman, 2004). Older adults have more illnesses than younger adults, despite the fact that many older adults report their health as good. Older adults see doctors more often, are hospitalized more often, and have longer hospital stays. Approximately one-third of the total health bill of the United States is for the care of adults 65 and over, who comprise only 12 percent of the population. The health-care needs of older adults are reflected in

A recent study in 21 countries revealed that older adults in Denmark reported the strongest control over their lives (HSBC Insurance, 2007).

ageism Prejudice against others because of their age, especially prejudice against older adults.

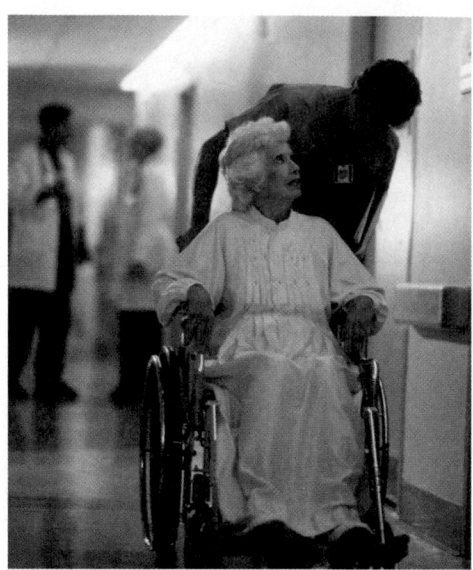

What are some concerns about health care for older adults?

Medicare, the program that provides health-care insurance to adults over 65 under the Social Security system (Butler & Schechter, 2007; Hsu & others, 2008). Of interest is the fact that the United States is the only industrialized nation that provides health insurance specifically for older adults rather than to the population at large, and the only industrialized nation currently without a national health-care system. Older adults themselves still pay about one-third of their total health-care costs. Thus, older adults as well as younger adults are adversely affected by rising medical costs (Zimmerman & Sloane, 2007; Williams, 2008).

A special concern is that while many of the health problems of older adults are chronic rather than acute, the medical system is still based on a "cure" rather than a "care" model (Stone, 2006). Chronic illness is long-term, often lifelong, and requires long-term, if not life-term, management (Garasen, Windspoll, & Johnsen, 2008; Nutting & others, 2007). Chronic illness often follows a pattern of an acute period that may require hospitalization, followed by a longer period of remission, and then repetitions of this pattern. The patient's home, rather than the hospital, often becomes the center of managing the patient's chronic illness. In a home-based system, a new type of cooperative relationship between doctors, nurses, patients, family members, and other service providers needs to be developed (May & others, 2004). Health-care personnel need to be trained and be available to provide home services, sharing authority with the patient and perhaps yielding it to them over the long term.

Eldercare   **Eldercare** is the physical and emotional caretaking of older members of the family, whether that care is day-to-day physical assistance or responsibility for arranging and overseeing such care. An important issue involving eldercare is how it can best be provided (Talley & Crews, 2007). With so many women in the labor market, who will replace them as caregivers? An added problem is that many caregivers are in their sixties, and many of them are ill themselves. They may find it especially stressful to be responsible for the care of relatives who are in their eighties or nineties.

Generational Inequity   Yet another policy issue involving aging is **generational inequity** (discussed initially in Chapter 1: The view that our aging society is being unfair to its younger members because older adults pile up advantages by receiving an inequitably large allocation of resources. Some authors have argued that generational inequity produces intergenerational conflict and divisiveness in the society at large (Longman, 1987). The generational equity issue raises questions about whether the young should be required to pay for the old (Svihula & Estes, 2008).

Income   Also of special concern are older adults who are poor (Chen & Colander, 2007; Wight & others, 2008). One analysis found that lower health-related quality of life in U.S. older adults was linked with income of $15,000 or less (Centers for Disease Control and Prevention, 2003).

Census data suggest that although the overall number of older people living in poverty has declined since the 1960s, the percentage of older persons living in poverty has consistently remained in the 10 to 12 percent range since the early 1980s (U.S. Census Bureau, 2004). More than 25 percent of older women who live alone live in poverty. Also, the number of older single women just above the poverty line remains substantial. Poverty rates among ethnic minorities are two to three times higher than the rate for non-Latino Whites. Combining sex and ethnicity, 60 percent of older African American women and 50 percent of older Latino women who live alone live in poverty. Also, the oldest-old are the age subgroup of older adults most likely to be living in poverty.

Many older adults are understandably concerned about their income (Holden & Hatcher, 2006). The average income of retired Americans is only about half of what they earned when they were fully employed. Although retired individuals need less income for job-related and social activities, adults 65 and over spend a greater proportion of their income for food, utilities, and health care. They spend a smaller proportion for transportation, clothing, pension and life insurance, and entertainment than do adults under the age of 65. Social Security is the largest contributor to the income

eldercare   Physical and emotional caretaking for older members of the family, whether by giving day-to-day physical assistance or by being responsible for overseeing such care.

generational inequity   The view that our aging society is being unfair to its younger members because older adults pile up advantages by receiving inequitably large allocations of resources.

of older Americans (38 percent), followed by assets, earnings, and pensions. There is a special concern about poverty in older women and the role of Social Security in providing a broad economic safety net for them (Calasanti, 2007).

Living Arrangements   One stereotype of older adults is that they are often residents in institutions—hospitals, mental hospitals, nursing homes, and so on. However, nearly 95 percent of older adults live in the community. Almost two-thirds of older adults live with family members—spouse, a child, a sibling, for example—and almost one-third live alone. The older people become, the greater are their odds for living alone. Half of older women 75 years and older live alone. The majority of older adults living alone are widowed, with three times as many of these individuals being women than men (U.S. Census Bureau, 2004). Older adults who live alone often report being more lonely than their counterparts who live with someone (Routasalo & others, 2006). However, as with younger adults, living alone as an older adult does not mean being lonely. Older adults who can sustain themselves while living alone often have good health and few disabilities, and they may have regular social exchanges with relatives, friends, and neighbors.

Technology   The Internet plays an increasingly important role in access to information and communication in adults as well as youth (Lindberg, Carstensen, & Carstensen, 2008; Sum & others, 2008). A recent study revealed that older adults are clearly capable of being trained to learn new technologies (Hickman, Rogers, & Fisk, 2007).

How well are older adults keeping up with changes in technology? Older adults are less likely to have a computer in their home and less likely to use the Internet than younger adults, but older adults are the fastest-growing segment of Internet users (Czaja & others, 2006). A 2003 survey indicated that 32 percent of 65 and older U.S. adults (about 11 million) and 61 percent of 50- to 64-year-olds are online (Harris Interactive, 2003). Older adults log more time on the Internet (an average of 8.3 hours per week), visit more Web sites, and spend more money on the Internet than their younger adult counterparts. They are especially interested in learning to use e-mail and going online for health information (Leung & others, 2007; Westlake & others, 2007). Increasing numbers of older adults use e-mail to communicate with relatives. As with children and younger adults, cautions about the accuracy of information—in areas such as health care—on the Internet need to always be kept in mind (Cutler, 2006).

Are older adults keeping up with changes in technology?

Review and Reflect: Learning Goal 2

 Describe Links Between Personality and Mortality, and Identify Changes in the Self and Society in Late Adulthood

REVIEW

- How are personality traits related to mortality in older adults?
- How does self-esteem change in late adulthood? What characterizes possible selves, self-acceptance, and self-control in older adults?
- How are older adults perceived and treated by society?

REFLECT

- What do you envision your life will be like as an older adult?

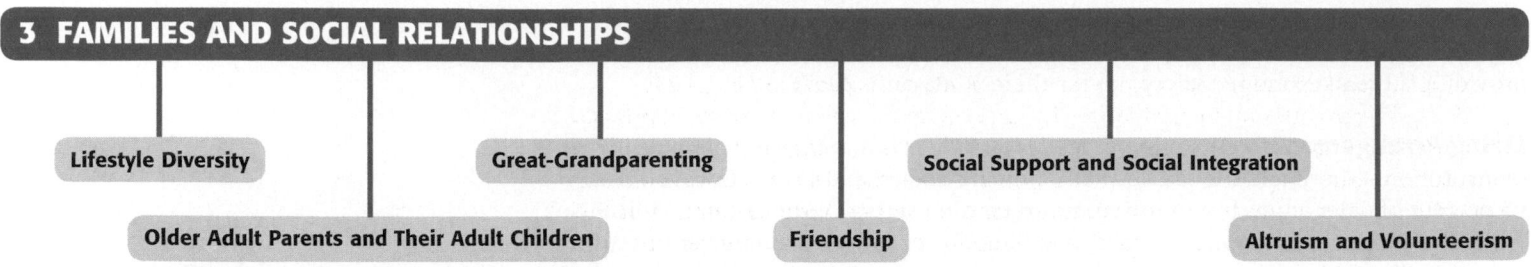

3 FAMILIES AND SOCIAL RELATIONSHIPS

Lifestyle Diversity

Great-Grandparenting

Social Support and Social Integration

Older Adult Parents and Their Adult Children

Friendship

Altruism and Volunteerism

Are the close relationships of older adults different from those of younger adults? What are the lifestyles of older adults like? What characterizes the relationships of older adult parents and their adult children? Is the role of great-grandparents different from the role of grandparents? What do friendships and social networks contribute to the lives of older adults? What type of social support do older adults need and want? How might older adults' altruism and volunteerism contribute to positive outcomes?

Lifestyle Diversity

The lifestyles of older adults are changing. Formerly, the later years of life were likely to consist of marriage for men and widowhood for women. With demographic shifts toward marital dissolution characterized by divorce, one-third of adults can now expect to marry, divorce, and remarry during their lifetime. Let's now explore some of the diverse lifestyles of older adults, beginning with those who are married or partnered.

Married Older Adults   In 2004, 56 percent of U.S. adults over 65 years of age were married (U.S. Census Bureau, 2006). Almost half of all older adult women were widows (45 percent). There were more than four times as many widows as widowers.

The time from retirement until death is sometimes referred to as the "final stage in the marriage process." A recent study revealed that marital satisfaction was greater in older adults than middle-aged adults (Henry & others, 2007). In this study, older adults perceived their spouse to be less hostile than did middle-aged adults.

Retirement alters a couple's lifestyle, requiring adaptation (Dickson, Christian, & Remmo, 2004). The greatest changes occur in the traditional family, in which the husband works and the wife is a homemaker. The husband may not know what to do with his time, and the wife may feel uneasy having him around the house all of the time. In traditional families, both partners may need to move toward more expressive roles. The husband must adjust from being the provider outside of the home to being a helper around the house; the wife must change from being the only homemaker to being a partner who shares and delegates household duties. Marital happiness as an older adult is also affected by each partner's ability to deal with personal conflicts, including aging, illness, and eventual death (Field, 1996).

Individuals who are married or partnered in late adulthood are usually happier and live longer than those who are single (Manzoli & others, 2007). One study found that older adults were more satisfied with their marriages than were young and middle-aged adults (Bookwala & Jacobs, 2004). Indeed, the majority of older adults evaluate their marriages as happy or very happy (Huyck, 1995). Marital satisfaction is often greater for women than for men, possibly because women place more emphasis on attaining satisfaction through marriage than men do. However, as more women develop careers, this sex difference may not continue. Also, a recent longitudinal study of adults 75 years of age and older revealed that individuals who were married were less likely to die across a span of seven years (Rasulo, Christensen, & Tomassini, 2005).

Divorced and Remarried Older Adults   Divorced and separated older adults represented only 8 percent of older adults in 2004 (U.S. Census Bureau, 2006). However, their numbers (2.6 million) have increased considerably since 1990 (1.5 million). Many of these individuals were divorced or separated before they entered late adulthood.

There are social, financial, and physical consequences of divorce for older adults (Mitchell, 2007). Divorce can weaken kinship ties when it occurs in later life, especially

What are some adaptations that many married older adults need to make?

in the case of older men (Cooney, 1994). Divorced older women are less likely to have adequate financial resources than married older women, and as earlier in adulthood, divorce is linked to more health problems in older adults (Lillard & Waite, 1995).

Rising divorce rates, increased longevity, and better health have led to an increase in remarriage by older adults (Ganong & Coleman, 2006). What happens when an older adult wants to remarry or does remarry? Researchers have found that some older adults perceive negative social pressure about their decision to remarry (McKain, 1972). These negative sanctions range from raised eyebrows to rejection by adult children (Ganong & Coleman, 2006). However, the majority of adult children support the decision of their older adult parents to remarry. Researchers have found that remarried parents and stepparents provide less support to adult stepchildren than parents in first marriages (White, 1994).

Cohabiting Older Adults An increasing number of older adults cohabit (Brown, Lee, & Bulanda, 2006). In 1960, hardly any older adults cohabited (Chevan, 1996). Today, approximately 3 percent of older adults cohabit (U.S. Census Bureau, 2004). It is expected that the number of cohabiting older adults will increase even further when baby boomers begin to turn 65 in 2010 and bring their historically more nontraditional values about love, sex, and relationships to late adulthood. In many cases, the cohabiting is more for companionship than for love. In other cases, for example, when one partner faces the potential for expensive care, a couple may decide to maintain their assets separately and thus not marry. One recent study found that older adults who cohabited had a more a more positive, stable relationship than younger adults who cohabited, although cohabiting older adults were less likely to have plans to marry their partner (King & Scott, 2005).

Does cohabiting affect an individual's health? One recent study of more than 8,000 51- to 61-year-old adults revealed that the health of couples who cohabited did not differ from the health of married couples (Waite, 2005). However, another recent study of individuals 50 years of age and older found that those who cohabited were more depressed than their married counterparts (Brown, Bulanda, & Lee, 2005).

Romance and Sex in Older Adults' Relationships Few of us imagine older couples taking an interest in sex or romantic relationships. We might think of them as being interested in a game of bridge or a conversation on the porch, but not much else. In fact, a number of older adults date. The increased health and longevity of older adults have resulted in a much larger pool of active older adults. And the increased divorce rate has added more older adults to the adult dating pool.

What are some ways that older adults retain their sexuality?

Regarding their sexuality, older adults may express their sexuality differently than younger adults, especially when engaging in sexual intercourse becomes difficult (Stones & Stones, 2007). Older adults especially enjoy touching and caressing as part of their sexual relationship. When older adults are healthy, they still may engage in sexual activities. For example, a recent study of older adults in Greece (age range 60 to 90, with a mean of 69 years) revealed that more than 50 percent reported having sexual desire and a frequency of intercourse of four times a month (Papaharitou & others, 2008). As expected, an increase in age was linked to a decrease in intercourse. With the increased use of drugs to treat erectile dysfunction, older adults can be expected to increase their sexual activity (Koulikov & others, 2007; Wessells & others, 2007). However, companionship often becomes more important than sexual activity in older adults. Older couples often emphasize intimacy over sexual prowess. One recent study of individuals 60 years and older revealed that attitudes had a stronger influence on sexual desire than biomedical factors (DeLamater & Sill, 2005).

Older Adult Parents and Their Adult Children

Approximately 80 percent of older adults have living children, many of whom are middle-aged. About 10 percent of older adults have children who are 65 years or older. Adult children are an important part of the aging parent's social network.

Researchers have found that older adults with children have more contacts with relatives than those without children (Johnson & Troll, 1992).

Increasingly, diversity characterizes older adult parents and their adult children (Pudrovska, Schieman, & Carr, 2006). Divorce, cohabitation, and nonmarital childbearing are more common in the history of older adults today than in the past (Allen, Blieszner, & Roberto, 2000). Also, one study found that only 10 of 45 older adults had adult children who were characterized as conventional in terms of marriage and parenting (Allen & others, 1999).

Gender plays an important role in relationships involving older adult parents and their children (Ward-Griffin & others, 2007). Adult daughters rather than adult sons are more likely to be involved in the lives of aging parents. For example, adult daughters are three times more likely than are adult sons to give parents assistance with daily living activities (Dwyer & Coward, 1991).

A valuable service that adult children can perform is to coordinate and monitor services for an aging parent who becomes disabled (Huyck, Ayalon, & Yoder, 2007). This might involve locating a nursing home and monitoring its quality, procuring medical services, arranging public service assistance, and handling finances. In some cases, adult children provide direct assistance with daily living, including such activities as eating, bathing, and dressing. Even less severely impaired older adults may need help with shopping, housework, transportation, home maintenance, and bill paying.

A recent study revealed that even when aging parents had health problems, they and their children generally described positive changes in their relationship in recent years (Fingerman & others, 2007). However, in most cases researchers have found that relationships between aging parents and their children are usually characterized by ambivalence. Perceptions include love, reciprocal help, and shared values on the positive side and isolation, family conflicts and problems, abuse, neglect, and caregiver stress on the negative side (Fowler, 1999). A study of 1,599 adult children's relationships with their older adult parents revealed that ambivalence was likely to be present when relationships involved in-laws, those in poor health, and adult children with poor parental relationships in early life (Wilson, Shuey, & Elder, 2003).

Great-Grandparenting

Because of increased longevity, more grandparents today than in the past are also great-grandparents. At the turn of the twentieth century, the three-generation family was common, but now the four-generation family is common. One contribution of great-grandparents is to transmit family history by telling their children, grandchildren, and great-grandchildren where the family came from, what their members achieved, what they endured, and how their lives changed over the years (Harris, 2002).

There has been little research on great-grandparenting. One study examined the relationship between young adults and their grandparents and great-grandparents (Roberto & Skoglund, 1996). The young adults interacted with, and participated in more activities with, their grandparents than great-grandparents. They also perceived their grandparents to have a more defined role and as more influential in their lives than great-grandparents.

Lillian Troll (2000) has found that older adults who are embedded in family relationships have much less distress than those who are family deprived. Next, we will consider these other aspects of social relationships in late adulthood: friendship, social support, and social integration.

Friendship

Aging expert Laura Carstensen (1998) concluded that people choose close friends over new friends as they grow older. And as long as they have several close people in their network, they seem content, says Carstensen. Supporting Cartensen's view, recall the recent study we described earlier in this chapter that compared with younger adults, older adults said they tended to experience less intense positive emotions with new

*B*eing embedded in a family is a positive aspect of life for many older adults.

—Lillian Troll
Contemporary Developmental Psychologist, University of California at San Francisco

At the beginning of the twentieth century, the three-generation family was common, but now the four-generation family is common as well. Thus, an increasing number of grandparents are also great-grandparents. The four-generation family shown here is the Jordans—author John Santrock's mother-in-law, daughter, granddaughter, and wife.

friends and equal levels of positive emotions with established friends (Charles & Piazza, 2007) (see Figure 19.7).

In one study of 128 married older adults, women were more depressed than men if they did not have a best friend, and women who did have a friend reported lower levels of depression (Antonucci, Lansford, & Akiyama, 2001). Similarly, women who did not have a best friend were less satisfied with life than women who did have a best friend.

Three recent studies documented the importance of friendship in older adults:

- A study of almost 1,700 U.S. adults 60 years and older revealed that friendships were more important than family relationships in predicting mental health (Fiori, Antonucci, & Cortina, 2006). Even when the researchers controlled for health, age, income, and other factors, older adults whose social contacts were mainly restricted to their family members were more likely to have depressive symptoms. Friends likely provide emotional intimacy and companionship, as well as integration into the community (Antonucci, Akiyama, & Sherman, 2007).

- A recent longitudinal study of adults 75 years of age and older revealed that individuals with close ties with friends were less likely to die across a seven-year age span (Rasulo, Christensen, & Tomassini, 2005). The findings were stronger for women than men.

- A recent study revealed that unmarried older adults embedded in a friend-focused network fared better physically and psychologically than unmarried older adults in a restricted network with little friend contact (Fiori, Smith, & Antonucci, 2007).

FIGURE 19.7 Happiness of Younger Adults and Older Adults with New and Established Friends. *Note:* The happiness scale ranged from 0 to 6 with participants rating how intensely they experienced happiness (0 = not at all, 6 = extremely intense). Older adults mean age 71; younger adults mean age 23.

Social Support and Social Integration

Social support and social integration play important roles in the physical and mental health of older adults (Fiori, Smith, & Antonucci, 2007). In the **convoy model of social relations**, individuals go through life embedded in a personal network of individuals to whom they give and from whom they receive social support (Antonucci, Akiyama, & Sherman, 2007). Social support can help individuals of all ages cope more effectively (Griffiths & others, 2007). For older adults, social support is related to their physical and mental health. It is linked with a reduction in symptoms of disease, with the ability to meet one's own health-care needs, and mortality (Rook & others, 2007). Social support also decreases the probability that an older adult will be institutionalized and is associated with a lower incidence of depression (Cacioppo & others, 2006).

Social support for older adults can be provided by different adults (Antonucci, Akiyama, & Sherman, 2007). Older adults who are married are less likely to need formal social supports, such as home nursing care, adult day care, and home-delivered meals, than nonmarried older adults. Families play important roles in social support for older adults, but friends also can provide invaluable resources for social support. Also, social support for older adults may vary across cultures. For example, in the United States, the focal support person for an older adult is most likely to be a daughter, whereas in Japan it is most likely to be a daughter-in-law.

Social integration also plays an important role in the lives of many older adults (Cavallero, Morino-Abbele, & Bertocci, 2007). Remember from our earlier discussion of socioemotional selectivity theory that many older adults choose to have fewer peripheral social contacts and more emotionally positive contacts with friends and family (Carstensen, 2006, 2008). Thus, a decrease in the overall social activity of many older adults may reflect their greater interest in spending more time in the small circle of friends and families where they are less likely to have negative emotional experiences. Researchers have found that a low level of social integration is linked with coronary heart disease in older adults (Loucks & others, 2006). Also, in one study, being part of a social network was related to longevity, especially for men (House, Landis, & Umberson, 1988). And in a longitudinal study, both women

What are some characteristics of older adults' friendships?

convoy model of social relations Individuals go through life embedded in a personal network of individuals to whom they give and from whom they receive support.

What role does social support play in the health of older adults?

Ninety-eight-year-old volunteer Iva Broadus plays cards with 10-year-old DeAngela Williams in Dallas, Texas. Iva recently was recognized as the oldest volunteer in the Big Sister program in the United States. Iva says that the card-playing helps to keep her memory and thinking skills good and can help DeAngela's as well.

and men with more organizational memberships lived longer than their counterparts with low participation in organizations (Tucker & others, 1999).

However, being lonely and socially isolated is a significant health risk factor in older adults (Cheung, Chau, & Yip, 2008; Mullins, 2007). In one longitudinal study, poor social connections, infrequent participation in social activities, and social disengagement predicted cognitive decline in older adults (Zunzunegui & others, 2003).

Altruism and Volunteerism

A common perception is that older adults need to be given help rather than give help themselves. However, researchers recently have found that when older adults engage in altruistic behavior and volunteering they benefit from these activities. One study followed 423 older adult couples for five years (Brown & others, 2003). At the beginning of the study, the couples were asked about the extent to which they had given or received emotional or practical help in the past year. Five years later, those who said they had helped others were half as likely to have died. One possible reason for this finding is that helping others may reduce the output of stress hormones, which improves cardiovascular health and strengthens the immune system.

A recent study of 21,000 individuals 50 to 79 years of age in 21 countries revealed that one-third give back to society, saying that they volunteer now or have volunteered in the past (HSBC Insurance, 2007). In this study, about 50 percent who volunteer reported that they do so for at least one-half day each week. And a recent study found that volunteering steadily increased from 57 to 85 years of age (Cornwell, Laumann, & Schumm, 2008).

Researchers also have found that volunteering as an older adult is associated with a number of positive outcomes (Harootyan, 2007). An early study of individuals 65 years and older found that volunteer workers compared with nonvolunteers were more satisfied with their lives and were less depressed and anxious (Hunter & Linn, 1980). A study of 2,000 older adults in Japan revealed that those who gave more assistance to others had better physical health than their elderly counterparts who gave less assistance (Krause & others, 1999). And in a recent study, being a volunteer as an older adult was associated with more positive affect and less negative affect (Greenfield & Marks, 2004). Among the reasons for the positive outcomes of volunteering are its provision of constructive activities and productive roles, social integration, and enhanced meaningfulness (Tan & others, 2007).

Review and Reflect: Learning Goal 3

3 **Characterize the Families and Social Relationships of Aging Adults**

REVIEW

- How would you profile the diversity of adult lifestyles?
- What characterizes the relationships of older adult parents and their adult children?
- Is the role of great-grandparents different than for grandparents?
- What is the friendship of older adults like?
- What roles do social support and social integration play in late adulthood?
- How are altruism and volunteerism linked to positive outcomes in older adults?

REFLECT

- If you were going to create a research study on close relationships in older adults, what topic would you want to study? Describe a study that you think would be interesting to conduct. Is it a correlational study or an experimental study? What type of measure (observation, interview, survey, for example) would you use?

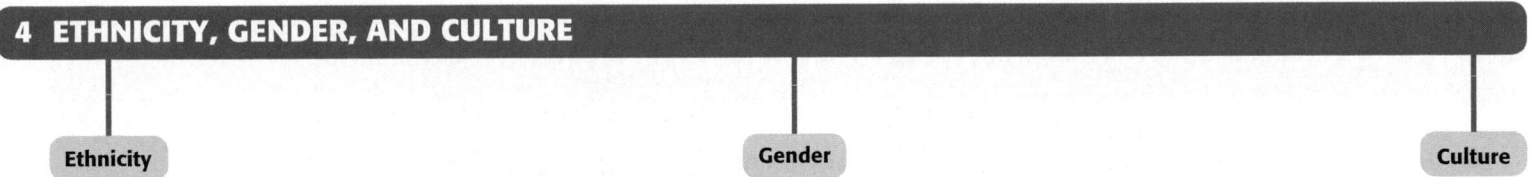

Ethnicity   Gender   Culture

How is ethnicity linked to aging? Do gender roles change in late adulthood? What are the social aspects of aging in different cultures?

Ethnicity

Of special concern are ethnic minority older adults, especially African Americans and Latinos, who are overrepresented in poverty statistics (Albert, 20007; Cornman & Freedman, 2008). Consider Harry, a 72-year-old African American who lives in a run-down hotel in Los Angeles. He suffers from arthritis and uses a walker. He has not been able to work for years, and government payments are barely enough to meet his needs.

Comparative information about African Americans, Latinos, and Whites indicates a possible double jeopardy for elderly ethnic minority individuals. They face problems related to *both* ageism and racism (Ciol & others, 2008). One study of more than 4,000 older adults found that African Americans perceived more discrimination than non-Latino Whites (Barnes & others, 2004). Both the wealth and the health of ethnic minority older adults decrease more rapidly than for elderly non-Latino Whites (Yee & Chiriboga, 2007). Older ethnic minority individuals are more likely to become ill but less likely to receive treatment (Hinrichsen, 2006). They also are more likely to have a history of less education, unemployment, worse housing conditions, and shorter life expectancies than their older non-Latino White counterparts (Himes, Hogan, & Eggebeen, 1996). And many ethnic minority workers never enjoy the Social Security and Medicare benefits to which their earnings contribute, because they die before reaching the age of eligibility for benefits.

Despite the stress and discrimination older ethnic minority individuals face, many of these older adults have developed coping mechanisms that allow them to survive in the dominant non-Latino White world (Markides & Rudkin, 1996). Extension of family networks helps older minority-group individuals cope with the bare essentials of living and gives them a sense of being loved (Karasik & Hamon, 2007). Churches in African American and Latino communities provide avenues for meaningful social participation, feelings of power, and a sense of internal satisfaction (Hill & others, 2006). And residential concentrations of ethnic minority groups give their older members a sense of belonging. Thus, it always is important to consider individual variations in the lives of aging minorities (Albert, 2007). To read about one individual who is providing help for aging minorities, see the *Careers in Life-Span Development* profile.

Gender

Do our gender roles change when we become older adults? Some developmentalists believe there is decreasing femininity in women and decreasing masculinity in men when they reach the late adulthood years (Gutmann, 1975). The evidence suggests that older men do become more feminine—nurturant, sensitive, and so on—but it appears that older women do not necessarily become more masculine—assertive, dominant, and so on (Turner, 1982). Keep in mind that cohort effects are especially important to consider in areas such as gender roles. As sociohistorical changes take place and are assessed more frequently in life-span investigations, what were once perceived to be age effects may turn out to be cohort effects (Schaie, 2007).

A possible double jeopardy also faces many women—the burden of *both* ageism and sexism (Slack & Jensen, 2008). The poverty rate for older adult females is almost double that of older adult males.

Careers in Life-Span Development

Norma Thomas, Social Work Professor and Administrator

Dr. Norma Thomas has worked for more than three decades in the field of aging. She obtained her undergraduate degree in social work from Pennsylvania State University and her doctoral degree in social work from the University of Pennsylvania, Thomas' activities are varied. Earlier in her career, as a social work practitioner, she provided services to older adults of color in an effort to improve their lives. She currently is a professor and academic administrator at Widener University in Chester, Pennsylvania, a fellow of the Institute of Aging at the University of Pennsylvania, and the chief executive officer and cofounder of the Center on Ethnic and Minority Aging (CEMA). CEMA was formed to provide research, consultation, training, and services to benefit aging individuals of color, their families, and their communities. Thomas has created numerous community service events that benefit older adults of color, especially African Americans and Latinos. She has also been a consultant to various national, regional, and state agencies in her effort to improve the lives of aging adults of color.

Norma Thomas.

Not only is it important to be concerned about older women's double jeopardy of ageism and sexism, but special attention also needs to be devoted to female ethnic minority older adults (Locher & others, 2005). They face what could be described as triple jeopardy—ageism, sexism, and racism (Markides, 1995). More information about being female, ethnic, and old appears in the *Diversity in Life-Span Development* interlude.

Diversity in Life-Span Development
Being Female, Ethnic, and Old

Part of the unfortunate history of ethnic minority groups in the United States has been the negative stereotypes against members of their groups (Fernandez & Goldstein, 2004). Many also have been hampered by their immigrant origins in that they are not fluent or literate in English, may not be aware of the values and norms involved in American social interaction, and may have lifestyles that differ from those of mainstream America (Organista, 1994). Often included in these cultural differences is the role of women in the family and in society. Many, but not all, immigrant ethnic groups traditionally have relegated the woman's role to family maintenance. Many important decisions may be made by a woman's husband or parents, and she is often not expected to seek an independent career or enter the workforce except in the case of dire financial need.

Some ethnic minority groups may define an older woman's role as unimportant, especially if she is unable to contribute financially. However, in some ethnic minority groups, an older woman's social status improves. For example, older African American women can express their own needs and can be given status and power in the community. Despite their positive status in the African American family and the African American culture, African American women over the age of 70 are the poorest population group in the United States. Three of five older African American women live alone; most of them are widowed. The low incomes of older African American women translate into less than adequate access to health care. Substantially lower incomes for African American older women are related to the kinds of jobs they hold, which either are not covered by Social Security or, in the case of domestic service, are not reported even when reporting is legally required.

A portrayal of older African American women in cities reveals some of their survival strategies. They highly value the family as a system of mutual support and aid, adhere to the American work ethic, and view religion as a source of strength (Perry & Johnson, 1994). The use of religion as a way of coping with stress has a long history in the African American culture, with roots in the slave experience. The African American church came to fulfill needs and functions once met by religion-based tribal and community organizations that African Americans brought from Africa. In one study, the older African American women valued church organizations more than their male counterparts did, especially valuing the church's group activities (Taylor, 1982).

In sum, older African American women have faced considerable stress in their lives (Locher & others, 2005). In the face of this stress, they have shown remarkable adaptiveness, resilience, responsibility, and coping skills.

Culture

What promotes a good old age in most cultures? A recent analysis indicated that these three factors are important in living the "good life" as an older adult: health, security, and kinship/support (Fry, 2007).

Another important question is: What factors are associated with whether older adults are accorded a position of high status in a culture? In one view, seven factors are most likely to predict high status for older adults in a culture (Sangree, 1989):

- Older persons have valuable knowledge.
- Older persons control key family/community resources.
- Older persons are permitted to engage in useful and valued functions as long as possible.
- There is role continuity throughout the life span.
- Age-related role changes involve greater responsibility, authority, and advisory capacity.
- The extended family is a common family arrangement in the culture, and the older person is integrated into the extended family.
- In general, respect for older adults is greater in collectivistic cultures (such as China and Japan) than in individualistic cultures (such as the United States). However, some researchers are finding that this collectivistic/individualistic difference in respect for older adults is not as strong as it used to be, and that in some cases older adults in individualistic cultures receive considerable respect (Antonucci, Vandewater, & Lansford, 2000).

A special concern is the stress faced by older African American women, many of whom view religion as a source of strength to help them cope. *What are some other characteristics of being female, ethnic, and old?*

Cultures vary in the prestige they give to older adults. In the Navajo culture, older adults are especially treated with respect because of their wisdom and extensive life experiences. *What are some other factors that are linked with respect for older adults in a culture?*

Review and Reflect: Learning Goal 4

4 **Summarize How Ethnicity, Gender, and Culture Are Linked with Aging**

REVIEW

- How does ethnicity modify the experience of aging?
- Do gender roles change in late adulthood? Explain.
- How is aging experienced in different cultures?

REFLECT

- What can America do to make being an older adult a more positive experience?

5 SUCCESSFUL AGING

John Glenn's space mission in his late sixties is emblematic of our rethinking of older adults in terms of successful aging.

For too long, the positive dimensions of late adulthood were ignored (Carstensen, 2008; Ram & others, 2009). Throughout this book, we have called attention to the positive aspects of aging. There are many robust, healthy older adults (Terry & others, 2008; Willcox & others, 2008). With a proper diet, an active lifestyle, mental stimulation and flexibility, positive coping skills, good social relationships and support, and the absence of disease, many abilities can be maintained or in some cases even improved as we get older (Gu & Conn, 2008; Lamond & others, 2008). Even when individuals develop a disease, improvements in medicine mean that increasing numbers of older adults can still lead active, constructive lives.

Being active is especially important to successful aging (Hillman, Erickson, & Kramer, 2008). Older adults who get out and go to meetings, participate in church activities, go on trips, and exercise regularly are more satisfied with their lives than their counterparts who disengage from society (Reichstadt & others, 2007). Older adults who are emotionally selective, optimize their choices, and compensate effectively for losses increase their chances of aging successfully (Baltes & Smith, 2008; Carstensen, 2008).

Successful aging also involves perceived control over the environment (HSBC Insurance, 2007). In Chapter 17, we described how perceived control over the environment had a positive effect on nursing home residents' health and longevity. In recent years, the term *self-efficacy* has often been used to describe perceived control over the environment and the ability to produce positive outcomes (Bandura, 2008, 2009). Researchers have found that many older adults are quite effective in maintaining a sense of control and have a positive view of themselves (Dunbar, Leventhal, & Leventhal, 2007). For example, one recent study of centenarians found that many were very happy and that self-efficacy and an optimistic attitude were linked to their happiness (Jopp & Rott, 2006). Examining the positive aspects of aging is an important trend in life-span development and is likely to benefit future generations of older adults (Baltes & Smith, 2008; Carstensen, 2008; Ram & others, 2009).

Review and Reflect: Learning Goal 5

5 **Explain How to Age Successfully**

REVIEW

• What factors are linked with aging successfully?

REFLECT

• How might aging successfully in late adulthood be related to what people have done earlier in their lives?

Socioemotional Development in Late Adulthood

1 THEORIES OF SOCIOEMOTIONAL DEVELOPMENT: DISCUSS FOUR THEORIES OF SOCIOEMOTIONAL DEVELOPMENT AND AGING

Erikson's Theory

- Erikson's eighth and final stage of development, which individuals experience in late adulthood, involves reflecting on the past and either integrating it positively or concluding that one's life has not been well spent. Life review is an important theme in Erikson's stage of integrity versus despair.

Activity Theory

- Activity theory states that the more active and involved older adults are, the more likely they are to be satisfied with their lives. This theory has been strongly supported.

Socioemotional Selectivity Theory

- Socioemotional selectivity theory states that older adults become more selective about their social networks. Because they place a high value on emotional satisfaction, they are motivated to spend more time with familiar individuals with whom they have had rewarding relationships. Knowledge-related and emotion-related goals change across the life span, with emotion-related goals being more important when individuals get older.

Selective Optimization with Compensation Theory

- Selective optimization with compensation theory states that successful aging is linked with three main factors: (1) selection, (2) optimization, and (3) compensation. These are especially likely to be relevant when loss occurs.

2 PERSONALITY, THE SELF, AND SOCIETY: DESCRIBE LINKS BETWEEN PERSONALITY AND MORTALITY, AND IDENTIFY CHANGES IN THE SELF AND SOCIETY IN LATE ADULTHOOD

Personality

- The personality traits of conscientiousness agreeableness increase in late adulthood. Low conscientiousness, high neuroticism, negative affect, pessimism, and a negative outlook on life are related to earlier death in late adulthood.

The Self and Society

- In one large-scale study, self-esteem increased through most of adulthood but declined in the seventies and eighties. Further research is needed to verify these developmental changes in self-esteem. The stability of self-esteem declines in older adults. Possible selves are what individuals might become, what they would like to become, and what they are afraid of becoming. Possible selves change during late adulthood and are linked to engagement in various activities and longevity. Changes in types of self-acceptance occur through the adult years as acceptance of ideal and future selves decreases with age and acceptance of past selves increases. Most older adults effectively maintain a sense of self-control, although self-regulation may vary by domain. For example, older adults often show less self-regulation in the physical domain than younger adults.

Older Adults in Society

- Ageism is prejudice against others because of their age. Too many negative stereotypes of older adults continue to exist. Social policy issues in an aging society include the status of the economy and the viability of the Social Security system, the provision of health care, eldercare, and generational inequity. Of special concern are older adults who are in poverty. Poverty rates are especially high among older women who live alone and ethnic minority older adults. Most older adults live in the community, not in institutions. Almost two-thirds of older adults live with family members. Older adults are less likely to have a computer in their home and less likely to use the Internet than younger adults, but they are the fastest-growing age segment of Internet users.

3   FAMILIES AND SOCIAL RELATIONSHIPS: CHARACTERIZE THE FAMILIES AND SOCIAL RELATIONSHIPS OF AGING ADULTS

Lifestyle Diversity

- Older adult men are more likely to be married than older adult women. Almost half of older adult women are widowed. Retirement alters a couple's lifestyle and requires adaptation. Married older adults are often happier than single older adults. There are social, financial, and physical consequences of divorce for older adults. More divorced older adults, increased longevity, and better health have led to an increase in remarriage by older adults. Some older adults perceive negative pressure about their decision to remarry, although the majority of adult children support the decision of their older adult parents to remarry. An increasing number of older adults cohabit. Older adults especially enjoy touching and caressing as part of their sexual relationship.

Older Adult Parents and Their Adult Children

- Approximately 80 percent of older adults have living children, many of whom are middle-aged. Increasingly, diversity characterizes older parents and their adult children. Adult daughters are more likely than adult sons to be involved in the lives of aging parents. An important task that adult children can perform is to coordinate and monitor services for an aging parent who becomes disabled. Ambivalence can characterize the relationships of adult children with their aging parents.

Great-Grandparenting

- Because of increased longevity, more grandparents today are also great-grandparents. One contribution of great-grandparents is family history. One research study found that young adults have a more involved relationship with grandparents than great-grandparents.

Friendship

- There is more continuity than change in friendship for older adults, although there is more change for males than for females.

Social Support and Social Integration

- Social support is linked with improved physical and mental health in older adults. Older adults who participate in more organizations live longer than their counterparts who have low participation rates. Older adults often have fewer peripheral social ties but a strong motivation to spend time in relationships with close friends and family members that are rewarding.

Altruism and Volunteerism

- Altruism is linked to having a longer life. Volunteering is associated with higher life satisfaction, less depression and anxiety, better physical health, and more positive affect and less negative affect.

4   ETHNICITY, GENDER, AND CULTURE: SUMMARIZE HOW ETHNICITY, GENDER, AND CULTURE ARE LINKED WITH AGING

Ethnicity

- Aging minorities face special burdens, having to cope with the double burden of ageism and racism. Nonetheless, there is considerable variation in aging minorities.

Gender

- There is stronger evidence that men become more feminine (nurturant, sensitive) as older adults than there is that women become more masculine (assertive). Older women face a double jeopardy of ageism and sexism.

Culture

- Historically, respect for older adults in China and Japan was high, but today their status is more variable. Factors that predict high status for the elderly across cultures range from their valuable knowledge to integration into the extended family.

5   SUCCESSFUL AGING: EXPLAIN HOW TO AGE SUCCESSFULLY

- Increasingly, the positive aspects of older adults are being studied. Factors that are linked with successful aging include an active lifestyle, positive coping skills, good social relationships and support, and the absence of disease.

KEY TERMS

integrity versus despair 589
activity theory 590
socioemotional selectivity
    theory 591

selective optimization with
    compensation theory 592
possible selves 596
ageism 597

eldercare 598
generational inequity 598
convoy model of social
    relations 603

KEY PEOPLE

Erik Erikson 589
Robert Butler 589

Laura Carstensen 591

Paul Baltes 592

Ursula Staudinger 593

E-LEARNING TOOLS

To help you master the material in this chapter, visit the Online Learning Center for *Life-Span Development*, twelfth edition, at **www.mhhe.com/santrockld12**.

Self-Assessment

Connect to **www.mhhe.com/santrockld12** to reflect on your life satisfaction by completing the self-assessment, *How Satisfied Am I with My Life?*

Taking It to the Net

Connect to **www.mhhe.com/santrockld12** to research the answers to these questions:

1. How much Social Security income can you expect to receive when you are normal retirement age? First, ascertain what will be your normal retirement age—it depends on the year in which you are born—and see how much you will receive. How much will you receive if you retire early? How much will you receive if you work past your normal retirement age?

2. Ted is the activities director at an adult retirement community. A friend who is a social worker suggested that Ted might want to develop a program in which the residents engage in reminiscence and life review. What benefits could the residents gain from such an activity?

3. Jessica, 33, a single mother of three, has been diagnosed with breast cancer. Just as a precaution, Jessica has made arrangements for her parents to raise the children if she dies. What types of services and financial assistance would be available to Jessica's parents if they need to take on the responsibility for their grandchildren?

Video Clips

The Online Learning Center includes a video for Chapter 19 called "Being in Love in Late Adulthood." This segment inquires into the sexual and emotional needs of older adults in various relationships. An older couple describe how the nature of their affection for each other has changed over the years.

Health and Well-Being, Parenting, and Education Exercises

Build your decision-making skills by trying your hand at the health and well-being, parenting, and education exercises. Connect to **www.mhhe.com/santrockld12** to research the answers and complete the exercises.

ENDINGS

*Years following years
steal something every
day; At last they steal us
from ourselves away.*

—ALEXANDER POPE
English Poet, 18th Century

Our life ultimately ends—when we approach life's grave

sustained and soothed with unfaltering trust or rave at the close

of day; when at last years steal us from ourselves; and when

we are linked to our children's children's children by an invisible

cable that runs from age to age. This final section contains one

chapter: "Death, Dying, and Grieving" (Chapter 20).

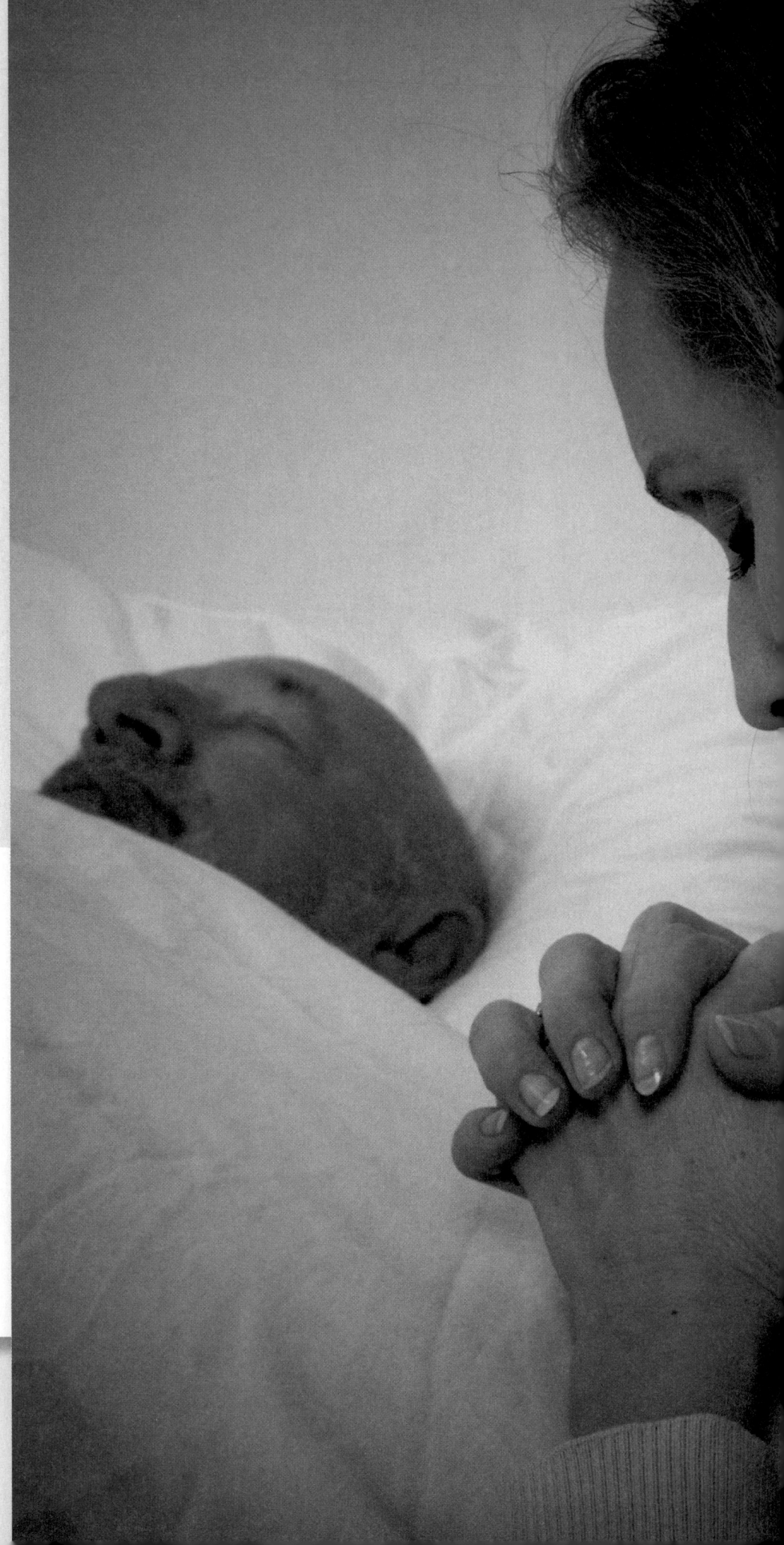

20

Sustained and soothed by an unfaltering trust, approach thy grave, Like one who wraps the drapery of his couch About him, and lies down to pleasant dreams.

—WILLIAM CULLEN BRYANT
American Poet, 19th Century

LEARNING GOALS

◆ Describe the death system and its cultural and historical contexts.

◆ Evaluate issues in determining death and decisions regarding death.

◆ Discuss death and attitudes about it at different points in development.

◆ Explain the psychological aspects involved in facing one's own death and the contexts in which people die.

◆ Identify ways to cope with the death of another person.

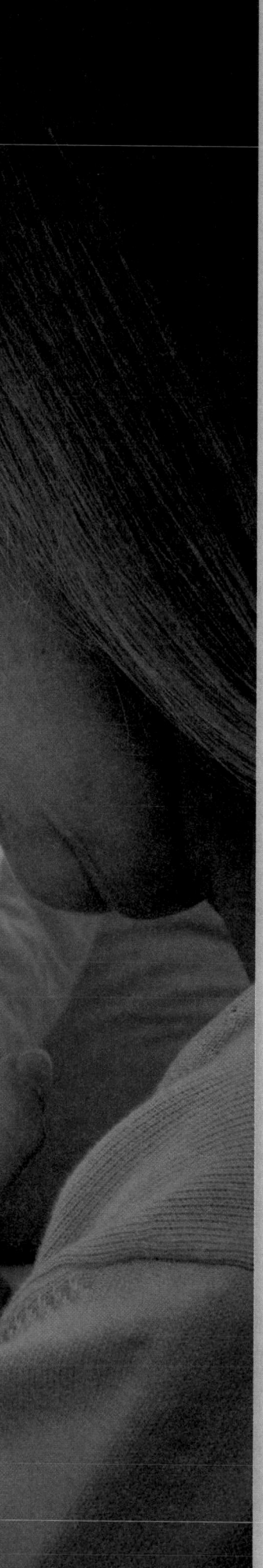

DEATH, DYING, AND GRIEVING

CHAPTER OUTLINE

1

THE DEATH SYSTEM AND CULTURAL CONTEXTS

The Death System and Its Cultural Variations

Changing Historical Circumstances

2

DEFINING DEATH AND LIFE/DEATH ISSUES

Issues in Determining Death

Decisions Regarding Life, Death, and Health Care

3

A DEVELOPMENTAL PERSPECTIVE ON DEATH

Causes of Death

Attitudes Toward Death at Different Points in the Life Span

4

FACING ONE'S OWN DEATH

Kübler-Ross' Stages of Dying

Perceived Control and Denial

The Contexts in Which People Die

5

COPING WITH THE DEATH OF SOMEONE ELSE

Communicating with a Dying Person

Grieving

Making Sense of the World

Losing a Life Partner

Forms of Mourning

Images of Life-Span Development
Paige Farley-Hackel and Ruth McCourt

Paige Farley-Hackel and her best friend Ruth McCourt teamed up to take McCourt's 4-year-old daughter, Juliana, to Disneyland. They were originally booked on the same flight from Boston to Los Angeles, but McCourt decided to use her frequent flyer miles and go on a different airplane. Both their flights exploded 17 minutes apart after terrorists hijacked them, then rammed them into the twin towers of the World Trade Center in New York City on 9/11/2001.

Forty-five-year-old Ruth McCourt was a homemaker from New London, Connecticut, who met Farley-Hackel at a day spa she used to own in Boston. McCourt gave up the business when she married, but the friendship between the two women lasted. They often traveled together and shared their passion for reading, cooking, and learning.

Forty-six-year-old Farley-Hackel was a writer, motivational speaker, and spiritual counselor who lived in Newton, Massachusetts. She was looking forward to the airing of the first few episodes of her new radio program, "Spiritually Speaking," and wanted to eventually be on "The Oprah Winfrey Show," said her husband, Allan Hackel. Following 9/11, Oprah included a memorial tribute to Farley-Hackel, McCourt, and Juliana.

> ### PREVIEW
> In this final chapter of the book, we will explore many aspects of death and dying. Among the questions that we will ask are: What characterizes the death system and its cultural and historical contexts? How can death be defined? What are some links between development and death? How do people face their own death? How do individuals cope with the death of someone they love?

1 THE DEATH SYSTEM AND CULTURAL CONTEXTS

| The Death System and Its Cultural Variations | Changing Historical Circumstances |

These children's parents died when they were swept away by the tsunami in Indonesia in 2004. The death system includes times such as the 2004 tsunami. *What are some other components of the death system?*

Every culture has a death system, and variations in this death system occur across cultures. Also, when, where, and how people die have changed historically in the United States.

The Death System and Its Cultural Variations

Robert Kastenbaum (2004, 2007) emphasizes that a number of components comprise the *death system* in any culture. The components include:

- *People.* Because death in inevitable, everyone is involved with death at some point, either their own death or the death of others. Some individuals have a more systematic role with death, such as those who work in the funeral industry and the clergy, as well as people who work in life-threatening contexts such as firemen and policemen.

- *Places or contexts.* These include hospitals, funeral homes, cemetaries, hospices, battle-fields, and memorials (such as the Vietnam Memorial Wall in Washington, D.C.).

- *Times.* Death involves times or occasions, such as Memorial Day in the United States, and the Day of the Dead in Mexico, which are times to honor those who have died. Also, anniversaries of disasters such as D-Day in World War II, 9/11/2001, and Hurricane Katrina in 2005, as well as the 2004 tsunami in Southeast Asia that took approximately 100,000 lives are times when those who died are remembered in special ways such as ceremonies.

- *Objects.* Many objects in a culture are associated with death, including caskets, various black objects such as clothes, arm bands, and hearses.

- *Symbols.* Symbols such as a skull and crossbones, as well as last rites in the Catholic religion and various religious ceremonies, are connected to death.

Kastenbaum (2004, 2007) also argues that the death system serves certain functions in a culture. These functions include *warnings and predictions* (such as weather forecasting services and the media, laboratories that analyze test results, and doctors that communicate with patients and their families); *preventing death* (this includes people such as firefighters, the police, physicians, and researchers who work to improve safety and find cures for diseases); *caring for the dying* (involves various health professionals such as physicians and nurses, as well as where dying individuals are cared for, such as in hospitals or hospices); *disposing of the dead* (removal of the body, whether the body is cremated, and so on); *social consolidation after death* (family members and friends of the deceased have to cope and adapt, often needing support and counseling); *making sense of the death* (how people in the society try to understand death); and *killing* (when, how, and for what reasons people in the culture can be killed, such as criminals and whether the death penalty should be given to some individuals). Figure 20.1 describes the functions of the death system in the context of Hurricane Katrina in 2005 (Kastenbaum, 2007).

What are some cultural variations in the death system? To live a full life and die with glory was the prevailing goal of the ancient Greeks. Individuals are more conscious of death in times of war, famine, and plague. Whereas Americans are conditioned from early in life to live as though they were immortal, in much of the world this fiction cannot be maintained. Death crowds the streets of Calcutta in daily overdisplay, as it does the scrubby villages of Africa's Sahel. Children live with the ultimate toll of malnutrition and disease, mothers lose as many babies as survive into adulthood, and it is rare that a family remains intact for many years. Even in peasant areas where life is better, and health and maturity may be reasonable expectations, the presence of dying people in the house, the large attendance at funerals, and the daily contact with aging adults prepare the young for death and provide them with guidelines on how to die. By contrast, in the United States it is not uncommon to reach adulthood without having seen someone die.

Most societies throughout history have had philosophical or religious beliefs about death, and most societies have a ritual that deals with death (Bruce, 2007). Death may be seen as a punishment for one's sins, an act of atonement, or a judgment of a just God. For some, death means loneliness; for others, death is a quest for happiness. For still others, death represents redemption, a relief from the trials and tribulations of the earthly world. Some embrace death and welcome it; others abhor and fear it. For those who welcome it, death may be seen as the fitting end to a fulfilled life. From this perspective, how we depart from Earth is influenced by how we have lived.

A body lies in the flooded streets of New Orleans in the aftermath of Hurricane Katrina.

Death System Function	Hurricane Katrina
Warnings and predictions	Long-standing recognition of vulnerability; clear advance warning of impending disaster.
Preventing death	The hurricane itself could not be prevented; loss of life, social disorganization, and massive property destruction could have been sharply reduced by better advanced planning and emergency response.
Caring for the dying	Medical care was interrupted and undermined by damage to hospitals and communications.
Disposing of the dead	Recovering bodies was delayed, and there were major problems in identifying bodies.
Social consolidation after death	Community cohesiveness and support was negatively impacted by evacuation, scattering of family members, and limited response by overwhelmed human service agencies.
Making sense of death	There was intense criticism of government agencies, whose alleged failures contributed to death and destruction.
Killing	The media reported spikes in lethal violence after the hurricane, but those reports were later found to be inaccurate.

FIGURE 20.1 Hurricane Katrina and Death System Functions

FIGURE 20.2 A Ritual Associated with Death. Family memorial day at the national cemetery in Seoul, South Korea.

In most societies, death is not viewed as the end of existence—though the biological body has died, the spiritual body is believed to live on (Morgan, 2003). This religious perspective is favored by most Americans as well (Gowan, 2003). Cultural variations in attitudes toward death include belief in reincarnation, which is an important aspect of the Hindu and Buddhist religions (Dillon, 2003). In the Gond culture of India, death is believed to be caused by magic and demons. The members of the Gond culture react angrily to death. In the Tanala culture of Madagascar, death is believed to be caused by natural forces. The members of the Tanala culture show a much more peaceful reaction to death than their counterparts in the Gond culture. Figure 20.2 shows a ritual associated with death in South Korea.

In many ways, we in the United States are death avoiders and death deniers (Norouzieh, 2005). This denial can take many forms:

- The tendency of the funeral industry to gloss over death and fashion lifelike qualities in the dead
- The adoption of euphemistic language for death—for example, *exiting, passing on, never say die,* and *good for life,* which implies forever
- The persistent search for a fountain of youth
- The rejection and isolation of the aged, who may remind us of death
- The adoption of the concept of a pleasant and rewarding afterlife, suggesting that we are immortal
- The medical community's emphasis on prolonging biological life rather than on diminishing human suffering

Changing Historical Circumstances

One historical change involves the age group in which death most often strikes. Two hundred years ago, almost one of every two children died before the age of 10, and one parent died before children grew up. Today, death occurs most often among older adults. Life expectancy has increased from 47 years for a person born in 1900 to 78 years for someone born today (U.S. Census Bureau, 2006). In 1900, most people died at home, cared for by their family. As our population has aged and become more mobile, more older adults die apart from their families. In the United States today, more than 80 percent of all deaths occur in institutions or hospitals. The care of a dying older person has shifted away from the family and minimized our exposure to death and its painful surroundings.

Review and Reflect: Learning Goal 1

 Describe the Death System and Its Cultural and Historical Contexts

REVIEW
- What characterizes the death system in a culture? What are some cultural variations in the death system?
- What are some changing sociohistorical circumstances regarding death?

REFLECT
- Describe how the United States is a death-denying culture. What could be done to change this?

2 DEFINING DEATH AND LIFE/DEATH ISSUES

Issues in Determining Death | Decisions Regarding Life, Death, and Health Care

Is there one point in the process of dying that is *the* point at which death takes place, or is death a more gradual process? What are some decisions individuals can make about life, death, and health care?

Issues in Determining Death

Twenty-five years ago, determining if someone was dead was simpler than it is today. The end of certain biological functions, such as breathing and blood pressure, and the rigidity of the body (rigor mortis) were considered to be clear signs of death. In recent decades, defining death has become more complex (Kendall & others, 2007; Quesnel & others, 2007).

Brain death is a neurological definition of death, which states that a person is brain dead when all electrical activity of the brain has ceased for a specified period of time. A flat EEG (electroencephalogram) recording for a specified period of time is one criterion of brain death. The higher portions of the brain often die sooner than the lower portions. Because the brain's lower portions monitor heartbeat and respiration, individuals whose higher brain areas have died may continue breathing and have a heartbeat. The definition of brain death currently followed by most physicians includes the death of both the higher cortical functions and the lower brain stem functions (Truog, 2007, 2008).

Some medical experts argue that the criteria for death should include only higher cortical functioning. If the cortical death definition were adopted, then physicians could claim a person is dead who has no cortical functioning, even though the lower brain stem is functioning. Supporters of the cortical death policy argue that the functions we associate with being human, such as intelligence and personality, are located in the higher cortical part of the brain. They believe that when these functions are lost, the "human being" is no longer alive.

Decisions Regarding Life, Death, and Health Care

In cases of catastrophic illness or accidents, patients might not be able to respond adequately to participate in decisions about their medical care. To prepare for this situation, some individuals make choices earlier.

Natural Death Act and Advance Directive   For many patients in a coma, it has not been clear what their wishes regarding termination of treatment might be if they still were conscious (Burck & others, 2007). Recognizing that terminally ill patients might prefer to die rather than linger in a painful or vegetative state, the organization "Choice in Dying" created the living will. This document is designed to be filled in while the individual can still think clearly; it expresses the person's desires regarding extraordinary medical procedures that might be used to sustain life when the medical situation becomes hopeless (Wolfson & Morgan, 2007).

Physicians' concerns over malpractice suits and the efforts of people who support the living will concept have produced natural death legislation in many states. For example, California's Natural Death Act permits individuals who have been diagnosed by two physicians as terminally ill to sign an *advance directive*, which states that life-sustaining procedures shall not be used to prolong their lives when death is imminent (Buford, 2008; Garrett & others, 2008). An advance directive must be signed while

brain death A neurological definition of death. A person is brain dead when all electrical activity of the brain has ceased for a specified period of time. A flat EEG recording is one criterion of brain death.

the individual still is able to think clearly (Abbo, Sobotka, & Meltzer, 2008). Laws in all fifty states now accept advance directives as reflecting an individual's wishes.

A recent study examined end-of-life health-care planning in 64- to 65-year-old adults (Carr & Khodyakov, 2007). Characteristics of these older adults who were more likely to engage in end-of-life planning (living will, durable power of attorney for health care, and discussion) included (1) being hospitalized in the year prior to the interview, (2) believing that patients rather than physicians should make health-care decisions, (3) having less death anxiety, and (4) having survived the painful death of a loved one.

Euthanasia   Euthanasia ("easy death") is the act of painlessly ending the lives of individuals who are suffering from an incurable disease or severe disability. Sometimes euthansia is called "mercy killing." Distinctions are made between two types of euthanasia: passive and active.

- **Passive euthanasia** occurs when a person is allowed to die by withholding available treatment, such as withdrawing a life-sustaining device. For example, this might involve turning off a respirator or a heart-lung machine.

- **Active euthanasia** occurs when death is deliberately induced, as when a lethal dose of a drug is injected.

Technological advances in life-support devices raise the issue of quality of life (Georges & others, 2008; Fenigsen, 2008). Nowhere was this more apparent in the highly publicized case of Terri Schiavo, who suffered severe brain damage related to cardiac arrest and a lack of oxygen to the brain. She went into a coma and spent 15 years in a vegetative state. Across the 15 years, whether passive euthanasia should be implemented or whether she should be kept in the vegetative state with the hope that her condition might change for the better was debated between family members and eventually at a number of levels in the judicial system. At one point toward the end of her life in early spring 2005, a court ordered her feeding tube be removed. However, subsequent appeals led to its reinsertion twice. The feeding tube was removed a third and final time on March 18, 2005, and she died 13 days later.

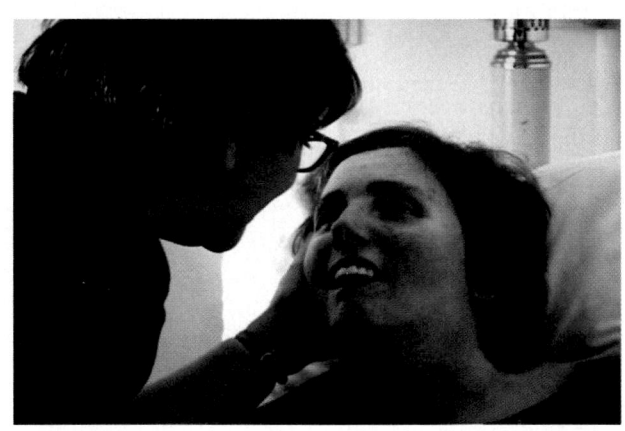

Terri Schiavo (*right*) shown with her mother in an undated photo. *What issues did the Terri Schiavo case raise?*

Should individuals like Terri Schiavo be kept alive in a vegetative state? The trend is toward acceptance of passive euthanasia in the case of terminally ill patients (Truog, 2008). The inflammatory argument that once equated this practice with suicide rarely is heard today. However, experts do not yet entirely agree on the precise boundaries or the exact mechanisms by which treatment decisions should be implemented (Asscher, 2008; Fenigsen, 2008). Can a comatose patient's life-support systems be disconnected when the patient has left no written instructions to that effect? Does the family of a comatose patient have the right to overrule the attending physician's decision to continue life-support systems? These questions have no simple or universally agreed-upon answers.

The most widely publicized cases of active euthanasia involve "assisted suicide" (Darr, 2007; Hertogh & others, 2007). Jack Kevorkian, a Michigan physician, has assisted a number of terminally ill patients to end their lives. After a series of trials, Kevorkian was convicted of second-degree murder and given 10- to 15-year sentence. He was released from prison at age 79 for good behavior in June 2007 and promised not to participate in any further assisted suicides.

Active euthanasia is a crime in most countries and in all states in the United States except one—Oregon. In 1994, the state of Oregon passed the Death with Dignity Act, which allows active euthanasia. Through 2001, ninety-one individuals were known to have died by active euthanasia in Oregon. In January 2006, the U.S. Supreme Court upheld Oregon's active euthanasia law. Active euthanasia is legal in the Netherlands and Uruguay (van der Heide & others, 2007; Vrakking & others, 2007). A recent Canadian

euthanasia The act of painlessly ending the lives of persons who are suffering from incurable diseases or severe disabilities; sometimes called "mercy killing."

passive euthanasia The withholding of available treatments, such as life-sustaining devices, allowing the person to die.

active euthanasia Death induced deliberately, as by injecting a lethal dose of a drug.

study assessed terminally ill cancer patients' views on physician-assisted suicide (Wilson & others, 2007). Slightly more than 60 percent thought that physician-assisted suicide should be legalized, but only 6 percent said they would make a request right away if it were legal. Patients who had a desire for a hastened death were less religious, had been diagnosed as having depression, and had a lower functional living status.

Needed: Better Care for Dying Individuals   Death in America is often lonely, prolonged, and painful (Schroepher, 2007). Dying individuals often get too little or too much care. Scientific advances sometimes have made dying harder by delaying the inevitable (Kaufman, 2005). Also, even though painkillers are available, too many people experience severe pain during the last days and months of life (Lo & Rubenfeld, 2005). Many health-care professionals have not been trained to provide adequate end-of-life care or to understand its importance (Lofmark & others, 2008).

End-of-life care should include respect for the goals, preferences, and choices of the patient and his or her family (Harrington & Smith, 2008; Mosenthal & others, 2008). Many patients who are nearing death want companionship.

Care providers are increasingly interested in helping individuals experience a "good death" (Brink & Smith, 2008; Lyall, 2007). One view is that a good death involves physical comfort, support from loved ones, acceptance, and appropriate medical care.

There are few fail-safe measures for avoiding pain at the end of life. Still, you can follow these suggestions (Cowley & Hager, 1995):

- Make a living will, and be sure there is someone who will draw your doctor's attention to it.

- Give someone the power of attorney, and make sure this person knows your wishes regarding medical care.

- Give your doctors specific instructions—from "Do not resuscitate" to "Do everything possible"—for specific circumstances.

- If you want to die at home, talk it over with your family and doctor.

- Check to see whether your insurance plan covers home care and hospice care.

Hospice is a program committed to making the end of life as free from pain, anxiety, and depression as possible (Gazelle, 2007; Harrison & Ford, 2007). Whereas a hospital's goals are to cure illness and prolong life, hospice care emphasizes **palliative care**, which involves reducing pain and suffering and helping individuals die with dignity (Kaasa, 2008; Miyashita & others, 2008). Health-care professionals work together to treat the dying person's symptoms, make the individual as comfortable as possible, show interest in the person and the person's family, and help them cope with death (White & others, 2008).

The hospice movement began toward the end of the 1960s in London, when a new kind of medical institution, St. Christopher's Hospice, opened. Little effort is made to prolong life at St. Christopher's—there are no heart-lung machines and there is no intensive care unit, for example. A primary goal is to bring pain under control and to help dying patients face death in a psychologically healthy way (McMillan & Small, 2007). The hospice also makes every effort to include the dying individual's family; it is believed that this strategy benefits not only the dying individual but family members as well, probably diminishing their guilt after the death (Kastenbaum, 2007).

The hospice movement has grown rapidly in the United States (Casarett & others, 2005). More than 1,500 community groups are involved nationally in establishing hospice programs. Hospices are more likely to serve people with terminal cancer than those with other life-threatening conditions (Kastenbaum, 2007). Hospice advocates underscore that it is possible to control pain for almost any dying individual and that it is possible to create an environment for the patient that is superior to that found in most hospitals (Hayslip, 1996).

Currently, approximately 90 percent of hospice care is provided in patients' homes (Hayslip & Hansson, 2007). In some cases, home-based care is provided by

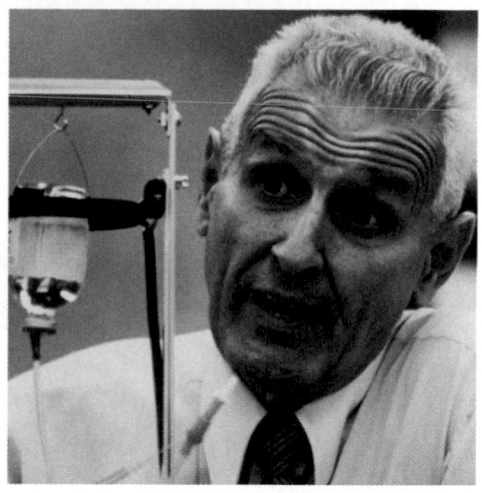

Dr. Jack Kevorkian assisted a number of people in Michigan to end their lives through active euthanasia. *Where do you stand on the use of active euthanasia?*

hospice A program committed to making the end of life as free from pain, anxiety, and depression as possible. The goals of hospice contrast with those of a hospital, which are to cure disease and prolong life.

palliative care Emphasized in hospice care, involves reducing pain and suffering and helping individuals die with dignity.

community-based health-care professionals or volunteers; in other cases, home-based care is provided by home-health-care agencies of Visiting Nurse Associations. Also, some hospice care is provided in free-standing, full-service hospice facilities and in hospice units in hospitals. To read about the work of a home hospice nurse, see the *Careers in Life-Span Development* profile.

Careers in Life-Span Development

Kathy McLaughlin, Home Hospice Nurse

Kathy McLaughlin is a home hospice nurse in Alexandria, Virginia. She provides care for individuals with terminal cancer, Alzheimer disease, and other diseases. There currently is a shortage of home hospice nurses in the United States.

McLaughlin says that she has seen too many people dying in pain, away from home, hooked up to needless machines. In her work as a home hospice nurse, she comments, "I know I'm making a difference, I just feel privileged to get the chance to meet this person who is not going to be around much longer. I want to enjoy the moment with this person. And I want them to enjoy the moment. They have great stories. They are better than novels" (McLaughlin, 2003, p. 1).

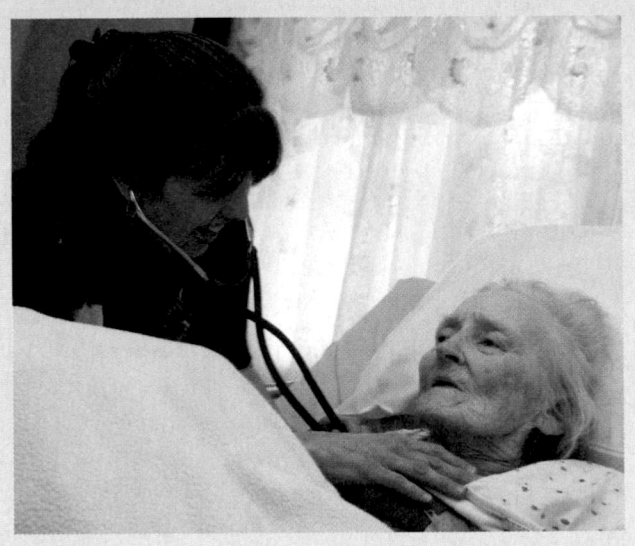

Kathy McLaughlin checks the vital signs of Kathryn Francis, 86, who is in an advanced stage of Alzheimer disease.

Researchers have found that family members provide more positive evaluations of a loved one's quality of life and better psychological adjustment themselves following the loved one's death when in-home hospice services are used than when the loved one is cared for in the final weeks of life in nursing homes, hospitals, or at home with home health nursing services (Teno & others, 2004). One study also revealed that hospice care reduced the increased mortality linked with bereavement by loved ones (Christakis & Iwashyna, 2003).

Review and Reflect: Learning Goal 2

 Evaluate Issues in Determining Death and Decisions Regarding Death

REVIEW

- What are some issues regarding the determination of death?
- What are some decisions to be made regarding life, death, and health care?

REFLECT

- Do you think assisted suicide should be legal? Explain your answer.

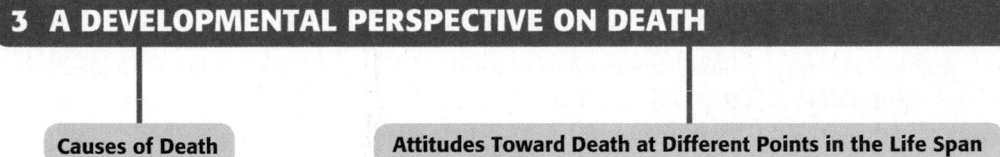

3 A DEVELOPMENTAL PERSPECTIVE ON DEATH

Causes of Death   **Attitudes Toward Death at Different Points in the Life Span**

Do the causes of death vary across the human life span? Do we have different expecta-tions about death as we develop through the life span? What are our attitudes toward death at different points in our development?

Causes of Death

Death can occur at any point in the human life span. Death can occur during prenatal development through miscarriages or stillborn births. Death can also occur during the birth process or in the first few days after birth, which usually happens because of a birth defect or because infants have not developed adequately to sustain life outside the uterus. In Chapter 4, "Physical Development in Infancy," we described *sudden infant death syn-drome (SIDS)*, in which infants stop breathing, usually during the night, and die without apparent cause (Keens & Gemmill, 2008). SIDS currently is the leading cause of infant death in the United States, with the risk highest at 2 to 4 months of age (NICHD, 2008).

In childhood, death occurs most often because of accidents or illness. Accidental death in childhood can be the consequence of such things as an automobile accident, drowning, poisoning, fire, or a fall from a high place. Major illnesses that cause death in children are heart disease, cancer, and birth defects.

Compared with childhood, death in adolescence is more likely to occur because of motor vehicle accidents, suicide, and homicide. Many motor vehicle accidents that cause death in adolescence are alcohol-related. We will examine suicide in greater depth shortly.

Older adults are more likely to die from chronic diseases, such as heart disease and cancer, whereas younger adults are more likely to die from accidents. Older adults' diseases often incapacitate before they kill, which produces a course of dying that slowly leads to death. Of course, many young and middle-aged adults die of diseases, such as heart disease and cancer.

Attitudes Toward Death at Different Points in the Life Span

The ages of children and adults influence the way they experience and think about death. A mature, adultlike conception of death includes an understanding that death is final and irreversible, that death represents the end of life, and that all living things die. Most researchers have found that as children grow, they develop a more mature approach to death (Hayslip & Hansson, 2003).

Childhood   Most researchers suggest that infants do not have even a rudimentary concept of death. However, as infants develop an attachment to a caregiver, they can experience loss or separation and an accompanying anxiety. But young children do not perceive time the way adults do. Even brief separations may be experienced as total losses. For most infants, the reappearance of the caregiver provides a continuity of existence and a reduction of anxiety. We know very little about the infant's actual experiences with bereavement, although the loss of a parent, especially if the care-giver is not replaced, can negatively affect the infant's health.

Even children 3 to 5 years of age have little or no idea of what death means. They may confuse death with sleep or ask in a puzzled way, "Why doesn't it move?" Pre-school-aged children rarely get upset by the sight of a dead animal or by being told that a person has died. They believe that the dead can be brought back to life spontaneously by magic or by giving them food or medical treatment. Young children often believe that only people who want to die, or who are bad or careless, actually die. They also may blame themselves for the death of someone they know well, illogically reasoning that the event may have happened because they disobeyed the person who died.

Sometime in the middle and late childhood years, more realistic perceptions of death develop. In one early investigation of children's perception of death, children 3 to 5 years of age denied that death exists, children 6 to 9 years of age believed that death exists but only happens to some people, and children 9 years of age and older recognized death's finality and universality (Nagy, 1948). In a review of research on children's conception of death, it was concluded that children probably do not view death as universal and irreversible until about 9 years of age (Cuddy-Casey & Orvaschel, 1997). Most children under 7 do not see death as likely. Those who do, perceive it as reversible.

An expert on death and dying, Robert Kastenbaum (2007) takes a different view on developmental dimensions of death and dying. He reasons that even very young children are acutely aware of and concerned about *separation* and *loss,* just as attachment theorist John Bowlby (1980) does. Kastenbaum also says that many children work hard at trying to understand death. Thus, instead of viewing young children as having illogical perceptions of death, Kastenbaum thinks a more accurate stance is to view them as having concerns about death and striving to understand it.

The following clarification of children's experience with the death of others was provided by Bert Hayslip and Robert Hansson (2003). They concluded that "experiences with the deaths of grandparents, friends, heros (sports figures, rock stars), and parents are particularly powerful influences on children's awareness of death, as are culturally relevant experiences such as the Columbine High School shootings in 1999, . . . the terrorist attack on the World Trade Center in 2001, and the deaths of such public figures as Kurt Cobain, Dale Earnhardt, Sr., Selena, Princess Diana, [and] John F. Kennedy" (Hayslip & Hansson, 2003, p. 440). The death of a parent is especially difficult for children (Sood & others, 2006). When a child's parent dies, the child's school performance and peer relationships often worsen. For some children, as well as adults, a parent's death can be devastating and result in a hypersensitivity about death, including a fear of losing others close to the individual. In some cases, loss of a sibling can result in similar negative outcomes (Sood & others, 2006). However, a number of factors, such as the quality of the relationship and type of the death (whether due to an accident, long-standing illness, suicide, or murder, for example), can influence the individual's development following the death of a person close to the individual.

Most psychologists emphasize that honesty is the best strategy in discussing death with children. Treating the concept as unmentionable is thought to be an inappropriate strategy, yet most of us have grown up in a society in which death is rarely discussed. In one study, the attitudes of 30,000 young adults toward death were evaluated (Shneidman, 1973). More than 30 percent said they could not recall any discussion of death during their childhood. An equal number said that, although death was discussed, the discussion took place in an uncomfortable atmosphere. Almost one of every two respondents said that the death of a grandparent was their first personal encounter with death.

In addition to honesty, what other strategies can be adopted in discussing death with children? The best response to the child's query about death might depend on the child's maturity level (Aiken, 2000). For example, the preschool child requires a less elaborate explanation than an older child. Death can be explained to preschool children in simple physical and biological terms. Actually, what young children need more than elaborate explanations of death is reassurance that they are loved and will not be abandoned. Regardless of children's age, adults should be sensitive and sympathetic, encouraging them to express their own feelings and ideas.

It is not unusual for terminally ill children to distance themselves from their parents as they approach the final phase of their illness. The distancing may be due to the depression that many dying patients experience, or it may be a child's way of protecting parents from the overwhelming grief they will experience at the death. Most dying children know they have a terminal illness. Their developmental level, social support, and coping skills influence how well they cope with knowing they will die.

Adolescence   In adolescence, the prospect of death, like the prospect of aging, is regarded as a notion so remote that it does not have much relevance. The subject of death may be avoided, glossed over, kidded about, neutralized, and controlled by a cool, spectator-like orientation. This perspective is typical of the adolescent's self-conscious thought; however, some adolescents do show a concern for death, both in trying to fathom its meaning and in confronting the prospect of their own demise (Baxter, Stuart, & Stewart, 1998).

Deaths of friends, siblings, parents, or grandparents bring death to the forefront of adolescents' lives. Deaths of peers who commit suicide "may be especially difficult for adolescents who feel . . . guilty for having failed to prevent the suicide or feel that they should have died, or . . . feel they are being rejected by their friends who hold them responsible for the death (Hayslip & Hansson, 2003, p. 441).

Adolescents develop more abstract conceptions of death than children do. For example, adolescents describe death in terms of darkness, light, transition, or nothingness (Wenestam & Wass, 1987). They also develop religious and philosophical views about the nature of death and whether there is life after death.

You will also recall (from Chapter 11, "Physical and Cognitive Development in Adolescence") the concepts of adolescent egocentrism and personal fable—adolescents' preoccupation with themselves and their belief that they are invincible and unique. Thus, it is not unusual for adolescents to think that they are somehow immune to death and that death is something that happens to other people but not to them.

Adulthood   There is no evidence that a special orientation toward death develops in early adulthood. An increase in consciousness about death accompanies individuals' awareness that they are aging, which usually intensifies in middle adulthood. In our discussion of middle adulthood, we indicated that midlife is a time when adults begin to think more about how much time is left in their lives. Researchers have found that middle-aged adults actually fear death more than do young adults or older adults (Kalish & Reynolds, 1976). Older adults, though, think about death more and talk about it more in conversation with others than do middle-aged and young adults. They also have more direct experience with death as their friends and relatives become ill and die (Hayslip & Hansson, 2003). Older adults are forced to examine the meanings of life and death more frequently than are younger adults.

Younger adults who are dying often feel cheated more than do older adults who are dying (Kalish, 1987). Younger adults are more likely to feel they have not had the opportunity to do what they want to with their lives. Younger adults perceive they are losing what they might achieve; older adults perceive they are losing what they have.

In old age, one's own death may take on an appropriateness it lacked in earlier years. Some of the increased thinking and conversing about death, and an increased sense of integrity developed through a positive life review, may help older adults accept death. Older adults are less likely to have unfinished business than are younger adults. They usually do not have children who need to be guided to maturity, their spouses are more likely to be dead, and they are less likely to have work-related projects that require completion. Lacking such anticipations, death may be less emotionally painful to them. Even among older adults, however, attitudes toward death vary. One 82-year-old woman declared that she had lived her life and was ready to see it come to an end. Another 82-year-old woman declared that death would be a regrettable interruption of her participation in activities and relationships.

What are children's and adolescents' attitudes about death?

How might older adults' attitudes about death differ from those of younger adults?

> *W*e keep on thinking and rethinking death after we have passed through childhood's hour.
>
> —ROBERT KASTENBAUM
> *Contemporary Gerontologist, Arizona State University*

Review and Reflect: Learning Goal 3

 3 **Discuss Death and Attitudes About It at Different Points in Development**

REVIEW

• What are some developmental changes in the cause of death?
• What are some attitudes about death at different points in development?

REFLECT

• What is your current attitude about death? Has it changed since you were an adolescent? If so, how?

4 FACING ONE'S OWN DEATH

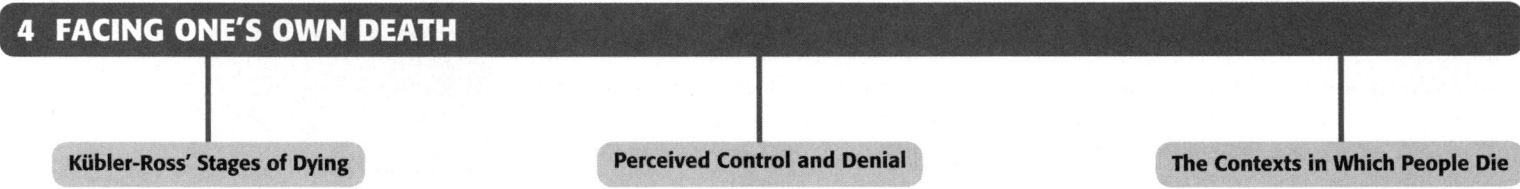

Kübler-Ross' Stages of Dying   Perceived Control and Denial   The Contexts in Which People Die

Knowledge of death's inevitability permits us to establish priorities and structure our time accordingly. As we age, these priorities and structurings change in recognition of diminishing future time. Values concerning the most important uses of time also change. For example, when asked how they would spend six remaining months of life, younger adults described such activities as traveling and accomplishing things they previously had not done; older adults described more inner-focused activities—contemplation and meditation, for example (Kalish & Reynolds, 1976).

Most dying individuals want an opportunity to make some decisions regarding their own life and death (Kastenbaum, 2007). Some individuals want to complete unfinished business; they want time to resolve problems and conflicts and to put their affairs in order.

A recent study examined the concerns of 36 dying individuals from 38 to 92 years of age with a mean age of 68 (Terry & others, 2006). The three areas of concern that consistently appeared were (1) privacy and autonomy, mainly in regard to their families; (2) inadequate information about physical changes and medication as they approached death; (3) the motivation to shorten their life, which was indicated by all patients.

Kübler-Ross' Stages of Dying

Might there be a sequence of stages we go through as we face death? Elisabeth Kübler-Ross (1969) divided the behavior and thinking of dying persons into five stages: denial and isolation, anger, bargaining, depression, and acceptance.

Denial and isolation is Kübler-Ross' first stage of dying, in which the person denies that death is really going to take place. The person may say, "No, it can't be me. It's not possible." This is a common reaction to terminal illness. However, denial is usually only a temporary defense. It is eventually replaced with increased awareness when the person is confronted with such matters as financial considerations, unfinished business, and worry about surviving family members.

Anger is Kübler-Ross' second stage of dying, in which the dying person recognizes that denial can no longer be maintained. Denial often gives way to anger, resentment, rage, and envy. The dying person's question is, "Why me?" At this point, the person becomes increasingly difficult to care for as anger may become displaced and

denial and isolation Kübler-Ross' first stage of dying, in which the dying person denies that she or he is really going to die.

anger Kübler-Ross' second stage of dying, in which the dying person's denial gives way to anger, resentment, rage, and envy.

projected onto physicians, nurses, family members, and even God. The realization of loss is great, and those who symbolize life, energy, and competent functioning are especially salient targets of the dying person's resentment and jealousy.

Bargaining is Kübler-Ross' third stage of dying, in which the person develops the hope that death can somehow be postponed or delayed. Some persons enter into a bargaining or negotiation—often with God—as they try to delay their death. Psychologically, the person is saying, "Yes, me, but . . ." In exchange for a few more days, weeks, or months of life, the person promises to lead a reformed life dedicated to God or to the service of others.

Depression is Kübler-Ross' fourth stage of dying, in which the dying person comes to accept the certainty of death. At this point, a period of depression or preparatory grief may appear. The dying person may become silent, refuse visitors, and spend much of the time crying or grieving. This behavior is normal and is an effort to disconnect the self from love objects. Attempts to cheer up the dying person at this stage should be discouraged, says Kübler-Ross, because the dying person has a need to contemplate impending death.

Acceptance is Kübler-Ross' fifth stage of dying, in which the person develops a sense of peace, an acceptance of one's fate, and in many cases, a desire to be left alone. In this stage, feelings and physical pain may be virtually absent. Kübler-Ross describes this fifth stage as the end of the dying struggle, the final resting stage before death. A summary of Kübler-Ross' dying stages is presented in Figure 20.3.

What is the current evaluation of Kübler-Ross' approach? According to Robert Kastenbaum (2007), there are some problems with Kübler-Ross' approach:

- The existence of the five-stage sequence has not been demonstrated by either Kübler-Ross or independent research.

- The stage interpretation neglected the patients' situations, including relationship support, specific effects of illness, family obligations, and institutional climate in which they were interviewed.

However, Kübler-Ross' pioneering efforts were important in calling attention to those who are attempting to cope with life-threatening illnesses. She did much to encourage attention to the quality of life for dying persons and their families.

Because of the criticisms of Kübler-Ross' stages, some psychologists prefer to describe them not as stages but as potential reactions to dying. At any one moment, a number of emotions may wax and wane. Hope, disbelief, bewilderment, anger, and acceptance may come and go as individuals try to make sense of what is happening to them.

In facing their own death, some individuals struggle until the end, desperately trying to hang on to their lives. Acceptance of death never comes for them. Some psychologists believe that the harder individuals fight to avoid the inevitable death they face and the more they deny it, the more difficulty they will have in dying peacefully and in a dignified way; other psychologists argue that not confronting death until the end may be adaptive for some individuals (Lifton, 1977).

The extent to which people have found meaning and purpose in their lives is linked with how they approach death. A study of 160 individuals with less than three months to live revealed that those who had found purpose and meaning in their lives felt the least despair in the final weeks, whereas dying individuals who saw no reason for living were the most distressed and wanted to hasten death (McClain, Rosenfeld, & Breitbart, 2003). In this and other studies, spirituality helped to buffer dying individuals from severe depression (Smith, McCullough, & Poll, 2003).

Perceived Control and Denial

Perceived control may work as an adaptive strategy for some older adults who face death. When individuals are led to believe they can influence and control events—such as prolonging their lives—they may become more alert and cheerful. Remember from Chapter 17 that giving nursing home residents options for control improved their attitudes and increased their longevity (Rodin & Langer, 1977).

FIGURE 20.3 Kübler-Ross' Stages of Dying. According to Elisabeth Kübler-Ross, we go through five stages of dying: denial and isolation, anger, bargaining, depression, and acceptance. *Does everyone go through these stages, or go through them in the same order? Explain.*

bargaining Kübler-Ross' third stage of dying, in which the dying person develops the hope that death can somehow be postponed.

depression Kübler-Ross' fourth stage of dying, in which the dying person comes to accept the certainty of her or his death. A period of depression or preparatory grief may appear.

acceptance Kübler-Ross' fifth stage of dying, in which the dying person develops a sense of peace, an acceptance of her or his fate, and, in many cases, a desire to be left alone.

*M*an is the only animal
that finds his own existence a
problem he has to solve and
from which he cannot escape.
In the same sense man is the
only animal who knows he
must die.

—ERICH FROMM
American Psychotherapist,
20th Century

Denial also may be a fruitful way for some individuals to approach death. It can be adaptive or maladaptive. Denial can be used to avoid the destructive impact of shock by delaying the necessity of dealing with one's death. Denial can insulate the individual from having to cope with intense feelings of anger and hurt; however, if denial keeps us from having a life-saving operation, it clearly is maladaptive. Denial is neither good nor bad; its adaptive qualities need to be evaluated on an individual basis.

The Contexts in Which People Die

For dying individuals, the context in which they die is important. More than 50 percent of Americans die in hospitals, and nearly 20 percent die in nursing homes. Some people spend their final days in isolation and fear (Clay, 1997). An increasing number of people choose to die in the humane atmosphere of a hospice.

Hospitals offer several important advantages to the dying individual; for example, professional staff members are readily available, and the medical technology present may prolong life. But a hospital may not be the best place for many people to die (Pantilat & Isaac, 2008). Most individuals say they would rather die at home (Kalish & Reynolds, 1976). Many feel, however, that they will be a burden at home, that there is limited space there, and that dying at home may alter relationships. Individuals who are facing death also worry about the competency and availability of emergency medical treatment if they remain at home.

Review and Reflect: Learning Goal 4

4 **Explain the Psychological Aspects Involved in Facing One's Own Death and the Contexts in Which People Die**

REVIEW

- What are Kübler-Ross' five stages of dying? What conclusions can be reached about them?
- What roles do perceived control and denial play in facing one's own death?
- What are the contexts in which people die?

REFLECT

- How do you think you will psychologically handle facing your own death?

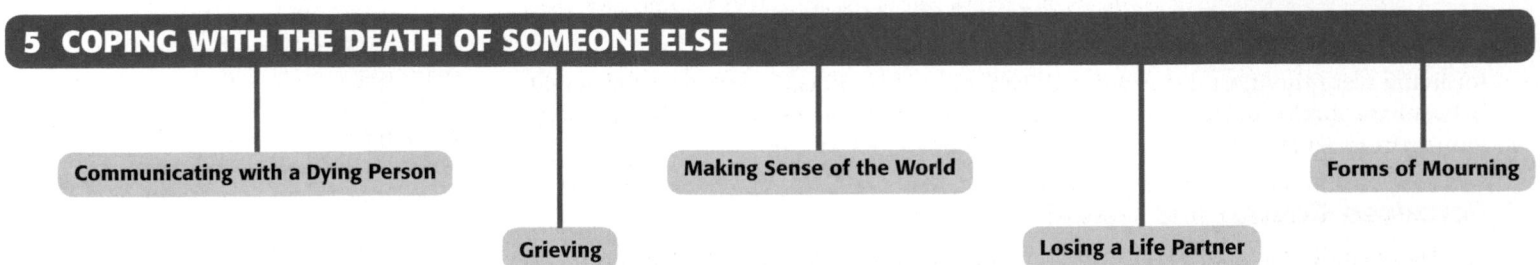

5 COPING WITH THE DEATH OF SOMEONE ELSE

Communicating with a Dying Person

Grieving

Making Sense of the World

Losing a Life Partner

Forms of Mourning

Loss can come in many forms in our lives—divorce, a pet's death, loss of a job—but no loss is greater than that which comes through the death of someone we love and care for—a parent, sibling, spouse, relative, or friend. In the ratings of life's stresses that require the most adjustment, death of a spouse is given the highest number. How should we communicate with a dying individual? How do we cope with the death of someone we love?

Communicating with a Dying Person

Most psychologists argue that it is best for dying individuals to know that they are dying and that significant others know they are dying so they can interact and communicate with each other on the basis of this mutual knowledge (Banja, 2005). What are some of the advantages of this open awareness for the dying individual? First, dying individuals can close their lives in accord with their own ideas about proper dying. Second, they may be able to complete some plans and projects, can make arrangements for survivors, and can participate in decisions about a funeral and burial. Third, dying individuals have the opportunity to reminisce, to converse with others who have been important in their life, and to end life conscious of what life has been like. And fourth, dying individuals have more understanding of what is happening within their bodies and what the medical staff is doing to them (Kalish, 1981).

In addition to keeping communication open, what are some suggestions for conversing with a dying individual? Some experts reason that conversation should not focus on mental pathology or preparation for death but should focus on strengths of the individual and preparation for the remainder of life. Since external accomplishments are not possible, communication should be directed more at internal growth. Keep in mind also that important support for a dying individual may come not only from mental health professionals, but also from nurses, physicians, a spouse, or intimate friends (DeSpelder & Strickland, 2005). In the *Applications in Life-Span Development* interlude, you can read further about effective communication strategies with a dying person.

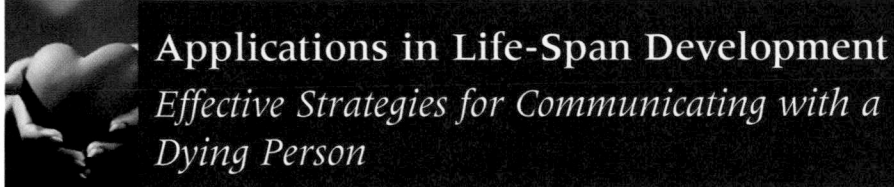

Applications in Life-Span Development
Effective Strategies for Communicating with a Dying Person

The following are effective strategies for communicating with a dying person:

1. Establish your presence, be at the same eye level; don't be afraid to touch the dying person—dying individuals are often starved for human touch.

2. Eliminate distraction—for example, ask if it is okay to turn off the TV. Realize that excessive small talk can be a distraction.

3. Dying individuals who are very frail often have little energy. If the dying person you are visiting is very frail, you may not want to visit for very long.

4. Don't insist that the dying person feel acceptance about death if the dying person wants to deny the reality of the situation; on the other hand, don't insist on denial if the dying individual indicates acceptance.

5. Allow the dying person to express guilt or anger; encourage the expression of feelings.

6. Don't be afraid to ask the person what the expected outcome for the illness is. Discuss alternatives, unfinished business.

7. Sometimes dying individuals don't have access to other people. Ask the dying person if there is anyone he or she would like to see that you can contact.

8. Encourage the dying individual to reminisce, especially if you have memories in common.

9. Talk with the individual when she or he wishes to talk. If this is impossible, make an appointment and keep it.

10. Express your regard for the dying individual. Don't be afraid to express love, and don't be afraid to say good-bye.

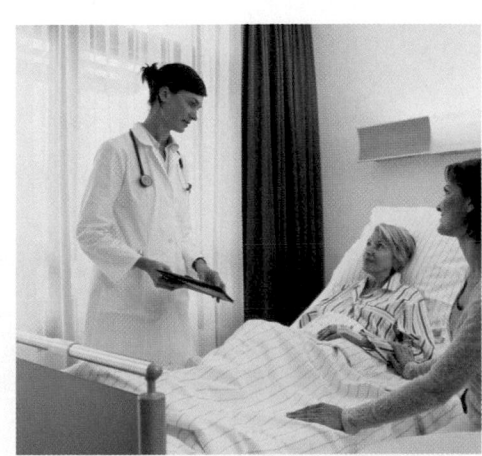

What are some good strategies for communicating with a dying person?

Grieving

Our exploration of grief focuses on dimensions of grieving, the dual-process model of coping with bereavement, and cultural diversity in healthy grieving.

Dimensions of Grieving   **Grief** is the emotional numbness, disbelief, separation anxiety, despair, sadness, and loneliness that accompany the loss of someone we love. Grief is not a simple emotional state but rather a complex, evolving process with multiple dimensions (Lund, 2007). In this view, pining for the lost person is one important dimension. Pining or yearning reflects an intermittent, recurrent wish or need to recover the lost person. A recent study revealed that the death of a loved one is most frequently followed by yearning and acceptance with most of the negative feelings associated with the death diminishing by six months after the death (Maciejewski & others, 2007). In this study, yearning was more common than depression following a loved one's death. Another important dimension of grief is separation anxiety, which not only includes pining and preoccupation with thoughts of the deceased person but also focuses on places and things associated with the deceased, as well as crying or sighing. Grief may also involve despair and sadness, which include a sense of hopelessness and defeat, depressive symptoms, apathy, loss of meaning for activities that used to involve the person who is gone, and growing desolation (Ringdal & others, 2001).

These feelings occur repeatedly shortly after a loss (Moules & others, 2004). As time passes, pining and protest over the loss tend to diminish, although episodes of depression and apathy may remain or increase. The sense of separation anxiety and loss may continue to the end of one's life, but most of us emerge from grief's tears, turning our attention once again to productive tasks and regaining a more positive view of life (Carrington & Bogetz, 2004).

The grieving process is more like a roller-coaster ride than an orderly progression of stages with clear-cut time frames (Lund, 2007). The ups and downs of grief often involve rapidly changing emotions, meeting the challenges of learning new skills, detecting personal weaknesses and limitations, creating new patterns of behavior, and forming new friendships and relationships (Feldon, 2003). For most individuals, grief becomes more manageable over time, with fewer abrupt highs and lows. But many grieving spouses report that even though time has brought some healing, they have never gotten over their loss. They have just learned to live with it.

Cognitive factors are involved in the severitiy of grief after a loved one has died. One study focused on 329 adults who had suffered the loss of a first-degree relative (Boelen, van den Bout, & van den Hout, 2003). The more negative beliefs and self-blame the adults had, the more servere were their symptoms of traumatic grief, depression, and anxiety.

Long-term grief is sometimes masked and can predispose individuals to become depressed and even suicidal (Kastenbaum, 2007). Good family communication can help reduce the incidence of depression and suicidal thoughts. For example, in one study, family members who communicated poorly with each other had more negative grief reactions six months later than those who communicated effectively with each other just after the loss of a family member (Schoka & Hayslip, 1999).

An estimated 80 to 90 percent of survivors experience normal or uncomplicated grief reactions that include sadness and even disbelief or considerable anguish. By six months after their loss, they accept it as a reality, are more optimistic about the future, and function competently in their everyday lives. However, six months after their loss, approximately 10 to 20 percent of survivors have difficulty moving on with their life, feel numb or detached, believe their life is empty without the deceased, and feel that the future has no meaning. Initially referred to as complicated grief, leading expert Holly Prigerson and her colleagues (Boelen & Prigerson, 2007; Maciejewski & others, 2007) recently have advocated use of the term **prolonged grief** to describe this type of grief that involves enduring despair and is still unresolved over an extended period of time. Prolonged grief usually has negative consequences on physical and mental

---

*E*veryone can master grief
but he who has it.

—WILLIAM SHAKESPEARE
English Playwright, 17th Century

---

grief The emotional numbness, disbelief, separation anxiety, despair, sadness, and loneliness that accompany the loss of someone we love.

prolonged grief Grief that involves enduring despair and is still unresolved over an extended period of time.

health (Bonanno & others, 2007; Piper & others, 2007; Wortman & Boerner, 2007). A person who loses someone he or she was emotionally dependent on is often at greatest risk for developing prolonged grief (Johnson & others, 2007). A recent study found that therapy focused on motivational interviewing, emotion coping, and communication skills was effective in reducing prolonged grief (Zuckoff & others, 2006).

Another type of grief is *disenfranchised grief*, which describes an individual's grief over a deceased person that is a socially ambiguous loss that can't be openly mourned or supported (Read & Elliott, 2007; Reilly & others, 2008). Examples of disenfranchised grief include a relationship that isn't socially recognized such as an ex-spouse, a hidden loss such as an abortion, and circumstances of the death that are stigmatized such as death because of AIDS. Disenfranchised grief may intensify an individual's grief because it cannot be publicly acknowledged. This type of grief may be hidden or repressed for many years, only to be reawakened by later deaths.

Dual-Process Model of Coping with Bereavement

The **dual-process model** of coping with bereavement consists of two main dimensions: (1) loss-oriented stressors, and (2) restoration-oriented stressors (Stroebe, Schut, & Stroebe, 2005). Loss-oriented stressors focus on the deceased individual and can include grief work and both positive and negative reappraisal of the loss. A positive reappraisal of the loss might include acknowledging that death brought relief at the end of suffering, whereas a negative reappraisal might involve yearning for the loved one and rumination about the death. Restoration-oriented stressors involve the secondary stressors that emerge as indirect outcomes of bereavement. They can include a changing identity (such as from "wife" to "widow") and mastering skills (such as dealing with finances). Restoration rebuilds "shattered assumptions about the world and one's own place in it."

In the dual-process model, effective coping with bereavement often involves an oscillation between coping with loss and coping with restoration (Wijnqaards-de Meij & others, 2008). Earlier models often emphasized a sequence of coping with loss through such strategies as grief work as an initial phase, followed by restoration efforts. However, in the dual-process model, coping with loss and engaging in restoration can be carried out concurrently (Richardson, 2007). According to this model, the person coping with death might be involved in grief group therapy while settling the affairs of the loved one. Oscillation might occur in the short term during a particular day as well as across weeks, months, and even years. Although loss and restoration coping can occur concurrently, over time there often is an initial emphasis on coping with loss followed by greater emphasis on restoration over time (Milberg & others, 2008).

Coping and Type of Death

The impact of death on surviving individuals is strongly influenced by the circumstances under which the death occurs (Hansson & Stroebe, 2007; Wortman & Boerner, 2007). Deaths that are sudden, untimely, violent, or traumatic are likely to have more intense and prolonged effects on surviving individuals and make the coping process more difficult for them (Murphy & others, 2003; Sveen & Walby, 2008). Such deaths often are accompanied by post-traumatic stress disorder (PTSD) symptoms, such as intrusive thoughts, flashbacks, nightmares, sleep disturbance, problems in concentrating, and others (Raphael, Taylor, & McAndrew, 2008).

Cultural Diversity in Healthy Grieving

Some approaches to grieving emphasize the importance of breaking bonds with the deceased and returning to autonomous lifestyles. People who persist in holding on to the deceased are believed to be in need of therapy. However, some doubt has been cast on whether this recommendation is always the best therapeutic advice (Reisman, 2001).

Analyses of non-Western cultures suggest that beliefs about continuing bonds with the deceased vary extensively. Maintenance of ties with the deceased is accepted and sustained in the religious rituals of Japan. In the Hopi of Arizona, the deceased are forgotten as quickly as possible and life is carried on as usual. Their funeral ritual concludes with a break-off between mortals and spirits. The diversity of grieving is nowhere

How might grieving vary across individuals and cultures?

dual-process model A model of coping with bereavement that emphasizes oscillation between two dimensions: (1) loss-oriented stressors, and (2) restoration-oriented stressors.

more clear than in two Muslim societies—one in Egypt, the other in Bali. In Egypt, the bereaved are encouraged to dwell at length on their grief, surrounded by others who relate similarly tragic accounts and express their own sorrow. By contrast, in Bali, the bereaved are encouraged to laugh and be joyful.

Consider also the responses of parents whose sons died in two Israeli wars, 13 and 4 years earlier (Rubin & Malkinson, 2001; Schuchter & Zisook, 1993). Even many years after the death of their sons, the Israeli parents showed a strong involvement with them. They idealized the lost sons in ways that were not present in the descriptions by a control group of parents of sons who had recently left home.

In sum, people grieve in a variety of ways (Hayes, Yeh, & Eisenberg, 2007). The diverse grieving patterns are culturally embedded practices. Thus, there is no one right, ideal way to grieve. There are many different ways to feel about a deceased person and no set series of stages that the bereaved must pass through to become well adjusted. The stoic widower may need to cry out over his loss at times. The weeping widow may need to put her husband's wishes aside as she becomes the financial manager of her estate. What is needed is an understanding that healthy coping with the death of a loved one involves growth, flexibility, and appropriateness within a cultural context.

Making Sense of the World

One beneficial aspect of grieving is that it stimulates many individuals to try to make sense of their world (Kalish, 1981). A common occurrence is to go over again and again all of the events that led up to the death. In the days and weeks after the death, the closest family members share experiences with each other, sometimes reminiscing over family experiences. In one study, women who became widowed in midlife were challenged by the crisis of their husband's death to examine meaningful directions for their lives (Danforth & Glass, 2001). Another study found that mourners who expressed positive themes of hope showed better adjustment than those who focused on negative themes of pain and suffering (Gamino & Sewell, 2004).

Each individual may offer a piece of death's puzzle. "When I saw him last Saturday, he looked as though he were rallying," says one family member. "Do you think it might have had something to do with his sister's illness?" remarks another. "I doubt it, but I heard from an aide that he fell going to the bathroom that morning," comments yet another. "That explains the bruise on his elbow," says the first individual. "No wonder he told me that he was angry because he could not seem to do anything right," chimes in a fourth family member. So it goes in the attempt to understand why someone who was rallying on Saturday was dead on Wednesday.

When a death is caused by an accident or a disaster, the effort to make sense of it is pursued more vigorously. As added pieces of news come trickling in, they are integrated into the puzzle. The bereaved want to put the death into a perspective that they can understand—divine intervention, a curse from a neighboring tribe, a logical sequence of cause and effect, or whatever it may be. A recent study of more than 1,000 college students found that making sense was an important factor in their grieving of a violent loss by accident, homicide, or suicide (Currier, Holland, & Neimeyer, 2006).

Losing a Life Partner

Those left behind after the death of an intimate partner often suffer profound grief and often endure financial loss, loneliness, increased physical illness, and psychological disorders, including depression (Kowalski & Bondmass, 2008; Zisook & Kendler, 2007). How surviving spouses cope varies considerably (Ott & others, 2007). A study

Mary Assanful (*front right* with other former restaurant workers) worked at Windows on the World restaurant located in the World Trade Center and lost her job when terrorist attacks came. She says that she still is not herself and regularly has nightmares. A Ghana native, Mary is still unemployed. She has joined several other workers who are now planning to return by opening a restaurant near Ground Zero. They hope the new restaurant will honor their coworkers who died and provide a focus and meaning for their still-unsettled lives. Mary says that since they have been working on this new project, her mind has calmed somewhat.

that included data from three years predeath to 18 months postdeath revealed that nearly half of surviving spouses experienced low levels of distress consistently over the $4\frac{1}{2}$ years (Bonanno, Wortman, & Nesse, 2004). Another study found that widowed individuals were more likely to increase their religious and spiritual beliefs following the death of a spouse, and this increase was linked with a lower level of grief (Brown & others, 2004). And a recent study concluded that chronic grief was more likely to characterize bereaved spouses who were highly dependent on their spouse (Ott & others, 2007).

Widows outnumber widowers by the ratio of 5 to 1, because women live longer than men, because women tend to marry men older than themselves, and because a widowed man is more likely to remarry. Widowed women are probably the poorest group in America. And the negative economic consequences for widowed women are greater for African American and Latino women than for non-Latino White women (Angel, Jimenez, & Angel, 2007). A recent study of Mexican Americans 65 years and older revealed that risk of death linked to widowhood was the highest in the first two years following the spouse's death (Stimpson & others, 2007). A study of African American widows found that storytelling was at the heart of widows' description of their bereavement experience (Rogers, 2004). Six themes were identified in their stories: awareness of death, caregiving, getting through, moving on, changing feelings, and financial security.

Many widows are lonely (Lund, 2007). The poorer and less educated they are, the lonelier they tend to be. The bereaved are also at increased risk for many health problems, including death (Ajdacic-Gross & others, 2008; Elwert & Christakis, 2008). The following *Research in Life-Span Development* interlude examines the relation of widowhood to health.

Research in Life-Span Development
The Women's Health Initiative Study of Widowhood and Health

One three-year longitudinal study of more than 130,000 women aged 50 to 79 years in the United States as part of the Women's Health Initiative examined the relation of widowhood to physical and mental health, health behaviors, and health outcomes (Wilcox & others, 2003). Women were categorized as (1) remaining married, (2) transitioning from married to widowed, (3) remaining widowed, and (4) transitioning from widowed to married. Widows were further subdivided into the recently widowed (widowed for less than one year) and longer-term widowed (widowed for more than one year).

The measures used to assess the older women's health were:

- *Physical health.* Blood pressure was assessed after five minutes of quiet rest using the average of two readings with 30 seconds between the readings. Hypertension was defined as more than 140/90. Body mass index (BMI) was calculated and used to determine whether a woman was obese. A health survey assessed physical function and health status.

- *Mental health.* Depressive symptoms were assessed by a six-item depression scale, with participants rating the frequency of their depressed thoughts during the past week. The participants' self-report of antidepressant medicine use was also obtained. Information about social functioning and mental health was based on participants' responses on the Social Functioning Scale (Ware, Kosinski, & Dewey, 2000).

- *Health behaviors.* Dietary behaviors were assessed with a modified version of the National Cancer Institute—Health Habits and History Questionnaire. Participants also were asked if they smoked tobacco, and if so, how much. To assess physical activity, participants were asked how often they walked outside the home each week and the extent to which they engaged in strenuous or moderate exercise. To assess health-care use, they were asked whether they had visited their doctor in the past year.

- *Health outcomes.* Cardiovascular disease and cancer occurrences were assessed annually and any overnight hospitalizations were noted.

At the beginning of the three-year study, married women reported better physical and mental health, and better health in general, than widowed women. Women who remained married over the three-year period of the study showed stability in mental health, recent widows experienced marked impairments in mental health, and longer-term widows showed stability or slight improvements in mental health. Both groups of widows (recent and longer-term) reported more unintentional weight loss across the three years. The findings underscore the resilience of older women and their capacity to reestablish connections but point to the need for services that strengthen social support for those who have difficulty during the transition from marriage to widowhood.

Optimal adjustment after a death depends on several factors. Women do better than men largely because, in our society, women are responsible for the emotional life of a couple, whereas men usually manage the finances and material goods (Fry, 2001). Thus, women have better networks of friends, closer relationships with relatives, and experience in taking care of themselves psychologically (Antonucci, Akiyama, & Sherman, 2007). Older widows do better than younger widows, perhaps because the death of a partner is more expected for older women. For their part, widowers usually have more money than widows do, and they are much more likely to remarry.

For either widows or widowers, social support helps them adjust to the death of a spouse (Schulz, Hebert, & Boerner, 2008; Walsh, 2008; Wortman & Boerner, 2007). The Widow-to-Widow program, begun in the 1960s, provides support for newly widowed women. Volunteer widows reach out to other widows, introducing them to others who may have similar problems, leading group discussions, and organizing social activities. The program has been adopted by the American Association of Retired Persons and disseminated throughout the United States as the Widowed Person's Service. The model has since been adopted by numerous community organizations to provide support for those going through a difficult transition. Other widow support groups also are often beneficial in reducing bereaved spouses' depression (Maruyama & Atencio, 2008).

Researchers have found that religiosity and coping skills are related to well-being following the loss of a spouse in late adulthood (Leighton, 2008). Further, a recent study revealed that compared with continually married counterparts, 50-year-old and older adults who experienced the death of a spouse reported a higher participation in volunteer work several years after the death (Li, 2007). The volunteer work helped to protect the spouses from depressive symptoms, and an increase in volunteer hours enhanced their self-efficacy. Another recent study also found that when older adults helped others following the death of a spouse, they experienced an accelerated decline in depressive symptoms (Brown & others, 2008).

Forms of Mourning

One decision facing the bereaved is what to do with the body. Approximately 80 percent of corpses are disposed of by burial, the remaining 20 percent by cremation (Cremation Association of America, 2000). Cremation is more popular in the Pacific region of the United States, less popular in the South. Cremation also is more popular in Canada than in the United States and most popular of all in Japan and many other Asian countries.

The funeral is an important aspect of mourning in many cultures. In one study, bereaved individuals who were personally religious derived more psychological benefits from a funeral, participated more actively in the rituals, and adjusted more positively to the loss (Hayslip, Edmondson, & Guarnaccia, 1999).

A widow leading a funeral procession in the United States.

A crowd gathered at a cremation ceremony in Bali, Indonesia, balancing decorative containers on their heads.

The funeral industry has been the source of controversy in recent years. Funeral directors and their supporters argue that the funeral provides a form of closure to the relationship with the deceased, especially when there is an open casket. Their critics claim that funeral directors are just trying to make money and that embalming is grotesque. One way to avoid being exploited during bereavement is to purchase funeral arrangements in advance. However, in one survey, only 24 percent of individuals 60 and over had made any funeral arrangements (Kalish & Reynolds, 1976).

In some cultures, a ceremonial meal is held after death; in others, a black armband is worn for one year following a death. Cultures vary in how they practice mourning. To learn about two cultures with extensive mourning systems, see the *Diversity in Life-Span Development* interlude.

Diversity in Life-Span Development
The Amish, Traditional Judaism, and Mourning

The family and the community have important roles in mourning in some cultures. Two of those cultures are the Amish and traditional Judaism (Worthington, 1989).

The Amish are a conservative group with approximately 80,000 members in the United States, Ontario, and several small settlements in South and Central America. The Amish live in a family-oriented society in which family and community support are essential for survival. Today, they live at the same unhurried pace as that of their ancestors, using horses instead of cars and facing death with the same steadfast faith as their forebears. At the time of death, close neighbors assume the responsibility of notifying others of the death. The Amish community handles virtually all aspects of the funeral.

The funeral service is held in a barn in warmer months and in a house during colder months. Calm acceptance of death, influenced by a deep religious faith, is an integral part of the Amish culture. Following the funeral, a high level of support is given to the bereaved family for at least a year. Visits to the family, special scrapbooks and handmade items for the family, new work projects started for the widow, and quilting days that combine fellowship and productivity are among the supports given to the bereaved family. A profound example of the Amish culture's religious faith and acceptance of death occurred after Charles Roberts shot and killed five Amish schoolgirls and then apparently took his own life in October 2006 in the small town of Bart Township, Pennsylvania. Soon after the murders and suicide, members of the Amish community visited his widow and offered their support and forgiveness.

A funeral procession of horse-drawn buggies on their way to the burial of five young Amish girls who were murdered in October 2006. A remarkable aspect of their mourning involved the outpouring of support and forgiveness they gave to the widow of the murderer.

The family and community also have specific and important roles in mourning in traditional Judaism. The program of mourning is divided into graduated time periods, each with its appropriate practices. The observance of these practices is required of the spouse and the immediate blood relatives of the deceased. The first period is *aninut,* the period between death and burial. The next two periods make up *avelut,* or mourning proper. The first of these is *shivah,* a period of seven days, which commences with the burial. It is followed by *sheloshim,* the 30-day period following the burial, including shivah. At the end of sheloshim, the mourning process is considered over for all but one's parents. For parents, mourning continues for 11 months, although observances are minimal.

The seven-day period of the shivah is especially important in traditional Judaism. The mourners, sitting together as a group through an extended period, have an opportunity to project their feelings to the group as a whole. Visits from others during shivah may help the mourner deal with feelings of guilt. After shivah, the mourner is encouraged to resume normal social interaction. In fact, it is customary for the mourners to walk together a short distance as a symbol of their return to society. In its entirety, the elaborate mourning system of traditional Judaism is designed to promote personal growth and to reintegrate the individual into the community.

Review and Reflect: Learning Goal 5

5 **Identify Ways to Cope with the Death of Another Person**

REVIEW

- What are some strategies for communicating with a dying person?
- What is the nature of grieving?
- How is making sense of the world a beneficial outcome of grieving?
- What are some characteristics and outcomes of losing a life partner?
- What are some forms of mourning? What is the nature of the funeral?

REFLECT

- Is there a best or worst way to grieve? Explain.

We have arrived at the end of this book. I hope this book and course have been a window to the life span of the human species and a window to your own personal journey in life.

Our study of the human life span has been long and complex. You have read about many physical, cognitive, and socioemotional changes that take place from conception through death. This is a good time to reflect on what you have learned. Which theories, studies, and ideas were especially interesting to you? What did you learn about your own development?

I wish you all the best in the remaining years of your journey though the human life span.

Death, Dying, and Grieving

1   THE DEATH SYSTEM AND CULTURAL CONTEXTS: DESCRIBE THE DEATH SYSTEM AND ITS CULTURAL AND HISTORICAL CONTEXTS

The Death System and Its Cultural Variations

- In Kastenbaum's view, every culture has a death system that involves these components: people, places, times, and objects and symbols. He also argues that the death system serves certain functions in a culture that include warnings and predictions, preventing death, caring for the dying, disposing of the dead, social consolidation after death, making sense of the death, and killing. Most cultures do not view death as the end of existence—spiritual life is thought to continue. Most societies throughout history have had philosophical or religious beliefs about death, and most societies have rituals that deal with death. The United States has been described as more of a death-denying and death-avoiding culture than most cultures.

Changing Historical Circumstances

- When, where, and why people die have changed historically. Today, death occurs most often among older adults. More than 80 percent of all deaths in the United States now occur in a hospital or other institution; our exposure to death in the family has been minimized.

2   DEFINING DEATH AND LIFE/DEATH ISSUES: EVALUATE ISSUES IN DETERMINING DEATH AND DECISIONS REGARDING DEATH

Issues in Determining Death

- Twenty-five years ago, determining if someone was dead was simpler than it is today. Brain death is a neurological definition of death, which states that a person is brain dead when all electrical activity of the brain has ceased for a specified period of time. Medical experts debate whether this should mean the higher and lower brain functions or just the higher cortical functions. Currently, most physicians define brain death as the death of both the higher cortical functions and the lower brain stem functions.

Decisions Regarding Life, Death, and Health Care

- Decisions regarding life, death, and health care can involve whether to have a living will, durable power of attorney for health care, the issue of euthanasia, and the availability of hospice care. Living wills and advance directives are increasingly used. Euthanasia ("mercy killing") is the act of painlessly ending the life of a person who is suffering from an incurable disease or disability. Distinctions are made between active and passive euthanasia. Hospice care emphasizes reducing pain and suffering rather than prolonging life.

3   A DEVELOPMENTAL PERSPECTIVE ON DEATH: DISCUSS DEATH AND ATTITUDES ABOUT IT AT DIFFERENT POINTS IN DEVELOPMENT

Causes of Death

- Although death is more likely to occur in late adulthood, death can come at any point in development. In children and younger adults, death is more likely to occur because of accidents or illness; in older adults, death is more likely to occur because of chronic diseases such as heart disease or cancer.

Attitudes Toward Death at Different Points in the Life Span

- Infants do not have a concept of death. Preschool children also have little concept of death. Preschool children sometimes blame themselves for a person's death. In the elementary school years, children develop a more realistic orientation toward death. Most psychologists argue that honesty is the best strategy for helping children cope with death. Death may be glossed over in adolescence. Adolescents have more abstract, philosophical views of death than children do. There is no evidence that a special orientation toward death emerges in early adulthood. Middle adulthood is a time when adults show a heightened consciousness about death and death anxiety. The deaths of some persons, especially children and younger adults, are often perceived to be more tragic than those of others, such as very old adults, who have had an opportunity to live a long life. Older adults often show less death anxiety than middle-aged adults, but older adults experience and converse about death more. Attitudes about death may vary considerably among adults of any age.

4   FACING ONE'S OWN DEATH: EXPLAIN THE PSYCHOLOGICAL ASPECTS INVOLVED IN FACING ONE'S OWN DEATH AND THE CONTEXTS IN WHICH PEOPLE DIE

Kübler-Ross' Stages of Dying

- Kübler-Ross proposed five stages: denial and isolation, anger, bargaining, depression, and acceptance. Not all individuals go through the same sequence.

Perceived Control and Denial

- Perceived control and denial may work together as an adaptive orientation for the dying individual. Denial can be adaptive or maladaptive, depending on the circumstance.

The Contexts in Which People Die

- Most deaths in the United States occur in hospitals; this has advantages and disadvantages. Most individuals say they would rather die at home, but they worry that they will be a burden and they worry about the lack of medical care.

5   COPING WITH THE DEATH OF SOMEONE ELSE: IDENTIFY WAYS TO COPE WITH THE DEATH OF ANOTHER PERSON

Communicating with a Dying Person

- Most psychologists recommend an open communication system with the dying. Communication should not dwell on pathology or preparation for death but should emphasize the dying person's strengths.

Grieving

- Grief is the emotional numbness, disbelief, separation anxiety, despair, sadness, and loneliness that accompany the loss of someone we love. Grief is multidimensional and in some cases may last for years. Prolonged grief involves enduring despair and is still unresolved after an extended period of time. In the dual-process model of coping with bereavement, oscillation occurs between two dimensions: (1) loss-oriented stressors, and (2) restoration-oriented stressors. Grief and coping vary with the type of death. There are cultural variations in grieving.

Making Sense of the World

- The grieving process may stimulate individuals to strive to make sense out of their world; each individual may contribute a piece to death's puzzle.

Losing a Life Partner

- Usually the most difficult loss is the death of a spouse. The bereaved are at risk for many health problems, although there are variations in the distress experienced by a surviving spouse. Social support benefits widows and widowers.

Forms of Mourning

- Forms of mourning vary across cultures. Approximately 80 percent of corpses are disposed of by burial, 20 percent by cremation. An important aspect of mourning in many cultures is the funeral. In recent years, the funeral industry has been the focus of controversy. In some cultures, a ceremonial meal is held after death.

KEY TERMS

brain death 619
euthanasia 620
passive euthanasia 620
active euthanasia 620

hospice 621
palliative care 621
denial and isolation 626
anger 626

bargaining 627
depression 627
acceptance 627
grief 630

prolonged grief 630
dual-process model 631

KEY PEOPLE

Robert Kastenbaum 616

Bert Hayslip and Robert
Hansson 624

Elisabeth Kübler-Ross 626

Holly Prigerson 630

E-LEARNING TOOLS

To help you master the material in this chapter, visit the Online Learning Center for *Life-Span Development,* twelfth edition, at **www.mhhe.com/santrockld12**.

Self-Assessment

Connect to **www.mhhe.com/santrockld12** to evaluate your anxiety about death, complete a living will, and complete the self-assessments, *How Much Death Anxiety Do I Have?* and *The Living Will.*

Taking It to the Net

Connect to **www.mhhe.com/santrockld12** to research the answers to these questions:

1. Herman's mother has Parkinson's disease. He wants her to make some difficult end-of-life decisions while she still can. He and his mother discuss the options of a health-care power of attorney, a living will, and/or a DNR. What are the different purposes of these documents, and what is the family's involvement in these decisions?

2. Ellen has taken care of her mother throughout her long, lingering illness that has just been diagnosed as terminal. Ellen does not think she alone can provide the type of care necessary to take care of her mother in her final weeks. Her neighbor suggested she contact the local hospice. What does a hospice offer to families in this situation and how is it different from a nursing home?

3. Since the death of her husband four months ago, 75-year-old Anna has had difficulty sleeping and eating. She spends her days staring out the living room window. Her daughter fears that she is clinically depressed. Her son thinks that she just needs time to go through the grieving process. Is there a typical grieving process? What are the differences between the physical symptoms of grieving and the symptoms of clinical depression?

Video Clips

The Online Learning Center includes two videos for Chapter 20 called "Fear of Dying at Age 72" and "On Dying at Age 71."

Health and Well-Being, Parenting, and Education Exercises

Build your decision-making skills by trying your hand at the health and well-being, parenting, and education exercises. Connect to **www.mhhe.com/santrockld12** to research the answers and complete the exercises.

GLOSSARY

A

acceptance Kübler-Ross' fifth stage of dying, in which the dying person develops a sense of peace, an acceptance of her or his fate, and, in many cases, a desire to be left alone.

accommodation Piagetian concept of adjusting schemes to fit new information and experiences.

active (niche-picking) genotype-environment correlations Correlations that exist when children seek out environments they find compatible and stimulating.

active euthanasia Death induced deliberately, as by injecting a lethal dose of a drug.

activity theory The theory that the more active and involved older adults are, the more likely they are to be satisfied with their lives.

addiction A pattern of behavior characterized by an overwhelming involvement with using a drug and securing its supply.

adolescent egocentrism The heightened self-consciousness of adolescents.

adoption study A study in which investigators seek to discover whether, in behavior and psychological characteristics, adopted children are more like their adoptive parents, who provided a home environment, or more like their biological parents, who contributed their heredity. Another form of the adoption study is to compare adoptive and biological siblings.

aerobic exercise Sustained exercise (such as jogging, swimming, or cycling) that stimulates heart and lung activity.

affectionate love In this type of love, also called companionate love, an individual desires to have the other person near and has a deep, caring affection for the other person.

affordances Opportunities for interaction offered by objects that fit within our capabilities to perform functional activities.

afterbirth The third stage of birth, when the placenta, umbilical cord, and other membranes are detached and expelled.

ageism Prejudice against others because of their age, especially prejudice against older adults.

Alzheimer disease A progressive, irreversible brain disorder characterized by a gradual deterioration of memory, reasoning, language, and eventually physical function.

amnion The life-support system that is a bag or envelope that contains a clear fluid in which the developing embryo floats.

amygdala The region of the brain that is the seat of emotions.

androgyny The presence of positive masculine and feminine characteristics in the same individual.

anger Kübler-Ross' second stage of dying, in which the dying person's denial gives way to anger, resentment, rage, and envy.

anger cry A variation of the basic cry, with more excess air forced through the vocal cords.

animism The belief that inanimate objects have lifelike qualities and are capable of action.

anorexia nervosa An eating disorder that involves the relentless pursuit of thinness through starvation.

A-not-B error Also called AB error, this occurs when infants make the mistake of selecting the familiar hiding place (A) rather than the new hiding place (B) as they progress into substage 4 in Piaget's sensorimotor stage.

anxious attachment style An attachment style that describes adults who demand closeness, are less trusting, and are more emotional, jealous, and possessive.

Apgar Scale A widely used method to assess the health of newborns at one and five minutes after birth. The Apgar Scale evaluates infants' heart rate, respiratory effort, muscle tone, body color, and reflex irritability.

aphasia A loss or impairment of language ability caused by brain damage.

arthritis Inflammation of the joints that is accompanied by pain, stiffness, and movement problems; especially common in older adults.

Asperger syndrome A relatively mild autism spectrum disorder in which the child has relatively good verbal language, milder nonverbal language problems, and a restricted range of interests and relationships.

assimilation Piagetian concept of using existing schemes to deal with new information or experiences.

assimilation The absorption of ethnic minority groups into the dominant group, which often involves the loss of some or virtually all of the behavior and values of the ethnic minority group.

attachment A close emotional bond between two people.

attention The focusing of mental resources on select information.

attention deficit hyperactivity disorder (ADHD) A disability in which children consistently show one or more of the following characteristics: (1) inattention, (2) hyperactivity, and (3) impulsivity.

authoritarian parenting A restrictive, punitive style in which parents exhort the child to follow their directions and to respect work and effort. The authoritarian parent places firm limits and controls on the child and allows little verbal exchange. Authoritarian parenting is associated with children's social incompetence.

authoritative parenting A parenting style in which parents encourage their children to be independent but still place limits and controls on their actions. Extensive verbal give-and-take is allowed, and parents are warm and nurturant toward the child. Authoritative parenting is associated with children's social competence.

autism spectrum disorders (ASD) Also called pervasive developmental disorders, they range from the severe disorder labeled autistic disorder to the milder disorder called Asperger syndrome. Children with these disorders are characterized by problems in social interaction, verbal and nonverbal communication, and repetitive behaviors.

autistic disorder A severe autism spectrum disorder that has its onset in the first three years of life and includes deficiencies in social relationships, abnormalities in communication, and restricted, repetitive, and stereotyped patterns of behavior.

autonomous morality In Piaget's theory, displayed by older children (about 10 years of age and older). The child becomes aware that rules and laws are created by people and that, in judging an action, one should consider the actor's intentions as well as the consequences.

average children Children who receive an average number of both positive and negative nominations from peers.

avoidant attachment style An attachment style that describes adults who are hesitant about getting involved in romantic relationships and once in a relationship tend to distance themselves from their partner.

B

bargaining Kübler-Ross' third stage of dying, in which the dying person develops the hope that death can somehow be postponed.

basic cry A rhythmic pattern usually consisting of a cry, a briefer silence, a shorter inspiratory whistle that is higher pitched than the main cry, and then a brief rest before the next cry.

Bayley Scales of Infant Development Scales developed by Nancy Bayley that are widely used in the assessment of infant development. The current version has three components: a mental scale, a motor scale, and an infant behavior profile.

behavior genetics The field that seeks to discover the influence of heredity and environment on individual differences in human traits and development.

Big Five factors of personality Emotional stability (neuroticism), extraversion, openness to experience, agreeableness, and conscientiousness.

biological processes Changes in an individual's physical nature.

blastocyst The inner layer of cells that develops during the germinal period. These cells later develop into the embryo.

bonding The formation of a close connection, especially a physical bond between parents and their newborn in the period shortly after birth.

brain death A neurological definition of death. A person is brain dead when all electrical activity of the brain has ceased for a specified period of time. A flat EEG recording is one criterion of brain death.

brainstorming A technique in which individuals are encouraged to come up with creative ideas in a group, play off each other's ideas, and say practically whatever comes to mind.

Brazelton Neonatal Behavioral Assessment Scale (NBAS) A measure that is used in the first month of life to assess the newborn's neurological development, reflexes, and reactions to people and objects.

breech position The baby's position in the uterus that causes the buttocks to be the first part to emerge from the vagina.

Broca's area An area in the brain's left frontal lobe involved in speech production.

Bronfenbrenner's ecological theory Maintains that development reflects the influence of five environmental systems: microsystem, mesosystem, exosystem, macrosystem, and chronosystem.

bulimia nervosa An eating disorder in which the individual consistently follows a binge-and-purge pattern.

C

care perspective The moral perspective of Carol Gilligan, which views people in terms of their connectedness with others and emphasizes interpersonal communication, relationships with others, and concern for others.

case study An in-depth look at a single individual.

cataracts Involve a thickening of the lens of the eye that causes vision to become cloudy, opaque, and distorted.

cellular clock theory Leonard Hayflick's theory that the maximum number of times that human cells can divide is about 75 to 80. As we age, our cells have less capability to divide.

centration The focusing of attention on one characteristic to the exclusion of all others.

cephalocaudal pattern The sequence in which the earliest growth always occurs at the top—the head—with physical growth in size, weight, and feature differentiation gradually working from top to bottom.

cesarean delivery The baby is removed from the mother's uterus through an incision made in her abdomen.

child-centered kindergarten Education that involves the whole child by considering both the child's physical, cognitive, and socioemotional development and the child's needs, interests, and learning styles.

child-directed speech Language spoken in a higher pitch than normal with simple words and sentences.

chromosomes Threadlike structures that come in 23 pairs, one member of each pair coming from each parent. Chromosomes contain the genetic substance DNA.

chronic disorders Disorders that are characterized by slow onset and long duration. They are rare in early adulthood, they increase during middle adulthood, and they become common in late adulthood.

climacteric The midlife transition in which fertility declines.

clique A small group that ranges from 2 to about 12 individuals, averaging about 5 to 6 individuals, and can form because adolescents engage in similar activities.

cognitive mechanics The "hardware" of the mind, reflecting the neurophysiological architecture of the brain as developed through evolution. Cognitive mechanics involve the speed and accuracy of the processes involving sensory input, visual and motor memory, discrimination, comparison, and categorization.

cognitive pragmatics The culture-based "software programs" of the mind. Cognitive pragmatics include reading and writing skills, language comprehension, educational qualifications, professional skills, and also the type of knowledge about the self and life skills that help us to master or cope with life.

cognitive processes Changes in an individual's thought, intelligence, and language.

cohort effects Describe effects due to a person's time of birth, era, or generation but not to actual age.

commitment Marcia's term for the part of identity development in which adolescents show a personal investment in identity.

connectedness Connectedness consists of two dimensions: mutuality (sensitivity to and respect for others' views) and permeability (openness to others' views).

conscience An internal regulation of standards of right and wrong that involves an integration of moral thought, feeling, and behavior.

consensual validation An explanation of why individuals are attracted to people who are similar to them. Our own attitudes and behavior are supported and validated when someone else's attitudes and behavior are similar to our own.

conservation In Piaget's theory, awareness that altering an object's or a substance's appearance does not change its basic properties.

constructive play Play that combines sensorimotor and repetitive activity with symbolic representation of ideas. Constructive play occurs when children engage in self-regulated creation or construction of a product or a solution.

constructivist approach A learner-centered approach that emphasizes the importance of individuals actively constructing their knowledge and understanding with guidance from the teacher.

contemporary life-events approach Emphasizes that how a life event influences the individual's development depends not only on the life event, but also on mediating factors, the individual's adaptation to the life event, the life-stage context, and the sociohistorical context.

continuity-discontinuity issue The issue regarding whether development involves gradual, cumulative change (continuity) or distinct stages (discontinuity).

controversial children Children who are frequently nominated both as someone's best friend and as being disliked.

conventional reasoning The second, or intermediate, level in Kohlberg's theory of moral development. At this level, individuals abide by certain standards but they are the standards of others such as parents or the laws of society.

convergent thinking Thinking that produces one correct answer and is characteristic of the kind of thinking tested by standardized intelligence tests.

convoy model of social relations Individuals go through life embedded in a personal network of individuals to whom they give and from whom they receive support.

coordination of secondary circular reactions Piaget's fourth sensorimotor substage, which develops between 8 and 12 months of age. Actions become more outwardly directed, and infants coordinate schemes and act with intentionality.

corpus callosum The location where fibers connect the brain's left and right hemispheres.

correlation coefficient A number based on statistical analysis that is used to describe the degree of association between two variables.

correlational research The goal is to describe the strength of the relationship between two or more events or characteristics.

creative thinking The ability to think in novel and unusual ways and to come up with unique solutions to problems.

crisis Marcia's term for a period of identity development during which the adolescent is exploring alternatives.

critical thinking Thinking reflectively and productively, as well as evaluating the evidence.

cross-cultural studies Comparisons of one culture with one or more other cultures.

These provide information about the degree to which children's development is similar, or universal, across cultures, and to the degree to which it is culture-specific.

cross-sectional approach A research strategy in which individuals of different ages are compared at one time.

crowd A larger group structure than a clique, a crowd is usually formed based on reputation and members may or may not spend much time together.

crystallized intelligence Accumulated information and verbal skills, which increase with in middle adulthood, according to Horn.

cultural-familial retardation Retardation that is characterized by no evidence of organic brain damage, but the individual's IQ is generally between 50 and 70.

culture The behavior patterns, beliefs, and all other products of a group that are passed on from generation to generation.

culture-fair tests Tests of intelligence that are designed to be free of cultural bias.

D

date or acquaintance rape Coercive sexual activity directed at someone with whom the perpetrator is at least casually acquainted.

deferred imitation Imitation that occurs after a delay of hours or days.

dementia A global term for any neurological disorder in which the primary symptoms involve a deterioration of mental functioning.

denial and isolation Kübler-Ross' first stage of dying, in which the dying person denies that she or he is really going to die.

depression Kübler-Ross' fourth stage of dying, in which the dying person comes to accept the certainty of her or his death. A period of depression or preparatory grief may appear.

descriptive research Has the purpose of observing and recording behavior.

development The pattern of movement or change that begins at conception and continues through the human life span.

developmental quotient (DQ) An overall score that combines subscores in motor, language, adaptive, and personal-social domains in the Gesell assessment of infants.

developmentally appropriate practice Education that focuses on the typical developmental patterns of children (age-appropriateness) and the uniqueness of each child (individual-appropriateness).

difficult child A child who tends to react negatively and cry frequently, engages in irregular daily routines, and is slow to accept change.

direct instruction approach A structured, teacher-centered approach that is characterized by teacher direction and control, mastery of academic skills, high expectations for students' progress, maximum time spent on learning tasks, and efforts to keep negative affect to a minimum.

dishabituation Recovery of a habituated response after a change in stimulation.

divergent thinking Thinking that produces many answers to the same question and is characteristic of creativity.

divided attention Concentrating on more than one activity at the same time.

DNA A complex molecule that contains genetic information.

doula A caregiver who provides continuous physical, emotional, and educational support for the mother before, during, and after childbirth.

Down syndrome A chromosomally transmitted form of mental retardation, caused by the presence of an extra copy of chromosome 21.

dual-process model A model of coping with bereavement that emphasizes oscillation between two dimensions: (1) loss-oriented stressors, and (2) restoration-oriented stressors.

dynamic systems theory The perspective on motor development that seeks to explain how motor behaviors are assembled for perceiving and acting.

dyslexia A category of learning disabilities involving a severe impairment in the ability to read and spell.

E

easy child A child who is generally in a positive mood, quickly establishes regular routines in infancy, and adapts easily to new experiences.

eclectic theoretical orientation An orientation that does not follow any one theoretical approach, but rather selects from each theory whatever is considered the best in it.

ecological view The view that perception functions to bring organisms in contact with the environment and to increase adaptation.

egocentrism The inability to distinguish between one's own perspective and someone else's (salient feature of the first substage of preoperational thought).

elaboration An important strategy that involves engaging in more extensive processing of information.

eldercare Physical and emotional caretaking for older members of the family, whether by giving day-to-day physical assistance or by being responsible for overseeing such care.

embryonic period The period of prenatal development that occurs two to eight weeks after conception. During the embryonic period, the rate of cell differentiation intensifies, support systems for the cells form, and organs appear.

emerging adulthood The transition from adolescence to adulthood (approximately 18 to 25 years of age) that involves experimentation and exploration.

emotion Feeling, or affect, that occurs when a person is in a state or interaction that is important to him or her. Emotion is characterized by behavior that reflects (expresses) the pleasantness or unpleasantness of the state a person is in or the transactions being experienced.

empty nest syndrome A decrease in marital satisfaction after children leave home, because parents derive considerable satisfaction from their children.

epigenetic view Emphasizes that development is the result of an ongoing, bidirectional interchange between heredity and environment.

episodic memory The retention of information about the where and when of life's happenings.

equilibration A mechanism that Piaget proposed to explain how children shift from one stage of thought to the next.

erectile dysfunction The inabilty to adequately achieve and maintain an erection that results in satisfactory sexual performance.

Erikson's theory Includes eight stages of human development. Each stage consists of a unique developmental task that confronts individuals with a crisis that must be resolved.

ethnic gloss Using an ethnic label such as African American or Latino in a superficial way that portrays an ethnic group as being more homogeneous than it really is.

ethnic identity An enduring, basic aspect of the self that includes a sense of membership in an ethnic group and the attitudes and feelings related to that membership.

ethnicity A characteristic based on cultural heritage, nationality, race, religion, and language.

ethology Stresses that behavior is strongly influenced by biology, is tied to evolution, and is characterized by critical or sensitive periods.

euthanasia The act of painlessly ending the lives of persons who are suffering from incurable diseases or severe disabilities; sometimes called "mercy killing."

evocative genotype-environment correlations Correlations that exist when the child's genotype elicits certain types of physical and social environments.

evolutionary psychology Emphasizes the importance of adaptation, reproduction, and "survival of the fittest" in shaping behavior.

executive attention Involves action planning, allocating attention to goals, error detection and compensation, monitoring progress on tasks, and dealing with novel or difficult circumstances.

experiment A carefully regulated procedure in which one or more of the factors believed to influence the behavior being studied are manipulated while all other factors are held constant.

explicit memory Memory of facts and experiences that individuals consciously know and can state.

F

fertilization A stage in reproduction whereby an egg and a sperm fuse to create a single cell, called a zygote.

fetal alcohol spectrum disorders (FASD) A cluster of abnormalities that appears in the offspring of mothers who drink alcohol heavily during pregnancy.

fetal period Lasting about seven months, the prenatal period between two months after conception and birth in typical pregnancies.

fine motor skills Motor skills that involve more finely tuned movements, such as finger dexterity.

first habits and primary circular reactions Piaget's second sensorimotor substage, which develops between 1 and 4 months of age. In this substage, the infant coordinates sensation and two types of schemes: habits and primary circular reactions.

fluid intelligence The ability to reason abstractly, which begins to decline from middle adulthood on, according to Horn.

fragile X syndrome A genetic disorder involving an abnormality in the X chromosome, which becomes constricted and often breaks.

free-radical theory A microbiological theory of aging that states that people age because inside their cells normal metabolism produces unstable oxygen molecules known as free radicals. These molecules ricochet around inside cells, damaging DNA and other cellular structures.

fuzzy trace theory States that memory is best understood by considering two types of memory representations: (1) verbatim memory trace, and (2) gist. In this theory, older children's better memory is attributed to the fuzzy traces created by extracting the gist of information.

G

games Activities engaged in for pleasure that include rules and often competition with one or more individuals.

gender Refers to the characteristics of people as males or females.

gender identity The sense of being male or female, which most children acquire by the time they are 3 years old.

gender role A set of expectations that prescribes how females or males should think, act, and feel.

gender schema theory The theory that gender-typing emerges as children develop gender schemas of their culture's gender-appropriate and gender-inappropriate behavior.

gender stereotypes Broad categories that reflect our impressions and beliefs about females and males.

generational inequity The view that our aging society is being unfair to its younger members because older adults pile up advantages by receiving inequitably large allocations of resources.

genes Units of hereditary information composed of short segments of DNA. Genes direct cells to reproduce themselves and manufacture the proteins that maintain life.

genotype A person's genetic heritage; the actual genetic material.

germinal period The period of prenatal development that takes place in the first two weeks after conception. It includes the creation of the zygote, continued cell division, and the attachment of the zygote to the uterine wall.

gifted Having above-average intelligence (an IQ of 130 or higher) and/or superior talent for something.

glaucoma Damage to the optic nerve because of the pressure created by a buildup of fluid in the eye.

gonads The sex glands—the testes in males and the ovaries in females.

goodness of fit Refers to the match between a child's temperament and the environmental demands with which the child must cope.

grasping reflex A neonatal reflex that occurs when something touches the infant's palms. The infant responds by grasping tightly.

grief The emotional numbness, disbelief, separation anxiety, despair, sadness, and loneliness that accompany the loss of someone we love.

gross motor skills Motor skills that involve large-muscle activities, such as walking.

H

habituation Decreased responsiveness to a stimulus after repeated presentations of the stimulus.

heritability The fraction of variance in a population that is attributed to genetics and is computed using correlational techniques.

heteronomous morality Kohlberg's first stage of preconventional reasoning in which moral thinking is tied to punishment.

heteronomous morality The first stage of moral development in Piaget's theory, occurring from approximately 4 to 7 years of age. Justice and rules are conceived of as unchangeable properties of the world, removed from the control of people.

hormonal stress theory The theory that aging in the body's hormonal system can lower resistance to stress and increase the likelihood of disease.

hormones Powerful chemical substances secreted by the endocrine glands and carried through the body by the bloodstream.

hospice A program committed to making the end of life as free from pain, anxiety, and depression as possible. The goals of hospice contrast with those of a hospital, which are to cure disease and prolong life.

hypothalamus A structure in the brain that monitors eating and sex.

hypotheses Specific assertions and predictions that can be tested to determine their accuracy.

hypothetical-deductive reasoning Piaget's formal operational concept that adolescents have the cognitive ability to develop hypotheses, or best guesses, about ways to solve problems, such as an algebraic equation.

I

identity achievement Marcia's term for the status of individuals who have undergone a crisis and have made a commitment.

identity diffusion Marcia's term for the status of individuals who have not yet experienced a crisis (explored meaningful alternatives) or made any commitments.

identity foreclosure Marcia's term for the status of individuals who have made a commitment but have not experienced a crisis.

identity moratorium Marcia's term for the status of individuals who are in the midst of a crisis, but their commitments are either absent or vaguely defined.

imaginary audience Involves adolescents' belief that others are as interested in them as they themselves are, as well as attention-getting behavior motivated by a desire to be noticed, visible, and "on stage."

immanent justice The concept that, if a rule is broken, punishment will be meted out immediately.

implicit memory Memory without conscious recollection; involves skills and routine procedures that are automatically performed.

inclusion Educating a child with special education needs full-time in the regular classroom.

individual differences The stable, consistent ways in which people are different from each other.

individualism, instrumental purpose, and exchange Kohlberg's second stage of preconventional reasoning. At this stage, individuals pursue their own interests but also let others do the same.

individuality Individuality consists of two dimensions: self-assertion (the ability to have and communicate a point of view) and separateness (the use of communication patterns to express how one is different from others).

individualized education plan (IEP) A written statement that spells out a program specifically tailored to a child with a disability.

indulgent parenting A style of parenting in which parents are highly involved with their children but place few demands or controls on them. Indulgent parenting is associated with children's social incompetence, especially a lack of self-control.

infinite generativity The ability to produce an endless number of meaningful sentences using a finite set of words and rules.

information-processing theory Emphasizes that individuals manipulate information, monitor it, and strategize about it. Central to this theory are the processes of memory and thinking.

insecure avoidant babies Babies that show insecurity by avoiding the caregiver.

insecure disorganized babies Babies that show insecurity by being disorganized and disoriented.

insecure resistant babies Babies that often cling to the caregiver, then resist her by fighting against the closeness, perhaps by kicking or pushing away.

integrity versus despair Erikson's eighth and final stage of development, which individuals experience in late adulthood. This involves reflecting on the past and either piecing together a positive review or concluding that one's life has not been well spent.

intelligence Problem-solving skills and the ability to learn from and adapt to the experiences of everyday life.

intelligence quotient (IQ) A person's mental age divided by chronological age, multiplied by 100.

intermodal perception The ability to relate and integrate information from two or more sensory modalities, such as vision and hearing.

internalization of schemes Piaget's sixth and final sensorimotor substage, which develops between 18 and 24 months of age. In this substage, the infant develops the ability to use primitive symbols.

intimacy in friendships Self-disclosure and the sharing of private thoughts.

intuitive thought substage Piaget's second substage of preoperational thought, in which children begin to use primitive reasoning and want to know the answers to all sorts of questions (between 4 and 7 years of age).

J

joint attention Occurs when individuals focus on the same object and an ability to track another's behavior is present, one individual directs another's attention, and reciprocal interaction is present.

justice perspective A moral perspective that focuses on the rights of the individual; individuals independently make moral decisions.

juvenile delinquent An adolescent who breaks the law or engages in behavior that is considered illegal.

K

kangaroo care Treatment for preterm infants that involves skin-to-skin contact.

Klinefelter syndrome A chromosomal disorder in which males have an extra X chromosome, making them XXY instead of XY.

kwashiorkor A condition caused by severe protein deficiency in which the child's abdomen and feet become swollen with water; usually appears between 1 to 3 years of age.

L

laboratory A controlled setting in which many of the complex factors of the "real world" are removed.

language A form of communication, whether spoken, written, or signed, that is based on a system of symbols.

language acquisition device (LAD) Chomsky's term that describes a biological endowment that enables the child to detect the features and rules of language, including phonology, syntax, and semantics.

lateralization Specialization of function in one hemisphere of the cerebral cortex or the other.

learning disability Describes a child who has difficulty in learning that involves understanding or using spoken or written language, and the difficulty can appear in listening, thinking, reading, writing, and spelling. A learning disability also may involve difficulty in doing mathematics. To be classified as a learning disability, the learning problem is not primarily the result of visual, hearing, or motor disabilities; mental retardation; emotional disorders; or due to environmental, cultural, or economic disadvantage.

least restrictive environment (LRE) A setting that is as similar as possible to the one in which children who do not have a disability are educated.

leisure The pleasant times after work when individuals are free to pursue activities and interests of their own choosing.

life expectancy The number of years that will probably be lived by the average person born in a particular year.

life span The upper boundary of life, the maximum number of years an individual can live. The maximum life span of human beings is about 120 to 125 years of age.

life-span perspective Views development as lifelong, multidimensional, multidirectional, plastic, multidisciplinary, and contextual, and as a process that involves growth, maintenance, and regulation of loss.

longitudinal approach A research strategy in which the same individuals are studied over a period of time, usually several years or more.

long-term memory A relatively permanent type of memory that holds huge amounts of information for a long period of time.

low birth weight infants An infant that weighs less than $5\frac{1}{2}$ pounds at birth.

M

macular degeneration A disease that involves deterioration of the macula of the retina, which corresponds to the focal center of the visual field.

major depression A mood disorder in which the individual is deeply unhappy, demoralized, self-derogatory, and bored. The person does not feel well, loses stamina easily, has poor appetite, and is listless and unmotivated. Major depression is so widespread that it has been called the "common cold" of mental disorders.

marasmus A wasting away of body tissues in the infant's first year, caused by severe protein-calorie deficiency.

matching hypothesis States that although we prefer a more attractive person in the abstract, in the real world we end up choosing someone who is close to our own level.

meaning-making coping Involves drawing on beliefs, values, and goals to change the meaning of a stressful situation, especially in times of chronic stress as when a loved one dies.

meiosis A specialized form of cell division that occurs to form eggs and sperm (or gametes).

memory A central feature of cognitive development, pertaining to all situations in which an individual retains information over time.

menarche A girl's first menstruation.

menopause Cessation of a woman's menstrual periods, usually in the late forties or fifties.

mental age (MA) Binet's measure of an individual's level of mental development, compared with that of others.

mental retardation A condition of limited mental ability in which an individual has a low IQ, usually below 70 on a traditional test of intelligence, and has difficulty adapting to everyday life.

metacognition Cognition about cognition, or knowing about knowing.

metalinguistic awareness Refers to knowledge about language, such as knowing what a preposition is or the ability to discuss the sounds of a language.

middle adulthood The developmental period that begins at approximately 40 to 45 years of age and extends to about 60 to 65 years of age.

mindset The cognitive view, either fixed or growth, that individuals develop for themselves.

mitochondrial theory The theory that aging is caused by the decay of mitochondria, tiny cellular bodies that supply energy for function, growth, and repair.

mitosis Cellular reproduction in which the cell's nucleus duplicates itself with two new cells being formed, each containing the same DNA as the parent cell, arranged in the same 23 pairs of chromosomes.

Montessori approach An educational philosophy in which children are given considerable freedom and spontaneity in choosing activities and are allowed to move from one activity to another as they desire.

moral development Development that involves thoughts, feelings, and behaviors regarding rules and conventions about what people should do in their interactions with other people.

Moro reflex A neonatal startle response that occurs in reaction to a sudden, intense noise or movement. When startled, the newborn arches its back, throws its head back, and flings out its arms and legs. Then the newborn rapidly closes its arms and legs to the center of the body.

morphology Units of meaning involved in word formation.

multi-infarct dementia Sporadic and progressive loss of intellectual functioning caused by repeated temporary obstruction of blood flow in cerebral arteries.

mutual interpersonal expectations, relationships, and interpersonal conformity Kohlberg's third stage of moral development. At this stage, individuals value trust, caring, and loyalty to others as a basis of moral judgments.

myelination The process by which the nerve cells are covered and insulated with a layer of fat cells, which increases the speed at which information travels through the nervous system.

N

natural childbirth Developed in 1914 by Dick-Read, this method attempts to reduce the mother's pain by decreasing her fear through education about childbirth and relaxation techniques during delivery.

naturalistic observation Observing behavior in real-world settings.

nature-nurture issue The issue that involves the extent to which development is influenced by nature and by nurture. The "nature" proponents claim biological inheritance is the most important influence on development; the "nurture" proponents claim that environmental experiences are the most important.

neglected children Children who are infrequently nominated as a best friend but are not disliked by their peers.

neglectful parenting A style of parenting in which the parent is very uninvolved in the child's life; it is associated with children's social incompetence, especially a lack of self-control.

Neonatal Intensive Care Unit Neurobehavioral Scale (NNNS) An "offspring" of the NBAS, the NNNS provides a more comprehensive analysis of the newborn's behavior, neurological and stress responses, and regulatory capacities.

neo-Piagetians Developmentalists who argue that Piaget got some things right but that his theory needs considerable revision. They have elaborated on Piaget's theory, giving more emphasis to information-processing, strategies, and precise cognitive steps.

neurogenesis The generation of new neurons.

neurons Nerve cells, which handle information processing at the cellular level in the brain.

nonnormative life events Unusual events that have a major impact on an individual's life.

nonshared environmental experiences The child's own unique experiences, both within the family and outside the family, that are not shared by another sibling. Thus, experiences occurring within the family can be part of the "nonshared environment."

normal distribution A symmetrical distribution with most scores falling in the middle of the possible range of scores and a few scores appearing toward the extremes of the range.

normative age-graded influences Describes influences that are similar for individuals in a particular age group.

normative history-graded influences Describes influences common to individuals of a particular generation because of historical circumstances.

O

object permanence The Piagetian term for understanding that objects and events continue to exist, even when they cannot directly be seen, heard, or touched.

operations In Piaget's theory, these are reversible mental actions that allow children to do mentally what they formerly did physically.

organic retardation Mental retardation that is caused by a genetic disorder or brain damage.

organization Piaget's concept of grouping isolated behaviors and thoughts into a higher-order, more smoothly functioning cognitive system.

organogenesis Organ formation that takes place during the first two months of prenatal development.

osteoporosis A chronic condition that involves an extensive loss of bone tissue and is the main reason many older adults walk with a marked stoop. Women are especially vulnerable to osteoporosis.

P

pain cry A sudden appearance of a long, initial loud cry without preliminary moaning, followed by breath holding.

palliative care Emphasized in hospice care, involves reducing pain and suffering and helping individuals die with dignity.

Parkinson disease A chronic, progressive disease characterized by muscle tremors, slowing of movement, and partial facial paralysis.

passive euthanasia The withholding of available treatments, such as life-sustaining devices, allowing the person to die.

passive genotype-environment correlations Correlations that exist when the natural parents, who are genetically related to the child, provide a rearing environment for the child.

perception The interpretation of what is sensed.

personal fable The part of adolescent egocentrism that involves an adolescent's sense of uniqueness and invincibility (or invulnerability).

perspective taking The ability to assume other people's perspectives and understand their thoughts and feelings.

phenotype The way an individual's genotype is expressed in observable and measurable characteristics.

phenylketonuria (PKU) A genetic disorder in which an individual cannot properly metabolize phenylalanine, an amino acid. PKU is now easily detected but, if left untreated, results in mental retardation and hyperactivity.

phonics approach The idea that reading instruction should teach the basic rules for translating written symbols into sounds.

phonology The sound system of the language, including the sounds that are used and how they may be combined.

Piaget's theory States that children actively construct their understanding of the world and go through four stages of cognitive development.

pituitary gland An important endocrine gland that controls growth and regulates other glands, including the gonads.

placenta A life-support system that consists of a disk-shaped group of tissues in which small blood vessels from the mother and offspring intertwine.

pluralism The coexistence of distinct ethnic and cultural groups in the same society, each of which maintains its cultural differences.

popular children Children who are frequently nominated as a best friend and are rarely disliked by their peers.

possible selves What individuals might become, what they would like to become, and what they are afraid of becoming.

postconventional reasoning The highest level in Kohlberg's theory of moral development. At this level, the individual recognizes alternative moral courses, explores the options, and then decides on a personal moral code.

postformal thought A form of thought that is qualitatively different from Piaget's formal operational thought. It involves understanding that the correct answer to a problem can require reflective thinking, that the correct answer can vary from one situation to another, and that the search for truth is often an ongoing, never-ending process. It also involves the belief that solutions to problems need to be realistic and that emotion and subjective factors can influence thinking.

postpartum depression Characteristic of women who have such strong feelings of sadness, anxiety, or despair that they have trouble coping with daily tasks in the postpartum period.

postpartum period The period after childbirth when the mother adjusts, both physically and psychologically, to the process of childbirth. This period lasts for about six weeks or until her body has completed its adjustment and returned to a near prepregnant state.

practice play Play that involves repetition of behavior when new skills are being learned or when physical or mental mastery and coordination of skills are required for games or sports.

pragmatics The appropriate use of language in different contexts.

preconventional reasoning The lowest level in Kohlberg's theory of moral development.

The individual's moral reasoning is controlled primarily by external rewards and punishment.

preoperational stage Piaget's second stage, lasting from about 2 to 7 years of age, during which children begin to represent the world with words, images, and drawings and symbolic thought goes beyond simple connections of sensory information and physical action; stable concepts are formed, mental reasoning emerges, egocentrism is present, and magical beliefs are constructed.

prepared childbirth Developed by French obstetrician Ferdinand Lamaze, this childbirth strategy is similar to natural childbirth but includes a special breathing technique to control pushing in the final stages of labor and a more detailed anatomy and physiology course.

pretense/symbolic play Play in which the child transforms the physical environment into a symbol.

preterm infants Those born before the completion of 37 weeks of gestation (the time between fertilization and birth).

primary circular reaction A scheme based on the attempt to reproduce an event that initially occurred by chance.

primary emotions Emotions that are present in humans and other animals and emerge early in life; examples are joy, anger, sadness, fear, and disgust.

Project Head Start A government-funded program that is designed to provide children from low-income families the opportunity to acquire the skills and experiences important for school success.

prolonged grief Grief that involves enduring despair and is still unresolved over an extended period of time.

prospective memory Involves remembering to do something in the future.

proximodistal pattern The sequence in which growth starts at the center of the body and moves toward the extremities.

psychoanalytic theories Describe development as primarily unconscious and heavily colored by emotion. Behavior is merely a surface characteristic, and the symbolic workings of the mind have to be analyzed to understand behavior. Early experiences with parents are emphasized.

psychoanalytic theory of gender A theory deriving from Freud's view that the preschool child develops a sexual attraction to the opposite-sex parent, by approximately 5 or 6 years of age renounces this attraction because of anxious feelings, and subsequently identifies with the same-sex parent, unconsciously adopting the same-sex parent's characteristics.

puberty A period of rapid physical growth involving hormonal and bodily changes that occurs mainly during early adolescence.

R

rape Forcible sexual intercourse with a person who does not consent to it.

rapport talk The language of conversation; it is a way of establishing connections and negotiating relationships.

reciprocal socialization Socialization that is bidirectional; children socialize parents, just as parents socialize children.

reflexes Built-in reactions to stimuli that govern the newborn's movements, which are automatic and beyond the newborn's control.

reflexive smile A smile that does not occur in response to external stimuli. It happens during the month after birth, usually during sleep.

rejected children Children who are infrequently nominated as a best friend and are actively disliked by their peers.

report talk Talk that is designed to give information and includes public speaking.

rite of passage A ceremony or ritual that marks an individual's transition from one status to another. Most rites of passage focus on the transition to adult status.

romantic love Also called passionate love, or eros, romantic love has strong sexual and infatuation components and often predominates in the early period of a love relationship.

rooting reflex A newborn's built-in reaction that occurs when the infant's cheek is stroked or the side of the mouth is touched. In response, the infant turns his or her head toward the side that was touched, in an apparent effort to find something to suck.

S

scaffolding Parents time interactions so that infants experience turn-taking with the parents.

schemes In Piaget's theory, actions or mental representations that organize knowledge.

scientific method An approach that can be used to obtain accurate information. It includes these steps: (1) conceptualize the problem, (2) collect data, (3) draw conclusions, and (4) revise research conclusions and theory.

secondary circular reactions Piaget's third sensorimotor substage, which develops between 4 and 8 months of age. In this substage, the infant becomes more object-oriented, moving beyond preoccupation with the self.

secure attachment style An attachment style that describes adults who have positive views of relationships, find it easy to get close to others, and are not overly concerned or stressed out about their romantic relationships.

securely attached babies Babies that use the caregiver as a secure base from which to explore the environment.

selective attention Focusing on a specific aspect of experience that is relevant while ignoring others that are irrelevant.

selective optimization with compensation theory The theory that successful aging is related to three main factors: selection, optimization, and compensation.

self-concept Domain-specific evaluations of the self.

self-conscious emotions Emotions that require self-awareness, especially consciousness and a sense of "me"; examples include jealousy, empathy, and embarrassment.

self-efficacy The belief that one can master a situation and produce favorable outcomes.

self-esteem The global evaluative dimension of the self. Self-esteem is also referred to as self-worth or self-image.

self-understanding The child's cognitive representation of self, the substance and content of the child's self-conceptions.

semantic memory A person's knowledge about the world—including a person's fields of expertise, general academic knowledge of the sort learned in school, and "everyday knowledge."

semantics The meaning of words and sentences.

sensation The product of the interaction between information and the sensory receptors—the eyes, ears, tongue, nostrils, and skin.

sensorimotor play Behavior engaged in by infants to derive pleasure from exercising their existing sensorimotor schemas.

sensorimotor stage The first of Piaget's stages, which lasts from birth to about 2 years of age; infants construct an understanding of the world by coordinating sensory experiences with motoric actions.

separation protest An infant's distressed crying when the caregiver leaves.

seriation The concrete operation that involves ordering stimuli along a quantitative dimension (such as length).

service learning A form of education that promotes social responsibility and service to the community.

sexually transmitted infections (STIs) Infections that are contracted primarily through sexual contact, including oral-genital and anal-genital contact.

shape constancy The recognition that an object's shape remains the same even though its orientation to us changes.

shared environmental experiences Siblings' common environmental experiences, such as their parents' personalities and intellectual orientation, the family's socioeconomic status, and the neighborhood in which they live.

short-term memory The memory component in which individuals retain information for up to 30 seconds, assuming there is no rehearsal of the information.

sickle-cell anemia A genetic disorder that affects the red blood cells and occurs most often in African Americans.

simple reflexes Piaget's first sensorimotor substage, which corresponds to the first month after birth. In this substage, sensation and action are coordinated primarily through reflexive behaviors.

size constancy The recognition that an object remains the same even though the retinal image of the object changes as you move toward or away from the object.

slow-to-warm-up child A child who has a low activity level, is somewhat negative, and displays a low intensity of mood.

small for date infants Also called small for gestational age infants, these infants' birth weights are below normal when the length of pregnancy is considered. Small for date infants may be preterm or full term.

social clock The timetable according to which individuals are expected to accomplish life's tasks, such as getting married, having children, or establishing themselves in a career.

social cognitive theory The view of psychologists who emphasize behavior, environment, and cognition as the key factors in development.

social cognitive theory of gender A theory that emphasizes that children's gender development occurs through the observation and imitation of gender behavior and through the rewards

and punishments children experience for gender-appropriate and gender-inappropriate behavior.

social constructivist approach An approach that emphasizes the social contexts of learning and that knowledge is mutually built and constructed. Vygotsky's theory reflects this approach.

social contract or utility and individual rights The fifth Kohlberg stage. At this stage, individuals reason that values, rights, and principles undergird or transcend the law.

social conventional reasoning Thoughts about social consensus and convention, in contrast to moral reasoning, which stresses ethical issues.

social play Play that involves social interactions with peers.

social policy The laws, regulations, and government programs designed to promote the welfare of its citizens.

social referencing "Reading" emotional cues in others to help determine how to act in a particular situation.

social role theory A theory that gender differences result from the contrasting roles of men and women.

social smile A smile in response to an external stimulus, which, early in development, typically is a face.

social systems morality The fourth stage in Kohlberg's theory of moral development. Moral judgments are based on understanding the social order, law, justice, and duty.

socioeconomic status (SES) Refers to a person's position within society based on occupational, educational, and economic characteristics.

socioemotional processes Changes in an individual's relationships with other people, emotions, and personality.

socioemotional selectivity theory The theory that older adults become more selective about their social networks. Because they place a high value on emotional satisfaction, older adults often spend more time with familiar individuals with whom they have had rewarding relationships.

source memory The ability to remember where one learned something.

stability-change issue Involves the degree to which early traits and characteristics persist through life or change.

standardized test A test with uniform procedures for administration and scoring. Many standardized tests allow a person's performance to be compared with the performance of other individuals.

Strange Situation An observational measure of infant attachment that requires the infant to move through a series of introductions, separations, and reunions with the caregiver and an adult stranger in a prescribed order.

stranger anxiety An infant's fear and wariness of strangers; it tends to appear in the second half of the first year of life.

strategies Deliberate mental activities to improve the processing of information.

sucking reflex A newborn's built-in reaction to automatically suck an object placed in its mouth. The sucking reflex enables the infant to get nourishment before he or she has associated a nipple with food and also serves as a self-soothing or self-regulating mechanism.

sudden infant death syndrome (SIDS) A condition that occurs when an infant stops breathing, usually during the night, and suddenly dies without an apparent cause.

sustained attention Focused and extended engagement with an object, task, event, or other aspect of environment.

sustained attention The state of readiness to detect and respond to small changes occurring at random times in the environment.

symbolic function substage Piaget's first substage of preoperational thought, in which the child gains the ability to mentally represent an object that is not present (between about 2 and 4 years of age).

syntax The ways words are combined to form acceptable phrases and sentences.

T

telegraphic speech The use of short and precise words without grammatical markers such as articles, auxiliary verbs, and other connectives.

temperament An individual's behavioral style and characteristic way of emotionally responding.

teratogen From the Greek word *tera*, meaning "monster." Any agent that causes a birth defect. The field of study that investigates the causes of birth defects is called teratology.

tertiary circular reactions, novelty, and curiosity Piaget's fifth sensorimotor substage, which develops between 12 and 18 months of age. In this substage, infants become intrigued by the many properties of objects and by the many things that they can make happen to objects.

theory An interrelated, coherent set of ideas that helps to explain phenomena and make predictions.

theory of mind Refers to the awareness of one's own mental processes and the mental processes of others.

top-dog phenomenon The circumstance of moving from the top position in elementary school to the lowest position in middle or junior high school.

transitivity The ability to logically combine relations to understand certain conclusions.

triarchic theory of intelligence Sternberg's theory that intelligence consists of analytical intelligence, creative intelligence, and practical intelligence.

trophoblast The outer layer of cells that develops in the germinal period. These cells provide nutrition and support for the embryo.

Turner syndrome A chromosomal disorder in females in which either an X chromosome is missing, making the person XO instead of XX, or part of one X chromosome is deleted.

twin study A study in which the behavioral similarity of identical twins is compared with the behavioral similarity of fraternal twins.

U

umbilical cord A life-support system containing two arteries and one vein that connects the baby to the placenta.

universal ethical principles The sixth and highest stage in Kohlberg's theory of moral development. Individuals develop a moral standard based on universal human rights.

V

visual preference method A method used to determine whether infants can distinguish one stimulus from another by measuring the length of time they attend to different stimuli.

Vygotsky's theory A sociocultural cognitive theory that emphasizes how culture and social interaction guide cognitive development.

W

Wernicke's area An area of the brain's left hemisphere that is involved in language comprehension.

whole-language approach An approach to reading instruction based on the idea that instruction should parallel children's natural language learning. Reading materials should be whole and meaningful.

wisdom Expert knowledge about the practical aspects of life that permits excellent judgment about important matters.

working memory The mental "workbench" where individuals manipulate and assemble information when decision making problem solving and comprehending language.

X

XYY syndrome A chromosomal disorder in which males have an extra Y chromosome.

Z

zone of proximal development (ZPD) Vygotsky's term for tasks too difficult for children to master alone but that can be mastered with the assistance of adults or more-skilled children.

zygote A single cell formed through fertilization.

REFERENCES

A

Aalsma, M., Lapsley, D. K., & Flannery, D. (2006). Narcissism, personal fables, and adolescent adjustment. *Psychology in the Schools, 43*, 481–491.

AARP. (2004). *The divorce experience: A study of divorce at midlife and beyond.* Washington, DC: Author.

Abbo, E. E., Sobotka, S., & Meltzer, D. O. (2008). Patient preference in instructional advance directives. *Journal of Palliative Medicine, 11*, 555–562.

Abbott, A. (2003). Restless nights, listless days. *Nature, 425*, 896–898.

Abbott, R. D., White, I. R., Ross, G. W., Masaki, K. H., Curb, J. D., & Petrovitch, H. (2004). Walking and dementia in physically capable elderly men. *Journal of the American Medical Association, 292*, 1447–1453.

ABC News. (2005, December 12). Larry Page and Sergey Brim. Retrieved June 24, 2006, from www. Montessori.org/enews/barbara Walters.html

Abdo, C. H., Afif-Abdo, J., Otani, F., & Machado, A. C. (2008, in press). Sexual satisfaction among patients with erectile dysfunction treated with counseling, sildenafil, or both. *Journal of Sexual Medicine.*

Aber, J. L., Bishop-Josef, S. J., Jones, S. M., McLern, T., & Phillips, D. A. (2006). *Child development and social policy.* Washington, DC: American Psychological Association.

Accornero, V. H., Amado, A. J., Morrow, C. E., Xue, L., Anthony, J. C., & Bandstra, E. S. (2007). Impact of prenatal cocaine exposure on attention and response inhibition as assessed by continuous performance tests. *Journal of Developmental and Behavioral Pediatrics, 28*, 195–205.

Accornero, V.H., Anthony, J. C., Morrow, C. E., Xue, L., & Bandstra, E. S. (2006). Prenatal cocaine exposure: An examination of childhood externalizing and internalizing behavior problems at age 7 years. *Epidemiology, Psychiatry, and Society, 15*, 20–29.

Adams, K. F., Schatzkin, A., Harris, T. B., Kipnis, V., Mouw, T., Ballard-Barbash, R., Hollenbeck, A., & Leitzmann, M. F. (2006). Overweight, obesity, and mortality in a large prospective cohort of persons 50 to 71 years old. *New England Journal of Medicine, 355*, 763–768.

Adams, S., Kuebli, J., Boyle, P. A., Fivush, R. (1995). Gender differences in parent-child conversations about past emotions: A longitudinal investigation. *Sex Roles, 33*, 309–323.

Adamson, L., & Frick, J. (2003). The still face: A history of a shared experimental paradigm. *Infancy, 4*, 451–473.

Adolph, K. E. (1997). Learning in the development of infant locomotion. *Monographs of the Society for Research in Child Development, 62* (3, Serial No. 251).

Adolph, K. E. (2008). Motor and physical development: Locomotion. In M. M. Haith & J. B. Benson (Eds.), *Encyclopedia of infant and early childhood development.* Oxford, UK: Elsevier.

Adolph, K. E., & Berger, S. E. (2005). Physical and motor development. In M. H. Bornstein & M. E. Lamb (Eds.), *Developmental psychology* (5th ed.). Mahwah, NJ: Erlbaum.

Adolph, K. E., & Joh, A. S. (2007). Motor development: How infants get into the act. In A. Slater & M. Lewis (eds.), *Infant Development* New York: Oxford University Press.

Adolph, K. E., & Joh, A. S. (2008, in press). Multiple learning mechanisms in the development of action. In A. Needham & A. Woodward (Eds.), *Learning and the infant mind.* New York: Oxford University Press.

Adolph, K. E., Vereijkeni, B., & Shrout, P. E. (2003). What changes in infant walking and why? *Child Development, 74*, 475–497.

Agency for Healthcare Research and Quality. (2007). *Evidence report/technology assessment number 153: Breastfeeding and maternal and health outcomes in developed countries.* Rockville, MD: U.S. Department of Health and Human Services.

Agras, W. S., & others. (2004). Report of the National Institutes of Health workshop on overcoming barriers to treatment research in anorexia nervosa. *International Journal of Eating Disorders, 35*, 509–521.

Ah, D. V., Kang, D. H., & Carpenter, J. S. (2007). Stress, optimism, and social support: Impact on immune responses in breast cancer. *Research in Nursing and Health, 30*, 72–83.

Ahluwalia, I. B., Tessaro, I., Grumer-Strawn, L. M., MacGowan, C., & Benton-Davis, S. (2000). Georgia's breastfeeding promotion program for low-income women. *Pediatrics, 105*, E-85–E-87.

Ahnert, L., & Lamb, M. E. (2009, in press). Child care and its impact on young children (2-5). In R. E. Tremblay, R. deV Peters, M. Boivan, & R. G. Barr (Eds.), *Encyclopedia on early childhood development.* Montreal: Center of Excellence for Early Childhood Development.

Ahrons, C. (2004). *We're still family.* New York: HarperCollins.

Ahrons, C. (2007). Family ties after divorce: Long-term implications for children. *Family Process, 46*, 53–65.

Aiken, L. (2000). *Dying, death, and bereavement* (4th ed.). Mahwah, NJ: Erlbaum.

Ainsworth, M. D. S. (1979). Infant-mother attachment. *American Psychologist, 34*, 932–937.

Ajdacic-Gross, V., Ring, M., Gadola, E., Lauber, C., Bopp, M., Gutzwiller, F., & Rossler, W. (2008). Suicide after bereavement: An overlooked problem *Psychology and Medicine, 38*, 673–676.

Akerblom, J., & others. (2008). Relation of plasma lipids to all-cause mortality in Caucasian, African-American, and Hispanic elders. *Age and Aging, 37*, 207–213.

Akhtar, N., & Herold, K. (2008). Pragmatic development. In M. M. Haith & J. B. Benson (Eds.), *Encyclopedia of infant and early childhood development.* Oxford, UK: Elsevier.

Akhter, M., Nishino, Y., Nakaya, N., Kurashima, K., Sato, Y., Kuriyama, S., Tsubono, Y., & Tsuji, I. (2007). Cigarette smoking and the risk of colorectal cancer among men: A prospective study in Japan. *European Journal of Cancer Prevention, 16*, 102–107.

Akiyama, H., & Antonucci, T. C. (1999, November). *Mother-daughter dynamics over the life course.* Paper presented at the meeting of the Gerontological Association of America, San Francisco.

Aktar, N., & Herold, K. (2008). Pragmatic development. In M. M. Haith & J. B. Benson (Eds.), *Encyclopedia of infant and early childhood development.*

Alan Guttmacher Institute. (2007). *Facts on sex education.* New York: Author.

Albert, S. M. (2007). Cultural and ethnic influences on aging. In J. E. Birren (Ed.), *Encyclopedia of gerontology* (2nd ed.). San Diego: Academic Press.

Alberts, E., Elkind, D., & Ginsberg, S. (2007). The personal fable and risk taking in early adolescence. *Journal of Youth and Adolescence, 36*, 71–76.

Aldwin, C. M., & Levenson, M. R. (2001). Stress, coping, and health at midlife: A developmental perspective. In M. E. Lachman (Ed.), *Handbook of midlife development.* New York: John Wiley.

Aldwin, C. M., Spiro, A., & Park, C. L. (2006). Health, behavior, and optimal aging. In J. E. Birren & K. W. Schaie (Eds.), *Handbook of the psychology of aging* (6th ed.). San Diego: Academic Press.

Alessandri, N., & others. (2007). Morphological and functional changes of cardiovascular system in postmenopausal women. *European Review for Medical and Pharmacological Sciences, 11*, 107–117.

Alessi, C. A. (2007). Sleep. In J. E. Birren (Ed.), *Encyclopedia of gerontology* (2nd ed.). San Diego: Academic Press.

Allemand, M., Zimprich, D., & Hendriks, A. A. J. (2008). Age differences in five personality domains across the life span. *Developmental Psychology, 44*, 758–770.

Allen, J. P. (2007, March). *A transformational perspective on the attachment system in adolescence.* Paper presented at the meeting of the Society for Research in Child Development, Boston.

Allen, J. P., & Antonishak, J. (2008). Adolescent peer influences: Beyond the dark side. In M. J. Prinstein & K. A. Dodge (Eds.), *Understanding peer influence in children and adolescents.* New York: Guilford.

Allen, J. P., Kuperminc, G. P., Moore, C. (2005, April). *Stability and predictors of change in attachment security across adolescence.* Paper presented at the meeting of the Society for Research on Child Development, Atlanta.

Allen, J. P., Philliber, S., Herring, S., & Kuperminc, G. P. (1997). Preventing teen pregnancy and academic failure: Experimental evaluation of a developmentally-based approach. *Child Development, 68*, 729–742.

Allen, J. P., Porter, M., McFarland, C., Boykin McElhaney, K., & Marsh, P. (2007). The relation of attachment security to adolescents' paternal and peer relationships, depression, and externalizing behavior. *Child Development, 78*, 1222–1239.

Allen, K. L., Byrne, S. M., McLean, N. J., & Davis, E.A. (2008, in press). Overconcern with weight and shape is not the same as body dissatisfaction: evidence from a prospective study of pre-adolescent boys and girls. *Body Image.*

Allen, K. R., Blieszner, R., & Roberto, K. A. (2000). Families in the middle and later years: A review and critique of research in the 1990s. *Journal of Marriage and the Family, 62*, 911–926.

Allen, K. R., Blieszner, R., Roberto, K. A., Farnsworth, E., & Wilcox, K. L. (1999). Older adults and their children: Family patterns of structural diversity. *Family Relations, 48*, 151–157.

Allen, M. C. (2008). Neurodevelopmental outcomes of preterm infants. *Current Opinion in Neurology, 21*, 123–128.

Allen, M., Brown, P., & Finlay, B. (1992). *Helping children by strengthening families.* Washington, DC: Children's Defense Fund.

Alm, B., Lagercrantz, H., & Wennergren, G. (2006). Stop SIDS—sleeping solitary supine, sucking smoother, stopping smoking substitutes. *Acta Paediatrica, 95*, 260–262.

Almeida, D., & Horn, M. (2004). Is daily life more stressful during middle adulthood? In G. Brim, C. D. Ryff, & R. Kessler (Eds.), *How healthy are we? A national study of well-being in midlife.* Chicago: University of Chicago Press.

Almeida, O. P., Garrido, G. J., Lautenschlager, N. T. Hulse, G. K., Jamrozik, K., & Flicker, L. (2008). Smoking is associated with reduced cortical gray matter density in brain regions associated with incipient Alzheimer disease. *American Journal of Geriatric Psychiatry, 16*, 92–98.

Als, H., & Butler, S. C. (2008). Screening, newborn, and maternal well-being. In M. M. Haith & J. B. Benson (Eds.), *Encyclopedia of infancy and early childhood development.* Oxford, UK: Elsevier.

Altarac, M., & Saroha, E. (2007). Lifetime prevalence of learning disability among U.S. children. *Pediatrics, 119* (Suppl. 1), S77–S83.

Altimer, L. (2008). Shaken baby syndrome. *Journal of Perinatal and Neonatal Nursing, 22*, 68–76.

Alvarez, A., & del Rio, P. (2007). Inside and outside the zone of proximal development: An ecofunctional reading of Vygotsky. In H. Daniels, J. Wertsch, & M. Cole (Eds.), *The Cambridge companion to Vygotsky.* New York: Cambridge University Press.

Alzheimer's Disease International. (2005). *Alzheimer's disease.* Retrieved, January 3, 2008, from http://www.alz.co.uk/

Amabile, T. M. (1993). Commentary. In D. Goleman, P. Kaufman, & M. Ray, *The creative spirit.* New York: Plume.

Amabile, T. M., & Hennesey, B. A. (1992). The motivation for creativity in children. In A. K. Boggiano & T. S. Pittman (Eds.), *Achievement and motivation.* New York: Cambridge University Press.

Amato, P. (2006). Historical trends in divorce and dissolution. In M. A. Fine & J. H. Harvey (Eds.), *Handbook of divorce and relationship dissolution.* Mahwah, NJ: Erlbaum.

Amato, P. R. (2006). Marital discord, divorce, and children's well-being: Results from a 20-year longitudinal study of two generations. In A. Clarke-Stewart & J. Dunn (Eds.), *Families count.* New York: Cambridge University Press.

Amato, P. R. (2007). Transformative processes in marriage: Some thoughts from a sociologist. *Journal of Marriage and the Family, 69*, 305–309.

Amato, P. R., & Booth, A. (1996). A prospective study of divorce and parent-child relationships. *Journal of Marriage and the Family, 58*, 356–365.

Amato, P. R., Booth, A., Johnson, D. R., & Rogers, S. J. (2007). *Alone together: How marriage in America is changing.* Cambridge, MA: Harvard University Press.

Amato, P. R., & Cheadle, J. (2005). The long reach of divorce: Divorce and child well-being across three generations. *Journal of Marriage an the Family, 67*, 191–206.

Amato, P., & Irving, S. (2006). Historical trends in divorce and dissolution. In M. A. Fine & J. H. Harvey (Eds.), *Handbook of divorce and relationship dissolution.* Mahwah, NJ: Erlbaum.

Amenta, F., & Tayebati, S. K. (2008). Pathways of acetylcholine synthesis, transport, and release as targets for treatment of adult-onset cognitive dysfunction. *Current Medicinal Chemistry, 15*, 488–498.

American Academy of Pediatrics (AAP) Work Group on Breastfeeding. (1997). Breastfeeding and the use of human milk. *Pediatrics, 100*, 1035–1039.

American Academy of Pediatrics Task Force on Infant Positioning and SIDS. (2000). Changing concepts of sudden infant death syndrome. *Pediatrics, 105*, 650–656.

American Association of University Women. (2006). *Drawing the line: Sexual harassment on campus.* Washington, DC: Author.

American College Health Association. (2008). American College Health Association National College Health Assessment spring 2007 reference group data report (abridged). *Journal of American College Health, 56*, 469–479.

American Psychological Association. (2003). *Psychology: Scientific problem solvers.* Washington, DC: Author.

American Psychological Association. (2007). *Stress in America.* Washington, DC: Author.

American Public Health Association. (2006). *Understanding the health culture of recent immigrants to the United States.* Retrieved February 10, 2006, from www.apha.org/ppp/red/Intro.htm

Amsterdam, B. K. (1968). *Mirror behavior in children under two years of age.* Unpublished doctoral dissertation. University of North Carolina, Chapel Hill.

Amuna, P., & Zotor, F. B. (2008). Epidemiological and nutrition transition in developing countries: Impact on human health and development. *Proceedings of the Nutrition Society, 67*, 82–90.

Anastasi, A., & Urbina, S. (1996). *Psychological testing* (7th ed.). Upper Saddle River, NJ: Prentice Hall.

Andel, R., Crowe, M., Pedersen, N. L., Fratiglioni, L., Johansson, B., & Gatz, M. (2008). Physical exercise at midlife and risk of dementia three decades later: Population-based study of Swedish twins. *Journals of Gerontology A: Biological Sciences and medical Sciences, 63*, 62–66.

Anderman, E. M., & Mueller, C. E. (2009, in press). Middle school transitions and adolescent development: Disentangling psychological, social, and biological effects. In J. Meece & J. Eccles (Eds.), *Handbook of research on schools, schooling, and human development.* Clifton, NJ: Psychology Press.

Anderson, D. R., Lorch, E. P., Field, D. E., Collins, P. A., & Nathan, J. G. (1985, April). *Television viewing at home: Age trends in visual attention and time with TV.* Paper presented at the biennial meeting of the Society for Research in Child Development, Toronto.

Anderson, E., Greene, S. M., Hetherington, E. M., & Clingempeel, W. G. (1999). The dynamics of parental remarriage. In E. M. Hetherington (Ed.), *Coping with divorce, single parenting, and remarriage.* Mahwah, NJ: Erlbaum.

Anderson, P. A. (2006). Sex differences that make a difference: Social evolution and reproduction. In K. Dindia & D. J. Canary (Eds.), *Sex differences and similarities in communication.* Mahwah, NJ: Erlbaum.

Anderson, R. M., & Weindruch, R. (2007). Metabolic reprogramming in dietary restriction. *Interdisciplinary Topics in Gerontology, 35*, 18–38.

Anderson, S. A., & Sabatelli, R. M. (2007). *Family interaction* (4th ed.). Boston: Allyn & Bacon.

Anderson, V., Jacobs, R., & Harvey, A. H. (2005). Prefrontal lesions and attentional skills in childhood. *Journal of the International Neuropsychological Society, 11*, 817–831.

Ang, S. & van Dyne, L. (2009, in press). *Handbook on cultural intelligence.* New York; M.E. Sharpe.

Angel, J. L., Jimenez, M. A., & Angel, R. J. (2007). The economic consequences of widowhood for older minority women. *Gerontologist, 47*, 224–234.

Anspaugh, D. J., Hamrick, M. H., & Rosato, F. D. (2009). *Wellness* (7th ed.). New York: McGraw-Hill.

Antonucci, T. C. (1989). Understanding adult social relationships. In K. Kreppner & R. M. Lerner (Eds.), *Family systems and life-span development.* Hillsdale, NJ: Erlbaum.

Antonucci, T. C., Akiyama, H., & Sherman, A. M. (2007). Social networks, support, and integration. In J. E. Birren (Ed.), *Encyclopedia of gerontology* (2nd ed.). San Diego: Academic Press.

Antonucci, T. C., Lansford, J. E., & Akiyama, H. (2001) The impact of positive and negative aspects of marital relationships and friendships on the well-being of older adults. In J. P. Reinhardt (Ed.), *Negative and positive support.* Mahwah, NJ: Erlbaum.

Antonucci, T. C., Vandewater, E. A., & Lansford, J. E. (2000). Adulthood and aging: Social processes and development. In A. Kazdin (Ed.), *Encyclopedia of psychology.* Washington, DC & New York: American Psychological Association and Oxford University Press.

Applebaum, M. (2008). Why diets fail—expert diet advice as a cause of diet failure. *American Psychologist, 63,* 200–202.

Archibald, A. B., Graber, J. A., & Brooks-Gunn, J. (1999). Associations among parent-adolescent relationships, pubertal growth, dieting, and body image in young adolescent girls: A short-term longitudinal study. *Journal of Research on Adolescence, 9,* 395–415.

Arehart, D. M., & Smith, P. H. (1990). Identity in adolescence: Influences on dysfunction and psychosocial task issues. *Journal of Youth and Adolescence, 19,* 63–72.

Ariceli, G., Castro, J., Cesena, J., & Toro, J. (2005). Anorexia nervosa in male adolescents: Body image, eating attitudes, and psychological traits. *Journal of Adolescent Health, 36,* 221–226.

Armour, S., & Haynie, D. L. (2007). Adolescent sexual debut and later delinquency. *Journal of Youth and Adolescence, 36,* 141–152.

Armstrong, D. G. Henson, K. T., & Savage, T. V. (2009). *Teaching today* (8th Ed.). Boston: Allyn & Bacon.

Armstrong, J. S. (2007). Mitochondrial medicine: Pharmacological targeting of mitochondria in disease. *British Journal of Pharmacology, 151,* 1154–1165.

Armstrong, M. L. (1995) Adolescent tattoos: Educating and pontificating. *Pediatric Nursing, 21* (6), 561–564.

Armstrong, M. L., Roberts, A. E., Owen, D. C., & Koch, J. R. (2004). Contemporary college students and body piercing. *Journal of Adolescent Health, 35,* 58–61.

Arnett, J. J. (1995, March). *Are college students adults?* Paper presented at the meeting of the Society for Research in Child Development, Indianapolis.

Arnett, J. J. (2004). *Emerging adulthood.* New York: Oxford University Press.

Arnett, J. J. (2006). Emerging adulthood: Understanding the new way of coming of age. In J. J. Arnett, J. L. Tanner (Eds.), *Emerging adults in America.* Washington, DC: American Psychological Association.

Arnett, J. J. (2007). Socialization in emerging adulthood. In J. E. Grusec & P. D. Hastings (Eds.), *Handbook of socialization.* New York: Guilford.

Aron, A., Aron, E., & Coupos, E. (2008). *Statistics for the behavioral and social sciences.* Upper Saddle River, NJ: Prentice Hall.

Aronow, W. S. (2007). Cardiovascular system. In J. E. Birren (Ed.), *Encylcopedia of gerontology* (2nd ed.). San Diego: Academic Press.

Aronson, E. (1986, August). *Teaching students things they think they already know about: The case of prejudice and desegregation.* Paper presented at the meeting of the American Psychological Association, Washington, DC.

Arpanantikul, M. (2004). Midlife experiences of Thai women. *Journal of Advanced Nursing, 47,* 49–56.

Arredondo, E. M., Elder, J. P., Ayala, G. X., Campbell, N., Baquero, B., & Duerksen, S. (2006). Is parenting style related to children's healthy eating and physical activity in Latino families? *Health Education Research, 21,* 862–871.

Arterberry, M. E. (2008). Perceptual development. In M. M. Haith & J. B. Benson (Eds.), *Encyclopedia of infant and early childhood development.* Oxford, UK: Elsevier.

Aschkenasy, M. T., & Rothenhaus, T. C. (2006). Trauma and falls in the elderly. *Emergency Clinics of North America, 24,* 413–432.

Asendorph, J. B. (2008). Shyness. In M. M. Haith & J. B. Benson (Eds.), *Encyclopedia of infant and early childhood development.* Oxford, UK: Elsevier.

Ash, P. (2006). Adolescents in adult court: Does the punishment fit the criminal? *The Journal of the American Academy of Psychiatry and the Law, 34,* 145–149.

Ash, P. (2008). Suicidal behavior in children and adolescents. *Journal of Psychosocial Nursing and Mental Health Services, 46,* 26–30.

Ashton, D. (2006). Prematurity—infant mortality: The scourge remains. *Ethnicity and Disease, 16.* (Suppl. 2), S3–S58.

Askham, J., Ferring, D., & Lamura, G. (2007). Personal relationships in later life. In J. Bond, S. Peace, F. Dittman-Kohli, & G. Westerhoff (Eds.), *Aging in society* (3rd ed.). Thousand Oaks, CA: Sage.

Aslin, R. N., & Lathrop, A. L. (2008). Visual perception. In M. M. Haith & J. B. Benson (Eds.), *Encyclopedia of infant and early childhood development.* Oxford, UK: Elsevier.

Aslin, R. N., Jusczyk, P. W., & Pisoni, D. B. (1998). Speech and auditory processing during infancy: Constraints on and precursors to language. In W. Damon (Ed.), *Handbook of child psychology* (5th ed., Vol. 2). New York: Wiley.

Assanand, S., Dias, M., Richardson, E., & Waxler–Morrison, N. (1990). The South Asians. In N. Waxler-Morrison, J. M. Anderson, & E. Richardson (Eds.), *Cross-cultural caring.* Vancouver, BC: UBC Press.

Asscher, J. (2008). The moral distinction between killing and letting die in medical cases. *Bioethics, 22,* 278–285.

Astington, J. W., & Dack, L. A. (2008). Theory of mind. In M. M. Haith & J. B. Benson (Eds.), *Encyclopedia of infant and early childhood development.* Oxford, UK: Elsevier.

Ata, R. N., Luden, A. B., & Lally, M. M. (2007). The effect of gender and family, friend, and media influences on eating behaviors and body image during adolescence. *Journal of Youth and Adolescence, 36,* 1024–1037.

Atchley, R. C. (2007). Retirement. In J. E. Birren (Ed.), *Encyclopedia of gerontology* (2nd ed.). San Diego: Academic Press.

Atkinson, R. M., Ryan, S. C., & Turner, J. A. (2001). Variation among aging alcoholic patients in treatment. *American Journal of Geriatric Psychiatry, 9,* 275–282.

Attie, L., & Brooks-Gunn, J. (1989). Development of eating problems in adolescent girls: A longitudinal study. *Developmental Psychology, 25,* 70–79.

Aubert, G., & Lansdorp, P. M. (2008). Telomeres and aging. *Physiological Review, 88,* 557–579.

Aucoin, K. J., Frick, P. J., & Bodin, S. D. (2006). Corporal punishment and child adjustment. *Journal of Applied Developmental Psychology, 27,* 527–541.

Aud, M. A., Bostick, J. E., Marek, K. D., & McDaniel, R. W. (2006). Introducing baccalaureate student nurses to gernotological nursing. *Journal of Professional Nursing, 22,* 73–78.

Avent, N. D., Plummer, Z. E., Madgett, T. E., Maddocks, D. G., & Soothill, P. W. (2008). Post-genomic studies and their application to non-invasive prenatal diagnosis. *Seminars in Fetal and Neonatal Medicine, 13,* 91–98.

Azmitia, M., Syed, M., & Radmacher, K. (Eds.) (2008). On the intersection of personal and social identities: Introduction and evidence from a longitudinal study of emerging adults. *The intersections of personal and social identities. New Directions in Child and Adolescent Development,* 1–16.

B

Bachman, J. G., O'Malley, P. M., Schulenberg, J. E., Johnston, L. D., Bryant, A. L., & Merline, A. C. (2002). *The decline of substance abuse in young adulthood.* Mahwah, NJ: Erlbaum.

Bachman, J. G., O'Malley, P. M., Schulenberg, J. E., Johnston, L. D., Freedman-Doan, P., & Messersmith, E. E. (2008). *The education-drug use connection.* Clifton, NJ: Psychology Press.

Backman, L., & Nyberg, L. (Eds.). (2009). *Memory, aging, and the brain.* Clifton, NJ: Psychology Press.

Backman, L., Small, B. J., & Wahlin, A. (2001). Aging and memory: Cognitive and behavioral processes. In J. E. Birren & K. W. Schaie (Eds.), *Handbook of the psychology of aging* (5th ed.). San Diego: Academic Press.

Badaly, D., & Adolph, K. E. (2008, in press). Beyond the average: Infants take steps longer than their leg length. *Infant Behavior and Development.*

Baddeley, A. (2000). Short-term and working memory. In E. Tulving & F. I. M. Craik (Eds.), *The Oxford handbook of memory.* New York: Oxford University Press.

Baddeley, A. D. (2006) Working memory: An overview. In S. Pickering (Ed.). *Working memory and education.* New York: Academic Press

Baddeley, A. D. (2007a). *Working memory, thought and action.* New York: Oxford University Press.

Baddeley, A. D. (2007b) Working memory: Multiple models, multiple mechanisms. In H. L. Roediger, Y. Dudai, & S. M. Fitzpatrick (Eds.). *Science of memory: concepts.* New York: Oxford University Press.

Baddock, S. A., Galland, B. C., Taylor, B. J., & Bolton, D. P. (2007). Sleep arrangements and behavior of bed-sharing families in the home setting. *Pediatrics, 119,* e200–e207.

Baehr, T. A., & Barnett, M. M. (2007). Examining retirement from a multi-level perspective. In K. S. Shultz & G. A. Adams (Eds.), *Aging and work in the 21st century.* Mahwah, NJ: Erlbaum.

Baezner, H., & others. (2008). Association of gait and balance disorders with age-related white matter changes: The LADIS Study. *Neurology, 70,* 935–942.

Bagwell, C. L. (2004). Friendships, peer networks, and antisocial behavior. In J. B. Kupersmidt & K. A. Dodge (Eds.), *Children's peer relations*. Washington. DC: American Psychological Association.

Bahrick, H. P. (1984). Semantic memory content in permastore: Fifty years of memory for Spanish learned in school. *Journal of Experimental Psychology: General, 113*, 1–35.

Bahrick, L. E., & Hollich, G. (2008). Intermodal perception. In M. M. Haith & J. B. Benson (Eds.), *Encyclopedia of infant and early childhood development*. Oxford, UK: Elsevier.

Baillargeon, R. (1995). The object concept revisited: New directions in the investigation of infants' physical knowledge, In C. E. Granrud (Ed.), *Visual perception and cognition in infancy*. Hillsdale, NJ: Erlbaum.

Baillargeon, R. (2004). The acquisition of physical knowledge in infancy: A summary in eight lessons. In U. Goswami (Ed.), *Blackwell handbook of childhood cognitive development*. Malden, MA: Blackwell.

Baillargeon, R., & Devo S. J. (1991). Object permanence in young children: Further evidence. *Child Development, 62*, 1227–1246.

Baillargeon, R. H., Zoccolillo, M., Keenna, K., Cote, S., Perusse, D., Wu, H-X., Boivin, M., & Tremblay, R. E. (2007). Gender differences in physical aggression: A prospective -population-based survey of children before and after two years of age. *Developmental Psychology, 43*, 13–26.

Baird, D. M. (2007). Telomeres. In J. E. Birren (Ed.), *Encyclopedia of gerontology* (2nd ed.). San Diego: Academic Press.

Bajanowski, T., Brinkmann, B, Mitchell, E. A., Vennemann, M. M., Leukel, H. W., Larsch, K. P., Beike, J., & the GeSID Group. (2007). Nicotine and cotinine in infants dying from sudden infant death syndrome. *International Journal of Legal Medicine, 122*, 23–28.

Bakeman, R., & Brown, J. V. (1980). Early interaction: Consequences for social and mental development at three years. *Child Development, 51*, 437–447.

Baker, D. A. (2007). Consequences of herpes simplex virus in pregnancy and their prevention. *Current Opinions in Infectious Diseases, 20*, 73–76.

Baker, S. R. (2006). Toward an idiopathic understanding of the role of social problem solving in daily event, mood, and health experiences: A prospective daily diary approach. *British Journal of Health Psychology, 11*, 513–531.

Bakermans-Kranenburg, M. J., Breddels-Van Bardewijk, F., Juffer, M. K., Velderman, M. H., & van IJzenddorn, M. H. (2007). Insecure mothers with temperamentally reactive infants. In F. Juffer, M. J. Bakermans-Kranenburg, & M. H. van IJzendoorn (Eds.), *Promoting positive parenting*. Mahwah, NJ: Erlbaum.

Balasubramanian, A., Koontz, J., & Reynolds, C. A. (2008). Genetics and inheritance. In M. M. Haith & J. B. Benson (Eds.), *Encyclopedia of infancy and early childhood*. Oxford, UK: Elsevier

Balchin, I., & Steer, P. J. (2007). Race, prematurity, and immaturity. *Early Human Development, 83*, 749–754.

Balchin, T., Hymer, B., & Matthews, D. (Eds.). (2009, in press). *International companion to gifted education*. London: Routledge.

Baldwin, J. D., & Baldwin, J. I. (1998). Sexual behavior. In H. S. Friedman (Ed.), *Encyclopedia of mental health* (Vol. 3). San Diego: Academic Press.

Baldwin, S., & Hoffman, J. P. (2002). The dynamics of self-esteem: A growth curve analysis. *Journal of Youth and Adolescence, 31*, 101–113.

Balkau, B., & others. (2007). International Day for the Evaluation of Abdominal Obesity (IDEA): A study of waist circumference, cardiovascular disease, and diabetes mellitus in 168,000 primary care patients in 63 countries. *Circulation, 116*, 1942–1951.

Ball, K., Edwards, J. D., & Ross, L. A. (2007). The impact of speed of process training on cognitive and everyday functions. *Journals of Gerontology B: Psychological Sciences and Social Sciences, 62*, P19–P31.

Ballantine, J. H., & Hammock, J. H. (2009). *The sociology of education* (6th ed.). Upper Saddle River, NJ: Prentice Hall.

Balsano, A., Phelps, E., Theokas, C., Lerner, J. V., & Lerner, R. M. (2008, in press). Patterns of early adolescents' participation in youth developing programs having positive youth development. *Journal of Research on Adolescence.*

Baltes, P. B. (1987). Theoretical propositions of lifespan developmental psychology: On the dynamics between growth and decline. *Developmental Psychology, 23*, 611–626.

Baltes, P. B. (2003). On the incomplete architecture of human ontogeny: Selection, optimization, and compensation as foundation for development theory, In U. M. Staudinger & U. Lindenberger (Eds.), *Understanding human development*. Boston: Kluwer.

Baltes, P. B. (2006). *Facing our limits: The very old and the future of aging.* Unpublished manuscript, Max Planck Institute, Berlin.

Baltes, P. B. (2009). Aging and wisdom. In D. C. Park & N. Schwarz (Eds.), Cognitive aging (2nd ed.). Clifton, NJ: Psychology Press.

Baltes, P. B., & Kunzmann, U. (2007). Wisdom and aging: The road toward excellence in mind and character. In D. C. Park & N. Schwarz (Eds.), *Cognitive aging: A primer* (2nd ed.). Philadelphia: Psychology Press.

Baltes, P. B., Lindenberger, U., & Staudinger, U. (2006). Lifespan theory in development psychology. In. W. Damon & R. Lerner (Eds.), *Handbook of child psychology* (6th ed.). New York: Wiley.

Baltes, P. B., Reuter-Lorenz, P., & Rösler, F. (Eds.). (2006). *Lifespan development and the brain.* New York: Cambridge University Press.

Baltes, P. B., & Smith, J. (2003). New frontiers in the future of aging: From successful aging of the young old to the dilemmas of the fourth age. *Gerontology, 49*, 123–135.

Baltes, P. B., & Smith, J. (2008). The fascination of wisdom: Its nature, ontogeny, and function. *Perspectives in Psychological Sciences, 3*, 56–64.

Bandura, A. (1986). *Social foundations of thought and action: A social cognitive theory.* Englewood Cliffs, NJ: Prentice Hall.

Bandura, A. (1998, August). *Swimming against the mainstream: Accentuating the positive aspects of humanity.*

Paper presented at the meeting of the American Psychological Association, San Francisco.

Bandura, A. (1999). Moral disengagement in the perpetuation of inhumanities. *Personality and Social Psychology Review, 3*, 193–209.

Bandura, A. (2001). Social cognitive theory. *Annual Review of Psychology.* Palo Alto, CA: Annual Reviews.

Bandura, A. (2002). Selective moral disengagement in the exercise of moral agency. *Journal of Moral Education, 31*, 101–119.

Bandura, A. (2004, May). *Toward a psychology of human agency.* Paper presented at the meeting of the American Psychological Society, Chicago.

Bandura, A. (2007a). Self-efficacy. In S. Clegg & J. Bailey (Eds.), *International encyclopedia of organization studies.* Thousand Oaks, CA: Sage.

Bandura, A. (2007b). Social cognitive theory. In W. Donsbach (Ed.), *International encyclopedia of communication.* Thousand Oaks, CA: Sage.

Bandura, A. (2008). Reconstrual of "free will" from the agentic perspective of social cognitive theory. In J. Baer, J. C., Kaufman, & R. F. Baumeister (Eds.), *Are we free? Psychology and free will.* Oxford, UK: Oxford University Press.

Bandura, A. (2009, in press). Social and policy impact of social cognitive theory. In M. Mark, S. Donaldson, & B. Campbell (Eds.), *Social psychology and program/policy evaluation.* New York: Guilford.

Banerjee, T. D., Middleton, F., & Faraone, S. V. (2007). Environmental risk factors for attention-deficit hyperactivity disorder. *Acta Pediatrica, 96*, 1269–1274.

Banja, J. (2005). Talking to the dying. *Case Manager, 16*, 37–39.

Bank, L., Burraston, B., & Snyder, J. (2004). Sibling conflict and ineffective parenting as predictors of adolescent boys' antisocial behavior and peer difficulties: additive and interactive effects. *Journal of Research on Adolescence, 14*, 99–125.

Banks, J. A. (2008). Introduction to multicultural education (4th ed.). Boston: Allyn & Bacon.

Banks, M. S. (2005). The benefits and costs of combining information between and within the senses. In J. J. Reiser, J. J. Lockman, & C. A. Nelson (Eds.), *The role of action in learning and development.* Mahwah, NJ: Erlbaum.

Barabasz, A., & Perez, N. (2007). Salient findings: Hypnotizability as core construct and the clinical utility of hypnosis. *International Journal of Clinical Hypnosis, 55*, 372–379.

Barajas, R. G., Philipsen, N., & Brooks-Gunn, J. (2008). Cognitive and emotional outcomes for children in poverty. In D. R. Crane & T. B. Heaton (Eds.), *Handbook of families and poverty.* Thousand Oaks, CA: Sage.

Barefoot, J. C., Mortensen, E. L., Helms, J., Avlund, K., & Schroll, M. (2001). A longitudinal study of gender differences in depressive symptoms from age 50 to 80. *Psychology and Aging, 16*, 342–345.

Barker, R., & Wright, H. F. (1951). *One boy's day.* New York: Harper & Row.

Barnes, L. L., de Leon, C. F., Lewis, T. T., Bienias, J. L., Wilson, R. S., & Evans, D. A. (2008). Perceived discrimination and mortality in a population-based study of older adults. *American Journal of Public Health, 98*, 1241–1247.

Barnes, L. L., Mendes de Leon, C. F., Wilson, R. S., Bienias, J. L., Bennett, D. A., & Evans, D. A. (2004). Racial differences in perceived discrimination in a community population of older Blacks and Whites. *Journal of Aging and Health, 16*, 315–317.

Barnett, R. C. (2001). Work-family balance. In J. Worell (Ed.), *Encyclopedia of women and gender.* San Diego: Academic Press.

Barnett, R. C., Gareis, K. C., James, J. B., & Steele, J. (2001, August). *Planning ahead: College seniors' concerns about work-family conflict.* Paper presented at the meeting of the American Psychological Association, San Francisco.

Baron, N. S. (1992). *Growing up with language.* Reading, MA: Addison-Wesley.

Baron-Cohen, S. (1995). *Mindblindness: An essay on autism and theory of mind.* Cambridge, MA: MIT Press.

Barrett, A. E., & Turner, R. J. (2005). Family structure and mental health: The mediating effects of socioeconomic status, family process, and social stress. *Journal of Health and Social Behavior, 46*, 156–169.

Barrett, D. E., Radke-Yarrow, M., & Klein, R. E. (1982). Chronic malnutrition and child behavior: Effects of calorie supplementation on social and emotional functioning at school age. *Developmental Psychology, 18*, 541–556.

Barrett, L. F., Mesquita, B., Ochsner, K. N., & Gross, J. J. (2007). The experience of emotion. *Annual Review of Psychology* (Vol. '58). Palo Alto, CA: Annual Reviews.

Barrett, T. M., Davis, E. F., & Needham, A. (2007). Learning about tools in infancy. *Developmental Psychology, 43*, 352–368.

Barrett, T. M., & Needham, A. (2008). Developmental differences in infants' use of an object's shape to grasp it securely. *Developmental Psychobiology, 50*, 97–106.

Barrett, T. M., Traupman, E., & Needham, A. (2008). Infants' visual anticipation of object structure in grasp planning. *Infant Behavior and Development, 31*, 1–9.

Barrio, J. R., Kepe, V., Satyamurthy, N., Huang, S. C., & Small, G. (2008). Amyloid and tau imaging, neuronal losses, and function in mild cognitive impairment. *Journal of Nutrition, Health, and Aging, 12* (Suppl. 1), 61S–65S.

Barron, J., Petrilli, F., Strath, L., & McCaffrey, R. (2007). Successful interventions for smoking cessation in pregnancy. *MCN American Journal of Maternal and Child Nursing, 32*, 42–47.

Bart, W. M., & Peterson, D. P. (2008). Stanford-Binet test. In N. J. Salkind (Ed.), *Encyclopedia of educational psychology.* Thousand Oaks, CA: Sage.

Bartle, C. (2007). Developing a service for children with iron deficiency anemia. *Nursing Standard, 21*, 44–49.

Bartsch, K., & Wellman, H. M. (1995). *Children talk about the mind.* Oxford University Press.

Basaran, A. (2007). Progesterone to prevent preterm delivery: Enigma or ready? *American Journal of Obstetrics and Gynecology, 197*, 686.

Bateman, B. T., & Simpson, L. L. (2006). Higher rate of stillbirth at the extremes of reproductive age:

A large nationwide sample of deliveries in the United States. *American Journal of Obstetrics and Gynecology, 194*, 840–845.

Bates, A. S., Fitzgerald, J. F., Dittus, R. S., & Wollinsky, F. D. (1994). Risk factors for underimmunization in poor urban infants. *Journal of the American Medical Association, 272*, 1105–1109.

Bates, E. (1990). Language about me and you: Pronominal reference and the emerging concept of self. In D. Cicchetti & M. Beeghly (Eds.), *The self in transition: Infancy to childhood.* Chicago: University of Chicago Press.

Bates, J. E. & Pettit, G. S. (2007). Temperament, parenting, and socialization. In J. E. Grusec & P. D. Hastings (Eds.), *Handbook of socialization.* New York: Guilford.

Bauer, P. J. (2007). *Remembering the times of our lives.* Mahwah, NJ: Erlbaum.

Bauer, P. J. (2008, in press). Learning and memory: Like a horse and carriage. In A. Netdham & A. Woodward (Eds.), *Learning and the infant Mind.* New York: Oxford University Press.

Bauer, P. J., Wenner, J. A., Dropik, P. I., & Wewerka, S. S. (2000). Parameters of remembering and forgetting in the transition from infancy to early childhood. *Monographs of the Society for Research in Child Development, 65* (4, Serial No. 263).

Bauer, P. J., Wiebe, S. A., Carver, L. J., Waters, J. M., & Nelson, C. A. (2003). Developments in long-term explicit memory late in the first year of life: Behavioral and electrophysiological indices. *Psychological Science, 14*, 629–635.

Bauman, K. E., Ennett, S. T., Foshee, V. A., Pemberton, M., King, T. S., & Koch, G. G. (2002). Influence of a family program on adolescent smoking and drinking prevalence. *Prevention Science, 3*, 35–42.

Bauman, W. P. (2008). Sexuality in later life. In R. Jacoby, C. Oppenheimer, T. Dening, & A. Thomas (Eds.). *Oxford textbook of old age psychiatry.* Oxford, UK: Oxford University Press.

Baumeister, R. F., Campbell, J. D., Krueger, J. I., & Vohs, K. D. (2003). Does high self-esteem cause better performance, interpersonal success, happiness, or healthier lifestyles? *Psychological Science in the Public Interest, 4* (No. 1), 1–44.

Baumeister, R. F., & Vohs, K. D. (2002). The pursuit of meaningfulness in life. In C. R. Snyder & S. J. Lopez (Eds.), *Handbook of positive psychology.* New York: Oxford University Press.

Baumrind, D. (1971). Current patterns of parental authority. *Developmental Psychology Monographs, 4* (1, Pt. 2).

Baumrind, D. (1999, November). Unpublished review of J. W. Santrock's *Child development,* 9th ed. (New York: McGraw-Hill.)

Bauserman, R. (2002). Child adjustment in joint-custody versus sole-custody arrangements: A meta-analytic review. *Journal of Family Psychology, 16*, 91–102.

Baxter, G. W., Stuart, W. J., & Stewart, W. J. (1998). *Death and the adolescent.* Toronto: University of Toronto Press.

Bayley, N. (1969). *Manual for the Bayley Scales of Infant Development.* New York: Psychological Corporation.

Bayley, N. (2005). *Bayley scales of infant and toddler development, third edition (Bayley—III).* Upper Saddle River, NJ: Pearson.

Bearman, P. S., & Moody, J. (2004). Suicide and friendships among American adolescents. *American Journal of Public Health, 94*, 89–95.

Bearman, S. K., Presnall, K., Martinez, E., & Stice, E. (2006). The skinny on body dissatisfaction: A longitudinal study of adolescent girls and boys. *Journal of Youth and Adolescence, 35*, 217–229.

Bechtold, A. G., Busnell, E. W., & Salapatek, P. (1979, April.), *Infants' visual localization of visual and auditory targets.* Paper presented at the meeting of the Society for Research in Child Development, San Francisco.

Beck, C. T. (2002). Theoretical perspectives of postpartum depression and their treatment implications. *American Journal of Maternal/Child Nursing, 27*, 282–287.

Beck, C. T. (2006). Postpartum depression: It isn't just the blues. *American Journal of Nursing, 106*, 40–50.

Beckmann, M. M., & Garrett, A. J. (2006). Antenatal perineal massage for reducing perineal trauma. *Cochrane Database of Systematic Reviews, 1*, CD005123.

Bednar, R. L., Wells, M. G., & Peterson, S. R. (1995). *Self-esteem* (2nd ed.). Washington, DC: American Psychological Association.

Beech, A. R., Ward, T., & Fisher, D. (2006). The identification of sexual and violent motivations in men who assault women: Implications for treatment. *Journal of Interpersonal Violence, 21*, 1635–1653.

Beeghly, M., Martin, B., Rose-Jacobs, R., Cahral, H., Heeren, T., Augustyn, M., Bellinger, D., & Frank, D. A. (2006). Prenatal cocaine exposure and children's language functioning at 6 and 9.5 years: Moderating effects of child age, birthweight, and gender. *Journal of Pediatric Psychology, 31*, 98–115.

Beets, M. W., & Foley, J. T. (2008). Association of father involvement and neighborhood quality with kindergartners' physical activity: A multilevel structural equation model. *American Journal of Health Promotion, 22*, 195–203.

Beghetto, R. A., & Kaufman, J. C. (2009, in press). *Nurturing creativity in the classroom.* New York: Cambridge University Press.

Beilin, L., & Huang, R. C. (2008). Childhood obesity, hypertension, the metabolic syndrome, and adult cardiovascular disease. *Clinical and Experimental Pharmacology and Physiology, 35*, 409–411.

Bell, M. A., & Fox, N. A. (1992). The relations between frontal brain electrical activity and cognitive development during infancy. *Child Development, 63*, 1142–1163.

Bell, M. A., & Wolfe, C. D. (2007). The cognitive neuroscience of early socioemotional development. In C. A. Brownell & C. B. Kopp (Eds.), *Socioemotional development in the toddler years.* New York: Guilford.

Bell, S. M., & Ainsworth, M. D. S. (1972). Infant crying and maternal responsiveness. *Child Development, 43*, 1171–1190.

Belleville, S., Sylvain-Roy, S., de Boysson, C., & Menard, M. C. (2008). Characterizing the memory changes in persons with mild cognitive impairment. *Progress in Brain Research, 169*, 365–375.

Belsky, J. (1981). Early human experience: A family perspective. *Developmental Psychology, 17*, 3–23.

Belsky, J. (2009a, in press). Social-contextual determinants of parenting. In R. E. Tremblay, R. deV Peters, M. Boivin, & R. G. Barr (Eds.), *Encyclopedia on early childhood development.* Montreal: Centre of Excellence for Early Childhood Development.

Belsky, J. (2009b, in press). Child care and its impact on young children (0-2). In R. E. Tremblay, R. deV Peters, M. Boivan, & R. G. Barr (Eds.), *Encyclopedia on early childhood development.* Montreal: Centre of Excellence for Early Childhood Development.

Belsky, J., Jaffe, S., Hsieh, K., & Silva, P. (2001). Child-rearing antecedents of intergenerational relations in young adulthood: A prospective study. *Developmental Psychology, 37*, 801–813.

Belsky, J., & Pasco Fearon, R. (2002). Early attachment security, subsequent maternal sensitivity, and later child development: Does continuity in development depend upon continuity of caregiving? *Attachment and Human Development, 4*, 361–387.

Belsky, J., Vandell, D. L., Burchinal, M., Clarke-Stewart, A., McCartney, K., Owen, M. T., & the NICHD Early Child Care Research Network. (2007). Are there long-term effects of early child care. *Child Development, 78*, 681–701.

Belson, W. (1978). *Television violence and the adolescent boy.* London: Saxon House.

Bem, S. L. (1977). On the utility of alternative procedures for assessing psychological androgyny. *Journal of Consulting and Clinical Psychology, 45*, 196–205.

Bender, H. L., Allen, J. P., McElhaney, K. B., Antonishak, J., Moore, C. M., Kello, H. O., & Davis, S. M. (2007). Use of harsh physical discipline and developmental outcomes in adolescence. *Development and Psychopathology, 19*, 227–242.

Bender, W. N. (2008). *Learning disabilities* (6th ed.). Boston: Allyn & Bacon.

Bendersky, M., & Sullivan, M. W. (2007). Basic methods in infant research. In A. Slater & M. Lewis (Eds.), *Introduction to infant development* (2nd ed.). New York: Oxford University Press.

Benenson, J. F., Apostolaris, N. H., & Parnass, J. (1997). Age and sex differences in dyadic and group interaction. *Developmental Psychology, 33*, 538–543.

Bengtson, H., & Psouni, E. (2008). Mothers' representations of caregiving and their adult children's representations of attachment: Intergenerational concordance and relations to beliefs about mothering. *Scandinavian Journal of Psychology, 49*, 247–257.

Bengtson, V. L. (1985). Diversity and symbolism in grandparental roles. In V. L. Gengtson & J. Robertson (Eds.), *Grandparenthood.* Newbury Park, CA: Sage.

Benjamins, M. R., & Finlayson, M. (2007). Using religious services to improve health. Findings from a sample of middle-aged and older adults with multiple sclerosis. *Journal of Aging and Health, 19*, 537–553.

Bennett, T., Szatmari, P., Bryson, S., Volden, J., Zwaigenbaum, L., Vaccarella, L., Duku, E., &

Boyle, M. (2007, in press). Differentiating autism and Asperger syndrome on the basis of language delay or impairment. *Journal of Autism and Developmental Disorders.*

Benninghoven, D., Tetsch, N., Kunzendorf, S., & Jantschek, G. (2007). Body image in patients with eating disorders and their mothers, and the role of family functioning. *Comprehensive Psychiatry, 48*, 118–123.

Benoit, D. (2009, in press). Efficacy of attachment-based interventions. In R. E. Tremblay, R. deV Peters, M. Boivin, & R. G. Barr (Eds.), *Encyclopedia on early childhood development.* Montreal: Centre of Excellence for Early Childhood Development.

Benoit, D., Coolbear, J., & Crawford, A. (2008). Abuse, neglect, and maltreatment of infants. In M. M. Haith & J. B. Benson (Eds.), *Encyclopedia of infant and early childhood development.* Oxford, UK: Elsevier.

Benokraitis, N. (2008). *Marriages and families* (6th ed.). Upper Saddle River, NJ: Prentice Hall.

Benson, A. C., Torode, M. E., & Fiatarone Singh, M. A. (2008, in press). The effects of high-intensity progressive resistance training on adiposity in children: A randomized controlled trial. *International Journal of Obesity.*

Benson, P. L., Roehlkepartain, E. C., & Hong, K. L. (2008, in press). Spiritual development. *New Directions for Youth Development.*

Bergen, D. (1988). Stages of play development. In D. Bergen (Ed.), *Play as a medium for learning and development.* Portsmouth, NH: Heinemann.

Berger, S., & Porell, F. (2008, in press). The association between low vision and function. *Journal of Aging and Health.*

Berk, L. E. (1994). Why children talk to themselves. *Scientific American, 271* (5), 78–83.

Berk, L. E., & Spuhl, S. T. (1995). Maternal interaction, private speech, and task performance in preschool children. *Early Childhood Research Quarterly, 10*, 145–169.

Berko, J. (1958). The child's learning of English morphology. *Word, 14*, 150–177.

Berko Gleason, J. (2003). Unpublished, review of J. W. Santrock's *Life-span development*, 9th Ed. (New York: McGraw-Hill).

Berko Gleason, J. (2005). The development of Language. In J. Berko Gleason, *The development of language* (6th ed.). Boston: Allyn & Bacon.

Berko Gleason, J. (2009). The development of language: An overview. In J. Berko Gleason & N. Ratner (Eds.), *The development of language* (7th ed.). Boston: Allyn & Bacon.

Berlyne, D. E. (1960). *Conflict, arousal, and curiosity.* New York: McGraw-Hill.

Bernard, K., & Dozier, M. (2008). Adoption and foster placement. In M. M. Haith & J. B. Benson (Eds.), *Encyclopedia of infant and early childhood development.* Oxford, UK: Elsevier.

Berndt, T. J. (2002). Friendship quality and social development. *Current Directions in Psychological Science, 11*, 7–10.

Berndt, T. J., & Perry, T. B. (1990). Distinctive features and effects of early adolescent friendships. In R. Montemayor (Ed.), *Advances in adolescent research.* Greenwich, CT: JAI Press.

Berninger, V. W. (2006). Learning disabilities. In W. Damon & R. Lerner (Eds.), *Handbook of child psychology* (6th ed.). New York: Wiley.

Berninger, V. W., & Abbott, R. (2005, April). *Paths leading to reading comprehension in at-risk and normally developing second-grade readers.* Paper presented at the meeting of the Society for Research in Child Development, Atlanta.

Bernstein, D., & Rubin, D. C. (2002). Emotionally charged autobiographical memories across the life span: The recall of happy, sad, traumatic, and involuntary memories. *Psychology and Aging, 17*, 636–652.

Berry, J. W. (2007). Acculturation. In J. E. Grusec & P. D. Hastings (Eds.), *Handbook of socialization.* New York: Guilford.

Bersamin, M. M., Walker, S., Fisher, D. A., & Grube, J. W. (2006). Correlates of oral sex and vaginal intercourse in early and middle adolescence. *Journal of Research on Adolescence, 16*, 59–68.

Berscheid, E. (1988). Some comments on love's anatomy: Or, whatever happened to old-fashioned lust? In R. J. Sternberg (Ed.), *Anatomy of love.* New haven, CT: Yale University Press.

Berscheid, E. (2000). Attraction. In A. Kazdin (Ed.), *Encyclopedia of psychology.* Washington, DC, & New York: American Psychological Association and Oxford University Press.

Berscheid, E., & Fei, J. (1977). Sexual jealousy and romantic love. In G. Clinton & G. Smith (Eds.), *Sexual jealousy.* Englewood Cliffs, NJ: Prentice Hall.

Berscheid, E., & Reis, H. T. (1998). Attraction and close relationships. In D. T. Gilbert, S. T. Fiske, & G. Lindzey (Eds.), *Handbook of social psychology* (4th ed., Vol. 2). New York: McGraw-Hill.

Bertenthal, B. L. (2008). Perception and action. In M. M. Haith & J. B. Benson (Eds.), *Encyclopedia of infant and early childhood development.* Oxford, UK: Elsevier.

Bertrand, R. M., & Lachman, M. E. (2003). Personality development in adulthood and old age. In I. B. Weiner (Ed.), *Handbook of psychology* (Vol. VI). New York: Wiley.

Bessey, P. Q., Arons, R. R., Dimaggio, C. J., & Yurt, R. W. (2006). The vulnerabilities of age: Burns in children and older adults. *Surgery, 140*, 705–715.

Bethell, J., & Roades, A. E. (2008). Adolescent depression and emergency department use: The roles of suicidality and deliberate self-harm. *Current Psychiatry Reports, 10*, 53–59.

Betz, C. L., & Sowden, L. A. (2008). *Mosby's pediatric nursing reference* (6th ed.). St. Louis: Mosby.

Beyene, Y. (1986). Cultural significance and physiological manifestations of menopause: A biocultural analysis. *Culture, Medicine and Psychiatry, 10*, 47–71.

Beyers, W., & Goossens, L. (2008). Dynamics of perceived parenting and identity formation in late adolescence. *Journal of Adolescence, 31*, 165–184.

Bhagwat, J., & Casasola, M. (2008). Semantic development. In M. M. Haith & J. B. Benson (Eds.), *Encyclopedia of infant and early childhood development.* Oxford, UK: Elsevier.

Bhatara, V. S., & Aparasu, R. R. (2007). Pharmacotherapy with atomoxetine for U.S. children and adolescents. *Annals of Clinical Psychiatry, 19*, 175–180.

Bhutta, Z. A., & others. (2008). What works? Interventions for maternal and child undernutrition and survival. *Lancet, 371*, 417–440.

Bialystok, E. (1993). Metalinguistic awareness: The development of children's representations in language. In C. Pratt & A Garton (Eds.), *Systems of representation in children.* London: Wiley.

Bialystok, E. (1997). Effects of bilingualism and biliteracy on children's emerging concepts of print. *Developmental Psychology, 33,* 429–440.

Bialystok, E. (1999). Cognitive complexity and attentional control in the bilingual mind. *Child Development, 70,* 537–804.

Bialystok, E. (2001). *Bilingualism in development: Language, literacy, and cognition.* New York: Cambridge University Press.

Bialystok, E. (2007). Acquisition of literacy in preschool children: A framework for research. *Language Learning, 57,* 45–77.

Bialystok, E. (2009, in press). Second-language acquisition and bilingualism at an early age and the impact on early cognitive development. In R. E. Tremblay, R. deV Peters, M. Boivin, & R. G. Barr (Eds.), *Encyclopedia on early childhood development.* Montreal: Centre of Excellence for Early Childhood Development.

Bianchi, S. M., & Spani, D. (1986). *American women in transition.* New York: Russell Sage Foundation.

Bianchi, S., Robinson, J., & Milkie, M. (2006). *Changing rhythms of American family life* (Rose series in sociology). New York: Russell Sage Foundation Publications.

Bianco, I. H., Carl, M., Russell, C., Clarke, J. D., & Wilson, S. W. (2008). Brain asymmetry is encoded at the level of axon terminal morphology. *Neural Development, 3,* 9.

Bibok, M. B., Carpendale, J. I. M., & Lewis, C. (2008). Social knowledge and social skill: An action-based view of social understanding. In U. Mueller, J. I. M. Carpendale, N. Budwig, & B. W. Sokol (Eds.), *Social life and social knowledge.* Philadelphia: Psychology Press.

Biederman, J. (2007). Advances in the neurobiology of ADHD. *CNS Spectrums, 12* (suppl. 4), S6–S7.

Biehl, M. C., Natsuaki, M. N., & Ge, X. (2007). The influence of pubertal timing on alcohol use and heavy drinking trajectories. *Journal of Youth and Adolescence, 36,* 153–167.

Bielak, A. A. M., Hughes, T. F., Small, B. J., & Dixon, R. A. (2007). It's never too late to engage in lifestyle activities: Significant concurrent but not change relationships between lifestyle activities and cognitive speed. *Journals of Gerontology B: Psychological Sciences and Social Sciences, 62,* P331–P339.

Bierman, K. L. (2004). *Peer rejection.* New York: Guilford.

Bill and Melinda Gates Foundation. (2008). *High Schools.* Retrieved June 6, 2008, from www.gates-foundation.org/UnitedStates/Education/TransformingHighSchools/

Billy, J. O. G., Rodgers, J. L., & Udry, J. R. (1984). Adolescent sexual behavior and friendship choice: *Social Forces, 62,* 653–678.

Binder, T., & Vavrinkova, B. (2008). Prospective randomized comparative study of the effect of bu-prenorphine, methadone, and heroin on the course of pregnancy, birthweight of newborns, early post-partum adaptation, and the course of neonatal abstinence syndrome (NAS). *Neuroendocrinology Letters, 29,* 80–86.

Birch, S., & Bloom, P. (2003). Children are cursed: An asymmetric bias in mental state attribution. *Psychological Science, 14,* 283–286.

Bird, T. D. (2008). Genetic aspects of Alzheimer's disease. *Genetics in Medicine, 10,* 231–239.

Birman, B. F., Le Floch, K. C., Klekotka, A., Ludwig, M., Taylor, J., Walters, K., Wayne, A., & Yoon, K-S. (2007). *State and local implementation of the "No Child Left Behind Act." Volume II—Teacher quality under "NCLB": Interim report.* Jessup, MD: U.S. Department of Education.

Birren, J.E. (Ed.). (1996). *Encyclopedia of gerontology.* San Diego: Academic Press.

Birren, J. E. (2002). Unpublished review of J. W. Santrock's *Life-span development,* 9th ed. (New York: McGraw-Hill).

Birren, J. E. (Ed.). (2007). *Encyclopedia of gerontology* (2nd ed.). San Diego: Academic Press.

Birren, J. E., Woods, A. M., & Williams, M. V. (1980). Behavioral slowing with age: Causes, organization, and consequences. In L. W. Poon (Ed.), *Aging in the 1980s: Psychological issues.* Washington, DC: American Psychological Association.

Bjorklund, D. F. (2006). Mother knows best: Epigenetic inheritance, maternal effects, and the evolution of human intelligence. *Developmental Review, 26,* 213–242.

Bjorklund, D. F. (2007). *Why youth is not wasted on the young.* Malden, MA: Blackwell.

Bjorklund, D. F. (2008). Advances in memory in childhood: Strategies, Knowledge, and meta cognition. In M. Courage & N. Cowan (Eds.), *The development of memory in infancy and childhood.* Philadelphia: Psychology Press.

Bjorklund, D. F., & Pellegrini, A. D. (2002). *The origins of human nature.* New York: Oxford University Press.

Black, M. M., & Hurley, K. M. (2007). Helping children develop healthy eating habits. In R. E. Tremblay, R. G. Barr, R. D. Peters, & M. Boivin (Eds.), *Encyclopedia of early childhood development.* Retrieved March 19, 2008, from www.child-encyclo-pedia.com/documents/Black-HurleyANGxp_rev-Eating.pdf.

Black, M. M., & Hurley, K. M. (2009, in press). Helping children develop healthy eating habits. In R.E. Tremblay, R. deV Peters, M. Boivin, & R.G. Barr (Eds.), *Encyclopedia of early childhood development.* Montreal: Centre of Excellence for Early Childhood Development.

Black, M. M., & Lozoff, B. (2008). Nutrition and diet. In M. M. Haith & J. B. Benson (Eds.), *Encyclopedia of infant and early childhood development.* Oxford, UK: Elsevier.

Blaine, S. M., & others (2008, in press). Interactive genetic counseling role-play: A novel educational strategy for family physicians. *Journal of Genetic Counseling.*

Blair, S. N., Kohl, H. W., Paffenbarger, R. S., Clark, D. G., Cooper, K. H., & Gibbons, L. W. (1989). Physical fitness and all-cause mortality: A prospective study of healthy men and women. *Journal of the American Medical Association, 262,* 2395–2401.

Blakemore, J. E. O., Berenbaum, S. A. & Liben, L. S. (2009). *Gender development.* Clifton, NJ: Psychology Press.

Blanchard-Fields, F., & Coats, A. (2007). *Emotions in everyday problems: Age differences in elicitation and regulation.* Paper submitted for publication. Atlanta: Department of Psychlogy, Georgia Tech University.

Blanchard-Fields, F., & Mienaltowski, A. (2007). Decision-making and everyday problem-solving. In J. E. Birren (Ed.), *Encyclopedia of gerontology* (2nd ed.). San Diego: Academic Press.

Blank, T., Nijhoit, I., & Spiess, J. (2007). Treatment strategies of age-related memory dysfunction by modulation of neuronal plasticity. *Mini Reviews in Medicinal Chemistry, 7,* 55–64.

Blass, E. (2008). Suckling. In M. M. Haith & J. B. Benson (Eds.), *Encyclopedia of infant and early childhood development.* Oxford, UK: Elsevier.

Block, J. H. (1993). Studying personality the long way. In D. Funder, R. D. Parke, C. Tomlinson-Keasey, & K. Widaman (Ed.), *Studying lives through time.* Washington, DC: American Psychological Association.

Block, J. H., & Block, J. (1980). The role of ego-control and ego-resiliency in the organization of behavior. In W. A. Collins (Ed.), *Minnesota symposium on child psychology* (Vol. 13). Minneapolis: University of Minnesota Press.

Bloom, B. (1985). *Developing talent in young people.* New York: Ballentine.

Bloom, B., & Dey, A. N. (2006). Summary health statistics for U.S. children: National Health Interview Survey, 2004. *Vital Health Statistics, 227,* 1–85.

Bloom, L., Lifter, K., & Broughton, J. (1985). The convergence of early cognition and language in the second year of life: Problems in conceptualization and measurement. In M. Barrett (Ed.), *Single word speech.* London: Wiley.

Bloom, P., & German, T. P. (2000). Two reasons to abandon the false belief task as a test of theory of mind. *Cognition, 77,* B25–B31.

Bloor, C., & White, F. (1983). *Unpublished manuscript.* La Jolla, CA: University of California at San Diego.

Blum, J. W., Beaudoin, C. M., & Caton-Lemos, L. (2005). Physical activity patterns and maternal well-being in postpartum women. *Maternal and Child Health Journal, 8,* 163–169.

Blum, R., & Nelson-Mmari, K. (2004). Adolescent health from an international perspective. In R. Lerner & L. Steinberg (Eds.), *Handbook of adolescent psychology.* New York: Wiley.

Blumenfeld, P. C., Kempler, T. M., & Krajcik, J. S. (2006). Motivation and cognitive engagement in learning environments. In R. K. Sawyer (Ed.), *The Cambridge handbook of the learning sciences.* New York: Cambridge University Press.

Blustein, D. L. (2008). The role of work in psychological health and well-being. *American Psychologist, 63,* 228–240.

Bodrova, E., & Leong, D. J. (2007). *Tools of the Mind* (2nd ed.). Geneva: International Bureau of Education, UNESCO.

Boelen, P. A., & Prigerson, H. G. (2007). The influence of symptoms of prolonged grief disorder, depression, and anxiety on quality of life among bereaved adults: A prospective study. *European Archives of Psychiatry and Clinical Neuroscience, 257,* 444–452.

Boelen, P. A., van den Bout, J., & van den Hout, M. A. (2003). The role of cognitive variables in psychological functioning after the death of a first degree relative. *Behavior Research and Therapy, 41,* 1123–1136.

Boeving, C. A., & Forsyth, B. (2008). AIDS and HIV. In M. M. Haith & J. B. Benson (Eds.), *Encyclopedia of infant and early childhood development.* Oxford, UK: Elsevier.

Bohannon, J. N. & Bonvillian, J. D. (2009). Theoretical approaches to language acquisition. In J. Berko Gleason & N. B. Ratner (eds.). *The development of language.* Boston: Allyn & Bacon.

Boles, R. E., & Roberts, M. C. (2008, in press). Supervising children during parental distractions. *Journal of Pediatric Psychology.*

Bolling, C. F., & Daniels, S. R. (2008). Obesity. In M. M. Haith & J. B. Benson (Eds.), *Encyclopedia of infant and early childhood development.* Oxford, UK: Elsevier.

Bombois, S., Debette, S., Bruandt, A., Delbeuck, X., Delmaire, C., Leys, D., & Pasquier, F. (2008, in press). Vascular subcortical hyperintensities predict conversion to vascular and mixed dementia MCI patients. *Stroke.*

Bonanno, G. A., Neria, Y., Mancini, A., Coiofman, K. G., Litz, B., & Insel, B. (2007). Is there more to complicated grief than depression and posttraumatic stress disorder? *Journal of Abnormal Psychology, 116,* 342–351.

Bonanno, G. A., Wortman, C. B., & Nesse, R. M. (2004). Prospective patterns of resilience and maladjustment during widowhood. *Psychology and Aging, 19,* 260–271.

Bondare, W. (2007). Brain and central nervous system. In J. E. Birren (Ed.), *Encyclopedia of gerontology* (2nd ed.). San Diego: Academic Press.

Bonvillian, J. (2005). Unpublished review of J. W. Santrock's *Topical life-span development,* 3rd ed. (New York: McGraw-Hill).

Bookwala, J., & Jacobs, J. (2004). Age, marital processes, and depressed affect. *The Gerontologist, 44,* 328–338.

Booth, A. (2006). Object function and categorization in infancy: Two mechanisms of facilitation. *Infancy, 10,* 145–169.

Booth, M. (2002). Arab adolescents facing the future: Enduring ideas and pressures to change. In B. B. Brown, R. W. Larson, & T. S. Saraswathi (eds.), *The world's youth.* New York: Cambridge University Press.

Bopp, K. L., & Verhaeghen, P. (2007). Age-related differences in control processes in verbal and visuospatial working memory: Storage, transformation, supervision, and coordination. *Journals of Gerontology B: Psychological Sciences and Social Sciences, 62,* P239–P246.

Bor, W., McGee, T. R., & Fagan, A. A. (2004). Early risk factors for adolescent antisocial behavior: An Australian longitudinal study: *Australian and New Zealand Journal of Psychiatry, 38,* 365–372.

Bornstein, M. H. (1975). Qualities of color vision in infancy. *Journal of Experimental Child Psychology, 19,* 401–409.

Bornstein, M. H., & Zlotnik, D. (2008). Parenting styles and their effects. In M. M. Haith & J. B. Benson (Eds.), *Encyclopedia of infant and early childhood development,* Oxford, UK: Elsevier.

Boron, J. B., Willis, S. L., & Schaie, K. W. (2007). Cognitive training gain as a predictor of mental

status. *Journals of Gerontology B: Psychological Sciences and Social Sciences, 62B,* P45–P52.

Bos, H. M. W., Sandfort, T. G. M., de Bruyn, E. H., & Kakvoort, E. M. (2008). Same-sex attraction, social relationships, psychosocial functioning, and school performance. *Developmental Psychology, 44,* 102–116.

Botwinick, J. (1978). *Aging and behavior* (2nd ed.). New York: Springer.

Bouchard, T. J., Lykken, D. T., McGue, M., Segal, N. L., & Tellegen, A. (1990). Source of human psychological differences. The Minnesota Study of Twins Reared Apart. *Science, 250,* 223–228.

Boucher, J. (2009). *The autistic spectrum.* Thousand Oaks, CA: Sage.

Boukydis, C. F., & Lester, B. M. (2008, in press). Mother-infant consultation during drug treatment: Research and innovative clinical practice. *Harm Reduction Journal.*

Boveris, A., & Navarro, A. (2008). Brain mitochondrial dysfunction in aging. *IUBMB Life, 60,* 308–314.

Bower, J. K., Hales, D. P., Tate, D. F., Rubin, D. A., Benjamin, S. E., & Ward, D. S. (2008). The childcare environment and children's physical activity. *American Journal of Preventive Medicine, 34,* 23–29.

Bower, T. G. R. (1966). Slant perception and shape constancy in infants. *Science, 151,* 832–834.

Bowlby, J. (1969). *Attachment and loss* (Vol. 1). London: Hogarth Press.

Bowlby, J. (1980). *Attachment and loss: Vol. 3. Loss, sadness, and depression.* New York: Basic Books.

Bowlby, J. (1989). *Secure and insecure attachment.* New York: Basic Books.

Bowman, M. A., Prelow, H. M., & Weaver, S. R. (2007). Parenting behaviors, association with deviant peers, and delinquency in African American adolescents: A mediated-moderation model. *Journal of Youth and Adolescence, 36,* 517–527.

Boyer, K., & Diamond, A. (1992). Development of memory for temporal order in infants and young children. In A. Diamond (Ed.), *Development and neural bases of higher cognitive function.* New York: New York Academy of Sciences.

Brabyn, J. A., Schneck, M. E., Haegerstrom-Portnoy, G., & Lott, L. (2001). The Smith-Kettlewell Institute (SKI). Longitudinal Study of Vision Function and Its Impact Among the Elderly: An Overview. *Ophthalmology and Vision Science, 78,* 2464–2469.

Bracken, M. B., Eskenazi, B., Sachse, K., McSharry, J., Hellenbrand, K., & Leo-Summers, L. (1990). Association of cocaine use with sperm concentration, motility, and morphology. *Fertility and Sterility, 53,* 315–322.

Bradley, R. E., & Webb, R. (1976). Age-related differences in locus of control orientation in three behavior domains. *Human Development, 19,* 49–55.

Bradley, R. H., & Corwyn, R. F. (2008). Infant temperament, parenting, and externalizing behavior in first grade: A test of the differential susceptibility hypothesis. *Journal of Child Psychology and Psychiatry, 49,* 124–131.

Bradley, R. H., & McKelvey, L. (2007). Managing the differences within: Immigration and early childhood education in the United States. In J. E.

Lansford, K. Deater-Deckhard, & M. H. Bornstein (Eds.), *Immigrant families in contemporary society.* New York: Guilford.

Brainerd, C. J., & Reyna, V. E. (1993). Domains of fuzzy-trace theory. In M. L. Howe & R. Pasnak (Eds.), *Emerging themes in cognitive development.* New York: Springer.

Branch, L. (2007). Health care system for older adults. In K. S. Markides (Ed.), *Encyclopedia of health and aging.* Thousand Oaks, CA: Sage.

Brandstädter, J., & Renner, G. (1990). Tenacious goal pursuit and flexible goal adjustment: Explication and age-related analysis of assimilative and accommodative strategies of coping. *Psychology and Aging, 5,* 58–67.

Bransford, J., & others. (2006). Learning theories in education. In P. A. Alexander & P. H. Winne (Eds.), *Handbook of educational psychology* (2nd ed.). Mahwah, NJ: Erlbaum.

Brazelton, T. B. (1956). Sucking in infancy. *Pediatrics, 17,* 400–404.

Brazelton, T. B. (2004). Preface: The Neonatal Intensive Care Unit Network Neurobehavioral Scale. *Pediatrics, 113.* (Suppl.) S632–S633.

Breaslau, N., Paneth N. S., & Lucia, V. C. (2004). The lingering academic deficits of low birth weight children. Pediatrics, 114, 1035–1040.

Brehm, S. S. (2002). *Intimate relationships* (3rd ed.). New York: McGraw-Hill.

Bremner, G. (2007). Perception and knowledge of the world. In A. Slater & M. Lewis (Eds.), *Introduction to infant development* (2nd ed.). Malden, MA: Blackwell.

Brenes, G. A., Williamson, J. D., Messier, S. P., Rejeski, W. J., Pahor, M., Ip, E., & Penninx, B. W. (2007). Treatment of minor depression in older adults: A pilot study comparing sertraline and exercise. *Aging and Mental Health, 11,* 61–68.

Bretherton, I., & Munholland, K. A. (2009). Internal working models in attachment relationships: Elaborating a central construct in attachment theory. In J. Cassidy & P.R. Shaver (Eds.), *Handbook of attachment* (2nd Ed.). New York: Guilford.

Bretherton, I., Stolberg, U., & Kreye, M. (1981). Engaging strangers in proximal interaction: Infants' social initiative. *Developmental Psychology, 17,* 746–755.

Brewster, K. L., & Harker Tillman, K. (2008). Who's doing it? Patterns and predictors of youths' oral sexual experiences. *Journal of Adolescent Health, 42,* 73–80.

Briem, V., Radeborg, K., Salo, I., & Bengtsson, H. (2004). Developmental aspects of children's behavior and safety while cycling. *Journal of Pediatric Psychology. 29,* 369–377.

Bril, B. (1999). Dires sur l'enfant selon les cultures. Etat des lieux et perspectives. In B. Brill, P. R. Dasen, C. Sabatier, & B. Krewer (Eds.), *Propos sur l'enfant et l'adolescent. Quels enfants pour quelles cultures?* Paris: L'Harmattan.

Brim, G. (1992, December 7). Commentary. *Newsweek,* p. 52.

Brim, G., Ryff, C. D., & Kessler, R. (Ed.). (2004). *How healthy are we? A national study of well-being at midlife.* Chicago: University of Chicago Press.

Brim, O. (1999). *The MacArthur Foundation study of midlife development.* Vero Beach, FL: MacArthur Foundation.

Brink, P., & Smith, T. F. (2008, in press). Determinants of home death in palliative home care: Using the interRAI palliative care to assess end-of-life care. *American Journal of Palliative Care*.

Brock, L. J., & Jennings, G. (2007). Sexuality and intimacy. In J. A. Blackburn & C. N. Dulmas (Eds.), *Handbook of gerontology*. New York: Wiley.

Broderick, R. (2003, July/August). A surgeon's saga. *Minnesota: The Magazine of the University of Minnesota Alumni Association*, 26–31.

Brody, N. (2000). Intelligence. In A. Kazdin (Ed.), *Encyclopedia of psychology*. Washington, DC, & New York: American Psychological Association and Oxford University Press.

Brody, N. (2007). Does education influence intelligence? In P. C. Kyllonen, R. D. Roberts, & L. Stankov (Eds.), *Extending intelligence*. Mahwah, NJ: Erlbaum.

Brodzinsky, D. M., & Pinderhughes, E. (2002). Parenting and child development in adoptive families. In M. H. Bornstein (Ed.), *Handbook of parenting* (Vol. 1). Mahwah, NJ: Erlbaum.

Bronfenbrenner, U. (1986). Ecology of the family as a context for human development: Research perspectives. *Developmental Psychology, 22*, 723–742.

Bronfenbrenner, U. (2004). *Making human beings human*. Thousand Oaks. CA: Sage.

Bronfenbrenner, U., & Morris, P. (1998). The ecology of developmental processes. In W. Damon (Ed.), *Handbook of child psychology* (5th ed., Vol. 1). New York: Wiley.

Bronfenbrenner, U., & Morris, P. A. (2006). The ecology of human development. In W. Damon & R. Lerner (Eds.), *Handbook of child psychology* (6th ed.). New York: Wiley.

Bronstein, P. (2006). The family environment: Where gender role socialization begins. In J. Worell & C. D. Goodheart (Eds.), *Handbook of girls' and women's psychological health*. New York: Oxford University Press.

Brook, J. S., Brook, D. W., Gordon, A. S., Whiteman, M., & Cohen, P. (1990). The psychological etiology of adolescent drug use: A family interactional approach. *Genetic psychology Monographs, 116*, no. 2.

Brook, J. S., Ning, Y., Balka, E. B., Brook, D. W., Lubliner, E. H., & Rosenberg, G. (2007). Grandmother and parent influences on self-esteem. *Pediatrics, 119*, e444–e451.

Brooker, R. J. (2009). *Genetics* (3rd ed.). New York: McGraw-Hill.

Brooks, J. G., & Brooks, M. G. (2001). *The case for constructivist classrooms*. (2nd ed.). Upper Saddle River, NJ: Erlbaum.

Brooks, R., & Meltzoff, A. N. (2005). The development of gaze in relation to language. *Developmental Science, 8*, 535–543.

Brooks-Gunn, J. (2003). Do you believe in magic?: What we can expect from early childhood programs. *Social Policy Report, Society for Research in Child Development, XVII* (No. 1), 1–13.

Brooks-Gunn, J., & Donahue, E. H. (2008). Introducing the issue. *Future of Children, 18 (No. 1)*, 3–10.

Brooks-Gunn, J., & Warren, M. P. (1989). The psychological significance of secondary sexual characteristics in 9- to 11-year-old girls. *Child Development, 59*, 161–169.

Brouwer, B. G., Visseren, F. L., Stolk, R. P., van der Graaf, Y., for the SMART Study Group. (2007). Abdominal fat and risk of coronary heart disease in patients with peripheral arterial disease. *Obesity, 15*, 1623–1630.

Brown, B. B. (1999). Measuring the peer environment of American adolescents. In S. L. Friedman & T. D. Wachs (Eds.), *Measuring environment across the life span*. Washington, DC: American Psychological Association.

Brown, B. B., Bakken, J. P., Ameriger, S. W., & Mahon, S. D. (2008). A comprehensive conceptualization of the peer influence process in adolescence. In M. J. Prinstein & K. A. Dodge (Eds.), *Understanding peer influence in children and adolescents*. New York: Guilford.

Brown, B. B., & Larson, R. W. (2002). The kaleidoscope of adolescence: Experiences of the world's youth at the beginning of the 21st century. In B. B. Brown, R. W. Larson, & T. S. Saraswathi (Eds.), *The world's youth*. New York: Cambridge University Press.

Brown, B. B., & Lohr, M. J. (1987). Peer-group affiliation and adolescent self-esteem: An integration of ego-identity and symbolic interaction theories. *Journal of Personality and Social Psychology, 52*, 47–55.

Brown, J. K. (1985). Introduction. In J. K. Brown & V. Kerns (Eds.). *In her prime: A new view of middle-aged women*. South Hadley, MA: Bergin & Garvey.

Brown, L. A., McKenzie, N. C., & Doan, J. B. (2005). Age-dependent differences in the attentional demands of obstacle negotiation. *Journals of Gerontology A: Biological Sciences and Medical Sciences, 60*, 924–927.

Brown, L. S. (1989). New voices, new visions: Toward a lesbian/gay paradigm for psychology. *Psychology of Women Quarterly, 13*, 445–458.

Brown, R. (1958). *Words and things*. Glencoe, IL: Free Press.

Brown, R. (1973). *A first language: The early stages*. Cambridge, MA: Harvard University Press.

Brown, S. L., Brown, R. M., House, J. S., & Smith, D. M. (2008). Coping with spousal loss: Potential buffering effects of self-reported helping behavior. *Personality and Social Psychology Bulletin, 34*, 849–861.

Brown, S. L., Bulanda, J. R., & Lee, G. R. (2005). The significance of nonmarital cohabitation: Marital status and mental health benefits among middle-aged and older adults. *Journals of Gerontology B: Psychological Sciences and Social Sciences, 60*, S21–S29.

Brown, S. L., Lee, G. R., & Bulanda, J. R. (2006). Cohabitation among older adults: A national portrait. *Journals of Gerontology B: Psychological Sciences and Social Sciences, 61*, S71–S79.

Brown, S. L., Nesse, R. M., House, J. S., & Utz, R. L. (2004). Religion and emotional compensation: Results from a prospective study of widowhood. *Personality and Social Psychology Bulletin, 30*, 1165–1174.

Brown, S. L., Nesse, R. M., Vinokur, A. D., & Smith, D. M. (2003). Providing social support may be more beneficial than receiving it: Results from a prospective study of mortality. *Psychological Science, 14*, 320–327.

Brown-Borg, H. M. (2007). Hormonal regulation of longevity in mammals. *Aging Research Reviews, 6*, 28–45.

Browne, C. V., & Braun, K. L. (2008). Globalization, women's migration, and the long-care workforce. *Gerontologist, 48*, 16–24.

Brownell, C. A., & Kopp, C. B. (Eds.). (2007). *Socioemotional development in the toddler years*. New York: Guilford.

Brownell, C. A., Ramani, G. B., & Zerwas, S. (2006). Becoming a social partner with peers: Cooperation and social understanding in one- and two-year-olds. *Child Development, 77*, 803–821.

Bruce, A. (2007). Time(lessness): Buddhist perspectives and end-of-life. *Nursing Philosophy, 8*, 151–157.

Bruce, J. M., Olen, K., & Jensen, S. J. (1999, April). *The role of emotion and regulation in social competence*. Paper presented at the meeting of the Society for Research in Child Development, Albuquerque.

Bruck, M., & Ceci, S. J. (1999). The suggestibility of children's memory. *Annual Review of Psychology, 50*, 419–439.

Bruck, M., Ceci, S. J., & Hembrooke, H. (1998). Reliability and credibility of young children's reports: From research to policy and practice. *American Psychologist, 53* (2), 136–151.

Bruck, M., Ceci, S. J., & Principe, G. F. (2006). The child and the law. In W. Damon & R. Lerner (Eds.), *Handbook of child psychology* (6 th ed.). New York: Wiley.

Bruck, M., & Melnyk, L. (2004). Individual differences in children's suggestibility: A review and a synthesis. *Applied Cognitive Psychology, 81*, 947–996.

Brune, C. W., & Woodward, A. L. (2007). Social cognition and social responsiveness in 10-month-old infants. *Journal of Cognition and Development, 2*, 3–27.

Brunstein Klomek, A., Marrocco, F., Kleinman, M., Schofeld, I. S., & Gould, M. S. (2007). Bullying, depression, and suicidality in adolescents. *Journal of the American Academy of Child and Adolescent Psychiatry, 46*, 40–49.

Bryant, D. P., Smith, D. D., & Bryant, B. R. (2008). *Teaching students with special needs in inclusive classrooms*. Boston: Allyn & Bacon.

Bryant, J. A. (Ed.). (2007). *The children's television community*. Mahwah, NJ: Erlbaum.

Bryant, J. B. (2009). Language in social contexts: Communication competence in the preschool years. In J. Berko Gleason & N. Ratner (Eds.), *The development of language* (7th ed.). Boston: Allyn & Bacon.

Bryce, J., Coitinho, D., Darnton-Hill, I., Pelletier, D., Pinstrup-Andersen, P., & the Maternal and Child Undernutrition Study Group. (2008). *Maternal and child undernutrition: Effective action at national level*. Lancet, 371, 510–526.

Brynes, J. P. (2008). Piaget's cognitive—developmental theory. In M. M. Haith & J. B. Benson (Eds.), *Encyclopedia of infancy and early childhood*. Oxford, UK: Elsevier.

Buchman, A. S., Boyle, P. A., Wilson, R. S., Bienias, J. L., & Bennett, D. A. (2007). Physical activity and motor decline in older persons. *Muscle and Nerve, 35*, 354–362.

Bucur, B., & Madden, D. J. (2007). Information processing/cognition. In J. E. Birren (Ed.), *Encyclopedia of gerontology* (2nd ed.). San Diego: Academic Press.

Bucx, F., van Wel, F., Knijn, T., & Hagendoorn, L. (2008). Intergenerational contact and the life course status of young adult children. *Journal of Marriage and the Family 70,* 144–156.

Buford, C. (2008, in press). Advancing an advance directive debate. *Bioethics.*

Bugental, D. B., & Grusec, J. E. (2006). Socialization processes. In W. Damon & R. Lerner (Eds.), *Handbook of child psychology* (6th ed.). New York: Wiley.

Buhrmester, D. (1998). Need fulfillment, interpersonal competence, and the developmental contexts of early adolescent friendship. In W. M. Bukowski & A. F. Newcomb (Eds.), *The company they keep: Friendship in childhood and adolescence:* New York: Cambridge University Press.

Buhrmester, D. (2001, April). *Romantic development: Does age at which romantic involvement start matter?* Paper presented at the meeting of the Society for Research in Child Development, Minneapolis.

Buhrmester, D. (2005, April). *The antecedents of adolescents' competence in close relationships: A six-year study.* Paper presented at the meeting of the Society for Research in Child Development, Atlanta.

Buhs, E. S., & Ladd, G. W. (2002). Peer rejection as antecedent of young children's school adjustment: An examination of mediating processes. *Developmental Psychology, 37,* 550–560.

Bukowski, R., & others. (2008, January). *Folic acid and preterm birth.* Paper presented at the meeting of the Society for Maternal-Fetal Medicine, Dallas.

Bukowski, W. M., Brendgen, M., & Vitaro, F. (2007). Peers and socialization: Effects on externalizing and internalizing problems. In J. E. Grusec & P. D. Hastings (Eds.), *Handbook of Socialization.* New York: Guilford.

Bukowski, W. M., Laursen, B., & Rubin, K. H. (Eds.). (2009). *Social and emotional development.* Clifton, NJ: Psychology Press.

Bukowski, W. M., Velasquez, A. M., & Brendgen, M. (2008). Variation in patterns of peer influence: Considerations of self and other. In M. J. Prinstein & K. A. Dodge (Eds.), *Understanding peer influence in children and adolescents.* New York: Guilford.

Bulik, C. M., Berkman, N. D., Brownley, K. A., Sedway, J. A., & Lohr, K. N. (2007). Anorexia nervosa treatment: A systematic review of randomized controlled trials. *International Journal of Eating Disorders, 40,* 310–320.

Bullock, R., & Dengiz, A. (2005). Cognitive performance in patients with Alzheimer's disease receiving cholinesterase inhibitors for up to 5 years. *International Journal of Clinical Practice, 59,* 817–822.

Bulthuis, Y., Drossaers-Bakker, K. W., Taal, E., Rasker, J., Oostveen, J., van't Pad Bosch, P., Oosterveld, F., & van de Laar, M. (2007). Arthritis patients show long-term benefits from 3 weeks intensive exercise training directly following hospital discharge. *Rheumatology, 46,* 1712–1717.

Bumpass, L. L., & Aquilino, W. (1994). *A social map of midlife: Family and work over the middle life course.* Center for Demography and Ecology, University of Wisconsin, Madison, WI.

Bumpass, L. L., & Lu, H. H. (2000). Trends in cohabitation and implications for children's family contexts in the United States. *Populations Studies, 54,* 29–41.

Bumpus, M. F., Crouter, A. C., & McHale, M. (2001). Parental autonomy granting during adolescence: Exploring gender differences in context. *Developmental Psychology, 37,* 163–173.

Burck, J. R., Vena, M., Jolicoeur, M., & Jolicoeur, L. E. (2007). At a threshold: Making decisions when you don't have all the answers. *Physical Medicine and Rehabilitation Clinics of North America, 18,* 1–25.

Burke, D. M., Shafto, M. A. (2004). Aging and language production. *Current Directions in Psychological Science, 13,* 21–24.

Burns, C., Dunn, A., Brady, M., Starr, N. B., & Blosser, C. (2008). *Pediatric primary care.* Oxford, UK: Elsevier.

Burns, L., Mattick, R. P., Lim, K., & Wallace, C. (2007). Methadone in pregnancy: Treatment retention and neonatal outcomes. *Addiction, 102,* 264–270.

Busby, D. M., Ivey, D. C., Harris, S. M., & Ates, C. (2007). Self-directed, therapist—directed, and assessment-based interventions for premarital couples. *Family Relations, 56,* 279–290.

Bushnell, I. W. R. (2003). Newborn face recognition. In O. Pascalis & A. Slater (Eds.), *The development of face processing in infancy and early childhood.* New York: NOVA Science.

Buss, D. M. (1995). Psychological sex differences: Origins through sexual selection. *American Psychologist, 50,* 164–168.

Buss, D. M. (2000). Evolutionary psychology. In A. Kazdin (Ed.), *Encyclopedia of psychology.* Washington, DC, & New York: American Psychological Association and Oxford University Press.

Buss, D. M. (2004). *Evolutionary psychology* (2nd ed.). Boston: Allyn & Bacon.

Buss, D. M. (2007). Foreword. In G. Geher & G. Miller (Eds.), *Mating intelligence.* Mahwah, NJ: Erlbaum.

Buss, D. M. (2008). *Evolutionary psychology* (3rd ed.). Boston: Allyn & Bacon.

Buss, D. M., & Barnes, M. (1986). Preferences in human mate selection. *Journal of personality and Social Psychology, 50,* 559–570.

Buss, D. M., & others. (1990). International preferences in selecting mates: A study of 37 cultures. *Journal of Cross-Cultural Psychology, 21,* 5–47.

Buss, K. A., & Goldsmith, H. H. (2007). Biobehavioral approaches to early socioemotional development. In C. A. Brownell & C. B. Kopp (Eds.), *Socioemotional development in the toddler years.* New York: Guilford.

Busse, E. W., & Blazer, D. G. (1996). *The American Psychiatric Press textbook of geriatric psychiatry* (2nd ed.). Washington, DC: American Psychiatric Press.

Bussey, K., & Bandura A. (1999). Social cognitive theory of gender development and differentiation. *Psychological Review, 106,* 676–713.

Butcher, K., Sallis, J. F., Mayer, J. A., & Woodruff, S. (2008). Correlates of physical activity guideline compliance for adolescents in 100 cities. *Journal of Adolescent Health, 42,* 360–368.

Butler, R. N. (2007). Life review. In J. E. Birren (Ed.), *Encyclopedia of gerontology* (2nd ed.). San Diego: Academic Press.

Butler, R. N., & Lewis, M. (2002). *The new love and sex after 60.* New York: Ballentine.

Butler, R. N., & Schechter, M. (2007). Medicare and Medicaid and economic policy of health care. In J.E. Birren (Ed.), *Encyclopedia of gerontology* (2nd ed.). San Diego: Academic Press.

Butterworth, G. (2004). Joint visual attention in infancy. In G. Bremner & A. Slater (Eds.), *Theories of infant development.* Malden, MA: Blackwell.

Buzwell, S., & Rosenthal, D. (1996). Constructing a sexual self: Adolescents' sexual self-perceptions and sexual risk-taking. *Journal of Research on Adolescence, 6,* 489–513.

Bybee, R. W., Powell, J. C., & Trowbridge, L. W. (2008). *Teaching secondary science* (9th ed.), Upper Saddle River, NJ: Prentice Hall.

Byrd, T. L., Chavez, R., & Wilson, K. M. (2007). Barriers and facilitators of cervical cancer screening among Hispanic women. *Ethnicity and Disease, 17,* 129–134.

Byrnes, H. F., Chen, M-J., Miller, B. A., & Maguin, E. (2007). The relative importance of mothers' and youths' neighborhood perceptions for youth alcohol use and delinquency. *Journal of Youth and Adolescence, 36,* 649–659.

Byrnes, J. P. (2008). Piaget's cognitive developmental theory. In M. M. Haith & J. B. Benson (Eds.), *Encyclopedia of infant and early childhood development.* Oxford, UK: Elsevier.

C

Cabeza, R. (2002). Hemispheric asymmetry reduction in older adults: The HAROLD model. *Psychology and Aging, 17,* 85–100.

Cabezon, C., Vigil, P., Rojas, I., Leiva, M. E., Riquelme, R., Aranda, W., & Garcia, C. (2005). Adolescent pregnancy prevention: An abstinence-centered randomized controlled intervention in a Chilean public high school. *Journal of Adolescent Health, 36,* 64–69.

Cabrera, N., Hutchens, R., & Peters, H. E. (Eds.). (2006). *From welfare to childcare.* Mahwah, NJ: Erlbaum.

Cacioppo, J. T., Hughes, M. E., Waite, L. J., Hawkley, L. C. & Thisted, R. A. (2006). Loneliness as a specific risk factor for depressive symptoms; Cross-sectional and longitudinal analyses. *Psychology and Aging, 21,* 140–151.

Calasanti, T. (2007). Gender roles. In J. E. Birren (Ed.), *Encyclopedia of gerontology* (2nd ed.). San Diego: Academic Press.

Caley, L., Syms, C., Robinson, L., Cederbaum, J., Henry, M., & Shipkey, N. (2008). What human service professionals know and want to know about fetal alcohol syndrome. *Canadian Journal of Clinical Pharmacology, 15,* e117–e123.

Calkins, S. D. (2007). The emergence of self-regulation: Biological and behavioral control mechanisms supporting toddler competencies. In C. A. Brownell & C. B. Kopp (Eds.), *Socioemotional development in the toddler years.* New York: Guilford.

Callaway, L. K., Lust, K., & McIntyre, H. D. (2005). Pregnancy outcomes in women of very advanced maternal age. *Obstetric and Gynecology Survey, 60,* 562–563.

Callisaya, M. L., Blizzard, L., Schmidt, M. D., McGinley, J. L., & Srikanth, V. K. (2008). Sex modifies the relationship between age and gait: A population-based study of older adults. *Journals of Gerontology A: Biological Sciences and Medical Sciences, 63,* 165–170.

Calvaresi, E., & Bryan, J. (2001). B vitamins, cognition, and aging: A review. *Journals of Gerontology B: Psychological Sciences, 56,* 327–339.

Caminis, A., Henrich, C., Ruchkin, V., Schwab-Stone, M., & Martin, A. (2007). Psychosocial predictors of sexual initiation and high-risk sexual behaviors in early adolescence. *Child and Adolescent Psychiatry and Mental Health, 1,* 14.

Campbell, D. A., Lake, M. F., Falk, M., & Backstrand, J. R. (2006). A randomized controlled trial of continuous support by a lay doula. *Journal of Obstetrics and Gynecology: Neonatal Nursing, 35,* 456–464.

Campbell, D., Scott, K. D., Klaus, M. H., & Falk, M. (2007). Female relatives or friends trained as labor doulas: Outcomes at 6 to 8 weeks postpartum. *Birth, 34,* 220–227.

Campbell, F. A. (2007). The malleability of the cognitive development of children of low-income African American families: Intellectual test performance over twenty-one years. In P. C. Kyllonen, R. D. Roberts, & L. Stankov (Eds.), *Extending intelligence.* Mahwah, NJ: Erlbaum.

Campbell, F. A., Pungello, E. P., Miller-Johnson, S., Burchinal, M., & Ramey, C. T. (2001). The development of cognitive and academic abilities: Growth curves from an early childhood educational experiment. *Developmental Psychology, 37,* 231–243.

Campbell, L., Campbell, B., & Dickinson, D. (2004). *Teaching and learning through multiple intelligence* (3rd ed.). Boston: Allyn & Bacon.

Campbell, S. S., & Murphy, P. J. (2007). The nature of spontaneous sleep across adulthood. *Journal of Sleep Research, 16,* 24–32.

Campos, J. J. (2005). Unpublished review of J. W. Santrock's *Life-span development,* 10th ed. (New York: McGraw-Hill).

Campos, J. J., Langer, A., & Krowitz, A. (1970). Cardiac responses on the visual cliff in prelocomotor human infants. *Science, 170,* 196–197.

Camras L. A., & others. (1998). Production of emotional facial expressions in European American, Japanese, and Chinese infants. *Developmental Psychology, 34,* 616–628.

Candore, G., & others. (2006). Immunogenetics, gender, and longevity. *Annals of the New York Academy of Sciences, 1089,* 516–537.

Canfield, J., & Hansen, M. V. (1995). *A second helping of chicken soup for the soul.* Deerfield Beach, FL: Health Communications.

Canfield, R. L., & Haith, M. M. (1991). Young infants' visual expectations for symmetric and asymmetric stimulus sequences. *Developmental Psychology, 27,* 198–208.

Canfield, R. L., & Jusko, T. A. (2008). Lead poisoning. In M. M. Haith & J. B. Benson (Eds.), *Encyclopedia of infant and early childhood development.* Oxford, UK: Elsevier.

Canterino, J. C., Ananth, C. V., Smulian, J., Harrigan, J. T., & Vintzileos, A. M. (2004). *Obstetrics and Gynecology Survey, 59,* 649–650. Maternal age and risk of fetal death in singleton gestation: United States, 1995–2000.

Cappeliez, P., & O'Rourke, N. (2006). Empirical validation of model of reminiscence and health in later life. *Journals of Gerontology B: Psychological and Social Sciences, 61,* P237–P244.

Cappeliez, P. O'Rourke, N. & Chaudhury, H. (2005). Functions of reminiscence and mental health in later life. *Aging and mental health 9,* 295–301.

Carcabelos, R. (2008). Pharmacogenomics in Alzheimer's disease. *Methods in Molecular Biology, 448,* 213–357.

Carlo, G. (2006). Care-based and altruistically-based morality. In M. Killen & J. Smetana (Eds.), *Handbook of moral development.* Mahwah, NJ: Erlbaum.

Carlsen, K. H., & Carlsen, K. C. (2008). Respiratory effects of tobacco smoking on infants and young children. *Pediatric Respiratory Review, 9,* 11–20.

Carlson, S. M., & Zelazo, P. D. (2008). Symbolic thought. In M. M. Haith & J. B. Benson (Eds.), *Encyclopedia of infant and early childhood development.* Oxford, UK: Elsevier.

Carnagey, N. L., Anderson, C. A., & Bushman, B. J. (2007, in press). The effect of video game violence on physiological desensitization to real-life violence. *Journal of Experimental Social Psychology.*

Carnegie Corporation. (1989). *Turning points: Preparing youth for the 21st century.* New York: Author.

Carnethon, M. R., Gidding, S. S., Nehgme, R., Sidney, S., Jacobs, D. R., & Liu, K. (2003). Cardiorespiratory fitness in young adulthood and the development of cardiovascular disease risk factors. *Journal of the American Medical Association, 290,* 3092–3100.

Carnethon, M. R., Gulati, M., & Greenland, P. (2005). Prevalence and cardiovascular disease correlates of low cardiorespiratory fitness in adolescents and adults. *Journal of the American Medical Association, 294,* 2981–2988.

Carpendale, J. I. M., & Chandler, M. J. (1996). On the distinction between false belief understanding and subscribing to an interpretive theory of mind. *Child Development, 67,* 1686–1706.

Carpendale, J. I. M., Muller, U., & Bibok, M. B. (2008). Piaget's theory of cognitive development. In N. J. Salkind (Ed.), *Encyclopedia of educational psychology.* Thousand Oaks, CA: Sage.

Carpenter, J., Nagell, K., & Tomasello, M. (1998). Social cognition, joint attention, and communicative competence from 9 to 15 months of age. *Monographs of the Society for Research in Child Development, 70* (1, Serial No. 279).

Carr, D., & Khodyakov, D. (2007). End-of-life health care planning among young-old adults: An assessment of psychosocial influences. *Journals of Gerontology B: Psychological Sciences and Social Sciences, 62,* S135–S141.

Carr, D., & Pudrovska, T. (2007). Mid-life and later-life crises. In J. E. Birren (Ed.), *Encyclopedia of gerontology* (2nd ed.). San Diego: Academic Press.

Carrington, N. A., & Bogetz, J. E. (2004). Normal grief and bereavement. *Journal of Palliative Medicine, 7,* 309–323.

Carroll, J. L. (2007). *Sexuality now* (2nd ed.). Belmont, CA: Wadsworth.

Carroll, J. S., & Doherty, W. J. (2003). Evaluating the effectiveness of premarital prevention programs: A meta-analytic review of outcome research. *Family Relations, 52,* 105–118.

Carskadon, M. A. (2004). Sleep difficulties in young people. *Archives of Pediatrics and Adolescent Medicine, 158,* 597–598.

Carskadon, M. A. (2005). Sleep and circadian rhythms in children and adolescents: Relevance for athletic performance of young people. *Clinical Sports Medicine, 24,* 319–328.

Carskadon, M. A. (2006, March). *Too little, too late: Sleep bioregulatory processes across adolescence.* Paper presented at the meeting of the Society for Research on Adolescence, San Francisco.

Carstensen, L. L. (1998). A life-span approach to social motivation. In J. Heckhausen & C. Dweck (Eds.), *Motivation and self-regulation across the life span.* New York: Cambridge University Press.

Carstensen, L. L. (2006). The influence of a sense of time on human development. *Science, 312,* 1913–1915.

Carstensen, L. L. (2008, May). *Long life in the 21st century.* Paper presented at the meeting of the Association of Psychological Science, Chicago.

Carstensen, L. L., Mikels, J. A., & Mather, M. (2006). Aging and the intersection of cognition, motivation, and emotion. In J. E. Birren & K. W. Schaie (Eds.), *Handbook of the psychology of aging* (6th ed.). San Diego: Academic Press.

Carter, N., Prater, M. A., & Dyches, T. T. (2009). *What every teacher should know about adaptations and accommodations for students with mild and moderate disabilities.* Upper Saddle River, NJ: Prentice Hall.

Cartwright, R., Agargun, M. Y., Kirkby, J., & Friedman, J. K. (2006). Relation of dreams to waking concerns. *Psychiatry Research, 141,* 261–270.

Carver, K., Joyner, K., & Udry, J. R. (2003). National estimates of romantic relationships. In P. Florsheim (Ed.), *Adolescent romantic relations and sexual behavior.* Mahwah, NJ: Erlbaum.

Carver, L. J, & Bauer, P. J. (2001). The dawning of a past: The emergence of long-term explicit memory in infancy. *Journal of Experimental Psychology: General, 130* (4), 726–745.

CASA. (2007). *The importance of family dinners IV.* New York: National Center for Addiction and Substance Abuse, Columbia University.

Casarett, D., Crowley, R., Stevenson, C., Xie, S., & Teno, J. (2005). Making difficult decisions about hospice enrollment: What do patients and families want to know? *Journal of the American Geriatric Society, 53,* 249–254.

Case, R., & Mueller, M. P. (2001). Differentiation, integration, and covariance mapping as fundamental processes in cognitive and neurological growth. In J. L. McClelland & R. S. Siegler (Eds.), *Mechanisms of cognitive development.* Mahwah, NJ: Erlbaum.

Casey, B. J., Getz, S., & Galvan, A. (2008). The adolescent brain. *Developmental Review, 28,* 42–77.

Casey, P. H. (2008). Growth of low birth weight preterm children. *Seminars in Perinatology, 32,* 20–27.

Cashman, K. D. (2008). Altered bone metabolism in inflammatory disease: Role for nutrition. *Proceedings of the Nutrition Society, 67,* 196–205.

Casper, L. M., & Bianchi, S. M. (2007). Cohabitation. In A. S. Skolnick & J. H. Skolnick

(Eds.), *Family in transition* (14th ed.). Boston: Allyn & Bacon.

Caspi, A. (1998). Personality development across the life course. In W. Damon (Ed.), *Handbook of child psychology* (Vol. 3). New York: Wiley.

Caspi, A., & Roberts, B. W. (2001). Personality development across the life course: The argument for change and continuity. *Psychological Inquiry, 12,* 49–66.

Caspi, A., & Shiner, R. L. (2006). Personality development. In W. Damon & R. Lerner (Eds.), *Handbook of child psychology* (6th ed.). New York: Wiley.

Cassidy, J. (2009). The nature of the child's ties. In J. Cassidy & P. R. Shaver (Eds.), *Handbook of attachment* (2nd ed.). New York: Guilford.

Castle, N. G. (2001). Innovation in nursing homes. *The Gerontologist, 41* (2), 161–172.

Cauffman, B. E. (1994, February). *The effects of puberty, dating, and sexual involvement on dieting and disordered eating in young adolescent girls.* Paper presented at the meeting of the Society for Research on Adolescence, San Diego.

Caughey, A. B., Hopkins, L. M., & Norton, M. E. (2006). Chorionic villus sampling compared with amniocentesis and the difference in the rate of pregnancy loss. *Obstetrics and Gynecology, 108,* 612–616.

Cavallero, P., Morino-Abbele, F., & Bertocci, B. (2007). The social relations of the elderly. *Archives of Gerontology and Geriatrics, 44,* Suppl. S97–S100.

Cavell, T. A., Hymel, S., Malcolm, K. T., & Seay, A. (2007). Socialization and interventions for antisocial youth. In J. E. Grusec & P. D. Hastings (Eds.), *Handbook of socialization.* New York: Gulford.

Ceci, S. J. (2000). Bronfenbrenner, Urie. In A. Kazdin (Ed.), *Encyclopedia of psychology.* Washington, DC, & New York: American Psychological Association and Oxford University Press.

Ceci, S. J., & Gilstrap, L. L. (2000). Determinants of intelligence: Schooling and intelligence. In A. Kazdin (Ed.), *Encyclopedia of Psychology.* Washington, DC, & New York: American Psychological Association and Oxford University Press.

Center for Survey Research at the University of Connecticut. (2000). *Hours on the job.* Storrs: University of Connecticut, Center for Survey Research.

Centers for Disease Control and Prevention. (2002). Author. *Adolescent pregnancy.* Atlanta:

Centers for Disease Control and Prevention. (2003). Public health and aging: Health-related quality of life among low-income persons aged 45–64 years—United State. *Morbidity and Mortality Weekly Reports, 21,* 1120–1124.

Centers for Disease Control and Prevention. (2006). *Health United States, 2006.* Atlanta: Author.

Centers for Disease Control and Prevention. (2007). *Autism and developmental disabilities monitoring (ADDM) network.* Retrieved May 30, 2008, from www.cdc.gov/hcbddd/autism/addm.htm

Centers for Disease Control and Prevention. (2007). *Body Mass index for children and teens.* Atlanta: Author.

Centers for Disease Control and Prevention. (2007, September 12). *U.S. life expectancy hits new high of nearly 78 years.* Atlanta: Author.

Centers for Disease Control and Prevention. (2008). *Body mass index for children and teens.* Atlanta: Centers for Disease Control and Prevention.

Centers for Disease Control and Prevention. (2008). *National Health Interview Study.* Atlanta: Author.

Centers for Disease Control and Prevention. (2008). *Sexually transmitted diseases.* Atlanta: Author.

Centers for Disease Control and Prevention. (2008). SIDS. Retrieved on May 28, 2008, from The Internet at www.cdc.gov/SIDS/index.htm

Centers for Disease Control and Prevention. (2008). Youth Risk Behavior Survey. Atlanta: Author.

Cepeda, M. S., Carr, D. B., Lau, J., & Alvarez, H. (2006). Music for pain relief. *Cochrane Database of Systematic Reviews, 2,* CD004843.

Cervino, A., Hosking, S. L., Montes-Mico, R., & Bates, k. (2007). Clinical ocular wavefront analyzers. *Journal of Refractive Surgery, 23,* 603–616.

Chaillet, N., & Dumont, A. (2007). Evidence-based strategies for reducing cesarean section rates: A meta-analysis. *Birth, 34,* 53–64.

Chand, P., & Litvan, I. (2007). Parkinson's disease. In J. E. Birren (Ed.), *Encyclopedia of gerontology* (2nd ed.). San Diego: Academic Press.

Chandler, M. (1973). Egocentrism and antisocial behavior: The assessment and training of social perspective-taking skills. *Developmental Psychology, 9,* 326–332.

Chang, M. Y., Chen, C. H., & Huang, K. F. (2006). A comparison of massage effects on labor pain using the McGill Pain Questionnaire. *Journal of Nursing Research, 14,* 190–197.

Chang, S. C., O'Brien, K. O., Nathanson, M. S., Mancini, J., & Witter, F. R. (2003). Characteristics and risk factors for adverse birth outcomes in pregnant black adolescents. *Journal of Obstetrics and Gynecology Canada, 25,* 751–759.

Chao, R. K. (2001). Extending research on the consequences of parenting style for Chinese Americans and European Americans. *Child Development, 72,* 1832–1843.

Chao, R. K. (2005, April). *The importance of* Guan *in describing control of immigrant Chinese.* Paper presented at the meeting of the Society for Research in Child Development, Atlanta.

Chao, R. K. (2007, March). *Research with Asian Americans: Looking back and moving forward.* Paper presented at the meeting of the Society for Research in Child Development, Boston.

Chao, R., & Tseng, V. (2002). Parenting of Asians. In M. H. Bornstein *Handbook of parenting* (2nd ed., Vol. 4). Mahwah, NJ: Erlbaum.

Charles, S. C., & Piazza, J. R. (2007). Memories of social interactions: Age differences in emotional intensity. *Psychology and Aging, 22,* 300–309.

Charles, S. T., & Carstensen, L. L. (2007). Emotion and aging. In J. J. Gross (Ed.), *Handbook of emotion regulation.* New York: Guilford.

Charles, S. T., Reynolds, C. A., & Gatz, M. (2001). Age-related differences and change in positive and negative affect over twenty-three years. *Journal of Personality and Social Psychology, 80,* 136–151.

Charlton, R. A., Morris, R. G., Nitkunan, A., & Markus, H. S. (2006). The cognitive profiles of CADASIL and sporadic small vessel disease. *Neurology, 66,* 1523–1526.

Charman, T. (2009, in press). Autism and its impact on child development. In R. E. Tremblay, R. deV Peters, M. Boivin, & R. G. Barr (Eds.), *Encyclopedia on early childhood development.* Montreal: Centre of Excellence for Early Childhood Development.

Charman, T., Ruffman, T., & Clements, W. (2002). Is there a gender difference in false belief developmental? *Social Development, 11,* 1–10.

Charness, N., & Bosman, E. A. (1992). Human factors and aging. In F. I. M. Craik & T. A. Salthouse (Eds.), *The handbook of aging and cognition.* Hillsdale, NJ: Erlbaum.

Charness, N., Czaja, S., & Sharit, J. (2007). Age and technology for work. In K. A. Schultz & G. A. Adams (Eds.), *Aging and work in the 21st century.* Mahwah, NJ: Erlbaum.

Chatoor, L., & Macaoay, M. (2008). Feeding development and disorders. In M. M. Haith & J. B. Benson (Eds.), *Encyclopedia of infant and early childhood development.* Oxford, UK: Elsevier.

Chattin-McNichols, J. (1992). *The Montessori controversy.* Albany, NY: Delmar.

Chatzimichael, A., Tsalkidis, A., Cassimos, D., Gardikis, S., Tripsianis, G., Deftereos, S. Ktenidou-Kartali, S., & Tsanaksas, I. (2007). The role of breastfeeding and passive smoking on the development of severe bronchiolitis in infants. *Minerva Pediatrica, 59,* 199–206.

Chauhuri, J. H., & Williams, P. H. (1999, April). *The contribution of infant temperament and parent emotional availability to toddler attachment.* Paper presented at the meeting of the Society for Research in Child Development, Albuquerque.

Chedraui, P. (2008). Pregnancy among young adolescents: trends, risk factors, and maternal-perinatal outcome. *Journal of Perinatal Medicine, 36,* 256–259.

Chehab, O., Ouertani, M., Souiden, Y., Chaieb, K., & Mahdouani, K. (2008, in press). Plasma antioxidants and human aging: A study on healthy elderly Tunisian population. *Molecular Biotechnology.*

Chen, D., & Guarente, L. (2007). SIR2: A potential target for calorie restriction mimetics. *Trends in Molecular Medicine, 13,* 64–71.

Chen, H., Tun, Y-C., Li, B., Iqbal, K., & Grundke-Iqbal, I. (2007). Trophic factors counteract elevated FGF-2-induced inhibition in adult neurogenesis. *Neurobiology of Aging, 28,* 1148–1162.

Chen, M., Yang, B., & Zhang, X. (2008). Effects of telomerase activity on carcinogenesis and survival in laryngeal carcinoma. *Journal of International Medicine Research, 36,* 336–342.

Chen, X., Hastings, P. D., Rubin, K. H., Chen, H., Cen, G., & Stewart, S. L. (1998). Child-rearing attitudes and behavioral inhibition in Chinese and Canadian toddlers: A cross-cultural study. *Developmental Psychology, 34,* 677–686.

Chen, X. K., Wen, S. W., Fleming, N., Demissie, K., Rhoads, G. G., & Walker, M. C. (2007a). Teenage pregnancy and adverse birth outcomes: A large population based retrospective cohort study. *International Journal of Epidemiology, 36,* 368–373.

Chen, X. K., Wen, S. W., Yang, Q., & Walker, M. C. (2007b). Adequacy of prenatal care and neonatal mortality in infants born to mothers with and without antenatal high-risk conditions. *Australian and New Zealand Journal of Obstetrics and Gynecology, 47,* 122–127.

Chen, Y.-P., & Colander, D. (2007). Economics: Society. In J. E. Birren (Ed.), *Encyclopedia of gerontology* (2nd ed.). San Diego: Academic Press.

Cheng, M-H., Lee, S-J, Wang, S-J., Wang, P.-H., & Fuh, J-L. (2007). Does menopausal transition affect the quality of life? A longitudinal study of middle-aged women in Kinmen. *Menopause, 14,* 885–890.

Cherkas, L. F., & others. (2008). The association between physical activity in leisure time and leukocyte telomere length. *Archives of Internal Medicine, 168,* 154–158.

Cherlin, A. J. (2007). The deinstitutionalization of marriage. In S. J. Ferguson (Ed.), *Shifting the center: Understanding contemporary families* (3rd ed.). New York: McGraw-Hill.

Cherlin, A. J., & Furstenberg, F. F. (1994). Stepfamilies in the United States: A reconsideration. In J. Blake & J. Hagen (Eds.), *Annual review of sociology.* Palo Alto, CA: Annual Reviews.

Cherniack, N. S., & Cherniack, E. P. (2007). Respiratory system. In J. E. Birren (Ed.), *Encyclopedia of gerontology* (2nd ed.). San Diego: Academic Press.

Chess, S., & Thomas, A. (1977). Temperamental individuality from childhood to adolescence. *Journal of Child Psychiatry, 16,* 218–226.

Chess, S., & Thomas, A. (1987). *Origins and evolution of behavior disorders.* Cambridge, MA: Harvard University Press.

Cheung, Y. T., Chau, P. H., & Yip, P. S. (2008, in press). A revisit of older adults' suicides and severe acute respiratory syndrome (SARS epidemic in Hong Kong. *International Journal of Psychiatry.*

Chevan, A. (1996 August). As cheaply as one: Cohabitation in the older population. *Journal of Marriage and the Family, 58,* 656–667.

Chi, M.T. (1978) Knowledge structures and memory development. In R. S. Siegler (Ed.), *children's thinking: What develops?* Hillsdale, NJ: Erlbaum.

Chia, E. M., Wang, J. J., Rochtchina, E., Cumming, R. R., Newall, P., & Mitchell, P. (2007). Hearing impairment and health-related quality of life: The Blue Mountains Hearing Study. *Ear and Hearing, 28,* 187–195.

Chia, P., Sellick, K., & Gan, S. (2006). The attitudes and practices of neonatal nurses in the use of kangaroo care. *Australian Journal of Advanced Nursing, 23,* 20–27.

Child Trends. (2006, April). *Fast facts at a glance* Washington, DC: Author.

Children's Defense Fund. (2007). *Children's welfare and mental health.* Retrieved January 6, 2007, from www.childrensdefense.org

Chiriboga, D. A. (1982). Adaptation to marital separation in later and earlier life. *Journal of Gerontology, 37,* 109–114.

Chiu, M. M. (2007). Families, economies, cultures, and science achievement in 41 countries: Country-, school-, and student-level analyses. *Journal of Family Psychology, 21,* 510–519.

Chodosh, J., Kado, D. M., Seeman, T. E., & Karlamangla, A. S. (2007). Depressive symptoms as a predictor of cognitive decline: MacArthur Studies of Successful Aging. *American Journal of Geriatric Psychiatry, 15,* 406–415.

Choi, S. H., Kim, S. Y., Na, H. R., Kim B. K., yang, D. W., Kwon, J. C., & Park, M. Y. (2008). Effect of ApoE genotype on response to donepezil in patients with Alzheimer's disease. *Dementia and Geriatric Cognitive Disorders, 25,* 445–450.

Chomsky, N. (1957). *Syntactic structures.* The Hague: Mouton.

Christakis, N. A., & Iwashyna, T. J. (2003). The Health Impact on Families of Health Care: A matched cohort study of hospice use by decedents and mortality outcomes in surviving, widowed spouses. *Social Science and Medicine, 57,* 465–475.

Church, D. K., Siegel, M. A., & Fowler, C. D. (1988). *Growing old in America.* Wylie, TX: Information Aids.

Church, T. S., Earnest, C. P., Skinner, J. S., & Blair, S. N. (2007). Effects of different doses of physical activity on cardiorespiratory fitness among sedentary, overweight, or obese postmenopausal women with elevated blood pressure: A randomized controlled trial. *Journal of the American Medical Association, 297,* 2081–2091.

Cicchetti, D., Toth, S. L., & Rogusch, F. A. (2005). *A prevention program for child maltreatment.* Unpublished manuscript, University of Rochester, Rochester, NY.

Cicirelli, V. G. (1991). Sibling relationships in adulthood. *Marriage and Family Review, 16,* 291–310.

Ciol, M. A., Shumway-Cook, A., Hoffman, J. M., Yorkston, K. M., Dudgeon, B. J., & Chan, L. (2008). Minority disparities in disability between Medicare beneficiaries. *Journal of the American Geriatrics Society, 56,* 444–453.

Cipriano, L. E., Rupar, C. A., & Zaric, G. S. (2007). The cost effectiveness of expanding newborn screening for up to 21 inherited metabolic disorders using tandem mass spectrometry: Results from a decision-analytic model. *Value Health, 10,* 83–97.

Cisneros-Cohernour, E. J., Moreno, R. P., & Cisneros, A. A. (2000). Curriculum reform in Mexico: Kindergarten teachers' challenges and dilemmas. Proceedings of the Lilian Katz Symposium. In D. Rothenberg (Ed.), *Issues in early childhood education: Curriculum reform, teacher education, and dissemination of information.* Urbana-Champaign: University of Illinois.

Clark, B. (2008). *Growing up gifted* (7th ed.). Upper Saddle River, NJ: Prentice Hall.

Clark, E. (1993). *The lexicon in acquisition.* New York: Cambridge University Press.

Clark, M. D., & Carroll, M. H. (2008). Acquaintance rape scripts of women and men: Similarities and differences. *Sex Roles, 58,* 616–625.

Clark-Cotton, M. R., Williams, R. K., & Goral, M. (2007). Language and communication in aging. In J. E. Birren (Ed.), *Encyclopedia of gerontology* (2nd ed.). San Diego: Academic Press.

Clarke, E. J., Preston, M., Raksin, J., & Bengtson, V. L. (1999). Type of conflicts and tensions between older adults and adult children. *Gerontologist, 39,* 261–270.

Clarke-Stewart, A. K. (2006). What have we learned: Proof that families matter, policies for families and children, prospects for future research. In A. Clarke-Stewart & J. Dunn (Eds.), *Families count.* New York: Cambridge University Press.

Clarke-Stewart, A. K., & Brentano, C. (2006). *Divorce: Causes and consequences.* New Haven, CT: Yale University Press.

Clarke-Stewart, A. K., & Dunn, J. (Eds.) (2006). *Families count.* New York: Cambridge University Press.

Clarke-Stewart, A. K., & Miner, J. L. (2008). Child and day care, effects of. In M. M. Haith & J. B. Benson (Eds.), *Encyclopedia of infant and early childhood development.* Oxford, UK: Elsevier.

Clark-Plaskie, M., & Lachman, M. E. (1999). The sense of control in midlife. In J. L. Willis & J. D. Reid (Eds.), *Life in the middle.* San Diego: Academic Press.

Clarkson-Smith, L., & Hartley, A. A. (1989). Relationships between physical exercise and cognitive abilities in older adults. *Psychology and Aging, 4,* 183–189.

Clausen, J. A. (1993). *American lives.* New York: Free Press.

Clay, R. A. (1997, April). Helping dying patients let go of life in peace. *APA Monitor,* p. 42.

Clearfield, M. W., Diedrich, F. J., Smith, L. B., & Thelen, E. (2006). Young infants reach correctly in A-not-B tasks: On the development of stability and perseveration. *Infant Behavior and Development, 29,* 435–444.

Cleary, P. D., Zaborksi, L. B., & Ayanian, J. Z. (2004). Sex differences in health over the course of midlife. In G. O. Brim, C. D. Ryff, & R. C. Kessler (Eds.), *How healthy are we?* Chicago: University of Chicago Press.

Cleveland, J. N., & Lim, A. S. (2007). Employee age and performance in organizations. In K. S. Shultz & G. A. Adams (Eds.), *Aging and work in the 21st century.* Mahwah, NJ: Erlbaum.

Cleveland, J. N., & Shore, L. M. (2007). Work and employment: Individual. In J. E. Birren (Ed.), *Encyclopedia of gerontology* (2nd ed.). San Diego: Academic Press.

Clifton, R. K., Morrongiello, B. A., Kulig, J. W., & Dowd, J. M. (1981). Developmental changes in auditory localization in infancy. In R. N. Aslin, J. R. Alberts, & M. R. Petersen (Eds.), *Development of perception* (Vol. 1). Orlando, FL: Academic Press.

Clifton, R. K., Muir, D. W., Ashmead, D. H., & Clarkson, M. G. (1993). Is visually guided reaching in early infancy a myth? *Child Development, 64,* 1099–1110.

Cloud, J. (2007, August 27). Failing our geniuses. *Time,* 40–47.

Coats, A., & Blanchard-Fields, F. (2008). Emotion regulation in interpersonal problems: The role of cognitive-emotional complexity, emotion regulation goals, and expressivity. *Psychology and Aging, 23,* 39–51.

Cochran, S. D., & Mays, V. M. (1990). Sex, lies, and HIV. *New England Journal of Medicine, 322*(11), 774–775.

Cohan, C., & Kleinbaum, S. (2002). Toward a greater understanding of the cohabitation effect: Premarital cohabitation and marital communication, *Journal of Marriage and Family 64*, 180–192.

Cohen, D., & Belsky, J. (2008). Avoidant romantic attachment and female orgasm: Testing an emotion-regulation hypothesis. *Attachment and Human Development, 10*, 1–10.

Cohen, F., Kemeny, M. E., Zegans, L. S., Johnson, P., Kearney, K. A., & Stites, D. P. (2007). Immune function declines with unemployment and recovers after stressor termination. *Psychosomatic Medicine, 69*, 225–234.

Cohen, L. B. (1995). Violent video games: Aggression, arousal, and desensitization in young adolescent boys. Doctoral dissertation, University of Southern California, 1995). *Dissertation Abstracts International, 57* (2-B), 1463. University Microfilms No. 9616947.

Cohen, N. J., Lojkasek, M., Zadeh, Z. Y., Pugliese, M., & Kiefer, H. (2008, in press). Children adopted in China: A prospective study of their growth and development. *Journal of Child Psychology and Psychiatry.*

Cohen, P., Kasen, S., Chen, H., Hartmark, C., & Gordon, K. (2003). Variations in patterns of developmental transitions in the emerging adulthood period. *Developmental Psychology, 39*, 657–669.

Cohn, E., & Harlow, K. (1993, October). *Elders as victims: Randomized studies in two states.* Paper presented at the meeting of the Gerontological Association of America, New Orleans.

Coie, J. (2004). The impact of negative social experiences on the development of antisocial behavior. In J. B. Kupersmidt & K. A. Dodge (Eds.), Children's peer relations: From development to intervention. Washington. DC: American Psychological Association.

Colby, A., Kohlberg, L., Gibbs, J., & Lieberman, M. (1983). A longitudinal study of moral judgment. *Monographs of the Society for Research in Child Development* (Serial No. 201).**Walker, L.** (1982). The sequentiality of Kohlberg's stages of moral development. *Child Development, 53*, 1130–1136.

Colcombe, S. J., Erickson, K. I., Scalf, P. E., Kim, J. S., Prakash, R., McAuely, E., Elavsky, S., Marquex, D. X., Hu, L., & Kramer, A. F. (2006). Aerobic exercise training increase brain volume in aging humans. *Journals of Gerontology A: Medical Sciences, 61*, 1166–1170.

Colcombe, S. J., & Kramer, A. F. (2003). Fitness effects on the cognitive function of older adults: A meta-analytic study. *Psychological Science, 14*, 125–130.

Cole, M. (2006). Culture and cognitive development in phylogenetic, historical, and ontogenetic perspective. In W. Damon & R. Lerner (Eds.), *Handbook of child psychology* (6th ed.). New York: Wiley.

Cole, M., & Gajdamaschko, N. (2007). Vygotsky and culture. In H. Daniels, J. Wertsch, & M. Cole (Eds.), *The Cambridge companion to Vygotsky.* New York: Cambridge University Press.

Cole, S. L., & Vassar, R. (2008, in press). Linking vascular disorders and Alzheimer's disease. *Neurobiology and Aging.*

Coleman, M., Ganong, L., & Fine, M. (2004). Communication in stepfamilies. In A. L. Vangelisti (Ed.), *Handbook of family communication.* Mahwah, NJ: Erlbaum.

Coleman, P. D. (1986, August). *Regulation of dendritic extent: Human aging brain and Alzheimer's disease.* Paper presented at the meeting of the American Psychological Association, Washington, DC.

Coleman, P. G., & Podolskij, A. (2007). Identity loss and recovery in the life stories of Soviet World War II veterans. *Gerontologist, 47*, 52–60.

Coleman, V. H., Erickson, K., Schulkin, J., Zinberg, S., & Sachs, B. P. (2005). Vaginal birth after cesarean delivery: Practice patterns of obstetricians-gynecologists. *Journal of Reproductive Medicine, 50*, 261–266.

Collaku, A., Rankinen, T., Rice, T., Leon, A. S. Rao, D. C., Skinner, J. S., Wilmore, J. H., & Bouchard, C. (2004). A genome-wide linkage scan for dietary energy and nutrient intakes. *American Journal of Clinical Nutrition, 79*, 881–886.

Collins, M. (1996, Winter). The job outlook for '96 grads. *Journal of Career Planning*, pp. 51–54.

Collins, R. L., Elliott, M. N., Berry, S. H., Kanocouse, D. E., Kunkel, D., Hunter, S. B., & Miu, A. (2004). Watching sex on television predicts adolescent initiation of sexual behavior. *Pediatrics, 114*, e280–e289.

Collins, W. A., & Steinberg, L. (2006). Adolescent development in Interpersonal Context. In W. Damon & R. Lerner (Eds.), *Handbook of child psychology* (6th ed.). New York: Wiley.

Collins, W. A., & van Dulmen, M. (2006). The significance of middle childhood peer competence for work and relationships in early childhood. In A. C. Huston & M. N. Ripke (Eds.), *Developmental contexts in middle childhood*: Bridges to adolescence and adulthood. New York: Cambridge University Press.

Colonna-Romano, G., Bulati, M., Aquino, A., Vitello, S., Lio, D., Candore, G., & Caruso, C. (2008). B cell immunosenescence in the elderly and in centenarians. *Rejuvenation Research, 11*, 433–439.

Coltrane, S. L., Parke, R. D., Schofield, T. J., Tsuha, S. J., Chavez, M., & Lio, S. (2008). Mexican American families and poverty. In D. R. Crane & T. B. Heaton (Eds.), *Handbook of families and poverty.* Thousand Oaks, CA: Sage.

Comer, J. (2004). *Leave no child behind.* New Haven, CT: Yale University Press.

Comer, J. (2006). Child development: The underweighted aspect of intelligence. In P. C. Kyllonen, R. D. Roberts, & L. Stankov (Eds.), *Extending intelligence.* Mahwah, NJ: Erlbaum.

Comer, J. P. (1988). Educating poor minority children. *Scientific American, 259*, 42–48.

Commoner, B. (2002). Unraveling the DNA myth: The spurious foundation of genetic engineering. *Harper's Magazine, 304*, 39–47.

Commons, M. L., & Bresette, L. M. (2006). Illuminating major creative scientific innovators with postformal stages. In C. Hoare (Ed.), *Handbook of adult development and learning.* New York: Oxford University Press.

Comstock, G., & Scharrer, E. (2006). Media and popular culture. In W. Damon & R. Lerner (Eds.), *Handbook of child psychology* (6th ed.). New York: Wiley.

Conger, R. D., & Chao, W. (1996). Adolescent depressed mood. In R. L. Simons (Ed.), *Understanding differences between divorced and intact families: Stress, interaction, and child outcome.* Thousand Oaks, CA: Sage.

Conger, R., & Conger, K. J. (2008). Understanding the processes through which economic hardship influences rural families and children. In D. R. Crane & T. B. Heaton (Eds.), *Handbook of families and poverty.* Thousand Oaks, CA: Sage.

Connides, I. A. (2009). *Family ties and aging* (2nd ed.). Thousand Oaks, CA: Sage.

Constantine, N. A. (2008). Editorial: Converging evidence leaves policy behind: Sex education in the United States. *Journal of Adolescent Health, 42*, 324–326.

Contemporary Research Press. (1993). *American working women: A statistical handbook.* Dallas: Author.

Conway, K. P., Swendsen, J. D., & Merikangas, K. R. (2003). Alcohol expectancies, alcohol consumption, and problem drinking: The moderating role of family history. *Addictive Behaviors, 28*, 823–836.

Conway, K. S., & Kutinova, A. (2006). Maternal health: Does prenatal care make a difference? *Health Economics, 15*, 461–488.

Cook, H. L., Patel, P. J., & Tufail, A. (2008). Age-related macular degeneration: Diagnosis and management. *British Medical Bulletin, 85*, 127–149.

Cook, I. A., Bookheimer, S. Y., Mickes, L., Leuchter, A. F., & Kumar, A. (2007). Aging and brain activation with working memory tasks: An fMRI study of connectivity. *International Journal of Geriatric Psychiatry, 22*, 332–342.

Cook, M., & Birch, R. (1984). Infant perception of the shapes of tilted plane forms. *Infant Behavior and Development, 7*, 389–402.

Cook, P. J., MacCoun, R., Muschkin, C., & Vigor, J. (2008). The negative impacts of starting middle school in the sixth grade. *Journal of Policy Analysis and Management, 27*, 104–121.

Cook, T. D., Deng, Y., & Morgano, E. (2007). Friendship influences during early adolescence: The special role of friends' grade point average. *Journal of Research on Adolescence, 17*, 325–356.

Cooney, T. M. (1994). Young adults' relations with parents: The influence of recent parental divorce. *Journal of Marriage and the Family, 56*, 45–56.

Coontz, S. (2007). The origins of modern divorce. *Family Process, 46*, 7–16.

Cooper, A. R., & Moley, K. H. (2008). Maternal tobacco use and its preimplantation effects on fertility: More reasons to stop smoking. *Seminars in Reproductive Medicine, 26*, 204–212.

Cooper, C. R., Behrens, R., & Trinh, N. (2008, in press). Identity development. In R. A. Shweder, T. R. Bidell, A. C. Daily, S. D. Dixon, P. J. Miller, & J. Model (Eds.), *The Chicago companion to the child.* Chicago: University of Chicago Press.

Cooper, C. R., & Grotevant, H. D. (1989, April). *Individuality and connectedness in the family and adolescent's self and relational competence.* Paper presented at the meeting of the Society for Research in Child Development, Kansas City.

Cooper, C. R., Grotevant, H. D., Moore, M. S., & Condon, S. M. (1982, August). *Family support and conflict: Both foster adolescent identity and role taking.* Paper presented at the meeting of the American Psychological Association, Washington, DC.

Cooper, C., Katona, C., Orrell, M., & Livingston, G. (2008, in press). Coping strategies, anxiety, and depression in caregivers of people with

Alzheimer's disease. *International Journal of Geriatric Psychiatry.*

Cooper, C., Selwood, A., & Livingston, G. (2008). The prevalence of elder abuse and neglect: A systematic review. *Age and Aging, 37,* 151–160.

Cooper, R., Mishra, G., Clennell, S., Guralnik, J., & Kuh, D. (2008, in press). Menopausal status and physical performance in midlife: Findings from a British cohort study. *Menopause.*

Corbett, T. (2007). Social indicators as policy tool: Welfare reform as a case study. In B. Brown (Ed.), *Key indicators of child and youth well-being.* Mahwah, NJ: Erlbaum.

Corbin, C. B., Welk, G. J., Corbin, W. R., & Welk, K. A. (2008). *Concepts of physical fitness* (14th ed.). New York: McGraw-Hill.

Cordier, S. (2008). Evidence for a role of paternal exposure in developmental toxicity. *Basic and Clinical Pharmacology and Toxicology, 102,* 176–181.

Cornelius, J. R., Clark, D. B., Reynolds, M., Kirisci, L., & Tarter, R. (2007). Early age of first sexual intercourse and affiliation with deviant peers predict development of SUD: A prospective longitudinal study. *Addictive Behavior, 32,* 850–854.

Cornman, J. C., & Freedman, V. A. (2008). Racial and ethnic disparities in mobility device use in late life. *Journals of Gerontology B: Psychological Sciences and Social Sciences, 63,* S34–S41.

Cornwell, B., Laumann, E. O., & Schumm, L. P. (2008). The social connectedness of older adults: A national profile. *American Sociological Review, 73,* 185–203.

Corso, J. F. (1977). Auditory perception and communication. In J. E. Birren & K. W. Schaie (Eds.), *Handbook of the psychology of aging.* (2nd ed.). New York: Van Nostrand Reinhold.

Costa, P. T., & McCrae, R. R., (1995). Solid ground on the wetlands of personality: A reply to Black. *Psychological Bulletin, 117,* 216–220.

Costa, P. T., & McCrae, R. R. (1998). Personality assessment. In H. S. Friedman (Ed.), *Encyclopedia of mental health* (Vol. 3). San Diego: Academic Press.

Costa, P. T., & McCrae, R. R. (2000). Contemporary personality psychology. In C. E. Coffey and J. L. Cummings (Eds.), *Textbook of geriatric neuropsychiatry.* Washington, DC: American Psychiatric Press.

Costello, D. M., Swendsen, J., Rose, J. S., & Dierker, L. C. (2008). Risk and protective factors associated with trajectories of depressed mood from adolescence to early adulthood. *Journal of Consulting and Clinical Psychology, 766,* 173–183.

Costello, E. J., Sung, M., Worthman, C., & Angold, A. (2007). Pubertal maturation and the development of alcohol use and abuse. *Drug and Alcohol Dependence, 88* (Suppl. 1), S50-S59.

Cote, J. E. (2006). Emerging adulthood as an institutionalized moratorium: Risks and benefits to identity formation. In J. J. Arnett & J. L. Tanner (Eds.), *Emerging adults in America.* Washington, DC: American Psychological Association.

Cotton, S., Zebracki, M. A., Rosenthal, S. L., Tsevat, J., & Drotar, D. (2006). Religion/spirituality and adolescent health outcomes: A review. *Journal of Adolescent Health, 38,* 472–480.

Council of Economic Advisors. (2000). *Teens and their parents in the 21st century: An examination of trends in teen behavior and the role of parent involvement.* Washington, DC: Author.

Courage, M. L., Howe, M. L., & Squires, S. E. (2004). Individual differences in 3.5 month olds' visual attention: What do they predict at 1 year? *Infant Behavior and Development, 127,* 19–30.

Courage, M. L., & Richards, J. E. (2008). Attention. In M. M. Haith & J. B. Benson (Eds.), *Encyclopedia of infant and early childhood development.* Oxford, UK: Elsevier.

Courtin, C. (2000). The impact of sign language on the cognitive development of deaf children: The case of theories of mind. *Journal of Deaf Studies and Deaf Education, 5,* 201–219.

Cousineau, T. M., Goldstein, M., & Franco, D. L. (2005). A collaborative approach to nutrition education for college students. *Journal of American College Health, 53,* 79–84.

Cowan, C. P., & Cowan, P. A. (2000). *When partners become parents.* Mahwah, NJ: Erlbaum.

Cowan, P., Cowan, C., Ablow, J., Johnson, V. K., and Measelle, J. (2005). *The family context of parenting in children's adaptation to elementaly school.* Mahwah, NJ: Lawrence Erlbaum Associates.

Cowley, G., & Hager, M. (1995, December 4). Terminal care: Too painful, too prolonged. *Newsweek,* pp. 74–75.

Cox, H., & Hammonds, A. (1998). Religiosity, aging, and life satisfaction. *Journal of Religion and Aging, 5,* 1–21.

Cox, J. (2006). Postnatal depression in fathers. *Lancet, 366,* 982.

Cox, M. J., Neilbron, N., Mills-Koonce, W. R., Pressel, A., Oppenheimer, C. W., & Szwedo, D. E. (2008). Marital relationship. In M. M. Haith & J. B. Benson (Eds.), *Encyclopedia of infant and early childhood development.* Oxford, UK: Elsevier.

Craik, F. I., Winocur, G., Palmer, H., Binns, M. A., Edwards, M., Bridges, K., Glazer, P., Chavannes, R., & Stuss, D. T. (2007). Cognitive rehabilitation in the elderly: Effects on memory. *Journal of the International Neuropsychological Society, 13,* 132–142.

Crane, D. R., & Heaton, T. B. (Eds.) (2008). *Handbook of Families and poverty.* Thousand Oaks, CA: Sage.

Crane, P. B., & Wallace, D. C. (2007). Cardiovascular risks and physical activity in middle-aged and elderly African American women. *Journal of Cardiovascular Nursing, 22,* 297–303.

Crean, H. F. (2008). Conflict in the Latino parent-youth dyad: the role of emotional support from the opposite parent. *Journal of Family Psychology, 22,* 484–493.

Cremation Association of America. (2000). *Fact sheet.* Milwaukee, WI: Author.

Creswell, J. W. (2008). *Educational research* (3rd ed.). Upper Saddle River, NJ: Prentice Hall.

Crick, N. R., Ostrov, J. M., & Werner, N. E. (2006). A longitudinal study of relational aggression, physical aggression, and children's social-psychological adjustment. *Journal of Abnormal Child Psychology, 34,* 131–142.

Crockenberg, S. B. (1986). Are temperamental differences in babies associated with predictable differences in caregiving? In J. V. Lerner & R. M. Lerner (Eds.), *Temperament and social interaction during infancy and childhood.* San Francisco: Jossey-Bass.

Crooks, R. L., & Baur, K. (2008). *Our sexuality* (10th ed.). Belmont, CA: Wadsworth.

Crosby, R. A., & Holtgrave, D. R. (2006). The protective value of social capital against teen pregnancy: A state–level analysis. *Journal of Adolescent Health, 38,* 556–559.

Crosnoe, R., Riegle-Crumb, C., Field, S., Frank, K., & Muller, C. (2008). Peer group contexts of girls' and boys' academic experiences. *Child Development, 79,* 139–155.

Crosnoe, R., & Trinitapoli, J. (2008). Shared family activities and the transition from childhood into adolescence. *Journal of Research on Adolescence, 18,* 23–48.

Crouter, A. C. (2006). Mothers and fathers at work. In A. Clarke-Stewart & J. Dunn (Eds.), *Families count.* New York: Cambridge University Press.

Crowley, K., Callahan, M. A., Tenenbaum, H. R., & Allen, E. (2001). Parents explain more to boys than to girls during shared scientific thinking. *Psychological Science, 12,* 258–261.

Crowley, M., Lichter, D. T., & Qian, Z. (2006). Beyond gateway cities: Economic -restructuring and poverty among Mexican immigrant families and children. *Family Relations, 55,* 345–360.

Csaba, A., Bush, M. C., & Saphier, C. (2006). How painful are amniocentesis and chorionic villus sampling? *Prenatal Diagnosis, 26,* 35–38.

Csikszentmihalyi, M. (1995). *Creativity.* New York: Harper Collins.

Csikszentmihalyi, M. (2000). Creativity: An overview. In A. Kazdin (Ed.), *Encyclopedia of psychology.* Washington, DC, & New York: American Psychological Association and Oxford University Press.

Cuddy-Casey, M., & Orvaschel, H. (1997). Children's understanding of death in relation to child suicidality and homicidality. *Death Studies, 17,* 33–45.

Cunningham, P.M. (2009). *Phonics they use* (5th Ed.). Boston: Allyn & Bacon.

Cunningham, P.M., & Hall, D.P. (2009). *Making words first grade.* Boston: Allyn & Bacon.

Cunningham, W., & Hyson, D. (2006). The skinny on high-protein, low-carbohydrate diets. *Preventive Cardiology, 9,* 166–171.

Cunningham-Sabo, L., Bauer, M., Pareo, S., Philips-Benally, S. Roanhorse, J., & Garcia, L. (2008, in press). Qualitative investigation of factors contributing to effective nutrition education for Navajo families. *Maternal and Child Health Journal.*

Cupertino, A. P. & Haan, M. N. (1999, November). *Religiosity and health among elderly Latinos.* Paper presented at the meeting of the Gerontological Society of America, San Francisco.

Curran, K., DuCette, J., Eisenstein, J., & Hyman, I. A. (2001, August). *Statistical analysis of the cross-cultural data: the third year.* Paper presented at the meeting of the American Psychological Association, San Francisco.

Currie, H. (2009, in press). Economic impact of Head Start. In R. E. Tremblay, R. deV Peters, M. Boivin, & R. G. Barr (Eds.), *Encyclopedia on early childhood development.* Montreal: Centre of Excellence for Early Childhood Development.

Currier, J. M., Holland, J. M., & Neimeyer, R. A. (2006). Sense-making, grief, and the experience of violent loss: Toward a mediational model. *Death Studies, 30,* 403–428.

Curtin, L. L. (2007). The perfect storm: Managed care, aging adults, and a nursing shortage. *Nursing Administration Quarterly, 31,* 105–114.

Cutler, S. J. (2006). Technological change and aging In R. H. Binstock & L. K. George (Eds.), *Handbook of aging and the social sciences* (6th ed.). San Diego: Academic Press.

Cuzon, V. C., Yeh, P. W., Yanagawa, Y., Obata, K., & Yeh, H. H. (2008). Ethanol consumption during early pregnancy alters the disposition of tangentially migrating GAB Aergic interneurons in the fetal cortex. *Journal of Neuroscience, 28,* 1854–1864.

Cyna, A. M., Andrew, M. I., & McAuliffe, G. L. (2006). Antenatal self-hypnosis for labor and child-birth: A pilot study. *Anesthesia and Intensive Care, 34,* 464–469.

Cyna, A. M., McAuliffe, G. L., & Andrew, M. I. (2004). Hypnosis for pain relief in labor and child-birth: A systematic review. *British Journal of Anesthesia, 93,* 505–511.

Czaja, S.J., Charness, N., Fisk, A. D., Hertzog, C., Nair, S. N., Rogers, W. A., & Sharit, J. (2006). Factors predicting the use of technology: Findings from the Center for Research and Education on Aging and Technology (CREATE). *Psychology and Aging, 21,* 333–352.

Czernochowski, D., Fabiani, M., & Friedman, D. (2007). Use it or lose it? SES mitigates age-related decline in a recency/recognition task. *Neurobiology of Aging, 29,* 945–958.

D

D'Amico, E. J., Edelen, M. O., Miles, J. N., & Morral, A. R. (2008). The longitudinal association between substance use and delinquency among high-risk youth. *Drug and Alcohol Dependence, 93,* 85–92.

D'Augelli, A. R. (1991). Gay men in college: Identity processes and adaptations. *Journal of College Student Development, 32,* 140–146.

D'Onofrio, B. M. (2008). Nature vs. nurture. In M. M. Haith & J. B. Benson (Eds.), *Encyclopedia of infancy and early childhood.* Oxford, UK: Elsevier.

D'Onofrio, B. M., & others. (2007). Intergenerational transmission of childhood conduct problems: A children of twins study. *Archives of General Psychiatry, 64,* 820–829.

Daadi, M. M. (2008). In vitro assays for neural stem cell differentiation: Induction of dopaminergic phenotype. *Methods in Molecular Biology, 438,* 205–212.

Daaleman, T. P., Perera, S., & Studenski, S. A. (2004). Religion, spirituality, and health status in geriatric outpatients. *Annals of Family Medicine, 2,* 49–53.

Dahl, R. E. (2004). Adolescent brain development: A period of vulnerabilities and opportunities. *Annals of the New York Academy of Sciences, 1021,* 1–22.

Daley, A. J., Macarthur, C., & Winter, H. (2007). The role of exercise in treating postpartum depression: A review of the literature. *Journal of Midwifery & Women's Health, 52,* 56–62.

Daley, S. E., & Hammen, C. (2002). Depressive symptoms and close relationships during the transition to adulthood: Perspectives from dysphoric women, their best friends, and their romantic partners. *Journal of Consulting and Clinical Psychology, 70,* 129–141.

Dalton, T. C., & Bergenn, V. W. (2007). *Early experience, the brain, and consciousness.* Mahwah, NJ: Erlbaum.

Damon, W. (1988). *The moral child.* New York: Free Press.

Danforth, M. M., & Glass, J. C. (2001). Listen to my words, give meaning to my sorrow: A study in cognitive constructs in middle-aged bereaved widows. *Death Studies, 25,* 513–548.

Daniels, H. (2007). Pedagogy. In H. Daniels, J. Wertsch, & M. Cole (Eds.), *The Cambridge companion to Vygotsky.* New York: Cambridge University Press.

Daniels, P., Noe, G. F., & Mayberry, R. (2006). Barriers to prenatal care among Black women of low socioeconomic status. *American Journal of Health Behavior, 30,* 188–198.

Danigelis, N. L. (2007. Leisure. In J. E. Birren (Ed.), *Encyclopedia of gerontology* (2nd ed.). San Diego: Academic Press.

Danne, T., & Becker, D. (2007). Pediatric diabetes: Achieving Practical, effective insulin therapy in type 1 and type 2 diabetes. *Acta Pediatrica, 96,* 1560–1570.

Danner D., Snowdon D., & Friesen W. (2001). *Positive emotions in early life and longevity: Findings from the Nun Study. Journal of Personality and Social Psychology,* 80(5), 814–813.

Darling-Hammond, L. (2007). Race, inequality, and educational accountability: The irony of "No Child Left Behind." *Race, Ethnicity, and Education, 10,* 245–260.

Darr, K. (2007). Physician-assisted suicide: Legal and ethical considerations. *Journal of Health and Law, 40,* 29–63.

Darwin, C. (1859). *On the origin of species.* London: John Murray.

Das, A. (2008, in press). Sexual harassment at work in the United States. *Archives of Sexual Behavior.*

Das, S., & O'Keefe, J. H. (2006). Behavioral cardiology: Recognizing and addressing the profound impact of psychosocial stress on cardiovascular health. *Current Atherosclerosis Reports, 8,* 111–118.

Daselaar, S. M., & Cabeza, R. (2008 in press). Episodic memory decline and healthy aging: Role of prefrontal and medial temporal lobe regions. In J. Byrne (Ed.), *Learning and memory: A comprehensive reference.* Oxford, UK: Elsevier.

Daselaar, S. M., Rice, H. J., Greenberg, D. L., Cabeza, R., LaBar, K. S., & Rubin, D. C. (2008). The spatiotemporal dynamics of autobiographical memory: Neural correlates of recall, emotional intensity, and reliving. *Cerebral Cortex, 18,* 217–229.

Dasen, P.R. (1977). Are cognitive processes universal? A contribution to cross-cultural Piagetian Psychology. In N. Warran (Ed.), *Studies in cross-cultural psychology* (Vol. 1). London: Academic Press.

Datar, A., & Sturm, R. (2004). Childhood overweight and parent- and teacher-reported behavior problems: Evidence from a prospective study of kindergartners. *Archives of Pediatric and Adolescent Medicine, 158,* 804–810.

Daubenmier, J. J., Weidner, G., Sumner, M. D., Mendell, N., Merritt-Worden, T., Studley, J., & Ornish, D. (2007). The contribution of changes in diet, exercise, and stress management to changes in coronary risk in women and men in the multisite cardiac lifestyle intervention program. *Annals of Behavior Medicine, 33,* 57–68.

Davidson, J. (2000). Giftedness. In A. Kazdin (Ed.), *Encyclopedia of psychology.* Washington, DC, & New York: American Psychological Association and Oxford University Press.

Davidson, M. R., London, M. L., & Ladewig, P. A. (2008). *Olds' maternal-newborn nursing and women's health across the lifespan* (8th ed.). Upper Saddle River, NJ: Prentice Hall.

Davies, J., & Brember, I. (1999). Reading and mathematics attainments and self-esteem in years 2 and 6 — an eight-year cross-sectional study. *Educational Studies, 25,* 145–157.

Davila, J., & Steinberg, S. J. (2006). Depression and romantic dysfunction during adolescence. In T. E. Joiner, J. S. Brown, & J. Kistner (Eds.), *The interpersonal, cognitive, and social nature of depression.* Mahwah, NJ: Erlbaum.

Davis, A. E., Hyatt, G., & Arrasmith, D. (1998, February). "I Have a Dream" program. *Class One Evaluation Report,* Portland, OR: Northwest Regional Education Laboratory.

Davis, B. E., Moon, R. Y., Sachs, M. C., & Ottolini, M. C. (1998). Effects of sleep position on infant motor development. *Pediatrics, 102,* 1135–1140.

Davis, C. L., Tomporowski, P. D., Boyle, C. A., Waller, J. L., Miller, P. H., Nagieri, J. A., & Gregoski, M. (2007). Effects of aerobic exercise on overweight children's cognitive functioning: A randomized controlled trial. *Research Quarterly for Exercise and Sport, 78,* 510–519.

Davis, D. K. (2005). Leading the midwifery renaissance. *RCM Midwives, 8,* 264–268.

Davis, E. P., Glynn, L. M. Schetter, C. D., Hobel, C., Chicz-Demet, A., & Sandman, C. A. (2007). Prenatal exposure to maternal depression and cortisol influences infant development. *Journal of the American Academy of Child and Adolescent Psychiatry, 46,* 737–746.

Davis, L., & Keyser, J. (1997). *Becoming the parent you want to be: A sourcebook of strategies for the first five years.* New York: Broadway Books.

Davison, G. C., & Neale, J. M. (2007). *Abnormal psychology* (10th ed.). New York: Wiley.

Day, N. L., Goldschmidt, L., & Thomas, C. A. (2006). Prenatal marijuana exposure contributes to the prediction of marijuana use at age 14. *Addiction, 101,* 1313–1322.

Day, R. H., & McKenzie, B. E. (1973). Perceptual shape constancy in early infancy. *Perception, 2,* 315–320.

De Boulle, K. L. (2007). Botulinum neurotoxin type A in facial aesthetics. *Expert Opinion on Pharmacotherapy, 8,* 1059–1072.

De Franciscis, P., Cobellis, L., Fornaro, F., Sepe, E., Torella, M., & Colarcurci, N. (2007). Low-dose hormone therapy in the perimenopause. *International Journal of Gynecology and Obstetrics, 98,* 138–142.

de Haan, M., & Martinos, M. (2008). Brain function. In M. M. Haith & J. B. Benson (Eds.), *Encyclopedia of infant and early childhood development.* Oxford, UK: Elsevier.

de Leo, D., & Heller, T. (2008). Social modeling in the transmission of suicidality. *Crisis, 29,* 11–19.

de Luis, D. A., Aller, R., Izaola, O., Gonzales Sagrado, M., Bellioo, D., & Conde, R. (2007). Effects of a low-fat versus a low-carbohydrate diet on adipocytokines in obese adults. *Hormone Research, 67,* 296–300.

de Onis, M., De Onis, M., Onyango, A. W., Borghi, E., Garza, C., & Yang, H. (2006). Comparison of the World Health Organization (WHO) child growth standards and the National Center for Health Statistics/WHO international growth reference: Implications for child health programs. *Public Health Nutrition, 9,* 942–947.

de Rosnay, M., Cooper, P. J., Tsigaras, N., & Murray, L. (2006). Transmission of social anxiety from mother to infant: An experimental study using a social referencing paradigm. *Behavior Research and Therapy, 44,* 1165–1175.

De Santis-Moniaci, D., & Altshuler, L. (2007). Comprehensive behavioral treatment of overweight and the pediatric practice. *Pediatric Annals, 36,* 102–108.

de Vries, P. (2005). Lessons from home: Scaffolding vocal improvisation and song acquisition in a 2-year-old. *Early Childhood Education Journal, 32,* 307–312.

Deary, I. J., & Der, G. (2005). Reaction time explains IQ's association with death. *Psychological Science, 16,* 64–69.

Deater-Deckard, K. & Dodge K. (1997). Externalizing behavior problems and discipline revisited: Non-linear effects and variation by culture, context and gender. *Psychological Inquiry, 8,* 161–75.

DeCasper, A. J., & Spence, M. J. (1986). Prenatal maternal speech influences newborn's perception of speech sounds. *Infant Behavior and Development, 9,* 133–150.

Declercq, E., Cunningham, D. K., Johnson, C., & Sakala, C. (2008). Mothers' reports of postpartum pain associated with vaginal and cesarean deliveries: Results of a national survey. *Birth, 35,* 16–24.

Deeg, D. J. H. (2005). The development of physical and mental health from late midlife to early old age. In S. L. Willis, & M. Martin (Eds.), *Middle adulthood.* Thousand Oaks, CA: Sage.

Deeny, S. P., & others. (2008, in press). Exercise, APOE, and working memory: MEG and behavioral evidence for benefit of exercise in epsilon4 carriers. *Biological Psychology.*

DeGarmo, D. S., & Martinez, C. R. (2006). A culturally informed model of academic well-being for Latino youth: The importance of discriminatory experiences and social support. *Family Relations, 55,* 267–278.

DeGenova, M. K., & Rice, F. P. (2008). *Intimate relationships, marriages, and families* (7th ed.). New York: McGraw-Hill.

DeLamater, J. D., & Sill, M. (2005). Sexual desire in later life. *Journal of Sex Research, 42,* 167–174.

DeLeon, C. W., & Karraker, K. H. (2007). Intrinsic and extrinsic factors associated with night waking in 9-month-old infants. *Infant Behavior and Development, 30,* 596–605.

Delmonico, M. J., & others. (2007). Alternative definitions of sarcopenia, lower extremity performance, and functional impairment with aging in older men and women. *Journal of the American Geriatric Association, 55,* 769–764.

DeLoache, J. S., Simcock, G., & Macari, S. (2007). Planes, trains, and automobiles—and tea sets: Extremely intense interests in very young children. *Developmental Psychology, 43,* 1579–1586.

Dement, W. C. (2005). History of sleep medicine. *Neurologic Clinics, 23,* 964–965.

Dempster, F. N. (1981). Memory span: Sources of individual and developmental differences. *Psychological Bulletin, 80,* 63–100.

Denham, S. A., Bassett, H. H., & Wyatt, T. (2007). The socialization of emotional competence. In J. E. Grusec & P. D. Hastings (Eds.), *Handbook of socialization.* New York: Guilford.

Denmark, F. L., Russo, N. F., Frieze, I. H., & Eschuzur, J. (1988). Guidelines for avoiding sexism in psychological research: A report of the ad hoc committee on nonsexist research. *American Psychologist, 43,* 582–585.

Denney, N. W. (1986, August). *Practical problem solving.* Paper presented at the meeting of the American Psychological Association, Washington, DC.

Denney, N. W. (1990). Adult age differences in traditional and practical problem solving. *Advances in Psychology, 72,* 329–349.

Dennis, N. A., & Cabeza, R. (2008). Neuroimaging of healthy cognitive aging. In F. I. M. Craik & T. A. Salthouse (Eds.), *Handbook of aging and cognition* (3rd ed.). Mahwah, NJ: Erlbaum.

Der Ananian, C., & Prohaska, T. R. (2007). Exercise and physical activity. In J. E. Birren (Ed.), *Encyclopedia of gerontology* (2nd ed.). San Diego: Academic Press.

Derbyshire, E. (2007a). Nutrition in pregnant teenagers: How nurses can help. *British Journal of Nursing, 16,* 144–145.

Derbyshire, E. (2007b). The importance of adequate fluid and fiber intake during pregnancy. *Nursing Standard, 21,* 40–43.

Derks, E. M., Hudziak, J. J., Dolan, C. V., van Beijsterveldt, T. C., Verhulst, F. C., & Boomsma, D. I. (2008). Genetic and environmental influences on the relation between attention problems and attention deficit hyperactivity disorder. *Behavior Genetics, 38,* 11–23.

DeRose, L., & Brooks-Gunn, J. (2008, in press). Pubertal development in early adolescence: Implications for affective processes. In N. B. Allen & L. Sheeber (Eds.), *Adolescent emotional development and the emergence of depressive disorders.* New York: Cambridge University Press.

DeRosier, M. E., & Marcus, S. R. (2005). Building friendships and combating bullying: Effectiveness of S. S. Grin at one-year follow-up. *Journal of Clinical Child and Adolescent Psychology, 34,* 140–150.

DeSantis, L. (1998). Building healthy communities with immigrants and refugees. *Journal of Transcultural Nursing, 9,* 20–31.

Deschesnes, M., Fines, P., & Demers, S. (2006). Are tattooing and body piercing indicators of risk-taking behaviours among high school students? *Journal of Adolescence, 29,* 379–393.

Deshpande, N., Metter, E. J., Ling, S., Conwit, R., & Ferruci, L. (2008). Physiological correlates of age-related decline in vibrotactile sensitivity. *Neurobiology of Aging, 29,* 765–773.

DeSpelder, L. A., & Strickland, A. L. (2005). *The last dance: Encountering death and dying* (6th ed., rev. update). Mountain View, CA: Mayfield.

Deutsch, F. M. (1991). Women's lives: The story not told by theories of development. *Contemporary Psychology, 36,* 237–238.

Devos, T. (2006). Implicit bicultural identity among Mexican American and Asian American college students. *Cultural Diversity and Ethnic Minority Psychology, 12,* 1381–1402.

Diamond, A. D. (1985). Development of the ability to use recall to guide action, as indicated by infants' performance on A–B. *Child Development, 56,* 868–883.

Diamond, A. D. (2007). Interrelated and interdependent. *Developmental Science, 10,* 152–158.

Diamond, L. M. (2008). Female bisexuality from adolescence to adulthood: Results from a 10-year longitudinal study. *Developmental Psychology, 44,* 5–14.

Dickson, F. C., Christian, A., & Remmo, C. J. (2004). Exploration of marital and family issues of the later-life adult. In C. Segrin & J. Flora (Eds.), *Family Communication.* Mahwah, NJ: Erlbaum.

Dickstein, D. L., Kabaso, D., Rocher, A. B., Luebke, J. I., Wearne, S. L., & Hof, P. R. (2007). Changes in the structural complexity of the aged brain. *Aging Cell, 6,* 275–284.

Diego, M. A., Field, T., & Hernandez-Reif, M. (2008). Temperature increases in preterm infants during massage therapy. *Infant Behavior and Development, 31,* 149–152.

Dillon, J. (2003). Reincarnation: The technology of death. In C. D. Bryant (Ed.), *Handbook of death and dying.* Thousand Oaks, CA: Sage.

Dindia, K. (2006). Men are from North Dakota, women are from South Dakota. In K. Dindia & D. J. Canary (Eds.), *Sex differences and similarities in communication.* Mahwah, NJ: Erlbaum.

Dishion, T. J., Piehler, T. F., & Myers, M. W. (2008). Dynamic and ecology of adolescent peer influence. In M. J. Prinstein & K. A. Dodge (Eds.), *Understanding peer influence in children and adolescents.* New York: Guilford.

Dittmann-Kohli, F. (2005). Middle age identity in cultural and lifespan perspective. In S. L. Willis & M. Martin (Eds.), *Middle adulthood.* Thousand Oaks, CA: Sage.

Divall, S. A., & Radovick, S. (2008). Pubertal development and menarche. *Annals of the New York Academy of Sciences, 1135,* 19-28.

Dixon, L., Browne, K., & Hamilton-Giachritsis, C. (2005). Risk factors of parents abused as children: A mediational analysis of the intergenerational continuity of child maltreatment (Part I). *Journal of Child Psychology and Psychiatry and Allied Disciplines, 46,* 47–57.

Dixon, R. A., Garrett, D. D., Lentz, T. L., MacDonald, S. W., Strauss, E., & Hultsch, D. F. (2007). Neurocognitive markers of cognitive impairment: Exploring the roles of speed and inconsistency. *Neuropsychology, 21,* 381–399.

Doblado, M., & Moley, K. H. (2007). Glucose metabolism in pregnancy and embryogenesis. *Current Opinion in Endocrinology, Diabetes, and Obesity, 14,* 488–493.

Dobrossy, M. D., & Dunnett, S. B. (2005). Optimizing plasticity: Environmental and training associated factors in transplant-mediated brain repair. *Review of Neuroscience, 16,* 1–21.

Dodge, K. A. (1983). Behavioral antecedents of peer social status. *Child Development, 54,* 1386–1399.

Dodge, K. A. (2001). The science of youth violence prevention: Progressing from developmental psychopathology to efficacy to effectiveness in public policy. *American Journal of Preventive Medicine, 20,* 63–70.

Dodge, K. A., & the Conduct Problems Prevention Research Group. (2007, March). *The impact of Fast Track on adolescent conduct disorder.* Paper presented at the meeting of the Society for Research in Child Development, Boston.

Dodge, K. A., Coie, J. D., & Lynam, D. R. (2006). Aggression and antisocial behavior in youth. In W. Damon & R. Lerner (Eds.), *Handbook of child psychology* (6th ed). New York: Wiley.

Dodson, C. S., Bawa, S., & Slotnick, S. D. (2007). Aging, Source memory, and misrecollections. *Journal of Experimental Psychology: Learning, Memory, and Cognition, 33,* 169–181.

Doherty, E. E., Green, K. M., & Ensminger, M. E. (2008). Investigating the long-term influence of adolescent delinquency on drug use initiation. *Drug and Alcohol Dependence, 93,* 72–84.

Doherty, M. (2008). *Theory of mind.* Philadelphia: Psychology Press.

Doherty, T., Chopra, M., Nkonki, L., Jackson, D., & Greiner, T. (2006). Effects of the HIV epidemic on infant feeding in South Africa: "When they see me coming with the tins they laugh at me." *Bulletin of the World Health Organization, 84,* 90–96.

Dohrenwend, B. S., & Shrout, P. E. (1985). "Hassles" in the conceptualization and measurement of life stress variables. *American Psychologist, 40,* 780–785.

Dondi, M., Simion, F., & Caltran, G. (1999). Can newborns discriminate between their own cry and the cry of another newborn infant? *Developmental Psychology, 35* (2), 418–426.

Dontigny, L., Arsenault, M.-Y., Martel, M.-J., Biringer, A., Cormier, J., Delaney, M., Gleason, T., Leduc, D., Penava, D., Polsky, Roggensack, A., Rowntree, C., & Wilson, A. K. (2008). Rubella in pregnancy. *Journal of Obstetrics and Gynecology Canada, 30,* 152–168.

Dorn, L. D., Dahl, R. E., Woodward, H. R., & Biro, F. (2006). Defining the boundaries of early adolescence: A user's guide to assessing pubertal status and pubertal timing in research with adolescents. *Applied Developmental Science, 10,* 30–56.

Doty, R. L., & Shah, M. (2008). Taste and smell. In M. M. Haith & J. B. Benson (Eds.), *Encyclopedia of infant and early childhood development.* Oxford, UK: Elsevier.

Dow, B. J., & Wood, J. (Eds.). (2006). *The Sage handbook of gender and communication.* Thousand Oaks, CA: Sage.

Dowker, A. (2006). What can functional brain imaging studies tell us about typical and atypical cognitive development in children. *Journal of Physiology, Paris, 99,* 333–341.

Draghi-Lorenz, R. (2007, July). *Self-conscious emotions in young infants and the direct perception of self and others in interaction.* Paper presented at the meeting of the International Society for Research on Emotions, Sunshine Coast, Australia.

Draghi-Lorenz, R., Reddy, V., & Costall, A. (2001). Re-thinking the development of "non-basic" emotions: A critical review of existing theories. *Developmental Review, 21,* 263–304.

Driscoll, A., & Nagel, N. G. (2008). *Early childhood education* (4th ed.). Boston: Allyn & Bacon.

Druzhyna, N. M., Wilson, G. L., & Ledoux, S. P. (2008, in press). Mitochondrial DNA repair in aging and disease. *Mechanisms of Aging and Development.*

Dryfoos, J. G. (1990). *Adolescents at risk: Prevalence or prevention.* New York: Oxford University Press.

Dryfoos, J. G., & Barkin, C. (2006). *Growing up in America today.* New York: Oxford University Press.

Dube, S., Boily, M. C., Mugurungi, O., Mahomva, A., Chikhata, F., & Gregson, F. (2008, in press). Estimating vertically acquired HIV infections and the impact of the prevention of mother-to-child transmission program in Zimbabwe: Insights from decision analysis models. *Journal of Acquired Immune Deficiency Syndrome.*

Dubois, J., & others. (2008). Microstructural correlates of infant functional development: Example of the visual pathways. *Journal of Neuroscience, 28,* 1943–1948.

Dubois, J., Dehaene-Lambertz, G., Perrin, M., Mangin, J. F., Cointepas, Y., Ducheesnay, E., Le Bihan, D., & Hertz-Pannier, L. (2007). Asynchrony of the early maturation of white matter bundles in healthy infants: Quantitative landmarks revealed noninvasively by diffusion tensor imaging. *Human Brain Mapping, 29,* 14–27.

Duggan, A., Fuddy, L., Burrell, L., Higman, S. M., McFarlane, E., Windham, A., & Sia, C. (2004). Randomized trial of statewide home visiting program to prevent child abuse: Impact in reducing parental risk factors. *Child Abuse and Neglect, 28,* 623–643.

Dumont, K. A., Widom, C. S., & Cazja, S. J. (2007). Predictors of resilience in abused and neglected children grown-up: The role of individual and neighborhood characteristics. *Child Abuse and Neglect, 31,* 255–274.

Dunbar, L., Leventhal, H., & Leventhal, E. A. (2007). Self-regulation, health, and behavior. In J. E. Birren (Ed.), *Encyclopedia of gerontology* (2nd ed.). San Diego: Academic Press.

Duncan, S. F., Holman, T. B., & Yang, C. (2007). Factors associated with involvement in marriage preparation programs. *Family Relations, 56,* 270–278.

Dundek, L. H. (2006). Establishment of a Somali doula program at a large metropolitan hospital. *Journal of Perinatal and Neonatal Nursing, 20,* 128–137.

Dunn, J. (1984). Sibling studies and the developmental impact of critical incidents. In P. B. Baltes & G. Brim (Eds.), *Life-span development and behavior* (Vol. 6). Orlando, FL: Academic Press.

Dunn, J. (2007). Siblings and socialization. In J. E. Grusec & P. D. Hastings (Eds.), *Handbook of socialization.* New York: Guilford.

Dunn, J., & Kendrick, C. (1982). *Siblings.* Cambridge, MA: Harvard University Press.

Dunn, N. F., Miller, R., Griffioen, A., & Lee, C. A. (2008, in press). Carrier testing in -haemophilia A and B: Adult carriers' and their partners' experiences and their views on the testing of young females. *Haemophilia.*

Dupre, M. E., & Meadows, S. O. (2007). Disaggregating the effects of marital trajectories on health. *Journal of Family Issues, 28,* 623–652.

Dupuy, A. M., Jaussent, I., Lacroux, A., Durant, R., Cristol, J. P., & Delcourt, C. (2007). Waist circumference adds to the variance in plasma C. reactive protein levels in elderly patients with metabolic syndrome. *Gerontology, 53,* 91–101.

Durrant, J. E. (2008). Physical punishment, culture, and rights: Current issues for professionals. *Journal of Developmental and Behavioral Pediatrics, 29,* 55–66.

Durston, S., & Casey, B. J. (2006). What have we learned about cognitive development from neuroimaging. *Neuropsychologia, 44,* 2149–2157.

Durston, S., Davidson, M. C., Tottenham, N. T., Galvan, A., Spicer, J., Fossella, J. A., & Casey, B. J. (2006). A shift from diffuse to focal cortical activity with development. *Developmental Science, 9,* 1–8.

Duvigneaud, N., & others. (2007). Socioeconomic and lifestyle factors associated with overweight in Flemish adult men and women. *BMC Public Health, 7,* 23.

Dweck, C. S. (2006). *Mindset.* New York: Random House.

Dworkin, S. L., & Santelli, J. (2007). Do abstinence-plus interventions reduce sexual risk behavior among youth? *PLoS Medicine, 4,* 1437–1439.

Dwyer, J. W., & Coward, R. T. (1991). A multivariate comparison of the involvement of adult sons versus daughters in the care of impaired parents. *Journals of Gerontology B: Psychological Sciences and Social Sciences, 46,* S259–S269.

Dyl, J., Kittler, J., Phillips, K. A., & Hunt, J. I. (2006). Body dysmorphic disorder and other clinically significant body image concerns in adolescent psychiatric inpatients: Prevalence and clinical characteristics. *Child Psychiatry and Human Development, 36,* 369–382.

E

Eagly, A. H. (2001). Social role theory of sex differences and similarities. In J. Worrell (Ed.), *Encyclopedia of women and gender.* San Diego: Academic Press.

Eagly, A. H. (2009, in press). Gender roles. In J. Levine & M. Hogg (Eds.), *Encyclopedia of group processes and intergroup relations.* Thousand Oaks, CA: Sage.

Eagly, A. H., & Crowley, M. (1986). Gender and helping: A meta-analytic review of the social psychological literature. *Psychological Bulletin, 108,* 233–256.

Eagly, A. H., & Steffen, V. J. (1986). Gender and aggressive behavior: A meta-analytic review of the social psychological literature. *Psychological Bulletin, 100,* 309–330.

Eastwick, P. W., & Finkel, E. J. (2008). Sex differences in mate preferences revisited: Do people know what they initially desire in a romantic partner? *Journal of Personality and Social Psychology, 94,* 245–264.

Eaton, D. K., & others. (2006). Youth risk behavior surveillance–United States, 2005. *MMWR Surveillance Summary, 55,* 1–108.

Eaton, D. K., & others (2008). Youth risk behavior surveillance—United States, 2007. *MMWR Surveillance Summaries, 57,* 1–131.

Eaton, W. O. (2008). Milestones: Physical. In M. M. Haith & J. B. Benson (Eds.), *Encyclopedia of infant and early childhood development.* Oxford, UK: Elsevier.

Ebbeling, C. A., & Ludwig, D. S. (2008). Tracking pediatric obesity. *Journal of the American Medical Association, 299,* 2442–2443.

Ebersole, P., Hess, P., & Luggen, A. S. (2004). *Toward healthy aging* (6th ed.). St. Louis: Mosby.

Eby, J. W., Herrell, A. L., & Jordan, M. L. (2009). *Teaching in elementary school: A reflective approach* (5th Ed.). Boston: Allyn & Bacon.

Eccles, J. S. (2007). Families, schools, and development achievement-related motivation and engagement. In J. E. Grusec & P. D. Hastings (Eds.), *Handbook of socialization.* New York: Guilford.

Eccles, J. S., Brown, B. V., & Templeton, J. (2008). A developmental framework for selecting indicators of well-being during the adolescent and young adult years. In B. V. Brown (Ed.), *Key indicators of child and youth well-being.* Clifton, NJ: Psychology Press.

Eccles, J. S., & Goodman, J. (Eds.). (2002). *Community programs to promote youth development.* Washington, DC: National Academy Press.

Echevarria, J., Vogt, M., & Short, D. J. (2008). *Making content comprehensible for English learners* (3rd ed.). Boston: Allyn & Bacon.

Eckerman, C., & Whitehead, H. (1999). How toddler peers generate coordinated action: A cross-cultural exploration. *Early Education and Development, 10,* 241–266.

Eckstein, K. C., Mikhail, L. M., Ariza, A. J., Thompson, J. S., Millard, S. C., Binns, H. J., & the Pediatric Practice Research Group. (2006). Parents' perceptions of their child's weight and health. *Pediatrics, 117,* 681–690.

Edelman, M. W. (1997, April). *Children, families and social policy.* Paper presented at the meeting of the Society for Research in Child Development, Washington, DC.

Edin, F., Macoveanu, J., Olesen, P., Tegner, J., & Klingberg, T. (2007). Stronger synaptic connectivity is a mechanism behind development of working memory-related brain activity during childhood. *Journal of Cognitive Neuroscience, 19,* 750–760.

Egeland, B. (2009, in press). Attachment-based interventions on the quality of attachment among infants and young children. In R. E. Tremblay, R. deV Peters, M. Boivin, & R. G. Barr (Eds.), *Encyclopedia on early childhood development.* Montreal: Centre of Excellence for Early Childhood Development.

Egeland, B., Jacobvitz, D., & Sroufe, L. A. (1988). Breaking the cycle of abuse. *New Directions for Child Development, 11,* 77–92.

Ehrlich, B. S., & Isaacowitz, D. M. (2002). Does subjective well-being increase with age? *Perspectives in Psychology, 5,* 20–26.

Eichorn, D. H., Clausen, J. A., Haan, N., Honzkik, M. P., & Mussen, P. H. (Eds.). (1981). *Present and post in middle life.* New York: Academic Press.

Eiferman, R. R. (1971). Social play in childhood. In R. Herron & B. Sutton-Smith (Eds.), *Child's play.* New York: Wiley.

Einarson, A., & Ito, S. (2007). Re: Use of contemporary antidepressants during breastfeeding: A proposal for a specific safety index. *Drug Safety, 30,* 643.

Einstein, G. O., McDaniel, M. A. (2005). Prospective memory. *Current Directions in Psychological Science, 14,* 286–290.

Eisdorfer, C. (1996, December). Interview. *APA Monitor,* p. 35.

Eisenberg, M. E., Bernat, D. H., Bearinger, L. H., & Resnick, M. D. (2008). Support for comprehensive sexuality education: Perspectives from parents of school-aged youth. *Journal of Adolescent Research, 42,* 352–359.

Eisenberg, N. (Ed.). (1982). *The development of prosocial behavior.* New York: Wiley.

Eisenberg, N., Fabes, R. A., & Spinrad, T. L. (2006). Prosocial development. In W. Damon & R. Lerner (Eds.), *Handbook of child psychology* (6th ed.). New York: Wiley.

Eisenberg, N., Martin, C. L., & Fabes, R. A. (1996). Gender development and gender effects. In D. C. Berliner & R. C. Calfee (Eds.), *Handbook of educational psychology.* New York: Macmillan.

Eisenberg, N., & Morris, A. S. (2004). Moral cognitions and social responding in adolescence. In R. Lerner & L. Steinberg (Eds.), *Handbook of adolescent psychology.* New York: Wiley.

Eisenberg, N., & others (2008). Understanding mother-adolescent conflict discussions: concurrent and across-time prediction from youths' dispositions and parenting. *Monographs of the Society for Research in Child Development, 73 (2),* 1–160.

Eisenberg, N., Spinrad, T. L., & Smith, C. L. (2004). Emotion-related regulation: Its conceptualization, relations to social functioning, and socialization. In P. Philippot & R. S. Feldman (Eds.), *The regulation of emotion.* Mahwah, NJ: Erlbaum.

Ekstrom, H. (2005). Trends in middle-aged women's reports of symptoms, use of hormone therapy and attitudes toward it. *Maturitas, 52,* 154–164.

Elder, G. H., & Shanahan, M. J. (2006). The life course and human development. In W. Damon & R. Lerner (Eds.), *Handbook of child -psychology* (6th ed.). New York: Wiley.

Elias, J. W., & Wagster, M. V. (2007). Developing context and background underlying cognitive intervention/training studies in older populations. *Journals of Gerontology B: Psychological Sciences and Social Sciences, 62,* 5–10.

Eliasieh, K., Liets, L. C., & Chalupa, L. M. (2007). Cellular reorganization in the human retina during normal aging. *Investigative Ophthalmology and Visual Science, 48,* 2824–2830.

Elkind, D. (1970, April 5). Erik Erikson's eight ages of man. *The New York Times Magazine.*

Elkind, D. (1976). *Child development and education: A Piagetian perspective.* New York: Oxford University Press.

Elliott, V. S. (2004). Methamphetamine use increasing. Retrieved Jan 16, 2005, from www.amaasson.org/amednews/2004/07/26/hlsc0726.htm.?

Ellis, L., & Ames, M. A. (1987). Neurohormonal functioning and sexual orientation. *Psychological Bulletin, 101,* 233–258.

Ellrichmann, G., Harati, A., & Müller, T. (2008). Deep brain stimulation improves -performance of complex instrumental paradigms. *European Neurology, 60,* 32–36.

Elwert, F., & Christakis, N. A. (2008, in press). The effect of widowhood on mortality by the causes of death of both spouses. *American Journal of Public Health.*

Emery, R. E. (1994). *Renegotiating family relationships.* New York: Guilford Press.

Enfield, A., & Collins, D. (2008). The relationship of service learning, social justice, multicultural competence, and civic engagement. *Journal of College Student Development, 49,* 95–109.

Enger, E., Ross, F. C., & Bailey, D. (2009). *Concepts in biology* (13th ed.). New York: McGraw-Hill.

Engler, A. J., Ludington-Hoe, S. M., Cusson, R. M., Adams, R., Bahnsen, M., Brumbaugh, E., Coates, P., Grief, J., McHargue, L., Ryan, D. L., Settle, M., & Williams, D. (2002). Kangaroo care: National survey of practice, knowledge, barriers, and perceptions. *American Journal of Maternal/child Nursing.* 27, 146–153.

Ennett, S. T., Bauman, K. E., Hussong, A., Faris, R., Foshee V. A., & Cai, L. (2006). The peer context of adolescent substance use: Findings from social network analysis. *Journal of Research on Adolescence, 16,* 159–186.

Epstein, J. L. (2007). Family and Community involvement. In K. Burman, S. Kahill, & B. Cotner (Eds.). *American high School.* Westport, CT: Greenwood.

Epstein, M., & Ward, L. M. (2008). "Always use protection": Communication boys receive about sex education from parents, peers, and the media. *Journal of Youth and Adolescence, 37,* 113–126.

Erickson, K. L., Colcombe, S. J., Wadhwa, R. Bherer, L., Peterson, M. S., Scalf, P. E., Kim, J. S., Alvarado, M., & Kramer, A. F. (2007). Training-induced plasticity in older adults: Effects of training on hemispheric asymmetry. *Neurobiology of Aging, 28,* 272–283.

Ericson, N. (2001, June). *Addressing the problem of juvenile bullying.* Washington, DC: Office of Juvenile Justice and Delinquency Prevention, Office of Justice Programs, U.S. Department of Justice.

Ericsson, K. A., Charness, N., Feltovich, P. J., & Hoffman, R. R. (Eds.). (2006). *The Cambridge handbook of expertise and expert performance.* New York: Cambridge University Press.

Ericsson, K. A., Krampe, R., & Tesch-Romer, C. (1993). The role of deliberate practice in the acquisition of expert performance. *Psychological Review, 100,* 363–406.

Erikson, E. H. (1950). *Childhood and society.* New York: W. W. Norton.

Erikson, E.H. (1968). *Identity: Youth and crisis.* New York: W. W. Norton.

Erixon-Lindroth, N., Farde, L., Wahlin, T. B., Sovago, J., Hallidin, C., & Backman, L. (2005). The role of the striatal dopamine transporter in cognitive aging. *Psychiatry Research, 138,* 1–12.

Escandon, S. (2006). Mexican American Intergenerational caregiving model. *Western Journal of Nursing, 28,* 564–585.

Escobar-Chaves, S. L., & Anderson, C. A. (2008). Media and risky behavior. *Future of Children, 18 (No. 1),* 147–180.

Espinola-Klein, C., & others. (2007). Impact of metabolic syndrome on atherosclerotic burden and cardiovascular prognosis. *American Journal of Cardiology, 9,* 1623–1628.

Etaugh, C., & Bridges, J. S. (2004). *The psychology of women* (2nd ed.). Boston: Allyn & Bacon.

Etaugh, C., & Bridges, J. S. (2006). *Women's lives: A topical approach.* Belmont, CA: Wadsworth.

Evans, G. W., & English, G. W. (2002). The environment of poverty. *Child Development, 73,* 1238–1248.

Evans, G. W., & Kim, P. (2007). Childhood poverty and health: Cumulative risk exposure and stress dysregulation. *Psychological Science, 18,* 953–957.

Evert, J., Lawler, E., Bogan, H., & Perls, T. (2003). Morbidity profiles of centenarians: Survivors, delayers, and escapers. *Journals of Gerontology A: Biological Sciences and Medical Sciences, 58,* 232–237.

Exploratorium. (2004). *Young in mind.* Retrieved February 16, 2004, from www.exploratorium.edu/exploring/exploring_-memory/memory_2.html

F

Fabiani, M., Low, K. A., Wee, E., Sable, J. J., & Gratton, G. (2006). Reduced suppression or labile memory? Mechanisms of inefficient filtering of irrelevant information in older adults. *Journal of Cognitive Neuroscience, 18,* 637–650.

Fagan, J. F. (1992). Intelligence: A theoretical viewpoint. *Current Directions in Psychological Science, 1,* 82–86.

Fagot, B. I., Rodgers, C. S., & Leinbach, M. D. (2000). Theories of gender socialization. In T. Eckes & H. M. Trautner (Eds.), *The developmental social psychology of gender.* Mahwah, NJ: Erlbaum.

Fahey, T. D. Insel, P. M., & Roth, W. T. (2009). *Fit and well* (8th ed.). New York: McGraw-Hill.

Fair, D., & Schlaggar, B. L. (2008). Brain development. In M. M. Haith & J. B. Benson (Eds.), *Encyclopedia of infant and early childhood development.* Oxford, UK: Elsevier.

Fakhoury, J., Nimmo, G. A., & Autexier, C. (2007). Harnessing telomerase in cancer therapeutics. *Anti-cancer Agents in Medicinal Chemistry, 7,* 475–483.

Falbo, T., & Poston, D. L. (1993). The academic, personality, and physical outcomes of only children in China. *Child Development, 64,* 18–35.

Falicov, C., & Karrer, B. (1980). Cultural variations in the family life cycle: The Mexican American family. In E. Carter & M. McGoldrick (Eds.), *The family life cycle: A framework for family therapy.* New York: Gardner Press.

Fantz, R. L. (1963). Pattern vision in newborn infants. *Science, 140,* 286–297.

Faraone, S. V. (2007). Stimulant therapy in the management of ADHD: Mixed -amphetamine salts (extended release). *Expert Opinion on Pharmacotherapy, 8,* 2127–2134.

Farlow, M. R.,, Miller, M. L., & Pejovic, V. (2008). Treatment options in Alzheimer's disease: Maximizing benefit, managing expectations. *Dementia and Geriatric Cognitive Disorders, 25,* 408–422.

Farrell, M. P. & Rosenberg, S. D. (1981). *Men at mid-life.* Boston: Auburn House.

Farrow, C. V., & Bissett, J. (2008). Controlling feeding practices: Cause or consequence of early child weight? *Pediatrics, 121,* e164–e169.

Fasig, L. (2000). Toddlers' understanding of ownership: Implications for self-concept development. *Social Development, 9,* 370–382.

Fassinger, R. E. (2008). Workplace diversity and public policy. *American Psychologist, 63,* 252–268.

Federal Interagency Forum on Child and Family Statistics. (2007). *American's Children: Key indicators of well-being 2007.* Washington, DC: U.S. Government Printing Office.

Feeney, B. C., & Collins, N. L. (2007). Interpersonal safe haven and secure base caregiving processes in adulthood. In W. S. Rholes & J. A. Simpson (Eds.), *Adult attachment.* New York: Guilford.

Feeney, J. A. (2009). Adult romantic attachment: Developments in the study of couple relationships. In J. Cassidy & P. R. Shaver (Eds.), *Handbook of attachment* (2nd ed.). New York: Guilford.

Feeney, J. A., & Monin, J. K. (2009). An attachment theoretical perspective on divorce. In J. Cassidy & P. R. Shaver (Eds.), *Handbook of attachment* (2nd ed.). New York: Guilford.

Fehr, B. (2000). The life cycle of friendships. In C. Hendrick, & S. S. Hendrick (Eds.), *Close relationships.* Thousand Oaks, CA: Sage.

Fein, G. G. (1986). Pretend play. In D. Görlitz & J. F. Wohlwill (Eds.), *Curiosity, imagination, and play.* Hillsdale, NJ: Erlbaum.

Feinberg, M. E., Button, T. M., Neiderhiser, J. M., Reiss, D., & Hetherington, E. M. (2007). Parenting and antisocial behavior and depression: Evidence of genotype x parenting environment interaction. *Archives of General Psychiatry, 64,* 457–465.

Feldman, R. (2007). Parent-infant synchrony. *Current Directions in Psychological Science, 16,* 340–345.

Feldman, R., & Eidelman, A. I. (2007). Maternal postpartum behavior and the emergence of infant-mother and infant-father synchrony in preterm and full-term infants: The role of neonatal vagal tone. *Developmental Psychobiology, 49,* 290–302.

Feldman, S. S., & Elliott, G. R. (1990). Progress and promise of research on normal adolescent development. In S. S. Feldman & G. Elliott (Eds.), *At the threshold: The developing adolescent.* Cambridge, MA: Harvard University Press.

Feldman, S. S., Turner, R., & Araujo, K. (1999). Interpersonal context as an influence on sexual timetables of youths: Gender and ethnic effects. *Journal of Research on Adolescence, 9,* 25–52.

Feldon, J. M. (2003). Grief as a transformative experience: Weaving through different lifeworlds after a loved one has committed suicide. *International Journal of Mental Health Nursing, 12,* 74–85.

Feng, L., Ng, T. P., Chuah, L., Niti, M., & Kua, E. H. (2006). Homocysteine, folate, And vitamin B-12 and cognitive performance in older Chinese adults: Findings from the Singapore Longitudinal Aging Study. *American Journal of Clinical Nutrition 84,* 1506–1512.

Fenigsen, R. (2008). Other people's lives: Reflections on medicine, ethics, and euthanasia. *Issues in Law and Medicine, 23,* 281–297.

Ferber, S. G., & Makhoul, I. R. (2008). Neurobehavioral assessment of skin-to-skin effects on reaction to pain in preterm infants: A randomized, controlled within-subject trial. *Acta Pediatrica, 97,* 171–176.

Ferguson, D. M., Harwood, L. J., & Shannon, F. T. (1987). Breastfeeding and subsequent social adjustment in 6- to 8-year-old children. *Journal of Child Psychology and Psychiatry, 28,* 378–386.

Fernandez, A., & Goldstein, L. (2004). Primary care physicians who treat blacks and whites. *New England Journal of Medicine, 351,* 2126–2127.

Fernandez, G. (2008). Progress in nutritional immunology. *Immunologic Research, 40,* 244–261.

Ferraro, K. F. (2006). Health and aging. In R. H. Binstock & L. K. George (Eds.), *Handbook of aging and the social sciences* (6th ed.). San Diego: Academic Press.

Ferrer-Blasco, T., Gonzalez-Meijome, J. M., & Montes-Mico, R. (2008). Age-related changes in the human visual system and -prevalence of refractive conditions in patients attending an eye clinic. *Journal of Cataract and Refractive Surgery, 34,* 424–432.

Ferrini, A. F., & Ferrini, R. (2008). *Health in the later years* (4th ed.). New York: McGraw-Hill.

Ferrucci, L., & Koh, C. (2007). Disabilty, functional status, and activities of daily living. In J. E. Birren (Ed.), *Encyclopedia of gerontology* (2nd ed.). San Diego: Academic Press.

Fidler, D. J. (2008). Down syndrome. In M. M. Haith & J. B. Benson (Eds.), *Encyclopedia of infancy and early childhood development.* Oxford, UK: Elsevier.

Field, A. E., Cambargo, C. A., Taylor, C. B., Berkey, C. S., Roberts, S. B., & Colditz, G. A. (2001). Peer, parent, and media influences on the development of weight concerns and frequent dieting among preadolescent and adolescent girls and boys. *Pediatrics, 107,* 54–60.

Field, D. (1996). Review of relationships in old age by Hansson & Carpenter. *Contemporary Psychology, 41,* 44–45.

Field, D. (1999). A cross-cultural perspective on continuity and change in social relations in old age: Introduction to a special issue. *International Journal of Aging and Human Development, 48,* 257–262.

Field, T. M. (2001). Massage therapy facilitates weight gain in preterm infants. *Current Directions in Psychological Science, 10,* 51–55.

Field, T. M. (2007). *The amazing infant.* Malden, MA: Blackwell.

Field, T. M. (2008, in press). Breastfeeding and antidepressants. *Infant Behavior and Development.*

Field, T. M., Diego, M., & Hernandez-Reif, M. (2007). Massage therapy research. *Developmental Review, 27,* 75–89.

Field, T. M., Diego, M., & Hernandez-Reif, M. (2008). Prematurity and potential predictors. *International Journal of Neuroscience, 118,* 277–289.

Field, T.M., Grizzle, N., Scafidi, F., & Schanberg, S. (1996). Massage and relaxation therapies' effects on depressed adolescent mothers. *Adolescence, 31,* 903–911.

Field, T. M., Henteleff, T., Hernandez-Reif, M., Martines, E., Mavunda, K., Kuhn, C., & Schanberg, S. (1998). Children with asthma have improved pulmonary functions after message therapy. *Journal of Pediatrics, 132,* 854–858.

Field, T. M., Hernandez-Reif, M., & Freedman, J. (2004, Fall). Stimulation programs for preterm infants. *SRCD Social Policy Reports, 28* (1), 1–20.

Field, T. M., Hernandez-Reif, M., Diego, M., Feijo, L., Vera, Y., & Gil, K. (2004). Massage therapy by parents improves early growth and development. *Infant Behavior and Development, 27,* 435–442.

Field, T. M., Hernandez-Reif, M., Feije, L., & Freedman, J. (2006). Prenatal, perinatal, and neonatal stimulation, *Infant Behavior and Development, 29,* 24–31.

Field, T. M., Hernandez-Reif, M., Taylor, S., Quinitino, O., & Burman, I. (1997). Labor pain is reduced by massage therapy. *Journal of Psychosomatic Obstetrics and Gynecology, 18,* 286–291.

Field, T. M., Lasko, D., Mundy, P., Henteleff, T., Kabat, S., Talpins, S., & Dowling, M. (1997). Brief report: Autistic children's attentiveness and responsivity improve after touch therapy. *Journal of Autism and Developmental Disorders, 27,* 333–338.

Field, T. M., Quintino, O., Hernandez-Reif, M., & Koslosky, G. (1998). Adolescents with attention deficit hyperactivity disorder benefit from massage therapy. *Adolescence, 33,* 103–108.

Field, T. M., & Hernandez-Reif, M. (2008). Touch and pain. In M. M. Haith & J. B. Benson (Eds.), *Encyclopedia of infant and early childhood development.* Oxford, UK: Elsevier.

Fiese, B. H., & Winter, M. A. (2008). Family influence. In M. M. Haith & J. B. Benson (Eds.), *Encyclopedia of infant and early childhood development.* Oxford, UK: Elsevier.

Fiese, B. H., & Winter, M. A. (2008). Family influences. In M. M. Haith & J. B. Benson (Eds.), *Encyclopedia of infant and early childhood development.* Oxford, UK: Elsevier.

Finch, C. E., & Seeman, T. E. (1999). Stress theories of aging. In V. L. Bengtson, & K. W. Schaie (Eds.). *Handbook of theories of aging.* New York: Springer.

Fincham, F. D., Stanley, S. M., & Beach, S. R. H. (2007). Transformative processes in marriage: An analysis of emerging trends. *Journal of Marriage and the Family, 69,* 275–292.

Fingerman, K. L. (2000). Age and generational differences in mothers' and daughters' descriptions of enjoyable visits. *Journals of Gerontology B: Psychological and Social Sciences, 55,* P95–P106.

Fingerman, K. L. (2006). Social relations. In J. E. Birren & K. W. Schaie (Eds.), *Handbook of the psychology of aging* (6th Ed.). San Diego: Academic Press.

Fingerman, K. L., Hay, E. L., Kamp Dush, C. M., Cichy, K. E., & Hosteman, S. J. (2007, in press). Parents' and offsprings' perceptions of change and continuity when parents the transition to old age. *Advances in Life Course Research.*

Fingerman, K. L., & Lang, F. R. (2004). Coming together: A perspective on relationships across the life span. In F. R. Lang & K. L. Fingerman (Eds.), *Growing together.* New York: Cambridge University Press.

Finkel, D., Reynolds, C. A., McArdle, J. J., & Pederson, N. L. (2007). Age changes in processing speed as a leading indicator of cognitive aging. *Psychology and Aging, 22,* 358–368.

Finkelstein, L. M., & Farrell, S. K. (2007). An expanded view of age bias in the workplace. In K. S. Shultz & G. A. Adams (Eds.), *Aging and work in the 21st century.* Mahwah, NJ: Erlbaum.

Finning, K. M., & Chitty., L. S. (2008). Non-invasive fetal sex determination: Impact on clinical practice. *Seminars in Fetal and Neonatal Medicine, 13,* 69–75.

Fiori, K. L., Antonucci, T. C., & Cortina, K. S. (2006). Social network typologies and mental health among older adults. *Journals of Gerontology B: Psychological Sciences and Social Sciences, 61,* P25–P32.

Fiori, K. L., Smith, J., & Antonucci, T. C. (2007). Social network types among older adults: A multidimensional approach. *Journals of Gerontology B: Psychological Sciences and Social Sciences, 62,* P322–P330.

Fischer, K. W., & Bidell, T. R. (2006). Dynamic development of action, thought, and emotion. In W. Damon & R. M. Lerner (Eds.), *Handbook of child psychology: Theoretical models of human development* (6th ed.). New York: Wiley.

Fischer, K. W., & Immordino-Yang, M. H. (2008, in press). The fundamental importance of the brain and learning for education. *The Jossey-Bass reader on the brain and learning.* San Francisco: Jossey-Bass.

Fischer, K. W., & Rose, S. P. (1995, Fall). Concurrent cycles in the dynamic development of brain and behavior. *SRCD Newsletter,* pp. 3–4, 15–16.

Fisher, B. S., Cullen, F. T., Turner, M. G. (2000). *The sexual victimization of college women.* Washington, DC: National Institute of Justice.

Fisher, C. B. (2009). *Decoding the ethics code* (2nd ed.). Thousand Oaks, CA: Sage.

Fisher, P. A. (2005, April). *Translational research on underlying mechanisms of risk among foster children: Implications for prevention science.* Paper presented at the meeting of the Society for Research in Child Development, Washington, DC.

Fivush, R. (1993). Developmental perspectives on autobiographical recall. In G. S. Goodman, & B. Bottoms (Eds.), *Child victims and child witnesses: Understanding and improving testimony.* New York: Guilford.

Flannery, D. J., Hussey, D., Biebelhausen, L., & Wester, K. (2003). Crime, delinquency, and youth gangs. In G. Adams & M. Berzonsky (Eds.), *Blackwell handbook of adolescence.* Malden, MA: Blackwell.

Flavell, J. H. (2004). Theory-of-mind development: Retrospect and prospect. *Merrill-Palmer Quarterly, 50,* 274–290.

Flavell, J. H., Friedrichs, A., & Hoyt, J. (1970). Developmental changes in memorization processes. *Cognitive Psychology, 1,* 324–340.

Flavell, J. H., Green, F. L., & Flavell, E. R. (1993). Children's understanding of the stream of consciousness. *Child Development, 64,* 95–120.

Flavell, J. H., Green, F. L., & Flavell, E. R. (1995). The development of children's knowledge about attentional focus. *Developmental Psychology, 31,* 706–712.

Flavell, J. H., Green, F. L., & Flavell, E. R. (1998). The mind has a mind of its own: Developing knowledge about mental uncontrollability. *Cognitive Development, 13,* 127–138.

Flavell, J. H., Green, F. L., & Flavell, E. R. (2000). Development of children's awareness of their own thoughts. *Journal of Cognition and Development, 1,* 97–112.

Flavell, J. H., & Miller, P. H. (1998). Social cognition. In W. Damon (Ed.), *Handbook of child psychology.* (5th ed.). New York: Wiley.

Flavell, J. H., Mumme, D., Green, F., and Flavell E. (1992). Young children's understanding of different types of beliefs. *Child Development, 63,* 960–977.

Flegal, W. A. (2007). Blood group genotyping in Germany. *Transfusion, 47* (Suppl. 1), S47–S53.

Fletcher, A. C., Steinberg, L., & Williams-Wheeler, M. (2004). Parental influences on adolescent problem behavior: Revisiting Stattin and Kerr. *Child Development, 75,* 781–796.

Fletcher, A. E., Breeze, E., & Shetty, P. S. (2003). Antioxidant vitamins and mortality in older persons. *American Journal of Nutrition, 78,* 999–1010.

Flint, M. S., Baum, A., Chambers, W. H., & Jenkins, F. J. (2007). Induction of DNA damage, alteration of DNA repair, and transcriptional activation by stress hormones. *Psychoneuroen-docrinology, 32,* 470–479.

Flom, R., & Pick, A. D. (2003). Verbal encouragement and joint attention in 18-month-old infants. *Infant Behavior and Development, 26,* 121–134.

Flora, S. J. (2007). Role of free radicals and antioxidants in health and disease. *Cellular and Molecular Biology, 53,* 1–2.

Floriani, V., & Kennedy, C. (2008). Promotion of physical activity in children. *Current Opinion in Pediatrics, 20,* 90–95.

Florsheim, P., Moore, D., & Edgington, C. (2003). Romantic relationships among pregnant and parenting adolescents. In P. Florsheim (Ed.), *Adolescent romantic relations and sexual behavior.* Mahwah, NJ: Erlbaum.

Floyd, P. A., Mimms, S. E., & Yelding, C. (2008). *Personal health* (4th ed.). Belmont, CA: Wadsworth.

Flynn, J. R. (1999). Searching for justice: The discovery of IQ gains over time. *American Psychologist, 54,* 5–20.

Flynn, J. R. (2007). The history of the American mind in the 20th century: A scenario to explain IQ gains over time and a case for the relevance of *g.* In P. C. Kyllonen, R. D. Roberts, & L. Stankov (Eds.), *Extending intelligence.* Mahwah, NJ: Erlbaum.

Flynn, L., Budd, M., & Modelski, J. (2008). Enhancing resource utilization among pregnant adolesecents. *Public Health Nursing, 25,* 140–148.

Fodor, I., G., & Franks, V. (1990). Women in midlife and beyond. The new prime of life? *Psychology of Women Quarterly, 14,* 445–449.

Fogelholm, M. (2008). How physical activity can work? *International Journal of Pediatric Obesity, 3* (Suppl. 1), S10–S14.

Fogoros, R. N. (2001). *Does stress really cause heart disease?* Retrieved October 10, 2001, from http://www.about.com

Follari, L. (2007). *Foundations and best practices in early childhood education.* Upper Saddle River, NJ: Prentice Hall.

Fonseca, E. B., Celik, E., Parra, M., Singh, M., Nicolaides, K. H., & the Fetal Medicine Foundation Second Trimester Screening Group. (2007). Progesterone and the risk of preterm birth among women with a short cervix. *New England Journal of Medicine, 357,* 462–469.

Fontana, L. (2008). Calorie restriction and cardio-metabolic health. *European Journal of Cardiovascular Prevention and Rehabilitation, 15,* 3–9.

Fontenot, H. B. (2007). Transition and adaptation to adoptive motherhood. *Journal of Obstetrics, Gynecologic, and Neonatal Nursing, 36,* 175–182.

Ford, E. S., & others. (2007). Explaining the decrease in U. S. deaths from coronary disease, 1980–2000. *New England Journal of Medicine, 356,* 2388–2398.

Forester, M. B., & Merz, R. D. (2007). Risk of selected birth defects with prenatal illicit drug use, Hawaii, 1986–2002. *Journal of Toxicology and Environmental Health, 70,* 7–18.

Forrester, M. B. (2007). Oxycodone abuse in Texas, 1998–2004. *Journal of Toxicology and Environmental Health A, 70,* 534–538.

Foster, H., & Brooks-Gunn, J. (2008, in press). Role strain in the transition to adolescence: Pubertal timing associations with behavior problems by gender and race/ethnicity. *Developmental Psychology.*

Foster-Cohen, S., Edgin, J. O., Champion, P. R., & Woodward, L. J. (2007). Early delayed language development in very preterm infants: Evidence from the MacArthur-Bates CDI. *Journal of Child Language, 34,* 655–675.

Fouad, N. A., & Bynner, J. (2008). Work transitions. *American Psychologist, 63,* 241–251.

Fowler, C. G., & Leigh-Paffenroth, E. D. (2007). Hearing. In J. E. Birren (Ed.), *Encyclopedia of gerontology* (2nd ed.). San Diego: Academic Press.

Fowler, G. (1999). *As we grow old: How adult children and their parents can face aging with candor and grace.* Valley Forge, PA: Judson Press.

Fox, M. K., Pac, S., Devaney, B., & Jankowski, L. (2004). Feeding infants and toddlers study: What foods are infants and toddlers eating? *American Dietetic Association Journal, 104,* (Suppl.), S22–S30.

Fozard, J. L. (1992, December 6). Commentary in "We can age successfully." *Parade Magazine,* pp. 14–15.

Fozard, J. L., & Gordon-Salant, S. (2001). Changes in vision and hearing with aging. In J. E. Birren & K. W. Schaie (Eds.), *Handbook of the psychology of aging* (5th ed.). San Diego: Academic Press.

Fraga, C. G., Motchnik, P. A., Shigenaga, M. K., Helbock, H. J., Jacob, R. A., & Ames, B. N. (1991). Ascorbic acid protects against endogenous oxidative DNA damage in human sperm. *Proceedings of the National Academy of Sciences of the United States, 88,* 11003–11006.

Francis, J., Fraser, G., & Marcia, J. E. (1989). *Cognitive and experimental factors in moratorium-achievement (MAMA) cycles.* Unpublished manuscript, Department of Psychology, Simon Fraser University, Burnaby, British Columbia.

Frankl, V. (1984). *Man's search for meaning.* New York: Basic Books.

Franz, C. E. (1996). The implications of preschool tempo and motoric activity level for personality decades later. Reported in A. Caspi, Personality development across-the life course, in W. Damon (Ed.), *Handbook of child psychology* (Vol. 3). New York: Wiley

Fraser, S. (Ed.). (1995). *The bell curve wars: Race, intelligence, and the future of America.* New York: Basic Books.

Fratelli, N., Papageorghiou, A. T., Prefumo, F., Bakalis, S., Homfray, T., & Thilaganathan, B.
(2007). Outcome of prenatally diagnosed agenesis of the corpus callosum. *Prenatal Diagnosis, 27,* 512–517.

Frederick, I. O., Williams, M. A., Sales, A. E., Martin, D. P., & Killien, M. (2008, in press). Prepregnancy body mass index, gestational weight gain, and other maternal characteristics in relation to infant birth weight. *Maternal Child Health Journal.*

Frederikse, M., Lu, A., Aylward, E., Barta, P., Sharma, T., & Pearlson, G. (2000). Sex differences in inferior lobule volume in schizophrenia. *American Journal of Psychiatry, 157,* 422–427.

Freedman, D. S., Mei, Z., Srinivasan, S. R., Berenson, G. S., & Dietz, W. H. (2007). Cardiovascular risk factors and excess adiposity among overweight children and adolescents in the Bogalusa Heart Study. *Journal of Pediatrics, 150,* 12–17.

Freeman, E. W., & Sherif, K. (2007). Prevalence of hot flushes and night sweats around the world: A systematic review. *Climacteric, 10,* 197–214.

French, D. C., Eisenberg, N., Vaughan, J., Purwono, U., & Suryanti, T. A. (2008). Religious involvement and the social competence and adjustment of Indonesian Muslim adolescents. *Developmental Psychology, 44,* 597–611.

Fretts, R. C., Zera, C., & Heffner, C. Z. (2008). Maternal age and pregnancy. In M. M. Haith & J. B. Benson (Eds.), *Encyclopedia of infancy and early childhood.* London, UK: Elsevier.

Freud, S. (1917). *A general introduction to psychoanalysis.* New York: Washington Square Press.

Freund, A. M., & Baltes, P. B. (2002). Life-management strategies of selection, optimization, and compensation: Measurement by self-report and construct validity. *Journal of Personality and Social Psychology, 82,* 642–662.

Frey, K. S., Hirschstein, M. K., Snell, J. L., Edstrom, L. V. S., & Broderick, C. J. (2005). Reducing playground bullying and supporting beliefs: An experimental trial of the Steps to Respect program. *Development Psychology, 41,* 479–790.

Frey, W. H. (2007). *Mapping the growth of older America: Seniors and boomers in the early 21st century.* Washington, DC: The Brookings Institution.

Friedlander, L., Connolly, J., Pepler, D. & Craig, W. (2007). Biological, familial, and peer influences on dating in early adolescence, *Archives of Sexual Behavior, 36,* 821–830.

Friedman, D. S., Hahn, S. R., Gelb, L., Tan, J., Shah, S. N., Kim, E. E., Zimmerman, T. J., & Quigley, H. A. (2008, in press). Doctor-patient communication, health-related beliefs, and adherence in glaucoma results from the Glaucoma Adherence and Persistence Study.

Friend, M. (2008). *Special education* (2nd ed.). Boston: Allyn & Bacon.

Frieske, D. A., & Park, D. C. (1999). Memory for news in young and old adults. *Psychology and aging. 14,* 90–98.

Frisina, R. D., & Walton, J. P. (2006). Age-related structural and functional changes in the cochlear nucleus. *Hearing Research, 217,* 216–223.

Fritsch, T., McClendon, M. J., Smyth, K. A., Lerner, A. J., Friedland, R. P., & Larson, J. D. (2007). Cognitive functioning in healthy aging: The role of reserve and lifestyle factors early in life. *Gerontologist, 47,* 307–322.

Fritschmann, N. S., & Solari, E. J. (2008). Learning disabilities. In N. J. Salkind (Ed.), *Encyclopedia of educational psychology.* Thousand Oaks, CA: Sage.

Frost, J. J., Darroch, J. E., & Ramez, L. (2008). Improving contraceptive use in the United States. *Issues Brief (Alan Guttmacher Institute), 1,* 1–8.

Fry, C. L. (2007). Comparative and cross-cultural studies. In J. E. Birren (Ed.). *Encyclopedia of gerontology* (2nd ed.). San Diego: Academic Press.

Fry, P. S. (2001). The unique contribution of key existential factors to the prediction of psychological well-being of older adults following spousal loss. *The Gerontologist, 41,* 69–81.

Frydenberg, E. (2007). *Adolescent coping.* Oxford, ENG: Routledge.

Frye, D. (1999). Development of intention: The relation of executive function of theory of mind. In P. D. Zelazo, J. W. Astington, & D. R. Olson (Eds.), *Developing theories of intention: Social understanding and self-control.* Mahwah, NJ: Erlbaum.

Fuligni, A. J., & Fuligni, A. S. (2007). Immigrant families and the educational achievement of their children. In J. E. Lansford, K. Deater-Deckhard, & M. H. Bornstein (Eds.), *Immigrant families in contemporary society.* New York: Guilford.

Fuligni, A. J., & Hardway, C. (2006). Daily variation in adolescents' sleep, activities, and psychological well-being. *Journal of Research on Adolescence, 16,* 353–378.

Fulmer, T., Guadagno, L., & Bolton, M. M. (2004). Elder mistreatment in women. *Journal of Obstetrics, Gynecological, and Neonatal Nursing, 33,* 657–663.

Funai, E. F., Evans, M., & Lockwood, C. J. (2008). *High risk obstetrics.* Oxford, UK: Elsevier.

Furman, E. (2005). *Boomerang nation.* New York: Fireside.

Furman, W. C. (2007, March). *The conceptualization of attachment in adolescents' relationships.* Paper presented at the meeting of the Society for Research in Child Development, Boston.

Furman, W. C., Ho, M., & Low, S. (2005, April). *Adolescent dating experiences and adjustment.* Paper presented at the meeting of the Society for Research in Child Development, Atlanta.

Furman, W. C., & Simon, V. A. (2008). Homophily in adolescent romantic relationships. In M. J. Prinstein & K. A. Dodge (Eds.), *Understanding peer influences in children and adolescents.* New York: Guilford.

Furstenberg, F. F. (2007). The future of marriage. In A. S. Skolnick & J. H. Skolnick (Eds.), *Family in transition* (14th ed.). Boston: Allyn & Bacon.

Furth, H. G., & Wachs, H. (1975). *Thinking goes to school.* New York: Oxford University Press.

G

Gable, S., Chang, Y., & Krull, J. L. (2007). Television watching and frequency of family meals are predictive of overweight onset and persistence in a national sample of preschool children. *Journal of the American Dietetic Association, 107,* 53–61.

Gaff, C. L. Williams, J. K., & McInerney, J. D. (2008, in press). Genetics in health practice and education special issue. *Journal of Genetic Counseling.*

Galinsky, E., & David, J. (1988). *The preschool years: Family strategies that work—from experts and parents.* New York: Times Books.

Gallagher, J. J. (2007). *Teaching science for understanding.* Upper Saddle River, NJ: Prentice Hall.

Gallo, L. C., Troxel, W. M., Matthews, K. A., & Kuller, L. W. (2003). Marital status and quality in middle-aged women: Associations with levels and trajectories of cardiovascular risk factors. *Health Psychology, 22,* 453–463.

Gallo, W. T., Bradley, E. H., Dubin, J. A., Jones, R. N., Falba, T. A., Teng, H. M., & Kasl, S. V. (2006). The persistence of depressive symptoms in older workers who experience involuntary job loss: Results from the health and retirement survey. *Journal of Gerontology B: Psychological Sciences and Social Sciences, 61,* S221–S228.

Galloway, J. C., & Thelen, E. (2004). Feet first: Object exploration in young infants. *Infant Behavior and Development, 27,* 107–112.

Gamble, T. K., & Gamble, M. (2008). *Communication Works* (9th ed.) New York: McGraw-Hill.

Gamino, L. A., & Sewell, K. W. (2004). Meaning constructs as predictors of bereavement adjustment: A report from the Scott & White Grief Study. *Death Studies, 28,* 397–421.

Gannon, L. (1998). Menopause. In H. S. Friedman (Ed.), *Encyclopedia of mental health* (Vol. 2). San Diego: Academic Press.

Gannon, T. A., Collie, R. M., Ward, T., & Thakker, J. (2008). Rape: Psychopathology, theory, and treatment. *Clinical Psychology Review, 28,* 982–1008.

Ganong, L., & Coleman, M. (2006). Obligations to stepparents acquired in later life: Relationship quality and acuity of needs. *Journals of Gerontology B: Psychological Sciences and Social Sciences, 61,* S80–S88.

Ganong, L., Coleman, M., & Hans, J. (2006). Divorce as prelude to stepfamily living and the consequences of re-divorce. In M. A. Fine & J. H. Harvey (Eds.), *Handbook of divorce and relationship dissolution.* Mahwah, NJ: Erlbaum.

Garasen, H., Windspoll, R., & Johnsen, R. (2008). Long-term patients' outcomes after intermediate care at a community hospital for elderly patients: 12-month follow-up of a randomized controlled trial. *Scandinavian Journal of Public Health, 36,* 197–204.

Garcia, E. E. (2008). Bilingual education in the United States. In J. Altarriba & R. R. Heredia (Eds.), *An introduction to bilingualism.* Philadelphia: Psychology Press.

Garcia Coll, C., & Pachter, L. M. (2002). Ethnic and minority parenting. In M. H. Bornstein (Ed.), *Handbook of parenting* (2nd ed., Vol. 4). Mahwah, NJ: Erlbaum.

Garcia-Bournissen, F., Tsur, L., Goldstein, L., Staroselsky, A., Avner, M., Asrar, F., BerkovitcH, M., Straface, G., Koren, G., & De Santis, M. (2008). Fetal exposure to isotretinoin—an international problem. *Reproductive Toxicology, 25,* 124–128.

Gardner, H. (1983). *Frames of mind.* New York: Basic Books.

Gardner, H. (1993). *Multiple intelligences.* New York: Basic books.

Gardner, H. (2002). The pursuit of excellence through education. In M. Ferrari (Ed.), *Learning from extraordinary minds.* Mahwah, NJ: Erlbaum.

Gardner, M., & Steinberg, L. (2005). Peer influence on risk taking, risk preference, and risky decision making in adolescence and adulthood. *Developmental Psychology, 41,* 625–635.

Garel, C. (2008). Fetal MRI: What is the future? *Ultrasound in Obstetrics and Gynecology, 31,* 123–128.

Gargiulo, R. M. (2009). *Special education in contemporary society.* Thousand Oaks, CA: Sage.

Garofalo, R., Wolf, R. C., Wissow, L. S., Woods, E. R., & Goodman, E. (1999). Sexual orientation and risk of suicide attempts among a representative sample of youth. *Archives of Pediatrics and Adolescent Medicine, 153,* 487–493.

Garrett, D. D., Tuokko, H., Stajduhar, K. I., Lindsay, J., & Buehler, S. (2008). Planning for end-of-life care: Findings from the Canadian Study of Health and Aging. *Canadian Journal of Aging, 27,* 11–21.

Garrett, N., & Martini, E. M. (2007). The boomers are coming: A total cost of care model of the impact of population aging on the cost of chronic conditions in the United States. *Disease Management, 10,* 51–60.

Garvey, C. (2000). *Play* (enlarged ed.). Cambridge, MA: Harvard University Press.

Gathercole, V. C. M., & Hoff, E. (2007). Input and the acquisition of language: Three questions. In E. Hoff & M. Shatz (Eds.), *Blackwell handbook of language development.* Malden, MA: Blackwell.

Gathwala, G., Singh, B., & Balhara, B. (2008). KMG facilitates mother baby attachment in low birth weight infants. *Indian Journal of Pediatrics, 75,* 43–47.

Gatz, M. (2006). Mental health and adjustment: In J. E. Birren & K. W. Schaie (Eds.), *Handbook of The Psychology of aging* (6th ed.). San Diego: Academic Press.

Gatz, M., Reynolds, C. A., Fratiglioni, L., Johansson, B., Mortimer, J. A., Berg, S., Fiske, A., & Pedersen, N. L. (2006). Role of genes and environments for explaining Alzheimer's disease. *Archives of General Psychiatry, 63,* 168–174.

Gaudernack, L. C., Forbord, S., & Hole, E. (2006). Acupuncture administered after spontaneous rupture of membranes at term significantly reduces the length of birth and use of oxytocin. *Acta Obstericia et Gynecologica Scandinavica, 85,* 1348–1353.

Gauvain, M, & Perez, S. M. (2007). The socialization of cognition. In J. E. Grusec & P. D. Hastings (Eds.), *Handbook of socialization.* Mahwah, NJ: Erlbaum.

Gauvain, M. (2008). Vygotsky's sociocultural theory. In M. M. Haith & J. B. Benson (Eds.), *Encyclopedia of infant and early childhood development.* Oxford, UK: Elsevier.

Gay, L. R., Mills, G., & Airasian, P. W. (2009). *Educational research* (9th ed.). Upper Saddle River, NJ: Prentice Hall.

Gazdinsky, S., Kornak, J., Weiner, M. W., & Meyerhoff, D. J. (2008, in press). Body mass index and magnetic resonance markers of brain integrity in adults. *Annals of Neurology.*

Gazelle, G. (2007). Understanding hospice—an underutilized option for life's final chapter. *New England Journal of Medicine, 357,* 321–324.

Gee, C. L., & Heyman, G. D. (2007). Children's evaluations of other people's self-descriptions. *Social Development, 16,* 800–818.

Geher, G., & Miller, G. (Eds.), (2007). *Mating intelligence.* Mahwah, NJ: Erlbaum.

Geissbuehler, V., Stein, S., & Eberhard, J. (2004). Waterbirths compared to landbirths: An observational study of nine years. *Journal of Perinatal Medicine, 32,* 308–314.

Gelhorn, H., Stallings, M., Young, S., Corley, R., Rhee, S. H., Christian, H., & Hewitt, J. (2006). Common and specific genetic influences on aggressive and nonaggressive conduct disorder domains. *Journal of the American Academy of Child and Adolescent Psychiatry, 45,* 570–577.

Gelman, R. (1969). Conservation acquisition: A problem of learning to attend to relevant attributes. *Journal of Experimental Child Psychology, 7,* 67–87.

Gelman, S. A., Heyman, G. D., & Legare, C. H. (2007). Developmental coherence of essentialist beliefs about psychological characteristics. *Child Development, 78,* 757–774.

Gelman, S. A., & Kalish, C. W. (2006). Conceptual development. In W. Damon & R. Lerner (Eds.), *Handbook of child psychology.* (6th ed.). New York: Wiley.

Gennetian, L. A., & Miller, C. (2002). Children and welfare reform: A view from an experimental welfare reform program in Minnesota. *Child Development, 73,* 601–620.

Gentzler, A. L., & Kerns, K. A. (2004). Associations between insecure attachment and sexual experiences. *Personal Relationships, 11,* 249–266.

George, L. K. (2006). Perceived quality of life. In R. H. Binstock & L. K. George (Eds.), *Handbook of aging and the Social sciences* (6th ed.). San Diego: Academic Press.

Georges, J. J., The, A. M., Onwuteaka-Philipsen, B. D., & van der Wal, G. (2008). Dealing with requests for euthanasia: A qualitative study investigating the experience of general practitioners. *Journal of Medical Ethics, 34,* 150–155.

Gerards, F. A., Twisk, J. W., Fetter, W. P., Wijnaendts, L. C., & van Vugt, J. M. (2008). Predicting pulmonary hypoplasia with 2- or 3-dimensional ultrasonography in complicated pregnancies. *American Journal of Gynecology and Obstetrics, 198,* e1–e6.

Gerrard, M., Gibbons, F. X., Houihan, A. E., Stock, M. L., & Pomery, E. A. (2008). A dual-process approach to health risk decision-making. *Developmental Review, 28,* 29–61.

Gerrotsen, M., Berg, I., Deelman, B., Visser-Keizer, A., & Jong, B. (2003). Speed of information processing after unilateral stroke. *Journal of Clinical and Experimental Neuropsychology, 25,* 1–13.

Gershoff, E. T. (2002). Corporal punishment by parents and associated child behaviors and experiences: A meta-analysis and theoretical review. *Psychological Bulletin, 128,* 539–579.

Gesell, A. (1934). *An atlas of infant behavior.* New Haven, CT: Yale University Press.

Gesell, A. L. (1934). *Infancy and human growth.* New York: Macmillan.

Gessert, C. E., Elliott, B. A., & Haller, I. V. (2003). Mortality patterns in middle and old age. *Journals of Gerontology A: Biological and Medical Sciences, 58,* B967.

Gewirtz, J. (1977). Maternal responding and the conditioning of infant crying: Directions of influence within the attachment-acquisition process. In B. C. Etzel, J. M. LeBlanc, & D. M. Baer (Eds.), *New developments in behavioral research.* Hillsdale, NJ: Erlbaum.

Ghetti, S., & Alexander, K. W. (2004). "If it happened, I would remember it": Strategic use of event memorability in the rejection of false autobiographical events. *Child Development, 75,* 542–561.

Giannarelli, F., Sonenstein, E., & Stagner, M. (2006). Child care arrangements and help for low-income families with young children: Evidence from the National Survey of America's Families. In N. Cabrera, R. Hutchens, & H. E. Peters (Eds.), *From welfare to childcare.* Mahwah, NJ: Erlbaum.

Giarrusso, R., & Bengtson, V. L. (2007). Self-esteem. In J. E. Birren (Ed.), *Encyclopedia of gerontology* (2nd ed.). San Diego: Academic Press.

Gibbons, F. X., Pomery, E. A., & Gerrard, M. (2008). Cognitive social influence: Moderation, mediation, and modification, and... the media. In M. J. Prinstein & K. A. Dodge (Eds.), *Understanding peer influence in children and adolescents.* New York: Guilford.

Gibbons, J., & Ng, S. H. (2004). Acting bilingual and thinking bilingual. *Journal of Language and Social Psychology, 23,* 4–6.

Gibbs, J. C., Basinger, K. S., Grime, R. L., & Snarey, J. R. (2007). Moral judgment development across cultures: Revisiting Kohlberg's universality claims. *Developmental Review, 27,* 443–500.

Gibson, E. J. (1969). *Principles of perceptual learning and development.* New York: Appleton-Century-Crofts.

Gibson, E. J. (1989). Exploratory behavior in the development of perceiving, acting, and the acquiring of knowledge. *Annual Review of Psychology, 39.* Palo Alto, CA: Annual Reviews.

Gibson, E. J. (2001). *Perceiving the affordances.* Mahwah, NJ: Erlbaum.

Gibson, E. J., Riccio, G., Schmuckler, M. A., Stoffregen, T. A., Rosenberg, D., & Taormina, J. (1987). Detection of the traversability of surfaces by crawling and walking infants. *Journal of Experimental Psychology: Human Perception and Performance, 13,* 533–544.

Gibson, E. J., & Walk, R. D. (1960). The "visual cliff." *Scientific American, 202,* 64–71.

Gibson, J. J. (1966). *The senses considered as perceptual systems.* Boston: Houghton Mifflin.

Gibson, J. J. (1979). *The ecological approach to visual perception.* Boston: Houghton Mifflin.

Gibson, L. Y., Bryne, S. M., Blair, E., Davis, E. A., Jacoby, P., & Zubrick, S. R. (2008). Clustering of psychological symptoms in overweight children. *Australian and New Zealand Journal of Psychiatry, 42,* 118–125.

Giedd, J. N. (2007, September, 27). Commentary in S. Jayson "Teens driven to distraction." *USA Today,* pp. D1–2.

Giedd, J. N. (2008). The teen brain: Insights from neuroimaging. *Journal of Adolescent Medicine, 42,* 335–343.

Giedd, J. N., & others. (2006). Puberty-related influences on brain development. *Molecular and Cellular Endocrinology, 25,* 154–162.

Gillen, M., Lefkowitz, E., & Shearer, C. (2006). Does body image play a role in risky sexual behavior and attitudes? *Journal of Youth and Adolescence, 35,* 230–242.

Gilligan, C. (1982). *In a different voice.* Cambridge, MA: Harvard University Press.

Gilligan, C. (1992, May). *Joining the resistance: Girls' development in adolescence.* Paper presented at the symposium on development and vulnerability in close relationships, Montreal, Quebec.

Gilligan, C. (1996). The centrality of relationships in psychological development: A puzzle, some evidence, and a theory. In G. G. Noam & K. W. Fischer (Eds.), *Development and vulnerability in close relationships,* Hillsdale, NJ: Erlbaum.

Gilligan, C., Spencer, R., Weinberg, M. K., & Bertsch, T. (2003). On the listening guide: A voice-centered relational model. In P. M. Carnic & J. E. Rhodes (Eds.), *Qualitative research in psychology* Washington, DC: American Psychological Association.

Gillum, R. F., & Ingram, D. D. (2007). Frequency of attendance at religious services, hypertension, and blood pressure: The third National Health and Nutrition Examination Survey. *Psychosomatic Medicine, 68,* 382–385.

Gillum, R. F., King, D. E., Obisesan, T. O., & Koenig, H. G. (2008). Frequency of attendance at religious services and mortality in a U. S. -national cohort. *Annals of Epidemiology, 18,* 124–129.

Girling, A. (2006). The benefits of using the Neonatal Behavioral Assessment Scale in health visiting practice. *Community Practice, 79,* 118–120.

Girls, Inc. (1991). *Truth, trusting, and technology: New research on preventing adolescent pregnancy.* Indianapolis: Author.

Given, L. M. (2008). Qualitative research methods. In N. J. Salkind (Ed.), *Encyclopedia of educational psychology.* Thousand Oaks, CA: Sage.

Gjerdingen, D., Katon, W., & Rich, D. E. (2008). Stepped care treatment of postpartum depression: A primary care-based management model. *Women's Health Issues, 18,* 44–52.

Glantz, J. C. (2005). Elective induction vs. sponta-neous labor associations and outcomes. *Journal of Reproductive Medicine, 50,* 235–240.

Glei, D. A. (1999). Measuring contraceptive use patterns among teenage and adult women. *Family Planning Perspectives, 31,* 73–80.

Glenn, N. D. (2005). *Fatherhood in America.* Report to the National Fatherhood Initiative, Washington, DC.

Gliori, G., Imm, P., Anderson, H. A., & Knobeloch, L. (2006). Fish consumption and advisory awareness among expectant women. *Wisconsin Medicine Journal, 105,* 41–44.

Gluck, J., & Bluck, S. (2007). Looking back across the life span: A life story account of the reminiscence bump. *Memory and Cognition, 35,* 1928–1939.

Glynn, L. M., Schetter, C. D., Hobel, C. J., & Sandman, C. A. (2008). Pattern of perceived stress and anxiety in pregnancy predicts preterm birth. *Health Psychology, 27,* 43–51.

Godding, V., Bonnier, C., Fiasse, L., Michel, M., Longueville, E., Lebecque, P., Robert, A., & Galanti, L. (2004). Does in utero exposure to heavy maternal smoking induce nicotine withdrawal symptoms in neonates? *Pediatric Research, 55,* 645–651.

Goffin, S. G., & Wilson, C. S. (2001). *Curriculum models and early childhood education.* Upper Saddle River, NJ: Prentice Hall.

Goh, V. I., & Koren, G. (2008). Folic acid in pregnancy and fetal outcomes. *Journal of Obstetrics and Gynecology, 28,* 3–13.

Gohel, P. S., Mandava, N., Olson, J. L., & Durairaj, V. D. (2008). Age-related macular degeneration: An update on treatment. *American Journal of Medicine, 121,* 279–281.

Goldberg, W. A., & Lucas-Thompson, R. (2008). Maternal and paternal employment, effects of. In M. M. Haith & J. B. Benson (Eds.), *Encyclopedia of infant and early childhood development.* Oxford, UK: Elsevier.

Goldenberg, R. L., & Culhane, J. F. (2007). Low birth weight in the United States. *American Journal of Clinical Nutrition, 85.* (Suppl.), S584–S590.

Goldenberg R. L., & Nagahwatte, N. T. (2008, in press). Poverty, mental health, and adverse pregnancy outcomes. *Annals of the New York Academy of Sciences.*

Goldfield, B. A., & Snow, C. A. (2009). Individual differences in language development. In J. Berko Gleason & N. Ratner (Eds.), *The development of language* (7th ed.). Boston: Allyn & Bacon.

Goldin-Meadow, S. (2008). Language acquisition theories. In M. M. Haith & J. B. Benson (Eds.), *Encyclopedia of infant and early childhood development.* Oxford, UK: Elsevier.

Goldschmidt, L., Richardson, G. A., Willford, J., & Day, N. L. (2008, in press). Prenatal marijuana exposure and intelligence test performance at age 6. *Journal of the American Academy of Child and Adolescent Psychiatry.*

Goldsmith, H. H. (2008). Behavior genetics. In M. M. Haith & J. B. Benson (Eds.), *Encyclopedia of infancy and early childhood development.* Oxford, UK: Elsevier.

Goldstein, M. H., King A. P., & West, M. J. (2003). Social interaction shapes babbling: Testing parallels between birdsong and speech. *Proceedings of the National Academy of Sciences, 100* (13), 8030–8035.

Goldston, D. B., Molock, S. D., Whitbeck, L. B., Murakami, J. L., Zayas, L. H., & Hall, G. C. (2008). Cultural considerations in adolescent suicide prevention and psychosocial treatment. *American Psychologist, 63,* 14–31.

Gollnick, D. M., & Chinn, P. C. (2009). *Multicultural education in a pluralistic society* (8th ed.). Boston: Allyn & Bacon.

Golombok, S., MacCallum, F., & Goodman, E. (2001). The "test-tube" generation: Parent-child relationships and the psychological well-being of in vitro fertilization children at adolescence. *Child Development, 72,* 599–608.

Gonzáles, P., Guzman, J. C., Partelow, L., Pahlke, E., Jocelyn, L., Kastberg, D., & Williams, T. (2004). *Highlights from the Trends in International Mathematics and Science Study (TIMSS) 2003.* Washington, DC: U.S. Government Printing Office.

Gonzales, V., Yawkey, T. D., & Minaya-Rowe, L. (2006). *English-as-a-second language (ESL) teaching and learning.* Boston: Allyn & Bacon.

Gonzalez, J. M. (Ed.) (2009). *Encyclopedia of bilingual education.* Thousand Oaks, CA: Sage.

Good, M., & Willoughby, T. (2008). Adolescence as a sensitive period for spiritual development. *Child Development Perspectives, 2,* 32–37.

Goodnow, J. J. (2009, in press). Sources, effects, and possible changes in parenting skills: Comments on Belsky, Grusec, and Sanders and Morawska. In R. E. Tremblay, R. deV Peters, M. Boivin, & R. G. Barr (Eds.), *Encyclopedia of early childhood development.* Montreal: Centre of Excellence for Early Childhood Development.

Goos, L. M., Ezzatian, P., & Schachar, R. (2007). Parent-of-origin effects in attention-deficit hyperactivity disorder. *Psychiatry Research, 149,* 1–9.

Gopnik, A., & Schulz, L. (Eds.). (2007). *Causal learning.* New York: Oxford University Press.

Goral, M., Clark-Cotton, M. R., & Albert, M. L. (2007). Language disorders: General. In J. E. Birren (ed.), *Encyclopedia of gerontology* (2nd ed.). San Diego: Academic Press.

Gordon-Salant, S., Yeni-Komshian, G. H., Fitzgibbons, P. J., & Barrett, J. (2006). Age-related differences in identification and discrimination of temporal cues in speech segments. *Journal of the Acoustical Society of America, 119,* 2455–2466.

Gosden, R. G. (2007). Menopause. In J. E. Birren (Ed.), *Encyclopedia of gerontology* (2nd ed.). San Diego: Academic Press.

Gostic, C. L. (2005). The crucial role of exercise and physical activity in weight management and functional improvement for seniors. *Clinical Geriatric Medicine, 21,* 747–756.

Gottlieb, G., Wahlsten, D., & Lickliter, R. (2006). The significance of biology for human development: A developmental psychobiological systems view. In W. Damon & R. Lerner (Eds.), *Handbook of child psychology* (6th ed.). New York: Wiley.

Gottlieb, G. (2007). Probabalistic epigenesis. *Developmental Science, 10,* 1–11.

Gottman, J. M. (1994). *What predicts divorce?* Mahwah, NJ: Erlbaum.

Gottman, J. M. (2006, April, 29). Secrets of long term love. *New Scientist, 2549,* 40.

Gottman, J. M. (2008). *Research on parenting.* Retrieved March 25, 2008, from www.gottman.com/parenting/research

Gottman, J. M., & DeClaire, J. (1997). *The heart of parenting: Raising an emotionally intelligent child.* New York: Simon & Schuster.

Gottman, J. M., & Gottman, J. S. (2009). Gottman method of couple therapy. In A. S. Gurman (Ed.), *Clinical handbook of couple therapy* (4th ed.). New York: Guilford.

Gottman, J. M., Gottman, J. S., & Declaire, J. (2006). *10 lessons to transform your marriage: America's love lab experts share their strategies for strengthening your relationship.* New York: Random House.

Gottman, J. M., & Parker, J. G. (Eds.). (1987). *conversations of friends.* New York: Cambridge University Press.

Gottman, J. M., Shapiro, A. F., Parthemer, J. (2004). Bringing baby home: A preventative intervention program for expectant couples. *International Journal of Childbirth Education, 19,* 28–30.

Gould, E. (2007). How widespread is neurogenesis in mammals? *Nature Review: Neuroscience, 8,* 481–488.

Gould, M. S., Greenberg, T., Velting, D. M., & Shaffer, D. (2003). Youth suicide risk and preventive interventions: A review of the past 10 years. *Journal of the American Academy of Child and Adolescent Psychiatry, 42,* 386–405.

Gould, S. J. (1981). *The mismeasure of man.* New York: W. W. Norton.

Gouldner, H., & Strong, M. M. (1987). *Speaking of friendship.* New York: Greenwood Press.

Gove, W. R., Style, C. B., & Hughes, M. (1990). The effect of marriage on the well-being of adults: A theoretical analysis. *Journal of Health and Social Behavior, 24,* 122–131.

Gow, A. J., Johnson, W., Pattie, A., Whiteman, M. C., Starr, J., & Deary, I. J. (2008, in press). Mental ability in childhood and cognitive aging. *Gerontology.*

Gowan, D. E. (2003). Christian beliefs concerning death and life after death. In C. D. Bryant (Ed.), *Handbook of death and dying.* Thousand Oaks, CA: Sage.

Grabe, S., & Hyde, J. S. (2006). Ethnicity and body dissatisfaction among women in the United States: A meta-analysis. *Psychological Bulletin, 132,* 622–640.

Graber, J. A. (2004). Internalizing problems during adolescence. In R. Lerner & L. Steinberg (Eds.), *Handbook of adolescent psychology.* New York: Wiley.

Graber, J. A. (2008, in press). Pubertal and neuroendocrine development and risk for depressive disorders. In N. B. Allen & L. Sheeber (Eds.), *Adolescent emotional development and the emergence of depressive disorders.* New York: Cambridge University Press.

Graber, J. A., & Brooks-Gunn, J. (2002). Adolescent girls' sexual development. In G. M. Wingood & R. J. DiClemente (Eds.), *Handbook of women's sexual and reproductive health.* New York: Kluwer Academic/Plenum Publishers.

Graber, J. A., Brooks-Gunn, J., & Warren, M. P. (2006). Pubertal effects on adjustment in girls: Moving from demonstrating effects to identifying pathways. *Journal of Youth and Adolescence, 35,* 391–401.

Grady, C. L. (2008). Cognitive neuroscience of aging. *Annals of the New York Academy of Sciences, 1124,* 127–144.

Graham, J. E., Christian, L. M., & Kiecolt-Glaser, J. K. (2006). Stress, age, and immune function: Toward a lifespan approach. *Journal of Behavioural Medicine, 29,* 389–400.

Graham, J. M., & Shaw, G. M. (2006). Gene-environment interactions in rare diseases that include common birth defects. *Birth defects Research, 73,* 865–867.

Graham, S. (2005, February 16). Commentary in *USA Today,* p.2D.

Graham, S. (Ed.). (2006). Our children too: A history of the first 25 years of the Black -caucus of the Society for Research in Child Development. *Monographs of the Society for Child Development, 71 (1, Serial No. 283).*

Grambs, J. D. (1989). *Women over forty* (rev. ed.), New York: Springer.

Gramling, L. F. (2007). Women in young and mid-adulthood: Theory advancement and retroduction. *ANS Advances in Nursing Science, 30,* 95–107.

Grant, J. (1993). *The state of the world's children.* New York: UNICEF and Oxford University Press.

Grant, J. P. (1997). *The state of the world's children.* New York: UNICEF and Oxford University Press.

Graven, S. (2006). Sleep and brain development. *Clinical Perinatology, 33,* 693–706.

Gray, K. A., Day, N. L., Leech, S., & Richardson, G. A. (2005). Prenatal marijuana exposure: Effect on child depressive symptoms at ten years of age. *Neurotoxicology and Teratology, 27,* 439–448.

Gray, M. J., & Acierno, R. (2002). Symptom presentation of older adult crime victim description of a clinical sample. *Journal of Anxiety Disorders, 16,* 299–309.

Gredler, M. E. (2008). Vygotsky's cultural historical theory of development. In N. J. Salkind (Ed.), *Encyclopedia of educational psychology.* Thousand Oaks, CA: Sage.

Green, R. J., & Mitchell, V. (2009). Gay and lesbian couples in therapy. In A. S. Gurman (Ed.), *Clinical handbook of couple therapy* (4th ed.). New York: Guilford.

Greene, V. L., Lovely, M. E., Miller, M. D., & Ondrich, J. I. (1995). Reducing nursing home use through community long-term care: An optimization analysis. *Journals of Gerontology B: Psychological Sciences and Social Sciences, 50,* S259–S268.

Greenfield, L. A., & Marks, N. F. (2004). Formal volunteering as a protective factor for older adults' psychological well-being. *Journal of Gerontology B: Psychological Sciences and Social Sciences, 59,* S258–S264.

Greenfield, P.M. (1966). On culture and conservation. In J. S. Bruner, R. P. Oliver, & P. M. Greenfield (Eds.), *Studies in cognitive growth.* New York: Wiley.

Greenough, A. (2007). Late respiratory outcomes after preterm birth. *Early Human Development, 83,* 785–788.

Greer, F. R., Sicherer, S. H., Burks, A. W., & the Committee on Nutrition and Section on Allergy and Immunology. (2008). Effects of early nutritional interventions on the development of atopic disease in infants and children: The role of maternal dietary restriction, breast feeding, timing of introduction of complementary foods, and hydrolyzed formulas. *Pediatrics, 121,* 183–191.

Greydanus, D. E., Pratt, H. D., & Patel, D. R. (2007). Attention deficit, hyperactivity disorder across the lifespan: The child, adolescent, and adult. *Disease-A-Month, 53,* 70–131.

Griffiths, R., Horsfall, J., Moore, M., Lane, D., Kroon, V., & Langdon, R. (2007). Assessment of health, well-being, and social connections: A survey of woman living in western Sydney. *International Journal of Nursing Practice, 13,* 3–13.

Grigorenko, E. (2000). Heritability and intelligence. In R. J. Sternberg (Ed.), *Handbook of intelligence.* New York: Cambridge University Press.

Grigoriadis, S., & Kennedy, S. H. (2002). Role of estrogen in the treatment of depression. *American Journal of Therapy, 9,* 503–509.

Grimes, J. N. (2007). Book review of A. Kupchip, *Judging juveniles. Journal of Youth and Adololescence, 36,* 1089–1091.

Gringart, E., Helmes, E., & Speelman, C. P. (2005). Exploring attitudes toward older workers among Australian employers: An empirical study. *Journal of Aging and Social Policy, 17,* 85–103.

Groer, M. W., & Morgan, K. (2007). Immune, health, and endocrine characteristics of depressed postpartum mothers. *Psycohoneuroimmunology, 32,* 133–138.

Gronlund, N. E., & Waugh, C. K. (2009). *Assessment of student achievement* (9th Ed.). Upper Saddle River, NJ: Prentice Hall.

Gropman, A. L., & Adams, D. R. (2007). Atypical patterns of inheritance. *Seminars in Pediatric Neurology, 14,* 34–45.

Grossi, E., Buscema, M. P., Snowdon, D., & Antuono, P. (2007). Neuropathological findings processed by artificial neural networks (ANNs) can perfectly distinguish Alzheimer's patients from controls in the Nun Study. *BMC Neurology, 21,* 15.

Grossman, K., & Grossman, K. E. (2009, in press). The impact of attachment to mother and father at an early age on children's psychosocial development through early adulthood. In R. E. Tremblay, R. deV Peters, M. Boivin, & R. G. Barr (Eds.). *Encyclopedia on early childhood development.* Montreal: Centre of Excellence for Early Childhood Development.

Grossmann, K., Grossmann, K. E., Spangler, G., Suess, G., & Unzner, L. (1985). Maternal sensitivity and newborns' orientation responses as related to quality of attachment in northern Germany. In I. Bretherton & E. Waters (Eds.), Growing points of attachment theory and research. *Monographs of the Society for Research in Child Development, 50* (1–2, Serial No. 209).

Grotevant, H. D., van Dulmen, M. H. M., Dunbar, N., Nelson-Christinedaughter, J., Christensen, M., Fan, X., & Miller, B. C. (2006). Antisocial behavior of adoptees and nonadoptees: Prediction from early history and adolescent relationships. *Journal of Research on Adolescence, 16,* 105–131.

Grusec, J. E. (2009, in press). Parents' attitudes and beliefs: Their impact on children's development. In R. E. Tremblay, R. deV Peters, M. Boivin, & R. G. Barr (Eds.), *Encyclopedia of early childhood development.* Montreal: Centre of Excellence for Early Childhood Development.

Grusec, J. E., & Davidov, M. (2007). Socialization in the family: The roles of parents. In J. E. Grusec & P. D. Hastings (Eds.), *Handbook of socialization.* New York: Guilford.

Gu, M. O., & Conn, V. S. (2008, in press). Meta-analysis of the effects of exercise interventions on functional status in older adults. *Research in Nursing and Health.*

Gualtieri, C. T., & Johnson, L. G. (2008, in press). Age-related cognitive decline in patients with mood disorders. *Progress in Neuro-psychopharmacology and Biological Psychiatry.*

Guarch, J., Marcos, T., Salamero, M., Gasto, C., & Blesa, R. (2008). Mild cognitive impairment: A risk indicator of later dementia, or a preclinical phase of the disease? *International Journal of Geriatric psychiatry, 23,* 257–265.

Gueldner, S. H., Grabo, T. N., Britton, G., Pierce, C., & Lombardi, B. (2007). Osteoporosis and aging related bone disorders. In. J. E. Birren (Ed.), *Encyclopedia of gerontology* (2nd ed.). Sand Diego: Academic Press.

Guelinckx, I., Devlieger, R., Beckers, K., & Vansant, G. (2008). Maternal obesity: Pregnancy complications, gestational weight gain, and nutrition. *Obesity Review, 9,* 140–150.

Guilford, J. P. (1967). *The structure of intellect.* New York: McGraw-Hill.

Gump, B., & Matthews, K. (2000 March). *Annual vacations, health, and death.* Paper presented at the meeting of American psychosomatic Society, Savannah, GA.

Gunderson, E. P., Rifas-Shiman, S. L., Oken, E., Rich-Edwards, J. W., Kleinman, K. P., Taveras, E. M., & Gilman, M. W. (2008). Association of fewer hours of sleep at 6 months postpartum with substantial weight retention at 1 year postpartum. *American Journal of Epidemiology, 167* 178–187.

Gunnar, M. R., Fisher, P. A., & the Early Experience, Stress, and Prevention Network. (2006). Bringing basis research on early experience and stress neurobiology to bear on preventive interventions for neglected and maltreated children. *Development and Psychopathology, 18,* 651–677.

Gunnar, M. R., Malone, S., & Fisch, R. O. (1987). The psychobiology of stress and coping in the human neonate: Studies of the adrenocortical activity in response to stress in the first week of life. In T. Field, P. McCabe, & N. Scheiderman (Eds.). *Stress and coping.* Hillsdale, NJ: Erlbaum.

Gunnar, M. R., & Quevado, K. (2007). The neurobiology of stress and development. *Annual Review of Psychology* (Vol. 58). Palo Alto, CA: Annual Reviews.

Gupta, A., Thornton, J. W., & Huston, A. C. (2008). Working families should be poor—the New Hope Program. In D. R. Crane & T. B. Heaton (Eds.), *Handbook of families and poverty.* Thousand Oaks, CA: Sage.

Gur, R. C., Mozley, L. H., Mozley, P. D., Resnick, S. M., Karp, J. S., Alavi, A., Arnold, S. E., & Gur, R. E. (1995). Sex differences in regional cerebral glucose metabolism during a resting state. *Science, 267,* 528–531.

Gurgan, T., & Demirol, A. (2007). Unresolved issues regarding assisted reproduction technology. *Reproductive Biomedicine Online, 14* (Suppl. 1), S40–S43.

Gurwitch, R. H. Silovksy, J. F., Schultz, S., Kees, M., & Burlingame, S. (2001). *Reactions and guidelines for children following trauma/disaster.* Norman: Department of Pediatrics, University of Oklahoma Health Sciences Center.

Gustafsson, J-E. (2007). Schooling and intelligence: Effects of track of study on level and profile of cognitive abilities. In P. C. Kyllonen, R. D. Roberts, & L. Stankov (Eds.), *Extending intelligence.* Mahwah, NJ: Erlbaum.

Gutchess, A. H., Welsch, R. C., Hedden, T., Bangert, A., Minear, M., Liu, L. L., & Park, D. C. (2005). Aging and the neural correlates of successful picture encoding: Frontal activations compensate for decreased medial-temporal activity. *Journal of Cognitive Neuroscience, 17,* 84–96.

Gutmann, D. L. (1975). Parenthood: A key to the comparative study of the life cycle. In N. Datan & L. Ginsberg (Eds.), *Life-span developmental psychology: Normative life crises.* New York: Academic Press.

H

Ha, J. H., & Ingersoll-Dayton, B. (2008). The effect of widowhood on intergenerational ambivalence. *Journals of Gerontology B: Psychological Sciences and Social Sciences, 63,* S49–S58.

Haber, D. (2007). Life review: Implementation, theory, research, and therapy. *International Journal of Aging and Human Development, 63,* 153–171.

Hagen, J. W., & Lamb-Parker, F. G. (2008). Head Start. In M. M. Haith & J. B. Benson (Eds.), *Encyclopedia of infant and early childhood development.* Oxford, UK: Elsevier.

Hagestad, G. O. (1985). Continuity and connectedness. In V. L. Bengston (Ed.), *Grandparenthood.* Beverly Hills, CA: Sage.

Hahn, C. S., & DiPietro, J. A. (2001). In vitro fertilization and the family: Quality of parenting, family functioning, and child psychosocial adjustment. *Developmental Psychology, 37,* 37–48.

Hahn, D. B., Payne, W. A., & Lucas, E. B. (2009). *Focus on health* (9th ed.). New York: McGraw-Hill.

Hahn, S., Zhong, X. Y., & Holzgreve, W. (2008). Recent progress in non-invasive prenatal diagnosis. *Seminars in Fetal and Neonatal Medicine, 13,* 57–62.

Hahn, W. K. (1987). Cerebral lateralization of function: From infancy through childhood. *Psychological Bulletin, 101,* 376–392.

Haight, B. K., & Haight, B. S. (2007). Reminiscence. In J. E. Birren (Ed.), *Encyclopedia of gerontology* (2nd ed.). San Diego: Academic Press.

Hair, E. C., Moore, K. A., Garrett, S. B., Ling, T., & Cleveland, K. (2008). The continued importance of quality parent-adolescent relationships during late adolescence. *Journal of Research on Adolescence, 18,* 187–200.

Haith, M. M., Hazen, C., & Goodman, G. S. (1988). Expectation and anticipation of dynamic visual events by 3.5 month old babies. *Child Development, 59,* 467–479.

Hakuta, K. (2000). Bilingualism. In A. Kazdin (ed.), *Encyclopedia of psychology.* Washington, DC, & New York: American Psychological Association and Oxford University Press.

Hakuta, K. (2001, April). *Key policy milestones and directions in the education of English language learners.* Paper prepared for the Rockefeller Foundation Symposium, Leveraging change: An Emerging Framework for educational equity, Washington, DC.

Hakuta, K. (2005, April). *Bilingualism at the intersection of research and public policy.* Paper presented at the meeting of the Society for Research in Child Development, Atlanta.

Hakuta, K., Butler, Y. G., & Witt, D. (2000). *How long does it take English learners to attain proficiency?* Berkeley, CA: The University of California Linguistic Minority Research Institute Policy Report 2000–1.

Halford, G. S. (2008). Cognitive developmental theories. In M. M. Haith & J. B. Benson (Eds.), *Encyclopedia of infancy and early childhood.* Oxford, UK: Elsevier.

Hall, G. S. (1904). *Adolescence* (Vols. 1 & 2). Englewood Cliffs, NJ: Prentice Hall.

Hall, L. (2009). *Autism spectrum disorders: From therapy to practice.* Boston: Allyn & Bacon.

Hallahan, D. P., & Kauffman, J. M. (2006). *Exceptional learners* (10th ed.). Boston: Allyn & Bacon.

Hallahan, D. P., Kauffman, J. M., & Pullen, P. C. (2009). *Exceptional learners* (11th ed.). Boston: Allyn & Bacon.

Halldin, M., Rosell, M., de Faire, U., & Hellenius, M. L. (2007). The metabolic syndrome: Prevalence and association to leisure-time and work-related physical activity in 60-year-old men and women. *Nutrition, Metabolism, and Cardiovascular Diseases, 17,* 349–357.

Halpern, D. F. (2006). Assessing gender gaps in learning and academic achievement. In P. A. Alexander & P. H. Wynne (Eds.), *Handbook of educational psychology* (2nd ed.). Mahwah, NJ: Erlbaum.

Halpern, D. F. (2007). The nature and nurture of critical thinking. In R. J. Sternberg, H. Roediger, & D. Halpern (Eds.), *Critical thinking in psychology.* New York: Cambridge University Press.

Halpern, D. F., Benbow, C. P., Geary, D. C., Gur, R. C., Hyde, J. S., & Gernsbacher, M. A. (2007). The science of sex differences in science and mathematics. *Psychological Science in the Public Interest, 8,* 1–51.

Hamlin, J. K., Hallinan, E. V., & Woodward, A. L. (2008, in press). Do as I do: 7-month-old infants selectively reproduce others' goals. *Developmental Science.*

Hampton, T. (2008). Scientists build map of imprinted genes. *Journal of the American Medical Association, 299,* 161.

Hancox, R. J., Milne, B. J., & Poulton, R. (2004). Association between child and adolescent television viewing and adult health: A longitudinal birth cohort study. *Lancet, 364,* 257–262.

Hankin, B. L., Kassel, J. D., & Abela, J. R. (2005). Adult attachment dimensions and specificity of emotional distress symptoms: Prospective investigations of cognitive risk and interpersonal stress generation as mediating mechanisms. *Personality and Social Psychology Bulletin, 31,* 136–151.

Hannish, L. D., & Guerra, N. G. (2004). Aggressive victims, passive victims, and bullies: Development continuity or developmental change? *Merrill-Palmer Quarterly, 50,* 17–38.

Hansen, M. L., Gunn, P. W., & Kaelber, D. C. (2007). Underdiagnosis of hypertension in children and adolescents. *Journal of the American Medical Association, 298,* 874–879.

Hansen, M., Janssen, I., Schiff, A., Zee, P. C., & Dubocovich, M. L. (2005). The impact of school daily schedule on adolescent sleep. *Pediatrics, 115,* 1555–1561.

Hansson, R. O., & Stroebe, M. S. (2007). *Bereavement in late life: Development, coping and adaptation.* Washington, DC: American Psychological Association.

Hardy, M. (2006). Older Workers. In R. H. Binstock & L. K. George (Eds.), *Handbook of aging and the social sciences* (6th ed.). San Diego: Academic Press.

Hargreaves, D. A., & Tiggemann, M. (2004). Idealized body images and adolescent body image: "Comparing" boys and girls. *Body Image, 1,* 351–361.

Harkins, S. W., Price, D. D., & Martinelli, M. (1986). Effects of age on pain perception. *Journal of Gerontology, 41,* 58–63.

Harkins, S. W., & Scott, R. B. (2007). Pain and presbyalgos. In J. E. Birren (Ed.), *Encyclopedia of aging* (2nd ed.). San Diego: Academic Press.

Harley, T. A. (2009). *The psychology of language.* Philadelphia: Psychology Press.

Harlow, H. F. (1958). The nature of love. *American Psychologist, 13,* 673–685.

Harman, S. M. (2007). Andropause. In J. E. Birren (Ed.), *Encyclopedia of gerontology* (2nd ed.). San Diego: Academic Press.

Harootyan, R. A. (2007). Volunteer activity in older adults. In J. E. Birren (Ed.), *Encyclopedia of gerontology* (2nd ed.). San Diego: Academic Press.

Harridge, S. D. R., & Saltin, B. (2007). Neuromuscular system. In J. E. Birren (Ed.), *Encyclopedia of gerontology* (2nd ed.). San Diego: Academic Press.

Harrington, S. E., & Smith, T. J. (2008). The role of chemotherapy at the end of life: "When is enough, enough?" *Journal of the American Medical Association, 299,* 2667–2678.

Harris Interactive. (2003, February 5). *Harris Poll # 8: Adults on the Internet.* Rochester, NY: Author.

Harris, G. (2002). *Grandparenting: How to meet its responsibilities.* Los Angeles: The Americas Group.

Harris, G., Thomas, A., & Booth, D. A. (1990). Development of salt taste in infancy. *Developmental Psychology, 26,* 534–538.

Harris, J. B. (1998). *The nurture assumption: Why children turn out the way they do: Parents matter less than you think and peers matter more.* New York: Free Press.

Harris, K. M., Gorden-Larsen, P., Chantala, K., & Udry, J. R. (2006). Longitudinal trends in race/ethnic disparities in leading health indicators from adolescence to young adulthood. *Archives of Pediatrics and Adolescent Medicine, 160,* 74–81.

Harris, L. (1975). *The myth and reality of aging in America.* Washington, DC: National Council on Aging.

Harris, P. L. (2000). *The work of the imagination.* Oxford University Press.

Harris, P. L. (2006). Social cognition. In W. Damon & R. Lerner (Eds.), *Handbook of child psychology* (6th ed.) New York: Wiley.

Harris, Y. R., & Graham, J. A. (2007). *The African American child,* New York: Springer.

Harrison, J. P., & Ford, D. (2007). A comprehensive community-based model for hospice care. *American Journal of Hospice and Palliative Care, 24,* 119–125.

Harrison-Hale, A. O., McLoyd, V. C., & Smedley, B. (2004). Racial and ethnic status: Risk and protective processes among African-American families. In K. L. Maton, C. J. Schellenbach, B. J. Leadbetter, & A. L. Solarz (Eds.), *Investing in children, families, and communities.* Washington, DC: American Psychological Association.

Hart, B., & Risley, T. R. (1995). *Meaningful differences in the everyday experience of young Americans.* Baltimore: Paul H. Brookes.

Hart, C. H., Yang, C., Charlesworth, R., & Burts, D. C. (2003, April). *Early childhood teachers' curriculum beliefs, classroom practices, and children's outcomes: What are the connections?* Paper presented at the biennial meeting of the Society for Research in Child Development, Tampa, FL.

Hart, D., Atkins, R., & Donnelly, T. M. (2006). Community service and moral development. In M. Killen & J. Smetana (Eds.), *Handbook of moral development.* Mahwah, NJ: Erlbaum.

Hart, D., Burock, D., London, B., & Atkins, R. (2003). Prosocial development, antisocial development, and moral development. In A. M. Slater & G. Bremner (Eds.), *An introduction to developmental psychology.* Malden, MA: Blackwell.

Hart, D., & Karmel, M. P. (1996). Self-awareness and self-knowledge in humans, great apes, and monkeys. In A. Russon, K. Bard, & S. Parker (Eds.), *Reaching into thought.* New York: Cambridge University Press.

Hart, D., Matsuba, M. K., & Atkins, R. (2008). The moral and civic effects of learning to serve. In L. Nucci & D. Narvaez (Eds.), *Handbook of moral and character education.* Clifton, NJ: Psychology Press.

Hart, K. A. (2007). The aging workforce: Implications for health care organizations. *Nursing Economics, 25,* 101–102.

Hart, S., & Carrington, H. (2002). Jealousy in 6-month-old infants. *Infancy, 3,* 395–402.

Harter, S. (2002). Unpublished review of J. W. Santrock's *Child development,* 10th ed. (New York: McGraw-Hill).

Harter, S. (2006). The self. In W. Damon & R. Lerner (Eds.), *Handbook of Child Psychology* (6th ed.). New York: Wiley.

Hartley, A. (2006). Changing role of the speed of processing construct in the cognitive psychology of human aging. In J. E. Birren & K. W. Schaie (Eds.), *Handbook of the psychology of aging* (6th ed.). San Diego: Academic Press.

Hartshorne, H., & May, M. S. (1928–1930). *Moral studies in the nature of character: Studies in the nature of character.* New York: Macmillan.

Hartup, W. W. (1983). The peer system. In P. H. Mussen (Ed.), *Handbook of child psychology* (4th ed., Vol. 4). New York: Wiley.

Hartup, W. W. (1996). The company they keep: friendships and their development significance. *Child Development, 67,* 1–13.

Hartup, W. W. (1999, April). *Peer relations and the growth of the individual child.* Paper presented at the meeting of the Society for Research in Child Development. Albuquerque.

Hartup, W. W., & Abecassis, M. (2004). Friends and enemies. In P. K. Smith & C. H. Hart (Eds.), *Blackwell handbook of childhood social development.* Malden, MA: Blackwell.

Hartwell, L. (2008). *Genetics* (3rd ed.). New York: McGraw-Hill.

Harvey, J. H., & Weber, A. L. (2002). *The odyssey of the heart* (2nd ed.). Mahwah, NJ: Erlbaum.

Harwood, R., Leyendecker, B., Carlson, V., Asencio, M., & Miller, A. (2002). Parenting among Latino families in the U.S. In M. H. Bornstein (Ed.), *Handbook of parenting* (2nd ed.). Mahwah, NJ: Erlbaum.

Hasche, L., & Morrow-Howell, N. (2007). Depression. In J. A. Blackburn & C. N. Dulmas (Eds.), *Handbook of gerontology.* New York: Wiley.

Hasher, L. (2003, February 28). Commentary in "The wisdom of the wizened." *Science, 299,* 1300–1302.

Hasher, L., Chung, C., May, C. P., & Foong, N. (2001). Age, time of testing, and proactive interference. *Canadian Journal of Experimental Psychology, 56,* 200–207.

Hastings, P. D., Utendale, W. T., & Sullivan, C. (2007). The socialization of prosocial development. In J. E. Grusec & P. D. Hastings (Eds.), *Handbook of socialization.* New York: Guilford.

Hattery A. J., & Smith, E. (2007). *African American families.* Thousand Oaks, CA: Sage.

Hattiangady, B., Shuai, B., Cai, J., Coksaygan, T., Rao, M. S., & Shetty, A. K. (2007). Increased dentate neurogenesis after grafting of glial restricted progenitors or neural stem cells in the aging hippocampus. *Stem Cells, 25,* 2104–2117.

Hauser, R. A., & Zesiewicz, T. A. (2007). Advances in the pharmacologic management of early Parkinson disease. *Neurologist, 13,* 126–132.

Hausman, B. L. (2005). Risky business: Framing childbirth in hospital settings. *Journal of Medical Ethics, 26,* 23–38.

Hawkes, C. (2006). Olfaction in neurogenerative disorder. *Advances in Otorhinollaryngology, 63,* 133–151.

Hawkins, N. M., & Dunn, F. G. (2006). The management of hypertension in ischemic heart disease. *Current Opinions in Cardiology, 21,* 273–278.

Hayes, J. A., Yeh, Y. J., & Eisenberg, A. (2007). Good grief and non-so-good grief: Countertransference in bereavement therapy. *Journal of Clinical Psychology, 63,* 345–355.

Hayes, S. M., & Cabeza, R. (2008). Imaging aging. In S. M. Hofer & D. F. Alwin (Eds.), *The handbook on cognitive aging: Interdisciplinary perspectives* Thousand Oaks, CA: Sage

Hayflick, L. (1977). The cellular basis for biological aging. In C. E. Finch & L. Hayflick (Eds.), *Handbook of the biology of aging.* New York: Van Nostrand.

Haykowsky, M., McGavock, J., Vonder, M. I., Koller, M., Mandie, S., Welsh, R., & Taylor, D. (2005). Effect of exercise training on peak aerobic power, left ventricular morphology, and muscle strength in older women. *Journals of Gerontology A: Biological Sciences and Medical Sciences, 60,* 307–311.

Haynes, R. L., Folkerth, R. D., Szweda, L. I., Volpe, J. J., & Kinney, H. C. (2006). Lipid peroxidation during cerebral myelination. *Journal of Neuropathology and Experimental Neurology, 65,* 894–904.

Hayslip, B. (1996). Hospice. In J. E. Birren (Ed.), *Encyclopedia of gerontology* (Vol. 1). San Diego: Academic Press.

Hayslip, B., Edmondson, R., & Guarnaccia, C. (1999, November). *Religiousness, perceptions of funerals, and bereavement adjustment in adulthood.* Paper presented at the meeting of the Gerontological Society of America, San Francisco.

Hayslip, B., & Hansson, R. (2003). Death awareness and adjustment across the life span. In C. D. Bryant (Ed.), *Handbook of death and dying.* Thousand Oaks, CA: Sage.

Hayslip, B., & Hansson, R. O. (2007). Hospice. In J. E. Birren (Ed.), *Encyclopedia of gerontology* (2nd ed.). San Diego: Academic Press.

Hazan, C., & Shaver, P. R. (1987). Romantic love conceptualized as an attachment process. *Journal of Personality and Social Psychology, 52,* 522–524.

Healey, J. F. (2009). *Race, ethnicity and class* (5th Ed.). Thousand Oaks, CA: Sage.

Health Management Resources. (2001). *Child health and fitness.* Boston: Author.

Hedden, T., Lautenschlager, G., & Park, D. C. (2005). Contributions of processing ability and knowledge to verbal memory tasks across the adult lifespan. *Quarterly Journal of Experimental Psychology, 58A,* 169–190.

Heimann, M., Strid, K., Smith, L., Tjus, T., Ulvund, S. E., & Melzoff, A. N. (2006). Exploring the relation between memory, gestural communication, and the emergence of language in infancy: A longitudinal study. *Infant and Child Development, 15,* 233–249.

Heitzler, C. D., Martin, S. L., Duke, J., & Huhman, M. (2006). Correlates of physical activity in a national sample of children aged 9–13 years. *Preventive Medicine, 42,* 254–260.

Helman, C. (2008). Inside T. Boone Pickens' brain. *Forbes.* Retrieved June 15, 2008, from http://www.forbes.com/billionaires/forbes/2008/0630/076.html

Helman, R., VanDerhei, J., & Copeland, C. (2007). the retirement system in transition: The 2007 Retirement Confidence Survey. *Employment Benefit Research Institute Issue Brief, 304* (1), 4–24.

Helmuth, L. (2003). The wisdom of the -wizened. *Science, 299,* 1300–1302.

Helson, R. (1997, August). *Personality change: When is it adult development?* Paper presented at the meeting of the American Psychological Association, Chicago.

Helson, R., & Wink, P. (1992). Personality change in women from the early 40s to early 50s. *Psychology and Aging, 7,* 46–55.

Henderson, A. J. (2008). The effects of tobacco smoke exposure on respiratory health in school-aged children. *Pediatric Respiratory Review, 9,* 21–28.

Hendry, J. (1995). *Understanding Japanese society.* London: Routledge.

Henriksen, T. B., Hjollund, N. H., Jensen, T. K., Bonde, J. P., Andersson, A. M., Kolstad, H., Ernst, E., Giwereman, A., Skakkebaek, N. E., & Olsen, J. (2004). Alcohol consumption at the time of conception and spontaneous abortion. *American Journal of Epidemiology, 160,* 661–667.

Henry, N. J. M., Berg, C. A., Smith, T. W., & Florsheim, P. (2007). Positive and negative characteristics of marital interaction and their association with marital satisfaction in middle aged and older couples. *Psychology and Aging, 22,* 428–441.

Henwood, T. R., Riek, S., & Taaffe, D. R. (2008). Strength versus muscle-power specific resistance training in community-dwelling older adults. *Journals of Gerontology A: Biological Sciences and Medical Sciences, 63,* 83–91.

Hepper, P. (2007). The foundations of development. In A. Slater & M. Lewis, *Introduction to infant development* (2nd ed.). New York: Oxford University Press.

Herbison, A. E., Porteus, R., Paper, J. R., Mora, J. M., & Hurst, P. R. (2008). Gonadotropin-releasing hormone neuron requirements for puberty, ovulation, and fertility. *Endocrinology, 149,* 597–604.

Herbst, M. A., Mercer, B. M., Beasley, D., Meyer, N., & Carr, T. (2003). Relationship of prenatal care and perinatal morbidity in low-birth-weight infants. *American Journal of Obstetrics and Gynecology, 189,* 930–933.

Herek, G. M. (2008, in press). Hate crimes and stigma-related experiences among sexual minority adults in the United States: Prevalence estimates from a national probability sample. *Journal of Interpersonal Violence.*

Herman, C. P., van Strien, T., & Polivy, J. (2008). Undereating or eliminating overeating. *American Psychologist, 63,* 202–203.

Herman, D. R., Harrison, G. G., Afifi, A. A., & Jenks, E. (2008). Effect of a target subsidy on intake of fruits and vegetables among low-income women in the Special Supplemental Nutrition Program for Women, Infants, and Children. *American Journal of Public Health, 98,* 98–105.

Hermann-Giddens, M. E. (2007). The decline. in the age of menarche in the United States: Should we be concerned? *Journal of Adolescent Health, 40,* 201–203.

Hermann-Giddens, M. E. (2006). Recent data on pubertal milestones in United States children: The secular trend toward earlier development. *International Journal of Andrology, 29,* 241–246.

Hernandez, D. J. (2007). Changes in the demographics of families over the course of American history. In A. S. Skolnick, & J. H. Skolnick (Eds.), *Family in transition* (14th ed.). Boston: Allyn & Bacon.

Hernandez, D. J., Denton, N. A., & Macartney, S. E. (2007). Family circumstances of children in immigrant families. In J. E. Lansford, K. Deater-Deckhard, & M. H. Bornstein (Eds.), *Immigrant families in contemporary society.* New York: Guilford.

Hernandez-Reif, M. (2007). Unpublished review of J. W. Santrock, *Life-span development,* 12th ed. (New York: McGraw-Hill).

Hernandez-Reif, M., Diego, M., & Field, T. (2007). Preterm infants show reduced stress behaviors and activity after 5 days of massage therapy. *Infant Behavior and Development, 30,* 557–561.

Heron, M. P., Hoyert, D. L., Xu, J., Scott, C. & Tejada-Vera, B. (2008, June 11). *Deaths: Preliminary data for 2006. National Vital Statistics Reports, 56* (No. 16), 1–52.

Herrera, V. M., Koss, M. P., Bailey, J., Yuan, N. P., & Lichter, E. L. (2006). Survivors of male violence. In J. Worell & C. D. Goodheart (Eds.), *Handbook of girls' and women's psychological health.* New York: Oxford University Press.

Herrmann, M., King, K., & Weitzman, M. (2008). Prenatal tobacco smoke and postnatal secondhand smoke exposure and child neurodevelopment. *Current Opinion in Pediatrics, 20,* 184–190.

Hertogh, C. M., de Boer, M. E., Droes, R. M., & Eefsting, J. A. (2007). Would we rather lose our life than lose our self? Lessons from the Dutch debate on euthanasia for patients with dementia. *American Journal of Bioethics, 7,* 48–56

Hertz-Picciotto, I., Park, H. Y., Dostal, M., Kocan, A., Trnovec, T., & Sram, R. (2008). Prenatal exposure to persistent and non-persistent organic compounds, and effects on immune system development. *Basic and Clinical Pharmacology and Toxicology, 102,* 146–154.

Hesmet, S., & Lo, K. C. (2006). Evaluation and treatment of ejaculatory duct obstruction in infertile men. *Canadian Journal of Urology, 13* (Suppl. 1), 18–21.

Hess, T. M. (2006). Attitudes toward aging and their effects on behavior. In J. E. Birren & K. W. Schaie (Eds.), *Handbook of the psychology of aging* (6th ed.). San Diego: Academic Press.

Hess, T. M., & Hinson, J. T. (2006). Age-related variation in the influences of stereotypes on memory in adulthood. *Psychology and Aging, 21,* 621–625.

Hess, T. M., Auman, C., Colcombe, S. J., & Rahhal, T. A. (2003). The impact of stereotype threat on age differences in memory performance. *Journals of Gerontology: Psychological and Social Sciences, 58B,* P3–P11.

Hetherington, E. M. (1989). Coping with family transitions: Winners, losers, and survivors. *Child Development, 60,* 1–14.

Hetherington, E. M. (1993). An overview of the Virginia Longitudinal Study of Divorce and Remarriage with a focus on early adolescence. *Journal of Family Psychology, 7,* 39–56.

Hetherington, E. M. (2000). Divorce. In A. Kazdin (Ed.), *Encyclopedia of psychology.* Washington, DC, & New York: American Psychological Association and Oxford University Press.

Hetherington, E. M. (2006). The influence of conflict, marital problem solving, and parenting on children's adjustment in nondivorced, divorced, and remarried families. In A. Clarke-Stewart & J. Dunn (Eds.), *Families count.* New York: Oxford University Press.

Hetherington, E. M., & Kelly, J. (2002). *For better or for worse: Divorce reconsidered.* New York: Norton.

Hetherington, E. M., & Stanley-Hagan, M. (2002). Parenting in divorced and remarried families. In M. H. Bornstein (Ed.), *Handbook of parenting* (2nd ed., Vol. 3). Mahwah, NJ: Erlbaum.

Hewlett, S. A. (2002). *Creating a life: Professional women and the quest for children.* New York: Talk Miramax Books.

Heyman, G. D., Fu, G., & Lee, K. (2007). Evaluating claims people make about themselves: the development of skepticism. *Child Development, 78,* 367–375.

Heyman, G. D., & Legare, C. H. (2005). Children's evaluation of sources of information about traits. *Developmental Psychology, 41,* 636–647.

Hibell, B., Andersson, B., Bjarnasson, T., & others. (2004). *The ESPAD report 2003: alcohol and other drug use among students in 35 European Countries,* The Swedish Council for Information on Alcohol and Other Drugs (CAN) and Council of Europe Pompidou Group.

Hick, P., & Thomas, G. (Eds.) (2009). *Inclusion and diversity in education.* Thousand Oaks, CA: Sage.

Hickman, J. M., Rogers, W. A., & Fisk, A. D. (2007). Training older adults to use a new technology. *Journals of Gerontology B: Psychological Sciences and Social Sciences, 62,* (Special Issue), P77–P84.

High/Scope Resource. (2005, Spring). The High/Scope Perry Preschool Study and the man who began it. *High/Scope Resource,* p. 9. Ypsilanti, MI: High/Scope Press.

Hijiya, N., & others. (2007). Cumulative incidence of secondary neoplasms as a first event after childhood acute lymphoblastic leukemia. *Journal of the American Medical Association, 297,* 1207–1215.

Hill, C. R., & Stafford, F. P. (1980). Parental care of children: Time diary estimate of quantity, predictability, and variety. *Journal of Human Resources, 15,* 219–239.

Hill, M. A. (2007). Early human development. *Clinical Obstetrics and Gynecology, 50,* 2–9.

Hill, T. D., Angel, J. L., Ellison, C. G., & Angel, R. J. (2005). Religious attendance and mortality: An 8-year follow-up of older Mexican Americans. *Journals of Gerontology B: Psychological Sciences and Social Sciences, 60,* S102–S109.

Hill, T. D., Burdetre, A. M., Angel, J. L., & Angel, R. J. (2006). Religious attendance and cognitive functioning, among older Mexican Americans, *Journals of Gerontology B: Psychological Sciences and Social Sciences, 61,* P3–P9.

Hillman, C. H., Erickson, K. I., & Kramer, A. F. (2008). Be smart, exercise your heart: Exercise effects on the brain and cognition. *Nature Reviews: Neuroscience, 9,* 58–65.

Himes, C. L., Hogan, D. P., & Eggebeen, D. J. (1996). Living arrangements of minority elders. *Journals of Gerontology, 51,* S42–S48.

Hingson, R. W., Heeren, T., & Winter, M. R. (2006). Age at drinking onset and alcohol dependence: Age at onset, duration, and severity. *Archives of Pediatric and Adolescent Medicine, 160,* 739–746.

Hinrichsen, G. A. (2006). Why multicultural issues matter for practitioners working with older adults. *Psychology and Aging, 37,* 29–35.

Hirsch, B. J., & Rapkin, B. D. (1987). The transition to junior high school: A longitudinal study of self-esteem, psychological symptomatology, school life, and social support. *Child Development, 58,* 1235–1243.

Hock, R. R. (2007). *Human Sexuality.* Upper Saddle River, NJ: Prentice Hall.

Hockenberry, M., & Wilson, D. (2009). *Wong's essentials of pediatric nursing.* Oxford, UK: Elsevier.

Hodapp, R. M., & Dykens, E. M. (2006). Mental retardation. In W. Damon & R. Lerner (Eds.), *Handbook of child psychology* (6th ed.) New York: Wiley.

Hoefnagles, M. (2009). *Biology concepts and investigations.* New York: McGraw-Hill.

Hoeger, W. W. K., & Hoeger, S. A. (2008). Principles and labs for physical fitness (6th ed.). New York: McGraw-Hill.

Hoek, H. W. (2006). Incidence, prevalence and mortality of anorexia nervosa and other eating disorders. *Current Opinion in Psychiatry, 19,* 389–394.

Hofer, A., Siedentopf, C. M., Ischebeck, A., Rettenbacher, M. A., Verius, M., Felber, S., & Fleischhacker, W. (2007a). Sex differences in brain activation patterns during processing of positively and negatively balanced emotional stimuli. *Psychological Medicine, 37,* 109–119.

Hofer A., Siedentopf, C. M., Ischebeck, A., Rettenbacher, M. A., Verius, M., Felber, S., & Fleischhacker, W. (2007b). Gender differences in regional cerebral activity during the perception of emotion: A functional MRI study. *Neuroimage, 132,* 854–862.

Hofer, S. M., & Piccinin, A. M. (2007). Longitudinal studies. In J. E. Birren (Ed.), *Encyclopedia of gerontology* (2nd ed.). San Diego: Academic Press.

Hofer, S. M., & Sliwinski, M. J. (2006). Design and analysis of longitudinal studies on aging. In J. E. Birren & K. W. Schaie (Eds.), *Handbook of the psychology of aging* (6th ed.). San Diego: Academic Press.

Hoff, E., Laursen, B., & Tardif, T. (2002). Socioeconomic status and parenting. In M. H. Bornstein (Ed.), *Handbook of parenting* (2nd ed.). Mahwah, NJ: Erlbaum.

Hofferth, S. L., & Reid, L. (2002). Early childbearing and children's achievement behavior over time. *Perspectives on sexual and reproductive health, 34,* 41–49.

Hoffman, M. L. (1970). Moral development. In P. H. Mussen (Ed.), *Manual of child psychology* (3rd ed., Vol. 2). New York: Wiley.

Hofheimer, J. A., & Lester, B. M. (2008). Neuropsychological assessment. In M. M. Haith & J. B. Benson (Eds.), *Encyclopedia of infancy and early childhood.* Oxford, UK: Elsevier.

Hogan, M. A., Glazebrook, R., Brancato, V., & Rogers, J. (2007). *Maternal-newborn nursing: Review and rationales* (2nd ed.). Upper Saddle River, NJ: Prentice Hall.

Holcombe, E., Carrier, D., Manlove, J., & Ryan, S. (2008, February). Contraceptive use patterns across teens' sexual relationships. *Child Fact Sheet.* Washington, DC: Child Trends.

Holden, K., & Hatcher, C. (2006). Economic status of the aged. In R. H. Binstock & L. K. George (Eds.), *Handbook of aging and the social science* (6th ed.). San Diego: Academic Press.

Hollich, G., Newman, R. S., & Jusczyk, P. W. (2005). Infants' use of synchronized visual information to separate streams of speech. *Child Development, 76,* 598–613.

Hollier, L., & Wendel, G. (2008). Third trimester antiviral prophylaxis for preventing maternal genital herpes simplex virus (HSV) recurrences and neonatal infection. *Cochrane Database of Systematic Reviews, 1,* CD004946.

Holmback, U., Fridman, J., Gustafsson, J., Proos, L., Sundelin, C., & Forslund, A. (2007). Overweight more prevalent among children than adolescents. *Acta Pediatrica, 96,* 577–581.

Holmes, T. H., & Rahe, R. H. (1967). The social readjustment rating scale. *Journal of Psychosomatic Research, 11,* 213–218.

Holstein, B. E., Due, P., Almind, G., & Avlund, K. (2007). Eight-year change in functional ability among 70- to 95-year-olds. *Scandinavian Journal of Public Health, 35,* 243–249.

Holzgrabe, U., Kapkova, P., Alptuzun, V., Scheiber, J., & Kugelmann, E. (2007). Targeting acetylcholinesterase to treat neurodegeneration. *Expert Opinion on Therapeutic Targets, 11,* 161–179.

Holzman, L. (2009). *Vygotsky at work and play.* Oxford, UK: Routledge.

Hong, Y., Jin, X., Lin, H. M., Duan, Y., Pu, M., Wolbrette, D. L., & Liao, D. (2007). Metabolic syndrome, its preeminent clusters, incident coronary heart disease, and all-cause mortality–results of prospective analysis for the Atherosclerosis Risk in Communities study. *Journal of Internal Medicine, 262,* 113–122.

Hongo, M., Itoi, E., Sinaki, M., Miyakoshi, N., Shimada, Y., Maekawa, S., Okada, K., & Mizutani, Y. (2007, in press). Effects of low-intensity back exercise on quality of life and back extensor strength in patients with -osteoporosis: A randomized controlled trial. *Osteoporosis International.*

Hooijmans, C. R., & Kiliaan, A. J. (2008, in press). Fatty acids, lipid metabolism, and Alzheimer pathology, *European Journal of Pharmacology.*

Hooper, S. R., & others (2008). Executive functions in young males with fragile X syndrome in comparison to mental age-matched controls: Baseline findings from a longitudinal study. *Neuropsychology, 22,* 36–47.

Hopkins, B. (1991). Facilitating early motor development: An intracultural study of West Indian mothers and their infants living in Britain. In J. K. Nugent, B. M. Lester, & T. B. Brazelton (Eds.), *The cultural context of infancy: Vol. 2. Multicultural and interdisciplinary approaches to parent-infant relations.* Norwood, NJ: Ablex.

Hopkins, B., & Westra, T. (1988). Maternal handling and motor development: An intracultural study. *Genetic Psychology Monographs, 14,* 377–420.

Hopkins, B., & Westra, T. (1990). Motor development, maternal expectations, and the role of handling. *Infant Behavior and Development, 13,* 117–122.

Hoppman, C., & Smith, J. (2007). Life-history related differences in possible selves in very old age. *International Journal of Aging and Human Development, 64,* 109–127.

Hoppmann, C. A., Gerstorf, D., Smith, J., & Klumb, P. L. (2007). Linking possible selves and behavior: Do domain-specific hopes and fears translate into daily activities in very old age? *Journals of Gerontology B: Psychological Sciences and Social Sciences, 62,* P104–P111.

Horn, J. (2007). Spearman, *g,* expertise, and the nature of human cognitive capacity. In P. C. Kyllonen, R. D. Roberts, & L. Stankov (Eds.), *Extending intelligence.* Mahwah, NJ: Erlbaum.

Horn, J. L., & Donaldson, G. (1980). Cognitive development II: Adulthood development of human abilities. In O. G. Brim & J. Kagan (Eds.), *Constancy and change in human development.* Cambridge, MA: Harvard University Press.

Horne, R. S., Franco, P., Adamson, T. M., Groswasser, J., & Kahn, A. (2002). Effects of body position on sleep and arousal characteristics in infants. *Early Human Development, 69,* 25–33.

Horowitz, J. A., & Cousins, A. (2006). Postpartum depression treatment rates for at-risk women. *Nursing Research, 55,* (Suppl. 2), S23–S27.

Horsthemke, B., & Bunting, K. (2008). Genomic imprinting and imprinting defects in humans. *Advances in Genetics, 61,* 225–246.

Horwitz, E. K. (2008). *Becoming a language teacher.* Boston: Allyn & Bacon.

Hosea Blewett, H. J., Cicalo, M. C., Holland, C. D., & Field, C. J. (2008). The immunological components of human milk. *Advances in Food and Nutrition Research, 54,* 45–80.

Hourigan, S. R., Nitz, J. C., Brauer, S. G., O'Neill, S., Wong, J., & Richardson, C. A. (2008, in press). Positive effects of exercise on falls and fracture risk in osteopathic women. *Osteoporosis International.*

House, J. S. (1998). Commentary: Age, work, and well-being, In K. W. Schaie & Schooler (Eds.), *The impact of work on older adults.* New York: Springer.

House, J. S., Landis, K. R., & Umberson, D. (1998). Social relationships and health. *Science, 241,* 540–545.

Howe, L. D., Huttly, S. R., & Abramsky, T. (2006). Risk factors for injuries in young children in four developing countries: The Young Lives Study. *Tropic Medicine and International Health, 11,* 1557–1566.

Howe, M. J. A., Davidson, J. W., Moore, D. G., & Sloboda, J. A. (1995). Are there early childhood signs of musical ability? *Psychology of Music, 23,* 162–176.

Howe, N., & Recchia, H. E. (2008). Siblings and sibling rivalry. In M. M. Haith & J. B. Benson (Eds.), *Encyclopedia of infant and early childhood development.* Oxford, UK: Elsevier.

Howe, N., & Recchia, H. E. (2009, in press). Sibling relations and their impact on children's development. In R. E. Tremblay, R. deV Peters, M. Boivin, & R. G. Barr (Eds.), *Encyclopedia of early childhood development.* Montreal: Centre of Excellence for Early Childhood Development.

Howes, C. (2008). Friends and peers. In M. M. Haith & J. B. Benson (Eds.), *Encyclopedia of infant and early childhood development.* Oxford, UK: Elsevier.

Howes, C. (2009, in press). The impact of child care on young children (0-2). In R. E. Tremblay, R. deV Peters, M. Boivan, & R. G. Barr (Eds.), *Encyclopedia on early childhood development.* Montreal: Centre of Excellence for Early Childhood Development.

Hoyer, W. J., & Roodin, P. A. (2003). *Adult development and aging* (5th ed.). New York: McGraw-Hill.

Hoyer, W. J., & Verhaeghen, P. (2006). Memory aging. In J. E. Birren & K. W. Schaie (Eds.), *Handbook of the psychology of aging* (6th ed.). San Diego: Academic Press.

Hoyert, D. L., Mathews, T. J., Menacker, F., Strobino, D. M., & Guyer, B. (2006). Annual summary of vital statistics: 2004, *Pediatrics, 117,* 168–183.

Hrabosky, J. I., Masheb, R. M., White, M. A., & Grilo, C. M. (2007). Overvaluation of shape and weight in binge eating disorder. *Journal of Consulting and Clinical Psychology, 75,* 175–180.

HSBC Insurance. (2007). *The future of retirement: The new old age-global report.* London: Author.

Hsu, H-C. (2004). Antecedents and consequences of separation anxiety in first-time mothers: infant, mother, and social-contextual characteristics. *Infant Behavior and Development, 27,* 113–133.

Hsu, J., Fung, V., Price, M., Huang, J., Brand, R., Hui, R., Fireman, B., & Newhouse, J. P. (2008). Medicare beneficiaries' knowledge of Part D prescription drug program benefits and responses to drug costs. *Journal of the American Medical Association, 299,* 1929–1936.

Hu, H., & others. (2006). Fetal lead exposure at each stage of pregnancy as a predictor of infant mental development. *Environmental Health Perspectives, 114,* 1730–1735.

Huang, C. M., Tung, W. S., Kuo, K. L., & Ying-Ju, C. (2004). Comparison of pain responses of premature infants to the heelstick between containment and swaddling. *Journal of Nursing Research, 12,* 31–40.

Huebner, A. M., & Garrod, A. C. (1993). Moral reasoning among Tibetan monks: A study of Buddhist adolescents and young adults in Nepal. *Journal of Cross-Cultural Psychology, 24,* 167–185.

Huerta, M., Cortina, L. M., Pang, J. S., Torges, C. M., & Magley, V. J. (2006). Sex and power in the academy: Modeling sexual harassment in the lives of college women. *Personality and Social Psychology Bulletin, 32,* 616–628.

Huesmann, L. R., Dubow, E. F., Eron, L. D., & Boxer, P. (2006). Middle childhood family-contextual and personal factors as predictors of adult outcomes. In A. C. Huston & M. N. Ripke (Eds.), *Developmental contexts in middle childhood: Bridges to adolescence and adulthood:* New York: Cambridge University Press.

Huesmann, L. R., Moise-Titus, J., Podolski, C., & Eron, L. D. (2003). Longitudinal relations between children's exposure to TV violence and their aggressive and violent behavior in young adulthood: 1977–1992. *Developmental Psychology, 39,* 201–221.

Hueston, W. J., Geesey, M. E., & Diaz, V. (2008). Prenatal care initiation among pregnant teens in the United States: An analysis over 25 years. *Journal of Adolescent Health, 42,* 243–248.

Huffman, D. M., Moellering, D. R., Grizzle, W. E., Stockard, C. R., Johnson, M. S., & Nagy, T. R. (2008, in press). Effect of exercise and calorie restriction on biomarkers in aging mice. *American Journal of Physiology: Regulatory, Integrative, and Comparative Physiology.*

Hughes, M. E., Waite, L. J., LaPierre, T. A., & Luo, Y. (2007). All in the family: The impact of caring for grandchildren on grandparents' health. *Journals of Gerontology B: Psychological Sciences and Social Sciences, 62,* S108–S119.

Huisman, T. A., & Kellenberger, C. J. (2008). MR imaging characteristics of the normal fetal gastrointestinal tract and abdomen. *European Journal of Radiology, 65,* 170–181.

Huizink, A. C., & Mulder, E. J. (2006). Maternal smoking, drinking, or cannibis use during pregnancy and neurobehavioral and cognitive functioning in human offspring. *Neuroscience and Biobehavioral Research, 30,* 24–41.

Hultsch, D. F., Hertzog, C., Small, B. J., & Dixon, R. A. (1999). Use it or lose it: Engaged lifestyle as a buffer of cognitive decline in aging? *Psychology and Aging, 14,* 245–263.

Humphreys, C. (2007). A health inequalities perspective on violence against women. *Health and Social Care in the Community, 15,* 120–127.

Hunter, K. I., & Linn, M. W. (1980). Psychological differences between elderly volunteers and non-volunteers. *International Journal of Aging and Human Development, 12,* 205–213.

Hurd Clarke, L. (2006). Older women and sexuality: Experiences in marital relationships across the life course. *Canadian Journal of Aging, 25,* 129–140.

Hurt, H., Brodsky, N. L., Roth, H., Malmud, F., & Giannetta, J. M. (2005). School performance of children with gestational cocaine exposure. *Neurotoxicology and Teratology, 27,* 203–211.

Hustedt, J. T., & Barnett, W. S. (2009, in press). Head Start policy. In R. E. Tremblay, R. deV Peters, M. Boivin, & R. G. Barr (Eds.), *Encyclopedia on early childhood development.* Montreal: Centre of Excellence for Early Childhood Development.

Huston, A. C., Epps, S. R., Shim, M. S., Duncan, G. J., Crosby, D. A., & Ripke, M. N. (2006). Effects of a poverty intervention program last from middle childhood to adolescence. In A. C. Huston & M. N. Ripke (Eds.), *Developmental contexts of middle childhood: Bridges to adolescence and adulthood.* New York: Cambridge University Press.

Huston, A. C., & Ripke, M. N. (2006). Experiences in middle childhood and children's development: A summary and integration of research. In A. C. Huston & M. N. Ripke (Eds.), *Developmental contexts in middle childhood.* New York: Cambridge University press.

Hutchinson, D. M., & Rapee, R. M. (2007). Do friends share similar body image and eating problems? The role of social networks and peer influences in early adolescence. *Behavior Research and Therapy, 45,* 1557–1577.

Hutson, R. A. (2008). Poverty. In N. J. Salkind (Ed.), *Encyclopedia of educational psychology.* Thousand Oaks, CA: Sage.

Huttenlocher, J., Haight, W., Bruk, A., Seltzer, M., & Lyons, T. (1991). Early vocabulary growth: Relation to language input and gender. *Developmental Psychology. 27,* 236–248.

Huttenlocher, P. R., & Dabholkar, A. S. (1997). Regional differences in synaptogenesis in human cerebral cortex. *Journal of Comparative Neurology, 37* (2), 167–178.

Huyck, M. H. (1995). Marriage and close relationships of the marital kind. In R. Blieszner & V. H. Bedford (Eds.), *Handbook of aging and the family.* Westport, CT: Greenwood Press.

Huyck, M. H., Ayalon, L., & Yoder, J. (2007). Using mixed methods to evaluate the use of caregiver strain measure to assess outcomes of a caregiver support program for caregivers of older adults. *International Journal of Geriatrics and Psychiatry, 22,* 160–165.

Huyck, M. H., & Hoyer, W. J. (1982). *Adult development and aging.* Belmont, CA: Wadsworth.

Hybels, C. F., & Blazer, D. G. (2004). Epidemiology of the late-life mental disorders. *Clinical Geriatric Medicine, 19,* 663–696.

Hyde, D. R. (2009). *Introduction to genetic principles.* New York: McGraw-Hill.

Hyde, J. S. (2005). The gender similarities hypothesis. *American Psychologist, 60,* 581–592.

Hyde, J. S. (2007a). *Half the human experience* (7th ed.). Boston: Houghton Mifflin.

Hyde, J. S. (2007b). New directions in the study of gender similarities and differences. *Current Directions in Psychological Science, 16,* 259–263.

Hyde, J. S., & Lindberg, S. M. (2007). Facts and assumptions about the nature of gender differences and their implications for gender equity. In S. Klein (Ed.), *Handbook for achieving gender equity through education.* Mahwah, NJ: Erlbaum.

Hyde, J. S., & DeLamater, J. D. (2008). *Understanding human sexuality* (10th ed.), New York: McGraw-Hill.

Hyde, J. S., Lindberg, S. M., Linn, M. C., Ellis, A. B., & Williams, C. C. (2008). Gender similarities characterize math performance. *Science, 321,* 494–495.

Hyde, J. S., & Price, M. (2007, November). *When two isn't better than one: Predictors of early sexual activity in adolescence using a cumulative risk model.* Paper presented at the meeting of the Society for the Scientific Study of Sexuality, Indianapolis.

Hyson, M. (2007). Curriculum. In R. New & M. Cochran (Eds.), *Early childhood education: An international encyclopedia of early childhood education.* New York: Greenwood.

Hyson, M. C., Copple, C., & Jones, J. (2006). Early childhood development and education. In W. Damon & R. Lerner (Eds.), *Handbook of child psychology* (6th ed.). New York: Wiley.

I

"I Have a Dream Foundation" (2008). *About us.* Retrieved January 5, 2008, from the Internet at www.ihaveadreamfoundation.org/html/

Iacoboni, M., & Dapretto, M. (2006). The mirror neuron system and the consequences of its dysfunction. *Nature Reviews: Neuroscience, 7,* 942–951.

Iacono, M. V. (2007). Osteoporosis: A national public health priority. *Journal of Perianesthesia Nursing, 223,* 175–180.

Idler, E. L., Kasl, S. V., & Hays, J. C. (2001). Patterns of religious practice and belief in the last year of life. *Journals of Gerontology B: Psychological Sciences and Social Sciences, 56,* S326–S334.

Ige, F., & Shelton, D. (2004). Reducing the risk of sudden infant death syndrome (SIDS) in African-American communities. *Journal of Pediatric Nursing, 19,* 290–292.

Ikeda, A., & others. (2007). Marital status and mortality among Japanese men and women: The Japanese Collaborative Cohort Study. *BMC Public Health, 7,* 73.

Ilola, L. M. (1990). Culture and health. In R. W. Brislin (Ed.), *Applied cross-cultural psychology.* Newbury park, CA: Sage.

Imada, T., Zhang, Y., Cheour, M., Taulu, S., Ahonen, A., & Kuhl, P. K. (2007). Infant speech perception activates Broca's area: A developmental magnetoencephalography study. *Neuroreport, 17,* 957–962.

Immordino-Yang, M. H., & Fischer, K. W. (2007). Dynamic development of hemispheric biases in three cases: Cognitive/hemispheric cycles, music, and hemispherectomy. In D. Coch, G. Dawson, & K. W. Fischer (Eds.), *Human behavior, learning, and the developing brain.* New York: Guilford.

Impett, E. A., Schoolder, D., Tolman, L., Sorsoli, L., & Henson, J. M. (2008). Girls' relationship authenticity and self-esteem across adolescence. *Developmental Psychology, 44,* 722–733.

Inglehart, R. (1990). *Culture shift in advanced industrial society.* Princeton, NJ: Princeton University Press.

Ingram, D. K., Young, J., & Mattison, J. A. (2007). Calorie restriction in nonhuman primates: Assessing effects on brain and behavioral aging. *Neuroscience, 145,* 1359–1364.

Insel, P. M., & Roth, W. T. (2008). *Core concepts in health* (10th ed.). New York: McGraw-Hill.

International Montessori Council. (2006). Much of their success on prime-time television. Retrieved March 24, 2006, from www.Montessori.org/enews/barbara_walters.html

Ip, S., Chung, M., Raman, G., Chew, P., Magula, N., Devine, D., Trikalinos, T., & Lau, J. (2007). Breastfeeding and maternal and infant health outcomes in developed countries. *Evidence Report/Technology Assessment, 153,* 1–86.

Irwin, C. E. (2004). Eating and physical activity during adolescence: Does it make a difference in adult health status? *Journal of Adolescent Health, 34,* 459–460.

Isella, V., Mapelli, C., Morielli, N., Pelati, O., Franceschi, M., Appollonio, I. M. (2008). Age-related quantitative and qualitative changes in decision-making ability. *Behavioral Neurology, 19,* 59–63.

Isen, J., & Baker, L. A. (2008). Genetic disorders: Sex-linked. In M. M. Haith & J. B. Benson (Eds.), *Encyclopedia of infancy and early childhood development.* Oxford, UK: Elsevier.

Ishii-Kuntz, M. (2004). Asian American families. In M. Coleman & L. Ganong (Eds.), *Handbook of contemporary families.* Thousand Oaks, CA: Sage.

Ito, A., Honmna, Y., Inamori, E., Yada, Y., Momoi, M. Y., & Nakamura, Y. (2006). Developmental outcome of very low birth weight twins conceived by assisted reproduction techniques. *Journal of Perinatology, 26,* 130–136.

J

Jackson, S. L. (2008). *Research methods.* Belmont, CA: Wadsworth.

Jacobs, J. E., & Tanner, J. L. (1999, August). *Stability and change in perceptions of parent-child relationships.* Paper presented at the meeting of the Gerontological Association of America, San Francisco.

Jacobs, J. M., Hammerman-Rozenberg, R., Cohen, A., & Stressman, J. (2008). Reading daily predicts reduced mortality among men from a cohort of community-dwelling 70-year-olds. *Journals of Gerontology B: psychological Sciences and Social Sciences, 63,* S73–S80.

Jacobs, N., Rijsdijk, F., Derom, C., Vlietinck, R., Delespaul, P., van Os, J., & Myin-Germeys, I. (2006). Genes making one feel blue in the flow of daily life: A momentary assessment study of gene-stress interaction. *Psychosomatic Medicine, 68,* 201–206.

Jacobs-Lawson, J. M., Hershey, D. A., & Neukam, K. A. (2005). Gender differences in factors that influence time spent planning for retirement. *Journal of Women and Aging, 16,* 55–69.

Jaddoe, V. W., Troe, E. J., Hofman, A., Mackenbach, J. P., Moll, H. A., Steegers, E. A., & Witteman, J. C. (2008). Active and passive smoking during pregnancy and the risks of low birthweight and preterm birth: The Generation R Study. *Pediatric and Perinatal Epidemiology, 22,* 162–171.

Jae, S. Y., Carnethon, M. R., Heffernan, K. S., Choi, Y. H., Lee, M. K., & Fernhall, B. (2007). Association between cardiorespiratory fitness and prevalence of carotid atherosclerosis among men with hypertension. *American Heart Journal, 153,* 1001–1005.

Jaffee, S. R., Caspi, A., Moffitt, T. E., Polo-Tomas, M., & Taylor, A. (2007). Individual, family, and neighborhood factors distinguish resilient from non-resilient maltreated children: A cumulative stressors model. *Child Abuse and Neglect, 31,* 231–253.

Jaffee, S., & Hyde, J. S. (2000). Gender differences in moral orientation: A meta-analysis. *Psychological Bulletin, 126,* 703–726.

Jalongo, M. R. (2007). *Early childhood language arts* (4th ed.). Boston: Allyn & Bacon.

James, A. H., Brancazio, L. R., & Price, T. (2008). Aspirin and reproductive outcomes. *Obstetrical and Gynecological Survey, 63,* 49–57.

James, D. C., & Dobson, B. (2005). Position of the American Dietetic Association: Promoting and supporting breastfeeding. *Journal of the American Dietetic Association, 105,* 810–818.

James, W. (1890/1950). *The principles of psychology.* New York: Dover.

James, W. H. (2005). Biological and psychosocial determinants of male and female human sexual orientation. *Journal of Biosocial Science, 37,* 555–567.

Jamshidi, Y., Snieder, H., Ge, D., Spector, T. D., & O'Dell, S. D. (2007). The SH2B gene is associated with serum leptin and body fat in normal female twins. *Obesity, 15,* 5–9.

Janacek, R. J., Anderson, N., Liu, M., Zheng, S., Yang, Q., & Tso, P. (2005). Effects of yo-yo diet, caloric restriction, and olestra on tissue distribution of hexachlorobenzene. *American Journal of Physiology and Gastrointestinal Liver Physiology, 288,* G292–G299.

Janssen, I., Craig, W. M., Boyce, W. F., & Picikett, W. (2004). Associations between overweight and obesity with bullying behaviors in school-aged children. *Pediatrics, 113,* 1187–1194.

Janssen, I., Katzmarzyk, P. T., Boyce, W. F., Vereecken, C., Mulvihill, C., Roberts, C., Currie, C., & Pickett, W. (2005). Comparison of overweight and obesity prevalence in school-aged youth from 34 countries and their relationships with physical activity and dietary patterns. *Obesity Reviews, 6,* 123–132.

Jasik, C. B., & Lustig, R. H. (2008). Adolescent obesity and puberty: the "perfect storm". *Annals of the New York Academy of Sciences, 1135,* 265–279.

Jaswal, V. K., & Fernald, A. (2007). Learning to communicate. In A. Slater & M. Lewis (Eds.), *Introduction to infant development* (2nd ed.). New York: Oxford University Press.

Jellinger, K. A., & Attems, J. (2007). Neuropatholgoical evaluation of mixed dementia. *Journal of the Neurological Sciences, 257,* 80–87.

Jenkins, J. M., & Astington, J. W. (1996). Cognitive factors and family structure associated with theory of mind development in young children. *Developmental Psychology, 32,* 70–78.

Jenni, O. G., & Carskadon, M. A. (2007). Sleep behavior and sleep regulation from infancy through adolescence: normative aspects. In O. G. Jenny & M. A. Carskadon (Eds), *Sleep Medicine Clinics: Sleep in Children and Adolescents.* Philadelphia: W.B. Saunders.

Jensen, P. S., & others. (2007). 3-year follow-up of the NIMH MTA study. *Journal of the American Academy of child and Adolescent Psychiatry, 46,* 989–1002.

Ji, B. T., Shu, X. O., Linet, M. S., Zheng, W., Wacholde, S., Gao, Y. T., Ying, D. M., & Jin, E. (1997). Paternal cigarette smoking and the risk of childhood cancer among offspring of nonsmoking mothers. *Journal of the National Cancer Institute, 89,* 238–244.

Ji, C. Y., & Chen, T. J. (2008, in press). Secular changes in stature and body mass index for Chinese youth in sixteen major cities, 1950s–2005. *American Journal of Human Biology.*

Jiao, S., Ji, G., & Jing, Q. (1996). Cognitive development of Chinese urban only children and children with siblings. *Child Development, 67,* 387–395.

Johansson, E. (2006). Children's morality: Perspectives and research. In B. Spodak & N. Saracho (Eds.), *Handbook of research on the education of young children* (2nd ed.). Mahwah, NJ: Erlbaum.

Johnson, A. A., & others. (2007). Determinants of inadequate prenatal care utilization by African American women. *Journal of Health Care for the Poor and Underserved, 18,* 620–636.

Johnson, A. D., Tarrant, K., & Brooks-Gunn J. (2008). Early childhood education and care: An opportunity to enhance the lives of poor children. In D. R. Crane & T. B. Heaton (Eds.), *Handbook of families and poverty.* Thousand Oaks, CA: Sage.

Johnson, A. N. (2007). Factors influencing implementation of kangaroo holding in a special care nursery. *MCN American Journal of Maternal Child Nursing, 32,* 25–29.

Johnson, C. L., & Troll, L. E. (1992). Family functioning in late life. *Journals of Gerontology, 47,* S66–S72.

Johnson, G. B. (2008). *The living world* (5th ed.). New York: McGraw-Hill.

Johnson, H. L., Erbelding, E. J., & Ghanem, K. G. (2007). Sexually transmitted infections during pregnancy. *Current Infectious Disease Reports, 9,* 125–133.

Johnson, J. G., Zhang, B., Greer, J. A., & Prigerson, H. G. (2007). Parental control, partner dependency, and complicated grief among widowed adults in the community. *Journal of Nervous and Mental Disease, 195,* 26–30.

Johnson, J. S., & Newport, E. L. (1991). Critical period effects on universal properties of language: The status of subjacency in the acquisition of a second language. *Cognition, 39,* 215–258.

Johnson, R. J. (2008). Advances in understanding and treating childhood sexual abuse: Implications for research and policy. *Family and Community Health, 31* (Suppl. 1), S24–S31.

Johnson, S. (2007). Cognitive and behavioral outcomes following very preterm birth. *Seminars in Fetal and Neonatal Medicine, 12,* 363–373.

Johnson, T. E., Lithow, G. J., Murakami, S., & Shook, D. R. (2007). Genetics. In J. E. Birren (Ed.), *Encyclopedia of gerontology* (2nd ed.). San Diego: Academic Press.

John-Steiner, V. (2007). Vygotsky on thinking and speaking. In H. Daniels, J. Wertsch, & M. Cole (Eds.), *The Cambridge companion to Vygotsky.* New York: Cambridge University Press.

Johnston, A. P., De Lisio, M., & Parise, G. (2008). Resistance training, sarcopenia, and the mitochondrial theory of aging. *Applied Physiology, Nutrition, and Metabolism, 33,* 191–199.

Johnston, B. B. (2008). Will increasing folic acid in fortified grain products further reduce neural tube defects without causing harm?: Consideration of the evidence. *Pediatric Research, 63,* 2–8.

Johnston, L. D., O'Malley, P. M., Bachman, J. G., & Schulenberg, J. E. (2007). *Monitoring the future national survey results on drug use, 1975–2006. Vol. II: College students and adults ages 19–45* (NIH Publication No. 07-6206). Bethesda, MD: National Institute on Drug Abuse.

Johnston, L. D., O'Malley, P. M., Bachman, J. G., & Schulenberg, J. E. (2008). *Monitoring the Future national results on adolescent drug use: Overview of key findings, 2007.* Bethesda, MD: National Institute on Drug Abuse.

Joint Economic Committee. (2007, February). *Investing in raising children.* Washington, DC: U.S. Senate.

Jolley, S. N., Ellmore, S., Barnard, K. E., & Carr, D. B. (2007). Dysregulation of the hypothalamic-pituitary-adrenal axis in postpartum depression. *Biological Research for Nursing, 8,* 210–222.

Jolly, C. A. (2005). Diet manipulation and prevention of aging, cancer, and autoimmune disease. *Current Opinions in Clinical Nutrition and Metabolic Care, 8,* 382–387.

Jones, D. C., Bain, N., & King, S. (2008). Weight and muscularity concerns as longitudinal predictors of body image among early adolescent boys: a test of the dual path model. *Body Image, 5,* 195–204.

Jones, H. W. (2007). Iatrogenic multiple births: A 2003 checkup. *Fertility and Sterility, 87,* 453–455.

Jones, M. C. (1965). Psychological correlates of somatic development. *Child Development, 36,* 899–911.

Jones, M. D., & Galliher, R. V. (2007). Ethnic identity and psychosocial functioning in Navajo adolescents. *Journal of Research on Adolescence, 17,* 683–696.

Jopp, D., & Rott, C. (2006). Adaptation in very old age: Exploring the role of resources and attitudes for centenarians' happiness. *Psychology and Aging, 21,* 266–280.

Jordan, S. J., & others. (2008, in press). Serious ovarian, fallopian tube, and primary peritoneal cancers: A comprehensive epidemiological analysis. *International Journal of Cancer.*

Jorgensen, M. E., Borch-Johnsen, K., & Bjerregaard, P. (2006). Lifestyle modifies obesity-associated risk of cardiovascular disease in a genetically homogeneous population. *American Journal of Clinical Nutrition, 84,* 29–36.

Joseph, J. (2006). *The missing gene.* New York: Algora.

Joshi, S., & Kotecha, S. (2007). Lung growth and development. *Early Human Development, 83,* 789–794.

Juffer, F., Bakermans-Kranenburg M. J., & van IJzendoorn, M. H. (2007). *Promoting positive parenting.* Mahwah, NJ: Erlbaum.

Juffer, F., & van IJzendoorn, M. H. (2005). Behavior problems and mental health referrals of international adoptees: A meta-analysis. *Journal of the American Medical Association, 293,* 2501–2513.

Juffer, F., & van IJzendoorn, M. H. (2007). Adoptees do not lack self-esteem: A meta—analysis of studies on self-esteem of transracial, international, and domestic adoptees. *Psychological Bulletin, 133,* 1067–1083.

Jumping-Eagle, S., Sheeder, J., Kelly, L. S., & **Stevens-Simon, C.** (2008). Association of conventional goals and perceptions of pregnancy with female teenagers' pregnancy avoidance behavior and attitudes. *Perspectives on Sexual and Reproductive Health, 40,* 74–80.

Jung, C. (1933). *Modern man in search of a soul.* New York: Harcourt Brace.

Jusczyk, P. W. (2000). *The discovery of spoken language.* Cambridge, MA: MIT Press.

Jusczyk, P. W., & Hohne, E. A. (1997). Infants' memory for spoken words. *Science, 277,* 1984–1986.

Juvonen, J., & Galvan, A. (2008). Peer influence in involuntary social groups: Lessons from research on bullying. In M. J. Prinstein & K. A. Dodge (Eds.), *Understanding peer influence in children and adolescents.* New York: Guilford.

K

Kaasa, S. (2008). Editorial: Palliative care research—time to intensify international collaboration. *Palliative Medicine, 22,* 301–302.

Kafai, Y. B. (2006). Constructivism. In R. K. Sawyer (Ed.), *The Cambridge handbook of the learning sciences.* New York: Cambridge University Press.

Kagan, J. (1987). Perspectives on infancy. In J. D. Osofsky (Ed.), *Handbook on infant development* (2nd ed.). New York: Wiley.

Kagan, J. (2002). Behavioral inhibition as a temperamental category. In R. J. Davidson, K. R. Scherer, & H. H. Goldsmith (Eds.), *Handbook of affective sciences.* New York: Oxford University Press.

Kagan, J. (2008). Fear and wariness. In M. M. Haith & J. B. Benson (Eds.), *Encyclopedia of infant and early childhood development.* Oxford, UK: Elsevier.

Kagan, J. (2009, in press). Temperament. In R. E. Tremblay, deV Peters, M. Boivan, & R. G. Barr (Eds.), *Encyclopedia on Early Childhood Development.* Montreal: Center of Excellence for Early Childhood Development.

Kagan, J., Snidman, N., Kahn, V., & Towsley, S. (2007). The preservation of two infant temperaments into adolescence. *Monographs of the Society for Research in Child Development, 72* (2), 1–75.

Kagan, J. J., Kearsley, R. B., & Zelazo, P. R. (1978). *Infancy: Its place in human development.* Cambridge, MA: Harvard University Press.

Kagan, S. H. (2008). Faculty profile, University of Pennsylvania School of Nursing. Retrieved January 5, 2008, from www.nursing.upenn.edu/faculty/profile.asp.

Kagan, S. L., & Kauerz, K. (2009, in press). Preschool programs: Effective curricula. In R. G. Tremblay, R. deV Peters, M. Boivin, & R. G. Barr (Eds.), *Encyclopedia of early childhood development.* Montreal: Centre for Early Childhood Development.

Kagan, S. L., & Scott-Little, C. (2004). Early learning standards. *Phi Delta Kappan, 82,* 388–395.

Kagitcibasi, C. (2007). *Family, self, and human development across cultures.* Mahwah, NJ: Erlbaum.

Kagiyama, S., & others. (2008). Association between blood pressure and mortality in 80-year-old subjects from a population-based prospective study in Japan. *Hypertension Research, 31,* 265–270.

Kail, R. V. (2007). Longitudinal evidence that increases in processing speed and working memory enhance children's reasoning. *Psychological Science, 18,* 312–313.

Kaleth, A. S., Chittenden, T. W., Hawkins, B. J., Hargens, T. A., Guill, S. G., Zedalis, D., Gregg, J. M., & Herbert, W. G. (2007). Unique cardiopulmonary exercise test responses in overweight middle-aged adults with obstructive sleep apnea. *Sleep Medicine, 8,* 160–168.

Kalick, S. M., & Hamilton, T. E. (1986). The matching hypothesis reexamined. *Journal of Personality and Social Psychology, 51,* 673–682.

Kalish, R. A. (1981). *Death, grief, and caring relationships.* Monterey, CA: Brooks/Cole.

Kalish, R. A. (1987). Death. In G. L. Maddox (Ed.), *Encyclopedia of aging.* New York: Springer.

Kalish, R. A., & Reynolds, D. K. (1976). *An overview of death and ethnicity.* Farmingdale, NY: Baywood.

Kammerman, S. B. (1989). Child care, women, work, and the family: An international overview of child-care services and related policies. In J. S. Lande, S. Scarr, & N. Gunzenhauser (Eds.), *Caring for children: Challenge to America.* Hillsdale, NJ: Erlbaum.

Kammerman, S. B. (2000a). Parental leave policies. *Social Policy Report of the Society for Research in Child Development, XIV* (No. 2), 1–15.

Kammerman, S. B. (2000b). From maternity to paternity child leave policies. *Journal of the Medical Women's Association, 55,* 98–99.

Kammerman, S. B. (2009, in press). Maternity, paternity, and parental leave policies. In R. E. Tremblay, deV Peters, M. Boivan, & R. G. Barr (Eds.), *Encyclopedia on Early Childhood Development.* Montreal: Center of Excellence for Early Childhood Development.

Kane, R. L. (2007). Health care and services. In J. E. Birren (Ed.), *Encyclopedia of gerontology* (2nd ed.). San Diego: Academic Press.

Kanner, A. D., Coyne, J. C., Schaefer, C., & **Lazarus, R. S.** (1981). Comparison of two modes of stress measurement: Daily hassles and uplifts versus major life events. *Journal of Behavioral Medicine, 4,* 1–39.

Kanoy, K., Ulku-Steiner, B., Cox, M., & **Burchinal, M.** (2003). Marital relationship and individual psychological characteristics that predict physical punishment of children. *Journal of Family Psychology, 17,* 20–28.

Kapornai, K., & Vetro, A. (2008). Depression in children. *Current Opinion in Psychiatry, 21,* 1–7.

Karasik, R. J., & Hamon, R. R. (2007). Cultural diversity and aging families. In B. S. Trask & R. R. Hamon (Eds.), *Cultural diversity and families.* Thousand Oaks, CA: Sage.

Karasu, S. R. (2007). The institution of marriage: Terminable or interminable? *American Journal of Psychotherapy, 61,* 1–16.

Karnes, F. A., & Stephens, K. R. (2008, in press). *Achieving excellence: Educating the gifted and talented.* Upper Saddle River, NJ: Prentice Hall.

Karney, B. R., & Bradbury, T. N. (2005). Contextual influences on marriage. *Current Directions in Psychological Science, 14,* 171–175.

Karney, B. R., Garvan, C. W., & Thomas, M. S. (2003). *Family formation in Florida: 2003 baseline survey of attitudes, beliefs, and demographics relating to marriage and family formation.* Gainesville, FL: University of Florida.

Karniol, R., Grosz, E., & Schorr, I. (2003). Caring, gender-role orientation, and volunteering. *Sex Roles, 49,* 11–19.

Karoly, L. A., & Bigelow, J. H. (2005). *The economics of investing in universal preschool education in California.* Santa Monica, CA: RAND Corporation.

Karp, H. (2002). *The happiest baby on the block.* New York: Bantam.

Karpov, Y. V. (2006). *The neo-Vygotskian approach to child development.* New York: Cambridge University Press.

Kastenbaum, R. J. (2004). *Death, society, and human experience* (8th ed.). Boston: Allyn & Bacon.

Kastenbaum, R. J. (2007). *Death, society, and human experience* (9th ed.). Boston: Allyn & Bacon.

Katakura, Y. (2006). Molecular basis for the cellular senescence program and its application to anticancer therapy. *Bioscience, Biotechnology, and Biochemistry, 70,* 1076–1081.

Kato, T. (2005). The relationship between coping with stress due to romantic break-ups and mental health. *Japanese Journal of Social Psychology, 20,* 171–180.

Katz, L. (1999). Curriculum disputes in early childhood education. *ERIC Clearinghouse on Elementary and Early Childhood Education,* Document EDO-PS-99–13.

Katzov, H. (2007). New insights into autism from a comprehensive genetic map. *Clinical Genetics, 72,* 186–187.

Kauffman, J. M., & Hallahan, D. P. (2005). *Special education: What it is and why we need it.* Boston: Allyn & Bacon.

Kauffman, J. M., McGee, K., & Brigham, M. (2004). Enabling or disabling? Observations on changes in special education. *Phi Delta Kappan, 85,* 613–620.

Kaufman, S. R. (2005)*... And a time to die.* New York: Scribner.

Kaur, G., Roberti, M., Raul, F., & Pendurthi, U. R. (2007). Suppression of human monocyte tissue factor induction by red wine phenoloics and synthetic derivatives of resveratrol. *Thrombosis Research, 119,* 247–256.

Kavanaugh, R. D. (2006). Pretend play. In B. Spodek & O. N. Saracho (Eds.), *Handbook of research on the education of young children* (2nd ed.). Mahwah, NJ: Erlbaum.

Kavsek, M. (2004). Predicting IQ from infant visual habituation and dishabituation: A meta-analysis. *Journal of Applied Developmental Psychology, 25,* 369–393.

Kazdin, A. E., & Benjet, C. (2003): Spanking children: Evidence and issues. *Current Directions in Psychological Science, 12,* 99–103.

Keating, D. P. (1990). Adolescent thinking. In S. S. Feldman & G. R. Elliott (Eds.), *At the threshold: The developing adolescent.* Cambridge, MA: Harvard University Press.

Keating, D. P. (2004). Cognitive and brain development. In R. Lerner & L. Steinberg (Ed.), *Handbook of Adolescent Psychology,* New York: Wiley.

Keating, D. P. (2007). Understanding adolescent development: Implications for driving safety. *Journal of Safety Research, 38,* 147–157.

Keen, R. (2005). Unpublished review of J. W. Santrock's *Topical life-span development,* 3rd ed. (New York: McGraw-Hill).

Keenan, K. (2009, in press). The development and socialization of aggression in the first five years of life. In R. E. Tremblay, R. deV Peters, M. Boivin, & R. G. Barr (Eds.), *Encyclopedia on early childhood development.* Montreal: Centre of Excellence for Early Childhood Development.

Keens, T. G., & Gemmill, D. R. (2008). SIDS. In M. M. Haith & J. B. Benson (Eds.), *Encyclopedia of infant and early childhood development.* Oxford, UK: Elsevier.

Keijer, J., & van Schothorst, E. M. (2008). Adipose tissue failure and mitochondria as a possible target for improvement by bioactive food components. *Current Opinion in Lipidology, 19,* 4–10.

Keller, A., Ford, L., & Meacham, J. (1978). Dimensions of self-concept in preschool children. *Developmental Psychology, 14,* 483–489.

Keller, H. (2007). *Cultures of infancy.* Mahwah, NJ: Erlbaum.

Kellman, P. J., & Arterberry, M. E. (2006). Infant visual perception. In W. Damon & R. Lerner (Eds.), *Handbook of child psychology* (6th ed.). New York: Wiley.

Kellman, P. J., & Banks, M. S. (1998). Infant visual perception. In W. Damon (Eds.), *Handbook of child psychology* (5th ed., Vol. 2). New York:

Kellogg, R. T. (2007). *Fundamentals of cognitive psychology.* Thousand Oaks, CA: Sage.

Kellough, R. D., & Carjuzaa, J. D. (2009). *Teaching in the middle and secondary schools* (9th Ed.). Boston: Allyn & Bacon.

Kelly, C., & Marshall, V. W. (2007). Politics of aging. In J. E. Birren (Ed.), *Encyclopedia of gerontology* (2nd ed.). San Diego: Academic Press.

Kelly, D. J., & others. (2005). Three-month-olds, but not newborns, prefer own-race faces. *Developmental Science, 8,* F31–F36.

Kelly, D. J., & others. (2007). Cross-race preferences for same-race faces extend beyond the African versus Caucasian contrast in 3-month-old infants. *Infancy, 11,* 87–95.

Kelly, G. F. (2008). *Sexuality today* (9th ed.). New York: McGraw-Hill.

Kelly, J. B. (2007). Children's living arrangements following separation and divorce: Insights from empirical and clinical research. *Family Process, 46,* 35–52.

Kelly, J. P., Borchert, J., & Teller, D. Y. (1997). The development of chromatic and achromatic sensitivity in infancy as tested with the sweep VEP. *Vision Research, 37,* 2057–2072.

Kempermann, G., Kuhn, H. G., & Gage, F. H. (1997). More hippocampal neurons in adult mice living in an enriched environment. *Nature, 386,* 493–495.

Kempermann, G., van Praag, H., & Gage, F. H. (2000). Activity-dependent regulation of neuronal plasticity and self repair. *Progress in Brain Research, 127,* 35–48.

Kendall, M., Harris, F., Boyd, K., Sheikh, A., Murray, S. A., Brown, D., Mallinson, I., Kearny,

N., & Worth, A. (2007). Key challenges and ways forward in researching the "good death": Qualitative in-depth interview and focus group study. *British Medical Journal, 334,* 485–486.

Kennell, J. H. (2006). Randomized controlled trial of skin-to-skin contact from birth versus conventional incubator for physiological stabilization in 1200 g to 2199 g newborns. *Acta Paediatica (Sweden), 95,* 15–16.

Kennell, J. H., & McGrath, S. K. (1999). Commentary: Practical and humanistic lessons from the third world for perinatal caregivers everywhere. *Birth, 26,* 9–10.

Kenner, C., Sugrue, N. M., & Finkelman, A. (2007). Poverty and neonatal outcomes: How nurses around the world can make a difference. *Nursing and Women's Health, 11,* 468–473.

Kessels, R. P., Boekhorst, S. T., & Postma, A. (2005). The contribution of implicit and explicit memory to the effects of errorless learning: A comparison between younger and older adults. *Journal of the international Neuropsychological Society, 11,* 144–151.

Kessen, W., Haith, M. M., & Salapatck, P. (1970). Human infancy. In P. H. Mussen (Ed.), *Manual of child psychology* (3rd ed., Vol. 1). New York: Wiley.

Kessler, R. C., & Walters, E. E. (1998). Epidemiology of *DSM-III-R* major depression and minor depression among adolescents and young adults in the National Comorbidity Survey. *Depression and Anxiety, 7,* 3–14.

Ketcham, C. J., & Stelmach, G. E. (2001). Age-related declines in motor control. In J. E. Birren & K. W. Schale (Eds.), *Handbook of the psychology of aging* (5th ed.). San Diego: Academic Press.

Key, J. D., Gebregziabher, M. G., Marsh, L. D., & O'Rourke, K.M. (2008). Effectiveness of an intensive, school-based intervention for teen mothers. *Journal of Adolescent Health, 42,* 394–400.

Keyes, C. L. M., & Ryff, C. D. (1998). Generativity in adult lives: Social structure contours and quality of life consequences. In D. P. McAdams & E. de St. Aubin (Eds.), *Generativity and adult development: How and why we care for the next generation.* Washington, DC: American Psychological Association.

Kiecolt-Glaser, J. K., & Glaser, R. (1988). Behavioral influences on immune function. In T. Field, P. McCabe, & N. Schneiderman (Eds.), *Stress and coping across development.* Hillsdale, NJ: Erlbaum.

Kiecolt-Glaser, J. K., McGuire, L., Robles, T. F., & Glaser, R. (2002). Psychoneuro-immunology and psychosomatic medicine: Back to the future. *Psychosomatic Medicine, 64,* 15–28.

Kiecolt-Glaser, J. K., Preacher, K. J., MacCallum, R. C., Atkinson, C., Malarkey, W. B., & Glaser, R. (2003). Chronic stress and age-related increases in the proinflammatory cytokine IL-6. *Proceedings of the National Academy of Sciences USA, 100,* 9090–9095.

Kilmartin, C., & Allison, J. (2007). *Men's violence against women.* Mahwah, NJ: Erlbaum.

Kim, J. A., Wei, Y., & Sowers, J. R. (2008). Role of mitochondrial dysfunction in insulin resistance. *Circulation Research, 102,* 401–414.

Kim, J. E., & Moen, P. (2002). Retirement transitions, gender, and psychological wellbeing: A life-course, ecological model. *Journals of Gerontology B: Psychological Sciences and Social Sciences, 57,* P212–P222.

Kim, J.E., & Cicchetti, D. (2006). Longitudinal trajectories of self-system processes and the depressive symptoms among maltreated and non-maltreated children. *Child Development, 77,* 624–639.

Kim, J.E., Peterson, K. E., Scanlon, K. S., Fitzmaurice, G. M., Must, A., Oken, E., Rifas-Shiman, S. L., Rich-Edwards, J. W., & Gillman, M. W. (2006). Trends in overweight from 1980 through 2001 among preschool-aged children enrolled in a health maintenance organization. *Obesity, 14,* 1107–1112.

Kim, S., Hasher, L. (2005). The attraction effect in decision making: Superior performance by older adults. *Quarterly Journal of Experimental Psychology, 58A,* 120–133.

Kim, S. C. (2008, in press). Sexual attitude and perception on sexual relationship among long-term users of sildenafil. *Journal of Sexual Medicine.*

Kim, S. K. (2007). Common aging pathways in worms, flies, mice, and humans. *Journal of Experimental Biology, 210,* 1607–1612.

Kim, S. Y., Su, J., Yancurra, L., & Yee, B. (2009). Asian American and Pacific Islander families. In N. Tewari & A. Alvarez (Eds.), *Asian American psychology.* Clifton, NJ: Psychology Press.

Kim, T. W., Wee, W. R., Lee, J. H., & Kim, M. K. (2007) Contrast sensitivity after LASIK, LASEK, and wavefront-guided LASEK with the VISX S4 laser. *Journal of Refractive Surgery, 23,* 355–361.

Kimber, L., McNabb, M., McCourt, C., Haines, A., & Brocklehurst, P. (2008, in press). Massage or music for pain relief in labor: A pilot randomized placebo controlled trial. *European Journal of Pain.*

Kimbro, R. T., Brooks-Gunn, J., & McClanahan, S. (2006). Racial and ethnic differences in overweight and obesity among 3-year-old children. *American Journal of Public Health, 97,* 298–305.

Kimmel, A. J. (2007). *Ethical issues in behavioral research.* Malden, MA: Blackwell.

King, A. A., DeBraun, M. R., & White, D. A. (2008). Need for cognitive rehabilitation for children with sickle-cell disease and strokes. *Expert Review of Neurotherapeutics, 8,* 291–296.

King, K. M., & Chassin, L. (2007). A prospective study of the effects of age of initiation of alcohol and drug use on young adult substance dependence. *Journal of Studies on Alcohol and Drugs, 68,* 256–265.

King, L. A., & Hicks, J. A. (2007). Whatever happened to "What might have been?" Regrets, happiness, and maturity. *American Psychologist, 62,* 625–636.

King, V., & Scott, M. E. (2005). A comparison of cohabiting relationships among older and younger adults. *Journal of Marriage and the Family, 67,* 271–285.

Kingston, N. (2008). Standardized tests. In N. J. Salkind (Ed.), *Encyclopedia of educational -psychology.* Thousand Oaks, CA: Sage.

Kinney, J. (2009). *Loosening The grip* (9th ed.). New York: McGraw-Hill.

Kirby, D., Laris, B. A., & Rolleri, L. A. (2007). Sex and HIV education programs: Their impact on sexual behaviors of young people throughout the world. *Journal of Adolescent Health, 40,* 206–217.

Kirsch, G., McVey, G., Tweed, S., & Katzman, D. K. (2007). Psychosocial profiles of young adolescent females seeking treatment for an eating disorder. *Journal of Adolescent Health, 40,* 351–356.

Kisilevsky, B. S., Hains, S. M., Lee, K., Xic, X., Huang, H., Ye, H. H., Zhang, K., & Wang, Z. (2003). Effects of Experiences on fetal voice recognition. *Psychological Science, 14,* 220–224.

Kisilevsky, S., Hains, S. M., Jacquet, A. Y., Granier-Deferre, C., & Lecanuet, J. P. (2004). Maturation of fetal responses to music. *Developmental Science, 7,* 550–559.

Kistner, J., A., David-Ferdon, C. F., Repper, K. K., & Joiner, T. E. (2006). Bias and accuracy of children's perceptions of peer acceptance: Prospective associations with depressive symptoms. *Journal of Abnormal Child Psychology, 34,* 349–361.

Kitchener, K. S., King, P. M., & DeLuca, S. (2006). The development of reflective judgment in adulthood. In C. Hoare (Ed.), *Handbook of adult development and learning.* New York: Oxford University Press.

Kitzmann, K. M. (2009, in press). Domestic violence and its impact on the social and emotional development of young children. In R. E. Tremblay, R. deV Peters, M. Boivin, & R. G. Barr (Eds.), *Encyclopedia of early childhood development.* Montreal: Centre of Excellence for Early Childhood Development.

Kivnik, H. Q., & Sinclair, H. M. (2007). Grandparenthood. In J. E. Birren (Ed.), *Encyclopedia of gerontology* (2nd ed.). San Diego: Academic Press.

Klaczynski, P. (2005). Metacognition and cognitive variability: A two-process model of decision making and its development. In J. Jacobs & P. Klaczynski (Eds.), *The development of decision making: cognitive, sociocultural, and legal perspectives.* Mahwah, NJ: Erlbaum.

Klaczynski, P. A., & Narasimham, G. (1998). Development of scientific reasoning biases: Cognitive versus ego-protective explanations. *Developmental Psychology, 34,* 175–187.

Klaus, M., & Kennell, H. H. (1976). *Maternal-infant bonding.* St. Louis: Mosby.

Klieger, C., Pollex, E., & Koren, G. (2008). Treating the mother—protecting the newborn: The safety of hypoglycemic drugs in pregnancy. *Journal of Maternal-Fetal and Neonatal Medicine, 21,* 191–196.

Kliegman, R. M., Behrman, R. E., Jenson, H. B., & Stanton, B. F. (2007). *Nelson textbook of pediatrics* (18th ed.). London: Elsevier.

Klimes-Dougan, B., & Zeman, J. (2007). Introduction to the special issue of social development: Emotion socialization in childhood and adolescence. *Social Development, 16,* 203–209.

Kline, D. W., & Scialfa, C. T. (1996). Visual and auditory aging. In J. E. Birren & K. W. Schaie (Eds.), *Handbook of the psychology of aging* (4th ed.). San Diego: Academic Press.

Kline, G. H., Stanley, S. M., Markman, H. J., Olmos-Gallo, P. A., S. Peters, M., Whitton, S. W., & Prado, L. M. (2004). Timing is everything: Pre-engagement cohabitation and -increased risk for poor marital outcomes. *Journal of Family Psychology, 18,* 311–318.

Kling, K. C., Hyde, J. S., Showers, C. J., & Buswell, B. N. (1999). Gender differences in self-esteem: A meta-analysis. *Psychological Bulletin, 125,* 470–500.

Klingman, A. (2006). Children and war trauma. In W. Damon & R. Lerner (Eds.), *Handbook of child psychology* (6th ed.). New York: Wiley.

Knight, B. G., Kaski, B., Shurgot, G. R., & Dave, J. (2006). Improving the mental health of older adults. In J. E. Birren & K. W. Schaie (Eds.), *Handbook of the psychology of aging.* (6th ed.). San Diego: Academic Press.

Knight, B. G., & Lee, L. (2007). Mental health. In J. E. Birren (Ed.), *Encyclopedia of gerontology* (2nd ed.). San Diego: Academic Press.

Knowles, R. (2004). *Alzheimer's disease.* Upper Saddle River, NJ: Prentice Hall.

Kochanska, G., & Aksan, N. (2007). Conscience in childhood: Past, Present, and future *Merrill-Palmer Quarterly, 50,* 299–310.

Kochanska, G., Aksan, N., Knaack, A., & Rhines, H. M. (2004). Maternal parenting and children's conscience: Early security as a moderator. *Child Development, 75,* 1229–1242.

Kochanska, G., Aksan, N., Prisco, T. R., & Adams, E. E. (2008). Mother-child and father-child mutually responsive orientation in the first two years and children's outcomes at preschool age: Mechanisms of influence. *Child Development, 79,* 30–44.

Koenig, H. G. (2001). Religion and medicine II: Religion, mental health, and related behaviors. *International Journal of Psychiatry. 31,* 97–109.

Koenig, H. G. (2007). Religion and remission of depression in medical inpatients with heart failure/pulmonary disease. *Journal of Nervous and Mental Disease, 195,* 389–395.

Koenig, H. G., & Blazer, D. G. (1996). Depression. In J. E. Birren (Ed.), *Encyclopedia of gerontology* (Vol. 1). San Diego: Academic Press.

Koenig, H. G., Cohen, H. J., Blazer, D. G., Pieper, C., Meador, K. G., Shelp, F., Goldi, V., & DiPasquale, R. (1992). Religious coping and depression in elderly hospitalized medically ill men. *American Journal of Psychiatry, 149,* 1693–1700.

Koenig, H. G., Smiley, M., & Gonzales, J. A. T. (1988). *Religion, health, and aging.* New York: greenwood Press.

Koenig, L. B., McGue, M., & Iacono, W. G. (2008). Stability and change in religiousness during emerging adulthood. *Developmental Psychology, 44,* 523–543.

Kohlberg, L. (1958). *The development of modes of moral thinking and choice in the years 10 to 16.* Unpublished doctoral dissertation. University of Chicago.

Kohlberg, L. (1969). Stage and sequence: The cognitive-developmental approach to socialization. In D. A. Goslin (Ed.), *Handbook of socialization theory and research.* Chicago: Rand McNally.

Kohlberg, L. (1986). A current statement of some theoretical issues. In S. Modgil & C. Modgil (Eds.), *Lawrence Kohlberg.* Philadelphia: Falmer.

Kohler, P. K., Manhart, L. E., & Lafferty, W. E. (2008). Abstinence-only and comprehensive sex education and the initiation of sexual activity and teen pregnancy. *Journal of Adolescent Health, 42,* 344–351.

Kohler, T. S., Kim, J., Feia, K., Bodi, J., Johnson, M., Makhlouf, A., & Monga, M. (2008). Prevalence of androgen deficiency in men with erectile dysfunction. *Urology, 71,* 693–697.

Koolhof, R., Loeber, R., Wei, E. H., Pardini, D., & D'escury, A. C. (2007). Inhibition deficits of serious delinquent boys of low intelligence. *Criminal Behavior and Mental Health, 17,* 274–292.

Kopp, C. B. (2008). Self-regulatory processes. In M. M. Haith & J. B. Benson (Eds.), *Encyclopedia of infant and early childhood development.* Oxford, UK: Elsevier.

Koppelman, K., & Goodheart, L. (2008). *Understanding human differences* (2nd ed.). Boston: Allyn & Bacon.

Korantzopoulos, P., Kolettis, T. M., Galaris, D., & Goudevenos, J. A. (2007). The role of oxidative stress in the pathogenesis and perpetuation of arterial fibrillation. *International Journal of Cardiology, 115,* 135–143.

Korrick, S. A., & Sagiv, S. K. (2008). Polychlorinated biphenyls, organopesticides, and neurodevelopment. *Current Opinion in Pediatrics, 20,* 198–204.

Kostelnik, M. J., Soderman, A. K., & Whiren, A. P. (2007). *Developmentally appropriate curriculum* (4th ed.). Upper Saddle River, NJ: Prentice Hall.

Koster, A., & others. (2008). Joint effects of adiposity and physical activity on incident mobility limitation in older adults. *Journal of the American Geriatric Society. 56,* 636–643.

Kostka, T., & Praczko, K. (2007). Interrelationship between physical activity, symptomatology of upper respiratory tract infections, and depression in elderly people. *Gerontology, 53,* 187–193.

Kotovsky, L., & Baillargeon, R. (1994). Calibration-based reasoning about collision events in 11-month-old infants. *Cognition, 51,* 107–129.

Kotre, J. (1984). *Outliving the self: Generativity and the interpretation of lives.* Baltimore: Johns Hopkins University Press.

Kottak, C. P. (2004). *Cultural anthropology* (10th ed.). New York: McGraw-Hill.

Koukoura, O., Sifakis, S., Stratoudakis, G., Manta, N., Kaminopetros, P., & Koumantakis, E. (2006). A case report of recurrent anencephaly and literature review. *Clinical and Experimental Obstetrics and Gynecology, 33,* 185–189.

Koulikov, D., Fridmans, A., Chertin, B., Shenfeld, O., Farkas, A., & Spitz, I. M. (2007). Is sildenafil citrate associated with an amelioration of the symptomatology of androgen decline in the aging male? *Journal of Urology, 177,* 2267–2271.

Kowalski, S. D., & Bondmass, M. D. (2008). Physiological and psychological symptoms of grief in widows. *Research in Nursing and Health, 31,* 23–30.

Kozol, J. (2005). *The Shame of the nation.* New York: Crown.

Krakoff, L. R. (2008). Older patients need better guidelines for optimal treatment of high blood pressure: I size fits few. *Hypertension, 51,* 817–818.

Kramer, A. F., & Erickson, K. I. (2007). Capitalizing on cortical plasticity: Influence of physical activity on cognition and brain functioning. *Trends in Cognitive Science, 11,* 342–348.

Kramer, A. F., Hahn, S., Cohen, N. J., Banich, M. T., McAuley, E., Harrison, C., Chason, J., Vakil, E., Bardell, L., Boileau, R., & Colcombe, A. (1999, July). Ageing, fitness, and neurocognitive function. *Nature, 400,* 418–419.

Kramer, A. F. & Madden, D. (2008). Attention. In F. I. M. Craik & T. A. Salthouse (Eds.), *The handbook of aging and cognition* (3rd ed.). Philadelphia: Psychology Press.

Kramer, A. F., & Morrow, D. (2009, in press). Cognitive training and expertise. In D. Park & N. Schwartz (Eds.), *Cognitive aging* (2nd ed.). Clifton, NJ: Psychology Press.

Kramer, L. (2006, July 10). Commentary in "How your siblings make you who you are" by J. Kluger. *Time,* pp. 46–55.

Kramer, L., & Perozynski, L. (1999). Parental beliefs about managing sibling conflict. *Developmental Psychology, 35,* 489–499.

Kramer, L., & Radey, C. (1997). Improving sibling relationships among young children: A social skills training model. *Family Relations, 46,* 237–246.

Kramer, M. (2003). Commentary: Breastfeeding and child health, growth, and survival. *International Journal of Epidemiology, 32,* 96–98.

Kramer, P. (1993). *Listening to Prozac.* New York: Penguin Books.

Kraska, M. (2008). Quantitative research methods. In N. J. Salkind (Ed.), *Encyclopedia of educational psychology.* Thousand Oaks, CA: Sage.

Krause, N. (2003). Religious meaning and subjective well-being in late life. *Journals of Gerontology B: Psychological Sciences and Social Sciences, 58,* S160–S170.

Krause, N., Ingersoll-Dayton, B., Liang, J., & Sugisawa, H. (1999). Religion social -behavior and health among the Japanese -elderly. *Journal of Health and Social Behavior, 40,* 405–421.

Kreutzer, M., Leonard, C., & Flavell, J. H. (1975). An interview study of children's knowledge about memory. *Monographs of the Society for Research in Child Development.* 40 (1, Serial No. 159).

Kroger, J. (2007). *Identity development: Adolescence through adulthood.* Thousand Oaks, CA: Sage.

Kruger, J., Blanck, H. M. & Gillespie, C. (2006). Dietary and physical activity behaviors among adults successful at weight loss management. *International Journal of Behavioral Nutrition and Physical Activity, 3,* 17.

Krueger, J. I., Vohs, K. D., & Baumeister, R. F. (2008). Is the allure of self-esteem a mirage after all? *American Psychologist, 63,* 64.

Ksir, C. J., Hart, C. L., & Ray, O. S. (2008). *Drugs, society, and human behavior* (12th ed.). New York: McGraw-Hill.

Kübler-Ross, E. (1969). *On death and dying.* New York: Macmillan.

Kuebli, J. (1994, March). Young children's understanding of everyday emotions. *Young Children,* pp. 36–48.

Kuhl, P. K. (1993). Infant speech perception: A window on psycholinguistic development. *International Journal of Psycholinguistics, 9,* 33–56.

Kuhl, P. K. (2000). A new view of language acquisition. *Proceedings of the National Academy of Science.* 97 (22), 11850–11857.

Kuhl, P. K. (2007). Is speech learning "gated" by the social brain? *Developmental Science, 10,* 110–120.

Kuhl, P. K. (2009). Linking infant speech perception to language acquisition: Phonetic learning predicts language growth. In J. Columbo, P. McCardle, & L. Freund (Eds.). *Infant pathways to language.* Clifton, NJ: Psychology Press.

Kuhl, P. K., Stevens, E., Hayashi, A., Deguchi, T., Kiritani, S., & Iverson, P. (2006). Infants show a facilitation for native language phonetic perception between 6 and 12 months. *Developmental Science, 9,* F13–F21.

Kuhn, D. (1998). Afterword to Volume 2: Cognition, perception, and language. In W. Damon (Ed.), *Handbook of child psychology* (5th ed., Vol. 2). New York: Wiley.

Kuhn, D. (1999). A developmental model of critical thinking. *Educational Researcher, 28,* 16–25.

Kuhn, D., & Franklin, S. (2006). The second decade: What develops (and how)? In W. Damon & R. Lerner (Eds.), *Handbook of child psychology* (6th ed.). New York: Wiley.

Kuhn, D., Cheney, R., & Weinstock, M. (2000). The development of epistemological understanding. *Cognitive Development, 15,* 309–328.

Kuhn, D., Schauble, L., & Garcia-Mila, M. (1992). Cross-domain development of scientific reasoning. *Cognition and Instruction, 9,* 285–327.

Kumar, R., & Burns, E. A. (2008). Age-related decline in immunity: Implications for vaccine responsiveness. *Expert Review of Vaccines, 7,* 467–479.

Kupersmidt, J. B., & Coie, J. D. (1990). Preadolescent peer status, aggression, and school adjustment as predictors of externalizing problems in adolescence. *Child Development, 61,* 1350–1363.

Kurdek, L. A. (1997). Adjustment to relationship dissolution in gay, lesbian, and heterosexual partners. *Personal Relationships, 4,* 145–161.

Kurdek, L. A. (2006). Differences between partners from heterosexual, gay, and lesbian cohabiting couples. *Journal of Marriage and the Family, 68,* 509–528.

Kurdek, L. A. (2007). The allocation of household labor between partners in gay and lesbian couples. *Journal of Family Issues, 28,* 132–148.

Kurian, A. K., & Cardarelli, K. M. (2007). Racial and ethnic differences in cardiovascular disease risk factors: A systematic review. *Ethnicity and Disease, 17,* 143–152.

Kurrle, S. E. (2006). Improving acute care services for older people: A collaborative trial is needed. *Medical Journal of Australia, 184,* 427–428.

Kurth, T., Everett, B. M., Buring, J. E., Kase, C. S., Ridker, P. M., & Gaziano, J. M. (2007). Lipid levels and the risk of ischemic stroke in women. *Neurology, 68,* 556–562.

Kyrous, I., & Tsigos, C. (2007). Stress mechanisms and metabolic complications. *Hormone and Metabolic Research, 39,* 430–438.

L

La Greca, A. M., & Harrison, H. M. (2005). Adolescent peer relations, friendships, and romantic relationships: Do they predict social anxiety and depression? *Journal of Clinical Child and Adolescent Psychology, 34,* 49–61.

Labouvie-Vief, G. (1986, August). *Modes of knowing and life-span cognition.* Paper presented at the meeting of the American Psychological Association, Washington, DC.

Labouvie-Vief, G. (2006). Emerging structures of adult thought. In J. J. Arnett & J. L. Tanner (Eds.), *Emerging adults in America.* Washington, DC: American Psychological Association.

Labouvie-Vief, G., & Diehl, M. (1999). Self and personality development. In J. C. Kavanaugh & S. K. Whitbourne (Eds.), *Gerontology: An interdisciplinary perspective.* New York: Oxford University Press.

Lacey, J., Cate, H., & Broadway, D. C. (2008, in press). Barriers to adherence with glaucoma medications: A qualitative research study. *Eye.*

Lachman, M. E. (2004). Development in midlife. *Annual Review of Psychology* (Vol. 55.). Palo Alto, CA: Annual Reviews.

Lachman, M. E. (2006). Perceived control over aging-related declines. *Current Directions in Psychological Science, 15,* 282–286.

Lachman, M. E., & Firth, K. (2004). The adaptive value of feeling in control during midlife. In G. O. Brim., C. D. Ryff, & R. C., Kessler (Eds.), How healthy are we?: A national study of well-being at midlife. Chicago: University of Chicago Press.

Lachman, M. E., Maier, H., & Budner, R. (2000). *A portrait of midlife.* Unpublished manuscript, Brandeis University, Waltham, MA.

Lachman, M. E., & Weaver, S. L. (1998). Sociodemographic variations in the sense of control by domain: Findings from the MacArthur Study of midlife. *Psychology and Aging, 13,* 553–562.

Ladd, G., Buhs, E., & Troop, W. (2004). School adjustment and social skills training. In P. K. Smith & C. H. Hart (Eds.), *Blackwell handbook of childhood social development.* Malden, MA: Blackwell.

Ladd, G. W., Herald, S. L., & Andrews R. K. (2006). Young children's peer relations and social competence. In B. Spodek & O. N. Sarancho (Eds.), *Handbook of research on the education of young children.* Mahwah, NJ: Erlbaum.

Laible, D. J., Carlo, G., & Raffaelli, M. (2000). The differential relations of parent and peer attachment to adolescent adjustment. *Journal of Youth and Adolescence, 29,* 45–53.

Laible, D., & Thompson, R. A. (2007). Early socialization: A relationship perspective. In J. E. Grusec & P. D. Hastings (Eds.), *Handbook of socialization.* New York: Guilford.

Laifer-Narin, S., Budorick, N. E., Simpson, L. L., & Platt, L. D. (2007). Fetal magnetic resonance imaging: A review. *Current Opinion in Obstetrics and Gynecology, 19,* 151–156.

Lainhart, J. E. (2006). Advances in autism neuroimaging research for the clinician and geneticist. *American Journal of Medical Genetics, C: Seminars in Medical Genetics, 142,* 33–39.

Laird, R. D., Criss, M. M., Pettit, G. S., Dodge, K. A., & Bates, J. E. (2008). Parents' monitoring knowledge attenuates the link between antisocial friends and adolescent delinquent behavior. *Journal of Abnormal Child Psychology, 36,* 299–310.

Lajunen, H. R., Keski-Rahkonen, A., Pulkkinen, L., Rose, R. J., Rissanen, A., & Kaprio, J. (2007). Are computer and cell phone use associated with body mass index and overweight? A population study among twin adolescents. *BMC Public Health, 26,* 24.

Lakey, S. L., Gray, S. L., Ciechanowski, P., Schwartz, S., & Logerfo, J. (2008). Antidepressant use in nonmajor depression: Secondary analysis of a program to encourage active, rewarding lives for seniors (PEARLS), a randomized controlled trial in older adults from 2000 to 2003. *American Journal of Pharmacotherapy, 6,* 12–20.

Lamb, C. S., Jackson, L. A., Cassiday, P. B., & Priest, D. J. (1993). Body figure preferences of men and women: A comparison of two generations. *Sex Roles, 28,* 345–358.

Lamb, M. E. (1994). Infant care practices and the application of knowledge. In C. B. Fisher & R. M. Lerner (Eds.), *Applied developmental psychology.* New York McGraw-Hill.

Lamb, M. E. (2000). The history of research on father involvement: An overview. *Marriage and Family Review, 29,* 23–42.

Lamb, M. E. (2005). Attachments, social networks, and developmental contexts. *Human Development, 48,* 108–112.

Lamb, M. E., Bornstein, M. H., & Teti, D. M. (2002). *Development in infancy* (4th ed.). Mahwah, NJ: Erlbaum.

Lamond, A. J., & others. (2008, in press). Measurement and predictors of resilience among community-dwelling older adults. *Journal of Psychiatric Research.*

Lamont, R. F., & Jaggat, A. N. (2007). Emerging drug therapies for preventing spontaneous labor and preterm birth. *Expert Opinion on Investigational Drugs, 16,* 337–345.

Land, K. C., & Yang, Y. (2006). Morbidity, disability, and mortality. In R. H. Binstock & L. K. George (Eds.), *Handbook of aging and the social sciences* (6th ed.). San Diego: Academic Press.

Landau, B., Smith, L., & Jones, S. (1998). Object perception and object naming in early development. *Trends in Cognitive Science, 2,* 19–24.

Landau, L. I. (2008). Tobacco smoke exposure and tracking of lung function into adult life. *Pediatric Respiratory Reviews, 9,* 39–44.

Landry, S. H. (2009, in press). The role of parents in early childhood learning. In R. E. Tremblay, R. deV Peters, M. Boivin, & R. G. Barr (Eds.), *Encyclopedia of early childhood development.* Montreal: Centre of Excellence for Early Childhood Development.

Lane, H. (1976). *The wild boy of Aveyron.* Cambridge, MA: Harvard University Press.

Lang, F. R., & Carstensen, L. L. (1994). Close emotional relationships in late life: Further support for proactive aging in the social domain. *Psychology and Aging, 9,* 315–324.

Langer, E. J. (2000). Mindful learning. *Current Directions in Psychological Science, 9,* 220–223.

Langer, E. J. (2007, August). *Counterclockwise: Mindfulness and aging.* Paper presented at the meeting of the American Psychological Association, San Francisco.

Lanham-New, S. A. (2008). Importance of calcium, vitamin D, and vitamin K for osteoporosis prevention and treatment. *Proceedings of the Nutrition Society, 67,* 163–176.

Lansford, J. E., Miller-Johnson, S., Berlin, L. J., Dodge, K. A., Bates, J. E., & Pettit, G. S. (2007). Early physical abuse and later violent delinquency: A prospective longitudinal study. *Child Maltreatment, 12,* 233–245.

Larbi, A., Franceschi, C., Mazzatti, D., Solana, R., Wikby, A., & Pawelec, G. (2008). Aging of the immune system as a prognostic factor for human longevity. *Physiology, 23,* 64–74.

Larson, K., Russ, S. A., Crall, J. J., & Halfon, N. (2008). Influence of multiple social risks on children's health. *Pediatrics, 121,* 337–344.

Larson, R. W. (2001). How U.S. children and adolescents spend their time: What it does (and doesn't) tell us about their development. *Current Directions in Psychological Science, 10,* 160–164.

Larson, R. W., & Verma, S. (1999). How children and adolescents spend time across the world: Work, play, and developmental opportunities. *Psychological Bulletin, 125,* 701–736.

Larson, R. W., & Wilson, S. (2004). Adolescence across place and time: Globalization and the changing, pathways to adulthood. In R. Lerner & L. Steinberg (Eds.), *Handbook of adolescent psychology.* New York: Wiley.

Larson, R., Pearce, N., Sullivan, P. & Jarrett, R. L. (2007). Participation in youth programs as a catalyst for negotiation of family autonomy with connection. *Journal of Youth and Adolescence, 36* (1), 31–45.

Larson-Meyer, D. E., & others. (2008, in press). Effect of 6-month calorie restriction and exercise on serum and liver lipids and markers of liver function. *Obesity.*

Lasker, J. N., Coyle, B., Li, K., & Ortynsky, M. (2005). Assessment of risk factors for low birth weight deliveries. *Health Care for Women International, 26,* 262–280.

Latham, N. K., Bennett, D. A., Stretton, C. M., & Anderson, C. S. (2004). Systematic review of resistance strength training in older adults. *Journals of Geronotology A: Biological Sciences and Medical Sciences, 59,* M48–M61.

Lauer, R., & Lauer, J. C. (2007). *Marriage and family: The quest for intimacy.* (6th ed.). New York: McGraw-Hill.

Laumann, E. O., West, S., Glasser, D., Carson, C., Rosen, R., & Kang, J. H. (2007). Prevalence and correlates of erectile dysfunction by race and ethnicity among men aged 40 or older in the United States: From the male attitudes regarding sexual health survey. *Journal of Sexual Medicine, 4,* 57–65.

Laurent, G., & others. (2008). Oxidative stress contributes to aging by enhancing angiogenesis and insulin signaling. *Cell Metabolism, 7,* 113–124.

Lawrence, R. A. (2008). Breastfeeding. In M. M. Haith & J. B. Benson (Eds.), *Encyclopedia of infant and early childhood development.* Oxford, UK: Elsevier.

Leadbeater, B. J. R., & Way, N. (2001). *Growing up fast.* Mahwah, NJ: Erlbaum.

Leaper, C., & Brown, C. S. (2008). Perceived experience of sexism among adolescent girls. *Child Development, 79,* 685–704.

Leaper, C., & Friedman, C. K. (2007). The socialization of gender. In J. E. Grusec & P. D. Davidson (Eds.), *Handbook of socialization.* New York: Guilford.

Leaper, C., & Smith, T. E. (2004). A meta-analytic review of gender variations in children's language use: Talkativeness, affiliative speech, and assertive speech. *Developmental Psychology, 40,* 993–1027.

Lee, A., & Chan, S. (2006). Acupuncture and anesthesia. *Best Practices in Research and Clinical Anesthesia, 20,* 303–314.

Lee, B. K., Glass, T. A., McAtee, M. J., Wand, G. S., Bandeen-Roche, K., Bolla, K. I., & Schwartz, B. S. (2007). Associations of salivary cortisol with cognitive function in the Baltimore Memory Study. *Archives of General Psychiatry, 64,* 810–818.

Lee, H. C., El-Sayed, Y. Y., & Gould, J. B. (2008, in press). Population trends in cesarean delivery for breech presentation in the United States, 1997–2003. *American Journal of Obstetrics and Gynecology.*

Lee, H. C., & Wei, Y. H. (2007). Oxidative stress, mitochondrial DNA mutation, and apoptosis in aging. *Experimental Biology and Medicine, 232,* 592–606.

Lee, I. M., Manson, J. E., Hennekens, C. H., & Paffenbarger, R. S. (1993). Bodyweight and mortality: A 27-year-follow-up. *Journal of the American Medical Association, 270,* 2823–2828.

Lee, I. M., & Skerrett, P. J, (2001). Physical activity and all-cause mortality: What is the dose-response relation? *Medical Science and Sports Exercise, 33* (Suppl 6), S459–S471.

Lee, K., Cameron, C. A., Doucette, J., & Talwar, V. (2002). Phantoms and fabrications: Young children's detection of implausible lies. *Child Development, 73,* 1688–1702.

Lee, Y., & Park, K. (2008). Does physical activity moderate the association between depressive symptoms and disability in older adults? *International Journal of Psychiatry, 23,* 249–256.

Lefkowitz, E. S., & Gillen, M. M. (2006). "Sex is just a normal part of life": Sexuality in emerging adulthood. In J. J. Arnett & J. L. Tanner (Eds.), *Emerging adults in America.* Washington, DC: American Psychological Association.

Legerstee, M. (1997). Contingency effects of people and objects on subsequent cognitive functioning in 3-month-old infants. *Social Development, 6,* 307–321.

Lehman, H. C. (1960). The age decrement in outstanding scientific creativity. *American Psychologist, 15,* 128–134.

Lehr, C. A., Hanson, A., Sinclair, M. F., & Christensen, S. L. (2003). Moving beyond dropout prevention towards school completion. *School Psychology Review, 32,* 342–364.

Lehrer, R., & Schauble, L. (2006). Scientific thinking and science literacy: Supporting developmental change in learning contexts. In W. Damon & R. Lerner (Eds.), *Handbook of child psychology* (6th ed.). New York: Wiley.

Leifer, A. D. (1973). *Television and the development of social behavior.* Paper presented at the meeting of the International Society for the Study of Behavioral Development, Ann Arbor, MI.

Leighton, S. (2008). Bereavement therapy with adolescents: Facilitating a process of spiritual growth. *Journal of Child and Adolescent Psychiatric Nursing, 21,* 24–34.

Lempers, J. D., Flavell, E. R., & Flavell, J. H. (1977). The development in very young children of tacit knowledge concerning visual perception. *Genetic Psychology Monographs, 95,* 3–53.

Lennon, E. M., Gardner, J. M., Karmel, B. Z., & Flory, M. J. (2008). Bayley Scales of Infant Development. In M. M. Haith & J. B. Benson (Eds.), *Encyclopedia of infant and early childhood development.* Oxford, UK: Elsevier.

Lenoir, C. P., Mallet, E., & Calenda, E. (2000). Siblings of sudden infant death syndrome and near miss in about 30 families: Is there a genetic link? *Medical Hypotheses, 54,* 408–411.

Lenroot, R. K., & Giedd, J. N. (2006). Brain development in children and adolescents: Insights from anatomical magnetic resonance imaging. *Neuroscience and Biobehavioral Reviews, 30,* 718–729.

Lenzi, T. A., & Johnson, T. R. B. (2008). Screening, prenatal. In M. M. Haith & J. B. Benson (Eds.), *Encyclopedia of infant and early childhood development.* Oxford, UK: Elsevier.

Leonard, B. (2004). Women's conditions occurring in men: breast cancer, osteoporosis, male menopause, and eating disorders. *Nursing Clinics of North America, 39,* 379–393.

Leonardi-Bee, J. A., Smyth, A. R., Britton, J., & Coleman, T. (2008, in press). Environmental tobacco smoke and fetal health: Systematic review and analysis. *Archives of Disease in Childhood: Fetal and Neonatal Edition.*

Leonards, U., Ibanez, V., & Giannakopoulos, P. (2002). The role of stimulus type in age-related changes of visual working memory. *Experimental Brain Research, 146,* 172–183.

Leon-Guerrero, A. (2009). *Social problems* (2nd ed.). Thousand Oaks, CA: Sage.

Leppanen, J. M., Moulson, M., Vogel-Farley, V. K., & Nelson, C. A. (2007). An ERP study of emotional face processing in the adult and infant brain. *Child Development, 78,* 232–245.

Lerner, H. G. (1989). *The dance of intimacy.* New York: Harper & Row.

Lerner, R. M., Boyd, M., & Du, D. (2008). Adolescent development. In I. B. Weiner & C. B. Craighead (Eds.), *Encyclopedia of psychology* (4th ed). Hoboken, NJ: Wiley.

Lerner, R. M., Roeser, R. W., & Phelps, E. (Eds.) (2009, in press). *Positive youth development and spirituality: From theory to research.* West Conshohocken, PA: Templeton Foundation press.

Lero, D. S. (2009, in press). Research on parental leave policies and children's development: Implications for policy makers and service providers. In R. E. Tremblay, R. deV Peters, M. Boivan, & R. G. Barr (Eds.), *Encyclopedia on Early Childhood Development.* Montreal: Center of Excellence for Early Childhood Development.

Lesaux, N. K., & Siegel, L. S. (2003). The development of reading in children who speak English as a second language. *Developmental Psychology, 39,* 1005–1019.

Lesley, C. (2005). *Burning Fence: A Western memoir of fatherhood.* New York: St. Martin's Press.

Lessow-Hurley, J. (2009). *The foundations of dual language instruction* (5th Ed.). Boston: Allyn & Bacon.

Lester, B. M., Tronick, E. Z., & Brazelton, T. B. (2004). The Neonatal Intensive Care Unit Network Neurobehavioral Scale procedures. *Pediatrics, 113.* (Suppl.) S641–S667.

Lester, B. M., Tronick, E. Z., LaGasse, L., Seifer, R., Bauer, C. R., Shankaran, S., Bada,

H. S., Wright, L. L., Smeriglio, V. L., Lu, J., Finnegan, L. P., & Maza, P. L. (2002). The maternal lifestyle study: Effects of substance exposure during pregnancy on neurodevelopmental outcome in 1-month-old infants. *Pediatrics, 110,* 1182–1192.

Leung, A., Ko, P., Chan, K.S., Chi, I., & Chow, N. (2007). Searching health information via the web: Hong Kong Chinese older adults' experience. *Public Health Nursing, 24,* 169–175.

Levant, R. F. (2002). Men and masculinity. In J. Worell (Ed.), *Encyclopedia of women and gender.* San Diego: academic Press.

LeVay, S. (1991). A difference in the hypothalamic structure between heterosexual and homosexual men. *Science, 253,* 1034–1037.

Levelt, W. J. M. (1989). *Speaking: From intention to articulation.* Cambridge, MA: MIT Press.

Leventhal, A. (1994, February). *Peer conformity during adolescence: An integration of developmental, situational, and individual characteristics.* Paper presented at the meeting of the Society for Research on Adolescence, San Diego.

Levine, B., Stuss, D. T., Winocur, G., Binns, M. A., Fahy, L., Mandic, M., Bridges, K., & Robertson, I. H. (2007). Cognitive rehabilitation in the elderly: Effects on strategic behavior in relation to goal management. *Journal of the International Neuropsychological Society, 13,* 143–152.

Levine, L. N., & McCloskey, M. L. (2009). *Teaching learners of English in a mainstream classrooms (K-8).* Boston: Allyn & Bacon.

LeVine, S. (1979). *Mothers and wives: Gusii women of East Africa.* Chicago: University of Chicago Press.

Levinson D. J. (1996). *Seasons of a woman's life.* New York: Alfred Knopf.

Levinson, D. J. (1978). *The seasons of a man's life.* New York: Knopf.

Levinson, S. (2009). Pragmatics, universals in. In P. Hogan (Ed.), *The Cambridge encyclopedia of language sciences.* Cambridge, UK: Cambridge University Press.

Levy, B. R., Slade, M. D., & Gill, T. (2006). Hearing decline predicted by elders' age stereotypes. *Journal of Gerontology B: Psychological Sciences and Social Sciences, 61,* P82–P87.

Levy, B. R., Slade, M. D., Kunkel, S. R., & Kasl, S. V. (2002). Longevity increased by positive self-perceptions of aging. *Journal of Personality and Social Psychology, 83,* 261–270.

Lewis, A. C. (2007). Looking beyond NCLB. *Phi Delta Kappan, 88,* 483–484.

Lewis, M. (2005). Selfhood. In B. Hopkins (Ed.). *The Cambridge Encyclopedia of child & development.* Cambridge, UK: Cambridge University Press.

Lewis, M. (2007). Early emotional development. In A. Slater & M. Lewis (Eds.), *Introduction to infant development* (2nd ed.). New York: Oxford University Press.

Lewis, M., & Brooks-Gunn, J. (1979). *Social cognition and the acquisition of the self.* New York: Plenum.

Lewis, M., Feiring, C., & Rosenthal, S. (2000). Attachment over time. *Child Development, 71,* 707–720.

Lewis, M., & Ramsay, D. S. (1999). Effect of maternal soothing and infant stress response. *Child Development, 70,* 11–20.

Li, C., Ford, E. S., McGuire, L. C., & Mokdad, A. H. (2007). Increasing trends in waist circumference and abdominal obesity among US adults. *Obesity, 15,* 216–224.

Li, C., Goran, M. I., Kauer, H., Nollen, N., & Ahluwalia, J. S. (2007). Developmental trajectories of overweight during childhood: Role of early life factors. *Obesity, 15,* 760–761.

Li, D. K., Willinger, M., Petitti, D. B., Odulil, R. K., Liu, L., & Hoffman, H.J. (2006). Use of a dummy (pacifier) during sleep and risk of sudden infant death syndrome (SIDS): Population based case-control study. *British Medical Journal, 332,* 18–22.

Li, S-C., Lindenberger, U., Hommel, B., Aschersleben, G., Prinz, W., & Baltes, P. B. (2004). Transformations in the couplings among intellectual abilities and constituent cognitive processes across the lifespan. *Psychological Science, 15,* 155–163.

Li, Y. (2007). Recovering from spousal bereavement in later life: Does volunteer participation play a role? *Journals of Gerontology B: Psychological Sciences and Social Sciences, 62,* S257–S266.

Li, Y., & Schellhorn, H. E. (2007). Can aging-related degenerative diseases be ameliorated through administration of vitamin C at pharmacological levels? *Medical Hypotheses, 68,* 1315–1317.

Liben, L. S. (1995). Psychology meets geography: Exploring the gender gap on the national geography bee. *Psychological Science Agenda, 8,* 8–9.

Libert, S., Cohen, D., & Guarente, L. (2008). Neurogenesis directed by Sirt 1. *Nature: Cell Biology, 10,* 373–374.

Lidral, A. C., & Murray, J. C. (2005). Genetic approaches to identify disease genes for birth defects with cleft lip/palate as a model. *Birth Defects Research, 70,* 893–901.

Lie, E., & Newcombe, N. (1999). Elementary school children's explicit and implicit memory of faces of preschool classmates. *Developmental Psychology, 35,* 102–112.

Lieberman, E., Davidson, K., Lee-Parritz, A., & Shearer, E. (2005). Changes in fetal position during labor and their association with epidural analgesia. *Obstetrics and Gynecology, 105,* 974–982.

Liegeois, F., Connelly, A., Baldeweg, T., & Vargha-Khadem, F. (2008, in press). Speaking with a single cerebral hemisphere: fMRI language organization after hemispherectomy in childhood. *Brain and Language.*

Lieven, E. (2008). Language development: Overview. In M. M. Haith & J. B. Benson (Eds.), *Encyclopedia of infant and early childhood development.* Oxford, UK: Elsevier.

Lifton, R. J. (1977). The sense of immortality: On death and the continuity of life In H. Feifel (Ed.), *New meanings of death.* New York: McGraw-Hill.

Lillard, A. (2006). Pretend play in toddlers. In C. A. Brownell & C. B. Kopp (Eds.), *Socioemotional development in the toddler year.* New York: Oxford University Press.

Lillard, L. A., & Waite, L. J. (1995). Til death do us part: Marital disruption and mortality. *American Journal of Sociology 100,* 1131–1156.

Lin, J. T., & Lane, J. M. (2008). Nonpharmacological management of osteoporosis to minimize fracture risk. *Nature Clinical Practice: Rheumatology, 4,* 20–25.

Lin, M., Johnson, J. E., & Johnson, K. M. (2003). Dramatic play in Montessori kindergartens in Taiwan and Mainland China. Unpublished manuscript, Department of Curriculum and Instruction, Pennsylvania State University, University Park, PA.

Lin, S. X., & Pi-Sunyer, E. X. (2007). Prevalence of metabolic syndrome among U.S. middle-aged and older adults with the without diabetes—a preliminary analysis of the NHANES 1999–2002. *Ethnicity and Disease, 17,* 35–39.

Lindau, S. T., Schumm, L. P., Laumann, E. O., Levinson, W., O'Muircheartaigh, C. A., & Waite, L. J. (2007). A study of sexuality and health among older adults in the United States. *New England Journal of Medicine, 357,* 762–774.

Lindberg, C., Carstensen, E. L., & Carstensen, L. L. (2008). *Lifelong learning and technology.* Paper prepared for the National Research Council's Committee on Learning Science in Informal Environments. Washington, DC: National Academies Press.

Lindwall, M., Rennemark, M., & Berggren, T. (2008). Movement in mind: The relationship of exercise with cognitive status for older adults in the Swedish National Study on Aging and Care (SNAC). *Aging and Mental Health, 12,* 212–220.

Lindwall, M., Rennemark, H., Halling, A., Berglun, J., & Hassmen, P. (2007). Depression and exercise in elderly men and women: Findings from the Swedish national study on aging and care. *Journal of Aging and Physical Activity, 15,* 41–55.

Lipovetzky, N., Hod, H., Roth, A., Kishon, Y., Sclarovksy, S., & Green, M. S. (2007). Emotional events and anger at the workplace as triggers for a first event of the acute coronary syndrome: A case-crossover study. *The Israel Medical Association Journal, 9,* 310–315.

Lippa, R. A. (2005). Gender, nature, and nurture (2nd ed.), Mahwah, NJ: Erlbaum.

Lippman, L. A., & Keith, J. D. (2006). The demographics of spirituality among youth: International perspectives. In E. Roehlkepartain, P. E. King, L. Wagener, & P. L. Benson (Eds.), *The handbook of spirituality in childhood and adolescence.* Thousand Oaks, CA: Sage.

Liu, A., Hu, X., Ma, G., Cui, Z., Pan, Y., Chang, S. Zhao, W., & Chen, C. (2008). Evaluations of a classroom-based physical activity promoting program. *Obesity Reviews, 9* (Suppl. 1), S130–S134.

Liu, C. H., Murakami, J., Iap, S., & Nagayama Hall, G. C. (2009). Who are Asian Americans? An overview of history, immigration, and communities. In N. Tewari & A. Alvarez (Eds.), *Asian American psychology.* Clifton, NJ: Psychology Press.

Liu, D., Wellman, H. M., Tardif, T., & Sabbagh, M. A. (2008). Theory of mind development in Chinese children: A meta-analysis of false-belief understanding across cultures and languages. *Developmental Psychology, 44,* 523–531.

Liu, W. M., & Hernandez, J. (2008). Social class and classism. In N. J. Salkind (Eds.), *Encyclopedia of educational psychology.* Thousand Oaks, CA: Sage.

Liu, X., Zhao, Z., Jia, C., & Buysse, D. J. (2008). Sleep patterns and problems among Chinese adolescents. *Pediatrics, 121,* 1173.

Liu, Y. J., Xiao, P., Xiong, D. H., Recker, R. R., & Deng, H. W. (2005). Searching for obesity genes: Progress and prospects. *Drugs Today, 41,* 345–362.

Lively, W., & Bromley, D. (1973). *Person perception in childhood and adolescence.* New York: Wiley.

Lo, B., & Rubenfeld, G. (2005). Palliative sedation in dying patients: "We turn to it when everything else hasn't worked." *Journal of the American Medical Association, 294,* 1810–1816.

Locher, J. L., Ritchle, C. S., Roth, D. I., Baker, P. S., Bodner, E. V., & Allman, R. M. (2005). Social isolation, support and capital and nulritional risk in an older sample: Ethnic and gender differences. *Social Science Medicine, 60,* 747–761.

Lochman, J., & the Conduct Problems Prevention Research Group. (2007, March). *Fast Track intervention outcomes in the middle school years.* Paper presented at the meeting of the Society for Research in Child Development, Boston.

Lock, A. (2004). Preverbal communication. In U. Goswami (Ed.), *Blackwell handbook of childhood cognitive development.* Malden, MA: Blackwell.

Lock, M. (1998). Menopause: Lessons from anthropology. *Psychosomatic Medicine, 60,* 410–419.

Lockenhoff, C. E., Costa, P. T., & Lane, R. D. (2008). Age differences in descriptions of emotional experiences in oneself and others. *Journals of Gerontology B: Psychological Sciences and Social Sciences, 63,* P62–P99.

Lockl, K., & Schneider, W. (2007). Knowledge about the mind: Links between theory of mind and later metamemory. *Child Development, 78,* 147–167.

Loebel, M., & Yali, A. M. (1999, August). *Effects of positive expectancies on adjustments to pregnancy.* Paper presented at the meeting of the American Psychological Association, Boston.

Loeber, R., Pardini, D. A., Stouthamer-Loeber, M., & Raine, A. (2007). Do cognitive, physiological, and psychosocial risk and promotive factors predict desistance from delinquency in males? *Development and Psychopathology, 19,* 867–887.

Loehlin, J. C., Horn, J. M., & Ernst, J. L. (2007). Genetic and environmental influences on adult life outcomes: Evidence from the Texas adoption project. *Behavior Genetics, 37,* 463–476.

Loessi, B., Valerius, G., Kopasz, M., Hornyak, M., Riemann, D., & Voderholzer, U. (2008, in press). Are adolescents chronically sleep-deprived? An investigation of sleep habits of adolescents in the Southwest of Germany. *Child Care Health and Development.*

Lofmark, R., & others. (2008). Physicians' experiences with end-of-life decision-making: Survey in 6 European countries and Australia. *BMC Medicine, 12,* 4.

London, M. L., Ladewig, P. A., Ball, J. W., & Bindler, R. A. (2007). *Maternal and child nursing care* (2nd ed.). Upper Saddle River, NJ. Prentice Hall.

Longman, P. (1987). *Born of pay: The new polities of aging in American.* Boston: Houghton-Mifflin.

Longo-Mbenza, B., Lukoki, L. E., & M'Buyamba-Kabangu, J. R. (2007). Nutritional Status, socioeconomic status, heart rate, and blood pressure in African school children and adolescents. *International Journal of Cardiology, 121,* 171–177.

Lopez-Lluch, G., & others. (2006). Calorie restriction induces mitochondrial biogenesis and bioenergetic efficiency. *Proceedings of the National Academy of Sciences USA, 103,* 1768–1773.

Lorenz, F. O., Wickrama, K. A., Conger, R. D., & Elder, G. H. (2006). The short-term and decade-long effects of divorce on women's midlife health. *Journal of Health and Social Behavior, 47,* 117–125.

Lorenz, K. Z. (1965). *Evolution and the modification of behavior.* Chicago: University of Chicago Press.

Loucks, E. B. & others. (2006). Association of educational level with inflammatory markers in the Framingham Offspring Study. *American Journal of Epidemiology, 163,* 622–628.

Loughlin, K. R. (2007). Urologic radiology during pregnancy. *Urology Clinics of North America, 34,* 23–26.

Loukas, A., Suizzo, M-A., & Prelow, H. M. (2007). Examining resource and protective factors in the adjustment of Latino youth in low income families: What role does maternal acculturation play? *Journal of Youth and Adolescence, 36,* 489–501.

Lovden, M., & Lindenberger, U. (2007). Intelligence. In J. E. Birren (Ed.), *Encyclopedia of gerontology* (2nd ed.). San Diego: Academic Press.

Lovden, M., Li, S.C., Shing, Y. L., & Lindenberger, U. (2007). Within-person trial-to-trial variability precedes and predicts cognitive decline in old and very old age: Longitudinal data from the Berlin Aging Study. *Neuropsychologia, 45,* 2827–2838.

Lovheim, H., Sandman, P. O., Karlsson, S., & Gustafson, Y. (208). Behavioral and psychological symptoms of dementia in relation to level of cognitive impairment. *International Psychogeriatrics, 17,* 1–13.

Lozoff, B., Corapci, F., Burden, M. J., Kaciroti, N., Angulo-Baaroso, R., Sazawal, S., & Black, M. (2007). Preschool-aged children with iron deficiency anemia show altered affect and behavior. *Journal of Nutrition, 137,* 683–689.

Lu, M. C., & Lu, J. S. (2008). Prenatal care. In M. M. Haith & J. B. Benson (Eds.), *Encyclopedia of infancy and early childhood development.* Oxford, UK: Elsevier.

Lucas, R. E., Clark, A. E., Yannis, G., & Diener, E. (2004). Unemployment alters the setpoint for life satisfaction. *Psychological Science, 15,* 8–13.

Luchsinger, J. A. (2008, in press). Adiposity, hyperinsulinemia, diabetes, and Alzheimer's disease: An epidemiological perspective. *European Journal of Pharmacology.*

Luders, E., Narr, K. L., Thompson, P. M., Rex, D. E., Jancke, L., Steinmetz, H., & Toga, A. W. (2004). Gender differences in cortical complexity. *Nature Neuroscience, 1,* 799–800.

Ludington-Hoe, S. M., Lewis, T., Morgan, K., Cong, X., Anderson, L., & Reese, S. (2006). Breast and infant temperatures with twins during kangaroo care. *Journal of Obstetric, Gynecologic, and Neonatal Nursing, 35,* 223–231.

Lund, D. A. (2007). Bereavement and loss. In J. E. Birren (Ed.), *Encyclopedia of gerontology* (2nd ed.). San Diego: Academic Press.

Lunkenheimer, E. S., Shields, A. M., & Cortina, K. S. (2007). Parental emotion coaching and dismissing in family interaction. *Social Development, 16,* 232–248.

Lunney, K. M., & others. (2008). HIV-positive poor women may stop breast-feeding early to protect their infants from HIV infection although available replacement diets are grossly inadequate. *Journal of Nutrition, 138,* 351–357.

Luo, L., Hendriks, T., & Craik, F. I. M. (2007). Age differences in recollection: Three patterns of enhanced encoding. *Psychology and Aging, 22,* 269–280.

Luria, A., & Herzog, E. (1985, April). *Gender segregation across and within settings.* Paper presented at the biennial meeting of the Society for Research in Child Development, Toronto.

Lust, B. (2009). Acquisition of language. In P. Hogan (Ed.), *The Cambridge encyclopedia of language sciences.* Cambridge, UK: Cambridge University Press.

Lust, R. (2007). *Child language.* New York: Cambridge University Press.

Luyckx, K., Schwartz, S. J., Goossens, L., Soenens, B., & Beyers, W. (2008a, in press). Developmental typologies of identity formation and adjustment in female emerging adults: A latent class growth analysis approach. *Journal of Research on Adolescence.*

Luyckx, K., Schwarz, S.J., Soenens, B., Vansteenkiste, M., & Goossens, L. (2008b, in press). The path from identity commitments to adjustment: Motivational underpinnings and mediating mechanisms. *Journal of Counseling and Development.*

Luyckx, K., Soenens, B., Goossens, L., & Vansteenkiste, M. (2007). Parenting, identity formation, and college adjustment: A mediation model with longitudinal data. *Identity, 7,* 309–330.

Luyckx, K., Soenens, B., Vansteenkiste, M., Goossens, L., & Berzonsky, M. D. (2008c, in press). Parental psychological control and dimensions of identity formation in emerging adulthood. *Journal of Family Psychology.*

Lyall, J. (2007). What is a good death? Nursing Older People, 19, 6–8.

Lykken, D. (2001). *Happiness: What studies on twins show us about nature, nurture, and the happiness set point.* New York: Golden Books.

Lyndaker, C., & Hulton, L. (2004). The influence of age on symptoms of perimenopause. *Journal of Obstetric, Gynecological, and Neonatal Nursing, 33,* 340–347.

Lyon, T. D., & Flavell, J. H. (1993). Young children's understanding of forgetting over time. *Child Development, 64,* 789–800.

Lyytinen, H., &Erskine, J. (2009, in press). Early identification and prevention of reading problems. In R. E. Tremblay, R. deV Peters, M. Boivin, & R. G. Barr (Eds.), *Encyclopedia on early childhood development.* Montreal: Centre of Excellence for Early Childhood Development.

M

Maas, C., Herrenkohl, T. I., & Sousa, C. (2008). Review of research on child maltreatment and violence in youth. *Trauma, Violence, and Abuse, 9,* 56–67.

Maas, J. (2008, March 4). Commentary in L. Szabo, "Parents with babies need time to reset inner clock." *USA Today,* p. 4D.

Mabbott, D. J., Noseworthy, M., Bouffet, E., Laughlin, S., & Rockel, C. (2006). White matter growth as a mechanism of cognitive development in children. *Neuroimage, 33,* 936–946.

Maccoby, E. E. (1987, November). Interview with Elizabeth Hall: All in the family. *Psychology Today,* pp. 54–60.

Maccoby, E. E. (1998). The two sexes: Growing up apart, coming together. Cambridge, MA: Harvard University Press.

Maccoby, E. E. (2002). Gender and group processes. *Current Directions in Psychological Science, 11,* 54–58.

Maccoby, E. E. (2007). Historical overview of socialization research and theory. In J. E. Grusec & P. D. Hastings (Eds.), *Handbook of socialization.* New York: Guilford.

Maccoby, E. E., & Jacklin, C. N. (1974). *The psychology of sex differences.* Palo Alto. CA: Stanford University Press.

Maccoby, E. E., & Martin, J. A. (1983). Socialization in the context of the family: Parent-child interaction. In P. H. Mussen (Ed.), *Handbook of child psychology* (4th ed., Vol. 4). New York: Wiley.

Maccoby, E. E., & Mnookin, R. H. (1992). *Dividing the child: Social and legal dilemmas of custody.* Cambridge, MA: Harvard University Press.

MacFarlane, J. A. (1975). Olfaction in the development of social preferences in the human neonate. In *Parent-infant interaction.* Ciba Foundation Symposium No. 33. Amsterdam: Elsevier.

MacGeorge, E. L. (2003). Gender differences in attributions and emotions in helping contexts. *Sex Roles, 48,* 175–182.

Maciejewski, P. K., Zhang, B., Block, S. D., & Prigerson, H. G. (2007). An empirical examination of the stage theory of grief. *Journal of the American Medical Association, 297,* 716–723.

Maciokas, J. B., & Crognale, M. A. (2003). Cognitive and attentional changes with age: Evidence from attentional blink deficits. *Experimental Aging Research, 29,* 137–153.

MacMillan, H. L. (2009, in press). Preventing child maltreatment. In R. E. Tremblay, R. deV Peters, & R. G. Barr (Eds.), *Encyclopedia of early childhood development.* Montreal: Centre of Excellence for Early Childhood Development.

Macononchie, N., Doyle, P., Prior, S., & Simmons, R. (2007). Risk factors for first trimester miscarriage—results from a UK-population-based case-control study. *British Journal of Obstetrics and Gynecology, 114,* 170–176.

Madden. D. J., Gottlob, L. R., Denny, L. L., Turkington, T. G., Provenzale, J. M., Hawk. T. C., et al. (1999). Aging and recognition memory: Changes in regional cerebral blood flow associated with components of reaction time distributions. *Journal of Cognitive Neuroscience, II,* 511–520.

Mader, S. M. (2009). *Concepts of biology.* New York: McGraw-Hill.

Magnusson, S. J., & Palinscar, A. S. (2005). Teaching to promote the development of scientific knowledge and reasoning about light at the elementary school level. In *How people learn.* Washington, DC: National Academies Press.

Magri, F., Cravello, L., Barili, L., Sarra, S., Cinchetti, W., Salmoiraghi, F., Micale, G., & Ferrari, E. (2006). Stress and dementia: The role of the hypothalamic-pituitary-adrenal axis. *Aging: Clinical and Experimental Research 18,* 167–170.

Mahler, M. (1979). *Separation-individuation* (Vol. 2). London: Jason Aronson.

Main, M. (2000). Attachment theory. In A. Kazdin. (Ed.), *Encyclopedia of psychology.* Washington, DC, & New York: American Psychological Association and Oxford University Press.

Malamitsi-Puchner, A., & Boutsikou, T. (2006). Adolescent pregnancy and perinatal outcome. *Pediatric Endocrinology Reviews, 3,* (Suppl. 1), 170–171.

Malatesta, V. J. (2007). Sexual problems, women, and aging: An overview. *Journal of Women and Aging, 19,* 139–154.

Malchiodi, C. A. (2008). A group art and play therapy program for children from violent homes. In C.A. Malchiodi (Ed.), *Creative interventions with traumatized children.* New York: Guilford.

Mamtani, M., Patel, A., & Kulkarni, H. (2008). Association of the pattern of transition between arousal states in neonates with the cord blood lead level. *Early Human Development, 84,* 231–235.

Mandara, J. (2006). The impact of family functioning on African American males' academic achievement: A review and clarification of the empirical literature. *Teachers College Record, 108,* 206–233.

Mandler, J. M. (2004). *The foundations of the mind: Origins of conceptual thought.* New York: Oxford University Press.

Mandler, J. M. (2006). *Jean Mandler.* Retrieved January 15, 2006, from http://cogsci.ucsd. edu/ ~jean/

Mandler, J. M., & McDonough, L. (1993). Concept formation in infancy. *Cognitive Development, 8,* 291–318.

Mangelsdorf, S. C., & Wong, M. S. (2008). Independence/dependence. In M. M. Haith & J. B. Benson (Eds.), *Encyclopedia of infant and early childhood development.* Oxford, UK: Elsevier.

Manheimer, R. J. (2007). Education and aging. In J. E. Birren. (Ed.), *Encyclopedia of gerontology* (2nd ed.). San Diego: Academic Press.

Mann, T., Tomiyama, A. J., Westling, E., Lew, A-M., Samuels, B., & Chatman, J. (2007). Medicare's search for effective obesity treatments. *American Psychologist, 62,* 220–233.

Manning, M. L., & Baruth, L. G. (2009). *Multicultural educational of children and adolescents* (5th ed.) Boston: Allyn & Bacon.

Manton, K. G. (2007). Life expectancy. In J. E. Birren (Ed.), *Encyclopedia of gerontology* (2nd ed.). San Diego: Academic Press.

Manton, K. G., Lowrimore, G. R., Ullian, A. D., Gu, X., & Tolley, H. D. (2007). From the cover: Labor force participation and human capital increases in an aging population and implications for U. S. research investment. *Proceedings of the National Academy of Sciences USA, 104,* 10802–10807.

Manton, K. I. (1989). The stress-buffering role of spiritual support: Cross-sectional and prospective investigations. *Journal for the Scientific Study of Religion, 28,* 310–323.

Manzoli, L., Villari, P., Pirone, M., & Boccia, A. (2007). Marital status and mortality in the elderly: A systematic review and meta-analysis. *Social Science Medicine, 64,* 77–94.

Marcell, T. J. (2003). Sarcopenia: Causes, consequences, and preventions. *Journals of Gerontology A: Biological and Medical Sciences, 58* M911–M916.

Marcia, J. E. (1980). Ego identity development. In J. Adelson (Ed.), *Handbook of adolescent psychology.* New York: Wiley.

Marcia, J. E. (1994). The empirical study of ego identity. In H. A. Bosma, T. L. G. Graafsma, H. D. Grotevant, & D. J. De Levita (Eds.), *Identity and development.* Newbury Park, CA: Sage.

Marcia, J. E. (2002). Identity and psychosocial development in adulthood. *Identity, 2,* 7–28.

Marcoen, A., Coleman, P., & O'Hanlon, A. (2007). Psychological aging. In J. Bond, S. Peace, F. Dittman-Kohli, & G. Westerhoff (Eds.), *Aging in society* (3rd ed.). Thousand Oaks, CA: Sage.

Marcovitch, H. (2004). Use of stimulants for attention deficit hyperactivity disorder: AGAINST. *British Medical Journal, 329,* 908–909.

Marcus, D. L., Mulrine, A., & Wong, K. (1999, September 13). How kids learn. *U.S. News & World Report,* pp. 44–50.

Marek, K. D., Popejoy, L., Petroski, G., Mehr, D., Rantz, M., & Lin, W. C. (2005). Clinical outcomes of aging in place. *Nursing Research, 54,* 202–211.

Markides, K. S. (1995). Aging and ethnicity. *Gerontologist, 35,* 276–277.

Markides, K. S., & Rudkin, L. (1996). Race and ethnic diversity. In J. E. Birren (Ed.), *Encyclopedia of gerontology* (Vol. 2). San Diego: Academic Press.

Markides, K. S., Rudkin, L., & Wallace, S. P. (2007). Ethnicity and minorities. In J. E. Birren (Ed.), *Encyclopedia of gerontology* (2nd ed.). San Diego: Academic Press.

Marko, M. G., Ahmed, T., Bunnell, S. C., Wu, D., Chung, H., Huber, B. T., & Meydani, S. N. (2007). Age-associated decline in effective immune synapse formation of CD4 (_) T cells is reversed by vitamin E supplementation. *Journal of Immunology, 178,* 1443–1449.

Markovic, K., Reulbach, U., Vassiliadu, A., Lunkenheimer, J., Lunkenheimer, B. Spannenberger, R., & Thuerauf, N. (2007). Good news for elderly persons: Olfactory pleasure increases at later stages of the life span. *Journals of Gerontology A: Biological Sciences and Medical Sciences, 62,* 1287–1293.

Markus, H. R., & Nurius, P. (1987). Possible selves: The interface between motivation and self-concept. In K. M. Yardley & T. M. Honess (Eds.), *Self and identity.* New York: Wiley.

Markus, H. R., Ryff, C. D., Curhan, K., & Palmersheim, K. (2004). In their own words: Well-being among high school and college-educated adults. In G. Brim, C. D. Ryff, & R. Kessler (Eds.), *How healthy are we? A national study of well-being in midlife.* Chicago: University of Chicago Press.

Marlow, N., Hennessy, E. M., Bracewell, M. A., Wolke, D., & the EPICure Study Group. (2007). Motor and executive function at 6 years of age after extremely preterm birth. *Pediatrics, 120,* 793–804.

Marsh, H., Ellis, L., & Craven, R. (2002). How do preschool children feel about themselves? Unraveling measurement and multidimensional self-concept structure. *Developmental Psychology, 38,* 376–393.

Marsh, R. L., Hicks, J. L., Cook, G. I., & Mayhorn, C. B. (2007). Comparing older and younger adults in an event-based prospective memory paradigm containing an output monitoring component. *Neuropsychology, Development, and Cognition, Section B: Aging, Neuropsychology, and Cognition, 14,* 168–188.

Marsiske, M., Klumb, P. L., & Baltes, M. M. (1997). Everyday activity patterns and sensory Functioning in old age. *Psychology and Aging, 12,* 444–457.

Martin, C. L., & Ruble, D. (2004). Children's search for gender cues. *Current Directions in Psychological Science, 13,* 67–70.

Martin, D. W. (2008). *Doing psychology experiments* (7th ed.). Belmont, CA: Wadsworth.

Martin, E. D., & Sher, K. J. (1994). Family history of alcoholism, alcohol use disorders, and the five-factor model of personality. *Journal of Studies in Alcohol, 55,* 81–90.

Martin, J. A., Hamilton, B. E., Menacker, F., Sutton, P. D., & Matthews, T. J. (2005, November 15). Preliminary births for 2004: Infant and maternal health. *Health E-Stats.* Atlanta: National Center for Health Statistics.

Martin, L. R., Friedman, H. S., & Schwartz, J. E. (2007). Personality and mortality risk across the life span: The importance of conscientiousness as a biopsychosocial attribute. *Health Psychology, 26,* 428–436.

Martin, M., Gruendahl, M., & Martin, P. (2001). Age differences in stress, social -resources, and well-being in middle and older age. *Journals of Gerontology: Psychological Sciences and Social Sciences, 56B,* P214–P222.

Martinez, E., & Halgunseth, L. (2004). Hispanics/Latinos. In M. Coleman & L. Ganong (Eds.), *Handbook of contemporary families.* Thousand Oaks, CA: Sage.

Martinez-Donate, M. P., Hovell, M. F., Hofsteer, C. R., Gonzalez-Perez, G. J., Adams, M. A., & Kotay, A. (2007). Correlates of home smoking bans among Mexican-Americans. *American Journal of Health Promotion, 21,* 229–236.

Martin-Matthews, A., & Davidson, K. (2007). Widowhood and widowerhood. In J. E. Birren (Ed.), *Encyclopedia of aging* (2nd ed.). San Diego: Academic Press.

Maruyama, N. C., & Atencio, C. V. (2008). Evaluating a bereavement support group. *Palliative Support and Care, 6,* 43–49.

Masley, S. C., Weaver, W., Peri, G., & Phillips, S. E. (2008). Efficacy of lifestyle changes in modifying practical markers of wellness and aging. *Alternative Therapies in Health and Medicine, 14,* 24–29.

Mason, W. A., Hitchings, J. E., & Spoth, R. L. (2007). Emergence of delinquency and depressed mood throughout adolescence as predictors of late adolescent problem substance use. *Psychology of Addictive Behaviors, 21,* 13–24.

Masoro, E. J. (2006). Are age-associated diseases an integral part of aging? In E. J. Masoro & S. N. Austad (Eds.), *Handbook of the biology of aging* (6th ed.). San Diego: Academic Press.

Massey, Z., Rising, S. S., & Ickovics, J. (2006). Centering Pregnancy group prenatal care: Promoting relationship-centered care. *Journal of Obstetric, Gynecologic, and Neonatal Nursing, 35,* 286–294.

Masten, A. S., Obradovic, J., & Burt, K. B. (2006). Resilience in emerging adulthood: Developmental perspectives on continuity and transformation. In J. J. Arnett & J. L. Tanner (Eds.), *Emerging adults in America.* Washington, DC: American Psychological Association.

Matlin, M. W. (2008). *The Psychology of women* (6th ed.). Belmont, CA: Wadsworth.

Matsumoto, D., & Juang, L. (2008). *Culture and psychology* (4th ed.). Belmont, CA: Wadsworth.

Matthews, C. E., Jurj, A. L., Shu, X.O., Yang, G., Li, Q., Gao, Y. T., & Zheng, W. (2007). Influence of exercise, walking, cycling, and overall nonexercise physical activity on mortality in Chinese women. *American Journal of Epidemiology, 165,* 1343–1350.

Matthews, J. D., & Cramer, E. P. (2006). Envisioning the adoption process to strengthen gay- and lesbian-headed families: Recommendations for adoption professionals. *Child Welfare, 85,* 317–340.

Mattison, J. A., Roth, G. S., Lane, M. A., & Ingram, D. K. (2007). Dietary restriction in aging nonhuman primates. *Interdisciplinary Topics in Gerontology, 35,* 137–158.

Mattson, M. P. (2000) Neuroprotective signaling and the aging brain: Take away my food and let me run. *Brain Research, 886,* 47–53.

Mattson, M. P. (2007). Mitochondrial regulation of neuronal plasticity. *Neurochemical Research, 32,* 707–715.

Maurer, D., & Salapatek, P. (1976). Developmental changes in the scanning of faces by young infants. *Child Development, 47,* 523–527.

Mausbach, B. T., & others. (2007). Stress-related reduction in personal mastery is associated with reduced immune cell beta2-adrenergic receptor sensitivity. *International Psychogeriatics, 4.* 1–13.

Mavandadi, S., & others. (2007). Effects of depression treatment on depressive symptoms in older adulthood: The moderating role of pain. *Journal of the American Geriatrics Association, 55,* 202–211.

May, C. P., Hasher, L., & Foong, N. (2005). Implicit memory, age, and time of day: Paradoxical priming effects. *Psychological Science, 16,* 96–100.

May, V., Onarcan, M., Oleschowski, C., & Mayron, Z. (2004). International perspectives on the role of home care and hospice in aging and long-term care. *Caring, 23,* 14–17.

Mayer, R. E. (2008). *Curriculum and instruction* (2nd ed.). Upper Saddle River, NJ: Prentice-Hall.

Mayers, L. B., & Chiffriller, S. H. (2008). Body art (body piercing and tattooing) among university undergraduate students: "Then and now". *Journal of Adolescent Health, 42,* 201–203.

Mayseless, O., & Scharf, M. (2007). Adolescents' attachment representations and their capacity for intimacy in close relationships. *Journal of Research in Adolescence, 17,* 23–50.

Mbonye, A. K., Neema, S., & Magnussen, P. (2006). Treatment-seeking practices for malaria in pregnancy among rural women in Mukono district, Uganda. *Journal of Biosocial Science, 38,* 221–237.

McAdams, D. P. (2001). Generativity in midlife. In M. E. Lachman (Ed.). *Handbook of midlife development.* New York: Wiley.

McAlister, A., & Peterson, C. (2007). A longitudinal study of child siblings and theory of mind development. *Cognitive Development, 22,* 258–270.

McAnarney, E. R. (2008). Editorial: Adolescent brain development: Forging new links? *Journal of Adolescent Health, 42,* 321–323.

McCarter, R. J. M. (2006). Differential aging among skeletal muscles. In E. J. Masoro & S. N. Austad (Eds.), *Handbook of the biology of aging* (6th ed.). San Diego: Academic Press.

McCarthy, J. (2007). Children with autism spectrum disorders and intellectual disability. *Current Opinion in Psychiatry, 20,* 472–476.

McCartney, K. (2003, July 16). Interview with Kathleen McCartney in A. Bucuvalas, "Child care and behavior." *HGSE News,* pp. 1–4. Cambridge, MA: Harvard Graduate School of Education.

McCartney, K. (2009, in press). Current research on childcare effects. In R. E. Tremblay, R. deV Peters, M. Boivan, & R. G. Barr (Eds.), *Encyclopedia on early childhood development.* Montreal: Center of Excellence for Early Childhood Development.

McCartney, K., Dearing, E., Taylor, B. A., & Bub, K. L. (2007). Quality child care supports the achievement of low-income children: Direct and indirect pathways through caregiving and the home environment. *Journal of Applied Developmental Psychology, 28,* 411–426.

McClain, C. S., Rosenfeld, B., & Breitbart, W. S. (2003, March). *The influence of spirituality on end-of-life despair in cancer patients close to death.* Paper presented at the meeting of American Psychosomatic Society, Phoenix.

McClellan, M. D. (2004, February 9). Captain Fantastic: The interview. *Celtic Nation,* pp. 1–9.

McCrae, R. R., & Costa, P. T. (1990). *Personality in adulthood.* New York: Guilford.

McCrae, R. R., & Costa, P. T. (2003). *Personality in adulthood* (2nd ed.). New York: Guilford.

McCrae, R. R., & Costa, P. T. (2006). Cross-cultural perspectives on adult personality trait development. In D. K. Mroczek & T. D. Little (Eds.), *Handbook of personality development.* Mahwah, NJ: Erlbaum.

McCullough, A. R., Steidle, C. P., Klee, B., & Tseng, L. J. (2008). Randomized, double-blind, cross-over trial of sildenafil in men with moderate erectile dysfunction: Efficacy at 8 and 12 hours postdose. *Urology, 71,* 686–692.

McCullough, J. L., & Kelly, K. M. (2006). Prevention and treatment of skin aging. *Annals of the New York Academy of Sciences, 1067,* 323–331.

McCullough, M. E., Enders, C. K., Brion, S. L., & Jain, A. R. (2005). The varieties of religious development in adulthood: A longitudinal investigation of religion and rational choice. *Journal of Personality and Social Psychology, 89,* 78–89.

McCullough, M. E., Hoyt, W. T., Larson, D. B., Koenig, H. G., & Thoresen, C. (2000). Religious involvement and mortality: A meta-analytic review. *Health psychology, 19,* 211–222.

McDonald, L. (2007). Abuse and neglect of elders. In J. E. Birren (Ed.), *Encyclopedia of gerontology* (2nd ed.). San Diego: Academic Press.

McDougall, G. J., Strauss, M. E., Holston, E. C., & Martin, M. (1999, November). *Memory self-efficacy and memory-anxiety as predictors of memory performance in at-risk elderly.* Paper presented at the meeting of the Gerontological Society of America, San Francisco.

McDowell, M. A., Brody, D. J., & Hughes, J. P. (2007). Has age of menarche changed? Results from the National Health and Nutrition Examination Survey. *Journal of Adolescent Health, 40,* 227–231.

McElwain, N. L., & Booth-LaForce, C. (2006). Maternal sensitivity to infant distress and nondistress as predictors of infant-mother attachment security. *Journal of Family Psychology, 2,* 247–255.

McFadden, S. H. (2007). Religion and spirituality. In J. E. Birren (Ed.), *Encyclopedia of gerontology* (2nd ed.). San Diego: Academic Press.

McGarvey, C., McDonnell, M., Hamilton, K., O'Regan, M., & Matthews, T. (2006). An 8-year study of risk factors for SIDS: Bed-sharing versus non-bed-sharing. *Archives of Disease in Childhood, 91,* 318–323.

McGee, L. M., & Richgels, D. J. (2008). *Literacy's beginnings* (5th ed.). Boston: Allyn & Bacon.

McGuire, L. C., Strine, T. W., Vachirasudlekha, S., Mokdad, A. H., & Anderson, L. A. (2008). The prevalence of depression in older U. S. women: 2006 -behavioral risk factor surveillance system. *Journal of Women's Health, 17,* 501–517.

McHale, J. (2007). *Charting the bumpy road of coparenthood.* Washington: Zero to Three Press.

McHale, J., Johnson, D., & Sinclair, R. (1999). Family dynamics, preschoolers' family representations, and preschool peer relationships. *Early Education and Development, 10,* 373–401.

McHale, J., & Sullivan, M. (2008). Family systems. In M. Hersen & A. Gross (Eds.), *Handbook of Clinical Psychology, Volume II: Children and Adolescents.* New York: Wiley.

McKain, W. C. (1972). A new look at older marriages. *The Family Coordinator, 21,* 61–69.

McKnight, A. J., & McKnight A. S. (1993). The effect of cellular phone use upon driver attention. *Accident Analysis and Prevention, 25,* 259–265.

McLaren, S., Gomez, R., Bailey, M., & Van Der Horst, R. K. (2007). The association of depression and sense of belonging with suicidal ideation among older adults: Applicability of resiliency models. *Suicide and Life Threatening Behavior, 37,* 89–102.

McLaughlin, K. (2003, December 30). Commentary in K. Painter, "Nurse dispenses dignity for dying." *USA Today,* Section D, pp. 1–2.

McLean, I. A., Balding, V., & White, C. (2005). Further aspects of male-on-male rape and sexual assault in greater Manchester. *Medical Science and Law, 45,* 225–232.

McMillan, J. H. (2008). *Educational research* (5th ed.). Boston: Allyn & Bacon.

McMillan, S. C., & Small, B. J. (2007). Using the COPE intervention for family caregivers to improve symptoms of hospice homecare patients: A clinical trial. *Oncology Nursing Forum, 34,* 313–321.

McMillen, I. C., MacLaughlin, S. M., Muhlhausler, B. S., Gentili, S., Duffield, J. L., & Morrison, J. L. (2008). Developmental origins of adult health and disease: The role of periconceptional and fetal nutrition. *Basic and Clinical Pharmacology and Toxicology 102,* 82–89.

McNamara, F., & Sullivan, C. E. (2000). Obstructive sleep apnea in infants. *Journal of Pediatrics, 136,* 318–323.

McNeil, G., & others. (2007). Effect of multivitamin and multiple supplementnation on cognitive function in men and women aged 65 years and over: A randomized controlled trial. *Nutrition Journal, 6,* 10.

McNeill, T. H., Davis, E. J., Hefti, F. F., & Collier, T. J. (2007). Neurotransmitters and neurotrophic factors. In J. E. Birren (Ed.), *Encyclopedia of gerontology* (2nd ed.). San Diego: Academic Press.

McNergney, R. F., & McNergney, J. M. (2009). *Education* (5th ed.). Upper Saddle River, NJ: Prentice Hall.

McNulty, J. K., Karney, B. R., & Neff, L. A. (2008). Beyond initial attraction: Physical -attractiveness in newlywed marriage. *Journal of Family Psychology, 22,* 135–143.

Meade, C., Kershaw, T. S., & Ickovics, J. R. (2008, in press). The intergenerational cycle of teenage motherhood: an ecological approach. *Health Psychology.*

Meerlo, P., Sgoifo, A., & Suchecki, D. (2008, in press). Restricted and disrupted sleep: Effects on autonomic function, neuroendocrine stress systems, and stress responsivity. *Sleep Medicine Review.*

Mehl, M. R., Vazire, S., Ramirez-Esparza, N., Slatcher, R. B., & Pennebaker, J. W. (2007). Are women really more talkative than men? *Science, 317,* 82.

Mehrotra, C. M., & Wagner, L. S. (2009). *Aging and diversity.* Clifton, NJ: Psychology Press.

Meier, A., & Allen, G. (2008, Spring). Intimate relationship development during the transition to adulthood: Differences by social class. *New Directions in Child and Adolescent Development, 119,* 25–39.

Meis, P. J., & Peaceman, A. M. (2003). Prevention of recurrent preterm delivery by 17-alpha-hydroxy-progesterone caproate. *New England Journal of Medicine, 348,* 2379–2385.

Melgar-Quinonez, H. R., & Kaiser, L. L. (2004). Relationship of child-feeding practices to overweight in low-income Mexican-American preschool-aged children. *Journal of the American Dietetic Association, 104,* 1110–1119.

Melov, S., Tarnopolsky, M., Beckman, K., Felkey, K., & Hubbard, A. (2007). Resistance exercise reverses aging in human skeletal muscle. *PLoS One, 23,* e465.

Meltzi, G., & Ely, R. (2009). Language development in the school years. In J. B. Gleason & N. Ratner (Eds.), *The development of language* (7th ed.). Boston: Allyn & Bacon.

Meltzoff, A. N. (1988). Infant imitation and memory: Nine-month-old infants in immediate and deferred tests. *Child Development, 59,* 217–225.

Meltzoff, A. N. (2004). Imitation as a mechanism of social cognition: Origins of empathy, theory of mind, and the representation of action. In U. Goswami (Ed.), *Blackwell handbook of childhood cognitive development.* Malden, MA: Blackwell.

Meltzoff, A. N. (2005). Imitation. In B. Hopkins (Ed.), *Cambridge encyclopedia of child development.* Cambridge: Cambridge University Press.

Meltzoff, A. N. (2007). "Like me": A foundation for social cognition. *Developmental Science, 10,* 126–134.

Meltzoff, A. N. (2007). Infants' causal learning. In A. Gopnik & L. Schulz (Eds.), *Casual learning*. New York: Oxford University Press.

Meltzoff, A. N. (2008). Unpublished review of J. W. Santrock's *Life-span development*, 12th ed. (New York: McGraw-Hill).

Meltzoff, A. N., & Brooks, R. (2006). Eyes wide shut: The importance of eyes in infant gaze following and understanding of other minds. In R. Flom, K. Lee, & D. Muir (Eds.), *Gaze following: Its development and significance*. Mahwah, NJ: Erlbaum.

Meltzoff, A. N., & Brooks, R. (2009). Social cognition: The role of gaze following in early word learning. In J. Colombo, P. McCardle, & L. Frend (Eds). *Infant pathways in language*. Clifton, NJ: Psychology Press.

Meltzoff, A. N., & Moore, M. K. (1998). Object representation, identity, and the paradox of early permanence: Steps toward a new framework. *Infant Behavior and Development, 21,* 201–235.

Meltzoff, A. N., & Moore, M. K. (1999). A new foundation for cognitive development in infancy: The birth of the representational infant. In E. K. Skolnick, K. Nelson, S. A. Gelman, & P. H. Miller (Eds.), *Conceptual development*. Mahwah, NJ: Erlbaum.

Meltzoff, A. N., & Williamson, R. A. (2008). Imitation and modeling. In M. M. Haith & J. B. Benson (Eds.), *Encyclopedia of infant and early childhood development*. Oxford, UK: Elsevier.

Mendle, J., Turkheimer, E., & Emery, R. E. (2007). Detrimental psychological outcomes associated with early pubertal timing in adolescent girls. *Developmental Review, 27,* 151–171.

Menec, V. H. (2003). The relation between everyday activities and successful aging: A 6-year longitudinal study. *Journal of Gerontology B: Psychological Sciences and Social Sciences, 58,* 574–582.

Menias, C. O., Elsayes, K. M., Peterson, C. M., Huete, A., Gratz, B. I., & Bhalla, S. (2007). CT of pregnancy-related complications. *Emergency Radiology, 13,* 299–306.

Menn, L., & Stoel-Gammon, C. (2005). Phonological development: Learning sounds and sound patterns. In J. Berko Gleason (Ed.), *The development of language* (6th ed.). Boston: Allyn & Bacon.

Menn L., & Stoel-Gammon, C. (2009). Phonological development: Learning sounds and sound patterns. In J. Berko Gleason & N. Ratner (Eds.), *The development of language* (7th ed.). Boston: Allyn & Bacon.

Mennuti, M. T. (2008). Genetic screening in reproductive health care. *Clinical Obstetrics and Gynecology, 51,* 3–23.

Menon, M., Tobin, D. D., Corby, B. C., Menon, M., Hodges, E. V. E., & Perry, D. G. (2007). The developmental costs of high self-esteem in aggressive children. *Child Development, 78,* 1627–1639.

Mensah, G. A., & Brown, D. W. (2007). An overview of cardiovascular disease burden in the United States. *Health Affairs, 26,* 38–48.

Menshikova, E. V., Ritov, B. V., Fairfull, L., Ferrell, R. E., Kelley, D. E., & Goodpaster, B. H. (2006). Effects of exercise on mitochondrial content and function in aging human skeletal muscle. *Journals of Gerontology A: Biological Sciences and Medical Sciences, 61,* 534–540.

Menyuk, P., Liebergott, J., & Schultz, M. (1995). *Early language development in full-term and premature infants*. Hillsdale, NJ: Erlbaum.

Meredith, N. V. (1978). Research between 1960 and 1970 on the standing height of young children in different parts of the world. In H. W. Reece & L. P. Lipsitt (Eds.), *Advances in child development and behavior* (Vol. 12). New York: Academic Press.

Merewood, A., Patel, B., Newton, K. N., MacAuley, L. P., Chamberlin, L. B., Francisco, P., & Metha, S. D. (2007). Breastfeeding duration rates and factors affecting continued breastfeeding among infants born at an inner-city U.S. baby-friendly hospital. *Journal of Human Lactation, 23,* 157–164.

Merrick, J., Morad, M., Halperin, I., & Kandel, I. (2005). Physical fitness and adolescence. *International Journal of Adolescent Medicine, 17,* 89–91.

Merrill, S. S., & Verbrugge, L. M. (1999). Health and disease in midlife. In S. L. Willis & J. D. Reid (Eds.), *Life in the middle: Psychological and social development in middle age*. San Diego: Academic Press.

Messinger, D. (2008). Smiling. In M. M. Haith & J. B. Benson (Eds.), *Encyclopedia of infant and early childhood development*. Oxford; UK: Elsevier.

Metsios, G. S., & others. (2008). Rheumatoid arthritis, cardiovascular disease, and physical exercise: A systematic review. *Rheumatology, 47,* 239–248.

Metts, S., & Cupach, W. R. (2007). responses to relational transgressions. In M. Tafoya & B. H. Spitzberg (Eds.), *The dark side of interpersonal communication*. Mahwah, NJ: Erlbaum.

Meyer, I. H. (2003). Prejudice, social stress, and mental health in gay, lesbian, and bisexual populations: Conceptual issues and research evidence. *Psychological Bulletin, 129,* 674–697.

Michael, R. T., Gagnon, J. H., Laumann, E. O., & Kolata, G. (1994). *Sex in America*. Boston: Little, Brown.

Middleton, L. E., Kirkland, S. A., Maxwel, C. J., Hogan, D. B., & Rockwood, K. (2007). Exercise: A potential contributing factor to the relationship between folate and dementia. *Journal of the American Geriatric Society, 55,* 1095–1098.

Mikkelsson, L., Kaprio, J., Kautiainen, H., Kujala, U., Mikkelsson, M., & Nupponen, H. (2006). School fitness tests as predictors of adult health-related fitness. *American Journal of Human Biology, 18,* 342–349.

Mikulincer, M., & Shaver, P. R. (2007). *Attachment in adulthood*. New York: Guilford.

Mikulincer, M., & Shaver, P. R. (2009). Adult attachment and affect regulation. In J. Cassidy & P. R. Shaver (Eds.), *Handbook of attachment* (2nd ed.). New York: Guilford.

Milberg, A., Olsson, E. C., Jakobsson, M., Olsson, M., & Friedrichsen, M. (2008). Family members' perceived needs for bereavement follow-up. *Journal of Pain and Symptom Management, 35,* 58–69.

Miles, M. F., & Williams, R. W. (2007). Meta-analysis for microarray studies of the genetics of complex traits. *Trends in Biotechnology, 25,* 45–47.

Miller, B. C., Fan, X., Christensen, M., Grotevant, H. D., & von Dulmen, M. (2000). Comparisons of adopted and nonadopted adolescents in a large, nationally representative sample. *Child Development, 71,* 1458–1473.

Miller, C. F., Lurye, L. E., Zosuls, K. M., & Ruble, D. N. (2007). *Content and accessibility of children's gender stereotypes: Girls are what they look like and boys are what they do*. Unpublished Manuscript. Department of Psychology, Princeton University, Princeton, NJ.

Miller, E. R., Pastor-Barriuso, R., Dalal, D., Riemersma, R. A., Appel, L. J., & Guallar, E. (2005). Meta-analysis: High-dosage vitamin E supplementation may increase all-cause mortality. *Annals of Internal Medicine. 142,* 37–46.

Miller, J. (2007). Cultural psychology of moral development. In S. Kitayama & D. Cohen (Eds.), *Handbook of cultural psychology*. New York: Guilford.

Miller, J. B. (1986). *Toward a new psychology of women* (2nd ed.). Boston: Beacon Press.

Miller, M. A., & Cappuccio, F. P. (2007). Inflammation, sleep, obesity, and cardiovascular disease. *Current Vascular Pharmacology, 5,* 92–102.

Miller, P. H, & Seier, W. I. (1994). strategy utilization deficiencies in children: When, where, and why. In H. W. Reese (Ed.), *Advances in child development and behavior* (Vol. 24). New York: Academic Press.

Miller, S. A. (2000). Children's understanding of preexisting differences in knowledge and belief. *Developmental Review, 20,* 227–282.

Miller, S. L., & others. (2008). Age-related memory impairment associated with parietal deactivation but preserved hippocampal activation. *Proceedings of the National Academy of Sciences USA 105,* 2181–2186.

Miller-Day, M. A. (2004). *Communication among grandmothers, mothers, and adult daughters*. Mahwah, NJ: Erlbaum.

Miller-Perrin, C. L., & Perrin, R. D. (2007). *Child maltreatment* (2nd ed.). Thousand Oaks, CA: Sage.

Mills, C. M. (2007). *Theory of mind*. Unpublished manuscript, University of Texas at Dallas, School of Behaviorial and Brain Sciences, Richardson, Tx.

Mills, D., & Mills, C. (2000). *Hungarian kindergarten curriculum translation*. London: Mills Production.

Minde, K., & Zelkowitz, P. (2008). Premature babies. In M. M. Haith & J. B. Benson (Eds.), *Encylopedia of infancy and early childhood development*. Oxford, UK: Elsevier.

Minino, A. M., Heron, M. P., & Smith, B. L. (2006, June 28). Deaths: Preliminary data for 2004. *National Vital Statistics Report, 54,* 1–49.

Minzenberg, M. J., Poole, J. H., & Vinogradov, S. (2006). Adult social attachment disturbance is related to childhood -maltreatment. *Journal of Nervous and Mental Disorders, 194,* 341–348.

Miranda, R., Scott, M., Hicks, R., Wilcox, H. C., Harris Munfakh, J. L., & Shaffer, D. (2008). Suicide attempt characteristics, diagnoses, and future attempts: Comparing multiple attempters to single attempters and ideators. *Journal of the American Academy of Child and Adolescent Psychiatry, 47,* 32–40.

Mischel, W. (2004). Toward an integrative science of the person. *Annual Review of Psychology* (Vol. 55). Palo Alto, CA: Annual Reviews.

Mitchell, B. A. (2007). Marriage and divorce. In J. E. Birren (Ed.), *Encyclopedia of gerontology* (2nd ed.). San Diego: Academic Press.

Mitchell, E. A. (2007). Recommendations for sudden infant death syndrome prevention: A discussion document. *Archives of Disease in Childhood, 92,* 155–159.

Mitchell, E. A., Stewart, A. W., Crampton, P., & Salmond, C. (2000). Deprivation and sudden infant death syndrome. *Social Science and Medicine, 51,* 147–150.

Mitchell, M. S., Koien, C. M., & Crow, S. M. (2008). Harassment: It's not (all) about sex! Part I: The evolving legal framework. *Health Care Management, 27,* 13–22.

Mitchell, V., & Helson, R. (1990). Women's prime of life: Is it the 50s? *Psychology of Women Quarterly, 14,* 451–470.

Miyake, K., Chen, S., & Campos, J. (1985). Infants' temperament, mothers' mode of interaction and attachment in Japan: An interim report. In I. Bretherton & F. Waters (Eds.), Growing points of attachment theory and research, *Monographs of the Society for Research in Child Development, 50* (1–2, Serial No. 109), 276–297.

Miyashita, M., Sato, K., Morita, T., Suzuki, M. (2008). Effect of a population-based educational intervention focusing on end-of-life home care, life-prolonging treatment, and knowledge about palliative care. *Palliative Medicine, 22,* 376–382.

MMWR. (2006, June 9). Youth risk behavior surveillance—United States 2005, Vol. 255. Atlanta: Centers for Disease Control and Prevention.

Moen, P. (2007). Unpublished review of J. W. Santrock's *Life-span development,* 12th ed. (New York: McGraw-Hill).

Moen, P., & Altobelli, J. (2007). Strategic selection as a retirement project: Will Americans develop hybrid arrangements? In J. James & P. Wink (Eds.), *The crown of life: Dynamics of the early post retirement period.* New York: Springer.

Moen, P., Kelly, E., and Magennis, R. (2008). Gender strategies: Social and institutional convoys, mystiques, and cycles of control. In M. C. Smith & T. G. Reio (Eds.) *Handbook of research on adult development and learning.* Mahwah: Erlbaum.

Moen, P., & Spencer, D. (2006). Converging divergences in age, gender, health, and well-being: Strategic selection in the third age. In R. H. Binstock & L. K. George (Eds.), *Handbook of Aging and the Social Sciences* (6th ed.). San Diego: Academic Press.

Moen, P., & Wethington, E. (1999). Midlife development in a life course context. In S. L. Willis & J. D. Reid (Eds.), *Life in the middle: Psychological and social development in middle age.* San Diego: Academic Press.

Mohr, J. J. (2009). Same-sex romantic attachment. In J. Cassidy & P. R. Shaver (Eds.), *Handbook of attachment* (2nd ed.). New York: Guilford.

Moise, K. J. (2005). Fetal RhD typing with free DNA I maternal plasma. *American Journal of Obstetrics and Gynecology, 192,* 663–665.

Mollenkopf, H. (2007). Mobility and flexibility. In J. E. Birren (Ed.), *Encyclopedia of gerontology* (2nd ed.). San Diego: Academic Press.

Molnar, B. E., Cerda, M., Roberts, A. L., & Buka, S. L. (2008). Effects of neighborhood resources on aggressive and delinquent behaviors among urban youths. *American Journal of Public Health, 98,* 1086–1093.

Monge, P., Wesseling, C., Guardado, J., Lundberg, II, Ahlbom, A., Cantor, K. P., Weiderpass, E., & Partanen, T. (2007). Parental occupation exposure to pesticides and the risk of childhood leukemia in Costa Rica. *Scandinavian Journal of Work, Environment, and Health, 33,* 293–303.

Monserud, M. A. (2008). Intergenerational relationships and affectual solidarity between grandparents and young adults. *Journal of Marriage and the Family, 70,* 182–195.

Montan, S. (2007). Increased risk in the elderly parturient. *Current Opinion in Obstetrics and Gynecology, 19,* 110–112.

Montemayor, R. (1982). The relationship between parent-adolescent conflict and the amount of time adolescents spend with parents, peers, and alone. *Child Development, 53,* 1512–1519.

Moore, A. (2007). Older people: We can work it out. *Health Services Journal, 117,* 24–26.

Moore, D. (2001). *The dependent gene.* New York: W. H. Freeman.

Moos, B. (2007, July 4). Who'll care for aging boomers? *Dallas Morning News,* pp. A1–A2.

Moos, M. K. (2006). Prenatal care: Limitations and opportunities. *Journal of Obstetric, Gynecologic, and Neonatal Nursing, 35,* 278–285.

Mora, F., Segovia, G., & del Arco, A. (2007). Aging, plasticity, and environmental enrichment: Structural changes and neurotransmitter dynamics in several areas of the brain. *Brain Research Review, 55,* 78–88.

Moran, S., & Gardner, H. (2006). Extraordinary achievements. In W. Damon & R. Lerner (Eds.), *Handbook of child psychology* (6th ed.). New York: Wiley.

Moran, S., & Gardner, H. (2007). Hill, skill, and will: Executive function from a multiple intelligences perspective. In L. Meltzer (Ed.), *Executive function in education.* New York: Guilford.

Moreno, A., Posada, G. E., & Goldyn, D. T. (2006). Presence and quality of touch influence coregulation in mother-infant dyads. *Infancy, 9,* 1–20.

Morgan, J. D. (2003). Spirituality. In C. D. Bryant (Ed.), *Handbook of death and dying.* Thousand Oaks, CA: Sage.

Morley J. E. (2003). Anorexia and weight loss in older persons. *Journals of Gerontology A: Biological and Medical Sciences, 58,* M131–M137.

Morokuma, S., & others. (2008). Developmental change in fetal response to repeated low-intensity sound. *Developmental Science, 11,* 47–52.

Morra, S., Gobbo, C., Marini, Z., & Sheese, R. (2008). *Cognitive development: Neo Piagetian perspectives.* Mahwah, NJ: Erlbaum.

Morrison, G. S. (2008). *Fundamentals of early childhood education* (5th ed.). Upper Saddle River, NJ: Prentice Hall.

Morrissey, M. V. (2007). Suffer no more in silence: Challenging the myths of women's mental health in childbearing. *International Journal of Psychiatric Nursing Research, 12,* 1429–1438.

Moschonis, G., Grammatikaki, E., & Manios, Y. (2008, in press). Perinatal predictors of overweight at infancy and preschool childhood: The GENESIS study. *International Journal of Obesity.*

Mosenthal, A. C., Murphy, P. A., Barker, L. K., Lavery, R., Retano, A., & Livingston, D. H. (2008). Changing the culture around end-of-life care in the trauma intensive care unit. *Journal of Trauma, 64,* 1587–1593

Mottershead, N. (2006). Hypnosis: Removing labor from birth. *Practicing Midwife, 9,* 26–27, 29.

Moules, N. J., Simonson, K., Prins, M., Angus, P., & Bell, J. M. (2004). Making room for grief. *Nursing Inquiry, 11,* 99–107.

Moulson, M. C., & Nelson, C. A. (2008). Neurological development. In M. M. Haith & J. B. Benson (Eds.), *Encyclopedia of infant and early childhood development.* Oxford, UK: Elsevier.

Mounts, N. S. (2002). Parental management of adolescent peer relationships in context: The role of parenting style. *Journal of Family Psychology, 16,* 58–69.

Moya, J., Bearer, C. F., & Etzel, R. A. (2004). Children's behavior and physiology and how it affects exposure to environmental contaminants. *Pediatrics, 113* (Suppl. 4), 996–1006.

Moyer, R. H., Hackett, J. K., & Everett, S. A. (2007). *Teaching science as investigations.* Upper Saddle River, NJ: Prentice Hall.

Mraz, M., Padak, N. D., & Rasinski, T. V. (2008). *Evidence-based instruction in reading.* Boston: Allyn & Bacon.

Mroczek, D. K. (2001). Age and emotion in adulthood. *Current Directions in Psychological Science, 10,* 87–90.

Mroczek, D. K., & Kolarz, C. M. (1998). The effect of age on positive and negative affect: A developmental perspective on happiness. *Journal of Personality and Social Psychology, 75,* 1333–1349.

Mroczek, D. K., & Spiro, A. (2007). Personality change influence mortality in older men. *Psychological Science, 18,* 371–376.

Mroczek, D. K., Spiro, A., & Griffin, P. W. (2006). Personality and aging. In J. E. Birren &. W. Schaie (Eds.), *Handbook of the psychology of aging* (6th ed.). San Diego: Academic Press.

Mueller, U., Carpendale, J. I. M., Budwig, N., & Sokol, B. W. (Eds.). (2008). *Social life and social knowledge.* Philadelphia: Psychology Press.

Mullins, L. C. (2007). Loneliness. In J. E. Birren (Ed.), *Encyclopedia of gerontology* (2nd ed.). San Diego: Academic Press.

Mullis, P. E., & Tonella, P. (2008). Regulation of fetal growth: Consequences and impact of being born small. *Best Practice Research: Clinical Endocrinology and Metabolism, 22,* 173–190.

Mulvaney, M. K., & Mebert, C. J. (2007). Parental corporal punishment predicts behavior problems in early childhood. *Journal of Family Psychology, 21,* 389–397.

Mundy, P., Block, J., Delgado, C., Pomares, Y., Van Hecke, A. V., & Parlade, M. V. (2007). Individual differences and the development of joint attention in infancy. *Child Development, 78,* 938–954.

Munkata, Y. (2006). Information processing: Approaches to development. In W. Damon & R. Lerner (Eds.), *Handbook of educational psychology.* New York: Wiley.

Murphy, M. C. (1996). Stressors on the college campus: A comparison of 1985 and 1993. *Journal of college Student Development, 37,* 20–28.

Murphy, M. M., & Mazzocco, M. M. (2008). Mathematics learning disabilities in girls with fragile X or Turner syndrome during late elementary school. *Journal of Learning Disabilities, 41,* 29–46.

Murphy, S. A., Johnson, L. C., Chung, I., & Beaton, R. D. (2003). The prevalence of PTSD following the violent death of a child and -predictors of change 5 years later. *Journal of Traumatic Stress, 16,* 17–25.

Murphy-Hoefer, R., Alder, S., & Higbee, C. (2004). Perceptions about cigarette smoking and risks among college students. *Nicotine and Tobacco Research, 6* (Suppl. 3), S371–S374.

Murray, E. A. (2007). Visual memory. *Annual Review of Neuroscience* (Vol. 29). Palo Alto, CA: Annual Reviews.

Murray, J. P. (2007). TV violence: Research and controversy. In N. Pecora, J. P. Murray, & E. A. Wartella (Eds.), *Children and television.* Mahwah, NJ: Erlbaum.

Murray, J. P., & Murray, A. D. (2008). Television: Uses and effects. In M. M. Haith & J. B. Benson (Eds.), *Encyclopedia of infant and early childhood development.* Oxford, UK: Elsevier.

Murray, K. E., & Zautra, A. J. (2007). Life events. In J. E. Birren (Ed.), *Encyclopedia of gerontology* (2nd ed.). San Diego: Academic Press.

Muskesh, B. N., Le, A., Dimitrov, P. N., Ahmed, S., Taylor, H. R., & McCarty, C. A. (2006). Development of cataract and associated risk factors: The visual Impairment Project. *Archives of Ophthalmology, 124,* 79–85.

Mussen, P. H., Honzik, M., & Eichorn, D. (1982). Early adult antecedents of life satisfaction at age 70. *Journal of Gerontology, 37,* 316–322.

Myers, D. G. (2000). *The American paradox.* New Haven, CT: Yale University Press.

Myers, D. L. (1999). *Excluding violent youths from juvenile court: The effectiveness of legislative waiver.* Doctoral dissertation, University of Maryland, College Park, MD.

Myerson, J., Rank, M. R., Raines, F. Q., & Schnitzler, M. A. (1998). Race and general cognitive ability: The myth of diminishing returns in education. *Psychological Science, 9,* 139–142.

N

Nabet, C., Lelong, N., Ancel, P. Y., Saurel-Cubizolles, M. J., & Kaminski, M. (2007). Smoking during pregnancy according to obstetric complications and parity: Results of the EUROPOP study. *European Journal of Epidemiology, 22,* 715–721.

Nader, K. (2001). Treatment methods for childhood trauma. In J. P. Wilson, M. J. Friedman, & J. Lindy (Eds.), *Treating psychological trauma and PTSD.* New York: Guilford Press.

Nader, P., O'Brien, M., Houts, R., Bradley, R., Belsky, J., Corsnoe, R., Friedman, S., Mei, Z., &

Susman, E. J. (2006). Identifying risk for obesity in early childhood. *Pediatrics, 118,* e594–e601.

NAEYC. (1997). *Principles of child development and learning that inform developmentally appropriate practice* [Position statement]. Washington, DC: Author.

NAEYC. (2002). *Early learning standards: Creating the conditions for success.* Washington, DC: Author.

NAEYC. (2005). *Critical facts about young children and early childhood in the United States.* Washington, DC: Author.

Nagel, H. T., Kneght, A. C, Kloosterman, M.D., Wildschut, H. I., Leschot, N. J., & Vandenbussche, F. P. (2007). Prenatal diagnosis in the Netherlands, 1991–2000: Number of invasive procedures, indications, abnormal results, and terminations of pregnancies. *Prenatal Diagnosis, 27,* 251–257.

Nagy, M. (1948). The child's theories concerning death. *Journal of Genetic Psychology, 73,* 3–27.

Naigles, L. R., & Swensen, L. D. (2007). Syntactic supports for word learning. In E. Hoff & M. Shatz (Eds.), *Blackwell handbook of language development.* Malden, MA: Blackwell.

Nakamura, K., Sheps, S., & Clara Arck, P. (2008, in press). Stress and reproductive failure: Past notions, present insights, and future directions. *Journal of Assisted Reproduction and Genetics.*

Nanovskaya, T. N., Nekhayeva, I. A., Hankins, G. D., & Ahmed, M. S. (2008). Transfer of methadone across the dually perfused preterm human placental lobule. *American Journal of Obstetrics and Gynecology, 198,* e1–e4.

Nansel, T. R., Overpeck, M., Pilla, R., Ruan, W., Simons-Morton, B., & Scheidt, P. (2001). Bullying behaviors among U.S. Youth. *Journal of the American Medical Association, 285,* 2094–2100.

Narberhaus, A., Segarra, D., Caldu, X., Gimenez, M., Junque, C., Pueyo, R., & Botet, F. (2007). Gestational age at preterm birth in relation to corpus callosum and general cognitive outcome in adolescents. *Journal of Child Neurology, 22,* 761–765.

Narberhaus, A., Segarra, D., Caldu, X., Gimenez, M., Pueyo, R., Botet, F., & Junque, C. (2008). Corpus collosum and prefrontal functions in adolescents with history of very preterm birth. *Neuropsychologia, 46,* 111–116.

Narvaez, D., & Lapsley, D. (Eds.) (2009, in press). Moral personality, identity, and character: An interdisciplinary future. New York: Cambridge University Press.

Nathalies, P., & Jean-Noel, O. (2008). Processing of amyloid precursor protein and amyloid peptide neurotoxicity. *Current Alzheimer Research, 5,* 92–99.

National Assessment of Educational Progress. (2005). *The nation's report card: 2005.* Washington, DC: U.S. Department of Education.

National Assessment of Educational Progress. (2007). *The nation's report card: 2007.* Washington, DC: U.S. Department of Education.

National Association for Sport and Physical Education. (2002). *Active start: A statement of physical activity guidelines for children birth to five years.* Reston, VA: Author.

National Cancer Institute. (2008a). *Cancer trends progress report.* Retrieved January 15, 2008, from http://progressreport.cancer.gov/highlights.asp

National Cancer Institute. (2008b). *Acute lymphoblastic leukemia in children.* Retrieved January 15, 2008, from www.cancer.gov/cancertopics/factsheet/ALLinchildren

National Center for Education Statistics. (2002). *Work during college.* Washington, DC: U.S. Office of Education.

National Center for Education Statistics. (2007). *Children with disabilities in public schools.* Washington, DC. U. S. Department of Education.

National Center for Education Statistics. (2007). *The condition of education 2007.* NCES 2007–064. Indicator 23. Washington, DC: U.S. Department of Education.

National Center for Health Statistics. (2000). *Health United States, 2000, with adolescent health chartbook.* Bethesda, MD: U.S. Department of Health and Human Services.

National Center for Health Statistics. (2002). *Sexual behavior and selected health measures: Men and women 15–44 years of age, United States, 2002,* PHS 2003–1250. Atlanta: Centers for Disease Control and Prevention.

National Center for Health Statistics. (2004) *Health United States.* Atlanta: Centers for Disease Control and Prevention.

National Center for Health Statistics. (2006). *Death Statistics.* Atlanta: Centers for Disease Control and Presentation.

National Center for Health Statistics. (2006). *Health United States.* Atlanta: Centers for Disease Control and Prevention.

National Center for Health Statistics. (2007). *Death rates.* Atlanta: Centers for Disease Control and Prevention.

National Center for Health Statistics. (2007). *Health United States, 2007.* Atlanta: Centers for Disease Control and Prevention.

National Center for Health Statistics. (2008, June 11). *U. S. mortality rate drops sharply in 2006, latest data show.* Atlanta: Centers for Disease Control and Prevention.

National Center for Juvenile Justice. (2006). *Juvenile offenders and victims: 2006 national report.* Pittsburgh: Author.

National Clearing House on Child Abuse and Neglect. (2004). *What is child abuse and neglect?* Washington, DC: U. S. Department of Health and Human Services.

National Council on Aging. (2000, March). *Myths and realities survey results.* Washington, DC: Author.

National Institute of Mental Health. (2004). *Autism spectrum disorders.* Bethesda, MD: Author.

National Institute of Mental Health. (2008). *Autism spectrum disorders (pervasive developmental disorders).* Retrieved January 6, 2008, from http://www.nimh.nih.gov/Publicat/autism.cfm.

National Institutes of Health. (2004). *Women's Health Initiative Hormone Therapy Study.* Bethesda, MD: Author.

National Institutes of Health. (2008). *Clinical trial. gov* Retrieved on April 22, 2008, from http://clinical-trials.gov/ct2/show/NCT00059293?cond=%22Intracranial1Embolism%22&r...

National Research Council. (1999). *How people learn.* Washington, DC: National Academy Press.

National Sleep Foundation. (2006). *2006 Sleep in America Poll.* Washington, DC: Author.

National Sleep Foundation (2007). *Sleep in America poll 2007.* Washington, DC: Author.

National Vital Statistics Report. (2004, March 7). *Deaths: Leading causes for 2002.* Atlanta: Centers for Disease Control and Prevention.

Nauck, B., & Suckow, J. (2006). Intergenerational relations in cross-cultural comparison: How social networks frame intergenerational relations between mothers and grandmothers in Japan, Korea, China, Indonesia, Israel, Germany, and Turkey. *Journal of Family Issues, 27,* 1159–1185.

Nava-Ocampo, A. A., & Koren, G. (2007). Human teratogens and evidence-based teratogen risk counseling: The Motherisk approach. *Clinical Obstetrics and Gynecology, 50,* 123–131.

Needham, A. (2008, in press). Learning in infants' object perception, object-directed action, and tool use. In A. Needham & A. Woodward (Eds.), *Learning and the infant mind.* New York: Oxford University Press.

Needham, A., Barrett, T., & Peterman, K. (2002). A pick-me-up for infants' exploratory skills: Early simulated experiences reaching for objects using "sticky mittens" enhances young infants' object exploration skills. *Infant Behavior and Development, 25,* 279–295.

Neisser, U., Boodoo, G., Bouchard, T. J., Boykin, A. W., Brody, N., Ceci, S. J., Halpern, D. F., Loehlin, J. C., Perloff, R. J., Sternberg, R., & Urbina, S. (1996). Intelligence: Knowns and unknowns. *American Psychologist, 51,* 77–101.

Nelson, C. A. (2003). Neural development and lifelong plasticity. In R. M. Lerner, F. Jacobs, & D. Wertlieb (Eds.), *Handbook of applied developmental science* (Vol. 1). Thousand Oaks, CA: Sage.

Nelson, C. A. (2006). Unpublished review of J. W. Santrock's *Topical life-span development,* 4th ed. (New York: McGraw-Hill).

Nelson, C. A. (2009). Brain development and behavior. In A. M. Rudolph, C. Rudolph, L. First, G. Lister, & A. A. Gersohon (Eds.), *Rudolph's pediatrics* (22nd ed.). New York: McGraw-Hill.

Nelson, C. A., Thomas, K. M., & de Haan, M. (2006). Neural bases of cognitive development. In W. Damon & R. Lerner (Eds.), *Handbook of child Psychology* (6th ed.). New York: Wiley.

Nelson, C. A., Zeanah, C., & Fox, N. A. (2007). The effects of early deprivation on brain-behavioral development: The Bucharest Early Intervention Project. In D. Romer & E. Walker (Eds.), *Adolescent psychopathology and the developing brain: Integrating brain and prevention science.* New York: Oxford University Press.

Nelson, D. B., Sammel, M. D., Feeman, E. W., Lin, H., Gracia, C. R., & Schmitz, K. H. (2008). Effect of physical activity on menopausal symptoms among urban women. *Medicine and Science in Sports and Exercise, 40,* 50–58.

Nelson, J. A., & Eckstein, D. (2008). A service-learning model for at-risk adolescents. *Education and Treatment of Children, 31,* 223–237.

Nelson, K. (1999). Levels and modes of representation: Issues for the theory of conceptual change and development. In E. K. Skolnick, K. Nelson, S. A. Gelman, & P. H. Miller (Eds.), *Conceptual development.* Mahwah, NJ: Erlbaum.

Nelson, L. J., Padilla-Walker, L. M., Carroll, J. S., Madsen, S. D., Barry, C. M., & Badger, S. (2007). "if you want me to treat you like an adult, start acting like one!" Comparing the criteria that emerging adults and their parents have for adulthood. *Journal of Family Psychology, 21,* 665–674.

Nelson, T. D. (2007). Ageism and discrimination. In J. E. Birren (Ed.), *Encyclopedia of gerontology* (2nd ed.). San Diego: Academic Press.

Nemund, H. K., & Kolland, F. (2007). Work and retirement. In J. Bond, S. Peace, F. Dittman-Kohli, & G. Westerhoff (Eds.), *Aging in society* (3rd ed.). Thousand Oaks, CA: Sage.

Ness, A., Dias, T., Damus, K., Burd, I., & Berghella, V. (2006). Impact of recent randomized trials on the use of progesterone to prevent preterm birth: A 2005 follow-up survey. *American Journal of Obsterics and Gynecology, 195,* 1174–1179.

Neugarten, B. L. (1986). The aging society. In A. Pifer & L. Bronte (Eds.), *Our aging society: Paradox and promise.* New York: W. W. Norton.

Neugarten, B. L. (1988, August). *Policy issues for an aging society.* Paper presented at the meeting of the American Psychological Association, Atlanta.

Neugarten, B. L., Havighurst, R. J., & Tobin, S. S. (1968). Personality and patterns of aging. In B. L. Neugarten (Ed.), *Middle age and aging.* Chicago. University of Chicago Press.

Neugarten, B. L., & Weinstein, K. K. (1964). The changing American grandparent, *Journal of Marriage and the Family, 26,* 199–204.

Neuman, S. B. (2007). Social contexts for literacy development. In K. A. Roskos & J. F. Christie (Eds.), *Play and literacy in early childhood.* Mawah, NJ: Erlbaum.

Neumark-Sztainer, D., Paxton S. J., Hannan, P. J., Haines, J., Story, M. (2006). Does body satisfaction matter? Five-year longitudinal associations between body satisfaction and health behaviours in adolescent females and males. *Journal of Adolescent Health, 39,* 244–251.

Neupert, S. D., Almeida, D. M., & Charles, S. T. (2007). Age differences in reactivity to daily stressors: The role of personal control. *Journals of Gerontology: Psychological Sciences and Social Sciences, 62B,* P316–P225.

Neville, H. J. (2006). Different profiles of plasticity within human cognition. In Y. Munakata & M. H. Johnson (Eds.), *Attention and Performance XXI: Processes of change in brain and cognitive development.* Oxford, UK: Oxford University Press.

New, R. (2005). The Reggio Emilia approach: Provocations and partnerships with U.S. early childhood educators. In J. L. Roopnarine & J. E. Johnson (Eds.), *Approaches to early childhood education* (4th ed.). Columbus, OH: Merrill/Prentice Hall.

New, R. (2007). Reggio Emilia as cultural activity theory in practice. *Theory into Practice, 46,* 5–13.

Newburg, D. S., & Walker, W. A. (2007). Protection of the neonate by the innate immune system of developing gut and of human milk. *Pediatric Research, 61,* 2–8.

Newcombe, N. (2008). The development of implicit and explicit memory. In N. Cowan & M. Courage (Eds.), *The development of memory in childhood.* Philadelphia: Psychology Press.

Newcombe, N. S. (2007). Developmental psychology meets the mommy wars. *Journal of Applied Developmental Psychology, 28,* 553–555.

Newell, K., Scully, D. M., McDonald, P. V., & Baillargeon, R. (1989). Task constraints and infant grip configurations, *Developmental Psychobiology, 22,* 817–832.

Newman, A. B., & others. (2006). Association of long-distance corridor walk performance with mortality, cardiovascular disease, mobility limitation, and disability. *Journal of the American Medical Association, 295,* 2018–2026.

Newman, B. M., & Newman, P. R. (2007). *Theories of human development.* Mahwah, NJ: Erlbaum.

Newman, M. B., & Bakay, R. A. (2008). Therapeutic potentials of human embryonic stem cells in Parkinson's disease. *Neurotherapeutics, 5,* 237–251.

Newman, M. L., Groom, C. J., Handelman, L. D., & Pennebaker, J. W. (2008, in press). *Discourse Perspectives.*

Newson, A. J. (2008). Ethical aspects arising from non-invasive fetal diagnosis. *Seminars in Fetal and Neonatal Medicine, 13,* 103–108.

Newton, A. W., & Vandeven, A. M. (2006). Unexplained infant death: A review of sudden infant death syndrome, sudden unexplained infant death, and child maltreatment facilities in shaken baby syndrome. *Current Opinions in Pediatrics, 18,* 196–200.

Newton, A. W., & Vandeven, A. M. (2008). Update on child maltreatment. *Current Opinion in Pediatrics, 20,* 205–212.

Newton, I. G., Forbes, M. E., Linville, M. C., Pang, H., Tucker, E. W., Riddle, D. R., & Brunso-Bechtoid, J. K. (2007, in press). Effects of aging and caloric restriction on dentate gyrus synapses and glutamate receptor subunits. *Neurobiology of Aging.*

Ney, D. M., Hull, A. K., van Calcar, S. C., Liu, X., & Etzel, M. R. (2008). Dietary glycomacropeptide supports growth and reduces the concentrations of phenylalanine in plasma and brain in a murine model of phenylketonuria. *Journal of Nutrition, 138,* 316–322.

NICHD. (2008). *SIDS facts.* Retrieved January 4, 2008, from www.nichd.nih/gov/sids

NICHD Early Child Care Research Network. (2000). Factors associated with fathers' caregiving activities and sensitivity with young children. *Developmental Psychology, 14,* 200–219.

NICHD Early Child Care Research Network. (2001). Nonmaternal care and family factors in early development: An overview of the NICHD study of Early Child Care. *Journal of Applied Developmental Psychology, 22,* 457–492.

NICHD Early Child Care Research Network. (2002). Structure _ Process _ Outcome: Direct and indirect effects of child care quality on young children's development. *Psychological Science, 13,* 199–206.

NICHD Early Child Care Research Network. (2003). Does amount of time spent in child care predict socioemotional adjustment during the transition to kindergarten? *Child Development, 74,* 976–1005.

NICHD Early Child Care Research Network. (2004). Type of child care and children's Development at 54 months. *Early Childhood Research Quarterly, 19,* 203–230.

NICHD Early Child Care Research Network. (2005). *Child care and development.* New York: Guilford.

NICHD Early Child Care Research Network. (2005). Duration and developmental timing of poverty and children's cognitive and social development from birth through third grade. *Child Development, 76,* 795–810.

NICHD Early Child Care Research Network, (2005). Predicting Individual differences in attention, memory, and planning in first graders from experiences at home, child care, and school. *Developmental Psychology, 41,* 99–114.

NICHD Early Child Care Research Network. (2006). Infant-mother attachment classification: Risk and protection in relation to changing maternal caregiving quality. *Developmental Psychology, 42,* 38–58.

Nielsen, S. J., Siega-Riz, A. M., & Popkin, B. M. (2002). Trends in energy intake in U. S. between 1977 and 1996: Similar shifts seen across age groups. *Obesity Research, 10,* 370–378.

Nisbett, R. (2003). *The geography of thought.* New York: Free Press.

Noddings, N. (2007). *When school reform goes wrong.* New York: Teachers College Press.

Nohr, E. A., Bech, B. H., Davies, M. J., Fryenberg, M., Henriksen, T. B., & Olsen, J. (2005). Prepregnancy obesity and fetal death: A study with the Danish National Birth Cohort. *Obstetrics and Gynecology, 106,* 250–259.

Noland, J. S., Singer, L. T., Short, E. J., Minnes, S., Arendt, R. E., Kirchner, H. L., & Bearer, C. (2005). Prenatal drug exposure and selective attention in preschoolers. *Neurotoxicology and Teratology, 27,* 429–438.

Nolen-Hoeksema, S. (2007). *Abnormal psychology* (4th ed.). New York: McGraw-Hill.

Norbury, G., & Norbury, C. J. (2008). Non-invasive prenatal diagnosis of single gene disorders: How close are we? *Seminars in Fetal and Neonatal Medicine, 13,* 76–83.

Nordberg, A. (2008). Amyloid plaque imaging in vivo: Current achievement and future prospects. *European Journal of Nuclear medicine and Molecular Imaging, 35* (Suppl. 1), S46–S50.

Norgard, B., Puho, E., Czeilel, A. E., Skriver, M. V., & Sorensen, H. T. (2006). Aspirin use during early pregnancy and the risk of congenital abnormalities. *American Journal of Obstetrics and Gynecology, 192,* 922–923.

Noriko, S. (2005). Identify development of pre– and post–empty nest women. *Japanese Journal of Developmental Psychology, 15,* 52–64.

Norman, J. F., Crabtree, C. E., Herrmann, M., Thompson, S. R., Shular, C. F., & Clayton, A. M. (2006). Aging and the perception of 3-D shape from dynamic patterns of binocular disparity. *Perception and Psychophysics, 68,* 94–101.

Norouzieh, K. (2005). Case management of the dying child. *Case Manager, 16,* 54–57.

Norris, J.E., Pratt, M. W., & Hebblewaite, S. (2007). Social cognition. In J. E. Birren (Ed.), *Encyclopedia of gerontology* (2nd ed.). San Diego: Academic Press.

Nottelmann, E. D., Susman, F. J., Blue, J. H., Inoff-Germain, G., Dorn, I. D., Loriaux, D. L., Cutler, G. B., & Chrousos, G. P. (1987). Gonadal and adrenal hormone correlates of adjustment in early adolescence. In R. M. Lerner & T. T. Foch (Eds.), *Biological-psychological interactions in early adolescence.* Hillsdale, NJ: Erlbaum.

Nsamenang, A. B. (2002). Adolescence in sub-Saharan Africa: An image constructed from Africa's triple heritage. In B. B. Brown, R. W. Larson, & T. S. Saraswathi (Eds.), *The world's youth.* New York: Cambridge University Press.

Nucci, L. (2006). Education for moral development. In M. Killen & J. Smetana (Eds.), *Handbook of moral development.* Mahwah, NJ: Erlbaum.

Nutting, P. A., Dickinson, W. P., Dickinson, L. M., Nelson, C. C., King, D. K., Crabtree, B. F., & Glasgow, R. E. (2007). Use of chronic care model elements is associated with higher-quality care for diabetes. *Annals of Family Medicine, 5,* 14–20.

Nylund, K., Bellmore, A., Nishina, A., & Graham, S. (2007). Subtypes, severity, and structural stability of peer victimization: What does latent class analysis say? *Child Development, 78,* 1706–1722.

O

O'Connor, A. B., & Roy, C. (2008). Electric power plant emissions and public health. *American Journal of Nursing, 108,* 62–70.

O'Connor, E., & McCartney, K. (2007). Attachment and cognitive skills: An investigation of mediating mechanisms. *Journal of Applied Developmental Psychology, 28,* 458–476.

O'Donnell, L., O'Donnell, C., Wardlaw, D. M., & Stueve, A. (2004). Risk and resiliency factors influencing suicidality among urban African American and Latino youth. *American Journal of Community Psychology, 33,* 37–49.

O'Neill, D. (1996). Two-year-old children's sensitivity to a parent's knowledge state when making requests. *Child Development, 67,* 659–677.

O'Rourke, M. F., & Hahimoto, J. (2007). Mechanical factors in arterial aging: A clinical perspective. *Journal of the American College of Cardiology, 50,* 1–13.

O'Sullivan, L. F., Cheng, M. M., Harris, K. M., & Brooks-Gunn, J. (2007). I wanna hold your hand: The progression of social, romantic, and sexual events in adolescent relationships. *Perspectives on Sexual and Reproductive Health, 39,* 100–107.

Oakes, L. M. (2008). Categorization skills and concepts. In M. M. Haith & J. B. Benson (Eds.), *Encyclopedia of infant and early childhood development.* Oxford, GB: Elsevier.

Oakes, L. M., Kannass, K. N., & Shaddy, D. J. (2002). Developmental changes in endogenous control of attention: The role of target familiarity on infants' distraction latency. *Child Development, 73,* 1644–1655.

Oates, R. K. (2009, in press). Child maltreatment and its impact of psychosocial development: Comments on Pollak, Toth and Cicchetti, and Trocme. In R. E. Tremblay, R. deV Peters, M. Boivin, & R. G. Barr (Eds.), *Encyclopedia of early childhood development.* Montreal: Centre of Excellence for Early Childhood Development.

Obenauer, S., & Maestre, L. A. (2008). Fetal MRI of lung hypoplasia: Imaging findings. *Clinical Imaging, 32,* 48–50.

Oberlander, S. E., Black, M. M., & Starr, R. H. (2007). African American adolescent mothers and grandmothers: A multigenerational approach to parenting. *American Journal of Community Psychology, 39,* 37–46.

Oberlander, T. F., Bonaguro, R. J., Misri, S., Papsdorf, M., Ross, C. J., & Simpson, E. M. (2008). Infant serotonin transporter (SLC6A4) promoter genotype is associated with adverse neonatal outcomes after prenatal exposure to serotonin reuptake inhibitor medications. *Molecular Psychiatry, 13,* 65–73.

Obler, L. K. (2005). Development in the older years. In J. Berko Gleason (Ed.), *The development of language* (6th ed.), Boston: Allyn & Bacon.

Obler, L. K. (2009). Developments in the adult years. In J. Berko Gleason & N. B. Ratner (Eds.), *The development of language* (7th ed.). Boston: Allyn & Bacon.

Occupational Outlook Handbook, 2006–2007. (2006). Washington, DC: U.S. Department of Labor, Bureau of Labor Statistics.

Occupational Outlook Handbook, 2008–2009. (2008). St. Paul, MN: JIST Publishing.

Offer, D., Ostrov E., Howard, K. I., & Atkinson, R. (1988). *The teenage world: Adolescents' self-image in ten countries.* New York: Plenum.

Ogbu, J. U. (1989, April). *Academic socialization of Black children: An inoculation against future failure?* Paper presented at the meeting of the Society for Research in Child Development, Kansas City.

Ogbu, J. U., & Stern, P. (2001). Caste status and intellectual ability. In R. J. Sternberg & E. L. Grigorenko (Eds.), *Environmental effects on cognitive abilities.* Mahwah, NJ: Erlbaum.

Ogden, C. L., Carroll, M. D., & Flegal, K. M. (2008). High body mass index for age among U. S. children and adolescents, 2003–2006. *Journal of the American Medical Association, 299,* 2401–2405.

Ohgi, S., Akiyama, T., Arisawa, K., & Shigemori, K. (2004). Randomised controlled trial of swaddling versus massage in the management of excessive crying in infants with cerebral injuries. *Archives of Diseases in Childhood. 89,* 212–216.

Oken, E., & Bellinger, D. C. (2008). Fish consumption, methylmercury, and child neurodevelopment. *Current Opinion in Pediatrics, 20,* 178–183.

Oksuzyan, A., Juel, K., Vaupel, J. W., & Christensen, K. (2008). Men: Good health and high mortality. Sex differences in health and aging. *Aging: Clinical and Experimental Research, 20,* 91–102.

Olson, H. C., King, S., & Jirikowic, T. (2008). Fetal alcohol spectrum disorders. In M. M. Haith & J. B. Benson (Eds.), *Encyclopedia of infancy and early childhood.* Thousand Oaks, CA: Sage.

Olweus, D. (2003). Prevalence estimation of school bullying with the Olweus bully/victim questionnaire. *Aggressive Behavior, 29*(3), 239–269.

Oman, D., & Thoresen, C. E. (2006). Do religion and spirituality influence health? In R. F. Paloutzian & C. L. Park (Eds.), *Handbook of the psychology of religion and spirituality.* New York: Guilford.

Onishi, K. H., & Baillargeon, R. (2005). Do 15-month-old infants understand false beliefs? *Science, 308,* 255–258.

Ono, M. Y., Farzin, F., & Hagerman, R. J. (2008). Fragile X syndrome. In M. M. Haith & J. B. Benson (Eds.), *Encyclopedia of infancy and early childhood development.* Oxford, UK: Elsevier.

Opitz, B., & Friederici, A. D. (2007). Neural basis of processing sequential and hierarchical structures. *Human Brain Mapping, 28,* 585–592.

Orbe, M. P. (2008). Theorizing multidimensional identity negotiation: Reflections on the lived experiences of first-generation college students. In M. Azmitia, M. Syed, & K. Radmacher (Eds.), *The intersections of personal and social identities. New Directions for Child and Adolescent Development, 120,* 81–95.

Orecchia, R., Lucignani, G., & Tosi, G. (2008). Prenatal irradiation and pregnancy: The effects of diagnostic imaging and radiation therapy. *Recent Results in Cancer Research, 178,* 3–20.

Organista, K. C. (1994). Overdue overview of elderly Latino mental health. *Contemparary Psychology, 39,* 61–62.

Orrange, Robert M. (2007). *Work, family, and leisure: Uncertainty in a risk society.* Boulder, CO: Rowman & Littlefield.

Osofsky, J. D. (Ed.). (2007). *Young children and trauma.* New York: Guilford.

Ott, C. H., Lueger, R. J., Kelber, S. T., & Prigerson, H. G. (2007). Spousal bereavement in older adults: Common, resilient, and chronic grief with defining characteristics. *Journal of Nervous and Mental Disease, 195,* 332–341.

Otto, B. W. (2008). *Literacy development in early childhood.* Upper Saddle River, NJ: Prentice Hall.

Ouldred, E., & Bryant, C. (2008). Dementia care. Part 2: Understanding managing behavioral challenges. *British Journal of Nursing, 17,* 242–247.

Owen, M. T. (2009, in press). Child care and the development of young children (0-2). In R. E. Tremblay, R. deV Peters, M. Boivan, & R. G. Barr (Eds.), *Encyclopedia on early childhood development.* Montreal: Centre of Excellence for Early Childhood Development.

Oxford, M. L., Gilchrist, L. D., Gillmore, M. R., & Lohr, M. J. (2006). Predicting variation in the life course of adolescent mothers as they enter adulthood. *Journal of Adolescent Health, 89,* 20–26.

P

Painter, K. (2008, June 16). Older, wiser, but less active. *USA Today.* p. 4D.

Pakpreo, P., Ryan, S., Auinger, P., & Aten, M. (2005). The association between parental lifestyle behaviors and adolescent knowledge, attitudes, intentions, and nutritional and physical activity behaviors. *Journal of Adolescent Health, 34,* 129–130.

Pallas, M., Verdaguer, E., Tajes, M., Gtierrez-Cuesta, J., & Camins, A. (2008). Modulation of sirtuins: New targets for antiaging. *Recent Patents on CNS Drug Discovery, 3,* 61–69.

Palmer, S. E. (2004). Custody and access issues with children whose parents are separated or divorced.

Canadian Journal of Community Mental Health, 4 (Suppl.) 25–38.

Palmore, E. B. (2004). Research note: Ageism in Canada and the United States. *Journal of Cross Cultural Gerontology, 19,* 41–46.

Palomaki, G. E., Steinort, K., Knight, G. J., & Haddow, J. E. (2006). Comparing three screening strategies for combining first- and -second-trimester Down syndrome markers. *Obstetrics and Gynecology, 107,* 1170.

Pan, B. A., Rowe, M. L., Singer, J. D., & Snow, C. E. (2005). Maternal correlates of growth in toddler vocabulary production in low-income families. *Child Development, 76,* 763–782.

Pan, B. A., & Uccelli, P. (2009). Semantic development. In J. Berko Gleason & N. Ratner (Eds.), *The development of language* (7th ed.). Boston: Allyn & Bacon.

Panneton, R., McIlreavy, M., & Bhullar, N. (2008). Preverbal development and speech production. In M. M. Haith & J. B. Benson (Eds.), *Encyclopedia of infant and early childhood development.* Oxford, UK: Elsevier.

Pantilat, S. Z., & Isaac, M. (2008). End-of-life care for the hospitalized patient. *Medical Clinics of North America, 92,* 349–370.

Papaharitou, S., Nakopoulou, E., Kirana, P., Giaglis, G., Moraitou, M., & Hatzichristou, D. (2008). Factors associated with sexuality in later life: An exploratory study in a group of Greek married older adults. *Archives of Gerontology and Geriatrics, 46,* 191–201.

Pardo, J. V., & others. (2007). Where the brain grows old: Decline in anterior cingulate and medial prefrontal function with normal aging. *Neuroimage, 35,* 1231–1237.

Parfitt, B., Mughal, M., & Thomas, H. (2008). Working together: A nursing development project in Tajikstan. *International Nursing Review, 55,* 205–211.

Paris, S. G., & Paris, A. H. (2006). Assessments of early reading. In W. Damon & R. Lerner (Eds.). *Handbook of child psychology* (6th ed.). New York: Wiley.

Park, C. L. (2005). Religion as a meaning-making systems. *Psychology of Religion Newsletter, 30* (No. 2), 1–9.

Park, C. L. (2007). Religiousness/spirituality and health: A meaning systems perspective. *Journal of Behavioral Medicine, 30,* 319–328.

Park, D. (2001). Commentary in Restak, R. *The secret life of the brain.* Washington, DC: Joseph Henry Press.

Park, D. C., & Gutchess, A. H. (2005). Long-term memory and aging: A cognitive neuroscience perspective. In R. Cabeza, L. Nyberg, & D. Park, (Eds.), *Cognitive neuroscience of aging: Linking cognitive and cerebral aging.* New York: Oxford University Press.

Park, D. C., Gutchess, A. H., Meade, M. L., & Stine-Morrow, E. A. L. (2007). Improving cognitive function in older adults: Nontraditional approaches. *Journals of Gerontology B: Psychological Sciences and Social Sciences, 62* (Special Issue I), P45–P52.

Park, D. C., & Schwarz, N. (Eds.) (2009). *Cognitive aging* (2nd ed.). Clifton, NJ: Psychology Press.

Park, J. H., Vincent, D., & Hastings-Tolsma, M. (2007). Disparity in prenatal care among women of color in the USA. *Midwifery, 23,* 28–37.

Park, M. J., Brindis, C. D., Chang, F., & Irwin, C. E. (2008). A midcourse review of the healthy people 2010: 21 critical health objectives for adolescents and young adults. *Journal of Adolescent Health, 42,* 329–334.

Park, M. J., Paul Mulye, T., Adams, S. H., Brindis, C. D., & Irwin, C. E. (2006). The health status of young adults in the United States. *Journal of Adolescent Health, 39,* 305–317.

Parke, R. D. (2004). Development in the family. *Annual Review of Psychology* (Vol. 55). Palo Alto, CA: Annual Reviews.

Parke, R. D., & Buriel, R. (2006). Socialization in the family: Ethnic and ecological perspectives. In W. Damon & R. Lerner (Eds.), *Handbook of child psychology* (6th ed.). New York: Wiley.

Parke, R. D., Leidy, M. S., Schofield, T. J., Miller, M. A., & Morris, K. L. (2008). Socialization. In M. M. Haith & J. B. Benson (Eds.), *Encyclopedia of infant and early childhood development.* Oxford, UK: Elsevier.

Parkes, K. R. (2006). Physical activity and self-rated health: Interactive effects of activity in work and leisure domains. *British Journal of Health Psychology, 11,* 533–550.

Parmalee, P. A. (2007). Depression. In J. E. Birren (Ed.), *Encyclopedia of gerontology* (2nd ed.). San Diego: Academic Press.

Parnes, H. S., & Sommers, D. G. (1994). Shunning retirement: Work experiences of men in their seventies and early eighties. *Journal of Gerontology, 49,* S117–S124.

Parra-Cardona, J. R., Bulock, L. A., Imig, D. R., Villarruel, F. A., & Gold, S. J. (2006). "Trabajanco duro todos los dias": Learning from the life experiences of Mexican-origin migrant families. *Family Relations, 55,* 361–375.

Partnership for a Drug-Free America. (2005). *Partnership Attitude Tracking Study.* New York: Author.

Partnership for Solutions. (2002). *Multiple chronic conditions: Complications in care and treatment.* Baltimore: Johns Hopkins University.

Pascalls, O., & Kelly, D. J. (2008). Face processing. In M. M. Haith & J. B. Benson (Eds.), *Encyclopedia of infant and early childhood development.* Oxford, UK: Elsevier.

Pasley, K., & Moorefield, B. S. (2004). Stepfamilies. In M. Coleman & L. Ganong (Eds.), *Handbook of contemporary families.* Thousand Oaks, CA: Sage.

Pasquini, E. S., Corriveau, K. H., Koenig, M., & Harris, P. L. (2007). Preschoolers monitor the relative accuracy of informants. *Developmental Psychology, 43,* 1216–1226.

Passuth, P. M., Maines, D. R., & Neugarten, B. L. (1984). *Age norms and age constraints twenty years later.* Paper presented at the annual meeting of the Midwest Sociological Society, Chicago.

Pate, R. R., Pfeiffer, K. A., Trost, S. G., Ziegler, P., & Dowda, M. (2004). Physical activity among children attending preschools. *Pediatrics, 114,* 1258–1263.

Patterson, C., Feightner, J. W., Garcia, A., Hsiung, G. Y., MacKnight, C., & Sadovnick, A. D. (2008). Diagnosis and treatment of dementia: 1. Risk assessment and primary prevention of Alzheimer's disease. *Canadian Medical Association Journal, 178,* 548–556.

Patterson, C. J. (2004). What differences does a civil union make? Changing public policies and the experiences of same-sex couples: Comment on Solomon, Rothblum, and Balsam (2004). *Journal of Family Psychology, 18,* 287–289.

Patterson, C. J., & Hastings, P. D. (2007). Socialization in the context of family diversity. In J. E. Grusec & P. D. Hastings (Eds.), *Handbook of socialization.* New York:

Paul, E. L., McManus, B., & Hayes, A. (2000). "Hookups": Characteristics and correlates of college students' spontaneous and anonymous sexual experiences. *The Journal of Sexual Research, 37,* 76–88.

Paul, P. (2003, Sept/Oct). The PermaParent trap. *Psychology Today, 36* (5), 40–53.

Pauley, S., Kopecky, B., Beisel, K., Soukup, G., & Fritzsch, B. (2008). Stem cells and molecular strategies to restore hearing. *Panminerva Medicine, 50,* 41–53.

Paulhus, D. L. (2008). Birth order. In M. M. Haith & J. B. Benson (Eds.), *Encyclopedia of infant and early childhood development.* Oxford, UK: Elsevier.

Paulson, J. F., Dauber, S., & Leiferman, J. A. (2006). Individual and combined effects of postpartum depression in mothers and fathers on parenting behavior. *Pediatrics, 118,* 659–668.

Paus, T., Toro, R., Leonard, G., Lerner, J. V., Lerner, R. M., Perron, M., Pike, G. B., Richer, L., Steinberg, L., Veillete, S., & Pausova, Z. (2008 in press). Morphological properties of the action-observation cortical network in adolescents with low and high resistance to peer influence. *Social Neuroscience.*

Pavone, C., Curto, F., Anello, G., Serretta, V., Almasio, P. L., & Pavone-Macaluso, M. (2008). Prospective, randomized crossover comparison of sublingual apopmorphine (3 mg) with oral sildenafil (50 mg) for male erectile dysfunction. *Journal of Urology, 179* (Suppl. 5), S92–S94.

Paxson, C., Donahue, E., Orleans, C. T., & Grisso, J. A. (2006). Introducing the issue. *Future of Children, 16* (No. 1) 3–17.

Payer, L. (1991). The menopause in various cultures. In H. Burger & M. Boulet (Eds.), *A portrait of the menopause.* Park Ridge, NJ: Parthenon.

Pederson, D. R., & Moran, G. (1996). Expressions of the attachment relationship outside of the Strange Situation. *Child Development, 67,* 915–927.

Pedroso, F. S. (2008). Reflexes. In M. M. Haith & J. B. Benson (Eds.), *Encyclopedia of infant and early childhood development.* Oxford, UK: Elsevier.

Pelayo, R., Owens, J., Mindell, J., & Sheldon, S. (2006). Bed sharing with unimpaired parents is not an important risk for sudden infant death syndrome: Letter to the editor. *Pediatrics, 117,* 993–994.

Pena, E., & Bedore, J. A. (2009). Bilingualism. In R. G. Schwartz (Ed.), *Handbook of child language disorders.* Clifton, NJ: Psychology Press.

Penagarikano, O., Mulle, J. G., & Warren, S. T. (2007). The pathophysiology of fragile X syndrome. *Annual Review of Genomics and Human Genetics, 8,* 109–129.

Pennick, V. E., & Young, G. (2007). Interventions for preventing and treating pelvic and back pain in pregnancy. *Cochrane Database of Systematic Reviews, 1,* CD001139.

Peplau, L. A., & Fingerhut, A. W. (2007). The close relationships of lesbians and gay men. *Annual Review of Psychology* (Vol. 58). Palo Alto, CA: Annual Reviews.

Peregoy, S. F., & Boyle O. F. (2009). *Reading, writing, and learning in ESL* (5th Ed.). Boston: Allyn & Bacon.

Pereira, A. C., & others. (2007). An in vivo correlate of exercise-induced neurogenesis in the adult dentate gyrus. *Proceedings of the National Academy of Sciences USA, 104,* 5638–5643.

Perez, S. M., & Gauvain, M. (2007). The sociocultural context of transitions in early socioemotional development. In C. A. Brownell & C. B. Kopp (Eds.), *Socioemotional development in the toddler years.* New York: Guilford.

Perez-Febles, A. M. (1992). *Acculturation and interactional styles of Latina mothers and their infants.* Unpublished honors thesis, Brown University, Providence, RI.

Perls, T. T. (2007). Centenarians. In J. E. Birren (Ed.), *Encyclopedia of gerontology* (2nd ed.). San Diego: Academic Press.

Perls, T. T., Lauerman, J. F., & Silver, M. H. (1999). *Living to 100.* New York: Basic Books.

Perner, J., Stummer, S., Sprung, M., & Doherty, M. (2002). Theory of mind finds its Piagetian perspective: Why alternative naming comes with understanding belief. *Cognitive Development, 17,* 1451–1472.

Perrig-Chiello, P., & Perren, S. (2005). The impact of past transitions on well-being in middle age. In S. L. Willis & M. Martin (Eds.), *Middle adulthood.* Thousand Oaks, CA: Sage.

Perry, C. M., & Johnson, C. L. (1994). Families and support networks among African American oldest-old. International *Journal of Aging on Human Development, 38,* 41–50.

Perry, W. G. (1999). *Forms of ethical and intellectual development in the college years: A scheme.* San Francisco: Jossey Bass.

Peskin, H. (1967). Pubertal onset and ego functioning. *Journal of Abnormal Psychology, 72,* 1–15.

Peskin, M. F., Tortolero, S. R., Markham, C. M., Addy, R. C., & Baumler, E. R. (2007). Bullying and victimization and internalizing symptoms among low-income Black and Hispanic students. *Journal of Adolescent Health, 40,* 372–375.

Peterson, B. E. (2002). Longitudinal analysis of midlife generativity, intergenerational roles, and caregiving. *Psychology and Aging, 17,* 161–168.

Petersen, B. E. (2006). Generativity and successful parenting: An analysis of young adult outcomes. *Journal of Personality, 74,* 847–869.

Peterson, B. E., & Stewart, A. J. (1996). Antecedents and contexts of generativity motivation at midlife. *Psychology and Aging, 11,* 21–33.

Peterson, C. C. (1996). The ticking of the social clock: Adults' beliefs about the timing of -transition events. *International Journal of Aging and Human Development, 42,* 189–203.

Peterson, C. C. (2005). Mind and body: Concepts of human cognition, physiology and false belief in children with autism or typical development. *Journal of Autism and Developmental Disorders, 35,* 487–497.

Peterson, M. B., Wang, Q., & Willems, P. J. (2008). Sex-linked deafness. *Clinical Genetics, 73,* 14–23.

Peterson, R. C., & Negash, S. (2008). Mild cognitive impairment: An overview. *CNS Spectrum, 13,* 45–53.

Petrill, S. A., Deater-Decklherd, K., Thompson, L. A., Dethorne, L. S., & Schatschneider, C. (2006). Reading skills in early readers: Genetic and shared environmental influences. *Journal of Learning Disabilities, 39,* 48–55.

Pfeifer, M. Goldsmith, H. H., Davidson, R. J., & Rickman, M. (2002). Continuity and change in inhibited and uninhibited children. *Child Development, 73,* 1474–1485.

Philipsen, N. M., Johnson, A. D., & Brooks-Gunn, J. (2009, in press). Poverty, effects on social and emotional development. *International Encyclopedia of Education.* Oxford, UK: Elsevier.

Phillips, A. C., Burns, V. E., & Lord, J. M. (2007). Stress and exercise: Getting the balance right for aging immunity. *Exercise and Sport Sciences Reviews, 35,* 35–39.

Phillipson, C., & Baars, J. (2007). Social -theory and social aging. In J. Bond, S. Peace, F. Dittman-Kohli, & G. Westerhoff (Eds.), *Aging in society* (3rd ed.). Thousand Oaks, CA: Sage.

Phinney, J. S. (2006). Ethnic identity exploration in emerging adulthood. In J. J. Arnett & J. L. Tanner (Eds.), *Emerging adults in America.* Washington, DC: American Psychological Association.

Phinney, J. S. (2008). *Bridging identities and disciplines: Advances and challenges in understanding multiple identities.* In M. Azmitia, M. Syed, & K. Radmacher (Eds.), *The intersections of personal and social identities. New Directions for Child and Adolescent Development, 120,* 81–95.

Piaget, J. (1932). *The moral judgment of the child.* New York: Harcourt Brace Jovanovich.

Piaget, J. (1952). *The origins of intelligence in children.* (M. Cook, Trans.). New York: International Universities Press.

Piaget, J. (1954). *The construction of reality in the child.* New York: Basic Books.

Piaget, J. (1962). *Play, dreams, and imitation.* New York. W. W. Norton.

Piaget, J., & Inhelder, B. (1969). *The child's conception of space* (F. J. Langdon & J. L. Lunger, Trans.). New York: W. W. Norton.

Pierce, G. F., Lillicrap, D., Pipe, S. W., & Vandenriessche, T. (2007). Gene therapy, bioengineered clotting factors, and novel technologies for hemophilia treatment. *Journal of Thrombosis and Haemostasis, 5,* 901–906.

Piggott, J. (2007). Cultivating creativity. *Mathematics Incorporating Micromath* (No. 202). 3–6.

Pinette, M., Wax, J. & Wilson, E. (2004). The risks of underwater birth. *American Journal of Obstetrics and Gynecology, 190,* 1211–1215.

Ping, H., & Hagopian, W. (2006). Environmental factors in the development of type 1 diabetes. *Reviews in Endocrine and Metabolic Disorders, 7,* 149–162.

Pinquart, M., & Sorensen, S. (2006). Gender differences in caregiver stressors, social -resources, and health: An updated meta—analysis. *Journals of Gerontology B: Psychological Sciences and Social Sciences, 61,* P33–P45.

Pinto, N. M., Marino, B. S., Wernovsky, G., de Ferranti, S. D., Walsh, A. Z., Laronde, M., Hyland, K., Dunn, S. O., & Cohen, M. S. (2007). Obesity is a common comorbidity in children with congenital and acquired heart disease. *Pediatrics, 120,* e1157–e1164.

Pipe M. (2008). Children as eye witnesses: Memory in the forensic context. *In M. Courage & N. Cowan (Eds.), The development of memory in Infancy and childhood. Philadelphia: Psychology Press.*

Piper, W. E., Ogrodniczuk, J. S., Joyce, A. S., Weideman, R., & Rosie, J. S. (2007). Group composition and group therapy for complicated grief. *Journal of Consulting and Clinical Psychology, 75,* 116–125.

Pitkanen, T., Lyyra, A. L., & Pulkkinen L. (2005). Age of onset of drinking and the use of alcohol in adulthood: A follow-up study from age 8–42 for females and males. *Addiction, 100,* 652–661.

Pitt-Catsouphes, M., Kossek, E. E., & Sweet, S. (Eds.). (2006). *The work and family handbook.* Mahwah, NJ: Erlbaum.

Plachta-Danielzik, S., Landsberg, B., Johannsen, M., Lange, D., & Muller, D. J. (2008). Association of different obesity indices with blood pressure and blood lipids in children and adolescents. *British Journal of Nutrition, 18,* 1–11.

Pleck, J. H. (1995). The gender-role strain paradigm. In R. F. Levant & W. S. Pollack (Eds.). *A new psychology of men.* New York: Basic Books.

Pliszka, S. R. (2007). Pharmacologic treatment of attention deficit hyperactivity disorder: Efficacy, safety, and mechanisms of action. *Neuropsychology Review, 17,* 61–72.

Plomin, R. (1999). Genetics and general cognitive ability. *Nature, 402* (Suppl.), C25–C29.

Plomin, R. (2004). Genetics and developmental psychology. *Merrill-Palmer Quarterly, 50,* 341–352.

Plomin, R., DeFries, J. C., & Fulker, D. W. (2007). *Nature and nurture during infancy and early childhood.* New York: Cambridge University Press.

Plomin, R., & Schalkwyk, L. C. (2007). Microarrays. *Developmental Science, 10,* 19–23.

Pollack, W. (1999). *Real boys.* New York: Owl Books.

Pollak, S. (2009, in press). The impact of child maltreatment on the psychosocial development of young children. In R. E. Tremblay, R. deV Peters, M. Boivin, & R. G. Barr (Eds.), *Encyclopedia of early childhood development.* Montreal: Centre of Excellence for Early Childhood Development.

Pollard, I. (2007). Neuropharmacology of drugs and alcohol in mother and fetus. *Seminars in Fetal and Neonatal Medicine, 12,* 106–113.

Pollitt, E. P., Gorman, K. S., Engle, P. L., Martorell, R., & Rivera, J. (1993). Early supplementary feeding and cognition. *Monographs of the Society for Research in Child Development, 58* (7, Serial No. 235).

Pomery, E. A., Gibbons, F. X., Ferrard, M., Cleveland, M. J., Brody, G. H., & Wills, T. A. (2005). Families and risk: Protective analyses of familial and social influences on adolescent substance abuse. *Journal of Family Psychology, 19,* 560–570.

Poole, D. A., & Lindsay, D. S. (1996). *Effects of parents' suggestions, interviewing techniques, and age on young children's event reports* Paper presented at the NATO Advanced Study Institute, Porte de Bourgenay, France.

Popenoe, D. (2007). *The state of our unions: 2007.* Piscataway, NJ: The National Marriage Project, Rutgers University.

Popenoe, D. (2008). *Cohabitation, marriage, and child wellbeing: A cross-national perspective.* Piscataway, NJ: The National Marriage Project, Rutgers University.

Popenoe, D., & Whitehead, B. D. (2006). *The state of our unions 2006.* New Brunswick, NJ: The National Marriage Project, Rutgers University.

Popenoe, D., & Whitehead, B. D. (2005). *The state of our unions: 2005.* Piscataway, NJ: The National Marriage Project, Rutgers University.

Posada, G. (2008). Attachment. In M. M. Haith & J. B. Benson (Eds.), *Encyclopedia of infancy and early childhood.* Oxford, UK: Elsevier.

Posner, M. I. (2003). Imaging a science of mind. *Trends in Cognitive Science, 7,* 450–453.

Posner, M. I., & Rothbart, M. K. (2007). *Educating the human brain.* Washington, DC: American Psychological Association.

Posner, M. I., & Rothbart, M. K. (2007). Research on attention networks as a model for the integration of psychological sciences. *Annual Review of Psychology, 58,* 1–23.

Postina, R. (2008). A closer look at alpha-secretase. *Current Alzheimer Research, 5,* 179–186.

Poulin, F., & Pedersen, S. (2007). Developmental changes in gender composition of friendship networks in adolescent girls and boys. *Developmental Psychology, 43,* 1484–1496.

Powell, S. D. (2009). *Introduction to teaching.* Upper Saddle River, NJ: Prentice Hall.

Power, F. C., Narvaez, D., Nuzzi, R., Lapsley, D., & Hunt, T., (Eds.). (2008). *Moral education: A handbook.* Westport, CT: Greenwood Publishing.

Pratt, C., & Bryant, P. E. (1990). Young children understand that looking leads to knowing (so long as they are looking in a single barrel): *Child Development, 61,* 973–982.

Pratt, M. W., Norris, J. E., Cressman, K., Lawford, H., & Hebblethwaite, S. (2008a). Parents' stories of grandparenting concerns in the three-generational family: Generativity, optimism, and forgiveness. *Journal of Personality, 76,* 581–604.

Pratt, M. W., Norris, J. E., Hebblethwaite, S., & Arnold, M. L. (2008b). Intergenerational transmission of values: Family generativity and adolescents' narratives of parent and grandparent value teaching. *Journal of Personality, 76,* 171–198.

Pressley, M. (2003). Psychology of literacy and literacy instruction. In I. B. Weiner (Ed.), *Handbook of psychology.* New York: Wiley.

Pressley, M. (2007). Achieving best practices. In L. B. Gambrell, L. M. Morrow, & M. Pressley, (Eds.), *Best practices in literary instruction:* New York: Guilford.

Pressley, M., Allington, R., Wharton-McDonald, R., Block, C. C., & Morrow, L. M. (2001). *Learning to read: Lessons from exemplary first grades.* New York: Guilford.

Pressley, M., Billman, A. K., Perry, K. H., Reffitt, K. E., & Reynolds, J. M. (Eds.). (2007). *Shaping literacy achievement.* New York: Guilford.

Pressley, M., Cariligia-bull, T., Deane, S., & Schneider, W. (1987). Short-term memory, verbal competence, and age as predictors of imagery instructional effectiveness. *Journal of Experimental child Psychology, 43,* 194–211.

Pressley, M., Dolezal, S. E., Raphael, L. M., Welsh, L. M., Bogner, K., & Roehrig, A. D. (2003). *Motivating primary-grades teachers.* New York: Guilford.

Pressley, M., & McCormick, C. B. (2007). *Child and adolescent development for educators.* New York: Guilford.

Pressley, M., Raphael, L. Gallagher, D., & DiBella, J. (2004). Providence–St. Mel School: How a school that works for African-American students works. *Journal of Educational Psychology, 96,* 216–235.

Presson, J. C., & Jenner, J. V. (2008). *Biology.* New York: McGraw-Hill.

Price, C. A., & Joo, E. (2005). Exploring the relationship between marital status and women's retirement satisfaction. *International Journal of Aging and Human Development, 61,* 37–55.

Price, D. L., & Gwin, J. F. (2008). *Pediatric nursing* (10th ed.). St. Louis: Mosby.

Prinstein, M. J., & Dodge, K. A. (Eds.) (2008). *Understanding peer influence in children and adolescents.* New York: Guilford.

Province, M. A., Hadley, E. C., Hornbrook, M. C., Lipitz, L. A., Miller, J. P., Mulrow, C. D., Ory, M. G., Sattin, R. W., Tinetti, M. E., & Wolf, S. L. (1995). The effects of exercise on falls in elderly patients. *Journal of the American Medical Association, 273,* 1341–1347.

Pryor, J. H. Y., Hurtado, S., Harkness, J., & Korn, W. S. (2007). *The American freshman: National norms for fall, 2007.* Los Angeles: Higher Education Research Institute, UCLA.

Pudrovska, T., Schieman, S., & Carr, D. (2006). Strains of singlehood in later life: Do race and gender matter? *Journals of Gerontology B: Psychological Sciences and Social Sciences, 61,* S315–S322.

Pueschel, S. M., Scola, P. S., Weidenman, L. E., & Bernier, J. C. (1995). *The special child.* Baltimore: Paul H. Brookes.

Putallaz, M., Grimes, C. L., Foster, K. J., Kupersmidt, J. B., Clie, J. D., & Dearing, K. (2007). Overt and relational aggression and victimization: Multiple perspectives within the school setting. *Journal of School Psychology, 45,* 523–547.

Putics, A., Vegh, E. M., Scermely, P., & Soti, C. (2008). Resveratrol induces the heat shock response and protects human cells from severe heatstress. *Antioxidants and Redox Signaling, 10,* 65–76.

Putnam Investments. (2006). *Survey of the working retired.* Franklin, MA: Author.

Putnam, S. P., Sanson, A. V., & Rothbart, M. K. (2002). Child temperament and parenting. In M. H. Bornstein (Ed.), *Handbook of parenting* (2nd ed.). Mahwah, NJ: Erlbaum.

Q

Quadrelli, R., Quadrelli, A., Mechoso, B., Laufer, M., Jaumandreu, C., & Vaglio, A. (2007). Parental decisions to abort or continue a pregnancy following prenatal diagnosis of chromosomal abnormalities in a setting where termination pregnancy is not legally available. *Prenatal Diagnosis, 27,* 228–232.

Quesnel, C., Fulgencio, J. P., Drie, C., Marro, B., Payen, L., Lembert, N., El Metaoua, S., & Bonnet, F. (2007). Limitations of computed tomographic angiography in the diagnosis of brain death. *Intensive Care Medicine, 33,* 2129–2135.

Quinn, P. C. (2007). Categorization. In A. Slater & M. Lewis (Eds.), *Introduction to infant development* (2nd ed.). New York: Oxford University Press.

Quinn, P. C., Bhatt, R. S., & Hayden, A. (2008, in press). What goes with what: Development of perceptual grouping in infancy. In B. H. Ross (Ed.), *Motivation* (Vol. 49). London: Elsevier.

Quinn, P. C., & Eimas, P. D. (1996). Perceptual cues that permit categorical differentiation of animal species by infants. *Journal of Experimental Child Psychology, 63,* 189–211.

Quiocho, A. L., & Ulanoff, S. H. (2009). *Differentiated literacy instruction for English language learners.* Boston: Allyn & Bacon.

R

Raabe, A., & Muller, W. U. (2008, in press). Radiation exposure during pregnancy. *Neurosurgery Review.*

Raffaelli, M., & Ontai, L. L. (2004). Gender socialization in Latino/a families: Results from two retrospective studies. *Sex Roles, 50,* 287–299.

Rahal, T. A., May, C. P., & Hasher, L. (2002). Truth and character: Sources that older adults can remember. *Psychological Science, 13,* 101–105.

Rajendran, G., & Mitchell, P. (2007). Cognitive theories of autism. *Developmental Review, 27,* 224–260.

Ram, K. T., Bobby, P., Hailpern, S. M., Lo, J. C., Schocken, M., Skurnick, J., & Santro, N. (2008). Duration of lactation is associated with lower prevalence of the metabolic syndrome in midlife—SWAN, the study of women's health across the nation. *American Journal of Obstetrics and Gynecology, 198,* e1–e6.

Ram, N., Morelli, S., Lindberg, C., & Carstensen, L. L. (2008, in press). From static to dynamic: The ongoing dialectic about human development. In K. W. Schaie & R. P. Abeles (Eds.), *Social structures and aging individuals: Continuing challenges.* Mahwah, NJ: Erlbaum.

Ramey, C. T., & Campbell, F. A. (1984). Preventive education for high-risk children: Cognitive consequences of the Carolina Abecedarian Project. *American Journal of Mental Deficiency, 88,* 515–523.

Ramey, C. T., & Ramey, S. L. (1998). Early Prevention and early experience. *American Psychologist, 53,* 109–120.

Ramey, C. T., Ramey, S. L., & Lanzi, R. G. (2001). Intelligence and experience. In R. J. Sternberg & E. I. Grigorenko (Eds.), *Environment effects on cognitive development.* Mahwah, NJ: Erlbaum.

Ramey, S. L. (2005). Human developmental science serving children and families: Contributions of the NICHD study of early child care. In NICHD Early Child Care Research Network (Eds.), *Child care and development.* New York: Guilford.

Ramsey-Rennels, J. L., & Langlois, J. H. (2007). How infants perceive and process faces. In A. Salter & M. Lewis (Eds.), *Introduction to infant development* (2nd ed.). Malden, MA: Blackwell.

Rapaport, S. (1994, November 28). Interview. *U. S. News & World Report,* p. 94.

Raphael, B., Taylor, M., & McAndrew, V. (2008). Women, catastrophe, and mental health. *Australia and New Zealand Journal of Psychiatry, 42,* 13–23.

Rasinski, T. V., & Padak, N. (2008). *From phonics to fluency* (2nd ed.). Boston: Allyn & Bacon.

Rasulo, D., Christensen, K., & Tomassini, C. (2005). The influence of social relations on mortality in later life: A study on elderly Danish twins. *Gerontologist, 45,* 601–608.

Ratey, J. (2006, March 27). Commentary in L. Szabo, "ADHD treatment is getting a workout." *USA Today,* 6D.

Rathunde, K., & Csikstentmihalyi M. (2006). The developing person: An Experiential perspective. In W. Damon's R. Lerner (Eds.), *Handbook of child psychology* (6th ed.). New York: Wiley.

Raven, P. H., Johnson, G. B., Mason, K. A., Losos, J., & Singer, S. (2008). *Biology* (8th ed.). New York: McGraw-Hill.

Rawlins, W. K. (2009). *The compass of friendship.* Thousand Oaks, CA: Sage.

Raymo, J. M., & Sweeney, M. M. (2006). Work-family conflict and retirement preferences. *Journals of Gerontology B: Psychological Sciences and Social Sciences, 61,* S161–S169.

Read, S., & Elliott, D. (2007). Exploring a continuum of support for bereaved people with intellectual disabilities: A strategic approach. *Journal of Intellectual Disabilities, 11,* 167–181.

Ream, G. L. & Savin-Williams, R. (2003). Religious development in adolescence. In G. Adams & M. Berzonsky (Eds.), *Blackwell handbook of adolescence.* Malden, MA: Blackwell.

Reddy, U. M., Wapner, R. J., Rebar, R. W., & Tasca, R. J. (2007). Infertility, assisted reproductive technology, and adverse pregnancy outcomes: Executive summary of the a National Institute of Child Health and Human Development workshop. *Obstetrics and Gynecology, 109,* 967–977.

Redgrave, G. W., Coughlin, J. W., Heinberg, L. J., & Guarda, A. S. (2007). First-degree relative history of alcoholism in eating disorder inpatients: Relationship to eating and substance abuse psychopathology. *Eating Behaviors, 8,* 15–22.

Redinbaugh, E. M., MacCallum, J., & Kiecolt-Glaser, J. K. (1995). Recurrent syndromal depression in caregivers. *Psychology and Aging, 10,* 358–368.

Redmond, N., & While, A. (2008). Age -related macular degeneration: Visual impairment with advancing age. *British Journal of Community Nursing, 13,* 68–75.

Reeb, B. C., Fox, N. A. Nelson, C. A., & Zeanah, C. H. (2008, in press). The effects of early institutionalization of social behavior and underlying neural correlates. In M. de Haan & M. Gunnar (Eds.), *Handbook of social developmental neuroscience.* Malden, MA: Blackwell.

Reece, E. A. (2008). Obesity, diabetes, and links to congenital defects: A review of the evidence and recommendations for intervention. *Journal of Maternal-Fetal and Neonatal Medicine, 21,* 173–180.

Reese, C. M., & Cherry, K. E. (2004). Practical memory concerns in adulthood. *International Journal of Aging and Human Development, 59,* 235–253.

Regalado, M., Sareen, H., Inkelas, M., Wissow, L. S., & Halfon, N. (2004). Parents' discipline of young children: Results from the National Survey of Early Childhood Health. *Pediatrics, 113,* 1952–1958.

Regan, P. C. (2008). *The mating game* (2nd ed.). Thousand Oaks, CA: Sage.

Regev, R. H., Lusky, A., Dolfin, T., Litmanovitz, I., Arnon, S., Reichman, B., & the Israel Neonatal Network. (2003). Excess mortality and morbidity among small-for-gestational-age premature infants: A population based study. *Journal of Pediatrics, 143,* 186–191.

Reichstadt, J., Depp, C. A., Palinkas, L. A., Folsom, D. P., & Jeste, D. V. (2007). Building blocks of successful aging: A focus group study of older adults' perceived contributors to successful aging. *American Journal of Geriatric Psychiatry, 15,* 194–201.

Reid, G., Fawcett, A., Manis, F., & Siegel, L. (Eds.) (2009). *The SAGE handbook of dyslexia.* Thousand Oaks, CA: Sage.

Reid, J. (2007). Centering pregnancy: A model for group prenatal care. *Nursing and Women's Health, 11,* 382–386.

Reid, P. T., & Zalk, S. R. (2001). Academic environments: Gender and ethnicity in U.S. higher education. In J. Worell (Ed.), *Encyclopedia of women and gender.* San Diego: Academic Press.

Reilly, D. E., Hastings, R. P., Vaughan, F. L., & Huws, J. C. (2008). Parental bereavement and the loss of a child with intellectual disabilities: A review of the literature. *Intellectual and Developmental Disabilities, 46,* 27–43.

Reilly, J. J. (2009, in press). Early prevention of obesity. In R. E. Tremblay, R. deV Peters, M. Boivin, & R. G. Barr (Eds.), *Encyclopedia of early childhood development.* Montreal: Centre of Excellence for Early Childhood Development.

Reinders, H., & Youniss, J. (2006). School-based required community service and civic development in adolescence. *Applied Developmental Science, 10,* 2–12.

Reisman, A. S. (2001). Death of a spouse: Basic assumptions and continuation of bonds. *Death Studies, 25,* 445–460.

Rejeski, W. J., King, A. C., Katula, J. A., Kritchevsky, S., Miller, M. E., Walkup, M. P., Glynn, N. W., Pahor, M., & LIFE investigators. (2008). Physical activity in prefrail older adults: Confidence and Satisfaction related to physical function. *Journals of Gerontology B: Psychological Sciences and Social Sciences, 63,* P19–P26.

Rendell, P. G., McDaniel, M. A., Forbes, R. D., & Einstein, G. O. (2007). Age-related effects in prospective memory are modulated by ongoing task complexity and relation to target cue. *Neuropsychology, Development, and Cognition, Section B: Neuropsychology and Cognition, 14,* 236–256.

Renner, P., Grofer Klinger, L., & Klinger, M. R. (2006). Exogenous and endogenous attention orienting in autism spectrum disorders. *Child Neuropsychology, 12,* 361–382.

Repacholi, B. M., & Gopnik, A. (1997). Early reasoning about desires: Evidence from 14- and 18-month-olds. *Developmental Psychology, 33,* 12–21.

Reusch, J. E., & Draznin, B. B. (2007). Atherosclerosis in diabetes and insulin resistance. *Diabetes, Obesity, and Metabolism, 9,* 455–463.

Reutzel, D.R., & Cooter, R.B. (2009). *Essentials of teaching to read* (2nd Ed.). Boston: Allyn & Bacon.

Reyna, C., Goodwin, E. J., & Ferrari, J. R. (2007). Older adult stereotypes among care providers in residential care facilities: Examining the relationship between contact, education, and ageism. *Journal of Gerontological Nursing, 33,* 50–55.

Reyna, V. F. (2004). How people make decisions that involve risk: A dual-process approach. *Current Directions in Psychological Science, 13,* 60–66.

Reyna, V. F., & Brainerd, C. J. (1995). Fuzzy-trace theory: An interim analysis. *Learning and Individual differences, 7,* 1–75.

Reyna, V. F., & Rivers, S. E. (2008). Current theories and rational decision making. *Developmental Review, 28,* 1–11.

Rholes, W. S., & Simpson, J. A. (2007). Introduction: New directions and emerging issues in adult attachment. In W. S. Rholes & J. A. Simpson (Eds.), *Adult attachment.* New York: Guilford.

Rice, D. P., & Fineman, N. (2004). Economic implications of increased longevity in the United States. *Annual Review of Public Health, 25,* 457–473.

Richardson, C. R., Faulkner, G., McDevitt, J., Skrinar, G. S., Hutchinson, D. S., & Piette, J. D. (2005). Integrating physical activity into mental health services for persons with serious mental illness. *Psychiatric Services, 56,* 324–331.

Richardson, G. A., Goldschmidt, L., & Larkby, C. (2008). Effects of prenatal cocaine exposure on growth: A longitudinal analysis. *Pediatrics, 120,* e1017–e1027.

Richardson, G. A., Goldschmidt, L., & Willford, J. (2008). The effects of prenatal cocaine use on infant development. *Neurotoxicology and Teratology, 30,* 96–106.

Richardson, V. E. (2007). A dual process model of grief counseling: Findings from the Changing Lives of Older Couples (CLOC) Study. *Journal of Gerontological Social Work, 48,* 311–329.

Richmond, E. J., & Royal, A. D. (2007). Male pubertal development and the role of androgen therapy. *Nature Clinical Practice: Endocrinology and Metabolism, 3,* 338–344.

Rickards, T., Moger, S., & Runco, M. (2009). *The Routledge companion to creativity.* Oxford, UK: Routledge.

Ridgeway, D., Waters, E., & Kuczaj, S. A. (1985). Acquisition of emotion-descriptive language: Receptive and productive vocabulary norms for ages 18 months to 6 years. *Developmental Psychology, 21,* 901–908.

Riebe, D., Garber, C. E., Rossi, J. S., Greaney, M. L., Nigg, C. R., Lees, F. D., Burbank, P. M., &

Clark, P. G. (2005). Physical activity, physical function, and stages of change in older adults. *American Journal of Health Behavior, 29,* 70–80.

Riediger, M., Li, S-C., & Lindenberger, U. (2006). Selection, optimization, and compensation as developmental mechanisms of adaptive resource allocation: Review and preview. In J. E. Birren & K. W. Schaie (Eds.), *Handbook of the psychology of aging* (6th ed.). San Diego: Academic Press.

Ries, M. L., Carlsson, C. M., Rowley, H. A., Sger, M. A., Gleason, C. E., Asthana, S., & Johnson, S. C. (2008, in press). Magnetic resonance imaging characterization of brain structure and function in mild cognitive impairment: A review. *Journal of the American Geriatric Society.*

Rifas-Shiman, S. L., Rich-Edwards, J. W., Willett, W. C., Kleinman, K. P., Oken, E., & Gillman, M. W. (2006). Changes in dietary intake from the first to the second trimester of pregnancy. *Pediatric and Perinatal Epidemiology, 20,* 35–42.

Rigaud, D., Verges, B., Colas-Linhart, N., Petiet, A., Moukkaddem, M., Van Wymelbeke, V., & Brondel, L. (2007). Hormonal and psychological factors linked to the increased thermic effect of food in malnourished fasting anorexia nervosa. *Journal of Clinical Endocrinology and Metabolism, 92,* 1623–1629.

Riley, E. H., Fuentes-Afflick, E., Jackson, R. A., Escobar, G. J., Brawarsky, P., Schreiber, M., & Haas, J. S. (2005). Correlates of prescription drug use during pregnancy. *Journal of Women's Health, 14,* 401–409.

Riley, K. P., Snowdon, D. A., Derosiers, M. F., & Markesbery, W. R. (2005). Early life linguistic ability, late life cognitive function, and neuropathology: Findings from the Nun Study. *Neurobiology of Aging, 26,* 341–347.

Riley, L. D., & Bowen, C. (2005). The sandwich generation: Challenges and coping strategies of multigenerational families. *Family Journal, 13,* 52–58.

Rimm, E. B., Stampfer, M. J., Ascherio, A., Giovannucci, E., Colditz, G. A., & Willett, W. C. (1993). Vitamin E consumption and the risk of coronary heart disease in men. *New England Journal of Medicine, 328,* 1450–1456.

Rimsza, M. E., & Kirk, G. M. (2005). Common medical problems of the college student. *Pediatric Clinics of North America, 52,* 9–24.

Ringdal, G. I., Jordhoy, M. S., Ringdal, K., & Kaasa, S. (2001). The first year of grief and bereavement in close family members to individuals who have died of cancer. *Palliative Medicine, 15,* 91–105.

Rink, J. E. (2009). *Designing the physical education curriculum.* New York: McGraw-Hill.

Rivera, C., & Collum, E. (Eds.). (2006). *State assessment policy and practice for English language learners.* Mahwah, NJ: Erlbaum.

Rivers, S. E., Reyna, V. F., & Mills, B. (2008). Risk taking under the influence: A fuzzy-trace theory of emotion in adolescence. *Developmental Review, 28,* 107–144.

Rizvi, A. A. (2007). Management of diabetes in older adults. *American Journal of Medical Science, 333,* 35–47.

Rizzo, M. S. (1999, May 8). Genetic counseling combines science with a human touch. *Kansas City Star,* p. 3.

Robbins, G., Powers, D., & Burgess, S. (2008). *A fit way of life.* New York: McGraw-Hill.

Roberto, K. A., & Skoglund, R. R. (1996). Interactions with grandparents and great— grandparents: A comparison of activities, influences, and relationships. *International Journal of Aging and Human Development, 43,* 107–117.

Roberts, B. W., Jackson, J. J. Fayard, J. V. Edmonds, G., & Meints, J. (2008a, in press). Conscientiousness. In M. Leary & R. Hoyle (Eds.), *Handbook of individual differences in social behavior.* New York: Guilford.

Roberts, B. W., & Mroczek, D. (2008). Personality trait change in adulthood. *Current Directions in Psychological Science, 17,* 31–35.

Roberts, B. W., Walton, K. E., & Bogg, T. (2005). Conscientiousness and health across the life course. *Review of General Psychology, 9,* 156–168.

Roberts, B. W., Walton, K. E., & Viechtbauer, W. (2006). Pattern of mean-level change in personality traits across the life course: A meta-analysis of longitudinal studies. *Psychological Bulletin, 132,* 1–25.

Roberts, B. W., & Wood, D. (2006). Personality development in the context of the Neo-Socioanalytic Model of personality. In D. Mroczek & T. Little (Eds.), *Handbook of Personality Development.* Mahwah, NJ: Erlbaum.

Roberts, B.W., Wood, D., & Caspi, a. (2008, in press). Personality development. In O. P. John, R. W. Robins, & L. A. Pervin (Eds.), *Handbook of personality* (3rd ed.). New York: Guilford.

Roberts, D. F., & Foehr, U. G. (2008). Trends in media use. *Future of Children, 18 (No. 1),* 11–37.

Roberts, D. F., Henrikson, L., & Foehr, V. G. (2004). Adolescents and the media. In R. Lerner & L. Steinberg (Eds.), *Handbook of adolescent psychology.* New York: Wiley.

Roberts, J. M. (2008). The parameters of prejudice: Knowledge of ethics and age bias. *Journal of Gerontological Social Work.*

Roberts, S. B., & Rosenberg, I. (2006). Nutrition and aging: Changes in the regulation of energy metabolism with aging. *Physiology Review, 86,* 651–667.

Roberts. B. W., Kuncel, N. R., Shiner, R., Caspi, A., & Goldberg, L. R. (2008b). The power of personality. *Perspectives on Psychological Science, 2,* 313–345.

Robins, R. W., Trzesniewski, K. H., Tracey, J. L., Potter, J., & Gosling, S. D. (2002). Age differences in self-esteem from age 9 to 90. *Psychology and Aging, 17,* 423–434.

Rochlen, A. B., McKelley, R. A., Suizzo, M-A., & Scaringi, V. (2008). Predictors of relationship satisfaction, psychological well-being, and life-satisfaction among stay-at-home fathers. *Psychology of Men and Masculinity, 9,* 17–28.

Rochlen, A. B., Suizzo, M. A., Scaringi, V., Bredow, A. McKelley, R. A. (2007, August) *A qualitative study of stay-at-home fathers.* Paper presented at the meeting of the American Psychological Association, San Francisco.

Rode, S. S., Change, P., Fisch, R. O., & Sroufe, L. A. (1981). Attachment patterns of infants separated at birth. *Developmental Psychology, 17,* 188–191.

Rodgers, W. (1982). Trends in reported happiness within demographically defined subgroups 1957–1978. *Social Forces, 60,* 826–842.

Rodin, J. (1983). Behavioral medicine: Beneficial effects of self-control training in aging. *International Review of Applied Psychology, 32,* 153–181.

Rodin, J., & Langer, E. J. (1977). Long-term effects of a control-relevant intervention with the institutionalized aged. *Journal of Personality and Social Psychology, 35,* 397–402.

Rodrigues, A. E., Hall, J. H., & Fincham, F. D. (2006). What predicts divorce and relationship dissolution. In M. A. Fine & J. H. Harvey (Eds.), *Handbook of divorce and relationship dissolution.* Mahwah, NJ: Erlbaum.

Roediger, H. L., & Geraci, L. (2007). Aging and the misinformation effect: A neuropsychological analysis. *Journal of Experimental Psychology: Learning, Memory, and Cognition, 33,* 321–334.

Roese, N. J., & Summerville, A. (2005). What we regret most... and why. *Personality and Social Psychology Bulletin, 31,* 1273–1285.

Rogers, L. S. (2004). Meaning of bereavement among older African American widows. *Geriatric Nursing, 25,* 10–16.

Rogoff, B., Moore, L., Najafi, B., Dexter, A., Correa-Chavez, M., & Solis, J. (2007). Children's development of cultural repertoires through participation in everyday routines and practices. In J. E. Grusec & P. D. Hastings (Eds.), *Handbook of socialization.* New York: Guilford.

Rohrer, J. F., Pierce, J. R., & Blackburn, C. (2005). Lifestyle and mental health. *Preventive Medicine, 40,* 438–443.

Roisman, G. I., Clausell, E., Holland, A., Fortuna, K., & Elieff, C. (2008). Adult romantic relationships as contexts of human development: A multimethod comparison of same-sex couples with opposite-sex dating, engaged, and married dyads. *Developmental Psychology, 44,* 91–101.

Rolls, B. J., & Drewnowski, A. (2007). Diet and nutrition. In J. E. Birren (Ed.), *Encyclopedia of gerontology* (2nd ed.). San Diego: Academic Press.

Rook, K. S., Mavandadi, S., Sorkin, D. h., & Zettel, L. A. (2007). Optimizing social relationships as a resource for health and wellbeing in later life. In C. M. Aldwin, C. L. Park, & A. Spiro (Eds.), *Handbook of health psychology and aging.* New York: Guilford.

Roopnarine, J. L., & Metindogan, A. (2006). Early childhood education research in cross-national perspective. In B. Spodek & O. N. Saracho (Eds.), *Handbook of research on the education of young children.* Mahwah, NJ: Erlbaum.

Rosano, G. M., Vitale, C., Marazzi, G., & Volterrani, M. (2007). Menopause and cardiovascular disease: The evidence. *Climacteric, 10* (Suppl. 1), S19–S24.

Rose, A. J., Carlson, W., & Waller, E. M. (2007). Prospective associations of co-rumination with friendship and emotional adjustment: Considering the socioemotional trade-offs of co-rumination. *Developmental Psychology, 43,* 1019–1031.

Rose, M. R., & Rauser, C. L. (2007). Evolution and comparative biology. In J. E. Birren (Ed.), *Encyclopedia of gerontology* (2nd ed.). San Diego: Academic Press.

Rose, S. A. (1990). Cross-modal transfer in human infants: What is being transferred? *Annals of the New York Academy of Sciences, 608,* 38–47.

Rose, S. A., Feldman, J. F., & Wallace, L. F. (1992). Infant Information processing in relation to six-year cognitive outcomes. *Child Development, 63,* 1126–1141.

Rosenberg, M. S., Westling, D. L., & McLeskey, J. (2008). *Special education for today's teachers.* Upper Saddle River, NJ: Prentice Hall.

Rosenberg, T. J., Garbers, S., Lipkind, H., & Chiasson, M. A. (2005). Maternal obesity and diabetes as risk factors for adverse pregnancy outcomes: Differences among 4 racial/ethnic groups. *American Journal of Public Health, 95,* 1545–1551.

Rosenblith, J. F. (1992). *In the beginning* (2nd ed.). Newbury Park, CA: Sage.

Rosenfeld, A., & Stark, E. (1987, May). The prime of our lives. *Psychology Today.* pp. 62–72.

Rosenstein, D., & Oster, H. (1988). Differential facial responses to four basic tastes in newborns. *Child Development, 59,* 1555-1568.

Roskos, K. A., & Christie, J. F. (Eds.). (2007) *Play and literacy in early childhood.* Mahwah, NJ: Erlbaum.

Rosnow, R. L., & Rosenthal, R. (2008). *Beginning behavioral research* (6th ed.). Upper Saddle River, NJ: Prentice Hall.

Rospenda, K. M., Richman, J. A., & Shannon, C. A. (2008, in press). Prevalence and mental health correlates of harassment and discrimination in the workplace: Results from a national study. *Journal of Interpersonal Violence.*

Ross, J. L., & others (2008, in press). Cognitive and motor development during childhood in boys with Klinefelter syndrome. *American Journal of Medical Genetics A.*

Ross, M. E. T., & Aday, L. A. (2006). Stress and coping in African American grandparents who are raising their children. *Journal of Family Issues, 27,* 912–932.

Rossi, A. S. (1989). A life-course approach to gender, aging, and intergenerational relations. In K. W. Schaie & C. Schooler (Eds.), *Social structure and aging.* Hillsdale, NJ: Erlbaum.

Rossi, S., Miniussi, C., Pasqualetti, P., Babilioni, C., Rossini, P. M., & Cappa, S. F. (2005). Age-related functional changes of prefrontal cortex in long-term memory: A repetitive transcranial magnetic stimulation study. *Journal of Neuroscience. 24,* 7939–7944.

Rossit, S., & Harvey, M. (2008). Age-related differences in corrected and inhibited pointing movements. *Experimental Brain Research, 185,* 1–10.

Rotermann, M. (2007). Marital breakdown and subsequent depression. *Health Reports, 18,* 33–44.

Roth, J. L., Brooks-Gunn, J., Murray, L., & Foster, W. (1998). Promoting healthy adolescents: Synthesis of youth development program evaluations. *Journal of Research on Adolescence, 8,* 423–459.

Rothbart, M. K. (2004). Temperament and the pursuit of an integrated developmental psychology. *Merrill-Palmer Quarterly, 50,* 492–505.

Rothbart, M. K. (2007). Temperament, development, and personality. *Current Directions in Psychological Science, 16,* 207–212.

Rothbart, M. K. (2009, in press). Early temperament and psychosocial development. In R. E. Tremblay, deV Peters, M. Boivan, & R. G. Barr (Eds.), *Encyclopedia on Early Childhood Development.* Montreal: Center of Excellence for Early Childhood Development.

Rothbart, M. K., & Gartstein, M. A. (2008). Temperament. In M. M. Haith & J. B. Benson (Eds.), *Encyclopedia of infant and early childhood development.* Oxford, UK: Elsevier.

Rothbart, M. K., & Putnam, S. P. (2002). Temperament and socialization. In L. Pulkkinen & A. Caspi (Eds.), *Paths to successful development.* New York: Cambridge University Press.

Rothbart, M. K., & Sheese, B. E. (2007). Temperament and emotion regulation. In J. J. Gross (Ed.), *Handbook of emotion regulation.* New York: Guilford Press.

Rothbaum, F., Poll, M., Azuma, H., Miyake, K., & Welsz, J. (2000). The development of close relationships in Japan and the United States: Paths of symbiotic harmony and generative tension. *Child Development, 71,* 1121–1142.

Rothbaum, F., & Trommsdorff, G. (2007). Do roots and wings complement or oppose one another?: The socialization of relatedness and autonomy in cultural context. In J. E. Grusec & P. D. Hastings (Eds.), *Handbook of socialization.* New York: Guilford.

Rouse, D. J., & others. (2007). A trial of 17 alpha-hyroxyprogesterone caproate to prevent prematurity in twins. *New England Journal of Medicine, 357,* 454–461.

Routasalo, P. E., Savikko, N., Tilvis, R. S., Strandberg, T. E., & Pitkala, k. H. (2006). Social contacts and their relationship to loneliness among aged people—a population-based study. *Gerontology, 52,* 181–187.

Rovee-Collier, C. (1987). Learning and memory in children. In J. D. Osofsky (Ed.), *Handbook of infant development* (2nd ed.). New York: Wiley.

Rovee-Collier, C. (2004). Infant learning and memory. In U. Goswami (Ed.), *Blackwell handbook of childhood cognitive development.* Malden, MA: Blackwell.

Rovee-Collier, C. (2008). The development of infant memory. In N. Cowan & M. Courage (Eds.), *The development of memory in childhood.* Philadelphia: Psychology Press.

Rovers, M. M., de Kok, I. M., & Schilder, A. G. (2006). Risk factors for otitis media: An international perspective. *International Journal of Otorhinolaryngology, 70,* 1251–1256.

Rowley, S. R., Kurtz-Costas, B., & Cooper, S. M. (2009, in press). The role of schooling in ethnic minority achievement and attainment. In J. Meece & J. Eccles (Eds.), *Handbook of research on schools, schooling, and human development.* Clifton, NJ: Psychology Press.

Rozzini, R., Ranhoff, A., & Trabucchi, M. (2007). Alcoholic beverage and long-term mortality in elderly people living at home. *Journals of Gerontology: Biological Sciences and Medical Sciences, 62A,* M1313–M1314.

Rubin, K. H., Bukowski, W., & Parker, J. G. (1998). Peer interactions, relationships, and groups. In N. Eisenberg (Ed.), *Handbook of child psychology* (5th ed., Vol. 3). New York: Wiley.

Rubin, K. H., Bukowski, W., & Parker, J. G. (2006). Peer interactions, relationships, and groups. In W. Damon & R. Lerner (Eds.), *Handbook of child psychology* (6th ed.). New York: Wiley.

Rubin, K., Fredstrom, B., & Bowker, J. (2008, in press). Future directions in friendship in childhood and early adolescence. *Social Development.*

Rubin, S., & Malkinson, R. (2001). *Parental response to child loss across the life-cycle.* Clinical and research perspectives. In M. Strocbe, R. Hansson, W. Stroebe & H. Schut (Eds.). *Handbook of bereavement research: consequences, coping and care.* Washington, DC: American Psychological Association.

Rubio-Aurioles, E., Casabe, A., Torres, L. O., Quinzanos, L., Glina, S., Filimon, I., Kopernicky, V., & Lenero, E. (2008, in press). Efficacy and safety of tadalafil in the treatment of Latin American men with erectile dysfunction: Results of integrated analysis. *Journal of Sexual Medicine.*

Ruble, D. (1983). The development of social comparison processes and their role in achievement-related self-socialization. In E. Higgins, D. Ruble, & W. Hartup (Eds.), *Social cognitive development: A social-cultural perspective.* New York: Cambridge University Press.

Ruble, D. N., Martin, C. L., & Berenbaum, S. (2006). Gender development. In W. Damon & R. Lerner (Eds.), *Handbook of child psychology* (6th ed.). New York: Wiley.

Rubnitz, J. E., Razzouk, B. I., Lensing, S., Pounds, S., Pui, C. H., & Ribeiro, R. C. (2006). Prognostic factors and outcome of recurrence in childhood acute myeloid leukemia. *Cancer, 109,* 157–163.

Ruckenhauser, G., Yazdani, F., & Ravaglia, G. (2007). Suicide in old age: Illness or autonomous decision of the will? *Archives of Gerontology and Geriatrics, 44 (Suppl.),* S355–S358.

Rudin, E., Rincon, M., Bauman, J., & Barzilai, N. (2007). Obesity. In J. E. Birren (Ed.), *Encyclopedia of gerontology* (2nd ed.). San Diego: Academic Press.

Ruel, M. T. & others. (2008). Age-based preventive targeting of food assistance and behavior change and communication for reduction of childhood undernutrition in Haiti: A cluster randomized trial. *Lancet, 371,* 588–595.

Ruff, H. A., & Capozzoli, M. C. (2003). Development of attention and distractibility in the first 4 years of life. *Developmental Psychology, 39,* 877–890.

Ruffman, T., Slade, L., & Crowe, E. (2002). The relation between children's and mothers' mental state language and theory-of-mind understanding. *Child Development, 73,* 734–751.

Rumberger, R. W. (1995). Dropping out of high school: The influence of race, sex, and family background. *American Educational Research Journal, 20,* 199–220.

Runquist, J. (2007). Persevering through postpartum fatigue. *Journal of Obsteric, Gynecologic, and Neonatal Nursing, 36,* 28–37.

Rupp, D. E., Vodanovich, S. J., & Crede, M. (2005). The multidimensional nature of ageism: Construct validity and group differences. *Journal of Social Psychology, 145,* 335–362.

Russell, S. T. & Joyner, K. (2001). Adolescent sexual orientation and suicide risk: Evidence from a national study. *American Journal of Public Health, 91,* 1276–1281.

Rutter, M. (2007). Gene-environment interdependence. *Developmental Science,10,* 12–18.

Rutter, M., & Schopler, E. (1987). Autism and pervasive developmental disorders: Concepts and diagnostic Issues. *Journal of Autism and Pervasive Developmental Disorders, 17,* 159–186.

Ryan, A. S., & Elahi, D. (2007). Body: Composition, weight, height, and build. In J. E. Birren (Ed.), *Encyclopedia of gerontology* (2nd ed.). San Diego: Academic Press.

Ryan, R. M., Fauth, R. C., & Brooks-Gunn, J. (2006). Childhood poverty: Implications for school readiness and early childhood education. In B. Spodek & O. N. Saracho (Eds.), *Handbook of research on the education of young children.* Mahwah, NJ: Erlbaum.

Ryan, S. D., Pearlmutter, S., & Groza, V. (2004). Coming out of the closet: Opening agencies to gay and lesbian adoptive parents. *Social Work, 49,* 85–95.

Ryan-Harshman, M., & Aldoori, W. (2008). Folic acid in pregnancy of neural tube defects. *Canadian Family Physician, 54,* 36–38.

Ryff, C. D. (1984). Personality development from the inside: The subjective experience of change in adulthood and aging. In P. B. Baltes & O. G. Brim (Eds.), *Life-span development and behavior.* New York: Academic Press.

Ryff, C. D. (1991). Possible selves in adulthood and old age: A tale of shifting horizons. *Psychology and Aging, 6,* 286–295.

Rypma, B., Eldreth, D. A., & Rebbechi, D. (2007). Age-related differences in activation-performance relations in delayed-response tasks: A multiple component analyses. *Cortex, 43,* 65–76.

S

Saarni, C. (1999). *The development of emotional competence.* New York: Guilford.

Saarni, C. (2002). Unpublished review of J. W. Santrock's *Life-span development,* 10th ed. (New York: McGraw-Hill).

Saarni, C., Campos, J., Camras, L. A., & Witherington, D. (2006). Emotional development. In W. Damon & R. Lerner (Eds.), *Handbook of child psychology* (6th ed.). New York: Wiley.

Sabbagh, M. A., Xu, F., Carlson, S. M., Moses, L. J., & Lee, K. (2006). The development of executive functioning and theory of mind: A comparison of Chinese and U.S. preschoolers. *Psychological Science, 17,* 74–81.

Sabia, S., Fournier, A., Mesrine, S., Boutron-Rualt, M. C., & Clavel-Chapelon, F. (2008, in press). Risk factors for onset of menopausal symptoms: Results from a large cohort study. *Maturitas.*

Sabiston, C. M., & Crocker, P. R. E. (2008). Examining an integrative model of physical activity and healthy eating self-perceptions and behaviors among adolescents. *Journal of Adolescent Health, 42,* 64–72.

Sachs, J. (2009). Communication development in infancy. In J. Berko Gleason & N. B. Ratner (Eds.). *The development of language* (7th ed.). Boston: Allyn & Bacon.

Sadeghi-Nejad, H., Seftel, A. D., & Munarriz, R. (2007). Erectile dysfunction. In J. E. Birren (Ed.). *Encyclopedia of gerontology* (2nd ed.). San Diego: Academic Press.

Sadeh, A. (2008). Sleep. In M. M. Haith & J. B. Benson (Eds.), *Encyclopedia of infant and early childhood development.* Oxford, UK: Elsevier.

Sadker, D. M., Sadker, M. P., & Zittleman, K. R. (2008). *Teachers, schools and society* (8th ed.) New York: McGraw-Hill

Saffran, J. R., Werker, J. F., & Werner, L. A. (2006). The infant's auditory world: Hearing, speech, and the beginnings of language. In W. Damon & R. Lerner (Eds.), *Handbook of child psychology* (6th ed.). New York: Wiley.

Sagiv, M., Goldmammer, E., Ben-Sira, D., & Amir, R. (2007). What maintains energy supply at peak aerobic exercise in trained and untrained older men? *Gerontology, 53,* 119–123.

Sakraida, T. J. (2005). Divorce transition differences of midlife women. *Issues in Mental Health nursing, 26,* 225–249.

Salmon, J., Campbell, K. J., & Crawford, D. A. (2006). Television viewing habits associated with obesity risk factors: A survey of Melbourne children. *Medical Journal of Australia, 184,* 64–67.

Salthouse, T. (2009). *Executive function.* In D. C. Park & N. Schwarz (Eds.), *Cognitive aging* (2nd ed.). Clifton, NJ: Psychology Press.

Salthouse, T. A. (1994). The nature of influence of speed on adult age differences in cognition. *Developmental Psychology, 30,* 240–259.

Salthouse, T. A. (2006). Mental exercise and mental aging: Evaluating the validity of the "use it or lose it" hypothesis. *Perspectives on Psychological Science, 1,* 68–87.

Salthouse, T. A. (2007). Reaction time. In J. E. Birren (Ed.), *Handbook of gerontology* (2nd ed.). San Diego: Academic press.

Salthouse, T. A., & Skovronek, E. (1992). Within-context assessment of working memory. *Journal of Gerontology, 47,* P110–P117.

Sanders, E. (2008). Medial art and play therapy with accident survivors. In C. A. Malchiodi (Ed.), *Creative interventions with traumatized children.* New York: Guilford.

Sandiford, R. (2006). Keeping it natural. *Nursing Times, 102,* 22–23.

Sando, S. B., & others. (2008). APOE epsilon4 lowers age at onset and is a high risk factor for Alzheimer's disease: A case-control study from central Norway. *BMC Neurology, 8,* 9.

Sands, R. G., & Goldberg-Glen, R. S. (2000). Factors associated with stress among -grandparents raising their grandchildren. *Family Relations, 49,* 97–105.

Sangree, W. H. (1989). Age and power: Life-course trajectories and age structuring of power relations in

East and West Africa. In D. I. Kertzer & K. W. Schaic (Eds.), *Age structuring in comparative perspective.* Hillsdale, NJ: Erlbaum.

Sann, C., & Streri, A. (2007). Perception of object shape and texture in human newborns: Evidence from cross-modal tasks. *Developmental Science, 10,* 399–410.

Sanson, A., & Rothbart, M. K. (1995). Child temperament and parenting. In M. H. Bornstein (Ed.), *Handbook of parenting* (Vol. 4). Hillsdale, NJ: Erlbaum.

Santelli, J. S., Lindberg, L. D., Finer, L. B., & Singh, S. (2007). Explaining recent declines in adolescent pregnancy in the United States: The contribution of abstinence and improved contraceptive use. *American Journal of Public Health, 97,* 150–156.

Santoro, N., Brockwell, S., Johnston, J., Crawford, S. L., Gold, E. B., Harlow, S. D., Matthews, K. A., & Sutton-Tyrrell, K. (2007). Helping midlife women predict the onset of the final menses: SWAN, the Study of Women's Health Across the Nation. *Menopause, 14,* 415–424.

Santrock, J. W., & Halonen, J. A. (2008). *Your guide to college success* (5th ed.). Belmont, CA: Wadsworth.

Santrock, J. W., Sitterle, K. A., & Warshak, R. A. (1988). Parent-child relationships in stepfather families. In P. Bronstein & C. P. Cowan (Eds.), *Fatherhood today: Men's changing roles in the family.* New York: Wiley.

Santrock, J. W., & Warshak, R. A. (1979). Father custody and social development in boys and girls. *Journal of Social Issues, 35,* 112–125.

Sarkisian, N., & Gerstel, N. (2008). Till marriage do us part: Adult children's relationship with their parents. *Journal of Marriage and the Family, 70,* 360–376.

Sarkisian, N., Gerena, M., & Gerstel, N. (2006). Extended family ties among Mexicans, Puerto Ricans, and Whites: Superintegration or disintegration? *Family Relations, 55,* 33–334.

Sausenthaler, S., Kompauer, I., Mielck, A., Borte, M., Herbarth, O., Schaaf, B., von Berg, A., & Heinrich, J. (2007). Impact of parental education and income equality on children's food intake. *public Health Nutrition, 10,* 24–33.

Savin-Williams, R. C. (2001). A critique of research on sexual minority youths. *Journal of Adolescence, 24,* 5–13.

Savin-Williams, R. C. (2006). *The new gay teenager.* Cambridge, MA: Harvard University Press.

Savin-Williams, R. C. (2007). Girl-on-girl sexuality. In B. J. R. Leadbeater & N. Way (Eds.), *Urban girls revisited: Building strengths* (pp. 301–318). New York: New York University Press.

Savin-Williams, R. C. (2008, in press). Who's gay? It depends on how you measure it. In D. A. Hope (Ed.), *Nebraska Symposium on Motivation: Contemporary perspectives on lesbian, gay, and bisexual identities.* Lincoln, NE: University of Nebraska Press.

Savin-Williams, R. C., & Cohen, K. M. (2007). Development of same-sex attracted youth. In I. H. Meyer & M. E. Northridge (Eds.), *The health of sexual minorities: Public health perspectives on lesbian, gay, bisexual and transgender populations* (pp. 27–47). New York: Springer.

Savin-Williams, R. C., & Diamond, L. (2004). Sex. In R. Lerner & L. Steinberg (Eds.), *Handbook of adolescent psychology.* New York: Wiley.

Savin-Williams, R. C., & Ream, G. L. (2007). Prevalence and stability of sexual orientation components during adolescence and young adulthood. *Archives of Sexual Behavior, 36,* 385–394.

Sawyer, R. K., & DeZutter, S. (2007). Improvisation: A lens for play and literacy research. In K. A. Roskos & J. F. Christie (Eds.), *Play and literacy in early childhood.* Mahwah, NJ: Erlbaum.

Sayal, K., Heron, J., Golding, J., & Emond, A. (2007). Prenatal alcohol exposure and gender differences in childhood mental health problems: A longitudinal population-based study. *Pediatrics, 119,* e426–e434.

Sayer, L. C. (2006). Economic aspects of divorce and relationship dissolution. In M. A. Fine & J. H. Harvey (Eds.), *Handbook of divorce and relationship dissolution.* Mahwah, NJ: Erlbaum.

Scarr, S. (1993). Biological and cultural diversity: The legacy of Darwin for development. *Child Development, 64,* 1333–1353.

Scarr, S., & Weinberg, R. A. (1983). The Minnesota adoption studies: Genetic differences and malleability. *Child Development, 54,* 182–259.

Schacter, E. P., & Ventura, J. J. (2008). Identity agents: Parents as active and reflective participants in their children's identity formation. *Journal of Research on Adolescence, 18,* 449–476.

Schaffer, H. R. (1996). *Social development.* Cambridge, MA: Blackwell.

Schaie, K. W. (1994). The life course of adult intellectual abilities. *American Psychologist, 49,* 304–313.

Schaie, K. W. (1996). *Intellectual development in adulthood: The Seattle Longitudinal Study.* New York: Cambridge University Press.

Schaie, K. W. (2000). Unpublished review of J. W. Santrock's *Life-span development,* 8th ed. (New York: McGraw-Hill).

Schaie, K. W. (2005). *Developmental influences on adult intelligence: The Seattle Longitudinal Study.* New York: Oxford University Press.

Schaie, K. W. (2007). Generational differences: The age-cohort period model. In J. E. Birren (Ed.), *Encyclopedia of gerontology* (2nd ed.). Oxford, UK: Elsevier.

Schaie, K. W. (2008). Historical processes and patterns of cognitive aging, In S. M. Hofer & D. F. Alwin (Eds.), *Handbook on cognitive aging: Interdisciplinary perspective.* Thousand Oaks, CA: Sage.

Schaie, K. W., & Elder, G. (2006). Historical influences on aging. In J. E. Birren & K. W. Schaie (Eds.), *Handbook of the Psychology of aging* (6th ed.). San Diego: Academic Press.

Schale, K. W., & Willis, S. L. (2000). A stage theory model of adult development revisited. In R. Rubinstein, M. Moss, & M. Kleban (Eds.), *The many dimensions of aging: Essays in honor of M. Powell Lawton.* New York: Springer.

Schattschneider, C., Fletcher, J. M., Francis, D. J., Carlson, C. D., & Foorman, B. R. (2004). Kindergarten prediction of reading skills: A longitudinal comparative analysis. *Journal of Educational Psychology, 96,* 265–282.

Schauble, L., Beane, D. B., Coates, G. D., Martin, L. M. W., & Sterling, P. V. (1996). Outside classroom walls: Learning in informal environments. In L. Schauble & R. Glaser (Eds.), *Innovations in learning.* Mahwah, NJ: Erlbaum.

Scheibe, S., Freund, A. M., & Baltes, P. B. (2007). Toward a developmental psychology of Sehnsucht (life-longings): The optimal (utopian) life. *Developmental Psychology, 43,* 778–795.

Scheibe, S., Kunzmann, U., & Baltes, P. B. (2007). Wisdom, life longings, and optimal development. In J. A. Blackburn & C. N. Dulmas (Ed.), *Handbook of gerontology.* New York: Wiley.

Scher, A., & Harel, J. (2008). Separation and stranger anxiety. In M. M. Haith & J. B. Benson (Eds.), *Encyclopedia of infant and early childhood development.* Oxford, UK: Elsevier.

Schieman, S., van Gundy, K., & Taylor, J. (2004). The relationship between age and depressive symptons: A test of competing explanatory and Suppression influences. *Journal of Aging Health, 14,* 260–285.

Schiff, W. J. (2009). *Nutrition for healthy living.* New York: McGraw-Hill. **Schiffman, S. S.** (2007). Smell and taste. In J. E. Birren (Ed.), *Encyclopedia of gerontology* (2nd ed.). San Diego: Academic Press.

Schindler, A. E. (2006). Climacteric symptoms and hormones. *Gynecological Endocrinology, 22,* 151–154.

Schlegel, M. (2000). All work and play. *Monitor on Psychology 31* (No. 11), 50–51.

Schmalz, D. L., Deane, G. D., Birch, L. L., & Davison, K. D. (2007). A longitudinal assessment of the links between physical activity and self-esteem in early adolescent non-Hispanic females. *Journal of Adolescent Health, 41,* 559–565.

Schmidt, J., Shumow, L., & Kackar, H. (2007). Adolescents' participation in service activities and its impact on academic, behavioral, and civic outcomes. *Journal of Youth and Adolescence, 36,* 127–140.

Schmidt, K. L., & Schulz, R. (2007). Emotions. In J. E. Birren (Ed.), *Encyclopedia of gerontology* (2nd ed.). San Diego: Academic Press.

Schmidt, S., & others. (2006). Cigarette smoking strongly modifies the association of LOC387715 and age-related macular degeneration. *American Journal of Human Genetics, 78,* 852–864.

Schmidt, U. (2003). Aetiology of eating disorders in the 21st century: New answers to old questions. *European Child and Adolescent Psychiatry, 12* (Suppl. 1), 1130–1137.

Schneider, W. (2004). Memory development in children. In U. Goswami (Ed.), *Blackwell handbook of childhood cognitive development.* Malden, MA: Blackwell.

Schneider, W., & Pressley, M. (1997). *Memory development between 2 and 20* (2nd ed.). Mahwah, NJ: Erlbaum.

Schneiderman, N., Antoni, M. H., Saab, P. G., & Ironson, G. (2001). Health psychology: Psychological and biobehavioral aspects of chronic disease management. *Annual Review of Psychology* (Vol. 52). Palo Alto, CA: Annual Reviews.

Schoka, E., & Hayslip, B. (1999, November). *Grief and the family system: The roles of communication,* *affect, and cohesion.* Paper presented at the meeting of the Gerontological Society of America, San Francisco.

Scholnick, E. K. (2008). Reasoning in early development. In M. M. Haith & J. B. Benson (Eds.), *Encyclopedia of infant and early childhood development.* Oxford, UK: Elsevier.

Schooler, C. (2007). Use it—and keep it, longer, probably: A reply to Salthouse (2006). *Perspectives on Psychological Science, 2,* 24–29.

Schooler, C., Mulatu, S., & Oates, G. (1999). The continuing effects of substantively complex work on the intellectual functioning of older workers. *Psychology and Aging. 14,* 483–506.

Schoppe-Sullivan, S. J., Mangelsdorf, S. C., Brown, G. L., & Sokolowski, M. S. (2007). Goodness-of-fit in family context: Infant temperament, marital quality, and early coparenting behavior. *Infant Behavior and Development, 30,* 82–96.

Schrag, S. G., & Dixon, R. L. (1985). Occupational exposure associated with male reproductive dysfunction. *Annual Review of Pharmacology and Toxicology, 25,* 467–592.

Schroepfer, T. A. (2007). Critical events in the dying process: The potential for physical and psychological suffering. *Journal of Palliative Medicine, 10,* 136–147.

Schroots, J. J. (2007). Time: Perception and concepts. In J. E. Birren (Ed.), *Encyclopedia of gerontology* (2nd ed.). San Diego: Academic Press.

Schuchter, S., & Zisook, S. (1993). The course of normal grief. In M. Stroebe, W. Stroebe, & R. O. Hanson (Eds.), *Handbook of bereavement.* New York: Cambridge University Press.

Schulenberg, J. E., Bryant, A., & O'Malley, P. (2004). Taking hold of some kind of life: How developmental tasks relate to trajectories of well-being during the transition to adulthood. *Development and Psychopathology, 16,* 1119–1140.

Schulenberg, J. E., O'Malley, P. M., Bachman, J. G., & Johnson, L. D. (2000). "Spread your wings and fly": The course of health and well-being during the transition to young adulthood. In L. Crockett & R. Silbereisen (Eds.), *Negotiating adolescence in times of social change.* New York: Cambridge University Press.

Schulenberg, J. E., & Zarrett, N. R. (2006). Mental health during emerging adulthood: Continuities and discontinuities in course, content, and meaning. In J. J. Arnett & J. Tanner (Eds.), *Advances in emerging adulthood.* Washington, DC: American Psychological Association.

Schultz, J. H., & Borowski, A. (2006). Economic security in retirement: Reshaping the public-private pension mix. In R. H. Binstock & L. K. George (Eds.), *Handbook of aging and the social sciences* (6th ed.). San Diego: Academic Press.

Schultz, R., & Curnow, C. (1988). Peak performance and age among super athletes: Track and field, swimming, baseball, tennis, and golf. *Journal of Gerontology, 43,* P113–P120.

Schulz, R., Hebert, R., & Boerner, K. (2008). Bereavement after caregiving. *Geriatrics, 63,* 20–22.

Schunk, D. H. (2008). *Learning theories: An educational perspective* (5th ed.). Upper Saddle River, NJ: Prentice Hall.

Schunk, D. H., Pintrich, P. R., & Meece, J. L. (2008). *Motivation in education: Theory, research, and applications* (3rd ed.). Upper Saddle River, NJ: Prentice Hall.

Schwab, P., & Klein, R. F. (2008). Nonpharmacological approaches to improve bone health and reduce osteoporosis. *Current Opinion in Rheumatology, 20,* 213–217.

Schwartz, M. A., & Scott, B. (2007). *Marriages and families* (5th ed.). Upper Saddle River, NJ: Prentice Hall.

Schwebel, D. C. (2008). Safety and childproofing. In M. M. Haith & J. B. Benson (Eds.), *Encyclopedia of infant and early childhood development.* Oxford, UK: Elsevier.

Schweinhart, L. J. (2009). Preschool programs. In R. E. Tremblay, R. deV Peters, M. Boivin, & R. G. Barr (Eds.), *Encyclopedia of early childhood development.* Montreal: Centre of Excellence for Early Childhood Development.

Schweinhart, L. J., Montie, J., Xiang, Z., Barnett, W. S., Belfield, C. R., & Nores, M. (2005). *Lifetime effects: The High/Scope Perry Preschool Study Through age 40.* Ypsilanti, MI: High/Scope Press.

Scialfa, C. T., & Fernie, G. R. (2006). Adaptive technology. In J. E. Birren & K. W. Schaie (Eds.), *Handbook of the psychology of aging* (6th ed.). San Diego: Academic Press.

Scialfa, C. T., & Kline, D. W. (2007). Vison. In J. E. Birren (Ed.), *Encyclopedia of gerontology* (2nd ed.). Sand Diego: Academic Press.

Science Daily. (2008, January 15). Human gene count tumbles again, p.l.

Scourfield, J., Van den Bree, M., Martin, N., & McGuffin, P. (2004). Conduct problems in children and adolescents: A twin study. *Archives of General Psychiatry, 61,* 489–496.

Sebastian-Galles, N. (2007). Biased to learn language. *Developmental Science, 10,* 713–718.

Seeman, T. E., Charpentier, P. A., Berkman, L. F., Tinetti, M. E., Guralnik, J. M., Albert, M., Blazer, D., & Rowe, J. W. (1994). Predicting changes in physical performance in a high-functioning elderly cohort: MacArthur Studies of Successful Aging. *Journal of Gerontology, 49,* M97–M108.

Seeman, T. E., & Chen, X. (2002). Risk and protective factors for physical functioning in older adults with and without chronic conditions: MacArthur Studies of Successful Aging. *Journals of Gerontology B: Psychological Sciences and Social Sciences, 57,* S135–S144.

Segal, B. (2007). Addiction: General. In J. E. Birren (ed.), *Encyclopedia of gerontology* (2nd ed.). San Diego: Academic Press.

Selim, A. J., Fincke, G., Berlowitz, D. R., Miller, D. R., Qian, S. X., Lee, A., Cong, Z., Rogers, W., Sileim, B. J., Ren, X. S., Spiro, A., Kazis, L. E. (2005). Comprehensive health status assessment of centenarians: Results from the 1999 Large Health Survey of Veteran Enrollees. *Journals of Gerontology A: Biological Sciences and Medical Sciences, 60,* 515–519.

Sellers, R. M., Copeland-Linder, N., Martin, P. P., & Lewis, R. L. (2006). Racial identity matters: The relationship between racial discrimination and psychological functioning in African American adolescents. *Journal of Research on Adolescence, 16,* 187–216.

Selman, R. (1980). *The growth of interpersonal understanding.* New York: Academic Press.

Senchina, D. S., & Kohut, M. L. (2007). Immunological outcomes of exercise in older adults. *Clinical Interventions in Aging, 2,* 3–16.

Sener, A., Terzioglu, R. G., & Karabulut E. (2007). Life satisfaction and leisure activities during men's retirement: A Turkish sample. *Aging and Mental health, 11,* 30–36

Shah, N. S., & Ershler, W. B. (2007). Immune system. In J. E. Birren (Ed.), *Encyclopedia of gerontology* (2nd ed.). San Diego: Academic Press.

Shah, R. S., Lee, H. G., Xiongwei, Z., Perry, G., Smith, M. A., & Catellani, R. J. (2008, in press). Current approaches in the treatment of Alzheimer's disease. *Biomedicine and Pharmacotherapy.*

Shaibi, G. Q., Ball, G. D., & Goran, M. I. (2006). Aerobic fitness among Caucasian, African–American, and Latino youth. *Ethnicity and Disease, 16,* 120–125.

Shakhatreh, F. M., & Mas'ad, D. (2006). Menopausal symptoms and health problems of women aged 50–65 years of age in southern Jordan. *Climacteric, 9,* 305–311.

Shamah, T., & Villalpando, S. (2006). The role of enriched foods in infant and child nutrition. *British Journal of Nutrition, 96* (Suppl. 1), S73–S77.

Shan, Z. Y., Liu, J. Z., Sahgal, V., Wang, B., & Yue, G. H. (2005). Selective atrophy of left hemisphere and frontal lobe of the brain in older men. *Journals of Gerontology A: Biological Sciences and Medical Sciences, 60,* A165–A174.

Shani, R., Fifer, W. P., & Myers, M. M. (2007). Identifying infants at risk for sudden infant death syndrome. *Current Opinion in Pediatrics, 19,* 145–149.

Shapiro, A. F., and Gottman, J. M. (2005). Effect on marriage of a psycho-education intervention with couples undergoing the transition to parenthood, evaluation at 1-year post-intervention. *Journal of Family Communication, 5,* 1–24.

Sharlip, I. D., Shumaker, B. P., Hakim, L. S., Goldfischer, E., Natanegra, F., & Wong, D. G. (2008). Tadalafil is efficacious and well tolerated in the treatment of erectile dysfunction (ED) in men over 65 years of age: Results from multiple observations in men with ED in -national tadalafil study in the United States. *Journal of Sexual Medicine, 5,* 716–725.

Sharma, A. R., McGue, M. K., & Benson, P. L. (1996). The emotional and behavioral adjustment of adopted adolescents: Part I: Age at adoption. *Children and Youth Services Review, 18,* 101–114.

Sharma, B. R. (2007). Sudden infant death syndrome: A subject of microlegal research. *American Journal of Forensic Medicine and Pathology, 28,* 69–72.

Shatz, M., & Gelman, R. (1973). The development of communication skills: Modifications in the speech of young children as a function of the listener. *Monographs of the Society for Research in Child Development, 38* (Serial No. 152).

Shaver, P. R. (1986, August). *Being lonely, falling in love: Perspectives from attachment theory.* Paper presented at the meeting of the American Psychological Association, Washington, DC.

Shaver, P. R., & Mikulincer, M. (2007). Attachment theory and research. In A. W. Kruglanski, & E. T. Higgins (Eds.), *Social psychology* (2nd ed.). New York: Guilford.

Shavers, V. L., & Shavers, B. S. (2006). Racism and health inequity among Americans. *Journal of the National Medical Association, 98*, 386–396.

Shaw, P., Eckstrand, K., Sharp, W., Blumenthal, J., Lerch, J. P., Greenstein, D., Clasen, L., Evans, A., Giedd, J., & Rapoport, J. L. (2007). Attention-deficit/hyperactivity disorder is characterized by a delay in cortical maturation. *proceedings of the National Academy of sciences, 104* (No. 49), 19649–19654.

Shay, J. W., & Wright, W. E. (2006). Telomerase therapeutics for cancer: Challenges and new directions. *Nature. Reviews: Drug Discovery, 5*, 577–584.

Shay, J. W., & Wright, W. E. (2007). Hallmarks of telomeres in aging research. *Journal of Pathology, 211*, 114–123.

Shaywitz, S. E., Gruen, J. R., & Shaywitz, B. A. (2007). Management of dyslexia, its rationale, and underlying neurobiology. *Pediatric Clinics of North America, 54*, 609–623.

Shaywitz, S. E., Morris, R., & Shaywitz, B. A. (2008). The education of dyslexic children from childhood to young adulthood. *Annual Review of Psychology, 59*. Palo Alto, CA: Annual Reviews.

Shea, A. K., & Steiner, M. (2008). Cigarette smoking during pregnancy. *Nicotine and Tobacco Research, 10*, 267–278.

Shea, A., Walsh, C., MacMillan, H., & Steiner, M. (2005). Child maltreatment and HPA axis dysregulation: Relationship to major depressive disorder and post traumatic stress disorder in females. *Psychoneuroendocrinology, 30*, 162–178.

Sheeber, L. B., Davis, B., Leve, C., Hops, H., & Tildesley, E. (2007). Adolescents' relationships with their mothers and fathers: Associations with depressive disorder and subdiagnostic symptomatology. *Journal of Abnormal Psychology, 116*, 144–154.

Shema, L, Ore, L., Ben-Shachar, M., Haj, M., & Linn, S. (2007). The association between breastfeeding and breast cancer occurrence among Jewish women: A case control study. *Journal of Cancer Research and Clinical Oncology, 133*, 903.

Sheridan, M., & Nelson, C. A. (2008, in press). Neurobiology of fetal and infant development: Implications for mental health. In C. H. Zeanah (Ed.), *Handbook of infant mental health* (3rd ed.). New York: Guilford.

Sherwin, B. B. (2007). Does estrogen protect against cognitive aging in women? *Current Directions in Psychological Science, 16*, 275–279.

Shields, S. A. (1991). Gender in the psychology of emotion: A selective research reviews. In K. T. Strongman (Ed.), *International review of studies on emotion* (Vol. 1). New York: Wiley.

Shiraev, E., & Levy, D. (2007). Cross-cultural Psychology (3rd ed.). Boston: Allyn & Bacon.

Shneidman, E. S. (1973). *Deaths of man.* New York: Quadrangle/New York Times.

Shore, L. M., & Goldberg, C. B. (2005). Age discrimination in the work place. In R. L. Dipobye & A. Colella (Eds.), *Discrimination at work.* Mahwah, NJ: Erlbaum.

Shulenberg J. E., & Zarett, N. R. (2006). Mental health during emerging adulthood: Continuity and discontinuity in courses, causes, and functions. In J. J. Arnett & J. L. Tanner (Eds.), *Emerging adults in*

America. Washington, DC: American Psychological Association.

Siedlecki, K. L. (2007). Investigating the structure and age invariance of episodic memory across the adult life span. *Psychology and Aging, 22*, 251–268.

Siegler, I. C., & Costa, P. T. (1999, August). *Personality change and continuity in midlife: UNC Alumni Heart Study.* Paper presented at the meeting of the American Psychological Association, Boston.

Siegler, I. C., Bosworth, H. B., & Poon, L. W. (2003). Disease, health, and aging, In I. B. Weiner (Eds.), *Handbook of psychology* (Vol. VI). New York: Wiley.

Siegler, I. C., Poon, L. W. Madden, D. J., Dilworth-Anderson P., Schaie, K. W., Willis, S. L., & Martin, P. (in press). Psychological aspects of normal aging. n D. G. Blazer & D. Steffens (Eds.), *Textbook of geriatric psychiatry* (4th ed.). Arlington, VA: American Psychiatric Publishing.

Siegler, R. S. (2006). Microgenetic analysis of learning. In W. Damon & R. Lerner (Eds.), *Handbook of child psychology* (6th ed.). New York: Wiley.

Siegler, R. S. (2007). Cognitive variability. *Developmental Science 10*, 104–109.

Sievert, L. L., Obermeyer, C. M., & Saliba, M. (2007). Symptom groupings at midlife: Cross-cultural variation and association with job, home, and life change. *Menopause, 14*, 798–807.

Sigman, M., Cohen, S. E., & Beckwith, L. (2000). Why does infant attention predict adolescent intelligence? In D. Muir & A. Slater (Eds.), *Infant development: Essential readings.* Malden, MA: Blackwell.

Signal, T. L., Gander, P. H., Sangalli, M. R., Travier, N., Firestone, R. T., & Tuohy, J. F. (2007). Sleep duration and quality in healthy nulliparous and multiparous women across pregnancy and post-partum. *Australian and New Zealand Journal of Obstetrics and Gynecology, 47*, 16–22.

Signore, R. J. (2004). Bradley method offers option for natural childbirth. *American Family Physician, 70*, 650.

Silberman, M. (2006). *Teaching actively.* Boston: Allyn & Bacon.

Silva, C. (2005, October 31). When teen dynamo talks, city listens, *Boston Globe*, pp. B1, B4.

Silverstein, M., Conroy, S. J., Wang, H., Giarrusso, R., & Bengtsson, V. L. (2002). Reciprocity in parent-child relation over the adult life course. *Journals of Gerontology: Psychological Sciences and Social Sciences. 57B*, S3–S13.

Silverstein, M., Gans, D., & Yang, F. M. (2006). Intergenerational support to aging parents. *Journal of Family Issues, 27*, 1068–1084.

Sim, T. N., & Ong, L. P. (2005). Parent punishment and child aggression in a Singapore Chinese preschool sample. *Journal of Marriage and the Family, 67*, 85–99.

Simhan, H. N., & Caritis, S. N. (2007). Prevention of preterm delivery. *New England Journal of Medicine, 375*, 477–487.

Simm, A., Nass, N., Bartling, B., Hofmann, B., Silber, R. E., & Navarrete Santos, A. (2008). Potential biomarkers of aging. *Biological Chemistry, 389*, 257–265.

Simmons, R. G., & Blyth, D. A. (1987). *Moving into adolescence.* Hawthorne, NY: Aldine.

Simonton, D. K. (1996). Creativity. In J. E. Birren (Ed.), *Encyclopedia of aging.* San Diego: Academic Press.

Simos, P. G., Fletcher, J. M., Sarkari, S., Billingsley, R. L., Denton, C., & Papanicolaou, A. C. (2007). Altering the brain circuits for reading through intervention: A magnetic source imaging study. *Neuropsychology, 21*, 485–496.

Simpkin, P., & Bolding, A. (2004). Update on nonpharmacological approaches to relieve labor pain and prevent suffering. *Journal of Midwifery and Women's Health, 49*, 489–504.

Simpkins, S. D., Fredricks, J. A., Davis-Kean, P. E., & Eccles, J. S. (2006). Healthy mind, healthy habits: The influence of activity involvement in middle childhood. In A. C. Huston & M. N. Ripke (Eds.), *Developmental contexts in middle childhood.* New York: Cambridge University Press.

Simpson, R. L., & LaCava, P. G. (2008). Autism spectrum disorders. In N. J. Salkind (Ed.), *Encyclopedia of educational psychology.* Thousand Oaks, CA: Sage.

Singh, N. A., Clements, K. M., & Fiatarone, M. A. (1997). A randomized controlled trial of progressive resistance training in depressed elders: *Journal of Gerontology, 52A*, M27–M35.

Singh, S., Wulf, D., Samara, R., & Cuca, Y. P. (2000). Gender differences in the timing of first intercourse. Data from 14 countries. *International Family Planning Perspectives, 26*, 21–28, 43.

Sinha, J. W., Cnaan, R. A., & Gelles, R. J. (2007). Adolescent risk behaviors and religion: Findings from a national study. *Journal of Adolescence, 30*, 231–249.

Sinnott, J. D. (2003). Postformal thought and adult development: Living in balance. In J. Demick & C. Andreoletti (Eds.), *Handbook of adult development.* New York: Kluwer.

Sirard, J. R., & Barr-Anderson, D. J. (2008). Editorial: Physical activity in adolescents: From associations to interventions. *Journal of Adolescent Health, 42*, 327–328.

Sivell, S., & others. (2008). How risk is perceived, constructed, and interpreted by clients in clinical genetics, and the effects on decision making: A review. *Journal of Genetic Counseling, 17*, 30–63.

Skinner, B. F. (1938). *The behavior of organisms: An experimental analysis.* New York: Appelton-Century-Crofts.

Skinner, B. F. (1957). *Verbal behavior.* New York: Appleton-Century-Crofts.

Skipper, J. I., Goldin-Meadow, S., Nusbaum, H. C., & Small, S. L. (2007). Speech-associated gestures, Broca's area, and the human mirror system. *Brain and Language, 101*, 260–277.

Skolnick, A. S. (2007). Grounds for marriage: How relationships succeed or fail. In A. S. Skolnick & J. H. Skolnick (Eds.), *Family in transition* (14th ed.). Boston: Allyn & Bacon.

Slack, T., & Jensen, L. (2008). Employment hardship among older workers: Does residential and gender inequality extend into old age? *Journals of Gerontology B: Psychological Sciences and Social Sciences, 63*, S15–S24.

Slater, A., Field, T., & Hernandez-Reif, M. (2007). The development of the senses. In A. Slater & M. Lewis (Eds.), *Introduction to infant development*, (2nd ed.) New York: Oxford University Press.

Slater, A., Morison, V., & Somers, M. (1988). Orientation discrimination and cortical function in the human newborn. *Perception, 17,* 597–602.

Sleet, D. A., & Mercy, J. A. (2003). Promotion of safety, security, and well-being. In M. H. Bornstein, L. Davidson, C. L. M., Keyes, & K. A. Moore (Eds.), *Well-being.* Mahwah, NJ: Erlbaum.

Slobin, D. (1972, July). Children and Language: They learn the same way around the world. *Psychology Today,* 71–76.

Slomkowski, C., Rende, R., Conger, K. J., Simons, R. L., & Conger, R. D. (2001). Sisters, brothers, and delinquency: Social influence during early and middle adolescence. *Child Development, 72,* 271–283.

Slough, N. M., McMahon, R. J., & the Conduct Problems Prevention Research Group (2008). Preventing serious conduct problems in school-aged youth: The Fast Track Program. *Cognitive and Behavioral Practice, 15,* 3–17.

Smetana, J. G. (2006). Social domain theory. In M. Killen & J. G. Smetana (Eds.), *Handbook of moral development.* Mahwah, NJ: Erlbaum.

Smith, A. D. (1996). Memory. In J. E. Birren (Ed.), *Encyclopedia of gerontology* (Vol. 2). San Diego: Academic Press.

Smith, A. D. (2007). Memory, In J. E. Birren (Ed.), *Encyclopedia of gerontology* (2nd ed.). San Diego: Academic Press.

Smith, B. (2007). *The psychology of sex and gender.* Boston: Allyn & Bacon.

Smith, C. A., Collins, C. T., Cyna, A. M., & Crowther, C. A. (2006). Complementary and alternative therapies for pain management in labor. *Cochrane Database of Systematic Reviews, 4,* CD003521.

Smith, C. A., & Crowther, C. A. (2004). Acupuncture for the induction of labor. *Cochrane Database of Systematic Review, 1,* CD0029262.

Smith, D. L. (2008). Birth complications and outcomes. In M. M. Haith & J. B. Benson (Eds.), *Encyclopedia of infancy and early childhood. development* Oxford, UK: Elsevier.

Smith, J., & Freund, A. M. (2002). The dynamics of possible selves in old age. *Journals of Gerontology B: Psychological Sciences and Social Sciences, 57,* P492–P500.

Smith, J., & Ross, H. (2007). Training parents to mediate sibling disputes affects children's negotiation and conflict understanding. *Child Development, 78,* 790–805.

Smith, L. B. (1999). Do infants possess innate knowledge structures? The con side. *Developmental Science, 2,* 133–144.

Smith, L. B., & Breazeal, C. (2007). The dynamic lift of developmental processes. *Developmental Science, 10,* 61–68.

Smith, L. M., Chang, L., Yonekura, M. L., Gilbride, K., Kuo, J., Poland, R. E., Walot, L., & Ernst, T. (2001). Brain proton magnetic resonance spectroscopy and imaging in children exposed to cocaine in utero. *Pediatrics, 107,* 227.

Smith, L. M., LaGasse, L., Derauf, C., Grant, P., Shah, R., Arria, A., Huestis, M., Haning, W., Strauss, A., Della Grotta, S., Fallone, M., Liu, J., & Lester, B. (2008). Prenatal methamphetamine use and neonatal neurobehavioral outcome. *Neurotoxicology and Teratology, 30,* 20–28.

Smith, L. M., & others. (2008). Prenatal methamphetamine use and neonatal neurobehavioral outcome. *Neurotoxicology and Teratology, 30,* 20–28.

Smith, T. B., McCullough, M. E., & Poll, J. (2003). Religiousness and depression: Evidence for a main effect and the moderating influence of stressful life events. *Psychological Bulletin, 129,* 614–636.

Smith, T. E. C., Polloway, E. A., Patton, J. R., & Dowdy, C. A. (2008). *Teaching students with special needs in inclusive settings* (5th ed.). Boston: Allyn & Bacon.

Smithbattle, L. (2007). Legacies of advantage and disadvantage: The case of teen mothers. *Public Health Nursing, 24,* 409–420.

Smoreda, Z., & Licoppe, C. (2000). Gender-specific use of the domestic telephone. *Social Psychology Quarterly, 63,* 238–252.

Snarey, J. (1987, June). A question of morality. *Psychology Today,* pp. 6–8.

Snijders, B. E., & others. (2007). Breast-feeding duration and infant atopic manifestations, by maternal allergic status, in the first two years of life (KOALA study.) *Journal of Pediatrics, 151,* 347–351.

Snow, C. E., & Yang, J. Y. (2006). Becoming bilingual, biliterate, and bicultural. In W. Damon & R. Lerner (Eds.), *Handbook of child psychology* (6th ed.). New York: Wiley.

Snowden, L. R., & Cheung, F. K. (1990). Use of inpatient mental health services by members of ethnic minority groups. *American Psychologist, 45,* 347–355.

Snowden, M., Steinman, L., & Frederick, J. (2008). Treating depression in older adults: Challenges to implementing the recommendations of an expert panel. *Prevention of Chronic Disorders, 5,* A26.

Snowdon, A. W., Hussein, A., High, L., Millar-Polgar, J., Patriack, L., & Ahmed, E. (2008). The effectiveness of a multimedia intervention on parents' knowledge and use of vehicle safety systems for children. *Journal of Pediatric Nursing, 23,* 126–139.

Snowdon, D. A. (1997). Aging and Alzheimer's disease: Lessons from the nun study. *Gerontologist, 37,* 150–156.

Snowdon, D. A. (2002). *Aging with grace: What the Nun Study teaches us about leading longer, healthier, and more meaningful lives.* New York: Bantam.

Snowdon, D. A. (2003). Healthy aging and dementia: Findings from the Nun study. *Annals of Internal Medicine, 139,* 450–454.

Snyder, A. R. (2008, in press). Silent no more: Expression of RNA from telomeres may regulate telomere length. *Cancer Biology and Therapy, 7.*

Snyder, K. A., & Torrence, C. M. (2008). Habituation and novelty. In M. M. Haith & J. B. Benson (Eds.), *Encyclopedia of infant and early childhood development.* Oxford, UK: Elsevier.

Soderman, A. K., & Farrell, P. (2008). *Creating literacy-rich preschools and kindergartens.* Boston: Allyn & Bacon.

Soderstrom, M. (2007). Beyond babytalk: Re-evaluating the nature and content of speech input to preverbal infants. *Developmental Review, 27,* 501–532.

Soenens, B., Vansteenkiste, M., Lens, W., Luyckx, K., Goossens, L., Beyers, W., & Ryan R. M. (2007). Conceptualizing parental autonomy support: Adolescent perceptions of promotion of independence versus promotion of volitional functioning. *Developmental Psychology, 43,* 633–646.

Soergel, P., Pruggmayer, M., Schwerdtfeger, R., Mulhaus, K., & Scharf, A. (2006). Screening for trisomy 21 with maternal age, fetal nuchal translucency, and maternal serum biochemistry at 11–14 weeks: A regional experience from Germany. *Fetal Diagnosis and Therapy, 21,* 264–268.

Solot, D., & Miller, M. (2002). *Unmarried to each other.* New York: Marlowe.

Sontag, L. M., Graber, J., Brooks-Gunn, J., & Warren, M. P. (2008, in press). Coping with social stress: Implications for psychopathology in young adolescent girls. *Journal of Abnormal Child Psychology.*

Sood, A. B., Razdan, A., Weller, E. B., & Weller, R. A. (2006). Children's reactions to parental and sibling death. *Current Psychiatry Reports, 8,* 115–120.

Sophian, C. (1985). Perseveration and infants' search: A comparison of two- and three- location tasks. *Developmental Psychology, 21,* 187–194.

Sorof, J. M., Lai, D., Turner, J., Poffenberger. T., & Portman, R. J. (2004). Overweight. ethnicity, and the prevalence of hypertension in school-aged children. *Pediatrics. 113,* 475–482.

South, M., Ozonoff, S., & McMahon, W. M. (2005). Repetitive behavior profiles in Asperger syndrome and high-functioning autism. *Journal of Autism and Developmental Disorders, 35,* 145–158.

Sowell, E. (2004, July). Commentary in M. Beckman, "Crime, culpability, and the adolescent brain. *Science Magazine, 305,* 599.

Sowell, E. R., Thompson, P. M., Leonard, C. M., Welcome, S. E., Kan, E., & Toga, A. W. (2004). Longitudinal mapping of cortical thickness and brain growth in children. *Journal of Neuroscience, 24,* 8223–8231.

Sparks, D. L., Hunsaker, J. C., Scheff, S. W., Kryscio, R. J., Henson, H., & Markesbery, W. R. (1990). Cortical senile plaques in coronary artery disease, aging, and Alzheimer's disease. *Neurobiology of Aging, 11,* 601–607.

Spelke, E. S. (1979). Perceiving bimodally specified events in infancy. *Developmental Psychology, 5,* 626–636.

Spelke, E. S. (1991). Physical knowledge in infancy: Reflections on Piaget's theory. In S. Carey & R. Gelman (Eds.), *The epigenesis of mind: Essays on biology and cognition.* Hillsdale, NJ: Erlbaum.

Spelke, E. S. (2000). Core knowledge. *American Psychologist, 55,* 1233–1243.

Spelke, E. S., Breinlinger, K., Macomber, J., & Jacobson, K. (1992). Origins of knowledge. *Psychological Review, 99,* 605–632.

Spelke, E. S., & Hespos, S. J. (2001). Continuity, competence, and the object concept. In E. Dupoux (Ed.), *Language, brain, and behavior.* Cambridge, MA: Bradford/MIT Press.

Spelke, E. S. & Kinzler, K. D. (2007a). Core knowledge. *Developmental Science 10,* 89–96.

Spelke, E. S. & Kinzler, K. D. (2007b). Core systems in human cognition. *Progress in Brain Research, 164,* 257–264.

Spelke, E. S., & Owsley, C. J. (1979). Intermodal exploration and knowledge in infancy. *Infant Behavior and Development, 2,* 13–28.

Spence, A. P. (1989). *Biology of human aging.* Englewood Cliffs, NJ: Prentice Hall.

Spence, J. T., & Helmreich, R. (1978). *Masculinity and feminity: Their psychological dimensions.* Austin: University of Texas Press.

Spencer, M. B. (1999). Social and cultural influences on school adjustment: The application of an identity-focused cultural ecological perspective. *Educational Psychologist, 34,* 43–57.

Spinetti, G., Wang, M., Monticone, R. E., & Lakatta, E. G. (2007). Atherosclerosis. In J. E. Birren (Ed.), *Encyclopedia of gerontology* (2nd ed.). San Diego: Academic Press.

Spiro, A. (2001). Health in midlife: Toward a lifespan view. In M. E. Lachman (Ed.), *Handbook of midlife development.* New York: John Wiley.

Spironelli, C., & Angrilli, A. (2008, in press). Developmental aspects of automatic word processing: Language lateralization of early ERP components in children, young adults, and middle-aged adults. *Biological Psychology.*

Sprei, J. E., & Courtois, C. A. (1988). The treatment of women's sexual dysfunctions arising from sexual assault. In R. A. Brown & J. R. Fields (Eds.), Treatment of sexual problems in individual and group therapy. Great Neck, NY: PMA.

Spring, J. (2008). *American education* (13th ed.). New York: McGraw-Hill.

Squire W. (2008). Shaken baby syndrome: The quest for evidence. *Developmental Medicine and Child Neurology, 50,* 10–14.

Srabstein, J. C., McCarter, R. J., Shao, C., & Huang, Z. J. (2006). Morbidities associated with bullying behaviors in adolescents: School based study of American adolescents. *International Journal of Adolescent Medicine and Health, 18,* 587–596.

Sroufe, L. A. (2000, Spring). The inside scoop on child development: Interview. *Cutting through the hype.* Minneapolis: College of Education and Human Development, University of Minnesota.

Sroufe, L. A. (2007). Commentary: The place of development in developmental psychology. In A. S. Masten (Ed.), *Multilevel dynamics in developmental psychology.* Mahwah, NJ: Erlbaum.

Sroufe, L. A., Egeland, B., Carlson, E., & Collins, W. A. (2005a). The place of early attachment in developmental context. In K. E. Grossman, K. Krossman, & E. Waters (Eds.). *The power of longitudinal attachment research: From infancy and childhood to adulthood.* New York: Guilford.

Sroufe, L. A., Egeland, B., Carlson, E., & Collins, W. A. (2005b). The place of early attachment in developmental context. In K. E. Grossman, K. Krossman, & E. Waters (Eds.), *The power of longitudinal attachment research: From infancy and childhood to adulthood.* New York: Guilford.

Sroufe, L. A., Waters, E., & Matas, L. (1974). Contextual determinants of infant affectional response. In M. Lewis & L. Rosenblum (Eds.), *Origins of fear.* New York: Wiley.

Stanley, S. M., Amato, P. R., Johnson, C. A., & Markman, H. J. (2006). Premarital education, marital quality, and marital stability: Findings from a large, household survey. *Journal of Family Psychology, 20,* 117–126.

Starr, L. R., & Davila, J. (2008, in press). Clarifying co-rumination: Association with internalizing symptoms and romantic involvement among adolescent girls. *Journal of Adolescence.*

Staudinger, U. M. (1996). Psychologische Produktivita und Selbstenfaltung im Alter. In M. M. Baltes & Montada (Eds.), *Produktives Leben im Alter.* Frankfurt: Campus.

Staudinger, U. M., & Bluck, S. (2001). *A view on midlife development from lifespan theory.* In M. E. Lachman (Ed.), *Handbook of midlife development.* New York: John Wiley.

Staudinger, U. M., & Dorner, J. (2007). Wisdom. In J. E. Birren (Ed.), *Encyclopedia of gerontology* (2nd ed.). San Diego Academic Press.

Steele, J., Waters, E., Crowell, J., & Treboux, D. (1998, June). *Self-report measures of attachment: Secure bonds to other attachment measures and attachment theory.* Paper presented at the meeting of the International Society for the Study of Personal Relationships, Saratoga Springs, NY.

Stein, M. T., Kennell, J. H., & Fulcher, A. (2004). Benefits of a doula present at the birth of a child. *Journal of Developmental and Behavioral Pediatrics, 25,* (Suppl. 5), S89–S92.

Steinberg, L. (2008). A social neuroscience perspective on adolescent risk-taking *Developmental Review, 28,* 78–106.

Steinberg, L. (2009). Adolescent development and juvenile justice. *Annual Review of clinical Psychology* (Vol. 5). Palo Alto, CA: Annual Reviews.

Steinberg, L., & Monahan, K. C. (2007). Age differences in resistance to peer influence. *Developmental Psychology, 43,* 1531–1543.

Steinberg, L., & Silk, J. S. (2002). Parenting adolescents. In M. Bornstein (Ed.), *Handbook of parenting* (2nd ed., Vol. 1). Mahwah, NJ: Erlbaum.

Steinberg, S. J., & Davila, J. (2008). Romantic functioning and depressive symptoms among early adolescent girls: The moderating role of parental emotional availability. *Journal of Clinical Child and Adolescent Psychology, 37,* 350–362.

Steiner, J. E. (1979). Human facial expressions in response to taste and smell stimulation. In H. Reese & L. Lipsitt (Eds.), *Advances in child development.* New York: Academic Press.

Steinhausen, H. C., Blattmann, B., & Pfund, F. (2007). Developmental outcome in children with intrauterine exposure to substances. *European Addiction Research, 13,* 94–100.

Stenklev, N. C., Vik, O., & Laukli, E. (2004). The aging ear. *Acta Otolaryngology, 124,* 69–76.

Stern, D. N., Beebe, B., Jaffe, J., & Bennett, S. L. (1977). The infant's stimulus world during social interaction: A study of caregiver behaviors with particular reference to repetition and timing. In H. R. Schaffer (Ed.), *Studies in mother-infant interaction.* London: Academic Press.

Sternberg, R. J. (1986). *Intelligence applied.* San Diego: Harcourt Brace Jovanovich.

Sternberg, R. J. (1988). *The triangle of love.* New York: Basic Books.

Sternberg, R. J. (2002). Intelligence: The triarchic theory of intelligence. In J. W. Gutherie (Ed.), *Encyclopedia of education* (2nd ed.). New York: Macmillan.

Sternberg, R. J. (2003). Contemporary theories of intelligence. In I. B. Weiner (Ed.), *Handbook of psychology* (Vol. 7). Ney York: Wiley.

Sternberg, R. J. (2004). Individual differences in cognitive development. In U. Goswami (Ed.), *Blackwell handbook of childhood cognitive development.* Malden, MA: Blackwell:

Sternberg, R. J. (2007a). *g, g's, or Jeez:* Which is the best model for developing abilities, competencies, and expertise? In P. C. Kyllonen, R. D. Roberts, & L. Stankov (Eds.), *Extending intelligence: Enhancement and new constructs* (pp. 250–265). Mahwah, NJ: Lawrence Erlbaum Associates.

Sternberg, R. J. (2007b). Finding students who are wise, practical, and creative. *The Chronicle of Higher Education, 53* (44), B11.

Sternberg, R. J. (2008a). Schools should nurture wisdom. In B. Z. Presseisen (Ed.), *Teaching for intelligence* (2nd ed.). Thousand Oaks, CA: Corwin.

Sternberg, R. J. (2008b, in press). Applying psychological theories to educational practice. *American Educational Research Journal.*

Sternberg, R. J. (2009a). *Cognitive psychology* (5th Ed.). Belmont, CA: Wadsworth.

Sternberg, R. J. (2009b, in press). Wisdom. In S. J. Lopez (Ed.). *Encyclopedia of positive psychology.* Malden, MA: Blackwell.

Sternberg, R. J. (2009c, in press). The triarchic theory of intelligence. In B. Kerr (Ed.), *Encyclopedia of giftedness, creativity, and talent.* Thousand Oaks, CA: Sage.

Sternberg, R. J. (2009d, in press). Teaching for creativity. In R. A. Beghetto & J. C. Kaufman (Eds.), *Nurturing creativity in the classroom.* New York: Cambridge University Press.

Sternberg, R. J. (2009e, in press). Successful intelligence as a framework for understanding cultural adaption. In S. Ang & L. van Dyne (Eds.), *Handbook on cultural intelligence.* New York: M.E. Sharpe.

Sternberg, R. J. (2009f, in press). Wisdom, intelligence, creativity, synthesized: A model of giftedness. In T. Balchin, B. Hymer, & D. Matthews (Eds.), *International companion to gifted education.* London: RoutledgeFalmer.

Sternberg, R. J., & Grigorenko, E. L. (2008, in press), Ability testing across cultures. In L. Suzuki. (Ed.), *Handbook of multicultural assessment* (3rd ed.). New York: Jossey-Bass

Sternberg, R. J., Jarvin, L., & Reznitskaya, A (2008, in press). Teaching for wisdom through history: Infusing wise thinking skills in the school curriculum. In M. Ferrari (Ed.) *Teaching for Wisdom.* Amsterdam: Springer.

Sternberg, R. J., Kaufman, J. C., & Grigorenko, E. (2008). *Applied intelligence.* New York: Cambridge University Press.

Sternberg, R. J., Lipka, J., Newman, T., Wildfeuer, S., & Grigorenko, E. L. (2007). Triarchically-based instruction and assessment of sixth-grade mathematics in a Yup'ik cultural setting in Alaska. *International Journal of Giftedness and Creativity, 21* (2), 6–19.

Sternberg, R. J., Roediger, H., & Halpern, D. (eds.). (2007). *Critical thinking in psychology.* Mahwah, NJ: Erlbaum.

Sternberg, R. J., & Williams, W. M. (1996). *How to develop student creativity.* Alexandria, VA: ASCD.

Sterns, H., & Huyck, M. H. (2001) The role of work in midlife. In M. Lachman (Ed.), *Handbook of Midlife development.* New York: Wiley.

Stetsenko, A. (2002). Adolescents in Russia: Surviving the turmoil and creating a brighter future. In B. B. Brown, R. W. Larson, & T. S. Saraswathi (Eds.), *The world's youth.* New York: Cambridge University Press.

Steur, F. B., Applefield, J. M., & Smith, R. (1971). Televised aggression and interpersonal aggression of preschool children. *Journal of Experimental Child Psychology, 11,* 442–447.

Stevenson, H. W. (1995). Mathematics achievement of American students: First in the world by 2000? In C. A. Nelson (Ed.), *Basic and applied perspectives in learning. cognition, and development.* Minneapolis: University of Minnesota Press.

Stevenson, H. W. (2000). Middle childhood: Education and schooling. In A. Kazdin (Ed.), *Encyclopedia of psychology.* Washington, DC, & New York: American Psychological Association and Oxford University Press.

Stevenson, H. W., & Hofer, B. K. (1999). Education policy in the United States and abroad: What we can learn from each other. In G. J. Cizek (Eds.), *Handbook of educational policy.* San Diego: Academic Press.

Stevenson, H. W., Lee, S., & Stigler, J. W. (1986). Mathematics achievement of Chinese, Japanese, and American children. *Science, 231,* 693–699.

Stevenson, H. W., Lee, S., Chen, C., Stigler, J. W., Hsu, C., & Kitamura, S. (1990). Contexts of achievement. *Monograph of the Society for Research in Child Development 55* (Serial No. 221).

Stevenson, H. W., & Newman, R. S. (1986). Long-term prediction of achievement and attitudes in mathematics and reading. *Child Development, 57,* 646–659.

Stewart, A., Livingston, M., & Dennison, S. (2008). Transitions and turning points: Examining the links between child maltreatment and juvenile offending. *Child Abuse and Neglect, 32,* 51–66.

Stewart, A. J., Ostrove, J. M., & Helson, R. (2001). Middle aging in women: Patterns of personality charge from the 30s to the 50s. *Journal of Adult Development, 8,* 23–37.

Stice, E., Presnell, K., Gau, J., & Shaw, H. (2007). Testing mediators of intervention effects in randomized controlled trials: An evaluation of two eating disorder programs. *Journal of Consulting and Clinical Psychology, 75,* 20–32.

Stiggins, R. (2008). *Introduction to student-involved assessment for learning* (5th ed.). Upper Saddle River, NJ: Prentice Hall.

Stimpson, J. P., Kuos, Y. F., Ray, L. A., Raji, M. A., & Peek, M. K. (2007). Risk of mortality related to widowhood in older Mexican Americans. *Annals of Epidemiology, 17,* 313–319.

Stine-Morrow, E. A. L. (2007). The Dumbledore hypothesis of cognitive aging. *Current Directions in Psychological Science, 16,* 295–299.

Stine-Morrow, E. A. L., Parisi, J. M., Morrow, d. G., Greene, J., & Park, D. C. (2007). An engagement model of cognitive optimization through adulthood. *Journals of Gerontology B: Psychological Sciences and Social Sciences, 62,* P62–P69.

Stinson, C. K., & Kirk, E. (2006). Structured reminiscence: An intervention to decrease depression and increase self-transcendence in older women. *Journal of Clinical Nursing, 15,* 208–218.

Stipek, D. (2005, February 16). Commentary in *USA Today,* p. 1D.

Stocker, C., & Dunn, J. (1990). Sibling relationships in adolescence: Links with friendships and peer relationships. *British Journal of Developmental Psychology, 8,* 227–244.

Stocker, C. M., Richmond, M. K., Rhoades, G. K., & Kiang, L. (2007). Family emotional processes and adolescent adjustment. *Social Development, 16,* 310–325.

Stone, R. I. (2006). Emerging issues in long-term care. In R. H. Binstock & L. K. George (Eds.), *Handbook of aging and the social sciences* (6th ed.). San Diego: Academic Press.

Stones, M., & Stones, L. (2007). Sexuality, sensuality, and intimacy. In J. E. Birren (Ed.), *Encyclopedia of gerontology* (2nd ed.). San Diego: Academic Press.

Stowe, R., & others. (2008). Dopamine agonist therapy in early Parkinson's disease. *Cochrane database of Systematic Reviews, 2,* CD006564.

Strandberg, T. E., Strandberg, A. Y., Slaomaa, V. V., Pitkala, K., Tilvis, R. S., & Miettinen, T. A. (2007). Alcoholic beverage preference, 29-year mortality, and quality of life in men in old age. *Journals of Gerontology A: Biological Sciences and Medical Sciences, 62,* M213–M218.

Strauss, M. A., Sugarman, D. B., & Giles-Sims, J. (1997). Spanking by parents and subsequent antisocial behavior in children. *Archives of Pediatrics and Adolescent Medicine, 151,* 761–767.

Streri, A. (1987). Tactile discrimination of shape and intermodal transfer in two- to three-month-old infants. *British Journal of Developmental Psychology, 5,* 213–220.

Striano, T., Reid, V. M., & Hoehl, S. (2006). Neural mechanisms of joint attention in infancy. *European Journal of Neuroscience, 23,* 2819–2823.

Striegel-Moore, R. H., & Bulik, C. M. (2007). Risk factors for eating disorders. *American Psychologist, 62,* 181–198.

Stringer, M., Ratcliffe, S. J., Evans, E. C., & Brown, L. P. (2005). The cost of prenatal care attendance and pregnancy outcomes in low-income working women. *Journal of Obstetrical, Gynecologic, and Neonatal Nursing, 34,* 551–560.

Stroebe, M., Schut, H., & Stroebe, W. (2005). Attachment in coping with bereavement: A theoretical integration. *Review of General Psychology, 9,* 48–66.

Strohmeir, D., & Schmitt-Rodermund, E. (Eds.) (2008). *Immigrant youth in European countries.* Clifton, NJ: Psychology Press.

Strong, B., DeVault, C., Sayad, B., & Yarber, W. (2008). *Human sexuality* (5th ed.). New York: McGraw-Hill.

Strong, B., Yarber, W., Sayad, B., & De Vault, C. (2008). *Human sexuality* (6th ed.). New York: McGraw-Hill.

Strong-Wilson, T., & Ellis, J. (2007). Children and place: Reggio Emilia's environment as a third teacher. *Theory into Practice, 46,* 40–47.

Studenski, S., Carlson, M. C., Fillet, H., Greenough, W. T., Kramer, A., F., & Rebok, G. W. (2006). From bedside to bench: Does mental and physical activity promote cognitive vitality in late life? *Science of Aging, Knowledge, and Environment, 10,* e21.

Stutts, J. C. (2007). Driving behavior. In J. E. Birren (Ed.), *Encyclopedia of gerontology* (2nd ed.). San Diego: Academic Press.

Substance Abuse and Mental Health Services Administration. (2002). *Aging and substance abuse.* Washington, DC: U.S. Department of Health and Human Services.

Suetta, C., Anderson, J. L., Dalgas, U., Berget, J., Koskinen, S. O., Aagaard, P., Magnusson, S. P., & Kjaer, M. (2008, in press). Resistance training induces qualitative changes in muscle morphology, muscle architecture, and muscle function in postoperative patients. *Journal of Applied Physiology.*

Sugar, J. A. (2007). Memory, strategies. In J. E. Birren (Ed.), *Encyclopedia of gerontology* (2nd ed.). San Diego: Academic Press.

Sugimoto, M., Kuze, M., & Uji, Y. (2008). Ultrasound bioimicroscopy for membranous congenital cataract. *Canadian Journal of Ophthalmology, 43,* 7–8.

Sugita, Y. (2004). Experience in early infancy is indispensable for color perception. *Current Biology, 14,* 1267-1271.

Sui, X., LaMonte, M. J., Laditka, J. N., Hardin, J. W., Chase, N., Hooker, S. P., & Blair, S. N. (2007). Cardiorespiratory fitness and adiposity as mortality predictors in older adults. *Journal of the American Medical Association, 298,* 2507–2516.

Sullivan, H. S. (1953). *The interpersonal theory of psychiatry.* New York: W. W. Norton.

Sullivan, K., & Sullivan, A. (1980). Adolescent-parent separation. *Developmental Psychology, 16,* 93–99.

Sum, S., Mathews, R. M., Hughes, I., & Campbell, A. (2008). Internet use and loneliness in older adults. *Cyberpsychology and Behavior, 11,* 208–211.

Suman, R. P., Udani, R., & Nanavati, R. (2008). Kangaroo mother care for low birth weight infants: A randomized controlled trial. *Indian Pediatrics, 45,* 17–23.

Sumaroka, M., & Bornstein, M. H. (2008). Play. In M. M. Haith & J. B. Benson (Eds.), *Encyclopedia of infant and early childhood development.* Oxford, UK: Elsevier.

Sumic, A., Michael, Y. L., Carlson, N. E., Howieson, D. B., & Kaye, J. A. (2007). Physical activity and the risk of dementia in oldest old. *Journal of Aging and Health, 19,* 242–259.

Sun, L. Y., & Bartke, A. (2007). Adult neurogenesis in the hippocampus of long-lived mice during aging. *Journal of Gerontology A: Biological Sciences and Medical Sciences, 62,* 117–125.

Sun, S. S., Liang, R., Huang, T. T., Daniels, S. R., Arsianian, S., Liu, K., Grave, G. D., & Siervogel, R. M. (2008). Childhood obesity predicts adult metabolic syndrome: The Fels Longitudinal Study. *Journal of Pediatrics, 152,* 191–200.

Sunstein, C. R. (2008). Adolescent risk-taking and social meaning: A commentary. *Developmental Review, 28,* 145–152.

Super, C., & Harkness, S. (1997). The cultural structuring of child development. In J. W. Berry, Y. H. Poortinga, & J. Pandey (Eds.), *Handbook of cross-cultural psychology: Theory and method.* Vol. 2. Boston: Allyn & Bacon.

Suris, J. C., Jeannin, A., Chossis, I., & Michaud, P. A. (2007). Piercing among -adolescents: Body art as a risk marker: A population-based study. *Journal of Family Practice, 56*, 126–130.

Sutterby, J. A., & Frost, J. (2006). Creating play environments for early childhood: Indoors and out. In B. Spodek & O. N. Saracho (Eds.), *Handbook of research on the education of young children* (2nd ed.). Mahwah, NJ: Erlbaum.

Suvas, S. (2008). Advancing age and immune cell dysfunction: Is it reversible or not? *Expert Opinion on Biological Therapy, 8*, 657–658.

Suzman, R. M., Harris, T., Hadley, E. C., Kovar, M. G., & Weindruch, R. (1992). The robust oldest old: Optimistic perspectives for increasing healthy life expectancy. In R. M. Suzman, D. P. Willis, & K. G. Manton (Eds.), *The oldest old.* New York: Oxford University Press.

Suzuki, A., Sekiguchi, S., Asano, S., & Itoh, M. (2008). Pharmacological topics of bone metabolism: Recent advances in pharmacological management of osteoporosis. *Journal of Pharmacological Science, 106*, 530–535.

Sveen, C. A., & Walby, F. A. (2008). Suicide survivors' mental health and grief reactions: A systematic review of controlled studies. *Suicide and Life Threatening Behavior, 38*, 13–29.

Svihula, J., & Estes, C. L. (2008). Social security politics: Ideology and reform. *Journals of Gerontology B: Psychological Sciences and Social Sciences, 62*, S79–S89.

Swaab, D. F., Chung, W. C., Kruijver, F. P., Hofman, M. A., & Ishunina, T. A. (2001). Structural and functional sex differences in the human hypothalamus. *Hormones and Behavior, 40*, 93–98.

Swahn, M., Bossarte, R. M., & Sullivent, E. E. (2008). Age of alcohol use initiation, suicidal behavior, and peer and dating violence victimization and perpetration among high-risk, seventh-grade adolescents. *Pediatrics, 121*, 297–305.

Swain, S. O. (1992). Men's friendships with women. In P. Nard: (Ed.), *Gender in intimate relationships.* Belmont, CA: Wadsworth.

Swamy, G. K., Ostbye, T., & Skjaerven, R. (2008). Association of preterm birth with long-term survival, reproduction, and next generation preterm birth. *Journal of the American Medical Association, 299*, 1429–1436.

Swanson, B. J., Roman-Shriver, C. R., Shriver, B. J., & Goodell, L. S. (2007). A comparison between improvers and non-improvers among children with anemia. enrolled in the WIC program. *Maternal and Child Health Journal, 11*, 447–459.

Swartz, T. T. (2008, Spring). Family capital and the invisible transfer of privilege: Intergenerational support and social class in early adulthood. *New Directions in Child and Adolescent Development, 119*, 11–24.

Sweet, S., Moen, P., & Meiksins, P. (2007) Dual earners in double jeopardy: Preparing for job loss in the new risk economy. In B. A. Rubin (Ed.), *Research in the Sociology of Work.* New York: Elsevier.

Sweeting, H. N. (2008). Gendered dimensions of obesity in childhood and adolescence. *Nutrition Journal, 14*, 1.

Syed, M., & Azmitia, M. (2008, in press). A narrative approach to ethnic identity in emerging adulthood: Bringing life to the identity status model. *Developmental Psychology.*

Sykes, C. J. (1995). *Dumbing down our kids: why American children feel good about themselves but can't read, write, or add.* New York: St. Martin's Press.

T

Taddio, A. (2008). Circumcision. In M. M. Haith & J. B. Benson (Eds.), *Encyclopedia of infant and early childhood development.* Oxford, UK: Elsevier.

Tafoya, M., & Spitzberg, B. H. (2007). The dark side of infidelity. In B. H. Spitzberg and W. R. Cupach (Eds.), *The dark side of interpersonal communication.* Mahwah, NJ: Erlbaum.

Tager-Flusberg, H. (2007). Theory of mind hypothesis of autism. *Current Directions in Psychological Science, 16*, 311–315.

Tager-Flusberg, H., & Zukowski, A. (2009). Putting words together: Morphology and syntax in the preschool years. In J. Berko Gleason & N. Ratner (Eds.), *The development of language* (7th ed.). Boston: Allyn & Bacon.

Taige, N. M., Neal, C., Glover, V., & the Early Stress, Translational Research and Prevention Science Network: Fetal and Neonatal Experience on Child and Adolescent Mental Health. (2007). Antenatal maternal stress and long-term effects on neurodevelopment: How and why? *Journal of Child Psychology and Psychiatry, 48*, 245–261.

Taige, N. M., & others. (2007). Antenatal maternal stress and long-term effects on child neurodevelopment: How and why? *Journal of Child Psychology and Psychiatry, 48*, 245–261.

Takai, Y., Sato, M., Tan, R., & Hirai, T. (2005). Development of stereoacuity: Longitudinal design using a computer-based random-dot stereo test. *Japanese Journal of Ophthalmology, 49*, 1–5.

Talaro, K. P. (2008). *Foundations of microbiology* (6th ed.). New York: McGraw-Hill.

Talley, R. C., & Crews, J. E. (2007). Framing the public health of caregiving. *American Journal of Public Health, 97*, 224–228.

Tam, W. H., & Chung, T. (2007). Psychosomatic disorders in pregnancy. *Current Opinion in Obstetrics and Gynecology, 19*, 126–132.

Tamis-LeMonda, C. S., & Rodriquez, E. T. (2009, in press). Parents' role in fostering young children's learning and language development. In R. E. Tremblay, R. deV Peters, M. Boivin, & R. G. Barr (Eds.), *Encyclopedia on early childhood development.* Montreal: Centre of Excellence for Early Childhood Development.

Tan, E. J., Xue, Q. L., Li, T., Carlson, M. C., & Fried, L. P. (2007). Volunteering: A physical activity intervention for older adults-the Experience Crops program in Baltimore. *Journal of Urban Health, 83*, 954–969.

Tang, K. L. (2008). Taking older people's rights seriously: The role of international law. *Journal of Aging and Social Policy, 20*, 99–117.

Tannen, D. (1990). *You just don't understand: Women and men in conversation.* New York: Ballantine.

Tannock, R. (2009, in press). Language development and literacy: Comments on Beitchman and Cohen. In R. E. Tremblay, R. deV Peters, M. Boivin, & R. G. Barr (Eds.), *Encyclopedia of early childhood development.* Montreal: Centre of Excellence for Early Childhood Development.

Tantillo, M., Kesick, C. M., Hynd, G. W., & Dishman, R. K. (2002). The effects of exercise on children with attention-deficit hyperactivity disorder. *Medical Science and Sports Exercise, 34*, 203–212.

Tappan, M. B. (1998). Sociocultural psychology and caring psychology: Exploring Vygotsky's "hidden curriculum." *Educational Psychologist, 33*, 23–33.

Tarokh, L., & Carskadon, M. A. (2008). Sleep in adolescents. In L. R. Squire (Ed.), *New encyclopedia of neuroscience.* Oxford, UK: Elsevier.

Tashiro, T., & Frazier, P. (2003). "I'll never be in a relationship like that again": Personal growth following romantic relationship breakups. *Personal Relationships, 10*, 113–128.

Tashiro, T., Frazier, P., & Berman, M. (2006). Stress related growth following divorce and relationship dissolution. In M. A. Fine & J. H. Harvey (Eds.) *Handbook of divorce and relationship dissolution.* Mahwah, NJ: Erlbaum.

Tasker, F. L., and Golombok, S. (1997). *Growing up in a lesbian family: Effects on child development.* New York: Guilford.

Tauman, R., & Gozal, D. (2006). Obesity and obstructive sleep apnea in children. *Pediatric Respiratory Reviews, 7*, 247–259.

Taveras, E. M., Rifas-Shiman, S. L., Oken, E., Gunderson, E. P., & Gillman, M. W. (2008). Short sleep duration in infancy and risk of childhood overweight. *Archives of Pediatric and Adolescent Medicine, 162*, 305–311.

Taylor, F. M. A., Ko, R., & Pan, M. (1999). Prenatal and reproductive health care. In E. J. Kramer, S. L. Ivey, & Y. W. Ying (Eds.), *Immigrant women's health.* San Francisco: Jossey-Bass.

Taylor, L. S., & Whittaker, C. R. (2009). *Bridging multiple worlds* (2nd ed.). Boston: Allyn & Bacon.

Taylor, P. (2007). Work and employment: Society. In J. E. Birren (ed.), *Encyclopedia of gerontology* (2nd ed.). San Diego: Academic Press.

Taylor, R. D., & Lopez, E. I. (2005). Family management practice, school achievement, and problem behavior in African American adolescents: Mediating processes. *Applied Developmental Psychology, 26*, 39–49.

Taylor, R. J., Chatters, L. M., & Jackson, J. S. (2007). Religious and spiritual involvement among older African Americas, Caribbean Blacks, and non-Hispanic Whites: Findings from the national Survey of American Life. *Journals of Gerontology B: Psychological Sciences and Social Sciences, 62*, S238–S250.

Taylor, R. L., Smiley, L., & Richards, S. B. (2009). *Exceptional students.* New York: McGraw-Hill.

Taylor, S. E., & Stanton, A. L. (2007). Coping resources, coping processes, and mental health. *Annual Review of Clinical Psychology* (Vol. 3). Palo Alto, CA: Annual Reviews.

Taylor, S. P. (1982). Mental health and successful coping among Black women. In R. C. Manuel (Ed.), *Minority aging.* Westport, CT: Greenwood Press.

te Velde, S. J., De Bourdeaudhuij, I., Throsdottir, I., Rasmussen, M., Hagstromer, M., Klepp, K. I., & Brug, J. (2007). Patterns in sedentary and exercise behaviors and associations with overweight in 9–14-year-old boys and girls–a cross-sectional study. *BMC Public Health, 7,* 16.

Teague, M. L., Mackenzie, S. L. C., & Rosenthal, D. M. (2009). *Your health today* (brief ed.). New York: McGraw-Hill.

Temple, B., Janzen, B. L., Chad, K., Bell, G., Reeder, B., & Martin, L. (2008). The health benefits of a physical activity program for older adults living in congregate housing. *Canadian Journal of Public Housing, 99,* 36–40.

Templeton, J. L., & Eccles, J. S. (2006). The relation between spiritual development and identity processes. In E. Roehlkepartain, P. E. King, L. Wagener, & P. L. Benson (Eds.), *The handbook of spirituality in childhood and adolescence.* Thousand Oaks, CA: Sage.

Teno, J. M., Clarridge, B. R., Casey, V., Welch, L. C., Wetie, T., Shield, R., & Mor, V. (2004). Family perspectives on end-of-life care at the last place of care. *Journal of the American Medical Association, 291,* 88–93.

Terman, L. (1925). Genetic studies of genius. Vol. I: *Mental and physical traits of a thousand gifted children.* Stanford, CA: Stanford University Press.

Terry, D. F., Sebastian, P., Andersen, P. S., & Perls, T. T. (2008). Disentangling the roles of disability and morbidity in survival to exceptional old age. *Archives of Internal Medicine, 168,* 277–283.

Terry, W., Olson, L. G., Wilss, L., & Boulton-Lewis, G. (2006). Experience of dying: Concerns of dying patients and of carers. *Internal Medicine Journal, 36,* 338–346.

Teti, D. (2001). Retrospect and prospect in the psychological study of sibling relationships. In J. P. McHale & W. S. Grolnick (Eds.). *Retrospect and prospect in the psychological study of families.* Mahwah, NJ: Erlbaum.

Teti, D. M., & Towe-Goodman, N. (2008). Postpartum depression, effects on infant. In M. M. Haith & J. B. Benson (Eds.), *Encyclopedia of infancy and early childhood.* Oxford, UK: Elsevier.

Thapar, A., Fowler, T., Rice, F., Scourfield, J., Van Den Bree, M., Thomas, S., Harold, G., & Hay, D. (2003). Maternal smoking during pregnancy and attention deficit hyperactivity disorder symptoms in offspring. *American Journal of Psychiatry, 160,* 1985–1989.

Tharp, R. G. (1994). Intergroup differences among Native Americans in socialization and child cognition: An erthogenetic analysis. In P. M. Greenfield & R. Cocking (Eds.), *Cross-cultural roots of minority child development.* Mahwah, NJ: Erlbaum.

Tharp, R. G., & Gallimore, R. (1988). *Rousing minds to life: Teaching, learning, and schooling in social context.* New York: Cambridge University Press.

Thavanati, R. K., Kanala, K. R., de Dios, A. E., & Cantu Garza, J. M. (2008). Age related correlation between antioxidant enzymes and DNA damage with smoking and body mass index. *Journals of Gerontology A: Biological Sciences and Medical Sciences, 63,* 360–364.

The Conduct Problems Prevention Research Group. (2007). The Fast Track randomized controlled trial to prevent externalizing psychiatric disorders: Findings from grades 3 to 9. *Journal of the American Academy of Child and Adolescent Psychiatry, 46,* 1250–1262.

The TADS Team. (2007). The Treatment for Adolescents with Depression Study: Long-term effectiveness and safety outcomes. *Archives of General Psychiatry, 64,* 1132–1143.

Thelen, E., (2000). Perception and motor development. In A. Kazdin (Ed.), *Encyclopedia of psychology.* Washington, DC, & New York: American Psychological Association and Oxford University Press.

Thelen, E., & Smith, L. B. (1998). Dynamic systems theory. In W. Damon (Ed.), *Handbook of child psychology* (5th ed., Vol. 1.). New York: Wiley.

Thelen, E., & Smith, L. B. (2006). Dynamic development of action and thought. In W. Damon & R. Lerner (Eds.), *Handbook of child psychology* (6th ed.). New York: Wiley.

Thelen, E., Corbetta, D., Kamm, K., Spencer, J. P., Schneider, K., & Zernicke, R. F. (1993). The transition to reaching: Mapping intention and intrinsic dynamics. *Child Development, 64,* 1058–1098.

Thiele, D. M., & Whelan, T. A. (2008). The relationship between grandparent satisfaction, reaming, and generativity. *International Journal of Aging and Human Development, 66,* 21–48.

Thomann, C. R., & Carter, A. S. (2008). Social and emotional development theories. In M. M. Haith & J. B. Benson (Eds.), *Encyclopedia of infant and early childhood development.* Oxford, UK: Elsevier.

Thomas, A., & Chess, S. (1991). Temperament in adolescence and its functional significance. In R. M. Lerner, A. C. Petersen, & J. Brooks-Gunn (Eds.), *Encyclopedia of adolescence* (Vol. 2). New York: Garland.

Thomas, M. S. C., & Johnson, M. H. (2008). New advances in understanding sensitive periods in brain development. *Current Directions in Psychological Science, 17,* 1–5.

Thomas, R. M., Hotsenpiller, G., & Peterson, D. A. (2007). Acute psychosocial stress reduces cell survival in adult hippocampal neurogenesis without altering proliferation. *Journal of Neuroscience, 27,* 2734–2743.

Thompson, D. R., Obarzanek, E., Franko, D. L., Barton, B. A., Morrison, J., Biro, F. M., Daniels, S. R., & Striegel-Moore, R. H. (2007). Childhood overweight and cardiovascular disease risk factors: The National Heart, Lung, and Blood Institute Growth and Health Study. *Journal of Pediatrics, 150,* 18–25.

Thompson, M. P., Ho, C. H., & Kingree, J. B. (2007). Prospective associations between delinquency and suicidal behaviors in a nationally representative sample. *Journal of Adolescent Health, 40,* 232–237.

Thompson, P. M., Giedd, J. N., Woods, R. P., MacDonald, D., Evans, A. C., & Toga, A. W. (2000). Growth patterns in the developing brain detected by using continuum mechanical tensor maps. *Nature, 404,* 190–193.

Thompson, R., & Murachver, T. (2001). Predicting gender from electronic discourse. *British Journal of Social Psychology, 40,* 193–208.

Thompson, R. A. (2006). The development of the person. In W. Damon & R. Lerner (Eds.), *Handbook of child psychology* (6th ed.). New York: Wiley.

Thompson, R. A. (2007). Unpublished review of J. W. Santrock's. *Children,* 10th ed. (New York: McGraw-Hill).

Thompson, R. A. (2008). Unpublished review of J. W. Santrock's *Life-span development,* 12th ed. (New York: McGraw-Hill).

Thompson, R. A. (2009a, in press). Emotional development. In R. A. Schweder (Ed.), *The Chicago companion to the child.* Chicago: University of Chicago Press.

Thompson, R. A. (2009b, in press). Early attachment and later development: Familiar questions, new answers. In J. Cassidy & P. R. Shaver (Eds.), *Handbook of attachment* (2nd Ed.). New York: Guilford.

Thompson, R. A., & Goodvin, R. (2005). The individual child: Temperament, emotion, self, and personality. In M. H. Bornstein & M. E. Lamb (Eds.), *Developmental Psychology* (5th ed.). Mahwah, NJ: Erlbaum.

Thompson, R. A., Meyer, S., & Jochem, R. (2008). Emotion regulation. In M. M. Haith & J. B. Benson (Eds.), *Encyclopedia of infant and early childhood development.* Oxford, UK: Elsevier.

Thompson, R. A., Meyer, S., & McGinley, M. (2006). Understanding values in relationships: The development of conscience. In M. Killen & J. Smetana (Eds.), *Handbook of moral development.* Mahwah, NJ: Erlbaum.

Thompson, R. A., & Nelson, C. A. (2001). Developmental science and the media. *American Psychologist, 56,* 5–15.

Thompson, R. A., & Newton, E. (2009, in press). Infant-caregiver communication. In H. T. Reis & S. Sprecher (Eds.), *Encyclopedia of human relationships.* Thousand Oaks, CA: Sage.

Thompson, R. A., & Virmani, E. A. (2009, in press). Creating persons: Culture, elf,p and personality development. In M. H. Bornstein (Ed.), *Handbook of cross- cultural developmental science.* Clifton, NJ: Psychology Press.

Thöni, A., & Moroder, L. (2004). Waterbirth: A safe and natural delivery method. Experience after 1355 waterbirths in Italy. *Midwifery Today, 70,* 44–48.

Thornton, J. G. (2007). Progesterone and preterm labor—Still no definite answers. *New England Journal of Medicine, 357,* 499–501.

Thornton, R., & Light, L. C. (2006). Aging and language. In J. E. Birren & K. W. Schaie (Eds.), *Handbook of the psychology of aging* (6th ed.). San Diego: Academic Press.

Thornton, W. J., & Dumke, H. A. (2005). Age differences in everyday problem-solving and decision-making effectiveness: A meta-analytic review. *Psychology and Aging, 20,* 85–99.

Thorton, A., & Camburn, D. (1989). Religious participation and sexual behavior and attitudes. *Journal of Marriage and the Family, 49,* 117–128.

Timmer, E., Westerhof, G. J., & Dittmann-Kohli, F. (2005). "When looking back on my past life I regret...": Retrospective regret in the second half of life. *Death Studies, 29,* 625–644,

Timmerman, K. L., & Volpe, E. (2008). Amino acid metabolism and regulatory effects in aging. *Current Opinion in Clinical Nutrition and Metabolic Care, 11,* 45–49.

Tinsley, B. J. (2003). *How Children learn to be healthy.* New York: Cambridge University Press.

Tobin, J. J., Wu, D. Y. H., & Davidson, D. H. (1989). *Preschool in three cultures.* New Haven, CT: Yale University Press.

Toga, A. W., Thompson, P. M., & Sowell, E. R. (2006). Mapping brain maturation, *Trends in Neuroscience, 29*, 148–159.

Tolani, N., & Brooks-Gunn, J. (2008). Family support, international trends. In M. M. Haith & J. B. Benson (Eds.), *Encyclopedia of infancy and early childhood.* Oxford, UK: Elsevier.

Tomasello, M. (2003). *Constructing a language: A usage-based theory of language acquisition.* Cambridge, MA: Harvard University Press.

Tomasello, M., & Carpenter, M. (2007). Shared intentionality. *Developmental Science, 10*, 121–125.

Tomasello, M., Carpenter, M., & Liszkowski, U. (2007). A new look at infant pointing. *Child Development, 78*, 705–722.

Toth, S. L. (2009, in press). Attachment-based interventions: Comments on Dozier, Egeland, and Benoit. In R. E. Tremblay, R. deV Peters, M. Boivin, & R. G. Barr (Eds.), *Encyclopedia on early childhood development.* Montreal: Centre of Excellence for Early Childhood Development.

Toth, S. L., & Cicchetti, D. (2009, in press). Child maltreatment and its impact on psychosocial development. In R. E. Tremblay, R. deV Peters, M. Boivin, & R. G. Barr (Eds.), *Encyclopedia of early childhood development.* Montreal: Centre of Excellence for Early Childhood Development.

Tough, S. C., Newburn-Cook, C., Johnston, D. W., Svenson, L. W., Rose, S., & Belik, J. (2002). Delayed childbearing and its impact on population rate changes in lower birth weight, multiple birth, and preterm delivery. *Pediatrics, 109*, 399–403.

Towse, J. (2008). *Working memory and cognitive development.* Philadelphia: Psychology Press.

Tozer, S. E., Senese, G., & Violas, P. C. (2006). *School and society* (5th ed.). New York: McGraw-Hill.

Trask, B. S., & Koivur, M. (2007). Trends in marriage and cohabitation. In B. S. Trask & R. R. Hamon (Eds.), *Cultural diversity and families.* Thousand Oaks, CA: Sage.

Trehub, S. E., Schneider, B. A., Thorpe, I. A., & Judge, P. (1991). Observational measures of auditory sensitivity in early infancy. *Developmental Psychology, 27*, 40–49.

Tremblay, R. E. (2009). Development of aggression from early childhood to adulthood. In R. E. Tremblay, R. deV Peters, M. Boivin, & R. G. Barr (Eds.), *Encyclopedia on early childhood development.* Montreal: Center of Excellence for Early Childhood Development.

Triche, E. W., & Hossain, N. (2007). Environmental factors implicated in the -causation of adverse pregnancy outcome. *Seminars in Perinatology, 31*, 240–242.

Trimble, J. E. (1988, August). *The enculturation of contemporary psychology.* Paper presented at the meeting of the American Psychological Association, New Orleans.

Troll, L. E. (2000). Transmission and transmutation. In J. E. Birren, & J. J. F. Schroots (Eds.), *A history of geropsychology in autobiography.* Washington, DC: American Psychological Association.

Trost, S. G., Fees, B., & Dzewaltowski, D. (2008). Feasibility and efficacy of "move and learn" physical activity curriculum in preschool children. *Journal of Physical Activity and Health, 5*, 88–103.

Truog, R. D. (2007). Brain death—too flawed to endure, too ingrained to abandon. *Journal of Law, Medicine, and Ethics, 35*, 273–281.

Truog, R. D. (2008). End-of-life decision-making in the United States. *European Journal of Anesthesiology, 42* (Suppl. 1), S43–S50.

Trzesniewski, K. H., Donnellan, M. B., Caspi, A., Moffitt, T. E., Robins, R. W., & Poultin, R. (2006). Adolescent low self-esteem is a risk factor for adult poor health, Criminal behavior, and limited economic prospects. *Developmental Psychology, 42*, 381–390.

Trzesniewski, K. H., Donnellan, M. B., & Robins, R. W. (2003). Stability of self-esteem across the life span. *Journal of Personality and Social Psychology, 84*, 205–220.

Tsukahara, K., & others, (2007). Comparison of age-related changes in facial wrinkles and sagging in the skin of Japanese, Chinese, and Thai women. *Journal of Dermatological Science, 47*, 19–28.

Tucker, J. S., Ellickson, P. L., & Klein, M. S. (2003). Predictors of the transition to regular smoking during adolescence and young adulthood. *Journal of Adolescent Health, 32*, 314–324.

Tucker, J. S., Schwartz, J. E., Clark, K. M., & Friedman, H. S. (1999). Age-related changes in the association of social network ties with mortality risk. *Psychology and Aging, 14*, 564–571.

Tulenko, T. N., Lapotofsky, D., & Mason, R. P. (2007). Cholesterol and plasma membranes. In J. E. Birren (Ed.), *Encyclopedia of gerontology* (2nd ed.). San Diego: Academic Press.

Turiel, E. (2006). The development of morality. In W. Damon & R. Lerner (Eds.), *Handbook of child psychology* (6th ed.), New York: Wiley.

Turkeltaub, P. E., Gareau, L., Flowers, D. L., Zeffiro, T. A., & Eden, G. F. (2003). Development of neural mechanisms for reading. *Nature Neuroscience, 6*, 767–773.

Turnbull, H. R., Huerta, N., & Stowe, M. (2009). *What every teacher should know about the Individuals with Disabilities Education Act as amended in 2004* (2nd Ed.). Upper Saddle River, NJ: Prentice Hall.

Turner, B. F. (1982). Sex-related differences in aging. In B. B. Wolman (Ed.), *Handbook of developmental psychology.* Englewood Cliffs, NJ: Prentice Hall.

Turvey, C. L., Carney, C., Arndt, S., & Wallace, R. B. (1999, November). *Conjugal loss and syndromal depression in a sample of elders ages 70 years and older.* Paper presented at the meeting of the Gerontological Society of America, San Francisco.

Tyas, S. L., Salazar, J. C., Snowdon, D. A., Desrosiers, M. F., Riley, K. P., Mendiondo, M. S., & Kryscio, R. J. (2007). Transitions to mild cognitive impairments, dementia, and death: Findings from the Nun Study. *American Journal of Epidemiology, 165*, 1231–1238.

U

U.S. Bureau of Labor Statistics. (2005). *People.* Washington, DC: U.S. Department of Labor.

U. S. Census Bureau. (2004). *Statistical abstracts of the United States.* Washington, DC: U.S. Government Printing Office.

U. S. Census Bureau. (2006). *Statistical abstracts of the United States.* Washington, DC: U. S. Government Printing Office.

U.S. Census Bureau. (2006). *American Community Survey.* Washington, DC: U.S. Department of Labor.

U.S. Department of Energy. (2001). *The human genome project.* Washington. DC: Author.

U. S. Department of Health and Human Services. (2005). *Child abuse and neglect statistics.* Washington, DC: Author.

U.S. Department of Health and Human Services. (2008). Retrieved May 26, 2008, from http://www.cdc.gov/ncbddd/folicacid/

U.S. Food and Drug Administration. (2004, March 19). *An important message for pregnant women and women of childbearing age who may become pregnant about the risk of mercury in fish.* Washington, DC: Author.

Uba, L. (1992). Cultural barriers to health care for Southeast Asian refugees. *Public Health Reports, 107*, 544–549.

Ubell, C. (1992, December 6). We can age successfully. *Parade,* pp. 14–15.

Uhlenberg, P., & Dannefer, D. (2007). Age stratification. In J. E. Birren (Ed.), *Encyclopedia of gerontology* (2nd ed.). San Diego: Academic Press.

Ulvund, S. E., & Smith, L. (1996). The predictive validity of nonverbal communicative skills in infants with perinatal hazards. *Infant Behavior and Development, 19*, 441–449.

Umana-Taylor, A. J. (2006, March). *Ethnic identity, acculturation, and enculturation: Considerations in methodology and theory.* Paper presented at the meeting of the Society for Research on Adolescence, San Francisco.

Umana-Taylor, A. J., Vargas-Changes, D., Garcia, C. D., & Gonzales-Backen, M. (2008). A longitudinal examination of Latino adolescents' ethnic identity, coping with discrimination, and self-esteem. *Journal of Early Adolescence, 28*, 16–50.

UNAIDS. (2006). *2006 report on the global AIDS epidemic.* Geneva: SWIT: UNICEF.

Underhill, K., Montgomery, P., & Operario, D. (2007). Sexual abstinence programs to prevent HIV infection in high-income countries. *British Medical Journal, 335*, 248.

Underwood, M. (2004). Sticks and stones and social exclusion: Aggression among boys and girls. In P. K. Smith & C. H. Hart (Eds.), *Blackwell handbook of childhood social development.* Malden, MA: Blackwell.

UNICEF. (2004). *The state of the world's children 2004.* Geneva: Author.

UNICEF. (2006). *The State of the world's Children, 2006.* Geneva: Author.

UNICEF. (2007). *The State of the world's Children, 2007.* Geneva: Author.

UNICEF. (2008). *The state of the world's children 2008.* Geneva: Author.

United Nations. (2002). *Improving the quality of life of girls.* New York: Author.

Urbano, M. T., & Tait, D. M. (2004). Can the irradiated uterus sustain a pregnancy? *Clinical Oncology, 16,* 24–28.

Urbina, E. M. (2008). Removing the mask: The danger of hidden hypertension. *Journal of Pediatrics, 152,* 455–456.

V

Vacca, J. A., Vacca, R. T., Gove, M. K., Burkey, L. C., Lenhart, L. A., & McKeon, C. A. (2009). *Reading and learning to read* (7th Ed.). Boston: Allyn & Bacon.

Vaillant, G. E. (1977). *Adaptation to life.* Boston: Little, Brown.

Vaillant, G. E. (1992). Is there a natural history of addiction? In C. P. O'Brien & J. H. Jaffe (Eds.), *Addictive states.* Cambridge, MA: Harvard University Press.

Vaillant, G. E. (2002). *Aging well.* Boston: Little, Brown.

Vallotton, C. D., & Fischer, K. W. (2008). Cognitive development. In M. M. Haith & J. B. Benson (Eds.), *Encyclopedia of infancy and early childhood.* Oxford, UK: Elsevier

Van Beveren, T. T. (2008, Janaury). *Personal conversation.* Richardson, TX: Department of Psychology, University of Texas at Dallas.

Van Buren, E., & Graham, S. (2003). *Redefining ethnic identity: Its relationship to positive and negative school adjustment outcomes for minority youth.* Paper presented at the meeting of the Society for Research in Child Development, Tampa.

van de Weijer-Bergsma, E., Wijnroks, L., & Jongmans, M. J. (2008, in press). Attention development in infants and preschool children born preterm: A review. *Infant Behavior and Development.*

van den Berg, P., Neumark-Sztainer, D., Hannan, P. J., & Haines, J. (2007). Is dieting advice from magazines helpful or harmful? Five-year associations with weight-control behaviors and psychological outcomes in adolescents. *Pediatrics, 119,* e30–e37.

van den Boom, D. C. (1989). Neonatal irritability and the development of attachment. In G. A. Kohnstamm, J. E. Bates, & M. K. Rothbart (Eds.), *Temperament in childhood.* New York: Wiley.

Van den Heuvel, A., & Marteau, T. M. (2008). Cultural variation in values attached to informed choice in the context of prenatal diagnosis. *Seminars in Fetal and Neonatal Medicine, 13,* 99–102.

van der Heide, A., & others. (2007). End-of-life practices in the Netherlands under the Euthanasia Act. *New England Journal of Medicine, 356,* 1957–1965.

van der Schoot, C. E., Hahn, S., & Chitty, L. S. (2008). Non-invasive prenatal diagnosis and determination of fetal Rh status. *Seminars in Fetal and Neonatal Medicine, 13,* 63–68.

van Hof, P., van der Kamp, J., & Savelsbergh, G. J. (2008). The relation between infants' perception of catchableness and the control of catching. *Developmental Psychology, 44,* 182–194.

van Hooren, S. A., Valentijn, A. M., Bosma, H., Ponds, R. W., van Boxtel, M. P., & Jolles, J. (2007). Cognitive functioning in healthy older adults aged 64–81: A cohort study into the effects of age, sex, and education. *Neuropsychology, Development, and Cognition B, 14,* 40–54.

van Hooren, S. A., Valentijn, S. A., Bosma, H., Ponds, R. W., van Boxtel, M. P., & Jolles, J. (2005). Relation between health status and cognitive functioning: A 6-year follow-up of the Maastricht Aging Study. *Journals of Gerontology B: Psychological Sciences and Social Sciences, 60,* 57–60.

van IJzendoorn, M. H., & Kroonenberg, P. M. (1988). Cross-cultural patterns of attachment: A meta-analysis of the Strange Situation. *Child Development, 59,* 147–156.

van IJzendoorn, M. H., & Sagi-Schwartz, A. (2009, in press). Cross-cultural patterns of attachment: Universal and contextual dimensions. In J. Cassidy & P.R. Shaver (Eds.), *Handbook of attachment* (2nd Ed.). New York: Guilford.

Van Orden, K. A., Witte, T. K., Gordon, K. H., Bender, T. W., & Joiner, T. E. (2008). Suicidal desire and the capability for suicide: Tests of the interpersonal-psychological theory of suicidal behavior among adults. *Journal of Consulting and Clinical Psychology, 76,* 72–83.

van Sleuwen, B. E. Engelberts, A. C., Boere-Boonekamp, M. M., Juis, W., Schulpen, T. W., & L'Hoir, M. P. (2007). Swaddling: A systematic review. *Pediatrics, 120,* e1097–e1106.

van Solinge, H., & Henkens, K. (2005). Couples' adjustment to retirement: A multiactor panel study. *Journals of Gerontology B: Psychological Sciences and Social Sciences, 60,* S11–S20.

Vandell, D. L. (2004). Early child care: The known and unknown. *Merrill-Palmer Quarterly, 50,* 387–414.

Vandell, D. L., & Wilson, K. S. (1988). Infants' interactions with mother, sibling, and peer: Contrasts and relations between interaction systems. *Child Development, 48,* 176–186.

Vandewater, E. A., Ostrove, J. M., & Stewart, A. J. (1997). Predicting women's well-being in midlife: The importance of personality development and social role involvements. *Journal of Personality and Social Development, 72,* 1147–1160.

Vasdev, G. (2008). *Obstetric anesthesia.* Oxford, UK: Elsevier.

Vasudevaraju, P., Bharathi, S., Garruto, R. M., Sambamurti, K., & Rao, K. S. (2008, in press). Role of DNA dynamics in Alzheimer's disease. *Brain Research: Brain Research Reviews.*

Vaughn Van Hecke, A., Mundy, P. C., Acra, C. F., Block, J. J., Delgado, E. F., Paralde, M. V., Meyer, J. A., Neal, A. R., & Pomares, Y. B. (2007). Infant joint attention, temperament, and social competence in preschool children. *Child Development, 78,* 53–69.

Vendittelli, F., Riviere, O., Crenn-Herbert, C., Rozan, M.A., Maria, B., Jacquetin, B., & the AUDIPOG Sentinel Network. (2008). Is a breech presentation at term more frequent in women with a history of caesarean delivery? *American Journal of Obstetrics and Gynecology, 198,* e1–e6.

Venners, S. A., Wang, X., Chen, C., Wang, L., Chen, D., Guang, W., Huang, A., Ryan, L., O'Conner, J., Lasley, B., Overstreet, J., Wilcox, A., & Xu, X. (2004). Paternal smoking and pregnancy loss: A prospective study using a biomarker of pregnancy. *American Journal of Epidemiology, 159,* 993–1001.

Ventura, A. K., Savage, J. S., May, A. L., & Birch, L. L. (2009, in press). Early behavioral, familial, and psychosocial predictors of overweight and obesity. In R. E. Tremblay, R. deV Peters, M. Boivin, & R. G. Barr (Eds.), *Encyclopedia of early childhood development.* Montreal: Centre of Excellence for Early Childhood Development.

Vermeersch, H., T'Sjoen, G., Kaufman, J.M., & Vincke, J. (2008). The role of testosterone in aggressive and non-aggressive risk-taking in boys. *Hormones and Behavior, 53,* 463–471.

Vernazza-Martin, S., Tricon, V., Martin, N., Mesure, S., Azulay, J. P., & Le Pellec Muller, A. (2008, in press). Effect of aging on coordination between equilibrium and movement: What changes? *Experimental Brain Research.*

Verret, L., Trouche, S., Zerwas, M., & Rampon, C. (2007). Hippocampal neurogenesis during normal and pathological aging. *Psychoneuroimmunology, 32,* 526–530.

Verster, J. C., van Duin, D., Volkerts, E. R., Schreueder, A. H., & Verbaten, M. N. (2003). Alcohol hangover effects on memory functioning and vigilance performance after an evening of binge drinking. *Neuropsychopharmacology, 28,* 740–746.

Vicario, A., Martinez, C. D., Baretto, D., Diaz Casale, A., & Nicolosi, L. (2005). Hypertension and cognitive decline: Impact of executive function. *Journal of Clinical Hypertension, 7,* 598–604.

Victor, E., Kellough, R. D., & Tai, R. H. (2008). *Science education* (11th ed.). Upper Saddle River, NJ: Prentice Hall.

Villegas, R., Gao, Y. T., Yang, G., Li, H. L., Elasy, T., Zheng, W., & Shu, X. O. (2008, in press). Duration of breast-feeding and the incidence of type 2 diabetes mellitus in the Shanghai Women's Health Study. *Diabetologia.*

Virnig, B., Huang, Z., Lurie, N., Musgrave, D., McBean, A. M., & Dowd, B. (2004). Does Medicare Managed care provide equal treatment for mental illness across race? *Archives of General Psychiatry, 61,* 201–205.

Virts, E. L., Phillips, J. A., & Thoman, M. L. (2006). A novel approach to thymic rejuvenation in the aged. *Rejuvenation Research, 9,* 134–142.

Visher, E., & Visher, J. (1989). Parenting coalitions after remarriage: Dynamics and therapeutic guidelines *Family Relations, 38,* 65–70.

Vitaro, F., Pedersen, S., & Brendgen, M. (2007). Children's disruptiveness, peer rejection, friends' deviancy, and delinquent behaviors: A process-oriented approach. *Development and Psychopathology, 19,* 433–453.

Vogler, G. P. (2006). Behavior genetics and aging. In J. E. Birren & K. W. Schaie (Eds.), *Handbook of the psychology of aging* (6th ed.) San Diego: Academic Press.

Vohr, B. R., & Boney, C. M. (2008). Gestational diabetes: The forerunner for the development of maternal and child obesity and metabolic syndrome? *Journal of Maternal-Fetal and Neonatal Medicine, 21,* 149–157.

Von Hofsten, C. (2008). Motor and physical development manual. In M. M. Haith & J. B. Benson (Eds.), *Encyclopedia of infant and early childhood development.* Oxford, UK: Elsevier.

Voorpostel, M., & Bliesner, R. (2008). Intergenerational solidarity and support between adult siblings. *Journal of marriage and the Family, 70,* 157–167.

Votruba-Drzal, E., Coley, R. L., & Chase-Lansdale, P. L. (2004). Child care and low-income children's development: Direct and moderated effects. *Child Development, 75,* 296–312.

Vrakking, A. M., van der Heid, A., Onwuteaka-Philipsen, B. D., van der Maas, P. J., & van der Wall, G. (2007). Regulating physician-assisted dying for minors in the Netherlands: Views of pediatricians and other physicians. *Acta Pediatrica, 96,* 117–121.

Vreeman, R. C., & Carroll, A. E. (2007). A systematic review of school-based interventions to prevent bullying. *Archives of Pediatric and Adolescent Medicine, 161,* 78–88.

Vurpillot, E. (1968). The development of scanning strategies and their relation to visual differentiation. *Journal of Experimental Child Psychology, 6,* 632–650.

Vygotsky, L. S. (1962). *Thought and language.* Cambridge, MA: MIT Press.

W

Wabitsch, M. (2009, in press). Preventing obesity in young children. In R. E. Tremblay, R. deV Peters, M. Boivin, & R. G. Barr (Eds.), *Encyclopedia of early childhood development.* Montreal: Centre of Excellence for Early Childhood Development.

Wachs, T. D. (1994). Fit, context and the transition between temperament and personality. In C. Halverson, G. Kohnstamm, & R. Martin (Eds.), *The developing structure of personality from infancy to adulthood.* Hillsdale, NJ: Erlbaum.

Wachs, T. D. (2000). *Necessary but not sufficient.* Washington, DC: American Psychological Association.

Wainryb, C. (2006). Moral development in culture: Diversity, tolerance, and justice. In M. Killen & J. G. Smetana (Eds.), *Handbook of moral development.* Mahwah, NJ: Erlbaum.

Waite, L. (2005, June). *The case for marriage.* Paper presented at the 9th annual Smart Marriages conference, Dallas.

Wakai, K., Marugame, T., Kuriyama, S., Sobue, T., Tamakoshi, A., Satoh, H., Tajima, K., Suzuki, T., & Tsugane, S. (2007). Decrease in risk of lung cancer death in Japanese men after smoking cessation by age at quitting: Pooled analysis of three large-scale cohort studies. *Cancer Science, 98,* 584–589.

Walden, T. (1991). Infant social referencing. In J. Garber & K. Dodge (Eds.), *The development of emotional regulation and dysregulation.* New York: Cambridge University Press.

Walji, S., & Badley, E. M. (2007). Arthritis and rheumatic diseases. In J. E. Birren (Ed.), *Encyclopedia of gerontology* (2nd ed.). San Diego: Academic Press.

Walker, L. J. (2002). In W. Damon (Ed.), *Bringing in a new era of character education.* Stanford, CA: Hoover Press.

Walker, L. J. (2004). Progress and prospects in the psychology of moral development. *Merrill-Palmer Quarterly, 50,* 546–557.

Walker, S. (2006). Unpublished review of J. W. Santrock's *Topical life-span development,* 3rd ed. (New York: McGraw-Hill.)

Wallace-Bell, M. (2003). The effects of passive smoking on adult and child health. *Professional Nurse, 19,* 217–219.

Wallerstein, J. S. (2008). Divorce. In M. M. Haith & J. B. Benson (Eds.), *Encyclopedia of infancy and early childhood.* Oxford, UK: Elsevier.

Walsh, D., & Bennett, N. (2004). *Why do they act that way?: A survival guide to the adolescent brain for you and your teen.* New York: Free Press.

Walsh, H. C. (2008). Caring for bereaved people 2: Nursing management. *Nursing Times, 104,* 32–33.

Walsh, L. A. (2000, Spring). The inside scoop on child development: Interview. *Cutting through the hype.* Minneapolis: College of Education and Human Development, University of Minnesota.

Walsh, L. V. (2006). Beliefs and rituals in traditional birth attendant practice in Guatemala. *Journal of Transcultural Nursing, 17,* 148–154.

Walters, M. W., Boggs, K. M., Ludington-Hoe, S., & Price, K. M. (2007). Kangaroo care at birth for full term infants: A pilot study. *MCN. The American Journal of Maternal Child Nursing, 32,* 375–381.

Wang, J. J. (2007). Group reminiscence therapy for cognitive and affective function of demented elderly in Taiwan. *International Journal of Geriatric Psychiatry, 22,* 1235–1240.

Wang, L. Y., Chyen, D., Lee, L., & Lowry, R. (2008, in press). The association between body mass index in adolescence and obesity in adulthood. *Journal of Adolescent Health, 42.*

Wang, X., Liang, X. B., Li, F. Q., Zhou, H. F., Liu, X. Y., Wang, J. J., & Wang, X. M. (2008, in press). Therapeutic strategies for Parkinson's disease. *Neurochemical Research.*

Wang, X. P., & Deng, H. L. (2008). Alzheimer's disease: Epidemiology, genetics, and beyond. *Neuroscience Bulletin, 24,* 105–109.

Ward, L. M., & Friedman, K. (2006). Using TV as a guide: Associations between television viewing and adolescents' sexual attitudes and behavior. *Journal of Research on Adolescence, 16,* 133–156.

Ward, W. F., Qi, W., Van Remmen, H., Zackert, W. E., Roberts, L. J., & Richardson, A. (2005). Effects of age and caloric restriction on lipid peroxidation: Measurement of oxidative stress by F-isoprostane levels. *Journals of Gerontology A: Biological Sciences and Medical Sciences, 60,* 847–851.

Ward-Griffin, C., Oudshoorn, A., Clark, K., & Bol, N. (2007). Mother-adult daughter relationship within dementia care: A critical analysis. *Journal of Family Nursing, 13,* 13–32.

Wardlaw, G. M., & Hampl, J. (2007). *Perspectives in nutrition* (7th ed.). New York: McGraw-Hill.

Wardlaw, G. M., & Smith, A. M. (2009). *Contemporary nutrition* (7th ed.). New York: McGraw-hill.

Ware, J. E., Kosinski, M., Dewey, J. E. (2000). *How to score Version 2 of the SF-36 Health Survey.* Boston: QualityMetric.

Waring, S. C., & Rosenberg, R. N. (2008). Genome-wide association studies in Alzheimer disease. *Archives in Neurology, 65,* 329–334.

Wark, G. R., & Krebs, D. L. (2000). The construction of moral dilemmas in everyday life. *Journal of Moral Education, 29,* 5–21.

Warr, P. (2004). Work, well-being, and mental health. In J. Baring, E. K. Kelloway, & M. R. Frone (Eds.), *Handbook of work stress.* Thousand Oaks, CA: Sage.

Warren, M. P. (2007). Historical perspectives on postmenopausal hormone therapy: Defining the right dose and duration. *Mayo Clinic Proceedings, 82,* 219–226.

Warshak, R. A. (2007, January). Personal communication, Department of Psychology, University of Texas at Dallas, Richardson.

Wasserman, M., Bender, D., & Lee, S. Y. (2007). Use of preventive maternal and child health services by Latina women: A review of published intervention studies. *Medical Care Research and Review, 64,* 4–45.

Watanabe, H., & Taga, G. (2006). General to specific development of movement patterns and memory for contingency between actions and events in young infants. *Infant Behavior and Development, 29,* 402–422.

Waterman, A. S. (1985). Identity in the context of adolescent psychology. In A. S. Waterman (Ed.), *Identity in adolescence: Processes and contents.* San Francisco: Jossey-Bass.

Waterman, A. S. (1999). Identity, the identity statuses, and identity status development: A contemporary statement. *Developmental Review, 19,* 591–621.

Watkins, N., Larson, R., & Sullivan, P. (2008, in press). Learning to bridge difference: Community youth programs as contexts for developing multicultural competencies. *American Behavioral Scientist.*

Watson, D. L., & Tharp, R. G. (2007). *Self-directed behavior* (9th ed.). Belmont, CA: Wadsworth.

Watson, J. A., Randolph, S. M., & Lyons, J. L. (2005). African-American grandmothers as health educators in the family. *International Journal of Aging and Human Development, 60,* 343–356.

Watson, J. B. (1928). *Psychological care of infant and child.* New York: W. W. Norton.

Watson, R., & DeMeo, P. (1987). Premarital cohabitation vs. traditional courtship and subsequent marital adjustment: A replication and follow-up. *Family Relations, 36,* 193–197.

Watts, C., & Zimmerman, C. (2002). Violence against women: Global scope and magnitude. *Lancet, 359,* 1232–1237.

Way, N., Santos, C., Niwa, E. Y., & Kim-Gervy, C. (2008). To be or not to be: An exploration of ethnic identity development in context. In M. Asmitia, M. Syed, & K. Radmacher (Eds.), *The intersections of personal and social identities. New Directions for Child and Adolescent Development, 120,* 61–79.

Weaver, R. F. (2008). *Molecular biology* (4th ed.). New York: McGraw-Hill.

Webb, J. T., Gore, J. L., Mend, E. R., & DeVries, A. R. (2007). *A parent's guide to gifted children.* Scottsdale, AZ: Great Potential Press.

Webster, N. S., & Worrell, F. C. (2008). Academically talented students' attitudes toward service in the community. *Gifted Child Quarterly, 52,* 170–179.

Wechsler, H., Davenport, A., Sowdall, G., Moetykens, B., & Castillo, S. (1994). Health and behavioral consequences of binge drinking in college. *Journal of the American Medical Association, 272,* 1672–1677.

Wechsler, H., Lee, J. E., Kuo, M., Seibring, M., Nelson, T. F., & Lee, H. (2002). Trends in college binge drinking during a period of increased prevention efforts: Findings from 4 Harvard School of Public Health college alcohol study surveys: 1993–2001. *Journal of American College Health, 50,* 203–217.

Wegman, M. E. (1987). Annual summary of vital statistics—1986. *Pediatrics, 80,* 817–827.

Wei, M., Fabrizio, P., Hu, J., Ge, H., Cheng, C., Li, L., & Longo, V. D. (2008). Life span extension by calorie restriction depends on Rim 15 and transcription factors downstream of Ras/PKA, Tor, and Sch9. *PloS Genetics, 4,* e13.

Weikert, D. P. (1993). [Long-term positive effects in the Perry Preschool Head Start Program.] Unpublished data, High Scope Foundation, Ypsilanti, MI.

Weil, R. (2008). Exercising the aging body. Part 2: Flexibility, balance, and diabetes control. *Diabetes Self Management, 25,* 42, 44, 47–50, 52.

Weinfield, N. S., Sroufe, L. A., Egeland, B., & Carlson, E. (2009). Individual differences in infant-caregiver attachment: Conceptual and empirical aspects of security. In J. Cassidy & P. R. Shaver (Eds.), *Handbook of attachment* (2nd ed.). New York: Guilford.

Weis, K., & Sternberg, R. J. (2008). The nature of love. In S. F. Davis & W. Buskist (Eds.), *21st century psychology: A reference handbook* (Vol. 2). Thousand Oaks, CA: Sage.

Weiss, L. A., & others. (2008). Association between microdeletion and microduplication at 16p 11.2 and autism. *New England Journal of Medicine, 358,* 667–675.

Weisz, A. N., & Black, B. M. (2002). Gender and moral reasoning: African American youth respond to dating dilemmas. *Journal of Human Behavior in the Social Environment, 5,* 35–52.

Wellman, H. M., Cross, D., & Watson, J. (2001). Meta-analysis of theory-of-mind development: The truth about false belief. *Child Development, 72,* 655–684.

Wellman, H. M., Lopez-Duran, S., Labounty, J., & Hamilton, B. (2008). Infant attention to intentional action predicts preschool theory of mind. *Developmental Psychology, 44,* 618–623.

Wellman, H. M., & Woolley, J. D. (1990). From simple desires to ordinary beliefs: The early development of everyday psychology. *Cognition, 35,* 245–275.

Wells, J. C., Hallal, P. C., Reichert, F. F., Menezes, A. M. Araujo, C. L., & Victora, C. G. (2008, in press). Sleep patterns and television viewing in relation to obesity and blood pressure: Evidence from an adolescent Brazilian cohort. *International Journal of Obesity.*

Wenestam, C. G., & Wass, H. (1987). Swedish and U.S. children's thinking about death: A qualitative study and cross-cultural comparison. *Death Studies, 11,* 99–121.

Weng, N. P. (2006). Aging of the human immune system: How much can the adaptive immune system adapt? *Immunity, 24,* 495–499.

Weng, X., Odouli, R., & Li, D. K. (2008, in press). Maternal caffeine consumption during pregnancy and the risk of miscarriage: A prospective cohort study. *American Journal of Obstetrics and Gynecology.*

Wenger, N.S., & others. (2003). The quality of medical care provided to vulnerable community-dwelling older patients. *Annals of Internal Medicine, 139,* 740–747.

Wengreen, H. J., & others. (2007). Antioxidant intake and cognitive function of elderly men and women: The Cache County Study. *Journal of Nutrition, Health, and Aging, 11,* 230–237.

Wentzel, K. R., & Asher, S. R. (1995). The academic lives of neglected, rejected, popular and controversial children. *Child Development, 66,* 754–763.

Wentzel, K. R, Barry, C. M., & Caldwell, K. A. (2004). Friendships in middle school: Influences on motivation and school adjustment. *Journal of Educational Psychology, 96,* 195–203.

Werker, J. F., & Tees, R. C. (2005). Speech perception as a window for understanding plasticity and commitment in language systems of the brain. *Developmental Psychobiology, 46,* 233–251.

Wertsch, J. V. (2007). Mediation. In H. Daniels, J. Wertsch, & M. Cole (Eds.), *The Cambridge companion to Vygotsky.* New York: Cambridge University Press.

Wessells, H., Joyce, G. F., Wise, M., & Wilt, T. J. (2007). Erectile dysfunction. *Journal of Urology, 177,* 1675–1681.

Westendorp, R. G., & Kirkwood, T. (2007). The biology of aging. In J. Bond, S. Peace, F. Dittman-Kohli, & G. Westerhoff (Eds.), *Aging in society* (3rd ed.). Thousand Oaks, CA: Sage.

Westlake, C., Evangelista, L. S., Stromberg, A., Ter-Galstanyan, A., Vazirani, S., & Dracup. K. (2007). Evaluation of a web-based education and counseling pilot for older heart failure patients. *Progress in Cardiovascular Nursing, 22,* 20–26.

Westling, E., Andrews, J. A., Hampson, S. E., & Peterson, M. (2008, in press). Pubertal timing and substance use: The effects of gender, parental monitoring, and deviant peers. *Journal of Adolescent Health.*

Weston, K. (2007). Exiles from kinship. In S. J. Ferguson (Ed.), *Shifting the center: Understanding contemporary families* (3rd ed.). New York: McGraw-Hill.

Wethington, E., Kessler, R. C., & Pixley, J. E. (2004). Turning points in adulthood. In O. G. Brim, C. D. Ryff, & R. C. Kessler, (Eds.), *How healthy are we?* Chicago: University of Chicago Press.

Weyman, A. (2003). Promoting sexual health to young people. *Journal of Research on Social Health, 123,* 6–7.

Wheeden, A., Scafidi, F. A., Field, T., Ironson, G., Valdeon, C. & Bandstra, E. (1993). Massage effects on cocaine-exposed preterm neonates. *Journal of Developmental and Behavioral Pediatrics, 14,* 318–322.

Whetstone, L. M., Morrissey, S. L., & Cummings, D. M. (2007). Children at risk: The association between perceived weight status and suicidal thoughts and attempts in middle school youth. *Journal of School Health, 77,* 59–66.

Whiffen, V. (2001). Depression. In J. Worell (Ed.), *Encyclopedia of women and gender.*San Diego: Academic Press.

Whincup, P. H., Papacosta, O., Lennon, L., & Haines, A. (2006). Carboxyhemoglobin levels and their determinants in older British men. *BMC Public Health, 18,* 189.

Whitbourne, S. K., & Connolly, L. A. (1999). The developing self in midlife. In S. L. Willis & J. D. Reid (Eds.), *Life in the middle.* San Diego: Academic Press.

White, C. B., & Catania, J. (1981). Psychoeducational intervention for sexuality with the aged, family members of the aged, and people who work with the aged. *International Journal of Aging and Human Development, 13,* 71–77.

White, C. D., Hardy, J. R., Gilshenan, K. S., Charles, M. A., & Pinkerton, C. R. (2008, in press). Randomized controlled trials of palliative care—a survey of the views of advanced cancer patients and their relatives. *European Journal of Cancer.*

White, J. W. (2001). Aggression and gender. In J. Worell (Ed.). *Encyclopedia of gender and women.* San Diego: Academic Press.

White, J. W., & Frabutt, J. M. (2006). Violence against girls and women. In J. Worell & C. D. Goodheart (Eds.), *Handbook of girls' and women's psychological health.* New York: Oxford University Press.

White, L. (1994). Stepfamilies over the life course: Social support. In A. Booth and J. Dunne (Eds.), *Stepfamilies: Who benefits and who does not.* Hillsdale, NJ: Erlbaum.

Whitehead, B. D., & Pupenue, D. (2003). *The state of our unions.* Piscataway, NJ: The National Marriage Project, Rutgers University.

Whitehouse, P. J. (2007a). Dementia. In J. E. Birren (Ed.), *Encyclopedia of gerontology* (2nd ed.). San Diego: Academic Press.

Whitehouse, P. J. (2007b). Dementia: Alzheimer's. In J. E. Birren (Ed.), *Encyclopedia of gerontology* (2nd ed.). San Diego: Academic Press.

Whitescarver, K. (2006, April). *Montessori rising: Montessori education in the United States, 1955–present.* Paper presented at the meeting of the American Education Research Association, San Francisco.

Whitesell, N. R., & Harter, S. (1989). Children's reports of conflict between simultaneous opposite-valence emotions. *Child Development, 60,* 637–682.

Whitfield, K. (2006). Health disparities and minority aging. In J. E. Birren & K. W. Schaie (Eds.), *Handbook of the psychology of aging* (6th ed.). Thousand Oaks, CA: Sage.

Whiting, J. (1981). Environmental constraint on infant care practices. In R. L. Munroe, R. M. Munroe, & B. B. Whiting (Eds.), *Handbook of cross-cultural human development.* New York: Garland STPM Press.

Wickelgren, I. (1999). Nurture helps to mold able minds. *Science, 283,* 1832–1834.

Wiesner, M., & Ittel, A. (2002). Relations of pubertal timing and depressing symptoms to substance use in early adolescence. *Journal of Early Adolescence, 22,* 5–23.

Wight, R. G., Cummings, J. R., Miller-Martinez, D., Karlamangla, A. S., Seeman, T. E., & Aneshensel, C. S. (2008). A multilevel analysis of urban neighborhood socioeconomic disadvantage and health in late life. *Social Science and Medicine, 66,* 862–872.

Wijngaards-de Meij, L., Stroebe, M., Schut, H., Stroebe, W., van den Bout, J., van der Heijden, P. G., & Dijkstra, I. (2008). Parents grieving the loss of their child: Interdependence in coping. *British Journal of Clinical Psychology, 47,* 31–42.

Wilcox, S., Evenson, K. R., Aragaki, A., Wassertheil-Smoller, S., Mouton, C. P., & Loevinger, B. L. (2003). The effects of widowhood on physical and mental health, health behaviors, and health outcomes: The women's health initiative. *Health Psychology, 22,* 513–522.

Wilkinson-Lee, A. M., Russell, S. T., Lee, F. C. H., & the Latina/o Teen Pregnancy Prevention Workgroup. (2006). Practitioners' perspectives on cultural sensitivity in Latina/o pregnancy prevention. *Family Relations, 55,* 376–389.

Willcox, B. J., Willcox, M. D., & Suzuki, M. (2002). *The Okinawa Program.* New York: Crown.

Willcox, D. C., Willcox, B. J., He, Q., Wang, N. C., & Suzuki, M. (2008). They really are that old: A validation study of centenarian prevalence in Okinawa. *Journals of Gerontology A: Biological Sciences and Medical Sciences, 63,* 338–349.

Willcox, D. C., Willcox, B. J., Sokolovsky, J., & Sakihara, S. (2007). The cultural context of "successful aging" among older women weavers in a Northern Okinawan village: The role of productive activity. *Journal of Cross Cultural Gerontology, 22,* 137–165.

Williams, D. R., & Sternthal, M. J. (2007). Spirituality, religion, and health: Evidence and research directions. *Medical Journal of Australia, 186* (Suppl.), S47–S50.

Williams, J. H., & Ross, L. (2007). Consequences of prenatal toxin exposure for mental health in children and adolescents: A systematic review. *European Child and Adolescent Psychiatry, 16,* 243–253.

Williams, M. H. (2005). *Nutrition for health, fitness, and sport* (7th ed.). New York: McGraw-Hill.

Williams, T. R. (2008). A cultural and global perspective of United States health care perspective. *Seminars in Radiation Oncology, 18,* 175–185.

Willis, S. L. & Martin, M. (2005). Preface. In S. L. Willis & M. Martin (Eds), *Middle adulthood.* Thousand Oaks, CA: Sage.

Willis, S. L., & Schaie, K. W. (1999). Intellectual functioning in midlife. In S. L. Willis & J. D. Reid (Eds.), *Life in the middle: Psychological and social development in middle age.* San Diego: Academic Press.

Willis, S. L. & Schaie, K. W. (2005). Cognitive trajectories in midlife and cognitive functioning in old age. In S. L. Willis & M. Martin (Eds.), *Middle adulthood.* Thousand Oaks, CA: Sage.

Willis, S. L., & Schaie, K. W. (2006). A co-constructionist view of the third age: The case of cognition. *Annual Review of Gerontology and Geriatrics, 26,* 131–152.

Willis, S. L., Temstedt, S. L., Marsiske, M., Ball, K., Elias, J., Koepke, K. M., Morris, J. N., Rebok, G. W., Unverzagt, F. W., Stoddar, A. M., & Wright, E., for the ACTIVE Study Group. (2006). Long-term effects of cognitive training on everyday functional outcomes in older adults. *Journal of the American Medical Association, 296,* 2805–2814.

Wilmoth, J. M., & Chen, P-C. (2003). Immigrant status, living arrangements, and depressive symptoms among middle-aged and older adults. *Journals of Gerontology B: Psychological Sciences and Social Sciences, 58,* S305–S313.

Wilson, A. E., Shuey, K. M., & Elder, G. H. (2003). Ambivalence in relationships of adult children to aging parents and in-laws. *Journal of Marriage and the Family, 65,* 1055–1072.

Wilson, B., & Smallwood, S. (2008). The proportion of marriages ending in divorce. *Population Trends, 131,* 28–36.

Wilson, B. J. (2008). Media and children's aggression, fear, and altruism. *Future of Children, 18* (No. 1), 87–118.

Wilson, D., & Hockenberry, M. J. (2008). *Wong's clinical manual of pediatric nursing* (7th ed.). St. Louis: Mosby.

Wilson, K. G., & others. (2007). Desire for euthanasia or physician-assisted suicide in palliative cancer care. *Health Psychology, 26,* 314–323.

Wilson, M. N. (2008). Poor fathers involvement in the lives of their children. In D. R. Crane & T. B. Heaton (Eds.), *Handbook of families and poverty.* Thousand Oaks, CA: Sage.

Wilson, R. S., Mendes de Leon, C. F., Barnes, L. L., Schneider, J. A., Bienias, J., Evans, D. A., & Bennett, D. A. (2002). Participation in cognitively stimulating activities and risk of incident Alzheimer disease. *Journal of the American Medical Association, 287,* 742–748.

Wilson, R. S., Mendes de Leon, C. F., Bienas, J. L., Evans, D. A., & Bennett, D. A. (2004). Personality and mortality in old age. *Journals of Gerontology B: Psychological Sciences and Social Sciences. 59,* P100–P116.

Windle, W. F. (1940). *Physiology of the human fetus.* Philadelphia: W. B. Saunders.

Wineberg, H. (1994). Marital reconciliation in the United States: Which couples are successful? *Journal of Marriage and the Family, 56,* 80–88.

Wing, R., Tate, D. F., Gorin, A. A., Raynor, H. A., Fava, J. L., & Machan, J. (2007). "STOP Regain": Are there negative effects of daily weighing? *Journal of Consulting and Clinical Psychology, 75,* 652–656.

Wink, P., & Dillon, M. (2002). Spiritual development across the adult life course: Findings from a longitudinal study. *Journal of Adult Development, 9,* 79–94.

Winner, E. (1986, August.). Where pelicans kiss seals. *Psychology Today,* pp. 24–35.

Winner, E. (1996). *Gifted children: Myths and realities.* New York: Basic Books.

Winner, E. (2006). Development in the arts. In W. Damon & R. Lerner (Eds.), *Handbook of child psychology* (6th ed.). New York: Wiley.

Winocur, G., & others. (2007). Cognitive rehabilitation in the elderly: Overview and future directions. *Journal of the International Neuropsychological Society, 13,* 166–171.

Winsler, A., Carlton, M. P., & Barry, M. J. (2000). Age-related changes in preschool children's systematic use of private speech in a natural setting. *Journal of Child Language, 27,* 665–687.

Wise, P. M. (2006). Aging of the female reproductive system. In E. J. Masoro & S. N. Austad (Eds.), *Handbook of the biology of aging* (6th ed.). San Diego: Academic Press.

Witkin, H. A., Mednick, S. A., Schulsinger, R., Bakkestrom, E., Christiansen, K. O., Goodenbough, D. R., Hirchhorn, K., Lunsteen, C., Owen, D. R., Philip, J., Ruben, D. B., & Stocking, M. (1976). Criminality in XYY and XXY men. *Science, 193,* 547–555.

Wittmeier, K. D., Mollar, R. C., & Kriellaars, D. J. (2008). Physical activity intensity and risk of overweight and adiposity in children. *Obesity, 16,* 415–420.

Wofford, L. G. (2008). Systematic review of childhood obesity prevention. *Journal of Pediatric Nursing, 23,* 5–19.

Wolff, J. L., & Kasper, J. D. (2006). Caregivers of frail elders: Updating a national profile. *Gerontologist, 46,* 344–356.

Wolfson, J., & Morgan, R. (2007). Health decisions and directives about the end of life. In J. A. Blackburn & C. N. Dulmus (Eds.), *Handbook of gerontology.* New York: Wiley.

Wolitzky-Taylor, K. B., Ruggiero, K. J., Danielson, C. K., Resnick, H. S., Hanson, R. F., Smith, D. W., Saunders, B. E., & Kilpatrick, D. G. (2008, in press). Prevalence and correlates of dating violence in a national sample of adolescents. *Journal of the American Academy of Child and Adolescent Psychiatry.*

Wong, A. M., Lin, Y. C., Chou, S. W., Tang, F. T., & Wong, P. Y. (2001). Coordination exercise and postural stability in elderly people: Effect of Tai Chi Chuan. *Archives of Physical Medicine and Rehabilitation, 82,* 608–612.

Wong, E. C., Kinzie, J. D., & Kinzie, M. (2009). Stress, refugees, and trauma. In N. Tewari & A. Alvarez (Eds.), *Asian American psychology.* Clifton, NJ: Psychology Press.

Wong, Y. J., & Rochlen, A. B. (2008). *The New Psychology of Men: The emotional.* Side Wesport, CT: Greenwood Publishing Group.

Wong Briggs, T. W. (2004, October 14). USA TODAY's 2004 all-USA teacher team. *USA TODAY,* pp. 6–7D.

Wood, A. C., Rijsdijk, F., Saudino, K. J., Asherson, P., & Kuntsi, J. (2008, in press). High heritability for a composite index of children's activity level Measures. *Behavior Genetics.*

Wood, J. T. (2001). *Gendered lives* (4th ed.). Belmont, CA: Wadsworth.

Wood, M. D., Read, J. P., Mitchell, R. E., & Brand, N. H. (2004). Do parents still matter? Parent and peer influences on alcohol involvement among recent high school graduates. *Psychology of Addictive Behaviors, 18,* 19–30.

Woodward, A. L., & Markman, E. M. (1998). Early word learning. In D. Kuhn & R. S. Siegler (Eds.). *Handbook of child psychology* (5th ed., Vol. 2). New York: Wiley.

Woollacott, M. (2007). Balance, posture, and gait. In J. E. Birren (Ed.), *Encyclopedia of gerontology* (2nd ed.). San Diego: Academic Press.

World Health Organization. (2000, February 2). *Adolescent health behavior in 28.* countries. Geneva: Author.

Worthington, E. L. (1989). Religious faith across the life span: Implications for counseling and research. *Counseling Psychologist, 17,* 555–612.

Wortman, C. B., & Boerner, K. (2007). Reactions to death of a loved one: Beyond the myths of coping with loss. In H. S. Friedman & R. C. Silver (Eds.), *Foundations of health psychology.* New York: Oxford University Press.

Writing Group for the British Menopause Society Counsel & others. (2008). Non–estrogen based treatments for menopausal symptoms. *Menopause International, 14,* 88–90.

Wrosch, C., Schultz, R., Miller, G. E., Lupien, S., & Dunne, E. (2007). Physical Health problems, depressive mood, and cortisol secretion in old age: Buffer effects of health engagement control strategies. *Health Psychology, 26,* 341–349.

Wu, L. T., Pilowsky, D. J., Schlenger, W. E., & Hasin, D. (2007). Alcohol use disorders and the use of treatment services among college-age young adults. *Psychiatric Services, 58,* 192–200.

X

Xie, J., Matthews, F. E., Jagger, C., Bond, J., & Brayne, C. (2008, in press). The oldest old in England and Wales: A descriptive analysis based on the MRC Cognitive Function and Aging Study. *Age and Aging.*

Xiong, G., & Doraiswamy, P. M. (2005). Combination drug therapy for Alzheimer's disease: What is evidence-based, and what is not? *Geriatrics, 60,* 22–26.

Xu, X., Hudspeth, C. D., & Bartkowski, J. P. (2006). The role of cohabitation in remarriage. *Journal of Marriage and the Family, 68,* 261–274.

Xue, F., Holzman, C., Rahbar, M. H., Trosko, K., & Fischer, L. (2007). Maternal fish consumption, mercury levels, and risk of preterm delivery. *Environmental Health Perspectives, 115,* 42–47.

Y

Yaari, R., & Corey-Bloom, J. (2007). Alzheimer's disease. *Seminars in Neurology, 27,* 32–41.

Yaffe, K., Barnes, D., Nevitt, M., Lui, L., & Covinsky, K. (2001). A prospective study of physical activity and cognitive decline in elderly women. *Archives of Internal Medicine, 161,* 1703–1708.

Yaffe, K., Haan, M., Blackwell, T., Cherkasova, E., Whitmer, R. A., & West, N. (2007). Metabolic syndrome and cognitive decline in elderly Latinos. *Journal of the American Geriatric Society, 55,* 758–762.

Yamamoto, M., & Schapira, A. H. (2008). Dopamine agonists against Parkinson's disease. *Expert Review of Neurotherapy, 8,* 671–677.

Yamasue, K., Hayashi, T., Ohshige, K., Tochikubo, O., & Souma, T. (2008). Masked hypertension in elderly managerial employees and retirees. *Clinical and Experimental Hypertension, 30,* 203–211.

Yang, C. K., Kim, J. K., Patel, S. R., & Lee, J. H. (2005). Age-related changes in sleep/wake patterns among Korean teenagers. *Pediatrics, 115* (Suppl. 1), S250–S256.

Yang, Q., Wen, S. W., Leader, A., Chen, X. K., Lipson, J. & Walker, M. (2007). Paternal age and birth defects: How strong is the association. *Human Reproduction, 22,* 696–701.

Yang, S., & Sternberg, R. J. (1997). Taiwanese Chinese people's conceptions of intelligence. *Intelligence, 25,* 21–36.

Yang, Y. (2008). Social inequalities in happiness in the United States, 1972–2004: An age-period-cohort analysis. *American Sociological Review, 73,* 204–226.

Yates, L. B., Djuousse, L., Kurth, T., Buring, J. E., & Gaziano, J. M. (2008). Exceptional longevity in men: Modifiable factors associated with survival and function to age 90 years. *Archives of Internal Medicine, 168,* 284–290.

Yee, B. W. K., & Chiriboga, D. A. (2007). Issues of diversity in health psychology and aging. In C. M. Aldwin, C. L. Park, & A. Spiro (Eds.), *Handbook of health psychology and aging.* New York: Guilford.

Yell, M. L., & Drasgow, E. (2009). *What every teacher should know about No Child Left Behind* (2nd Ed.). Upper Saddle River, NJ: Prentice Hall.

Yellone, E., Piras, G., Talucci, C., & Cohen, M. Z. (2008). Quality of life for caregivers of people with Alzheimer's disease. *Journal of Advanced Nursing, 61,* 222–231.

Yoo, H. J., Choi, K. M., Ryu, O. H., Suh, S. I., Kim, N. H., Baik, S. H., & Choi, D. S. (2006). Delayed puberty due to pituitary stalk dysgenesis and ectopic neuorphyophysis. *Korean Journal of Internal Medicine, 21,* 68–72.

Yoon, D. P., & Lee, E. K. (2007). The impact of religiousness, spirituality, and social support on psychological well-being among older adults in rural areas. *Journal of Gerontological Social Work. 48,* 281–298.

Yoshida, S., Kozu, T., Gotoda, T., & Saito, D. (2006). Detection and treatment of early cancer in high-risk populations. *Best Practice and Research: Clinical Gastroenterology, 20,* 745–765.

You, T., & others. (2008). The metabolic syndrome is associated with circulating adipokines in older adults across a wide range of adiposity. *Journals of Gerontology A: Biological Sciences and Medical Sciences, 63,* 414–419.

Young, E. L., Boye, A. E., & Nelson, D. A. (2006). Relational aggression: understanding, identifying, and responding in schools. *Psychology in the Schools, 43,* 297–312.

Young, K. T. (1990). American conceptions of infant development from 1955 to 1984: What the experts are telling parents. *Child Development, 61,* 17–28.

Youniss, J., McLellan, J. A., & Yates, M. (1999). Religion, community service, and identity in American youth. *Journal of Adolescence, 22,* 243–253.

Yuan, T. F. (2008). GABA effects on neurogenesis: An arsenal of regulation. *Science Signaling, 1,* jcl.

Z

Zaborowska, E., & others. (2007). Effects of acupuncture, applied relaxation, estrogens, and placebo on hot flushes in postmenopausal women:

An analysis of two prospective, parallel, randomized studies. *Climacteric, 10,* 38–45.

Zalc, B. (2006). The acquisition of myelin: A success story. *Novartis Foundation Symposium, 276,* 15–21.

Zanardo, F., De Beni, R., & Moe, A. (2006). Influence of other-beliefs on self-beliefs and on everyday memory self-report in the elderly. *Aging: Clinical and Experimental Research, 18,* 425–432.

Zangl, R., & Mills, D. L. (2007). Increased brain activity to infant-directed speech in 6- and 13-month-old infants. *Infancy, 11,* 31–62.

Zarit, S. H., & Knight, B. G. (Eds.). (1996). *A guide to psychotherapy and aging.* Washington, DC: American Psychological Association.

Zeifman, D., & Hazan, C. (2009). Pair bonds as attachments: Reevaluating the evidence. In J. Cassidy & P. R. Shaver (Eds.), *Handbook of attachment* (2nd ed.). New York: Guilford.

Zelazo, P. D. & Müller, U. (2004). Executive function in typical and atypical development. In U. Goswami (Ed.), *Blackwell handbook of cognitive development.* Malden, MA: Blackwell.

Zelazo, P. D., Müller, U., Frye, D., & Marcovitch, S. (2003). The development of executive function in early childhood. *Monographs of the Society for Research in Child Development, 68* (3, Serial No. 274).

Zelinski, E. M., & Kennison, R. F. (2007). Not your parents' test scores: Cohort reduces psychometric aging effects. *Psychology and Aging, 22,* 546–557.

Zeller, M. H., Reiter-Purtill, J., & Ramey, C. (2008, in press). Negative peer perceptions of obese children in the classroom environment. *Obesity.*

Zentall, S. S. (2006). *ADHD and education.* Upper Saddle River, NJ: Prentice Hall.

Zeskind, P. S. (2009, in press). Impact of the cry of the infant at risk on psychosocial development. In R. E. Tremblay, R. deV Peters, M. Boivan, & R. G. Barr (Eds.), *Encyclopedia on Early Childhood Development.* Montreal: Center of Excellence for Early Childhood Development.

Zeskind, P. S., Klein, L., & Marshall, T. R. (1992). Adults' perceptions of experimental modifications of durations and expiratory sounds in infant crying. *Developmental Psychology, 28,* 1153–1162.

Zhang, L.-F., & Sternberg, R. J. (2008, in press). Learning in a cross-cultural perspective. In T. Husén & T. N. Postlethwaite (Eds.), *International encyclopedia of education* (3rd ed.), *Learning and cognition.* Oxford: Elsevier.

Zhao, Y., Hoshiyama, H., Shay, J. W., & Wright, W. E. (2008). Quantitative telomeric overhang determination using a double-strand specific nuclease. *Nucleic Acids Research, 36,* e14.

Zigler, E. (2009, in press). Head Start policy—comments on Currie, and Hustedt and Barnett. In R. E. Tremblay, R. deV Peters, M. Boivin, & R. G. Barr (Eds.), *Encyclopedia on early childhood development.* Montreal: Centre of Excellence for Early Childhood Development.

Zigler, E. F., Gilliam, W. S., & Jones, S. M. (2006). *A vision for universal preschool education.* New York: Cambridge University Press.

Zigler, E. F., & Styfco, S. J. (1994). Head Start: Criticisms in a constructive context. *American Psychologist, 49,* 127–132.

Zimmer-Gembeck, M. J., & Helfand, M. (2008). Ten years of longitudinal research on U. S. adolescent sexual behavior: Developmental correlates of sexual intercourse, and the importance of age, gender, and ethnic background. *Developmental Review, 28,* 153–224.

Zimmerman, P. (2007, March). *Attachment in adolescence.* Paper presented at the meeting of the Society for Research in Child Development, Boston.

Zimmerman, R. S., Khoury, E., Vega, W. A. Gil, A. G., & Warheit, G. J. (1995). Teacher and student perceptions of behavior problems among a sample of African American, Hispanic, and non-Hispanic White students. *American Journal of Community Psychology, 23,* 181–197.

Zimmerman, S., & Sloane, P. D. (2007). Long term care. In J. E. Birren (Ed.), *Encyclopedia of gerontology* (2nd ed.). San Diego: Academic Press.

Zinn, M. B., & Wells, B. (2000). Diversity within Latino families: New lessons for family social science. In D. M. Demo, K. R. Allen, & M. A. Fine (Eds.), *Handbook of family diversity.* New York: Oxford Press University.

Zisook, S., & Kendler, K. S. (2007). Is bereavement-related depression different than non-bereavement-related depression? *Psychological Medicine, 19,* 1–31.

Zittleman, K. (2006, April). *Being a girl and being a boy: The voices of middle schoolers.* Paper presented at the meeting of the American Educational Research Association, San Francisco.

Zosuls, K. M., Lurye, L. E., & Ruble, D. N. (2008). Gender: Awareness, identity, and -stereotyping. In M. M. Haith & J. B. Benson (Eds.), *Encyclopedia of infancy and early childhood.* Oxford UK: Elsevier.

Zubenko, G. S., Zubenko, W. N., Maher, B. S., & Wolf, N. S. (2007). Reduced age-related cataracts among elderly persons who reach age 90 with preserved cognition: A biomarker of successful aging? *Journals of Gerontology A: Biological Sciences and Medical Sciences, 62,* 500–506.

Zucker, A. N., Ostrove, J. M., & Stewart A. J. (2002). College educated women's personality development in adulthood: Perceptions and age differences. *Psychology and Aging, 17,* 236–244.

Zuckoff, A., Shear, K., Frank, E., Daley, D. C., Seligman, K., & Silowash, R. (2006). Treating complicated grief and substance use disorders: A pilot study. *Journal of Substance Abuse and Treatment, 30,* 205–211.

Zunzunegui, M., Alvarado, B. E., Del Ser, T., & Vtero, A. (2003). Social networks, social integration, and social engagement determine cognitive decline in community-dwelling Spanish older adults. *Journals of Gerontology B: Psychological Sciences and Social Sciences, 58,* S93–S100.

CREDITS

Photo Credits

Section Openers

1: © Chuck Savage/Corbis; 2: © Petit Format/Nestle/ Photo Researchers; 3: © Elizabeth Hathon/Corbis; 4: © Ariel Skelley/Corbis; 5: © Ariel Skelley/Corbis; 6: © David Young-Wolff/Stone/Getty Images: 7: © Ariel Skelley/Corbis; 8: © Barros & Barros/The Image Bank/ Getty Images; 9: © Adamsmith/Superstock; 10: © Dennis Stock/Magnum Photos

Chapter 1

Opener: © Bob Torrz/Stone/Getty Images; p. 6 (top): © Seana O'Sullivan/Corbis/Sygma; p. 6 (bottom): © AP/Wide World Photos; p. 8: © Ryan McVay/Photodisc/Getty RF; p. 9: Courtesy of Paul Baltes, Margaret Baltes Foundation; p. 10 (top): © Adam Tanner/Reuters/Corbis; p. 10 (bottom): © Paul Bartan/Corbis; p. 11: Courtesy of Luis Vargas; p. 12 (top): © Nancy Agostini; p. 12 (bottom): © James Pozarik; p. 13: Courtesy of Marian Wright Edelman, The Children's Defense Fund, photograph by Rick Reinhard; p. 14 (top): © Nathan Benn/Corbis; p. 14 (bottom): © Dennis Brack Ltd./Black Star/Stock Photo; 1.7 (prenatal): Courtesy of Landrum Shettles, MD; (infancy): John Santrock; (early childhood): © Joe Sohm/The Image Works; (middle/late childhood): © Corbis RF; (adolescence): © James L. Shaffer; (early adulthood): © Vol. 155/Corbis RF; (middle adulthood): © Corbis RF; (late adulthood): © Corbis RF; p. 17: © iStock; p. 19 (top): © Jay Syverson/Corbis; p. 19 (bottom): © Owaki-Kulla/Corbis; p. 20: © Joel Gordon 1995; p. 22: © Bettmann/Corbis; p. 23: © Bettmann/Corbis; p. 24: © Yves de Braine/Black Star/Stock Photo; p. 25: A.R. Lauria/Dr. Michael Cole, Laboratory of Human Cognition, University of California, San Diego; p. 26: © AP/Wide World Photos; p. 27: Courtesy Albert Bandura, Stanford University; p. 28: Photo by Nina Leen/Timepix/Getty Images; p. 29: Courtesy of Urie Bronfenbrenner; p. 30: © Ray Stott/The Image Works; p. 32 (top): © Bettmann/Corbis; p. 32 (bottom): © S. Fraser/ Photo Researchers; p. 35 (top): © AP/Wide World Photos; p. 35 (bottom): © Lawrence Migdale/Photo Researchers; p. 37: Courtesy of Pam Trotman Reid; p. 38 (left): © AFP/Getty Images; p. 38 (right): © Stuart McClymont/Stone/Getty Images

Chapter 2

Opener: © Hua China Tourism Press, Shao/The Image Bank/Getty Images; p. 52 © Enrico Ferorelli Enterprises; p. 54 © Frans Lemmens/Corbis; p. 54: © Alan and Sandy Carey/Getty RF; p. 55: © David Wilkie; p. 56: © Rick Rickman; 2.4: © Science Source/Photo Researchers; 2.5a&b: © Custom Medical Stock Photo; p. 60 © Joel Gordon 1989; p. 60 (bottom): From R. Simensen and R. Curtis Rogers, "Fragile X Syndrome," *American Family Physician*, 39 (5): 186, May 1989. © American Academy of Family Physicians.; p. 61: © Andrew Eccles/JBGPHOTO.COM; p. 62: Courtesy of Holly Ishmael; p. 63: © Jacques Pavlousky/Sygma/Corbis; 2.8: © Larry Berman; p. 64: © Science Source/Photo Researchers; p. 66: © AP/Wide World Photos; p. 68: © Randy Santos/ SuperStock; p. 69: © Myrleen Ferguson Cate/Photo Edit; p. 71: © Duomo/Corbis

Chapter 3

Opener: Photo Lennart Nilsson/Albert Bonniers Forlag AB, *A Child is Born*, Dell Publishing Company; p. 78: © John Santrock; 3.3 (top, middle, bottom): Photo Lennart Nilsson/Albert Bonniers Forlag AB., *A Child is Born*, Dell Publishing Company; 3.4: © Lennart Nilsson/Albert Bonniers Forlag AB; p. 83 (bottom): 2006 Spina Bifida camp photo; p. 85 (top): Courtesy of Ann Streissguth; p. 85 (bottom): © Will & Deni McIntyre/Photo Researchers; p. 86: © John Chiasson; p. 87: © R.I.A. Novosti/Gamma/ H.P.P./Eyedea; p. 88: © Betty Press/Woodfin Camp & Associates; p. 89 (top): © iStock Photos; p. 89 (bottom): © Alon Reininger/Contract Press Images; p. 90: © David Butow/Corbis/SABA; p. 91 (top): © Roger Tully/Stone/Getty; p. 91 (bottom): © Sharon Schindler Rising, Centering Pregnancy Program; p. 92: © Vivian Moos/Corbis; p. 94 (top): © SIU/ Peter Arnold, Inc.; p. 94 (bottom): © Marjorie Shostak/Anthro-Photo; p. 95: © Corbis RF; p. 96: Courtesy of Linda Pugh; p. 97: © Dr. Holly Beckwith; 3.7: © Stephen Marks, Inc./The Image Bank/Getty Images; p. 100: © Charles Gupton/Stock Boston; p. 101: Courtesy of Dr. Susan M. Ludington; p. 102: Courtesy of Dr. Tiffany Field; p. 105: © Ariel Skelley/Corbis; p. 106: © James White

Chapter 4

Opener: © Stockbyte/Getty RF; p. 114 (top): © Wendy Stone/Corbis; p. 114 (bottom): © Dave Bartruff/Corbis; 4.2: © 1999 Kenneth Jarecke/ Contact Press Images; 4.3: © A. Glauberman/Photo Researchers; 4.8 (left & right): Courtesy of Dr. Harry T. Chugani, Children's Hospital of Michigan; 4.9a: © David Grubin Productions, Inc. Reprinted by permission.; 4.9b: Image courtesy of Dana Boatman, Ph.D., Department of Neurology, John Hopkins University, reprinted with permission from *The Secret Life of the Brain*, Joseph Henry Press; p. 121: © C Squared Studios/Getty RF; p. 122 (top): © SuperStock; p. 122 (bottom): © McGraw-Hill Companies, photographer Jill Braaten; p. 124: © Bruce McAllister/Image Works; p. 125: © Bob Dammrich/The Image Works; p. 126 (top): Courtesy of T. Berry Brazelton; p. 126 (bottom): Hawaiian Family Support Healthy Start Program; lp. 127: Courtesy of Esther Thelen; p. 128 (top): © Elizabeth Crews/The Image Works; p. 128 (bottom): © Petit Format/Photo Researchers; p. 129 (top): © PictureQuest/Stockbyte RF; p. 129 (bottom): © Fabio Caardosa/zefa/Corbis; 4.14 (top & bottom): Courtesy Dr. Karen Adolph, New York University; p. 132 (top): © Michael Greenlar/The Image Works; p. 132 (middle): © Frank Baily Studios; p. 132 (bottom): © Newstockimages/SuperStock RF; p. 133: Courtesy Amy Needham, Duke University; p. 134: © Mika/zefa/Corbis; 4.17: Adapted from "The Origin of Form and Perception" by R.L. Fantz © 1961 by *Scientific American*. Photo © by David Linton; 4.19 (all): Courtesy of Dr. Charles Nelson; 4.21: © Enrico Ferorelli Enterprises; 4.22a: © Michael Siluk; 4.22b: © Dr. Melanie Spence, University of Texas; 4.23: © Jean Guichard/Sygma/Corbis; 4.24 (a–c): From D. Rosenstein and H. Oster "Differential Facial Responses to Four Basic Tastes in Newborns," *Child Development*, Vol. 59, 1988. © Society for Research in Child Development, Inc.; p. 142: © Philip Kaake/Corbis

Chapter 5

Opener: © Spencer Grant/Photo Edit; p. 149: © Laura Dwight/Corbis; p. 150: © Elyse Lewin/Brand X/Corbis RF; p. 152: © PunchStock; 5.2a & b: © Doug Goodman/Photo Researchers; p. 155 (top): © Joe McNally; p. 155 (bottom): © Don Mason/ Corbis; 5.4: Courtesy of Dr. Carolyn Rovee-Collier; 5.5a & b: Photos from: Meltzoff, A. N., & Brooks, R. (2007). Intersubjectivity before language: Three windows on preverbal sharing. In S. Bråten (Ed.), On being moved: From mirror neurons to empathy (pp. 149–174). Philadelphia, PA: John Benjamins.; p. 158 (left): © Tom Stewart/Corbis; 5.7: © Andrew Meltzoff; 5.8: From Jean Mandler, University of California, San Diego. Reprinted by permission of Oxford University Press, Inc.; p. 161 (top) and 162 (top): © John Santrock; p. 162 (bottom): Bayley Scales of Infant and Toddler Development - Third Edition (Bayley - III). Copyright © 2006 by NCS Pearson, Inc. Reproduced with permission. All rights reserved.; 5.11a & b: © 2003 University of Washington, Institute for Learning and Brain Sciences (I-LABS).; p. 167: © Niki Mareschal/Photographers Choice/Getty Images; 5.13: © ABPL Image Library /Animals Animals/Earth Scenes; p. 168 (bottom): © Tim Davis/Corbis; 5.15: © Michael Goldstein, Cornell University; p. 172: © John Carter/ Photo Researchers

Chapter 6

Opener: © Jamie Marcial/SuperStock; p. 180: © Rick Gomez/Corbis; p. 181: © Zen Sekizawa/Getty Images; 6.1 (all): © Michael Lewis, Institute for the Study of Child Development, Robert Wood Johnson Medical School; 6.2: © Sybil L. Hart, Texas Tech University; p. 183: © Andy Cox/Stone/Getty Images; 6.3: © Dr. Daniel Messinger, University of Miami, FL; p. 184: © Romilly Lockyer/The Image Bank/Getty Images; p. 186: © Michael Tcherevkoff/The Image Bank/Getty Images; p. 187: © Judith Oddie/Photo Edit; p. 189 (top): © Charles Gullung/Photonica/Getty Images; p. 189 (bottom): © Vol. 63 Photodisc/Getty RF; p. 190: © Britt Erlanson/Image Bank/Getty; 6.6: Courtesy Celia A. Brownell, University of Pittsburgh; 6.7: © Martin Rogers/Stock Boston; p. 194: © David Young-Wolff/Photo Edit; p. 195: © Penny Tweedie/ Stone/Getty Images; p. 196: © BrandXPictues/Getty Images RF; p. 197: © Corbis RF; 6.10a: © National Geographic/Getty RF; 6.10b: © Stephanie Rausser/ Taxi/Getty Images; p. 198 (bottom): © John Henley/ Corbis; p. 199: © Schwartzwald Lawrence/Corbis; p. 200: Courtesy of Rashmi Nakhre, The Hattie Daniels Day Care Center; p. 201: © Lawrence Migdale/Stone/Getty Images

Chapter 7

Opener: © Ariel Skelley/The Stock Market/Corbis; p. 210: From 'Open Window' © 1994 Municipality of Reggio Emilia Infant-toddler Centers and Preschools Published by Reggio Children; p. 211: © Bob Daemmrich/The Image Works; 7.1: © Photo Researchers; p. 212: © Joel Gordon 1993; p. 213 (top): © Felicia Martinez/Photo Edit; p. 213 (bottom): © istock; p. 214: © Michael Newman/Photo Edit; p. 216: © AP/Wide World Photos; 7.6: © Paul Fusco/Magnum Photos; 7.8: © Elizabeth Crews/The Image Works; p. 221 (top): © James Wertsch/Washington University at St. Louis; p. 221 (bottom): © Gabe Palmer/Corbis; 7.9: Images courtesy of E. Bodrova and D.J. Leong, from

Tools of the Mind, 2007; 7.10a: A. R. Lauria/Dr. Michael Cole, Laboratory of Human Cognition, University of California, San Diego; 7.10b: © Bettmann/Corbis; p. 224 (bottom): © Ariel Skelley/Corbis; p. 226: © 2005 JAMESKAMP.COM; p. 227: © Nita Winter; p. 228: © John Flavell; p. 230: © Joe Baker, Images.com/Corbis; p. 231: © AP/Wide World Photos; p. 233: © Ellen Senisi/The Image Works; p. 235 (top): © image100/Corbis RF; p. 235 (bottom): © AP/Wide World Photos; p. 237: Courtesy of Yolanda Garcia; p. 238 © Ronnie Kaufman/The Stock Market/Corbis; p. 239 (left): © Karen Kasmauski/Corbis; p. 239 (right): © SOS Children's Villages (www.sos-usa.org)

Chapter 8

Opener: © Ariel Skelley/Corbis; p. 248: © Corbis RF; p. 249 (top): © Michael Lewis, Institute for the Study of Child Development, Robert Wood Johnson Medical School; p. 249 (bottom): © LWA-Dann Tardif/zefa/Corbis; p. 250: © Catherine Ledner/Stone/Getty Images; p. 251: © Randy Faris/Corbis; p. 252: © Corbis RF; p. 253: © BigStock Photos; p. 254: © Digital Stock; 8.2: © Ariel Skelley/Corbis; p. 259: © Jose Luis Pelaez/Corbis; p. 260: © PunchStock RF; p. 261 (top): Courtesy of Darla Botkin; p. 261 (bottom): © David M. Wells/Corbis; p. 262: © Prevent Child Abuse America. Also reprinted by permission of Grant and Tamia Hill; p. 263 (top): © Don Hammond/Design Pics/Corbis RF; p. 263 (bottom): © Ariel Skelley/Corbis; p. 264: © Ariel Skelley/Corbis; p. 265: © PunchStock RF; p. 267: © Shelly Gazin/The Image Works; p. 268: © Karen Kasmauski/Woodfin Camp; p. 269: © Spencer Grant/Photo Edit; p. 270: © Ariel Skelley/Corbis; p. 271: © BigStock Photos; p. 272 (top): © Richard Hutchings/Photo Edit; p. 272 (bottom): © Bryan Peterson; p. 274: © Franco Vogt/Corbis

Chapter 9

Opener: © Michael Pole/Corbis; p. 284: © Aerial Skelley/Corbis; p. 286 (top): Courtesy of Sharon McLeod; p. 286 (bottom): © L. Perez/zefa/Corbis; p. 287 (top): © Jules Frazier/Getty RF; p. 287 (bottom): © Corbis RF; p. 289: © AP/Wide World Photos; p. 289 (bottom): © David Young-Wolff/Photo Edit; p. 290: © Michael Macor/San Francisco Chronicles/Corbis; p. 291: © Will McIntyre/Photo Researchers; p. 293: © M & E Bernheim/Woodfin Camp & Associates; p. 294: © Brand X Pictures/PunchStock RF; p. 297 (top): © Francisco Cruz/SuperStock; p. 297 (bottom): © Stan Godlewski Photography; p. 298 (top): © John Flavell; p. 298 (bottom): © Ellen Senis/The Image Works; p. 300: Courtesy of Robert Sternberg; p. 301 (top): © Jay Gardner, 1998; p. 301 (bottom): © Joe McNally; p. 305: © Jill Cannefax/EKM-Nepenthe; p. 306: © Koichi Kamoshida/Newsmakers/Getty Images; p. 307: © Doug Wilson/Corbis; p. 308: © Richard Howard; p. 310 (top): © Kenji Hakuta, Stanford University; p. 310 (bottom): © Elizabeth Crews

Chapter 10

Opener: © Juice Images/Corbis RF; p. 318: © Joseph Sohm/Visions of America/Corbis; p. 319: © Paul Edmondson/Corbis; p. 320: © Ron Chapple Stock/Corbis RF; p. 321 (top): © Jose Luis Pelaez/Corbis; p. 321 (bottom): © Jim Craigmyle/Corbis; p. 322: © Christopher Thomas/Getty; p. 323 (top): © Reutuers/NewMedia Inc./Corbis; p. 323 (middle): © AP/Wide World Photos; p. 326: © Raghu-Rai/Magnum Photos; p. 327: © Keith Carter Photography; p. 328: © Norbert Schaefer/Corbis; p. 330: © Roy McMahon/Crobis RF; p. 332: © Catherine Gehm; p. 333: © Ariel Skelley/Corbis; p. 334: © Michael Newman/Photo Edit; p. 336: © Royalty-Free/Corbis; p. 338: © Stone/Getty Images; p. 339: © Rolf Bruderer/Corbis; p. 340: © Elizabeth Crews; p. 341 (top): © Martin Poole/Getty Images; p. 341 (bottom) © Bob Daemmrich/The Image Works; p. 342: © 2004, USA Today. Reprinted with permission; p. 343: © Michael Conroy/AP Wide World Photos; p. 344: © Jose Luis Pelaez/Corbis; p. 345: © John S. Abbott; p. 346: © Journal Sentinel, photographer Mary Zahn

Chapter 11

Opener: © Rob Melnychuk/Brand X/Corbis RF; p. 355: © M. Regine/The Image Bank/Getty Images; p. 356: © Value RF/Corbis RF; p. 358: © Jon Feingersh/The Stock Market/Corbis; p. 359: © Corbis RF; p. 360: © Davis Turner-Pool/Getty Images; p. 361 (top): © Joel Gordon 1995; p. 361 (bottom): © Marilyn Humphries; p. 362: © Lawrence Migdale/Stock Boston; p. 363: © Michael Ray; p. 364: Courtesy of Lynn Blankinship; p. 365: © 1998 Frank Fournier; p. 367 (top): © Jim LoScalzo; p. 367 (bottom): © Kyle Ericson/AP Wide World Photos; p. 369: © Daniel Allan/Taxi/Getty; p. 370: © Tony Freeman/Photo Edit; p. 372: © David Young-Wolff/Photo Edit; p. 373: © Stewart Cohen/Stone/Getty Images; p. 374: © Big Cheese Photo/SuperStock/SuperStock RF; p. 377: Courtesy I Have a Dream Program, Texas; p. 378: © David Young-Wolff/Photo Edit

Chapter 12

Opener: © George Disario/The Stock Market/Corbis; p. 384: © Matthew J. Lee, The Boston Globe; p. 385: © Dominic Rouse/The Image Bank/Getty Images; p. 387: © John Henley/Corbis; p. 388 (top): © Mike Watson Images/Corbis RF; p. 388 (bottom): © USA Today Library, photo by Robert Deutsch; p. 389: © Stone/Getty Images; p. 390: © Bob Daemmrich/The Image Works; p. 391: © Myrleen Ferguson Cate/Photo Edit; p. 392 (top): © Pat Vasquez-Cunningham 1999; p. 392 (bottom): © Jeffry W. Myers/Stock Boston; 12.3: © Spencer Grant/Photo Edit; p. 394: © Tony Freeman/Photo Edit; p. 395: © Michael Siluk/The Image Works; p. 396 (top): © Tessa Codrington/Stone/Getty Images; p. 396 (bottom): © Tom & Dee Ann McCarthy/Corbis; p. 397: © David De Lossy/The Image Bank/Getty Images; p. 398 (top): © Dain Gair Photographic/Index Stock; p. 398 (middle): © AFP/Getty Images; p. 398 (bottom): © AP/Wide World Photos; p. 399 (top): © Getty RF; p. 399 (bottom): © Daniel Laine; p. 400: © USA Today Library, photo by H. Darr Beiser; p. 402: © Corbis RF; p. 403: © Chuck Savage/Corbis; p. 404: Courtesy of Rodney Hammond; p. 405: © Jim Smith/Photo Researchers; p. 407: © David Young-Wolff/Stone/Getty Images

Chapter 13

Opener: © Ariel Skelley/Corbis; p. 416: © AP/Wide World Photos; p. 417: © Michael Maddaus, University of Minnesota, Division of Thoracic & Foregut Surgery; p. 418: © David Young-Wolff/Stone/Getty Images; p. 419: Courtesy of Grace Leaf; p. 421: © Ausloser/zefa/Corbis; p. 422: © Michael A. Kelle/zefa/Corbis; p. 423: © Randy M. Ury/Corbis; p. 424: © Joe Raelle/Newsmakers/Getty Images; p. 425: © Randy Faris/Corbis; p. 428 (top): © PunchStock RF; p. 428 (middle): © Corbis RF; p. 428 (bottom): © 1996 Rob Lewine/The Stock Market/Corbis; p. 430: © Photomorgana/Corbis; p. 433: © Johnny Le Fortune/zefa/Corbis; p. 434: Courtesy Mihaly Csikszentmihalyi; p. 437: © LWA-Dann Tardif/Corbis; p. 438: © Ariel Skelley/Corbis

Chapter 14

Opener: © Ariel Skelley/Corbis; p. 445 (top): © Grace/zefa/Corbis; p. 445 (middle): © LWA-Sharie Kennedy/Corbis; p. 447: © Corbis RF; p. 451 (top): © David Young-Wolff/Photo Edit; p. 451 (middle): © Tony Freeman/Photo Edit; p. 451 (bottom): © Scott A. Woodward/Corbis RF; p. 453: © Carol Ford/Stone/Getty Images; p. 455 (left): © Steve Cole/Getty RF; p. 455 (right): © PunchStock RF; p. 457a: © Mats Widen/Johner Images/Getty RF; p. 457b: © Ali Jarekji/Reuters/Corbis; p. 457c: © David Hanover/Stone/Getty Images; p. 460 (top): © Courtesy Dr. John Gottman, The Gottman Institute; p. 460 (bottom): © Ronald Mackechnie/Stone/Getty Images; p. 461: © Corbis RF; p. 462: Courtesy of Janis Keyser; p. 463: © Grace/zefa/Corbis; p. 466: © EyeWire EP036/Getty Images RF

Chapter 15

Opener: © Zephyr Pictures/Index Stock/Photolibrary; p. 475: © Paul Barton/Corbis; p. 477 (top): © Bettmann/Corbis; p. 477 (bottom): © Matthew Mendelsohn/Corbis; p. 478: © George V. Mann, M.D.; p. 479 (top): © Ryan McVay/Photodisc/Getty RF; p. 479 (bottom): © Randy M. Ury/Corbis; 15.3: © Eye of Science/Photo Researchers; p. 481 (top): © PunchStock RF; p. 481 (middle): © Corbis RF; p. 481 (bottom): © Taxi/Getty Images; p. 483: © 1998 Tom & Dee McCarthy/The Stock Market/Corbis; p. 484: © McGraw-Hill Companies/Suzie Ross, Photographer; 15.5: © Vol. 155/Corbis RF; p. 488: Courtesy K. Warner Schaie; p. 489: © Reuters Newsmedia Inc/Corbis; p. 491: © Chris Cheadle/Stone/Getty Images; p. 492: © Tony Freeman/Photo Edit; p. 493: © PunchStock RF; p. 494: © Michael Prince/Corbis

Chapter 16

Opener: © Savin Patrick/Sygma/Corbis; 16.3 (top): © CORBIS RF; 16.3 (middle): © Eyewire/Getty RF; 16.3 (bottom): © Vol. 67/PhotoDisc/Getty RF; p. 506 (top): © Bettmann/Corbis; p. 506 (bottom): © EyeWire/Getty RF; p. 507 (top): © Rhoda Sidney/Photo Edit; p. 507 (bottom): © Betty Press/Woodfin Camp & Associates; p. 510: © Francine Fleischer/Corbis; p. 511: © Bettmann/Corbis; p. 512: © LWA-Dann Tardif/Corbis; p. 513: © Stock4B/Getty Images; p. 514: © Stephanie Grewet/zefa/Corbis; p. 515: © Jose Luis Pelaez, Inc./Corbis; p. 517: © Reza/National Geographic/Getty; p. 518: © William Hubbell/Woodfin Camp & Associates; p. 519: © Steve Casimro/The Image Bank/Getty Images; p. 520: Courtesy of Lillian Troll

Chapter 17

Opener: © Chuck Savage/Corbis; p. 528: © John Goodman; p. 529: © Ingram Publishing/SuperStock RF; p. 531 (left): Courtesy New England Centenarian Study at Boston University Medical Center; p. 531 (middle): © Waldo McBurney; p. 531 (right): Courtesy New England Centenarian Study at Boston University Medical Center; p. 532: © USA Today, Paul Wiseman, photographer; p. 533 (left): © Pascal Parrot/Sygma/CORBIS; p. 533 (right): © Thomas Del Brase; 17.3: Courtesy of Dr. Jerry Shay, PhD., UT Southwestern Medical Center; 17.4: © Photo Researchers; 17.5 (top & bottom): Courtesy of Dr. Fred Gage; 17.6: From R. Cabeza, et al., "Age-related differences in neural activity during memory encoding and retrieval: A positron emission tomography study" in *Journal of Neuroscience*, 17, 391–400, 1997; 17.7 (top): Courtesy of Denise Park, University of Texas at Dallas Center for Brain Health; 17.7 (bottom: © Michael O'Brien; 17.8 (top & bottom): © James Balog; p. 540: © Argentum/Photo Researchers; p. 541: © Image Source/Punchstock RF; p. 542: © Emma Rian/zefa/Corbis; p. 544: © George Gardner/The Image Works; p. 545: © Norbert Schaefer/Corbis; p. 546: © Bob Daemmrich/Stock Boston; 17.18: Courtesy of Colin Bloor; 17.20a & b: © Ethan Hill; p. 550: © AP Photo/Jacqueline Larma; p. 552: © Rex Curry

Chapter 18

Opener: © George Shelley/Corbis; p. 558: © Cornell Capa/Magnum Photos; p. 564: © Elizabeth Crews; p. 566 (top): © Barbara Stitzer/ Photo Edit; p. 566 (middle): © Paul Barton/Corbis; p. 566 (bottom): © Jeff Zaruba/Corbis; p. 567: © Jeff Derose; p. 567 (bottom): © David Buffington/Blend Images/Getty RF; p. 568: © Corbis RF; p. 570: © Image Shop/Corbis RF; p. 571: © Greg Sailor; p. 573 (top): © Chuck Savage/Corbis; p. 573 (bottom): © Walter Hodges/Stone/Getty; p. 575: © G. Baden/zefa/Corbis; 18.6a & b: © Alfred Pasieka/Science Photo Library/Photo Researchers, Inc.; p. 577: © Bettmann/Corbis; p. 578: Courtesy of Jan W. Weaver; p. 579: © AP/Wide World Photos; p. 580: Courtesy of Donna Polisar; p. 581: © Bryan Peterson/The Stock Market/Corbis

Chapter 19

Opener: © Chuck Savage/Corbis; p. 588 (left): © AP/Wide World Photos; p. 588 (right): Photo by Steve Lipofsky BasketballPhoto.com; 19.1: © Sarah Putman/Picture Cube/Index Stock; p. 590 (top): © Owen Franken/Corbis; p. 590 (bottom): © Chuck Savage/Corbis; p. 591: Courtesy of Laura Carstensen; 19.4 (25 to 34 years): © Eyewire/Getty Images RF; (35 to 54 years): © PhotoDisc/Getty RF; (55 to 65 years): © Corbis RF; (70 to 84 years): © PhotoDisc/Getty RF; (85 to 105 years): © Vol. 34/Corbis RF; p. 597 (top): © Soren Hald/Stone/Getty; p. 597 (bottom): © Steve Prezant/Corbis; p. 599: © Peter Dazeley/zefa/Corbis; p. 600: © Ronnie Kaufman/Corbis; p. 601: © Tom & Dee Ann McCarthy/Corbis; p. 602: John Santrock; p. 603: © George Shelley/Corbis; p. 604 (top): © Frank Conaway/Index Stock; p. 604 (bottom): © Dallas Morning News, photographer Jim Mahoney; p. 606: Courtesy of Dr. Norma Thomas; p. 607 (top): © G. Wayne Floyd/Unicorn Stock Photos; p. 607 (bottom): © Suzi Moore-McGregor/Woodfin Camp & Associates; p. 608: © NASA/Liaison Agency/Getty Images News Service

Chapter 20

Opener: © Loretta Hostettler/iStockphoto; p. 616: © Lynsey Addario/Corbis; p. 617: © Robert Galbrait/Reuters/Corbis; p. 618: © Patrick Ward/Stock Boston; p. 620: © Handout Courtesy of the Schaivo Family/Corbis; p. 621: © Reprinted with permission from The Detroit News; p. 622: © USA Today, photographer Tim Dillon; p. 625 (top): © Mika/zefa/Corbis; p. 625 (bottom): © Norbert Schaefer/Corbis; p. 627: © Eastcott Momatinck/The Image Works; p. 629: © M. Thomsen/zefa/Corbis; p. 631: © Phyllis Picarci/Image State; p. 632: © Jennifer S. Altman; p. 635 (left): © Russell/Underwood/Corbis; p. 635 (right): © Paul Almasy/Corbis; p. 636: Courtesy of The Baltimore Sun Company, Inc. All Rights Reserved

Text and Line Art Credits

Chapter 1

Figure 1.3: From "Percentage of Children 7 to 18 Years of Age Around the World Who Have Never Been to School of Any Kind," 2004, *The State of the World's Children*, Geneva, Switzerland: UNICEF, Fig. 5, p. 27. **Figure 1.14:** From "Bronfenbrenner's Ecological Theory of Development," in C. B. Kopp & J. B. Krakow, 1982, *Child Development in the Social Context*, p. 648. Addison-Wesley Longman, Inc. Reprinted by permission of Pearson Education, Inc. **Figure 1.17:** From Santrock *Children*, 9/e, Figure 2.12. Copyright © 2007 The McGraw-Hill Companies. Reproduced with permission by The McGraw-Hill Companies.

Chapter 2

Figure 2.2: From P. B. Baltes, U. M. Staudinger, & U. Lindenberger, 1999, "Lifespan Psychology," Reprinted with permission from the *Annual Review of Psychology*, Volume 50 © 1999 by Annual Reviews. www.annualreviews.org **Figure 2.3:** From Santrock, *Psychology*, 7/e. Copyright © 2003 The McGraw-Hill Companies. Reproduced with permission by The McGraw-Hill Companies. **Figure 2.10:** From Santrock, *Children*, 9/e, Figure 3.10. Copyright © 2007 The McGraw-Hill Companies. Reproduced with permission by The McGraw-Hill Companies. **Chp. 2, pp. 66–68:** From *Handbook of Parenting Vol. 1: Children and Parenting* by D. Brodzinsky and E. Pinderhughes. Copyright 2002 by Taylor & Francis Group LLC — Books. Reproduced with permission of Taylor & Francis Group L.L.C — Books in the format Textbook via Copyright Clearance Center.

Chapter 3

Figure 3.3: From Santrock, *Children*, 9/e, Figure 4.3. Copyright © 2007 The McGraw-Hill Companies. Reproduced with permission of The McGraw-Hill Companies. **Figure 3.5:** Adapted from K. L. Moore and T. V. N. Persaud from *Before We Are Born*, p. 130.

© 1993, with permission from Elsevier. **Figure 3.6:** From Santrock, *Children*, 9/e, Figure 4.6. Copyright © 2007 The McGraw-Hill Companies. Reproduced with permission of The McGraw-Hill Companies. **Figure 3.7a:** From Virginia A. Apgar, 1975. "A Proposal for a New Method of Evaluation of a Newborn Infant," in *Anesthesia and Analgesia*, Vol. 32, pp. 260–267. Reprinted by permission of Lippincott Williams & Wilkins. **Figure 3.8:** From Santrock, *Children*, 10/e. Copyright © 2008 The McGraw-Hill Companies. Reproduced with permission by The McGraw-Hill Companies. **Figure 3.10:** Reprinted from *Infant Behavior and Development*, Vol. 30, M. Hernandez-Reif, M. Diego, and T. Field, "Preterm Infants Show Reduced Stress Behaviors and Activity After 5 Days of Massage Therapy," Figure 1. Copyright © 2007, with permission from Elsevier. **Figure 3.12:** From Santrock, *Child Development*, 10/e, Figure 4.11. Copyright © 2004 The McGraw-Hill Companies. Reproduced with permission by The McGraw-Hill Companies.

Chapter 4

Figure 4.1: From Santrock, *Children*, 9/e, Figure 6.1. Copyright © 2007 The McGraw-Hill Companies. Reproduced with permission by The McGraw-Hill Companies. **Figure 4.5:** From Santrock, *Child Development*, 10/e, Figure 5.2. Copyright © 2004 The McGraw-Hill Companies. Reproduced with permission by The McGraw-Hill Companies. **Figure 4.7:** From Santrock, *Child Development*, 11/e, Figure 5.11. Copyright © 2007 The McGraw-Hill Companies. Reproduced with permission by The McGraw-Hill Companies. **Figure 4.10:** From Santrock, *Child Development*, 11/e, Figure 5.13. Copyright © 2007 The McGraw-Hill Companies. Reproduced with permission by The McGraw-Hill Companies. **Figure 4.11:** From J. Kim (2006). *Obesity*, 14, 1107–1112. Reprinted by permission from Macmillan Publishers Ltd. **Figure 4.12:** From Santrock, *Child Development*, 10/e, Figure 5.11. Copyright © 2004 The McGraw-Hill Companies. Reproduced with permission by The McGraw-Hill Companies. **Figure 4.15:** Reprinted from *Journal of Pediatrics*, Vol. 71, W. K. Frankenburg and J. B. Dobbs, "The Denver Development Screening Test," pp. 181–191. Copyright © 1967, with permission from Elsevier. **Figure 4.17a:** Adapted from "The Origin of Form Perception" by R. L. Frantz. Copyright © 1961 by Scientific American, Inc. **Figure 4.18a and b:** From A. Slater, V. Morison, & M. Somers, 1988, "Orientation Discrimination and Cortical Functions in the Human Newborn," *Perception*, Vol. 17, pp. 597–602, Fig. 1 and Table 1. Reprinted by permission of Pion, Ltd. London. **Figure 4.20:** From Santrock, *Child Development*, 10/e, Figure 5.18. Copyright © 2004 The McGraw-Hill Companies. Reproduced with permission by The McGraw-Hill Companies.

Chapter 5

Figure 5.3: From R. Baillargeon & J. DeVoe, "Using the Violation of Expectations Method to Study Object Permanence in Infants," 1991, "Object Permanence in Young Children: Further Evidence," *Child Development*, 62, pp. 1227–1246. Reprinted by permission of Blackwell Publishing. **Figure 5.6:** From Santrock, *A Topical Approach to Life-Span Development*, 4/e, Figure 7.7. Copyright © 2008 The McGraw-Hill Companies. Reproduced with permission by The McGraw-Hill Companies. **Figure 5.9:** From DeLoache, Simcock, and Macari, "Planes, Trains and Automobiles," *Developmental Psychology* 43: 1579–1586. Copyright © 2007 by the American Psychological Association. **Figure 5.10:** From "The Rule Systems of Language," from S. L. Haight, *Language Overview*. Reprinted by permission. **Figure 5.12:** From Santrock, *A Topical Approach to Life Span Development*, 4/e, Figure 9.3. Copyright © 2008 The McGraw-Hill Companies. Reproduced with permission by The McGraw-Hill Companies. **Figure 5.13:** From Santrock, *Children*, 9/e, Figure 7.11. Copyright © 2007 The McGraw-Hill Companies. Reproduced with permission by The McGraw-Hill Companies. **Figure 5.14:** From Santrock, *Child Development*, 10/e, Figure 10.2. Copyright ©

2004 The McGraw-Hill Companies. Reproduced with permission by The McGraw-Hill Companies. **Figure 5.16a and b:** From Hart & Risley (1995), *Meaningful Differences in the Everyday Experiences of Young American Children*, Baltimore: Paul H. Brookes Publishing Co. Reprinted by permission of Paul H. Brookes Publishing Co. **Ch. 5, p. 148:** From J. Piaget, *The Origins of Intelligence*, pp. 27, 159, 225, 273, 339. Reprinted with permission of International Universities Press, Inc. and Taylor & Francis Books.

Chapter 6

Figure 6.5: From Santrock, *Life-Span Development*, 4/e. Copyright © 1999 The McGraw-Hill Companies. Reproduced with permission by The McGraw-Hill Companies. **Figure 6.8:** From van Ijzendoorn & Kroonenberg, 1988, "Cross Cultural Patterns of Attachment," *Child Development*, 59, 147–156. Adapted by permission of Blackwell Publishing. **Figure 6.9:** From Jay Belksy, "Early Human Experiences: A Family Perspective," in *Developmental Psychology*, Vol. 17, pp. 3-23. Copyright © 1981 by the American Psychological Association.

Chapter 7

Figure 7.4: From Santrock, *Psychology*, 7/e. Copyright © 2003 The McGraw-Hill Companies. Reproduced with permission by The McGraw-Hill Companies. **Figure 7.5:** "The Symbolic Drawings of Young Children," reprinted courtesy of D. Wolf and J. Nove. Reprinted by permission of Dennie Palmer Wolf, Annenberg Institute, Brown University. **Figure 7.9a and b:** Elena Bodrova, Deborah J. Leong. **Figure 7.11:** From Santrock, *Children*, 7/e. Copyright © 2003 The McGraw-Hill Companies. Reproduced with permission by The McGraw-Hill Companies. **Figure 7.14:** From U. Frith, 1989. *Autism: Explaining the Enigma*, p. 83. Used by permission of Blackwell Publishing. **Figure 7.16:** From Jean Berko, 1958, "The Child's Learning of English Morphology," in *Word*, Vol. 14, p. 154. Reprinted courtesy of Jean Berko Gleason. **Figure 7.17:** Adapted and excerpted, by permission, from S. Bredekamp and C. Copple, "Developmentally Appropriate Practice for 3- through 5-Year-Olds," in *Developmentally Appropriate Practice in Early Childhood Programs*, Rev. ed., eds. S. Bredekamp and C. Copple (Washington, DC: NAEYC, 1997), 123–38. Reprinted with permission from the National Association for the Education of Young Children. **Ch 7, p. 234 (art):** From Berko Gleason, Jean. *The Development of Language*, 3/e. Published by Allyn and Bacon, Boston, MA. Copyright © 1993 by Pearson Education. Reprinted by permission of the publisher. **Chap. 7 text, p. 226:** From Bruck and Ceci, "The Suggestibility of Children's Memory" in *Annual Review of Psychology*, 50, pp. 429–430. Used with permission by M. Bruck.

Chapter 8

Figure 8.1: From Santrock, *Child Development*, 10/e, Figure 13.3. Copyright © 2004 The McGraw-Hill Companies. Reproduced with permission by The McGraw-Hill Companies. **Chap. 8 text: p. 246:** From *Burning Fence* by Craig Lesley. Copyright © 2005 by author and reprinted by permission of St. Martin's Press, LLC.

Chapter 9

Figure 9.1: From Santrock, *Children*, 9/e, Figure 9.3. Copyright © 2007 The McGraw-Hill Companies. Reproduced with permission by The McGraw-Hill Companies. **Figure 9.6:** From Shaw et al. (2007). "Attention Deficit/Hyperactivity Disorder is Characterized by a Delay in Cortical Maturation," *Proceedings of the National Academy of Sciences*, Vol. 104, p. 19650, Fig. 2. Copyright © 2007 National Academy of Sciences, U.S.A. Used with permission. **Figure 9.8:** From *Children's Thinking: What Develops?* by M.T.H. Chi in F.S. Seigler. Copyright 1978 by Taylor & Francis Group LLC—Books. Reproduced with permission of Taylor & Francis Group LLC—Books in the format Textbook via Copyright Clearance Center.

Chapter 10

Figure 10.2: From Colby et al., "A Longitudinal Study of Moral Judgment," *Monographs of the Society for Research in Child Development,* Serial No. 201. Reprinted with permission by Blackwell Publishing. **Figure 10.3:** From Santrock, *A Topical Approach to Life-Span Development,* 3/e, Figure 12.4. Copyright © 2007 The McGraw-Hill Companies. Reproduced with permission by The McGraw-Hill Companies. **Figure 10.4:** Reproduced by special permission of the Publisher, Mind Garden, Inc.; www.mindgarden.com from the *Bem Sex Role Inventory* by Sandra Bem. Copyright 1978 by Consulting Psychologists Press, Inc. All rights reserved. Further reproduction is prohibited without the Publisher's written consent. **Figure 10.5:** From Nansel et al., 2001, "Bullying Behaviors Among U.S. Youth," *Journal of the American Medical Association,* Vol. 285, pp. 2094–2100. **Figure 10.6:** From Stevenson et al., 1986, Figure 6, "Mathematics Achievement of Chinese, Japanese, and American Children, *Science,* Vol. 231, pp. 693–699. Reprinted with permission from AAAS.

Chapter 11

Figure 11.1: From J. M. Tanner et al., "Standards from Birth to Maturity for Height, Weight, Height Velocity: British Children in 1965" in *Archives of Diseases in Childhood* 41, 1966. With permission from BMJ Publishing Group. **Figure 11.2:** From A. F. Roache, "Secular Trends in Stature, Weight and Maturation," *Monographs of the Society for Research in Child Development,* n. 179. © Blackwell Publishing. Used with permission. **Figure 11.3:** From R. B. Simmons, D. A. Blyth, and K. L. McKinney, "The Social and Psychological Effects of Puberty on White Females. In J. Brooks-Gunn & A. C. Petersen (eds). *Girls at Puberty: Biological and Psychological Perspectives,* pp. 229–272, 1983. With kind permission of Springer Science and Business Media. **Figure 11.4:** From Santrock, *Essentials of Life-Span Development,* 1/e. Copyright © 2008 The McGraw-Hill Companies. Reproduced with permission by The McGraw-Hill Companies. **Figure 11.6:** From Santrock, *Child Development,* 10/e, Figure 6.14. Copyright © 2004 The McGraw-Hill Companies. Reproduced with permission by The McGraw-Hill Companies. **Figure 11.7:** From Santrock, *Children,* 4/e. Copyright © 1995 The McGraw-Hill Companies. Reproduced with permission by The McGraw-Hill Companies. **Figure 11.8:** From "Trends in Drug Use by U.S. Eighth-, Tenth-, and Twelfth-Grade Students," by Johnston and others, 2008, *The Monitoring of the Future: National Results on Adolescent Drug Use,* Washington DC: National Institute on Drug Abuse. **Figure 11.9:** From "Young Adolescents' Reports of Alcohol use in the Family Matters Program," from K.E. Bauman, S.T. Ennett, et al., 2002, "Influence of a Family Program on Adolescent Smoking and Drinking Prevalence," *Prevention Science* 3, 2002, pp. 35–42. With kind permission of Springer Science and Business Media. **Figure 11.10:** From Santrock, *Children,* 10/e, Figure 15.3. Copyright © 2004 The McGraw-Hill Companies. Reproduced with permission by The McGraw-Hill Companies.

Chapter 12

Figure 12.4: From Santrock, *Child Development,* 11/e, Figure 16.4. Copyright © 2007 The McGraw-Hill Companies. Reproduced with permission by The McGraw-Hill Companies. **Figure 12.6:** "Percentage of U.S. 9th to 12th Grade Students Who Seriously Considered Attempting Suicide in the Previous 12 Months from 1991 to 2005," National Risk Behavior Survey 1991–2005: Trends in the Prevalence of Suicide Ideating and Attempts. Centers for Disease Control and Prevention. **Figure 12.7:** From D.B. Goldston et al., "Cultural Considerations in Adolescent Suicide Prevention and Psychosocial Treatment" *American Psychologist,* 63, 14–31. Copyright © 2008 American Psychological Association.

Chapter 13

Figure 13.2: Reprinted from *Journal of Adolescent Health,* Vol. 39, M. Jane Park, et al., "The Health Status of Young Adults in the United States," pp. 305–317. Copyright © 2006, with permission from Elsevier. **Figure 13.1:** From The American College Health Association National College Health Assessment Spring 2007 Reference Group Data Report (abridged). *Journal of American College Health,* 56, Table 17, p. 478. Used with permission by American College Health Association. **Figure 13.3:** Centers for Disease Control and Prevention, 2006. Based on data collected in the 2005 National Health Interview Study. **Figure 13.4:** From J. Kruger, H. M. Blanck, and C. Gillespie (2006). "Dietary and Physical Activity Behaviors Among Adults Successful at Weight Loss Management" *International Journal of Behavioral Nutrition and Physical Activity,* 3, 17. **Figure 13.6:** From *Sex in America* by John Gagnon. Copyright © 1994 by CSG Enterprises, Inc., Edward O. Laumann, Robert T. Michael, and Gina Kolata. By permission of Little, Brown & Company and Brockman, Inc. **Figure 13.7:** From Santrock, *Children,* 9/e, Figure 15.8. Copyright © 2007 The McGraw-Hill Companies. Reproduced with permission by The McGraw-Hill Companies.

Chapter 14

Figure 14.1: From *Developing Structure of Temperament and Personality from Infancy to Adulthood* by T.D. Wachs in C. Halverson, et al. Copyright 1994 by Taylor & Francis Group LLC — Books. Reproduced with permission by Taylor 7 Francis Group LLC — Books in the format Textbook via Copyright Clearance Center. **Figure 14.3:** From "Examples of Positive Changes in the Aftermath of a Romantic Breakup" by T. Tashiro & P. Frazier, 2003, "I'll Never Be in a Relationship Like That Again: Personal Growth Following Romantic Relationship Breakups," *Personal Relationships,* 10, after Table 1, p. 120. Reprinted with permission from Blackwell Publishing. **Figure 14.5:** From Popenoe, David and Barbara DaFoe Whitehead. *The State of Our Unions: The Social Health of Marriage in America, 2005,* copyright 2005 by The National Marriage Projects at Rutgers University. Reprinted by permission of the National Marriage Project. **Figure 14.6:** From B. R. Karney & T. N. Bradbury, "Contextual Influences on Marriage," 2005, *Current Directions in Psychological Science,* 14, pp. 171–175, Figure 2. Reprinted with permission from Blackwell Publishing. **Chap. 14 text: p. 444:** From *The Dance of Intimacy* by Harriet Goldhor Lerner, pp. 44–45. Copyright © 1989 by Harriet Goldhor Lerner. Reprinted by permission of HarperCollins Publishers. **Chap. 14 text: pp. 463–464:** From *For Better Or For Worse: Divorce Reconsidered* by E. Mavis Hetherington & John Kelly. Copyright © 2002 by E. Mavis Hetherington and John Kelly. Used by permission of W. W. Norton & Company, Inc.

Chapter 15

Figure 15.1: Adapted from *Newsweek,* "Health for Life," Special Section, Fall/Winter 2001. Copyright © Newsweek, Inc. All rights reserved. Used with permission by PARS International Corp., Inc. **Figure 15.2:** Adapted from *Newsweek,* "Health for Life," Special Section, Fall/Winter 2001. Copyright © Newsweek, Inc. All rights reserved. Used with permission by PARS International Corp., Inc. **Figure 15.5 graph:** From *Sex in America* by John Gagnon. Copyright © 1994 by CSG Enterprises, Inc., Edward O. Laumann, Robert T. Michael, and Gina Kolata. By permission of Little, Brown & Company and Brockman, Inc. **Chap. 15 lyrics p. 474:** From Jim Croce, "Time in a Bottle." Copyright © 1972, 1985 Denjac Music, Co. Reprinted with permission.

Chapter 16

Figure 16.1: From "Changes in Generativity and Identity Certainty from the 30s through the 50s," from Stewart, Osgrove & Helson, 2002, "Middle Aging in Women: Patterns of Personality Change from the 30s to the 50s," Fig. 3, *Journal of Adult Development,* Vol. 8, pp. 23–37. With kind permission of Springer Science and Business Media. **Figure 16.2:** From "Items used to Assess Generativity and Identity Certainty," from Steward, Osgrove 7 Helson, 2002, "Middle Aging in Women: Patterns of Personality Change from the 30s to the 50s," Table II, *Journal of Adult Development,* Vol. 8, pp. 23–37. With kind permission of Springer Science and Business Media. **Figure 16.4:** From Santrock, *A Topical Approach to Life-Span Development,* 3/e, Figure 11.12. Copyright © 2007 The McGraw-Hill Companies. Reproduced with permission by The McGraw-Hill Companies. **Figure 16.5:** From Nansel et al., 2001. "Bullying Behaviors Among U.S. Youth," *Journal of the American Medical Association,* Vol. 285, pp. 2094–2100. **Figure 16.8 graph:** From "Individuals' Conceptions of the Right Age for Major Life Events and Achievements: Late 1950s and Late 1970s," from D. F. Hultsch and J. K. Plemons, "Life Events and Life Span Development" in *Life Span Development and Behavior,* Vol. 2, by P. B. Baltes and O.G. Brun (eds). **Figure 16.9:** From Santrock, *Psychology,* 7/e, Figure 12.11. Copyright © 2003 The McGraw-Hill Companies. Reproduced with permission by The McGraw-Hill Companies.

Chapter 17

Figure 17.1: From *The Psychology of Death, Dying and Bereavement,* by Richard Schultz. Copyright © 1978 The McGraw-Hill Companies. Reproduced with permission by The McGraw-Hill Companies. **Figure 17.2:** From *The Okinawa Diet Plan* by Bradley J. Willcox, M. D, D. Craig Willcox, Ph.D., and Makoto Suzuki, M. D. with Leah Feldon, copyright © 2004 by Bradley J. Willcox and D. Craig Willcox. Used by permission of Clarkson Potter/Publishers, a division of Random House, Inc. **Figure 17.8:** Adapted from *Newsweek,* "Health for Life," Special Section, Fall/Winter 2001. Copyright © Newsweek, Inc. All rights reserved. Used with permission by PARS International Corp., Inc. **Figure 17.14:** From Partnership for Solutions (2002). Baltimore: Johns Hopkins University. Used with permission by Dr. Gerard Anderson. **Figure 17.16:** From "Age and the Consumption of Five or More Drinks on at Least One Day in the United States," from National Center for Health Statistics, 2002.

Chapter 18

Figure 18.1: From S.-C. Li et al., 2004, *Psychological Science,* 15, p. 158. Reprinted by permission of Blackwell Publishing. **Figure 18.2:** From M. Lovden & U. Lindenberger, 2007, *Intelligence,* Fig. 3, p. 765 in J.E. Birren (ed.) *Encyclopedia of Gerontology,* 2/e. Adapted from S. C. Li, U. Lindenberger, B. Hommel, G. Ascherslaben, W. Prinz, and P. B. Baltes, 2004, *Psychological Science,* 15, 158. **Figure 18.5:** After data presented by HBSC Insurance (2007). *The Future of Retirement.* London: HSBC Holdings Ltd.

Chapter 19

Figure 19.2: From L. Carstensen, et al., "The Social Context of Emotion" in the *Annual Review of Geriatrics and Gerontology* by Schaie/Lawton, 1997, Vol. 17, p. 331. Copyright © 1997 by Springer Publishing Company. Adapted by permission of Springer Publishing Company, LLC, New York, NY 10036. **Figure 19.3:** From "Changes in Positive and Negative Emotion Across the Adult Years," from D. Mroczek and C. M. Kolarz, "The Effect of Age in Positive and Negative Affect" in *Journal of Personality and Social Psychology,* Vol. 75, pp. 1333–1349. Copyright © 1998 by the American Psychological Association. Reprinted by permission. **Chap. 19 questionnaire, p. 592:** From R. C. Kessler et al. (2002). "Short Screening Scales to Monitor Population Prevalences and Trends in Nonspecific Psychological Distress," *Psychological Medicine,* 32, 959–976. Reprinted with the permission of Cambridge University Press.

SUBJECT INDEX